11. Format for Bank Reconciliation:

Cash balance according to bank statement		$xxx
Add: Additions by depositor not on bank statement	$xx	
Bank errors	xx	xx
		$xxx
Deduct: Deductions by depositor not on bank statement	$xx	
Bank errors	xx	xx
Adjusted balance		$xxx
Cash balance according to depositor's records		$xxx
Add: Additions by bank not recorded by depositor	$xx	
Depositor errors	xx	xx
		$xxx
Deduct: Deductions by bank not recorded by depositor	$xx	
Depositor errors	xx	xx
Adjusted balance		$xxx

12. Inventory Costing Methods:

1. First-in, First-out (fifo)
2. Last-in, First-out (lifo)
3. Average Cost

13. Interest Computations:

Interest = Face Amount (or Principal) × Rate × Time

14. Methods of Determining Annual Depreciation:

STRAIGHT-LINE: $\frac{\text{Cost} - \text{Estimated Residual Value}}{\text{Estimated Life}}$

DECLINING-BALANCE: Rate* × Book Value at Beginning of Period

*Rate is commonly twice the straight-line rate (1 ÷ Estimated Life).

15. Cash Provided by Operations on Statement of Cash Flows (indirect method):

Net income, per income statement		$xx
Add: Depreciation of plant assets	$xx	
Amortization of bond payable discount and intangible assets	xx	
Decreases in current assets (receivables, inventories, prepaid expenses)	xx	
Increases in current liabilities (accounts and notes payable, accrued liabilities)	xx	
Losses on disposal of assets and retirement of debt	xx	xx
Deduct: Amortization of bond payable premium	$xx	
Increases in current assets (receivables, inventories, prepaid expenses)	xx	
Decreases in current liabilities (accounts and notes payable, accrued liabilities)	xx	
Gains on disposal of assets and retirement of debt	xx	xx
Net cash flow from operating activities		$xx

16. Contribution Margin Ratio

$$\text{Contribution Margin Ratio} = \frac{\text{Sales} - \text{Variable Costs}}{\text{Sales}}$$

17. Break-Even Sales (Units)

$$\text{Break-Even Sales (Units)} = \frac{\text{Fixed Costs}}{\text{Unit Contribution Margin}}$$

18. Sales (Units)

$$\text{Sales (Units)} = \frac{\text{Fixed Costs} + \text{Target Profit}}{\text{Unit Contribution Margin}}$$

19. Margin of Safety

$$\text{Margin of Safety} = \frac{\text{Sales} - \text{Sales at Break-Even Point}}{\text{Sales}}$$

20. Operating Leverage

$$\text{Operating Leverage} = \frac{\text{Contribution Margin}}{\text{Operating Income}}$$

21. Variances

$$\text{Direct Materials Price Variance} = (\text{Actual Price per Unit} - \text{Standard Price}) \times \text{Actual Quantity Used}$$

$$\text{Direct Materials Quantity Variance} = (\text{Actual Quantity Used} - \text{Standard Quantity}) \times \text{Standard Price per Unit}$$

$$\text{Direct Labor Rate Variance} = (\text{Actual Rate per Hour} - \text{Standard Rate}) \times \text{Actual Hours Worked}$$

$$\text{Direct Labor Time Variance} = (\text{Actual Hours Worked} - \text{Standard Hours}) \times \text{Standard Rate per Hour}$$

$$\text{Variable Factory Overhead Controllable Variance} = \text{Actual Variable Factory Overhead} - \text{Budgeted Variable Factory Overhead for Actual Amount Produced}$$

$$\text{Fixed Factory Overhead Volume Variance} = (\text{100\% of Normal Capacity} - \text{Std. Capacity for Amount Produced}) \times \text{Std. Fixed Factory Overhead Rate}$$

22. Rate of Return on Investment (ROI)

$$\text{Rate of Return on Investment (ROI)} = \frac{\text{Controllable Operating Income}}{\text{Invested Assets}}$$

Alternative ROI Computation:

$$\text{ROI} = \frac{\text{Controllable Operating Income}}{\text{Sales}} \times \frac{\text{Sales}}{\text{Invested Assets}}$$

23. Capital Investment Analysis Methods:

1. Methods That Ignore Present Values:
   - A. Average Rate of Return Method
   - B. Cash Payback Method
2. Methods That Use Present Values:
   - A. Net Present Value Method
   - B. Internal Rate of Return Method

24. Average Rate of Return

$$\text{Average Rate of Return} = \frac{\text{Estimated Average Annual Income}}{\text{Average Investment}}$$

25. Present Value Index

$$\text{Present Value Index} = \frac{\text{Total Present Value of Net Cash Flow}}{\text{Amount to Be Invested}}$$

26. Present Value Factor for an Annuity of $1

$$\text{Present Value Factor for an Annuity of \$1} = \frac{\text{Amount to Be Invested}}{\text{Equal Annual Net Cash Flows}}$$

Warren/Fess/Reeve
Accounting, 18e

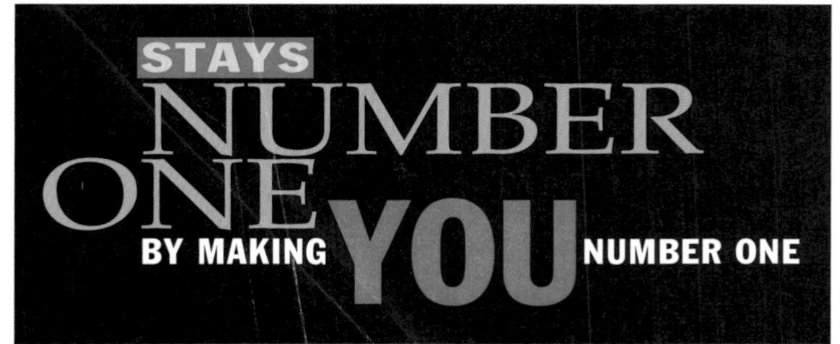

IN ITS SEVENTH DECADE OF PUTTING STUDENTS *FIRST.*

Accounting, 18e...

THE STUDENT-APPROVED PACKAGE FOR LEARNING ACCOUNTING

IN ITS SEVENTH DECADE OF PUTTING STUDENTS *FIRST.*

MORE THAN 10 MILLION STUDENTS LEARNED THEIR FOUNDATION IN BUSINESS RIGHT HERE.

Accounting, 18e, is the time-tested leader for teaching accounting in an interesting and understandable way. This renowned learning system continues to be the preferred teaching tool on campuses coast to coast. Through generations of users, *Accounting* has focused on the most current and relevant topics and applications ... providing you with the accounting you need to know as you enter the business world.

Five tips for a top grade

Accounting, 18e, can help you succeed in your chosen profession from finance and marketing to production and management. Read on to find out how your accounting class can be the beginning of a rewarding and stimulating field of study.

1. **Read the chapter** prior to your instructor's lecture.
2. **Work the problems** assigned by your instructor.
3. **Complete the Continuing Problem** in Chs. 1 - 4 so you'll understand an accounting basic — the accounting cycle.
4. **Review the illustrative problems** in each chapter to test your knowledge of the concepts presented and prepare yourself for your assignments.
5. **Attend class!** Note-taking during lectures coupled with reading your text will make your accounting experience a successful one.

MAKES ACCOUNTING RELEVANT FOR BOTH ACCOUNTING AND NON-ACCOUNTING MAJORS.

Accounting, 18e, is a flexible learning system, presenting accounting in a manner appropriate for every major, every profession, every student. Less theory and more reality makes the material interesting and applicable not just to accounting majors, but to all students. Numerous examples of accounting "at work" in real companies add to the appeal of this popular learning package.

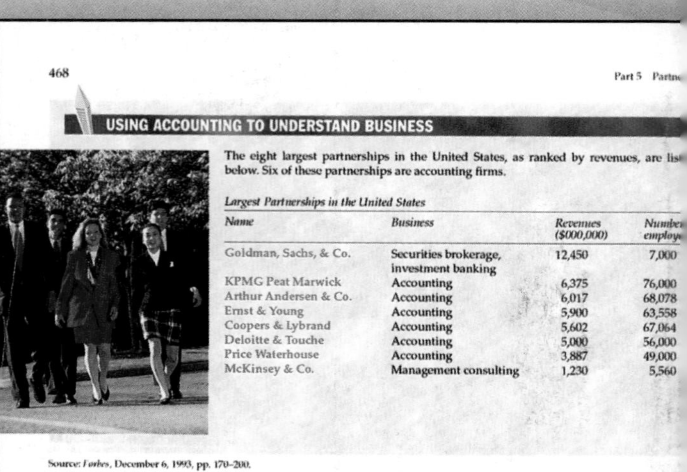

468 Part 5 Partn

USING ACCOUNTING TO UNDERSTAND BUSINESS

The eight largest partnerships in the United States, as ranked by revenues, are lis below. Six of these partnerships are accounting firms.

Largest Partnerships in the United States

Name	*Business*	*Revenues ($000,000)*	*Number employ*
Goldman, Sachs, & Co.	Securities brokerage, investment banking	12,450	7,000
KPMG Peat Marwick	Accounting	6,375	76,000
Arthur Andersen & Co.	Accounting	6,017	68,078
Ernst & Young	Accounting	5,900	63,558
Coopers & Lybrand	Accounting	5,602	67,064
Deloitte & Touche	Accounting	5,000	56,000
Price Waterhouse	Accounting	3,887	49,000
McKinsey & Co.	Management consulting	1,230	5,560

Source: *Forbes*, December 6, 1993, pp. 170–200.

This reporting is done on information returns. The partners must, in turn, r their share of partnership income on their personal tax returns.

A partnership is created by a contract. It is not necessary that the contract writing, nor even that its terms be specifically expressed. However, good bus practice requires that the contract be in writing and that it clearly expresses th tentions of the partners. The contract is known as the partnership agreement **ticles of partnership.** It should include statements regarding such matte amounts to be invested, limits on withdrawals, distributions of income and l and admission and withdrawal of partners.

ADVANTAGES AND DISADVANTAGES OF PARTNERSHIPS

ACCOUNTING, 18E, IS THE LEARNING SYSTEM THAT'S CURRENT WITH TODAY.

This learning package is current in its content, its style of teaching, and as a flexible learning system. It's the culmination of our asking instructors what they need for teaching, what works with students, and which teaching tools really make a difference in the classroom. Count on ***Accounting*** to be the learning package that will help you succeed in the accounting portion of your business curriculum.

WHAT CAN YOU EXPECT?

Content that's relevant to you. A format and writing style that students like you told us you like. And examples that make accounting more interesting, more pertinent, more real world. We even bring you video lecture tapes and a Student Tutorial Software in case you miss class or need extra help. We want you to succeed so we offer an unparalleled supplemental learning package to help you do just that. That's why *Accounting, 18e,* stays number one —— by making you number one!

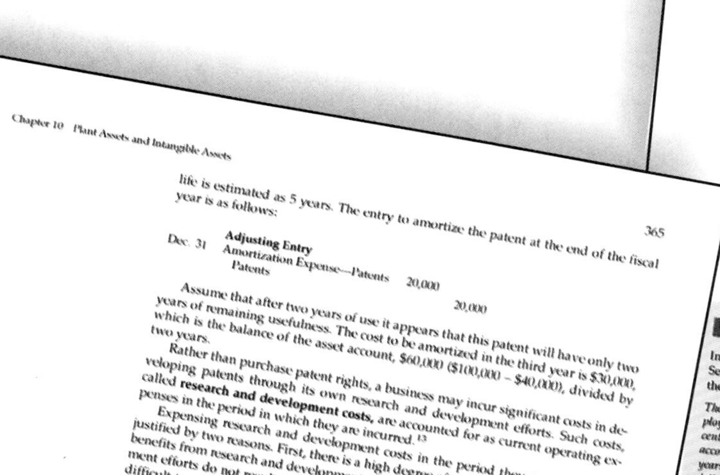

Chapter 11 Payroll, Notes Payable, and Other Current Liabilities 389

both the schedule of future tax rates and the maximum amount subject to tax are revised often by Congress, such changes have little effect on the basic payroll system.[1] In this text, we will use a combined rate of 7.5% on the first $70,000 of annual earnings and a rate of 1.5% on annual earnings in excess of $70,000.

To illustrate, assume that John T. McGrath's annual earnings prior to the current payroll period total $69,150. Assume also that the current period earnings are $1,150. The FICA tax of $68.25 is determined as follows:[2]

Earnings subject to 7.5% FICA tax ($70,000 – $69,150)	$ 850	
FICA tax rate	× 7.5%	
FICA tax		$63.75
Earnings subject to 1.5% FICA tax ($69,150 + $1,150 – $70,000)	$ 300	
FICA tax rate	× 1.5%	
FICA tax		4.50
Total FICA tax		$68.25

YOUR SOCIAL SECURITY TAXES

In its 1936 publication, *Security in Your Old Age*, the Social Security Board set forth the following explanation of how the social security tax would affect a worker's paycheck:

The taxes called for in this law will be paid both by your employer and by you. For the next 3 years you will pay maybe 15 cents a week, maybe 25 cents a week, maybe 30 cents or more, according to what you earn. That is to say, during the next 3 years, beginning January 1, 1937, you will pay 1 cent for every dollar you earn, and at the same time your employer will pay 1 cent for every dollar you earn, up to $3,000 a year. Twenty-six million other workers and their employers will be paying at the same time.

After the first 3 years—that is to say, beginning in 1940—you will pay, and your employer will pay, 1 1/2 cents for each dollar you earn, up to $3,000 a year. This will be the tax for 3 years, and then beginning in 1943, you will pay 2 cents, and so will your employer, for every dollar you earn for the next three years. After that, you and your employer will each pay half a cent more for 3 years, and finally, beginning in 1949, twelve years from now, you and your employer will each pay 3 cents on each dollar you earn, up to $3,000 a year. That is the most you will ever pay.

The rate on January 1, 1995, was 7.65 cents per dollar earned (7.65%). The social security portion was 6.2% on the first $61,200 of earnings. The Medicare portion is 1.45% on all earnings.

Source: Arthur Lodge, "That Is the Most You Will Ever Pay," *Journal of Accountancy*, October 1985, p. 44.

INCOME TAXES

Except for certain types of employment, all employers must withhold a portion of employee earnings for payment of the employees' federal income tax. As a basis for determining the amount to be withheld, each employee completes and submits to the employer an "Employee's Withholding Allowance Certificate," often called a W-4. Exhibit 1 on the next page is an example of a completed W-4 form.

You may recall filling out a W-4 form. On the W-4, an employee indicates marital status, the number of withholding allowances, and whether any additional withholdings are authorized. A single employee may claim one withholding allowance. A married employee may claim an additional allowance for a spouse. An

[1] The FICA ...

Chapter 10 Plant Assets and Intangible Assets 365

life is estimated as 5 years. The entry to amortize the patent at the end of the fiscal year is as follows:

	Adjusting Entry		
Dec. 31	Amortization Expense—Patents	20,000	
	Patents		20,000

Assume that after two years of use it appears that this patent will have only two years of remaining usefulness. The cost to be amortized in the third year is $30,000, which is the balance of the asset account, $60,000 ($100,000 – $40,000), divided by two years.

Rather than purchase patent rights, a business may incur significant costs in developing patents through its own research and development efforts. Such costs, called **research and development costs,** are accounted for as current operating expenses in the period in which they are incurred.[13]

Expensing research and development costs in the period they are incurred is justified by two reasons. First, there is a high degree of uncertainty about the future benefits from research and development efforts. In fact, most research and development efforts do not result in patents. Second, even if a patent is granted, it may be difficult to objectively estimate its cost. If many research projects are in process at the same time, for example, it is difficult to separate the costs of one project from another.

Whether patent rights are purchased or developed internally, a business often incurs significant legal fees related to patents. For example, legal fees may be incurred in filing for patents or in defending the legal rights to patents. Such fees should be debited to an asset account and then amortized over the years of usefulness of the patents.

COPYRIGHTS

The exclusive right to publish and sell a literary, artistic, or musical composition is granted by a **copyright.** Copyrights are issued by the federal government and extend for 50 years beyond the author's death. The costs of a copyright include all costs of creating the work plus any administrative or legal costs of obtaining the copyright. A copyright that is purchased from another should be recorded at the price paid for it. Because of the uncertainty regarding the useful life of a copyright, it is normally amortized over a short period of time. For example, the copyright costs of this text are amortized over 3 years.

GOODWILL

In business, goodwill refers to an intangible asset of a business that is created from such favorable factors as location, product quality, reputation, and managerial skill. Goodwill allows a business to earn a rate of return on its investment that is often in excess of the normal rate for other firms in the same business.

Generally accepted accounting principles permit the recording of goodwill in the accounts only if it is objectively determined by a transaction. An example of such a transaction is the purchase or sale of a business. In addition, goodwill should be amortized over its estimated useful life, which cannot exceed 40 years.[14] For example, in its 1994 annual report, La-Z-Boy Chair Company reported that it amortizes goodwill from acquired companies over a period of 30 years.

The exclusive right to sell a creative work like "The Lion King" is granted by a copyright issued by the federal government.

[13] Statement of Financial Accounting Standards, No. 2, "Accounting for Research and Development Costs" (Stamford: Financial Accounting Standards Board, 1974), par. 12.
[14] Opinions of the Accounting Principles Board, No. 17, "Intangible Assets," op. cit., par. 29.

LEARN TO USE ACCOUNTING TO UNDERSTAND AND SUCCEED IN BUSINESS.

IN ITS SEVENTH DECADE OF PUTTING STUDENTS *FIRST.*

*A*CCOUNTING, *18E*, IS FULL OF FEATURES TO HELP YOU UNDERSTAND HOW ACCOUNTING FUNCTIONS IN TODAY'S BUSINESS WORLD. FROM COVER TO COVER, YOU'LL FIND VALUABLE INFORMATION NO MATTER WHAT CAREER PATH YOU CHOOSE. TAKE A LOOK AT SOME OF THE MANY RELEVANT AND INTERESTING TOPICS THAT LIE AHEAD.

NEW!

"Using Accounting To Understand Business"

Accounting, 18e, puts accounting into real-world context. Each chapter includes one or more informative examples that clearly connect accounting to the business environment and show how, as a future business person, you will use accounting information. See pgs. 14, 91, 135, 388, 544, 679.

Real World Examples

BMW, JCPenney Co., General Electric, Coca-Cola, and numerous other business examples demonstrate how accounting is used in organizations and how it affects businesses worldwide. Integrated throughout the chapters and in the end-of-chapter cases and problems, these examples add concrete meaning to concepts and principles. See pgs. 9, 15, 44, 111, 144, 264, 365, 538.

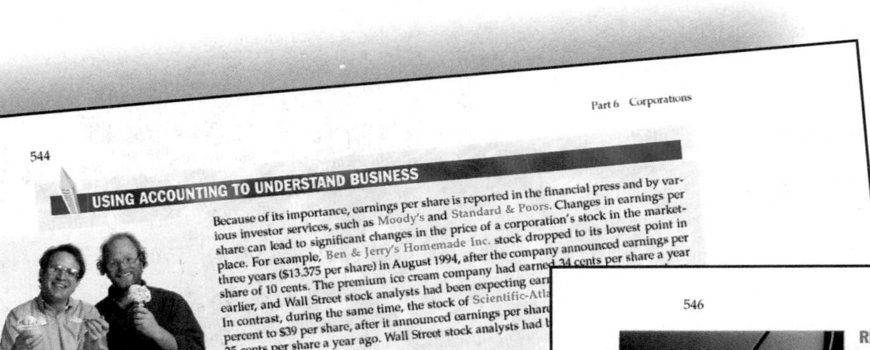

544 Part 6 Corporations

USING ACCOUNTING TO UNDERSTAND BUSINESS

Because of its importance, earnings per share is reported in the financial press and by various investor services, such as Moody's and Standard & Poors. Changes in earnings per share can lead to significant changes in the price of a corporation's stock in the marketplace. For example, Ben & Jerry's Homemade Inc. stock dropped to its lowest point in three years ($13.375 per share) in August 1994, after the company announced earnings per share of 10 cents. The premium ice cream company had earned 34 cents per share a year earlier, and Wall Street stock analysts had been expecting ear[...] In contrast, during the same time, the stock of Scientific-Atla[...] percent to $39 per share, after it announced earnings per shar[...] 25 cents per share a year ago. Wall Street stock analysts had b[...] share of 41 cents.

Source: *The New York Times*, August 6, 1994.

If a company has only common stock outstandin[...] common stock is determined by dividing net incom[...] shares outstanding. If preferred stock is outstanding[...] duced by the amount of any preferred dividend req[...] the number of common shares outstanding.

The effect of unusual items should be consider[...] share. Otherwise, a single earnings per share amou[...] be misleading. For example, assume that Jones Corp[...] statement was presented in Exhibit 1, reported ne[...] Also assume that no extraordinary or other specia[...] The corporation had 200,000 common shares outs[...] The earnings per share is $3.50 ($700,000 ÷ 200,000[...] 200,000) for 1997. Comparing the two earnings p[...] 1997 suggests that operations had significantly i[...] year's per share amount that is comparable to $3.[...] from continuing operations of $690,000 divided[...] stock outstanding. This latter amount indicates a[...] mal operations.

When unusual items exist, earnings per share [...] ing items:

1. Income from continuing operations.
2. Income before extraordinary items and the c[...] counting principle.
3. The cumulative effect of a change in account[...]

546 Part 6 Corporation[...]

Some foreign companies like BMW have begun to build manufacturing plants in the U.S. to, in part, avoid currency exchange gains and losses.

REALIZED CURRENCY EXCHANGE GAINS AND LOSSES

When a U.S. company receives foreign currency, the amount must be converted t[...] its equivalent in U.S. dollars for recording in the accounts. When payment is to b[...] made in a foreign currency, U.S. dollars must be exchanged for the foreign currenc[...] for payment. To illustrate, assume that a U.S. company purchases merchandis[...] from a British company that requires payment in British pounds. In this case, U.S[...] dollars ($) must be exchanged for British pounds (£) to pay for the merchandis[...] This exchange of one currency for another involves using an exchange rate. Th[...] exchange rate is the rate at which one unit of currency (the dollar, for example) ca[...] be converted into another currency (the British pound, for example).

To continue the example, assume that the U.S. company had purchased me[...] chandise for £1,000 from a British company on June 1, when the exchange rate wa[...] $1.40 per British pound. Thus, $1,400 must be exchanged for £1,000 to make th[...] purchase.[14] The U.S. company records the transaction in dollars, as follows:

June 1	Merchandise Inventory	1,400	
	Cash		1,400
	Payment of Invoice No. 1725 from W. A. Sterling Co., £1,000; exchange rate, $1.40 per British pound.		

Instead of a cash purchase, the purchase may be made on account. In this cas[...] the exchange rate may change between the date of purchase and the date of pay[...] ment of the account payable in the foreign currency. In practice, exchange rat[...] vary daily.

To illustrate, assume that the preceding purchase was made on account. Th[...] entry to record it is as follows:

June 1	Merchandise Inventory	1,400	
	Accounts Payable—W. A. Sterling Co.		1,400

Excerpts From Popular Journals

What's "in the news" is in this text. Brief excerpts from *The Wall Street Journal, Forbes, Business Week,* and other periodicals generate stimulating discussions and help you see accounting in the current business press.

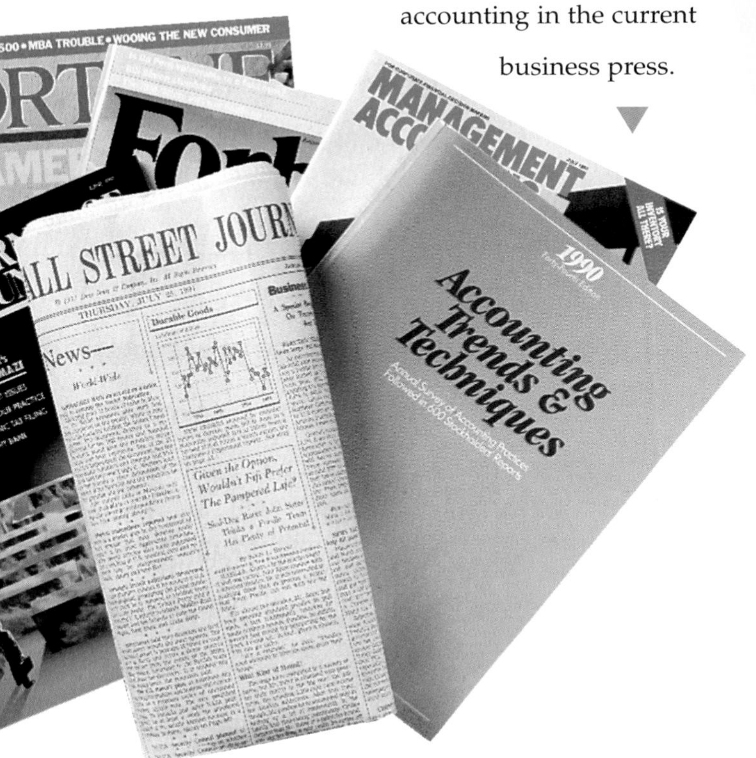

Take a look at just a few of the numerous companies cited throughout the text.

Anheuser-Busch
Apple Computer, Inc.
AT&T
BMW
British-Petroleum
Campbell Soup Company
Coca-Cola Enterprises Inc.
Delta Air Lines, Inc.
Fisher Price
Ford
Gillette
Goodyear
Harley-Davidson
Hershey Foods Corporation
Hewlett-Packard
La-Z-Boy
Mercedes-Benz
Microsoft Inc.
Orion Pictures
PepsiCo, Inc.
Pier 1 Imports, Inc.
Price Waterhouse
RCA
The Limited, Inc.
Time Incorporated
U-Haul
Walt Disney Co.
Zenith

"You And Accounting"

Found at the beginning of each chapter, these short "stories" relate your personal experience to the chapter's topic, making the material more enjoyable to read and easier to grasp. See pgs. 8, 42, 89, 124, 282, 572, 743.

13

Partnership Formation, Income Division, and Liquidation

YOU AND ACCOUNTING

Assume that you and a friend have an idea for startin a part-time business to earn some extra money.

What does it take to start a business operated b two or more individuals? How much money shoul each individual (you and your friend) contribute t start the business? How will the profits be divided? Can you withdraw money from the business whenever you want, or do you have to have your friend's (partner's) approval? Can your friend bring someone else into the business as a partner without your approval? Could you or your friend quit the business at any time? Will you be liable for commitments made b your partner, even if they were made without knowledge? Is the amount you can lose in th ness, if it's not successful, limited to the am initially invested?

The partnership form of business organization allows two or m combine capital, managerial talent, and experience with a minim form is widely used by small businesses. In many cases, the onl partnership form of organization is the corporate form. Some not permit the corporate form for certain types of businesse cians, attorneys, and certified public accountants often or Medical and legal partnerships made up of 20 or more par the number of partners in some national CPA firms exc

The preceding chapters focused on the accounting chapter describes and illustrates the accounting for zation, which is the form you and your friend w business. The answers to the questions above ar will be addressed throughout this discussion.

466

"What's Wrong With This?"

These unique exercises will challenge you to

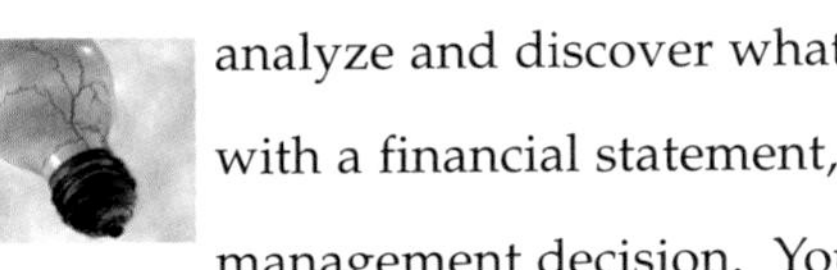

analyze and discover what is wrong with a financial statement, report, or management decision. You'll gain practical experience and critical-thinking skills that will assist you in the business world. See pgs. 31, 84, 148, 271, 523, 764.

PUT ACCOUNTING INTO PRACTICE

IN ITS SEVENTH DECADE OF PUTTING STUDENTS *FIRST.*

EVEN MORE EXERCISES AND ACTIVITIES HELP YOU APPLY WHAT YOU'VE LEARNED FROM *ACCOUNTING, 18E.*

NEW! Cases

Cases in every chapter are designed to help you use accounting to make business decisions and develop your critical thinking. ▶

- Ethics cases stimulate discussion on ethical dilemmas in business. See pgs. 86, 202, 343.
- *NEW!* Financial analysis cases based on the annual report of Hershey Foods Corporation help you develop analytical skills. See pgs. 87, 311, 534.
- *NEW!* Managerial analysis cases require you to use analytical tools in a decision-making setting. See pgs. 772, 859, 894.

Chapter 9 Inventories 34

CASES

CASE 9–1
Hanley Co.
Determining quantities in inventory

Hanley Co. is experiencing a decrease in sales and operating income for the fiscal year ending December 31, 1997. Jill Rizzoli, controller of Hanley Co., has suggested that all orders received before the end of the fiscal year be shipped by midnight, December 31, 1997, eve if the shipping department must work overtime. Since Han ley Co. ships all merchandise FOB shipping point, it woul record all such shipments as sales for the year ending Decem ber 31, 1997, thereby offsetting some of the decreases in sale and operating income.

→ Discuss whether Jill Rizzoli is behaving in a ethical manner.

CASE 9–2
Walgreen Co.
Fifo vs. lifo

The following footnote was taken from the 1994 financial statements of Walgreen Co.:

Inventories are valued on a . . . last-in, first-out (LIFO) cost . . . basis. At August 31, 1994 and 1993, inventories would have been greater by $393,568,000 and $388,464,000 respectively, if they had been valued on a lower of first-in, first-out (FIFO) cost or market basis.

Additional data are as follows:

Earnings before income taxes, 1994	$ 458,421,00
Total lifo inventories, August 31, 1994	1,263,400,00

Based on the preceding data, determine (a) what the total in ventories at August 31, 1994, would have been, using the fif method, and (b) what the earnings before income taxes fo the year ended August 31, 1994, would have been if fifo ha been used instead of lifo.

CASE 9–3
Oakey Wholesale Co.
Lifo and inventory flow

The following is an excerpt from a conversation between Leo Kagle, the warehouse manager for Oakey Wholesale Co., and its accountant, Megan Goodman. Oakey Wholesale operates a large regional warehouse that supplies grocery stores in smaller communities with produce and other grocery products.

Leo: Megan, can you explain what's going on here with these monthly statements?
Megan: Sure, Leo. How can I help you?
Leo: I don't understand this last-in, first-out inventory procedure. It just doesn't make sense.
Megan: Well, what it means is that we assume that the las goods we receive are the first ones sold. So the inventor is made up of the items we purchased first.
Leo: Yes, but that's my problem. It doesn't work that way! W always distribute the oldest produce first. Some of tha produce is perishable! We can't keep any of it very long o it'll spoil.
Megan: Leo, you don't understand. We only *assume* that th products we distribute are the last ones received. W don't actually have to distribute the goods in this way.
Leo: I always thought that accounting was supposed to show what really happened. It all sounds like "make believe" t me! Why not report what really happens?

→ Respond to Leo's concerns.

CASE 9–4
Hershey Foods Corporation
Financial analysis

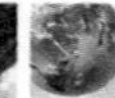

A merchandising business should keep enough inventory on hand to meet the needs of its customers. At the same time, however, too much inventory reduces solvency by tying up funds, and it increases expenses such as storage expense. Moreover, excess inventory increases the risk of losses due to prices declining or the inventory becoming obsolete.

As with many types of financial analyses, it is possible t determine more than one measure to express the relationshi between the cost of merchandise sold (cost of sales) and in ventory. Two such measures are the inventory turnover an the number of days' sales in inventory. The inventor turnover is computed as follows:

$$\textbf{Inventory turnover} = \frac{\textbf{Cost of merchandise sold}}{\textbf{Average inventory}}$$

The average inventory can be determined by dividing th sum of the inventories at the beginning and end of the yea by 2.

NEW! Continuing Problem in Chs. 1-4

Here's a great opportunity to practice what you're learning.

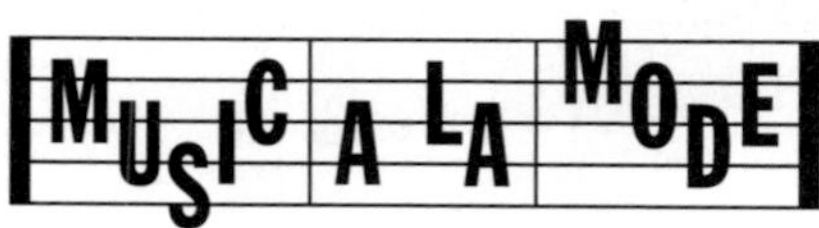

As you study each step of the accounting cycle, you can follow a single company, Music A La Mode, from its transactions to the effect of those transactions on its financial statements. See pgs. 38, 85, 120, 157.

Communication Items ▲

Communication items at the end of chapters help you develop essential communication skills, key to your business success. See pgs. 112, 121, 341.

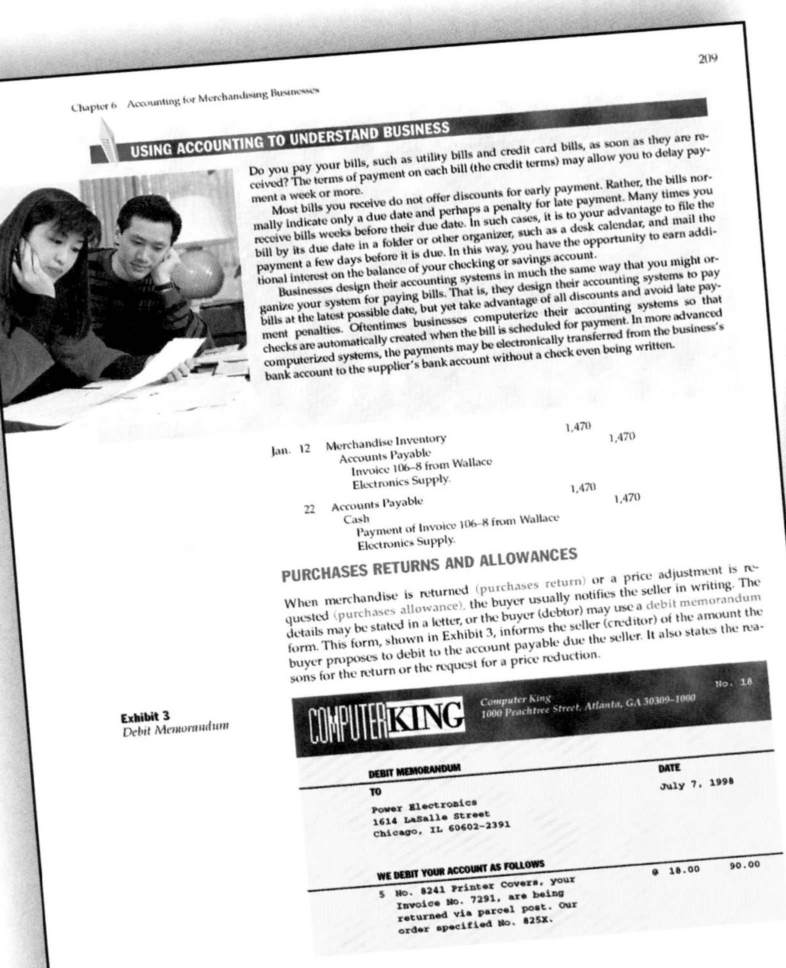

USING ACCOUNTING TO UNDERSTAND BUSINESS

Do you pay your bills, such as utility bills and credit card bills, as soon as they are received? The terms of payment on each bill (the credit terms) may allow you to delay payment a week or more.

Most bills you receive do not offer discounts for early payment. Rather, the bills normally indicate only a due date and perhaps a penalty for late payment. Many times you receive bills weeks before their due date. In such cases, it is to your advantage to file the bill by its due date in a folder or other organizer, such as a desk calendar, and mail the payment a few days before it is due. In this way, you have the opportunity to earn additional interest on the balance of your checking or savings account.

Businesses design their accounting systems in much the same way that you might organize your system for paying bills. That is, they design their accounting systems to pay bills at the latest possible date, but yet take advantage of all discounts and avoid late payment penalties. Oftentimes businesses computerize their accounting systems so that checks are automatically created when the bill is scheduled for payment. In more advanced computerized systems, the payments may be electronically transferred from the business's bank account to the supplier's bank account without a check even being written.

Jan.	12	Merchandise Inventory	1,470	
		Accounts Payable		1,470
		Invoice 106–8 from Wallace Electronics Supply.		
	22	Accounts Payable	1,470	
		Cash		1,470
		Payment of Invoice 106–8 from Wallace Electronics Supply.		

PURCHASES RETURNS AND ALLOWANCES

When merchandise is returned (purchases return) or a price adjustment is requested (purchases allowance), the buyer usually notifies the seller in writing. The details may be stated in a letter, or the buyer (debtor) may use a debit memorandum form. This form, shown in Exhibit 3, informs the seller (creditor) of the amount the buyer proposes to debit to the account payable due the seller. It also states the reasons for the return or the request for a price reduction.

Exhibit 3
Debit Memorandum

COMPUTER KING
Computer King
1000 Peachtree Street, Atlanta, GA 30309–1000
No. 18

DEBIT MEMORANDUM
DATE July 7, 1998

TO
Power Electronics
1614 LaSalle Street
Chicago, IL 60602-2391

WE DEBIT YOUR ACCOUNT AS FOLLOWS
5 No. 8241 Printer Covers, your Invoice No. 7291, are being returned via parcel post. Our order specified No. 825X. @ 18.00 90.00

The **Internal Revenue Service (IRS)** oversees the laws and re
preparing federal tax returns. These laws and regulations determine h
reported for federal income tax purposes. These rules sometimes conf
erally accepted accounting principles for preparing financial statemen
Other regulatory agencies exercise a major influence over the accou
ples of the industries under their jurisdiction. For example, the Con
Currency and the Federal Deposit Insurance Corporation greatly influ
ally accepted accounting principles used by banks. In rare situations, C
also enact special laws that require firms to use specific accounting met

International Accounting Standards

The United States economy, as well as the economies of other nations t
the world, is becoming more global in nature. For example, more and
vestors are investing in companies outside the United States. Likewise,
other financial institutions frequently loan monies on an international s
many companies are involved in international transactions with custo
suppliers.

Currently, accounting concepts and principles differ greatly among
These differences exist because of differences in cultures, legal systems, pol
tems, economies, and the processes by which concepts and principles are de
As a result of the increasing global business activity, attention has been
on developing uniform international accounting standards. The primary g
volved in this effort is the International Accounting Standards Committee
The IASC was formed in 1973 by the leading professional accounting bodies
nations: Australia, Canada, France, Germany, Japan, Mexico, the Netherlan
United Kingdom, and Ireland.[3] At the present time, over 101 accounting or
tions from 77 different countries make up the IASC.

The IASC functions very similarly to the FASB, which we described
For example, after studying an issue, the IASC prepares a preliminary dra
new standard, which is exposed among its members for comments. After re
the proposed standard for any comments, the IASC votes for or against its r
as an *International Accounting Standard*. Currently, over thirty Standards
been issued.

The IASC has no enforcement powers. Instead, the members pledge to use
best efforts to advocate the adoption of the *Standards* in their own countries. As
sult, accounting concepts and principles still differ significantly among count
For example, in the United States and Germany, research and development
are treated as expenses when incurred. In Japan and the United Kingdom, they
treated as assets when incurred and then amortized as expenses in future peri
Over time, however, as the economies throughout the world become more
more interdependent, the trend towards more uniformity will continue.

The need for developing uniform international accounting standards arose from the increase in global business activities in nations throughout the world.

Statements of Financial Accounting Concepts

Objective 2
Describe the *Statements of Financial Accounting Concepts.*

As we mentioned in the preceding section, the FASB's *Statements of Financial A*
counting Concepts are the framework for financial accounting. Four of these *State*
ments are relevant to our discussions of accounting for business and are summa
rized in Exhibit 1.[4]

[3] The United States was represented by the AICPA.
[4] Of the six *Statements* that have been issued to date, one has been superseded and the other focuses on accounting for nonbusiness organizations.

Computer King 

Computer King, a company introduced in Ch. 1 and used in Chs. 2-7, helps you tie together elements of the accounting cycle. See pgs. 44, 93, 212.

"What Do You Think?" Exercises

Found in the end-of-chapter material, these exercises require analyses beyond the material included in the text. Real companies like Ford and Delta are presented. See pgs. 86, 121.

Comprehensive Problems

Found at the end of Chs. 4, 6, 11, and 16, these learning applications integrate and summarize concepts and principles of several chapters to test your comprehension and help you prepare for and pass your midterm and final exams. You may complete these problems manually or use the available Solutions Software. See pgs. 158, 244, 419.

The Basics

You'll find this handy review of basic accounting facts conveniently located on the inside front cover of your text.

TOOLS TO BUILD YOUR SKILLS FOR THE BUSINESS WORLD.

IN ITS SEVENTH DECADE OF PUTTING STUDENTS *FIRST.*

ACCOUNTING, 18E, HAS THE TECHNOLOGIES THAT YOU'LL NEED TO KNOW FOR THE WORKPLACE. LEARNING THESE EASY-TO-USE, AFFORDABLE TECHNOLOGIES WILL SEND YOU INTO THE BUSINESS WORLD WITH THE SKILLS AND CONFIDENCE TO HELP YOU SUCCEED.

Solutions Software

The best selling educational general ledger package is now available for Windows®. Solving end-of-chapter and comprehensive problems, as well as five practice sets, is as easy as clicking icons with a mouse.

Solutions Software for Windows (ISBN 0-538-85165-1)

Solutions Software for IBM, 3.5" Version (ISBN 0-538-83940-6)

Solutions Software for IBM, 5.25" Version (ISBN 0-538-83939-2)

New! Homework Assistant Tutorial (HAT)

This new, user-friendly software for Windows visually teaches you the relationships between journals, ledgers, and financial statements as you solve many end-of-chapter problems. A built-in tutor function includes numerous hints and help screens.

HAT for Windows (ISBN 0-538-85034-5)

Your instructor may already have selected these items as part of your course materials. Or, you may add to your own library by contacting your bookstore manager with the ISBN provided.

Spreadsheet Applications Software

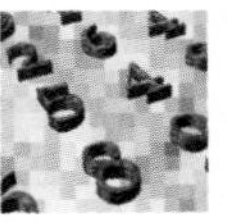

Dozens of problems can be solved using most standard spreadsheet packages, such as Lotus 1-2-3®, Quattro®, or Excel®. Alternative "What-if" scenarios are also presented. **Ask your instructor for a free copy of this software.**

***Accounting* Template for IBM, Chs. 1 - 17, 5.25" Version** (ISBN 0-538-83978-3)

***Accounting* Template for IBM, Chs. 18 - 26, 5.25" Version** (ISBN 0-538-83979-1)

Decision Tools Software

A set of managerial accounting problems can be solved using this easy-to-use software, shifting emphasis from computation to "What-if" analysis of data and results. You'll develop analytical skills as you learn more about the "real world" uses of decision tools.

***Managerial Accounting* Decision Tools for IBM, 3.5" Version** (ISBN 0-538-84862-6)

Additional Student Supplements

Study Guide, Chs. 1 - 13 (ISBN 0-538-83936-8)

Study Guide, Chs. 13 - 26 (ISBN 0-538-83937-6)

Study Guide, Chs. 1-13, with Illustrative Problems Video (ISBN 0-538-85161-9)

Study Guide, Chs. 13-26, with Illustrative Problems Video (ISBN 0-538-85163-5)

18E

ACCOUNTING

CARL S. WARREN, Ph.D., C.P.A., C.M.A., C.I.A.
Professor of Accounting
University of Georgia, Athens

PHILIP E. FESS, Ph.D., C.P.A.
Professor Emeritus of Accountancy
University of Illinois, Champaign-Urbana

JAMES M. REEVE, Ph.D., C.P.A.
Professor of Accounting
University of Tennessee, Knoxville

SOUTH-WESTERN College Publishing

An International Thomson Publishing Company

Sponsoring Editor: David L. Shaut
Senior Developmental Editor: Ken Martin
Production Editor: Mark Sears
Production House: Litten Editing and Production
Cover and Internal Design: Craig LaGesse Ramsdell
Cover Illustration ©1995 Glenn Mitsui
Photo Researcher: Kathryn A. Russell, Pix Inc.
Internal Icons: Alan Brown/Photonics
Marketing Manager: Sharon Oblinger
Media and Technology Editor: Diane M. Van Bakel
For preliminary pages i-viii and xii-xiii:
Writer: Creative Solutions, Judy Smyth
Designer: Bruce Design, Seana Hue & Karen Melaragno
Project Manager: Emilie Copeland D'Agostino
Cover illustration acknowledgements:
Microsoft logo is reprinted with permission of Microsoft Corporation.
L. L. Bean catalog cover reprinted with permission of L. L. Bean, Inc. 1-800-809-7057.
Dodge Caravan reproduced courtesy of Chrysler Corporation.
McDonald's golden arches reproduced with permission of McDonald's Corporation.
Southwest aircraft reproduced courtesy of Southwest Airlines Co.
Sony portable CD player reproduced courtesy of Sony Electronics, Inc.
HERSHEY'S® is a registered trademark and used with permission by Hershey Foods Corporation.
Coca-Cola boxes are reproduced courtesy of Coca-Cola. "Coca Cola" is a trademark of The Coca-Cola Company.
Wal-Mart storefront is reproduced courtesy of Wal-Mart Stores, Inc.

AB70SA

International Thomson Publishing

South-Western College Publishing is an ITP Company.
The ITP trademark is used under license.

Library of Congress Cataloging-in-Publication Data

Warren, Carl S.
Accounting / Carl S. Warren, Philip E. Fess, James M. Reeve.—
18th ed.
p. cm.
Rev. ed. of: Accounting principles / Philip E. Fess, Carl S.
Warren. 17th ed. c1993.
Includes index.
ISBN 0-538-83933-3
1. Accounting. I. Fess, Philip E. II. Reeve, James M.,
III. Fess, Philip E. Accounting principles. IV. Title.
HF5635.W265 1995
657—dc20 95-8635
CIP

ISBN 0-538-83933-3

4 5 6 7 VH 1 0 9 8 7 6

Printed in the United States of America

ABOUT THE AUTHORS

CARL S. WARREN

Dr. Carl S. Warren is the Arthur Andersen & Co. Alumni Professor of Accounting at the J.M. Tull School of Accounting at the University of Georgia, Athens. Professor Warren received his Ph.D. from Michigan State University in 1973. Dr. Warren's experience in listening to users of his texts sharpens his keen focus on helping students learn. When he is not teaching classes or writing textbooks, Dr. Warren enjoys golf, racquetball, and fishing.

PHILIP E. FESS

Dr. Philip E. Fess is the Arthur Andersen & Co. Alumni Professor of Accountancy Emeritus at the University of Illinois, Champaign-Urbana. He received his Ph.D. from the University of Illinois. Dr. Fess has been involved in writing textbooks for over twenty-five years, and his knowledge of how to make texts user-friendly is reflected on the pages of this edition. Dr. Fess plays golf and tennis, and he has represented the United States in international tennis competition.

JAMES M. REEVE

Dr. James M. Reeve is Professor of Accounting at the University of Tennessee, Knoxville. He received his Ph.D. from Oklahoma State University in 1980. Dr. Reeve is founder of the Cost Management Institute and a member of the Institute for Productivity Through Quality faculty at the University of Tennessee. In addition to his teaching experience, Dr. Reeve brings to this text a wealth of experience consulting on managerial accounting issues with numerous companies, including Procter and Gamble, AMOCO, Rockwell International, Harris Corporation, and Freddie Mac. Dr. Reeve's interests outside the classroom and the business world include golf, skiing, reading, and travel.

INSTRUCTION FOR THE CL

FINANCIAL ACCOUNTING, 6E, IS AT THE FOREFRONT OF TEACHING WITH THE BROADEST SPECTRUM OF SUPPORT, FROM TRADITIONAL MATERIALS TO THE LATEST INTEGRATED CLASSROOM TECHNOLOGY — NUMEROUS SUPPLEMENTS TO CHOOSE FROM FOR YOU AND YOUR STUDENTS.

NEW! South-Western Integrated Media Manager (SWIMM)

This new Windows software program brings together a wide array of computerized presentation tools into one seamless easy-to-use package. You can switch between the presentation tools and software applications with just a single click of the mouse to create compelling in-class presentations. You can incorporate your own presentation materials or select from South-Western's Presentation Library, which includes:

THE LEGEND
Millions of students strong.

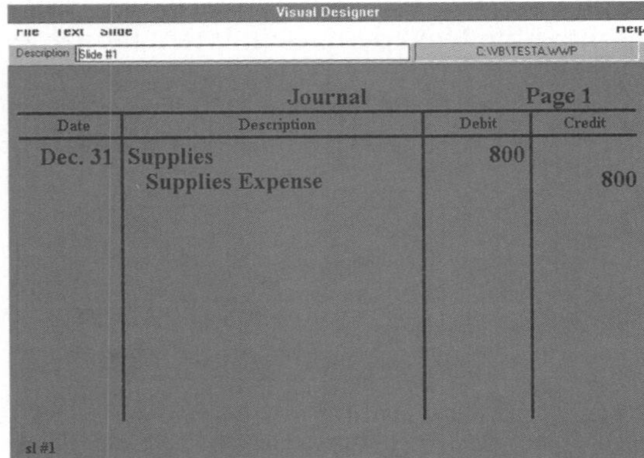

- **Presenting Accounting**
  Journal entries, T-accounts, ledgers, financial statements, and definitions from the text.

- ***PowerPoint*® Transparencies**
  Transparencies of learning objectives, points to emphasize, definitions, and illustrations from South-Western's library of transparency files.

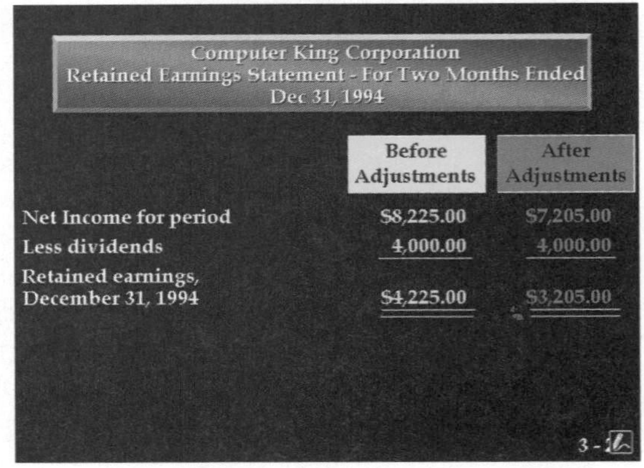

ASSROOM OF TOMORROW

Accounting Principles Videotapes

South-Western also provides a videotape package second-to-none, with illustrative problem videos conveniently packaged with the study guide, mini-cases, ethics cases, part-opener videos, *Setting the Stage* videos, and the fascinating Luca Pacioli historical video to provoke classroom discussion and assist students outside the classroom.

Distance Learning Package

A complete videotape course is available for Distance Learning, using more media-intensive resources than any other accounting telecourse to date.

THE INNOVATOR

The vision to change.

You're Online with South-Western

Instructor resources and software technical support are now available on-line. Reach us at:

- Internet **(cd_hotline@swpco.com)**
- Gopher **(gopher.thomson.com)**
- World Wide Web **(http: //www.thomson. com/swcp.html)**

Download demonstration software, presentation resources, 10-K reports, and other accounting-related resources.

Software Technical Support

South-Western's Technical Support Hotline is available via electronic mail (see left). Reach us by phone:

- New dial-up Bulletin Board System (BBS) **(800/ 544-3101)**
- HotFax service **(513/527-6235)**
- Toll-free Instructor support **(800/543-0174)**

PAC Hotline

Contact our Preferred Accounting Customer Hotline for special requests at **(800/342-8798).**

SOUTH-WESTERN College Publishing

An International Thomson Publishing Company

Summary of Contents and Changes

The most significant changes made in the 18th Edition of Accounting were reducing the number of chapters from 28 to 26. This reduction was accomplished by condensing three corporate equity chapters into two, and integrating much of the financial statement analysis material into cases at the end of the financial chapters. Below you'll find a chapter-by-chapter account of the changes made in the 18th Edition of Accounting. You'll see how Warren/Fess/Reeve have streamlined coverage and expanded other areas for a greater understanding of accounting principles. You'll also find a continued adherence to AECC recommendations that help your students excel in their learning and help you emphasize important aspects in your classroom. Who ever said change isn't good?

Chapter 1
Introduction to Accounting Concepts and Practice 8

Financial and managerial accounting are emphasized in the discussion of specialized accounting fields. The format of the statement of owner's equity was revised to show a beginning balance of zero for a start-up business.

Chapter 2
Analyzing Transactions 42

Chapter 3
The Matching Concept and the Adjusting Process 89

A new exhibit was added to illustrate the difference between deferrals and accruals.

Chapter 4
Completing the Accounting Cycle 124

Chapter 5
Accounting Systems, Internal Control, and Special Journals 162

The section on internal control framework was revised to follow the recommendations of the Committee of Sponsoring Organizations (COSO) of the Treadway Commission. The special journals section of this chapter was recast in the context of a service business, rather than a merchandising business. By presenting simple revenue, purchases, cash payments, and cash receipts journals, the emphasis on special journals is reduced. A new exhibit illustrating a computerized accounts receivable system was added.

Chapter 6
Accounting for Merchandising Businesses 205
Merchandising is covered in one chapter, rather than two. Purchases are discussed prior to sales. The perpetual inventory system is emphasized, which simplifies the recording of purchases and sales transactions. Purchases are recorded at their net amount. The work sheet and closing entries are covered in a chapter appendix. The periodic inventory system is covered in an end-of-text appendix.

Chapter 7
Cash 250
The discussion of internal controls for cash was moved to the beginning of the chapter. The voucher register and the check register are no longer illustrated.

Chapter 8
Receivables and Temporary Investments 282
The discussion of accounts receivable and uncollectible receivables was moved to the beginning of the chapter. The discussion of temporary investments was updated to reflect FASB 115.

Chapter 9
Inventories 313
The discussion of inventory costing under a perpetual system is presented prior to the discussion of inventory costing under a periodic system.

Chapter 10
Plant Assets and Intangible Assets 346
A new exhibit summarizing the costs of acquiring plant assets was added. The sum-of-the-years-digits method of depreciation is covered in a chapter appendix.

Chapter 11
Payroll, Notes Payable, and Other Current Liabilities 386
The illustration of income-sharing bonuses was eliminated. Form 941 is now a transparency master in the Instructor's Resource package. The pension discussion was revised to present pensions as either defined contribution plans or defined benefit plans.

Chapter 12
Concepts and Principles 426
Sections on international accounting standards and the role of auditing of financial statements were added.

Chapter 13
Partnership Formation, Income Division, and Liquidation 466

Chapter 14
Corporations: Organization and Equity Rights 498
A section on forming a corporation, including the discussion of organization costs, was added at the beginning of the chapter. The discussion of stock subscriptions was eliminated. The discussions of stock splits, cash dividends, stock dividends, appropriations of retained earnings, and reporting retained earnings were moved from former Chapter 16. The discussion of the statement of stockholders' equity was moved from former Chapter 18.

Chapter 15
Corporate Earnings, International Transactions, and Investments in Stocks 537
The discussions of corporate income taxes, unusual items that affect the income statement and retained earnings statement, and earnings per share were moved from former Chapter 16. The discussion of equity per share was retained from former Chapter 15. The coverage of consolidated financial statements was significantly reduced.

Chapter 16
Bonds Payable and Investments in Bonds 572
Amortization of premium and discount by the interest method was moved to a chapter appendix. The coverage of bond sinking funds was significantly reduced.

Chapter 17
Statement of Cash Flows 605

Chapter 18
Managerial Accounting Concepts and Principles 662
The discussion of the characteristics of managerial accounting reports was integrated into the chapter. The section on cost terminology was eliminated and the terms defined as they are introduced in subsequent chapters. A hypothetical printing company is used in this chapter to introduce managerial accounting. The income statement illustration was revised to reflect a perpetual inventory system. The appendix on traditional versus JIT systems was incorporated into new Chapter 20. A new end-of-text appendix on periodic inventory systems for manufacturing businesses was added.

Chapter 19
Job Order Cost Systems 699
The hypothetical printing company introduced in Chapter 18 is used to illustrate a job order costing system. A section on selecting an activity base for allocating factory overhead was added. A section on using job order costing in decision making was added. The appendix on activity-based costing at the end of former Chapter 23 was condensed and moved to the end of new Chapter 19.

Chapter 20
Process Cost Systems 743
A new exhibit comparing job order and process cost systems was added. A new exhibit illustrating the physical flows for a process manufacturer was added. The discussion of equivalent units was revised to emphasize a step-by-step calculation. The cost of production report format was revised. A section on using the cost of production report for decision making was added. The coverage of joint products and by-products was eliminated. The illustration of the average cost method was eliminated.

Chapter 21
Cost Behavior and Cost-Volume-Profit Analysis 776

Chapter 22
Budgeting 820
The discussion of standard costs was moved to new Chapter 23. A section on human behavior and budgeting was added. The terms "static budget" and "flexible budget" are introduced prior to the discussion of the master budget. The illustration of the cash budget was expanded.

Chapter 23
Performance Evaluation Using Variances from Standard Costs 862
This is a new chapter on standard costs that expands on the discussion in former Chapter 25. A new section on nonfinancial performance measures was added at the end of the chapter.

Chapter 24
Performance Evaluation for Decentralized Operations 897
The discussion of responsibility accounting for profit centers was revised to focus on operating income, service department charges, and controllable operating income. The discussion of investment centers was revised to use terminology consistent with that of profit centers.

Chapter 25
Differential Analysis and Product Pricing 934
The discussion of the economic theory of product pricing was eliminated. A new section on profitability and pricing under production bottlenecks was added.

Chapter 26
Capital Investment Analysis 967
A brief discussion of present value concepts was added.

Contents

Practice Set: First Designs Inc.
This set is available with transactions in narrative form. It provides practice in accounting for a merchandising corporation that operates a departmentalized business and uses a periodic inventory system and special journals. It may also be solved using the Solutions Software.

Acknowledgments

Throughout the textbook, relevant professional statements of the Financial Accounting Standards Board and the Institute of Management Accountants and other authoritative publications are discussed, quoted, paraphrased, or footnoted. We are indebted to the American Accounting Association, the American Institute of Certified Public Accountants, the Financial Accounting Standards Board, and the Institute of Management Accountants for material from their publications.

The following faculty reviewed manuscript for this edition and provided helpful comments:

Karen Adamson
Central Washington University

Sheila Ammons
Austin Community College

Diana Anderson
Baker College

Dan Best
Craven Community College

Verne Bryers
Fox Valley Technical College

Paul Concilio
McLennon Community College

John Crain
Southeastern Louisiana University

Steven Daulton
Newberry College

Paul Doran, Jr.
Jefferson State Community College

Lester Downing
Indiana Vocational Technical College

Robert Francis
Herkimer County Community College

Debra Goorbin
Westchester Community College

Mary Govan
Sinclair Community College

Gary Guinn
Skagit Valley College

Curt Gustafson
South Dakota State University

Leonard Hausenbauer
North Harris County College

James L. Haydon
East Los Angeles Community College

James Heely
Monmouth College

Stephen Hester
State Technical Institute of Memphis

Zach Holmes
Oakland Community College

Sharon Hoover
Scott Community College

Steven Jarett
Saint Joseph College

Mary Thomas Keim
Indiana University of Pennsylvania

James Lentz
Moraine Valley Community College

Daniel Luna
Raritan Valley Community College

Irving Mason
Herkimer County Community College

Patrick O'Shaughnessy
Central Washington University

Phyllis Palmer
Seminole Community College

Bobby Phillips
Johnston Community College

Sharyll Plato
University of Central Oklahoma

Ronald Richard
Westark Community College

Jill Russell
Camden County College

Karlene Sanborn
Butler County Community College

Mary Scott
Grambling State University

Jack Sterrett
Brunswick College

Ron Strittmater
North Hennepin Community College

Kathy Tam
Tulsa Junior College

Richard Vuolo
Columbia-Greene Community College

Charles Wellens
Fitchburg State College

Adelle Yeakel-Ziemer
Lehigh County Community College

Marilyn Young
Tulsa Junior College

We especially thank the following faculty who provided comments on a regular basis as they taught their courses:

Boyd Binde
Dickinson State University

Joseph Colmie
Thomas Nelson Community College

Pat Conn
Atlantic Community College

Sue Counte
Moraine Valley Community College

Michael Cravatta
Richland Community College

James Genseal
Joliet Junior College

Zach Holmes
Oakland Community College

James Lentz
Moraine Valley Community College

Florence McGovern
Bergen Community College

Salah Negm
Prince George's Community College

Lois Slutsky
Broward Community College

Nelson White
College of the Albermarle

We also received useful comments from the following faculty:

Michael Blue
Bloomsburg University

Sam Dean
Macon College

David Keys
Macon College

Jack Klett
Indian River Community College

We are most grateful for this input, and we continue to welcome your comments and suggestions.

We also deeply express our appreciation to the South-Western staff—editorial, production, art, advertising, marketing, and sales—for their input and assistance in helping us offer you this refreshing view of accounting.

Carl S. Warren
Philip E. Fess
James M. Reeve

Photo Credits

Page 7 © 1992 Ralph Mercer
Page 8 © Michael Grecco/Stock Boston
Page 10 © 1992 Peter Hendrie/The Image Bank
Page 14 © John Abbott
Page 15 © Bill Bachmann/Stock, Boston
Page 16 © Tim Brown/Tony Stone Images
Page 22 Superstock
Page 42 © Paul Chauncey/The Stock Market
Page 44 Tony Stone Images
Page 44 Erik Von Fischer/Photonics
Page 89 © Glennon Donahue/Tony Stone Images
Page 91 The Image Bank
Page 99 Photo Courtesy of KI
Page 124 © Rohan/Tony Stone Images
Page 135 Churchill & Klehr
Page 161 © 1992 Ralph Mercer
Page 162 © David J. Sams/Stock, Boston
Page 165 © Keith Olson/Tony Stone Images
Page 166 © Bob Daemmrich/Stock, Boston
Page 171 © Blair Seitz/Photo Researchers, Inc.
Page 209 © 1992 Frank Siteman/Stock, Boston
Page 214 © Wendt Worldwide. All Rights Reserved.
Page 249 © Ralph Mercer
Page 252 © Bob Peterson/FPG International
Page 260 © Churchill & Klehr
Page 263 Bob Daemmrich/Stock, Boston
Page 264 © John A. Schakel, Jr./Unicorn Stock Photos
Page 282 © Churchill & Klehr
Page 290 Tony Stone Images
Page 313 © Bill Gallery/Stock, Boston
Page 315 © Amy C. Etra/PhotoEdit
Page 321 New York Stock Exchange/
Edward Topple, Staff Photographer
Page 326 © 1994 Churchill & Klehr
Page 329 C.L.&M. Photo/FPG International
Page 346 © 1987 Joe Baraban/The Stock Market
Page 349 © 1992 Jose Pelaez/The Stock Market
Page 358 © Obremski/The Image Bank
Page 365 © 1994 Walt Disney/The Kobal Collection
Page 388 Wide World Photos
Page 399 © DC Comics Inc./The Kobal Collection
Page 401 © 1994 Don Mason/The Stock Market

Page 402 Courtesy of General Motors Corporation
Page 425 © Ralph Mercer
Page 428 Courtesy of Financial Accounting Foundation
Page 429 © 1993 Romilly Lockyer/The Image Bank
Page 432 Stock, Boston
Page 437 © Paul Steel/The Stock Market
Page 440 © 1994 Torleif Svensson/The Stock Market
Page 465 © Ralph Mercer/Tony Stone Images
Page 466 © 1987 John Lewis Stage/The Image Bank
Page 468 Courtesy of Deloitte & Touche
Page 469 Courtesy of Coopers & Lybrand
Page 470 © Chad Ehlers/Tony Stone Images
Page 497 © 1993 Ralph Mercer
Page 498 © Ralph Mercer/Tony Stone Images
Page 505 Courtesy of Bethlehem Steel
Page 506 Churchill & Klehr
Page 511 © Rich LaSalle/Tony Stone Images
Page 512 © 1992 Antonio M. Rosario/The Image Bank
Page 537 © Philip Temple/Tony Stone Images
Page 543 © 1991 Stephen Derr/The Image Bank
Page 544 Courtesy of Ben & Jerry's Homemade, Inc.
Page 546 © Wendt Worldwide. All Rights Reserved.
Page 554 Churchill & Klehr
Page 572 © Wendt Worldwide. All Rights Reserved.
Page 575 © Wendt Worldwide. All Rights Reserved.
Page 581 Churchill & Klehr
Page 606 © Lawrence Migdale/Stock, Boston
Page 614 © 1993 William Trufic/The Stock Market
Page 615 © 1990 Henley & Savage/The Stock Market
Page 661 © Ralph Mercer/Tony Stone Images
Page 662 © Roy Morsch/The Stock Market
Page 666 © 1994 Jerry Wachter/Focus on Sports
Page 669 © 1986 C. A. Giampiccolo/FPG International
Page 671 Churchill & Klehr
Page 679 © Michael Iamborrino/FPG International
Page 681 © Henley & Savage/The Stock Market
Page 699 © Dallas & John Heaton/West Light
Page 701 © Robert Essel/The Stock Market
Page 705 © Henley & Savage/Tony Stone Images
Page 719 Hewlett-Packard Company
Page 743 © Brent Bear/West Light
Page 747 American Iron and Steel Institute
Page 752 GENCORP
Page 758 Photo Courtesy Oregon Cutting Systems Div., Blount, Inc.
Page 775 © 1991 Ralph Mercer
Page 776 © Tony Freeman/Photo Edit
Page 780 © 1992 Bill Horsman/Stock, Boston
Page 788 © Deborah Davis/Photo Edit
Page 795 © COMNET/West Light
Page 820 Australian Picture Library/John Carnemoll/West Light
Page 823 Jay Payton/Georgia Tech Sports Information
Page 827 © Tom McCarthy/Photo Edit
Page 834 Courtesy of Emerson Electric Co., St. Louis, MO
Page 862 © Vic Bider/PhotoEdit
Page 863 Courtesy of Limited Stores, Inc.
Page 866 © Bob Daemmrich/Stock Boston
Page 871 © 1994 Erika Svensson/The Stock Market
Page 873 © Will Van Overbeek
Page 899 Courtesy © PepsiCo, Inc.
Page 902 © R. Landau/West Light
Page 908 Churchill & Klehr
Page 910 Courtesy of Analog Devices, Inc.
Page 933 © 1993 Ralph Mercer
Page 934 © 1992 The Stock Market
Page 935 Mercedes-Benz of North America, Inc.
Page 940 © 1992 David Burnett/Contact Press/The Stock Market
Page 943 Courtesy American Airlines
Page 967 © 1993 Jon Feingersh/The Stock Market
Page 968 Toyota Motor Manufacturing, U.S.A., Inc.
Page 971 Churchill & Klehr
Page 976 Marriott International, Inc.
Page 979 Churchill & Klehr

Learning Objectives of Accounting

After studying this text, you should be able to:

Objective 1
Summarize the basic nature of the accounting profession.

Objective 2
Define and apply financial and managerial accounting terms.

Objective 3
Summarize basic financial and managerial accounting concepts and principles.

Objective 4
Analyze, record, and report transactions for service, merchandising, and manufacturing businesses organized as:

sole proprietorships
partnerships
corporations.

Objective 5
Use cost information to support operating decisions and strategic decisions regarding products, customers, and technology.

A Brief Look at Accounting—Its Past, Present, and Future

Accounting is a profession similar to law and medicine. Such professions continually evolve and change as society and the needs of society change. In recent years, for example, the practice of medicine has changed significantly with the invention and use of lasers. Likewise, the practice of law has changed to reflect new specializations, such as environmental law.

The objective of this introduction is to make you aware of how accounting has changed over the years. This awareness will help you better understand the role and the importance of accounting in society and in your everyday life.

EARLY ACCOUNTING

Just as you may keep a record of the money you spend, people throughout history have maintained records of their business activities. Some of these records were clay tablets that indicated the payment of wages in Babylon around 3600 B.C. Record keeping also existed in ancient Egypt and in the Greek city-states. Some of the earliest English records were compiled by William the Conqueror in the eleventh century. These early accounting records included only some of the financial activities of an entity. A systematic recording of all activities of an entity developed later in response to the needs of the commercial republics of Italy.

DOUBLE-ENTRY SYSTEM

How did the early recording of financial activities evolve into a system of accounting? The basic system of accounting, which is still used today, was invented by Luca Pacioli, a Franciscan monk. Pacioli was a mathematician who taught in various universities in Perugia, Naples, Pisa, and Florence. He was a close friend of Leonardo da Vinci, with whom he collaborated on a mathematics book. Pacioli wrote the text and da Vinci drew the illustrations.

Pacioli invented what is known as the double-entry system of accounting. A description of the double-entry system was first published in Italy in 1494. This system was strongly influenced by the financial needs of the Venetian merchants. Goethe, the German poet, novelist, and scientist, described the double-entry system as "one of the most beautiful inventions of the human spirit, and every good businessman should use it in his economic undertakings."[1]

What is so special about the double-entry system? It is unique because it records financial activities in such a way that an equilibrium is created within the records. For example, assume that you borrow $1,000 from a bank. Within a double-entry system, the loan is recorded as $1,000 of cash received, and at the same time, an obligation is recorded for the eventual repayment of the $1,000. Each of the $1,000 amounts is balanced by the other. In a complex business environment, in which an entity may be involved in thousands of transactions daily, this balancing is a valuable control that ensures the accuracy of the recording process.

In spite of the enormous changes in business operations and their complexity since 1494, the basic elements of the double-entry system have remained virtually unchanged. This is a lasting tribute to the significance of Pacioli's invention and his contribution to society.

INDUSTRIAL REVOLUTION

In addition to the invention of the double-entry system, other major events significantly influenced the evolution of accounting. One such event was the Industrial Revolution. The Industrial Revolution occurred in England from the mid-eighteenth to the mid-nineteenth centuries. It changed the method of producing marketable goods from a handicraft method to a factory system.

The handicraft method of producing goods involved the coordinating of a network of independent artisans. For example, a textile business would coordinate separate weaving, spinning, and assembly artisans in order to finish completed garments. The final product price would be determined from the sum of the individual artisan rates for work completed plus some profit to the manager for coordinating the activity. There is little need for cost accounting or managerial accounting information in such an environment. The manager only needed a book of accounts to record transactions with the independent artisans and to record receipts for sales from customers.

Under the factory system, businesses took advantage of economies of scale by assembling machinery and labor into a centralized location under the control of a single manager. **Economies of scale** refers to the benefit obtained by spreading the cost of physical assets over a large quantity of production. The result was an increasing growth in productivity that only "size" could accomplish. For example, it was during this period that the early steel industry developed.

The factory system, however, introduced a new challenge for managers. No longer were the managers merely coordinators of independent artisans. Instead, the independent artisans were replaced with employees paid according to daily

[1] Johann Wolfgang von Goethe, *Samtliche Werke,* edited by Edward von der Hellen (Stuttgart and Berlin: J. G. Cotta, 1902–07), Vol. XVII, p. 37.

wage rates. In turn, single-manager businesses were replaced by large factories with several layers of management, where senior managers had responsibility over junior managers. As a result, internal reporting measures were needed to guide management in identifying the cost of their products and monitoring the results of operations. The fields of cost accounting and managerial accounting developed to meet these needs.

Even today, the fields of cost accounting and managerial accounting continue to undergo major changes as accountants attempt to more accurately record, estimate, and report information for manufacturing operations.

CORPORATE ORGANIZATION

As you might expect, the Industrial Revolution created a demand for large amounts of money or capital to build factories and purchase machinery. To meet this need for capital, the corporate form of organization was developed. The corporate form of organization was first established in England in 1845. It soon spread rapidly to the United States, which became one of the world's leading industrial nations shortly after the Civil War. In the United States, large amounts of capital were essential for the development of new industries, such as steel, transportation, mining, electric power, and communications. As in England, the corporation was the primary vehicle for raising the capital that was needed.

How does the corporate form of organization raise capital? If you answered "by issuing stock," you are correct. Corporate ownership is divided into shares of stock that can be readily transferred. The stockholders of a corporation normally do not exercise direct control over the operations of the corporation. The management runs day-to-day operations, and the stockholders only indirectly control the corporation through the election of a board of directors. The board of directors sets general policies and selects the officers who actively manage the corporation.

So how did the corporate form of organization affect accounting? The corporate form affected the evolution of accounting because the stockholders needed information about how well management was running the corporation. Since stockholders are not directly involved in day-to-day operations, they must rely on accounting reports in evaluating management's performance. These reports created additional demands upon accounting.

As corporations grew larger, the number of individuals and institutions relying on accounting reports increased. Potential shareholders and creditors needed information. Government agencies required information for purposes of taxation and regulation. Employees, union representatives, and customers requested information to judge the stability and profitability of corporations. Thus, largely due to the use of the corporate form of organization, accounting had to expand from serving the needs of a few owners to a public role of meeting the needs of a variety of interested parties.

PUBLIC ACCOUNTING

The corporate form of organization also created a need for an independent review or audit of reports prepared by the corporation's management. This audit was necessary to provide some assurance to users of the information that the reports were reliable. This audit function, called the **attest function,** was responsible for the development and growth of the public accounting profession. Unlike private accountants who work for a specific business entity, public accountants are self-employed. In this sense, they are independent of the businesses whose reports they audit.

All states currently provide for the regulation and licensing of certified public accountants (CPAs). In 1944, fifty years after the enactment of the first CPA law, there were approximately 25,000 CPAs in the United States. During the next four decades, the number increased tenfold. Currently the number exceeds 300,000 and is continuing to increase.

Although auditing is still a major service offered by CPAs, much of their time is also spent assisting in the planning and controlling of clients' operations. Such consulting services have increased dramatically in recent years. Today, consulting services are a major part of the practice of many public accounting firms.

INCOME TAX

All of us are affected by income taxes. Since income taxes are based upon records of financial activities, the development of the income tax significantly affected the evolution of accounting, as you might expect.

The development of the federal income tax was made possible by the Sixteenth Amendment to the Constitution of the United States. The first federal income tax law was passed by the United States Congress in 1913. Currently, all businesses organized as corporations or partnerships, as well as many individuals and organizations, are required to file income tax returns. To meet this requirement properly, filers must maintain adequate financial records. Because of the complexity of the tax laws and regulations, more and more organizations and individuals depend upon accountants. In addition to preparing tax returns, accountants advise clients on how to minimize their taxes.

GOVERNMENT INFLUENCE

Local, state, and federal governments also have had a significant influence on the evolution of accounting. Current accounting systems must record and report financial data for a variety of governmental laws and regulations. You are probably aware of some examples of such laws and regulations at the local, state, and federal levels. At the local level, commissions and boards levy property and sales taxes based upon accounting data. At the state level, public service commissions often approve utility rates. Such rate-making processes use and analyze accounting data. At the federal level, in addition to the income tax, the Social Security and Medicare laws require accounting record keeping and reporting by almost all businesses and many individuals.

ACCOUNTING'S FUTURE

As the preceding paragraphs emphasize, accounting touches all our lives in one way or another. Although long-range predictions are risky, there are three areas of accounting that are undergoing intense study and review. These areas, which will likely change significantly in the future, are international accounting, socioeconomic accounting, and managerial accounting.

International Accounting

As we discussed, accounting changes to meet the needs of society. As a result, accounting rules and regulations differ significantly among countries, each of which has unique cultural and societal needs. These differences create major accounting problems when a firm has foreign operations in more than one country. In such cases, the firm must adapt its accounting system to the rules and regulations of each country. This increases the costs of recording accounting data and preparing accounting reports. Also, there is potential for confusing the users of accounting reports. To overcome these problems, the accounting profession is seeking to develop uniform international accounting standards.

Socioeconomic Accounting

Accounting traditionally focuses on recording and reporting financial activities of businesses or other specific entities. Recently, there has been a suggestion that accounting should also record and report the impact of organizations on society. This area of accounting is called socioeconomic accounting.

As socioeconomic accounting has evolved, three main areas have been identified for study. The first area is recording and reporting the impact of various organizations on matters that affect the overall quality of life in society. The second area is recording and reporting the impact of government programs on achieving specific social objectives. The third area is recording and reporting the impact of corporate social performance. Corporate social performance refers to the corporation's responsibilities in such areas as water and air quality, conservation of natural resources, and equal employment practices.

The concept of socioeconomic accounting is relatively simple as a theory. However, additional study and research are needed before socioeconomic costs and benefits of various activities can be recorded and reported. For example, the overall impact of a public utility's proposal to build a nuclear power plant is difficult to measure, record, and report.

Managerial Accounting

The role of managerial accounting is evolving as the information needs of managers change. One of the reasons for the change in information needs is **total quality management.** This new management concept is challenging many of the traditional methods of managing businesses.

Total quality management focuses on two major objectives. First, the business's primary objective is to earn customer loyalty by providing them with superior products and service. Second, the business should attempt to earn customer loyalty by continually improving employees, business processes, and products. This latter emphasis is called **continuous process improvement.**

Continuous process improvement extends traditional cost accounting and managerial accounting concepts beyond an emphasis of just the products that customers buy to everything that is done by the employees of the business. Under this philosophy, accountants are expected to provide information that will help managers and employees continually improve and re-engineer the business systems of which they are a part. As a result, cost accounting and managerial accounting systems are being revised to provide new and innovative types of information and reports.

DO YOU USE ACCOUNTING?

As this introduction suggests, we all use accounting to some degree. For some of us, accounting involves recording checks in our checkbooks. For others, it may involve preparing our tax returns. As you begin your study of accounting, keep in mind the importance of accounting to your everyday life as well as its importance for your business career.

PART ONE

Basic Accounting Systems

1. *Introduction to Accounting Concepts and Practice*

2. *Analyzing Transactions*

3. *The Matching Concept and the Adjusting Process*

4. *Completing the Accounting Cycle*

1

Introduction to Accounting Concepts and Practice

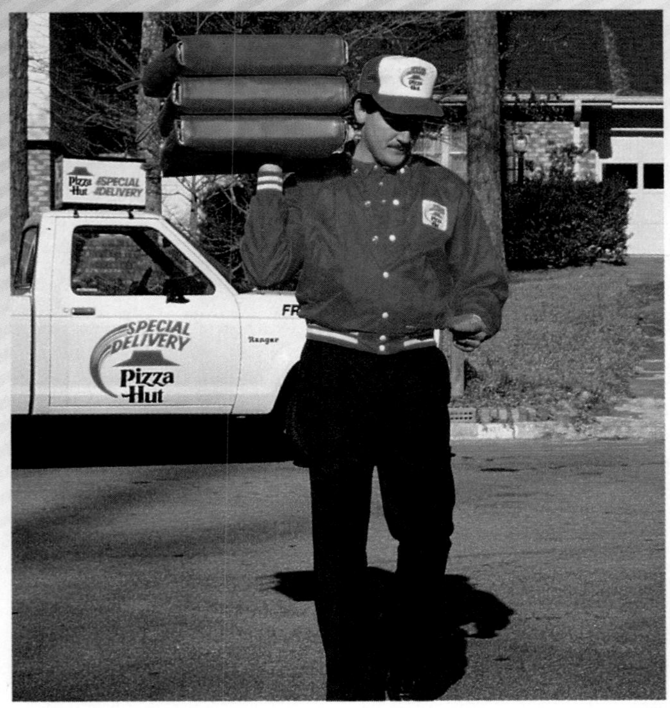

YOU AND ACCOUNTING

Is accounting important to you? Do you use accounting information? The answer to both questions is yes. We all use accounting information in one form or another. For example, if you are thinking about buying a new car, you use accounting information to determine whether you can afford the monthly payments. Similarly, your decision to attend college implies that you considered the benefits (the ability to obtain a higher-paying or more desirable job). Most likely, you also considered the related costs of attending college (the costs of tuition, textbooks, and so on).

Managers of businesses make decisions similar to this everyday. For example, a manager of a chain of pizza restaurants must decide whether to acquire delivery cars. Accounting information about the pizza restaurants will be a major factor in determining whether the cars should be acquired. Also, this information will be used in determining whether a loan can be obtained to finance the purchase of the cars.

This chapter discusses the accounting framework by which businesses gather and report economic data. These data are then used in making decisions such as the ones described above.

Our primary objective in this text is to describe and illustrate basic accounting principles and concepts that will help you in your personal, as well as professional, lives. Accounting will be important to you, even though you may not be an accountant or a manager. If you are an engineer designing a product, for example, you should consider the costs of alternative manufacturing processes. If you are a lawyer, you will use accounting data in tax cases and in settling lawsuits.

In this text, we will focus primarily upon businesses organized for profit. However, the principles apply to organizations that are not organized for profit, such as churches, charities, and governmental agencies.

After studying this chapter, you should be able to:

Objective 1
Define accounting as an information system.

Objective 2
Describe the profession of accounting and list its specialized fields.

Objective 3
Summarize the development of accounting principles and relate them to practice.

Objective 4
List the characteristics of a business transaction.

Objective 5
State the accounting equation and define each element of the equation.

Objective 6
Explain how business transactions can be stated in terms of the resulting changes in the three basic elements of the accounting equation.

Objective 7
Describe the financial statements of a sole proprietorship and explain how they interrelate.

Accounting as an Information System

Objective 1
Define accounting as an information system.

Accounting[1] may be defined as an information system that provides reports to various individuals or groups about economic activities of an organization or other entity. You might think of accounting as the "language of business," because it is the means by which most business information is communicated. For example, companies distribute accounting reports that summarize their financial performance to their owners, creditors, government regulators, and potential investors.

The process of using accounting to provide information to users is illustrated in Exhibit 1. First, accountants must identify user groups and their information needs. These needs determine which economic data and activities are recorded by the accounting system. Finally, accountants prepare reports that summarize this information for users.

Because individuals make decisions based upon the data in accounting reports, accounting has a major impact upon our economic and social system. For example, the management of Delta Airlines may decide to lay off 500 pilots in Atlanta based upon accounting projections and reports. Likewise, Congress and state legislatures allocate monies to various programs, based at least partially upon accounting reports.

Profession of Accounting

Objective 2
Describe the profession of accounting and list its specialized fields.

The demand for accounting services has increased with the increase in number, size, and complexity of businesses. In addition, new laws and regulations have also created an increased demand for accounting.

You may wonder whether there are career opportunities in accounting. The answer is yes. Employment opportunities in the profession of accountancy are expected to continue to grow and expand. In a report prepared by the U.S. Department of Labor, the accounting profession is projected to increase by 39.8% between the late 1980s and the year 2000.[2]

[1] A glossary of terms appears at the end of each chapter. A complete glossary is included at the end of the text. The terms included in each glossary are printed in color the first time they are defined in the text.
[2] U.S. Department of Labor, Bureau of Labor Statistics, *Occupational Projections and Training Data: 1991 Edition*, U.S. Government Printing Office, Washington, April 1991.

Exhibit 1
Accounting as a Process of Providing Information to Users

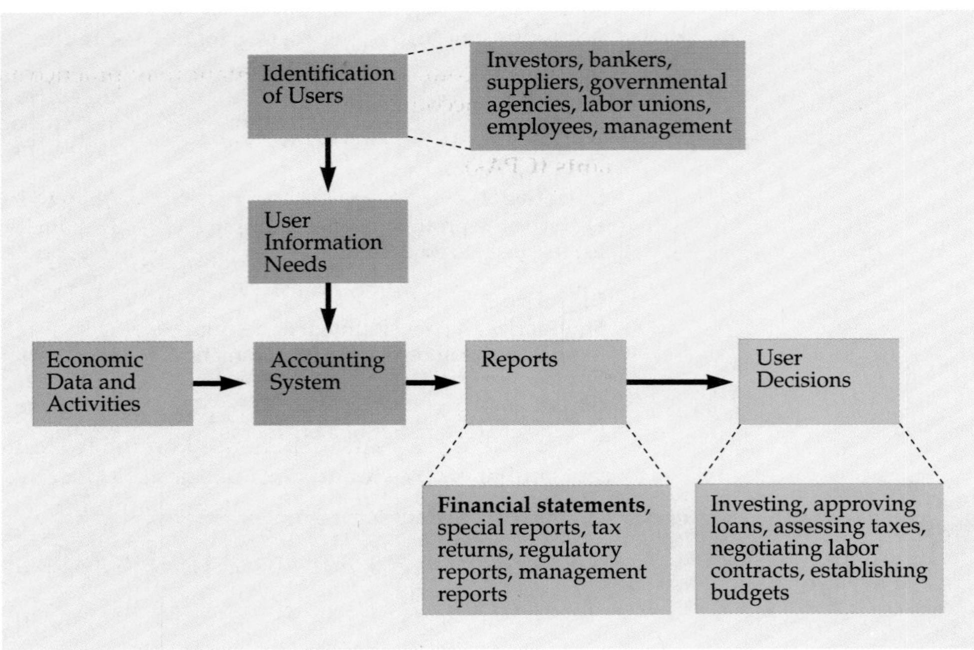

The scope of activities and duties of accountants varies widely and provides excellent training for top management positions.

Accountants are engaged in either (1) private accounting or (2) public accounting. Accountants employed by a business firm or not-for-profit organization are said to be engaged in **private accounting**. Accountants and their staff who provide services on a fee basis are said to be engaged in **public accounting**.

Experience in private and public accounting has long been recognized as excellent training for top management positions. Many positions in industry and in state and federal agencies are held by individuals with education and experience in accounting. For example, in its 1990 Special Bonus Issue on "The Corporate Elite," *Business Week* reported that 31% of the chief executives of the 1,000 largest public corporations followed a finance-accounting career path. Merchandising-marketing was the career path for 27%, and engineering-technical was the career path for 22% of the chief executives.

PRIVATE ACCOUNTING

The scope of activities and duties of private accountants varies widely. Private accountants are frequently called management accountants. If they are employed by a manufacturing concern, they may be called industrial or cost accountants. The chief accountant in a business may be called the **controller.** Various state and federal agencies and other not-for-profit agencies also employ accountants.

The Institute of Certified Management Accountants, an affiliate of the Institute of Management Accountants (IMA), sponsors the **Certified Management Accountant (CMA)** program. The CMA certificate is evidence of competence in management accounting. To become a CMA requires a college degree, two years of experience, and successful completion of a two-day examination. Continuing professional education is required for renewal of the CMA certificate.

The Institute of Internal Auditors sponsors a similar program for internal auditors. Internal auditors are accountants who review the accounting and operating procedures prescribed by their firms. Accountants who specialize in internal auditing may be granted the **Certified Internal Auditor (CIA)** certificate.

PUBLIC ACCOUNTING

In public accounting, an accountant may practice as an individual or as a member of a public accounting firm. Public accountants who have met a state's education, experience, and examination requirements may become **Certified Public Accountants (CPAs).**

The requirements for obtaining a CPA certificate differ among the various states.[3] All states require a college education in accounting, and most states now require 150 semester hours of college credit. In addition, a candidate must pass a two-day examination prepared by the American Institute of Certified Public Accountants (AICPA). How difficult is the CPA examination? Approximately 30% of the candidates pass each of the four parts of the CPA examination. Only about 10% to 20% pass the entire examination at one time.

Most states do not permit individuals to practice as CPAs until they have had from one to three years' experience in public accounting. Some states, however, accept similar employment in private accounting as equivalent experience.

All states require CPAs to obtain continuing professional education. CPAs who do not comply may lose their certificates and their right to practice. Although the details of this requirement may vary, most states require at least 40 hours of continuing education per year.

PROFESSIONAL ETHICS FOR ACCOUNTANTS

What are ethics? Ethics are moral principles that guide the conduct of individuals. In some cases, individuals may differ as to what is "right" or "wrong" in a given situation. For example, you may believe that it is unethical to copy another student's homework and hand it in as your own. Other students may feel that it is acceptable to copy homework, unless the instructor has told the class that it is prohibited. Likewise, business managers are often in situations where they may feel pressure to "bend the rules." For example, managers of Sears automotive service departments were accused of recommending unnecessary repairs and overcharging customers for actual repairs in order to meet company goals and earn bonuses. In another example, Hertz overcharged customers for repairs on damaged automobiles.

Regardless of differences among individuals, proper ethical conduct implies a behavior that considers the impact of one's actions on society and others. In other words, proper ethical conduct implies that you not only consider what's in your best interests, but also what's in the best interests of others.

Ethical conduct is good business. A survey of top managers by the accounting firm of Deloitte & Touche reports that "an enterprise actually strengthens its competitive position by maintaining high ethical standards."[4] For example, an automobile manufacturer that fails to correct a safety defect to save costs may later lose sales from the loss of consumer confidence. Likewise, the management of a business that pollutes the environment may find itself the focus of lawsuits and customer boycotts.

Why is ethical conduct so important for accountants? As we indicated earlier, individuals, businesses, governmental agencies, and others rely on accounting reports in making decisions. Therefore, it is critical that such reports be prepared accurately and with minimal bias. In some cases, accountants may be pressured by supervisors to report activities or financial results that are more favorable than warranted by the facts. Accountants must resist such pressures. For example, a company's accountant might be pressured to delay recording a loss until after a bank

[3] Information on a state's requirements is available from that state's Board of Accountancy.
[4] *Ethics in Business,* Deloitte & Touche (formerly Touche Ross), January 1988.

has approved the company's loan. Providing misleading information would be unethical and, in this case, illegal.

Accountants in both private and public practice have developed ethical standards to guide them.[5] The Institute of Management Accountants (IMA) has prepared **standards of ethical conduct** to guide management accountants in serving their employers, their profession, and the public. As stated in these standards, management accountants have a responsibility to:[6]

1. Maintain an appropriate level of professional competence.
2. Refrain from disclosing confidential information.
3. Avoid conflicts of interest.
4. Communicate information fairly and objectively.

The American Institute of Certified Public Accountants (AICPA) has also developed standards to guide its members. The purpose of these standards, called **codes of professional conduct** or **codes of professional ethics,** is to instill public confidence in the public accounting profession. The standards require CPAs to:[7]

1. Exercise sensitive professional and moral judgment.
2. Act in a way that will serve the public interest, honor the public trust, and demonstrate commitment to professionalism.
3. Perform all professional responsibilities with integrity.
4. Maintain objectivity and be free of conflicts of interest.
5. Observe the profession's technical and ethical standards and continually improve competency.
6. Determine the scope and nature of professional services according to ethical standards.

The AICPA and state societies of CPAs can revoke a CPA's membership in their organizations for violations of the code of professional conduct. A state board of accountancy, the Securities and Exchange Commission (SEC), or other regulatory agencies may revoke or limit the CPA's ability to practice. This combination of review by the AICPA, state societies of CPAs, the SEC, and other regulatory agencies encourages ethical behavior by CPAs.

Codes of professional conduct change as society changes. However, ethical conduct is more than simply conforming to written standards of professional behavior. In a true sense, ethical conduct requires a personal commitment to honorable behavior.

SPECIALIZED ACCOUNTING FIELDS

You may think that all accounting is the same. However, you will find several specialized fields of accounting in practice. The two most common are financial accounting and managerial accounting. Other fields include cost accounting, environmental accounting, tax accounting, systems, international accounting, not-for-profit accounting, and social accounting.

Financial accounting is primarily concerned with the recording and reporting of economic data and activities for an entity. Although such reports provide useful information for managers, they are the principal reports for owners, creditors, governmental agencies, and the public. Financial accountants follow **generally accepted accounting principles (GAAP)** in preparing reports for stockholders and

[5] An ethics discussion case is provided at the end of each chapter to focus attention on meaningful ethical situations that accountants often face in practice.

[6] The text of the *Standards of Ethical Conduct for Management Accountants* (Institute of Management Accountants, Montvale, New Jersey, 1992) is reproduced in Appendix B.

[7] The text of the *Code of Professional Conduct* (American Institute of Certified Public Accountants, New York, 1992) is reproduced in Appendix B.

the investing public. These rules of accounting ensure that reports for different companies can be compared. For example, the ability to compare financial reports is essential for an investor who is deciding between investing in one company or another.

Managerial accounting, often called **management accounting,** uses both financial accounting and estimated data to aid management in running day-to-day operations and in planning future operations. The focus of managerial accounting is providing managers with relevant and timely information and reports. Unlike financial accountants, management accountants are not restricted to using generally accepted accounting principles. Instead, management accountants use the basic principle of gathering and reporting information that is useful to management. Thus, managerial reports can differ widely in form and content.

Management accountants are often concerned with identifying alternative courses of action and preparing reports evaluating the impact of each alternative. For example, the president of a company might request an analysis of alternative plans for financing the construction of a new office building.

Generally Accepted Accounting Principles

Objective 3
Summarize the development of accounting principles and relate them to practice.

What are generally accepted accounting principles (GAAP)? They are principles and concepts that are used by accountants in preparing financial reports. GAAP are necessary so that users of these reports can compare the financial condition and operating results across companies. If the management of a company could record and report transactions as they saw fit, then comparability between companies would be difficult, if not impossible.

Accounting principles and concepts develop from research, accepted accounting practices, and pronouncements of authoritative bodies. Currently, the **Financial Accounting Standards Board (FASB)** has the primary responsibility for developing accounting principles. The FASB and its staff research issues in financial accounting. Generally, after publishing discussion memoranda and preliminary proposals and evaluating comments from interested parties, the FASB publishes *Statements of Financial Accounting Standards*. These Standards become part of generally accepted accounting principles. To explain, clarify, or elaborate on existing Standards, the FASB also publishes *Interpretations,* which have the same authority as the Standards. Since its inception in 1973, the FASB has published over 100 Statements and Interpretations.[8]

Because generally accepted accounting principles impact how and what companies report to external users, managers and others are interested in the establishment of these principles. For example, the FASB recently proposed a Standard on how to account for options granted employees and managers to purchase shares of ownership in the company. The proposal is being opposed because it would impact negatively the financial results of many companies. Managers and others, including the United States Senate, have urged the FASB to amend or drop the proposed Standard.[9]

In this chapter and throughout this text, we emphasize accounting principles and concepts. It is through this emphasis on the "why" of accounting as well as the "how" that you will gain an understanding of the full significance of accounting. In the following paragraphs, we discuss the business entity concept and the cost principle.

[8] The FASB is also developing a broad conceptual framework for financial accounting. This framework is expected to take many years to complete. Six *Statements of Financial Accounting Concepts* have been published to date.

[9] Glenn Alan Cheney, "Senate Rips FASB on Stock Options," *Accounting Today,* May 23, 1994.

USING ACCOUNTING TO UNDERSTAND BUSINESS

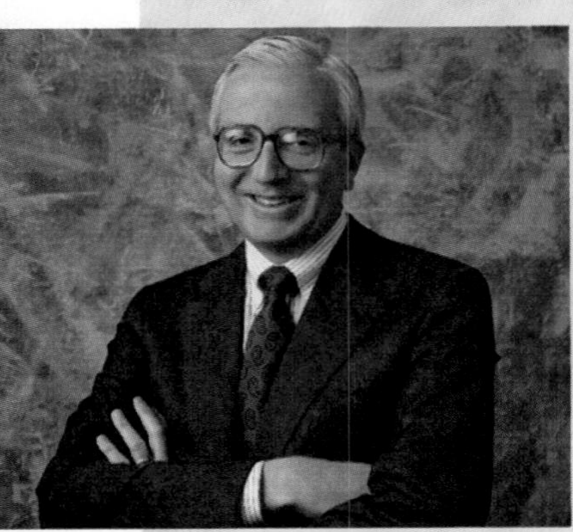

In an editorial in *The Wall Street Journal,* Dennis R. Beresford, Chairman of the Financial Accounting Standards Board, discussed the role of generally accepted accounting principles. He asserted that the primary role of accounting principles should be to truthfully portray the economic consequences of events on the financial statements of a business enterprise. In doing so, Mr. Beresford asserted, ". . . the truth will set investors free." Mr. Beresford goes on to state that ". . . Truth in accounting means telling it like it is, without bias or intent to encourage any particular mode of behavior by the user of the information."

Source: "In Accounting, Truth Above All," Letters to the Editor, *The Wall Street Journal,* March 21, 1994.

BUSINESS ENTITY CONCEPT

The **business entity concept** is based on identifying the individual economic units for which economic data are needed. Once the entity is identified, the accountant can determine which economic data and activities should be analyzed, recorded, and summarized in reports. The business entity could be an individual, a not-for-profit organization such as a church, or a profit enterprise such as a real estate agency.

This textbook focuses on accounting concepts and principles for profit-making businesses. Such businesses are normally organized as sole proprietorships, partnerships, or corporations. A **sole proprietorship** is owned by one individual. A **partnership** is owned by two or more individuals. A **corporation** is organized under state or federal statutes as a separate legal entity. The ownership of a corporation is divided into shares of stock. The sole proprietorship is the most common business form. However, corporations receive over 90% of the total dollars of business receipts. These facts are shown in Exhibit 2.

Exhibit 2
Profit-Making Businesses

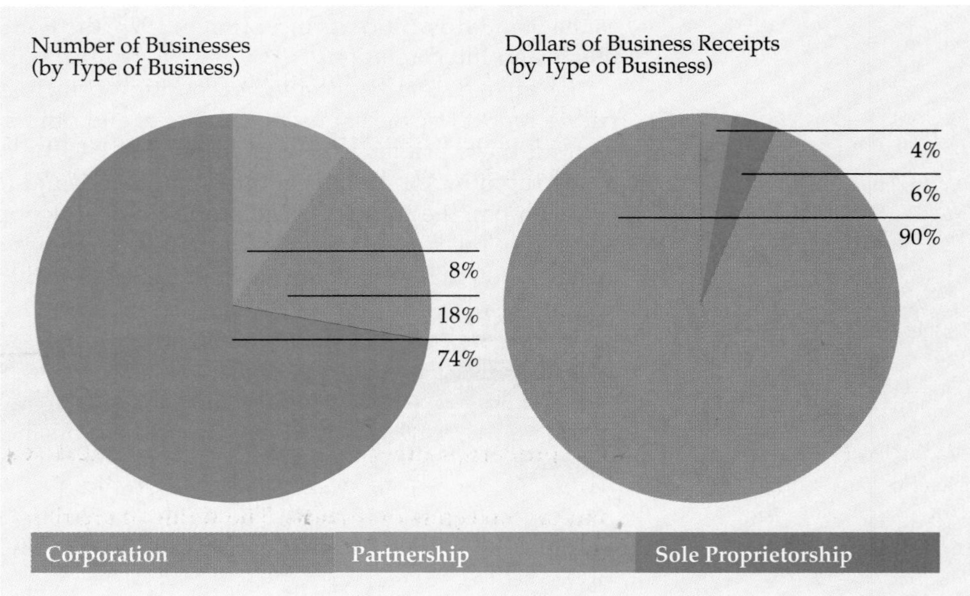

Source: U.S. Bureau of the Census, *Statistical Abstract of the United States,* 114th edition, Washington, DC, 1994.

THE COST PRINCIPLE

The cost of an automobile is the amount agreed on between the buyer and the dealer.

The **cost principle** determines the amount entered into the accounting records for purchases of properties and services. For example, if a building is bought for $150,000, that amount should be entered into the buyer's accounting records. The seller may have been asking $170,000 for the building up to the time of the sale. The buyer may have initially offered $130,000 for the building. The building may have been assessed at $125,000 for property tax purposes. The buyer may have received an offer of $175,000 for the building the day after it was acquired. These latter amounts have no effect on the accounting records because they did not result in an exchange of the building from the seller to the buyer. *The exchange price, or cost, of $150,000 is the amount used in the accounting records for the building.*

Continuing the illustration, the $175,000 offer received by the buyer the day after the building was acquired indicates that it was a bargain purchase at $150,000. To use $175,000 in the accounting records, however, would record an illusory or unrealized profit. If, after buying the building, the buyer accepts the offer and sells the building for $175,000, a profit of $25,000 is then realized and recorded. The new owner would record $175,000 as the cost of the building.

In exchanges between buyer and seller, both try to get the best price. Only the final amount agreed on is objective enough for accounting purposes. If the amounts for which properties were recorded were constantly revised upward and downward based on offers, appraisals, and opinions, accounting reports would soon become unstable and unreliable.

Business Transactions

Objective 4
List the characteristics of a business transaction.

Are all economic events affecting a business entity recorded in an accounting system? No, for example, a change in a business's credit rating by an agency such as **Dun and Bradstreet** is not recorded in the accounting records. Only business transactions are recorded in the accounting records.

A **business transaction** is an economic event or condition that directly changes the entity's financial position or directly affects its results of operations. For example, the payment of a monthly telephone bill of $68 affects the entity's financial position because the entity now has less cash on hand. Likewise, the purchase of land for $50,000 is a business transaction that should be recorded. In contrast, the change in an entity's credit rating does not directly affect cash or any other element of the entity's financial position.

A business transaction may lead to an event or a condition that results in another transaction. For example, the purchase of $1,750 of merchandise on credit will be followed by the payment to the creditor. Each time a portion of the merchandise is sold, another transaction occurs. Each of these events must be recorded.

Assets, Liabilities, and Owner's Equity

Objective 5
State the accounting equation and define each element of the equation.

The properties owned by a business are called **assets**. The rights or claims to the properties are normally divided into two principal types: (1) the rights of creditors and (2) the rights of owners. The rights of creditors represent debts of the business and are called **liabilities**. The rights of the owners are called **owner's equity**. The relationship between the two may be stated in the form of an equation, as follows:

Assets = Liabilities + Owner's Equity

The preceding equation is known as the accounting equation. It is usual to place liabilities before owner's equity in the accounting equation because creditors have first rights to the assets. The claim of the owners is sometimes given greater emphasis by transposing liabilities to the other side of the equation, yielding:

Assets – Liabilities = Owner's Equity

To illustrate, if the assets owned by a business amount to $100,000 and the liabilities amount to $30,000, the owner's equity is equal to $70,000, as shown below:

Assets – Liabilities = Owner's Equity
$100,000 – $30,000 = $70,000

Transactions and the Accounting Equation

Objective 6
Explain how business transactions can be stated in terms of the resulting changes in the three basic elements of the accounting equation.

COMPUTER KING

All business transactions can be stated in terms of changes in the three elements of the accounting equation. You will see how business transactions affect the accounting equation by studying some typical transactions. For example, assume that on November 1, 1996, Pat King begins a sole proprietorship to be known as Computer King. Using Pat's knowledge of microcomputers, the business will offer computer consulting services for a fee. Each transaction or group of similar transactions during the first month of operations is described as follows. The effects of the transaction on the accounting equation are then shown.

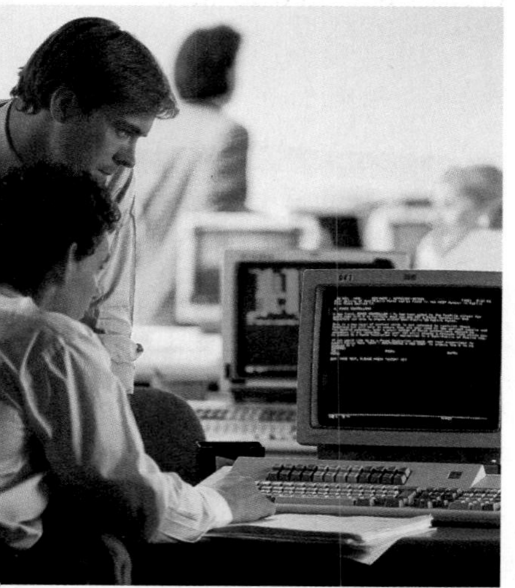

Computer King offers computer consulting services for a fee. Each transaction will affect Computer King's accounting equation.

Transaction a. Pat King deposits $15,000 in a bank account in the name of Computer King. The effect of this transaction is to increase the asset (cash), on the left side of the equation, by $15,000. To balance the equation, the owner's equity, on the right side of the equation, is increased by the same amount. The equity of the owner is referred to by using the owner's name and "Capital," such as "Pat King, Capital." The effect of this transaction on Computer King's accounting equation is shown below.

	Assets		*Owner's Equity*	
	Cash	=	Pat King, Capital	
a.	15,000		15,000	Investment by Pat King

Note that the equation relates only to the business, Computer King. Pat King's personal assets, such as a home or personal bank account, and personal liabilities are excluded from the equation. The business is treated as a separate entity, with cash of $15,000 and owner's equity of $15,000.

Transaction b. Computer King's next transaction is to buy land for $10,000 cash. The land is located near a shopping mall that contains three microcomputer stores. Pat King plans to rent office space and equipment for several months. If the business is a success, the company will build on the land.

The purchase of the land changes the makeup of the assets but does not change the total assets. The items in the equation prior to this transaction and the effect of the transaction are shown next. The new amounts or *balances* of the items are also shown.

	Assets				*Owner's Equity*
	Cash	+	Land	=	Pat King, Capital
	15,000				15,000
b.	–10,000		+10,000		
Bal.	5,000		10,000		15,000

Transaction c. During the month, Computer King buys supplies for $1,350, agreeing to pay the supplier in the near future. This type of transaction is called a purchase *on account.* The liability created is termed an **account payable.** Items such as supplies that will be used in the business in the future are called **prepaid expenses,** which are assets.

In practice, each purchase is normally recorded separately. However, to simplify this illustration, all the purchases of supplies are recorded together. The effect is to increase assets and liabilities by $1,350, as follows:

	Assets					=	*Liabilities*	+	*Owner's Equity*
	Cash	+	Supplies	+	Land	=	Accounts Payable	+	Pat King, Capital
Bal.	5,000				10,000				15,000
c.			+1,350				+1,350		
Bal.	5,000		1,350		10,000		1,350		15,000

Transaction d. The amount charged to customers for goods or services sold to them is called **revenue.** Special terms may be used for certain kinds of revenue, such as *sales* for the sale of merchandise. Revenue from providing services is called *fees earned.* For example, a physician would record fees earned for services to patients. Other examples of revenue terms include *rent earned* for the use of real estate or other property and *interest earned* for a bank.

The amount of revenue earned during a period is measured by the amount of assets received from customers for the goods sold or services rendered to them. Earning revenue through business operations increases owner's equity. Thus, revenue increases assets and increases owner's equity.

During its first month of operations, Computer King earns fees of $7,500, receiving the amount in cash. These transactions increase cash and the owner's equity by $7,500, as shown here.

	Assets					=	*Liabilities*	+	*Owner's Equity*	
	Cash	+	Supplies	+	Land	=	Accounts Payable	+	Pat King, Capital	
Bal.	5,000		1,350		10,000		1,350		15,000	
d.	+7,500								+7,500	Fees earned
Bal.	12,500		1,350		10,000		1,350		22,500	

Instead of requiring the payment of cash at the time services are provided or goods are sold, a business may accept payment at a later date. Such revenues are called **fees on account** or **sales on account.** In such cases, the firm has an **account receivable,** which is a claim against the customer. An account receivable is an asset, and the revenue is earned as if cash had been received. When customers pay their accounts, there is an exchange of one asset for another. Cash increases and accounts receivable decreases.

Transaction e. The amount of assets or services used in the process of earning revenue is called **expense.** Expenses include supplies used, wages of employees, and other assets and services used in operating the business. As you might have guessed, the effect of expenses on owner's equity is the opposite of the effect of revenues. Expenses decrease owner's equity.

For Computer King, the expenses paid during the month were as follows: wages, $2,125; rent, $800; utilities, $450; and miscellaneous, $275. Miscellaneous expenses include small amounts paid for such items as postage due, coffee, and newspaper and magazine purchases. This group of transactions reduces cash and owner's equity, as shown.

	Assets					=	*Liabilities*	+	*Owner's Equity*	
	Cash	+	Supplies	+	Land	=	Accounts Payable	+	Pat King, Capital	
Bal.	12,500		1,350		10,000		1,350		22,500	
e.	−3,650								−2,125	Wages expense
									− 800	Rent expense
									− 450	Utilities expense
									− 275	Misc. expense
Bal.	8,850		1,350		10,000		1,350		18,850	

Transaction f. During the month, Computer King pays $950 to creditors on account, thereby reducing both assets and liabilities. The effect on the equation is as follows:

	Assets					=	*Liabilities*	+	*Owner's Equity*
	Cash	+	Supplies	+	Land	=	Accounts Payable	+	Pat King, Capital
Bal.	8,850		1,350		10,000		1,350		18,850
f.	−950						−950		
Bal.	7,900		1,350		10,000		400		18,850

You should note that paying an amount on account is different from paying an amount for an expense. The payment of an expense reduces owner's equity, as illustrated in transaction (e). Paying an amount on account reduces the amount owed on a liability.

Transaction g. At the end of the month, the cost of the supplies on hand is $550. The remainder of the supplies ($1,350 – $550) was used in the operations of the business and is treated as an expense. This decrease of $800 in supplies and owner's equity is shown as follows:

	Assets					=	*Liabilities*	+	*Owner's Equity*	
	Cash	+	Supplies	+	Land	=	Accounts Payable	+	Pat King, Capital	
Bal.	7,900		1,350		10,000		400		18,850	
g.			− 800						− 800	Supplies expense
Bal.	7,900		550		10,000		400		18,050	

Transaction h. At the end of the month, Pat King withdraws $2,000 in cash from the business for personal use. This transaction is the exact opposite of an investment in the business by the owner. Cash and owner's equity are decreased. The cash payment is not a business expense but a withdrawal of a part of the owner's equity. The effect of the $2,000 withdrawal is shown as follows:

	Assets					=	*Liabilities*	+	*Owner's Equity*	
	Cash	+	Supplies	+	Land	=	Accounts Payable	+	Pat King, Capital	
Bal.	7,900		550		10,000		400		18,050	
h.	−2,000								−2,000	Withdrawal
Bal.	5,900		550		10,000		400		16,050	

You should be careful not to confuse withdrawals by the owner with expenses. Withdrawals do not represent assets consumed or services used in the process of earning revenues. The owner's equity decrease from the withdrawals is listed in the equation under Capital. This is because withdrawals are considered a distribution of capital to the owner.

Summary. The transactions of Computer King are summarized as follows. The transactions are identified by letter, and the balance of each item is shown after each transaction.

	Assets					=	*Liabilities*	+	*Owner's Equity*	
	Cash	+	Supplies	+	Land	=	Accounts Payable	+	Pat King, Capital	
a.	+15,000								+15,000	Investment by Pat King
b.	−10,000				+10,000					
Bal.	5,000				10,000				15,000	
c.			+1,350				+1,350			
Bal.	5,000		1,350		10,000		1,350		15,000	
d.	+ 7,500								+ 7,500	Fees earned
Bal.	12,500		1,350		10,000		1,350		22,500	
e.	− 3,650								− 2,125	Wages expense
									− 800	Rent expense
									− 450	Utilities expense
									− 275	Misc. expense
Bal.	8,850		1,350		10,000		1,350		18,850	
f.	− 950						− 950			
Bal.	7,900		1,350		10,000		400		18,850	
g.			− 800						− 800	Supplies expense
Bal.	7,900		550		10,000		400		18,050	
h.	− 2,000								− 2,000	Withdrawal
Bal.	5,900		550		10,000		400		16,050	

In reviewing the preceding illustration, you should note the following, which apply to all types of businesses:

1. The effect of every transaction is an increase or a decrease in one or more of the accounting equation elements.
2. The two sides of the accounting equation are always equal.
3. The owner's equity is increased by amounts invested by the owner and is decreased by withdrawals by the owner. In addition, the owner's equity is increased by revenues and is decreased by expenses. The effects of these four types of transactions on owner's equity are illustrated in Exhibit 3.

Exhibit 3
Effects of Transactions on Owner's Equity

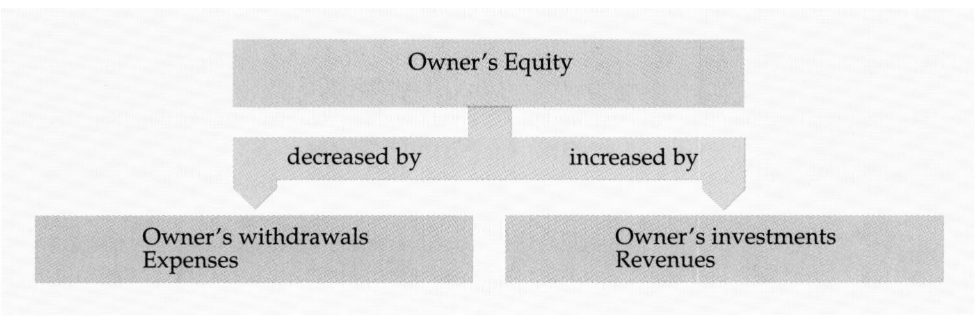

Financial Statements

Objective 7
Describe the financial statements of a sole proprietorship and explain how they interrelate.

After transactions have been recorded and summarized, reports are prepared for users. The accounting reports that provide this information are called **financial statements.** The principal financial statements of a sole proprietorship are the income statement, the statement of owner's equity, the balance sheet, and the statement of cash flows. The nature of the entity's data presented in each statement is as follows:

- Income statement—A summary of the revenue and expenses *for a specific period of time,* such as a month or a year.
- Statement of owner's equity—A summary of the changes in the owner's equity that have occurred *during a specific period of time,* such as a month or a year.
- Balance sheet—A list of the assets, liabilities, and owner's equity *as of a specific date,* usually at the close of the last day of a month or a year.
- Statement of cash flows—A summary of the cash receipts and cash payments *for a specific period of time,* such as a month or a year.

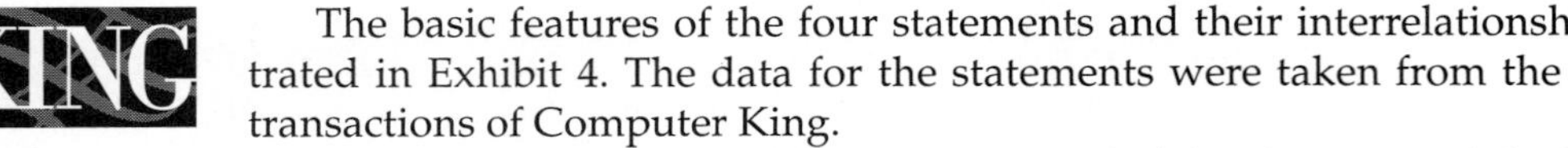

The basic features of the four statements and their interrelationships are illustrated in Exhibit 4. The data for the statements were taken from the summary of transactions of Computer King.

All financial statements should be identified by the name of the business, the title of the statement, and the *date* or *period of time.* The data presented in the income statement, the statement of owner's equity, and the statement of cash flows are for a period of time. The data presented in the balance sheet are for a specific date.

You should note the use of indentions, captions, dollar signs, and rulings in the financial statements. They aid the reader by emphasizing the sections of the statements.

INCOME STATEMENT

The excess of the revenue over the expenses incurred in earning the revenue is called net income or **net profit.** If the expenses of the business exceed the revenue, the excess is a net loss. It is impractical to determine the exact amount of expense for each revenue transaction. Therefore, the net income or the net loss is reported for a period of time, such as a month or a year, rather than for each revenue transaction.

The net income (or net loss) is determined using a matching process involving two steps. First, revenue is recorded during the period. Second, expenses used in generating the revenue are matched against the revenue to determine the net income or the net loss. Generally, the revenue for providing a service is recorded after the service has been provided to the customer. The expenses incurred in generating revenue during a period are then recorded and are thus matched against the revenue.

The effects of revenue earned and expenses incurred during the month for Computer King were shown in the equation as increases and decreases in owner's equity (capital). Net income for a period has the effect of increasing owner's equity (capital) for the period, whereas a net loss has the effect of decreasing owner's equity (capital) for the period.

The revenue, expenses, and net income of $3,050 for Computer King are reported in the income statement in Exhibit 4. The order in which the expenses are listed in the income statement varies among businesses. One method is to list them in order of size, beginning with the larger items. Miscellaneous expense is usually shown as the last item, regardless of the amount.

Exhibit 4
Financial Statements

Computer King
Income Statement
For the Month Ended November 30, 1996

Fees earned		$7 5 0 0 00
Operating expenses:		
Wages expense	$2 1 2 5 00	
Rent expense	8 0 0 00	
Supplies expense	8 0 0 00	
Utilities expense	4 5 0 00	
Miscellaneous expense	2 7 5 00	
Total operating expenses		4 4 5 0 00
Net income		$3 0 5 0 00

Computer King
Statement of Owner's Equity
For the Month Ended November 30, 1996

Pat King, capital, November 1, 1996		$ 0
Investment on November 1, 1996	$15 0 0 0 00	
Net income for November	3 0 5 0 00	
	$18 0 5 0 00	
Less withdrawals	2 0 0 0 00	
Increase in owner's equity		16 0 5 0 00
Pat King, capital, November 30, 1996		$16 0 5 0 00

Computer King
Balance Sheet
November 30, 1996

Assets		**Liabilities**	
Cash	$ 5 9 0 0 00	Accounts payable	$ 4 0 0 00
Supplies	5 5 0 00	**Owner's Equity**	
Land	10 0 0 0 00	Pat King, capital	16 0 5 0 00
		Total liabilities and	
Total assets	$16 4 5 0 00	owner's equity	$16 4 5 0 00

Computer King
Statement of Cash Flows
For the Month Ended November 30, 1996

Cash flows from operating activities:		
Cash received from customers	$ 7 5 0 0 00	
Deduct cash payments for expenses and payments to creditors	4 6 0 0 00	
Net cash flow from operating activities		$ 2 9 0 0 00
Cash flows from investing activities:		
Cash payments for acquisition of land		(10 0 0 0 00)
Cash flows from financing activities:		
Cash received as owner's investment	$15 0 0 0 00	
Deduct cash withdrawal by owner	2 0 0 0 00	
Net cash flow from financing activities		13 0 0 0 00
Net cash flow and Nov. 30, 1996 cash balance		$ 5 9 0 0 00

USING ACCOUNTING TO UNDERSTAND BUSINESS

Financial statements such as those illustrated in Exhibit 4 are used to evaluate the current financial position of a business and to predict its future operating results and cash flows. For example, bank loan officers use an entity's financial statements in deciding whether to grant a loan to the entity. Once the loan is granted, the borrower may be required to maintain a level of assets in excess of liabilities. The entity's financial statements will be used to monitor this condition.

STATEMENT OF OWNER'S EQUITY

Changes in the owner's equity of a sole proprietorship for a period are reported in the statement of owner's equity. This statement links the balance sheet and the income statement.

Three types of transactions affected owner's equity for Computer King during November: (1) the original investment of $15,000, (2) the revenue and expenses that resulted in net income of $3,050 for the month, and (3) a withdrawal of $2,000 by the owner. This information is summarized in the statement of owner's equity for Computer King in Exhibit 4.

BALANCE SHEET

The amounts of Computer King's assets, liabilities, and owner's equity at the end of November are taken from the last line of the summary of transactions presented earlier. With the addition of a heading, the balance sheet is prepared as shown in Exhibit 4. This form of balance sheet, called the **account form,** resembles the basic format of the accounting equation, with assets on the left side and the liabilities and owner's equity sections on the right side. An alternative form of balance sheet, called the **report form,** presents the liabilities and owner's equity sections below the assets section. We illustrate this form of balance sheet in a later chapter.

The assets section of the balance sheet normally presents assets in the order that they will be converted into cash or used in operations. Cash is presented first, followed by receivables, supplies, prepaid insurance, and other assets. Then, the assets of a more permanent nature are shown, such as land, buildings, and equipment.

In the liabilities section of the balance sheet in Exhibit 4, accounts payable is the only liability. When there are two or more categories of liabilities, each should be listed and the total amount of liabilities presented as shown below.

Liabilities		
Accounts payable	$12,900	
Wages payable	2,570	
Total liabilities		$15,470

STATEMENT OF CASH FLOWS

The statement of cash flows in Exhibit 4 consists of three sections: (1) operating activities, (2) investing activities, and (3) financing activities. Each of these sections is briefly described below.

CASH FLOWS FROM OPERATING ACTIVITIES. This section reports a summary of cash receipts and cash payments from operations. The net cash flow from operating activities will normally differ from the amount of net income for the period. This difference occurs because revenues and expenses may not be recorded at the same time that cash is received from customers and cash is paid to creditors.

CASH FLOWS FROM INVESTING ACTIVITIES. This section reports the cash transactions for the acquisition and sale of relatively long-term or permanent-type assets.

CASH FLOWS FROM FINANCING ACTIVITIES. This section reports the cash transactions related to cash investments by the owner, borrowings, and cash withdrawals by the owner.

Preparing the statement of cash flows requires an understanding of concepts that we have not discussed in this chapter. Therefore, we will illustrate the preparation of the statement of cash flows in a later chapter.

KEY POINTS

Objective 1. Define accounting as an information system.
The goal of accounting is to record, report, and interpret economic data for use by decision makers. Accounting is often called the language of business. Accounting can be viewed as an information system that provides essential information about the economic activities of an entity to various individuals or groups.

Accounting provides the framework for gathering economic data and reporting these data to various users. Examples of users of accounting information include investors, bankers, creditors, government agencies, employees, and managers of the entity.

Objective 2. Describe the profession of accounting and list its specialized fields.
Accountants are engaged in either (1) private accounting or (2) public accounting. Accountants in both private and public accounting must adhere to codes of professional ethics.

Specialized fields in accounting have evolved as a result of technological advances and economic growth. The most common accounting fields are financial accounting and managerial accounting.

Objective 3. Summarize the development of accounting principles and relate them to practice.
Generally accepted accounting principles have evolved to form a basis for accounting practice. The Financial Accounting Standards Board issues authoritative pronouncements on accounting principles.

The business entity concept is based on applying accounting to individual economic units in society. Profit-making businesses are normally organized as sole proprietorships, partnerships, or corporations.

The cost principle requires that properties and services bought by a business be recorded in terms of actual cost.

Objective 4. List the characteristics of a business transaction.
A business transaction is an economic event or a condition that must be recorded by an entity. Some business transactions cause future events or conditions that must also be recorded as transactions.

Objective 5. State the accounting equation and define each element of the equation.
The properties owned by a business and the rights or claims to properties may be stated in the form of an equation, as follows:

Assets = Liabilities + Owner's Equity.

Objective 6. Explain how business transactions can be stated in terms of the resulting changes in the three basic elements of the accounting equation.
All transactions can be stated in terms of the change in one or more of the three elements of the accounting equation. That is, the effect of every transaction can be stated in terms of increases or decreases in one or more of these elements, while maintaining the equality between the two sides of the equation.

Objective 7. Describe the financial statements of a sole proprietorship and explain how they interrelate.

The principal financial statements of a sole proprietorship are the income statement, the statement of owner's equity, the balance sheet, and the statement of cash flows. The income statement reports a net income or net loss for the period, which also appears on the statement of owner's equity. The ending owner's capital reported on the statement of owner's equity is also reported on the balance sheet. The ending cash balance is reported on the balance sheet and the statement of cash flows.

GLOSSARY OF KEY TERMS

Account form. The form of balance sheet with the assets section presented on the left-hand side and the liabilities and owner's equity sections presented on the right-hand side. *Objective 7*

Account payable. A liability created by a purchase made on credit. *Objective 6*

Account receivable. A claim against a customer for services rendered or goods sold on credit. *Objective 6*

Accounting. The process of identifying, measuring, and communicating economic information to permit informed judgments and decisions by users of the information. *Objective 1*

Accounting equation. The expression of the relationship between assets, liabilities, and owner's equity; it is most commonly stated as Assets = Liabilities + Owner's Equity. *Objective 5*

Assets. Properties owned by a business. *Objective 5*

Balance sheet. A financial statement listing the assets, liabilities, and owner's equity of a business entity as of a specific date. *Objective 7*

Business entity concept. The concept that accounting applies to individual economic units and that each unit is separate from the persons who supply its assets. *Objective 3*

Business transaction. The occurrence of an economic event or a condition that must be recorded in the accounting records. *Objective 4*

Corporation. A separate legal entity that is organized in accordance with state or federal statutes and in which ownership is divided into shares of stock. *Objective 3*

Cost principle. The principle that the monetary record for properties and services purchased by a business should be maintained in terms of actual cost. *Objective 3*

Expense. The amount of assets or services used in the process of earning revenue. *Objective 6*

Financial Accounting Standards Board (FASB). An authoritative body for the development of accounting principles. *Objective 3*

Generally accepted accounting principles (GAAP). Generally accepted guidelines for the preparation of financial statements. *Objective 2*

Income statement. A summary of the revenues and expenses of a business entity for a specific period of time. *Objective 7*

Liabilities. Debts of a business. *Objective 5*

Matching. The concept that expenses incurred in generating revenue should be matched against the revenue in determining the net income or net loss for the period. *Objective 7*

Net income. The final figure in the income statement when revenues exceed expenses. *Objective 7*

Net loss. The final figure in the income statement when expenses exceed revenues. *Objective 7*

Owner's equity. The rights of the owners in a business. *Objective 5*

Partnership. An unincorporated business owned by two or more individuals. *Objective 3*

Prepaid expenses. Purchased commodities or services that have not been used up at the end of an accounting period. *Objective 6*

Private accounting. The profession whose members are accountants employed by a business firm or not-for-profit organization. *Objective 2*

Public accounting. The profession whose members render accounting services on a fee basis. *Objective 2*

Report form. The form of balance sheet with the liabilities and owner's equity sections presented below the assets section. *Objective 7*

Revenue. The gross increase in owner's equity as a result of business and professional activities that earn income. *Objective 6*

Sole proprietorship. An unincorporated business owned by one individual. *Objective 3*

Statement of cash flows. A summary of the major cash receipts and cash payments for a period. *Objective 7*

Statement of owner's equity. A summary of the changes in the owner's equity of a business that have occurred during a specific period of time. *Objective 7*

ILLUSTRATIVE PROBLEM

On July 1 of the current year, the assets and liabilities of Cecil Jameson, Attorney-at-Law, are as follows: cash, $1,000; accounts receivable, $3,200; supplies, $850; land, $10,000; accounts payable, $1,530. Cecil Jameson, Attorney-at-Law, is a sole proprietorship owned and operated by Cecil Jameson. Currently, office space and office equipment are being rented, pending the construction of an office complex on land purchased last year. Business transactions during July are summarized as follows:

a. Received cash from clients for services, $3,928.
b. Paid creditors on account, $1,055.
c. Received cash from Cecil Jameson as an additional investment, $3,700.
d. Paid office rent for the month, $1,200.
e. Charged clients for legal services on account, $2,025.
f. Purchased office supplies on account, $245.
g. Received cash from clients on account, $3,000.
h. Received invoice for paralegal services from Legal Aid Inc. for July (to be paid on August 10), $1,635.
i. Paid the following: wages expense, $850; answering service expense, $250; utilities expense, $325; and miscellaneous expense, $75.
j. Determined that the cost of office supplies on hand was $980; therefore, the cost of supplies used during the month was $115.
k. Jameson withdrew $1,000 in cash from the business for personal use.

Instructions

1. Determine the amount of owner's equity (Cecil Jameson's capital) as of July 1 of the current year.
2. State the assets, liabilities, and owner's equity as of July 1 in equation form similar to that shown in this chapter. In tabular form below the equation, indicate the increases and decreases resulting from each transaction and the new balances after each transaction. Explain the nature of each increase and decrease in owner's equity by an appropriate notation at the right of the amount.
3. Prepare an income statement for July, a statement of owner's equity for July, and a balance sheet as of July 31.

Solution

1. **Assets – Liabilities = Owner's Equity (Cecil Jameson, capital)**
$15,050 – $1,530 = Owner's Equity (Cecil Jameson, capital)
$13,520 = Owner's Equity (Cecil Jameson, capital)

2.

	Assets				=	*Liabilities*	+	*Owner's Equity*	
	Cash	+ Accounts Receivable	+ Supplies	+ Land	=	Accounts Payable	+	Cecil Jameson, Capital	
Bal.	1,000	3,200	850	10,000		1,530		13,520	
a.	+3,928							+ 3,928	Fees earned
Bal.	4,928	3,200	850	10,000		1,530		17,448	
b	–1,055					–1,055			
Bal.	3,873	3,200	850	10,000		475		17,448	
c.	+3,700							+ 3,700	Investment
Bal.	7,573	3,200	850	10,000		475		21,148	
d.	–1,200							– 1,200	Rent expense
Bal.	6,373	3,200	850	10,000		475		19,948	
e.		+2,025						+ 2,025	Fees earned
Bal.	6,373	5,225	850	10,000		475		21,973	
f.			+ 245			+ 245			
Bal.	6,373	5,225	1,095	10,000		720		21,973	
g.	+3,000	–3,000							
Bal.	9,373	2,225	1,095	10,000		720		21,973	
h.						+1,635		– 1,635	Paralegal exp.
Bal.	9,373	2,225	1,095	10,000		2,355		20,338	
i.	–1,500							– 850	Wages exp.
								– 250	Answ. svc. exp.
								– 325	Utilities exp.
								– 75	Misc. exp.
Bal.	7,873	2,225	1,095	10,000		2,355		18,838	
j.			– 115					– 115	Supplies exp.
Bal.	7,873	2,225	980	10,000		2,355		18,723	
k.	–1,000							– 1,000	Withdrawal
	6,873	2,225	980	10,000		2,355		17,723	

3.

Cecil Jameson, Attorney-at-Law
Income Statement
For the Month Ended July 31, 19—

Fees earned		$5,953.00
Operating expenses:		
Paralegal expense	$1,635.00	
Rent expense	1,200.00	
Wages expense	850.00	
Utilities expense	325.00	
Answering service expense	250.00	
Supplies expense	115.00	
Miscellaneous expense	75.00	
Total operating expenses		4,450.00
Net income		$1,503.00

Cecil Jameson, Attorney-at-Law
Statement of Owner's Equity
For the Month Ended July 31, 19—

Cecil Jameson, capital, July 1, 19—		$13,520.00
Additional investment by owner	$3,700.00	
Net income for the month	1,503.00	
	$5,203.00	
Less withdrawals	1,000.00	
Increase in owner's equity		4,203.00
Cecil Jameson, capital, July 31, 19—		$17,723.00

Cecil Jameson, Attorney-at-Law
Balance Sheet
July 31, 19—

Assets		Liabilities	
Cash	$ 6,873.00	Accounts payable	$ 2,355.00
Accounts receivable	2,225.00	**Owner's Equity**	
Supplies	980.00	Cecil Jameson, capital	17,723.00
Land	10,000.00	Total liabilities and	
Total assets	$20,078.00	owner's equity	$20,078.00

SELF-EXAMINATION QUESTIONS (ANSWERS AT END OF CHAPTER)

1. A profit-making business that is a separate legal entity and in which ownership is divided into shares of stock is known as a:
   A. sole proprietorship
   B. single proprietorship
   C. partnership
   D. corporation

2. The properties owned by a business are called:
   A. assets
   B. liabilities
   C. the accounting equation
   D. owner's equity

3. A list of assets, liabilities, and owner's equity of a business entity as of a specific date is:
   A. a balance sheet
   B. an income statement
   C. a statement of owner's equity
   D. a statement of cash flows

4. If total assets increased $20,000 during a period of time and total liabilities increased $12,000 during the same period, the amount and direction (increase or decrease) of the period's change in owner's equity is:
   A. $32,000 increase
   B. $32,000 decrease
   C. $8,000 increase
   D. $8,000 decrease

5. If revenue was $45,000, expenses were $37,500, and the owner's withdrawals were $10,000, the amount of net income or net loss would be:
   A. $45,000 net income
   B. $7,500 net income
   C. $37,500 net loss
   D. $2,500 net loss

DISCUSSION QUESTIONS

1. Name some of the categories of individuals and institutions who use accounting information.

2. Distinguish between private accounting and public accounting.
3. Describe in general terms the requirements that an individual must meet for (a) the CMA certificate and (b) the CPA certificate.
4. What are ethics?
5. Name the two most common specialized fields in accounting.
6. Identify each of the following abbreviations:
   a. AICPA
   b. CIA
   c. CMA
   d. CPA
   e. GAAP
7. Identify what the abbreviation FASB stands for and describe how the FASB sets generally accepted accounting principles.
8. a. Name the three principal forms of profit-making business organizations.
   b. Which of these forms is identified with the greatest number of businesses?
   c. Which of these forms is the dominant form in terms of dollars of business activity?
9. What is meant by the cost principle?
10. On February 8, Allen Delivery Service extended an offer of $90,000 for land that had been priced for sale at $100,000. On February 20, Allen Delivery Service accepted the seller's counteroffer of $95,000. Describe how Allen Delivery Service should record the land.
11. a. Land with an assessed value of $60,000 for property tax purposes is acquired by a business for $75,000. Ten years later, the plot of land has an assessed value of $110,000 and the business receives an offer of $150,000 for it. Should the monetary amount assigned to the land in the business records now be increased?
    b. Assuming that the land acquired in (a) was sold for $175,000, how would the various elements of the accounting equation be affected?
12. What are the two principal rights to the properties of a business?
13. Name the three elements of the accounting equation.
14. Describe the difference between an account receivable and an account payable.
15. A business had revenues of $112,000 and operating expenses of $120,000. Did the business (a) incur a net loss or (b) realize a net income?
16. A business had revenues of $202,500 and operating expenses of $170,000. Did the business (a) incur a net loss or (b) realize a net income?
17. Name the two types of transactions that increase the owner's equity of a sole proprietorship.
18. List a sole proprietorship's four major financial statements illustrated in this chapter, and briefly describe the nature of the information provided by each.
19. Indicate whether the data in each of the following financial statements (a) cover a period of time or (b) are for a specific date:
    1. balance sheet
    2. income statement
    3. statement of owner's equity
    4. statement of cash flows
20. What particular item of financial or operating data appears on (a) both the income statement and the statement of owner's equity and (b) both the balance sheet and the statement of owner's equity?
21. Name the three types of activities reported in the statement of cash flows.

EXERCISES

EXERCISE 1–1
Professional ethics
Objective 2

A fertilizer manufacturing company wants to relocate to Collier County. A 13-year-old report from a fired researcher at the company says the company's product is releasing toxic by-products. The company has suppressed that report. A second report commissioned by the company shows there is no problem with the fertilizer.

Should the company's chief executive officer reveal the context of the unfavorable report in discussions with Collier County representatives? Discuss.

Source: "Business Leaders Ponder Ethical Questions," *Naples Daily News*, May 12, 1991, p. 1E.

EXERCISE 1–2
Accounting equation
Objective 5

Determine the missing amount for each of the following:

	Assets	=	*Liabilities*	+	*Owner's Equity*
a.	X	=	$10,500	+	$31,500
b.	$62,750	=	X	+	20,000
c.	57,000	=	18,000	+	X

EXERCISE 1–3
Accounting equation
Objectives 5, 7

Diana Morley is the sole owner and operator of Dyn-A-Mo, a motivational consulting business. As of the end of its accounting period, December 31, 1996, Dyn-A-Mo has assets of $125,000 and liabilities of $85,000. Using the accounting equation and considering each case independently, determine the following amounts:

a. Diana Morley, capital, as of December 31, 1996.
b. Diana Morley, capital, as of December 31, 1997, assuming that during 1997, assets increased by $34,000 and liabilities increased by $21,000.
c. Diana Morley, capital, as of December 31, 1997, assuming that during 1997, assets decreased by $5,000 and liabilities increased by $6,000.
d. Diana Morley, capital, as of December 31, 1997, assuming that during 1997, assets increased by $45,000 and liabilities decreased by $15,000.
e. Net income (or net loss) during 1997, assuming that as of December 31, 1997, assets were $180,000, liabilities were $105,000, and there were no additional investments or withdrawals.

EXERCISE 1–4
Asset, liability, owner's equity items
Objective 6

Indicate whether each of the following is identified with (1) an asset, (2) a liability, or (3) owner's equity:

a. fees earned
b. supplies
c. wages expense
d. land
e. accounts payable
f. cash

EXERCISE 1–5
Effect of transactions on accounting equation
Objective 6

Describe how the following business transactions affect the three elements of the accounting equation.

a. Invested cash in business.
b. Received cash for services performed.
c. Purchased supplies for cash.
d. Paid for utilities used in the business.
e. Purchased supplies on account.

EXERCISE 1–6
Effect of transactions on accounting equation
Objective 6

a. A vacant lot acquired for $50,000, on which there is a balance owed of $35,000, is sold for $65,000 in cash. What is the effect of the sale on the total amount of the seller's (1) assets, (2) liabilities, and (3) owner's equity?
b. After receiving the $65,000 cash in (a), the seller pays the $35,000 owed. What is the effect of the payment on the total amount of the seller's (1) assets, (2) liabilities, and (3) owner's equity?

EXERCISE 1–7
Effect of transactions on owner's equity
Objective 6

Indicate whether each of the following types of transactions will (a) increase owner's equity or (b) decrease owner's equity:

1. owner's investments
2. revenues
3. expenses
4. owner's withdrawals

EXERCISE 1–8
Transactions
Objective 6

The following selected transactions were completed by Pronto Delivery Service during July:

1. Paid advertising expense, $625.
2. Received cash from owner as additional investment, $25,000.
3. Paid creditors on account, $250.
4. Received cash from cash customers, $6,250.
5. Billed customers for delivery services on account, $2,900.

6. Paid rent for July, $2,500.
7. Purchased supplies for cash, $750.
8. Received cash from customers on account, $900.
9. Determined that the cost of supplies on hand was $180; therefore, $570 of supplies had been used during the month.
10. Paid cash to owner for personal use, $1,000.

Indicate the effect of each transaction on the accounting equation by listing the numbers identifying the transactions, (1) through (10), in a vertical column, and inserting at the right of each number the appropriate letter from the following list:

a. Increase in an asset, decrease in another asset.
b. Increase in an asset, increase in a liability.
c. Increase in an asset, increase in owner's equity.
d. Decrease in an asset, decrease in a liability.
e. Decrease in an asset, decrease in owner's equity.

EXERCISE 1–9
Nature of transactions
Objective 6

Kim Regis operates her own catering service. Summary financial data for March are presented in equation form as follows. Each line designated by a number indicates the effect of a transaction on the equation. Each increase and decrease in owner's equity, except transaction (5), affects net income.

	Cash	+ *Supplies*	+ *Land*	= *Liabilities*	+ *Owner's Equity*
Bal.	5,500	750	19,000	3,750	21,500
1.	+9,000				+ 9,000
2.	−4,000		+ 4,000		
3.	−3,250				− 3,250
4.		+600		+ 600	
5.	−1,950				− 1,950
6.	−2,300			−2,300	
7.		−800			− 800
Bal.	3,000	550	23,000	2,050	24,500

a. Describe each transaction.
b. What is the amount of net decrease in cash during the month?
c. What is the amount of net increase in owner's equity during the month?
d. What is the amount of the net income for the month?
e. How much of the net income for the month was retained in the business?

EXERCISE 1–10
Net income and owner's withdrawals
Objective 7

The income statement of a sole proprietorship for the month of February indicates a net income of $15,000. During the same period, the owner withdrew $25,000 in cash from the business for personal use.

Would it be correct to say that the business incurred a net loss of $10,000 during the month? Discuss.

EXERCISE 1–11
Net income and owner's equity for four businesses
Objective 7

Four different sole proprietorships, A, B, C, and D, show the same balance sheet data at the beginning and end of a year. These data, exclusive of the amount of owner's equity, are summarized as follows:

	Total Assets	*Total Liabilities*
Beginning of the year	$425,000	$180,000
End of the year	570,000	225,000

On the basis of the above data and the following additional information for the year, determine the net income (or loss) of each company for the year. (Suggestion: First determine the amount of increase or decrease in owner's equity during the year.)

Company A: The owner had made no additional investments in the business and had made no withdrawals from the business.

Company B: The owner had made no additional investments in the business but had withdrawn $30,000.

Company C: The owner had made an additional investment of $110,000 but had made no withdrawals.

Company D: The owner had made an additional investment of $110,000 and had withdrawn $30,000.

EXERCISE 1–12
Balance sheet items
Objective 7

From the following list of selected items taken from the records of Magic Appliance Service as of a specific date, identify those that would appear on the balance sheet:

1. Utilities Expense
2. Fees Earned
3. Supplies
4. Wages Expense
5. Accounts Payable
6. Cash
7. Supplies Expense
8. Land
9. Susan Copperfield, Capital
10. Wages Payable

EXERCISE 1–13
Income statement items
Objective 7

Based on the data presented in Exercise 1–12, identify those items that would appear on the income statement.

EXERCISE 1–14
Statement of owner's equity
Objective 7

Financial information related to Kelvinator Company, a sole proprietorship, for the month ended June 30, 1997, is as follows:

Net income for June	$11,750
Kelvin Baer's withdrawals during June	8,000
Kelvin Baer, capital, June 1, 1997	79,950

Prepare a statement of owner's equity for the month ended June 30, 1997.

EXERCISE 1–15
Income statement
Objective 7

Leasing Services was organized on April 1. A summary of the revenue and expense transactions for April are as follows:

Fees earned	$15,400
Wages expense	7,700
Miscellaneous expense	250
Rent expense	2,500
Supplies expense	1,250

Prepare an income statement for the month ended April 30.

EXERCISE 1–16
Missing amounts from balance sheet and income statement data
Objective 7

One item is omitted in each of the following summaries of balance sheet and income statement data for four different sole proprietorships, I, II, III, and IV.

	I	*II*	*III*	*IV*
Beginning of the year:				
Assets	$370,000	$95,000	$90,000	(d)
Liabilities	260,000	45,000	76,000	$32,750
End of the year:				
Assets	355,000	125,000	94,000	99,000
Liabilities	165,000	35,000	87,000	42,000
During the year:				
Additional investment in the business	(a)	22,000	5,000	25,000
Withdrawals from the business	30,000	8,000	(c)	15,000
Revenue	97,750	(b)	88,100	99,000
Expenses	72,750	52,000	89,600	78,000

Determine the amounts of the missing items, identifying them by letter. (Suggestion: First determine the amount of increase or decrease in owner's equity during the year.)

EXERCISE 1–17
Balance sheets, net income
Objective 7

Financial information related to the sole proprietorship of Kate Interiors for March and April of the current year is as follows:

	March 31, 19—	*April 30, 19—*
Accounts payable	$ 5,720	$ 6,900
Accounts receivable	9,300	10,400
Kate Lynch, capital	?	?
Cash	10,150	12,050
Supplies	975	550

a. Prepare balance sheets for Kate Interiors as of March 31 and as of April 30 of the current year.
b. Determine the amount of net income for April, assuming that the owner made no additional investments or withdrawals during the month.
c. Determine the amount of net income for April, assuming that the owner made no additional investments but withdrew $2,000 during the month.

EXERCISE 1–18
Financial statements
Objective 7

Each of the following items is shown in the financial statements of Exxon Corporation. Identify the financial statement (balance sheet or income statement) in which each item would appear.

a. Operating expenses
b. Crude oil inventory
c. Income taxes payable
d. Sales
e. Investments
f. Marketable securities
g. Exploration expenses
h. Notes and loans payable
i. Cash equivalents
j. Long-term debt
k. Selling expenses
l. Notes receivable
m. Equipment
n. Accounts payable
o. Prepaid taxes

EXERCISE 1–19
Statement of cash flows
Objective 7

Indicate whether each of the following activities would be reported on the statement of cash flows as (a) an operating activity, (b) an investing activity, or (c) a financing activity:

1. Cash received as owner's investment
2. Cash paid for land
3. Cash received from fees earned
4. Cash paid for expenses

EXERCISE 1–20
Financial statements
Objective 7

Pastel Realty, organized March 1, 1997, as a sole proprietorship, is owned and operated by Erin Jones. How many errors can you find in the following financial statements for Pastel Realty, prepared after its second month of operations?

Pastel Realty
Income Statement
April 30, 1997

Sales commissions		$16,100.00
Operating expenses:		
Office salaries expense	$3,150.00	
Rent expense	2,800.00	
Automobile expense	750.00	
Miscellaneous expense	550.00	
Supplies expense	225.00	
Total operating expenses		7,475.00
Net income		$ 8,650.00

Erin Jones
Statement of Owner's Equity
April 30, 1996

Erin Jones, capital, April 1, 1997	$ 8,450.00
Less withdrawals during April	2,000.00
	$ 6,450.00
Additional investment during April	2,500.00
	$ 8,950.00
Net income for the month	8,650.00
Erin Jones, capital, April 30, 1997	$17,600.00

Balance Sheet
For the Month Ended April 30, 1997

Assets	
Cash	$ 8,350.00
Accounts payable	1,300.00
Total assets	$ 9,650.00
Liabilities	
Accounts receivable	$ 9,200.00
Supplies	1,325.00
Owner's Equity	
Erin Jones, capital	17,600.00
Total liabilities and owner's equity	$28,125.00

PROBLEMS SERIES A

PROBLEM 1–1A
Transactions
Objective 6

On June 1 of the current year, Linda Yoke established a business to manage rental property. She completed the following transactions during June:

a. Opened a business bank account with a deposit of $28,000.
b. Purchased supplies (stationery, stamps, pencils, etc.) on account, $1,950.
c. Received cash from fees earned, $5,500.
d. Paid rent on office and equipment for the month, $3,000.
e. Paid creditors on account, $975.
f. Billed customers for fees earned, $2,250.
g. Paid automobile expenses (including rental charges) for month, $980, and miscellaneous expenses, $775.
h. Paid office salaries, $1,500.
i. Determined that the cost of supplies on hand was $925; therefore, the cost of supplies used was $1,025.
j. Withdrew cash for personal use, $1,000.

Instructions

1. Indicate the effect of each transaction and the balances after each transaction, using the following tabular headings:

Assets	=	*Liabilities*	+	*Owner's Equity*
Cash + Accounts Receivable + Supplies	=	Accounts Payable	+	Linda Yoke, Capital

Explain the nature of each increase and decrease in owner's equity by an appropriate notation at the right of the amount.

2. Briefly explain why the owner's investment and revenues increased owner's equity, while withdrawals and expenses decreased owner's equity.

PROBLEM 1–2A
Financial statements
Objective 7

Following are the amounts of the assets and liabilities of Tursan Travel Agency, a sole proprietorship, at December 31, 1997, the end of the current year, and its revenue and expenses for the year ended on that date. The items are listed in alphabetical order. The capital of Joel

Tursan, owner, was $14,500 on January 1, 1997, the beginning of the current year. During the current year, Joel withdrew $25,000.

Accounts payable	$ 1,200
Cash	26,490
Miscellaneous expense	1,750
Rent expense	34,000
Revenue earned	114,530
Supplies	865
Supplies expense	2,125
Utilities expense	4,500
Wages expense	35,500

Instructions

1. Prepare an income statement for the current year ended December 31, 1997.
2. Prepare a statement of owner's equity for the current year ended December 31, 1997.
3. Prepare a balance sheet as of December 31, 1997.

PROBLEM 1–3A
Financial statements
Objective 7

Peggy Arnold established Arnold Services on May 1 of the current year. Arnold Services offers financial planning advice to its clients. The effect of each transaction and the balances after each transaction for May are as follows:

	Assets			=	*Liabilities*	+	*Owner's Equity*	
	Cash	+ Accounts Receivable	+ Supplies	=	Accounts Payable	+	Peggy Arnold, Capital	
a.	+15,000						+15,000	Investment
b.			+725		+725			
Bal.	15,000		725		725		15,000	
c.	– 225				–225			
Bal.	14,775		725		500		15,000	
d.	+ 6,750						+ 6,750	Fees earned
Bal.	21,525		725		500		21,750	
e.	– 2,800						– 2,800	Rent expense
Bal.	18,725		725		500		18,950	
f.	– 1,600						– 1,250	Auto expense
							– 350	Misc. expense
Bal.	17,125		725		500		17,350	
g.	– 1,900						– 1,900	Salaries expense
Bal.	15,225		725		500		15,450	
h.			–450				– 450	Supplies expense
Bal.	15,225		275		500		15,000	
i.		+4,350					+ 4,350	Fees earned
Bal.	15,225	4,350	275		500		19,350	
j.	– 2,000						– 2,000	Withdrawal
Bal.	13,225	4,350	275		500		17,350	

Instructions

1. Prepare an income statement for the month ended May 31.
2. Prepare a statement of owner's equity for the month ended May 31.
3. Prepare a balance sheet as of May 31.

PROBLEM 1–4A
Transactions; financial statements
Objectives 6, 7

On September 1 of the current year, Jill Ivey established a real estate agency as a sole proprietorship under the name Ivey Realty. Ivey completed the following transactions during the month of September:

a. Opened a business bank account with a deposit of $7,500.
b. Purchased supplies (stationery, stamps, pencils, etc.) on account, $900.

c. Paid creditor on account, $500.
d. Earned sales commissions, receiving cash, $15,200.
e. Paid rent on office and equipment for the month, $2,000.
f. Withdrew cash for personal use, $3,000.
g. Paid automobile expenses (including rental charge) for month, $1,900, and miscellaneous expenses, $350.
h. Paid office salaries, $4,150.
i. Determined that the cost of supplies on hand was $350; therefore, the cost of supplies used was $550.

Instructions

1. Indicate the effect of each transaction and the balances after each transaction, using the following tabular headings:

Assets	=	*Liabilities*	+	*Owner's Equity*
Cash + Supplies	=	Accounts Payable	+	Jill Ivey, Capital

   Explain the nature of each increase and decrease in owner's equity by an appropriate notation at the right of the amount.
2. Prepare an income statement for September, a statement of owner's equity for September, and a balance sheet as of September 30.

PROBLEM 1–5A
Transactions; financial statements
Objectives 6, 7

Stansell Dry Cleaners is a sole proprietorship owned and operated by Joan Stansell. Currently, a building and equipment are being rented, pending expansion to new facilities. The actual work of dry cleaning is done by another company at wholesale rates. The assets and the liabilities of the business on July 1 of the current year are as follows: Cash, $8,250; Accounts Receivable, $12,100; Supplies, $1,200; Land, $25,000; Accounts Payable, $6,800. Business transactions during July are summarized as follows:

a. Received cash from cash customers for dry cleaning sales, $9,750.
b. Paid rent for the month, $2,000.
c. Purchased supplies on account, $750.
d. Paid creditors on account, $6,800.
e. Charged customers for dry cleaning sales on account, $5,920.
f. Received monthly invoice for dry cleaning expense for July (to be paid on August 10), $4,700.
g. Paid the following: wages expense, $2,400; truck expense, $1,580; utilities expense, $960; miscellaneous expense, $630.
h. Received cash from customers on account, $8,100.
i. Determined that the cost of supplies on hand was $900; therefore, the cost of supplies used during the month was $1,050.

Instructions

1. Determine the amount of Joan Stansell's capital as of July 1 of the current year.
2. State the assets, liabilities, and owner's equity as of July 1 in equation form similar to that shown in this chapter. In tabular form below the equation, indicate increases and decreases resulting from each transaction and the new balances after each transaction. Explain the nature of each increase and decrease in owner's equity by an appropriate notation at the right of the amount.
3. Prepare an income statement for July, a statement of owner's equity for July, and a balance sheet as of July 31.

PROBLEM 1–6A
Financial statements
Objective 7

Kervar Services is an architectural firm operated as a sole proprietorship. Following are the amounts of the assets and liabilities of Kervar Services at December 31, the end of the current year, and its revenue and expenses for the year ended on that date. The capital of Thomas Kervar, owner, was $120,450 at January 1, the beginning of the current year, and the owner withdrew $50,000 during the current year.

Cash	$ 27,200
Accounts receivable	41,000
Supplies	2,750
Land	80,000
Accounts payable	13,100
Wages payable	1,500
Fees earned	129,250
Wages expense	29,700
Rent expense	12,000
Utilities expense	8,100
Supplies expense	4,800
Taxes expense	4,500
Advertising expense	3,000
Miscellaneous expense	1,250

Instructions

1. Prepare an income statement for the current year ended December 31.
2. Prepare a statement of owner's equity for the current year ended December 31.
3. Prepare a balance sheet as of December 31 of the current year.

PROBLEMS SERIES B

PROBLEM 1–1B
Transactions
Objective 6

Jane Myers established an insurance agency as a sole proprietorship on March 1 of the current year and completed the following transactions during March:

a. Opened a business bank account with a deposit of $15,000.
b. Purchased supplies on account, $850.
c. Paid creditors on account, $625.
d. Received cash from fees earned, $4,250.
e. Paid rent on office and equipment for the month, $1,500.
f. Paid automobile expenses for month, $780, and miscellaneous expenses, $250.
g. Paid office salaries, $1,800.
h. Determined that the cost of supplies on hand was $275; therefore, the cost of supplies used was $575.
i. Billed insurance companies for sales commissions earned, $3,350.
j. Withdrew cash for personal use, $2,000.

Instructions

1. Indicate the effect of each transaction and the balances after each transaction, using the following tabular headings:

Assets	=	*Liabilities*	+	*Owner's Equity*
Cash + Accounts Receivable + Supplies	=	Accounts Payable	+	Jane Myers, Capital

   Explain the nature of each increase and decrease in owner's equity by an appropriate notation at the right of the amount.
2. Briefly explain why the owner's investment and revenues increased owner's equity, while withdrawals and expenses decreased owner's equity.

PROBLEM 1–2B
Financial statements
Objective 7

Following are the amounts of the assets and liabilities of VIP Travel Service, a sole proprietorship, at April 30, 1997, the end of the current year, and its revenue and expenses for the year ended on that date. The capital of J. F. Pierce, owner, was $15,000 at May 1, 1996, the beginning of the current year, and the owner withdrew $20,000 during the current year.

Cash	$24,725
Supplies	1,675
Accounts payable	6,100
Fees earned	97,775
Wages expense	34,900
Rent expense	19,900
Utilities expense	9,500
Supplies expense	3,550
Taxes expense	2,800
Miscellaneous expense	1,825

Instructions

1. Prepare an income statement for the current year ended April 30, 1997.
2. Prepare a statement of owner's equity for the current year ended April 30, 1997.
3. Prepare a balance sheet as of April 30, 1997.

PROBLEM 1–3B
Financial statements
Objective 7

Ed Seaquist established Ed's Computer Services on August 1 of the current year. The effect of each transaction and the balances after each transaction for August are as follows:

	Assets					=	*Liabilities*	+	*Owner's Equity*	
	Cash	+	Accounts Receivable	+	Supplies	=	Accounts Payable	+	Ed Seaquist, Capital	
a.	+12,500								+12,500	Investment
b.					+550		+550			
Bal.	12,500				550		550		12,500	
c.	+ 5,000								+ 5,000	Fees earned
Bal.	17,500				550		550		17,500	
d.	– 1,500								– 1,500	Rent expense
Bal.	16,000				550		550		16,000	
e.	– 250						–250			
Bal.	15,750				550		300		16,000	
f.			+2,750						+ 2,750	Fees earned
Bal.	15,750		2,750		550		300		18,750	
g.	– 1,155								– 780	Auto expense
									– 375	Misc. expense
Bal.	14,595		2,750		550		300		17,595	
h.	– 2,500								– 2,500	Salaries expense
Bal.	12,095		2,750		550		300		15,095	
i.					–125				– 125	Supplies expense
Bal.	12,095		2,750		425		300		14,970	
j.	– 1,200								– 1,200	Withdrawal
Bal.	10,895		2,750		425		300		13,770	

Instructions

1. Prepare an income statement for the month ended August 31.
2. Prepare a statement of owner's equity for the month ended August 31.
3. Prepare a balance sheet as of August 31.

PROBLEM 1–4B
Transactions; financial statements
Objectives 6, 7

On May 1 of the current year, Lee Box established a sole proprietorship under the name Box Realty. Box completed the following transactions during the month of May:

a. Opened a business bank account with a deposit of $10,000.
b. Purchased supplies (stationery, stamps, pencils, etc.) on account, $825.
c. Paid creditor on account, $500.

d. Earned sales commissions, receiving cash, $13,500.
e. Paid rent on office and equipment for the month, $4,600.
f. Withdrew cash for personal use, $2,000.
g. Paid automobile expenses (including rental charge) for month, $900, and miscellaneous expenses, $550.
h. Paid office salaries, $3,950.
i. Determined that the cost of supplies on hand was $400; therefore, the cost of supplies used was $425.

Instructions

1. Indicate the effect of each transaction and the balances after each transaction, using the following tabular headings:

Assets	=	*Liabilities*	+	*Owner's Equity*
Cash + Supplies	=	Accounts Payable	+	Lee Box, Capital

   Explain the nature of each increase and decrease in owner's equity by an appropriate notation at the right of the amount.
2. Prepare an income statement for May, a statement of owner's equity for May, and a balance sheet as of May 31.

PROBLEM 1–5B
Transactions; financial statements
Objectives 6, 7

Habana Dry Cleaners is a sole proprietorship owned and operated by Cibo Habana. Currently, a building and equipment are being rented, pending expansion to new facilities. The actual work of dry cleaning is done by another company at wholesale rates. The assets and the liabilities of the business on November 1 of the current year are as follows: Cash, $5,400; Accounts Receivable, $8,750; Supplies, $1,560; Land, $15,000; Accounts Payable, $5,880. Business transactions during November are summarized as follows:

a. Paid rent for the month, $2,450.
b. Charged customers for dry cleaning sales on account, $7,150.
c. Paid creditors on account, $1,680.
d. Purchased supplies on account, $840.
e. Received cash from cash customers for dry cleaning sales, $4,600.
f. Received cash from customers on account, $4,750.
g. Received monthly invoice for dry cleaning expense for November (to be paid on December 10), $3,400.
h. Paid the following: wages expense, $1,800; truck expense, $725; utilities expense, $510; miscellaneous expense, $190.
i. Determined the cost of supplies on hand was $1,500; therefore, the cost of supplies used during the month was $900.

Instructions

1. Determine the amount of Cibo Habana's capital as of November 1 of the current year.
2. State the assets, liabilities, and owner's equity as of November 1 in equation form similar to that shown in this chapter. In tabular form below the equation, indicate increases and decreases resulting from each transaction and the new balances after each transaction. Explain the nature of each increase and decrease in owner's equity by an appropriate notation at the right of the amount.
3. Prepare an income statement for November, a statement of owner's equity for November, and a balance sheet as of November 30.

PROBLEM 1–6B
Financial statements
Objective 7

Following are the amounts of the assets and liabilities of Yamada Consultants at March 31, 1997, the end of the current year, and its revenue and expenses for the year ended on that date. The items are listed in alphabetical order. The capital of Mort Yamada, owner, was $157,890 on April 1, 1996, the beginning of the current year. During the current year, the owner withdrew $60,000.

Accounts payable	$ 78,000
Accounts receivable	69,750
Advertising expense	30,000
Cash	64,515
Fees earned	727,500
Land	150,000
Miscellaneous expense	8,125
Rent expense	155,000
Supplies	6,250
Supplies expense	19,750
Taxes expense	33,500
Utilities expense	65,750
Wages expense	312,000
Wages payable	11,250

Instructions

1. Prepare an income statement for the current year ended March 31, 1997.
2. Prepare a statement of owner's equity for the current year ended March 31, 1997.
3. Prepare a balance sheet as of March 31, 1997.

CONTINUING PROBLEM

Julian Felipe enjoys listening to all types of music and owns countless CDs, tapes, and records. Over the years, Julian has gained a local reputation for his knowledge of music from classical to rap and the ability to put together sets of recordings that appeal to all ages.

During the last several months, Julian served as a guest disc jockey on a local radio station. In addition, he has entertained at several friends' parties as the host deejay.

On November 1, 1996, Julian established a sole proprietorship known as Music A La Mode. Using his extensive collection of CDs, tapes, and records, Julian will serve as a disc jockey on a fee basis for weddings, college parties, and other events. During November, Julian entered into the following transactions:

Nov. 1. Deposited $1,000 in a checking account in the name of Music A La Mode.
2. Received $500 from a local radio station to serve as the guest disc jockey for November.
2. Agreed to share office space with a local real estate agency, Picasso Realty. Music A La Mode will pay 1/4 of the rent. In addition, Music A La Mode agreed to pay $110 a month toward the salary of the receptionist and to pay 1/4 of the utilities. Paid $250 for the rent of the office.
3. Purchased supplies (blank cassette tapes, poster board, extension cords, etc.) from Ideal Office Supply Co. for $150. Agreed to pay $100 within 10 days and the remainder by December 3, 1996.
5. Paid $75 to a local radio station to advertise the services of Music A La Mode twice daily for two weeks.
8. Paid $300 to a local electronics store for rent on two CD players, two cassette players, and eight speakers.
12. Paid $100 (music expense) to The Music Store for the use of its current demo CDs and tapes to make cassette tapes of various music sets.
13. Paid Ideal Office Supply Co. $100 on account.
16. Received $40 from a dentist for providing two music sets for the dentist to play for her patients.
22. Served as disc jockey for a wedding party. The father of the bride agreed to pay $350 the 1st of December.
25. Received $150 from a friend for serving as the disc jockey for a cancer charity ball hosted by the local hospital.
29. Paid $120 (music expense) to Crescendo Music for the use of its library of demo CDs, tapes, and records.

Nov. 30. Received $300 for serving as disc jockey for a local club's monthly dance.
30. Paid Picasso Realty $110 for Music A La Mode's share of the receptionist's salary for November.
30. Paid Picasso Realty $100 for Music A La Mode's share of the utilities for November.
30. Determined that the cost of supplies on hand is $70. Therefore, the cost of supplies used during the month was $80.
30. Paid for miscellaneous expenses, $65.
30. Withdrew $75 of cash from Music A La Mode for personal use.

Instructions

1. Indicate the effect of each transaction and the balances after each transaction, using the following tabular headings:

Assets	=	*Liabilities* + *Owner's Equity*
Cash + Accounts Receivable + Supplies	=	Accounts Payable + Julian Felipe, Capital

   Explain the nature of each increase and decrease in owner's equity by an appropriate notation at the right of the amount.
2. Prepare an income statement for Music A La Mode for the month ended November 30, 1996.
3. Prepare a statement of owner's equity for Music A La Mode for the month ended November 30, 1996.
4. Prepare a balance sheet for Music A La Mode as of November 30, 1996.

CASES

CASE 1–1
Kelley Enterprises
Financial statements

Joan Kelley, president of Kelley Enterprises, applied for a $100,000 loan from Pioneer National Bank. The bank requested financial statements from Kelley Enterprises as a basis for granting the loan. Joan Kelley has told her accountant to provide the bank with a balance sheet. Joan Kelley has decided to omit the other financial statements because there was a net loss during the past year.

Discuss whether Joan Kelley is behaving in an ethical manner by omitting some of the financial statements.

CASE 1–2
Second Opinion
Net income

On January 3, 1996, Dr. Avery Bacall established Second Opinion, a medical practice organized as a sole proprietorship. The following conversation occurred the following August between Dr. Bacall and a former medical school classmate, Dr. June Ivy, at an American Medical Association convention in Bermuda.

Dr. Ivy: Avery, good to see you again. Why didn't you call when you were in Denver? We could have had dinner together.

Dr. Bacall: Actually, I never made it to Colorado this year. My wife and kids went up to our Vail condo twice, but I got stuck in Chicago. I opened a new consulting practice this January and I haven't had any time for myself since.

Dr. Ivy: I heard about it ... Second ... something ... right?

Dr. Bacall: Yea, Second Opinion. My wife chose the name.

Dr. Ivy: I've thought about doing something like that. Are you making any money? I mean, is it worth your time?

Dr. Bacall: You wouldn't believe it. I started by opening a bank account of $15,000, and my July bank statement has a balance of $125,000. Not bad for seven months—all pure profit.

Dr. Ivy: Maybe I'll try it in Denver. Let's have breakfast together tomorrow and you can fill me in on the details.

Comment on Dr. Bacall's statement that the difference between the opening bank balance ($15,000) and the July statement balance ($125,000) is pure profit.

CASE 1–3
Hershey Foods Corporation
Financial analysis

The relationship between liabilities and owner's (stockholder's) equity is often used in analyzing a corporation's ability to withstand adverse business conditions. It is also used to indicate the margin of safety for creditors. The ratio is computed as follows:

$$\textbf{Ratio of liabilities to stockholders' equity} = \frac{\textbf{Total liabilities}}{\textbf{Total stockholders' equity}}$$

The lower the ratio, the better the corporation can withstand poor business conditions and still meet its commitments to creditors. Moreover, the lower the ratio, the greater is the protection to the creditors. For example, a ratio of 1:1 indicates that the liabilities and stockholders' equity are equal and that the protection to the creditors is 100%. If the ratio decreases to 0.5:1, the protection to the creditors is 200%; that is, the corporation may suffer a loss equal to 200% of liabilities before the amount of the assets drops below the amount of the liabilities.

1. Determine the ratio of liabilities to stockholders' equity for Hershey Foods Corporation at the end of 1993 and 1992. (The financial statements for Hershey Foods Corporation are presented at the end of the text.)
2. What conclusions regarding the margin of protection to the creditors can be drawn from your analysis?

CASE 1–4
Village Tennis Services
Transactions and financial statements

Tega Hearst, a junior in college, has been seeking ways to earn extra spending money. As an active sports enthusiast, Tega plays tennis regularly at the Village Tennis Club, where her family has a membership. The president of the club recently approached Tega with the proposal that she manage the club's tennis courts on weekends. Tega's primary duty would be to supervise the operation of the club's four indoor and six outdoor courts, including court reservations.

In return for her services, the club would pay Tega $75 per weekend, plus Tega could keep whatever she earned from lessons and the fees from the use of the ball machine. The club and Tega agreed to a one-month trial, after which both would consider an arrangement for the remaining two years of Tega's college career. On this basis, Tega organized Village Tennis Services. During September, Tega managed the tennis courts and entered into the following transactions:

a. Opened a business account by depositing $500.
b. Paid $150 for tennis supplies (practice tennis balls, etc.).
c. Paid $75 for the rental of videotape equipment to be used in offering lessons during September.
d. Arranged for the rental of two ball machines during September for $100. Paid $60 in advance, with the remaining $40 due October 1.
e. Received $850 for lessons given during September.
f. Received $150 in fees from the use of the ball machines during September.
g. Paid $350 for salaries of part-time employees who answered the telephone and took reservations while Tega was giving lessons.
h. Paid $75 for miscellaneous expenses.
i. Received $300 from the club for managing the tennis courts during September.
j. Determined that the cost of supplies on hand at the end of the month totaled $80; therefore, the cost of supplies used was $70.
k. Withdrew $600 for personal use on September 30.

As a friend and accounting student, you have been asked by Tega to aid her in assessing the venture.

1. Indicate the effect of each transaction and the balances after each transaction, using the following tabular headings:

Assets	=	*Liabilities*	+	*Owner's Equity*
Cash + Supplies	=	Accounts Payable	+	Tega Hearst, Capital

   Explain the nature of each increase and decrease in owner's equity by an appropriate notation at the right of the amount.
2. Prepare an income statement for September.
3. Prepare a statement of owner's equity for September.
4. Prepare a balance sheet as of September 30.
5. a. Assume that Tega Hearst could earn $6 per hour working 20 hours each of the four weekends as a waitress. Evaluate which of the two alternatives, working as a waitress or operating Village Tennis Services, would provide Tega with the most income per month.
   b. Discuss any other factors that you believe Tega should consider before discussing a long-term arrangement with Village Tennis Club.

ANSWERS TO SELF-EXAMINATION QUESTIONS

1. **D** A corporation, organized in accordance with state or federal statutes, is a separate legal entity in which ownership is divided into shares of stock (answer D). A sole proprietorship, sometimes called a single proprietorship (answers A and B), is an unincorporated business owned by one individual. A partnership (answer C) is an unincorporated business owned by two or more individuals.
2. **A** The properties owned by a business are called assets (answer A). The debts of the business are called liabilities (answer B), and the equity of the owners is called owner's equity (answer D). The relationship between assets, liabilities, and owner's equity is expressed as the accounting equation (answer C).
3. **A** The balance sheet is a listing of the assets, liabilities, and owner's equity of a business at a specific date (answer A). The income statement (answer B) is a summary of the revenue and expenses of a business for a specific period of time. The statement of owner's equity (answer C) summarizes the changes in owner's equity for a sole proprietorship or partnership during a specific period of time. The statement of cash flows (answer D) summarizes the cash receipts and cash payments for a specific period of time.
4. **C** The accounting equation is:

   Assets = Liabilities + Owner's Equity

   Therefore, if assets increased by $20,000 and liabilities increased by $12,000, owner's equity must have increased by $8,000 (answer C), as indicated in the following computation:

Assets	=	*Liabilities + Owner's Equity*
$20,000	=	$12,000 + Owner's Equity
$20,000 – $12,000	=	Owner's Equity
$8,000	=	Owner's Equity

5. **B** Net income is the excess of revenue over expenses, or $7,500 (answer B). If expenses exceed revenue, the difference is a net loss. Withdrawals by the owner are the opposite of the owner's investing in the business and do not affect the amount of net income or net loss.

2 Analyzing Transactions

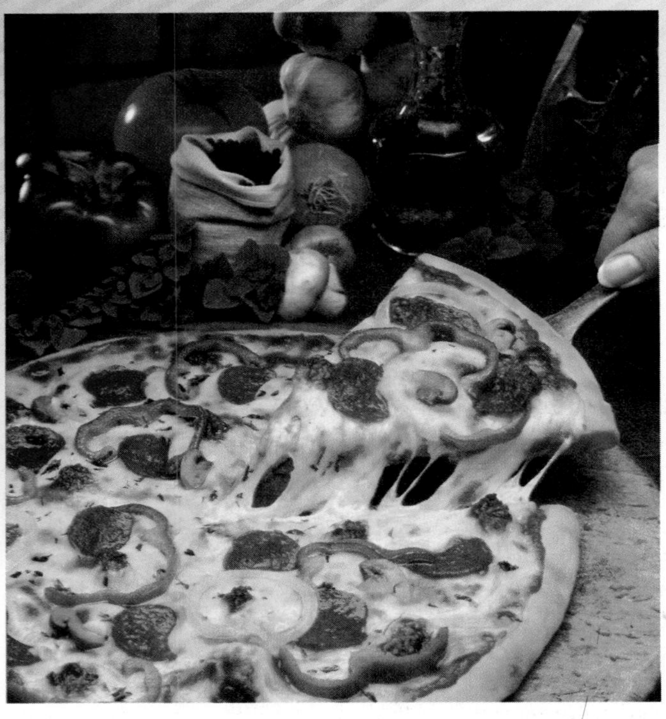

YOU AND ACCOUNTING

Assume that you have been hired by a pizza restaurant to deliver pizzas, using your own car. You will be paid $5.00 per hour plus $0.20 per mile plus tips. What is the best way for you to determine how many miles you have driven each day in delivering pizzas?

One method would be to record the odometer mileage before work and then at quitting time. The difference would be the miles driven. For example, if the odometer read 56,743 at the start of work and 56,889 at the end of work, you have driven 146 miles. However, this method is subject to error if you copy down the wrong reading or make a math error.

In running a business, managers need to have similar information readily available. Such information is useful for analyzing the effects of transactions on the business and for making decisions. For example, the manager of your neighborhood dry cleaners needs to know how much cash is available, how much has been spent, and what services have been provided customers.

In Chapter 1, we analyzed and recorded this kind of information by using the accounting equation, Assets = Liabilities + Owner's Equity. Since such a format is not practical for most businesses, we will study, in Chapter 2, more practical methods of recording transactions. We will conclude this chapter by discussing how accounting errors may occur and how they may be detected by the accounting process.

After studying this chapter, you should be able to:

Objective 1
Explain why accounts are used to record and summarize the effects of transactions on financial statements.

Objective 2
Explain the characteristics of an account.

Objective 3
List the rules of debit and credit and the normal balances of accounts.

Objective 4
Analyze and summarize the financial statement effects of transactions.

Objective 5
Prepare a trial balance and explain how it can be used to discover errors.

Objective 6
Discover errors in recording transactions and correct them.

Usefulness of an Account

Objective 1
Explain why accounts are used to record and summarize the effects of transactions on financial statements.

Before making a major cash purchase, such as buying a CD player, you need to know the balance of your bank account. Likewise, managers need timely, useful information in order to make good decisions about their businesses. An accounting system must be designed to provide this information.

How are accounting systems designed to provide information? We illustrated a very simple design in Chapter 1, where transactions were recorded and summarized in the accounting equation format. However, this format is awkward and cumbersome for recording thousands of daily transactions. Thus, accounting systems are designed to show the increases and decreases in each financial statement item in a separate record. This record is called an **account**. For example, since cash appears on the balance sheet, a separate record is kept of the increases and decreases in cash. Likewise, a separate record is kept of the increases and decreases for supplies, land, accounts payable, and the other balance sheet items. Similar records would be kept for income statement items, such as fees earned, wages expense, and rent expense.

A group of accounts for a business entity is called a **ledger**. A list of the accounts in the ledger is called a **chart of accounts**. The accounts are normally listed in the order in which they appear in the financial statements. The balance sheet accounts are usually listed first, in the order of assets, liabilities, and owner's equity. The income statement accounts are then listed in the order of revenues and expenses. Each of these major account classifications is briefly described below.

Assets are physical items (tangible) or rights (intangible) that have value and that are owned by the business entity. Examples of tangible assets include cash, accounts receivable, supplies, prepaid expenses (such as insurance), buildings, equipment, and land. An example of an intangible asset is patent rights.

Liabilities are debts owed to outsiders (creditors). Liabilities are often identified on the balance sheet by titles that include the word *payable*. Examples of liabilities include accounts payable, notes payable, and wages payable. Revenue received in advance, such as magazine subscriptions received by a publisher or tuition received by a college, is also classified as a liability. Revenue received in advance is often called *unearned* revenue.

Owner's equity is the owner's right to assets of the business. For a sole proprietorship, the owner's equity on the balance sheet is represented by the balance of the owner's *capital* account. A **drawing** account represents the amount of withdrawals made by the owner of a sole proprietorship.

Revenues are increases in owner's equity as a result of rendering services or selling products to customers. Examples of revenues include fees earned, fares earned, commissions revenue, and rent revenue, often called rent income.

USING ACCOUNTING TO UNDERSTAND BUSINESS

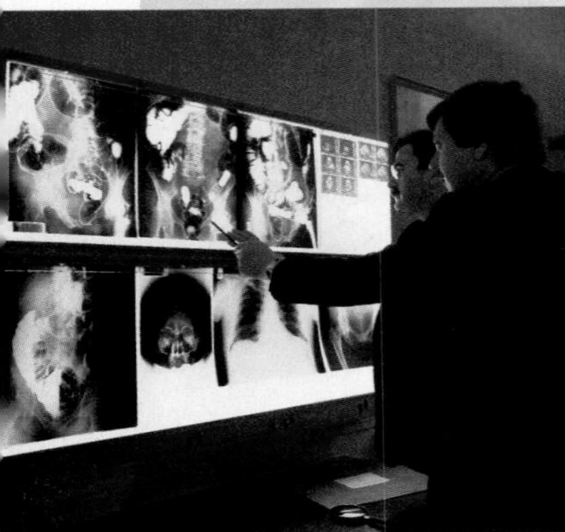

A review of the chart of accounts can provide a quick overview of a business's operations. For example, some revenue and expense accounts taken from the chart of accounts of a hospital include the following:

- Revenue Accounts:
  - Pulmonary Laboratory
  - Emergency Department
  - Radiology
  - Anesthesiology
  - Physical Therapy
  - Cardiovascular Center
  - Radiation—Oncology
  - Diabetic Clinic
  - Cafeteria Sales
- Expense Accounts:
  - Nursing Administration
  - Pulmonary Laboratory
  - Cafeteria
  - Security
  - Depreciation
  - Insurance
  - Education and Training
  - Housekeeping
  - Laundry
  - Linen

These accounts tell us that the hospital offers radiation, cardiovascular, and diabetic services, among others. In addition, the accounts reflect some of the decision-making needs of management. For example, comparing the revenues from the pulmonary laboratory with its related expenses assists management in determining whether the pulmonary laboratory is profitable. A loss from operating the laboratory might lead management to consider discontinuing the laboratory or increasing laboratory fees.

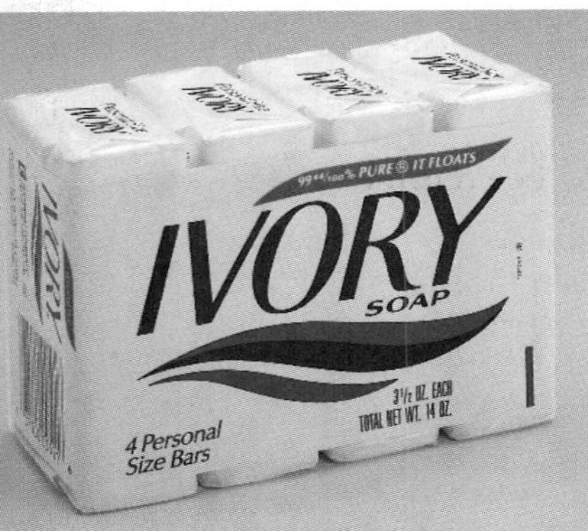

Procter and Gamble's account numbers have over 30 digits to reflect its different operations and regions. This can be typical for very large businesses.

Assets used up or services consumed in the process of generating revenues are **expenses**. Examples of typical expenses include wages expense, rent expense, utilities expense, supplies expense, and miscellaneous expense.

Accounts are numbered for use as references. Although accounts may be in numeric order, as are the pages of this book, a flexible system of indexing is desired. Such a system has the advantage of allowing new accounts to be added in their proper order without affecting other account numbers.

In designing the chart of accounts for a company, the company's expected operations and volume of business must be analyzed. In addition, the extent to which reports are needed for taxes, managerial decisions, and credit purposes must also be considered. For example, the type and number of accounts for a small retailer would be different from those needed by an attorney or a real estate agency. For a large enterprise with many departments or operations, it is common for each account number to have four or more digits. For example, **Procter and Gamble's** account numbers have over 30 digits to reflect different operations and regions.

Exhibit 1 is Computer King's chart of accounts that we will be using in this chapter. Additional accounts will be introduced in later chapters. In Exhibit 1, each account number has two digits. The first digit indicates the major classification of the ledger in which the account is located. Accounts beginning with 1 represent assets; 2, liabilities; 3, owner's equity; 4, revenue; and 5, expenses. The second digit indicates the location of the account within its class.

Exhibit 1
Chart of Accounts for Computer King

Balance Sheet Accounts	*Income Statement Accounts*
1. Assets	4. Revenue
11 Cash	41 Fees Earned
12 Accounts Receivable	5. Expenses
14 Supplies	51 Wages Expense
15 Prepaid Insurance	52 Rent Expense
17 Land	54 Utilities Expense
18 Office Equipment	55 Supplies Expense
2. Liabilities	59 Miscellaneous Expense
21 Accounts Payable	
23 Unearned Rent	
3. Owner's Equity	
31 Pat King, Capital	
32 Pat King, Drawing	

Characteristics of an Account

Objective 2
Explain the characteristics of an account.

The simplest form of an account has three parts. First, each account has a title, which is the name of the item recorded in the account. Second, each account has a space for recording increases in the amount of the item. Third, each account has a space for recording decreases in the amount of the item. The account form presented below is called a **T account** because it is similar to the letter T.

Title	
Left side *debit*	Right side *credit*

The left side of the account is called the debit side, and the right side is called the credit side.[1] Amounts entered on the left side of an account, regardless of the account title, are called **debits** to the account. When debits are entered in an account, the account is said to be **debited** (or charged). Amounts entered on the right side of an account are called **credits,** and the account is said to be **credited.** Debits and credits are sometimes abbreviated as *Dr.* and *Cr.*

In the cash account shown at the top of the next page, transactions involving receipts of cash are listed vertically on the debit side of the account. The transactions involving cash payments have been listed in similar fashion on the credit side of the account. If at any time the total of the cash receipts is needed, the entries on the debit side of the account may be added and the total ($10,950) inserted below the last debit.[2] The total of the cash payments, $6,850 in the example, may be inserted on the credit side in a similar manner. Subtracting the smaller sum from the larger, $10,950 – $6,850, identifies the amount of cash on hand, $4,100. This amount is called the **balance of the account.** It may be inserted in the account, next to the total of the debit column. In this way, the balance is identified as a **debit balance.** If a balance sheet were to be prepared at this time, cash of $4,100 would be reported.

[1] The terms *debit* and *credit* are derived from the Latin *debere* and *credere.*
[2] This amount, called a memorandum balance, should be written in small figures or identified in some other way to avoid mistaking the amount for an additional debit.

Cash

		Debit	Credit		
Debit Side of Account		3,750	850		Credit Side of Account
		4,300	1,400		
		2,900	700		
	4,100	*10,950*	2,900		
			1,000		
			6,850		

Analyzing and Summarizing Transactions in Accounts

Objective 3
List the rules of debit and credit and the normal balances of accounts.

In this section, we will use the Computer King transactions from Chapter 1, with dates added, as the basis for discussing how transactions are analyzed and summarized in accounts. First, we illustrate how transactions (a), (b), (c), and (f) are analyzed and summarized in balance sheet accounts. Next, we illustrate how transactions (d), (e), and (g) are analyzed and summarized in income statement accounts. Finally, we illustrate how the withdrawal of cash by Pat King, transaction (h), is analyzed and summarized in the accounts.

BALANCE SHEET ACCOUNTS

Balance sheet accounts consist of the assets, liabilities, and owner's equity accounts. Pat King's first transaction (a) was to deposit $15,000 in a bank account on November 1 in the name of Computer King. After the deposit, the balance sheet for the business is as follows:

Computer King
Balance Sheet
November 1, 1996

Assets		Owner's Equity	
Cash	$15,000	Pat King, Capital	$15,000

Every business transaction affects a business's financial statements and at least two accounts. The effect of the above transaction on the balance sheet is to increase cash and owner's equity. This effect is shown in the accounts as a $15,000 debit to Cash and a $15,000 credit to Pat King, Capital.

The effects of a transaction on a business and its accounts is initially entered in a record called a journal. In the journal, the transaction's effects are stated in a formal manner. The title of the account to be debited is listed first, followed by the amount to be debited. The title of the account to be credited is listed below and to the right of the debit, followed by the amount to be credited. This process of recording a transaction in the journal is called journalizing. The form of presentation is called a **journal entry,** as shown below.

Entry A.

Nov. 1	Cash	15,000	
	Pat King, Capital		15,000

The effects of this transaction are shown in the accounts by transferring the amount and the date of the journal entry to Cash and Pat King, Capital, as follows:

Cash		Pat King, Capital	
Nov. 1 15,000			Nov. 1 15,000

The amount of the asset, which is reported on the left side of the balance sheet, is transferred to the left (debit) side of Cash. The owner's equity in the business, which is reported on the right side of the balance sheet, is transferred to the right (credit) side of Pat King, Capital. When other assets are acquired, the increases will also be recorded as debits to asset accounts. Likewise, other increases in owner's equity will be recorded as credits to owner's equity accounts.

On November 5 (transaction b), Computer King bought land for $10,000, paying cash. This transaction increases one asset account and decreases another. It can be expressed as a $10,000 increase (debit) to Land and a $10,000 decrease (credit) to Cash. The journal entry for this transaction is shown below.

Entry B.

Nov. 5	Land	10,000	
	Cash		10,000

The effect of this entry is shown in the accounts of Computer King as follows:

Cash		Land		Pat King, Capital	
Nov. 1 15,000	Nov. 5 10,000	Nov. 5 10,000			Nov. 1 15,000

On November 10 (transaction c), Computer King purchased supplies on account for $1,350. This transaction increases an asset account and increases a liability account. It can be expressed as a $1,350 increase (debit) to Supplies and a $1,350 increase (credit) to Accounts Payable. The journal entry for this transaction is shown below. To simplify the illustration, the effect of entry (c) and the remaining journal entries for Computer King will be shown in the accounts later.

Entry C.

Nov. 10	Supplies	1,350	
	Accounts Payable		1,350

On November 30 (transaction f), Computer King paid creditors on account, $950. This transaction decreases a liability account and decreases an asset account. It can be expressed as a $950 decrease (debit) to Accounts Payable and a $950 decrease (credit) to Cash. The journal entry for this transaction is shown below.

Entry F.

Nov. 30	Accounts Payable	950	
	Cash		950

In the preceding examples, you should observe that the left side of asset accounts is used for recording increases and the right side is used for recording decreases. Also, the right side of liability and owner's equity accounts is used to record increases. It naturally follows that the left side of such accounts is used to record decreases. The left side of all accounts, whether asset, liability, or owner's equity, is the debit side, and the right side is the credit side. Thus, a debit may be either an increase or a decrease, depending on the account affected. A credit may likewise be either an increase or a decrease, depending on the account. The general rules of debit and credit for balance sheet accounts may therefore be stated as follows:

	Debit	Credit
Asset accounts	Increase (+)	Decrease (–)
Liability accounts	Decrease (–)	Increase (+)
Owner's equity (capital) accounts	Decrease (–)	Increase (+)

The rules of debit and credit may also be stated in relationship to the accounting equation, as shown below.

Balance Sheet Accounts

ASSETS Asset Accounts		LIABILITIES Liability Accounts	
Debit for increases	Credit for decreases	Debit for decreases	Credit for increases
		OWNER'S EQUITY Owner's Equity Accounts	
		Debit for decreases	Credit for increases

INCOME STATEMENT ACCOUNTS

The analysis of business transactions affecting the income statement focuses on how each transaction affects owner's equity. Transactions that increase revenue will increase owner's equity. Just as increases in owner's equity are recorded as credits, increases in revenue accounts are recorded as credits. Transactions that increase expense will decrease owner's equity. Just as decreases in owner's equity are recorded as debits, increases in expense accounts are recorded as debits.

Computer King's transactions (d), (e), and (g) illustrate the analysis of transactions and the rules of debit and credit for revenue and expense accounts. On November 18 (transaction d), Computer King received fees of $7,500 from customers for services. This transaction increases an asset account and increases a revenue account. It can be expressed as a $7,500 increase (debit) to Cash and a $7,500 increase (credit) to Fees Earned. The journal entry for this transaction is shown below.

Entry D.

Nov. 18	Cash	7,500	
	Fees Earned		7,500

Throughout the month, Computer King incurred the following expenses: wages, $2,125; rent, $800; utilities, $450; and miscellaneous, $275. To simplify the illustration, the entry to journalize the payment of these expenses is recorded on November 30 (transaction e), as shown below. This transaction increases various expense accounts and decreases an asset account.

Entry E.

Nov. 30	Wages Expense	2,125	
	Rent Expense	800	
	Utilities Expense	450	
	Miscellaneous Expense	275	
	Cash		3,650

Regardless of the number of accounts, the sum of the debits is always equal to the sum of the credits in a journal entry. This equality of debit and credit for each transaction is inherent in the accounting equation: Assets = Liabilities + Owner's Equity. It is also because of this double equality that the system is known as **double-entry accounting.**

On November 30, Computer King recorded the amount of supplies used in the operations during the month (transaction g). This transaction increases an expense account and decreases an asset account. The journal entry for transaction (g) is shown below.

Entry G.

Nov. 30	Supplies Expense	800	
	Supplies		800

The general rules of debit and credit for analyzing transactions affecting income statement accounts are stated below.

	Debit	Credit
Revenue accounts	Decrease (–)	Increase (+)
Expense accounts	Increase (+)	Decrease (–)

The rules of debit and credit for income statement accounts may also be summarized in relationship to the owner's equity in the accounting equation, as shown below.

Income Statement Accounts			
Debit for decreases in owner's equity		*Credit for increases in owner's equity*	
Expense Accounts		Revenue Accounts	
Debit for increases	Credit for decreases	Debit for decreases	Credit for increases

WITHDRAWALS BY THE OWNER

The owner of a sole proprietorship may withdraw cash from the business for personal use. This practice is common if the owner devotes full time to the business. In this case, the business may be the owner's main source of income. Such withdrawals have the effect of decreasing owner's equity. Just as decreases in owner's equity are recorded as debits, increases in withdrawals are recorded as debits. Withdrawals are debited to an account with the owner's name followed by *Drawing* or *Personal*.

In transaction (h), Pat King withdrew $2,000 in cash from Computer King for personal use. The effect of this transaction is to increase the drawing account and decrease the cash account. The journal entry for transaction (h) is shown below.

Entry H.

Nov. 30	Pat King, Drawing	2,000	
	Cash		2,000

NORMAL BALANCES OF ACCOUNTS

The sum of the increases recorded in an account is usually equal to or greater than the sum of the decreases recorded in the account. For this reason, the normal balances of all accounts are positive rather than negative. For example, the total debits (increases) in an asset account will ordinarily be greater than the total credits (decreases). Thus, asset accounts normally have debit balances.

The rules of debit and credit and the normal balances of the various types of accounts are summarized as follows:

	Increase (Normal Balance)	*Decrease*
Balance sheet accounts:		
Asset	**Debit**	Credit
Liability	**Credit**	Debit
Owner's Equity:		
Capital	**Credit**	Debit
Drawing	**Debit**	Credit
Income statement accounts:		
Revenue	**Credit**	Debit
Expense	**Debit**	Credit

When an account that normally has a debit balance actually has a credit balance, or vice versa, an error may have occurred or an unusual situation may exist. For example, a credit balance in the office equipment account could result only from an error. On the other hand, a debit balance in an accounts payable account could result from an overpayment.

Illustration of Analyzing and Summarizing Transactions

Objective 4
Analyze and summarize the financial statement effects of transactions.

How does a transaction occur in a business? A transaction is initiated by the action of a manager or other authorized employee, who normally generates a business document. For example, a purchase order is a business document used in purchasing supplies.[3] A billing statement or invoice is a business document used for billing customers for services or goods provided. On the basis of business documents, the effects of transactions on the financial statements are analyzed and recorded. As we discussed in the preceding section, a transaction is first recorded in a journal. Periodically the journal entries are transferred to the accounts in the ledger. This process of transferring the debits and credits from the journal entries to the accounts is called **posting**. The flow of a transaction from its authorization to its posting in the accounts is shown in the diagram below.

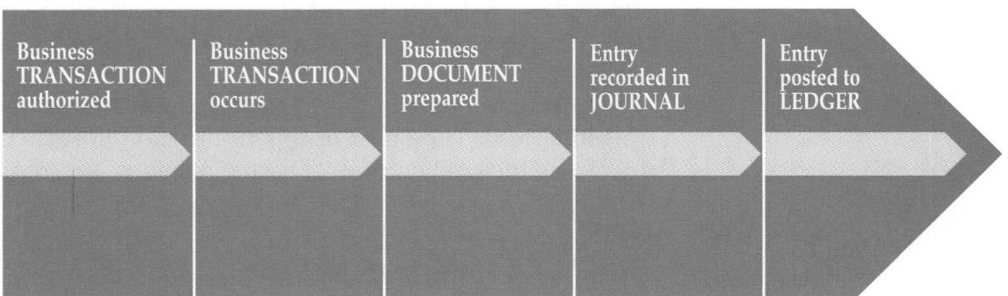

The ability to analyze the effects of transactions on financial statements is an essential skill for a successful career in business. As we illustrated earlier in the chapter, the double-entry accounting system is a very powerful tool in this analysis.

[3] In computerized accounting systems, some transactions are automatically authorized when certain events occur. For example, the salaries of managers may be paid automatically at the end of each pay period.

Using this system to analyze transactions can be summarized as follows:

1. Determine whether an asset, a liability, owner's equity, revenue, or expense account is affected by the transaction.
2. For each account affected by the transaction, determine whether the account increases or decreases.
3. Determine whether each increase or decrease should be recorded as a debit or a credit.

In practice, businesses use a variety of formats for recording journal entries. A business may use one all-purpose journal, sometimes called a two-column journal, or it may use several journals. In the latter case, each journal is used to record different types of transactions, such as cash receipts or cash payments. The journals may be part of either a manual accounting system or a computerized accounting system.[4]

COMPUTER KING

To illustrate recording a transaction in an all-purpose journal and posting in a manual accounting system, we will use the December transactions of Computer King. The first transaction in December occurred on December 1.

Dec. 1. Computer King paid a premium of $2,400 for a comprehensive insurance policy covering liability, theft, and fire. The policy covers a two-year period.

ANALYSIS: Advance payments of expenses such as insurance are prepaid expenses, which are assets. For Computer King, the asset acquired for the cash payment is insurance protection for 24 months. The asset Prepaid Insurance increases and is debited for $2,400. The asset Cash decreases and is credited for $2,400.

The recording of this transaction in an all-purpose journal and its posting to accounts in the ledger is shown in Exhibit 2.

Exhibit 2
Diagram of the Recording and Posting of a Debit and a Credit

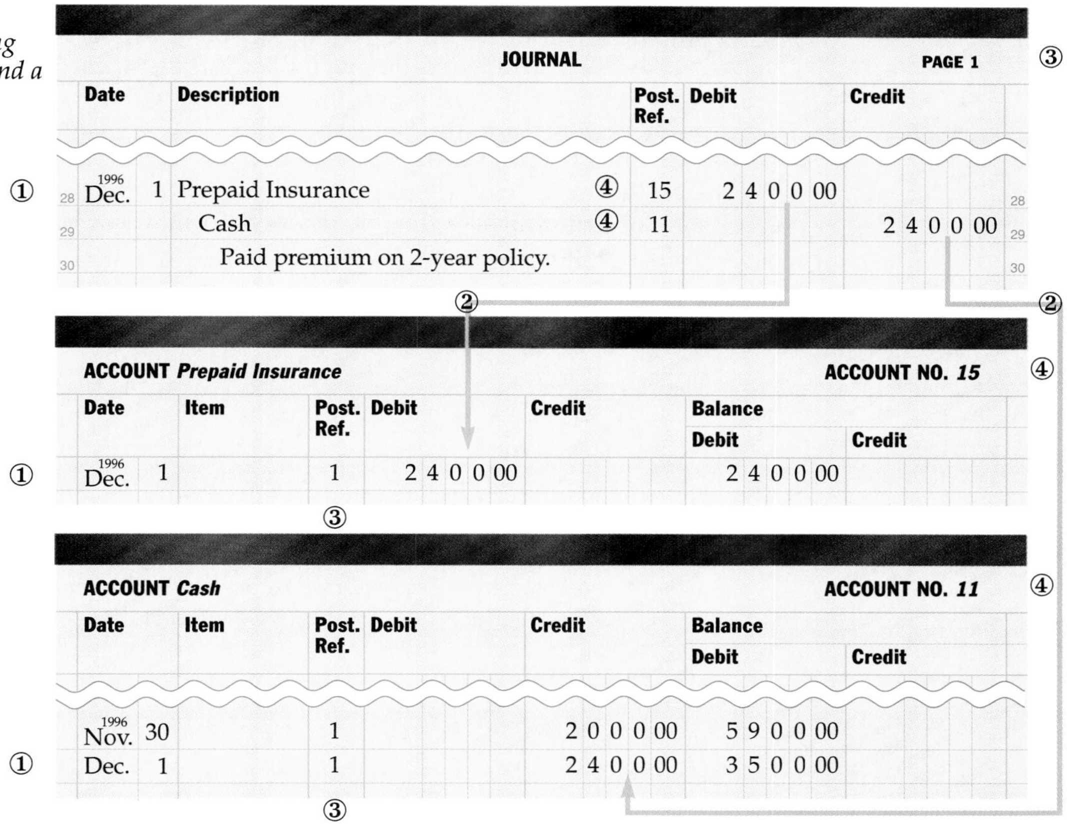

JOURNAL — PAGE 1 ③

Date		Description	Post. Ref.	Debit	Credit
① 1996 Dec.	1	Prepaid Insurance ④	15	2 4 0 0 00	
		Cash ④	11		2 4 0 0 00
		Paid premium on 2-year policy.			

②

ACCOUNT *Prepaid Insurance* — **ACCOUNT NO.** *15* ④

Date		Item	Post. Ref.	Debit	Credit	Balance Debit	Balance Credit
① 1996 Dec.	1		1 ③	2 4 0 0 00		2 4 0 0 00	

ACCOUNT *Cash* — **ACCOUNT NO.** *11* ④

Date		Item	Post. Ref.	Debit	Credit	Balance Debit	Balance Credit
1996 Nov.	30		1		2 0 0 0 00	5 9 0 0 00	
① Dec.	1		1 ③		2 4 0 0 00	3 5 0 0 00	

[4] The use of special journals and computerized accounting systems are discussed in later chapters, after the basics of accounting systems have been presented.

In the journal, you should note where the date of the transaction is recorded. Also note that the entry is explained as the payment of an insurance premium. Such explanations are normally used only for unusual entries when the nature of the transaction is not obvious. For complex transactions, such as a long-term rental arrangement, the journal entry explanation may include a reference to the rental agreement or other business document.

You will note that the T account form is not used in this illustration. Although the T account clearly separates debit entries and credit entries, it is inefficient for summarizing a large quantity of transactions. In practice, the T account is usually replaced with the standard form shown in Exhibit 2.

The debits and credits for each journal entry are posted to the accounts in the order that they occur in the journal. In posting to the standard account, ① the date is entered, and ② the amount of the entry is entered. For future reference, ③ the journal page number is inserted in the Posting Reference column of the account, and ④ the account number is inserted in the Posting Reference column of the journal.

The remaining December transactions for Computer King are analyzed in the following paragraphs. These transactions are posted to the ledger in Exhibit 3, shown later. To simplify and reduce repetition, some of the December transactions are stated in summary form. For example, cash received for services is normally recorded on a daily basis. In this example, however, only summary totals are recorded at the middle and end of the month. Likewise, all fees earned on account during December are recorded at the middle and end of the month. In practice, each fee earned is recorded separately.

Dec. 1. Computer King paid rent for December, $800. The company from which Computer King is renting its store space now requires the payment of rent on the 1st of each month, rather than at the end of the month.

ANALYSIS: Similar to the advance payment of the insurance premium in the preceding transaction, the advance payment of rent is an asset. However, the asset Prepaid Insurance will not completely expire for 24 months, while the asset Prepaid Rent will expire in one month. When an asset that is purchased will be used up in a short period of time, such as a month, it is normal to debit an expense account initially. This avoids having to transfer the balance from an asset account (Prepaid Rent) to an expense account (Rent Expense) at the end of the month. Thus, when the rent for December is prepaid at the beginning of the month, Rent Expense is debited for $800 and Cash is credited for $800.

Date		Description	Post. Ref.	Debit	Credit
Dec.	1	Rent Expense	52	800 00	
		Cash	11		800 00

Dec. 1. Computer King received an offer from a local retailer to rent the land purchased on November 5. The retailer plans to use the land as a parking lot for its employees and customers. Computer King agreed to rent the land for three months, payable in advance. Computer King received $360 for three months' rent beginning December 1.

ANALYSIS: By agreeing to rent the land and accepting the $360, Computer King has incurred an obligation (liability) to the retailer. This obligation is to make the land available for use for three months and not to interfere with its use. The liability created by receiving the revenue in advance is called **unearned revenue.** Thus, the $360 received is an increase in an asset and is debited to Cash.

The liability account Unearned Rent increases and is credited for $360. As time passes, the unearned rent liability will decrease and will become revenue.

You will note that an explanation has been added to this journal entry. This is because the transaction is unusual for Computer King, which is not in the business of renting land.

JOURNAL **PAGE 2**

Date		Description	Post. Ref.	Debit	Credit
1996 Dec.	1	Cash	11	360 00	
		Unearned Rent	23		360 00
		Received advance payment			
		for three months' rent.			

Dec. 4. Purchased office equipment on account from Executive Supply Co. for $1,800.

ANALYSIS: The asset account Office Equipment increases and is therefore debited for $1,800. The liability account Accounts Payable increases and is credited for $1,800.

Date		Description	Post. Ref.	Debit	Credit
	4	Office Equipment	18	1 800 00	
		Accounts Payable	21		1 800 00

Dec. 6. Paid $180 for a newspaper advertisement.

ANALYSIS: An expense increases and is debited for $180. The asset Cash decreases and is credited for $180. Expense items that are expected to be minor in amount are normally included as part of the miscellaneous expense. Thus, Miscellaneous Expense is debited for $180.

Date		Description	Post. Ref.	Debit	Credit
	6	Miscellaneous Expense	59	180 00	
		Cash	11		180 00

Dec.11. Paid creditors $400.

ANALYSIS: This payment decreases the liability account Accounts Payable, which is debited for $400. Cash also decreases and is credited for $400.

Date		Description	Post. Ref.	Debit	Credit
	11	Accounts Payable	21	400 00	
		Cash	11		400 00

Dec.13. Paid receptionist and part-time assistant $950 for two weeks' wages.

ANALYSIS: This transaction is similar to the December 6 transaction, where an expense account is increased and Cash is decreased. Thus, Wages Expense is debited for $950 and Cash is credited for $950.

Date	Description	Post. Ref.	Debit	Credit
13	Wages Expense	51	950 00	
	Cash	11		950 00

Dec.16. Received $3,100 from fees earned for the first half of December.

ANALYSIS: Cash increases and is debited for $3,100. The revenue account Fees Earned increases and is credited for $3,100.

Date	Description	Post. Ref.	Debit	Credit
16	Cash	11	3100 00	
	Fees Earned	41		3100 00

Dec.16. Fees earned on account totaled $1,750 for the first half of December.

ANALYSIS: When a business agrees that payment for services provided or goods sold can be accepted at another date, the firm has an **account receivable,** which is a claim against the customer. The account receivable is an asset, and the revenue is earned even though no cash has been received. Thus, Accounts Receivable increases and is debited for $1,750. The revenue account Fees Earned increases and is credited for $1,750.

Date	Description	Post. Ref.	Debit	Credit
16	Accounts Receivable	12	1750 00	
	Fees Earned	41		1750 00

Dec. 20. Paid $900 to Executive Supply Co. on the $1,800 debt owed from the December 4 transaction.

ANALYSIS: Similar to transaction of December 11.

Date	Description	Post. Ref.	Debit	Credit
20	Accounts Payable	21	900 00	
	Cash	11		900 00

Dec. 21. Received $650 from customers in payment of their accounts.

ANALYSIS: When customers pay amounts owed for services they have previously received, one asset increases and another asset decreases. Thus, Cash is debited for $650, and Accounts Receivable is credited for $650.

Date	Description	Post. Ref.	Debit	Credit
21	Cash	11	650 00	
	Accounts Receivable	12		650 00

Dec. 23. Paid $1,450 for supplies.

ANALYSIS: The asset account Supplies increases and is debited for $1,450. The asset account Cash decreases and is credited for $1,450.

Date	Description	Post. Ref.	Debit	Credit
23	Supplies	14	1 450 00	
	Cash	11		1 450 00

Dec. 27. Paid receptionist and part-time assistant $1,200 for two weeks' wages.

ANALYSIS: Similar to transaction of December 13.

Date	Description	Post. Ref.	Debit	Credit
27	Wages Expense	51	1 200 00	
	Cash	11		1 200 00

Dec. 31. Paid $310 telephone bill for the month.

ANALYSIS: Similar to transaction of December 6. The expense account Utilities Expense is debited for $310, and Cash is credited for $310.

JOURNAL **PAGE 3**

Date		Description	Post. Ref.	Debit	Credit
1996 Dec.	31	Utilities Expense	54	310 00	
		Cash	11		310 00

Dec. 31. Paid $225 electric bill for the month.

ANALYSIS: Similar to the preceding transaction.

Date	Description	Post. Ref.	Debit	Credit
31	Utilities Expense	54	225 00	
	Cash	11		225 00

Dec. 31. Received $2,870 from fees earned for the second half of December.

ANALYSIS: Similar to transaction of December 16.

Date	Description	Post. Ref.	Debit	Credit
31	Cash	11	2870 00	
	Fees Earned	41		2870 00

Dec. 31. Fees earned on account totaled $1,120 for the second half of December.

ANALYSIS: Similar to transaction of December 16.

Date	Description	Post. Ref.	Debit	Credit
31	Accounts Receivable	12	1120 00	
	Fees Earned	41		1120 00

Dec. 31. Pat King withdrew $2,000 for personal use.

ANALYSIS: The transaction resulted in an increase in the amount of withdrawals and is recorded by a $2,000 debit to Pat King, Drawing. The decrease in business cash is recorded by a $2,000 credit to Cash.

Date	Description	Post. Ref.	Debit	Credit
31	Pat King, Drawing	32	2000 00	
	Cash	11		2000 00

The journal for Computer King since it was organized on November 1 is shown in Exhibit 3. Exhibit 3 also shows the ledger after the transactions for both November and December have been posted.

Exhibit 3
Journal and Ledger—Computer King

JOURNAL **PAGE 1**

Date		Description	Post. Ref.	Debit	Credit
1996 Nov.	1	Cash	11	15000 00	
		Pat King, Capital	31		15000 00
	5	Land	17	10000 00	
		Cash	11		10000 00
	10	Supplies	14	1350 00	
		Accounts Payable	21		1350 00
	18	Cash	11	7500 00	
		Fees Earned	41		7500 00
	30	Wages Expense	51	2125 00	
		Rent Expense	52	800 00	
		Utilities Expense	54	450 00	
		Miscellaneous Expense	59	275 00	
		Cash	11		3650 00
	30	Accounts Payable	21	950 00	
		Cash	11		950 00

Exhibit 3 *(continued)*

Date		Description	Post. Ref.	Debit	Credit
	30	Supplies Expense	55	800 00	
		Supplies	14		800 00
	30	Pat King, Drawing	32	2000 00	
		Cash	11		2000 00
Dec.	1	Prepaid Insurance	15	2400 00	
		Cash	11		2400 00
	1	Rent Expense	52	800 00	
		Cash	11		800 00

JOURNAL **PAGE 2**

Date		Description	Post. Ref.	Debit	Credit
1996 Dec.	1	Cash	11	360 00	
		Unearned Rent	23		360 00
	4	Office Equipment	18	1800 00	
		Accounts Payable	21		1800 00
	6	Miscellaneous Expense	59	180 00	
		Cash	11		180 00
	11	Accounts Payable	21	400 00	
		Cash	11		400 00
	13	Wages Expense	51	950 00	
		Cash	11		950 00
	16	Cash	11	3100 00	
		Fees Earned	41		3100 00
	16	Accounts Receivable	12	1750 00	
		Fees Earned	41		1750 00
	20	Accounts Payable	21	900 00	
		Cash	11		900 00
	21	Cash	11	650 00	
		Accounts Receivable	12		650 00
	23	Supplies	14	1450 00	
		Cash	11		1450 00
	27	Wages Expense	51	1200 00	
		Cash	11		1200 00

Exhibit 3 *(continued)*

JOURNAL PAGE 3

Date		Description	Post. Ref.	Debit	Credit
1996 Dec.	31	Utilities Expense	54	310 00	
		Cash	11		310 00
	31	Utilities Expense	54	225 00	
		Cash	11		225 00
	31	Cash	11	2870 00	
		Fees Earned	41		2870 00
	31	Accounts Receivable	12	1120 00	
		Fees Earned	41		1120 00
	31	Pat King, Drawing	32	2000 00	
		Cash	11		2000 00

LEDGER

ACCOUNT *Cash* ACCOUNT NO. *11*

Date		Item	Post. Ref.	Debit	Credit	Balance Debit	Balance Credit
1996 Nov.	1		1	15000 00		15000 00	
	5		1		10000 00	5000 00	
	18		1	7500 00		12500 00	
	30		1		3650 00	8850 00	
	30		1		950 00	7900 00	
	30		1		2000 00	5900 00	
Dec.	1		1		2400 00	3500 00	
	1		1		800 00	2700 00	
	1		2	360 00		3060 00	
	6		2		180 00	2880 00	
	11		2		400 00	2480 00	
	13		2		950 00	1530 00	
	16		2	3100 00		4630 00	
	20		2		900 00	3730 00	
	21		2	650 00		4380 00	
	23		2		1450 00	2930 00	
	27		2		1200 00	1730 00	
	31		3		310 00	1420 00	
	31		3		225 00	1195 00	
	31		3	2870 00		4065 00	
	31		3		2000 00	2065 00	

Exhibit 3 *(continued)*

ACCOUNT ***Accounts Receivable*** **ACCOUNT NO. *12***

Date		Item	Post. Ref.	Debit	Credit	Balance Debit	Balance Credit
1996 Dec.	16		2	1,750.00		1,750.00	
	21		2		650.00	1,100.00	
	31		3	1,120.00		2,220.00	

ACCOUNT ***Supplies*** **ACCOUNT NO. *14***

Date		Item	Post. Ref.	Debit	Credit	Balance Debit	Balance Credit
1996 Nov.	10		1	1,350.00		1,350.00	
	30		1		800.00	550.00	
Dec.	23		2	1,450.00		2,000.00	

ACCOUNT ***Prepaid Insurance*** **ACCOUNT NO. *15***

Date		Item	Post. Ref.	Debit	Credit	Balance Debit	Balance Credit
1996 Dec.	1		1	2,400.00		2,400.00	

ACCOUNT ***Land*** **ACCOUNT NO. *17***

Date		Item	Post. Ref.	Debit	Credit	Balance Debit	Balance Credit
1996 Nov.	5		1	10,000.00		10,000.00	

ACCOUNT ***Office Equipment*** **ACCOUNT NO. *18***

Date		Item	Post. Ref.	Debit	Credit	Balance Debit	Balance Credit
1996 Dec.	4		2	1,800.00		1,800.00	

ACCOUNT ***Accounts Payable*** **ACCOUNT NO. *21***

Date		Item	Post. Ref.	Debit	Credit	Balance Debit	Balance Credit
1996 Nov.	10		1		1,350.00		1,350.00
	30		1	950.00			400.00
Dec.	4		2		1,800.00		2,200.00
	11		2	400.00			1,800.00
	20		2	900.00			900.00

Exhibit 3 *(continued)*

ACCOUNT ***Unearned Rent*** — **ACCOUNT NO.** ***23***

Date		Item	Post. Ref.	Debit	Credit	Balance Debit	Balance Credit
1996 Dec.	1		2		360 00		360 00

ACCOUNT ***Pat King, Capital*** — **ACCOUNT NO.** ***31***

Date		Item	Post. Ref.	Debit	Credit	Balance Debit	Balance Credit
1996 Nov.	1		1		15 000 00		15 000 00

ACCOUNT ***Pat King, Drawing*** — **ACCOUNT NO.** ***32***

Date		Item	Post. Ref.	Debit	Credit	Balance Debit	Balance Credit
1996 Nov.	30		1	2 000 00		2 000 00	
Dec.	31		3	2 000 00		4 000 00	

ACCOUNT ***Fees Earned*** — **ACCOUNT NO.** ***41***

Date		Item	Post. Ref.	Debit	Credit	Balance Debit	Balance Credit
1996 Nov.	18		1		7 500 00		7 500 00
Dec.	16		2		3 100 00		10 600 00
	16		2		1 750 00		12 350 00
	31		3		2 870 00		15 220 00
	31		3		1 120 00		16 340 00

ACCOUNT ***Wages Expense*** — **ACCOUNT NO.** ***51***

Date		Item	Post. Ref.	Debit	Credit	Balance Debit	Balance Credit
1996 Nov.	30		1	2 125 00		2 125 00	
Dec.	13		2	950 00		3 075 00	
	27		2	1 200 00		4 275 00	

ACCOUNT ***Rent Expense*** — **ACCOUNT NO.** ***52***

Date		Item	Post. Ref.	Debit	Credit	Balance Debit	Balance Credit
1996 Nov.	30		1	800 00		800 00	
Dec.	1		1	800 00		1 600 00	

Exhibit 3 *(concluded)*

ACCOUNT ***Utilities Expense*** **ACCOUNT NO. *54***

Date		Item	Post. Ref.	Debit	Credit	Balance Debit	Balance Credit
1996 Nov.	30		1	450 00		450 00	
Dec.	31		3	310 00		760 00	
	31		3	225 00		985 00	

ACCOUNT ***Supplies Expense*** **ACCOUNT NO. *55***

Date		Item	Post. Ref.	Debit	Credit	Balance Debit	Balance Credit
1996 Nov.	30		1	800 00		800 00	

ACCOUNT ***Miscellaneous Expense*** **ACCOUNT NO. *59***

Date		Item	Post. Ref.	Debit	Credit	Balance Debit	Balance Credit
1996 Nov.	30		1	275 00		275 00	
Dec.	6		2	180 00		455 00	

Trial Balance

Objective 5
Prepare a trial balance and explain how it can be used to discover errors.

How can you be sure that you have not made an error in posting the debits and credits to the ledger? One way is to determine the equality of the debits and credits in the ledger. This equality should be proved at the end of each accounting period, if not more often. Such a proof, called a **trial balance,** may be in the form of a computer printout or in the form shown in Exhibit 4.[5]

The first step in preparing the trial balance is to determine the balance of each account in the ledger. When the standard account form is used, the balance of each account appears in the balance column on the same line as the last posting to the account.

The trial balance does not provide complete proof of the accuracy of the ledger. It indicates only that the debits and the credits are equal. This proof is of value, however, because errors often affect the equality of debits and credits. If the two totals of a trial balance are not equal, an error has occurred. In the remainder of this chapter, we will discuss procedures for discovering and correcting errors.

[5] A trial balance is not a formal statement, but is used by the accountant to verify the accuracy of the accounting records. Thus, financial statement captions, subtotals, and dollar signs are normally omitted from a trial balance.

Exhibit 4
Trial Balance

Computer King Trial Balance December 31, 1996		
Cash	2 0 6 5 00	
Accounts Receivable	2 2 2 0 00	
Supplies	2 0 0 0 00	
Prepaid Insurance	2 4 0 0 00	
Land	10 0 0 0 00	
Office Equipment	1 8 0 0 00	
Accounts Payable		9 0 0 00
Unearned Rent		3 6 0 00
Pat King, Capital		15 0 0 0 00
Pat King, Drawing	4 0 0 0 00	
Fees Earned		16 3 4 0 00
Wages Expense	4 2 7 5 00	
Rent Expense	1 6 0 0 00	
Utilities Expense	9 8 5 00	
Supplies Expense	8 0 0 00	
Miscellaneous Expense	4 5 5 00	
	32 6 0 0 00	32 6 0 0 00

Discovery and Correction of Errors

Objective 6
Discover errors in recording transactions and correct them.

Errors will sometimes occur in journalizing and posting transactions. In the following paragraphs, we describe and illustrate how errors may be discovered and corrected. In some cases, however, an error might not be significant enough to affect the decisions of management or others. In such cases, the **materiality concept** implies that the error may be treated in the easiest possible way. For example, an error of a few dollars in recording an asset as an expense for a business with millions of dollars in assets would be considered immaterial, and a correction would not be necessary. In the remaining paragraphs, we assume that errors discovered are material and should be corrected.

DISCOVERY OF ERRORS

As mentioned previously, the trial balance is one of the primary ways for discovering errors in the ledger. However, it indicates only that the debits and credits are equal. If the two totals of the trial balance are not equal, it is probably due to one or more of the following types of errors:

1. Error in preparing the trial balance, such as:
   a. One of the columns of the trial balance was incorrectly added.
   b. The amount of an account balance was incorrectly recorded on the trial balance.
   c. A debit balance was recorded on the trial balance as a credit, or vice versa, or a balance was omitted entirely.
2. Error in determining the account balances, such as:
   a. A balance was incorrectly computed.
   b. A balance was entered in the wrong balance column.

3. Error in recording a transaction in the ledger, such as:
   a. An erroneous amount was posted to the account.
   b. A debit entry was posted as a credit, or vice versa.
   c. A debit or a credit posting was omitted.

Among the types of errors that will not cause an inequality in the trial balance totals are the following:

1. Failure to record a transaction or to post a transaction.
2. Recording the same erroneous amount for both the debit and the credit parts of a transaction.
3. Recording the same transaction more than once.
4. Posting a part of a transaction correctly as a debit or credit but to the wrong account.

It is obvious that care should be used in recording transactions in the journal and in posting to the accounts. The need for accuracy in determining account balances and reporting them on the trial balance is equally obvious.

Errors in the accounts may be discovered in various ways: (1) by audit procedures, (2) by chance, or (3) by looking at the trial balance. If the two trial balance totals are not equal, the amount of the difference between the totals should be determined before searching for the error.

The amount of the difference between the two totals of a trial balance sometimes gives a clue as to the nature of the error or where it occurred. For example, a difference of 10, 100, or 1,000 between two totals is often the result of an error in addition. A difference between totals can also be due to omitting a debit or a credit posting. If the difference is divisible evenly by 2, the error may be due to the posting of a debit as a credit, or vice versa. For example, if the debit total is $20,640 and the credit total is $20,236, the difference of $404 may indicate that a credit posting of $404 was omitted or that a credit of $202 was incorrectly posted as a debit.

Two other common types of errors are known as transpositions and slides. A **transposition** is the erroneous rearrangement of digits, such as writing $542 as $452 or $524. In a **slide,** the entire number is erroneously moved one or more spaces to the right or the left, such as writing $542.00 as $54.20 or $5,420.00. If an error of either type has occurred and there are no other errors, the difference between the two trial balance totals can be evenly divided by 9.

If an error is not revealed by the trial balance, the steps in the accounting process must be retraced, beginning with the last step and working back to the entries in the journal. Usually, errors causing the trial balance totals to be unequal will be discovered before all of the steps are retraced. While there are no standard rules for searching for errors, the steps presented below are usually followed:

1. Prove the accuracy of the trial balance totals by re-adding the columns.
2. Compare the listings in the trial balance with the balances shown in the ledger. Make certain that no accounts have been omitted.
3. Recompute the balance of each account in the ledger.
4. Trace the postings in the ledger back to the journal. Place a small check mark beside each item in the ledger and also in the journal. If the error is not found, examine each account to see if there is an entry without a check mark. Do the same with the entries in the journal.
5. Prove the equality of the debits and the credits in the journal.

CORRECTION OF ERRORS

When errors in journalizing and posting transactions are discovered, the procedures used to correct them vary according to the nature of the error and when the error is discovered. We will discuss these procedures in the following paragraphs.

An error in an account title or amount in the journal may be discovered before the entry is posted. In this case, the correction may be made by drawing a line through the error and inserting the correct title or amount directly above. If there is any chance of questions arising later, the person responsible may initial the correction.

An entry in the journal may be prepared correctly but posted incorrectly to the account. In this case, the incorrect posting may be corrected by drawing a line through the error and posting the item correctly. As indicated above, if there is any chance of questions arising later, the person responsible may initial the correction.

An incorrect account title may appear in a journal entry and the error may not be discovered until after posting is completed. In this case, it is best to journalize and post a correcting entry. To illustrate, assume that on May 5 a purchase of office equipment was incorrectly journalized and posted as a $12,500 debit to Supplies. The credit was correctly journalized and posted as a $12,500 credit to Accounts Payable. Before a correcting entry is made, it is best to determine (1) the debit(s) and credit(s) of the entry in which the error occurred and (2) the debit(s) and credit(s) that should have been recorded. T accounts may be helpful in making this analysis, as in the following example:

Entry in which error occurred:

Supplies		Accounts Payable	
12,500			12,500

Entry that should have been recorded:

Office Equipment		Accounts Payable	
12,500			12,500

Comparing the two sets of T accounts shows that the incorrect debit of $12,500 to Supplies may be corrected by debiting Office Equipment for $12,500 and crediting Supplies for $12,500. The following correcting entry is then journalized and posted:

JOURNAL PAGE 30

	Date		Description	Post. Ref.	Debit	Credit	
1	1996 May	5	Office Equipment	18	12 5 0 0 00		1
2			Supplies	14		12 5 0 0 00	2
3			To correct erroneous debit to				3
4			Supplies on May 5. See invoice				4
5			from Bell Office Equipment Co. *CW*				5

The procedures for correcting errors are summarized in Exhibit 5.

Exhibit 5
Procedures for Correcting Errors

Error	*Correction Procedure*
Journal entry incorrect but not posted.	Draw line through the error and insert correct title or amount.
Journal entry correct but posted incorrectly.	Draw line through the error and post correctly.
Journal entry incorrect and posted.	Journalize and post a correcting entry.

KEY POINTS

Objective 1. Explain why accounts are used to record and summarize the effects of transactions on financial statements.
The record used for the purpose of recording individual transactions is an account. A group of accounts is called a ledger.

The system of accounts that make up a ledger is called a chart of accounts. The accounts are numbered and listed in the order in which they appear in the balance sheet and the income statement.

Objective 2. Explain the characteristics of an account.
The simplest form of an account, a T account, has three parts. First, each account has a title, which is the name of the item recorded in the account. Second, each account has a left side, called the debit side. Third, each account has a right side, called the credit side. Amounts entered on the left side of an account, regardless of the account title, are called debits to the account. Amounts entered on the right side of an account are called credits. Periodically, the debits and the credits in an account are summed and the balance of the account is determined.

Objective 3. List the rules of debit and credit and the normal balances of accounts.
General rules of debit and credit have been established for recording increases or decreases in asset, liability, owner's equity, revenue, expense, and drawing accounts. Each transaction is recorded so that the sum of the debits is always equal to the sum of the credits. Transactions are initially entered in a record called a journal.

The sum of the increases recorded in an account is usually equal to or greater than the sum of the decreases recorded in the account. For this reason, the normal balance of an account is indicated by the side of the account (debit or credit) that receives the increases.

The rules of debit and credit and normal account balances are summarized in the following table:

	Increase (Normal Balance)	*Decrease*
Balance sheet accounts:		
Asset	**Debit**	Credit
Liability	**Credit**	Debit
Owner's Equity:		
Capital	**Credit**	Debit
Drawing	**Debit**	Credit
Income statement accounts:		
Revenue	**Credit**	Debit
Expense	**Debit**	Credit

Objective 4. Analyze and summarize the financial statement effects of transactions.
A two-column journal with a debit column and a credit column is used for recording initial transactions in an accounting system. In practice, the T account is usually replaced with the standard account form. Journal entries are periodically posted to the accounts.

Objective 5. Prepare a trial balance and explain how it can be used to discover errors.
A trial balance is prepared by listing the accounts from the ledger and their balances. If the two totals of the trial balance are not equal, an error has occurred.

Objective 6. Discover errors in recording transactions and correct them.
Errors may be discovered (1) by audit procedures, (2) by chance, or (3) by looking at the trial balance. The procedures for correcting errors are summarized in Exhibit 5.

GLOSSARY OF KEY TERMS

Account. The form used to record additions and deductions for each individual asset, liability, owner's equity, revenue, and expense. *Objective 1*

Assets. Physical items (tangible) or rights (intangible) that have value and that are owned by the business entity. *Objective 1*

Balance of the account. The amount of difference between the debits and the credits that have been entered into an account. *Objective 2*

Chart of accounts. The system of accounts that make up the ledger for a business. *Objective 1*

Credit. (1) The right side of an account; (2) the amount entered on the right side of an account; (3) to enter an amount on the right side of an account. *Objective 2*

Debit. (1) The left side of an account; (2) the amount entered on the left side of an account; (3) to enter an amount on the left side of an account. *Objective 2*

Double-entry accounting. A system for recording transactions, based on recording increases and decreases in accounts so that debits always equal credits. *Objective 3*

Drawing. The amount of withdrawals made by the owner of a sole proprietorship. *Objective 1*

Expenses. Assets used up or services consumed in the process of generating revenues. *Objective 1*

Journal. The initial record in which the effects of a transaction on accounts are recorded. *Objective 3*

Journalizing. The process of recording a transaction in a journal. *Objective 3*

Ledger. The group of accounts used by a business. *Objective 1*

Liabilities. Debts owed to outsiders (creditors). *Objective 1*

Owner's equity. The owner's right to the assets of the business after the total liabilities are deducted. *Objective 1*

Posting. The process of transferring debits and credits from a journal to the accounts. *Objective 4*

Revenues. Increases in owner's equity as a result of providing services or selling products to customers. *Objective 1*

Slide. The erroneous movement of all digits in a number, one or more spaces to the right or the left, such as writing $542 as $5,420. *Objective 6*

T account. A form of account resembling the letter T. *Objective 2*

Transposition. The erroneous arrangement of digits in a number, such as writing $542 as $524. *Objective 6*

Trial balance. A summary listing of the titles and balances of the accounts in the ledger. *Objective 5*

ILLUSTRATIVE PROBLEM

J. F. Outz, M.D., has been practicing as a cardiologist for three years. During April, Outz completed the following transactions in her practice of cardiology.

April 1. Paid office rent for April, $800.
3. Purchased equipment on account, $2,100.
5. Received cash on account from patients, $3,150.
8. Purchased X-ray film and other supplies on account, $245.
9. One of the items of equipment purchased on April 3 was defective. It was returned with the permission of the supplier, who agreed to reduce the account for the amount charged for the item, $325.
12. Paid cash to creditors on account, $1,250.
17. Paid cash for renewal of a six-month property insurance policy, $370.
20. Discovered that the balance of the cash account and of the accounts payable account as of April 1 were overstated by $200. A payment of that amount to a creditor in March had not been recorded. Journalize the $200 payment as of April 20.
24. Paid cash for laboratory analysis, $545.
27. Paid cash from business bank account for personal and family expenses, $1,250.
30. Recorded the cash received in payment of services (on a cash basis) to patients during April, $1,720.
30. Paid salaries of receptionist and nurses, $1,725.
30. Paid various utility expenses, $360.
30. Recorded fees charged to patients on account for services performed in April, $5,145.
30. Paid miscellaneous expenses, $132.

Outz's account titles, numbers, and balances as of April 1 (all normal balances) are listed as follows: Cash, 11, $4,123; Accounts Receivable, 12, $6,725; Supplies, 13, $290; Prepaid Insurance, 14, $465; Equipment, 18, $19,745; Accounts Payable, 22, $765; J. F. Outz, Capital, 31, $30,583; J. F. Outz, Drawing, 32; Professional Fees, 41; Salary Expense, 51; Rent Expense, 53; Laboratory Expense, 55; Utilities Expense, 56; Miscellaneous Expense, 59.

Instructions

1. Open a ledger of standard four-column accounts for Dr. Outz as of April 1 of the current year. Enter the balances in the appropriate balance columns and place a check mark (✓) in the posting reference column. (It is advisable to verify the equality of the debit and credit balances in the ledger before proceeding with the next instruction.)
2. Journalize each transaction in a two-column journal.
3. Post the journal to the ledger, extending the month-end balances to the appropriate balance columns after each posting.
4. Prepare a trial balance as of April 30.

Solution

2. and 3.

JOURNAL PAGE 27

Date		Description	Post. Ref.	Debit	Credit
19— April	1	Rent Expense	53	800 00	
		Cash	11		800 00
	3	Equipment	18	2 100 00	
		Accounts Payable	22		2 100 00
	5	Cash	11	3 150 00	
		Accounts Receivable	12		3 150 00
	8	Supplies	13	245 00	
		Accounts Payable	22		245 00
	9	Accounts Payable	22	325 00	
		Equipment	18		325 00
	12	Accounts Payable	22	1 250 00	
		Cash	11		1 250 00
	17	Prepaid Insurance	14	370 00	
		Cash	11		370 00
	20	Accounts Payable	22	200 00	
		Cash	11		200 00
	24	Laboratory Expense	55	545 00	
		Cash	11		545 00
	27	J. F. Outz, Drawing	32	1 250 00	
		Cash	11		1 250 00
	30	Cash	11	1 720 00	
		Professional Fees	41		1 720 00

JOURNAL PAGE 28

Date		Description	Post. Ref.	Debit	Credit
19— April	30	Salary Expense	51	1 725 00	
		Cash	11		1 725 00
	30	Utilities Expense	56	360 00	
		Cash	11		360 00
	30	Accounts Receivable	12	5 145 00	
		Professional Fees	41		5 145 00
	30	Miscellaneous Expense	59	132 00	
		Cash	11		132 00

1. and 3.

ACCOUNT *Cash* **ACCOUNT NO.** *11*

Date		Item	Post. Ref.	Debit	Credit	Balance Debit	Balance Credit
19— April	1	Balance	✓			4 1 2 3 00	
	1		27		8 0 0 00	3 3 2 3 00	
	5		27	3 1 5 0 00		6 4 7 3 00	
	12		27		1 2 5 0 00	5 2 2 3 00	
	17		27		3 7 0 00	4 8 5 3 00	
	20		27		2 0 0 00	4 6 5 3 00	
	24		27		5 4 5 00	4 1 0 8 00	
	27		27		1 2 5 0 00	2 8 5 8 00	
	30		27	1 7 2 0 00		4 5 7 8 00	
	30		28		1 7 2 5 00	2 8 5 3 00	
	30		28		3 6 0 00	2 4 9 3 00	
	30		28		1 3 2 00	2 3 6 1 00	

ACCOUNT *Accounts Receivable* **ACCOUNT NO.** *12*

Date		Item	Post. Ref.	Debit	Credit	Balance Debit	Balance Credit
19— April	1	Balance	✓			6 7 2 5 00	
	5		27		3 1 5 0 00	3 5 7 5 00	
	30		28	5 1 4 5 00		8 7 2 0 00	

ACCOUNT *Supplies* **ACCOUNT NO.** *13*

Date		Item	Post. Ref.	Debit	Credit	Balance Debit	Balance Credit
19— April	1	Balance	✓			2 9 0 00	
	8		27	2 4 5 00		5 3 5 00	

ACCOUNT *Prepaid Insurance* **ACCOUNT NO.** *14*

Date		Item	Post. Ref.	Debit	Credit	Balance Debit	Balance Credit
19— April	1	Balance	✓			4 6 5 00	
	17		27	3 7 0 00		8 3 5 00	

ACCOUNT *Equipment* **ACCOUNT NO.** *18*

Date		Item	Post. Ref.	Debit	Credit	Balance Debit	Balance Credit
19— April	1	Balance	✓			19 7 4 5 00	
	3		27	2 1 0 0 00		21 8 4 5 00	
	9		27		3 2 5 00	21 5 2 0 00	

ACCOUNT ***Accounts Payable*** **ACCOUNT NO. *22***

Date		Item	Post. Ref.	Debit	Credit	Balance Debit	Balance Credit
19— April	1	Balance	✓				7 6 5 00
	3		27		2 1 0 0 00		2 8 6 5 00
	8		27		2 4 5 00		3 1 1 0 00
	9		27	3 2 5 00			2 7 8 5 00
	12		27	1 2 5 0 00			1 5 3 5 00
	20		27	2 0 0 00			1 3 3 5 00

ACCOUNT ***J. F. Outz, Capital*** **ACCOUNT NO. *31***

Date		Item	Post. Ref.	Debit	Credit	Balance Debit	Balance Credit
19— April	1	Balance	✓				30 5 8 3 00

ACCOUNT ***J. F. Outz, Drawing*** **ACCOUNT NO. *32***

Date		Item	Post. Ref.	Debit	Credit	Balance Debit	Balance Credit
19— April	27		27	1 2 5 0 00		1 2 5 0 00	

ACCOUNT ***Professional Fees*** **ACCOUNT NO. *41***

Date		Item	Post. Ref.	Debit	Credit	Balance Debit	Balance Credit
19— April	30		27		1 7 2 0 00		1 7 2 0 00
	30		28		5 1 4 5 00		6 8 6 5 00

ACCOUNT ***Salary Expense*** **ACCOUNT NO. *51***

Date		Item	Post. Ref.	Debit	Credit	Balance Debit	Balance Credit
19— April	30		28	1 7 2 5 00		1 7 2 5 00	

ACCOUNT ***Rent Expense*** **ACCOUNT NO. *53***

Date		Item	Post. Ref.	Debit	Credit	Balance Debit	Balance Credit
19— April	1		27	8 0 0 00		8 0 0 00	

ACCOUNT ***Laboratory Expense*** **ACCOUNT NO. *55***

Date		Item	Post. Ref.	Debit	Credit	Balance Debit	Balance Credit
19— April	24		27	5 4 5 00		5 4 5 00	

ACCOUNT ***Utilities Expense*** **ACCOUNT NO. *56***

Date		Item	Post. Ref.	Debit	Credit	Balance Debit	Balance Credit
19— April	30		28	360 00		360 00	

ACCOUNT ***Miscellaneous Expense*** **ACCOUNT NO. *59***

Date		Item	Post. Ref.	Debit	Credit	Balance Debit	Balance Credit
19— April	30		28	132 00		132 00	

4.

J. F. Outz, M.D.
Trial Balance
April 30, 19—

Cash	2 361 00	
Accounts Receivable	8 720 00	
Supplies	535 00	
Prepaid Insurance	835 00	
Equipment	21 520 00	
Accounts Payable		1 335 00
J. F. Outz, Capital		30 583 00
J. F. Outz, Drawing	1 250 00	
Professional Fees		6 865 00
Salary Expense	1 725 00	
Rent Expense	800 00	
Laboratory Expense	545 00	
Utilities Expense	360 00	
Miscellaneous Expense	132 00	
	38 783 00	38 783 00

SELF-EXAMINATION QUESTIONS (ANSWERS AT END OF CHAPTER)

1. A debit may signify:
   A. an increase in an asset account
   B. a decrease in an asset account
   C. an increase in a liability account
   D. an increase in the owner's capital account

2. The type of account with a normal credit balance is:
   A. an asset C. a revenue
   B. drawing D. an expense

3. A debit balance in which of the following accounts would indicate a likely error?
   A. Accounts Receivable C. Fees Earned
   B. Cash D. Miscellaneous Expense

4. The receipt of cash from customers in payment of their accounts would be recorded by a:
   A. debit to Cash; credit to Accounts Receivable
   B. debit to Accounts Receivable; credit to Cash
   C. debit to Cash; credit to Accounts Payable
   D. debit to Accounts Payable; credit to Cash

5. The form listing the titles and balances of the accounts in the ledger on a given date is the:
   A. income statement C. statement of owner's equity
   B. balance sheet D. trial balance

DISCUSSION QUESTIONS

1. What is an account?
2. Differentiate between an account and a ledger.
3. What is the name of the listing of accounts in the ledger?
4. Describe in general terms the sequence of accounts in the ledger.
5. Do the terms *debit* and *credit* signify increase or decrease, or may they signify either? Explain.
6. What is the name of the record in which a transaction is initially entered?
7. Define posting.
8. Explain why the rules of debit and credit are the same for liability accounts and owner's equity accounts.
9. What is the effect (increase or decrease) of debits to expense accounts (a) in terms of owner's equity and (b) in terms of expense?
10. What is the effect (increase or decrease) of credits to revenue accounts (a) in terms of owner's equity and (b) in terms of revenue?
11. Liebrandt Company adheres to a policy of depositing all cash receipts in a bank account and making all payments by check. The cash account as of June 30 has a credit balance of $575, and there is no undeposited cash on hand. (a) Assuming that there were no errors in journalizing or posting, what is the explanation of this unusual balance? (b) Is the $575 credit balance in the cash account an asset, a liability, owner's equity, a revenue, or an expense?
12. Rearrange the following in proper sequence: (a) entry is posted to ledger, (b) business transaction occurs, (c) entry is recorded in journal, (d) business document is prepared, (e) business transaction is authorized.
13. Describe the three procedures required to post the credit portion of the following journal entry (Fees Earned is account no. 41):

JOURNAL **PAGE 32**

Date		Description	Post. Ref.	Debit	Credit
19— June	11	Accounts Receivable	12	875 00	
		Fees Earned			875 00

14. In examining an entry that has been recorded in the journal, what indicates that the entry has been posted to the accounts?
15. Justice Company performed services in June for a specific customer, and the fee was $6,200. Payment was received the following July. (a) Was the revenue earned in June or July? (b) What accounts should be debited and credited in (1) June and (2) July?
16. a. Describe the form known as a trial balance.
    b. What proof is provided by a trial balance?
17. If the two totals of a trial balance are equal, does it mean that there are no errors in the accounting records? Explain.
18. Assume that a trial balance is prepared with an account balance of $36,750 listed as $3,675 and an account balance of $4,500 listed as $5,400. Identify the transposition and the slide.
19. When a purchase of supplies of $690 for cash was recorded, both the debit and the credit were journalized and posted as $960. (a) Would this error cause the trial balance to be out of balance? (b) Would the answer be the same if the $690 entry had been journalized correctly, but the credit to Cash had been posted as $960?
20. How is a correction made when an error in an account title or amount in the journal is discovered before the entry is posted?
21. In journalizing and posting the entry to record the purchase of supplies on account, the accounts receivable account was credited in error. What is the preferred procedure to correct the error?

22. Banks rely heavily upon customers' deposits as a source of funds. Demand deposits normally pay interest to the customer, who is entitled to withdraw at any time without prior notice to the bank. Checking and NOW (negotiable order of withdrawal) accounts are the most common form of demand deposits for banks. Assume that The Exquisite Company has a checking account at First Savings Bank. What type of account (asset, liability, owner's equity, revenue, expense, drawing) does the account balance of $8,500 represent from the viewpoint of (a) The Exquisite Company and (b) First Savings Bank?

EXERCISES

EXERCISE 2–1
Chart of accounts
Objective 1

Maurice Interiors is owned and operated by Maurice Katz, an interior decorator. In the ledger of Maurice Interiors, the first digit of the account number indicates its major account classification (1—assets, 2—liabilities, 3—owner's equity, 4—revenues, 5—expenses). The second digit of the account number indicates the specific account within each of the preceding major account classifications.

Match each of the following account numbers with its most likely account in the list below.

Account Numbers: 11, 12, 13, 21, 31, 32, 41, 51, 52, 53

Accounts:

Accounts Payable	Maurice Katz, Capital
Accounts Receivable	Maurice Katz, Drawing
Cash	Miscellaneous Expense
Fees Earned	Supplies Expense
Land	Wages Expense

EXERCISE 2–2
Chart of accounts
Objective 1

The Charm Shop is a newly organized business that teaches young people how to behave in a socially acceptable way. The list of accounts to be opened in the general ledger is as follows:

Accounts Payable	Miscellaneous Expense
Accounts Receivable	Prepaid Insurance
Anni Vogel, Capital	Rent Expense
Anni Vogel, Drawing	Supplies
Cash	Supplies Expense
Equipment	Unearned Rent
Fees Earned	Wages Expense

List the accounts in the order in which they should appear in the ledger of The Charm Shop and assign account numbers. Each account number is to have two digits: the first digit is to indicate the major classification (*1* for assets, etc.), and the second digit is to identify the specific account within each major classification (*11* for Cash, etc.).

EXERCISE 2–3
Identifying transactions
Objectives 2, 3

Pioneer Co. is a travel agency. The nine transactions recorded by Pioneer during April, its first month of operations, are indicated in the following T accounts:

Cash		Supplies		Accounts Payable	
(1) 20,000	(2) 2,500	(2) 2,500	(9) 1,450	(6) 6,000	(3) 12,000
(7) 9,500	(3) 3,000				
	(4) 2,725				
	(6) 6,000				
	(8) 2,500				

Accounts Receivable		Equipment		Davy Crocket, Capital	
(5) 12,500	(7) 9,500	(3) 15,000			(1) 20,000

Davy Crocket, Drawing	
(8) 2,500	

Service Revenue	
	(5) 12,500

Operating Expenses	
(4) 2,725	
(9) 1,450	

Indicate for each debit and each credit: (a) whether an asset, liability, owner's equity, drawing, revenue, or expense account was affected and (b) whether the account was increased (+) or decreased (–). Present your answers in the following form [transaction (1) is given as an example]:

	Account Debited		*Account Credited*	
Transaction	*Type*	*Effect*	*Type*	*Effect*
(1)	asset	+	owner's equity	+

EXERCISE 2–4
Journal entries
Objectives 3, 4

Based upon the T accounts in Exercise 2–3, prepare the nine journal entries from which the postings were made.

EXERCISE 2–5
Trial balance
Objective 5

Based upon the data presented in Exercise 2–3, prepare a trial balance, listing the accounts in their proper order.

EXERCISE 2–6
Normal entries for accounts
Objective 3

During the month, City Labs Co. has a substantial number of transactions affecting each of the following accounts. State for each account whether it is likely to have (a) debit entries only, (b) credit entries only, or (c) both debit and credit entries.

1. Fees Earned
2. Cash
3. Miscellaneous Expense
4. Accounts Payable
5. Beth Wilson, Drawing
6. Accounts Receivable
7. Supplies Expense

EXERCISE 2–7
Normal balances of accounts
Objective 3

Identify each of the following accounts of Roberts Services Co. as asset, liability, owner's equity, revenue, or expense, and state in each case whether the normal balance is a debit or a credit.

a. Accounts Payable
b. Equipment
c. Salary Expense
d. E. F. Roberts, Drawing
e. Cash
f. Accounts Receivable
g. Fees Earned
h. E. F. Roberts, Capital
i. Supplies
j. Rent Expense

EXERCISE 2–8
Rules of debit and credit
Objective 3

The following table summarizes the rules of debit and credit. For each of the items (a) through (l), indicate whether the proper answer is a debit or a credit.

	Increase	*Decrease*	*Normal Balance*
Balance sheet accounts:			
Asset	Debit	Credit	(a)
Liability	(b)	(c)	(d)
Owner's Equity:			
Capital	Credit	(e)	(f)
Drawing	(g)	(h)	Debit
Income statement accounts:			
Revenue	Credit	(i)	(j)
Expense	(k)	Credit	(l)

EXERCISE 2–9
Capital account balance
Objective 2

As of January 1, Karen Kahan, Capital had a credit balance of $12,000. During the year, withdrawals totaled $10,000 and the business incurred a net loss of $5,000.

a. Calculate the balance of Karen Kahan, Capital as of the end of the year.
b. Assuming that there have been no recording errors, will the balance sheet prepared at December 31 balance? Explain.

EXERCISE 2–10
Cash account balance
Objective 2

During the month, a business received $597,500 in cash and paid out $525,000 in cash.

a. Do the data indicate that the business earned $72,500 during the month? Explain.
b. If the balance of the cash account was $41,300 at the beginning of the month, what was the cash balance at the end of the month?

EXERCISE 2–11
Account balances
Objective 2

a. On March 1, the cash account balance was $8,750. During March, cash receipts totaled $16,500 and the March 31 balance was $11,150. Determine the cash payments made during March.
b. On March 1, the accounts receivable account balance was $23,900. During March, $21,000 was received from customers on account. If the March 31 balance was $27,500, determine the fees billed to customers on account during March.
c. During March, $40,500 was paid to creditors on account and purchases on account were $57,700. If the March 31 balance of Accounts Payable was $45,000, determine the account balance on March 1.

EXERCISE 2–12
Transactions
Objectives 3, 4

The Wildlife Co. has the following accounts in its ledger: Cash; Accounts Receivable; Supplies; Office Equipment; Accounts Payable; Jay Wren, Capital; Jay Wren, Drawing; Fees Earned; Rent Expense; Advertising Expense; Utilities Expense; Miscellaneous Expense.

Journalize the following selected transactions in a two-column journal:

May 1. Paid rent for the month, $2,500.
2. Paid advertising expense, $500.
4. Paid cash for supplies, $770.
5. Purchased office equipment on account, $7,200.
8. Received cash from customers on account, $3,600.
12. Paid creditor on account, $2,150.
15. Withdrew cash for personal use, $1,000.
25. Paid cash for repairs to office equipment, $120.
30. Paid telephone bill for the month, $195.
31. Fees earned and billed to customers for the month, $11,150.
31. Paid electricity bill for the month, $430.

EXERCISE 2–13
Journalizing and posting
Objectives 3, 4

On April 2, 1997, Magnetic Co. purchased $3,150 of supplies on account. In Magnetic Co.'s chart of accounts, the supplies account is No. 15 and the accounts payable account is No. 21.

a. Journalize the April 2, 1997 transaction on page 10 of Magnetic Co.'s two-column journal. Include an explanation of the entry.
b. Prepare a four-column account for Supplies. Enter a debit balance of $2,200 as of April 2, 1997. Place a check mark (✓) in the posting reference column.
c. Prepare a four-column account for Accounts Payable. Enter a credit balance of $11,734 as of April 2, 1997. Place a check mark (✓) in the posting reference column.
d. Post the April 2, 1997 transaction to the accounts.

EXERCISE 2–14
Transactions and T accounts
Objectives 2, 3, 4

The following selected transactions were completed during February of the current year:

1. Billed customers for fees earned, $3,210.
2. Purchased supplies on account, $520.
3. Received cash from customers on account, $2,100.
4. Paid creditors on account, $400.

a. Journalize the foregoing transactions in a two-column journal, using the appropriate number to identify the transactions.
b. Post the entries prepared in (a) to the following T accounts: Cash, Supplies, Accounts Receivable, Accounts Payable, Fees Earned. To the left of each amount posted in the accounts, place the appropriate number to identify the transactions.

EXERCISE 2–15
Trial balance
Objective 5

The accounts in the ledger of Asbury Park Co. as of March 31 of the current year are listed in alphabetical order as follows. All accounts have normal balances. The balance of the cash account has been intentionally omitted.

Accounts Payable	$ 13,710	Notes Payable	$ 27,000
Accounts Receivable	10,500	Prepaid Insurance	3,150
Cash	?	Rent Expense	48,000
Bob Dillon, Capital	110,290	Supplies	4,100
Bob Dillon, Drawing	18,000	Supplies Expense	5,900
Fees Earned	315,000	Unearned Rent	4,000
Insurance Expense	5,000	Utilities Expense	41,500
Land	125,000	Wages Expense	190,000
Miscellaneous Expense	9,900		

Prepare a trial balance, listing the accounts in their proper order and inserting the missing figure for cash.

EXERCISE 2–16
Effect of errors on trial balance
Objective 5

Indicate which of the following errors, each considered individually, would cause the trial balance totals to be unequal:

a. A payment of $950 to a creditor was posted as a debit of $950 to Accounts Payable and a debit of $950 to Cash.
b. Payment of a cash withdrawal of $2,000 was journalized and posted as a debit of $200 to Salary Expense and a credit of $200 to Cash.
c. A payment of $5,000 for equipment purchased was posted as a debit of $5,000 to Equipment and a credit of $50,000 to Cash.
d. A receipt of $500 from an account receivable was journalized and posted as a debit of $500 to Cash and a credit of $500 to Fees Earned.
e. A fee of $2,500 earned and due from a client was not debited to Accounts Receivable or credited to a revenue account, because the cash had not been received.

EXERCISE 2–17
Errors in trial balance
Objective 5

The following preliminary trial balance of The Cowboy Co., a sports ticket agency, does not balance:

The Cowboy Co.
Trial Balance
December 31, 19—

Cash	83,000	
Accounts Receivable	26,200	
Prepaid Insurance		3,300
Equipment	4,500	
Accounts Payable		10,050
Unearned Rent		1,480
Emmitt Smith, Capital	68,550	
Emmitt Smith, Drawing	10,000	
Service Revenue		64,940
Wages Expense		33,400
Advertising Expense	5,200	
Miscellaneous Expense		1,380
	197,450	114,550

When the ledger and other records are reviewed, you discover the following: (1) the debits and credits in the cash account total $83,000 and $65,300, respectively; (2) a billing of $1,100 to a customer on account was not posted to the accounts receivable account; (3) a payment of $2,100 made to a creditor on account was not posted to the accounts payable account; (4) the balance of the unearned rent account is $1,840; (5) the correct balance of the equipment account is $45,000; and (6) each account has a normal balance. Prepare a corrected trial balance.

EXERCISE 2–18
Effect of errors on trial balance
Objective 5

The following errors occurred in posting from a two-column journal:

1. A credit of $250 to Cash was posted as $520.
2. A debit of $1,200 to Supplies was posted twice.
3. A credit of $500 to Accounts Payable was posted as a debit.
4. A debit of $1,000 to Cash was posted to Wages Expense.
5. An entry debiting Accounts Receivable and crediting Fees Earned for $4,500 was not posted.
6. A debit of $1,575 to Wages Expense was posted as $1,755.
7. A credit of $1,130 to Accounts Receivable was not posted.

Considering each case individually (i.e., assuming that no other errors had occurred), indicate: (a) by "yes" or "no" whether the trial balance would be out of balance; (b) if answer to (a) is "yes," the amount by which the trial balance totals would differ; and (c) whether the debit or credit column of the trial balance would have the larger total. Answers should be presented in the following form [error (1) is given as an example]:

Error	*(a)* *Out of Balance*	*(b)* *Difference*	*(c)* *Larger Total*
1.	yes	$270	credit

EXERCISE 2–19
Errors in trial balance
Objective 5

How many errors can you find in the following trial balance? All accounts have normal balances.

The Buffalo Co.
Trial Balance
For the Month Ending July 31, 19—

Cash	3,010	
Accounts Receivable		16,400
Prepaid Insurance	2,400	
Equipment	41,200	
Accounts Payable	1,850	
Salaries Payable		750
J. Kelly, Capital		34,600
J. Kelly, Drawing		5,000
Service Revenue	67,900	
Salary Expense	28,400	
Advertising Expense	7,200	
Miscellaneous Expense	1,490	
	153,450	153,450

EXERCISE 2–20
Entries to correct errors
Objective 6

Errors in journalizing and posting transactions are described as follows:

a. A withdrawal of $2,000 by J. Madden, owner of the business, was recorded as a debit to Miscellaneous Expense and a credit to Cash.
b. Rent of $1,800 paid for the current month was recorded as a debit to Accounts Payable and a credit to cash.

Journalize the entries to correct the errors.

EXERCISE 2–21
Entries to correct errors
Objective 6

Errors in journalizing and posting transactions are described as follows:

a. A $750 purchase of supplies on account was recorded as a debit to Cash and a credit to Accounts Payable.
b. Cash of $1,350 received on account was recorded as a debit to Accounts Payable and a credit to Cash.

Journalize the entries to correct the errors.

PROBLEMS SERIES A

PROBLEM 2–1A
Entries into T accounts and trial balance
Objectives 2, 3, 5

David Colletti, an architect, opened an office on August 1 of the current year. During the month, he completed the following transactions connected with his professional practice:

a. Transferred cash from a personal bank account to an account to be used for the business, $20,000.
b. Paid August rent for office and workroom, $2,500.
c. Purchased used automobile for $11,500, paying $2,500 cash and giving a non-interest-bearing note for the remainder.
d. Purchased office and drafting room equipment on account, $6,000.
e. Paid cash for supplies, $900.
f. Paid cash for insurance policies, $1,050.
g. Received cash from client for plans delivered, $3,100.
h. Paid cash for miscellaneous services, $75.
i. Paid cash to creditors on account, $3,000.
j. Paid installment due on note payable, $400.
k. Received invoice for blueprint service, due in September, $310.
l. Recorded fee earned on plans delivered, payment to be received in September, $4,150.
m. Paid salary of assistant, $1,250.
n. Paid gas, oil, and repairs on automobile for August, $115.

Instructions

1. Record the foregoing transactions directly in the following T accounts, without journalizing: Cash; Accounts Receivable; Supplies; Prepaid Insurance; Automobiles; Equipment; Notes Payable; Accounts Payable; David Colletti, Capital; Professional Fees; Rent Expense; Salary Expense; Automobile Expense; Blueprint Expense; Miscellaneous Expense. To the left of the amount entered in the accounts, place the appropriate letter to identify the transaction.
2. Determine the balances of the T accounts having two or more debits or credits. A memorandum balance should be inserted in accounts having both debits and credits, in the manner illustrated in the chapter. For accounts with entries on one side only (such as Professional Fees), there is no need to insert the memorandum balance in the item column. For accounts containing only a single debit and a single credit (such as Notes Payable), the memorandum balance should be inserted in the appropriate item column. Accounts containing a single entry only (such as Prepaid Insurance) do not need a memorandum balance.
3. Prepare a trial balance for David Colletti, Architect, as of August 31 of the current year.

PROBLEM 2–2A
Journal entries and trial balance
Objectives 2, 3, 5

On July 1 of the current year, Diane Nehring established Oasis Realty, which completed the following transactions during July:

a. Diane Nehring transferred cash from her personal bank account to an account to be used for the business, $15,000.
b. Paid rent on office and equipment for the month, $3,500.
c. Purchased supplies on account, $1,500.
d. Paid creditor on account, $900.
e. Earned sales commissions, receiving cash, $19,750.
f. Paid automobile expenses (including rental charge) for month, $2,900, and miscellaneous expenses, $1,250.
g. Paid office salaries, $3,000.
h. Determined that the cost of supplies used was $1,125.
i. Withdrew cash for personal use, $1,000.

Instructions

1. Journalize entries for transactions (a) through (i), using the following account titles: Cash; Supplies; Accounts Payable; Diane Nehring, Capital; Diane Nehring, Drawing; Sales Commissions; Office Salaries Expense; Rent Expense; Automobile Expense; Supplies Expense; Miscellaneous Expense.

2. Prepare T accounts, using the account titles in (1). Post the journal entries to these accounts, placing the appropriate letter to the left of each amount to identify the transactions. Determine the account balances, after all posting is complete, for all accounts having two or more debits or credits. A memorandum balance should also be inserted in accounts having both debits and credits, in the manner illustrated in the chapter. For accounts with entries on one side only, there is no need to insert a memorandum balance in the item column. For accounts containing only a single debit and a single credit, the memorandum balance should be inserted in the appropriate item column.
3. Prepare a trial balance as of July 31, 19—.
4. Determine the following:
   a. Amount of total revenue recorded in the ledger.
   b. Amount of total expenses recorded in the ledger.
   c. Amount of net income for July.

PROBLEM 2–3A
Journal entries and trial balance
Objectives 3, 4, 5

On June 5 of the current year, Juan Sanchez established a sole proprietorship to be known as Progressive Designs. During the remainder of the month, Juan completed the following transactions related to his interior decorating business:

June 5. Juan transferred cash from a personal bank account to an account to be used for the business, $15,000.
5. Paid rent for period of June 5 to end of month, $1,950.
7. Purchased office equipment on account, $6,250.
8. Purchased a used truck for $16,000, paying $9,500 cash and giving a note payable for the remainder.
10. Purchased supplies for cash, $725.
12. Received cash for job completed, $1,600.
15. Paid wages of employees, $800.
20. Paid premiums on property and casualty insurance, $725.
22. Recorded jobs completed on account and sent invoices to customers, $1,950.
24. Received an invoice for truck expenses, to be paid in July, $310.
26. Received cash for job completed, $1,650. This job had not been recorded previously.
28. Purchased supplies on account, $590.
29. Paid utilities expense, $490.
29. Paid miscellaneous expenses, $195.
30. Received cash from customers on account, $1,200.
30. Paid wages of employees, $1,200.
30. Paid creditor a portion of the amount owed for equipment purchased on June 7, $1,500.
30. Withdrew cash for personal use, $500.

Instructions

1. Journalize each transaction in a two-column journal, referring to the following chart of accounts in selecting the accounts to be debited and credited. (Do not insert the account numbers in the journal at this time.)

11 Cash	41 Fees Earned
12 Accounts Receivable	51 Wages Expense
13 Supplies	53 Rent Expense
14 Prepaid Insurance	54 Utilities Expense
16 Equipment	55 Truck Expense
18 Truck	59 Miscellaneous Expense
21 Notes Payable	
22 Accounts Payable	
31 Juan Sanchez, Capital	
32 Juan Sanchez, Drawing	

2. Post the journal to a ledger of four-column accounts, inserting appropriate posting references as each item is posted. Extend the balances to the appropriate balance columns after each transaction is posted.
3. Prepare a trial balance for Progressive Designs as of June 30.

PROBLEM 2–4A
Journal entries and trial balance
Objectives 3, 4, 5

Reynaldo Realty acts as an agent in buying, selling, renting, and managing real estate. The account balances at the end of March of the current year are as follows:

11	Cash	26,150	
12	Accounts Receivable	38,750	
13	Prepaid Insurance	1,100	
14	Office Supplies	715	
16	Land	0	
21	Accounts Payable		11,175
22	Notes Payable		0
31	K. Hamlet, Capital		39,840
32	K. Hamlet, Drawing	1,000	
41	Fees Earned		124,500
51	Salary and Commission Expense	94,100	
52	Rent Expense	5,500	
53	Advertising Expense	3,900	
54	Automobile Expense	2,750	
59	Miscellaneous Expense	1,550	
		175,515	175,515

The following business transactions were completed by Reynaldo Realty during April of the current year:

April 1. Paid rent on office for month, $2,500.
3. Purchased office supplies on account, $1,375.
5. Paid insurance premiums, $1,650.
7. Received cash from clients on account, $28,200.
15. Paid salaries and commissions for the first half of the month, $16,650.
15. Purchased land for a future building site for $45,000, paying $15,000 in cash and giving a note payable for the remainder.
15. Recorded revenue earned and billed to clients during first half of month, $20,100.
18. Paid creditors on account, $7,150.
20. Returned a portion of the office supplies purchased on April 3, receiving full credit for their cost, $275.
23. Received cash from clients on account, $16,700.
24. Paid advertising expense, $1,550.
27. Discovered an error in computing a commission; received cash from the salesperson for the overpayment, $350.
28. Paid automobile expense (including rental charges for an automobile), $715.
29. Paid miscellaneous expenses, $215.
30. Recorded revenue earned and billed to clients during second half of the month, $18,300.
30. Paid salaries and commissions for the second half of the month, $19,850.
30. Withdrew cash for personal use, $2,500.

Instructions

1. Record the April 1 balance of each account in the appropriate balance column of a four-column account, write *Balance* in the item section, and place a check mark (✓) in the posting reference column.
2. Journalize the transactions for April in a two-column journal.
3. Post to the ledger, extending the account balance to the appropriate balance column after each posting.
4. Prepare a trial balance of the ledger as of April 30.

PROBLEM 2–5A
Errors in trial balance
Objectives 5, 6

If the working papers correlating with this textbook are not used, omit Problem 2–5A.

The following records of Duncan TV Repair are presented in the working papers:

- Journal containing entries for the period March 1–31.
- Ledger to which the March entries have been posted.
- Preliminary trial balance as of March 31, which does not balance.

Locate the errors, supply the information requested, and prepare a corrected trial balance according to the following instructions. The balances recorded in the accounts as of March 1 and the entries in the journal are correctly stated. If it is necessary to correct any posted amounts in the ledger, a line should be drawn through the erroneous figure and the correct amount inserted above. Corrections or notations may be inserted on the preliminary trial balance in any manner desired. It is not necessary to complete all of the instructions if equal trial balance totals can be obtained earlier. However, the requirements of instructions (6) and (7) should be completed in any event.

Instructions

1. Verify the totals of the preliminary trial balance, inserting the correct amounts in the schedule provided in the working papers.
2. Compute the difference between the trial balance totals.
3. Compare the listings in the trial balance with the balances appearing in the ledger, and list the errors found in the space provided in the working papers.
4. Verify the accuracy of the balance of each account in the ledger, and list the errors found in the space provided in the working papers.
5. Trace the postings in the ledger back to the journal, using small check marks to identify items traced. Correct any amounts in the ledger that may be necessitated by errors in posting, and list the errors in the space provided in the working papers.
6. Journalize as of March 31 the payment of $180 for advertising expense. The bill had been paid on March 31 but was inadvertently omitted from the journal. Post to the ledger. (Revise any amounts necessitated by posting this entry.)
7. Prepare a new trial balance.

PROBLEM 2–6A
Corrected trial balance
Objectives 5, 6

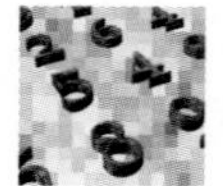

Anatole Carpet Installation, a sole proprietorship, has the following trial balance as of March 31 of the current year:

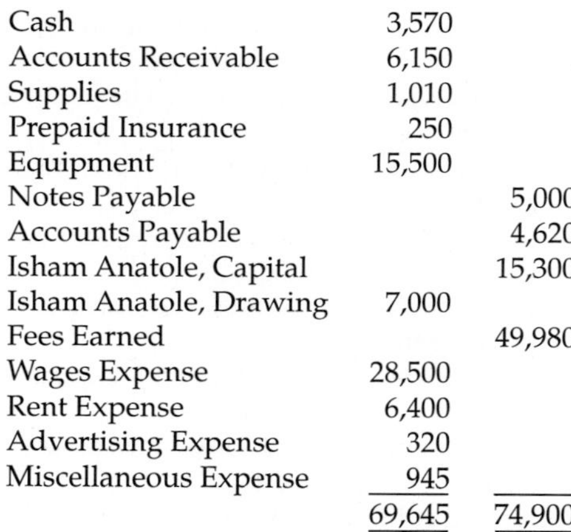

Cash	3,570	
Accounts Receivable	6,150	
Supplies	1,010	
Prepaid Insurance	250	
Equipment	15,500	
Notes Payable		5,000
Accounts Payable		4,620
Isham Anatole, Capital		15,300
Isham Anatole, Drawing	7,000	
Fees Earned		49,980
Wages Expense	28,500	
Rent Expense	6,400	
Advertising Expense	320	
Miscellaneous Expense	945	
	69,645	74,900

The debit and credit totals are not equal as a result of the following errors:

a. The balance of cash was overstated by $750.
b. A cash receipt of $2,100 was posted as a debit to Cash of $1,200.
c. A debit of $1,000 for a withdrawal by the owner was posted as a credit to Isham Anatole, Capital.
d. The balance of $3,200 in Advertising Expense was entered as $320 in the trial balance.
e. A debit of $975 to Accounts Receivable was not posted.
f. A return of $125 of defective supplies was erroneously posted as a $215 credit to Supplies.
g. The balance of Notes Payable was understated by $5,000.
h. An insurance policy acquired at a cost of $150 was posted as a credit to Prepaid Insurance.
i. Gas, Electricity, and Water Expense, with a balance of $3,150, was omitted from the trial balance.
j. A debit of $710 in Accounts Payable was overlooked when determining the balance of the account.

Instructions

1. Prepare a corrected trial balance as of March 31 of the current year.
2.  Does the fact that the trial balance in (1) is balanced mean that there are no errors in the accounts? Explain.

PROBLEMS SERIES B

PROBLEM 2–1B
Entries into T accounts and trial balance
Objectives 2, 3, 5

Julie Stein, an architect, opened an office on June 1 of the current year. During the month, she completed the following transactions connected with her professional practice:

a. Transferred cash from a personal bank account to an account to be used for her business, $25,000.
b. Purchased used automobile for $18,300, paying $5,300 cash and giving a non-interest-bearing note for the remainder.
c. Paid June rent for office and workroom, $2,200.
d. Paid cash for supplies, $225.
e. Purchased office and drafting room equipment on account, $4,200.
f. Paid cash for insurance policies on automobile and equipment, $810.
g. Received cash from a client for plans delivered, $2,725.
h. Paid cash to creditors on account, $2,100.
i. Paid cash for miscellaneous expenses, $65.
j. Received invoice for blueprint service, due in following month, $275.
k. Recorded fee earned on plans delivered, payment to be received in July, $3,500.
l. Paid salary of assistant, $1,500.
m. Paid cash for miscellaneous expenses, $68.
n. Paid installment due on note payable, $500.
o. Paid gas, oil, and repairs on automobile for June, $170.

Instructions

1. Record the foregoing transactions directly in the following T accounts, without journalizing: Cash; Accounts Receivable; Supplies; Prepaid Insurance; Automobiles; Equipment; Notes Payable; Accounts Payable; Julie Stein, Capital; Professional Fees; Rent Expense; Salary Expense; Automobile Expense; Blueprint Expense; Miscellaneous Expense. To the left of each amount entered in the accounts, place the appropriate letter to identify the transaction.
2. Determine the balances of the T accounts having two or more debits or credits. A memorandum balance should be inserted in accounts having both debits and credits, in the manner illustrated in the chapter. For accounts with entries on one side only (such as Professional Fees), there is no need to insert the memorandum balance in the item column. For accounts containing only a single debit and a single credit (such as Notes Payable), the memorandum balance should be inserted in the appropriate item column. Accounts containing a single entry only (such as Prepaid Insurance) do not need a memorandum balance.
3. Prepare a trial balance for Julie Stein, Architect, as of June 30 of the current year.

PROBLEM 2–2B
Journal entries and trial balance
Objectives 2, 3, 5

On March 1 of the current year, Augie Ackman established Ace Realty, which completed the following transactions during the month:

a. Augie Ackman transferred cash from his personal bank account to an account to be used for the business, $10,000.
b. Paid rent on office and equipment for the month, $5,500.
c. Purchased supplies on account, $2,900.
d. Paid creditor on account, $1,000.
e. Earned sales commissions, receiving cash, $21,500.
f. Withdrew cash for personal use, $1,000.
g. Paid automobile expenses (including rental charge) for month, $1,900, and miscellaneous expenses, $1,050.
h. Paid office salaries, $4,000.
i. Determined that the cost of supplies used was $1,250.

Instructions

1. Journalize entries for transactions (a) through (i), using the following account titles: Cash; Supplies; Accounts Payable; Augie Ackman, Capital; Augie Ackman, Drawing; Sales Commissions; Rent Expense; Office Salaries Expense; Automobile Expense; Supplies Expense; Miscellaneous Expense.
2. Prepare T accounts, using the account titles in (1). Post the journal entries to these accounts, placing the appropriate letter to the left of each amount to identify the transactions. Determine the account balances, after all posting is complete, for all accounts having two or more debits or credits. A memorandum balance should be inserted in accounts having both debits and credits, in the manner illustrated in the chapter. For accounts with entries on one side only, there is no need to insert a memorandum balance in the item column. For accounts containing only a single debit and a single credit, the memorandum balance should be inserted in the appropriate item column.
3. Prepare a trial balance as of March 31, 19—.
4. Determine the following:
   a. Amount of total revenue recorded in the ledger.
   b. Amount of total expenses recorded in the ledger.
   c. Amount of net income for March.

PROBLEM 2–3B
Journal entries and trial balance
Objectives 3, 4, 5

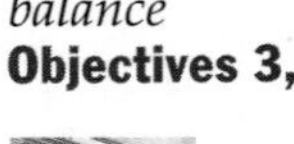

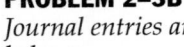

On July 10 of the current year, Cecil Montoya established a sole proprietorship to be known as Deco Designs. During the remainder of the month, Montoya completed the following transactions related to her interior decorating business:

July 10. Cecil transferred cash from a personal bank account to an account to be used for the business, $20,000.
10. Paid rent for period of July 10 to end of month, $900.
11. Purchased a truck for $15,000, paying $7,000 cash and giving a note payable for the remainder.
12. Purchased equipment on account, $3,700.
14. Purchased supplies for cash, $885.
14. Paid premiums on property and casualty insurance, $750.
15. Received cash for job completed, $1,200.
16. Purchased supplies on account, $1,240.
17. Paid wages of employees, $600.
21. Paid creditor for equipment purchased on July 12, $3,700.
24. Recorded jobs completed on account and sent invoices to customers, $3,100.
26. Received an invoice for truck expenses, to be paid in August, $225.
26. Received cash for job completed, $1,050. This job had not been recorded previously.
27. Paid utilities expense, $1,205.
27. Paid miscellaneous expenses, $173.
28. Received cash from customers on account, $1,420.
31. Paid wages of employees, $1,350.
31. Withdrew cash for personal use, $1,500.

Instructions

1. Journalize each transaction in a two-column journal, referring to the following chart of accounts in selecting the accounts to be debited and credited. (Do not insert the account numbers in the journal at this time.)

11 Cash	41 Fees Earned
12 Accounts Receivable	51 Wages Expense
13 Supplies	53 Rent Expense
14 Prepaid Insurance	54 Utilities Expense
16 Equipment	55 Truck Expense
18 Truck	59 Miscellaneous Expense
21 Notes Payable	
22 Accounts Payable	
31 Cecil Montoya, Capital	
32 Cecil Montoya, Drawing	

2. Post the journal to a ledger of four-column accounts, inserting appropriate posting references as each item is posted. Extend the balances to the appropriate balance columns after each transaction is posted.
3. Prepare a trial balance for Deco Designs as of July 31.

PROBLEM 2–4B
Journal entries and trial balance
Objectives 3, 4, 5

Macbeth Realty acts as an agent in buying, selling, renting, and managing real estate. The account balances at the end of April of the current year are as follows:

11 Cash	29,500	
12 Accounts Receivable	38,600	
13 Prepaid Insurance	750	
14 Office Supplies	625	
16 Land	0	
21 Accounts Payable		13,250
22 Notes Payable		0
31 K. Lear, Capital		63,025
32 K. Lear, Drawing	10,000	
41 Fees Earned		157,750
51 Salary and Commission Expense	122,100	
52 Rent Expense	19,000	
53 Advertising Expense	8,900	
54 Automobile Expense	3,950	
59 Miscellaneous Expense	600	
	234,025	234,025

The following business transactions were completed by Macbeth Realty during May of the current year:

May 1. Paid rent on office for month, $2,500.
2. Purchased office supplies on account, $925.
3. Paid insurance premiums, $1,925.
9. Received cash from clients on account, $19,500.
15. Paid salaries and commissions for the first half of the month, $20,650.
15. Purchased land for a future building site for $60,000, paying $10,000 in cash and giving a note payable for the remainder.
15. Recorded revenue earned and billed to clients during first half of month, $30,900.
18. Paid creditors on account, $7,650.
20. Returned a portion of the office supplies purchased on May 2, receiving full credit for their cost, $150.
29. Received cash from clients on account, $28,200.
29. Paid advertising expense, $2,150.
29. Discovered an error in computing a commission; received cash from the salesperson for the overpayment, $500.
30. Paid automobile expense (including rental charges for an automobile), $850.
30. Paid miscellaneous expenses, $215.
31. Recorded revenue earned and billed to clients during the second half of the month, $15,300.
31. Paid salaries and commissions for the second half of the month, $20,850.
31. Withdrew cash for personal use, $5,000.

Instructions

1. Record the May 1 balance of each account in the appropriate balance column of a four-column account, write *Balance* in the item section, and place a check mark (✓) in the posting reference column.
2. Journalize the transactions for May in a two-column journal.
3. Post to the ledger, extending the account balance to the appropriate balance column after each posting.
4. Prepare a trial balance of the ledger as of May 31.

PROBLEM 2–5B
Errors in trial balance
Objectives 5, 6

If the working papers correlating with this textbook are not used, omit Problem 2–5B.

The following records of Duncan TV Repair are presented in the working papers:

- Journal containing entries for the period March 1–31.
- Ledger to which the March entries have been posted.
- Preliminary trial balance as of March 31, which does not balance.

Locate the errors, supply the information requested, and prepare a corrected trial balance according to the following instructions. The balances recorded in the accounts as of March 1 and the entries in the journal are correctly stated. If it is necessary to correct any posted amounts in the ledger, a line should be drawn through the erroneous figure and the correct amount inserted above. Corrections or notations may be inserted on the preliminary trial balance in any manner desired. It is not necessary to complete all of the instructions if equal trial balance totals can be obtained earlier. However, the requirements of instructions (6) and (7) should be completed in any event.

Instructions

1. Verify the totals of the preliminary trial balance, inserting the correct amounts in the schedule provided in the working papers.
2. Compute the difference between the trial balance totals.
3. Compare the listings in the trial balance with the balances appearing in the ledger, and list the errors found in the space provided in the working papers.
4. Verify the accuracy of the balance of each account in the ledger, and list the errors found in the space provided in the working papers.
5. Trace the postings in the ledger back to the journal, using small check marks to identify items traced. Correct any amounts in the ledger that may be necessitated by errors in posting, and list the errors in the space provided in the working papers.
6. Journalize as of March 31 the payment of $150 for gas and electricity. The bill had been paid on March 31 but was inadvertently omitted from the journal. Post to the ledger. (Revise any amounts necessitated by posting this entry.)
7. Prepare a new trial balance.

PROBLEM 2–6B
Corrected trial balance
Objectives 5, 6

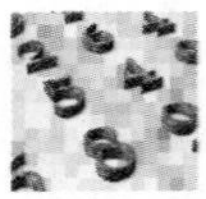

Halpern Photography, a sole proprietorship, has the following trial balance as of December 31 of the current year:

Cash	5,225	
Accounts Receivable	9,350	
Supplies	1,277	
Prepaid Insurance	330	
Equipment	12,500	
Notes Payable		10,000
Accounts Payable		3,025
Jennifer Halpern, Capital		12,540
Jennifer Halpern, Drawing	6,700	
Fees Earned		80,750
Wages Expense	48,150	
Rent Expense	750	
Advertising Expense	5,250	
Gas, Electricity, and Water Expense	3,150	
	92,682	106,315

The debit and credit totals are not equal as a result of the following errors:

a. The balance of cash was understated by $1,500.
b. A cash receipt of $1,200 was posted as a debit to Cash of $2,100.
c. A debit of $750 to Accounts Receivable was not posted.
d. A return of $252 of defective supplies was erroneously posted as a $225 credit to Supplies.
e. An insurance policy acquired at a cost of $310 was posted as a credit to Prepaid Insurance.
f. The balance of Notes Payable was overstated by $2,500.

g. A credit of $75 in Accounts Payable was overlooked when the balance of the account was determined.
h. A debit of $800 for a withdrawal by the owner was posted as a credit to Jennifer Halpern, Capital.
i. The balance of $7,500 in Rent Expense was entered as $750 in the trial balance.
j. Miscellaneous Expense, with a balance of $915, was omitted from the trial balance.

Instructions

1. Prepare a corrected trial balance as of December 31 of the current year.
2. Does the fact that the trial balance in (1) is balanced mean that there are no errors in the accounts? Explain.

CONTINUING PROBLEM

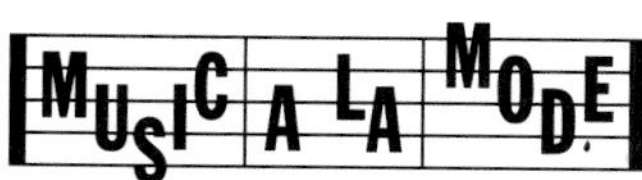

The transactions completed by Music A La Mode during November 1996 were described at the end of Chapter 1. The following transactions were completed during December, the second month of the business's operations:

Dec. 1. Julian Felipe made an additional investment in Music A La Mode by depositing $2,000 in Music A La Mode's checking account.
1. Instead of continuing to share office space with a local real estate agency, Julian decided to rent office space near a local music store. Paid rent for December, $720.
1. Paid a premium of $1,680 for a comprehensive insurance policy covering liability, theft, and fire. The policy covers a two-year period.
2. Received $350 on account.
3. On behalf of Music A La Mode, Julian signed a contract with a local radio station, KPRG, to provide guest spots for the next three months. The contract requires Music A La Mode to provide a guest disc jockey for 40 hours per month for a monthly fee of $500. Any additional hours beyond 40 will be billed to KPRG at $15 per hour. In accordance with the contract, Julian received $1,500 from KPRG as an advance payment for the first three months.
3. Paid $50 on account.
4. Paid an attorney $75 for reviewing (on December 2) the contract with KPRG. (Record as Miscellaneous Expense.)
5. Purchased office equipment on account from One-Stop Office Mart, $2,500.
8. Paid for a newspaper advertisement, $100.
11. Received $300 for serving as a disc jockey for a college fraternity party.
13. Paid $250 to a local audio electronics store for rental of various equipment (speakers, CD players, etc.).
14. Paid wages of $400 to receptionist and part-time assistant.
16. Received $550 for serving as a disc jockey for a wedding reception.
18. Purchased miscellaneous supplies on account, $375.
21. Paid $120 to The Music Store for use of its current demo CDs and tapes in making cassettes of various music sets.
22. Paid $50 to a local radio station to advertise the services of Music A La Mode twice daily for the remainder of December.
23. Served as disc jockey for an annual holiday party for $780. Received $200, with the remainder due January 6, 1997.
27. Paid electric bill, $280.
28. Paid wages of $400 to receptionist and part-time assistant.
29. Paid miscellaneous expenses, $88.
30. Served as a disc jockey for a pre-New Year's Eve charity ball for $600. Received $300, with the remainder due on January 10, 1997.
31. Received $1,000 for serving as a disc jockey for a New Year's Eve party.
31. Withdrew $400 cash from Music A La Mode for personal use.

Music A La Mode's chart of accounts and the balance of accounts as of December 1, 1996 (all normal balances), are as follows:

11 Cash	$ 695
12 Accounts Receivable	350
14 Supplies	70
15 Prepaid Insurance	—
17 Office Equipment	—
21 Accounts Payable	50
23 Unearned Revenue	—
31 Julian Felipe, Capital	1,000
32 Julian Felipe, Drawing	75
41 Fees Earned	1,340
50 Wages Expense	110
51 Office Rent Expense	250
52 Equipment Rent Expense	300
53 Utilities Expense	100
54 Music Expense	220
55 Advertising Expense	75
56 Supplies Expense	80
59 Miscellaneous Expense	65

Instructions

1. Enter the December 1, 1996 account balances in the appropriate balance column of a four-column account. Write *Balance* in the Item column, and place a check mark (✓) in the Posting Reference column. (It is advisable to verify the equality of the debit and credit balances in the ledger before proceeding with the next instruction.)
2. Analyze and journalize each transaction in a two-column journal. Omit journal entry explanations.
3. Post the journal to the ledger, extending the account balance to the appropriate balance column after each posting.
4. Prepare a trial balance as of December 31, 1996.

CASES

CASE 2–1

Metro Services Co.

Errors in trial balance

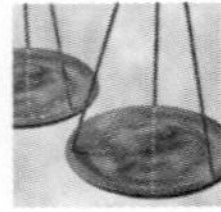

At the end of the current month, Jill Smith prepared a trial balance for Metro Services Co. The credit side of the trial balance exceeds the debit side by a significant amount. Jill has decided to add the difference to the balance of the miscellaneous expense account in order to complete the preparation of the current month's financial statements by a 5 o'clock deadline. Jill will look for the difference next week when there is more time.

Discuss whether Jill Smith is behaving in an ethical manner.

CASE 2–2

State College

Accounting for revenue

State College requires students to pay tuition each term before classes begin. Students who have not paid their tuition are not allowed to enroll or to attend classes.

What journal entry do you think would be used by State College to record the receipt of the students' tuition payments? Describe the nature of each account in the entry.

CASE 2–3

Prodata Company

Recording transactions

The following discussion took place between Jacob Mandy, the office manager of Prodata Company, and a new accountant, Harold Hartly.

Harold: I've been thinking about our method of recording entries. It seems that it's inefficient.

Jacob: In what way?

Harold: Well—correct me if I'm wrong—it seems like we have unnecessary steps in the process. We could very easily develop a trial balance by posting our transactions directly into the ledger and by-passing the journal altogether. In this way we could combine the recording and posting process into one step and save ourselves a lot of time. What do you think?

Jacob: We need to have a talk.

What should Jacob say to Harold?

CASE 2–4

Beaverdam Construction Co.

Debits and credits

The following is an excerpt from a conversation between Derrick Rawlins, the president and chief operating officer of Beaverdam Construction Co., and his neighbor, Carrie Crymes.

Carrie: Derrick, I'm taking a course in night school, "Intro to Accounting." I was wondering—could you answer a couple of questions for me?

Derrick: Well, I will if I can.

Carrie: Okay, our instructor says that it's critical we understand the basic concepts of accounting, or we'll never get beyond the first test. My problem is with those rules of debit and credit . . . you know, assets increase with debits, decrease with credits, etc.

Derrick: Yes, pretty basic stuff. You just have to memorize the rules. It shouldn't be too difficult.

Carrie: Sure, I can memorize the rules, but my problem is I want to be sure I understand the basic concepts behind the rules.

For example, why can't assets be increased with credits and decreased with debits like revenue? As long as everyone did it that way, why not? It would seem easier if we had the same rules for all increases and decreases in accounts.

Also, why is the left side of an account called the debit side? Why couldn't it be called something simple . . . like the "LE" for Left Entry? The right side could be called just "RE" for Right Entry.

Finally, why are there just two sides to an entry? Why can't there be three or four sides to an entry?

Help Derrick answer Carrie's questions.

CASE 2–5

Hershey Foods Corporation

Financial analysis

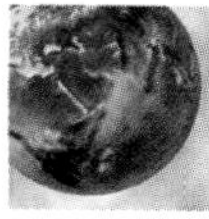

A single item appearing in a financial statement is often useful in interpreting the financial results of a business. However, comparing this item in a current statement with the same item in the prior statement often enhances the usefulness of the financial information. Such comparisons often take two forms: (1) the amount of the increase or decrease and (2) the percent of the increase or decrease for the current item when compared to the same item in the prior period. For example, the amount of the prior period's revenue and the amount of the change and the percent of change determined is indicated in the following table:

			Increase (Decrease)	
	1994	*1993*	*Amount*	*Percent*
Revenues	$120,000	$100,000	$20,000	20%

a. For Hershey Foods Corporation, comparing 1993 with 1992, determine the amount of change and the percent of change for
   1. net sales (revenues) and
   2. selling, marketing, and administrative expenses.

b. What conclusions can be drawn from this analysis of the net sales and the selling, marketing, and administrative expenses?

CASE 2–6

Ace Caddy Service

Transactions and income statement

During June through August, Yu Li is planning to manage and operate Ace Caddy Service at Greenwich Golf and Country Club. Yu will rent a small maintenance building from the country club for $150 per month and will offer caddy services, including cart rentals, to golfers. Yu has had no formal training in record keeping. During June, he kept notes of all receipts and expenses in a shoe box.

An examination of Yu's shoe box records for June revealed the following:

June 1. Withdrew $2,000 from personal bank account to be used to operate the caddy service.
1. Paid rent to Greenwich Golf and Country Club, $150.
2. Paid for golf supplies (practice balls, etc.), $200.
2. Paid miscellaneous expenses, $75.
3. Arranged for the rental of forty regular (pulling) golf carts and ten gasoline-driven carts for $1,000 per month. Paid $750 in advance, with the remaining $250 due June 20.
7. Purchased supplies, including gasoline, for the golf carts on account, $325. Greenwich Golf and Country Club has agreed to allow Yu to store the gasoline in one of its fuel tanks at no cost.
15. Received cash for services from June 1–15, $990.
15. Accepted IOUs from customers on account for services from June 1–15, $210.
15. Paid wages of part-time employees, $120.
17. Paid cash to creditors on account, $180.
20. Paid remaining rental on golf carts, $250.
22. Purchased supplies, including gasoline, on account, $280.
25. Received cash in payment of IOUs on account, $150.

June 28. Paid miscellaneous expenses, $60.
30. Received cash for services from June 16–30, $1,475.
30. For June 16–30, accepted IOUs from customers on account, $150.
30. Paid electricity (utilities) expense, $55.
30. Paid telephone (utilities) expense, $30.
30. Paid wages of part-time employees, $110.
30. Supplies on hand at the end of June, $180.

Yu has asked you several questions concerning his financial affairs to date, and he has asked you to assist with his record keeping and reporting of financial data.

a. To assist Yu with his record keeping, prepare a chart of accounts that would be appropriate for Ace Caddy Service.
b. Prepare an income statement for June in order to help Yu assess the profitability of Ace Caddy Service. For this purpose, the use of T accounts may be helpful in analyzing the effects of each June transaction.
c. Based on Yu's records of receipts and payments, calculate the amount of cash on hand on June 30. For this purpose, a T account for cash may be useful.
d. A count of the cash on hand on June 30 totaled $2,135. Briefly discuss the possible causes of the difference between the amount of cash computed in (c) and the actual amount of cash on hand.

ANSWERS TO SELF-EXAMINATION QUESTIONS

1. **A** A debit may signify an increase in an asset account (answer A) or a decrease in a liability or owner's capital account. A credit may signify a decrease in an asset account (answer B) or an increase in a liability or owner's capital account (answers C and D).
2. **C** Liability, capital, and revenue (answer C) accounts have normal credit balances. Asset (answer A), drawing (answer B), and expense (answer D) accounts have normal debit balances.
3. **C** Accounts Receivable (answer A), Cash (answer B), and Miscellaneous Expense (answer D) would all normally have debit balances. Fees Earned should normally have a credit balance. Hence, a debit balance in Fees Earned (answer C) would indicate a likely error in the recording process.
4. **A** The receipt of cash from customers on account increases the asset Cash and decreases the asset Accounts Receivable, as indicated by answer A. Answer B has the debit and credit reversed, and answers C and D involve transactions with creditors (accounts payable) and not customers (accounts receivable).
5. **D** The trial balance (answer D) is a listing of the balances and the titles of the accounts in the ledger on a given date, so that the equality of the debits and credits in the ledger can be verified. The income statement (answer A) is a summary of revenue and expenses for a period of time. The balance sheet (answer B) is a presentation of the assets, liabilities, and owner's equity on a given date. The statement of owner's equity (answer C) is a summary of the changes in owner's equity for a period of time.

3 The Matching Concept and the Adjusting Process

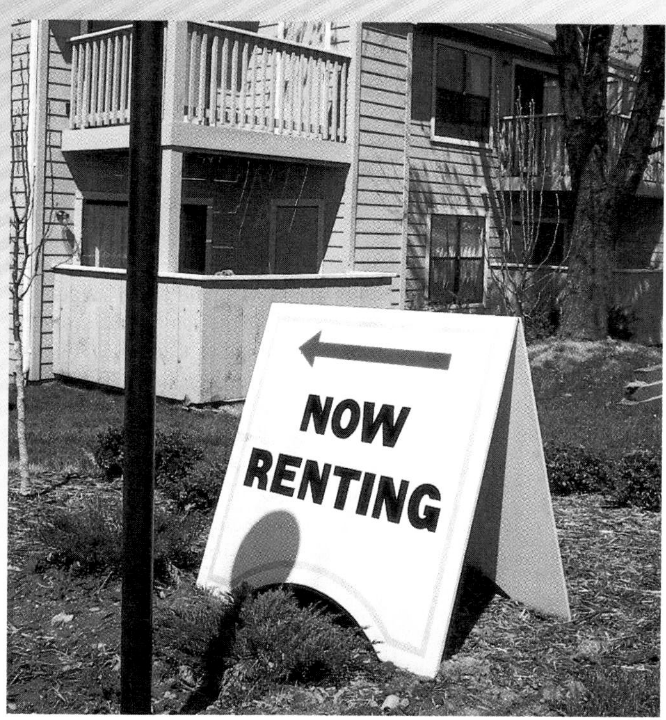

YOU AND ACCOUNTING

Assume that you rented an apartment last month and signed a nine-month lease. When you signed the lease agreement, you were required to pay the final month's rent of $500. This amount is not returnable to you.

You are now applying for a student loan at a local bank. The loan application requires a listing of all your assets. Should you list the $500 deposit as an asset?

The answer to this question is "yes." The deposit is an asset to you until you receive the use of the apartment in the ninth month.

A business faces similar accounting problems at the end of a period. A business must determine what assets, liabilities, and owner's equity should be reported on its balance sheet. It must also determine what revenues and expenses should be reported on its income statement.

As we illustrated in previous chapters, transactions are normally recorded as they occur. Periodically, financial statements are prepared, summarizing the effects of the transactions on the financial position and the operations of the business.

At any one point in time, however, the accounting records may not reflect all transactions. For example, most businesses do not record the daily usage of supplies. Likewise, revenue may have been earned from providing services to customers, but the customers have not been billed when the accounting period ends. Thus, at the end of the period, the revenue and the receivable accounts must be updated.

In this chapter, we describe and illustrate this updating process. We will focus on accounts that normally require updating and the journal entries that update these accounts. We will also briefly discuss how some accountants use work sheets to aid them at the end of an accounting period.

After studying this chapter, you should be able to:

Objective 1
Explain how the matching concept relates to the accrual basis of accounting.

Objective 2
Explain why adjustments are necessary and list the characteristics of adjusting entries.

Objective 3
Journalize entries for accounts requiring adjustment.

Objective 4
Enter adjustments on a work sheet and prepare an adjusted trial balance.

The Matching Concept

Objective 1
Explain how the matching concept relates to the accrual basis of accounting.

When accountants prepare monthly, quarterly, and yearly financial statements, they are assuming that the economic life of the business can be divided into time periods. Using this **accounting period concept,** accountants must determine in which period the revenues and expenses of the business should be reported. To determine the appropriate period, accountants will use either (1) the **cash basis** of accounting or (2) the **accrual basis** of accounting.

Under the cash basis, revenues and expenses are reported in the income statement in the period in which cash is received or paid. For example, fees are recorded when cash is received from clients, and wages are recorded when cash is paid to employees. The net income (or net loss) is the difference between the cash receipts (revenues) and the cash payments (expenses). Most individuals and many small service businesses use the cash basis of accounting.

Under the accrual basis, the **revenue recognition principle** leads to reporting revenues in the income statement in the period in which they are earned. For example, revenue is normally reported in the period in which the services are provided to customers. Cash may or may not be received from customers during this period.

Under the accrual basis, expenses are reported in the same period as the revenues to which they relate. For example, employee wages are reported as an expense in the period in which the employees provided services to customers and not when the wages are paid.

The accounting principle that requires the matching of revenues and expenses is called the **matching concept** or **matching principle.** Under the matching concept, the income statement will match the revenues earned and the expenses incurred, and it will report the resulting income or loss for the period.

Generally accepted accounting principles require the use of the accrual basis. However, small service businesses may use the cash basis because they have few receivables and payables. For example, practicing accountants, attorneys, physicians, and real estate agents often use the cash basis. For such enterprises, the cash basis will yield financial statements similar to those prepared under the accrual basis.

For most large businesses, the cash basis will not provide accurate financial statements for user needs. For this reason, we will emphasize the accrual basis in the remainder of this text. The accrual basis and its related matching concept require an analysis and updating of some accounts when financial statements are prepared. In the following paragraphs, we will describe and illustrate this process, called the **adjusting process.**

USING ACCOUNTING TO UNDERSTAND BUSINESS

An understanding of the difference between the accrual and cash basis of accounting can be extremely important for many types of businesses. For example, a bank loan officer requires an individual, who normally keeps records on a cash basis, to list assets, such as automobiles, homes, investments, etc., on an application for a loan or a line of credit. In addition, the application often asks for an estimate of the individual's liabilities, such as credit card amounts outstanding and balances of automobile loans. In a sense, a loan application converts an individual from a cash-basis accounting system to an estimated accrual basis. Other information, such as the amount of life insurance policies in force, estimated wages and other sources of income, and major monthly expenses, is also requested. In this way, the completed loan application provides the loan officer with information that can be used in assessing the individual's ability to repay the loan.

Nature of the Adjusting Process

Objective 2
Explain why adjustments are necessary and list the characteristics of adjusting entries.

At the end of an accounting period, many of the balances of accounts in the ledger can be reported, without change, in the financial statements. For example, the balance of the cash account is normally the amount reported on the balance sheet as the cash on hand at the end of the accounting period.

Some accounts in the ledger, however, require updating. For example, the balances listed for prepaid expenses are normally overstated because the use of these assets is not recorded on a day-to-day basis. The balance of the supplies account usually represents the cost of supplies at the beginning of the period plus the cost of supplies acquired during the period. To record the daily use of supplies would require many entries with small amounts. In addition, the total amount of supplies is small relative to other assets, and managers usually do not require day-to-day information on the amount of supplies on hand.

Another example of a prepaid expense account that requires updating is Prepaid Insurance. The balance in Prepaid Insurance represents the beginning balance plus the cost of insurance policies acquired during the period. Journal entries are not made daily for the premiums as they expire. To make such entries would be costly and unnecessary.

The journal entries at the end of an accounting period to bring the accounts up to date and to properly match revenues and expenses are called **adjusting entries.** By their nature, *all adjusting entries affect at least one income statement account and one balance sheet account.* Thus, an adjusting entry will always involve a revenue or an expense account and an asset or a liability account.

Is there an easy way to know when an adjusting entry is needed? Yes, two basic classifications of items require adjusting entries. The first class of items, **deferrals,** is created by recording a transaction in a way that delays or defers the recognition of an expense or a revenue. Deferrals may be either deferred expenses or deferred revenues, as described below.

Deferred expenses are items that have been initially recorded as assets but are expected to become expenses over time or through the normal operations of the business. The supplies and prepaid insurance discussed in the preceding paragraphs are examples of deferred expenses. The supplies become an expense as they are used, and the prepaid insurance becomes an expense as time passes and the insurance expires. Deferred expenses are often called **prepaid expenses.**

Deferred revenues are items that have been initially recorded as liabilities but are expected to become revenues over time or through the normal operations of the business. Examples of deferred revenues include tuition received by a college at the beginning of the term and magazine subscriptions received in advance by a publisher. The tuition is earned throughout the term as students attend class. The subscriptions are earned as the magazines are published and distributed. Deferred revenues are often called **unearned revenues.**

The second class of items that give rise to adjusting entries is accruals. Accruals are created by the failure to record an expense that has been incurred or a revenue that has been earned. Accruals may be either accrued expenses or accrued revenues, as described below.

Accrued expenses are expenses that have been incurred *but have not been recorded* in the accounts. Examples of accrued expenses include unrecorded wages owed to employees at the end of a period and unrecorded interest owed on loans. Accrued expenses are often called **accrued liabilities.**

Accrued revenues are revenues that have been earned *but have not been recorded* in the accounts. Examples of accrued revenues include unrecorded fees earned by an attorney or unrecorded commissions earned by a real estate agent. Accrued revenues are often called **accrued assets.**

How do you tell the difference between deferrals and accruals? Deferrals normally arise when cash is received or paid in the current period but the related revenue or expense is to be recorded in a future period. Accruals normally arise when a revenue or expense is recorded in the current period but the related cash is received or paid in a future period. These differences are illustrated in Exhibit 1.

Exhibit 1
Deferrals and Accruals

	Current Period	*Future Period*
Deferral	Cash received or paid	Revenue or expense recorded
Accrual	Revenue or expense recorded	Cash received or paid

Recording Adjusting Entries

Objective 3
Journalize entries for accounts requiring adjustment.

The examples of adjusting entries in the following paragraphs are based on the ledger of Computer King as reported in the December 31, 1996 trial balance in Exhibit 2. An expanded chart of accounts for Computer King is shown in Exhibit 3. The additional accounts that will be used in this chapter are shown in color. To simplify the examples, T accounts are used. The adjusting entries are shown in color in the accounts to separate them from other transactions.

Exhibit 2
Unadjusted Trial Balance for Computer King

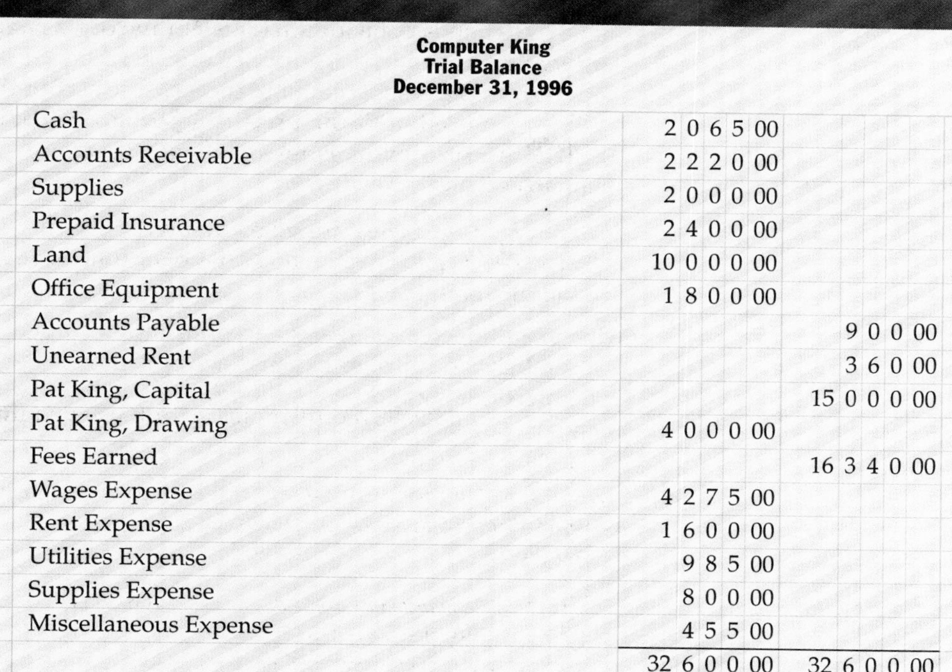

Computer King
Trial Balance
December 31, 1996

Cash	2 0 6 5 00	
Accounts Receivable	2 2 2 0 00	
Supplies	2 0 0 0 00	
Prepaid Insurance	2 4 0 0 00	
Land	10 0 0 0 00	
Office Equipment	1 8 0 0 00	
Accounts Payable		9 0 0 00
Unearned Rent		3 6 0 00
Pat King, Capital		15 0 0 0 00
Pat King, Drawing	4 0 0 0 00	
Fees Earned		16 3 4 0 00
Wages Expense	4 2 7 5 00	
Rent Expense	1 6 0 0 00	
Utilities Expense	9 8 5 00	
Supplies Expense	8 0 0 00	
Miscellaneous Expense	4 5 5 00	
	32 6 0 0 00	32 6 0 0 00

Exhibit 3
Expanded Chart of Accounts for Computer King

Balance Sheet Accounts	*Income Statement Accounts*
1. Assets	4. Revenue
11 Cash	41 Fees Earned
12 Accounts Receivable	42 Rent Income
14 Supplies	5. Expenses
15 Prepaid Insurance	51 Wages Expense
17 Land	52 Rent Expense
18 Office Equipment	53 Depreciation Expense
19 Accumulated Depreciation	54 Utilities Expense
2. Liabilities	55 Supplies Expense
21 Accounts Payable	56 Insurance Expense
22 Wages Payable	59 Miscellaneous Expense
23 Unearned Rent	
3. Owner's Equity	
31 Pat King, Capital	
32 Pat King, Drawing	

DEFERRED EXPENSES (PREPAID EXPENSES)

The concept of adjusting the accounting records was introduced in Chapters 1 and 2 in the illustration for Computer King. In that illustration, supplies were purchased on November 10 (transaction c). The supplies used during November were recorded on November 30 (transaction g). In practice, this matching of revenues and expenses is part of the normal adjusting process that takes place only at the end of the accounting period, which is typically monthly and at least yearly.

The balance in Computer King's supplies account on December 31 is $2,000. Some of these supplies (computer diskettes, paper, envelopes, etc.) were used during December, and some are still on hand. If either amount is known, the other can be readily determined. It is normally easier to determine the cost of the supplies on hand at the end of the month than it is to keep a record of those used daily. Assuming that the inventory of supplies on December 31 is $760, the amount to be transferred from the asset account to the expense account is $1,240, computed as follows:

Supplies available (balance of account)	$2,000
Supplies on hand (inventory)	760
Supplies used (amount of adjustment)	$1,240

As we discussed in Chapter 2, increases in expense accounts are recorded as debits and decreases in asset accounts are recorded as credits. Hence, at the end of December, the supplies expense account should be debited for $1,240 and the supplies account should be credited for $1,240 to record the supplies used during December. The adjusting journal entry and T accounts for Supplies and Supplies Expense are as follows:

Supplies Expense	1,240	
Supplies		1,240

Supplies

Bal.	2,000	Dec. 31	1,240
760			

Supplies Expense

Bal.	800		
Dec. 31	1,240		
	2,040		

After the adjustment has been recorded and posted, the supplies account has a debit balance of $760. This balance represents an asset that will become an expense in a future period.

The debit balance of $2,400 in Computer King's prepaid insurance account represents a December 1 prepayment of insurance for 24 months. At the end of December, the insurance expense account should be increased (debited) and the prepaid insurance account should be decreased (credited) by $100, the insurance for one month. The adjusting journal entry and the T accounts for Prepaid Insurance and Insurance Expense are as follows:

Insurance Expense	100	
Prepaid Insurance		100

Prepaid Insurance

Bal.	2,400	Dec. 31	100
2,300			

Insurance Expense

Dec. 31	100		

After the adjustment has been recorded and posted, the prepaid insurance account has a debit balance of $2,300. This balance represents an asset that will become an expense in future periods. The insurance expense account has a debit balance of $100, which is an expense of the current period.

What is the effect of omitting adjusting entries? If the preceding adjustments for supplies ($1,240) and insurance ($100) are not recorded, the financial statements prepared as of December 31 will be misstated. On the income statement, Supplies Expense and Insurance Expense will be understated by a total of $1,340 and net income will be overstated by $1,340. On the balance sheet, Supplies and Prepaid Insurance will be overstated by a total of $1,340. Since net income increases owner's equity, Pat King, Capital will also be overstated by $1,340 on the balance sheet. The effects of omitting these adjusting entries on the income statement and balance sheet are as follows:

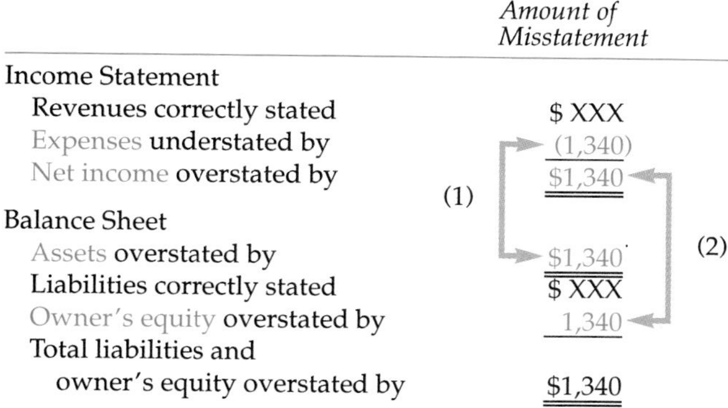

	Amount of Misstatement
Income Statement	
Revenues correctly stated	$ XXX
Expenses understated by	(1,340)
Net income overstated by	$1,340
Balance Sheet	
Assets overstated by	$1,340
Liabilities correctly stated	$ XXX
Owner's equity overstated by	1,340
Total liabilities and owner's equity overstated by	$1,340

Arrows (1) and (2) indicate how omitting adjusting entries affects both the income statement and the balance sheet. Arrow (1) indicates the effects on the expenses and assets. Arrow (2) indicates the effect of the overstated net income on owner's equity. On the balance sheet, the assets and the total liabilities and owner's equity are misstated by the same amount.

Supplies and prepaid insurance are two examples of prepaid expenses that may require adjustment at the end of an accounting period. Other examples of prepaid expenses that may require adjustment are prepaid advertising and prepaid interest.

Prepayments of expenses are sometimes made at the beginning of the period in which they will be *entirely consumed.* On December 1, for example, Computer King paid rent of $800 for the month. On December 1, the rent payment represents the asset prepaid rent. The prepaid rent expires daily, and at the end of December, the entire amount has become an expense (rent expense). In cases such as this, the initial payment is recorded as an expense rather than as an asset. Thus, if the payment is recorded as a debit to Rent Expense, no adjusting entry is needed at the end of the period.[1]

DEFERRED REVENUE (UNEARNED REVENUE)

According to Computer King's trial balance on December 31, the balance in the unearned rent account is $360. This balance represents the receipt of three months' rent on December 1 for December, January, and February. At the end of December, the unearned rent account should be decreased by $120 (debited) and the rent income account should be increased by $120 (credited). The $120 represents the rental income for one month ($360 ÷ 3). The adjusting journal entry and T accounts are shown below.

Unearned Rent	120	
Rent Income		120

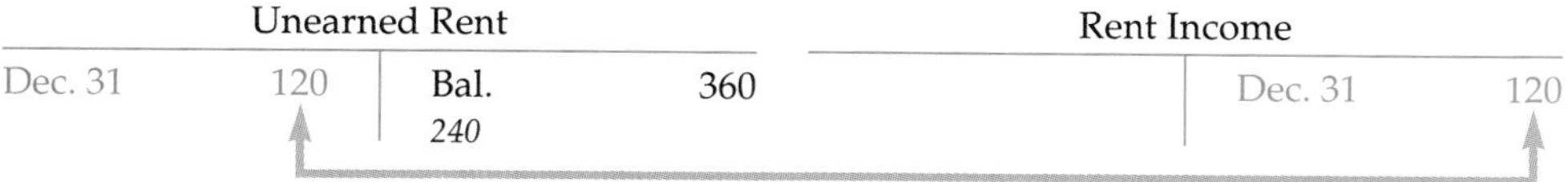

Unearned Rent
Dec. 31 120
Bal. 360
240
Rent Income
Dec. 31 120

After the adjustment has been recorded and posted, the unearned rent account, which is a liability, has a credit balance of $240. This balance represents a deferral that will become revenue in a future period. The rent income account has a balance of $120, which is revenue of the current period.

[1] This alternative treatment of recording the cost of supplies, rent, and other prepayments of expenses is discussed in Appendix C.

If the preceding adjustment of unearned rent and rent income is not recorded, the financial statements prepared on December 31 will be misstated. On the income statement, Rent Income and the net income will be understated by $120. On the balance sheet, Unearned Rent will be overstated by $120, and Pat King, Capital will be understated by $120. The effects of omitting this adjusting entry are shown below.

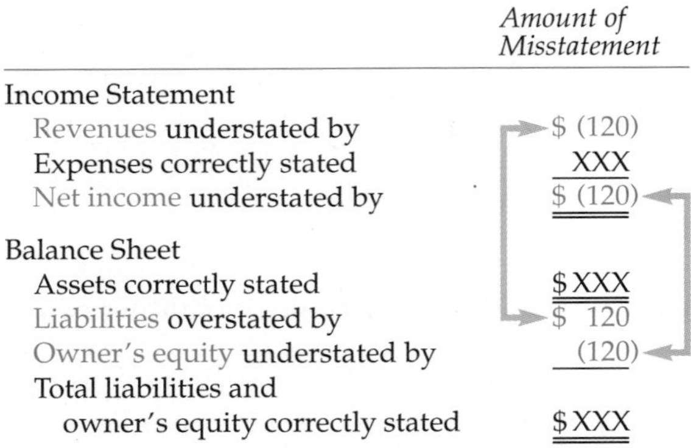

	Amount of Misstatement
Income Statement	
Revenues understated by	$ (120)
Expenses correctly stated	XXX
Net income understated by	$ (120)
Balance Sheet	
Assets correctly stated	$XXX
Liabilities overstated by	$ 120
Owner's equity understated by	(120)
Total liabilities and owner's equity correctly stated	$XXX

The only unearned revenue for Computer King was unearned rent. Other examples of unearned revenue that may require adjustment include tuition received in advance by a school, an annual retainer fee received by an attorney, premiums received in advance by an insurance company, and amounts received in advance by an advertising firm for advertising services to be rendered in the future.[2]

ACCRUED EXPENSES (ACCRUED LIABILITIES)

Some types of services, such as insurance, are normally paid for before they are used. These prepayments are deferrals. Other types of services are paid for *after* the service has been performed. For example, wages expense accumulates or *accrues* hour by hour and day by day, but payment may be made only weekly, biweekly, or monthly. The amount of such an accrued but unpaid item at the end of the accounting period is both an expense and a liability. For this reason, such accruals are called **accrued expenses** or **accrued liabilities.** In the case of wages expense, if the last day of a pay period is not the last day of the accounting period, the accrued expense and the related liability must be recorded in the accounts by an adjusting entry. This adjusting entry is necessary so that expenses are properly matched to the period in which they were incurred.

At the end of December, accrued wages for Computer King were $250. This amount is an additional expense of December and is debited to the wages expense account. It is also a liability as of December 31 and is credited to Wages Payable. The adjusting journal entry and T accounts are shown below.

Wages Expense	250	
Wages Payable		250

Wages Expense			Wages Payable		
Bal.	4,275			Dec. 31	250
Dec. 31	250				
	4,525				

[2] An alternative treatment of recording revenues received in advance of their being earned is discussed in Appendix C.

After the adjustment has been recorded and posted, the debit balance of the wages expense account is $4,525, which is the wages expense for the two months, November and December. The credit balance of $250 in Wages Payable is the amount of the liability for wages owed as of December 31.

The accrual of the wages expense for Computer King is summarized in Exhibit 4. You should note that Computer King paid wages of $950 on December 13 and $1,200 on December 27. These payments represent biweekly payroll payments made on alternate Fridays for the pay periods ending on those days. The wages of $250 earned for Monday and Tuesday, December 30 and 31, are accrued at December 31. The wages paid on January 10 totaled $1,275, which included the $250 accrued wages of December 31.

Exhibit 4
Accrued Wages

1. Wages are paid on the second and fourth Fridays for the two-week periods ending on those Fridays. The payments were $950 on December 13 and $1,200 on December 27.
2. The wages accrued for Monday and Tuesday, December 30 and 31, are $250.
3. Wages paid on Friday, January 10, total $1,275.

December

	S	M	T	W	T	F	S	
	1	2	3	4	5	6	7	
	8	9	10	11	12	13	14	Wages expense (paid), $950
	15	16	17	18	19	20	21	
	22	23	24	25	26	27	28	Wages expense (paid), $1,200
Wages expense (accrued), $250	29	30	31					

January

	S	M	T	W	T	F	S
				1	2	3	4
Wages expense (paid), $1,275	5	6	7	8	9	10	11

What would be the effect on the financial statements if the adjustment for wages ($250) is not recorded? The income statement for the period and the balance sheet as of December 31 will be misstated. On the income statement, Wages Expense will be understated by $250, and the net income will be overstated by $250. On the balance sheet, Wages Payable will be understated by $250, and Pat King, Capital will be overstated by $250. These effects of omitting the adjusting entry are shown below.

	Amount of Misstatement
Income Statement	
Revenues correctly stated	$ XXX
Expenses understated by	(250)
Net income overstated by	$ 250
Balance Sheet	
Assets correctly stated	$ XXX
Liabilities understated by	$ (250)
Owner's equity overstated by	250
Total liabilities and owner's equity correctly stated	$ XXX

Accrued wages is an example of an accrued expense that must be recorded by an adjusting entry. Other accrued expenses include accrued interest on notes payable and accrued taxes.

ACCRUED REVENUES (ACCRUED ASSETS)

All assets belonging to a business at the end of an accounting period and all revenue earned during a period should be recorded in the ledger. During an accounting period, some revenues are recorded only when cash is received. Thus, at the end of an accounting period, there may be items of revenue that have been earned *but have not been recorded*. In such cases, the amount of the revenue should be recorded by debiting an asset account and crediting a revenue account. Because of the dual nature of such accruals, they are called **accrued revenues** or **accrued assets.**

To illustrate, assume that Computer King signed an agreement with Dankner Co. on December 15. The agreement provides that Computer King will be on call to answer questions and render assistance to Dankner Co.'s employees concerning computer problems. The services provided will be billed to Dankner Co. on the fifteenth of each month at a rate of $20 per hour. As of December 31, Computer King had provided 25 hours of assistance to Dankner Co. Although the revenue of $500 (25 hours × $20) will be billed and collected in January, Computer King earned the revenue in December. The adjusting journal entry and T accounts to record the claim against the customer (an account receivable) and the revenue earned in December are shown below.

	Debit	Credit
Accounts Receivable	500	
Fees Earned		500

Accounts Receivable

Debit		Credit
Bal.	2,220	
Dec. 31	500	
	2,720	

Fees Earned

Debit	Credit	
	Bal.	16,340
	Dec. 31	500
		16,840

If the adjustment for the accrued asset ($500) is not recorded, the income statement for the period and the balance sheet as of December 31 will be misstated. On the income statement, Fees Earned and the net income will be understated by $500. On the balance sheet, Accounts Receivable and Pat King, Capital will be understated by $500. These effects of omitting the adjusting entry are shown below.

	Amount of Misstatement
Income Statement	
Revenues understated by	$ (500)
Expenses correctly stated	XXX
Net income understated by	$ (500)
Balance Sheet	
Assets understated by	$ (500)
Liabilities correctly stated	$ XXX
Owner's equity understated by	(500)
Total liabilities and owner's equity understated by	$ (500)

Accrued attorney's fees in a law firm is an example of an accrued revenue that must be recorded by an adjusting entry to properly match revenues and expenses. Other accruals that would require similar treatment include commissions earned by a travel agent but not billed, accrued interest on notes receivable, and accrued rent on property rented to others.

Computer King's plant assets such as office equipment and furniture will decrease in usefulness, or depreciate, over time.

PLANT ASSETS

Tangible assets that are owned by a business, are permanent or have a long life, and are used in the business are called **plant assets** or **fixed assets.** In a sense, plant assets are a type of long-term deferred expense. However, because of their nature and long life, they are discussed separately from other deferred expenses, such as supplies and prepaid insurance.

Computer King's plant assets include office equipment that is used much like the supplies are used to generate revenue. Unlike supplies, however, there is no visible reduction in the quantity of the equipment. Instead, as time passes, the equipment loses its ability to provide useful services. This decrease in usefulness is called *depreciation.*

All plant assets, except land, lose their usefulness. Any decrease in an asset used to generate revenue is an expense. However, it is difficult to objectively measure the decrease in usefulness of a plant asset. For this reason, **depreciation** in accounting is the systematic allocation of a plant asset's cost to expense. This allocation occurs over the asset's estimated life during which it is expected to generate revenue. Methods of computing depreciation are discussed and illustrated in a later chapter.

The adjusting entry to record depreciation is similar to the adjusting entry for supplies used, in which an expense account is debited and an asset account is credited. The account debited is a depreciation expense account. However, the asset account Office Equipment is not credited because both the original cost of a plant asset and the amount of depreciation recorded since its purchase are normally reported on the balance sheet. The account credited is an **accumulated depreciation account,** which is reported on the balance sheet as a deduction from the asset account. Accumulated depreciation accounts are called **contra accounts** or **contra asset accounts** because they are reported as deductions from the related asset accounts.

Normal titles for plant asset accounts and their related contra asset accounts are as follows:

Plant Asset	*Contra Asset*
Land	None—Land is not depreciated.
Buildings	Accumulated Depreciation—Buildings
Equipment	Accumulated Depreciation—Equipment

The ledger could have a separate account for each of a number of buildings. Equipment may also be subdivided according to function, such as Delivery Equipment, Store Equipment, and Office Equipment, with a related accumulated depreciation account for each plant asset account.

The adjusting entry to record depreciation for December for Computer King is illustrated in the following journal entry and T accounts. The estimated amount of depreciation for the month is assumed to be $50.

Depreciation Expense	50	
Accumulated Depreciation—Office Equipment		50

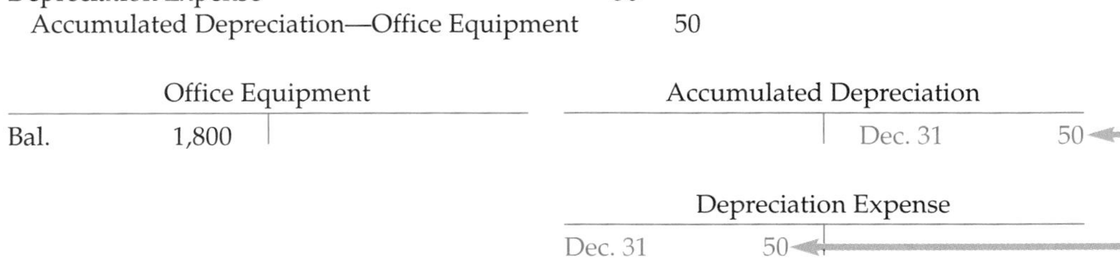

The $50 increase in the accumulated depreciation account is subtracted from the $1,800 cost recorded in the related plant asset account. The difference between the two balances is the unexpired, undepreciated, or unallocated cost. This amount ($1,750) is called the book value of the asset. The book value may be presented on the balance sheet in the following manner:

Office equipment	$1,800	
Less accumulated depreciation	50	$1,750

You should note that the market value of a plant asset normally differs from its book value. This is because depreciation is an allocation method, not a valuation method. That is, depreciation allocates the cost of a plant asset to expense over its estimated life. Depreciation does not attempt to measure changes in market values, which may vary significantly from year to year.

If the previous adjustment for depreciation ($50) is not recorded, the financial statements as of December 31 will be misstated. On the income statement, Depreciation Expense will be understated by $50, and the net income will be overstated by $50. On the balance sheet, the book value of the office equipment and Pat King, Capital will be overstated by $50. The effects of omitting the adjustment for depreciation are shown below.

	Amount of Misstatement
Income Statement	
Revenues correctly stated	$ XX
Expenses understated by	(50)
Net income overstated by	$ 50
Balance Sheet	
Assets overstated by	$ 50
Liabilities correctly stated	$ XX
Owner's equity overstated by	50
Total liabilities and owner's equity overstated by	$ 50

Work Sheet

Objective 4
Enter adjustments on a work sheet and prepare an adjusted trial balance.

Before adjusting entries such as those described above can be prepared, the relevant data must be assembled. For example, the cost of supplies on hand and the wages accrued at the end of the period must be determined. Such data and analysis are summarized by accountants in **working papers.**

A working paper often used by accountants to summarize adjusting entries and assist in preparing the financial statements is the work sheet. The name of the business, the type of working paper (work sheet), and the period of time should be listed at the top of the work sheet, as shown in Exhibit 5. Such work sheets are normally not prepared in computerized accounting systems, since computer programs automatically post to the accounts and prepare financial statements after the adjusting entries are entered into the program.

TRIAL BALANCE COLUMNS

The trial balance discussed in Chapter 2 may be prepared directly on the work sheet. The work sheet in Exhibit 5 shows the trial balance for Computer King at December 31, 1996.

Computer King
Work Sheet
For the Two Months Ended December 31, 1996

Account Title	Trial Balance		Adjustments		Adjusted Trial Balance		Income Statement		Balance Sheet	
	Dr.	Cr.	Dr.	Cr.	Dr.	Cr.	Dr.	Cr.	Dr.	Cr.
Cash	2,065									
Accounts Receivable	2,220									
Supplies	2,000									
Prepaid Insurance	2,400									
Land	10,000									
Office Equipment	1,800									
Accounts Payable		900								
Unearned Rent		360								
Pat King, Capital		15,000								
Pat King, Drawing	4,000									
Fees Earned		16,340								
Wages Expense	4,275									
Rent Expense	1,600									
Utilities Expense	985									
Supplies Expense	800									
Miscellaneous Expense	455									
	32,600	32,600								

Exhibit 5
Work Sheet with Trial Balance Entered

The work sheet is used for assembling data and summarizing the effects of adjusting entries. It also aids in the preparation of financial statements.

ADJUSTMENTS COLUMNS

The adjustment data are entered on the work sheet in the Adjustments columns. Both the debit and the credit amounts are inserted for the proper accounts for each adjustment. Cross-referencing the debit and credit of each adjustment by letters is useful in reviewing the work sheet. It is also helpful when the adjusting entries are recorded in the journal.

The order in which the adjustments are entered on the work sheet is not important. Most accountants enter the adjustments in the order in which the data are assembled. If the titles of some of the accounts to be adjusted do not appear in the trial balance, they should be inserted in the Account Title column, below the trial balance totals, as needed. The adjustments for Computer King that were explained and illustrated earlier in the chapter have been entered on the work sheet in Exhibit 6.

Explanations for the entries in the Adjustments columns of the work sheet follow:

(a) **Supplies.** The supplies account has a debit balance of $2,000. The cost of the supplies on hand at the end of the period is $760. Therefore, the supplies expense for December is the difference between the two amounts, or $1,240. The adjustment is entered by writing (1) $1,240 in the Adjustments Debit column on the same line as Supplies Expense and (2) $1,240 in the Adjustments Credit column on the same line as Supplies.

(b) **Prepaid Insurance.** The prepaid insurance account has a debit balance of $2,400, which represents the prepayment of insurance for 24 months beginning December 1. Thus, the insurance expense for December is $100 ($2,400 ÷ 24). The adjustment is entered by writing (1) Insurance Expense in the Account Title

Exhibit 6
Work Sheet with Trial Balance and Adjustments Entered

Computer King
Work Sheet
For the Two Months Ended December 31, 1996

Account Title	Trial Balance Dr.	Trial Balance Cr.	Adjustments Dr.	Adjustments Cr.	Adjusted Trial Balance Dr.	Adjusted Trial Balance Cr.	Income Statement Dr.	Income Statement Cr.	Balance Sheet Dr.	Balance Sheet Cr.
Cash	2,065									
Accounts Receivable	2,220		(e) 500							
Supplies	2,000			(a)1,240						
Prepaid Insurance	2,400			(b) 100						
Land	10,000									
Office Equipment	1,800									
Accounts Payable		900								
Unearned Rent		360	(c) 120							
Pat King, Capital		15,000								
Pat King, Drawing	4,000									
Fees Earned		16,340		(e) 500						
Wages Expense	4,275		(d) 250							
Rent Expense	1,600									
Utilities Expense	985									
Supplies Expense	800		(a)1,240							
Miscellaneous Expense	455									
	32,600	32,600								
Insurance Expense			(b) 100							
Rent Income				(c) 120						
Wages Payable				(d) 250						
Depreciation Expense			(f) 50							
Accumulated Depreciation				(f) 50						
			2,260	2,260						

Accounts are added, as needed, to complete the adjustments.

(a) Supplies used, $1,240 ($2,000 – $760).
(b) Insurance expired, $100.
(c) Rent earned from amount received in advance, $120.
(d) Wages accrued but not paid, $250.
(e) Fees earned but not received, $500.
(f) Depreciation of office equipment, $50.

column, (2) $100 in the Adjustments Debit column on the same line as Insurance Expense, and (3) $100 in the Adjustments Credit column on the same line as Prepaid Insurance.

(c) **Unearned Rent.** The unearned rent account has a credit balance of $360, which represents the receipt of three months' rent, beginning with December. Thus, the rent income for December is $120. The adjustment is entered by writing (1) $120 in the Adjustments Debit column on the same line as Unearned Rent, (2) Rent Income in the Account Title column, and (3) $120 in the Adjustments Credit column on the same line as Rent Income.

(d) **Wages.** Wages accrued but not paid at the end of December total $250. This amount is an increase in expenses and an increase in liabilities. The adjustment is entered by writing (1) $250 in the Adjustments Debit column on the same line as Wages Expense, (2) Wages Payable in the Account Title column, and (3) $250 in the Adjustments Credit column on the same line as Wages Payable.

(e) **Accrued Fees.** Fees accrued at the end of December but not recorded total $500. This amount is an increase in an asset and an increase in revenue. The adjustment is entered by writing (1) $500 in the Adjustments Debit column on the same line as Accounts Receivable and (2) $500 in the Adjustments Credit column on the same line as Fees Earned.

(f) **Depreciation.** Depreciation of the office equipment is $50 for December. The adjustment is entered by writing (1) Depreciation Expense in the Account Title column, (2) $50 in the Adjustments Debit column on the same line as Depreciation Expense, (3) Accumulated Depreciation in the Account Title column, and (4) $50 in the Adjustments Credit column on the same line as Accumulated Depreciation.

The Adjustments columns are totaled to verify the mathematical accuracy of the adjustment data. The total of the Debit column must equal the total of the Credit column.

ADJUSTED TRIAL BALANCE COLUMNS

The data in the Trial Balance columns are added to or subtracted from the adjustments data and extended to the Adjusted Trial Balance columns, as shown on the work sheet in Exhibit 7. For example, the cash account is extended at its original amount of $2,065, since no adjustments affected Cash. Accounts Receivable has an initial balance of $2,220 and a debit adjustment (increase) of $500. The amount to be extended is the debit balance of $2,720. The same procedure is continued until all

Exhibit 7
Work Sheet with Trial Balance, Adjustments, and Adjusted Trial Balance Entered

Computer King
Work Sheet
For the Two Months Ended December 31, 1996

	Trial Balance		Adjustments		Adjusted Trial Balance		Income Statement		Balance Sheet	
Account Title	**Dr.**	**Cr.**	**Dr.**	**Cr.**	**Dr.**	**Cr.**	**Dr.**	**Cr.**	**Dr.**	**Cr.**
Cash	2,065				2,065					
Accounts Receivable	2,220		(e) 500		2,720					
Supplies	2,000			(a)1,240	760					
Prepaid Insurance	2,400			(b) 100	2,300					
Land	10,000				10,000					
Office Equipment	1,800				1,800					
Accounts Payable		900				900				
Unearned Rent		360	(c) 120			240				
Pat King, Capital		15,000				15,000				
Pat King, Drawing	4,000				4,000					
Fees Earned		16,340		(e) 500		16,840				
Wages Expense	4,275		(d) 250		4,525					
Rent Expense	1,600				1,600					
Utilities Expense	985				985					
Supplies Expense	800		(a)1,240		2,040					
Miscellaneous Expense	455				455					
	32,600	32,600								
Insurance Expense			(b) 100		100					
Rent Income				(c) 120		120				
Wages Payable				(d) 250		250				
Depreciation Expense			(f) 50		50					
Accumulated Depreciation				(f) 50		50				
			2,260	2,260	33,400	33,400				

The adjusted trial balance amounts are determined by extending the trial balance amounts plus or minus the adjustments. For example, the Wages Expense debit of $4,525 is the trial balance amount of $4,275 plus the $250 adjustment debit.

account balances have been extended to the Adjusted Trial Balance columns. The Debit and Credit columns are then totaled to verify the equality of the Debit and Credit columns.

COMPLETING THE WORK SHEET

We will complete the work sheet, including the use of the Income Statement and Balance Sheet columns, in Chapter 4. Also, we will discuss the use of the work sheet in preparing financial statements and the journalizing and posting of the adjusting entries. Finally, we will illustrate how to prepare the accounting records for the next accounting period.

KEY POINTS

Objective 1. Explain how the matching concept relates to the accrual basis of accounting.
The accrual basis of accounting requires the use of an adjusting process at the end of the accounting period to match revenues and expenses properly. Revenues are reported in the period in which they are earned, and expenses are matched with the revenues they generate.

Objective 2. Explain why adjustments are necessary and list the characteristics of adjusting entries.
At the end of an accounting period, some of the amounts listed on the trial balance are not necessarily current balances. For example, amounts listed for prepaid expenses are normally overstated because the use of these assets has not been recorded on a daily basis. A delay of the recognition of an expense already paid or a revenue already received is called a deferral.

Some revenues and expenses related to a period may not be recorded at the end of the period, since these items are normally recorded only when cash has been received or paid. A revenue or expense that has not been paid or recorded is called an accrual.

The entries required at the end of an accounting period to bring accounts up to date and to ensure the proper matching of revenues and expenses are called adjusting entries. Adjusting entries require a debit or a credit to a revenue or an expense account and an offsetting debit or credit to an asset or a liability account.

Adjusting entries affect amounts reported in the income statement and the balance sheet. Thus, if an adjusting entry is not recorded, these financial statements will be incorrect (misstated).

Objective 3. Journalize entries for accounts requiring adjustment.
Adjusting entries illustrated in this chapter include deferred (prepaid) expenses, deferred (unearned) revenues, accrued expenses (accrued liabilities), and accrued revenues (accrued assets). In addition, the adjusting entry necessary to record depreciation on plant assets was illustrated.

Objective 4. Enter adjustments on a work sheet and prepare an adjusted trial balance.
The work sheet illustrated in this chapter has trial balance, adjustments, adjusted trial balance, income statement, and balance sheet columns. Adjustments are entered on the work sheet in the Adjustments columns. The adjustments are added to or subtracted from the trial balance amounts, and the resulting amounts are extended to the Adjusted Trial Balance columns. The Debit and Credit columns are then totaled to verify the equality of the Debit and Credit columns.

GLOSSARY OF KEY TERMS

Accounting period concept. An accounting principle that requires accounting reports be prepared at periodic intervals. *Objective 1*

Accrual basis. Revenues are recognized in the period earned, and expenses are recognized in the period incurred in the process of generating revenues. *Objective 1*

Accruals. Expenses that have been incurred or revenues that have been earned but have not been recorded. *Objective 2*

Accrued expenses. Expenses that have been incurred but not recorded in the accounts. Sometimes called accrued liabilities. *Objective 2*

Accrued revenues. Revenues that have been earned but not recorded in the accounts. Sometimes called accrued assets. *Objective 2*

Accumulated depreciation account. The contra asset account used to accumulate the depreciation recognized to date on plant assets. *Objective 3*

Adjusting entries. Entries required at the end of an accounting period to bring the ledger up to date. *Objective 2*

Adjusting process. The process of updating the accounts at the end of a period. *Objective 1*

Book value of the asset. The difference between the balance of a plant asset account and its related accumulated depreciation account. *Objective 3*

Cash basis. Revenue is recognized in the period cash is received, and expenses are recognized in the period cash is paid. *Objective 1*

Contra accounts. Accounts that are offset against other accounts. *Objective 3*

Deferrals. Delays in the recognition of expenses that have been incurred or revenues that have been received. *Objective 2*

Deferred expenses. Items that are initially recorded as assets but are expected to become expenses over time or through the normal operations of the business. Sometimes called prepaid expenses. *Objective 2*

Deferred revenues. Items that are initially recorded as liabilities but are expected to become revenues over time or through the normal operations of the business. Sometimes called unearned revenues. *Objective 2*

Depreciation. In a general sense, the decrease in usefulness of plant assets other than land. In accounting, refers to the systematic allocation of a plant asset's cost to expense. *Objective 3*

Matching concept. The concept that all expenses incurred should be matched with the revenue they generate during a period of time. *Objective 1*

Plant assets. Tangible assets that are owned by a business, are permanent or have a long life, and are used in the business. *Objective 3*

Revenue recognition principle. The principle by which revenues are recognized in the period in which they are earned. *Objective 1*

Work sheet. A working paper used to summarize adjusting entries and assist in the preparation of financial statements. *Objective 4*

ILLUSTRATIVE PROBLEM

Three years ago, T. Roderick organized Harbor Realty. At July 31, 1997, the end of the current year, the trial balance of Harbor Realty is as follows:

Cash	3,425	
Accounts Receivable	7,000	
Supplies	1,270	
Prepaid Insurance	620	
Office Equipment	51,650	
Accumulated Depreciation		9,700
Accounts Payable		925
Unearned Fees		1,250
T. Roderick, Capital		29,000
T. Roderick, Drawing	5,200	
Fees Earned		59,125
Wages Expense	22,415	
Rent Expense	4,200	
Utilities Expense	2,715	
Miscellaneous Expense	1,505	
	100,000	100,000

The data needed to determine year-end adjustments are as follows:

a. Supplies on hand at July 31, 1997, $380.
b. Insurance premiums expired during the year, $315.
c. Depreciation of equipment during the year, $4,950.
d. Wages accrued but not paid at July 31, 1997, $440.
e. Accrued fees earned but not recorded at July 31, 1997, $1,000.
f. Unearned fees on July 31, 1997, $750.

Instructions

1. Enter the July 31, 1997 trial balance on a work sheet.
2. Using the adjustment data, enter the necessary adjustments on the work sheet.
3. Extend the adjustment data on the work sheet to the Adjusted Trial Balance columns.

Solution

1., 2., and 3.

Harbor Realty
Work Sheet
For the Year Ended July 31, 1997

Account Title	Trial Balance		Adjustments		Adjusted Trial Balance	
	Debit	Credit	Debit	Credit	Debit	Credit
Cash	3 4 2 5 00				3 4 2 5 00	
Accounts Receivable	7 0 0 0 00		(e)1 0 0 0 00		8 0 0 0 00	
Supplies	1 2 7 0 00			(a) 8 9 0 00	3 8 0 00	
Prepaid Insurance	6 2 0 00			(b) 3 1 5 00	3 0 5 00	
Office Equipment	51 6 5 0 00				51 6 5 0 00	
Accumulated Depreciation		9 7 0 0 00		(c)4 9 5 0 00		14 6 5 0 00
Accounts Payable		9 2 5 00				9 2 5 00
Unearned Fees		1 2 5 0 00	(f) 5 0 0 00			7 5 0 00
T. Roderick, Capital		29 0 0 0 00				29 0 0 0 00
T. Roderick, Drawing	5 2 0 0 00				5 2 0 0 00	
Fees Earned		59 1 2 5 00		(e)1 0 0 0 00		60 6 2 5 00
				(f) 5 0 0 00		
Wages Expense	22 4 1 5 00		(d) 4 4 0 00		22 8 5 5 00	
Rent Expense	4 2 0 0 00				4 2 0 0 00	
Utilities Expense	2 7 1 5 00				2 7 1 5 00	
Miscellaneous Expense	1 5 0 5 00				1 5 0 5 00	
	100 0 0 0 00	100 0 0 0 00				
Supplies Expense			(a) 8 9 0 00		8 9 0 00	
Insurance Expense			(b) 3 1 5 00		3 1 5 00	
Depreciation Expense			(c)4 9 5 0 00		4 9 5 0 00	
Wages Payable				(d) 4 4 0 00		4 4 0 00
			8 0 9 5 00	8 0 9 5 00	106 3 9 0 00	106 3 9 0 00

SELF-EXAMINATION QUESTIONS (ANSWERS AT END OF CHAPTER)

1. Which of the following items represents a deferral?
   A. Prepaid insurance
   B. Wages payable
   C. Fees earned
   D. Accumulated depreciation

2. If the supplies account, before adjustment on May 31, indicated a balance of $2,250, and supplies on hand at May 31 totaled $950, the adjusting entry would be:
   A. debit Supplies, $950; credit Supplies Expense, $950
   B. debit Supplies, $1,300; credit Supplies Expense, $1,300
   C. debit Supplies Expense, $950; credit Supplies, $950
   D. debit Supplies Expense, $1,300; credit Supplies, $1,300

3. The balance in the unearned rent account for Jones Co. as of December 31 is $1,200. If Jones Co. failed to record the adjusting entry for $600 of rent earned during December, the effect on the balance sheet and income statement for December is:
   A. assets understated $600; net income overstated $600
   B. liabilities understated $600; net income understated $600
   C. liabilities overstated $600; net income understated $600
   D. liabilities overstated $600; net income overstated $600

4. If the estimated amount of depreciation on equipment for a period is $2,000, the adjusting entry to record depreciation would be:
   A. debit Depreciation Expense, $2,000; credit Equipment, $2,000
   B. debit Equipment, $2,000; credit Depreciation Expense, $2,000
   C. debit Depreciation Expense, $2,000; credit Accumulated Depreciation, $2,000
   D. debit Accumulated Depreciation, $2,000; credit Depreciation Expense, $2,000

5. If the equipment account has a balance of $22,500 and its accumulated depreciation account has a balance of $14,000, the book value of the equipment is:
   A. $36,500
   B. $22,500
   C. $14,000
   D. $8,500

DISCUSSION QUESTIONS

1. How are revenues and expenses reported on the income statement under (a) the cash basis of accounting and (b) the accrual basis of accounting?
2. Fees for services provided are billed to a customer during 1996. The customer remits the amount owed in 1997. During which year would the revenues be reported on the income statement under (a) the cash basis? (b) the accrual basis?
3. Employees performed services in 1996 but the wages were not paid until 1997. During which year would the wages expense be reported on the income statement under (a) the cash basis? (b) the accrual basis?
4. Is the matching concept related to (a) the cash basis of accounting or (b) the accrual basis of accounting?
5. Is the balance listed for cash on the trial balance, before the accounts have been adjusted, the amount that should normally be reported on the balance sheet? Explain.
6. Is the balance listed for supplies on the trial balance, before the accounts have been adjusted, the amount that should normally be reported on the balance sheet? Explain.
7. Why are adjusting entries needed at the end of an accounting period?
8. What is the difference between *adjusting entries* and *correcting entries*?
9. Identify the five different categories of adjusting entries frequently required at the end of an accounting period.
10. If the effect of the credit portion of an adjusting entry is to increase the balance of a liability account, which of the following statements describes the effect of the debit portion of the entry?
    a. Increases the balance of a revenue account.
    b. Increases the balance of an expense account.
    c. Increases the balance of an asset account.
11. Does every adjusting entry have an effect on the determination of the amount of net income for a period? Explain.
12. What is the nature of the balance in the prepaid insurance account at the end of the accounting period (a) before adjustment? (b) after adjustment?
13. On May 1 of the current year, a business paid the May rent on the building that it occupies. (a) Do the rights acquired at May 1 represent an asset or an expense? (b) What is the justification for debiting Rent Expense at the time of payment?
14. What are plant assets?
15. What is depreciation?
16. In accounting for depreciation on equipment, what is the name of the account that would be referred to as a contra asset account?
17. (a) Explain the purpose of the two accounts: Depreciation Expense and Accumulated Depreciation. (b) What is the normal balance of each account? (c) Is it customary for the balances of the two accounts to be equal in amount? (d) In what financial statements, if any, will each account appear?
18. What term is applied to the difference between the balance of a plant asset account and its related accumulated depreciation account?
19. What is a work sheet?
20. What purpose do the Adjusted Trial Balance columns serve in a work sheet?

EXERCISES

EXERCISE 3–1
Classifying accruals and deferrals
Objectives 2, 3

Classify the following items as (a) deferred expense (prepaid expense), (b) deferred revenue (unearned revenue), (c) accrued expense (accrued liability), or (d) accrued revenue (accrued asset).

1. Utilities owed but not yet paid.
2. Fees received but not yet earned.
3. Salary owed but not yet paid.
4. A two-year premium paid on a fire insurance policy.
5. Fees earned but not yet received.
6. Taxes owed but payable in the following period.
7. Supplies on hand.
8. Tuition collected in advance by a university.

EXERCISE 3–2
Classifying adjusting entries
Objectives 2, 3

The following accounts were taken from the unadjusted trial balance of Wingrich Co., a congressional lobbying firm. Indicate whether or not each account would normally require an adjusting entry. If the account normally requires an adjusting entry, use the following notation to indicate the type of adjustment:

AE—Accrued Expense
AR—Accrued Revenue
DE—Deferred Expense
DR—Deferred Revenue

To illustrate, the answers for the first two accounts are shown below:

Account	*Answer*
Abe Drew, Drawing	Does not normally require adjustment.
Accounts Receivable	Normally requires adjustment (AR).
Accumulated Depreciation	
Cash	
Insurance Expense	
Interest Payable	
Interest Receivable	
Land	
Office Equipment	
Prepaid Rent	
Supplies Expense	
Unearned Fees	
Wages Expense	

EXERCISE 3–3
Adjusting entry for supplies
Objective 3

The balance in the supplies account, before adjustment at the end of the year, is $1,725. Journalize the adjusting entry required if the amount of supplies on hand at the end of the year is $420.

EXERCISE 3–4
Determining supplies purchased
Objective 3

The supplies and supplies expense accounts at December 31, after adjusting entries have been posted at the end of the first year of operations, are shown in the following T accounts:

Supplies			Supplies Expense		
Bal.	375		Bal.	1,750	

Determine the amount of supplies purchased during the year.

EXERCISE 3–5
Effect of omitting adjusting entry
Objective 3

At December 31, the end of the first *month* of the year, the usual adjusting entry transferring supplies used to an expense account is omitted. Which items will be incorrectly stated, because of the error, on (a) the income statement for December and (b) the balance sheet as of December 31? Also indicate whether the items in error will be overstated or understated.

EXERCISE 3–6
Adjusting entries for prepaid insurance
Objective 3

The balance in the prepaid insurance account, before adjustment at the end of the year, is $6,650. Journalize the adjusting entry required under each of the following *alternatives* for determining the amount of the adjustment: (a) the amount of insurance expired during the year is $1,900; (b) the amount of unexpired insurance applicable to future periods is $4,750.

EXERCISE 3–7
Adjusting entries for prepaid insurance
Objective 3

The prepaid insurance account had a balance of $3,750 at the beginning of the year. The account was debited for $1,150 for premiums on policies purchased during the year. Journalize the adjusting entry required at the end of the year for each of the following situations: (a) the amount of unexpired insurance applicable to future periods is $2,300; (b) the amount of insurance expired during the year is $2,150.

EXERCISE 3–8
Adjusting entries for unearned fees
Objective 3

The balance in the unearned fees account, before adjustment at the end of the year, is $9,000. Journalize the adjusting entry required if the amount of unearned fees at the end of the year is $2,500.

EXERCISE 3–9
Effect of omitting adjusting entry
Objective 3

At the end of January, the first *month* of the year, the usual adjusting entry transferring rent earned to a revenue account from the unearned rent account was omitted. Indicate which items will be incorrectly stated, because of the error, on (a) the income statement for January and (b) the balance sheet as of January 31. Also indicate whether the items in error will be overstated or understated.

EXERCISE 3–10
Adjusting entries for accrued salaries
Objective 3

Jones Realty Co. pays weekly salaries of $7,500 on Friday for a five-day week ending on that day. Journalize the necessary adjusting entry at the end of the accounting period, assuming that the period ends (a) on Tuesday, (b) on Wednesday.

EXERCISE 3–11
Determining wages paid
Objective 3

The wages payable and wages expense accounts at December 31, after adjusting entries have been posted at the end of the first year of operations, are shown in the following T accounts:

Wages Payable			Wages Expense		
	Bal.	420	Bal.	21,800	

Determine the amount of wages paid during the year.

EXERCISE 3–12
Effect of omitting adjusting entry
Objective 3

Accrued salaries of $3,000 owed to employees for December 30 and 31 are not taken into consideration in preparing the financial statements for the year ended December 31. Indicate which items will be erroneously stated, because of the error, on (a) the income statement for the year and (b) the balance sheet as of December 31. Also indicate whether the items in error will be overstated or understated.

EXERCISE 3–13
Effect of omitting adjusting entry
Objective 3

Assume that the error in Exercise 3–12 was not corrected and that the $3,000 of accrued salaries was included in the first salary payment in January. Indicate which items will be erroneously stated, because of failure to correct the initial error, on (a) the income statement for the month of January and (b) the balance sheet as of January 31.

EXERCISE 3–14
Adjusting entries for prepaid and accrued taxes
Objective 3

Edwards Financial Planning Co. was organized on April 1 of the current year. On April 2, Edwards prepaid $1,080 to the city for taxes (license fees) for the *next* 12 months and debited the prepaid taxes account. Edwards is also required to pay in January an annual tax (on property) for the *previous* calendar year. The estimated amount of the property tax for the current year (April 1 to December 31) is $13,600. (a) Journalize the two adjusting entries required to bring the accounts affected by the two taxes up to date as of December 31, the end of the current year. (b) What is the amount of tax expense for the current year?

EXERCISE 3–15
Effects of errors on financial statements
Objective 3

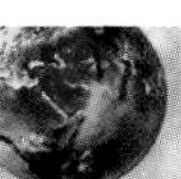

The balance sheet for **Circuit City Stores, Inc.** as of February 28, 1994, includes the following accrued expenses as liabilities:

Accrued expenses	$86,826,000
Accrued income taxes	38,582,000

The net income for Circuit City Stores, Inc. for the year ended February 28, 1994, was $132,400,000. (a) If the accruals had not been recorded at February 28, 1994, by how much would net income have been misstated for the fiscal year ended February 28, 1994? (b) What is the percentage of the misstatement in (a) to the reported net income of $132,400,000?

EXERCISE 3–16
Effects of errors on financial statements
Objective 3

The accountant for Econoline Medical Co., a medical services consulting firm, mistakenly omitted adjusting entries for (a) unearned revenue ($2,500) and (b) accrued wages ($850). Indicate the effect of each error, considered individually, on the income statement for the current year ended December 31. Also indicate the effect of each error on the December 31 balance sheet. Set up a table similar to the following, and record your answers by inserting the dollar amount in the appropriate spaces. Insert a zero if the error does not affect the item.

	Error (a)		*Error (b)*	
	Over-stated	*Under-stated*	*Over-stated*	*Under-stated*
1. Revenue for the year would be	$	$	$	$
2. Expenses for the year would be	$	$	$	$
3. Net income for the year would be	$	$	$	$
4. Assets at December 31 would be	$	$	$	$
5. Liabilities at December 31 would be	$	$	$	$
6. Owner's equity at December 31 would be	$	$	$	$

EXERCISE 3–17
Effects of errors on financial statements
Objective 3

If the net income for the current year had been $31,700 in Exercise 3–16, what would be the correct net income if the proper adjusting entries had been made?

EXERCISE 3–18
Adjusting entry for accrued fees
Objective 3

At the end of the current year, $1,150 of fees have been earned but have not been billed to clients.

a. Journalize the adjusting entry to record the accrued fees.
b. If the cash basis rather than the accrual basis had been used, would an adjusting entry have been necessary? Explain.

EXERCISE 3–19
Adjusting entries for unearned and accrued fees
Objective 3

The balance in the unearned fees account, before adjustment at the end of the year, is $11,300. Of these fees, $8,500 have been earned. In addition, $2,750 of fees have been earned but have not been billed. Journalize the adjusting entries (a) to adjust the unearned fees account and (b) to record the accrued fees.

EXERCISE 3–20
Effect on financial statements of omitting adjusting entry
Objective 3

The adjusting entry for accrued fees was omitted at December 31, the end of the current year. Indicate which items will be in error, because of the omission, on (a) the income statement for the current year and (b) the balance sheet as of December 31. Also indicate whether the items in error will be overstated or understated.

EXERCISE 3–21
Adjusting entry for depreciation
Objective 3

The estimated amount of depreciation on equipment for the current year is $4,100. Journalize the adjusting entry to record the depreciation.

EXERCISE 3–22
Determining plant asset's book value
Objective 3

The balance in the equipment account is $115,000, and the balance in the accumulated depreciation—equipment account is $80,000.

a. What is the book value of the equipment?
b. Does the balance in the accumulated depreciation account mean that the equipment's loss of value is $80,000? Explain.

EXERCISE 3–23
Book value of plant assets
Objective 3

Microsoft Corporation reported *Property, Plant, and Equipment* of $1,181 million and *Accumulated Depreciation* of $314 million at June 30, 1994.

a. What was the book value of the plant assets at June 30, 1994?
b. Would the book value of Microsoft Corporation's plant assets normally approximate their fair market values?

EXERCISE 3–24
Adjusting entries for depreciation; effect of error
Objective 3

On December 31, a business estimates depreciation on equipment used during the first year of operations to be $1,800. (a) Journalize the adjusting entry required as of December 31. (b) If the adjusting entry in (a) were omitted, which items would be erroneously stated on (1) the income statement for the year and (2) the balance sheet as of December 31?

EXERCISE 3–25
Entering adjustments data on work sheet
Objective 4

The unadjusted trial balance for Coral Services Co. has been prepared on the following work sheet for the year ended December 31, 1996.

Coral Services Co.
Work Sheet
For the Year Ended December 31, 1996

	Unadjusted Trial Balance		Adjustments		Adjusted Trial Balance	
Account Title	Dr.	Cr.	Dr.	Cr.	Dr.	Cr.
Cash	6					
Accounts Receivable	18					
Supplies	4					
Prepaid Insurance	6					
Land	12					
Equipment	20					
Accumulated Depr.—Equip.		3				
Accounts Payable		13				
Wages Payable		0				
Jill Tolbert, Capital		40				
Jill Tolbert, Drawing	4					
Fees Earned		34				
Wages Expense	12					
Rent Expense	4					
Insurance Expense	0					
Utilities Expense	2					
Depreciation Expense	0					
Supplies Expense	0					
Miscellaneous Expense	2					
Totals	90	90				

The data for year-end adjustments are as follows:

a. Fees earned but not yet billed, $5.
b. Supplies on hand, $1.
c. Insurance premiums expired, $4.
d. Depreciation expense, $2.
e. Wages accrued but not paid, $1.

Set up the above work sheet on separate paper, enter the adjustments data, and extend the balances to the Adjusted Trial Balance columns.

EXERCISE 3–26
Work sheet
Objective 4

The accountant for All-Washed-Up Laundry prepared the following portion of a work sheet. Assume that all balances in the unadjusted trial balance are correct in amount. How many errors can you find in the accountant's work?

All-Washed-Up Laundry
Work Sheet
For the Year Ended August 31, 1997

	Trial Balance		Adjustments		Adjusted Trial Balance	
Account Title	Dr.	Cr.	Dr.	Cr.	Dr.	Cr.
Cash	17,790				7,790	
Laundry Supplies	4,750		(a) 3,910		8,660	
Prepaid Insurance	2,825			(b) 1,500	1,325	
Laundry Equipment		85,600				85,600
Accumulated Depreciation	55,700		(c) 5,720		61,420	
Accounts Payable		4,950				4,950
Jim Lee, Capital		30,900				30,900
Jim Lee, Drawing	8,000				8,000	
Laundry Revenue		76,900				76,900
Wages Expense	24,500		(d) 850		24,500	
Rent Expense	15,575				15,575	
Utilities Expense	8,500				5,800	
Miscellaneous Expense	910					
	138,550	198,350				
Laundry Supplies Expense			(a) 3,910		3,910	
Insurance Expense					1,500	
Depreciation Expense				(c) 5,720	5,720	
Wages Payable			(d) 850			850
			15,240	7,220	144,200	199,200

PROBLEMS SERIES A

PROBLEM 3–1A
Adjusting entries
Objective 3

On December 31, the end of the current year, the following data were accumulated to assist the accountant in preparing the adjusting entries for Wyckoff Realty:

a. The supplies account balance on December 31 is $2,450. The supplies on hand on December 31 are $490.
b. The unearned rent account balance on December 31 is $2,400, representing the receipt of an advance payment on December 1 of three months' rent from tenants.
c. Wages accrued but not paid at December 31 are $1,500.
d. Fees accrued but unbilled at December 31 are $7,500.
e. Depreciation on office equipment for the year is $850.

Instructions

1. Journalize the adjusting entries required at December 31.
2. Briefly explain the difference between adjusting entries and entries that would be made to correct errors.

PROBLEM 3–2A
Adjusting entries
Objective 3

Selected account balances before adjustment for Omni Realty at December 31, the end of the current year, are as follows:

	Debits	Credits
Accounts Receivable	$11,250	
Supplies	4,750	
Prepaid Rent	27,000	
Equipment	42,500	
Accumulated Depreciation		$10,900
Wages Payable		—
Unearned Fees		5,000
Fees Earned		87,950
Wages Expense	29,400	
Rent Expense	—	
Depreciation Expense	—	
Supplies Expense	—	

Data needed for year-end adjustments are as follows:

a. Unbilled fees at December 31, $3,650.
b. Supplies on hand at December 31, $1,275.
c. Rent expired during year, $24,000.
d. Depreciation of equipment during year, $2,750.
e. Unearned fees at December 31, $1,250.
f. Wages accrued but not paid at December 31, $1,150.

Instructions

Journalize the six adjusting entries required at December 31, based upon the data presented.

PROBLEM 3–3A
Adjusting entries
Objectives 3, 4

If the working papers correlating with this textbook are not used, omit Problem 3–3A.

A portion of the work sheet for Millennium Services for the current year ending December 31 is presented in the working papers.

Instructions

1. Enter the data for the six adjustments in the two Adjustments columns of the work sheet. (Although the sequence in which the accounts are analyzed is not important, it is suggested that the analysis begin with Cash and proceed downward in the order that the accounts are listed on the work sheet.) Cross-reference the debit and credit for each adjustment by letters. Total the adjustments columns after all adjustment data have been entered.
2. Assume that the adjusting entries were omitted for (a) supplies used and (b) accrued wages. Indicate the effect of each error, considered individually, on net income for the current year and on assets, liabilities, and owner's equity at December 31. Set up a table similar to the following, and record your answers by inserting the dollar amount in the appropriate spaces. Insert a zero if the error does not affect the item.

	Error (a)		*Error (b)*	
	Over-stated	*Under-stated*	*Over-stated*	*Under-stated*
1. Net income for the year would be	$	$	$	$
2. Assets at December 31 would be	$	$	$	$
3. Liabilities at December 31 would be	$	$	$	$
4. Owner's equity at December 31 would be	$	$	$	$

PROBLEM 3–4A
Adjusting entries
Objective 3

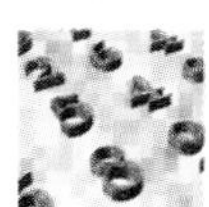

Octavius Company specializes in the repair of music equipment and is owned and operated by Cecil Virgil. On June 30, 1997, the end of the current year, the accountant for Octavius Company prepared a trial balance and an adjusted trial balance. The two trial balances are as follows:

Octavius Company
Trial Balance
June 30, 1997

	Unadjusted		Adjusted	
Cash	11,825		11,825	
Accounts Receivable	29,500		29,500	
Supplies	6,950		2,635	
Prepaid Insurance	3,750		1,150	
Equipment	92,150		92,150	
Accumulated Depreciation—Equipment		53,480		61,270
Automobiles	36,500		36,500	
Accumulated Depreciation—Automobiles		18,250		22,900
Accounts Payable		8,310		9,730
Salaries Payable		—		2,400
Unearned Service Fees		5,000		1,225
C. Virgil, Capital		55,470		55,470
C. Virgil, Drawing	5,000		5,000	
Service Fees Earned		244,600		248,375
Salary Expense	172,300		174,700	
Rent Expense	18,000		18,000	
Supplies Expense	—		4,315	
Depreciation Expense—Equipment	—		7,790	
Depreciation Expense—Automobiles	—		4,650	
Utilities Expense	4,700		6,120	
Taxes Expense	2,725		2,725	
Insurance Expense	—		2,600	
Miscellaneous Expense	1,710		1,710	
	385,110	385,110	401,370	401,370

Instructions

Journalize the seven entries that adjusted the accounts at June 30. None of the accounts were affected by more than one adjusting entry.

PROBLEM 3–5A
Adjusting entries
Objective 3

Blair Company, an electronics repair store, prepared the following trial balance at the end of its first year of operations:

Blair Company
Trial Balance
November 30, 19—

Cash	1,150	
Accounts Receivable	5,500	
Supplies	1,800	
Equipment	17,900	
Accounts Payable		750
Unearned Fees		2,000
G. Orwell, Capital		10,000
G. Orwell, Drawing	1,500	
Fees Earned		35,250
Wages Expense	8,500	
Rent Expense	8,000	
Utilities Expense	2,750	
Miscellaneous Expense	900	
	48,000	48,000

For preparing the adjusting entries, the following data were assembled:

a. Fees earned but unbilled on November 30 were $1,550.
b. Supplies on hand on November 30 were $480.

c. Depreciation of equipment was estimated to be $1,100 for the year.
d. The balance in unearned fees represented the September 1 receipt in advance for services to be provided. Only $800 of the services was provided between September 1 and November 30.
e. Unpaid wages accrued on November 30 were $275.

Instructions

Journalize the adjusting entries necessary on November 30.

PROBLEM 3–6A
Work sheet and adjusting entries
Objectives 3, 4

Twain Company is a small editorial services company owned and operated by Tom Sawyer. Twain Company's accounting clerk prepared the following trial balance on December 31, the end of the current year:

Twain Company
Trial Balance
December 31, 19—

Cash	6,700	
Accounts Receivable	23,800	
Prepaid Insurance	3,400	
Supplies	1,950	
Land	50,000	
Building	141,500	
Accumulated Depreciation—Building		91,700
Equipment	90,100	
Accumulated Depreciation—Equipment		65,300
Accounts Payable		7,500
Unearned Rent		6,000
Tom Sawyer, Capital		81,500
Tom Sawyer, Drawing	10,000	
Fees Earned		218,400
Salaries and Wages Expense	80,200	
Utilities Expense	28,200	
Advertising Expense	19,000	
Repairs Expense	11,500	
Miscellaneous Expense	4,050	
	470,400	470,400

The data needed to determine year-end adjustments are as follows:

a. Unexpired insurance at December 31, $800.
b. Supplies on hand at December 31, $450.
c. Depreciation of building for the year, $1,620.
d. Depreciation of equipment for the year, $5,500.
e. Rent unearned at December 31, $1,500.
f. Accrued salaries and wages at December 31, $2,000.
g. Fees earned but unbilled on December 31, $2,750.

Instructions

1. Enter the trial balance on a work sheet.
2. Enter the data for the seven adjustments in the Adjustments columns of the work sheet. Add additional accounts as needed.
3. Complete the Adjusted Trial Balance columns in the work sheet.
4. On the basis of the adjustment data in the work sheet, journalize the adjusting entries.

PROBLEM 3–7A
Adjusting entries and errors
Objective 3

At the end of June, the first month of operations, the following selected data were taken from the financial statements of K. Martin, an attorney:

Net income for June	$ 39,750
Total assets at June 30	189,700
Total liabilities at June 30	20,200
Total owner's equity at June 30	169,500

In preparing the financial statements, adjustments for the following data were overlooked:

a. Supplies used during June, $1,750.
b. Unbilled fees earned at June 30, $2,900.
c. Depreciation of equipment for June, $2,500.
d. Accrued wages at June 30, $1,500.

Instructions

1. Journalize the entries to record the omitted adjustments.
2. Determine the correct amount of net income for June and the total assets, liabilities, and owner's equity at June 30. In addition to indicating the corrected amounts, indicate the effect of each omitted adjustment by setting up and completing a columnar table similar to the following. Adjustment (a) is presented as an example.

	Net Income	*Total Assets*	*Total Liabilities*	*Total Owner's Equity*
Reported amounts	$39,750	$189,700	$20,200	$169,500
Corrections:				
Adjustment (a)	–1,750	–1,750	0	–1,750
Adjustment (b)	______	______	______	______
Adjustment (c)	______	______	______	______
Adjustment (d)	______	______	______	______
Corrected amounts	______	______	______	______

PROBLEMS SERIES B

PROBLEM 3–1B
Adjusting entries
Objective 3

On December 31, the end of the current year, the following data were accumulated to assist the accountant in preparing the adjusting entries for Millburn Realty:

a. Fees accrued but unbilled at December 31 are $5,250.
b. The supplies account balance on December 31 is $3,100. The supplies on hand at December 31 are $1,050.
c. Wages accrued but not paid at December 31 are $1,350.
d. The unearned rent account balance at December 31 is $4,500, representing the receipt of an advance payment on December 1 of three months' rent from tenants.
e. Depreciation of office equipment for the year is $900.

Instructions

1. Journalize the adjusting entries required at December 31.
2. Briefly explain the difference between adjusting entries and entries that would be made to correct errors.

PROBLEM 3–2B
Adjusting entries
Objective 3

Selected account balances before adjustment for Centrex Realty at December 31, the end of the current year, are as follows:

	Debits	Credits
Accounts Receivable	$ 9,250	
Supplies	2,700	
Prepaid Rent	21,000	
Equipment	50,500	
Accumulated Depreciation		$16,900
Wages Payable		—
Unearned Fees		6,500
Fees Earned		99,850
Wages Expense	40,750	
Rent Expense	—	
Depreciation Expense	—	
Supplies Expense	—	

Data needed for year-end adjustments are as follows:

a. Supplies on hand at December 31, $825.
b. Depreciation of equipment during year, $3,950.
c. Rent expired during year, $18,000.
d. Wages accrued but not paid at December 31, $1,525.
e. Unearned fees at December 31, $2,250.
f. Unbilled fees at December 31, $3,750.

Instructions

Journalize the six adjusting entries required at December 31, based upon the data presented.

PROBLEM 3–3B
Adjusting entries
Objectives 3, 4

If the working papers correlating with this textbook are not used, omit Problem 3–3B.

A portion of the work sheet for Millennium Services for the current year ending December 31 is presented in the working papers.

Instructions

1. Enter the data for the six adjustments in the two Adjustments columns of the work sheet. (Although the sequence in which the accounts are analyzed is not important, it is suggested that the analysis begin with Cash and proceed downward in the order that the accounts are listed on the work sheet.) Cross-reference the debit and credit for each adjustment by letters. Total the Adjustments columns after all adjustment data have been entered.
2. Assume that the adjusting entries were omitted for (a) insurance expired and (b) accrued service revenue. Indicate the effect of each error, considered individually, on net income for the current year and on assets, liabilities, and owner's equity at December 31. Set up a table similar to the following, and record your answers by inserting the dollar amount in the appropriate spaces. Insert a zero if the error does not affect the item.

	Error (a)		*Error (b)*	
	Over-stated	*Under-stated*	*Over-stated*	*Under-stated*
1. Net income for the year would be	$	$	$	$
2. Assets at December 31 would be	$	$	$	$
3. Liabilities at December 31 would be	$	$	$	$
4. Owner's equity at December 31 would be	$	$	$	$

PROBLEM 3–4B
Adjusting entries
Objective 3

Aneid Company specializes in the maintenance and repair of signs, such as billboards. On December 31, the end of the current year, the accountant for Aneid Company prepared a trial balance and an adjusted trial balance. The two trial balances are as follows:

Aneid Company
Trial Balance
December 31, 19—

	Unadjusted		Adjusted	
Cash	9,750		9,750	
Accounts Receivable	20,400		20,400	
Supplies	7,880		1,460	
Prepaid Insurance	2,700		700	
Land	47,500		47,500	
Buildings	107,480		107,480	
Accumulated Depreciation—Buildings		79,600		85,100
Trucks	72,000		72,000	
Accumulated Depreciation—Trucks		32,800		43,900
Accounts Payable		8,920		9,420
Salaries Payable		—		1,450
Unearned Service Fees		7,500		920
V. Homer, Capital		93,890		93,890
V. Homer, Drawing	8,000		8,000	
Service Fees Earned		152,680		159,260
Salary Expense	81,200		82,650	
Depreciation Expense—Trucks	—		11,100	
Rent Expense	9,600		9,600	
Supplies Expense	—		6,420	
Utilities Expense	6,200		6,700	
Depreciation Expense—Buildings	—		5,500	
Taxes Expense	1,720		1,720	
Insurance Expense	—		2,000	
Miscellaneous Expense	960		960	
	375,390	375,390	393,940	393,940

Instructions

Journalize the seven entries that adjusted the accounts at December 31. None of the accounts were affected by more than one adjusting entry.

PROBLEM 3–5B
Adjusting entries
Objective 3

Western Trout Co., an outfitter store for fishing treks, prepared the following trial balance at the end of its first year of operations:

Western Trout Co.
Trial Balance
June 30, 19—

Cash	1,150	
Accounts Receivable	3,500	
Supplies	1,300	
Equipment	9,900	
Accounts Payable		750
Unearned Fees		2,000
Erich Remarque, Capital		10,500
Erich Remarque, Drawing	1,000	
Fees Earned		36,750
Wages Expense	19,500	
Rent Expense	9,000	
Utilities Expense	3,750	
Miscellaneous Expense	900	
	50,000	50,000

For preparing the adjusting entries, the following data were assembled:

a. Supplies on hand on June 30 were $275.
b. Fees earned but unbilled on June 30 were $1,025.

c. Depreciation of equipment was estimated to be $750 for the year.
d. Unpaid wages accrued on June 30 were $510.
e. The balance in unearned fees represented the May 1 receipt in advance for services to be provided. Only $1,200 of the services were provided between May 1 and June 30.

Instructions

Journalize the adjusting entries necessary on June 30.

PROBLEM 3–6B
Work sheet and adjusting entries
Objectives 3, 4

Phelps Service Co., which specializes in appliance repair services, is owned and operated by Silas Loftus. Phelps Service Co.'s accounting clerk prepared the following trial balance at December 31, the end of the current year:

Phelps Service Co.
Trial Balance
December 31, 19—

Cash	3,200	
Accounts Receivable	17,200	
Prepaid Insurance	3,900	
Supplies	2,450	
Land	50,000	
Building	141,500	
Accumulated Depreciation—Building		95,700
Equipment	90,100	
Accumulated Depreciation—Equipment		65,300
Accounts Payable		7,500
Unearned Rent		4,000
Silas Loftus, Capital		65,900
Silas Loftus, Drawing	5,000	
Fees Earned		218,400
Salaries and Wages Expense	78,700	
Utilities Expense	28,200	
Advertising Expense	19,000	
Repairs Expense	13,500	
Miscellaneous Expense	4,050	
	456,800	456,800

The data needed to determine year-end adjustments are as follows:

a. Unexpired insurance at December 31, $825.
b. Supplies on hand at December 31, $700.
c. Depreciation of building for the year, $1,500.
d. Depreciation of equipment for the year, $5,500.
e. Rent unearned at December 31, $3,000.
f. Accrued salaries and wages at December 31, $1,250.
g. Fees earned but unbilled on December 31, $1,950.

Instructions

1. Enter the trial balance on a work sheet.
2. Enter the data for the seven adjustments in the Adjustments columns of the work sheet. Add additional accounts as needed.
3. Complete the Adjusted Trial Balance columns in the work sheet.
4. On the basis of the adjustment data in the work sheet, journalize the adjusting entries.

PROBLEM 3–7B
Adjusting entries and errors
Objective 3

At the end of July, the first month of operations, the following selected data were taken from the financial statements of Addison Garwood, III, an attorney:

Net income for July	$ 70,500
Total assets at July 31	177,250
Total liabilities at July 31	36,500
Total owner's equity at July 31	140,750

In preparing the financial statements, adjustments for the following data were overlooked:

a. Unbilled fees earned at July 31, $6,500.
b. Supplies used during July, $3,100.
c. Depreciation of equipment for July, $5,300.
d. Accrued wages at July 31, $2,250.

Instructions

1. Journalize the entries to record the omitted adjustments.
2. Determine the correct amount of net income for July and the total assets, liabilities, and owner's equity at July 31. In addition to indicating the corrected amounts, indicate the effect of each omitted adjustment by setting up and completing a columnar table similar to the following. Adjustment (a) is presented as an example.

	Net Income	*Total Assets*	*Total Liabilities*	*Total Owner's Equity*
Reported amounts	$70,500	$177,250	$36,500	$140,750
Corrections:				
Adjustment (a)	+6,500	+6,500	0	+6,500
Adjustment (b)				
Adjustment (c)				
Adjustment (d)				
Corrected amounts				

CONTINUING PROBLEM

The trial balance that you prepared for Music A La Mode at the end of Chapter 2 should appear as follows:

Music A La Mode
Trial Balance
December 31, 1996

Cash	2,282	
Accounts Receivable	880	
Supplies	445	
Prepaid Insurance	1,680	
Office Equipment	2,500	
Accounts Payable		2,875
Unearned Revenue		1,500
Julian Felipe, Capital		3,000
Julian Felipe, Drawing	475	
Fees Earned		4,570
Wages Expense	910	
Office Rent Expense	970	
Equipment Rent Expense	550	
Utilities Expense	380	
Music Expense	340	
Advertising Expense	225	
Supplies Expense	80	
Miscellaneous Expense	228	
	11,945	11,945

The data needed to determine adjustments for the two-month period ending December 31, 1996, are as follows:

a. During December, Music A La Mode provided guest disc jockeys for KPRG for a total of 70 hours. For information on the amount of the accrued revenue to be billed to KPRG, see the contract described in the December 3, 1996 transaction at the end of Chapter 2.

b. Supplies on hand at December 31, $320.
c. The balance of the prepaid insurance account relates to the December 1, 1996 transaction at the end of Chapter 2.
d. Depreciation of the office equipment is $40.
e. The balance of the unearned revenue account relates to the contract between Music A La Mode and KPRG, described in the December 3, 1996 transaction at the end of Chapter 2.
f. Accrued wages as of December 31, 1996, were $80.

Instructions

1. Enter the unadjusted trial balance on a ten-column work sheet. Include the following additional accounts in the unadjusted trial balance:

   18 Accumulated Depreciation—Office Equipment
   22 Wages Payable
   57 Insurance Expense
   58 Depreciation Expense

2. Enter the data for the adjustments in the Adjustments columns of the work sheet.
3. Complete the Adjusted Trial Balance columns in the work sheet.

CASES

CASE 3–1
Sunrise Real Estate Co.
Cash basis versus accrual basis

Addison Stein opened Sunrise Real Estate Co., a small sole proprietorship, on January 11 of the current year. A CPA friend explained the accrual basis of reporting revenue and expenses, noted that it was the most widely used method, and suggested its use for Sunrise Real Estate Co. Addison decided that the accrual basis was too complicated and unnecessary for her business. She decided to use the cash basis for preparing financial statements, even though some receivables and payables existed at the end of the year.

Discuss whether Addison Stein behaved in an ethical manner by using the cash basis for preparing the financial statements for Sunrise Real Estate Co.

CASE 3–2
Ford Motor Co.
Accrued expense

On December 30, 1996, you buy a Ford Explorer. It comes with a three-year, 50,000-mile warranty. On January 21, 1997, you return the Explorer to the dealership for some basic repairs covered under the warranty. The cost of the repairs to the dealership is $150. In what year, 1996 or 1997, should Ford Motor Co. recognize the cost of the warranty repairs as an expense?

CASE 3–3
Delta Airlines
Accrued revenue

The following is an excerpt from a conversation between Margaret Nelms and Dave Jerkins just before they boarded a flight to Jamaica on Delta Airlines. They are going to Jamaica to attend their company's annual sales conference.

Margaret: Dave, aren't you taking an introductory accounting course at Metro College?

Dave: Yes, I decided it's about time I learned something about accounting. You know, our annual bonuses are based upon the sales figures that come from the Accounting Department.

Margaret: I guess I never really thought about it.

Dave: You should think about it! Last year, I placed a $100,000 order on December 21. But when I got my bonus, the $100,000 sale wasn't included. They said it hadn't been shipped until January 3, so it would have to count in next year's bonus.

Margaret: A real bummer!

Dave: Right! I was counting on that bonus including the $100,000 sale.

Margaret: Did you complain?

Dave: Yes, but it didn't do any good. Elmer, the head accountant, said something about matching revenues and expenses. Also, something about not recording revenues until the sale is final. I figure I'd take the accounting course and find out whether he's just jerking me around.

Margaret: I never really thought about it. When do you think Delta Airlines will record its revenues from this flight?

Dave: Mmm . . . I guess it could record the revenue when it sells the ticket . . . or . . . when the boarding passes are taken at the door . . . or . . . when we get off the plane . . . or when our company pays for the tickets . . . or . . . I don't know. I'll ask my accounting instructor.

Discuss when Delta Airlines should recognize the revenue from ticket sales to properly match revenues and expenses.

CASE 3–4
Hershey Foods Corporation
Financial analysis

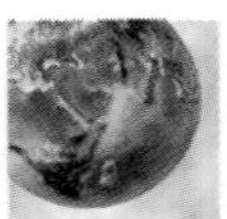

Analytical procedures can take many forms. One form would be comparing an item on the current statement with the same item on a prior statement. For example, the net income for the current year may be compared to the net income of the prior year. Also, an item in the current statement may be compared to other items in the same statement. For example, the amount of the net income for the current year can be compared with the amount of the revenues for the same year.

a. Determine for Hershey Foods Corporation:
   1. The amount of the change and percent of change in net income for the year ended December 31, 1993.
   2. The percentage relationship between net income and net sales (net income divided by net sales) for the years ended December 31, 1993 and 1992.

b. What conclusions can be drawn from the analysis performed in (a)?

CASE 3–5
Niki Television Repair
Adjustments and financial statements

Several years ago, your father opened Niki Television Repair. He made a small initial investment and added money from his personal bank account as needed. He withdrew money for living expenses at irregular intervals. As the business grew, he hired an assistant. He is now considering adding more employees, purchasing additional service trucks, and purchasing the building he now rents. To secure funds for the expansion, your father submitted a loan application to the bank and included the most recent financial statements (shown at right) prepared from accounts maintained by a part-time bookkeeper.

After reviewing the financial statements, the loan officer at the bank asked your father if he used the accrual basis of accounting for revenues and expenses. Your father responded that he did and that is why he included an account for "Amounts Due from Customers." The loan officer then asked whether or not the accounts were adjusted prior to the preparation of the statements. Your father answered that they had not been adjusted.

a. Why do you think the loan officer suspected that the accounts had not been adjusted prior to the preparation of the statements?

b. Indicate possible accounts that might need to be adjusted before an accurate set of financial statements could be prepared.

Niki Television Repair
Income Statement
For the Year Ended December 31, 19—

Service revenue		$66,900
Less: Rent paid	$18,000	
Wages paid	16,500	
Supplies paid	7,000	
Utilities paid	3,100	
Insurance paid	3,000	
Miscellaneous payments	2,150	49,750
Net income		$17,150

Niki Television Repair
Balance Sheet
December 31, 19—

Assets	
Cash	$ 3,750
Amounts due from customers	2,100
Truck	25,000
Total assets	$30,850
Equities	
Owner's capital	$30,850

ANSWERS TO SELF-EXAMINATION QUESTIONS

1. **A** A deferral is the delay in recording an expense already paid, such as prepaid insurance (answer A). Wages payable (answer B) is considered an accrued expense or accrued liability. Fees earned (answer C) is a revenue item. Accumulated depreciation (answer D) is a contra account to a plant asset.
2. **D** The balance in the supplies account, before adjustment, represents the amount of supplies available. From this amount ($2,250) is subtracted the amount of supplies on hand ($950) to determine the supplies used ($1,300). Since increases in expense accounts are recorded by debits and decreases in asset accounts are recorded by credits, answer D is the correct entry.
3. **C** The failure to record the adjusting entry debiting unearned rent, $600, and crediting rent income, $600, would have the effect of overstating liabilities by $600 and understating net income by $600 (answer C).
4. **C** Since increases in expense accounts (such as depreciation expense) are recorded by debits and it is customary to record the decreases in usefulness of plant assets as credits to accumulated depreciation accounts, answer C is the correct entry.
5. **D** The book value of a plant asset is the difference between the balance in the asset account and the balance in the related accumulated depreciation account, or $22,500 – $14,000, as indicated by answer D ($8,500).

4 Completing the Accounting Cycle

YOU AND ACCOUNTING

Have you ever ridden in a taxicab? When you get in, you tell the driver where you want to go, and the driver lowers the meter lever (flag) to start the meter running. At the end of the trip, the driver stops the meter. You then pay the driver for the amount indicated on the meter. As the next passenger is picked up, the driver lowers the lever, and the cycle starts all over again.

Businesses also go through a cycle of activities. At the beginning of the cycle, management plans where it wants the business to go and begins the necessary actions to achieve its operating goals. Throughout the cycle, which is normally one year, the accountant records the operating activities (transactions) of the business. At the end of the cycle, the accountant prepares financial statements, which summarize the operating activities for the year. The accountant then prepares the accounts for the recording of the operating activities in the next cycle.

We begin this chapter by completing our discussion of how to use the work sheet in preparing financial statements. We then describe and illustrate the journalizing and posting of adjusting entries and how we should go about preparing the accounting records for the next accounting period.

We will also discuss how assets are classified according to their ability to be converted to cash and how liabilities are classified by their due date. These classifications are important because a company must be able to pay its debts as they come due. If it has a large amount of assets invested in equipment, for example, that cannot be readily converted to cash, the company may have difficulty paying its debts on time.

After you have finished studying this chapter, we will have covered all the basic steps in the accounting process. We conclude the chapter by summarizing these steps.

After studying this chapter, you should be able to:

Objective 1
Prepare a work sheet.

Objective 2
Prepare financial statements from a work sheet.

Objective 3
Journalize and post the adjusting entries.

Objective 4
Journalize and post the closing entries and prepare a post-closing trial balance.

Objective 5
Explain what is meant by the fiscal year and the natural business year.

Objective 6
List the seven basic steps of the accounting cycle.

Work Sheet

Objective 1
Prepare a work sheet.

In Chapter 3, we illustrated the use of a work sheet for assembling data and summarizing the effects of adjusting entries on the accounts. The December 31, 1996 trial balance for Computer King was prepared directly on the work sheet, as shown in Exhibit 1 on page 128B. The adjustments were then entered in the Adjustments Debit and Credit columns, and the Trial Balance amounts were extended through these columns to the Adjusted Trial Balance columns, as shown in the first transparency overlay (Exhibit 2). In the following paragraphs, we describe how the extension of the Adjusted Trial Balance amounts to Income Statement and Balance Sheet columns can aid in the preparation of financial statements.

INCOME STATEMENT AND BALANCE SHEET COLUMNS

The Income Statement Debit and Credit columns are directly to the right of the Adjusted Trial Balance columns in the work sheet. The Balance Sheet Debit and Credit columns are directly to the right of the Income Statement columns.

The work sheet may be expanded to include Statement of Owner's Equity columns. However, because of the few accounts affected (Capital and Drawing), separate columns for the statement of owner's equity are normally not included in the work sheet. Instead, the owner's equity accounts are extended to the Balance Sheet columns.

COMPLETING THE WORK SHEET

The work sheet is completed by extending the Adjusted Trial Balance amounts to the Income Statement and Balance Sheet columns. The amounts for assets, liabilities, owner's capital, and drawing are extended to the Balance Sheet columns. The amounts for revenues and expenses are extended to the Income Statement columns.

In the Computer King work sheet, the first account listed is Cash and the balance appearing in the Adjusted Trial Balance Debit column is $2,065. This amount should be extended to the proper column. Cash is an asset, it is listed on the balance sheet, and it has a debit balance. Thus, the $2,065 is extended to the Debit column of the Balance Sheet section. The $2,720 balance of Accounts Receivable is extended in similar fashion. The same procedure is continued until all account balances have been extended to the proper columns, as shown in the second transparency overlay (Exhibit 3). The balances of the capital and drawing accounts are extended to the Balance Sheet columns because this work sheet does not provide for separate Statement of Owner's Equity columns.

After all of the balances have been extended, each of the four statement columns is added, as shown in the third transparency overlay (Exhibit 4). The difference between the two Income Statement column totals is the amount of the net income or the net loss for the period. Likewise, the difference between the two Balance Sheet column totals is also the amount of the net income or net loss for the period.

If the Income Statement Credit column total (representing total revenue) is greater than the Income Statement Debit column total (representing total expenses), the difference is the net income. If the Income Statement Debit column total is greater than the Income Statement Credit column total, the difference is a net loss. For Computer King, the computation of net income is as follows:

Total of Credit column (revenues)	$16,960
Total of Debit column (expenses)	9,755
Net income (excess of revenues over expenses)	$ 7,205

As shown in Exhibit 4, the amount of the net income, $7,205, is inserted in the Income Statement Debit column and the Balance Sheet Credit column. The term *Net income* is inserted in the Account Title column. If there had been a net loss instead of net income, the amount would have been entered in the Income Statement Credit column and the Balance Sheet Debit column. The term *Net loss* would then have been inserted in the Account Title column. Inserting the net income or net loss into the statement columns on the work sheet shows the effect of transferring the net balance of the revenue and expense accounts to the owner's capital account. Journalizing this transfer is discussed later in this chapter.

After the net income or net loss has been entered on the work sheet, each of the four statement columns is totaled. The totals of the two Income Statement columns must be equal. The totals of the two Balance Sheet columns must also be equal.

Financial Statements

Objective 2
Prepare financial statements from a work sheet.

The work sheet is an aid in preparing the income statement, the statement of owner's equity, and the balance sheet, which are presented in Exhibit 5 on page 128C. In the following paragraphs, we discuss these financial statements for Computer King, prepared from the completed work sheet in Exhibit 4. The basic form of the statements is similar to those presented in Chapter 1.

INCOME STATEMENT

The income statement is normally prepared directly from the accounts listed in the work sheet. However, the order of the expenses may be changed. One method used in preparing the income statement is to list the expenses in order of size, beginning with the larger items. Miscellaneous expense is usually shown as the last item, regardless of the amount. This is the method that we will follow in this text.

STATEMENT OF OWNER'S EQUITY

The first item normally presented on the statement of owner's equity is the balance of the proprietor's capital account at the beginning of the period. On the work sheet, however, the amount listed as capital does not always represent the account balance at the beginning of the period. The proprietor may have invested additional assets in the business during the period. Hence, for the beginning balance and any additional investments, it is necessary to refer to the capital account in the ledger. The amount of net income (or net loss) and the amount of the drawings are then used to determine the ending capital account balance. The net income (or net loss) and the drawings amounts can be taken from the Balance Sheet columns of the work sheet.

The basic form of the statement of owner's equity is shown in Exhibit 5. For Computer King, the amount of drawings by the owner was less than the net income. If the owner's withdrawals had exceeded the net income, the order of the net income and the withdrawals would have been reversed. The difference between the two items would then be deducted from the beginning capital account balance. Other factors, such as additional investments or a net loss, also require some change in the form, as shown in the following example:

Allan Johnson, capital, January 1, 19—	$39,000	
Additional investment during the year	6,000	
Total		$45,000
Net loss for the year	$ 5,600	
Withdrawals	9,500	
Decrease in owner's equity		15,100
Allan Johnson, capital, December 31, 19—		$29,900

BALANCE SHEET

The balance sheet in Exhibit 5 was expanded by the addition of subsections for current assets, plant assets, and current liabilities. Such a balance sheet may sometimes be described as a *classified* balance sheet. In the following paragraphs, we describe some of the sections and subsections that may be used in a balance sheet. We will introduce additional sections in later chapters.

Assets

Assets are commonly divided into classes for presentation on the balance sheet. Two of these classes are (1) current assets and (2) plant assets.

CURRENT ASSETS. Cash and other assets that are expected to be converted to cash or sold or used up usually within one year or less, through the normal operations of the business, are called current assets. In addition to cash, the current assets usually owned by a service business are notes receivable, accounts receivable, supplies, and other prepaid expenses. Notes receivable and accounts receivable are current assets because they will usually be converted to cash within one year or less.

Notes receivable are written claims against debtors who promise to pay the amount of the note, and possibly interest at an agreed rate, to a specified person or bearer. Accounts receivable are also claims against debtors but are less formal than notes and do not provide for interest. Accounts receivable normally arise from providing services or selling merchandise on account.

PLANT ASSETS. The plant assets section may also be described as **property, plant, and equipment.** Plant assets include equipment, machinery, buildings, and land. With the exception of land, such assets depreciate over a period of time, as we discussed in Chapter 3. The cost, accumulated depreciation, and book value of each major type of plant asset is normally reported on the balance sheet.

Liabilities

Liabilities are debts of the business entity owed to outsiders (creditors). The two most common classes of liabilities are (1) current liabilities and (2) long-term liabilities.

CURRENT LIABILITIES. Liabilities that will be due within a short time (usually one year or less) and that are to be paid out of current assets are called **current liabilities.** The most common liabilities in this group are notes payable and accounts payable. These liabilities are like their receivable counterparts, except that the debtor-creditor relationship is reversed. Other current liability accounts commonly found in the ledger are Wages Payable, Interest Payable, Taxes Payable, and Unearned Fees.

LONG-TERM LIABILITIES. Liabilities that will not be due for a long time (usually more than one year) are called **long-term liabilities.** If Computer King had long-term liabilities, they would be reported below the current liabilities. As long-term liabilities come due and are to be paid within one year, they are classified as current liabilities. If they are to be renewed rather than paid, they would continue to be classified as long-term. When an asset is pledged as security for a liability, the obligation may be called a *mortgage note payable* or a *mortgage payable.*

Owner's Equity

The owner's right to the assets of the business entity is presented on the balance sheet below the liabilities section. The owner's equity is added to the total liabilities, and this total must be equal to the total assets.

Journalizing and Posting Adjusting Entries

Objective 3
Journalize and post the adjusting entries.

At the end of the accounting period, the adjustment data appearing in the work sheet are normally used to record the adjusting entries in the journal. After all the adjusting entries have been posted, the ledger is in agreement with the data reported on the financial statements. The adjusting entries are dated as of the last day of the period, even though they are usually recorded at a later date. Each entry may be supported by an explanation, but a caption above the first adjusting entry is acceptable.

The adjusting entries for Computer King are as follows. The accounts to which they have been posted appear in the ledger in Exhibit 7 (pages 129–133).

JOURNAL **PAGE 4**

Date		Description	Post. Ref.	Debit	Credit
		Adjusting Entries			
1996 Dec.	31	Supplies Expense	55	1 2 4 0 00	
		Supplies	14		1 2 4 0 00
	31	Insurance Expense	56	1 0 0 00	
		Prepaid Insurance	15		1 0 0 00
	31	Unearned Rent	23	1 2 0 00	
		Rent Income	42		1 2 0 00
	31	Wages Expense	51	2 5 0 00	
		Wages Payable	22		2 5 0 00
	31	Accounts Receivable	12	5 0 0 00	
		Fees Earned	41		5 0 0 00

17	31	Depreciation Expense	53	5 0 00	
18		Accumulated Depreciation—			
19		Office Equipment	19		5 0 00

Nature of the Closing Process

Objective 4
Journalize and post the closing entries and prepare a post-closing trial balance.

At the end of an accounting period, the revenue and expense account balances are reported in the income statement. The expenses are deducted from revenues to determine the net income or net loss for the period. Since revenues and expenses are reported for each period, the balances of these accounts should be zero at the beginning of the next period. The zero balances allow the next period's revenues and expenses to be recorded separately from the preceding period. Because the balances of revenue and expense accounts are not carried forward, they are sometimes called **temporary accounts** or **nominal accounts.** The balances of the accounts reported in the balance sheet are carried forward from year to year. Because of their permanent nature, balance sheet accounts are sometimes called **real accounts.**

How are the end-of-period balances of the temporary accounts converted to zero? To begin, the revenue and expense account balances are transferred to an account called **Income Summary.** The balance of Income Summary is then transferred to the owner's capital account.

At the end of an accounting period, the balance of the owner's drawing account is reported on the statement of owner's equity. The owner's withdrawals are deducted from the net income or added to the net loss for the period to determine the net increase or decrease in owner's equity. Since withdrawals are reported for each period, the balance of the owner's drawing account should be zero at the beginning of the next period. Thus, the owner's drawing account is also a temporary account. Its balance is transferred to the owner's capital account at the end of the period.

JOURNALIZING AND POSTING CLOSING ENTRIES

Revenue, expense, and drawing account balances are transferred to the owner's capital account by a series of entries called **closing entries.** This transfer process is called the **closing process**. Four closing entries are required at the end of the period. For a sole proprietorship, these entries are as follows:

1. Each revenue account is debited for the amount of its balance, and Income Summary is credited for the total revenue.
2. Each expense account is credited for the amount of its balance, and Income Summary is debited for the total expense.
3. Income Summary is debited for the amount of its balance (net income), and the capital account is credited for the same amount. (The accounts debited and credited are reversed if there is a net loss.)
4. The drawing account is credited for the amount of its balance, and the capital account is debited for the same amount.

The account titles and balances needed in preparing the closing entries may be obtained from either the (1) work sheet, (2) income statement and statement of owner's equity, or (3) ledger. If a work sheet is used, the data for the first two entries appear in the Income Statement columns. The amount for the third entry is the net income or net loss appearing at the bottom of the work sheet. The drawing account balance appears in the Balance Sheet Debit column of the work sheet.

The closing entries for Computer King are shown at the top of page 128D.

Exhibit 1
Work Sheet with Trial Balance Entered

Computer King
Work Sheet
For the Two Months Ended December 31, 1996

	Trial Balance		Adjustments		Adjusted Trial Balance		Income Statement		Balance Sheet	
Account Title	**Dr.**	**Cr.**	**Dr.**	**Cr.**	**Dr.**	**Cr.**	**Dr.**	**Cr.**	**Dr.**	**Cr.**
Cash	2,065									
Accounts Receivable	2,220									
Supplies	2,000									
Prepaid Insurance	2,400									
Land	10,000									
Office Equipment	1,800									
Accounts Payable		900								
Unearned Rent		360								
Pat King, Capital		15,000								
Pat King, Drawing	4,000									
Fees Earned		16,340								
Wages Expense	4,275									
Rent Expense	1,600									
Utilities Expense	985									
Supplies Expense	800									
Miscellaneous Expense	455									
	32,600	32,600								

The work sheet is used for assembling data and summarizing the effects of adjusting entries. It also aids in the preparation of financial statements.

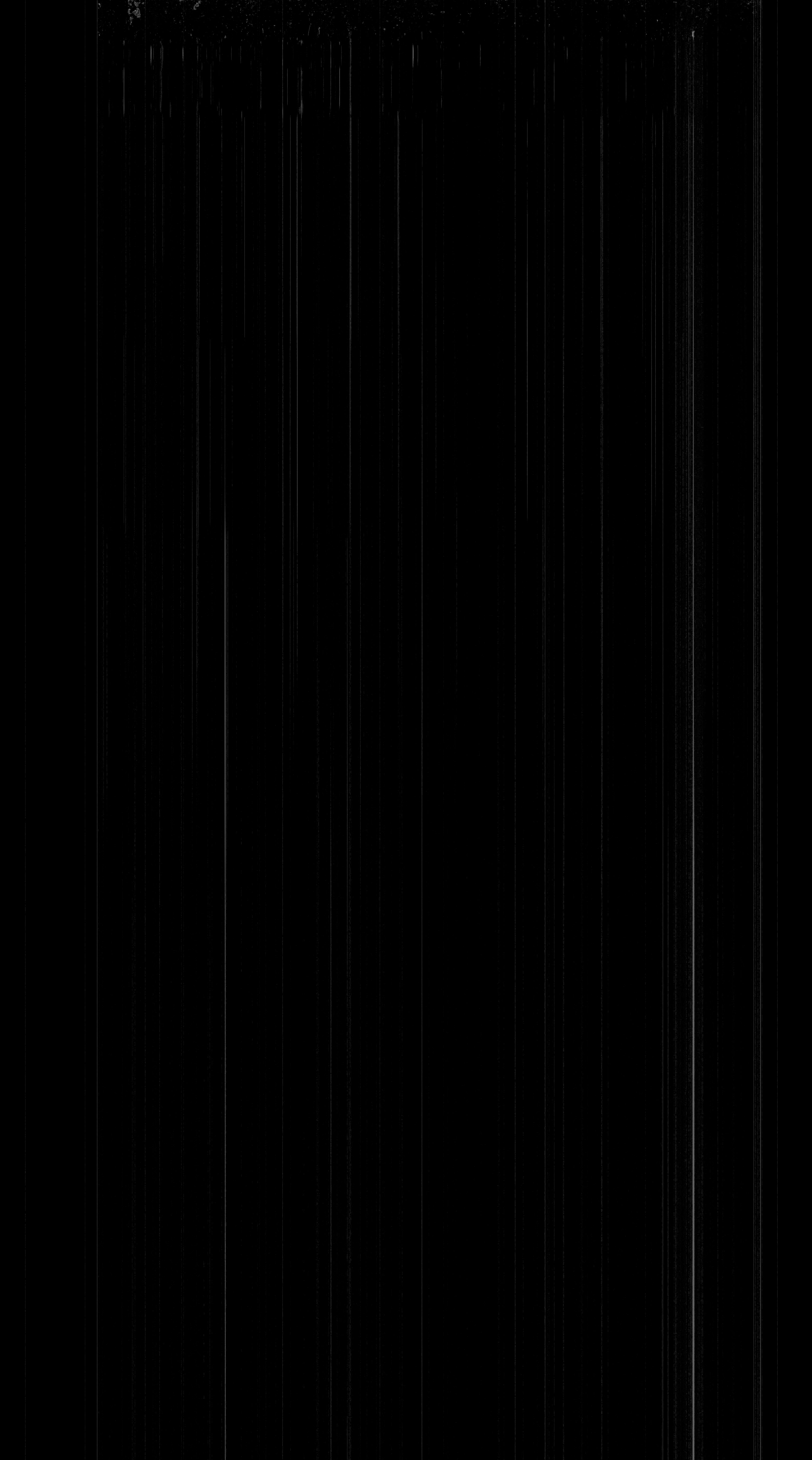

Exhibit 2

Work Sheet with Adjustments and Trial Balance Entered

Exhibit 5
Financial Statements Prepared from Work Sheet

Computer King
Income Statement
For the Two Months Ended December 31, 1996

Fees earned	$16 840 00	
Rent income	120 00	
Total revenues		$16 960 00
Expenses:		
Wages expense	$ 4 525 00	
Supplies expense	2 040 00	
Rent expense	1 600 00	
Utilities expense	985 00	
Insurance expense	100 00	
Depreciation expense	50 00	
Miscellaneous expense	455 00	
Total expenses		9 755 00
Net income		$ 7 205 00

Computer King
Statement of Owner's Equity
For the Two Months Ended December 31, 1996

Pat King, capital, November 1, 1996		$ 0
Investment on November 1, 1996	$15 000 00	
Net income for November and December	7 205 00	
	$22 205 00	
Less withdrawals	4 000 00	
Increase in owner's equity		18 205 00
Pat King, capital, December 31, 1996		$18 205 00

Computer King
Balance Sheet
December 31, 1996

Assets				Liabilities		
Current assets:				Current liabilities:		
Cash		$ 2 065 00		Accounts payable	$ 900 00	
Accounts receivable		2 720 00		Wages payable	250 00	
Supplies		760 00		Unearned rent	240 00	
Prepaid insurance		2 300 00		Total liabilities		$ 1 390 00
Total current assets			$ 7 845 00			
Plant assets:						
Land		$10 000 00				
Office equipment	$1,800			**Owner's Equity**		
Less accum. depr.	50	1 750 00		Pat King, Capital		18 205 00
Total plant assets			11 750 00	Total liabilities and		
Total assets			$19 595 00	owner's equity		$19 595 00

JOURNAL				PAGE 5
Date	**Description**	**Post. Ref.**	**Debit**	**Credit**
	Closing Entries			
1996 Dec. 31	Fees Earned	41	16 8 4 0 00	
	Rent Income	42	1 2 0 00	
	Income Summary	33		16 9 6 0 00
31	Income Summary	33	9 7 5 5 00	
	Wages Expense	51		4 5 2 5 00
	Rent Expense	52		1 6 0 0 00
	Depreciation Expense	53		5 0 00
	Utilities Expense	54		9 8 5 00
	Supplies Expense	55		2 0 4 0 00
	Insurance Expense	56		1 0 0 00
	Miscellaneous Expense	59		4 5 5 00
31	Income Summary	33	7 2 0 5 00	
	Pat King, Capital	31		7 2 0 5 00
31	Pat King, Capital	31	4 0 0 0 00	
	Pat King, Drawing	32		4 0 0 0 00

A flowchart of the closing process for Computer King is shown in Exhibit 6. The balances in the accounts are those shown in the Trial Balance columns of the work sheet in Exhibit 1.

After the closing entries have been posted to the ledger, the balance in the capital account will agree with the amount reported on the statement of owner's equity and the balance sheet. In addition, the revenue, expense, and drawing accounts will have zero balances.

You should note that Income Summary is used only at the end of the period. At the beginning of the closing process, Income Summary has no balance. During the closing process, Income Summary will be debited and credited for various amounts. At the end of the closing process, Income Summary will again have no balance. Because Income Summary has the effect of clearing the revenue and expense accounts of their balances, it is sometimes called a **clearing account**. Other titles used for this account include Revenue and Expense Summary, Profit and Loss Summary, and Income and Expense Summary.[1]

The ledger of Computer King after the adjusting and closing entries have been posted appears in Exhibit 7. Each posting of an adjusting entry and a closing entry is identified in the item section of the account as an aid. It is not necessary that this be done in actual practice.

After the entry to close an account has been posted, a line should be inserted in both balance columns opposite the final entry. The next period's transactions for the revenue, expense, and drawing accounts will be posted directly below the closing entry.

[1] It is possible to close the temporary revenue and expense accounts without using a clearing account such as Income Summary. In this case, the balances of the revenue and expense accounts are debited directly to the owner's capital account.

Exhibit 6
Flowchart of Closing Process for Computer King

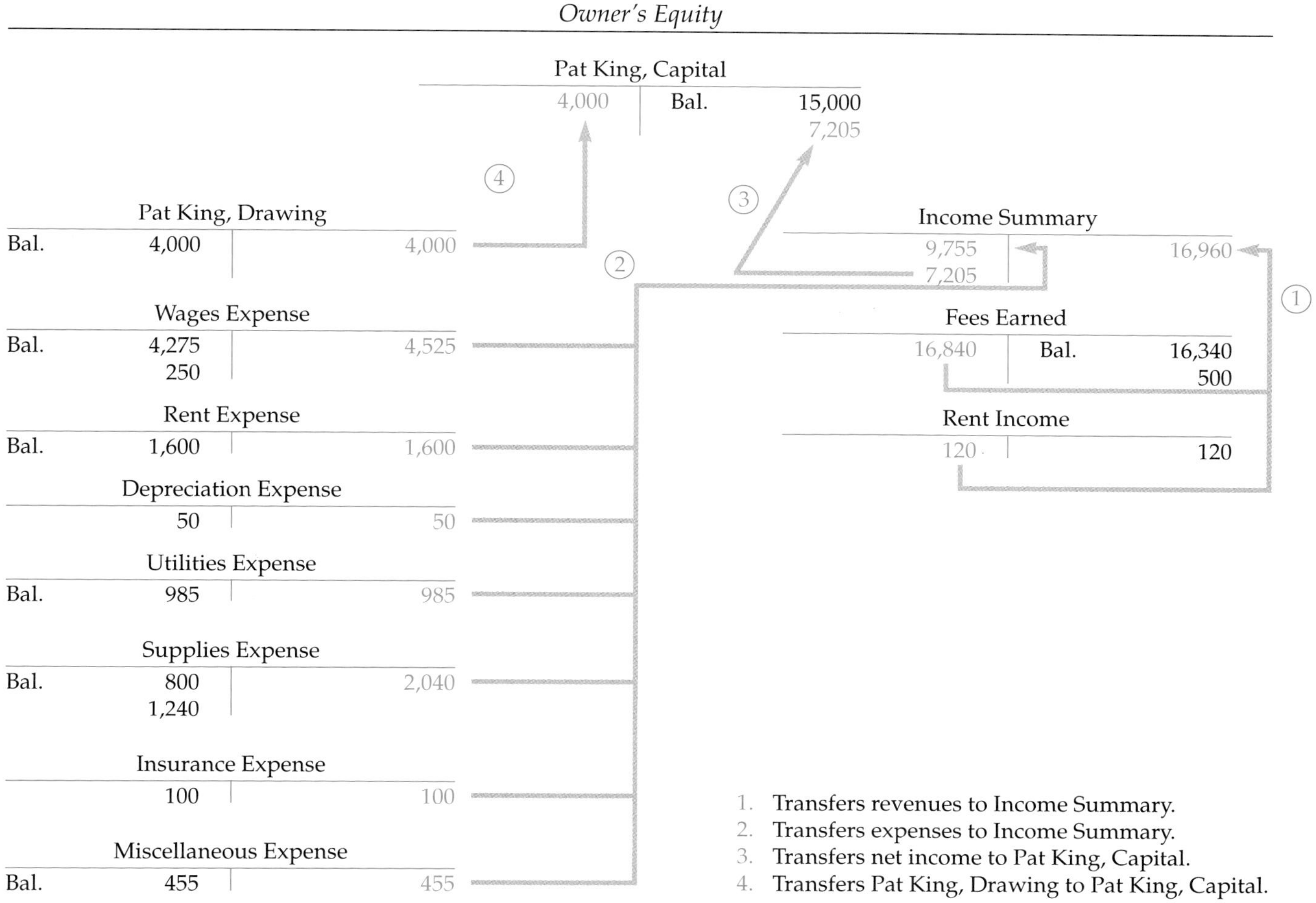

Owner's Equity

Pat King, Capital

	Debit		Credit
	4,000	Bal.	15,000
			7,205

Pat King, Drawing

	Debit	Credit
Bal.	4,000	4,000

Wages Expense

	Debit	Credit
Bal.	4,275	4,525
	250	

Rent Expense

	Debit	Credit
Bal.	1,600	1,600

Depreciation Expense

	Debit	Credit
	50	50

Utilities Expense

	Debit	Credit
Bal.	985	985

Supplies Expense

	Debit	Credit
Bal.	800	2,040
	1,240	

Insurance Expense

	Debit	Credit
	100	100

Miscellaneous Expense

	Debit	Credit
Bal.	455	455

Income Summary

Debit	Credit
9,755	16,960
7,205	

Fees Earned

Debit		Credit
16,840	Bal.	16,340
		500

Rent Income

Debit	Credit
120	120

1. Transfers revenues to Income Summary.
2. Transfers expenses to Income Summary.
3. Transfers net income to Pat King, Capital.
4. Transfers Pat King, Drawing to Pat King, Capital.

Exhibit 7
Ledger for Computer King

ACCOUNT *Cash* **ACCOUNT NO. *11***

Date		Item	Post. Ref.	Debit	Credit	Balance Debit	Balance Credit
1996 Nov.	1		1	15,000 00		15,000 00	
	5		1		10,000 00	5,000 00	
	16		1		950 00	4,050 00	
	18		1	7,500 00		11,550 00	
	30		1		3,650 00	7,900 00	
	30		1		2,000 00	5,900 00	
Dec.	1		2		2,400 00	3,500 00	
	1		2		800 00	2,700 00	
	1		2	360 00		3,060 00	
	6		2		180 00	2,880 00	
	11		2		400 00	2,480 00	
	13		2		950 00	1,530 00	
	16		2	3,100 00		4,630 00	
	20		2		900 00	3,730 00	

(Cash account continues)

Exhibit 7 ***(continued)***
Ledger for Computer King

Date		Item	Post. Ref.	Debit	Credit	Balance Debit	Balance Credit
1996 Dec.	20	Bal. fwd.				3 7 3 0 00	
	21		2	6 5 0 00		4 3 8 0 00	
	23		2		1 4 5 0 00	2 9 3 0 00	
	27		2		1 2 0 0 00	1 7 3 0 00	
	31		3		3 1 0 00	1 4 2 0 00	
	31		3		2 2 5 00	1 1 9 5 00	
	31		3	2 8 7 0 00		4 0 6 5 00	
	31		3		2 0 0 0 00	2 0 6 5 00	

ACCOUNT ***Accounts Receivable*** **ACCOUNT NO.** ***12***

Date		Item	Post. Ref.	Debit	Credit	Balance Debit	Balance Credit
1996 Dec.	16		2	1 7 5 0 00		1 7 5 0 00	
	21		2		6 5 0 00	1 1 0 0 00	
	31		3	1 1 2 0 00		2 2 2 0 00	
	31	Adjusting	4	5 0 0 00		2 7 2 0 00	

ACCOUNT ***Supplies*** **ACCOUNT NO.** ***14***

Date		Item	Post. Ref.	Debit	Credit	Balance Debit	Balance Credit
1996 Nov.	10		1	1 3 5 0 00		1 3 5 0 00	
	30		1		8 0 0 00	5 5 0 00	
Dec.	23		2	1 4 5 0 00		2 0 0 0 00	
	31	Adjusting	4		1 2 4 0 00	7 6 0 00	

ACCOUNT ***Prepaid Insurance*** **ACCOUNT NO.** ***15***

Date		Item	Post. Ref.	Debit	Credit	Balance Debit	Balance Credit
1996 Dec.	1		2	2 4 0 0 00		2 4 0 0 00	
	31	Adjusting	4		1 0 0 00	2 3 0 0 00	

ACCOUNT ***Land*** **ACCOUNT NO.** ***17***

Date		Item	Post. Ref.	Debit	Credit	Balance Debit	Balance Credit
1996 Nov.	5		1	10 0 0 0 00		10 0 0 0 00	

ACCOUNT ***Office Equipment*** **ACCOUNT NO.** ***18***

Date		Item	Post. Ref.	Debit	Credit	Balance Debit	Balance Credit
1996 Dec.	4		2	1 8 0 0 00		1 8 0 0 00	

Exhibit 7 *(continued)*
Ledger for Computer King

ACCOUNT ***Accumulated Depreciation*** — **ACCOUNT NO. *19***

Date		Item	Post. Ref.	Debit	Credit	Balance Debit	Balance Credit
1996 Dec.	31	Adjusting	4		5 0 00		5 0 00

ACCOUNT ***Accounts Payable*** — **ACCOUNT NO. *21***

Date		Item	Post. Ref.	Debit	Credit	Balance Debit	Balance Credit
1996 Nov.	10		1		1 3 5 0 00		1 3 5 0 00
	16		1	9 5 0 00			4 0 0 00
Dec.	4		2		1 8 0 0 00		2 2 0 0 00
	11		2	4 0 0 00			1 8 0 0 00
	20		2	9 0 0 00			9 0 0 00

ACCOUNT ***Wages Payable*** — **ACCOUNT NO. *22***

Date		Item	Post. Ref.	Debit	Credit	Balance Debit	Balance Credit
1996 Dec.	31	Adjusting	4		2 5 0 00		2 5 0 00

ACCOUNT ***Unearned Rent*** — **ACCOUNT NO. *23***

Date		Item	Post. Ref.	Debit	Credit	Balance Debit	Balance Credit
1996 Dec.	1		2		3 6 0 00		3 6 0 00
	31	Adjusting	4	1 2 0 00			2 4 0 00

ACCOUNT ***Pat King, Capital*** — **ACCOUNT NO. *31***

Date		Item	Post. Ref.	Debit	Credit	Balance Debit	Balance Credit
1996 Nov.	1		1		15 0 0 0 00		15 0 0 0 00
Dec.	31	Closing	5		7 2 0 5 00		22 2 0 5 00
	31	Closing	5	4 0 0 0 00			18 2 0 5 00

ACCOUNT ***Pat King, Drawing*** — **ACCOUNT NO. *32***

Date		Item	Post. Ref.	Debit	Credit	Balance Debit	Balance Credit
1996 Nov.	30		1	2 0 0 0 00		2 0 0 0 00	
Dec.	31		3	2 0 0 0 00		4 0 0 0 00	
	31	Closing	5		4 0 0 0 00	—	—

Exhibit 7 ***(continued)***
Ledger for Computer King

ACCOUNT ***Income Summary*** — **ACCOUNT NO.** ***33***

Date		Item	Post. Ref.	Debit	Credit	Balance Debit	Balance Credit
1996 Dec.	31	Closing	5		16,960.00		16,960.00
	31	Closing	5	9,755.00			7,205.00
	31	Closing	5	7,205.00		—	—

ACCOUNT ***Fees Earned*** — **ACCOUNT NO.** ***41***

Date		Item	Post. Ref.	Debit	Credit	Balance Debit	Balance Credit
1996 Nov.	18		1		7,500.00		7,500.00
Dec.	16		2		3,100.00		10,600.00
	16		2		1,750.00		12,350.00
	31		3		2,870.00		15,220.00
	31		3		1,120.00		16,340.00
	31	Adjusting	4		500.00		16,840.00
	31	Closing	5	16,840.00		—	—

ACCOUNT ***Rent Income*** — **ACCOUNT NO.** ***42***

Date		Item	Post. Ref.	Debit	Credit	Balance Debit	Balance Credit
1996 Dec.	31	Adjusting	4		120.00		120.00
	31	Closing	5	120.00		—	—

ACCOUNT ***Wages Expense*** — **ACCOUNT NO.** ***51***

Date		Item	Post. Ref.	Debit	Credit	Balance Debit	Balance Credit
1996 Nov.	30		1	2,125.00		2,125.00	
Dec.	13		2	950.00		3,075.00	
	27		2	1,200.00		4,275.00	
	31	Adjusting	4	250.00		4,525.00	
	31	Closing	5		4,525.00	—	—

ACCOUNT ***Rent Expense*** — **ACCOUNT NO.** ***52***

Date		Item	Post. Ref.	Debit	Credit	Balance Debit	Balance Credit
1996 Nov.	30		1	800.00		800.00	
Dec.	1		2	800.00		1,600.00	
	31	Closing	5		1,600.00	—	—

Exhibit 7 *(concluded)*
Ledger for Computer King

ACCOUNT ***Depreciation Expense*** **ACCOUNT NO. *53***

Date		Item	Post. Ref.	Debit	Credit	Balance Debit	Balance Credit
1996 Dec.	31	Adjusting	4	50 00		50 00	
	31	Closing	5		50 00	—	—

ACCOUNT ***Utilities Expense*** **ACCOUNT NO. *54***

Date		Item	Post. Ref.	Debit	Credit	Balance Debit	Balance Credit
1996 Nov.	30		1	450 00		450 00	
Dec.	31		3	310 00		760 00	
	31		3	225 00		985 00	
	31	Closing	5		985 00	—	—

ACCOUNT ***Supplies Expense*** **ACCOUNT NO. *55***

Date		Item	Post. Ref.	Debit	Credit	Balance Debit	Balance Credit
1996 Nov.	30		1	800 00		800 00	
Dec.	31	Adjusting	4	1240 00		2040 00	
	31	Closing	5		2040 00	—	—

ACCOUNT ***Insurance Expense*** **ACCOUNT NO. *56***

Date		Item	Post. Ref.	Debit	Credit	Balance Debit	Balance Credit
1996 Dec.	31	Adjusting	4	100 00		100 00	
	31	Closing	5		100 00	—	—

ACCOUNT ***Miscellaneous Expense*** **ACCOUNT NO. *59***

Date		Item	Post. Ref.	Debit	Credit	Balance Debit	Balance Credit
1996 Nov.	30		1	275 00		275 00	
Dec.	6		2	180 00		455 00	
	31	Closing	5		455 00	—	—

POST-CLOSING TRIAL BALANCE

The last accounting procedure for a period is to prepare a trial balance after the closing entries have been posted. The purpose of the **post-closing** (after closing) **trial balance** is to make sure that the ledger is in balance at the beginning of the next period. The accounts and amounts should agree exactly with the accounts and amounts listed on the balance sheet at the end of the period. The post-closing trial balance for Computer King is shown in Exhibit 8.

Exhibit 8
Post-Closing Trial Balance

Computer King
Post-Closing Trial Balance
December 31, 1996

Cash	2,065 00	
Accounts Receivable	2,720 00	
Supplies	760 00	
Prepaid Insurance	2,300 00	
Land	10,000 00	
Office Equipment	1,800 00	
Accumulated Depreciation		50 00
Accounts Payable		900 00
Wages Payable		250 00
Unearned Rent		240 00
Pat King, Capital		18,205 00
	19,645 00	19,645 00

Instead of preparing a formal post-closing trial balance, it is possible to list the accounts directly from the ledger, using a printing calculator or a computer. The calculator tape or computer printout, in effect, becomes the post-closing trial balance. Without such a tape or printout, there are no efficient means of determining the cause of an inequality of trial balance totals.

Fiscal Year

Objective 5
Explain what is meant by the fiscal year and the natural business year.

The maximum length of an accounting period is usually one year, which includes a complete cycle of business activities. Income, property taxes, and other financial reporting requirements are often based on yearly periods.

In the Computer King illustration, the length of the accounting period was for two months, November and December. Computer King began operations November 1, and a sole proprietorship, except in rare cases, is required by the federal income tax law to maintain the same accounting period as its owner. Since Pat King maintains a calendar-year accounting period for tax purposes, Computer King must also close its accounts on December 31, 1996. In future years, the financial statements for Computer King will be prepared for twelve months ending on December 31 each year.

The annual accounting period adopted by a business is known as its **fiscal year**. Fiscal years begin with the first day of the month selected and end on the last day of the following twelfth month. The period most commonly used is the calendar year. Other periods are not unusual, especially for businesses organized as corporations. For example, a corporation may adopt a fiscal year that ends when business activities have reached the lowest point in the corporation's annual operating cycle. Such a fiscal year is called the **natural business year**.

The 1994 edition of *Accounting Trends & Techniques*, published by the American Institute of Certified Public Accountants, reported the following results of a survey

USING ACCOUNTING TO UNDERSTAND BUSINESS

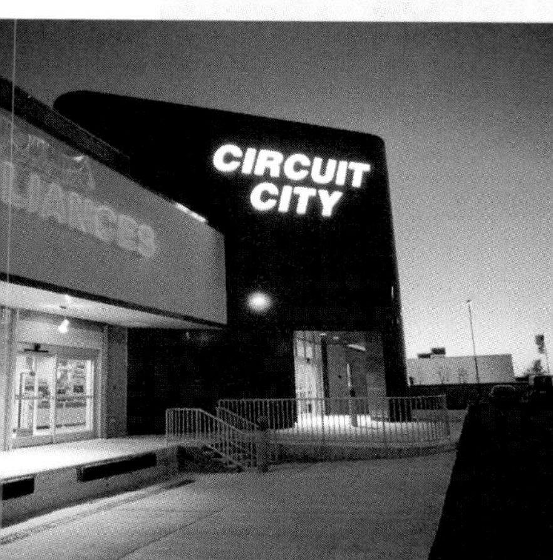

Companies whose business operations are highly seasonal often select their accounting period to coincide with the lowest point in their normal operations. At this point, they have more time to analyze the results of operations and to prepare financial statements. Circuit City Stores, Inc., is an example of a company whose fiscal year is other than the calendar year. Circuit City's 1994 fiscal year-end was February 28, 1994. This should not surprise you, since you would expect that Circuit City experiences a high volume of sales around the December holiday season, followed by relatively low sales in January and February.

Because companies with fiscal years often have highly seasonal operations, investors and others should be careful in interpreting partial-year reports for such companies. That is, you should expect the results of operations for these companies to vary significantly throughout the fiscal year. For example, during its 1994 fiscal year, Circuit City reported the following net sales and operating revenues:

	Net Sales and Operating Revenue (in thousands of dollars)
First Quarter	$ 798,950
Second Quarter	906,678
Third Quarter	1,018,051
Fourth Quarter	1,406,736

of 600 industrial and merchandising companies concerning the month of their fiscal year-end.

Percentage of Companies with Fiscal Years Ending in the Month of:

January	4%	July	2%
February	1	August	3
March	3	September	6
April	1	October	4
May	3	November	3
June	10	December	60

The financial history of a business may be shown by a series of balance sheets and income statements. If the life of a business is expressed by a line moving from left to right, the series of balance sheets and income statements may be graphed as follows:

Balance Sheet dated Dec. 31, 1995	Balance Sheet dated Dec. 31, 1996	Balance Sheet dated Dec. 31, 1997	Balance Sheet dated Dec. 31, 1998
	Income Statement for Fiscal Year 1996	Income Statement for Fiscal Year 1997	Income Statement for Fiscal Year 1998

Accounting Cycle

Objective 6
List the seven basic steps of the accounting cycle.

The primary accounting procedures of a fiscal period have been presented in this chapter and Chapters 2 and 3. This sequence of procedures is called the accounting cycle. It begins with the analysis and the journalizing of transactions and ends with the post-closing trial balance. The most important output of the accounting cycle is the financial statements.

An understanding of the steps of the accounting cycle is essential for further study of accounting. The following basic steps of the cycle are shown, by number, in the flowchart in Exhibit 9.

1. Transactions are analyzed and recorded in journal.
2. Transactions are posted to ledger.
3. Trial balance is prepared, adjustment data are assembled, and work sheet is completed.
4. Financial statements are prepared.
5. Adjusting entries are journalized and posted to ledger.
6. Closing entries are journalized and posted to ledger.
7. Post-closing trial balance is prepared.

Exhibit 9
Accounting Cycle

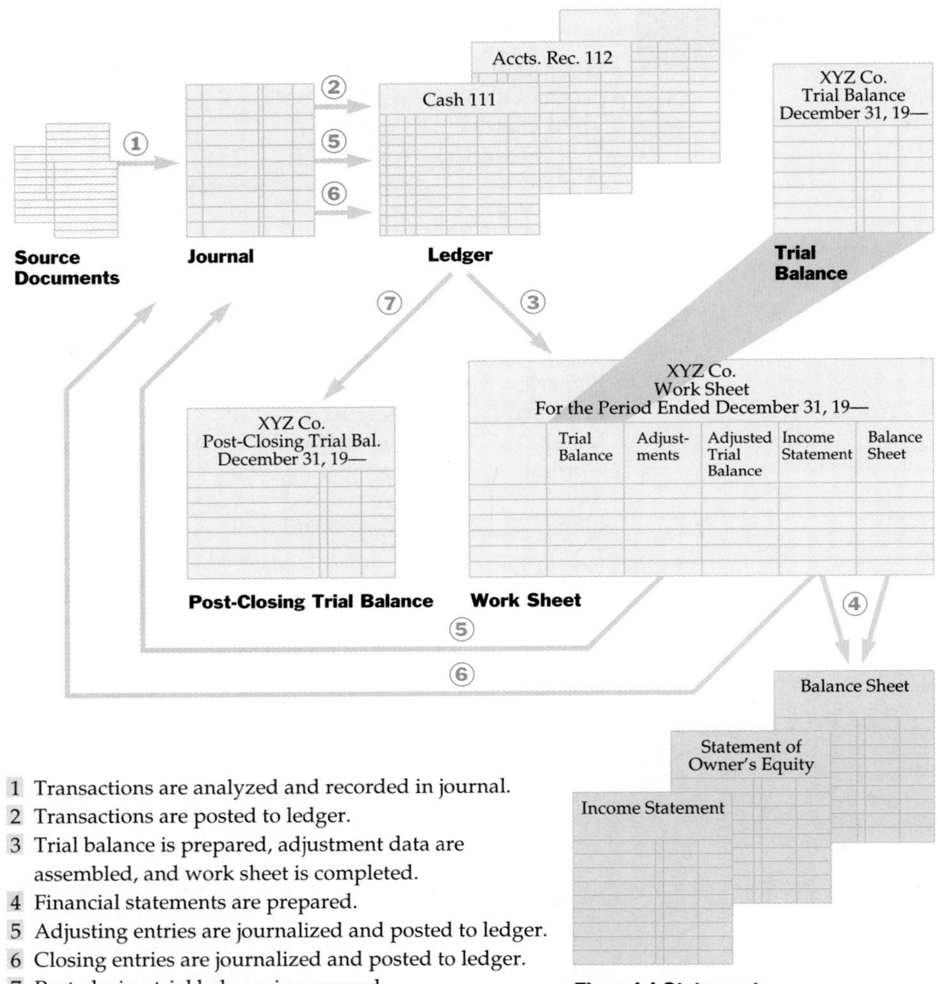

Appendix: Reversing Entries

Some of the adjusting entries recorded at the end of an accounting period have an important effect on otherwise routine transactions that occur in the following period. A typical example is accrued wages owed to employees at the end of a period.

If there has been an adjusting entry for accrued wages expense, the first payment of wages in the following period will include the accrual. In the absence of some special provision, Wages Payable must be debited for the amount owed for the earlier period, and Wages Expense must be debited for the portion of the payroll that represents expense for the later period. However, an *optional* entry—the reversing entry—may be used to simplify the analysis and recording of this first payroll entry in a period. As the term implies, a **reversing entry** is the exact reverse of the adjusting entry to which it relates. The amounts and accounts are the same as the adjusting entry; the debits and credits are reversed.

We will illustrate the use of reversing entries by using the data for Computer King's accrued wages, which were presented in Chapter 3. These data are summarized in Exhibit 10.

Exhibit 10
Accrued Wages

1. Wages are paid on the second and fourth Fridays for the two-week periods ending on those Fridays.
2. The wages accrued for Monday and Tuesday, December 30 and 31, are $250.
3. Wages paid on Friday, January 10, total $1,275.

December

	S	M	T	W	T	F	S	
	1	2	3	4	5	6	7	
	8	9	10	11	12	13	14	Wages expense (paid), $950
	15	16	17	18	19	20	21	
	22	23	24	25	26	27	28	Wages expense (paid), $1,200
Wages expense (accrued), $250	29	30	31					

January

				1	2	3	4
Wages expense (paid), $1,275	5	6	7	8	9	10	11

The adjusting entry for the accrued wages of December 30 and 31 is as follows:

3	Dec. 31	Wages Expense	51	2 5 0 00		3
4		Wages Payable	22		2 5 0 00	4

After the adjusting entry has been posted, Wages Expense will have a debit balance of $4,525 ($4,275 + $250), and Wages Payable will have a credit balance of $250. After the closing process is completed, Wages Expense will have a zero balance and will be ready for entries in the next period. Wages Payable, on the other hand, has a balance of $250. Without the use of a reversing entry, it is necessary to record the $1,275 payroll on January 10 as a debit of $250 to Wages Payable, a debit of $1,025 to Wages Expense, and a credit of $1,275 to Cash. The employee who records this entry must refer to the prior period's adjusting entries to determine the amount of the debits to Wages Payable and Wages Expense.

Because the January 10th payroll is not recorded in the usual manner, there is a greater chance that an error may occur. This chance of error is reduced by recording a reversing entry as of the first day of the fiscal period. For example, the reversing entry for the accrued wages expense is as follows:

Date		Description	Post. Ref.	Debit	Credit
1997 Jan.	1	Wages Payable	22	2 5 0 00	
		Wages Expense	51		2 5 0 00

The reversing entry transfers the $250 liability from Wages Payable to the credit side of Wages Expense. The nature of the $250 is unchanged—it is still a liability. When the payroll is paid on January 10, Wages Expense is debited and Cash is credited for the entire amount of the payment, $1,275. After this entry is posted, Wages Expense has a debit balance of $1,025. This amount is the wages expense for the period January 1–10. The sequence of entries, including adjusting, closing, and reversing entries, is illustrated in the following accounts:

ACCOUNT *Wages Payable* **ACCOUNT NO. *22***

Date		Item	Post. Ref.	Debit	Credit	Balance Debit	Balance Credit
1996 Dec.	31	Adjusting	4		2 5 0 00		2 5 0 00
1997 Jan.	1	Reversing	6	2 5 0 00		—	—

ACCOUNT *Wages Expense* **ACCOUNT NO. *51***

Date		Item	Post. Ref.	Debit	Credit	Balance Debit	Balance Credit
1996 Nov.	30		1	2 1 2 5 00		2 1 2 5 00	
Dec.	13		2	9 5 0 00		3 0 7 5 00	
	27		2	1 2 0 0 00		4 2 7 5 00	
	31	Adjusting	4	2 5 0 00		4 5 2 5 00	
	31	Closing	5		4 5 2 5 00	—	—
1997 Jan.	1	Reversing	6		2 5 0 00		2 5 0 00
	10		6	1 2 7 5 00		1 0 2 5 00	

In addition to accrued expenses (accrued liabilities), reversing entries may be journalized for accrued revenues (accrued assets). For example, the following reversing entry could be recorded for Computer King's accrued fees earned:

Date		Description	Post. Ref.	Debit	Credit
Jan.	1	Fees Earned	41	5 0 0 00	
		Accounts Receivable	12		5 0 0 00

Reversing entries may also be journalized for prepaid expenses that are initially recorded as expenses and unearned revenues that are initially recorded as revenues. These situations are described and illustrated in Appendix C.

As mentioned, the use of reversing entries is optional. However, with the increased use of computerized accounting systems, data entry personnel may be inputting routine accounting entries. In such an environment, reversing entries may be useful, since these individuals may not recognize the impact of adjusting entries on the related transactions in the following period.

KEY POINTS

Objective 1. Prepare a work sheet.
The work sheet is prepared by first entering a trial balance in the Trial Balance columns. The adjustments are then entered in the Adjustments Debit and Credit columns. The Trial Balance accounts plus or minus the adjustments are extended to the Adjusted Trial Balance columns. The work sheet is completed by extending the Adjusted Trial Balance amounts of assets, liabilities, owner's capital, and drawing to the Balance Sheet columns. The Adjusted Trial Balance amounts of revenues and expenses are extended to the Income Statement columns. The net income (or net loss) for the period is entered on the work sheet in the Income Statement Debit (or Credit) column and the Balance Sheet Credit (or Debit) column. Each of the four statement columns is then totaled.

Objective 2. Prepare financial statements from a work sheet.
The income statement is normally prepared directly from the accounts listed in the work sheet. On the income statement, the expenses are normally presented in the order of size, from largest to smallest.

The basic form of the statement of owner's equity is prepared by listing the beginning balance of owner's equity, adding investments in the business and net income during the period, and deducting the owner's withdrawals. The amount listed on the work sheet as the capital of a sole proprietor does not always represent the account balance at the beginning of the accounting period. The proprietor may have invested additional assets in the business during the period. Hence, for the beginning balance and any additional investments, it is necessary to refer to the capital account.

Various sections and subsections are often used in preparing a balance sheet. Two common classes of assets are current assets and plant assets. Cash and other assets that are normally expected to be converted to cash or sold or used up within one year or less are called current assets. Plant assets may also be called property, plant, and equipment. The cost, accumulated depreciation, and book value of each major type of plant asset are normally reported on the balance sheet.

Two common classes of liabilities are current liabilities and long-term liabilities. Liabilities that will be due within a short time (usually one year or less) and that are to be paid out of current assets are called current liabilities. Liabilities that will not be due for a long time (usually more than one year) are called long-term liabilities.

The owner's claim against the assets is presented below the liabilities section and added to the total liabilities. The total liabilities and total owner's equity must equal the total assets.

Objective 3. Journalize and post the adjusting entries.
At the end of the accounting period, the adjusting entries appearing in the work sheet are recorded in the journal and posted to the ledger. This brings the ledger into agreement with the data reported on the financial statements.

Objective 4. Journalize and post the closing entries and prepare a post-closing trial balance.
The four entries required in closing the temporary accounts of a sole proprietorship are:

1. Each revenue account is debited for the amount of its balance, and Income Summary is credited for the total revenue.
2. Each expense account is credited for the amount of its balance, and Income Summary is debited for the total expense.
3. Income Summary is debited for the amount of its balance (net income), and the capital account is credited for the same amount. (Debit and credit are reversed if there is a net loss.)
4. The drawing account is credited for the amount of its balance, and the capital account is debited for the same amount.

After the closing entries have been posted to the ledger, the balance in the capital account will agree with the amount reported on the statement of owner's equity and balance sheet. In addition, the revenue, expense, and drawing accounts will have zero balances.

The last step of the accounting cycle is to prepare a post-closing trial balance. The purpose of the post-closing trial balance is to make sure that the ledger is in balance at the beginning of the next period.

Objective 5. Explain what is meant by the fiscal year and the natural business year.
The annual accounting period adopted by a business is known as its fiscal year. A business may adopt a fiscal year that ends when business activities have reached the lowest point in its annual operating cycle. Such a fiscal year is called the natural business year.

Objective 6. List the seven basic steps of the accounting cycle.
The basic steps of the accounting cycle are:

1. Transactions are analyzed and recorded in a journal.
2. Transactions are posted to the ledger.
3. Trial balance is prepared, adjustment data are assembled, and work sheet is completed.
4. Financial statements are prepared.
5. Adjusting entries are journalized and posted to ledger.
6. Closing entries are journalized and posted to ledger.
7. Post-closing trial balance is prepared.

GLOSSARY OF KEY TERMS

Accounting cycle. The sequence of basic accounting procedures during a fiscal period. *Objective 6*

Closing entries. Entries necessary to eliminate the balances of temporary accounts in preparation for the following accounting period. *Objective 4*

Current assets. Cash or other assets that are expected to be converted to cash or sold or used up, usually within a year or less, through the normal operations of a business. *Objective 2*

Current liabilities. Liabilities that will be due within a short time (usually one year or less) and that are to be paid out of current assets. *Objective 2*

Fiscal year. The annual accounting period adopted by a business. *Objective 5*

Income Summary. The account used in the closing process for transferring the revenue and expense account balances to the owner's capital account at the end of the period. *Objective 4*

Long-term liabilities. Liabilities that are not due for a long time (usually more than one year). *Objective 2*

Natural business year. A year that ends when a business's activities have reached the lowest point in its annual operating cycle. *Objective 5*

Nominal accounts. Revenue or expense accounts that are periodically closed to the income summary account; temporary owner's equity accounts. *Objective 4*

Post-closing trial balance. A trial balance prepared after all of the temporary accounts have been closed. *Objective 4*

Real accounts. Balance sheet accounts. *Objective 4*

Temporary accounts. Revenue or expense accounts that are periodically closed to the income summary account; nominal accounts. *Objective 4*

ILLUSTRATIVE PROBLEM

Three years ago, T. Roderick organized Harbor Realty. At July 31, 1997, the end of the current fiscal year, the trial balance of Harbor Realty is as follows:

Harbor Realty
Trial Balance
July 31, 1997

Cash	3 4 2 5 00	
Accounts Receivable	7 0 0 0 00	
Supplies	1 2 7 0 00	
Prepaid Insurance	6 2 0 00	
Office Equipment	51 6 5 0 00	
Accumulated Depreciation		9 7 0 0 00
Accounts Payable		9 2 5 00
Unearned Fees		1 2 5 0 00
T. Roderick, Capital		29 0 0 0 00
T. Roderick, Drawing	5 2 0 0 00	
Fees Earned		59 1 2 5 00
Wages Expense	22 4 1 5 00	
Rent Expense	4 2 0 0 00	
Utilities Expense	2 7 1 5 00	
Miscellaneous Expense	1 5 0 5 00	
	100 0 0 0 00	100 0 0 0 00

The following adjustment data have been entered on the 10-column work sheet.

a. Supplies on hand at July 31, 1997, are $380.
b. Insurance premiums expired during the year are $315.
c. Depreciation of equipment during the year is $4,950.
d. Wages accrued but not paid at July 31, 1997, are $440.
e. Accrued fees earned but not recorded at July 31, 1997, are $1,000.
f Unearned fees on July 31, 1997, are $750.

Instructions

1. Complete the 10-column work sheet.
2. Prepare an income statement, a statement of owner's equity (no additional investments were made during the year), and a balance sheet.

3. On the basis of the adjustment data in the work sheet, journalize the adjusting entries.
4. On the basis of the data in the work sheet, journalize the closing entries.

Solution

1.

Harbor Realty
Work Sheet
For the Year Ended July 31, 1997

	Trial Balance		Adjustments		Adjusted Trial Balance		Income Statement		Balance Sheet	
Account Title	**Dr.**	**Cr.**	**Dr.**	**Cr.**	**Dr.**	**Cr.**	**Dr.**	**Cr.**	**Dr.**	**Cr.**
Cash	3,425				3,425				3,425	
Accounts Receivable	7,000		(e)1,000		8,000				8,000	
Supplies	1,270			(a) 890	380				380	
Prepaid Insurance	620			(b) 315	305				305	
Office Equipment	51,650				51,650				51,650	
Accumulated Depreciation		9,700		(c)4,950		14,650				14,650
Accounts Payable		925				925				925
Unearned Fees		1,250	(f) 500			750				750
T. Roderick, Capital		29,000				29,000				29,000
T. Roderick, Drawing	5,200				5,200				5,200	
Fees Earned		59,125		(e)1,000 (f) 500		60,625		60,625		
Wages Expense	22,415		(d) 440		22,855		22,855			
Rent Expense	4,200				4,200		4,200			
Utilities Expense	2,715				2,715		2,715			
Miscellaneous Expense	1,505				1,505		1,505			
	100,000	100,000								
Supplies Expense			(a) 890		890		890			
Insurance Expense			(b) 315		315		315			
Depreciation Expense			(c)4,950		4,950		4,950			
Wages Payable				(d) 440		440				440
			8,095	8,095	106,390	106,390	37,430	60,625	68,960	45,765
Net income							23,195			23,195
							60,625	60,625	68,960	68,960

2.

Harbor Realty
Income Statement
For the Year Ended July 31, 1997

Fees earned		$60 6 2 5 00
Operating expenses:		
Wages expense	$22 8 5 5 00	
Depreciation expense	4 9 5 0 00	
Rent expense	4 2 0 0 00	
Utilities expense	2 7 1 5 00	
Supplies expense	8 9 0 00	
Insurance expense	3 1 5 00	
Miscellaneous expense	1 5 0 5 00	
Total operating expenses		37 4 3 0 00
Net income		$23 1 9 5 00

Harbor Realty
Statement of Owner's Equity
For the Year Ended July 31, 1997

T. Roderick, capital, August 1, 1996		$29 0 0 0 00
Net income for the year	$23 1 9 5 00	
Less withdrawals	5 2 0 0 00	
Increase in owner's equity		17 9 9 5 00
T. Roderick, capital, July 31, 1997		$46 9 9 5 00

Harbor Realty
Balance Sheet
July 31, 1997

Assets			Liabilities		
Current assets:			Current liabilities:		
Cash	$3 4 2 5 00		Accounts payable	$ 9 2 5 00	
Accounts receivable	8 0 0 0 00		Unearned fees	7 5 0 00	
Supplies	3 8 0 00		Wages payable	4 4 0 00	
Prepaid insurance	3 0 5 00		Total liabilities		$ 2 1 1 5 00
Total current assets		$12 1 1 0 00			
Plant assets:			**Owner's Equity**		
Office equipment	$51 6 5 0 00		T. Roderick, capital		46 9 9 5 00
Less accumulated depr.	14 6 5 0 00	37 0 0 0 00	Total liabilities and		
Total assets		$49 1 1 0 00	owner's equity		$49 1 1 0 00

3.

JOURNAL PAGE

Date		Description	Post. Ref.	Debit	Credit
		Adjusting Entries			
1997 July	31	Supplies Expense		8 9 0 00	
		Supplies			8 9 0 00
	31	Insurance Expense		3 1 5 00	
		Prepaid Insurance			3 1 5 00
	31	Depreciation Expense		4 9 5 0 00	
		Accumulated Depreciation			4 9 5 0 00
	31	Wages Expense		4 4 0 00	
		Wages Payable			4 4 0 00
	31	Accounts Receivable		1 0 0 0 00	
		Fees Earned			1 0 0 0 00
	31	Unearned Fees		5 0 0 00	
		Fees Earned			5 0 0 00

4.

JOURNAL **PAGE**

Date		Description	Post. Ref.	Debit	Credit
		Closing Entries			
1997 July	31	Fees Earned		60 6 2 5 00	
		Income Summary			60 6 2 5 00
	31	Income Summary		37 4 3 0 00	
		Wages Expense			22 8 5 5 00
		Rent Expense			4 2 0 0 00
		Utilities Expense			2 7 1 5 00
		Miscellaneous Expense			1 5 0 5 00
		Supplies Expense			8 9 0 00
		Insurance Expense			3 1 5 00
		Depreciation Expense			4 9 5 0 00
	31	Income Summary		23 1 9 5 00	
		T. Roderick, Capital			23 1 9 5 00
	31	T. Roderick, Capital		5 2 0 0 00	
		T. Roderick, Drawing			5 2 0 0 00

SELF-EXAMINATION QUESTIONS (ANSWERS AT END OF CHAPTER)

1. Which of the following accounts would be extended from the Adjusted Trial Balance columns of the work sheet to the Balance Sheet columns?
   A. Utilities Expense
   B. Rent Income
   C. M. E. Jones, Drawing
   D. Miscellaneous Expense

2. Which of the following accounts would be classified as a current asset on the balance sheet?
   A. Office Equipment
   B. Land
   C. Accumulated Depreciation
   D. Accounts Receivable

3. Which of the following entries closes the owner's drawing account at the end of the period?
   A. Debit the drawing account, credit the income summary account.
   B. Debit the owner's capital account, credit the drawing account.
   C. Debit the income summary account, credit the drawing account.
   D. Debit the drawing account, credit the owner's capital account.

4. Which of the following accounts would not be closed to the income summary account at the end of a period?
   A. Fees Earned
   B. Wages Expense
   C. Rent Expense
   D. Accumulated Depreciation

5. Which of the following accounts would not be included in a post-closing trial balance?
   A. Cash
   B. Fees Earned
   C. Accumulated Depreciation
   D. J. C. Smith, Capital

DISCUSSION QUESTIONS

1. Is the work sheet a substitute for the financial statements? Discuss.
2. In the Income Statement columns of the work sheet, the Debit column total is greater than the Credit column total before the amount for the net income or net loss has been included. Would the income statement report a net income or a net loss? Explain.
3. In the Balance Sheet columns of the work sheet for McReynolds Co. for the current year, the Debit column total is $91,500 greater than the Credit column total before the amount

for net income or net loss has been included. Would the income statement report a net income or a net loss? Explain.

4. Describe the nature of the assets that compose the following sections of a balance sheet: (a) current assets, (b) plant assets.
5. What is the difference between a current liability and a long-term liability?
6. What types of accounts are referred to as temporary accounts?
7. Are adjusting and closing entries in the journal dated as of the last day of the fiscal period or as of the day the entries are actually made? Explain.
8. Why are closing entries required at the end of an accounting period?
9. What is the difference between adjusting entries and closing entries?
10. Describe the four entries that close the temporary accounts.
11. What type of accounts are closed by transferring their balances (a) as a debit to Income Summary, (b) as a credit to Income Summary?
12. To what account is the income summary account closed?
13. To what account is the owner's drawing account closed?
14. What is the purpose of the post-closing trial balance?
15. What term is applied to the annual accounting period adopted by a business?
16. What is the natural business year?
17. Why might a department store select a fiscal year ending January 31, rather than a fiscal year ending December 31?
18. The fiscal years for several well-known companies were as follows:

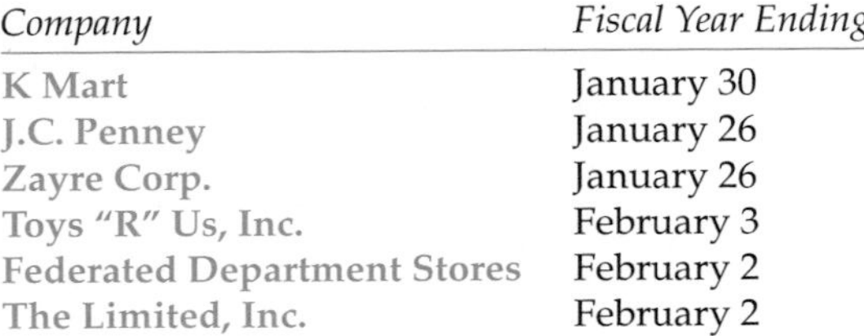

Company	*Fiscal Year Ending*
K Mart	January 30
J.C. Penney	January 26
Zayre Corp.	January 26
Toys "R" Us, Inc.	February 3
Federated Department Stores	February 2
The Limited, Inc.	February 2

What general characteristic shared by these companies explains why they do not have fiscal years ending December 31?

EXERCISES

EXERCISE 4–1
Extending accounts in a work sheet
Objective 1

The balances for the accounts listed below appeared in the Adjusted Trial Balance columns of the work sheet. Indicate whether each balance should be extended to (a) the Income Statement columns or (b) the Balance Sheet columns.

1. J. C. Eddie, Capital
2. Fees Earned
3. Accounts Payable
4. Wages Expense
5. Supplies
6. Unearned Fees
7. Utilities Expense
8. J. C. Eddie, Drawing
9. Accounts Receivable
10. Wages Payable

EXERCISE 4–2
Classifying accounts
Objective 1

Balances for each of the following accounts appear in the Adjusted Trial Balance columns of the work sheet. Identify each as (a) asset, (b) liability, (c) revenue, or (d) expense.

1. Unearned Rent
2. Supplies
3. Salary Expense
4. Rent Income
5. Prepaid Advertising
6. Insurance Expense
7. Accounts Receivable
8. Land
9. Fees Earned
10. Supplies Expense
11. Salary Payable
12. Prepaid Insurance

EXERCISE 4–3
Steps in completing a work sheet
Objective 1

The steps performed in completing a work sheet are listed below in random order.

a. Add or deduct adjusting entry data to trial balance amounts and extend amounts to the Adjusted Trial Balance columns.

b. Extend the adjusted trial balance amounts to the Income Statement columns and the Balance Sheet columns.
c. Enter the amount of net income or net loss for the period in the proper Income Statement column and Balance Sheet column.
d. Add the Debit and Credit columns of the Balance Sheet and Income Statement columns of the work sheet to verify that the totals are equal.
e. Add the Debit and Credit columns of the Adjusted Trial Balance columns of the work sheet to verify that the totals are equal.
f. Add the Debit and Credit columns of the Adjustments columns of the work sheet to verify that the totals are equal.
g. Enter the adjusting entries into the work sheet, based upon the adjustment data.
h. Add the Debit and Credit columns of the unadjusted Trial Balance columns of the work sheet to verify that the totals are equal.
i. Add the Debit and Credit columns of the Balance Sheet and Income Statement columns of the work sheet to determine the amount of net income or net loss for the period.
j. Enter the unadjusted account balances from the general ledger into the unadjusted Trial Balance columns of the work sheet.

Indicate the order in which the preceding steps would be performed in preparing and completing a work sheet.

EXERCISE 4–4
Adjustments data on work sheet
Objective 1

Sanitize Services Co. offers cleaning services to business clients. The trial balance for Sanitize Services Co. has been prepared on the following work sheet for the year ended December 31, 1996.

Sanitize Services Co.
Work Sheet
For the Year Ended December 31, 1996

	Trial Balance		Adjustments		Adjusted Trial Balance	
Account Title	Dr.	Cr.	Dr.	Cr.	Dr.	Cr.
Cash	6					
Accounts Receivable	25					
Supplies	4					
Prepaid Insurance	6					
Land	10					
Equipment	12					
Accumulated Depr.—Equip.		1				
Accounts Payable		13				
Wages Payable		0				
Joe Camarillo, Capital		41				
Joe Camarillo, Drawing	4					
Fees Earned		27				
Wages Expense	7					
Rent Expense	4					
Insurance Expense	0					
Utilities Expense	2					
Depreciation Expense	0					
Supplies Expense	0					
Miscellaneous Expense	2					
Totals	82	82				

The data for year-end adjustments are as follows:

a. Fees earned, but not yet billed, $3.
b. Supplies on hand, $3.
c. Insurance premiums expired, $4.
d. Depreciation expense, $1.
e. Wages accrued, but not paid, $2.

Enter the adjustments data, and extend balances to the Adjusted Trial Balance columns.

EXERCISE 4–5
Completing a work sheet
Objective 1

Sanitize Services Co. offers cleaning services to business clients. The following is a partially completed work sheet for Sanitize Services Co.

Sanitize Services Co.
Work Sheet
For the Year Ended December 31, 1996

	Adjusted Trial Balance		Income Statement		Balance Sheet	
Account Title	Dr.	Cr.	Dr.	Cr.	Dr.	Cr.
Cash	6					
Accounts Receivable	28					
Supplies	3					
Prepaid Insurance	2					
Land	10					
Equipment	12					
Accumulated Depr.—Equip.		2				
Accounts Payable		13				
Wages Payable		2				
Joe Camarillo, Capital		41				
Joe Camarillo, Drawing	4					
Fees Earned		30				
Wages Expense	9					
Rent Expense	4					
Insurance Expense	4					
Utilities Expense	2					
Depreciation Expense	1					
Supplies Expense	1					
Miscellaneous Expense	2					
Totals	88	88				
Net Income (Loss)						

Complete the work sheet.

EXERCISE 4–6
Financial statements
Objective 2

Based upon the data in Exercise 4–5, prepare an income statement, statement of owner's equity, and balance sheet for Sanitize Services Co.

EXERCISE 4–7
Adjusting entries
Objective 3

Based upon the data in Exercise 4–4, prepare the adjusting entries for Sanitize Services Co.

EXERCISE 4–8
Closing entries
Objective 4

Based upon the data in Exercise 4–5, prepare the closing entries for Sanitize Services Co.

EXERCISE 4–9
Income statement
Objective 2

The following account balances were taken from the Adjusted Trial Balance columns of the work sheet for The Courier Co., a delivery service firm, for the current fiscal year ended April 30:

Fees Earned	$112,500
Salaries Expense	47,100
Rent Expense	18,000
Utilities Expense	7,500
Supplies Expense	2,050
Miscellaneous Expense	1,350
Insurance Expense	1,500
Depreciation Expense	3,100

Prepare an income statement.

EXERCISE 4–10
Income statement; net loss
Objective 2

The following revenue and expense account balances were taken from the ledger of Custom Services Co. after the accounts had been adjusted on January 31, the end of the current fiscal year:

Depreciation Expense	$ 7,500
Insurance Expense	3,900
Miscellaneous Expense	2,250
Rent Expense	34,000
Service Revenue	81,200
Supplies Expense	3,100
Utilities Expense	8,500
Wages Expense	46,750

Prepare an income statement.

EXERCISE 4–11
Statement of owner's equity
Objective 2

Newcomer Services Co. offers its services to new arrivals in the Chicago area. Selected accounts from the ledger of Newcomer Services Co. for the current fiscal year ended December 31 are as follows:

F. Henri, Capital

Dec. 31	10,000	Jan. 1	122,500
		Dec. 31	33,250

F. Henri, Drawing

Mar. 31	2,500	Dec. 31	10,000
June 30	2,500		
Sep. 30	2,500		
Dec. 31	2,500		

Income Summary

Dec. 31	578,150	Dec. 31	611,400
31	33,250		

Prepare a statement of owner's equity for the year.

EXERCISE 4–12
Statement of owner's equity; net loss
Objective 2

Selected accounts from the ledger of News Services Co. for the current fiscal year ended July 31 are as follows:

C. Chang, Capital

July 31	20,000	Aug. 1	360,500
31	10,500		

C. Chang, Drawing

Oct. 31	5,000	July 31	20,000
Jan. 31	5,000		
Apr. 30	5,000		
July 31	5,000		

Income Summary

July 31	723,400	July 31	712,900
		31	10,500

Prepare a statement of owner's equity for the year.

EXERCISE 4–13
Classifying assets
Objective 2

Identify each of the following as (a) a current asset or (b) a plant asset:

1. Supplies
2. Cash
3. Building
4. Accounts receivable
5. Equipment
6. Land

EXERCISE 4–14
Balance sheet classification
Objective 2

At the balance sheet date, a business owes a mortgage note payable of $300,000, the terms of which provide for monthly payments of $5,000.

Explain how the liability should be classified on the balance sheet.

EXERCISE 4–15
Balance sheet
Objective 2

Shape Up Co. offers personal weight reduction consulting services to individuals. After all the accounts have been closed on April 30, the end of the current fiscal year, the balances of selected accounts from the ledger of Shape Up Co. are as follows:

Accounts Payable	$12,750
Accounts Receivable	29,920
Accumulated Depreciation—Equipment	21,100
Cash	6,150
Equipment	80,600
J. Fonda, Capital	87,820
Prepaid Insurance	4,100
Prepaid Rent	2,400
Salaries Payable	3,750
Supplies	4,750
Unearned Fees	2,500

Prepare a classified balance sheet.

EXERCISE 4–16
Balance sheet
Objective 2

List the errors you can find in the following balance sheet. Prepare a corrected balance sheet.

Healthcare Services Co.
Balance Sheet
For the Year Ended August 31, 1996

Assets			Liabilities	
Current assets:			Current liabilities:	
Cash	$ 6,170		Accounts receivable	$ 5,390
Accounts payable	5,390		Accum. depr.—building	23,525
Supplies	590		Accum. depr.—equipment	17,340
Prepaid insurance	845		Net loss	15,500
Land	20,000		Total liabilities	$ 61,755
Total current assets		$ 32,995		
			Owner's Equity	
Plant assets:			Wages payable	$ 975
Building		$ 55,500	Wally Olstein, capital	69,515
Equipment		28,250	Total owner's equity	$ 70,490
Total plant assets		$ 99,250	Total liabilities and	
Total assets		$132,245	owner's equity	$132,245

EXERCISE 4–17
Adjusting entries from work sheet
Objective 3

Smog Purifier Co. is a consulting firm specializing in pollution control. The entries in the Adjustments columns of the work sheet for Smog Purifier Co. are shown below.

	Adjustments	
	Dr.	*Cr.*
Accounts Receivable	1,200	
Supplies		975
Prepaid Insurance		1,100
Accumulated Depreciation—Equipment		500
Wages Payable		636
Unearned Rent	2,500	
Fees Earned		1,200
Wages Expense	636	
Supplies Expense	975	
Rent Income		2,500
Insurance Expense	1,100	
Depreciation Expense	500	

Prepare the adjusting journal entries.

EXERCISE 4–18
Identifying accounts to be closed
Objective 4

From the following list, identify the accounts that should be closed to Income Summary at the end of the fiscal year:

a. Accounts Payable
b. Salaries Payable
c. Fees Earned
d. Salaries Expense
e. Depreciation Expense—Buildings
f. Supplies
g. Equipment
h. Supplies Expense
i. D. Thorton, Capital
j. D. Thorton, Drawing
k. Land
l. Accumulated Depreciation—Buildings

EXERCISE 4–19
Closing entries
Objective 4

Prior to the completion of the closing process, Income Summary had total debits of $257,500 and total credits of $318,000.

Briefly explain the purpose served by the income summary account and the nature of the entries that resulted in the $257,500 and the $318,000.

EXERCISE 4–20
Closing entries
Objective 4

After all revenue and expense accounts have been closed at the end of the fiscal year, Income Summary has a debit of $695,500 and a credit of $787,500. At the same date, Lee Sassier, Capital has a credit balance of $139,500, and Lee Sassier, Drawing has a balance of $25,000. (a) Journalize the entries required to complete the closing of the accounts. (b) Determine the amount of Lee Sassier, Capital at the end of the period.

EXERCISE 4–21
Closing entries
Objective 4

Image Services Co. offers its services to individuals desiring to improve their personal images. After the accounts have been adjusted at August 31, the end of the fiscal year, the following balances were taken from the ledger of Image Services Co.

W. J. Disney, Capital	$795,300
W. J. Disney, Drawing	40,000
Fees Earned	355,000
Wages Expense	221,500
Rent Expense	39,000
Supplies Expense	15,500
Miscellaneous Expense	2,000

Journalize the four entries required to close the accounts.

EXERCISE 4–22
Identifying permanent account
Objective 4

Which of the following accounts will usually appear in the post-closing trial balance?

a. Accounts Receivable
b. Accumulated Depreciation
c. Cash
d. Supplies
e. Depreciation Expense
f. Wages Payable
g. Equipment
h. Wages Expense
i. S. A. McDermott, Capital
j. Fees Earned
k. S. A. McDermott, Drawing

EXERCISE 4–23
Post-closing trial balance
Objective 4

An accountant prepared the following post-closing trial balance:

Cheatham Repairs Co.
Post-Closing Trial Balance
October 31, 19—

Cash	9,400	
Accounts Receivable	11,250	
Supplies		1,800
Equipment		31,500
Accumulated Depreciation—Equipment	15,130	
Accounts Payable	7,250	
Salaries Payable		1,500
Unearned Rent	4,000	
Joe Harris, Capital	26,070	
	73,100	34,800

Prepare a corrected post-closing trial balance. Assume that all accounts have normal balances and that the amounts shown are correct.

EXERCISE 4–24
Steps in the accounting cycle
Objective 6

Rearrange the following steps in the accounting cycle in proper sequence:

a. Adjusting entries are journalized and posted to ledger.
b. Post-closing trial balance is prepared.
c. Closing entries are journalized and posted to ledger.
d. Transactions are analyzed and recorded in journal.
e. Financial statements are prepared.
f. Trial balance is prepared, adjustment data are assembled, and work sheet is completed.
g. Transactions are posted to ledger.

APPENDIX EXERCISE 4–25
Adjusting and reversing entries

On the basis of the following data, (a) journalize the adjusting entries at December 31, 1996, the end of the current fiscal year, and (b) journalize the reversing entries on January 1, 1997, the first day of the following year.

1. Sales salaries are uniformly $15,000 for a five-day workweek, ending on Friday. The last payday of the year was Friday, December 26.
2. Accrued fees earned but not recorded at December 31, $5,750.

APPENDIX EXERCISE 4–26
Entries posted to the wages expense account

Portions of the wages expense account of a business are as follows:

ACCOUNT *Wages Expense* ACCOUNT NO. *53*

Date		Item	Post. Ref.	Dr.	Cr.	Balance Dr.	Balance Cr.
19—							
Dec.	26	(1)	51	15,000		245,500	
	31	(2)	52	9,000		254,500	
	31	(3)	53		254,500	—	—
19—							
Jan.	1	(4)	54		9,000		9,000
	2	(5)	55	15,000		6,000	

a. Indicate the nature of the entry (payment, adjusting, closing, reversing) from which each numbered posting was made.
b. Journalize the complete entry from which each numbered posting was made.

PROBLEMS SERIES A

PROBLEM 4–1A
Work sheet and related items
Objectives 1, 2, 3, 4

The trial balance of The Washboard Laundromat at March 31, 1997, the end of the current fiscal year, and the data needed to determine year-end adjustments are as follows:

The Washboard Laundromat
Trial Balance
March 31, 1997

Cash	6,290	
Laundry Supplies	5,850	
Prepaid Insurance	2,400	
Laundry Equipment	96,750	
Accumulated Depreciation		52,700
Accounts Payable		3,950
Lee Cheswick, Capital		37,450
Lee Cheswick, Drawing	3,000	
Laundry Revenue		66,900
Wages Expense	22,900	
Rent Expense	14,400	
Utilities Expense	8,500	
Miscellaneous Expense	910	
	161,000	161,000

a. Laundry supplies on hand at March 31 are $1,040.
b. Insurance premiums expired during the year are $1,700.
c. Depreciation of equipment during the year is $5,220.
d. Wages accrued but not paid at March 31 are $850.

Instructions

1. Record the trial balance on a ten-column work sheet, and complete the work sheet.
2. Prepare an income statement, a statement of owner's equity (no additional investments were made during the year), and a balance sheet.
3. On the basis of the adjustment data in the work sheet, journalize the adjusting entries.
4. On the basis of the data in the work sheet, journalize the closing entries.

PROBLEM 4–2A
Adjusting and closing entries; statement of owner's equity
Objectives 2, 3

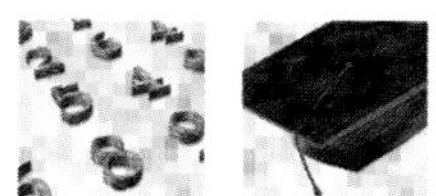

Grail Company is an investigative services firm that is owned and operated by S. Launcelot. On November 30, 19—, the end of the current fiscal year, the accountant for Grail Company prepared a trial balance, journalized and posted the adjusting entries, prepared an adjusted trial balance, prepared the financial statements, and completed the other procedures required at the end of the accounting cycle. The two trial balances as of November 30, one before adjustments and the other after adjustments, are as follows:

Grail Company
Trial Balance
November 30, 19—

	Unadjusted		*Adjusted*	
Cash	7,325		7,325	
Accounts Receivable	16,900		20,500	
Supplies	6,920		1,610	
Prepaid Insurance	4,275		1,350	
Equipment	69,750		69,750	
Accumulated Depreciation—Equipment		29,395		32,185
Accounts Payable		4,310		5,030
Salaries Payable		—		3,480
Taxes Payable		—		2,200
Unearned Rent		3,750		1,500
S. Launcelot, Capital		31,345		31,345
S. Launcelot, Drawing	7,500		7,500	
Service Fees Earned		181,200		184,800
Rent Income		—		2,250
Salary Expense	116,385		119,865	
Rent Expense	15,600		15,600	
Supplies Expense	—		5,310	
Depreciation Expense—Equipment	—		2,790	
Utilities Expense	2,720		3,440	
Taxes Expense	915		3,115	
Insurance Expense	—		2,925	
Miscellaneous Expense	1,710		1,710	
	250,000	250,000	262,790	262,790

Instructions

1. Journalize the eight entries that were required to adjust the accounts at November 30. None of the accounts were affected by more than one adjusting entry.
2. Journalize the entries that were required to close the accounts at November 30.
3. Prepare a statement of owner's equity for the fiscal year ended November 30, 19—. There were no additional investments during the year.
4. If the balance of S. Launcelot, Drawing had been $75,000 instead of $7,500, what would the balance of S. Launcelot, Capital have been on November 30, 19—? Explain how this balance would be reported on the balance sheet.

If the working papers correlating with this textbook are not used, omit Problem 4–3A.

PROBLEM 4–3A
Ledger accounts, work sheet, and related items
Objectives 1, 2, 3, 4

The ledger and trial balance of Huckleberry Company as of January 31, 1997, the end of the first month of its current fiscal year, are presented in the working papers.

Instructions

1. Complete the ten-column work sheet. Data needed to determine the necessary adjusting entries are as follows:
   a. Service revenue accrued at January 31 is $900.
   b. Supplies on hand at January 31 are $550.
   c. Insurance premiums expired during January are $100.
   d. Depreciation of the building during January is $110.
   e. Depreciation of equipment during January is $115.
   f. Unearned rent at January 31 is $100.
   g. Wages accrued at January 31 are $275.
2. Prepare an income statement, a statement of owner's equity, and a balance sheet. (*Note:* The owner made an additional investment during the period.)
3. Journalize and post the adjusting entries, inserting balances in the accounts affected.
4. Journalize and post the closing entries. Indicate closed accounts by inserting a line in both Balance columns opposite the closing entry.
5. Prepare a post-closing trial balance.

PROBLEM 4–4A
Work sheet and financial statements
Objectives 1, 2

Beacon Company maintains and repairs warning lights, such as those found on radio towers and lighthouses. Beacon Company prepared the following trial balance at May 31, 1997, the end of the current fiscal year:

Beacon Company
Trial Balance
May 31, 1997

Cash	7,500	
Accounts Receivable	16,500	
Prepaid Insurance	2,600	
Supplies	1,950	
Land	60,000	
Building	100,500	
Accumulated Depreciation—Building		81,700
Equipment	72,400	
Accumulated Depreciation—Equipment		63,800
Accounts Payable		6,100
Unearned Rent		1,500
Iris Cuttner, Capital		60,700
Iris Cuttner, Drawing	4,000	
Fees Revenue		161,200
Salaries and Wages Expense	60,200	
Advertising Expense	19,000	
Utilities Expense	18,200	
Repairs Expense	8,100	
Miscellaneous Expense	4,050	
	375,000	375,000

The data needed to determine year-end adjustments are as follows:

a. Fees revenue accrued at May 31 is $1,200.
b. Insurance expired during the year is $1,250.
c. Supplies on hand at May 31 are $450.
d. Depreciation of building for the year is $1,620.
e. Depreciation of equipment for the year is $3,160.

f. Accrued salaries and wages at May 31 are $1,450.
g. Unearned rent at May 31 is $500.

Instructions

1. Record the trial balance on a ten-column work sheet, and complete the work sheet.
2. Prepare an income statement for the year ended May 31.
3. Prepare a statement of owner's equity for the year ended May 31. No additional investments were made during the year.
4. Prepare a balance sheet as of May 31.
5. Compute the percent of net income to total revenue for the year.

PROBLEM 4–5A
Ledger accounts, work sheet, and related items
Objectives 1, 2, 3, 4

The trial balance of Fix-It Repairs at March 31, 1997, the end of the current year, and the data needed to determine year-end adjustments are as follows:

Fix-It Repairs
Trial Balance
March 31, 1997

11 Cash	6,950	
13 Supplies	4,295	
14 Prepaid Insurance	2,735	
16 Equipment	40,650	
17 Accumulated Depreciation—Equipment		11,209
18 Trucks	36,300	
19 Accumulated Depreciation—Trucks		6,400
21 Accounts Payable		2,015
31 Jay Hammer, Capital		40,426
32 Jay Hammer, Drawing	5,000	
41 Service Revenue		89,950
51 Wages Expense	33,925	
53 Rent Expense	9,600	
55 Truck Expense	8,350	
59 Miscellaneous Expense	2,195	
	150,000	150,000

a. Supplies on hand at March 31 are $1,302.
b. Insurance premiums expired during year are $1,050.
c. Depreciation of equipment during year is $3,380.
d. Depreciation of trucks during year is $4,400.
e. Wages accrued but not paid at March 31 are $650.

Instructions

1. For each account listed in the trial balance, enter the balance in the appropriate Balance column of a four-column account and place a check mark (√) in the Posting Reference column.
2. Record the trial balance on a ten-column work sheet, and complete the work sheet.
3. Prepare an income statement, a statement of owner's equity (no additional investments were made during the year), and a balance sheet.
4. Journalize and post the adjusting entries, inserting balances in the accounts affected. The following additional accounts from Fix-It's chart of accounts should be used: Wages Payable, 22; Supplies Expense, 52; Depreciation Expense—Equipment, 54; Depreciation Expense—Trucks, 56; Insurance Expense, 57.
5. Journalize and post the closing entries. (Income Summary is account #33 in the chart of accounts.) Indicate closed accounts by inserting a line in both Balance columns opposite the closing entry.
6. Prepare a post-closing trial balance.

PROBLEMS SERIES B

PROBLEM 4–1B
Work sheet and related items
Objectives 1, 2, 3, 4

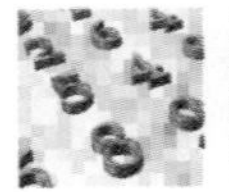

The trial balance of Tidal Wave Laundry at August 31, 1997, the end of the current fiscal year, and the data needed to determine year-end adjustments are as follows:

Tidal Wave Laundry
Trial Balance
August 31, 1997

Cash	13,100	
Laundry Supplies	6,560	
Prepaid Insurance	4,490	
Laundry Equipment	100,100	
Accumulated Depreciation		45,200
Accounts Payable		6,100
Sylvia Akai, Capital		37,800
Sylvia Akai, Drawing	2,000	
Laundry Revenue		140,900
Wages Expense	51,400	
Rent Expense	36,000	
Utilities Expense	13,650	
Miscellaneous Expense	2,700	
	230,000	230,000

a. Laundry supplies on hand at August 31 are $2,050.
b. Insurance premiums expired during the year are $2,800.
c. Depreciation of equipment during the year is $4,600.
d. Wages accrued but not paid at August 31 are $1,750.

Instructions

1. Record the trial balance on a ten-column work sheet, and complete the work sheet.
2. Prepare an income statement, a statement of owner's equity (no additional investments were made during the year), and a balance sheet.
3. On the basis of the adjustment data in the work sheet, journalize the adjusting entries.
4. On the basis of the data in the work sheet, journalize the closing entries.

PROBLEM 4–2B
Adjusting and closing entries; statement of owner's equity
Objectives 2, 3

Merlin Company is a financial planning services firm owned and operated by K. Arthur. As of December 31, the end of the current fiscal year, the accountant for Merlin Company prepared a trial balance, journalized and posted the adjusting entries, prepared an adjusted trial balance, prepared the financial statements, and completed the other procedures required at the end of the accounting cycle. The two trial balances as of December 31, one before adjustments and the other after adjustments, are as shown on the following page.

Instructions

1. Journalize the nine entries that were required to adjust the accounts at December 31. None of the accounts were affected by more than one adjusting entry.
2. Journalize the entries that were required to close the accounts at December 31.
3. Prepare a statement of owner's equity for the fiscal year ended December 31. There were no additional investments during the year.
4. If the balance of K. Arthur, Drawing had been $140,000 instead of $10,000, what would the balance of K. Arthur, Capital have been on December 31? Explain how this balance would be reported on the balance sheet.

Merlin Company
Trial Balance
December 31, 19––

	Unadjusted		*Adjusted*	
Cash	3,650		3,650	
Accounts Receivable	20,380		23,960	
Supplies	11,760		3,380	
Prepaid Insurance	2,400		800	
Land	42,500		42,500	
Buildings	116,000		116,000	
Accumulated Depreciation—Buildings		77,600		82,400
Equipment	82,000		82,000	
Accumulated Depreciation—Equipment		32,800		50,900
Accounts Payable		7,120		7,640
Salaries Payable		—		1,450
Taxes Payable		—		2,920
Unearned Rent		1,900		300
K. Arthur, Capital		114,900		114,900
K. Arthur, Drawing	10,000		10,000	
Service Fees Earned		140,680		144,260
Rent Income		—		1,600
Salary Expense	71,200		72,650	
Depreciation Expense—Equipment	—		18,100	
Rent Expense	9,000		9,000	
Supplies Expense	—		8,380	
Utilities Expense	4,550		5,070	
Depreciation Expense—Buildings	—		4,800	
Taxes Expense	600		3,520	
Insurance Expense	—		1,600	
Miscellaneous Expense	960		960	
	375,000	375,000	406,370	406,370

If the working papers correlating with this textbook are not used, omit Problem 4–3B.

PROBLEM 4–3B
Ledger accounts and work sheet and related items
Objectives 1, 2, 3, 4

The ledger and trial balance of Huckleberry Company as of January 31, 1997, the end of the first month of its current fiscal year, are presented in the working papers.

Instructions

1. Complete the ten-column work sheet. Data needed to determine the necessary adjusting entries are as follows:
   a. Service revenue accrued at January 31 is $650.
   b. Supplies on hand at January 31 are $710.
   c. Insurance premiums expired during January are $90.
   d. Depreciation of the building during January is $125.
   e. Depreciation of equipment during January is $95.
   f. Unearned rent at January 31 is $100.
   g. Wages accrued but not paid at January 31 are $575.
2. Prepare an income statement, a statement of owner's equity, and a balance sheet. (*Note:* The owner made an additional investment during the period.)
3. Journalize and post the adjusting entries, inserting balances in the accounts affected.
4. Journalize and post the closing entries. Indicate closed accounts by inserting a line in both Balance columns opposite the closing entry. Insert the new balance of the capital account.
5. Prepare a post-closing trial balance.

PROBLEM 4–4B
Work sheet and financial statements
Objectives 1, 2

Supreme Company offers legal consulting advice to death-row inmates. Supreme Company prepared the following trial balance at April 30, 1997, the end of the current fiscal year:

Supreme Company
Trial Balance
April 30, 1997

Cash	3,200	
Accounts Receivable	10,500	
Prepaid Insurance	3,800	
Supplies	1,950	
Land	50,000	
Building	137,500	
Accumulated Depreciation—Building		51,700
Equipment	90,100	
Accumulated Depreciation—Equipment		35,300
Accounts Payable		7,500
Unearned Rent		3,000
Jean Ginsburg, Capital		164,100
Jean Ginsburg, Drawing	10,000	
Fees Revenue		198,400
Salaries and Wages Expense	80,200	
Advertising Expense	38,200	
Utilities Expense	19,000	
Repairs Expense	11,500	
Miscellaneous Expense	4,050	
	460,000	460,000

The data needed to determine year-end adjustments are as follows:

a. Accrued fees revenue at April 30 are $1,500.
b. Insurance expired during the year is $2,600.
c. Supplies on hand at April 30 are $450.
d. Depreciation of building for the year is $1,620.
e. Depreciation of equipment for the year is $3,500.
f. Accrued salaries and wages at April 30 are $1,800.
g. Unearned rent at April 30 is $1,000.

Instructions

1. Record the trial balance on a ten-column work sheet, and complete the work sheet.
2. Prepare an income statement for the year ended April 30.
3. Prepare a statement of owner's equity for the year ended April 30. No additional investments were made during the year.
4. Prepare a balance sheet as of April 30.
5. Compute the percent of net income to total revenue for the year.

PROBLEM 4–5B
Ledger accounts, work sheet, and related items
Objectives 1, 2, 3, 4

The trial balance of Like-New Repairs at December 31, 1997, the end of the current year, is shown at the top of the next page. The data needed to determine year-end adjustments are as follows:

a. Supplies on hand at December 31 are $1,360.
b. Insurance premiums expired during year are $2,050.
c. Depreciation of equipment during year is $6,080.
d. Depreciation of trucks during year is $5,500.
e. Wages accrued but not paid at December 31 are $500.

Like-New Repairs
Trial Balance
December 31, 1997

11	Cash	6,825	
13	Supplies	4,820	
14	Prepaid Insurance	3,500	
16	Equipment	42,200	
17	Accumulated Depreciation—Equipment		9,050
18	Trucks	45,000	
19	Accumulated Depreciation—Trucks		27,100
21	Accounts Payable		4,015
31	S. Driver, Capital		29,885
32	S. Driver, Drawing	3,000	
41	Service Revenue		99,950
51	Wages Expense	42,010	
53	Rent Expense	10,100	
55	Truck Expense	9,350	
59	Miscellaneous Expense	3,195	
		170,000	170,000

Instructions

1. For each account listed in the trial balance, enter the balance in the appropriate Balance column of a four-column account and place a check mark (√) in the Posting Reference column.
2. Record the trial balance on a ten-column work sheet, and complete the work sheet.
3. Prepare an income statement, a statement of owner's equity (no additional investments were made during the year), and a balance sheet.
4. Journalize and post the adjusting entries, inserting balances in the accounts affected. The following additional accounts from Like-New's chart of accounts should be used: Wages Payable, 22; Supplies Expense, 52; Depreciation Expense—Equipment, 54; Depreciation Expense—Trucks, 56; Insurance Expense, 57.
5. Journalize and post the closing entries. (Income Summary is account #33 in the chart of accounts.) Indicate closed accounts by inserting a line in both Balance columns opposite the closing entry.
6. Prepare a post-closing trial balance.

CONTINUING PROBLEM

The unadjusted trial balance of Music A La Mode as of December 31, 1996, along with the adjustment data for the two months ended December 31, 1996, are shown in the work sheet that you began preparing at the end of Chapter 3.

Instructions

1. Complete the ten-column work sheet for Music A La Mode.
2. Prepare an income statement, a statement of owner's equity, and a balance sheet. (*Note:* Julian Felipe made investments in Music A La Mode on November 1 and December 1, 1996.)
3. Journalize and post the adjusting entries, inserting balances in the accounts affected.
4. Add the income summary account (#33) to the ledger of Music A La Mode. Journalize and post the closing entries. Indicate closed accounts by inserting a line in both Balance columns opposite the closing entry.
5. Prepare a post-closing trial balance.

COMPREHENSIVE PROBLEM 1

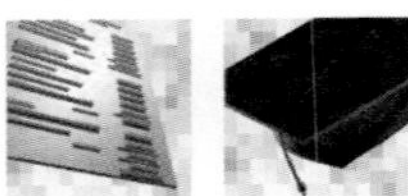

For the past several years, Damon Carnegie has operated a consulting business from his home on a part-time basis. As of September 1, 1997, Damon decided to move to rented quarters and to operate the business, which was to be known as Impact Consulting, on a full-time basis. Impact Consulting entered into the following transactions during September:

Sept. 1. The following assets were received from Damon Carnegie: cash, $5,000; accounts receivable, $1,500; supplies, $1,250; and office equipment, $7,200. There were no liabilities received.
2. Paid three months' rent on a lease rental contract, $2,400.
2. Paid the premiums on property and casualty insurance policies, $1,800.
4. Received cash from clients as an advance payment for services to be performed and recorded them as unearned fees, $3,500.
5. Purchased additional office equipment on account from Payne Company, $1,800.
6. Received cash from clients on account, $800.
10. Paid cash for a newspaper advertisement, $120.
11. Paid Payne Company for part of the debt incurred on September 5, $900.
12. Recorded services performed on account for the period September 1–12, $1,200.
13. Paid part-time receptionist for two weeks' salary, $400.
17. Recorded cash from cash clients for fees earned during the first half of September, $2,100.
18. Paid cash for supplies, $750.
20. Recorded services performed on account for the period September 13–20, $1,100.
24. Recorded cash from cash clients for fees earned for the period September 17–24, $1,850.
25. Received cash from clients on account, $1,300.
27. Paid part-time receptionist for two weeks' salary, $400.
29. Paid telephone bill for September, $130.
30. Paid electricity bill for September, $200.
30. Recorded cash from cash clients for fees earned for the period September 25–30, $850.
30. Recorded services performed on account for the remainder of September, $500.
30. Damon withdrew $1,000 for personal use.

Instructions

1. Journalize each transaction in a two-column journal, referring to the following chart of accounts in selecting the accounts to be debited and credited. (Do not insert the account numbers in the journal at this time.)

11 Cash	31 Damon Carnegie, Capital
12 Accounts Receivable	32 Damon Carnegie, Drawing
14 Supplies	41 Fees Earned
15 Prepaid Rent	51 Salary Expense
16 Prepaid Insurance	52 Rent Expense
18 Office Equipment	53 Supplies Expense
19 Accumulated Depreciation	54 Depreciation Expense
21 Accounts Payable	55 Insurance Expense
22 Salaries Payable	59 Miscellaneous Expense
23 Unearned Fees	

2. Post the journal to a ledger of four-column accounts.
3. Prepare a trial balance as of September 30, 1997, on a ten-column work sheet, listing all the accounts in the order given in the ledger. Complete the work sheet, using the following adjustment data:
   a. Insurance expired during September is $150.
   b. Supplies on hand on September 30 are $1,320.
   c. Depreciation of office equipment for September is $250.
   d. Accrued receptionist salary on September 30 is $100.
   e. Rent expired during September is $800.
   f. Unearned fees on September 30 are $1,100.

4. Prepare an income statement, a statement of owner's equity, and a balance sheet.
5. Journalize and post the adjusting entries.
6. Journalize and post the closing entries. (Income Summary is account #33 in the chart of accounts.) Indicate closed accounts by inserting a line in both Balance columns opposite the closing entry.
7. Prepare a post-closing trial balance.

CASES

CASE 4–1

Visual Co.

Classifying account receivable

Visual Co. is a graphics arts design consulting firm. Joel Pazer, its treasurer and vice-president of finance, has prepared a classified balance sheet as of March 31, 1997, the end of its fiscal year. This balance sheet will be submitted with Visual's loan application to Metro Trust & Savings Bank.

In the Current Assets section of the balance sheet, Joel reported a $30,000 receivable from Susan Eisenberg, the president of Visual, as a trade account receivable. Susan borrowed the money from Visual Co. in February 1996 for a down payment on a new home. She has orally assured Joel that she will pay off the account receivable within the next year. Joel reported the $30,000 in the same manner on the preceding year's balance sheet.

Evaluate whether it is ethical for Joel Pazer to prepare the March 31, 1997 balance sheet in the manner indicated above.

CASE 4–2

Ecological Supplies Co.

Financial statements

The following is an excerpt from a telephone conversation between Janice Sequoia, president of Ecological Supplies Co., and Fred Spruce, who is owner of Cameo Employment Co.

Janice: Fred, you're going to have to do a better job of finding me a new computer programmer. That last guy was great at programming, but he didn't have any common sense.

Fred: What do you mean? The guy had a master's degree with straight A's.

Janice: Yes, well, last month he developed a new financial reporting system. He said we could do away with manually preparing a work sheet and financial statements. The computer would automatically generate our financial statements with "a push of a button."

Fred: So what's the big deal? Sounds to me like it would save you time and effort.

Janice: Right! The balance sheet showed a minus for supplies!

Fred: Minus supplies? How can that be?

Janice: That's what I asked.

Fred: So, what did he say?

Janice: Well, after he checked the program, he said that it must be right. The minuses were greater than the pluses. . .

Fred: Didn't he know that supplies can't have a credit balance—it must have a debit balance?

Janice: He asked me what a debit and credit were.

Fred: I see your point.

1. Comment on (a) the desirability of computerizing Ecological Supplies Co.'s financial reporting system, (b) the elimination of the work sheet in a computerized accounting system, and (c) the computer programmer's lack of accounting knowledge.
2. Explain to the programmer why supplies could not have a credit balance.

CASE 4–3

Hershey Foods Corporation

Financial analysis

The ability of a business to meet its financial obligations (debts) as they come due is called solvency. There are many ways in which financial statement data can be analyzed to provide insight into the solvency of a business. One financial measure that relates to a business's ability to pay its debts is working capital. Working capital is the excess of the current assets of a business over its current liabilities, as follows:

Working capital = Current assets – Current liabilities

Working capital is especially useful in making monthly or other period-to-period comparisons for a company.

1. Determine the working capital for Hershey Foods Corporation as of December 31, 1993 and 1992.
2. What conclusions concerning the company's ability to meets its financial obligations can you draw from these data?

CASE 4–4
No-Pest
Financial statements

Assume that you recently accepted a position with the First Union National Bank as an assistant loan officer. As one of your first duties, you have been assigned the responsibility of evaluating a loan request for $50,000 from No-Pest, a small sole proprietorship. In support of the loan application, Nancy Roach, owner, submitted the shown "Statement of Accounts" (trial balance) for the first year of operations ended December 31, 1997.

No-Pest
Statement of Accounts
December 31, 1997

Cash	4,120	
Billings Due from Others	8,740	
Supplies (chemicals, etc.)	14,950	
Trucks	32,750	
Equipment	26,150	
Amounts Owed to Others		5,700
Investment in Business		47,500
Service Revenue		107,650
Wages Expense	60,100	
Utilities Expense	6,900	
Rent Expense	4,800	
Insurance Expense	1,400	
Other Expenses	940	
	160,850	160,850

1. Explain to Nancy Roach why a set of financial statements (income statement, statement of owner's equity, and balance sheet) would be useful to you in evaluating the loan request.
2. In discussing the "Statement of Accounts" with Nancy Roach, you discovered that the accounts had not been adjusted at December 31. Through analysis of the "Statement of Accounts," indicate possible adjusting entries that might be necessary before an accurate set of financial statements could be prepared.
3. Assuming that an accurate set of financial statements will be submitted by Nancy Roach in a few days, what other considerations or information would you require before making a decision on the loan request?

ANSWERS TO SELF-EXAMINATION QUESTIONS

1. **C** The drawing account, M. E. Jones, Drawing (answer C), would be extended to the Balance Sheet columns of the work sheet. Utilities Expense (answer A), Rent Income (answer B), and Miscellaneous Expense (answer D) would all be extended to the Income Statement columns of the work sheet.
2. **D** Cash or other assets that are expected to be converted to cash or sold or used up within one year or less, through the normal operations of the business, are classified as current assets on the balance sheet. Accounts Receivable (answer D) is a current asset, since it will normally be converted to cash within one year. Office Equipment (answer A), Land (answer B), and Accumulated Depreciation (answer C) are all reported in the plant asset section of the balance sheet.
3. **B** The entry to close the owner's drawing account is to debit the owner's capital account and credit the drawing account (answer B).
4. **D** Since all revenue and expense accounts are closed at the end of the period, Fees Earned (answer A), Wages Expense (answer B), and Rent Expense (answer C) would all be closed to Income Summary. Accumulated Depreciation (answer D) is a contra asset account that is not closed.
5. **B** Since the post-closing trial balance includes only balance sheet accounts (all of the revenue, expense, and drawing accounts are closed), Cash (answer A), Accumulated Depreciation (answer C), and J. C. Smith, Capital (answer D) would appear on the post-closing trial balance. Fees Earned (answer B) is a temporary account that is closed prior to the preparation of the post-closing trial balance.

PART TWO

Advanced Accounting Systems

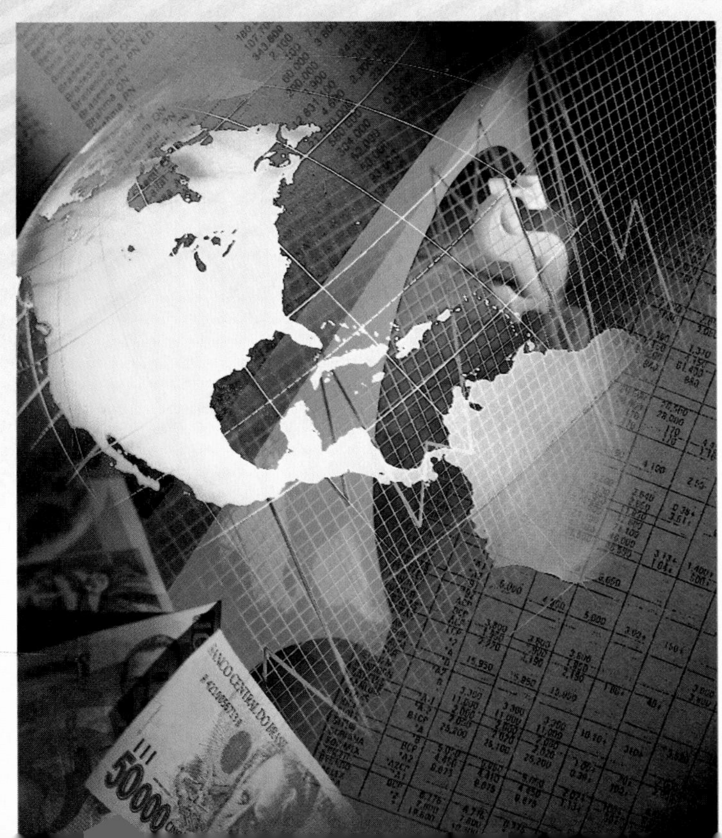

5 Accounting Systems, Internal Controls, and Special Journals

YOU AND ACCOUNTING

Controls are a part of your everyday life. At one extreme, laws are used to govern your behavior. However, you are also affected by many informal controls. For example, professors use exams as a control to verify that you have studied the material. A college or university may use SAT scores as a control to verify a minimum level of academic knowledge prior to your being accepted as a student. Banks give you a personal identification number (PIN) as a control to prevent unauthorized access to your cash from an automated teller machine. Dairies use "freshness dating" on their milk containers as a control to prevent you from buying soured milk.

Just as there are many examples of controls throughout society, businesses must also implement controls to help guide the behavior of their employees toward enterprise objectives. This is one aspect of accounting systems that we will discuss in this chapter.

In the previous chapter, we discussed completing the accounting cycle and preparing financial statements for Computer King. This is a major part of the accounting system of a business. In this chapter, we will discuss controls that can be used to provide assurance about the reliability of these statements. We will apply the principles of accounting system design to manual systems, using special journals and subsidiary ledgers. We will then conclude the chapter by describing the basic design elements of a computer-based accounting system.

After studying this chapter, you should be able to:

Objective 1
Describe the basic principles of accounting systems.

Objective 2
List and describe the three phases of accounting systems installation and revision.

Objective 3
List the three objectives of internal control and define and give examples of the five elements of an internal control framework.

Objective 4
Journalize and post transactions, using subsidiary ledgers and the following special journals:

Revenue journal
Cash receipts journal
Purchases journal
Cash payments journal

Objective 5
Describe and give examples of additional subsidiary ledgers and modified special journals.

Objective 6
Describe the basic features of a computerized accounting system.

Principles of Accounting Systems

Objective 1
Describe the basic principles of accounting systems.

The methods and procedures for recording and reporting financial information make up a business's **accounting system**. The accounting system for most businesses, however, is more complex than we have illustrated in the preceding chapters. One reason for this complexity is that the accounting system is uniquely designed for a business because of differences in management's information needs, the type and number of transactions to be recorded, and the information needs of external users of financial statements. For example, how would an accounting system for a law firm differ from that for a college or university? The accounting system for a law firm would be profit-oriented and would emphasize fees earned and expenses incurred. The accounting system for a college or university would be non-profit-oriented and would emphasize the budgeting of cash receipts and payments. Accounting systems will also vary, depending on whether a business uses a manual system or a computerized system. However, the basic principles that we discuss in the following paragraphs are applicable to all types of systems.

COST-BENEFIT BALANCE

An accounting system must be designed to meet the specific information needs of a business. However, providing information is costly. Thus, a major consideration in designing an accounting system is balancing the benefits against the cost of the information. In general, the benefits should be at least equal to the cost of producing the information.

EFFECTIVE REPORTS

To be effective, the reports generated by an accounting system must be prepared in a timely, clear, and concise manner. When these reports are prepared, the needs and knowledge of the user should be considered. For example, managers may need a variety of detailed reports for planning and controlling operations on a daily or weekly basis. In contrast, regulatory agencies such as the Securities and Exchange Commission and the Internal Revenue Service often require uniform reports at established intervals, such as quarterly or yearly.

ABILITY TO ADAPT TO FUTURE NEEDS

Businesses operate in a changing environment. This environment may include changes beyond the control of a business, such as new government regulations, changes in accounting principles, or changes in computer technology. An accounting system must be able to adapt to the changing information needs in such an environment. For example, regulatory agencies often change the information and reports they require of businesses.

Accounting systems reflect the organizational structure and the information needs of individuals within the business. As individuals or lines of authority and responsibility within a business change, the accounting system must also adapt and change. To be effective, the accounting system must support all levels of management.

ADEQUATE INTERNAL CONTROLS

An accounting system provides information that management reports to owners, creditors, and other interested parties. In addition, the system should aid management in planning and controlling operations. The detailed policies and procedures used to direct operations toward desired goals, ensure accurate financial reports, and ensure compliance with applicable laws and regulations are called **internal controls**. The general principles for an adequate internal control structure are discussed later in this chapter.

Accounting Systems Installation and Revision

Objective 2
List and describe the three phases of accounting systems installation and revision.

Designing and installing an accounting system for a business requires a thorough knowledge of the business's operations. In addition, accounting systems must be continually reviewed for possible revisions in order to keep pace with the changing information needs of businesses. For example, some areas of the system, such as the types and design of forms and the number and titles of accounts, continually change as the business grows and adapts to its environment. This process of installing or changing an accounting system is made up of three phases: (1) analysis, (2) design, and (3) implementation.

SYSTEMS ANALYSIS

Systems analysis usually begins with a review of the organizational structure and the job descriptions of personnel. This review is followed by a study of the forms, records, procedures, processing methods, and reports used by the business. The source of such information is usually found in the firm's *Systems Manual*.

The goal of systems analysis is to determine information needs, the sources of information, any weaknesses in the procedures, and the data processing methods being used. In addition to analyzing and reviewing the current system, the systems analyst should also assess management's plans for changes in operations (volume, products, territories, etc.). Such changes usually require changes in the current system.

SYSTEMS DESIGN

Accounting systems are changed as a result of the kind of systems analysis described above. Such changes may involve only minor changes from the existing system, such as revision of a particular form and the related procedures and processing methods. In contrast, a complete revision of the entire system may be required. Many companies are completely revising their systems to be more integrated. For example, Oracle, SAP, and D & B software companies have developed integrated systems in which data are entered only once into a database that is shared by all system components. A **database** contains the financial and nonfinancial data needed by a business to satisfy its information needs.

System designers must have a general knowledge of different accounting systems and methods of processing transactions, both manual and computerized. A successful systems design depends upon the creativity, imagination, and ability of the systems designer to evaluate alternatives. The basic principles of accounting systems are also necessary for a successful design.

SYSTEMS IMPLEMENTATION

The final phase of systems installation is to carry out, or implement, the systems design. New or revised forms, records, procedures, and equipment must be installed, and any that are no longer useful must be withdrawn. All personnel responsible for operating the system must be carefully trained and supervised until the system is fully operational.

Major revisions of a system, such as changing from a centralized computer system to a decentralized, micro-computer-based data processing system, must be carefully planned. Managers must have reasonable assurance that the new system will provide complete and accurate information. Therefore, many companies implement new or revised systems in stages over a period of time. Weaknesses and conflicting or unnecessary elements in the design are easier to detect when the implementation is gradual rather than all at once. In addition, this approach reduces the chances that essential operating information will be unavailable during the systems implementation.

Another approach to new system implementation is to conduct a parallel test. In a parallel test, the old and new systems are run at the same time. The outputs of both systems are then compared. Parallel tests are costly, since two systems are being run. However, many managers believe this additional cost is worth the assurance that the new system is complete and accurate. In addition, this approach guarantees that essential operating information will be available from the old system if the new system does not function properly.

ACCOUNTING SYSTEMS, PROFIT MEASUREMENT, AND MANAGEMENT

A Greek restaurant owner in Canada had his own system of accounting. He kept his accounts payable in a cigar box on the left-hand side of his cash register, his daily cash returns in the cash register, and his receipts for paid bills in another cigar box on the right.

When his youngest son graduated as an accountant, he was appalled by his father's primitive methods. "I don't know how you can run a business that way," he said. "How do you know what your profits are?"

"Well, son," the father replied, "when I got off the boat from Greece, I had nothing but the pants I was wearing. Today, your brother is a doctor. You are an accountant. Your sister is a speech therapist. Your mother and I have a nice car, a city house, and a country home. We have a good business, and everything is paid for...."

"So, you add all that together, subtract the pants, and there's your profit!"

Internal Control

Objective 3
List the three objectives of internal control and define and give examples of the five elements of an internal control framework.

Managing a lawn care business would require the use of internal controls to guide its operations and achieve desired goals.

One of the key aspects of systems analysis, design, and implementation is a business's internal control. Businesses use internal controls to guide their operations. For example, assume that you own and manage a lawn care service during the summer months. Assume further that your business employs several teams, each with a vehicle and lawn equipment that you provide. What are some of the issues you would face as a manager in controlling the operations of this business? Below are some examples.

- Lawn care needs to be provided on schedule.
- The quality of lawn care services must meet customer expectations.
- Employees must provide work for the hours they are paid.
- Lawn care equipment should be used for business purposes only.
- Customers must be billed and bills collected for services rendered.
- Vehicles should be used for business purposes only.

How would you address some of these control issues? You could, for example, have "surprise" inspections by arriving on site at random times to verify that the teams are working on schedule. You could develop a schedule at the beginning of each day and then inspect the work at the end of the day to verify its completion and quality. You could require the work teams to return the vehicles and equipment to a central location to prevent unauthorized use. You could bill customers after you inspected the work, and you could monitor collection of all receivables. You could keep a log of odometer readings at the end of each day to verify that the vehicle has not been used for "joy riding." All of these are examples of internal control.

OBJECTIVES OF INTERNAL CONTROL

The objectives of internal control are to provide reasonable assurance that:

1. operations are managed to achieve desired goals.
2. financial reports are accurate.
3. laws and regulations are complied with.[1]

Internal control can prevent loss of resources, provide information about how the business is performing, and help guide it in the planned direction. Unfortunately, internal control cannot eliminate all bad decisions or unexpected events. Internal control provides managers with assurance that their business is in compliance with external financial reporting standards and applicable laws and regulations. Examples of such standards and laws include generally accepted accounting principles (GAAP), environmental regulations, contract terms, and safety regulations.

ELEMENTS OF INTERNAL CONTROL

How does management achieve internal control? Internal control consists of five major elements: (1) the control environment, (2) risk assessment, (3) control procedures, (4) monitoring, and (5) information and communication.[2] These elements form the **internal control framework** for achieving the three objectives identified above.

[1] The source for the material in this section is *Internal Control—Integrated Framework* by the Committee of Sponsoring Organizations of the Treadway Commission (COSO). This 1992 document provides a professionally sponsored framework for internal control.
[2] Ibid., pp. 12–14.

The internal control framework is illustrated in Exhibit 1. In this exhibit, the elements of internal control form a pyramid. The base of the pyramid is the business's control environment, upon which the remaining elements are built. Information and communication occur between each element and management, who is responsible for achieving the three internal control objectives. In the following paragraphs, we discuss each of these elements.

Exhibit 1
Elements of Internal Control

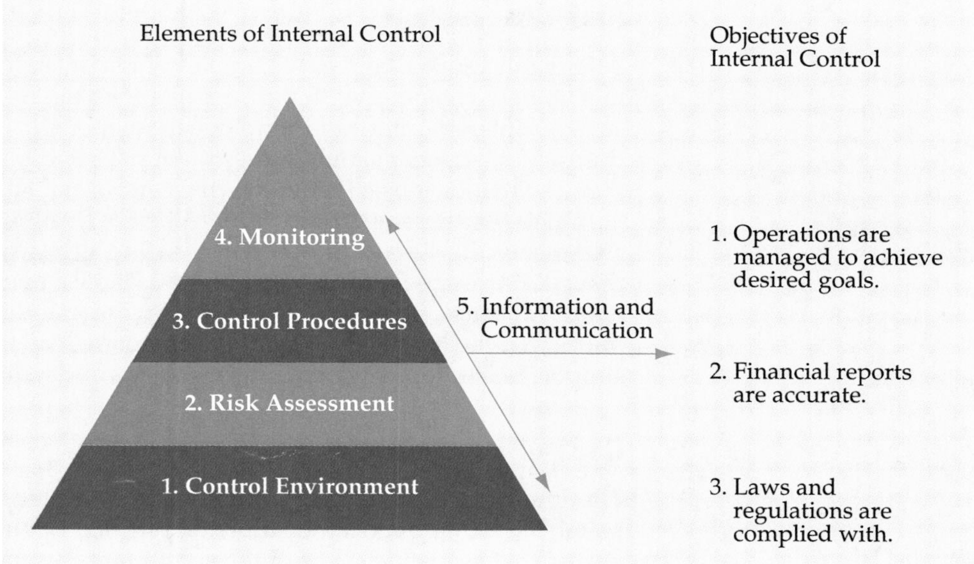

Control Environment

A business's control environment is the overall attitude of management and employees about the importance of controls. One of the factors that influences the control environment is management's philosophy and operating style. A management that overemphasizes operating goals may indirectly encourage employees to overstate or misreport operating data. For example, in the early 1990s, Sears had a policy of paying bonuses to its automobile department managers, based on the amount of work provided. This bonus arrangement created incentives for service department managers to overstate the amount of service work required by customers. Thus, customers were being charged for work that they did not need. A lawsuit was initiated in California and caused Sears to suffer significant negative publicity from this incident and to eliminate the bonus policy nationwide.

A management that often deviates from established control policies and procedures may also be indicating to employees that controls are not important. For example, if management routinely ignores a policy requiring that safety glasses be worn in the plant, it may cause other employees to interpret the policy as "optional," thereby creating an unsafe plant environment. On the other hand, a management that emphasizes the importance of controls and encourages adherence to control policies will create an effective control environment.

Another factor that influences the control environment is the business's organizational structure, which is the framework for planning and controlling operations. For example, a department store chain might organize each of its stores as relatively separate business units. Each store manager is given full authority over pricing and other operating activities. In such a structure, each store manager has the responsibility for establishing an effective control environment.

Personnel policies and procedures also affect the control environment. Personnel policies involve the hiring, training, evaluating, compensating, and promoting of employees. The human resource area also includes the development of job descriptions, employee codes of ethics, and conflict-of-interest policies. For example, Teledyne Inc. has developed a code of business conduct that establishes ethical guidelines for governmental contracting, employee hiring and development, environmental management, and international business. Such policies and procedures can enhance the internal control environment if they provide reasonable assurance that only competent, honest employees are hired and retained.

Risk Assessment

All organizations face risks. Examples of risk include changes in customer requirements, new competitive threats, regulatory changes, changes in economic factors such as interest rates, and employee violations of company policies and procedures. Management should assess these risks and take necessary actions to control them, so that the objectives of internal control can be achieved.

Once risks are identified, they can be analyzed to estimate their significance, to assess their likelihood of occurring, and to determine actions that will minimize them. For example, the manager of a warehouse operation may analyze the risk of employee back injuries, which might give rise to lawsuits. If the manager determines that the risk is significant, the company may take action by purchasing back support braces for its warehouse employees and requiring them to wear the braces.

Control Procedures

The importance of control procedures is indicated by the results of a survey of members of the American Institute of Certified Public Accountants. This survey reported that as many as 38% of the accountants responding witnessed fraud during the past year.[3]

Control procedures are established to provide reasonable assurance that enterprise goals will be achieved and fraud will be prevented. In the following paragraphs, we will briefly discuss control procedures that can be integrated throughout the accounting system.

COMPETENT PERSONNEL, ROTATING DUTIES, AND MANDATORY VACATIONS. The successful operation of an accounting system requires procedures to ensure that people are able to perform the duties to which they are assigned. Hence, it is necessary that all accounting employees be adequately trained and supervised in performing their jobs. It may also be advisable to rotate clerical personnel periodically from job to job. In addition to increasing their understanding of the system, the knowledge that an employee's work may be performed by others encourages adherence to prescribed procedures. For nonclerical personnel such as managers, mandatory vacations normally are used rather than job rotations. During vacation periods, the relevant job responsibilities are performed by other managers.

Rotating duties and mandating vacations may prevent errors or detect existing errors and fraud. For example, an accounts receivable clerk should be periodically rotated to another job or required to take a vacation. If the clerk steals customers' cash payments, the thefts will likely be discovered when a new clerk bills customers for amounts they have already paid.

ASSIGNING RESPONSIBILITY. If employees are to work efficiently, their responsibilities must be clearly defined. Control procedures should provide assurance that no overlapping or undefined areas of responsibility exist and that employees are held accountable for their responsibilities. For example, if a certain cash register is to be

[3] John P. Rice, et al, "Old Fashioned Fraud Is Alive and Well: Results of a Survey of Practicing CPAs," *CPA Journal*, September 1988, pp. 74–77.

used by two or more salesclerks, the clerks should be assigned separate cash drawers and register keys. In this way, the clerks are held responsible for their individual cash drawers, and a daily proof of cash can be obtained for each clerk.

SEPARATING RESPONSIBILITIES FOR RELATED OPERATIONS. To decrease the possibility of inefficiency, errors, and fraud, responsibility for a sequence of related operations should be divided among two or more persons. For example, the responsibilities for purchasing, receiving, and paying for computer supplies should be divided among three persons or departments. If the same person orders supplies, verifies the receipt of the supplies, and pays the supplier, the following abuses are possible:

1. Orders may be placed on the basis of friendship with a supplier, rather than on price, quality, and other objective factors.
2. The quantity and quality of supplies received may not be verified.
3. Supplies may be stolen by the employee.
4. The validity and accuracy of invoices may be verified carelessly, thus causing the payment of false or inaccurate invoices. For example, it has been estimated that the typical company pays one of every one hundred invoices more than once.[4]

The "checks and balances" provided by dividing responsibilities among various departments requires no duplication of effort. The business documents prepared by one department are designed to coordinate and support those prepared by other departments.

SEPARATING ACCOUNTING, CUSTODY OF ASSETS, AND OPERATIONS. Control policies and procedures should establish the responsibilities for various business activities. To reduce the possibility of errors and fraud, the following functions should be separated:

1. Accounting for the business's transactions.
2. Custody of the firm's assets.
3. Engaging in the firm's operating activities.

When these functions are separated, the accounting records serve as an independent check on the individuals who have custody of the assets and who engage in the business operations. For example, the employees entrusted with handling cash receipts from credit customers should not record cash receipts in the accounting records. To do so would allow employees to borrow or steal cash and hide the theft in the records. Likewise, if those engaged in operating activities also record the results of operations, they could distort the accounting reports to show favorable results. For example, a store manager whose year-end bonus is based upon operating profits might be tempted to record fictitious sales in order to receive a larger bonus.

When responsibilities for the functions above are not separated, a company is more vulnerable to employee theft. For example, one individual, who called himself David Shelton, was hired as a bookkeeper at a number of firms, where he stole thousands of dollars and then disappeared. Shelton's main method was to steal cash receipts, while changing the books to hide the shortage. Separating the cash-handling function from the bookkeeping function would have reduced the likelihood of this type of theft.[5]

PROOFS AND SECURITY MEASURES. Proofs and security measures should be used to safeguard business assets and ensure reliable accounting data. This control procedure applies to many different techniques, such as authorization, approval, and

[4] *Checkers, Simon, and Rosner—Client Report*, Spring 1994 (Issue 3).

[5] J. R. Emshwiller, "Looking for a New Bookkeeper? Beware of this One," *Wall Street Journal*, April 19, 1994, pp. B1–B2.

reconciliation procedures. For example, employees who travel on company business could be required to obtain a department manager's approval on a travel request form.

Other examples of control procedures include the use of bank accounts and other measures to ensure the safety of cash and other valuable documents. Using a cash register that displays the amount recorded for each sale and provides for the customer a printed receipt can be an effective part of the internal control structure. An all-night convenience store could use the following security measures to deter robberies:

1. Locate the cash register near the door, so that it is fully visible from outside the store; have two employees work late hours, or employ a security guard.
2. Deposit cash in the bank daily before 5 p.m.
3. Keep only small amounts of cash on hand after 5 p.m. by depositing excess cash in a store safe that can't be opened by employees on duty.
4. Install cameras and alarm systems.

Companies may obtain insurance to protect against losses from employee fraud. Such insurance, called a fidelity bond, normally requires background checks on all employees covered. If a claim is paid, insurance companies normally take legal action against the employees responsible. Such legal action tends to deter employee fraud and enhances the internal control structure.

Monitoring

Monitoring the internal control system locates deficiencies and improves control effectiveness. The internal control system may be monitored through either ongoing efforts by management or separate evaluations. Ongoing monitoring efforts may include observing both employee behavior and warning signs from the accounting system.[6] The following employee activities may be clues to dishonest behavior:

1. Abrupt change in lifestyle (without winning the lottery).
2. Close social relationships with suppliers.
3. Refusal to take vacation.
4. Frequent borrowing from other employees.
5. Excessive use of alcohol or drugs.

The following warning signs from the accounting system may indicate the presence of fraud:

1. Missing documents or gaps in transaction numbers (could mean documents are being used for fraudulent transactions).
2. An unusual increase in customer refunds (they may be phony).
3. Discrepancies between daily cash receipts and bank deposits (could mean receipts are pocketed before being deposited).
4. Sudden increase in slow payments (employee may be pocketing the payment).
5. Backlog in recording transactions (possibly an attempt to delay detection of fraud).

Separate evaluations are generally performed periodically when there are major changes in strategy, senior management, corporate structure, or operations. In large businesses, internal auditors who are independent of operations normally are responsible for monitoring the internal control system. In addition, external auditors also evaluate internal control as a normal part of their annual financial statement audit.

Often the internal auditor's review will be noted in a company's annual report, as shown in the following excerpt from the management letter to **Rose's Stores Inc.'s** stockholders:

[6] Edwin C. Bliss, "Employee Theft," *Boardroom Reports*, July 15, 1994, pp. 5–6.

To meet its responsibilities with respect to financial information, management maintains and enforces internal accounting policies, procedures, and controls which are designed to provide reasonable assurance that assets are safeguarded and that transactions are properly recorded and executed in accordance with management's authorization. The concept of reasonable assurance is based on the recognition that the cost of controls should not exceed the expected benefits. Management maintains an internal audit function and an internal control function which are responsible for evaluating the adequacy and application of financial and operating controls and for testing compliance with Company policies and procedures.

Information and Communication

Information and communication are essential elements of an organization's internal control. Information about the control environment, risk assessment, control procedures, and monitoring are needed by management to guide operations and ensure compliance with reporting, legal, and regulatory requirements. For example, the management of CSX Transportation, a large eastern U.S. railroad, uses a weekly on-the-job injury report to assess employee safety.

Information can also be acquired from sources outside of the firm. Management can use this information to assess external standards, laws, regulations, events, and conditions that impact decision making and external reporting. For example, management uses information from the Financial Accounting Standards Board (FASB) to assess the impact of possible changes in reporting standards.

USING ACCOUNTING TO UNDERSTAND BUSINESS

Internal Control Failure	*What Happened When Internal Control Failed?*
Recording cash received as revenue, even though future services are required.	Jiffy Lube franchises 10-minute automobile oil change centers. Up-front fees paid by franchisees for these centers were recorded immediately by Jiffy Lube as revenue, even though future services to the franchisees were required. The company was forced to restate earnings, causing a 75% reduction in previously reported profits. The stock price dropped by approximately 90% during this period.
Recording revenue before it is earned.	Datapoint Corporation, a computer company, recorded revenue before it had been earned. In 1981, the Securities and Exchange Commission charged the company with overstating earnings. This event began a long slide in the company's stock price from $120 per share in 1981 to around $4 per share in 1990.
Improperly recording expenses as assets.	DeLaurentis Entertainment Group (DEG), a movie production company, improperly recorded $1.3 million of selling, administrative, and interest costs as assets rather than expenses. This caused the income to be grossly overstated. DEG agreed to settle a government case against it by preparing and adhering to new internal control policies.
Recording a refund from a supplier as revenue.	L.A. Gear manufactures and sells athletic sportswear. The SEC charged L.A. Gear with improperly recording $4.7 million of cash received from suppliers for returned merchandise as revenue. The company was forced to restate its reported income and record a loss. As a result, L.A. Gear's stock price decreased from $50 to $20 per share in one year's time.

The examples and categories are from Howard M. Schmilit's book, *Financial Shenanigans*, McGraw-Hill, Inc., New York, 1993.

Subsidiary Ledgers and Special Journals

Objective 4
Journalize and post transactions, using subsidiary ledgers and the following special journals:

Revenue journal
Cash receipts journal
Purchases journal
Cash payments journal

In preceding chapters, all transactions for Computer King were manually recorded in an all-purpose (two-column) journal. The journal entries were then posted individually to the accounts in the ledger. Such manual accounting systems are simple to use and easy to understand. Manually kept records may serve a business reasonably well when the amount of data collected, stored, and used by a business is relatively small. For a large business with a large database, however, such manual processing is too costly and too time-consuming. For example, a large company such as AT&T has millions of long distance telephone fees earned on account with millions of customers daily. Each telephone fee on account requires an entry debiting Accounts Receivable and crediting Fees Earned. In addition, a record of each customer's receivable must be kept. Clearly, a simple manual system would not serve the business needs of AT&T.

When a business has a large number of similar transactions, using an all-purpose journal is inefficient and impractical. In such cases, subsidiary ledgers and special journals are useful. In addition, the manual system can be supplemented or replaced by a computerized system. Although we will illustrate the manual use of subsidiary ledgers and special journals, the basic principles described in the following paragraphs also apply to a computerized accounting system.

SUBSIDIARY LEDGERS

An accounting system should be designed to provide information on the amounts due from various customers (accounts receivable) and amounts owed to various creditors (accounts payable). A separate account for each customer and creditor could be added to the ledger. However, as the number of customers and creditors increases, the ledger becomes unwieldy when a separate account for each customer and creditor is included.

When there are a large number of individual accounts with a common characteristic, they can be grouped together in a separate ledger called a **subsidiary ledger**. The primary ledger, which contains all of the balance sheet and income statement accounts, is then called the **general ledger**. Each subsidiary ledger is represented in the general ledger by a summarizing account, called a **controlling account**. The sum of the balances of the accounts in a subsidiary ledger must equal the balance of the related controlling account. Thus, you may think of a subsidiary ledger as a secondary ledger that supports a controlling account in the general ledger.

The individual accounts with customers are arranged in alphabetical order in a subsidiary ledger called the **accounts receivable subsidiary ledger** or **customers ledger**. The controlling account in the general ledger that summarizes the debits and credits to the individual customer accounts is Accounts Receivable. The individual accounts with creditors are arranged in alphabetical order in a subsidiary ledger called the **accounts payable subsidiary ledger** or **creditors ledger**. The related controlling account in the general ledger is Accounts Payable. The relationship between the general ledger and these subsidiary ledgers is illustrated in Exhibit 2.

SPECIAL JOURNALS

One method of processing data more efficiently in a manual accounting system is to expand the all-purpose two-column journal to a multicolumn journal. Each column in a multicolumn journal is used only for recording transactions that affect a certain

Exhibit 2
General Ledger and Subsidiary Ledgers

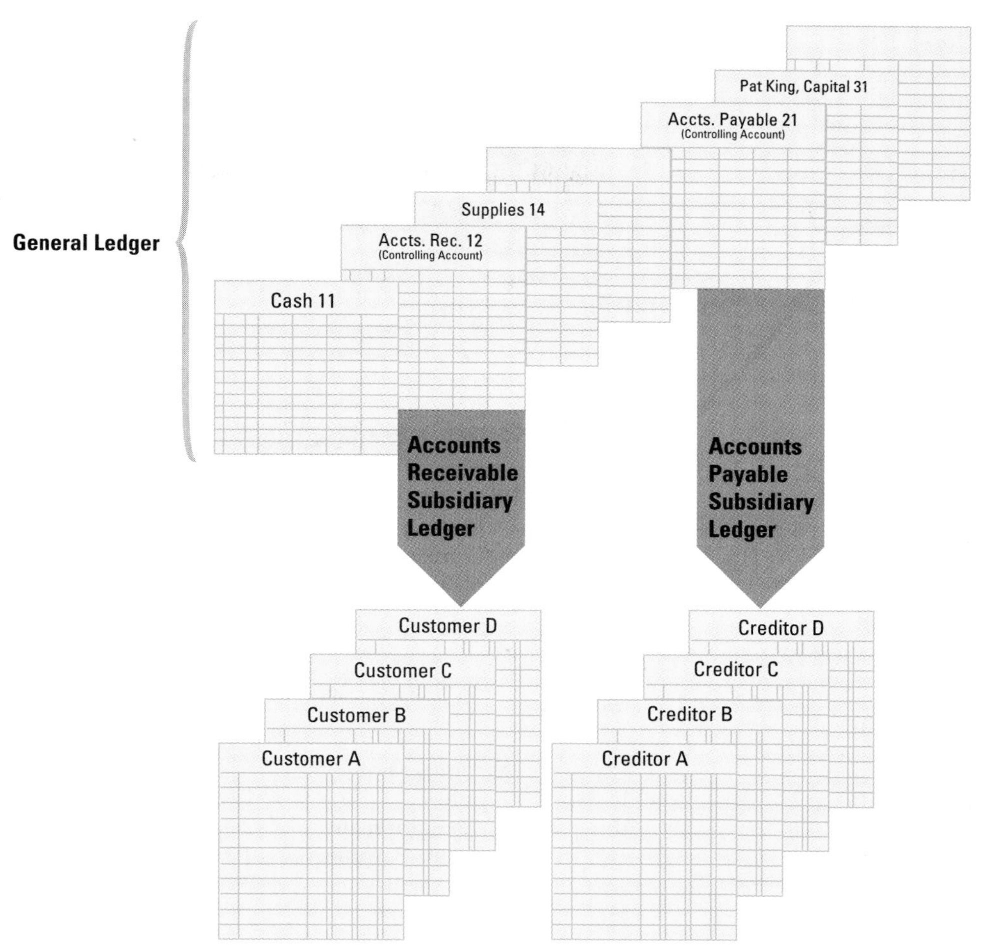

account. For example, a special column could be used only for recording debits to the cash account, and another special column could be used only for recording credits to the cash account. The addition of the two special columns would eliminate the writing of *Cash* in the journal for every receipt and payment of cash. Also, there would be no need to post each individual debit and credit to the cash account. Instead, the *Cash Dr.* and *Cash Cr.* columns could be totaled periodically and only the totals posted. In a similar way, special columns could be added for recording credits to Fees Earned, debits and credits to Accounts Receivable and Accounts Payable, and for other entries that are often repeated.

An all-purpose multicolumn journal may be adequate for a small business that has many transactions of a similar nature. However, a journal that has many columns for recording many different types of transactions is impractical for larger businesses.

The next logical extension of the accounting system is to replace the single multicolumn journal with several **special journals**. Each special journal is designed to be used for recording a single kind of transaction that occurs frequently. For example, since most businesses have many transactions in which cash is paid out, they will likely use a special journal for recording cash payments. Likewise, they will use another special journal for recording cash receipts.

The format and number of special journals that a business uses depends upon the nature of the business. A business that renders services to customers on account might use a special journal designed for recording only revenue from services provided on credit. On the other hand, a business that does not give credit would have no need for such a journal. In other cases, record-keeping costs may be reduced by using supporting documents as special journals.

The transactions that occur most often in a medium-sized service business and the special journals in which they are recorded are as follows:

Rendering of services *on account*	**recorded in**	Revenue (sales) journal
Receipt of cash from *any* source	**recorded in**	Cash receipts journal
Purchase of items *on account*	**recorded in**	Purchases journal
Payment of cash for *any* purpose	**recorded in**	Cash payments journal

The all-purpose two-column journal, called the general journal or simply the **journal**, can be used for entries that do not fit into any of the special journals. For example, adjusting and closing entries are recorded in the general journal.

In the following sections, we illustrate the use of special journals and subsidiary ledgers for Computer King. We will use a minimum number of transactions in order to simplify the illustration. We will assume that Computer King had the following selected general ledger balances on March 1, 1997:

Account Number	*Account*	*Balance*
11	Cash	$6,200
12	Accounts Receivable	3,400
14	Supplies	2,500
18	Office Equipment	2,500
21	Accounts Payable	1,230
52	Rent Expense	3,200
54	Utilities Expense	2,000

REVENUE JOURNAL

The revenue journal is used only for recording **fees earned on account.** *If there were cash fees earned, they would be recorded in the cash receipts journal.* We will compare the use of a revenue journal with a general journal by assuming that Computer King recorded the following revenue transactions in a general journal:

1997				
Mar.	2	Accounts Receivable—Handler Co.	2,200	
		Fees Earned		2,200
	6	Accounts Receivable—Jordan Co.	1,750	
		Fees Earned		1,750
	18	Accounts Receivable—Kenner Co.	2,650	
		Fees Earned		2,650
	27	Accounts Receivable—Handler Co.	3,000	
		Fees Earned		3,000

For these four transactions, Computer King recorded eight account titles and eight amounts. In addition, Computer King made 12 postings to the ledgers—four to Accounts Receivable in the general ledger, four to the accounts receivable subsidiary ledger, and four to Fees Earned in the general ledger. In contrast, these transactions could be recorded more efficiently in a revenue journal as shown in Exhibit 3.

In each revenue transaction, the amount of the debit to Accounts Receivable is the same as the amount of the credit to Fees Earned. Therefore, only a single amount column is necessary. The date, invoice number, customer name, and amount are entered separately for each transaction.

Exhibit 3
Revenue Journal

REVENUE JOURNAL — PAGE 35

	Date		Invoice No.	Account Debited	Post. Ref.	Accts. Rec. Dr. Fees Earned Cr.	
1	1997 Mar.	2	615	Handler Co.		2 2 0 0 00	1
2		6	616	Jordan Co.		1 7 5 0 00	2
3		18	617	Kenner Co.		2 6 5 0 00	3
4		27	618	Handler Co.		3 0 0 0 00	4
5		31				9 6 0 0 00	5

Each transaction recorded in a revenue journal must be posted individually to the customer accounts in the accounts receivable subsidiary ledger. A single monthly total is posted to Accounts Receivable and Fees Earned in the general ledger. The basic procedure of posting from a revenue journal to the accounts receivable subsidiary ledger and the general ledger is shown in Exhibit 4.

The individual amounts in Exhibit 4, such as the $2,200 debit to Handler Co., are posted frequently to the accounts receivable subsidiary ledger. In this way, management has information on the current balance of each customer's account. Since the balances in the customer accounts are usually debit balances, the three-column account form shown in the exhibit is often used.

Exhibit 4
Revenue Journal Postings to Ledgers

REVENUE JOURNAL — PAGE 35

Date		Invoice No.	Account Debited	Post. Ref.	Accts. Rec. Dr. Fees Earned Cr.
1997					
March	2	615	Handler Co.	✓	2,200
	6	616	Jordan Co.	✓	1,750
	18	617	Kenner Co.	✓	2,650
	27	618	Handler Co.	✓	3,000
	31				9,600
					(12) (41)

GENERAL LEDGER

ACCOUNT Accounts Receivable — Account No. 12

Date	Item	Post. Ref.	Dr.	Cr.	Balance Dr.	Balance Cr.
1997						
March 1	Balance	✓			3,400	
31		R35	9,600		13,000	

ACCOUNT Fees Earned — Account No. 41

Date	Item	Post. Ref.	Dr.	Cr.	Balance Dr.	Balance Cr.
1997						
March 31		R35		9,600		9,600

ACCOUNTS RECEIVABLE SUBSIDIARY LEDGER

NAME: Handler Co.

Date	Item	Post. Ref.	Dr.	Cr.	Balance
1997					
March 2		R35	2,200		2,200
27		R35	3,000		5,200

NAME: Jordan Co.

Date	Item	Post. Ref.	Dr.	Cr.	Balance
1997					
March 6		R35	1,750		1,750

NAME: Kenner Co.

Date	Item	Post. Ref.	Dr.	Cr.	Balance
1997					
March 1	Balance	✓			3,400
18		R35	2,650		6,050

The source of the entries posted to the subsidiary ledger is indicated in the Posting Reference column of each account by inserting the letter *R* and the page number of the revenue journal. A check mark (✓) instead of a number is then inserted in the Posting Reference column of the revenue journal, as shown in Exhibit 4.

The customer accounts in the subsidiary ledger are maintained in alphabetical order. They are usually not numbered because the order changes each time a new account is inserted or an old account is removed. If a customer's account has a credit balance, that fact should be indicated by an asterisk or parentheses in the Balance column. When an account's balance is zero, a line may be drawn in the Balance column.

At the end of each month, the amount column of the revenue journal is totaled and ruled. This total is equal to the sum of the month's debits to the individual accounts in the subsidiary ledger. It is posted in the general ledger as a debit to Accounts Receivable and a credit to Fees Earned, as shown in Exhibit 4. The respective account numbers are then inserted below the total in the revenue journal to indicate that the posting is completed, as shown in Exhibit 4. In this way, all of the transactions for fees earned during the month are posted to the general ledger only once—at the end of the month, greatly simplifying the posting process.

CASH RECEIPTS JOURNAL

All transactions that involve the receipt of cash are recorded in a cash receipts journal. Thus, the cash receipts journal has a column entitled *Cash Dr.*, as shown in Exhibit 5. All transactions recorded in the cash receipts journal will involve an entry in the Cash Dr. column. For example, on March 28 Computer King received cash of $2,200 from Handler Co. and entered that amount in the Cash Dr. column.

The kinds of transactions in which cash is received and how often they occur determine the titles of the other columns. For Computer King, the most frequent source of cash is collections from customers. Thus, Computer King's cash receipts journal has an *Accounts Receivable Cr.* column.

The Other Accounts Cr. column in Exhibit 5 is used for recording credits to any account for which there is no special credit column. For example, Computer King received cash on March 1 for rent. Since no special column exists for Rent Income, *Rent Income* is written in the Account Credited column and $400 is entered in the Other Accounts Cr. column.

The flow of data from the cash receipts journal to the ledgers of Computer King is also shown in Exhibit 5. At regular intervals, each amount in the Other Accounts Cr. column is posted to the proper account in the general ledger. The posting is indicated by inserting the account number in the Posting Reference column of the cash receipts journal. The posting reference *CR* and the proper page number are inserted in the Posting Reference columns of the accounts.

The amounts in the Accounts Receivable Cr. column are posted at frequent intervals to the customer accounts in the accounts receivable subsidiary ledger. These customers are identified in the Account Credited column of the cash receipts journal. The posting reference *CR* and the proper page number are inserted in the Posting Reference column of each customer's account. A check mark is placed in the Posting Reference column of the cash receipts journal to show that each amount has been posted. None of the individual amounts in the Cash Dr. column is posted separately.

At the end of the month, all of the amount columns are totaled and ruled. The equality of the debits and credits should be verified. Because each amount in the Other Accounts Cr. column has been posted individually to a general ledger account, a check mark is inserted below the column total to indicate that no further action is needed. The totals of the Accounts Receivable Cr. and Cash Dr. columns are posted to the proper accounts in the general ledger, and their account numbers are inserted below the totals to show that the postings have been completed.

Exhibit 5
Cash Receipts Journal and Postings

CASH RECEIPTS JOURNAL PAGE 14

Date		Account Credited	Post. Ref.	Other Accounts Cr.	Accounts Receivable Cr.	Cash Dr.
1997						
March	1	Rent Income	42	400		400
	19	Kenner Co.	✓		3,400	3,400
	28	Handler Co.	✓		2,200	2,200
	30	Jordan Co.	✓		1,750	1,750
	31			400	7,350	7,750
				(✓)	(12)	(11)

GENERAL LEDGER

ACCOUNT Rent Income — Account No. 42

Date		Item	Post. Ref.	Dr.	Cr.	Balance Dr.	Balance Cr.
1997							
March	1		CR14		400		400

ACCOUNT Accounts Receivable — Account No. 12

Date		Item	Post. Ref.	Dr.	Cr.	Balance Dr.	Balance Cr.
1997							
March	1	Balance	✓			3,400	
	31		R35	9,600		13,000	
	31		CR14		7,350	5,650	

ACCOUNT Cash — Account No. 11

Date		Item	Post. Ref.	Dr.	Cr.	Balance Dr.	Balance Cr.
1997							
March	1	Balance	✓			6,200	
	31		CR14	7,750		13,950	

ACCOUNTS RECEIVABLE SUBSIDIARY LEDGER

NAME: Handler Co.

Date		Item	Post. Ref.	Dr.	Cr.	Balance
1997						
March	2		R35	2,200		2,200
	27		R35	3,000		5,200
	28		CR14		2,200	3,000

NAME: Jordan Co.

Date		Item	Post. Ref.	Dr.	Cr.	Balance
1997						
March	6		R35	1,750		1,750
	30		CR14		1,750	—

NAME: Kenner Co.

Date		Item	Post. Ref.	Dr.	Cr.	Balance
1997						
March	1	Balance	✓			3,400
	18		R35	2,650		6,050
	19		CR14		3,400	2,650

ACCOUNTS RECEIVABLE CONTROL AND SUBSIDIARY LEDGER

After all posting has been completed for the month, the sum of the balances in the accounts receivable subsidiary ledger should be compared with the balance of the accounts receivable controlling account in the general ledger. If the controlling account and the subsidiary ledger do not agree, the error or errors must be located and corrected. The balances of the individual customer accounts may be summarized in a schedule. The total of Computer King's schedule, $5,650, agrees with the balance of its accounts receivable controlling account on March 31, 1997, as shown below.

Accounts Receivable (Controlling Account)		*Computer King Schedule of Accounts Receivable March 31, 1997*	
Balance, March 1, 1997	$3,400	Handler Co.	$3,000
Debit from R35	9,600	Jordan Co.	0
Credit from CR14	(7,350)	Kenner Co.	2,650
Balance, March 31, 1997	$5,650	Total accounts receivable	$5,650

Internal control is enhanced by separating the function of recording credit sales in the revenue journal from recording cash collections in the cash receipts journal. Thus, for example, one person could not hide the embezzlement of cash collections by not recording the original sale.

PURCHASES JOURNAL

The purchases journal is designed for recording all items purchased on account. Thus, the purchases journal has a column entitled **Accounts Payable Cr.** *Cash purchases are recorded in the cash payments journal.* The purchases journal used by Computer King, along with postings to the accounts payable subsidiary ledger and general ledger accounts, is shown in Exhibit 6.

The purchases journal also includes special columns for recording debits to accounts most often affected. Since Computer King makes frequent debits to its supplies account, a Supplies Dr. column is identified for these transactions.

Exhibit 6
Purchases Journal and Postings

PURCHASES JOURNAL **PAGE 11**

Date	Account Credited	Post. Ref.	Accounts Payable Cr.	Supplies Dr.	Other Accounts Dr.	Post. Ref.	Amount
1997							
March 3	Howard Supplies	✓	600	600			
7	Donnelly Supplies	✓	420	420			
12	Jewett Business Systems	✓	2,800		Office Equipment	18	2,800
19	Donnelly Supplies	✓	1,450	1,450			
27	Howard Supplies	✓	960	960			
31			6,230	3,430			2,800
			(21)	(14)			(✓)

GENERAL LEDGER

ACCOUNT Accounts Payable **Account No. 21**

Date	Item	Post. Ref.	Dr.	Cr.	Balance
1997					
March 1	Balance	✓			1,230
31		P11		6,230	7,460

ACCOUNT Supplies **Account No. 14**

Date	Item	Post. Ref.	Dr.	Cr.	Balance
1997					
March 1	Balance	✓			2,500
31		P11	3,430		5,930

ACCOUNT Office Equipment **Account No. 18**

Date	Item	Post. Ref.	Dr.	Cr.	Balance
1997					
March 1	Balance	✓			2,500
12		P11	2,800		5,300

ACCOUNTS PAYABLE SUBSIDIARY LEDGER

NAME: Donnelly Supplies

Date	Item	Post. Ref.	Dr.	Cr.	Balance
1997					
March 7		P11		420	420
19		P11		1,450	1,870

NAME: Grayco Supplies

Date	Item	Post. Ref.	Dr.	Cr.	Balance
1997					
March 1	Balance	✓			1,230

NAME: Howard Supplies

Date	Item	Post. Ref.	Dr.	Cr.	Balance
1997					
March 3		P11		600	600
27		P11		960	1,560

NAME: Jewett Business Systems

Date	Item	Post. Ref.	Dr.	Cr.	Balance
1997					
March 12		P11		2,800	2,800

The Other Accounts Dr. column in Exhibit 6 is used to record purchases, on account, of any item for which there is no special debit column. The title of the account to be debited is entered in the Other Accounts Dr. column, and the amount is entered in the Amount column. A separate Posting Reference column is provided for this section of the purchases journal. For Computer King, office equipment purchased on account on March 12 was recorded in the Other Accounts Dr. column.

The flow of the data from the purchases journal of Computer King to the ledgers is also shown in Exhibit 6. The principles used in posting the purchases journal are similar to those used in posting the revenue and cash receipts journals. The source of the entries posted to the subsidiary and general ledgers is indicated in the Posting Reference column of each account by inserting the letter *P* and the page number of the purchases journal. A check mark (✓) is inserted in the Posting Reference column of the purchases journal after each credit is posted to a creditor's account in the accounts payable subsidiary ledger.

At regular intervals, the amounts in the Other Accounts Dr. column are posted to the accounts in the general ledger. As each amount is posted, the related general ledger account number is inserted in the Posting Reference column of the Other Accounts section.

At the end of each month, the purchases journal is totaled and ruled. Before the totals are posted to the general ledger, the sum of the totals of the two debit columns should be compared with the total of the credit column to prove their equality.

The totals of the Accounts Payable Cr. and Supplies Dr. columns are posted to the appropriate general ledger accounts in the usual manner, with the related account numbers inserted below the column totals. Because each amount in the Other Accounts Dr. column was posted individually, a check mark is placed below the $2,800 total to show that no further action is needed.

CASH PAYMENTS JOURNAL

The special columns for the **cash payments journal** are determined in the same manner as for the revenue, cash receipts, and purchases journals. The determining factors are the kinds of transactions to be recorded and how often they occur.

The cash payments journal has a Cash Cr. column as shown in Computer King's cash payments journal in Exhibit 7. Payments to creditors on account happen often enough to require an Accounts Payable Dr. column. Debits to creditor accounts for invoices paid are recorded in the Accounts Payable Dr. column, and credits for the amounts paid are recorded in the Cash Cr. column.

Computer King makes all payments by check. As each transaction is recorded in the cash payments journal, the related check number is entered in the column at the right of the Date column. The check numbers are helpful in controlling cash payments, and they provide a useful cross-reference.

The Other Accounts Dr. column is used for recording debits to any account for which there is no special column. For example, Computer King paid $1,600 on March 2 for rent. The transaction was recorded by writing *Rent Expense* in the space provided and $1,600 in the Other Accounts Dr. and Cash Cr. columns.

The flow of data from the cash payments journal to the ledgers of Computer King is also shown in Exhibit 7. At frequent intervals during the month, the amounts entered in the Accounts Payable Dr. column are posted to the creditor accounts in the accounts payable subsidiary ledger. After each posting, *CP* and the page number of the journal are inserted in the Posting Reference column of the account. A check mark is placed in the Posting Reference column of the cash payments journal to indicate that each amount has been posted.

The items in the Other Accounts Dr. column are also posted to the accounts in the general ledger at regular intervals. The posting is indicated by writing the account numbers in the Posting Reference column of the cash payments journal.

Exhibit 7
Cash Payments Journal and Postings

CASH PAYMENTS JOURNAL **PAGE 7**

Date	Ck. No.	Account Debited	Post. Ref.	Other Accounts Dr.	Accounts Payable Dr.	Cash Cr.
1997						
March 2	150	Rent Expense	52	1,600		1,600
15	151	Grayco Supplies	✓		1,230	1,230
21	152	Jewett Business Systems	✓		2,800	2,800
22	153	Donnelly Supplies	✓		420	420
30	154	Utilities Expense	54	1,050		1,050
31	155	Howard Supplies	✓		600	600
31				2,650	5,050	7,700
				(✓)	(21)	(11)

GENERAL LEDGER

ACCOUNT Accounts Payable **Account No. 21**

Date	Item	Post. Ref.	Dr.	Cr.	Balance
1997					
March 1	Balance	✓			1,230
31		P11		6,230	7,460
31		CP7	5,050		2,410

ACCOUNT Cash **Account No. 11**

Date	Item	Post. Ref.	Dr.	Cr.	Balance
1997					
March 1	Balance	✓			6,200
31		CR14	7,750		13,950
31		CP7		7,700	6,250

ACCOUNT Rent Expense **Account No. 52**

Date	Item	Post. Ref.	Dr.	Cr.	Balance
1997					
March 1	Balance	✓			3,200
2		CP7	1,600		4,800

ACCOUNT Utilities Expense **Account No. 54**

Date	Item	Post. Ref.	Dr.	Cr.	Balance
1997					
March 1	Balance	✓			2,000
30		CP7	1,050		3,050

ACCOUNTS PAYABLE SUBSIDIARY LEDGER

NAME: Donnelly Supplies

Date	Item	Post. Ref.	Dr.	Cr.	Balance
1997					
March 7		P11		420	420
19		P11		1,450	1,870
22		CP7	420		1,450

NAME: Grayco Supplies

Date	Item	Post. Ref.	Dr.	Cr.	Balance
1997					
March 1	Balance	✓			1,230
15		CP7	1,230		—

NAME: Howard Supplies

Date	Item	Post. Ref.	Dr.	Cr.	Balance
1997					
March 3		P11		600	600
27		P11		960	1,560
31		CP7	600		960

NAME: Jewett Business Systems

Date	Item	Post. Ref.	Dr.	Cr.	Balance
1997					
March 12		P11		2,800	2,800
21		CP7	2,800		—

At the end of the month, each of the amount columns in the cash payments journal is totaled. The sum of the two debit totals is compared with the sum of the credit total to determine their equality, and the journal is ruled. A check mark is placed below the total of the Other Accounts Dr. column to indicate that it is not posted. When each of the totals of the other two columns is posted to a general ledger account, the account numbers are inserted below the column totals.

ACCOUNTS PAYABLE CONTROL AND SUBSIDIARY LEDGER

After all posting has been completed for the month, the sum of the balances in the accounts payable subsidiary ledger should be compared with the balance of the accounts payable controlling account in the general ledger. If the controlling account and the subsidiary ledger do not agree, the error or errors must be located and corrected. The balances of the individual supplier accounts may be summarized in a schedule. The total of Computer King's schedule, $2,410, agrees with the balance of the accounts payable controlling account on March 31, 1997, as shown below.

Accounts Payable (Controlling Account)		*Computer King Schedule of Accounts Payable March 31, 1997*	
Balance, March 1, 1997	$1,230	Donnelly Supplies	$1,450
Credit from P11	6,230	Grayco Supplies	0
Debit from CP7	(5,050)	Howard Supplies	960
		Jewett Business Systems	0
Balance, March 31, 1997	$2,410	Total	$2,410

Internal control is enhanced by separating the function of recording purchases in the purchases journal from recording cash payments in the cash payments journal. Separating duties in this way would prevent an individual from recording fictitious purchases and then collecting payments for these purchases that were never delivered.

Adapting Accounting Systems

Objective 5
Describe and give examples of additional subsidiary ledgers and modified special journals.

The preceding sections of this chapter illustrate subsidiary ledgers and special journals that are common for a medium-sized business. Many businesses use subsidiary ledgers for other accounts, in addition to Accounts Receivable and Accounts Payable. Also, special journals are often adapted or modified in practice to meet the specific needs of a business. In the following paragraphs, we describe other subsidiary ledgers and modified special journals.

ADDITIONAL SUBSIDIARY LEDGERS

Generally, subsidiary ledgers are used for accounts that consist of a large number of individual items, each of which has unique characteristics. For example, businesses may use a subsidiary equipment ledger to keep track of each item of equipment purchased, its cost, location, and other data. Such ledgers are similar to the accounts receivable and accounts payable subsidiary ledgers that we illustrated in this chapter.

MODIFIED SPECIAL JOURNALS

A business may modify its special journals by adding one or more columns for recording transactions that occur frequently. For example, a business may collect sales taxes that must be remitted periodically to the taxing authorities. Thus, the business may add a special column for Sales Taxes Payable in its revenue journal, as shown below.

REVENUE JOURNAL **PAGE 40**

	Date		Invoice No.	Account Debited	Post. Ref.	Accts. Rec. Dr.	Fees Earned Cr.	Sales Taxes Payable Cr.	
1	1997 Nov.	2	842	Litten Co.	✓	4 7 7 0 00	4 5 0 0 00	2 7 0 00	1
2		3	843	Kauffman Supply Co.	✓	1 1 6 6 00	1 1 0 0 00	6 6 00	2

Some other examples of how special journals may be modified for a variety of different types of businesses are:

- **Farm**
  The purchases journal may be modified to include columns for various types of seeds (corn, wheat), livestock (cows, hogs, sheep), fertilizer, and fuel.
- **Automobile Repair Shop**
  The revenue journal may be modified to include columns for each major type of repair service. In addition, columns for warranty repairs, credit card charges, and sales taxes may be added.
- **Hospital**
  The cash receipts journal may be modified to include columns for receipts from patients on account, from Blue Cross/Blue Shield or other major insurance reimbursers, and Medicare.
- **Movie Theater**
  The cash receipts journal may be modified to include columns for revenues from admissions, gift certificates, and concession sales.
- **Restaurant**
  The purchases journal may be modified to include columns for food, linen, silverware and glassware, and kitchen supplies.

Regardless of how a special journal is modified, the basic principles and procedures discussed in this chapter apply. For example, special journals are normally totaled and ruled at periodic intervals. The totals of the debit and credit columns are then compared to verify their equality before the totals are posted to the general ledger accounts.

Computerized Accounting Systems

Objective 6
Describe the basic features of a computerized accounting system.

Computerized accounting systems have become more widely used as the cost of computer hardware and software has declined. Given this wide usage, why did we study manual accounting systems? The reason is that the concepts we described for a manual system also apply to computerized systems.

Computerized accounting systems have three main advantages. First, in a computerized accounting system, transactions are simultaneously recorded in journals and posted electronically to general and subsidiary ledger accounts. The posting process is done without manual effort, since the original transactions include the required information for posting to the ledger. Thus, computerized accounting systems simplify the record-keeping process. Second, computerized accounting systems are generally more accurate than manual systems. Computer systems will not make common mistakes, such as math errors, posting errors, and journal recording errors. Thus, computerized systems avoid the time lost in correcting common errors. Third, computerized systems provide management current account balance information, since account balances are posted as the transactions occur. Thus, a computerized accounting system provides management more current information to support decision making.

How do computerized accounting systems work? Computerized accounting systems consist of various subsystems. Examples include the accounts receivable and the accounts payable subsystems. We illustrate the computerized accounts receivable subsystem for Computer King in Exhibit 8.

Assume that Pat King renders services to four customers on May 5. These four customers need to be billed (invoiced) for the services. A computer operator sits at a console and enters billing data for each customer into the computer. The data include the date, customer's account number, and the amount billed. An electronic

Exhibit 8 *Computerized Accounts Receivable System*

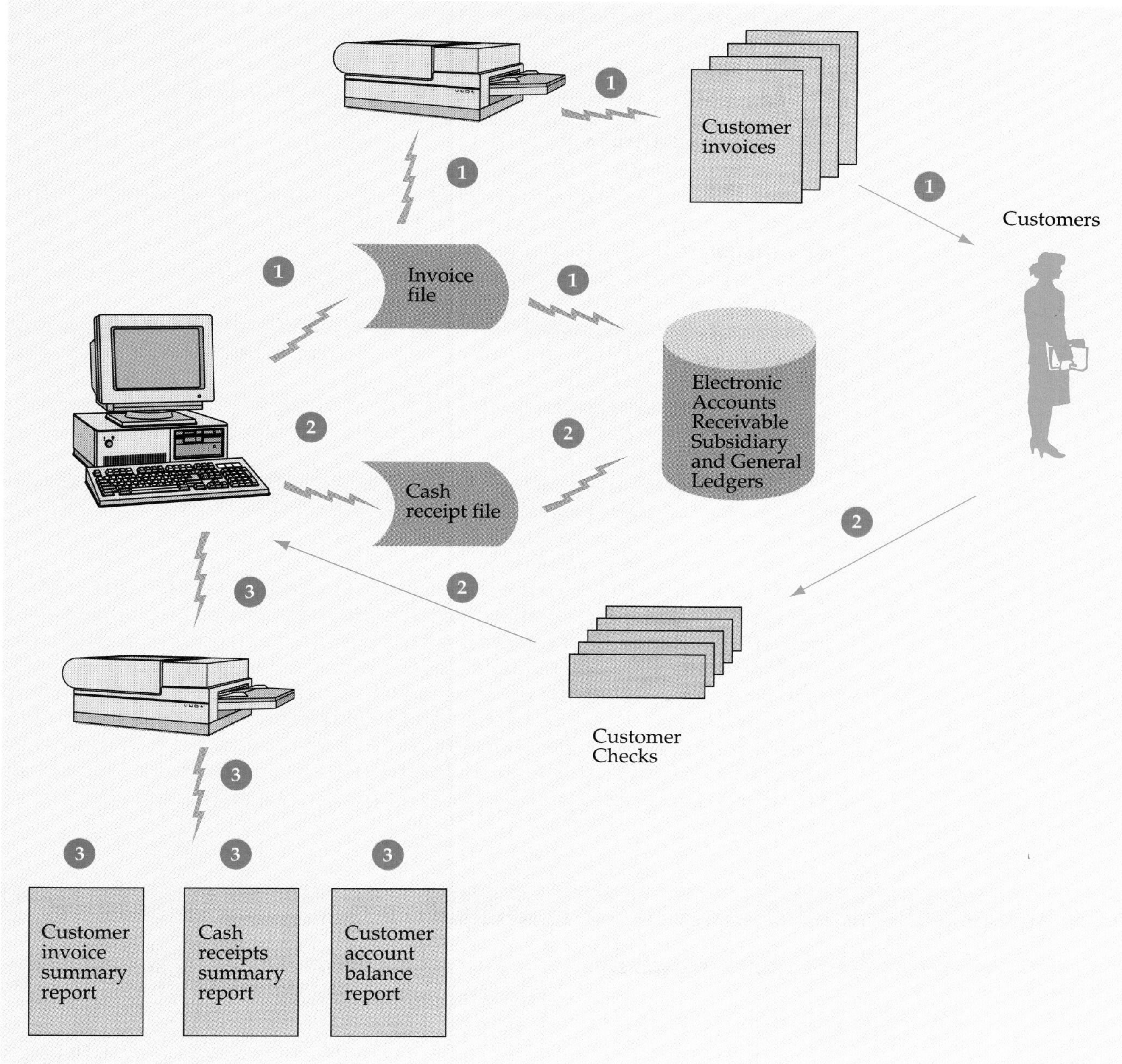

listing of this information in the computer is termed an invoice file. This process is much like recording information in a revenue journal in a manual system. The computer uses the invoice file information to print bills for mailing to the customers. In addition, the computer electronically posts each of the four amounts in the invoice file as debits to the appropriate customer accounts in the subsidiary ledger and to Accounts Receivable in the general ledger. At the same time, a credit is electronically posted to the fees earned account in the general ledger. The posting is automatic. The accounting software is programmed to take the information in the invoice file and automatically create the appropriate debits and credits in the electronic ledger. These steps are indicated by the number *1* in Exhibit 8.

Assume that Computer King also received five checks from customers on May 5 in payment for services rendered in April. The computer operator inputs the check information into the computer before depositing the checks at the bank. The data include the date of receipt, customer's account number, and amount of the check. An electronic listing of this information in the computer is termed a cash receipts file. This process is much like recording information in a cash receipts journal in a manual system. The computer uses this information to electronically post each of the five checks as credits to the appropriate customer accounts in the subsidiary ledger and to Accounts Receivable in the general ledger. At the same time, a debit is electronically posted to Cash in the general ledger. These steps are indicated by the number 2 in Exhibit 8.

Periodically, management may need reports to use in making decisions. Three common reports from the accounts receivable system are the customer invoice summary report, cash receipts summary report, and customer account balance report. These reports, which can be printed out at any time, are indicated by the number 3 in Exhibit 8.

The **customer invoice summary report** is a summary of the invoice files for a period of time. The customer invoice summary report is often similar in format to the revenue journal in a manual system.

The **cash receipts summary report** is a summary of the cash receipts files for a period of time. The cash receipts summary report is similar in format to the cash receipts journal in the manual system.

The **customer account balance report** is a listing of all of the accounts receivable balances from the electronic accounts receivable subsidiary ledger. Since the accounts are posted electronically from the invoice and cash receipts file information, the balances are always current.

We have illustrated the accounts receivable system in a computerized environment to help you understand how a portion of a computerized accounting system is constructed. Although a description of a complete computerized accounting system is beyond our scope, a thorough understanding of this chapter provides a solid foundation for applying the concepts in either a manual or a computer environment. In addition, an understanding of manual accounting systems assists managers in recognizing the interrelationships that exist between accounting data and accounting reports. This recognition, in turn, enables managers to better anticipate how decisions may affect operations and the financial statements and other reports of a business.

KEY POINTS

Objective 1. Describe the basic principles of accounting systems.

Although accounting systems vary from business to business, the following principles apply to all systems:

1. The cost of the information must be balanced against its benefits.
2. Reports must be prepared with the needs and the knowledge of the user considered.
3. The system must be able to adapt to changing needs.
4. Internal controls must be adequate.

Objective 2. List and describe the three phases of accounting systems installation and revision.

The three phases of accounting systems installation are (1) analysis of information needs, (2) design of the system, and (3) implementation of the systems design.

Objective 3. List the three objectives of internal control and define and give examples of the five elements of an internal control framework.

The three objectives of internal control are to provide reasonable assurance that (1) operations are managed to achieve desired goals, (2) financial reports are accurate, and (3) laws and regulations are complied with.

The five elements of an internal control framework are the control environment, risk assessment, control procedures, monitoring, and information and communication. The control environment is the overall attitude of management and employees about the importance of controls. The existence of employee codes of ethics and conflict-of-interest policies contributes to the effectiveness of a control environment. Management must continually assess and attempt to reduce the influence of risk. Risk assessment includes evaluating competitor threats, regulatory changes, and changes in economic factors. Control procedures are established to provide reasonable assurance that enterprise goals will be achieved. Control procedures include rotating duties and mandatory vacations. The internal control system should be monitored periodically. Monitoring can be provided by an internal audit staff or by external auditors. Information and communication provide feedback about internal control. Information includes reports about business operations.

Objective 4. Journalize and post transactions, using subsidiary ledgers and the following special journals:

Revenue journal
Cash receipts journal
Purchases journal
Cash payments journal

Subsidiary ledgers may be used to maintain separate records for each customer (the accounts receivable subsidiary ledger) and creditor (the accounts payable subsidiary ledger). When subsidiary ledgers are used, each subsidiary ledger is represented in the general ledger by a summarizing account, called a controlling account. The sum of the balances of the accounts in a subsidiary ledger must agree with the balance of the related controlling account.

Special journals may be used to reduce the processing time and expense of recording a large number of similar transactions. The revenue journal is used to record the sale of services on account. The cash receipts journal is used to record all receipts of cash. The purchases journal is used to record purchases on account. The cash payments journal is used to record all payments of cash. The general journal is used for recording transactions that do not fit in any of the special journals. The use of each special journal and the accounts receivable and accounts payable subsidiary ledgers is illustrated in the chapter.

Objective 5. Describe and give examples of additional subsidiary ledgers and modified special journals.

Subsidiary ledgers may be maintained for a variety of accounts, such as plant assets, as well as accounts receivable and accounts payable. Special journals may be modified by adding columns in which to record frequently occurring transactions. For example, an additional column is often added to the revenue journal for recording sales taxes payable.

Objective 6. Describe the basic features of a computerized accounting system.

Computerized accounting systems are similar to manual accounting systems. The main advantages of a computerized accounting system are the simultaneous recording and posting of transactions, the high degree of accuracy, and the timeliness of reporting. An example of an accounts receivable computer subsystem is provided in the chapter.

GLOSSARY OF KEY TERMS

Accounting system. The methods and procedures used by a business to record and report financial data for use by management and external users. *Objective 1*

Accounts payable subsidiary ledger. The subsidiary ledger containing the individual accounts with suppliers (creditors). *Objective 4*

Accounts receivable subsidiary ledger. The subsidiary ledger containing the individual accounts with customers (debtors). *Objective 4*

Cash payments journal. The journal in which all cash payments are recorded. *Objective 4*

Cash receipts file. An electronic listing of customer cash receipts information. *Objective 6*

Cash receipts journal. The journal in which all cash receipts are recorded. *Objective 4*

Controlling account. The account in the general ledger that summarizes the balances of the accounts in a subsidiary ledger. *Objective 4*

General journal. The two-column form used for entries that do not "fit" in any of the special journals. *Objective 4*

General ledger. The primary ledger, when used in conjunction with subsidiary ledgers, that contains all of the balance sheet and income statement accounts. *Objective 4*

Internal control framework. Consists of five major elements: (1) the control environment, (2) risk assessment, (3) control procedures, (4) monitoring, and (5) information and communication. *Objective 3*

Internal controls. The detailed policies and procedures used to direct operations, ensure accurate reports, and ensure compliance with laws and regulations. *Objective 1*

Invoice file. An electronic listing of customer billing information in a computer. *Objective 6*

Purchases journal. The journal in which all items purchased on account are recorded. *Objective 4*

Revenue journal. The journal in which all sales of services on account are recorded. *Objective 4*

Special journals. Journals designed to be used for recording a single type of transaction. *Objective 4*

Subsidiary ledger. A ledger containing individual accounts with a common characteristic. *Objective 4*

ILLUSTRATIVE PROBLEM

Selected transactions of O'Malley Co. for the month of May are as follows:

May
a. 1. Issued Check No. 1001 in payment of rent for May, $1,200.
b. 2. Purchased office supplies on account from McMillan Co., $3,600.
c. 4. Issued Check No. 1003 in payment of transportation charges on the supplies purchased on May 2, $320.
d. 8. Rendered services on account to Waller Co., Invoice No. 51, $4,500.
e. 9. Issued Check No. 1005 for office supplies purchased, $450.

May
f. 10. Received cash for office supplies sold to employees at cost, $120.
g. 11. Purchased office equipment on account from Fender Office Products, $15,000.
h. 12. Issued Check No. 1010 in payment of the supplies purchased from McMillan Co. on May 2, $3,600.
i. 16. Rendered services on account to Riese Co., Invoice No. 58, $8,000.
j. 18. Received $4,500 from Waller Co. in payment of May 8 invoice.
k. 20. Invested additional cash in the business, $10,000.
l. 25. Rendered services for cash, $15,900.
m. 30. Issued Check No. 1040 for withdrawal of cash for personal use, $1,000.
n. 30. Issued Check No. 1041 in payment of electricity and water bills, $690.
o. 30. Issued Check No. 1042 in payment of office and sales salaries for May, $15,800.
p. 31. Journalized adjusting entries from the work sheet prepared for the fiscal year ended May 31.

O'Malley Co. maintains a revenue journal, a cash receipts journal, a purchases journal, a cash payments journal, and a general journal. In addition, accounts receivable and accounts payable subsidiary ledgers are used.

Instructions

1. Indicate the journal in which each of the preceding transactions, (a) through (p), would be recorded.
2. Indicate whether an account in the accounts receivable or accounts payable subsidiary ledgers would be affected for each of the preceding transactions.
3. Journalize transactions (b), (c), (d), (h), and (j) in the appropriate journals.

Solution

1. *Journal*	2. *Subsidiary Ledger*
a. Cash payments journal	
b. Purchases journal	Accounts payable ledger
c. Cash payments journal	
d. Revenue journal	Accounts receivable ledger
e. Cash payments journal	
f. Cash receipts journal	
g. Purchases journal	Accounts payable ledger
h. Cash payments journal	Accounts payable ledger
i. Revenue journal	Accounts receivable ledger
j. Cash receipts journal	Accounts receivable ledger
k. Cash receipts journal	
l. Cash receipts journal	
m. Cash payments journal	
n. Cash payments journal	
o. Cash payments journal	
p. General journal	

3.

Transaction (b):

PURCHASES JOURNAL

Date	Account Credited	Post. Ref.	Accounts Payable Cr.	Office Supplies Dr.	Other Accounts Dr.	Post. Ref.	Amount
May 2	McMillan Co.		3,600.00	3,600.00			

Transactions (c) and (h):

CASH PAYMENTS JOURNAL

Date		Ck. No.	Account Debited	Post. Ref.	Other Accounts Dr.	Accounts Payable Dr.	Cash Cr.
May	4	1003	Transportation In		3 2 0 00		3 2 0 00
	12	1010	McMillan Co.			3 6 0 0 00	3 6 0 0 00

Transaction (d):

REVENUE JOURNAL

Date		Invoice No.	Account Debited	Post. Ref.	Accts. Rec. Dr. Fees Earned Cr.
May	8	51	Waller Co.		4 5 0 0 00

Transaction (j):

CASH RECEIPTS JOURNAL

Date		Account Credited	Post. Ref.	Other Accounts Cr.	Accounts Receivable Cr.	Cash Dr.
May	18	Waller Co.			4 5 0 0 00	4 5 0 0 00

SELF-EXAMINATION QUESTIONS (ANSWERS AT END OF CHAPTER)

1. The final phase of the installation of an accounting system that involves carrying out the proposals for changes in the system is called:
   A. systems analysis
   B. systems design
   C. systems implementation
   D. systems training

2. The detailed procedures used by management to direct operations toward desired goals are called:
   A. internal controls
   B. systems analysis
   C. systems design
   D. systems implementation

3. A payment of cash for the purchase of services should be recorded in the:
   A. purchases journal
   B. cash payments journal
   C. revenue journal
   D. cash receipts journal

4. When there are a large number of individual accounts with a common characteristic, it is common to place them in a separate ledger called:
   A. a subsidiary ledger
   B. a creditors ledger
   C. an accounts payable ledger
   D. an accounts receivable ledger

5. The controlling account in the general ledger that summarizes the debits and credits to the individual customer accounts in the subsidiary ledger is entitled:
   A. Accounts Payable
   B. Accounts Receivable
   C. Fees Earned
   D. Rent Expense

DISCUSSION QUESTIONS

1. Why is the accounting system of a business an information system?
2. What are internal controls?
3. What is the objective of systems analysis?
4. What is included in a firm's *Systems Manual*?
5. What are the three objectives of internal control?
6. Name and describe the five elements of the internal control framework.
7. Should management attempt to assess risk associated with embezzlement?
8. How does a policy of rotating clerical employees from job to job aid in strengthening the control procedures within the control environment?
9. Why should the responsibility for a sequence of related operations be divided among different persons?
10. Why should the employee who handles cash receipts not have the responsibility for maintaining the accounts receivable records?
11. Why should the employee who handles cash receipts not be responsible for approving refunds to customers?
12. In an attempt to improve operating efficiency, one employee was made responsible for all purchasing, receiving, and storing of supplies. Is this organizational change wise from an internal control standpoint? Explain.
13. In an attempt to improve operating efficiency, one employee was made responsible for maintaining all personnel records, for timekeeping, for preparing payroll records, and for distributing payroll checks. Is this organizational change wise from an internal control standpoint? Explain.
14. The ticket seller at a movie theater doubles as a ticket taker for a few minutes each day while the ticket taker is on a break. Which control procedure of a business's system of internal control is violated in this situation?
15. Why should the responsibility for maintaining the accounting records be separated from the responsibility for operations?
16. How can the use of a fidelity bond aid internal control?
17. How does a periodic review by internal auditors strengthen the internal control framework?
18. How does management use information and communication in the internal control framework?
19. What is the term applied (a) to the ledger containing the individual customer accounts and (b) to the single account summarizing accounts receivable?
20. What are the major advantages of the use of special journals?
21. Environmental Services Co. uses the special journals described in this chapter. Which journal will be used to record fees earned (a) for cash, (b) on account?
22. In recording 250 fees earned on account during a single month, how many times will it be necessary to write *Fees Earned* (a) if each transaction, including fees earned, is recorded individually in a two-column general journal; (b) if each transaction for fees earned is recorded in a revenue journal?
23. How many individual postings to Fees Earned for the month would be needed in Question 22 if the procedure described in (a) had been used; if the procedure described in (b) had been used?
24. As illustrated in this chapter, what does a check mark (✓) in the Posting Reference column of the cash receipts journal signify (a) when the account credited is an account receivable; (b) when the account credited is Fees Earned?
25. During the current month, the following errors occurred in recording transactions in the purchases journal or in posting from it:
    a. An invoice for $900 of supplies from Hoffman Co. was recorded as having been received from Hoffer Co., another supplier.
    b. A credit of $840 to JPC Company was posted as $480 in the subsidiary ledger.
    c. An invoice for equipment of $6,500 was recorded as $5,500.
    d. The Accounts Payable column of the purchases journal was overstated by $2,000.

    How will each error come to the bookkeeper's attention, other than by chance discovery?
26. The Accounts Payable and Cash columns in the cash payments journal were unknowingly overstated by $100 at the end of the month. (a) Assuming no other errors in recording or posting, will the error cause the trial balance totals to be unequal? (b) Will the creditors ledger agree with the accounts payable controlling account?

27. Assuming the use of a two-column general journal, a purchases journal, and a cash payments journal as illustrated in this chapter, indicate the journal in which each of the following transactions should be recorded:
    a. Purchase of supplies for cash.
    b. Purchase of office supplies on account.
    c. Payment of cash on account to creditor.
    d. Purchase of store equipment on account.
    e. Payment of cash for office supplies.

28. In the **Equity Funding** fraud, approximately $2 billion of insurance policies that were claimed to have been sold by the company were bogus. The bogus policies, which were supported by falsified policy applications, were listed along with real policies on Equity Funding's computer tapes (records). These computer tapes were kept in a separate room where they were easily accessible by Equity Funding personnel, including the computer programmers. In addition, computer programmers and other company personnel had access to the computer. What general weaknesses in Equity Funding's internal controls contributed to the occurrence and the size of the fraud?

EXERCISES

EXERCISE 5–1
Internal controls
Objective 3

Karen Byers has recently been hired as the manager of Jenny's Deli. Jenny's is a national chain of franchised delicatessens. During her first month as store manager, Karen encountered the following internal control situations:

a. Jenny's has one cash register. Prior to Karen's joining the deli, each employee working on a shift would take a customer order, accept payment, and then prepare the order. Karen made one employee on each shift responsible for taking orders and accepting the customer's payment. Other employees prepare the orders.
b. Since only one employee uses the cash register, that employee is responsible for counting the cash at the end of the shift and verifying that the cash in the drawer matches the amount of cash sales recorded by the cash register. Karen expects each cashier to balance the drawer to the penny **every** time—no exceptions.
c. Karen caught an employee putting a box of 100 single-serving bags of potato chips in his car. Not wanting to create a scene, Karen smiled and said, "I don't think you're putting those chips on the right shelf. Don't they belong inside the deli?" The employee returned the chips to the stockroom.

State whether you agree or disagree with Karen's handling of each situation and explain your answer.

EXERCISE 5–2
Internal controls
Objective 3

Gypsy Fashions is a retail store specializing in women's clothing. The store has established a liberal return policy for the holiday season in order to encourage gift purchases. Any item purchased during November and December may be returned through January 31, with a receipt, for cash or exchange. If the customer does not have a receipt, cash will still be refunded for any item under $25. If the item is more than $25, a check is mailed to the customer.

Whenever an item is returned, a store clerk completes a return slip, which the customer signs. The return slip is placed in a special box. The store manager visits the return counter approximately once every two hours to authorize the return slips. Clerks are instructed to place the returned merchandise on the proper rack on the selling floor as soon as possible.

This year, returns at Gypsy Fashions have reached an all-time high. There are a large number of returns under $25 without receipts.

a. How can sales clerks employed at Gypsy Fashions use the store's return policy to steal money from the cash register?
b. 1. What internal control weaknesses do you see in the return policy that make cash thefts easier?
   2. Would issuing a store credit in place of a cash refund for all merchandise returned without a receipt reduce the possibility of theft? List some advantages and disadvantages of issuing a store credit in place of a cash refund.
   3. Assume that Gypsy Fashions is committed to the current policy of issuing cash refunds without a receipt. What changes could be made in the store's procedures regarding customer refunds in order to improve internal control?

EXERCISE 5–3
Internal controls for bank lending
Objective 3

Las Cruz Bank provides loans to businesses in the community through its Commercial Lending Department. Small loans (less than $100,000) may be approved by an individual loan officer, while larger loans (greater than $100,000) must be approved by a board of loan officers. Once a loan is approved, the funds are made available to the loan applicant under agreed terms. The president of Las Cruz Bank has instituted a policy whereby she has the individual authority to approve loans up to $5,000,000. The president believes that this policy will allow flexibility to approve loans to valued clients much quicker than under the previous policy.

As an internal auditor of Las Cruz Bank, how would you respond to this change in policy?

EXERCISE 5–4
Identifying postings from revenue journal
Objective 4

Using the following revenue journal for J. A. Bach Co., identify each of the posting references, indicated by a letter, as representing (1) a posting to a general ledger account, (2) a posting to a subsidiary ledger account, or (3) a posting to two general ledger accounts.

REVENUE JOURNAL

Date		Invoice No.	Account Debited	Post. Ref.	
19—					
Nov.	1	772	Environmental Safety Co.	(a)	$1,700
	10	773	Greenberg Co.	(b)	795
	20	774	Smith and Smith	(c)	900
	27	775	Envirolab	(d)	540
	30				$3,935
					(e)

EXERCISE 5–5
Accounts receivable ledger
Objective 4

Based upon the data presented in Exercise 5-4, (a) set up a T account for Accounts Receivable and T accounts for the four accounts needed in the customers ledger, (b) post to the T accounts, (c) determine the balance in the accounts, if necessary, and (d) prepare a schedule of accounts receivable at November 30.

EXERCISE 5–6
Identifying journals
Objective 4

Assuming the use of a two-column (all-purpose) general journal, a revenue journal, and a cash receipts journal as illustrated in this chapter, indicate the journal in which each of the following transactions should be recorded:

a. Investment of additional cash in the business by the owner.
b. Receipt of cash refund from overpayment of taxes.
c. Rendering of services for cash.
d. Rendering of services on account.
e. Receipt of cash from sale of office equipment.
f. Receipt of cash on account from a customer.
g. Sale of office supplies on account, at cost, to a neighboring business.
h. Adjustment to record accrued salaries at the end of the year.
i. Closing of drawing account at the end of the year.
j. Receipt of cash for rent.

EXERCISE 5–7
Identifying journals
Objective 4

Assuming the use of a two-column (all-purpose) general journal, a purchases journal, and a cash payments journal as illustrated in this chapter, indicate the journal in which each of the following transactions should be recorded:

a. Payment of six months' rent in advance.
b. Purchase of office supplies on account.
c. Purchase of an office computer on account.
d. Purchase of office supplies for cash.
e. Advance payment of a one-year fire insurance policy on the office.
f. Adjustment to prepaid rent at the end of the month.
g. Adjustment to record accrued salaries at the end of the period.
h. Adjustment to prepaid insurance at the end of the month.
i. Adjustment to record depreciation at the end of the month.
j. Purchase of office equipment for cash.
k. Purchase of services on account.

EXERCISE 5–8
Identifying transactions in accounts receivable ledger
Objective 4

The debits and credits from three related transactions are presented in the following customer's account taken from the accounts receivable subsidiary ledger:

NAME *Future Environmental Services*
ADDRESS *1319 Main Street*

Date	Item	Post. Ref.	Debit	Credit	Balance
19—					
Sep. 3		R50	6,000		6,000
9		J9		700	5,300
13		CR38		5,300	—

Describe each transaction, and identify the source of each posting.

EXERCISE 5–9
Identifying postings from purchases journal
Objective 4

Using the following purchases journal, identify each of the posting references, indicated by a letter, as representing (1) a posting to a general ledger account, (2) a posting to a subsidiary ledger account, or (3) that no posting is required.

PURCHASES JOURNAL **Page 49**

Date	Account Credited	Post. Ref.	Accounts Payable Cr.	Store Supplies Dr.	Office Supplies Dr.	Other Accounts Dr. Account	Post. Ref.	Amount
19—								
June 4	Coastal Insurance Co.	(a)	4,525			Prepaid Insurance	(b)	4,525
6	Porter Supply Co.	(c)	3,000			Office Equipment	(d)	3,000
11	Baker Products	(e)	1,950	1,500	450			
13	Wilson and Wilson	(f)	6,800		6,800			
20	Cowen Supply	(g)	3,775	3,775				
27	Porter Supply Co.	(h)	9,100			Store Equipment	(i)	9,100
30			29,150	5,275	7,250			16,625
			(j)	(k)	(l)			(m)

EXERCISE 5–10
Identifying postings from cash payments journal
Objective 4

Using the following cash payments journal, identify each of the posting references, indicated by a letter, as representing (1) a posting to a general ledger account, (2) a posting to a subsidiary ledger account, or (3) that no posting is required.

CASH PAYMENTS JOURNAL **Page 46**

Date	Ck. No.	Account Debited	Post. Ref.	Other Accounts Dr.	Accounts Payable Dr.	Cash Cr.
19—						
July 3	611	Aquatic Systems Co.	(a)		4,000	4,000
5	612	Utilities Expense	(b)	325		325
10	613	Prepaid Rent	(c)	3,200		3,200
17	614	Coe Bros.	(d)		2,500	2,500
20	615	Office Equipment	(e)	2,100		2,100
22	616	Advertising Expense	(f)	400		400
25	617	Office Supplies	(g)	250		250
27	618	Evans Co.	(h)		5,500	5,500
31	619	Salaries Expense	(i)	1,750		1,750
31				8,025	12,000	20,025
				(j)	(k)	(l)

EXERCISE 5–11
Identifying transactions in accounts payable ledger account
Objective 4

The debits and credits from three related transactions are presented in the following creditor's account taken from the accounts payable ledger:

NAME *Echo Co.*
ADDRESS *1717 Kirby Street*

Date	Item	Post. Ref.	Debit	Credit	Balance
19—					
July 6		P34		10,500	10,500
10		J10	500		10,000
16		CP37	10,000		—

Describe each transaction, and identify the source of each posting.

EXERCISE 5–12
Error in accounts payable ledger and schedule of accounts payable
Objective 4

After Wittier Company had completed all postings for October in the current year, the sum of the balances in the following accounts payable ledger did not agree with the balance of the appropriate controlling account in the general ledger.

NAME *C. D. Cali Co.*
ADDRESS *1240 W. Main Street*

Date	Item	Post. Ref.	Debit	Credit	Balance
19—					
Oct. 1	Balance	✓			4,750
10		CP22	4,750		—
17		P30		3,250	3,250
25		J7	250		2,000

NAME *Cutler and Powell*
ADDRESS *717 Elm Street*

Date	Item	Post. Ref.	Debit	Credit	Balance
19—					
Oct. 1	Balance	✓			6,100
18		CP23	6,100		—
29		P31		9,500	9,500

NAME *C. D. Greer and Son*
ADDRESS *972 S. Tenth Street*

Date	Item	Post. Ref.	Debit	Credit	Balance
19—					
Oct. 17		P30		3,750	3,750
27		P31		7,000	10,750

NAME *Taber Supply*
ADDRESS *1170 Mattis Avenue*

Date	Item	Post. Ref.	Debit	Credit	Balance
19—					
Oct. 1	Balance	✓			8,250
7		P30		4,900	13,050
12		J7	250		12,800
20		CP23	5,700		7,100

NAME *L. L. Weiss Co.*
ADDRESS *915 E. Walnut Street*

Date	Item	Post. Ref.	Debit	Credit	Balance
19—					
Oct. 5		P30		2,750	2,750

Assuming that the controlling account balance of $33,200 has been verified as correct, (a) determine the error(s) in the preceding accounts and (b) prepare a schedule of accounts payable from the corrected accounts payable subsidiary ledger.

EXERCISE 5–13
Identifying postings from special journals
Objective 4

Tracy Company makes most of its sales and purchases on credit. It uses the five journals described in this chapter (revenue, cash receipts, purchases, cash payments, and general journals). Identify the journal most likely used in recording the postings for selected transactions indicated by letter in the following T accounts:

Cash

	Dr.		Cr.
a.	9,650	b.	8,325

Prepaid Rent

	Dr.		Cr.
		g.	400

Accounts Receivable

	Dr.		Cr.
c.	10,950	d.	9,200

Accounts Payable

	Dr.		Cr.
h.	7,600	i.	7,790

Office Supplies

	Dr.		Cr.
e.	7,790		
f.	1,725		

Fees Earned

	Dr.		Cr.
		j.	10,950
		k.	450

Rent Expense

	Dr.		Cr.
l.	400		

EXERCISE 5–14
Cash receipts journal
Objective 4

The following cash receipts journal headings have been suggested for a small service firm. How many errors can you find in the headings?

CASH RECEIPTS JOURNAL — **PAGE**

Date	Account Credited	Post. Ref.	Fees Earned Cr.	Accounts Rec. Cr.	Cash Cr.	Other Accounts Dr.

EXERCISE 5–15
Modified special journals
Objectives 4, 5

Wellguard Testing Services was established on June 15 of the current year. Wellguard collects a 5% sales tax on all testing services provided.

June 16. Provided testing services to A. Sommerfeld on account, Invoice No. 1, $160 plus tax.
19. Provided testing services to B. Lin, Invoice No. 2, $40 plus tax.
21. Provided testing services to J. Koss, Invoice No. 3, $60 plus tax.
22. Provided testing services to D. Jeffries, Invoice No. 4, $100 plus tax.
24. Provided testing services to K. Sallinger in exchange for testing supplies, $200 plus tax.
26. Provided testing services to J. Koss, Invoice No. 5, $120 plus tax.
28. Provided testing services to B. Lin, Invoice No. 6, $80 plus tax.
30. Provided testing services to D. Finnigan, Invoice No. 7, $180 plus tax.

a. Journalize the transactions for June, using a three-column revenue journal and a two-column general journal. Post the customer accounts in the accounts receivable subsidiary ledger, and insert the balance immediately after recording each entry.
b. Post the general journal and the revenue journal to the following general ledger accounts, inserting account balances only after the last postings:

12 Accounts Receivable
14 Testing Supplies
22 Sales Tax Payable
41 Fees Earned

c. 1. What is the sum of the balances in the accounts receivable subsidiary ledger at June 30?
2. What is the balance of the controlling account at June 30?

PROBLEMS SERIES A

PROBLEM 5–1A
Revenue journal; accounts receivable and general ledgers
Objective 4

Horowitz and Sons Co. was established on May 20 of the current year to provide advertising services. It rendered services during the remainder of the month as follows:

May 21. Rendered services on account to Dunlop Co., Invoice No. 1, $1,200.
22. Rendered services on account to Stark Co., Invoice No. 2, $2,750.
24. Rendered services on account to Morris Co., Invoice No. 3, $3,175.
27. Rendered services on account to Mintz Co., Invoice No. 4, $2,500.
28. Rendered services on account to Benner Co., Invoice No. 5, $1,500.
28. Received a $3,600 note receivable from Brown Co. for services rendered.
30. Rendered services on account to Stark Co., Invoice No. 6, $2,925.
31. Rendered services on account to Morris Co., Invoice No. 7, $995.

Instructions

1. Journalize the transactions for May, using a single-column revenue journal and a two-column general journal. Post to the following customer accounts in the accounts receivable ledger, and insert the balance immediately after recording each entry: Benner Co.; Dunlop Co.; Mintz Co.; Morris Co.; Stark Co.
2. Post the revenue journal and the general journal to the following accounts in the general ledger, inserting the account balances only after the last postings:

   12 Accounts Receivable
   13 Notes Receivable
   41 Fees Earned

3. a. What is the sum of the balances of the accounts in the subsidiary ledger at May 31?
   b. What is the balance of the controlling account at May 31?
4. Assume that on June 1, the state in which Horowitz and Sons operates begins requiring that sales tax be collected on advertising services. Briefly explain how the revenue journal may be modified to accommodate sales of services on account that require the collection of a state sales tax.

PROBLEM 5–2A
Revenue and cash receipts journals; accounts receivable and general ledgers
Objective 4

Transactions related to revenue and cash receipts completed by Environmental Services of Collier County during the period June 15–30 of the current year are as follows:

June 15. Issued Invoice No. 793 to Yamura Co., $8,320.
16. Received cash from AGI Co. for the balance owed on its account.
19. Issued Invoice No. 794 to Hardy Co., $4,210.
20. Issued Invoice No. 795 to Ross and Son, $5,570.
Post all journals to the accounts receivable ledger.
23. Received cash from Hardy Co. for the balance owed on June 15.
24. Issued Invoice No. 796 to Hardy Co., $3,190.
Post all journals to the accounts receivable ledger.
25. Received cash from Yamura Co. for the balance due on invoice of June 15.
28. Received cash from Hardy Co. for invoice of June 19.
28. Issued Invoice No. 797 to AGI Co., $1,890.
30. Received $5,000 of supplies for services rendered to Hang Company.
30. Recorded cash fees received for the second half of the month, $10,400.
Post all journals to the accounts receivable ledger.

Instructions

1. Insert the following balances in the general ledger as of June 1:

11	Cash	$14,380
12	Accounts Receivable	10,440
14	Supplies	8,000
41	Fees Earned	—

2. Insert the following balances in the accounts receivable ledger as of June 15:

AGI Co.	$ 7,890
Hardy Co.	11,410
Ross and Son	—
Yamura Co.	—

3. In a single-column revenue journal and a cash receipts journal, insert *June 15 Total(s) Forwarded* on the left side of the first line of the journal. Use the following column headings for the cash receipts journal: Other Accounts, Fees Earned, Accounts Receivable, and Cash. The Fees Earned column is used to record cash fees. Insert a check mark (✓) in the Post. Ref. column, and the following dollar figures in the respective amount columns:

   Revenue journal: 28,460
   Cash receipts journal: 3,260; 11,820; 19,600; 34,680.

4. Using the two special journals and the two-column general journal, journalize the transactions for the remainder of June. Post to the accounts receivable ledger, and insert the balances at the points indicated in the narrative of transactions. *Determine the balance in the customer's account before recording a cash receipt.*
5. Total each of the columns of the special journals, and post the individual entries and totals to the general ledger. Insert account balances after the last posting.
6. Determine that the subsidiary ledger agrees with the controlling account in the general ledger.

PROBLEM 5–3A
Purchases, accounts payable account, and accounts payable ledger
Objective 4

Lee Landscaping Services designs and installs landscaping. Office supplies are used by the landscape designers and office staff, while field supplies (rock, bark, etc.) are used in the actual landscaping. Purchases on account completed by Lee Landscaping during May of the current year are as follows:

May 1. Purchased field supplies on account from Yin Co., $5,430.
4. Purchased office supplies on account from Lapp Co., $2,600.
9. Purchased field supplies on account from Nelson Co., $1,240.
13. Purchased field supplies on account from Yin Co., $980.
14. Purchased office equipment on account from Emerald Computers Co., $8,900.
17. Purchased office supplies on account from J-Mart Supplies Co., $2,040.
20. Purchased office equipment on account from Cencor Co., $9,500.
24. Purchased field supplies on account from Nelson Co., $1,020.
29. Purchased office supplies on account from J-Mart Supplies Co., $3,560.
31. Purchased field supplies on account from Nelson Co., $2,040.

Instructions

1. Insert the following balances in the general ledger as of May 1:

14	Field Supplies	$ 3,120
15	Office Supplies	1,760
18	Office Equipment	28,600
21	Accounts Payable	7,600

2. Insert the following balances in the accounts payable ledger as of May 1:

Cencor Co.	$ 3,250
Emerald Computers Co.	—
J-Mart Supplies Co.	1,780
Lapp Co.	2,570
Nelson Co.	—
Yin Co.	—

3. Journalize the transactions for May, using a purchases journal similar to the one illustrated in this chapter. Prepare the purchases journal with columns for Accounts Payable,

Field Supplies, Office Supplies, and Other Accounts. Post to the creditor accounts in the accounts payable ledger immediately after each entry.

4. Post the purchases journal to the accounts in the general ledger.
5. a. What is the sum of the balances in the subsidiary ledger at May 31?
   b. What is the balance of the controlling account at May 31?

PROBLEM 5–4A
Purchases and cash payments journals; accounts payable and general ledgers
Objective 4

Desai Water Testing Service was established on June 16 of the current year. Desai uses field equipment and field supplies (chemicals and other supplies) to analyze water for unsafe contaminants in streams, lakes, and ponds. Transactions related to purchases and cash payments during the remainder of June are as follows:

June 16. Issued Check No. 1 in payment of rent for the remainder of June, $1,200.
16. Purchased field equipment on account from Harper Equipment Co., $6,890.
16. Purchased field supplies on account from Heath Supply Co., $12,340.
17. Issued Check No. 2 in payment of field supplies, $3,450, and office supplies, $240.
18. Purchased office equipment on account from Chavez Co., $2,090.
19. Purchased office supplies on account from Aztec Supply Co., $980.
Post the journals to the accounts payable ledger.
23. Issued Check No. 3 to Harper Equipment Co. in payment of invoice, $6,890.
24. Issued Check No. 4 to Heath Supply Co. in payment of invoice, $12,340.
25. Issued Check No. 5 to purchase land, $24,000.
26. Issued Check No. 6 to Chavez Co. in payment of the balance owed.
27. Purchased office supplies on account from Aztec Supply Co., $1,340.
Post the journals to the accounts payable ledger.
30. Purchased the following from Harper Equipment Co. on account: field supplies, $3,400, and field equipment, $11,280.
30. Issued Check No. 7 to Aztec Supply Co. in payment of invoice, $980.
30. Purchased field supplies on account from Heath Supply Co., $8,670.
30. Issued Check No. 8 in payment of salaries, $5,400.
30. Acquired land in exchange for field equipment having a cost of $10,500.
Post the journals to the accounts payable ledger.

Instructions

1. Journalize the transactions for June. Use a purchases journal and a cash payments journal, similar to those illustrated in this chapter, and a two-column general journal. Refer to the following partial chart of accounts:

   11 Cash
   14 Field Supplies
   15 Office Supplies
   17 Field Equipment
   18 Office Equipment
   19 Land
   21 Accounts Payable
   61 Salary Expense
   71 Rent Expense

   At the points indicated in the narrative of transactions, post to the following accounts in the accounts payable ledger:

   Aztec Supply Co.
   Chavez Co.
   Harper Equipment Co.
   Heath Supply Co.

2. Post the individual entries (Other Accounts columns of the purchases journal and the cash payments journal and both columns of the general journal) to the appropriate general ledger accounts.
3. Total each of the columns of the purchases journal and the cash payments journal, and post the appropriate totals to the general ledger. (Because the problem does not include transactions related to cash receipts, the cash account in the ledger will have a credit balance.)
4. Prepare a schedule of accounts payable.

PROBLEM 5–5A
All journals and general ledger; trial balance
Objective 4

The transactions completed by Miles Delivery Company during July, the first month of the current fiscal year, were as follows:

July 1. Issued Check No. 610 for July rent, $1,200.
2. Purchased a vehicle on account from Browning Transportation, $15,680.
3. Purchased office equipment on account from Gunter Computer Co., $5,360.
5. Issued Invoice No. 940 to Capps Co., $1,400.
6. Received check from Pease Co. for $3,100 invoice.
6. Issued Check No. 611 for fuel expense, $750.
9. Issued Invoice No. 941 to Collins Co., $2,570.
10. Issued Check No. 612 for $1,860 to Hoy Enterprises in payment of invoice.
10. Received check from Sokol Co. for $4,450 invoice.
10. Issued Check No. 613 to Burks Co. for $4,400 invoice.
11. Issued Invoice No. 942 to Joy Co., $4,180.
11. Issued Check No. 614 for $1,030 to Porter Co. in payment of account.
12. Received check from Capps Co. for $1,400 invoice.
13. Issued Check No. 615 to Browning Transportation in payment of $15,680 balance.
16. Issued Check No. 616 for $6,000 for cash purchase of a vehicle.
16. Cash fees earned for July 1–16, $14,370.
17. Purchased maintenance supplies on account from Burks Co., $3,200.
18. Issued Check No. 617 for miscellaneous administrative expense, $700.
18. Received check for rental of office space, $1,200.
19. Purchased the following on account from McClain Co.: maintenance supplies, $3,260; office supplies, $1,540.
20. Used $3,450 maintenance supplies to repair delivery vehicles.
20. Issued Check No. 618 in payment of advertising expense, $2,250.
23. Issued Invoice No. 943 to Sokol Co., $3,490.
24. Purchased office supplies on account from Hoy Enterprises, $1,020.
25. Issued Invoice No. 944 to Collins Co., $8,350.
25. Received check for $7,280 from Pease Co. in payment of balance.
26. Issued Check No. 619 to Gunter Computer Co. in payment of $5,360 invoice of July 3.
27. Issued Check No. 620 to D. D. Miles as a personal withdrawal, $3,000.
30. Issued Check No. 621 for monthly salaries as follows: driver salaries, $1,400; office salaries, $2,600.
31. Cash fees earned for July 17–31, $8,300.
31. Issued Check No. 622 in payment for office supplies, $360.

Instructions

1. Enter the following account balances in the general ledger as of July 1:

11	Cash	$12,450
12	Accounts Receivable	14,830
14	Maintenance Supplies	3,240
15	Office Supplies	1,430
16	Office Equipment	8,900
17	Accumulated Depreciation—Office Equipment	300
18	Vehicles	42,000
19	Accumulated Depreciation—Vehicles	4,200
21	Accounts Payable	7,290
31	D. D. Miles, Capital	71,060
32	D. D. Miles, Drawing	—
41	Fees Earned	—
42	Rent Income	—
51	Driver Salaries Expense	—
52	Maintenance Supplies Expense	—
53	Fuel Expense	—
61	Office Salaries Expense	—
62	Rent Expense	—
63	Advertising Expense	—
64	Miscellaneous Administrative Expense	—

2. Journalize the transactions for July, using the following journals similar to those illustrated in this chapter: purchases journal (with columns for Accounts Payable, Maintenance Supplies, Office Supplies, and Other Accounts), cash receipts journal, single-column revenue journal, cash payments journal, and two-column general journal. Assume that an assistant makes daily postings to the individual accounts in the accounts payable ledger and the accounts receivable ledger.
3. Post the appropriate individual entries to the general ledger.
4. Total each of the columns of the special journals and post the appropriate totals to the general ledger; insert the account balances.
5. Prepare a trial balance.
6. Verify the agreement of each subsidiary ledger with its controlling account. The sum of the balances of the accounts in the subsidiary ledgers as of July 31 are as follows:

   Accounts receivable: $18,590
   Accounts payable: $9,020

PROBLEMS SERIES B

PROBLEM 5–1B
Revenue journal; accounts receivable and general ledgers
Objective 4

Durbin Company was established on May 15 of the current year to provide accounting services. It rendered services during the remainder of the month as follows:

May 18. Rendered services on account to Jay Co., Invoice No. 1, $1,500.
20. Rendered services on account to Reese Co., Invoice No. 2, $3,250.
22. Rendered services on account to Innis Co., Invoice No. 3, $3,375.
27. Rendered services on account to D. L. Victor Co., Invoice No. 4, $3,125.
28. Rendered services on account to Bower Co., Invoice No. 5, $500.
28. Received a $5,000 note receivable from Taylor Co. for services rendered.
30. Rendered services on account to Reese Co., Invoice No. 6, $1,800.
31. Rendered services on account to Innis Co., Invoice No. 7, $1,495.

Instructions

1. Journalize the transactions for May, using a single-column revenue journal and a two-column general journal. Post to the following customer accounts in the accounts receivable ledger, and insert the balance immediately after recording each entry: Bower Co.; Innis Co.; Jay Co.; Reese Co.; D. L. Victor Co.
2. Post the revenue journal to the following accounts in the general ledger, inserting the account balances only after the last postings:

   12 Accounts Receivable
   13 Notes Receivable
   41 Fees Earned

3. a. What is the sum of the balances of the accounts in the subsidiary ledger at May 31?
   b. What is the balance of the controlling account at May 31?
4. Assume that on June 1, the state in which Durbin Company operates begins requiring that sales tax be collected on accounting services. Briefly explain how the revenue journal may be modified to accommodate sales of services on account requiring the collection of a state sales tax.

PROBLEM 5–2B
Revenue and cash receipts journals; accounts receivable and general ledgers
Objective 4

Transactions related to revenue and cash receipts completed by Jayco Co. during the period June 15–30 of the current year are as follows:

June 15. Issued Invoice No. 717 to Yamura Co., $6,780.
16. Received cash from AGI Co. for the balance owed on its account.
17. Issued Invoice No. 718 to Hardy Co., $5,340.
18. Issued Invoice No. 719 to Ross and Son, $6,500.
Post all journals to the accounts receivable ledger.
21. Received cash from Hardy Co. for the balance owed on June 15.
24. Issued Invoice No. 720 to Hardy Co., $2,960.
Post all journals to the accounts receivable ledger.

June 25. Received cash from Yamura Co. for the balance due on invoice of June 15.
27. Received cash from Hardy Co. for invoice of June 17.
29. Issued Invoice No. 721 to AGI Co., $1,600.
30. Recorded cash sales for the second half of the month, $11,340.
30. Received $4,000 of supplies for services rendered to Breck Company.
Post all journals to the accounts receivable ledger.

Instructions

1. Insert the following balances in the general ledger as of June 1:

11	Cash	$13,560
12	Accounts Receivable	8,800
14	Supplies	6,000
41	Fees Earned	—

2. Insert the following balances in the accounts receivable ledger as of June 15:

AGI Co.	$ 6,340
Hardy Co.	10,680
Ross and Son	—
Yamura Co.	—

3. In a single-column revenue journal and a cash receipts journal, insert *June 15 Total(s) Forwarded* on the left side of the first line of the journal. Use the following column headings for the cash receipts journal: Other Accounts, Fees Earned, Accounts Receivable, and Cash. The Fees Earned column is used to record cash fees. Insert a check mark (✓) in the Post. Ref. column and the following dollar figures in the respective amount columns:

   Revenue journal: 26,790
   Cash receipts journal: 4,120; 9,980; 18,570; 32,670.

4. Using the two special journals and the two-column general journal, journalize the transactions for the remainder of June. Post to the accounts receivable ledger, and insert the balances at the points indicated in the narrative of transactions. *Determine the balance in the customer's account before recording a cash receipt.*
5. Total each of the columns of the special journals, and post the individual entries and totals to the general ledger. Insert account balances after the last posting.
6. Determine that the subsidiary ledger agrees with the controlling account in the general ledger.

PROBLEM 5–3B
Purchases, accounts payable account, and accounts payable ledger
Objective 4

Robbins Surveyors provides survey work for construction projects. Office supplies are used by the office staff, while field supplies are used by surveying crews at construction sites. Purchases on account completed by Robbins Surveyors during May of the current year are as follows:

May 1. Purchased field supplies on account from Wendell Co., $4,230.
3. Purchased office supplies on account from Lassiter Co., $3,120.
8. Purchased field supplies on account from Trent Supply, $1,640.
12. Purchased field supplies on account from Wendell Co., $1,890.
13. Purchased office equipment on account from Gore Computers Co., $7,500.
15. Purchased office supplies on account from J-Mart Co., $940.
19. Purchased office equipment on account from Eskew Co., $11,400.
23. Purchased field supplies on account from Trent Supply, $2,340.
26. Purchased office supplies on account from J-Mart Co., $1,250.
30. Purchased field supplies on account from Trent Supply, $6,780.

Instructions

1. Insert the following balances in the general ledger as of May 1:

14	Field Supplies	$ 4,570
15	Office Supplies	2,050
18	Office Equipment	19,500
21	Accounts Payable	8,210

2. Insert the following balances in the accounts payable ledger as of May 1:

Eskew Co.	$ 2,860
Gore Computers Co.	—
J-Mart Co.	1,030
Lassiter Co.	4,320
Trent Supply	—
Wendell Co.	—

3. Journalize the transactions for May, using a purchases journal similar to the one illustrated in this chapter. Prepare the purchases journal with columns for Accounts Payable, Field Supplies, Office Supplies, and Other Accounts. Post to the creditor accounts in the accounts payable ledger immediately after each entry.
4. Post the purchases journal to the accounts in the general ledger.
5. a. What is the sum of the balances in the subsidiary ledger at May 31?
   b. What is the balance of the controlling account at May 31?

PROBLEM 5–4B
Purchases and cash payments journals; accounts payable and general ledgers
Objective 4

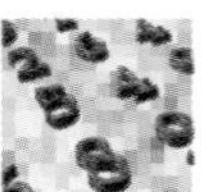

Cruz Exploration Co. was established on March 15 of the current year to provide oil-drilling services. Cruz uses field equipment (rigs, pipe, drill bits) and field supplies in its operations. Transactions related to purchases and cash payments during the remainder of March are as follows:

Mar. 16. Issued Check No. 1 in payment of rent for March, $800.
16. Purchased field equipment on account from Harper Equipment Co., $7,400.
17. Purchased field supplies on account from Culver Supply Co., $4,780.
18. Issued Check No. 2 in payment of field supplies, $3,450, and office supplies, $450.
19. Purchased office equipment on account from Lacy Co., $8,950.
20. Purchased office supplies on account from Ange Supply Co., $1,460.
Post the journals to the accounts payable ledger.
24. Issued Check No. 3 to Harper Equipment Co. in payment of invoice, $7,400.
26. Issued Check No. 4 to Culver Supply Co. in payment of invoice, $4,780.
28. Issued Check No. 5 to purchase land from the owner, $19,000.
28. Issued Check No. 6 to Lacy Co. in payment of the balance owed.
28. Purchased office supplies on account from Ange Supply Co., $860.
Post the journals to the accounts payable ledger.
30. Purchased the following from Harper Equipment Co. on account: field supplies, $2,300, and office equipment, $7,230.
30. Issued Check No. 7 to Ange Supply Co. in payment of invoice, $1,460.
30. Purchased field supplies on account from Culver Supply Co., $7,320.
31. Issued Check No. 8 in payment of salaries, $1,750.
31. Acquired land in exchange for field equipment having a cost of $4,800.
Post the journals to the accounts payable ledger.

Instructions

1. Journalize the transactions for March. Use a purchases journal and a cash payments journal, similar to those illustrated in this chapter, and a two-column general journal. Refer to the following partial chart of accounts:

11	Cash
14	Field Supplies
15	Office Supplies
17	Field Equipment
18	Office Equipment
19	Land

21 Accounts Payable
61 Salary Expense
71 Rent Expense

At the points indicated in the narrative of transactions, post to the following accounts in the accounts payable ledger:

Ange Supply Co.
Culver Supply Co.
Harper Equipment Co.
Lacy Co.

2. Post the individual entries (Other Accounts columns of the purchases journal and the cash payments journal; both columns of the general journal) to the appropriate general ledger accounts.
3. Total each of the columns of the purchases journal and the cash payments journal, and post the appropriate totals to the general ledger. (Because the problem does not include transactions related to cash receipts, the cash account in the ledger will have a credit balance.)
4. Prepare a schedule of accounts payable.

PROBLEM 5–5B
All journals and general ledger; trial balance
Objective 4

The transactions completed by Davis Courier Company during May, the first month of the current fiscal year, were as follows:

May 1. Issued Check No. 205 for May rent, $900.
2. Purchased a vehicle on account from Bunting Co., $21,400.
3. Purchased office equipment on account from Gill Computer Co., $6,400.
5. Issued Invoice No. 91 to Carlton Co., $970.
6. Received check from Pease Co. for $2,450 invoice.
6. Issued Check No. 206 for vehicle fuel, $700.
9. Issued Invoice No. 92 to Collins Co., $1,860.
10. Received check from Sing Co. for $5,630 invoice.
10. Issued Check No. 207 to Haber Enterprises in payment of $2,140 invoice.
10. Issued Check No. 208 to Bastille Co. in payment of $3,420 invoice.
11. Issued Invoice No. 93 to Joy Co., $3,560.
11. Issued Check No. 209 to Porter Co. in payment of $1,370 invoice.
12. Received check from Carlton Co. for $970 invoice.
13. Issued Check No. 210 to Bunting Co. in payment of $21,400 invoice.
16. Cash fees earned for May 1–16, $17,680.
16. Issued Check No. 211 for purchase of a vehicle, $8,000.
17. Purchased maintenance supplies on account from Bastille Co., $2,680.
18. Issued Check No. 212 for miscellaneous administrative expenses, $1,000.
18. Received check for rent income on office space, $1,500.
19. Purchased the following on account from Master Co.: maintenance supplies, $1,250, and office supplies, $3,250.
20. Issued Check No. 213 in payment of advertising expense, $3,500.
20. Used maintenance supplies with a cost of $4,580 to overhaul vehicle engines.
23. Issued Invoice No. 94 to Sing Co., $5,400.
24. Purchased office supplies on account from Haber Enterprises, $850.
25. Received check from Pease Co. for $1,760 invoice.
25. Issued Invoice No. 95 to Collins Co., $2,780.
26. Issued Check No. 214 to Gill Computer Co. in payment of $6,400 invoice.
27. Issued Check No. 215 to C. Davis as a personal withdrawal, $2,800.
30. Issued Check No. 216 in payment of driver salaries, $1,900.
31. Issued Check No. 217 in payment of office salaries, $2,950.
31. Issued Check No. 218 for office supplies, $1,850.
31. Cash sales for May 17–31, $21,400.

Instructions

1. Enter the following account balances in the general ledger as of May 1:

11	Cash	$14,680
12	Accounts Receivable	9,840
14	Maintenance Supplies	4,210
15	Office Supplies	2,100
16	Office Equipment	12,400
17	Accumulated Depreciation—Office Equipment	2,000
18	Vehicles	62,000
19	Accumulated Depreciation—Vehicles	12,400
21	Accounts Payable	6,930
31	C. Davis, Capital	83,900
32	C. Davis, Drawing	—
41	Fees Earned	—
42	Rent Income	—
51	Driver Salaries Expense	—
52	Maintenance Supplies Expense	—
53	Fuel Expense	—
61	Office Salaries Expense	—
62	Rent Expense	—
63	Advertising Expense	—
64	Miscellaneous Administrative Expense	—

2. Journalize the transactions for May, using the following journals similar to those illustrated in this chapter: single-column revenue journal, cash receipts journal, purchases journal (with columns for Accounts Payable, Maintenance Supplies, Office Supplies, and Other Accounts), cash payments journal, and two-column general journal. Assume that an assistant makes daily postings to the individual accounts in the accounts payable ledger and the accounts receivable ledger.
3. Post the appropriate individual entries to the general ledger.
4. Total each of the columns of the special journals, and post the appropriate totals to the general ledger; insert the account balances.
5. Prepare a trial balance.
6. Verify the agreement of each subsidiary ledger with its controlling account. The sum of the balances of the accounts in the subsidiary ledgers as of May 31 are as follows:

   Accounts receivable: $13,600
   Accounts payable: $8,030

CASES

CASE 5–1
Gunthorpe Security Co.
Internal controls

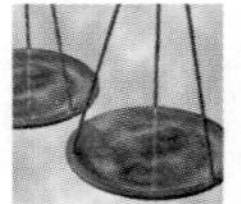

Lee Baskin sells security systems for Gunthorpe Security Co. Baskin has a monthly sales quota of $40,000. If Baskin exceeds this quota, he is awarded a bonus. In measuring the quota, a sale is credited to the salesperson when a customer signs a contract for installation of a security system. Through the 25th of the current month, Baskin has sold $30,000 in security systems.

Vortex Co., a business rumored to be on the verge of bankruptcy, contacted Baskin on the 26th of the month about having a security system installed. Baskin estimates that the contract would yield about $14,000 of business for Gunthorpe Security Co. In addition, this contract would be large enough to put Baskin "over the top" for a bonus in the current month. However, Baskin is concerned that Vortex Co. will not be able to make the contract payment after the security system is installed. In fact, Baskin has heard rumors that a competing security services company refused to install a system for Vortex Co. because of these concerns.

Upon further consideration, Baskin concluded that his job is to sell security systems and that it's someone else's problem to collect the resulting accounts receivable. Thus, Baskin wrote the contract with Vortex Co. and received a bonus for the month.

Discuss whether Lee Baskin was acting in an ethical manner. How might Gunthorpe Security Co. use internal controls to prevent this scenario from occurring?

CASE 5–2
Lafont Co.
Manual vs. computerized accounting systems

The following conversation took place between Lafont Co.'s bookkeeper, Gerry Monroe, and the accounting supervisor, Lyn Hargrove.

Lyn: Gerry, I'm thinking about bringing in a new computerized accounting system to replace our manual system. I guess this will mean that you will need to learn how to do computerized accounting.
Gerry: What does computerized accounting mean?
Lyn: I'm not sure, but you'll need to prepare for this new way of doing business.
Gerry: I'm not so sure we need a computerized system. I've been looking at some of the sample reports from the software vendor. It looks to me like the computer will not add much to what we are already doing.
Lyn: What do you mean?
Gerry: Well, look at these reports. This Customer Invoice Summary Report looks like our revenue journal, and the Cash Receipts Summary Report looks like our cash receipts journal. Granted, they are typed by the computer, so they look much neater than my special journals, but I don't see that we're gaining much from this change.
Lyn: Well, surely there's more to it than nice-looking reports. I've got to believe that a computerized system will save us time and effort someplace.
Gerry: I don't see how. We still need to key in transactions into the computer. If anything, there may be more work when it's all said and done.

Do you agree with Gerry? Why might a computerized environment be preferred over the manual system?

CASE 5–3
Hitchcock Company
Internal controls

Like most businesses, when Hitchcock Company renders services to another business, it is typical that the service is rendered "on account," rather than as a cash transaction. As a result, Hitchcock Company has an account receivable for the service provided. Likewise, the company receiving the service has an account payable for the amount owed for services received. At a later date, Hitchcock Company will receive cash from the customer to satisfy the accounts receivable balance. However, when individuals conduct transactions with each other, it is common for the transaction to be satisfied with cash. For example, when you buy a pizza, you often pay with cash.

Why is it unusual for businesses such as Hitchcock Company to engage in cash transactions, while for individuals it is more common?

CASE 5–4
Hershey Foods Corporation
Financial analysis

Corporations generally issue annual reports to their stockholders and other interested parties. These annual reports include a Management Responsibility (or Management Report) section as well as financial statements. The Management Responsibility section discusses responsibility for the financial statements and normally includes an assessment of the company's internal control system.

What does the annual report for Hershey Foods Corporation indicate about the internal control system?

CASE 5–5
Rockland Landscaping Services
Design of accounting systems

For the past few years, your client, Rockland Landscaping Services (RLS), has operated a small landscaping business. RLS's current annual revenues are $420,000. Because the accountant has been spending more and more time each month recording all transactions in a two-column journal and preparing the financial statements, RLS is considering improving the accounting system by adding special journals and subsidiary ledgers. RLS has asked you to help with this project and has compiled the following information:

Type of Transaction	*Estimated Frequency per Month*
Fees earned on account	240
Purchase of landscaping supplies on account	190
Cash receipts from customers on account	175
Cash receipts from customers at time services rendered	120
Purchase of office supplies on account	15
Cash purchases of office supplies	6
Purchase of fuel on account	5
Purchase of landscaping equipment on account	4
Cash payments for office salaries	3
Cash payments for utilities expense	3

A local sales tax is collected on all customer bills, and monthly financial statements are prepared.

1. Briefly discuss the circumstances under which special journals would be used in place of a two-column (all-purpose) journal. Include in your answer your recommendations for RLS's business.
2. Assume that RLS has decided to use a revenue journal and purchases journal. Design the format for each journal, giving special consideration to the needs of the landscaping business.
3. Which subsidiary ledgers would you recommend for the landscaping business?

ANSWERS TO SELF-EXAMINATION QUESTIONS

1. **C** The task of installing an accounting system is composed of three phases. Systems analysis (answer A) is the initial phase of determining the informational needs, sources of such information, and deficiencies in the procedures and data processing methods currently employed. Systems design (answer B) is the phase in which proposals for changes are developed. Systems implementation (answer C) is the final phase involving carrying out or implementing the proposals for changes. Systems training (answer D) is not a separate phase of installing an accounting system but is considered part of the systems implementation.
2. **A** The policies and procedures that are established to provide reasonable assurance that the enterprise's goals will be achieved are called internal controls (answer A). The three phases of installing or changing an accounting system are (1) analysis (answer B), (2) design (answer C), and (3) implementation (answer D). Systems analysis is determining the informational needs, sources of such information, and deficiencies in the procedures and data processing methods presently used. Systems design refers to the design of a new system or change in the present system based on the systems analysis. The carrying out of proposals for the design of a system is called systems implementation.
3. **B** All payments of cash for any purpose are recorded in the cash payments journal (answer B). Only purchases of services or other items on account are recorded in the purchases journal (answer A). All sales of services on account are recorded in the revenue journal (answer C), and all receipts of cash are recorded in the cash receipts journal (answer D).
4. **A** The general term used to describe the type of separate ledger that contains a large number of individual accounts with a common characteristic is a subsidiary ledger (answer A). The creditors ledger (answer B), sometimes called the accounts payable ledger (answer C), is a specific subsidiary ledger containing only individual accounts with creditors. Likewise, the accounts receivable ledger (answer D), also called the customers ledger, is a specific subsidiary ledger containing only individual accounts with customers.
5. **B** The controlling account for the customers ledger (the ledger that contains the individual accounts with customers) is Accounts Receivable (answer B). The accounts payable account (answer A) is the controlling account for the creditors ledger. There are no subsidiary ledgers for the fees earned (answer C) and rent expense (answer D) accounts.

6 Accounting for Merchandising Businesses

INGLES #426
ATHENS GA

10/02/96

GROCERY	2.99L
GROCERY	1.00L
FZ FOOD	1.29L
SUBTOTAL	5.28
TAX	.32
TOTAL	5.60
CASH	10.00
CHANGE	4.40
# ITEMS 3	

THANK YOU C123 R03 T12:38

YOU AND ACCOUNTING

Assume that you bought groceries at a store and received the receipt shown here. This receipt indicates that you purchased three items totaling $5.28, the sales tax was $.32 (6%), the total due was $5.60, you gave the clerk $10.00, and you received change of $4.40. The receipt also indicates that the sale was made by Store #426 of the Ingles chain, located in Athens, Georgia. The date and time of the sale and other data used internally by the store are also indicated.

Whether you are buying groceries, textbooks, school supplies, or an automobile, you are doing business with a retail or merchandising business. As you might imagine, the accounting for a merchandising business is more complex than for a service business. For example, the accounting system for a merchandiser must be designed to record the receipt of goods for resale, keep track of the goods on hand and available for sale, and record the eventual sale and cost of the goods sold. Any special price reductions to customers who pay their bills early or who return damaged merchandise must also be recorded. Likewise, the accounting system must be designed to ensure prompt payments to suppliers and to keep a record of the amounts paid.

In this chapter, we will focus on the accounting principles and concepts for merchandising businesses. We begin our discussion by highlighting the basic differences in the activities of such businesses and service businesses. We then describe and illustrate the proper recording of purchases and sales transactions for merchandising businesses. We conclude the chapter by illustrating the preparation of financial statements for merchandisers.

After studying this chapter, you should be able to:

Objective 1
Compare a service business's income statement to a merchandising business's income statement.

Objective 2
Journalize the entries for merchandise transactions, including:

a. Merchandise purchases
b. Merchandise sales
c. Merchandise transportation costs

Objective 3
Journalize the entries for merchandise transactions from both the buyer's and the seller's point of view.

Objective 4
Prepare a chart of accounts for a merchandising business.

Objective 5
Prepare an income statement for a merchandising business.

Objective 6
Describe the accounting cycle for a merchandising business.

Nature of Merchandising Businesses

Objective 1
Compare a service business's income statement to a merchandising business's income statement.

How do the revenue activities of Computer King, an attorney, and an architect, which are service businesses, differ from those of **Wal-Mart** or **K Mart**, which are merchandising businesses? These differences are highlighted in the following condensed income statements:

Service Business	
Fees earned	$XXX
Operating expenses	XXX
Net income	$XXX

Merchandising Business	
Sales	$XXX
Cost of merchandise sold	XXX
Gross profit	$XXX
Operating expenses	XXX
Net income	$XXX

The revenue-generating activities of a service business involve providing services to customers. On the income statement for a service business, the revenues from services are reported as fees earned. The operating expenses incurred in providing the services are subtracted from the fees earned to arrive at net income.

In contrast, the revenue-generating activities of a merchandising business involve the buying and selling of merchandise. A merchandising business must first purchase merchandise to sell to its customers. When this merchandise is sold, the revenue is reported as sales, and its cost is recognized as an expense called the cost of merchandise sold. For many merchandising businesses, the cost of merchandise sold is the largest expense. For example, the approximate percentage of cost of merchandise sold to sales is 70% for **Toys "R" Us, Inc.**, 70% for **Winn-Dixie Stores, Inc.**, and 73% for **Circuit City Stores, Inc.**

The cost of merchandise sold is subtracted from sales to arrive at **gross profit**. This amount is called gross profit because from it the operating expenses are deducted to arrive at net income.

Merchandise that is not sold at the end of an accounting period is called **merchandise inventory**. Merchandise inventory is reported as a current asset on the balance sheet.

We discuss in the remainder of this chapter the transactions that affect these identifying features of a merchandising business's financial statements—sales, cost of merchandise sold, and gross profit on the income statement, and merchandise inventory on the balance sheet. We will illustrate these transactions for Computer King, assuming that Computer King opened a retail store in January 1998.

Merchandise transactions are recorded in the accounts, using the rules of debit and credit that we described and illustrated in earlier chapters. Special journals, such as those we described and illustrated for service businesses in the previous chapter, may be used by merchandising businesses. Alternatively, transactions may be entered, recorded, and posted to the accounts electronically. Although transactions are not recorded manually in such systems, we will use a two-column general journal format in the remainder of this chapter in order to simplify the illustrations.

Accounting for Purchases

Objective 2a
Journalize the entries for merchandise purchases.

There are two systems for accounting for merchandise purchased for sale: perpetual and periodic. In the **perpetual inventory system,** each purchase and sale of merchandise is recorded in an inventory account. In this way, the inventory records always (perpetually) disclose the amount of merchandise on hand and the amount sold. In the **periodic inventory system,** no attempt is made to keep detailed inventory records of the amounts on hand throughout the period. Instead, a detailed listing of the merchandise on hand (called a **physical inventory**) at the end of the accounting period is prepared. This physical inventory listing is used to determine the cost of the inventory on hand at the end of the period and the cost of the merchandise sold during the period.

Large retailers and many small merchandising businesses use computerized perpetual inventory systems. Such systems normally use bar codes, such as the one on the back of this textbook. An optical scanner reads the bar code to initiate the recording of merchandise purchased for resale and sales of merchandise to customers. Examples of such retailers are K Mart, Sears, and Wal-Mart and grocery store chains such as Winn Dixie and Kroger. Because the perpetual inventory system is widely used, we illustrate it in this chapter. We describe and illustrate the periodic inventory system in an appendix at the end of this text.

Under the perpetual inventory system, purchases of merchandise for sale are recorded in the merchandise inventory account in the ledger. When purchases are made for cash, the transaction is recorded as follows:

Jan.	3	Merchandise Inventory	2,510	
		Cash		2,510
		Purchases from supplier, Bowen Co.		

Purchases of merchandise on account are recorded as follows:

Jan.	4	Merchandise Inventory	9,250	
		Accounts Payable		9,250
		Purchases from supplier, Thomas Corporation.		

PURCHASES DISCOUNTS

The terms of a purchase are normally indicated on the **invoice,** or bill, that the seller sends to the buyer. An example of such an invoice is shown in Exhibit 1.

The terms agreed on by the buyer and the seller as to when payments for merchandise are to be made are called the **credit terms.** If payment is required on delivery, the terms are said to be *cash* or *net cash*. Otherwise, the buyer is allowed an amount of time, known as the **credit period,** in which to pay.

Exhibit 1
Invoice

Wallace Electronics Supply 3800 Mission Street
San Francisco, CA 94110–1732

Made in USA.

SOLD TO		CUSTOMER'S ORDER NO. & DATE	
Computer King 1000 Peachtree Street Atlanta, GA 30309-1000		412 Jan. 10, 1998 **REFER TO INVOICE NO.** 106-8	
DATE SHIPPED	**HOW SHIPPED AND ROUTE**	**TERMS**	**INVOICE DATE**
Jan. 12, 1998	Western Trucking Co.	2/10, n/30	Jan. 12,1998
FROM	**F.O.B.**	**PREPAID OR COLLECT?**	
San Francisco	Atlanta	Prepaid	
QUANTITY	**DESCRIPTION**	**UNIT PRICE**	**AMOUNT**
20	392E Monitors	75.00	1,500.00

The credit period usually begins with the date of the sale as shown on the invoice. If payment is due within a stated number of days after the date of the invoice, such as 30 days, the terms are said to be *net 30 days*. These terms may be written as *n/30*.[1] If payment is due by the end of the month in which the sale was made, it may be written as *n/eom*.

As a means of encouraging payment before the end of the credit period, the seller may offer a discount to the buyer for the early payment of cash. For example, a seller may offer a buyer a 2% discount if payment is received within 10 days of the invoice date. If the buyer does not take the discount, the total amount is due within 30 days. These terms are expressed as *2/10, n/30* and are read as *2% discount if paid within 10 days, net amount due within 30 days*. The credit terms of 2/10, n/30 are summarized in Exhibit 2.

Exhibit 2
Credit Terms

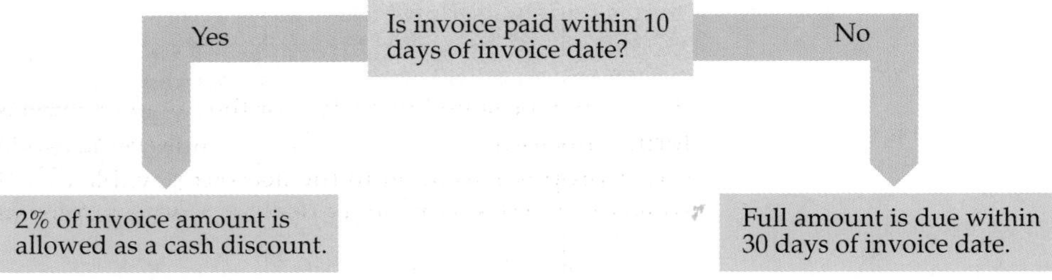

Discounts taken by the buyer for early payment of an invoice are called **purchases discounts**. These discounts are viewed as a reduction in the cost of the merchandise purchased. Most businesses design their accounting systems so that all available discounts are taken. Thus, throughout this chapter, we assume that all discounts are taken.[2]

Since most buyers will take advantage of purchases discounts, buyers using perpetual inventory systems normally record merchandise purchases at their net cost. *Net cost* is the invoice price less any discounts. For example, for the invoice in Exhibit 1, the net cost is $1,470 [$1,500 – (.02 × $1,500)]. The entries recorded by Computer King for this invoice in Exhibit 1 and its payment at the end of the discount period are as shown on the next page.

[1] The word *net* as used here does not have the usual meaning of a number after deductions have been subtracted, as in *net income*.
[2] In the next chapter, we will discuss the accounting for discounts not taken.

USING ACCOUNTING TO UNDERSTAND BUSINESS

Do you pay your bills, such as utility bills and credit card bills, as soon as they are received? The terms of payment on each bill (the credit terms) may allow you to delay payment a week or more.

Most bills you receive do not offer discounts for early payment. Rather, the bills normally indicate only a due date and perhaps a penalty for late payment. Many times you receive bills weeks before their due date. In such cases, it is to your advantage to file the bill by its due date in a folder or other organizer, such as a desk calendar, and mail the payment a few days before it is due. In this way, you have the opportunity to earn additional interest on the balance of your checking or savings account.

Businesses design their accounting systems in much the same way that you might organize your system for paying bills. That is, they design their accounting systems to pay bills at the latest possible date, but yet take advantage of all discounts and avoid late payment penalties. Oftentimes businesses computerize their accounting systems so that checks are automatically created when the bill is scheduled for payment. In more advanced computerized systems, the payments may be electronically transferred from the business's bank account to the supplier's bank account without a check even being written.

Jan.	12	Merchandise Inventory	1,470	
		Accounts Payable		1,470
		Invoice 106–8 from Wallace Electronics Supply.		
	22	Accounts Payable	1,470	
		Cash		1,470
		Payment of Invoice 106–8 from Wallace Electronics Supply.		

PURCHASES RETURNS AND ALLOWANCES

When merchandise is returned (purchases return) or a price adjustment is requested (purchases allowance), the buyer usually notifies the seller in writing. The details may be stated in a letter, or the buyer (debtor) may use a debit memorandum form. This form, shown in Exhibit 3, informs the seller (creditor) of the amount the buyer proposes to debit to the account payable due the seller. It also states the reasons for the return or the request for a price reduction.

Exhibit 3
Debit Memorandum

COMPUTER KING
Computer King
1000 Peachtree Street, Atlanta, GA 30309–1000
No. 18

DEBIT MEMORANDUM

TO
Power Electronics
1614 LaSalle Street
Chicago, IL 60602-2391

DATE
July 7, 1998

WE DEBIT YOUR ACCOUNT AS FOLLOWS

5	No. 8241 Printer Covers, your Invoice No. 7291, are being returned via parcel post. Our order specified No. 825X.	@ 18.00	90.00

The buyer may use a copy of the debit memorandum as the basis for an entry or may wait for confirmation from the seller. The seller confirms the return or allowance by issuing a **credit memorandum**. In either event, Accounts Payable must be debited, and Merchandise Inventory must be credited. To illustrate, the entry by Computer King to record the return of the merchandise indicated in the debit memo in Exhibit 3 is as follows:

July	7	Accounts Payable	90	
		Merchandise Inventory		90
		Debit Memo No. 18.		

When merchandise subject to a purchase discount is returned, the amount of the entry is for the net cost of the merchandise returned. For example, assume that on May 2, Computer King purchases $5,000 of merchandise subject to terms 2/10, n/30. On May 4, Computer King returns $3,000 of the merchandise, and on May 12, Computer King pays the original invoice less the return. The entries to record the preceding transactions are as follows:

May	2	Merchandise Inventory	4,900	
		Accounts Payable		4,900
		[$5,000 – (2% × $5,000)]		
	4	Accounts Payable	2,940	
		Merchandise Inventory		2,940
		[$3,000 – (2% × $3,000)]		
	12	Accounts Payable	1,960	
		Cash		1,960
		($4,900 – $2,940)		

Accounting for Sales

Objective 2b
Journalize the entries for merchandise sales.

Revenue from merchandise sales is usually identified in the ledger as *Sales*. Sometimes a business will use a more exact title, such as *Sales of Merchandise*.

A business may sell merchandise for cash. Cash sales are normally rung up (entered) on a cash register. At the end of the day, the sales can be recorded as follows:

Jan.	3	Cash	1,800	
		Sales		1,800
		Cash sales for the day.		

Under the perpetual inventory system, the cost of merchandise sold and the reduction in merchandise inventory can also be recorded at the end of the day. In this way, the merchandise inventory account will indicate the amount of merchandise that should be on hand. At the end of the period, the balance of the cost of merchandise sold account is reported on the income statement, along with the related sales for the period. To illustrate, assume that the cost of merchandise sold on January 3 was $1,200. The entry to record the cost of merchandise sold and the reduction in the merchandise inventory is as follows:

Jan.	3	Cost of Merchandise Sold	1,200	
		Merchandise Inventory		1,200
		Cost of merchandise sold for the day.		

How do retailers record sales made with the use of MasterCard or VISA? Sales to customers who use such bank credit cards are usually treated as cash sales. The credit card receipts (slips) for these sales are deposited by the seller directly into the bank. The credit card slips, cash, and checks received for the sales make up the total deposit.

Normally, banks charge service fees for handling credit card sales. These service fees should be debited to an expense account. An entry at the end of a month to record the payment of service charges on bank credit card sales is shown here.

Jan. 31	Bank Credit Card Expense	48	
	Cash		48
	Service charges on bank credit card sales for the month.		

Sales may also be made by accepting a customer's nonbank credit card (such as **American Express**). These sales must be reported directly to the card company before cash is received. Therefore, such sales create a receivable with the card company. Before the card company pays cash, it normally deducts a service fee. For example, assume that nonbank credit card sales of $1,000 are made and reported to the card company on January 20. The cost of the merchandise sold was $550. On January 27, the card company deducts a service fee of $50 and sends $950 to the seller. These transactions are recorded by the seller as follows:

Jan. 20	Accounts Receivable	1,000	
	Sales		1,000
	American Express credit card sales.		
20	Cost of Merchandise Sold	550	
	Merchandise Inventory		550
	Cost of merchandise sold on American Express credit card sales.		
27	Cash	950	
	Nonbank Credit Card Expense	50	
	Accounts Receivable		1,000
	Receipt of cash from American Express for sales reported on January 20.		

A business may sell merchandise on account. Such sales result in a debit to Accounts Receivable and a credit to Sales. An example of an entry for a sale on account of $510 follows. The cost of merchandise sold was $280.

Jan. 12	Accounts Receivable	510	
	Sales		510
	Invoice No. 7172 to Sims Co.		
12	Cost of Merchandise Sold	280	
	Merchandise Inventory		280
	Cost of merchandise sold on Invoice No. 7172 to Sims Co.		

SALES DISCOUNTS

As we mentioned in our discussion of purchase transactions, a seller may offer the buyer credit terms that include a discount for early payment, such as 2/10, n/30. Such discounts are referred to by the seller as **sales discounts.** When a buyer takes advantage of such a discount by paying within the discount period, the seller debits the sales discounts account. For example, if cash is received within the discount period (10 days) from the credit sale of $1,500, shown on the invoice

USING ACCOUNTING TO UNDERSTAND BUSINESS

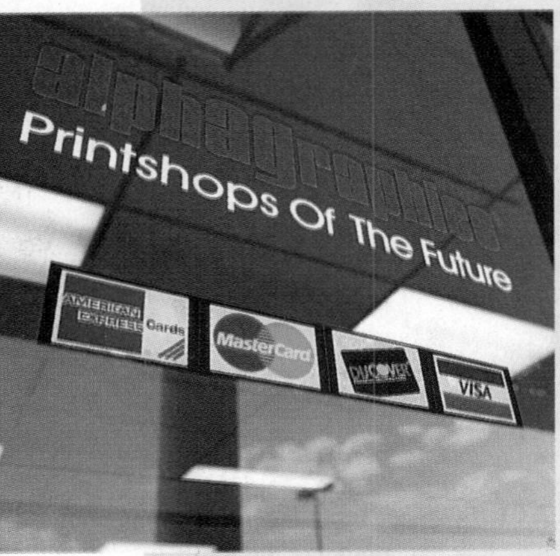

Have you ever wondered why some retailers accept one type of credit card and not another? For example, a retailer may accept MasterCard or VISA but not American Express. Also, some retailers will offer you a discount if you pay in cash.

The service fees that credit card companies charge retailers is the primary reason why businesses do not accept all credit cards. For example, American Express Co.'s service fees are normally higher than MasterCard's or VISA's. As a result, some retailers choose not to accept American Express cards. The primary disadvantage of this practice for retailers is that they may lose customers to competitors who do accept American Express cards.

in Exhibit 1, the transaction would be recorded by Wallace Electronics Supply as follows:

Jan. 22	Cash	1,470	
	Sales Discounts	30	
	Accounts Receivable		1,500
	Collection on Invoice No. 106–8 to Computer King, less discount.		

Sales discounts are considered to be a reduction in the amount initially recorded in Sales. In this sense, the balance of the sales discounts account is viewed as a contra (or offsetting) account to Sales.

SALES RETURNS AND ALLOWANCES

Merchandise sold may be returned to the seller **(sales return)**. In addition, the buyer may be allowed a reduction from the initial price at which the goods were sold because of defects or for other reasons **(sales allowance)**. If the return or allowance is for a sale on account, the seller usually issues the buyer a **credit memorandum**. This memorandum shows the amount and the reason for which the buyer's account receivable is to be credited. A credit memorandum is illustrated in Exhibit 4.

Exhibit 4
Credit Memorandum

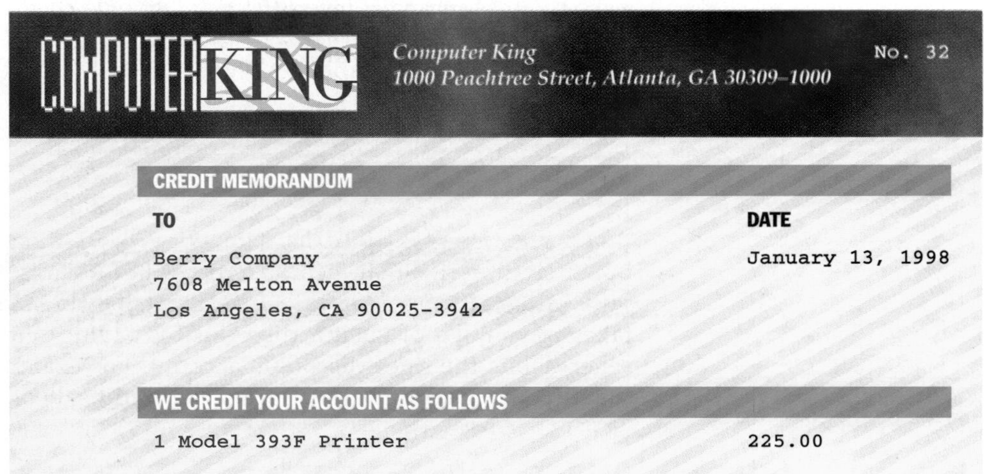
COMPUTER KING

Computer King
1000 Peachtree Street, Atlanta, GA 30309–1000

No. 32

CREDIT MEMORANDUM

TO	DATE
Berry Company 7608 Melton Avenue Los Angeles, CA 90025-3942	January 13, 1998

WE CREDIT YOUR ACCOUNT AS FOLLOWS

1 Model 393F Printer	225.00

The effect of a sales return or allowance is to reduce sales revenue and cash or accounts receivable. To reduce sales, the sales account could be debited. However, the balance of the sales account would then represent net sales for the period. Because of the loss in revenue and the related expense that may result from returns and allowances, management closely monitors the amount of returns and allowances. If it becomes too large, management may take appropriate action to reduce returns and allowances. For this reason, sales returns and allowances are recorded in a separate account entitled *Sales Returns and Allowances*. Because sales returns and allowances reduce the amount initially recorded in Sales, the sales returns and allowances account is a contra (or offsetting) account to Sales.

Sales Returns and Allowances is debited for the amount of the return or allowance. If the original sale is on account, Accounts Receivable is credited. Since the merchandise inventory is kept up to date in a perpetual system, the cost of the merchandise returned is added to the merchandise inventory account. The cost of merchandise returned must also be credited to the cost of merchandise sold account, since this account was debited when the original sale was recorded.

To illustrate, assume that the cost of the merchandise returned in Exhibit 4 was $140. The credit memo in Exhibit 4 would be recorded by Computer King as follows:

Jan. 13	Sales Returns and Allowances	225	
	Accounts Receivable		225
	Credit Memo No. 32.		
13	Merchandise Inventory	140	
	Cost of Merchandise Sold		140
	Cost of merchandise returned, Credit Memo No. 32.		

What if the buyer pays for the merchandise and the merchandise is later returned? In this case, the seller may issue a credit and apply it against other accounts receivable owed by the buyer, or the cash may be refunded. If the credit is to be applied against the buyer's other receivables, entries similar to the preceding are recorded. If cash is refunded for merchandise returned or for an allowance, Sales Returns and Allowances is debited and Cash is credited.

SALES TAXES

Almost all states and many other taxing units levy a tax on sales of merchandise.[3] The liability for the sales tax is incurred at the time the sale is made.

At the time of a cash sale, the seller collects the sales tax. When a sale is made on account, the tax is charged to the buyer by debiting Accounts Receivable. The seller credits the sales account for only the amount of the sale and credits the tax to Sales Tax Payable. For example, a sale of $100 on account, subject to a tax of 6%, is recorded by the following entry:

Aug. 12	Accounts Receivable	106	
	Sales		100
	Sales Tax Payable		6
	Invoice No. 339.		

The amount of the sales tax that has been collected is normally paid to the taxing unit on a regular basis. An entry to record such a payment is as follows:

[3] Businesses that purchase merchandise for resale to others are normally exempt from paying sales taxes on their purchases. Only *final* buyers of merchandise normally pay sales taxes.

Sep. 15	Sales Tax Payable	2,900	
	Cash		2,900
	Payment for sales taxes collected during August.		

TRADE DISCOUNTS

Many wholesalers of merchandise publish periodic catalogs that are used by buyers in ordering merchandise. Rather than updating their catalogs frequently, wholesalers publish price updates, which may involve large discounts from the list prices in their catalogs. In addition, sellers frequently offer certain classes of buyers, such as government agencies or buyers who order large quantities, special discounts. These special discounts or discounts for large quantities purchased are called **trade discounts**.

Sellers and buyers do not normally record the list prices of merchandise and the related trade discounts in their accounts. For example, assume that a seller offers for sale an item with a list price of $1,000 and a 40% trade discount. The seller records the sale of the item at $600 [$1,000 less the trade discount of $400 ($1,000 × 40%)]. Likewise, the buyer records the purchase at $600. For accounting purposes, only the final price—$600 in this example—is important.

Transportation Costs

Objective 2c
Journalize the entries for merchandise transportation costs.

A sales agreement should indicate when the title of the merchandise passes from the seller to the buyer, because that determines who must pay the transportation costs.

The terms of a sales agreement between a buyer and a seller should indicate when the ownership (title) of the merchandise passes to the buyer. The point at which the title of the merchandise passes to the buyer determines which party, the buyer or the seller, must pay the transportation costs.[4]

The ownership of the merchandise may pass to the buyer when the seller delivers the merchandise to the transportation company or freight carrier. For example, **Chrysler Corp.** records the sale and the transfer of ownership of its vehicles to dealers when the vehicles are shipped. In this case, the terms are said to be **FOB shipping point**. This shipping term means that Chrysler delivers the merchandise *free on board* to the shipping point. The dealer pays the transportation costs to the final destination.

The ownership of the merchandise may pass to the buyer when the merchandise is received by the buyer. In this case, the terms are said to be **FOB destination**. This shipping term means that the seller delivers the merchandise *free on board* to the buyer's final destination. The seller pays the transportation costs to the final destination.

Sometimes FOB shipping point and FOB destination are expressed in terms of the location at which the title to the merchandise passes to the buyer. For example, assume that a seller located in Philadelphia ships merchandise to a buyer located in Chicago. In this case, the terms FOB shipping point could be expressed as *FOB Philadelphia*. Likewise, the terms FOB destination could be expressed as *FOB Chicago*.

Shipping terms, the passage of title, and whether the buyer or seller is to pay the transportation costs are summarized as follows:

	FOB Shipping Point	*FOB Destination*
Ownership (title) passes to buyer when merchandise is	delivered to freight carrier	delivered to buyer
Transportation costs are paid by.	buyer	seller

[4] The passage of title also determines whether the buyer or seller must pay other costs, such as the cost of insurance while the merchandise is in transit.

When merchandise is purchased on terms of FOB shipping point, the transportation costs are paid by the buyer. Such costs are part of the total cost of acquiring inventory and should be added to the cost of the inventory by debiting the merchandise inventory account.

When the terms of shipment are FOB destination, the amounts paid by the seller for delivery are debited to Transportation Out, Delivery Expense, or a similarly titled account. The total of such costs incurred during a period is reported on the seller's income statement as an expense.

As a convenience or courtesy to the buyer, the seller may prepay the transportation costs even though the terms are FOB shipping point. For example, the seller often prepays the transportation costs when the merchandise is shipped by parcel post. The seller will then add the transportation costs to the invoice. The buyer will debit Merchandise Inventory for the total amount of the invoice, including transportation costs.

To illustrate, assume that on June 10, Computer King sells merchandise to Reese Company on account, $900, terms FOB shipping point, n/30. Computer King pays the transportation costs of $50 and adds them to the invoice. The cost of the merchandise sold is $480. The entries by Computer King (the seller) are shown here.

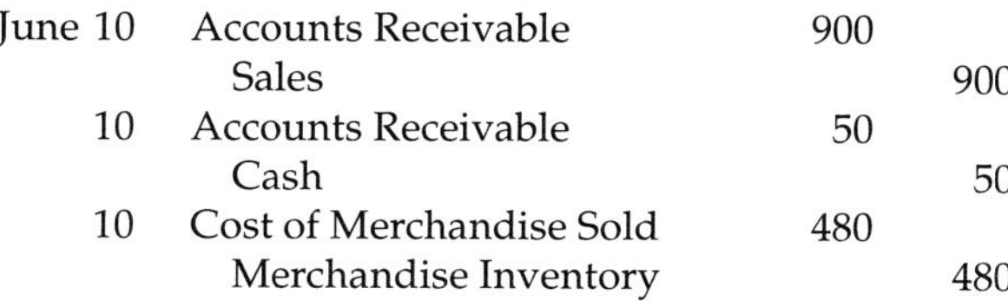

June 10	Accounts Receivable	900	
	Sales		900
10	Accounts Receivable	50	
	Cash		50
10	Cost of Merchandise Sold	480	
	Merchandise Inventory		480

The entry by Reese Company (the buyer) on receipt of the invoice is as follows:

June 10	Merchandise Inventory	950	
	Accounts Payable		950

Transportation costs are not subject to sales or purchase discounts. Thus, if the terms had been 2/10, n/30 in the preceding illustration, the payment by Reese Company would have been $932, computed as follows:

Invoice from Computer King, including prepaid transportation of $50		$950
Amount subject to discount	$900	
Rate of discount	× 2%	
Amount of purchases discount		18
Amount of payment		$932

Illustration of Accounting for Merchandise Transactions

Objective 3
Journalize the entries for merchandise transactions from both the buyer's and the seller's point of view.

Each merchandising transaction, as described in the preceding paragraphs, affects a buyer and a seller. The following illustration summarizes the principles and concepts of accounting for merchandising transactions by presenting the entries that the seller and the buyer would record. In this example, the seller is Scully Company and the buyer is Burton Co.

ransaction	Scully Company (Seller)			Burton Co. (Buyer)		
July 1. Scully Company sold merchandise on account to Burton Co., $5,000, terms FOB destination, n/30. The cost of the merchandise sold was $3,500.	Accounts Receivable Sales Cost of Merchandise Sold Merchandise Inventory	5,000 3,500	 5,000 3,500	Merchandise Inventory Accounts Payable	5,000	 5,000
July 3. Scully Company paid transportation costs of $250 for delivery of merchandise sold to Burton Co. on July 1.	Transportation Out Cash	250	 250	No entry.		
July 9. Scully Company issued Burton Co. a credit memorandum for merchandise returned, $1,000. The merchandise had been purchased by Burton Co. on account on July 1. The cost of the merchandise returned was $700.	Sales Returns & Allowances Accounts Receivable Merchandise Inventory Cost of Merchandise Sold	1,000 700	 1,000 700	Accounts Payable Merchandise Inventory	1,000	 1,000
July 11. Scully Company received payment from Burton Co. for purchase of July 1.	Cash Accounts Receivable	4,000	 4,000	Accounts Payable Cash	4,000	 4,000
July 13. Scully Company sold merchandise on account to Burton Co., $12,000, terms FOB shipping point, 2/15, n/eom. Scully Company prepaid transportation costs of $500, which were added to the invoice. The cost of the merchandise sold was $7,200.	Accounts Receivable Sales Accounts Receivable Cash Cost of Merchandise Sold Merchandise Inventory	12,000 500 7,200	 12,000 500 7,200	Merchandise Inventory Accounts Payable [$12,000 – (2% × $12,000) + $500]	12,260	 12,260
July 28. Scully Company received payment from Burton Co. for purchase of July 13, less discount (2% × $12,000).	Cash Sales Discounts Accounts Receivable	12,260 240	 12,500	Accounts Payable Cash	12,260	 12,260
July 30. Scully Company sold merchandise on account to Burton Co., $7,500, terms FOB shipping point, n/45. The cost of the merchandise sold was $4,500.	Accounts Receivable Sales Cost of Merchandise Sold Merchandise Inventory	7,500 4,500	 7,500 4,500	Merchandise Inventory Accounts Payable	7,500	 7,500
July 31. Burton Co. paid transportation charges of $150 on July 30 purchase from Scully Company.	No entry.			Merchandise Inventory Cash	150	 150

Chart of Accounts for a Merchandising Business

Objective 4
Prepare a chart of accounts for a merchandising business.

The chart of accounts for a merchandising business should reflect the types of transactions described in the preceding paragraphs. We will use Computer King as a basis for illustrating a merchandiser's chart of accounts.

When Computer King opened a merchandising outlet selling microcomputers and software on January 1, 1998, it stopped providing consulting services. As a result of this change in the type of its transactions, Computer King's chart of accounts changed. A new chart of accounts for Computer King is shown in Exhibit 5. The accounts related to merchandising transactions are shown in color.

Computer King is now using three-digit account numbers, which are assigned in a manner that permits the addition of new accounts as they are needed. The first digit indicates the major financial statement classification (1 for assets, 2 for liabilities, and so on). The second digit indicates the subclassification (e.g., 11 for current assets, 12 for noncurrent assets). The third digit identifies the specific account (e.g., 110 for Cash, 123 for Store Equipment).

Computer King is using a more complex numbering system because it has a greater variety of transactions. As a business grows, the types of transactions and the complexities of transactions usually increase. For example, a rapidly growing business may borrow funds to expand its operations by issuing notes payable. It may also accept notes receivable from major customers for sales of merchandise. Interest expense may be incurred on the notes payable, and interest income may be earned on the notes receivable. Thus, such transactions would require including Notes Receivable, Notes Payable, Interest Income, and Interest Expense in the chart of accounts.

Exhibit 5
Chart of Accounts for Computer King, Merchandising Business

Balance Sheet Accounts		*Income Statement Accounts*	
	100 Assets		400 Revenues
110	Cash	410	Sales
111	Notes Receivable	411	Sales Returns and Allowances
112	Accounts Receivable	412	Sales Discounts
113	Interest Receivable		500 Costs and Expenses
115	Merchandise Inventory	510	Cost of Merchandise Sold
116	Office Supplies	520	Sales Salaries Expense
117	Prepaid Insurance	521	Advertising Expense
120	Land	522	Depreciation Expense—Store Equipment
123	Store Equipment	529	Miscellaneous Selling Expense
124	Accumulated Depreciation—Store Equipment	530	Office Salaries Expense
125	Office Equipment	531	Rent Expense
126	Accumulated Depreciation—Office Equipment	532	Depreciation Expense—Office Equipment
	200 Liabilities	533	Insurance Expense
210	Accounts Payable	534	Office Supplies Expense
211	Salaries Payable	539	Misc. Administrative Expense
212	Unearned Rent		600 Other Income
215	Notes Payable	610	Rent Income
	300 Owner's Equity	611	Interest Income
310	Pat King, Capital		700 Other Expense
311	Pat King, Drawing	710	Interest Expense
312	Income Summary		

The growth of a business also creates a need for more detailed information for use in managing it. For example, a wages expense account may be adequate for managing a small service business with one or two employees. However, a merchandising business normally uses two or more payroll accounts, such as Sales Salaries Expense and Office Salaries Expense.

Income Statement for a Merchandising Business

Objective 5
Prepare an income statement for a merchandising business.

In this section, we emphasize the income statement of a merchandising business because merchandising transactions primarily affect this financial statement. The balance sheet is only affected to the extent that merchandise inventory is reported as a current asset.

There are two widely used formats for preparing an income statement: multiple step and single step. The 1994 edition of Accounting Trends & Techniques reported that 67% of the 600 industrial and merchandising companies surveyed use the multiple-step form. The single-step form was used by 33% of the companies surveyed.

MULTIPLE-STEP FORM

The **multiple-step income statement** contains several sections, subsections, and subtotals. The amount of detail presented in these sections varies from company to company. For example, instead of reporting gross sales, sales returns and allowances, and sales discounts, some companies just report net sales.

We use Computer King's income statement, shown in Exhibit 6, as a basis for illustrating the multiple-step form for a merchandising business. We discuss each of the sections of the income statement in the following paragraphs.

Revenue from Sales

The total amount charged customers for merchandise sold, for cash and on account, is reported in this section. Sales returns and allowances and sales discounts are deducted from this total to yield net sales.

Cost of Merchandise Sold

The cost of merchandise sold during the period may also be called the **cost of goods sold** or the **cost of sales.**

Gross Profit

The excess of net sales over cost of merchandise sold is called **gross profit.** It is sometimes called **gross profit on sales** or **gross margin.**

Operating Expenses

Most merchandising businesses classify operating expenses as either selling expenses or administrative expenses. However, depending on the decision-making needs of managers and other users of the financial statements, other classifications could be used.

Expenses that are incurred directly in the selling of merchandise are **selling expenses.** They include such expenses as salespersons' salaries, store supplies used, depreciation of store equipment, and advertising.

Exhibit 6
Multiple-Step Income Statement

Computer King
Income Statement
For the Year Ended December 31, 1998

Revenue from sales:			
Sales		$720 1 8 5 00	
Less: Sales returns and allowances	$ 6 1 4 0 00		
Sales discounts	5 7 9 0 00	11 9 3 0 00	
Net sales			$708 2 5 5 00
Cost of merchandise sold			525 3 0 5 00
Gross profit			$182 9 5 0 00
Operating expenses:			
Selling expenses:			
Sales salaries expense	$60 0 3 0 00		
Advertising expense	10 8 6 0 00		
Depr. expense—store equipment	3 1 0 0 00		
Miscellaneous selling expense	6 3 0 00		
Total selling expenses		$ 74 6 2 0 00	
Administrative expenses:			
Office salaries expense	$21 0 2 0 00		
Rent expense	8 1 0 0 00		
Depr. expense—office equipment	2 4 9 0 00		
Insurance expense	1 9 1 0 00		
Office supplies expense	6 1 0 00		
Misc. administrative expense	7 6 0 00		
Total administrative expenses		34 8 9 0 00	
Total operating expenses			109 5 1 0 00
Income from operations			$ 73 4 4 0 00
Other income:			
Interest income	$ 3 8 0 0 00		
Rent income	6 0 0 00		
Total other income		$ 4 4 0 0 00	
Other expense:			
Interest expense		2 4 4 0 00	1 9 6 0 00
Net income			$ 75 4 0 0 00

Expenses incurred in the administration or general operations of the business are **administrative expenses** or **general expenses.** Examples of these expenses are office salaries, depreciation of office equipment, and office supplies used. Bank credit card expense is also normally classified as an administrative expense.

Expenses that are related to both administrative and selling functions may be divided between the two classifications. In small businesses, however, such expenses as rent, insurance, and taxes are commonly reported as administrative expenses. Transactions for small, infrequent expenses are often reported as Miscellaneous Selling Expense or Miscellaneous Administrative Expense.

Income from Operations

The excess of gross profit over total operating expenses is called **income from operations** or **operating income.** The relationships of income from operations to total assets and to net sales are important factors in judging the efficiency and profitability of operations. If operating expenses are greater than the gross profit, the excess is called a **loss from operations.**

Other Income and Other Expense

Revenue from sources other than the primary operating activity of a business is classified as other income or **nonoperating income.** In a merchandising business, these items include income from interest, rent, and gains resulting from the sale of plant assets.

Expenses that cannot be traced directly to operations are identified as other expense or **nonoperating expense.** Interest expense that results from financing activities and losses incurred in the disposal of plant assets are examples of these items.

Other income and other expense are offset against each other on the income statement. If the total of other income exceeds the total of other expense, the difference is added to income from operations. If the reverse is true, the difference is subtracted from income from operations.

Net Income

The final figure on the income statement is called **net income** (or **net loss**). It is the net increase (or net decrease) in the owner's equity as a result of the period's profit-making activities.

SINGLE-STEP FORM

In the single-step income statement, the total of all expenses is deducted *in one step* from the total of all revenues. Such a statement is shown in Exhibit 7 for Computer King. The statement has been condensed to focus attention on its primary features. Such condensing is not essential for the single-step form.

Exhibit 7
Single-Step Income Statement

Computer King
Income Statement
For the Year Ended December 31, 1998

Revenues:		
Net sales		$708 2 5 5 00
Interest income		3 8 0 0 00
Rent income		6 0 0 00
Total revenues		$712 6 5 5 00
Expenses:		
Cost of merchandise sold	$525 3 0 5 00	
Selling expenses	74 6 2 0 00	
Administrative expenses	34 8 9 0 00	
Interest expense	2 4 4 0 00	
Total expenses		637 2 5 5 00
Net income		$ 75 4 0 0 00

The single-step form has the advantage of emphasizing total revenues and total expenses as the factors that determine net income. A criticism of the single-step form is that such amounts as gross profit and income from operations are not readily available for analysis.

The Accounting Cycle for a Merchandising Business

Objective 6
Describe the accounting cycle for a merchandising business.

Earlier in this chapter, we described and illustrated the chart of accounts and the analysis and recording of transactions for a merchandising business. We also illustrated the preparation of an income statement for a merchandiser, Computer King, at the end of an accounting cycle. In the remainder of this chapter, we describe the other elements of the accounting cycle for a merchandising business. In this discussion, we will focus primarily on the elements of this cycle that are likely to differ from those of a service business.

MERCHANDISE INVENTORY SHRINKAGE

What is merchandise **inventory shrinkage?** Under the perpetual inventory system, a separate merchandise inventory account is maintained in the ledger. Throughout the accounting period, this account shows the amount of merchandise that should be on hand at any time. However, merchandising businesses may experience some loss of inventory due to shoplifting, employee theft, or errors in recording or counting inventory. As a result, the physical inventory taken at the end of the accounting period may differ from the amount of inventory shown in the inventory records. Normally, the amount of merchandise that should be on hand, as indicated by the balance of the merchandise inventory account, is larger than the total amount of merchandise counted during the physical inventory. For this reason, the difference is often called **inventory shrinkage** or **inventory shortage.**

To illustrate, Computer King's inventory records indicate that $63,950 of merchandise should be on hand on December 31, 1998. The physical inventory taken on December 31, 1998, however, indicates that only $62,150 of merchandise is actually on hand. Thus, the inventory shrinkage for the year ending December 31, 1998, is $1,800 ($63,950 – $62,150). This amount is recorded by the following adjusting entry:

	Adjusting Entry		
Dec. 31	Cost of Merchandise Sold	1,800	
	Merchandise Inventory		1,800

After this entry has been recorded and posted, the accounting records agree with the actual physical inventory at the end of the period. Since no system of procedures and safeguards can totally eliminate it, inventory shrinkage is often considered a normal cost of operations. If the amount of the shrinkage is abnormally large, it may be disclosed separately on the income statement, below the cost of merchandise sold. In such cases, the shrinkage may be recorded in a separate account, such as Loss From Merchandise Inventory Shrinkage.

WORK SHEET

Merchandising businesses that use a perpetual inventory system are also likely to use a computerized accounting system. In a computerized system, the adjusting entries are recorded and financial statements prepared without using a work sheet. Therefore, in this chapter, we do not illustrate the preparation of a work sheet. The appendix at the end of the chapter, however, illustrates the work sheet and the adjusting entries for a merchandising business that uses a manual accounting system.

STATEMENT OF OWNER'S EQUITY

The statement of owner's equity for Computer King is shown in Exhibit 8. This statement is prepared in the same manner that we described previously for a service business.

Exhibit 8
Statement of Owner's Equity for Merchandising Business

Computer King
Statement of Owner's Equity
For the Year Ended December 31, 1998

Pat King, capital, January 1, 1998		$153 8 0 0 00
Net income for year	$75 4 0 0 00	
Less withdrawals	18 0 0 0 00	
Increase in owner's equity		57 4 0 0 00
Pat King, capital, December 31, 1998		$211 2 0 0 00

BALANCE SHEET

As we discussed and illustrated in previous chapters, the balance sheet may be presented with assets on the left-hand side and the liabilities and owner's equity on the right-hand side. This form of the balance sheet is called the **account form.** The balance sheet may also be presented in a downward sequence in three sections. The total of the Assets section equals the combined total of the Liabilities and Owner's Equity sections. This form of balance sheet is called the **report form.** The report form of balance sheet for Computer King is shown in Exhibit 9. In this balance sheet, note that merchandise inventory at the end of the period is reported as a current asset and that the current portion of the note payable is $5,000.

CLOSING ENTRIES

The closing entries for a merchandising business are similar to those for a service business. The first entry closes the temporary accounts with credit balances, such as Sales, to the income summary account. The second entry closes the temporary accounts with debit balances, including Sales Returns and Allowances, Sales Discounts, and Cost of Merchandise Sold, to the income summary account. The third entry closes the balance of the income summary account to the owner's capital account. The fourth entry closes the owner's drawing account to the owner's capital account.

In a computerized accounting system, the closing entries are prepared automatically. Therefore, in this chapter, we do not illustrate the closing entries for a merchandising business. The closing entries for Computer King are illustrated in the appendix.

Exhibit 9
Report Form of Balance Sheet

Computer King
Balance Sheet
December 31, 1998

Assets			
Current assets:			
Cash		$52 9 5 0 00	
Notes receivable		40 0 0 0 00	
Accounts receivable		60 8 8 0 00	
Interest receivable		2 0 0 00	
Merchandise inventory		62 1 5 0 00	
Office supplies		4 8 0 00	
Prepaid insurance		2 6 5 0 00	
Total current assets			$219 3 1 0 00
Plant assets:			
Land		$10 0 0 0 00	
Store equipment	$27 1 0 0 00		
Less accumulated depreciation	5 7 0 0 00	21 4 0 0 00	
Office equipment	$15 5 7 0 00		
Less accumulated depreciation	4 7 2 0 00	10 8 5 0 00	
Total plant assets			42 2 5 0 00
Total assets			$261 5 6 0 00
Liabilities			
Current liabilities:			
Accounts payable		$22 4 2 0 00	
Note payable (current portion)		5 0 0 0 00	
Salaries payable		1 1 4 0 00	
Unearned rent		1 8 0 0 00	
Total current liabilities			$ 30 3 6 0 00
Long-term liabilities:			
Note payable (final payment due 2002)			20 0 0 0 00
Total liabilities			$ 50 3 6 0 00
Owner's Equity			
Pat King, capital			211 2 0 0 00
Total liabilities and owner's equity			$261 5 6 0 00

Appendix: Work Sheet and Adjusting and Closing Entries for a Merchandising Business

A merchandising business that does not use a computerized accounting system may use a work sheet in assembling the data for preparing financial statements and adjusting and closing entries. In this appendix, we illustrate such a work sheet, along with the adjusting and closing entries for a merchandising business.

The work sheet in Exhibit 10 is for Computer King on December 31, 1998, the end of its first year of operations as a merchandiser. In this work sheet, we list all of the accounts, including the accounts that have no balances, in the order that they appear in Computer King's ledger.

Exhibit 10
Work sheet for Merchandising Business

Computer King
Work Sheet
For the Year Ended December 31, 1998

Account Title	Trial Balance Dr.	Trial Balance Cr.	Adjustments Dr.	Adjustments Cr.	Adjusted Trial Balance Dr.	Adjusted Trial Balance Cr.	Income Statement Dr.	Income Statement Cr.	Balance Sheet Dr.	Balance Sheet Cr.
Cash	52,950				52,950				52,950	
Notes Receivable	40,000				40,000				40,000	
Accounts Receivable	60,880				60,880				60,880	
Interest Receivable			(a) 200		200				200	
Merchandise Inventory	63,950			(b)1,800	62,150				62,150	
Office Supplies	1,090			(c) 610	480				480	
Prepaid Insurance	4,560			(d)1,910	2,650				2,650	
Land	10,000				10,000				10,000	
Store Equipment	27,100				27,100				27,100	
Accum. Depr.—Store Equip.		2,600		(e)3,100		5,700				5,700
Office Equipment	15,570				15,570				15,570	
Accum. Depr.—Office Equip.		2,230		(f) 2,490		4,720				4,720
Accounts Payable		22,420				22,420				22,420
Salaries Payable				(g)1,140		1,140				1,140
Unearned Rent		2,400	(h) 600			1,800				1,800
Notes Payable (final payment due 2002)		25,000				25,000				25,000
Pat King, Capital		153,800				153,800				153,800
Pat King, Drawing	18,000				18,000				18,000	
Sales		720,185				720,185		720,185		
Sales Returns and Allowances	6,140				6,140		6,140			
Sales Discounts	5,790				5,790		5,790			
Cost of Merchandise Sold	523,505		(b)1,800		525,305		525,305			
Sales Salaries Expense	59,250		(g) 780		60,030		60,030			
Advertising Expense	10,860				10,860		10,860			
Depr. Exp.—Store Equip.			(e)3,100		3,100		3,100			
Miscellaneous Selling Expense	630				630		630			
Office Salaries Expense	20,660		(g) 360		21,020		21,020			
Rent Expense	8,100				8,100		8,100			
Depr. Exp.—Office Equip.			(f) 2,490		2,490		2,490			
Insurance Expense			(d)1,910		1,910		1,910			
Office Supplies Expense			(c) 610		610		610			
Misc. Administrative Expense	760				760		760			
Rent Income				(h) 600		600		600		
Interest Income		3,600		(a) 200		3,800		3,800		
Interest Expense	2,440				2,440		2,440			
	932,235	932,235	11,850	11,850	939,165	939,165	649,185	724,585	289,980	214,580
Net Income							75,400			75,400
							724,585	724,585	289,980	289,980

(a) Interest earned but not received on notes receivable, $200.
(b) Merchandise inventory shrinkage for period, $1,800 ($63,950 – $62,150).
(c) Office supplies used, $610 ($1,090 – $480).
(d) Insurance expired, $1,910.
(e) Depreciation of store equipment, $3,100.
(f) Depreciation of office equipment, $2,490.
(g) Salaries accrued but not paid (sales salaries, $780; office salaries, $360), $1,140.
(h) Rent earned from amount received in advance, $600.

The data needed for adjusting the accounts of Computer King are as follows:

Interest accrued on notes receivable on December 31, 1998			$ 200
Physical merchandise inventory on December 31, 1998			62,150
Office supplies on hand on December 31, 1998			480
Insurance expired during 1998			1,910
Depreciation during 1998 on:	Store equipment		3,100
	Office equipment		2,490
Salaries accrued on December 31, 1998:	Sales salaries	$780	
	Office salaries	360	1,140
Rent income earned during 1998			600

There is no specific order in which to analyze the accounts in the work sheet, assemble the adjustment data, and make the adjusting entries. However, you can normally save time by selecting the accounts in the order in which they appear on the trial balance. Using this approach, the adjustment for accrued interest is listed first {entry (a) on the work sheet}, followed by the adjustment for merchandise inventory shrinkage {entry (b) on the work sheet}, and so on.

After all the adjustments have been entered on the work sheet, the Adjustments columns are totaled to prove the equality of debits and credits. As we illustrated in previous chapters, the balances of the accounts in the Trial Balance columns and the amount of any adjustments are extended to the Adjusted Trial Balance columns.[5] The Adjusted Trial Balance columns are then totaled to prove the equality of debits and credits.

The process of extending the balances, as adjusted, to the statement columns usually begins with Cash and moves down the work sheet, item by item. After all the items have been extended to the statement columns, the four columns are totaled, and the net income or net loss is determined. For Computer King, the difference between the credit and debit columns of the Income Statement section is $75,400, the amount of the net income. The difference between the debit and credit columns of the Balance Sheet section is also $75,400, which is the increase in owner's equity as a result of the net income. Agreement between the two balancing amounts is evidence of debit-credit equality and mathematical accuracy.

After all account balances have been extended, the income statement, statement of owner's equity, and balance sheet are prepared from the work sheet in a manner similar to that of a service business. The Adjustments columns in the work sheet provide the data for journalizing the adjusting entries. Computer King's adjusting entries at the end of 1998 are as follows:

JOURNAL **PAGE 28**

Date		Description	Post. Ref.	Debit	Credit
1998		Adjusting Entries			
Dec.	31	Interest Receivable	113	200 00	
		Interest Income	611		200 00
	31	Cost of Merchandise Sold	510	1,800 00	
		Merchandise Inventory	115		1,800 00
	31	Office Supplies Expense	534	610 00	
		Office Supplies	116		610 00

[5] Some accountants prefer to eliminate the Adjusted Trial Balance columns and to extend the adjusted balances directly to the statement columns. Such a work sheet is often used if there are only a few adjustment items.

Date		Description	Post. Ref.	Debit	Credit
Dec.	31	Insurance Expense	533	1 9 1 0 00	
		Prepaid Insurance	117		1 9 1 0 00
	31	Depreciation Expense—			
		Store Equipment	522	3 1 0 0 00	
		Accumulated Depreciation—			
		Store Equipment	124		3 1 0 0 00
	31	Depreciation Expense—			
		Office Equipment	532	2 4 9 0 00	
		Accumulated Depreciation—			
		Office Equipment	126		2 4 9 0 00
	31	Sales Salaries Expense	520	7 8 0 00	
		Office Salaries Expense	530	3 6 0 00	
		Salaries Payable	211		1 1 4 0 00
	31	Unearned Rent	212	6 0 0 00	
		Rent Income	610		6 0 0 00

The Income Statement columns of the work sheet provide the data for preparing the closing entries. The closing entries for Computer King at the end of 1998 are as follows:

JOURNAL **PAGE 29**

Date		Description	Post. Ref.	Debit	Credit
1998		Closing Entries			
Dec.	31	Sales	410	720 1 8 5 00	
		Rent Income	610	6 0 0 00	
		Interest Income	611	3 8 0 0 00	
		Income Summary	312		724 5 8 5 00
	31	Income Summary	312	649 1 8 5 00	
		Sales Returns and Allowances	411		6 1 4 0 00
		Sales Discounts	412		5 7 9 0 00
		Cost of Merchandise Sold	510		525 3 0 5 00
		Sales Salaries Expense	520		60 0 3 0 00
		Advertising Expense	521		10 8 6 0 00
		Depr. Expense—Store Equipment	522		3 1 0 0 00
		Miscellaneous Selling Expense	529		6 3 0 00
		Office Salaries Expense	530		21 0 2 0 00
		Rent Expense	531		8 1 0 0 00
		Depr. Expense—Office Equipment	532		2 4 9 0 00
		Insurance Expense	533		1 9 1 0 00
		Office Supplies Expense	534		6 1 0 00
		Misc. Administrative Expense	539		7 6 0 00
		Interest Expense	710		2 4 4 0 00

Date		Description	Post. Ref.	Debit	Credit
Dec.	31	Income Summary	312	75 4 0 0 00	
		Pat King, Capital	310		75 4 0 0 00
	31	Pat King, Capital	310	18 0 0 0 00	
		Pat King, Drawing	311		18 0 0 0 00

The balance of Income Summary, after the first two closing entries have been posted, is the net income or net loss for the period. The third closing entry transfers this balance to the owner's capital account. Computer King's income summary account after the closing entries have been posted is as follows:

ACCOUNT *Income Summary* **ACCOUNT NO. *312***

Date		Item	Post. Ref.	Debit	Credit	Balance Debit	Balance Credit
1998 Dec.	31	Revenues	29		724 5 8 5 00		724 5 8 5 00
	31	Expenses	29	649 1 8 5 00			75 4 0 0 00
	31	Net income	29	75 4 0 0 00		—	—

After the closing entries have been prepared and posted to the accounts, a post-closing trial balance may be prepared to verify the debit-credit equality. The only accounts that should appear on the post-closing trial balance are the asset, contra asset, liability, and owner's capital accounts with balances. These are the same accounts that appear on the end-of-period balance sheet.

KEY POINTS

Objective 1. Compare a service business's income statement to a merchandising business's income statement.

The primary differences between a service business and a merchandising business relate to revenue activities. Merchandising businesses purchase merchandise for selling to customers.

On a merchandising business's income statement, revenue from selling merchandise is reported as sales. The cost of the merchandise sold is subtracted from sales to arrive at gross profit. The operating expenses are subtracted from gross profit to arrive at net income.

Merchandise inventory, which is merchandise not sold, is reported as a current asset on the balance sheet.

Objective 2a. Journalize the entries for merchandise purchases.

Purchases of merchandise for cash or on account are recorded by debiting Merchandise Inventory. For purchases of merchandise on account, the credit terms may allow cash discounts for early payment. Such purchases discounts are viewed as a reduction in the cost of the merchandise purchased. Since most buyers will take advantage of purchases discounts, merchandise purchases are normally recorded at their net cost. Net cost is the invoice price less any discounts.

When merchandise is returned or a price adjustment is granted, the buyer credits Merchandise Inventory.

Objective 2b. Journalize the entries for merchandise sales.

Sales of merchandise for cash or on account are recorded by crediting Sales. The cost of merchandise sold and the reduction in merchandise inventory are also recorded for the sale.

For sales of merchandise on account, the credit terms may allow sales discounts for early payment. Such discounts are recorded by the seller as a debit to Sales Discounts. Sales discounts are reported as a deduction from the amount initially recorded in Sales. Likewise, when merchandise is returned or a price adjustment is granted, the seller debits Sales Returns and Allowances.

The liability for sales tax is incurred at the time the sale is made and is recorded by the seller as a credit to the sales tax payable account. When the amount of the sales tax is paid to the taxing unit, Sales Tax Payable is debited and Cash is credited.

Many wholesalers offer trade discounts, which are discounts off the list prices of merchandise. Normally, neither the seller nor the buyer records the list price and the related trade discount in the accounts.

Objective 2c. Journalize the entries for merchandise transportation costs.
When merchandise is shipped FOB shipping point, the buyer pays the transportation costs and debits Merchandise Inventory. When merchandise is shipped FOB destination, the seller pays the transportation costs and debits Transportation Out, Delivery Expense, or a similarly titled account. If the seller prepays transportation costs as a convenience to the buyer, the seller debits Accounts Receivable for the costs.

Objective 3. Journalize the entries for merchandise transactions from both the buyer's and the seller's point of view.
The illustration in this chapter summarizes the principles and concepts of accounting for merchandising transactions by presenting the entries that the seller and the buyer would record.

Objective 4. Prepare a chart of accounts for a merchandising business.
The chart of accounts for a merchandising business is more complex than that for a service business and normally includes accounts such as Sales, Sales Discounts, Sales Returns and Allowances, Cost of Merchandise Sold, and Merchandise Inventory.

Objective 5. Prepare an income statement for a merchandising business.
The income statement of a merchandising business reports sales, cost of merchandise sold, and gross profit. The income statement can be prepared in either the multiple-step form or the single-step form.

Objective 6. Describe the accounting cycle for a merchandising business.
The accounting cycle for a merchandising business is similar to that of a service business. However, a merchandiser is likely to experience inventory shrinkage, which must be recorded. The normal adjusting entry is to debit Cost of Merchandise Sold and credit Merchandise Inventory for the amount of the shrinkage.

The balance sheet may be prepared in either the account form or the report form. Regardless of the form used, merchandise inventory should be reported as a current asset.

GLOSSARY OF KEY TERMS

Account form of balance sheet. A form of balance sheet with assets on the left-hand side and liabilities and owner's equity on the right-hand side. *Objective 6*

Administrative expenses. Expenses incurred in the administration or general operations of a business. *Objective 5*

Credit memorandum. The form issued by a seller to inform a buyer that a credit has been posted to the buyer's account receivable. *Objective 2b*

Debit memorandum. The form issued by a buyer to inform a seller that a debit has been posted to the seller's account payable. *Objective 2a*

FOB destination. Terms of agreement between buyer and seller whereby ownership passes when merchandise is received by the buyer, and the seller pays the transportation costs. *Objective 2c*

FOB shipping point. Terms of agreement between buyer and seller whereby ownership passes when merchandise is delivered to the freight carrier, and the buyer pays the transportation costs. *Objective 2c*

Gross profit. The excess of net sales over the cost of merchandise sold. *Objective 1*

Income from operations. The excess of gross profit over total operating expenses. *Objective 5*

Inventory shrinkage. Loss of inventory due to shoplifting, employee theft, or errors in recording or counting inventory. *Objective 6*

Invoice. The bill provided by the seller (who refers to it as a *sales invoice*) to a buyer (who refers to it as a *purchase invoice*) for items purchased. *Objective 2a*

Merchandise inventory. Merchandise on hand and available for sale to customers. *Objective 1*

Multiple-step income statement. An income statement with several sections, subsections, and subtotals. *Objective 5*

Other expense. An expense that cannot be traced directly to operations. *Objective 5*

Other income. Revenue from sources other than the primary operating activity of a business. *Objective 5*

Periodic inventory system. A system of inventory accounting in which only the revenue from sales is recorded each time a sale is made. The cost of merchandise on hand at the end of a period is determined by a detailed listing (physical inventory) of the merchandise on hand. *Objective 2a*

Perpetual inventory system. A system of inventory accounting in which both the revenue from sales and the cost of merchandise sold are recorded each time a sale is made, so that the records continually disclose the amount of the inventory on hand. *Objective 2a*

Physical inventory. The detailed listing of merchandise on hand. *Objective 2a*

Purchases discounts. An available discount taken by a buyer for early payment of an invoice. *Objective 2a*

Purchases returns and allowances. Reductions in purchases, resulting from merchandise being returned to the seller or from the seller's reduction in the original purchase price. *Objective 2a*

Report form of balance sheet. A form of balance sheet with the liabilities and owner's equity sections below the assets section. *Objective 6*

Sales discounts. An available discount granted by a seller for early payment of an invoice; a contra account to Sales. *Objective 2b*

Sales returns and allowances. Reductions in sales, resulting from merchandise being returned by customers or from the seller's reduction in the original sales price; a contra account to Sales. *Objective 2b*

Selling expenses. Expenses incurred directly in the sale of merchandise. *Objective 5*

Single-step income statement. An income statement in which the total of all expenses is deducted in one step from the total of all revenues. *Objective 5*

Trade discounts. Special discounts from published list prices offered by sellers to certain classes of buyers. *Objective 2b*

ILLUSTRATIVE PROBLEM

The following transactions were completed by Montrose Company during May of the current year. Montrose Company uses a perpetual inventory system.

May 3. Purchased merchandise on account from Floyd Co., $4,000, terms FOB shipping point, 2/10, n/30, with prepaid transportation costs of $120 added to the invoice.
5. Purchased merchandise on account from Kramer Co., $8,500, terms FOB destination, 1/10, n/30.
6. Sold merchandise on account to C. F. Howell Co., list price $4,000, trade discount 30%, terms 2/10, n/30. The cost of the merchandise sold was $1,125.
8. Purchased office supplies for cash, $150.
10. Returned merchandise purchased on May 5 from Kramer Co., $1,300.
13. Paid Floyd Co. on account for purchase of May 3, less discount.
14. Purchased merchandise for cash, $10,500.
15. Paid Kramer Co. on account for purchase of May 5, less return of May 10 and discount.
16. Received cash on account from sale of May 6 to C. F. Howell Co., less discount.
19. Sold merchandise on nonbank credit cards and reported accounts to the card company, $2,450. The cost of the merchandise sold was $980.
22. Sold merchandise on account to Comer Co., $3,480, terms 2/10, n/30. The cost of the merchandise sold was $1,400.
24. Sold merchandise for cash, $4,350. The cost of the merchandise sold was $1,750.
25. Received merchandise returned by Comer Co. from sale on May 22, $1,480. The cost of the returned merchandise was $600.
31. Received cash from card company for nonbank credit card sales of May 19, less $140 service fee.

Instructions

1. Journalize the preceding transactions.
2. Journalize the adjusting entry for merchandise inventory shrinkage, $3,750.

Solution

1.

May	3	Merchandise Inventory	4,040	
		Accounts Payable		4,040
		[$4,000 – (2% × $4,000) + $120]		
	5	Merchandise Inventory	8,415	
		Accounts Payable		8,415
		[$8,500 – (1% × $8,500)]		
	6	Accounts Receivable	2,800	
		Sales		2,800
		[$4,000 – (30% × $4,000)]		
	6	Cost of Merchandise Sold	1,125	
		Merchandise Inventory		1,125
	8	Office Supplies	150	
		Cash		150
	10	Accounts Payable	1,287	
		Merchandise Inventory		1,287
		[$1,300 – (1% × $1,300)]		

May 13	Accounts Payable	4,040	
	Cash		4,040
14	Merchandise Inventory	10,500	
	Cash		10,500
15	Accounts Payable	7,128	
	Cash		7,128
	($8,415 – $1,287)		
16	Cash	2,744	
	Sales Discounts	56	
	Accounts Receivable		2,800
19	Accounts Receivable	2,450	
	Sales		2,450
19	Cost of Merchandise Sold	980	
	Merchandise Inventory		980
22	Accounts Receivable	3,480	
	Sales		3,480
22	Cost of Merchandise Sold	1,400	
	Merchandise Inventory		1,400
24	Cash	4,350	
	Sales		4,350
24	Cost of Merchandise Sold	1,750	
	Merchandise Inventory		1,750
25	Sales Returns and Allowances	1,480	
	Accounts Receivable		1,480
25	Merchandise Inventory	600	
	Cost of Merchandise Sold		600
31	Cash	2,310	
	Credit Card Collection Expense	140	
	Accounts Receivable		2,450

2.

May 31	Cost of Merchandise Sold	3,750	
	Merchandise Inventory		3,750

SELF-EXAMINATION QUESTIONS (ANSWERS AT END OF CHAPTER)

1. If merchandise purchased on account is returned, the buyer may inform the seller of the details by issuing:
   A. a debit memorandum C. an invoice
   B. a credit memorandum D. a bill

2. If merchandise is sold on account to a customer for $1,000, terms FOB shipping point, 1/10, n/30, and the seller prepays $50 in transportation costs, the amount of the discount for early payment would be:
   A. $0 C. $10.00
   B. $5.00 D. $10.50

3. The income statement in which the total of all expenses is deducted from the total of all revenues is termed:
   A. multiple-step form C. account form
   B. single-step form D. report form

4. On a multiple-step income statement, the excess of net sales over the cost of merchandise sold is called:
   A. operating income C. gross profit
   B. income from operations D. net income

5. Which of the following expenses would normally be classified as Other expense on a multiple-step income statement?
   A. Depreciation expense—office equipment C. Insurance expense
   B. Sales salaries expense D. Interest expense

DISCUSSION QUESTIONS

1. What distinguishes a merchandising business from a service business?
2. Can a business earn a gross profit but incur a net loss? Explain.
3. In which type of system for accounting for merchandise held for sale is there no attempt to record the cost of merchandise sold until the end of the period, when a physical inventory is taken?

4. What is the name of the account in which purchases of merchandise are recorded in a perpetual inventory system?
5. What is the name of the account in which sales of merchandise are recorded?
6. How does the accounting for sales to customers using bank credit cards, such as MasterCard and VISA, differ from accounting for sales to customers using nonbank credit cards, such as American Express?
7. The credit period during which the buyer of merchandise is allowed to pay usually begins with what date?
8. Boyd Company ordered $1,000 of merchandise from Smith Company on April 1, terms 2/10, n/30. Although Smith Company shipped the merchandise on April 6, the merchandise was not received by Boyd Company until April 7. The invoice received with the merchandise was dated April 6. What is the last date Boyd Company could pay the invoice and still receive the discount?
9. What is the meaning of (a) 1/10, n/60; (b) n/30; (c) n/eom?
10. What is the term applied to discounts for early payment of an invoice (a) by the seller, (b) by the buyer?

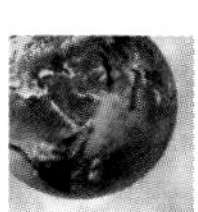

11. It is not unusual for a customer to drive into some Texaco, Mobil, or BP gasoline stations and discover that the cash price per gallon is 3 or 4 cents less than the credit price per gallon. As a result, many customers pay cash rather than use their credit cards. Why would a gasoline station owner establish such a policy?
12. What is the nature of (a) a credit memorandum issued by the seller of merchandise, (b) a debit memorandum issued by the buyer of merchandise?
13. Who bears the transportation costs when the terms of sale are (a) FOB shipping point, (b) FOB destination?
14. Name at least three accounts that would normally appear in the chart of accounts of a merchandising business but would not appear in the chart of accounts of a service business.
15. Differentiate between the multiple-step and the single-step forms of the income statement.
16. What major advantages and disadvantages does the single-step form of income statement have in comparison to the multiple-step statement?
17. What type of revenue is reported in the Other income section of the multiple-step income statement?
18. The Furniture Accessory Co., which uses a perpetual inventory system, experienced a normal inventory shrinkage of $32,000. What accounts would be debited and credited to record the adjustment for the inventory shrinkage at the end of the accounting period?
19. Assume that The Furniture Accessory Co. in Question 18 experienced an abnormal inventory shrinkage of $232,000. The Furniture Accessory Co. has decided to record the abnormal inventory shrinkage so that it would be separately disclosed on the income statement. What account would be debited for the abnormal inventory shrinkage?
20. Differentiate between the account form and the report form of balance sheet.

EXERCISES

EXERCISE 6–1
Determining gross profit
Objective 1

During the current year, merchandise is sold for $230,000 cash and for $415,000 on account. The cost of the merchandise sold is $430,000.

a. What is the amount of the gross profit?
b. Will the income statement necessarily report a net income? Explain.

EXERCISE 6–2
Determining cost of merchandise sold
Objective 1

Sales were $310,000, and the gross profit was $190,000. What was the amount of the cost of merchandise sold?

EXERCISE 6–3
Purchase-related transaction
Objective 2

Blair Company purchased merchandise on account from a supplier for $3,000, terms 2/10, n/30. Blair Company returned $800 of the merchandise and received full credit.

a. If Blair Company pays the invoice within the discount period, what is the amount of cash required for the payment?
b. Under a perpetual inventory system, what account is credited by Blair Company to record the return?

EXERCISE 6–4
Determining amounts to be paid on invoices
Objective 2

Determine the amount to be paid in full settlement of each of the following invoices, assuming that credit for returns and allowances was received prior to payment and that all invoices were paid within the discount period.

	Merchandise	*Transportation Paid by Seller*	*Terms*	*Returns and Allowances*
a.	$6,000	—	FOB shipping point, 1/10, n/30	$1,500
b.	1,000	$50	FOB shipping point, 2/10, n/30	600
c.	8,000	—	FOB destination, n/30	400
d.	4,000	75	FOB shipping point, 1/10, n/30	100
e.	5,000	—	FOB destination, 2/10, n/30	—

EXERCISE 6–5
Purchase-related transactions
Objective 2

A retailer is considering the purchase of ten units of a specific item from either of two suppliers. Their offers are as follows:

X: $600 a unit, total of $6,000, 2/10, n/30, plus transportation costs of $375.
Y: $630 a unit, total of $6,300, 1/10, n/30, no charge for transportation.

Which of the two offers, X or Y, yields the lower price?

EXERCISE 6–6
Purchase-related transactions
Objective 2

The debits and credits from four related transactions are presented in the following T accounts. Describe each transaction.

Cash

		(2)	200
		(4)	4,900

Accounts Payable

(3)	980	(1)	5,880
(4)	4,900		

Merchandise Inventory

(1)	5,880	(3)	980
(2)	200		

EXERCISE 6–7
Purchase-related transactions
Objective 2

Madeline Co., a women's clothing store, purchased $12,000 of merchandise from a supplier on account, terms FOB destination, 2/10, n/30. Madeline Co. returned $2,500 of the merchandise, receiving a credit memorandum, and then paid the amount due within the discount period. Journalize Madeline Co.'s entries in a two-column general journal to record (a) the purchase, (b) the merchandise return, and (c) the payment.

EXERCISE 6–8
Purchase-related transactions
Objective 2

Journalize, in a two-column general journal, entries for the following related transactions of Restoration Company:

a. Purchased $20,000 of merchandise from Veneer Co. on account, terms 2/10, n/30.
b. Paid the amount owed on the invoice within the discount period.
c. Discovered that $5,000 of the merchandise was defective and returned items, receiving credit.
d. Purchased $4,000 of merchandise from Veneer Co. on account, terms 2/10, n/30.
e. Received a check for the balance owed from the return in (c), after deducting for the purchase in (d).

EXERCISE 6–9
Sales-related transactions, including the use of credit cards
Objective 2

Journalize, in a two-column general journal, the entries for the following transactions:

a. Sold merchandise for cash, $10,500. The cost of the merchandise sold was $7,500.
b. Sold merchandise on account, $9,500. The cost of the merchandise sold was $6,000.
c. Sold merchandise to customers who used MasterCard and VISA, $5,750. The cost of the merchandise sold was $2,850.
d. Sold merchandise to customers who used American Express, $4,100. The cost of the merchandise sold was $1,860.
e. Paid an invoice from First National Bank for $350, representing a service fee for processing MasterCard and VISA sales.
f. Received $3,890 from American Express Company after a $210 collection fee had been deducted.

EXERCISE 6–10
Sales returns and allowances
Objective 2

During the year, sales returns and allowances totaled $112,150. The cost of the merchandise returned was $67,300. The accountant recorded all the returns and allowances by debiting the sales account and crediting Cost of Merchandise Sold for $112,150.

Was the accountant's method of recording returns acceptable? Explain. In your explanation, include the advantages of using a sales returns and allowances account.

EXERCISE 6–11
Sales-related transactions
Objective 2

After the amount due on a sale of $7,000, terms 2/10, n/eom, is received from a customer within the discount period, the seller consents to the return of the entire shipment. (a) What is the amount of the refund owed to the customer? (b) Journalize the entry made by the seller to record the return and the refund.

EXERCISE 6–12
Sales-related transactions
Objective 2

The debits and credits for three related transactions are presented in the following T accounts. Describe each transaction.

Cash			
(5)	6,930		

Sales			
		(1)	8,000

Accounts Receivable			
(1)	8,000	(3)	1,000
		(5)	7,000

Sales Discounts			
(5)	70		

Merchandise Inventory			
(4)	750	(2)	6,000

Sales Returns and Allowances			
(3)	1,000		

Cost of Merchandise Sold			
(2)	6,000	(4)	750

EXERCISE 6–13
Sales-related transactions
Objective 2

Merchandise is sold on account to a customer for $20,000, terms FOB shipping point, 3/10, n/30. The seller paid the transportation costs of $500. Determine the following: (a) amount of the sale, (b) amount debited to Accounts Receivable, (c) amount of the discount for early payment, and (d) amount due within the discount period.

EXERCISE 6–14
Sales tax
Objective 2

A sale of merchandise on account for $500 is subject to a 6% sales tax. (a) Should the sales tax be recorded at the time of sale or when payment is received? (b) What is the amount of the sale? (c) What is the amount debited to Accounts Receivable? (d) What is the title of the account to which the $30 is credited?

EXERCISE 6–15
Sales tax transactions
Objective 2

Journalize, in a two-column general journal, the entries to record the following selected transactions:

a. Sold $11,500 of merchandise on account, subject to a sales tax of 4%. The cost of the merchandise sold was $7,000.
b. Paid $1,250 to the state sales tax department for taxes collected.

EXERCISE 6–16
Sales-related transactions
Objectives 2, 3

Coyles Co., a furniture wholesaler, sells merchandise to Westbury Co. on account, $6,900, terms 2/15, n/30. The cost of the merchandise sold is $3,900. Coyles Co. issues a credit memorandum for $750 for merchandise returned and subsequently receives the amount due within the discount period. The cost of the merchandise returned is $450. Journalize, in a two-column general journal, Coyles Co.'s entries for (a) the sale, including the cost of the merchandise sold, (b) the credit memorandum, including the cost of the returned merchandise, and (c) the receipt of the check for the amount due from Westbury Co.

EXERCISE 6–17
Purchase-related transactions
Objectives 2, 3

Based on the data presented in Exercise 6-16, journalize, in a two-column general journal, Westbury Co.'s entries for (a) the purchase, (b) the return of the merchandise for credit, and (c) the payment of the invoice within the discount period.

EXERCISE 6–18
Normal balances of merchandise accounts
Objective 2

What is the normal balance of the following accounts: (a) Sales Returns and Allowances, (b) Merchandise Inventory, (c) Sales Discounts, (d) Transportation Out, (e) Sales, (f) Cost of Merchandise Sold?

EXERCISE 6–19
Chart of accounts
Objective 4

Las Posas Co. is a newly organized business with the following list of accounts, arranged in alphabetical order:

Accounts Payable
Accounts Receivable
Accumulated Depreciation—Office Equipment
Accumulated Depreciation—Store Equipment
Advertising Expense
A. E. Carmen, Capital
A. E. Carmen, Drawing
Cash
Cost of Merchandise Sold
Depreciation Expense—Office Equipment
Depreciation Expense—Store Equipment
Income Summary
Insurance Expense
Interest Expense
Interest Income
Interest Receivable
Land
Merchandise Inventory
Miscellaneous Administrative Expense
Miscellaneous Selling Expense
Notes Payable (short-term)
Notes Receivable (short-term)
Office Equipment
Office Salaries Expense
Office Supplies
Office Supplies Expense
Prepaid Insurance
Rent Expense
Salaries Payable
Sales
Sales Discounts
Sales Returns and Allowances
Sales Salaries Expense
Store Equipment
Store Supplies
Store Supplies Expense

Construct a chart of accounts, assigning account numbers and arranging the accounts in balance sheet and income statement order, as illustrated in Exhibit 5. Each account number is to comprise three digits: the first digit is to indicate the major classification ("1" for assets, and so on); the second digit is to indicate the subclassification ("11" for current assets, and so on); and the third digit is to identify the specific account ("110" for Cash, and so on).

EXERCISE 6–20
Income statement for merchandiser
Objective 5

For the fiscal year, sales were $1,230,000, sales discounts were $20,100, sales returns and allowances were $60,000, and the cost of merchandise sold was $825,000. What was the amount of net sales and gross profit?

EXERCISE 6–21
Income statement for merchandiser
Objective 5

The following expenses were incurred by a merchandising business during the year. In which expense section of the income statement should each be reported: (a) selling, (b) administrative, or (c) other?

1. Interest expense on notes payable.
2. Salaries of office personnel.
3. Advertising expense.
4. Insurance expense on store equipment.
5. Rent expense on office building.
6. Depreciation expense on office equipment.
7. Office supplies used.
8. Salary of sales manager.

EXERCISE 6–22
Determining amounts for items omitted from income statement
Objective 5

Two items are omitted in each of the following four lists of income statement data. Determine the amounts of the missing items, identifying them by letter.

Sales	$ (a)	$600,000	$800,000	$757,500
Sales returns and allowances	12,000	17,000	(e)	30,500
Sales discounts	5,000	8,000	10,000	(g)
Net sales	250,000	(c)	765,000	(h)
Cost of merchandise sold	150,000	345,000	(f)	540,000
Gross profit	(b)	(d)	300,000	170,000

EXERCISE 6–23
Multiple-step income statement
Objective 5

How many errors can you find in the following income statement?

Enclosures Company
Income Statement
For the Year Ended December 31, 19—

Revenue from sales:			
Sales		$1,000,000	
Add: Sales returns and allowances	$18,000		
Sales discounts	4,500	22,500	
Gross sales			$1,022,500
Cost of merchandise sold			495,000
Income from operations			$ 527,500
Operating expenses:			
Selling expenses		$ 145,000	
Transportation on merchandise sold		5,300	
Administrative expenses		87,200	
Total operating expenses			237,500
Gross profit			$ 290,000
Other expense:			
Interest expense			27,500
Net loss			$ 262,500

EXERCISE 6–24
Single-step income statement
Objective 5

Summary operating data for Orthodontics Company during the current year ended April 30, 1997, are as follows: cost of merchandise sold, $825,000; administrative expenses, $125,000; interest expense, $17,500; rent income, $30,000; net sales, $1,600,000; and selling expenses, $200,000. Prepare a single-step income statement.

EXERCISE 6–25
Multiple-step income statement
Objectives 5, 6

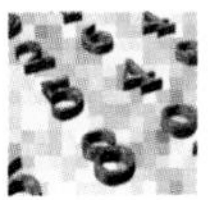

At the end of the year, selected accounts and related amounts appearing in the ledger of Carriage Company, a furniture wholesaler, are listed in alphabetical order as follows:

Administrative Expenses	$ 74,500
Building	512,500
Cash	48,500
Cost of Merchandise Sold	636,300

J. I. Ford, Capital	$180,000
J. I. Ford, Drawing	15,000
Interest Expense	7,500
Merchandise Inventory	130,000
Notes Payable	25,000
Office Supplies	10,600
Salaries Payable	3,220
Sales	975,000
Sales Discounts	10,200
Sales Returns and Allowances	24,300
Selling Expenses	132,700
Store Supplies	7,700

All selling expenses have been recorded in the account entitled *Selling Expenses*, and all administrative expenses have been recorded in the account entitled *Administrative Expenses*.

a. Prepare a multiple-step income statement for the year ended December 31.
b. Compare the major advantages and disadvantages of the multiple-step and single-step forms of income statements.

EXERCISE 6–26
Adjusting entry for merchandise inventory shrinkage
Objective 6

Wilkes Inc. perpetual inventory records indicate that $129,500 of merchandise should be on hand on December 31, 1997. The physical inventory indicates that $127,300 of merchandise is actually on hand. Journalize, in a two-column general journal, the adjusting entry for the inventory shrinkage for Wilkes Inc. for the year ended December 31, 1997.

EXERCISE 6–27
Closing the accounts of a merchandiser
Objective 6

From the following list, identify the accounts that should be closed to Income Summary at the end of the fiscal year: (a) Accounts Receivable, (b) Cost of Merchandise Sold, (c) Merchandise Inventory, (d) Sales, (e) Sales Discounts, (f) Sales Returns and Allowances, (g) Supplies, (h) Supplies Expense, (i) Salaries Expense, (j) Salaries Payable.

APPENDIX EXERCISE 6–28
Closing entries

Based on the data presented in Exercise 6–25, journalize the closing entries in a two-column general journal.

PROBLEMS SERIES A

PROBLEM 6–1A
Purchase-related transactions
Objective 2

The following selected transactions were completed by Bizcomp Company during March of the current year:

Mar. 1. Purchased merchandise from Kohl Co., $6,100, terms FOB destination, n/30.
4. Purchased merchandise from Laufer Co., $8,000, terms FOB shipping point, 2/10, n/eom. Prepaid transportation costs of $150 were added to the invoice.
5. Purchased merchandise from Faber Co., $5,000, terms FOB destination, 2/10, n/30.
8. Issued debit memorandum to Faber Co. for $1,000 of merchandise returned from purchase on March 5.
14. Paid Laufer Co. for invoice of March 4, less discount.
15. Paid Faber Co. for invoice of March 5, less debit memorandum of March 8 and discount.
19. Purchased merchandise from Porcelain Co., $6,250, terms FOB shipping point, n/eom.
19. Paid transportation charges of $120 on March 19 purchase from Porcelain Co.
20. Purchased merchandise from Hatcher Co., $3,500, terms FOB destination, 1/10, n/30.
30. Paid Hatcher Co. for invoice of March 20, less discount.
31. Paid Kohl Co. for invoice of March 1.
31. Paid Porcelain Co. for invoice of March 19.

Instructions
Journalize, in a two-column general journal, the entries to record the transactions of Bizcomp Company for March.

PROBLEM 6–2A
Sales-related transactions
Objective 2

The following selected transactions were completed by Mallory Supply Co. Mallory Supply Co. sells office supplies primarily to wholesalers but occasionally sells to retail customers.

Oct. 1. Sold merchandise on account to Beckman Co., $4,200, terms FOB destination, 2/10, n/30. The cost of the merchandise sold was $2,400.
1. Paid transportation costs of $125 on merchandise sold on October 1.
2. Sold merchandise for $620 plus 5% sales tax to cash customers. The cost of merchandise sold was $350.
4. Sold merchandise on account to Atlas Co., $2,400, terms FOB shipping point, n/eom. The cost of merchandise sold was $1,800.
5. Sold merchandise for $1,400 plus 5% sales tax to customers who used MasterCard. Deposited credit card receipts into the bank. The cost of merchandise sold was $750.
9. Sold merchandise on account to Atlas Co., $1,450, terms FOB shipping point, n/eom. The cost of merchandise sold was $900.
11. Received check for amount due from Beckman Co. for sale on October 1.
14. Sold merchandise to customers who used American Express cards, $3,600. The cost of merchandise sold was $2,100.
15. Sold merchandise on account to Monroe Co., $6,500, terms FOB shipping point, 1/10, n/30. The cost of merchandise sold was $3,900.
17. Issued credit memorandum for $500 to Monroe Co. for merchandise returned from sale on October 15. The cost of the merchandise returned was $300.
17. Sold merchandise on account to Davis Co., $10,000, terms FOB destination, 2/15, n/30. The cost of merchandise sold was $6,000.
18. Sold merchandise on account to Braggs Co., $7,500, terms FOB shipping point, 1/10, n/30. Added $85 to the invoice for transportation costs prepaid. The cost of merchandise sold was $4,500.
25. Received check for amount due from Monroe Co. for sale on October 15 less credit memorandum of October 17 and discount.
26. Issued credit memorandum for $250 to Davis Co. for allowance for damaged merchandise sold on October 17.
26. Received $9,410 from American Express for $10,000 of sales reported during the week of October 11-17.
28. Received check for amount due from Braggs Co. for sale of October 18.
31. Received check for amount due from Atlas Co. for sales of October 4 and October 9.
31. Paid Fast Delivery Service $770 for merchandise delivered during October to local customers under shipping terms of FOB destination.

Nov. 4. Paid First National Bank $480 for service fees for handling MasterCard sales during October.
10. Paid $875 to state sales tax division for taxes owed on October sales.
16. Received check for amount due from Davis Co. for sale of October 17, less credit memorandum of October 26.

Instructions

Journalize, in a two-column general journal, the entries to record the transactions of Mallory Supply Co.

PROBLEM 6–3A
Sales-related and purchase-related transactions
Objective 2

The following were selected from among the transactions completed by The Accessories Company during April of the current year:

Apr. 3. Purchased office supplies for cash, $320.
4. Purchased merchandise on account from Anchor Co., list price $15,000, trade discount 40%, terms FOB destination, 2/10, n/30.
5. Sold merchandise for cash, $3,950. The cost of the merchandise sold was $2,450.
7. Purchased merchandise on account from Mattox Co., $6,400, terms FOB shipping point, 2/10, n/30, with prepaid transportation costs of $190 added to the invoice.
7. Returned $2,500 of merchandise purchased on April 4 from Anchor Co.
11. Sold merchandise on account to Bowles Co., list price $2,250, trade discount 20%, terms 1/10, n/30. The cost of the merchandise sold was $880.
14. Paid Anchor Co. on account for purchase of April 4, less return of April 7 and discount.
15. Sold merchandise on nonbank credit cards and reported accounts to the card company, $5,850. The cost of the merchandise sold was $3,900.

Apr. 17. Paid Mattox Co. on account for purchase of April 7, less discount.
20. Purchased merchandise for cash, $6,500.
21. Received cash on account from sale of April 11 to Bowles Co., less discount.
25. Sold merchandise on account to Clemons Co., $3,200, terms 1/10, n/30. The cost of the merchandise sold was $2,025.
28. Received cash from card company for nonbank credit card sales of April 15, less $280 service fee.
30. Received merchandise returned by Clemons Co. from sale on April 25, $1,700. The cost of the returned merchandise was $810.

Instructions
Journalize the transactions in a two-column general journal.

PROBLEM 6–4A
Sales-related and purchase-related transactions for seller and buyer
Objectives 2, 3

The following selected transactions were completed during July between Spivey Company and C. K. Barker Co.:

July 3. Spivey Company sold merchandise on account to C. K. Barker Co., $9,500, terms FOB destination, 2/15, n/eom. The cost of the merchandise sold was $6,000.
3. Spivey Company paid transportation costs of $400 for delivery of merchandise sold to C. K. Barker Co. on July 3.
10. Spivey Company sold merchandise on account to C. K. Barker Co., $12,000, terms FOB shipping point, n/eom. The cost of the merchandise sold was $9,000.
11. C. K. Barker Co. returned $2,000 of merchandise purchased on account on July 3 from Spivey Company. The cost of the merchandise returned was $1,200.
14. C. K. Barker Co. paid transportation charges of $200 on July 10 purchase from Spivey Company.
17. Spivey Company sold merchandise on account to C. K. Barker Co., $18,000, terms FOB shipping point, 1/10, n/30. Spivey Company paid transportation costs of $1,500, which were added to the invoice. The cost of the merchandise sold was $10,800.
18. C. K. Barker Co. paid Spivey Company for purchase of July 3, less discount and less return of July 11.
27. C. K. Barker Co. paid Spivey Company on account for purchase of July 17, less discount.
31. C. K. Barker Co. paid Spivey Company on account for purchase of July 10.

Instructions
Journalize, in a two-column general journal, the July transactions for (1) Spivey Company and (2) C. K. Barker Co.

PROBLEM 6–5A
Multiple-step income statement and report form of balance sheet
Objectives 5, 6

The following selected accounts and their normal balances appear in the ledger of The Attache Co. for the fiscal year ended March 31, 1997:

Cash	$ 18,000
Notes Receivable	120,000
Accounts Receivable	92,000
Merchandise Inventory	100,000
Office Supplies	5,600
Prepaid Insurance	3,400
Office Equipment	55,000
Accumulated Depreciation—Office Equipment	12,800
Store Equipment	113,000
Accumulated Depreciation—Store Equipment	24,200
Accounts Payable	45,600
Salaries Payable	2,400
Note Payable (final payment due 2010)	56,000
J. Hartmann, Capital	291,000
J. Hartmann, Drawing	15,000
Sales	1,400,000
Sales Returns and Allowances	12,100
Sales Discounts	11,900
Cost of Merchandise Sold	1,050,000

Sales Salaries Expense	$113,200
Advertising Expense	32,800
Depreciation Expense—Store Equipment	6,400
Miscellaneous Selling Expense	1,600
Office Salaries Expense	51,150
Rent Expense	16,350
Depreciation Expense—Office Equipment	12,700
Insurance Expense	3,900
Office Supplies Expense	1,300
Miscellaneous Administrative Expense	1,600
Interest Income	11,000
Interest Expense	6,000

Instructions

1. Prepare a multiple-step income statement.
2. Prepare a statement of owner's equity.
3. Prepare a report form of balance sheet, assuming that the current portion of the note payable is $15,000.
4. Briefly explain (a) how multiple-step and single-step income statements differ and (b) how report-form and account-form balance sheets differ.

PROBLEM 6–6A
Single-step income statement and account form of balance sheet
Objectives 5, 6

Selected accounts and related amounts for The Attache Co. for the fiscal year ended March 31, 1997, are presented in Problem 6–5A.

Instructions

1. Prepare a single-step income statement in the format shown in Exhibit 7.
2. Prepare a statement of owner's equity.
3. Prepare an account form of balance sheet, assuming that the current portion of the note payable is $15,000.

APPENDIX PROBLEM 6–7A
Work sheet, financial statements, and adjusting and closing entries

The accounts and their balances in the ledger of The Bag Co. on December 31 of the current year are as follows:

Cash	$ 38,175
Accounts Receivable	112,500
Merchandise Inventory	230,000
Prepaid Insurance	9,700
Store Supplies	4,250
Office Supplies	2,100
Store Equipment	132,000
Accumulated Depreciation—Store Equipment	40,300
Office Equipment	50,000
Accumulated Depreciation—Office Equipment	17,200
Accounts Payable	66,700
Salaries Payable	—
Unearned Rent	1,200
Note Payable (final payment due 2008)	105,000
C. Tote, Capital	175,510
C. Tote, Drawing	40,000
Income Summary	—
Sales	895,000
Sales Returns and Allowances	11,900
Sales Discounts	7,100
Cost of Merchandise Sold	476,200
Sales Salaries Expense	76,400
Advertising Expense	25,000
Depreciation Expense—Store Equipment	—
Store Supplies Expense	—
Miscellaneous Selling Expense	1,335

Office Salaries Expense	$44,000
Rent Expense	26,000
Insurance Expense	—
Depreciation Expense—Office Equipment	—
Office Supplies Expense	—
Miscellaneous Administrative Expense	1,650
Rent Income	—
Interest Expense	12,600

The data needed for year-end adjustments on December 31 are as follows:

Physical merchandise inventory on December 31		$220,000
Insurance expired during the year		6,260
Supplies on hand on December 31:		
Store supplies		1,300
Office supplies		750
Depreciation for the year:		
Store equipment		7,500
Office equipment		3,800
Salaries payable on December 31:		
Sales salaries	$3,750	
Office salaries	1,150	4,900
Unearned rent on December 31		400

Instructions

1. Prepare a work sheet for the fiscal year ended December 31. List all accounts in the order given.
2. Prepare a multiple-step income statement.
3. Prepare a statement of owner's equity.
4. Prepare a report form of balance sheet, assuming that the current portion of the note payable is $15,000.
5. Journalize the adjusting entries.
6. Journalize the closing entries.

PROBLEMS SERIES B

PROBLEM 6–1B
Purchase-related transactions
Objective 2

The following selected transactions were completed by Babcock Co. during August of the current year:

Aug. 1. Purchased merchandise from Pickron Co., $7,750, terms FOB destination, n/30.
4. Purchased merchandise from Jones Co., $8,000, terms FOB shipping point, 2/10, n/eom. Prepaid transportation costs of $150 were added to the invoice.
5. Purchased merchandise from Rice Co., $5,000, terms FOB destination, 1/10, n/30.
7. Issued debit memorandum to Rice Co. for $1,000 of merchandise returned from purchase on August 5.
14. Paid Jones Co. for invoice of August 4, less discount.
15. Paid Rice Co. for invoice of August 5, less debit memorandum of August 7 and discount.
18. Purchased merchandise from Robbins Company, $7,250, terms FOB shipping point, n/eom.
18. Paid transportation charges of $120 on August 18 purchase from Robbins Company.
19. Purchased merchandise from Hatcher Co., $7,500, terms FOB destination, 2/10, n/30.
29. Paid Hatcher Co. for invoice of August 19, less discount.
31. Paid Pickron Co. for invoice of August 1.
31. Paid Robbins Company for invoice of August 18.

Instructions

Journalize, in a two-column general journal, the entries to record the transactions of Babcock Co. for August.

PROBLEM 6–2B
Sales-related transactions
Objective 2

The following selected transactions were completed by Acoustical Supplies Co., which sells electrical supplies primarily to wholesalers but occasionally sells to retail customers.

May 1. Sold merchandise on account to Boyd Company, $15,000, terms FOB destination, 1/10, n/30. The cost of merchandise sold was $9,200.
1. Paid transportation costs of $155 on merchandise sold on May 1.
2. Sold merchandise for $1,800 plus 6% sales tax to cash customers. The cost of merchandise sold was $950.
3. Sold merchandise on account to Cramer Co., $2,500, terms FOB shipping point, n/eom. The cost of merchandise sold was $1,300.
7. Sold merchandise for $1,150 plus 6% sales tax to customers who used VISA Cards. Deposited credit card receipts into the bank. The cost of merchandise sold was $800.
9. Sold merchandise on account to Cramer Co., $3,500, terms FOB shipping point, n/eom. The cost of merchandise sold was $2,700.
11. Received check for amount due from Boyd Company for sale on May 1.
13. Sold merchandise to customers who used American Express cards, $4,500. The cost of merchandise sold was $2,600.
14. Sold merchandise on account to Monroe Co., $6,500, terms FOB shipping point, 1/10, n/30. The cost of merchandise sold was $4,000.
16. Issued credit memorandum for $500 to Monroe Co. for merchandise returned from sale on May 13. The cost of the merchandise returned was $360.
16. Sold merchandise on account to Lester Co., $5,400, terms FOB destination, 2/15, n/30. The cost of merchandise sold was $3,000.
18. Sold merchandise on account to Stockton Company, $7,500, terms FOB shipping point, 1/10, n/30. Paid $110 for transportation costs and added them to the invoice. The cost of merchandise sold was $5,000.
24. Received check for amount due from Monroe Co. for sale on May 14 less credit memorandum of May 16 and discount.
24. Issued credit memorandum for $850 to Lester Co. for allowance for damaged merchandise sold on May 16.
27. Received $7,680 from American Express for $8,000 of sales reported during the week of May 12–18.
28. Received check for amount due from Stockton Company for sale of May 18.
30. Received check for amount due from Cramer Co. for sales of May 3 and May 9.
31. Paid Anywhere Delivery Service $1,050 for merchandise delivered during May to local customers under shipping terms of FOB destination.

June 3. Paid First National Bank $425 for service fees for handling MasterCard sales during May.
10. Paid $580 to state sales tax division for taxes owed on May sales.
15. Received check for amount due from Lester Co. for sale of May 16, less credit memorandum of May 24.

Instructions

Journalize, in a two-column general journal, the entries to record the transactions of Acoustical Supplies Co.

PROBLEM 6–3B
Sales-related and purchase-related transactions
Objective 2

The following were selected from among the transactions completed by Stevens Company during March of the current year:

Mar. 2. Purchased merchandise on account from Doyle Co., list price $15,000, trade discount 20%, terms FOB shipping point, 2/10, n/30, with prepaid transportation costs of $720 added to the invoice.
4. Purchased merchandise on account from Annex Co., $6,000, terms FOB destination, 1/10, n/30.
6. Sold merchandise on account to C. F. Howell Co., list price $4,000, trade discount 30%, terms 2/10, n/30. The cost of the merchandise sold was $1,125.
7. Purchased office supplies for cash, $350.
9. Returned $1,300 of merchandise purchased on March 4 from Annex Co.
12. Paid Doyle Co. on account for purchase of March 2, less discount.
13. Purchased merchandise for cash, $18,000.
14. Paid Annex Co. on account for purchase of March 4, less return of March 9 and discount.

Mar. 16. Received cash on account from sale of Mar. 6 to C. F. Howell Co., less discount.
19. Sold merchandise on nonbank credit cards and reported accounts to the card company, $3,450. The cost of the merchandise sold was $1,950.
22. Sold merchandise on account to Comer Co., $3,480, terms 2/10, n/30. The cost of the merchandise sold was $1,400.
24. Sold merchandise for cash, $4,350. The cost of the merchandise sold was $1,750.
25. Received merchandise returned by Comer Co. from sale on March 22, $1,480. The cost of the returned merchandise was $600.
31. Received cash from card company for nonbank credit card sales of March 19, less $340 service fee.

Instructions
Journalize the transactions in a two-column general journal.

PROBLEM 6–4B
Sales-related and purchase-related transactions for seller and buyer
Objectives 2, 3

The following selected transactions were completed during November between Selby Company and Bristol Company:

Nov. 3. Selby Company sold merchandise on account to Bristol Company, $10,500, terms FOB shipping point, 2/10, n/30. Selby Company paid transportation costs of $600, which were added to the invoice. The cost of the merchandise sold was $7,500.
8. Selby Company sold merchandise on account to Bristol Company, $12,000, terms FOB destination, 1/15, n/eom. The cost of the merchandise sold was $9,500.
8. Selby Company paid transportation costs of $650 for delivery of merchandise sold to Bristol Company on November 8.
12. Bristol Company returned $4,000 of merchandise purchased on account on November 8 from Selby Company. The cost of the merchandise returned was $2,500.
13. Bristol Company paid Selby Company for purchase of November 3, less discount.
23. Bristol Company paid Selby Company for purchase of November 8, less discount and less return of November 12.
24. Selby Company sold merchandise on account to Bristol Company, $6,000, terms FOB shipping point, n/eom. The cost of the merchandise sold was $4,000.
27. Bristol Company paid transportation charges of $150 on November 24 purchase from Selby Company.
30. Bristol Company paid Selby Company on account for purchase of November 24.

Instructions
Journalize, in a two-column general journal, the November transactions for (1) Selby Company and (2) Bristol Company.

PROBLEM 6–5B
Multiple-step income statement and report form of balance sheet
Objectives 5, 6

The following selected accounts and their normal balances appear in the ledger of Renwick Co. for the fiscal year ended June 30, 1997:

Cash	$ 38,000
Notes Receivable	50,000
Accounts Receivable	62,000
Merchandise Inventory	100,000
Office Supplies	1,600
Prepaid Insurance	6,800
Office Equipment	54,000
Accumulated Depreciation—Office Equipment	10,800
Store Equipment	107,500
Accumulated Depreciation—Store Equipment	48,900
Accounts Payable	27,000
Salaries Payable	1,700
Note Payable (final payment due 2008)	30,000
J. Lucas, Capital	194,010
J. Lucas, Drawing	15,000
Sales	1,257,000
Sales Returns and Allowances	19,000
Sales Discounts	8,500
Cost of Merchandise Sold	870,300

Sales Salaries Expense	$108,000
Advertising Expense	28,300
Depreciation Expense—Store Equipment	4,600
Miscellaneous Selling Expense	1,000
Office Salaries Expense	50,900
Rent Expense	22,150
Insurance Expense	12,750
Depreciation Expense—Office Equipment	8,700
Office Supplies Expense	900
Miscellaneous Administrative Expense	1,150
Interest Income	5,400
Interest Expense	3,660

Instructions

1. Prepare a multiple-step income statement.
2. Prepare a statement of owner's equity.
3. Prepare a report form of balance sheet, assuming that the current portion of the note payable is $5,000.
4. Briefly explain (a) how multiple-step and single-step income statements differ and (b) how report-form and account-form balance sheets differ.

PROBLEM 6–6B
Single-step income statement and account form of balance sheet
Objectives 5, 6

Selected accounts and related amounts for Renwick Co. for the fiscal year ended June 30, 1997, are presented in Problem 6–5B.

Instructions

1. Prepare a single-step income statement in the format shown in Exhibit 7.
2. Prepare a statement of owner's equity.
3. Prepare an account form of balance sheet, assuming that the current portion of the note payable is $5,000.

APPENDIX PROBLEM 6–7B
Work sheet, financial statements, and adjusting and closing entries

The accounts and their balances in the ledger of The Luggage Co. on December 31 of the current year are as follows:

Cash	$ 49,575
Accounts Receivable	116,100
Merchandise Inventory	235,000
Prepaid Insurance	10,600
Store Supplies	3,750
Office Supplies	1,700
Store Equipment	125,000
Accumulated Depreciation—Store Equipment	40,300
Office Equipment	62,000
Accumulated Depreciation—Office Equipment	17,200
Accounts Payable	66,700
Salaries Payable	—
Unearned Rent	1,200
Note Payable (final payment due 2005)	105,000
J. Samsonite, Capital	220,510
J. Samsonite, Drawing	40,000
Income Summary	—
Sales	1,007,500
Sales Returns and Allowances	15,500
Sales Discounts	6,000
Cost of Merchandise Sold	571,200
Sales Salaries Expense	86,400
Advertising Expense	29,450
Depreciation Expense—Store Equipment	—
Store Supplies Expense	—
Miscellaneous Selling Expense	1,885

Office Salaries Expense	$60,000
Rent Expense	30,000
Insurance Expense	—
Depreciation Expense—Office Equipment	—
Office Supplies Expense	—
Miscellaneous Administrative Expense	1,650
Rent Income	—
Interest Expense	12,600

The data needed for year-end adjustments on December 31 are as follows:

Physical merchandise inventory on December 31		$220,000
Insurance expired during the year		7,200
Supplies on hand on December 31:		
Store supplies		1,050
Office supplies		750
Depreciation for the year:		
Store equipment		8,500
Office equipment		4,500
Salaries payable on December 31:		
Sales salaries	$3,250	
Office salaries	1,550	4,800
Unearned rent on December 31		400

Instructions

1. Prepare a work sheet for the fiscal year ended December 31. List all accounts in the order given.
2. Prepare a multiple-step income statement.
3. Prepare a statement of owner's equity.
4. Prepare a report form of balance sheet, assuming that the current portion of the note payable is $15,000.
5. Journalize the adjusting entries.
6. Journalize the closing entries.

COMPREHENSIVE PROBLEM 2

The Bike Co. is a merchandising business. The account balances for The Bike Co. as of May 1, 1997 (unless otherwise indicated) are as follows:

110	Cash	$ 29,160
111	Notes Receivable	—
112	Accounts Receivable	50,220
113	Interest Receivable	—
115	Merchandise Inventory	123,900
116	Prepaid Insurance	3,750
117	Store Supplies	2,550
123	Store Equipment	54,300
124	Accumulated Depreciation	12,600
210	Accounts Payable	38,500
211	Salaries Payable	—
310	F. R. Schwinn, Capital, June 1, 1996	173,270
311	F. R. Schwinn, Drawing	25,000
312	Income Summary	—
410	Sales	731,600
411	Sales Returns and Allowances	13,600
412	Sales Discounts	5,200
510	Cost of Merchandise Sold	497,540

520	Sales Salaries Expense	$74,400
521	Advertising Expense	18,000
522	Depreciation Expense	—
523	Store Supplies Expense	—
529	Miscellaneous Selling Expense	2,800
530	Office Salaries Expense	29,400
531	Rent Expense	24,500
532	Insurance Expense	—
539	Miscellaneous Administrative Expense	1,650
611	Interest Income	—

During May, the last month of the fiscal year, the following transactions were completed:

May 1. Paid rent for May, $2,400.
1. Received a $10,000 note receivable from a customer on account.
2. Purchased merchandise on account, terms 2/10, n/30, FOB shipping point, $25,000.
3. Paid transportation charges on purchase of May 2, $750.
4. Purchased merchandise on account, terms n/20, FOB destination, $18,200.
5. Sold merchandise on account, terms 2/10, n/30, FOB shipping point, $8,500. The cost of the merchandise sold was $5,000.
7. Received $16,900 cash from customers on account, no discount.
10. Sold merchandise for cash, $18,300. The cost of the merchandise sold was $11,000.
11. Paid $12,800 to creditors on account.
12. Paid for merchandise purchased on May 2, less discount.
13. Received merchandise returned on sale of May 5, $1,000. The cost of the merchandise returned was $600.
14. Paid advertising expense for last half of May, $2,500.
15. Received cash from sale of May 5, less return of May 13 and discount.
18. Paid sales salaries of $1,500 and office salaries of $500.
19. Purchased merchandise for cash, $7,400.
19. Paid $13,150 to creditors on account.
20. Sold merchandise on account, terms 1/10, n/30, FOB shipping point, $16,000. The cost of the merchandise sold was $9,600.
21. For the convenience of the customer, paid shipping charges on sale of May 20, $600.
21. Received $30,380 cash from customers on account, after discounts of $620 had been deducted.
21. Purchased merchandise on account, terms 1/10, n/30, FOB destination, $15,000.
22. Paid for merchandise purchased on May 4.
24. Returned $3,000 of damaged merchandise purchased on May 21, receiving credit from the seller.
25. Refunded cash on sales made for cash, $750. The cost of the merchandise returned was $480.
27. Paid sales salaries of $1,200 and office salaries of $400.
28. Sold merchandise on account, terms 2/10, n/30, FOB shipping point, $25,700. The cost of the merchandise sold was $15,000.
29. Purchased store supplies for cash, $350.
30. Received cash from sale of May 20, less discount, plus transportation paid on May 21.
31. Paid for purchase of May 21, less return of May 24 and discount.
31. Sold merchandise on account, terms 2/10, n/30, FOB shipping point, $17,400. The cost of the merchandise sold was $10,000.
31. Purchased merchandise on account, terms 1/10, n/30, FOB destination, $15,700.

Instructions (*Note:* If the work sheet described in the appendix is used, follow the alternative instructions.)

1. Enter the balances of each of the accounts in the appropriate balance column of a four-column account. Write *Balance* in the item section, and place a check mark (✓) in the Posting Reference column.
2. Journalize the transactions for May in a two-column general journal.
3. Journalize the adjusting entries, using the following adjustment data:

a.	Interest accrued on notes receivable on May 31		$ 100
b.	Merchandise inventory on May 31		145,000
c.	Insurance expired during the year		1,250
d.	Store supplies on hand on May 31		1,050
e.	Depreciation for the current year		8,860
f.	Accrued salaries on May 31:		
	Sales salaries	$400	
	Office salaries	140	540

4. Post the journal to the ledger, extending the month-end balances to the appropriate balance columns after all posting is completed.
5. Prepare a multiple-step income statement, a statement of owner's equity, and a report form of balance sheet.
6. Journalize and post the closing entries. Indicate closed accounts by inserting a line in both balance columns opposite the closing entry. Insert the new balance in the owner's capital account.
7. Prepare a post-closing trial balance.

Alternative Instructions

1. Enter the balances of each of the accounts in the appropriate balance column of a four-column account. Write *Balance* in the item section, and place a check mark (✓) in the Posting Reference column.
2. Journalize the transactions for May in a two-column general journal.
3. Post the journal to the ledger, extending the month-end balances to the appropriate balance columns after all posting is completed.
4. Prepare a trial balance as of May 31 on a ten-column work sheet, listing all accounts in the order given in the ledger. Complete the work sheet for the fiscal year ended May 31, using the following adjustment data:

a.	Interest accrued on notes receivable on May 31		$ 100
b.	Merchandise inventory on May 31		145,000
c.	Insurance expired during the year		1,250
d.	Store supplies on hand on May 31		1,050
e.	Depreciation for the current year		8,860
f.	Accrued salaries on May 31:		
	Sales salaries	$400	
	Office salaries	140	540

5. Prepare a multiple-step income statement, a statement of owner's equity, and a report form of balance sheet.
6. Journalize and post the adjusting entries.
7. Journalize and post the closing entries. Indicate closed accounts by inserting a line in both balance columns opposite the closing entry. Insert the new balance in the owner's capital account.
8. Prepare a post-closing trial balance.

CASES

CASE 6–1
Field Company
Purchases discounts

On March 1, 1997, Field Company, a garden retailer, purchased $5,000 of corn seed, terms 1/10, n/30, from Dynacorn Co. Even though the discount period had expired on March 15, 1997, Ed Farmer subtracted the discount of $50 when he processed the documents for payment.

Discuss whether Ed Farmer behaved in an ethical manner by subtracting the discount, even though the discount period had expired.

CASE 6–2
The Home Store Co.
Purchases discounts and accounts payable

The Home Store Co. is owned and operated by Julius Billups. The following is an excerpt from a conversation between Julius Billups and JoAnn Sims, the chief accountant for The Home Store.

Julius: JoAnn, I've got a question about this recent balance sheet.
JoAnn: Sure, what's your question?
Julius: Well, as you know, I'm applying for a bank loan to finance our new store in Kirksville, and I noticed that the accounts payable are listed as $750,000.
JoAnn: That's right. Approximately $720,000 of that represents amounts due our suppliers, and the remainder is miscellaneous payables to creditors for utilities, office equipment, supplies, etc.
Julius: That's what I thought. But as you know, we normally receive a 2% discount from our suppliers for earlier payment, and we always try to take the discount.
JoAnn: That's right. I can't remember the last time we missed a discount.
Julius: Well, in that case, it seems to me the accounts payable should be listed minus the 2% discount. Let's list the accounts payable due suppliers as $705,600, rather than $720,000. Every little bit helps. You never know. It might make the difference between getting the loan and not.

How would you respond to Julius Billups' request?

CASE 6–3
Audio-Tec versus Powerhouse Electronics
Determining cost of purchase

The following is an excerpt from a conversation between Joe Hitachi and Kim Kenwood. Joe is debating whether to buy a stereo system from Audio-Tec, a locally owned electronics store, or Powerhouse Electronics, a mail-order electronics company.

Joe: Kim, I don't know what to do about buying my new stereo.
Kim: What's the problem?
Joe: Well, I can buy it locally at Audio-Tec for $689.95. However, Powerhouse Electronics has the same system listed for $699.99.
Kim: So what's the big deal? Buy it from Audio-Tec.
Joe: It's not quite that simple. Powerhouse said something about not having to pay sales tax, since I was out-of-state.
Kim: Yes, that's a good point. If you buy it at Audio-Tec, they'll charge you 6% sales tax.
Joe: But Powerhouse Electronics charges $15 for shipping and handling. If I have them send it next-day air, it'll cost an additional $20 for shipping and handling.
Kim: I guess it is a little confusing.
Joe: That's not all. Audio-Tec will give an additional 2% discount if I pay cash. Otherwise, they will let me use my MasterCard, or I can pay it off in three monthly installments.
Kim: Anything else???
Joe: Well...Powerhouse says I have to charge it on my MasterCard. They don't accept checks.
Kim: I am not surprised. Many mail-order houses don't accept checks.
Joe: I give up. What would you do?

1. Assuming that Powerhouse Electronics doesn't charge sales tax on the sale to Joe, which company is offering the best buy?
2. What might be some considerations other than price that might influence Joe's decision on where to buy the stereo system?

CASE 6–4
Hershey Foods Corporation
Financial analysis

Profitability refers to a business's ability to earn profits or net income. This ability depends on the efficiency of operations as well as the assets available to the business. Thus, profitability analysis focuses primarily on the relationship between the operating results (the income statement) and the assets used (the balance sheet).

One ratio that may be used to assess profitability is the ratio of net sales to assets. It indicates how effectively a firm uses its assets and is computed as follows:

$$\textbf{Ratio of net sales to assets} = \frac{\textbf{Net sales}}{\textbf{Total assets}}$$

1. Using total assets at the end of each year, determine the ratio of net sales to total assets for Hershey Foods Corporation for the years ended December 31, 1992 and 1993.
2. What conclusions can be drawn from these ratios concerning the trend in profitability?

CASE 6–5

Escapade Video Company

Sales discounts

Your sister operates Escapade Video Company, a videotape distributorship that is in its third year of operation. The following income statement was recently prepared for the year ended October 31, 1997:

Escapade Video Company
Income Statement
For the Year Ended October 31, 1997

Revenues:		
Net sales		$450,000
Interest income		2,500
Total revenues		$452,500
Expenses:		
Cost of merchandise sold	$310,000	
Selling expenses	46,000	
Administrative expenses	24,000	
Interest expense	5,000	
Total expenses		385,000
Net income		$ 67,500

Your sister is considering a proposal to increase net income by offering sales discounts of 2/15, n/30, and by shipping all merchandise FOB shipping point. Currently, no sales discounts are allowed and merchandise is shipped FOB destination. It is estimated that these credit terms will increase net sales by 10%. The ratio of the cost of merchandise sold to net sales is expected to be 70%. All selling and administrative expenses are expected to remain unchanged, except for store supplies, miscellaneous selling, office supplies, and miscellaneous administrative expenses, which are expected to increase proportionately with increased net sales. The amounts of these preceding items for the year ended October 31, 1997, were as follows:

Store supplies expense	$2,000
Miscellaneous selling expense	1,000
Office supplies expense	800
Miscellaneous administrative expense	1,500

The other income and other expense items will remain unchanged. The shipment of all merchandise FOB shipping point will eliminate all transportation-out expenses, which for the year ended October 31, 1997, were $18,000.

1. Prepare a projected single-step income statement for the year ending October 31, 1998, based on the proposal.
2. a. Based on the projected income statement in (1), would you recommend the implementation of the proposed changes?
   b. Describe any possible concerns you may have related to the proposed changes described in (1).

ANSWERS TO SELF-EXAMINATION QUESTIONS

1. **A** A debit memorandum (answer A), issued by the buyer, indicates the amount the buyer proposes to debit to the accounts payable account. A credit memorandum (answer B), issued by the seller, indicates the amount the seller proposes to credit to the accounts receivable account. An invoice (answer C) or a bill (answer D), issued by the seller, indicates the amount and terms of the sale.
2. **C** The amount of discount for early payment is $10 (answer C), or 1% of $1,000. Although the $50 of transportation costs paid by the seller is debited to the customer's account, the customer is not entitled to a discount on that amount.
3. **B** The single-step form of income statement (answer B) is so named because the total of all expenses is deducted in one step from the total of all revenues. The multiple-step form (answer A) includes numerous sections and subsections with several subtotals. The account form (answer C) and the report form (answer D) are two common forms of the balance sheet.
4. **C** Gross profit (answer C) is the excess of net sales over the cost of merchandise sold. Operating income (answer A) or income from operations (answer B) is the excess of gross profit over operating expenses. Net income (answer D) is the final figure on the income statement after all revenues and expenses have been reported.
5. **D** Expenses such as interest expense (answer D) that cannot be associated directly with operations are identified as *Other expense* or *Nonoperating expense*. Depreciation expense—office equipment (answer A) is an administrative expense. Sales salaries expense (answer B) is a selling expense. Insurance expense (answer C) is a mixed expense with elements of both selling expense and administrative expense. For small businesses, insurance expense is usually reported as an administrative expense.

PART THREE

Assets and Liabilities

7 Cash

YOU AND ACCOUNTING

When you receive the monthly statement for your checking account, you may simply accept the bank statement as correct. However, banks can make mistakes. For example, at the bottom right-hand corner of each check returned from the bank is a magnetic coding that has been entered by a bank clerk. This coding indicates the amount of the check. If the clerk enters the coding incorrectly, then the check will be processed for a wrong amount. To illustrate, the following check written for $25 was incorrectly processed as $250:

Ed Smith
1026 3rd Ave., So.
Lansing, Wisconsin 58241

7406
7/23 19 97
64-7088/2611

PAY TO THE ORDER OF Jones Co. $ 25 00/100
Twenty-Five Dollars and no/100 DOLLARS

FIRST FEDERAL
SAVINGS BANK
OF WISCONSIN
LANSING, WISCONSIN

FOR Ed Smith

⑆261170889⑆ 04 33 503662⑈ 7406 ⑈0000025000⑈

We are all concerned about controlling our cash. Likewise, businesses need to control cash. Inadequate controls can and often do lead to theft, misappropriation, or otherwise embarrassing situations. For example, in one of the biggest errors in banking history, **Chemical Bank** incorrectly deducted customer automated teller machine (ATM) withdrawals twice from each customer's account. For instance, if a customer withdrew $100 from his or her account, the customer actually had $200 deducted from the account balance. Before the error was discovered, Chemical Bank mistakenly deducted about $15 million from more than 100,000 customer accounts. The error was caused by inadequate controls over the changing of its computer programs. Chemical Bank corrected the error, but it was obviously quite embarrassed by it.[1]

Not only can banks make errors, but so can you. To detect such errors, control procedures should be used by both you and the bank. In a prior chapter, we described basic internal control concepts and procedures. In this chapter, we will apply these concepts to the control of cash. We begin by describing methods used by businesses to control cash receipts and cash payments. We then illustrate how these methods may be applied. For example, we illustrate how businesses reconcile their monthly bank statements as a means of accounting for and controlling cash. You may want to use this illustration as a guide for reconciling your own bank statement to your checking account.

[1] Saul Hansell, "Cash Machines Getting Greedy at a Big Bank," *The Wall Street Journal,* February 18, 1994.

After studying this chapter, you should be able to:

Objective 1
Describe the nature of cash and the importance of internal control over cash.

Objective 2
Summarize basic procedures for achieving internal control over cash receipts, including the use of cash change funds and the cash short and over account.

Objective 3
Summarize basic procedures for achieving internal control over cash payments, including the use of a voucher system, a discounts lost account, and a petty cash account.

Objective 4
Describe the nature of a bank account and its use in controlling cash.

Objective 5
Prepare a bank reconciliation and journalize any necessary entries.

Objective 6
Summarize how cash is presented on the balance sheet.

Objective 7
Define electronic funds transfer and give an example of how it is used to process cash transactions.

Nature of Cash and Importance of Controls Over Cash

Objective 1
Describe the nature of cash and the importance of internal control over cash.

Cash includes coins, currency (paper money), checks, money orders, and money on deposit that is available for unrestricted withdrawal from banks and other financial institutions. Normally, you can think of cash as anything that a bank would accept for deposit in your account. For example, a check made payable to you could normally be deposited in a bank and thus is considered cash. If, however, a check is dated in the future (post-dated), the bank would not accept the check for deposit. In this case, the check is not cash, but instead represents a type of receivable. That is, the party writing the check to you is promising to pay you the amount of the check in the future. For the check to be considered cash, it must be due and payable immediately.

In practice, a business normally has several cash accounts in its ledger. For example, it may maintain separate ledger accounts for cash on hand and cash used for special purposes, such as travel reimbursements and small payments. It may also maintain a ledger account for each of its bank accounts, such as one for general cash payments and another for payroll. To simplify, we will assume in this chapter that a business maintains only one bank account, represented in the ledger as *Cash in Bank*. We will introduce other nonbank cash accounts throughout the chapter.

As you might expect, because of the ease with which money can be transferred, cash is the asset most likely to be diverted and used improperly by employees. In addition, many transactions either directly or indirectly affect the receipt or the payment of cash. A business must therefore design and use controls that safeguard cash and authorize cash transactions. In the following paragraphs, we will discuss these controls.

Internal Control of Cash Receipts

Objective 2
Summarize basic procedures for achieving internal control over cash receipts, including the use of cash change funds and the cash short and over account.

To protect cash from theft and misuse, a business must control cash from the time it is received until it can be deposited in a bank. Such procedures are called **protective controls**.

Procedures that are designed to detect theft or misuse of cash are called **detective controls**. In a sense, detective controls are also preventive in nature, since employees are less likely to steal or misuse cash if they know there is a good chance they will be detected.

Retail businesses normally receive cash from two main sources: (1) over the counter from cash customers and (2) by mail from credit customers making payments on account. For example, fast-food restaurants such as McDonald's, Wendy's, and Burger King receive cash primarily from over-the-counter sales to customers. Mail-order retailers such as Lands' End, Orvis, and L.L. Bean receive cash primarily through the mail and from credit card companies. Wholesalers receive the majority of their cash through the mail. Regardless of the source of cash receipts, every business must properly safeguard and record its cash receipts.

One of the most important controls to protect cash received in over-the-counter sales is a cash register. You have noticed that when the clerk (cashier) enters the amount of the sale, the cash register normally displays the amount. You, the customer, may also receive a paper receipt, which helps you verify the accuracy of the purchase and serves as an additional control.

One way a retail business such as a fast-food restaurant receives cash is from over-the-counter sales to customers.

At the end of the day or work shift, the cashiers count the cash in their cash drawers and record the amounts on cash or sales memorandum forms. The cashiers' supervisor removes the cash register tapes on which total receipts were recorded. The supervisor counts the cash and compares the total with the memorandums and the tapes, noting any differences. Normally, the cash is then placed in a store safe until it can be deposited in the bank. The tapes and memorandums are forwarded to the Accounting Department, where they become the basis for journal entries.

Cash is received in the mail when customers pay their bills. This cash is usually in the form of checks and money orders. Most companies' invoices are designed so that customers return a remittance advice with these payments. The employee who opens the incoming mail should initially compare the amount of cash received with the amount shown on the remittance advice. As a protective control, the employee may also stamp the checks and money orders "For Deposit Only."

If a customer does not return a remittance advice, an employee prepares one on a form designed for such use. Like the cash register, this record of cash received establishes the initial accountability for the cash. It also helps ensure that the posting to the customer's account is accurate.

All cash received in the mail is sent to the Cashier's Department. An employee there combines it with the receipts from cash sales and prepares a bank deposit ticket. The remittance advices and their summary totals are delivered to the Accounting Department. An accounting clerk then prepares the journal entries and posts them to the customer accounts in the subsidiary ledger.

After the cash is deposited in the bank, the duplicate deposit tickets or other bank receipt forms are returned to the Accounting Department. An accounting clerk then compares the total amount deposited with the amount recorded as the cash receipt. This control helps ensure that all the cash is deposited and that no cash is lost or stolen on the way to the bank. Any shortages are thus promptly detected.

The separation of the duties of the Cashier's Department, which handles cash, and the Accounting Department, which records cash, is a preventive control. If Accounting Department employees both handled and recorded cash, an employee could steal cash and change the accounting records to hide the theft.

CASH CHANGE FUNDS

Retail stores and other businesses that receive cash directly from customers must keep some currency and coins on hand in order to make change. This cash is recorded in a cash change fund account.

The cash change fund may be established by drawing a check for the required amount, debiting Cash on Hand, and crediting Cash in Bank. No additional charges or credits to the cash on hand account are necessary unless the amount of the fund is increased or decreased.

The cash on hand may be divided up among the various cash registers. The amount in each cash register is recorded for later use in reconciling cash sales for the day. The total amount of cash received during the day is deposited, and the original amount of the change fund is retained. The desired makeup of the fund is maintained by exchanging bills or coins at the bank.

CASH SHORT AND OVER

The amount of cash on hand at the end of each day should be the beginning amount of cash in each cash register plus the cash sales for the day. However, the amount of actual cash on hand at the end of the day often differs from this amount. This occurs because of errors in recording cash sales or errors in making change.

Differences in the amount of cash counted and the amount of cash in the records are normally recorded in an account entitled Cash Short and Over. For example, the following entry records one day's cash sales, when the actual cash received is less than the amount indicated by the cash register tally:

Cash in Bank	4,577.60	
Cash Short and Over	3.16	
Sales		4,580.76

If there is a debit balance in the cash short and over account at the end of a period, it may be included as a miscellaneous administrative expense in the income statement. If there is a credit balance, it may be listed in the Other income section. If the balance becomes larger than may be accounted for by minor errors in making change, management should take any necessary corrective measures.

Internal Control of Cash Payments

Objective 3
Summarize basic procedures for achieving internal control over cash payments, including the use of a voucher system, a discounts lost account, and a petty cash account.

Regardless of the size of the company, the control over cash payments often can be improved. For example, Howard Schultz & Associates (HS&A) reviews the cash payments made by its client companies. HS&A searches for errors, such as duplicate payments, failures to take discounts, and inaccurate calculations. The typical amount recovered for a client is about one-tenth of 1 percent of the total payments made to suppliers. This averages to about $300,000 per client. In one case, HS&A recovered over $4.5 million for a client.[2]

Internal control over cash payments should provide reasonable assurance that payments are made for only authorized transactions. In addition, controls should ensure that cash is used efficiently. For example, controls should ensure that all available discounts, such as purchase and trade discounts, are taken, and thus cash is not wasted.

In the following paragraphs, we describe controls that address these issues. We also discuss how controls are often modified for small cash payments when the cost of more elaborate controls is not worthwhile.

BASIC FEATURES OF THE VOUCHER SYSTEM

In a small business, an owner/manager may sign all checks, based upon personal knowledge of all goods and services purchased. In a large business, however, checks are prepared by employees who do not likely have such a complete knowledge of the transactions. In such businesses, the duties of issuing purchase orders,

[2] Thomas Buell, Jr., "Demand Grows for Auditor," *The Naples Daily News,* January 12, 1992, p. 14F.

inspecting goods received, and verifying invoices are divided among the employees of several departments. These activities must be coordinated with the final issuance of checks to creditors. One system used for this purpose is the voucher system.

A **voucher system** is a set of methods and procedures for authorizing and recording liabilities and cash payments. A voucher system normally uses (1) vouchers, (2) a file for unpaid vouchers, and (3) a file for paid vouchers.

The term voucher is widely used in accounting. Generally, a voucher is any document that serves as proof of authority to pay cash, such as an invoice approved for payment. In some businesses, a **voucher** is a special form on which is recorded relevant data about a liability and the details of its payment. An example of such a form is shown in Exhibit 1.

Vouchers are normally prenumbered for control purposes. Each voucher provides space for the name and address of the creditor, the date, and a summary of the basic details of the supporting document. Such basic details in the voucher shown include the invoice number and the amount and terms of the invoice. One half of the back of the voucher is devoted to the account distribution and the other half to summaries of the voucher and the details of payment. Spaces are also provided for the signature or initials of certain employees.

A voucher is normally prepared in the Accounting Department by an accounts payable clerk and is based on an invoice or other supporting document. For example, when a voucher is prepared for the purchase of merchandise, the voucher should be supported by the supplier's invoice, a purchase order, and a receiving report. In preparing the voucher, the accounts payable clerk should verify the quantity, price, and mathematical accuracy of the supporting documents. This procedure provides reasonable assurance that what is being paid for was properly ordered and received.

After a voucher such as the one shown in Exhibit 1 has been prepared, the invoice or other supporting evidence is attached to the voucher. The voucher is then given to the proper official for approval.

COMPUTER KING

After a voucher has been approved, it is recorded as a credit to Accounts Payable and a debit to the appropriate account or accounts. For example, Computer King's entry to record the voucher illustrated in Exhibit 1 (No. 451), is as follows:

Merchandise Inventory	1,470	
Accounts Payable		1,470

Exhibit 1
Voucher

(face)

COMPUTER KING — VOUCHER

Date July 1, 1998 Voucher No. 451

Payee Allied Manufacturing Company
683 Fairmont Road
Chicago, IL 60630-3168

Date	Details	Amount
June 28, 1998	Invoice No. 4693-C, $1,500, FOB Chicago, 2/10, n/30	1,470.00

Attach Supporting Documents

(back)

ACCOUNT DISTRIBUTION

DEBIT	AMOUNT	
MERCHANDISE INVENTORY	1470	00
SUPPLIES		
ADVERTISING EXPENSE		
DELIVERY EXPENSE		
MISC. SELLING EXPENSE		
MISC. ADMIN. EXPENSE		
CREDIT ACCOUNTS PAYABLE	1470	00

DISTRIBUTION APPROVED L. Donnelly

NO. 451
DATE 7/1/98 DUE 7/8/98

PAYEE
Allied Manufacturing Company
683 Fairmont Road
Chicago, IL 60630-3168

VOUCHER SUMMARY

AMOUNT	1500	00
ADJUSTMENT		
DISCOUNT	30	00
NET	1470	00

APPROVED M.C. Leshen CONTROLLER
RECORDED W.B.

PAYMENT SUMMARY

DATE 7/8/98
AMOUNT 1470.00
CHECK NO. 863
APPROVED Pat King
RECORDED L.K.R. A.S.

After a voucher has been recorded, it is filed in an unpaid voucher file by due date. The amount due on each voucher represents the credit balance of an account payable.

When a voucher is to be paid, it is removed from the unpaid voucher file. The date, the number, and the amount of the check written in payment are listed on the back of the voucher. Paid vouchers and supporting documents should be stamped PAID or otherwise canceled to prevent accidental or intentional reuse.

The payment of a voucher is recorded in the same manner as the payment of an account payable. For example, Computer King's entry to record the check issued in payment of the voucher in Exhibit 1 is as follows:

Accounts Payable	1,470	
Cash in Bank		1,470

After payment, vouchers are usually filed in numerical order in a paid voucher file. They are then readily available for examination by employees needing information about a certain expenditure.

A voucher system not only provides effective accounting controls over cash payments but also aids management in fulfilling its responsibilities. For example, a voucher system may be used in predicting future cash requirements. This enables management to make the best use of cash resources.

PURCHASES DISCOUNTS LOST

In previous examples, we assumed that all invoices subject to a purchases discount were paid within the discount period. Even if the buyer has to borrow to make the payment within the discount period, it is normally to the buyer's advantage to do so. To illustrate, assume that Computer King borrows money to pay the invoice shown in Exhibit 1. The last day of the discount period in which the $30 discount can be taken is July 8, 1998. The money is borrowed for the remaining 20 days of the credit period. If an annual interest rate of 12% and a 360-day year are assumed, the interest on the loan of $1,470 ($1,500 – $30) is $9.80 ($1,470 × 12% × 20/360). The net savings to Computer King is $20.20, computed as follows:

Discount of 2% on $1,500	$30.00
Interest for 20 days at rate of 12% on $1,470	9.80
Savings from borrowing	$20.20

The approximate interest rate earned on taking a discount on a purchase with credit terms of 2/10, n/30 is 36%. As shown in the following calculation, this rate is estimated by annualizing 2% for 20 days.

$$2\% \times \frac{\textbf{360 days}}{\textbf{20 days}} = \mathbf{2\% \times 18 = 36\%}$$

In this example, as long as Computer King can borrow the necessary amount at a rate of less than 36%, it should take advantage of the discount and pay within the discount period.

In practice, companies should use a control system, such as a voucher system, that provides for the timely payment of all invoices within the discount period. However, purchase discounts may be missed due to oversight, errors in recording due dates, or other reasons. Controls should also exist to monitor missed discounts. If the amount of missed discounts becomes large, management may then take corrective action, such as revising the manner in which due dates are recorded or changing personnel.

The amount of a discount not taken should be debited to an expense account called *Discounts Lost*.[3] The balance of this account represents the cost of failing to take purchase discounts. To illustrate, assume that the discount on the invoice in Exhibit 1 is not taken. If the invoice is paid on July 28, the payment would be recorded as follows:

July 28	Accounts Payable	1,470	
	Discounts Lost	30	
	Cash in Bank		1,500

PETTY CASH

As in your own day-to-day life, most businesses frequently need cash to pay small amounts, such as postage due or for small purchases of urgently needed supplies. Normal control procedures, which might require payment by check, could result in unnecessary delay and expense in such cases. Yet, these small payments may occur frequently enough to add up to a significant total amount. Thus, it is desirable to retain some control over such payments. For this purpose, a special cash fund called a **petty cash fund** is used.

A petty cash fund is established by first estimating the amount of cash needed for payments from the fund during a period, such as a week or a month. If a voucher system is used, a voucher is prepared for this amount. The voucher is recorded as a debit to Petty Cash and a credit to Accounts Payable. The check drawn to pay the voucher is recorded as a debit to Accounts Payable and a credit to Cash in Bank.

The money obtained from cashing the check is placed in the custody of a specific employee who is authorized to disburse monies from the fund. Restrictions may also be placed on the maximum amount and the nature of fund disbursements. Each time monies are disbursed from the fund, the fund custodian records the essential details on a petty cash receipt form. In addition, the signature of the payee and the initials of the custodian of the fund are written on the form as proof of the payment. A typical petty cash receipt is illustrated in Exhibit 2.

A petty cash fund is normally replenished at periodic intervals or when it is depleted or reaches a minimum amount. When a petty cash fund is replenished, the accounts debited are determined by summarizing the petty cash receipts. If a

Exhibit 2
Petty Cash Receipt

PETTY CASH RECEIPT

No. 121 **Date** August 1, 1997

Paid to Metropolitan Times **Amount** 3 | 70

For Daily newspaper

Charge to Miscellaneous Administrative Expense

Payment received:

S.O. Hall **Approved by** N.E.R.

[3] Some companies debit Cost of Merchandise Sold or Merchandise Inventory for any discounts lost. However, debiting such accounts will not allow management to easily identify the amount of discounts lost.

voucher system is used, the voucher is recorded as a debit to the various expense and asset accounts and a credit to Accounts Payable. The check in payment of the voucher is recorded in the usual manner.

To illustrate the entries that would be made in accounting for petty cash, assume that a voucher system is used and that a petty cash fund of $100 is established on August 1. At the end of August, the petty cash receipts indicate expenditures for the following items: office supplies, $28; postage (office supplies), $22; store supplies, $35; and daily newspapers (miscellaneous administrative expense), $3.70. The entries to establish and replenish the petty cash fund are as follows:

Aug.	1	Petty Cash	100.00	
		Accounts Payable		100.00
	1	Accounts Payable	100.00	
		Cash in Bank		100.00
	31	Office Supplies	50.00	
		Store Supplies	35.00	
		Miscellaneous Administrative Expense	3.70	
		Accounts Payable		88.70
	31	Accounts Payable	88.70	
		Cash in Bank		88.70

Replenishing the petty cash fund restores it to its original amount of $100. You should note that there is no entry in Petty Cash when the fund is replenished. Petty Cash is debited only when the fund is initially set up or when the permanent amount of the fund is increased at some later time.

OTHER CASH FUNDS

Cash funds may also be established to meet other special needs of a business. For example, money may be advanced for travel expenses as needed. Periodically, after expense reports have been received, the expenses are recorded and the fund is replenished. A similar procedure may be used to provide a cash operating fund for a sales office located in another city. The amount of the fund may be deposited in a local bank, and the sales representative may be authorized to draw checks for payment of rent, salaries, and other operating expenses. Each month, the representative sends the invoices, paid checks, and other business documents to the home office. The data are audited, the expenditures are recorded, and a replenishing check is returned for deposit in the local bank.

Like petty cash funds, disbursements from other cash funds are not recorded in the accounts until the funds are replenished. To bring the accounts up to date, such funds should always be replenished at the end of an accounting period. The amount of monies in these funds will then agree with the balances in the fund accounts. At the same time, the expenses and the assets for which payments have been made will be recorded in the proper period.

Bank Accounts: Their Nature and Use as a Control Over Cash

Objective 4
Describe the nature of a bank account and its use in controlling cash.

Most of you are already familiar with bank accounts. You have a checking account at a local bank, credit union, savings and loan association, or other financial institution. In this section, we discuss the nature of a bank account maintained by a business. The features of such accounts will be similar to your own bank account. We then discuss the use of bank accounts as an additional control over cash.

BUSINESS BANK ACCOUNTS

As we mentioned earlier in the chapter, a business often maintains several bank accounts. The forms used with such accounts are a signature card, deposit ticket, check, and record of checks drawn. We briefly describe each of these forms below.

Signature Card

When you open a checking account, you sign a **signature card**. This card is used by the bank to verify the signature on checks that you have written. Also, when you open an account, the bank assigns an identifying number to the account.

Deposit Ticket

The details of a deposit are listed by the depositor on a printed form supplied by the bank. These **deposit tickets** may be prepared in duplicate. The bank teller stamps or initials a copy of the deposit ticket and gives it to the depositor as a receipt. Other types of receipts may also be used to give the depositor written proof of the date and the total amount of the deposit.

Check

A **check** is a written instrument signed by the depositor, ordering the bank to pay a sum of money to an individual or entity. There are three parties to a check—the drawer, the drawee, and the payee. The **drawer** is the one who signs the check, ordering payment by the bank. The **drawee** is the bank on which the check is drawn. The **payee** is the party to whom payment is to be made.

When checks are issued to pay bills, they are recorded as credits to Cash on the day issued. The credit to Cash is recorded, even though the checks will not be presented by the payee to the drawer's bank until a later date. Likewise, when checks are received from customers, they are recorded as debits to Cash.

The name and the address of the depositor are often printed on each check. In addition, checks are normally prenumbered, so that they can easily be kept track of as an aid to internal control. Most banks use automatic sorting and posting equipment. This equipment requires that the bank's identification number and the depositor's account number be printed on each check. These numbers are usually printed along the lower margin in machine-readable magnetic ink. When the check is presented for payment, the amount for which it is drawn is inserted next to the account number, which is also in magnetic ink. At the beginning of this chapter, we illustrated a check that had been processed by a bank.

Record of Checks Drawn

A record of the basic details of a check should be prepared at the time the check is written. A copy of each check written or a stub from which the check is detached may be used as the basis for recording cash payments. A small booklet called a **transactions register** may also be used.

The invoice number or other data may be inserted in spaces provided on the check or on an attachment to the check. Normally, checks issued to a creditor on account are sent with a form that identifies the specific invoice that is being paid. The purpose of this form, sometimes called a **remittance advice,** is to make sure that proper credit is recorded in the accounts of the creditor. In this way, mistakes are less likely to occur. A check and remittance advice is shown in Exhibit 3.

Before depositing the check at the bank, the payee removes the remittance advice. The remittance advice may then be used by the payee as written proof of the details of the cash receipt.

Exhibit 3
Check and Remittance Advice

MONROE COMPANY 363

813 Greenwood Street Detroit, MI 48206-4070 April 12 19 97 9-42/720

Pay to the Order of Hammond Office Products $ 921.20

Nine hundred twenty-one 20/100---------------------------- Dollars

ANB AMERICAN NATIONAL BANK OF DETROIT
DETROIT, MI 48201-2500 (313)933-8547 MEMBER FDIC

K.R. Simons Treasurer

Earl M. Hartman Vice President

⑆0720004 23⑆ 1627042 363⑈

DETACH THIS PORTION BEFORE CASHING

Date	Description	Gross Amount	Deductions	Net Amount
4/12/97	Invoice No. 529482	940.00	18.80	921.20

MONROE COMPANY

BANK STATEMENT

Banks usually maintain a record of all checking account transactions. A summary of all transactions, called a **statement of account**, is mailed to the depositor, usually once each month. Like any account with a customer or a creditor, the bank statement shows the beginning balance, additions, deductions, and the balance at the end of the period.

The depositor's checks received by the bank during the period may accompany the bank statement, arranged in the order of payment. The paid or canceled checks are perforated or stamped "Paid," together with the date of payment. Debit or credit memorandums describing other entries in the depositor's account may also be enclosed with the statement. For example, the bank may have debited the depositor's account for service charges or for deposited checks returned because of insufficient funds. It may have credited the account for receipts from notes receivable left for collection, for loans to the depositor, or for interest.[4] A typical bank statement is shown in Exhibit 4.

BANK ACCOUNTS AS A CONTROL OVER CASH

A bank account is one of the primary tools a business can use to control cash. For example, businesses often require that all cash receipts be initially deposited in a bank account. Likewise, all cash payments are often disbursed from one or more bank accounts. When such a system is used, there is a double record of cash transactions—one by the business and the other by the bank.[5]

[4] Although interest-bearing checking accounts are common for individuals, Federal Reserve Regulation Q prohibits the paying of interest on corporate checking accounts.
[5] The cash in bank account in the business's (the depositor's) ledger is an asset account with a debit balance. This same account is shown in the bank's records as a liability.

Exhibit 4
Bank Statement

PAGE 1

ANB
AMERICAN NATIONAL BANK
OF DETROIT
MEMBER FDIC
DETROIT, MI 48201-2500 (313)933-8547

MONROE COMPANY
813 GREENWOOD STREET
DETROIT, MI 48206-4070

ACCOUNT NUMBER		1627042
FROM 6/30/97	TO	7/31/97
	BALANCE	4,218.60
22	DEPOSITS	13,749.75
52	WITHDRAWALS	14,698.57
3	OTHER DEBITS AND CREDITS	90.00CR
	NEW BALANCE	3,359.78

--CHECKS AND OTHER DEBITS---			---DEPOSITS--*	--DATE--*	--BALANCE--*
819.40	122.54		585.75	07/01	3,862.41
369.50	732.26	20.15	421.53	07/02	3,162.03
600.00	190.70	52.50	781.30	07/03	3,100.13
25.93	160.00		662.50	07/05	3,576.70
36.80	NSF 300.00		503.18	07/07	3,743.08
32.26	535.09		932.00	07/29	3,404.40
21.10	126.20		705.21	07/30	3,962.31
	SC 18.00		MS 408.00	07/30	4,352.31
26.12	1,615.13		648.72	07/31	3,359.78

EC--ERROR CORRECTION
MS--MISCELLANEOUS
NSF--NOT SUFFICIENT FUNDS
OD--OVERDRAFT
PS--PAYMENT STOPPED
SC--SERVICE CHARGE

*** *** ***

THE RECONCILEMENT OF THIS STATEMENT WITH YOUR RECORDS IS ESSENTIAL.
ANY ERROR OR EXCEPTION SHOULD BE REPORTED IMMEDIATELY.

If a depositor uses the night depository, there will probably be a time lag between the date of the deposit and the date that it is recorded by the bank.

A bank statement allows a business to compare the cash transactions recorded in the accounting records to those recorded by the bank. The cash balance shown by a bank statement is usually different from the cash in bank balance shown in the accounting records of the business. The difference may be the result of a delay by either party in recording transactions. For example, there is a time lag of one day or more between the date a check is written and the date that it is presented to the bank for payment. If the depositor mails deposits to the bank or uses the night depository, a time lag between the date of the deposit and the date that it is recorded by the bank is also probable. Conversely, the bank may debit or credit the depositor's account for transactions about which the depositor will not be informed until later. Examples are service or collection fees charged by the bank and the proceeds of notes receivable sent to the bank for collection.

The difference may also be the result of errors by either party in recording transactions. For example, a depositor may incorrectly post to Cash in Bank a check written for $4,500 as $450. Likewise, a bank may incorrectly enter the amount of a check, as we illustrated at the beginning of this chapter.

To enhance internal control, the difference between the bank statement and the ledger account for cash in the bank should be reconciled. This reconciliation should be prepared by an employee who does not take part in or record cash transactions. Without a proper separation of these duties, mistakes are likely to occur and it is more likely that cash will be stolen or otherwise misapplied. For example, an employee who takes part in all of these duties could prepare and cash an unauthorized check, omit it from the accounts, and omit it from the reconciliation.

Bank Reconciliation

Objective 5
Prepare a bank reconciliation and journalize any necessary entries.

A bank reconciliation is a listing of items and amounts that cause the cash balance reported in the bank statement to differ from the cash in bank account balance. It is usually divided into two sections. The first section begins with the cash balance according to the bank statement and ends with the adjusted balance. The second section begins with the cash balance according to the depositor's records and ends with the adjusted balance. The two amounts designated as the adjusted balance must be equal. The form and the content of the bank reconciliation are outlined as follows:

Cash balance according to bank statement			$XXX
Add:	Additions by depositor not on bank statement	$XX	
	Bank errors	XX	XX
			$XXX
Deduct:	Deductions by depositor not on bank statement	$XX	
	Bank errors	XX	XX
Adjusted balance			$XXX
Cash balance according to depositor's records			$XXX
Add:	Additions by bank not recorded by depositor	$XX	
	Depositor errors	XX	XX
			$XXX
Deduct:	Deductions by bank not recorded by depositor	$XX	
	Depositor errors	XX	XX
Adjusted balance			$XXX

The following steps are useful in finding the reconciling items and determining the adjusted balance of Cash in Bank:

1. Compare individual deposits listed on the bank statement with unrecorded deposits appearing in the preceding period's reconciliation and with deposit receipts or other records of deposits. *Add deposits not recorded by the bank to the balance according to the bank statement.*
2. Compare paid checks with outstanding checks appearing on the preceding period's reconciliation and with checks recorded. *Deduct checks outstanding that have not been paid by the bank from the balance according to the bank statement.*
3. Compare bank credit memorandums to entries in the journal. For example, a bank would issue a credit memorandum for a note receivable and interest that it collected for a customer. *Add credit memorandums that have not been recorded to the balance according to the depositor's records.*
4. Compare bank debit memorandums to entries recording cash payments. For example, a bank normally issues debit memorandums for service charges and check printing charges. A bank also issues debit memorandums for not-sufficient-funds checks. A **not-sufficient-funds (NSF) check** is a customer's check that was recorded and deposited but was not paid when it was presented to the customer's bank for payment. NSF checks are normally charged back to the customer's account receivable. *Deduct debit memorandums that have not been recorded from the balance according to the depositor's records.*
5. Listed separately on the reconciliation are any errors discovered during the preceding steps. For example, if an amount has been recorded incorrectly by the depositor, the amount of the error should be added to or deducted from the cash balance according to the depositor's records. Similarly, errors by the bank should be added to or deducted from the cash balance according to the bank statement.

To illustrate a bank reconciliation, we will use the bank statement for Monroe Company in Exhibit 4. This bank statement shows a balance of $3,359.78 as of July 31. The balance in Cash in Bank in Monroe Company's ledger as of the same date is $2,549.99. The following reconciling items are revealed by using the steps outlined above:

Deposit of July 31 not recorded on bank statement	$ 816.20
Checks outstanding: No. 812, $1,061.00; No. 878, $435.39; No. 883, $48.60	1,544.99
Note plus interest of $8 collected by bank (credit memorandum), not recorded in the journal	408.00
Check from customer (Thomas Ivey) returned by bank because of insufficient funds (NSF)	300.00
Bank service charges (debit memorandum) not recorded in the journal	18.00
Check No. 879 for $732.26 to Taylor Co. on account, recorded in the journal as $723.26	9.00

The bank reconciliation based on the bank statement and the reconciling items is as follows:

Monroe Company
Bank Reconciliation
July 31, 1997

Cash balance according to bank statement		$3,359.78
Add deposit of July 31, not recorded by bank		816.20
		$4,175.98
Deduct outstanding checks:		
No. 812	$1,061.00	
No. 878	435.39	
No. 883	48.60	1,544.99
Adjusted balance		$2,630.99
Cash balance according to depositor's records		$2,549.99
Add note and interest collected by bank		408.00
		$2,957.99
Deduct: Check returned because of insufficient funds	$ 300.00	
Bank service charges	18.00	
Error in recording Check No. 879	9.00	327.00
Adjusted balance		$2,630.99

No entries are necessary on the depositor's records as a result of the information included in the first section of the bank reconciliation. This section begins with the cash balance according to the bank statement. However, the bank should be notified of any errors that need to be corrected on its records.

Any addition or deduction items in the second section of the bank reconciliation must be recorded in the depositor's accounts. This section begins with the cash balance according to the depositor's records. Entries should be made for bank memorandums not recorded by the depositor and any depositor's errors.

USING ACCOUNTING TO UNDERSTAND BUSINESS

Many of us reconcile our bank account each month after we receive our bank statements. In reconciling our accounts, most of us first scan the bank statement for any bank entries that we have not yet recorded. Examples of such entries include service charges (a debit entry) and interest earned (a credit entry). We then enter these amounts in our check book (register) and determine the balance of our account. Many individuals stop at this point. If you do so, you are assuming that the bank hasn't made any errors.

If you decide to continue and fully reconcile your account, you then must examine your check book to determine items that the bank has not yet recorded. Such items normally include (1) deposits in transit and (2) outstanding checks. Deposits in transit should be added to the bank balance and outstanding checks should be subtracted from the bank balance. The result is an adjusted bank balance which should agree with the balance of your check book. If the two are not equal, an error has occurred by either you or the bank.

The entries for Monroe Company, based on its bank reconciliation, are as follows:

July 31	Cash in Bank	408	
	Notes Receivable		400
	Interest Income		8
	Note collected by bank.		
31	Accounts Receivable—Thomas Ivey	300	
	Miscellaneous Administrative Expense	18	
	Accounts Payable—Taylor Co.	9	
	Cash in Bank		327
	NSF check, bank service charges, and error in recording Check No. 879.		

After the above entries have been posted, Cash in Bank will have a debit balance of $2,630.99. This balance agrees with the adjusted cash balance shown on the bank reconciliation. It is the amount of cash available as of July 31 and the amount that would be reported on the balance sheet on that date.

Although businesses may reconcile their bank accounts in a slightly different format from what we described above, the objective is the same: to control cash by reconciling the company's records to the records of an independent outside source, the bank. In doing so, any errors or misappropriations of cash may be detected.

Presentation of Cash on the Balance Sheet

Objective 6
Summarize how cash is presented on the balance sheet.

Cash is the most liquid asset, and therefore it is listed as the first asset in the Current Assets section of the balance sheet. Most companies combine all their cash accounts and present only a single cash amount on the balance sheet.

A company may have cash in excess of its operating needs. In such cases, it may invest in highly liquid investments in order to earn interest. These investments are called cash equivalents.[6] Examples of cash equivalents include United States Treasury Bills, notes issued by major corporations (referred to as commercial paper), and money market funds. Companies that have invested excess cash in cash equivalents usually report *Cash and cash equivalents* as one amount on the balance sheet.

Cash and cash equivalents normally do not require special disclosures in the notes to the financial statements. However, if the ability to withdraw cash is restricted, the restrictions should be disclosed. For example, companies with foreign operations often have cash deposits in foreign banks. These deposits may be subject to foreign laws that limit withdrawals to certain amounts. Such limitations should be disclosed in the notes to the financial statements.

A bank often requires a business to maintain in a bank account a minimum cash balance. Such a balance is called a **compensating balance**. This requirement is generally imposed by the bank as a part of a loan agreement or line of credit. A line of credit is a pre-approved amount the bank is willing to lend to a customer upon request. Compensating balance requirements should be disclosed in notes to the financial statements. An example of such a note is shown below for K Mart Corporation:

. . . In support of lines of credit, it is expected that compensating balances will be maintained on deposit with the banks, which will average 10% of the line to the extent that it is not in use and an additional 10% on the portion in use, whereas other lines require fees in lieu of compensating balances. . . .

Electronic Funds Transfer

Objective 7
Define electronic funds transfer and give an example of how it is used to process cash transactions.

With rapidly changing technology, new systems are being devised to more efficiently record and transfer cash among companies. Such systems often use electronic funds transfer (EFT). In an EFT system, computerized information, rather than paper (money, checks, etc.), are used to effect cash transactions. For example, a business may pay its employees by means of EFT. Under such a system, employees may authorize the deposit of their payroll checks directly into checking accounts. Each pay period, the business electronically transfers the employees' net pay to their checking accounts through the use of computer systems and telephone lines.

More and more companies are using EFT systems to process cash transactions. For example, the treasurer for Chevron U.S.A. reported that Chevron is making more than 5,800 electronic payments a month to suppliers, nearly 14% of the checks it once wrote.[7] Some attempts are also being made to use EFT systems in retailing. For example, in a point-of-sale (POS) system, a customer pays for goods at the time of purchase by presenting a plastic card. The card authorizes the transfer of cash from the customer's checking account to the retailer's bank account at the time of the sale.

Although EFT systems generally reduce the cost of processing cash transactions, some difficulties have arisen in the use of EFT. For example, concerns have arisen over protecting privacy of information transferred over public telephone lines, documenting transactions, and controlling access to funds.[8]

Many companies use EFT systems to process cash transactions. Chevron, for example, is making more than 5,800 electronic payments a month to its suppliers.

[6] To be classified as a cash equivalent, the investment is expected to be converted to cash within 90 days.

[7] Fred R. Bleakley, "Fast Money: Electronic Payments Now Supplant Checks at More Large Firms," *The Wall Street Journal*, April 3, 1994.

[8] Michael J. Fischer, "Electronic Funds Transfers: Controlling the Risk," *The Journal of Accountancy*, June 1988, pp. 130–134.

KEY POINTS

Objective 1. Describe the nature of cash and the importance of internal control over cash.
Cash includes coins, currency (paper money), checks, money orders, and money on deposit that is available for unrestricted withdrawal from banks and other financial institutions. Because of the ease with which money can be transferred, businesses should design and use controls that safeguard cash and authorize cash transactions.

Objective 2. Summarize basic procedures for achieving internal control over cash receipts, including the use of cash change funds and the cash short and over account.
One of the most important controls to protect cash received in over-the-counter sales is a cash register. A remittance advice is a protective control for cash received through the mail. The separation of the duties of handling cash and recording cash is also a protective control.

Retail stores and other businesses that receive cash directly from customers must keep some currency and coins in a cash change fund in order to make change. Differences in the amount of cash counted and the amount of cash in the records are normally recorded in Cash Short and Over.

Objective 3. Summarize basic procedures for achieving internal control over cash payments, including the use of a voucher system, a discounts lost account, and a petty cash account.
A voucher system is a set of methods and procedures for authorizing and recording liabilities and cash payments. A voucher system uses vouchers, a file for unpaid vouchers, and a file for paid vouchers.

Because of the importance of taking advantage of all purchases discounts, a business may use a separate account, called Discounts Lost, to account for any discounts not taken during the discount period.

A petty cash fund may be used by a business to make small payments that occur frequently. The money in a petty cash fund is placed in the custody of a specific employee, who authorizes payments from the fund. Periodically or when the amount of money in the fund is depleted or reduced to a minimum amount, the fund is replenished.

Objective 4. Describe the nature of a bank account and its use in controlling cash.
The forms used with bank accounts are a signature card, deposit ticket, check, and record of checks drawn. Each month, the bank usually sends a bank statement to the depositor, summarizing all of the transactions for the month. The bank statement allows a business to compare the cash transactions recorded in the accounting records to those recorded by the bank.

Objective 5. Prepare a bank reconciliation and journalize any necessary entries.
The first section of the bank reconciliation begins with the cash balance according to the bank statement. This balance is adjusted for the depositor's changes in cash that do not appear on the bank statement and for any bank errors. The second section begins with the cash balance according to the depositor's records. This balance is adjusted for the bank's changes in cash that do not appear on the depositor's records and for any depositor errors. The adjusted balances for the two sections must be equal.

No entries are necessary on the depositor's records as a result of the information included in the first section of the bank reconciliation. However, the items in the second section must be journalized on the depositor's records.

Objective 6. Summarize how cash is presented on the balance sheet.
Cash is listed as the first asset in the Current Assets section of the balance sheet. Companies that have invested excess cash in highly liquid investments usually report *Cash and cash equivalents* on the balance sheet.

Objective 7. Define electronic funds transfer and give an example of how it is used to process cash transactions.
Electronic funds transfer (EFT) is a payment system that uses computerized information rather than paper (money, checks, etc.) to effect cash transactions. EFT may be used in processing cash payments and cash receipts and in processing retail sales.

GLOSSARY OF KEY TERMS

Bank reconciliation. The analysis that details the items responsible for the difference between the cash balance reported in the bank statement and the balance of the cash account in the ledger. *Objective 5*

Cash. Coins, currency (paper money), checks, money orders, and money on deposit that is available for unrestricted withdrawal from banks or other financial institutions. *Objective 1*

Cash equivalents. Highly liquid investments that are usually reported on the balance sheet with cash. *Objective 6*

Electronic funds transfer (EFT). A payment system that uses computerized information rather than paper (money, checks, etc.) to effect a cash transaction. *Objective 7*

Petty cash fund. A special cash fund used to pay relatively small amounts. *Objective 3*

Voucher. A document that serves as evidence of authority to pay cash. *Objective 3*

Voucher system. Records, methods, and procedures used in verifying and recording liabilities and paying and recording cash payments. *Objective 3*

ILLUSTRATIVE PROBLEM

The bank statement for Urethane Company for June 30 indicates a balance of $9,143.11. Urethane Company uses a voucher system in controlling cash payments. All cash receipts are deposited each evening in a night depository, after banking hours. The accounting records indicate the following summary data for cash receipts and payments for June:

Cash balance as of June 1	$ 3,943.50
Total cash receipts for June	28,971.60
Total amount of checks issued in June	28,388.85

Comparison of the bank statement and the accompanying canceled checks and memorandums with the records reveals the following reconciling items:

a. The bank had collected for Urethane Company $1,030 on a note left for collection. The face of the note was $1,000.
b. A deposit of $1,852.21, representing receipts of June 30, had been made too late to appear on the bank statement.
c. Checks outstanding totaled $5,265.27.
d. A check drawn for $139 had been erroneously charged by the bank as $157.
e. A check for $30 returned with the statement had been recorded in the depositor's records as $240. The check was for the payment of an obligation to Avery Equipment Company for the purchase of office supplies on account.
f. Bank service charges for June amounted to $18.20.

Instructions

1. Prepare a bank reconciliation for June.
2. Journalize the entries that should be made by Urethane Company.

Solution

1.

Urethane Company
Bank Reconciliation
June 30, 19—

Cash balance according to bank statement		$ 9,143.11
Add: Deposit of June 30 not recorded by bank	$1,852.21	
Bank error in charging check as $157 instead of $139	18.00	1,870.21
		$11,013.32
Deduct: Outstanding checks		5,265.27
Adjusted balance		$ 5,748.05
Cash balance according to depositor's records		$ 4,526.25*
Add: Proceeds of note collected by bank, including $30 interest	$1,030.00	
Error in recording check	210.00	1,240.00
		$ 5,766.25
Deduct: Bank service charges		18.20
Adjusted balance		$ 5,748.05

*$3,943.50 + $28,971.60 – $28,388.85

2.

Cash in Bank	1,240.00	
Notes Receivable		1,000.00
Interest Income		30.00
Accounts Payable		210.00
Miscellaneous Administrative Expense	18.20	
Cash in Bank		18.20

SELF-EXAMINATION QUESTIONS (ANSWERS AT END OF CHAPTER)

1. A voucher system is used and all vouchers for purchases are recorded at the net amount. When a purchase of merchandise is made for $500 under terms 1/10, n/30:
   A. Merchandise Inventory would be debited for $495.
   B. Discounts Lost would be debited for $5 if the voucher is not paid within the discount period.
   C. the discount lost would be reported as an expense on the income statement if the voucher is not paid until after the discount period has expired.
   D. all of the above would occur.

2. A petty cash fund is:
   A. used to pay relatively small amounts.
   B. established by estimating the amount of cash needed for disbursements of relatively small amounts during a specified period.
   C. reimbursed when the amount of money in the fund is reduced to a predetermined minimum amount.
   D. all of the above.

3. The bank erroneously charged Tropical Services' account for $450.50 for a check that was correctly written and recorded by Tropical Services as $540.50. To reconcile the bank account of Tropical Services at the end of the month, you would:
   A. add $90 to the cash balance according to the bank statement.
   B. add $90 to the cash balance according to Tropical Services' records.
   C. deduct $90 from the cash balance according to the bank statement.
   D. deduct $90 from the cash balance according to Tropical Services' records.

4. In preparing a bank reconciliation, the amount of checks outstanding would be:
   A. added to the cash balance according to the bank statement.
   B. deducted from the cash balance according to the bank statement.
   C. added to the cash balance according to the depositor's records.
   D. deducted from the cash balance according to the depositor's records.

5. Journal entries based on the bank reconciliation are required for:
   A. additions to the cash balance according to the depositor's records.
   B. deductions from the cash balance according to the depositor's records.
   C. both A and B.
   D. neither A nor B.

DISCUSSION QUESTIONS

1. Why is cash the asset that often warrants the most attention in the design of an effective internal control structure?
2. Most retail businesses maintain cash change funds. (a) What is the purpose of such funds, and (b) what entry is made to establish a cash change fund?
3. The combined cash count of all cash registers at the close of business is $4 less than the cash sales indicated by the cash register tapes. (a) In what account is the cash shortage recorded? (b) Are cash shortages debited or credited to this account?
4. In which section of the income statement would a credit balance in Cash Short and Over be reported?
5. What is meant by the term *voucher* as applied to the voucher system?
6. Before a voucher for the purchase of merchandise is approved for payment, supporting documents should be compared to verify the accuracy of the liability. Name an example of a supporting document for the purchase of merchandise.
7. After a voucher has been approved for payment, it is recorded as a credit to what account?
8. The controller approves all vouchers before they are submitted to the treasurer for payment. What procedure can the controller add to the system to ensure that the documents accompanying the vouchers and supporting the payments are not "reused" to support future vouchers improperly?
9. The accounting clerk pays all obligations by prenumbered checks. What are the strengths and weaknesses in the internal control over cash payments in this situation?
10. In what order are vouchers ordinarily filed (a) in the unpaid voucher file and (b) in the paid voucher file? Give reasons for the answers.
11. What is the advantage of recording missed discounts in the discounts lost account?
12. Quality Wholesale Co. purchased $10,000 of merchandise, 2/15, n/30. Due to an oversight, Quality Wholesale failed to pay the supplier within the discount period. What accounts would be debited when Quality Wholesale pays the $10,000?

13. As a general rule, all cash payments should be made by check. Explain why some cash payments are made in coins and currency from a petty cash fund.
14. What account or accounts are debited when recording the voucher (a) establishing a petty cash fund and (b) replenishing a petty cash fund?
15. The petty cash account has a debit balance of $500. At the end of the accounting period, there is $93 in the petty cash fund, along with petty cash receipts totaling $407. Should the fund be replenished as of the last day of the period? Discuss.
16. Distinguish between the drawer and the payee of a check.
17. What name is often given to the notification, attached to a check, that indicates the specific invoice being paid?
18. The balance of Cash in Bank is likely to differ from the cash balance reported by the bank statement. What two factors are likely to be responsible for the difference?
19. What is the purpose of preparing a bank reconciliation?
20. Do items reported on the bank statement as credits represent (a) additions made by the bank to the depositor's balance, or (b) deductions made by the bank from the depositor's balance?
21. What entry should be made if a check received from a customer and deposited is returned by the bank for lack of sufficient funds (an NSF check)?
22. a. What is meant by the term *cash equivalents?*
    b. How are cash equivalents reported in the financial statements?
23. a. What is meant by the term *compensating balance* as applied to the checking account of a firm?
    b. How is the compensating balance reported in the financial statements?
24. What is meant by *electronic funds transfer?*

EXERCISES

EXERCISE 7–1
Internal control of cash receipts
Objective 2

The procedures used for over-the-counter receipts are as follows. At the close of each day's business, the sales clerks count the cash in their respective cash drawers, after which they determine the amount recorded by the cash register and prepare the memorandum cash form, noting any discrepancies. An employee from the cashier's office counts the cash, compares the total with the memorandum, and takes the cash to the cashier's office.

a. Indicate the weak link in internal control.
b. How can the weakness be corrected?

EXERCISE 7–2
Internal control over cash receipts
Objective 2

Ed Pinto works at the drive-through window of Dominick's Burgers. Occasionally, when a drive-through customer orders, Ed fills the order and pockets the customer's money. He does not ring up the order on the cash register.

Identify the internal control weaknesses that exist at Dominick's Burgers, and discuss what can be done to prevent this theft.

EXERCISE 7–3
Internal control of cash receipts
Objective 2

The mailroom employees send all remittances and remittance advices to the cashier. The cashier deposits the cash in the bank and forwards the remittance advices and duplicate deposit slips to the Accounting Department.

a. Indicate the weak link in internal control in the handling of cash receipts.
b. How can the weakness be corrected?

EXERCISE 7–4
Entry for cash sales
Objective 2

The actual cash received from cash sales was $12,839.79, and the amount indicated by the cash register total was $12,853.16. Journalize the entry, in general journal form, to record the cash receipts and cash sales.

EXERCISE 7–5
Internal control of cash payments
Objective 3

Montclair Co. is a medium-size merchandising company. When its current income statement was reviewed, it was noted that the amount of purchases discounts lost was disproportionately large in comparison with earlier periods. Further investigation revealed that in spite of a sufficient bank balance, a significant amount of available cash discounts had been lost because of failure to make timely payments. In addition, it was discovered that several purchases invoices had been paid twice.

Outline procedures for the payment of vendors' invoices, so that the possibilities of losing available cash discounts and of paying an invoice a second time will be minimized.

EXERCISE 7–6
Internal control of cash payments
Objective 3

NYCOM Company, a communications equipment manufacturer, recently fell victim to an embezzlement scheme masterminded by one of its employees. To understand the scheme, it is necessary to review NYCOM's procedures for the purchase of services.

The purchasing agent is responsible for ordering services (such as repairs to a photocopy machine or office cleaning) after receiving a service requisition from an authorized manager. However, since no tangible goods are delivered, a receiving report is not prepared. When the Accounting Department receives an invoice billing NYCOM for a service call, the accounts payable clerk calls the manager who requested the service in order to verify that it was performed.

The embezzlement scheme involves Judy Bell, the manager of plant and facilities. Judy arranged for her uncle's company, Advo Industrial Supply and Service, to be placed on NYCOM's approved vendor list. Judy did not disclose the family relationship.

On several occasions, Judy would submit a requisition for services to be provided by Advo's Industrial Supply and Service. However, the service requested was really not needed, and it was never performed. Advo would bill NYCOM for the service and then split the cash payment with Judy.

Explain what changes should be made to NYCOM's procedures for ordering and paying for services in order to prevent such occurrences in the future.

EXERCISE 7–7
Internal control of cash
Objectives 1, 3

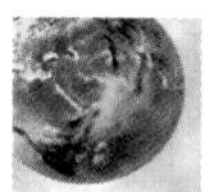

Between September 3 and September 22, seventeen prenumbered checks totaling $1,129,232.39 were forged and cashed on the accounts of Perini Corporation, a construction company based in the Boston suburb of Framingham. Perini Corporation kept its supply of blank prenumbered checks in an unlocked storeroom with items such as styrofoam coffee cups. Every clerk and secretary had access to this storeroom. It was later discovered that someone had apparently stolen two boxes of prenumbered checks. The numbers of the missing checks matched the numbers of the out-of-sequence checks cashed by the banks.

What fundamental principle of control over cash was violated in this case?

EXERCISE 7–8
Entries for purchases and discounts lost
Objective 3

Journalize, in general journal form, the following related transactions, assuming that any discounts lost are recorded separately.

Aug. 3. Voucher No. 963 is prepared for merchandise purchased from Baker Co., $8,000, terms 1/10, n/30.
12. Voucher No. 1010 is prepared for merchandise purchased from Butcher Co., $7,500, terms 2/10, n/30.
22. Check No. 410 is issued in payment of Voucher No. 1010.
Sept. 2. Check No. 423 is issued in payment of Voucher No. 963.

EXERCISE 7–9
Purchases discounts lost
Objective 3

Journalize the entries to record the following transactions by Dill Inc.:

a. Purchased merchandise on October 1, terms 3/10, n/30, $10,000.
b. Paid the invoice on October 31.

EXERCISE 7–10
Borrowing to take a purchases discount
Objective 3

From the data in Exercise 7–9, compute the following:

a. The net savings to Dill Inc. from borrowing at 12% to take the discount.
b. The approximate interest rate earned on taking a discount on a purchase with credit terms of 3/10, n/30.

EXERCISE 7–11
Petty cash fund entries
Objective 3

Journalize the entries to record the following:

a. Voucher No. 10002 is prepared to establish a petty cash fund of $450.
b. Check No. 2511 is issued in payment of Voucher No. 10002.
c. The amount of cash in the petty cash fund is now $87.30. Voucher No. 10127 is prepared to replenish the fund, based on the following summary of petty cash receipts: office supplies, $115.83; miscellaneous selling expense, $125.60; miscellaneous administrative expense, $118.10. (Since the amount of the check to replenish the fund plus the balance in the fund do not equal $450, record the discrepancy in the cash short and over account.)
d. Check No. 2555 is issued by the disbursing officer in payment of Voucher No. 10127. The check is cashed, and the money is placed in the fund.

EXERCISE 7–12
Cash change fund entries with voucher system
Objectives 2, 3

Journalize the entries for the following transactions:

a. Voucher No. 130 is prepared to establish a change fund of $800.
b. Check No. 1170 is issued in payment of Voucher No. 130.
c. Cash sales for the day, according to the cash register tapes, were $7,358.10, and cash on hand is $8,162.90. A bank deposit ticket was prepared for $7,362.90.

EXERCISE 7–13
Bank reconciliation
Objective 5

Identify each of the following reconciling items as: (a) an addition to the cash balance according to the bank statement, (b) a deduction from the cash balance according to the bank statement, (c) an addition to the cash balance according to the depositor's records, or (d) a deduction from the cash balance according to the depositor's records. (None of the transactions reported by bank debit and credit memorandums have been recorded by the depositor.)

1. Check for $36 charged by bank as $63.
2. Check drawn by depositor for $25 but recorded as $250.
3. Outstanding checks, $6,515.50.
4. Deposit in transit, $5,279.12.
5. Note collected by bank, $5,200.00.
6. Check of a customer returned by bank to depositor because of insufficient funds, $712.50.
7. Bank service charges, $20.10.

EXERCISE 7–14
Entries based on bank reconciliation
Objective 5

Which of the reconciling items listed in Exercise 7–13 necessitate an entry in the depositor's accounts?

EXERCISE 7–15
Bank reconciliation
Objective 5

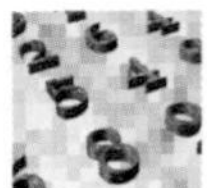

The following data were accumulated for use in reconciling the bank account of The Skin Care Co. for May:

a. Cash balance according to the depositor's records at May 31, $8,530.20.
b. Cash balance according to the bank statement at May 31, $11,100.50.
c. Checks outstanding, $4,276.20.
d. Deposit in transit, not recorded by bank, $1,780.40.
e. A check for $230 in payment of a voucher was erroneously recorded in the check register as $320.
f. Bank debit memorandum for service charges, $15.50.

Prepare a bank reconciliation.

EXERCISE 7–16
Entries for bank reconciliation
Objective 5

Using the data presented in Exercise 7–15, journalize, in general journal form, the entry or entries that should be made by the depositor.

EXERCISE 7–17
Entries for note collected by bank
Objective 5

Accompanying a bank statement for Profumeria Company is a credit memorandum for $12,255, representing the principal ($12,000) and interest ($255) on a note that had been collected by the bank. The depositor had been notified by the bank at the time of the collection, but had made no entries. In general journal form, journalize the entry that should be made by the depositor to bring the accounting records up to date.

EXERCISE 7–18
Bank reconciliation
Objective 5

An accounting clerk for The Emporium Co. prepared the following bank reconciliation:

The Emporium Co.
Bank Reconciliation
January 31, 1997

Cash balance according to depositor's records		$12,100.75
Add: Outstanding checks	$3,557.12	
Error by the Emporium Co. in recording Check No. 345 as $760 instead of $670	90.00	
Note for $1,500 collected by bank, including interest	1,620.00	5,267.12
		$17,367.87
Deduct: Deposit in transit on January 31	$1,150.00	
Bank service charges	25.60	1,175.60
Cash balance according to bank statement		$16,192.27

a. Using the data in the above bank reconciliation, prepare a bank reconciliation for The Emporium Co. in the format shown in the chapter.
b. If a balance sheet were prepared for The Emporium Co. on January 31, 1997, what amount should be reported for cash in bank?

EXERCISE 7–19
Using bank reconciliation to determine cash receipts stolen
Objective 5

Desktop Co. records all cash receipts on the basis of its cash register tapes. Desktop Co. discovered during June 1997 that one of its sales clerks had stolen an undetermined amount of cash receipts when he took the daily deposits to the bank. The following data have been gathered for June:

Cash in bank according to the general ledger	$10,773.22
Cash according to the June 30, 1997 bank statement	12,271.14
Outstanding checks as of June 30, 1997	1,889.37
Bank service charge for June	18.60
Note receivable, including interest collected by bank in June	1,060.00

No deposits were in transit on June 30, which fell on a Sunday.

a. Determine the amount of cash receipts stolen by the sales clerk.
b. What accounting controls would have prevented or detected this theft?

EXERCISE 7–20
Bank reconciliation
Objective 5

How many errors can you find in the following bank reconciliation prepared as of the end of the current month?

Abracadabra Co.
Bank Reconciliation
For the Month Ended June 30, 19—

Cash balance according to bank statement			$13,767.76
Add outstanding checks:			
No. 3721		$ 345.95	
3739		172.75	
3743		359.60	
3744		601.50	1,479.80
			$15,247.56
Deduct deposit of June 30, not recorded by bank			1,010.06
Adjusted balance			$10,237.50
Cash balance according to depositor's records			$10,739.32
Add: Proceeds of note collected by bank:			
Principal	$2,500.00		
Interest	75.00	$2,575.00	
Service charges		19.50	2,594.50
			$13,333.82
Deduct: Check returned because of insufficient funds		$ 266.80	
Error in recording May 15 deposit of $1,859 as $1,589		270.00	536.80
Adjusted balance			$12,797.02

PROBLEMS SERIES A

PROBLEM 7–1A
Evaluating internal control of cash
Objectives 1, 2, 3

The following procedures were recently installed by Kato Company:

a. The bank reconciliation is prepared by the cashier, who works under the supervision of the treasurer.
b. All mail is opened by the mail clerk, who forwards all cash remittances to the cashier. The cashier prepares a listing of the cash receipts and forwards a copy of the list to the accounts receivable clerk for recording in the accounts.
c. At the end of each day, an accounting clerk compares the duplicate copy of the daily cash deposit slip with the deposit receipt obtained from the bank.

d. The accounts payable clerk prepares a voucher for each disbursement. The voucher along with the supporting documentation is forwarded to the treasurer's office for approval.
e. After necessary approvals have been obtained for the payment of a voucher, the treasurer signs and mails the check. The treasurer then stamps the voucher and supporting documentation as paid and returns the voucher and supporting documentation to the accounts payable clerk for filing.
f. Along with petty cash expense receipts for postage, office supplies, etc., several post-dated employee checks are in the petty cash fund.
g. At the end of each day, any deposited cash receipts are placed in the bank's night depository.
h. At the end of the day, cash register clerks are required to use their own funds to make up any cash shortages in their registers.

Instructions

Indicate whether each of the procedures of internal control over cash represents (1) a strength or (2) a weakness. For each weakness, indicate why it exists.

PROBLEM 7–2A
Transactions for petty cash, advances to salespersons fund; cash short and over
Objectives 2, 3

Phoenix Company has just adopted the policy of depositing all cash receipts in the bank and of making all payments by check in conjunction with the voucher system. The following transactions were selected from those completed in August of the current year:

Aug. 2. Recorded Voucher No. 1 to establish a petty cash fund of $400 and a change fund of $500.
2. Issued Check No. 719 in payment of Voucher No. 1.
3. Recorded Voucher No. 5 to establish an advances to salespersons fund of $2,000.
5. Issued Check No. 722 in payment of Voucher No. 5.
17. The cash sales for the day, according to the cash register tapes, totaled $2,970.60. The combined count of all cash on hand (including the change fund) totaled $3,473.20.
29. Recorded Voucher No. 44 to reimburse the petty cash fund for the following disbursements, each evidenced by a petty cash receipt:
    Aug. 3. Store supplies, $21.50.
    5. Express charges on merchandise purchased, $16.00.
    8. Office supplies, $12.75.
    11. Office supplies, $9.20.
    17. Postage stamps, $52 (Office Supplies).
    19. Repair to office calculator, $37.50 (Miscellaneous Administrative Expense).
    22. Postage due on special delivery letter, $1.05 (Miscellaneous Administraive Expense).
    23. Express charges on merchandise purchased, $35.
    27. Office supplies, $11.10.
29. Issued Check No. 752 in payment of Voucher No. 44.
30. The cash sales for the day, according to the cash register tapes, totaled $3,055.50. The count of all cash on hand (including the change fund) totaled $3,551.60.
31. Recorded Voucher No. 49 to replenish the advances to salespersons fund for the following expenditures for travel: Mark May, $312.50; Joe Wolf, $556.50; Tony Sacca, $372.10.
31. Issued Check No. 760 in payment of Voucher No. 49.

Instructions

Journalize the transactions.

PROBLEM 7–3A
Entries for voucher system, discounts lost, petty cash
Objective 3

The following selected transactions were completed by a company that uses a voucher system and a perpetual inventory system and records all invoices at their net price.

Sept. 3. Recorded Voucher No. 540 for $800, payable to Jones Supply Co., for office supplies purchased, terms n/eom.
8. Recorded Voucher No. 542 for $9,000, payable to Cox Co., for merchandise purchased, terms 1/10, n/30.
9. Recorded Voucher No. 548 for $1,400, payable to Collins Co., for merchandise purchased, terms 2/10, n/30.
19. Issued Check No. 264 in payment of Voucher No. 548.

Sept. 29. Recorded Voucher No. 560 for $255.14 to replenish the petty cash fund for the following disbursements: store supplies, $92.88; office supplies, $84.95; miscellaneous administrative expense, $42.45; miscellaneous selling expense, $34.86.
30. Issued Check No. 270 in payment of Voucher No. 560.
30. Issued Check No. 277 in payment of Voucher No. 542.
30. Issued Check No. 289 in payment of Voucher No. 540.

Instructions

Journalize the transactions.

PROBLEM 7–4A
Bank reconciliation and entries
Objective 5

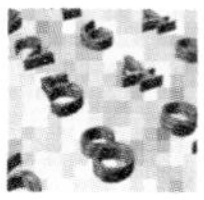

The cash in bank account for Zashy Carpets at November 30 of the current year indicated a balance of $15,100.30. The bank statement indicated a balance of $21,016.30 on November 30. Comparison of the bank statement and the accompanying canceled checks and memorandums with the records revealed the following reconciling items:

a. Checks outstanding totaled $8,169.75.
b. A deposit of $3,917.75, representing receipts of November 30, had been made too late to appear on the bank statement.
c. The bank had collected $3,150 on a note left for collection. The face of the note was $3,000.
d. A check for $1,500 returned with the statement had been incorrectly recorded by Zashy Carpets as $1,050. The check was for the payment of an obligation to Morgan Co. for the purchase of office equipment on account.
e. A check drawn for $600 had been erroneously charged by the bank as $1,600.
f. Bank service charges for June amounted to $36.00.

Instructions

1. Prepare a bank reconciliation.
2. Journalize the necessary entries. The accounts have not been closed. The voucher system is used.

PROBLEM 7–5A
Bank reconciliation and entries
Objective 5

The cash in bank account for Conner Co. at August 1 of the current year indicated a balance of $18,443.90. During August, the total cash deposited was $30,650.75, and checks written totaled $31,770.25. The bank statement indicated a balance of $26,465.50 on August 31. Comparison of the bank statement, the canceled checks, and the accompanying memorandums with the records revealed the following reconciling items:

a. Checks outstanding totaled $8,003.84.
b. A deposit of $2,148.21, representing receipts of August 31, had been made too late to appear on the bank statement.
c. The bank had collected for Conner Co. $3,650 on a note left for collection. The face of the note was $3,500.
d. A check for $470 returned with the statement had been incorrectly charged by the bank as $740.
e. A check for $84.20 returned with the statement had been recorded by Conner Co. as $8.42. The check was for the payment of an obligation to Bartles Co. on account.
f. Bank service charges for August amounted to $18.75.

Instructions

1. Prepare a bank reconciliation as of August 31.
2. Journalize the necessary entries. The accounts have not been closed.

PROBLEM 7–6A
Bank reconciliation and entries
Objective 5

The Español Company uses the voucher system in controlling cash payments. All cash receipts are deposited each Wednesday and Friday in a night depository, after banking hours. The data required to reconcile the bank statement as of June 30 have been taken from various documents and records and are reproduced as follows. The sources of the data are printed in capital letters.

CASH IN BANK ACCOUNT:	
Balance as of June 1	$7,317.40
CASH RECEIPTS FOR MONTH OF JUNE:	7,579.58

DUPLICATE DEPOSIT TICKETS:
Date and amount of each deposit in June:

Date	*Amount*	*Date*	*Amount*	*Date*	*Amount*
June 1	$908.50	June 10	$ 896.61	June 22	$897.34
3	854.17	15	882.95	24	942.71
8	840.50	17	1,046.74	29	310.06

CHECKS WRITTEN:
Number and amount of each check issued in June:

Check No.	*Amount*	*Check No.*	*Amount*	*Check No.*	*Amount*
740	$237.50	747	Void	754	$249.75
741	495.15	748	$450.90	755	172.75
742	501.90	749	640.13	756	113.95
743	671.30	750	276.77	757	407.95
744	506.88	751	299.37	758	359.60
745	117.25	752	537.01	759	701.50
746	298.66	753	380.95	760	486.39

Total amount of checks issued in June: $7,905.66

JUNE BANK STATEMENT:

PAGE 1

ANB
AMERICAN NATIONAL BANK
MEMBER FDIC

ACCOUNT NUMBER

FROM 6/01/19–	TO	6/30/19–
BALANCE		7,447.20
9 DEPOSITS		10,944.77
20 WITHDRAWALS		7,145.91
4 OTHER DEBITS AND CREDITS		326.30
NEW BALANCE		10,919.76

THE ESPANOL COMPANY

----CHECKS AND OTHER DEBITS---		---DEPOSITS-*	-DATE-*	--BALANCE--*
No.731 162.15	No.738 251.40	690.25	06/01	7,723.90
No.739 60.55	No.740 237.50	908.50	06/02	8,334.35
No.741 495.15	No.742 501.90	854.17	06/04	8,191.47
No.743 671.30	No.744 506.88	840.50	06/09	7,853.79
No.745 117.25	No.746 298.66	MS 2,500.00	06/09	9,937.88
No.748 450.90	No.749 640.13	MS 125.00	06/09	8,971.85
No.750 276.77	No.751 299.37	896.61	06/11	9,292.32
No.752 537.01	No.753 380.95	882.95	06/16	9,257.31
No.754 249.75	No.756 113.95	1,406.74	06/18	10,300.35
No.757 407.95	No.760 486.39	897.34	06/23	10,303.35
		942.71	06/25	11,246.06
	NSF 291.90		06/28	10,954.16
	SC 34.40		06/30	10,919.76

EC--ERROR CORRECTION OD--OVERDRAFT
MS--MISCELLANEOUS PS--PAYMENT STOPPED
NSF--NOT SUFFICIENT FUNDS SC--SERVICE CHARGE

*** *** ***

THE RECONCILEMENT OF THIS STATEMENT WITH YOUR RECORDS IS ESSENTIAL.
ANY ERROR OR EXCEPTIONS SHOULD BE REPORTED IMMEDIATELY.

BANK RECONCILIATION FOR PRECEDING MONTH:

The Español Company
Bank Reconciliation
May 31, 19—

Cash balance according to bank statement		$7,447.20
Add deposit for May 31, not recorded by bank		690.25
		$8,137.45
Deduct outstanding checks:		
No. 731	$162.15	
736	345.95	
738	251.40	
739	60.55	820.05
Adjusted balance		$7,317.40
Cash balance according to depositor's records		$7,352.50
Deduct service charges		35.10
Adjusted balance		$7,317.40

Instructions

1. Prepare a bank reconciliation as of June 30. If errors in recording deposits or checks are discovered, assume that the errors were made by the company. Assume that all deposits are from cash sales. All checks are in payment of vouchers.
2. Journalize the necessary entries. The accounts have not been closed.
3. What is the amount of Cash in Bank that should appear on the balance sheet as of June 30?
4. If in preparing the bank reconciliation you note that a canceled check for $250 has been incorrectly recorded by the bank as $520, briefly explain how the error would be included in the bank reconciliation and how it should be corrected.

PROBLEMS SERIES B

PROBLEM 7–1B
Evaluating internal control of cash
Objectives 1, 2, 3

The following procedures were recently installed by Jafra Company:

a. The bank reconciliation is prepared by the accountant.
b. Each cashier is assigned a separate cash register drawer, to which no other cashier has access.
c. All sales are rung up on the cash register, and a receipt is given to the customer. All sales are recorded on a tape locked inside the cash register.
d. At the end of a shift, each cashier counts the cash in his or her cash register, unlocks the tape, and compares the amount of cash with the amount on the tape to determine cash shortages and overages.
e. Checks received through the mail are given daily to the accounts receivable clerk for recording collections on account and for depositing in the bank.
f. Disbursements are made from the petty cash fund only after a petty cash receipt has been completed and signed by the payee.
g. Vouchers and all supporting documents are perforated with a PAID designation after being paid by the treasurer.

Instructions

Indicate whether each of the procedures of internal control over cash represents (1) a strength or (2) a weakness. For each weakness, indicate why it exists.

PROBLEM 7–2B
Transactions for petty cash, advances to salespersons fund; cash short and over
Objectives 2, 3

Physical Dynamics Company has just adopted the policy of depositing all cash receipts in the bank and of making all payments by check in conjunction with the voucher system. The following transactions were selected from those completed in April of the current year:

April 1. Recorded Voucher No. 1 to establish a petty cash fund of $350 and a change fund of $500.
1. Issued Check No. 299 in payment of Voucher No. 1.

April 5. Recorded Voucher No. 5 to establish an advances to salespersons fund of $1,500.
6. Issued Check No. 302 in payment of Voucher No. 5.
15. The cash sales for the day, according to the cash register tapes, totaled $1,995.60. The combined count of all cash on hand (including the change fund) totaled $2,498.20.
26. Recorded Voucher No. 38 to reimburse the petty cash fund for the following disbursements, each evidenced by a petty cash receipt:
  April 4. Store supplies, $26.50.
  6. Express charges on merchandise purchased, $15.50.
  8. Office supplies, $14.75.
  9. Office supplies, $9.20.
  12. Postage stamps, $52.00 (Office Supplies).
  16. Repair to adding machine, $39.50 (Miscellaneous Administrative Expense).
  20. Repair to typewriter, $31.50 (Miscellaneous Administrative Expense).
  22. Postage due on special delivery letter, $1.05 (Miscellaneous Administrative Expense).
  24. Express charges on merchandise purchased, $19.50.
26. Issued Check No. 337 in payment of Voucher No. 38.
30. The cash sales for the day, according to the cash register tapes, totaled $2,009.50. The count of all cash on hand (including the change fund) totaled $2,505.60.
30. Recorded Voucher No. 43 to replenish the advances to salespersons fund for the following expenditures for travel: Susan Hilgenberg, $119.50; Al Del Greco, $433.40; Alice McKyer, $375.10.
30. Issued Check No. 340 in payment of Voucher No. 43.

Instructions
Journalize the transactions.

PROBLEM 7–3B
Entries for voucher system, discounts lost, petty cash
Objective 3

The following selected transactions were completed by a company that uses a voucher system and a perpetual inventory system, and records all invoices at their net price.

Jan. 3. Recorded Voucher No. 1015 for $2,500, payable to Edwards Supply Co., for office supplies purchased, terms n/30.
5. Recorded Voucher No. 1020 for $8,000, payable to Fair Co., for merchandise purchased, terms 2/10, n/eom.
10. Recorded Voucher No. 1028 for $2,500, payable to Clinton Co., for merchandise purchased, terms 1/10, n/30.
20. Issued Check No. 795 in payment of Voucher No. 1028.
30. Recorded Voucher No. 1040 for $239.84 to replenish the petty cash fund for the following disbursements: store supplies, $92.88; office supplies, $69.95; miscellaneous administrative expense, $42.45; miscellaneous selling expense, $34.56.
31. Issued Check No. 806 in payment of Voucher No. 1040.
31. Issued Check No. 821 in payment of Voucher No. 1020.
31. Issued Check No. 835 in payment of Voucher No. 1015.

Instructions
Journalize the transactions.

PROBLEM 7–4B
Bank reconciliation and entries
Objective 5

The cash in bank account for Intercom Systems at March 31 of the current year indicated a balance of $17,460. The bank statement indicated a balance of $23,391.40 on March 31. Comparison of the bank statement and the accompanying canceled checks and memorandums with the records reveals the following reconciling items:

a. Checks outstanding totaled $3,943.90.
b. A deposit of $1,215.50, representing receipts of March 31, had been made too late to appear on the bank statement.
c. The bank had collected $2,600 on a note left for collection. The face of the note was $2,500.
d. A check for $180 returned with the statement had been incorrectly recorded by Intercom Systems as $810. The check was for the payment of an obligation to Optel Co. for the purchase of office supplies on account.
e. A check drawn for $75 had been incorrectly charged by the bank as $57.
f. Bank service charges for March amounted to $45.

Instructions

1. Prepare a bank reconciliation.
2. Journalize the necessary entries. The accounts have not been closed. The voucher system is used.

PROBLEM 7–5B
Bank reconciliation and entries
Objective 5

The cash in bank account for Powlen Co. at June 1 of the current year indicated a balance of $12,881.40. During June, the total cash deposited was $40,500.40, and checks written totaled $38,850.47. The bank statement indicated a balance of $18,880.45 on June 30. Comparison of the bank statement, the canceled checks, and the accompanying memorandums with the records revealed the following reconciling items:

a. Checks outstanding totaled $4,180.27.
b. A deposit of $2,481.70, representing receipts of June 30, had been made too late to appear on the bank statement.
c. A check for $190 had been incorrectly charged by the bank as $100.
d. A check for $570.45 returned with the statement had been recorded by Powlen Co. as $750.45. The check was for the payment of an obligation to Scott and Son on account.
e. The bank had collected for Powlen Co. $2,400 on a note left for collection. The face of the note was $2,000.
f. Bank service charges for June amounted to $19.45.

Instructions

1. Prepare a bank reconciliation as of June 30.
2. Journalize the necessary entries. The accounts have not been closed.

PROBLEM 7–6B
Bank reconciliation and entries
Objective 5

Trevino Interiors uses the voucher system in controlling cash payments. All cash receipts are deposited each Wednesday and Friday in a night depository, after banking hours. The data required to reconcile the bank statement as of August 31 have been taken from various documents and records and are reproduced as follows. The sources of the data are printed in capital letters.

CASH IN BANK ACCOUNT:
Balance as of August 1 $10,578.00

CASH RECEIPTS FOR MONTH OF AUGUST 6,132.60

DUPLICATE DEPOSIT TICKETS:
Date and amount of each deposit in August:

Date	*Amount*	*Date*	*Amount*	*Date*	*Amount*
Aug. 2	$619.50	Aug. 12	$780.70	Aug. 23	$731.45
5	701.80	16	600.10	26	601.50
9	819.24	19	701.26	31	577.05

CHECKS WRITTEN:
Number and amount of each check issued in August:

Check No.	*Amount*	*Check No.*	*Amount*	*Check No.*	*Amount*
614	$243.50	621	$409.50	628	$ 737.70
615	650.10	622	Void	629	329.90
616	279.90	623	Void	630	882.80
617	395.50	624	707.01	631	1081.56
618	535.40	625	658.63	632	62.40
619	230.10	626	550.03	633	310.08
620	238.87	627	318.73	634	203.30

Total amount of checks issued in August: $8,825.01

ANB AMERICAN NATIONAL BANK MEMBER FDIC

TREVINO INTERIORS

		PAGE	1
	ACCOUNT NUMBER		
	FROM 8/01/19—	TO	8/31/19—
	BALANCE		10,422.80
9	DEPOSITS		11,436.35
20	WITHDRAWALS		8,514.11
4	OTHER DEBITS AND CREDITS		249.50
	NEW BALANCE		13,095.54

CHECKS AND OTHER DEBITS					DEPOSITS	DATE	BALANCE
No.580	310.10	No.612	92.50		780.80	08/01	10,801.00
No.613	137.50	No.614	243.50		619.50	08/03	11,039.50
No.615	650.10	No.616	279.90		701.80	08/06	10,811.30
No.617	395.50	No.618	535.40		819.24	08/11	10,699.64
No.619	320.10	No.620	238.87		780.70	08/13	10,921.37
No.621	409.50	No.624	707.01		MS 5000.00	08/14	14,804.86
No.625	658.63	No.626	550.03		MS 100.00	08/14	13,696.20
No.627	318.73	No.629	329.90		600.10	08/17	13,647.67
No.630	882.80	No.631	1081.56	NSF 225.40		08/20	11,457.91
No.632	62.40	No.633	310.08		701.26	08/21	11,786.69
					731.45	08/24	12,518.14
					601.50	08/28	13,119.64
		SC	24.10			08/31	13,095.54

EC--ERROR CORRECTION OD--OVERDRAFT
MS--MISCELLANEOUS PS--PAYMENT STOPPED
NSF--NOT SUFFICIENT FUNDS SC--SERVICE CHARGE

*** *** ***

THE RECONCILEMENT OF THIS STATEMENT WITH YOUR RECORDS IS ESSENTIAL. ANY ERROR OR EXCEPTIONS SHOULD BE REPORTED IMMEDIATELY.

BANK RECONCILIATION FOR PRECEDING MONTH:

Trevino Interiors Company
Bank Reconciliation
July 31, 19—

Cash balance according to bank statement		$10,422.80
Add deposit of July 31, not recorded by bank		780.80
		$11,203.60
Deduct outstanding checks:		
No. 580	$310.10	
No. 602	85.50	
No. 612	92.50	
No. 613	137.50	625.60
Adjusted balance		$10,578.00
Cash balance according to depositor's records		$10,605.70
Deduct service charges		27.70
Adjusted balance		$10,578.00

Instructions

1. Prepare a bank reconciliation as of August 31. If errors in recording deposits or checks are discovered, assume that the errors were made by the company. Assume that all deposits are from cash sales. All checks are in payment of vouchers.

2. Journalize the necessary entries. The accounts have not been closed.
3. What is the amount of Cash in Bank that should appear on the balance sheet as of August 31?
4. Assume that in preparing the bank reconciliation, you note that a canceled check for $570 has been incorrectly recorded by the bank as $750. Briefly explain how the error would be included in the bank reconciliation and how it should be corrected.

CASES

CASE 7–1
The Cosmetics Co.
Bank reconciliation

During the preparation of the bank reconciliation for The Cosmetics Co., Karen Kay, the assistant controller, discovered that Avon National Bank erroneously recorded a $1,700 check written by The Cosmetics Co. as $700. Karen has decided not to notify the bank, but to wait for the bank to detect the error. Karen plans to record the $1,000 error as Other Income if the bank fails to detect the error within the next three months.

Discuss whether Karen is behaving in an ethical manner.

CASE 7–2
Regents Computer Co.
Internal controls

The following is an excerpt from a conversation between two sales clerks, Carol Morrow and Will Fleming. Both Carol and Will are employed by Regents Computer Co., a locally owned and operated computer retail store.

Carol: Did you hear the news?
Will: What news?
Carol: Agatha and Bailey were both arrested this morning.
Will: What? Arrested? You're putting me on!
Carol: No, really! The police arrested them first thing this morning. Put them in handcuffs, read them their rights—the whole works. It was unreal!
Will: What did they do?
Carol: Well, apparently they were filling out merchandise refund forms for fictitious customers and then taking the cash.
Will: I guess I never thought of that. How did they catch them?
Carol: The store manager noticed that returns were twice that of last year and seemed to be increasing. When he confronted Agatha, she became flustered and admitted to taking the cash, apparently over $2,000 in just three months. They're going over the last six months' transactions to try to determine how much Bailey stole. He apparently started stealing first.

Suggest appropriate control procedures that would have prevented or detected the theft of cash.

CASE 7–3
Friendly Grocery Stores
Internal controls

The following is an excerpt from a conversation between the store manager of Friendly Grocery Stores, Kim Hennsley, and Myles Cockren, president of Friendly Grocery Stores.

Myles: Kim, I'm concerned about this new scanning system.
Kim: What's the problem?
Myles: Well, how do we know the clerks are ringing up all the merchandise?
Kim: That's one of the strong points about the system. The scanner automatically rings up each item, based on its bar code. We update the prices daily, so we're sure that the sale is rung up for the right price.
Myles: That's not my concern. What keeps a clerk from pretending to scan items and then simply not charging his friends? If his friends were buying 10-15 items, it would be easy for the clerk to pass through several items with his finger over the bar code or just pass the merchandise through the scanner with the wrong side showing. It would look normal for anyone observing. In the old days, we at least could hear the cash register ringing up each sale.
Kim: I see your point.

Suggest ways that Friendly Grocery Stores could prevent or detect the theft of merchandise as described.

CASE 7–4
Sunrise Markets
Internal controls

Leo Reckler and Deborah Getman are both cash register clerks for Sunrise Markets. Jo Calloway is the store manager for Sunrise Markets. The following is an excerpt of a conversation between Leo and Deborah:

Leo: Debbie, how long have you been working for Sunrise Markets?
Deborah: Almost five years this September. You just started two weeks ago . . . right?
Leo: Yes. Do you mind if I ask you a question?
Deborah: No, go ahead.
Leo: What I want to know is, have they always had this rule that if your cash register is short at the end of the day you have to make up the shortage out of your own pocket?
Deborah: Yes, as long as I've been working here.
Leo: Well, it's the pits. Last week I had to pay in almost $60.
Deborah: It's not that big a deal. I just make sure that I'm not short at the end of the day.
Leo: How do you do that?
Deborah: I just short-change a few customers early in the day. There are a few jerks that deserve it anyway. Most of the time, their attention is elsewhere and they don't think to check their change.
Leo: What happens if you're over at the end of the day?
Deborah: Jo lets me keep it as long as it doesn't get to be too large. I've not been short in over a year. I usually clear about $10 to $40 extra per day.

Discuss the ethics of this case from the viewpoints of Deborah, Leo, and Jo.

CASE 7–5
Hershey Foods Corporation
Financial analysis

Corporations generally issue annual reports to their stockholders and other interested parties. These annual reports include a Management Responsibility (or Management Report) section as well as financial statements. The Management Responsibility section discusses responsibility for the financial statements and normally includes an assessment of the company's internal control system. The financial statements also report the company's cash and cash equivalents.

1. What does the annual report for Hershey Foods Corporation indicate about the internal control system?
2. What is Hershey's amount of cash and cash equivalents at December 31, 1993?
3. What is the makeup of Hershey's cash equivalents at December 31, 1993?
4. In which financial statement for Hershey Foods Corporation are the major inflows and outflows of cash and cash equivalents for 1993 reported?

CASE 7–6
Interscope Company
Bank reconciliation and internal control

The records of Interscope Company indicate a May 31 cash in bank balance of $22,631.05, which includes undeposited receipts for May 30 and 31. The cash balance on the bank statement as of May 31 is $20,004.95. This balance includes a note of $3,000 plus $150 interest collected by the bank but not recorded in the journal. Checks outstanding on May 31 were as follows: No. 470, $950.20; No. 479, $510; No. 490, $616.50; No. 796, $127.40; No. 797, $520; and No. 799, $351.50.

On May 3, the cashier resigned, effective at the end of the month. Before leaving on May 31, the cashier prepared the following bank reconciliation:

Cash balance per books, May 31		$22,631.05
Add outstanding checks:		
No. 796	$127.40	
797	520.00	
799	351.50	798.90
		$24,129.95
Less undeposited receipts		3,425.00
Cash balance per bank, May 31		$20,004.95
Deduct unrecorded note with interest		3,150.00
True cash, May 31		$16,854.95

Calculator Tape of Outstanding Checks

0.00 *
127.40 +
520.00 +
351.50 +
798.90 *

Subsequently, the owner of Interscope Company discovered that the cashier had stolen all undeposited receipts in excess of the $3,425 on hand on May 31. The owner, a close family friend, has asked your help in determining the amount that the former cashier has stolen.

1. Determine the amount the cashier stole from Interscope Company. Show your computations in good form.
2. How did the cashier attempt to conceal the theft?
3. a. Identify two major weaknesses in internal controls, which allowed the cashier to steal the undeposited cash receipts.
   b. Recommend improvements in internal controls, so that similar types of thefts of undeposited cash receipts can be prevented.

ANSWERS TO SELF-EXAMINATION QUESTIONS

1. **D** A major advantage of recording purchases at the net amount (answer A) is that the cost of failing to take discounts is recorded in the accounts (answer B) and then reported as an expense on the income statement (answer C).
2. **D** To avoid the delay, annoyance, and expense that is associated with paying all obligations by check, relatively small amounts (answer A) are paid from a petty cash fund. The fund is established by estimating the amount of cash needed to pay these small amounts during a specified period (answer B), and it is then reimbursed when the amount of money in the fund is reduced to a predetermined minimum amount (answer C).
3. **C** The error was made by the bank, so the cash balance according to the bank statement needs to be adjusted. Since the bank deducted $90 ($540.50 – $450.50) too little, the error of $90 should be deducted from the cash balance according to the bank statement (answer C).
4. **B** On any specific date, the cash in bank account in a depositor's ledger may not agree with the account in the bank's ledger because of delays and/or errors by either party in recording transactions. The purpose of a bank reconciliation, therefore, is to determine the reasons for any differences between the two account balances. All errors should then be corrected by the depositor or the bank, as appropriate. In arriving at the adjusted (correct) cash balance according to the bank statement, outstanding checks must be deducted (answer B) to adjust for checks that have been written by the depositor but that have not yet been presented to the bank for payment.
5. **C** All reconciling items that are added to and deducted from the cash balance according to the depositor's records on the bank reconciliation (answer C) require that journal entries be made by the depositor to correct errors made in recording transactions or to bring the cash account up to date for delays in recording transactions.

8 Receivables and Temporary Investments

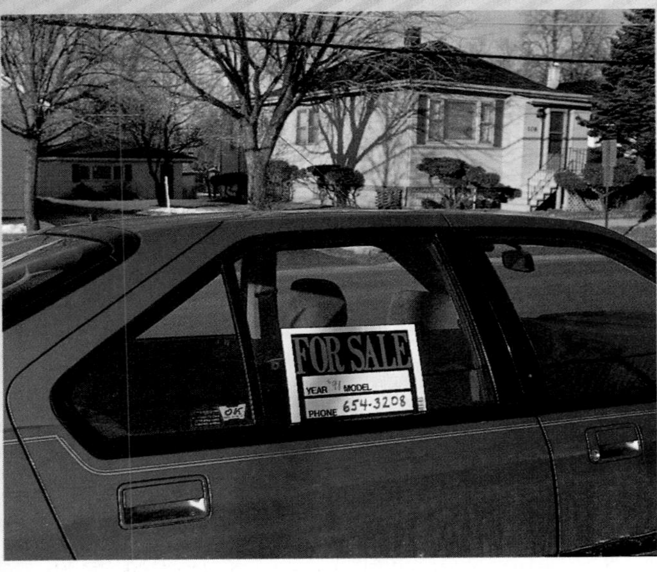

YOU AND ACCOUNTING

Assume that you have decided to sell your car to a neighbor for $7,500. Your neighbor agrees to pay you $1,500 immediately and the remaining $6,000 in a year. How much should you charge your neighbor for interest?

You could determine an appropriate interest rate by asking some financial institutions what they currently charge their customers. Using this information as a starting point, you could then negotiate with your neighbor and agree upon a rate. Assuming that the agreed-upon rate is 8%, you will receive interest totalling $480 for the one-year loan.

In this chapter, we will describe and illustrate how interest is computed. In addition, we will discuss the accounting for receivables, including uncollectible receivables. Most of these receivables result from a business rendering services or selling merchandise on account. We conclude this chapter with a discussion of temporary investments of excess cash.

After studying this chapter, you should be able to:

Objective 1
List the common classifications of receivables.

Objective 2
Summarize and provide examples of internal control procedures that apply to receivables.

Objective 3
Describe the nature of and the accounting for uncollectible receivables.

Objective 4
Journalize the entries for the allowance method of accounting for uncollectibles, and estimate uncollectible receivables based on sales and on an analysis of receivables.

Objective 5
Journalize the entries for the direct write-off of uncollectible receivables.

Objective 6
State the accounting implications of promissory notes.

Objective 7
Journalize the entries for notes receivable transactions, including discounted notes receivable and dishonored notes receivable.

Objective 8
Define temporary investments.

Objective 9
Prepare the Current Assets section of the balance sheet that includes temporary investments and receivables.

Classification of Receivables

Objective 1
List the common classifications of receivables.

The term **receivables** includes all money claims against other entities, including people, business firms, and other organizations. Receivables are normally classified as accounts receivable, notes receivable, or other receivables. These receivables are usually a significant portion of the total current assets. For example, the 1994 annual report of La-Z-Boy Chair Company reports that receivables make up over 60% of La-Z-Boy's current assets.

ACCOUNTS RECEIVABLE

The most common transaction giving rise to a receivable is selling merchandise or services on credit. The receivable is recorded as a debit to the accounts receivable account. Such **accounts receivable** are normally expected to be collected within a relatively short period, such as 30 or 60 days, and are classified on the balance sheet as a current asset.

NOTES RECEIVABLE

A business may grant credit to customers on the basis of a formal instrument of credit, called a promissory note. A promissory note, often simply called a note, is a written promise to pay a sum of money on demand or at a definite time. Notes are often used for credit periods of more than sixty days, such as an installment plan for equipment sales. Notes may also be used to settle a customer's account receivable. The acceptance of a note is recorded as a debit to the notes receivable account. As long as a note is expected to be collected within a year, it is normally classified on the balance sheet as a current asset.

Notes and accounts receivable that originate from sales transactions are sometimes called **trade receivables.** Unless otherwise described, we will assume that accounts and notes receivable have originated from credit sales in the usual course of business.

OTHER RECEIVABLES

Other receivables include interest receivable, taxes receivable, and receivables from officers or employees. Other receivables are unusual and are normally listed separately on the balance sheet. If such receivables are expected to be collected within one year, they are normally classified as a current asset on the balance sheet. If collection is expected beyond one year, they are classified as a noncurrent asset and reported under the caption *Investments*.

Internal Control of Receivables

Objective 2
Summarize and provide examples of internal control procedures that apply to receivables.

The principles of internal control discussed in prior chapters can be used to establish procedures to safeguard receivables. These controls include separating the business operations from the accounting for receivables. In this way, the accounting records can serve as an independent check on operations. Thus, the employee who handles the accounting for notes and accounts receivables should not be involved with the operating aspects of approving credit or collecting receivables. Separating these functions reduces the possibility of errors and misusing funds. For example, if the accounts receivable billing clerk has access to cash receipts from customers, the clerk could steal the cash but report the receipt only on the customer's monthly statement. The customer would not complain and the theft would go undetected.

To further illustrate the internal control principle of separating related operating functions, assume that salespersons have authority to approve credit. If the salespersons are paid salaries plus commissions, say 10% of sales, they can increase their commissions by approving poor credit risks. Thus, the credit approval function is normally assigned to an individual outside the sales area.

Within the accounting function, related functions should also be separated. In this way, the work of one employee serves as a check on the work of another employee. For example, the responsibilities for maintaining the accounts receivable customers' (subsidiary) ledger and the general ledger should be separated. The work of the accounts receivable clerk can be checked by comparing the total of the individual account balances in the customers' (subsidiary) ledger with the balance of the accounts receivable controlling account that is maintained by the general ledger clerk. If one individual performed both functions, this control would be lacking.

For most businesses, the primary receivables are notes receivable and accounts receivable. As we mentioned in the preceding section, notes receivable are normally recorded in a single general ledger account. If there are many notes, the general ledger account can be supported by a notes receivable register or a subsidiary ledger. The register would contain details of each note, such as the name of the maker, place of payment, amount, term, interest rate, and due date. When a note is due for payment, the maker of the note can be notified, and the risk that the maker will overlook the due date is minimized.

Control over accounts receivable begins with the proper credit approval of the sale by an authorized company official. Procedures for granting credit should be developed by the credit department of the company. Likewise, procedures for authorizing adjustments of accounts receivable, such as for sales returns and allowances and sales discounts, should be developed. Collection procedures should also be established to ensure timely collection of accounts receivable and to minimize losses from uncollectible accounts.

Uncollectible Receivables

Objective 3
Describe the nature of and the accounting for uncollectible receivables.

In prior chapters, we described and illustrated the accounting for transactions involving sales of merchandise or services on credit. The primary accounting issue that we have not yet discussed is uncollectible receivables.

As we discussed in the preceding section, companies attempt to limit the number and amount of uncollectible accounts by using control procedures. The primary focus of controls in this area is the credit-granting function. These controls normally involve investigating customer credit-worthiness, using references and running background checks. For example, most of us have completed credit application forms requiring such information. Companies may also impose credit limits on new customers. For example, you may have been limited to a maximum of $1,000 when your credit card was first issued to you. Such limits are designed to control potentially uncollectible amounts.

Once an account is past due, companies should use procedures to maximize the collection of the account. After repeated attempts at collection, such procedures may include turning an account over to a collection agency.

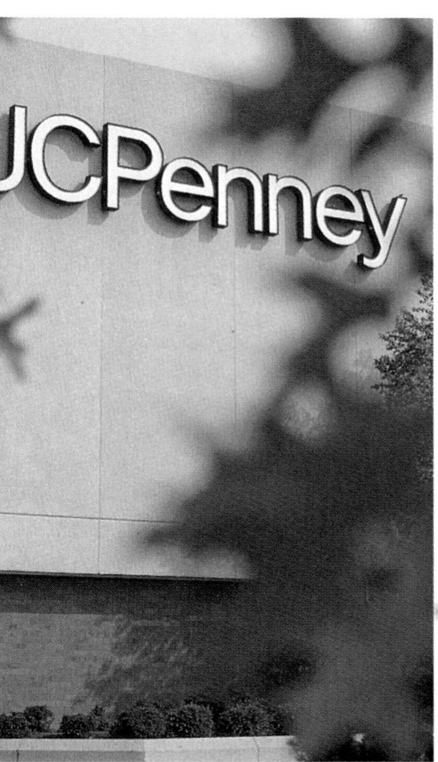

Some retailers such as Penney's have developed their own credit cards to minimize the risk of uncollectible receivables.

Retail businesses often attempt to shift the risk of uncollectible accounts to other companies. For example, some retailers do not accept sales on account, but will only accept cash or credit cards. Such policies effectively shift the risk to the credit card companies. Other retailers, such as Macy's, Sears, and Penney's, have developed their own credit cards. However, these retailers often sell their credit card receivables to other companies.

The selling of a company's receivables is called **factoring** the receivables, and the purchaser of the receivable is called a **factor.** One advantage of factoring its receivables is that the company receives immediate cash for operations and other needs. In addition, depending upon the factoring agreement, some of the risk of uncollectible accounts may be shifted to the factor.[1]

Regardless of the care used in granting credit and the collection procedures used, a part of the claims from sales to customers on credit will normally not be collectible. The operating expense incurred because of the failure to collect receivables is called an expense or a loss from **uncollectible accounts, doubtful accounts,** or **bad debts.**[2]

When does an account or a note become uncollectible? There is no general rule for determining when an account becomes uncollectible. The fact that a debtor fails to pay an account according to a sales contract or dishonors a note on the due date does not necessarily mean that the amount will be uncollectible. Bankruptcy of the debtor is one of the most significant indications of partial or complete uncollectibility. Other indications include the closing of the customer's business and the failure of repeated attempts to collect.

There are two methods of accounting for receivables that appear to be uncollectible. The allowance method provides an expense for uncollectible receivables in advance of their write-off.[3] The other procedure, called the direct write-off method or **direct charge-off method,** recognizes the expense only when certain accounts are judged to be worthless. We will discuss each of these methods in the following paragraphs.

[1] The accounting for the factoring of accounts receivable, with and without recourse, is beyond the scope of our discussion in this chapter. The accounting for such transactions is discussed in advanced accounting texts.
[2] If both notes and accounts are involved, both may be included in the expense account title, as in *Uncollectible Notes and Accounts Expense,* or *Uncollectible Receivables Expense.* Because of its wide usage and simplicity, we will use *Uncollectible Accounts Expense* in this text.
[3] The allowance method is not acceptable for determining the federal income tax of most taxpayers.

Allowance Method of Accounting for Uncollectibles

Objective 4
Journalize the entries for the allowance method of accounting for uncollectibles, and estimate uncollectible receivables based on sales and on an analysis of receivables.

Most large businesses estimate the uncollectible portion of their trade receivables. An adjusting entry at the end of a fiscal period records the expense for future uncollectibility. As with all periodic adjustments, this entry serves two purposes. First, it reduces the value of the receivables to the amount of cash expected to be realized in the future, called the **net realizable value.** Second, it matches the uncollectible expense of the current period with the related revenues of the period.

To illustrate the allowance method, we will use assumed data for a new business, Richards Company. The business began in August and chose to use the calendar year as its fiscal year. The accounts receivable account, shown below, has a balance of $105,000 at the end of the period.

ACCOUNT ***Accounts Receivable*** — **ACCOUNT NO.** ***114***

Date		Item	Post. Ref.	Debit	Credit	Balance Debit	Balance Credit
19— Aug.	31			20 0 0 0 00		20 0 0 0 00	
Sept.	30			25 0 0 0 00		45 0 0 0 00	
	30				15 0 0 0 00	30 0 0 0 00	
Oct.	31			40 0 0 0 00		70 0 0 0 00	
	31				25 0 0 0 00	45 0 0 0 00	
Nov.	30			38 0 0 0 00		83 0 0 0 00	
	30				23 0 0 0 00	60 0 0 0 00	
Dec.	31			75 0 0 0 00		135 0 0 0 00	
	31				30 0 0 0 00	105 0 0 0 00	

The customer accounts making up the $105,000 balance in Accounts Receivable include some that are past due. No specific accounts are believed to be totally uncollectible at this time. However, it seems likely that some will be collected only in part and that others will become worthless. Based on a careful study, Richards estimates that a total of $3,000 will eventually be uncollectible. The net realizable value of the accounts receivable is therefore $102,000 ($105,000 – $3,000). The $3,000 reduction in value is the uncollectible accounts expense for the period.

Because the $3,000 reduction in accounts receivable is an estimate, it cannot be credited to specific customer accounts or to the accounts receivable controlling account. Instead, a contra asset account entitled Allowance for Doubtful Accounts is credited. The adjusting entry to record the expense and the reduction in the asset is as follows:

	Adjusting Entry			
Dec. 31	Uncollectible Accounts Expense	717	3,000	
	Allowance for Doubtful Accounts	115		3,000

The two accounts to which the entry is posted are as follows:

ACCOUNT ***Uncollectible Accounts Expense*** — **ACCOUNT NO.** ***717***

Date		Item	Post. Ref.	Debit	Credit	Balance Debit	Balance Credit
19— Dec.	31	Adjusting		3 0 0 0 00		3 0 0 0 00	

ACCOUNT *Allowance for Doubtful Accounts*					ACCOUNT NO. *115*
Date	Item	Post. Ref.	Debit	Credit	Balance	
					Debit	Credit
19— Dec. 31	Adjusting			3 0 0 0 00		3 0 0 0 00

The debit balance of $105,000 in Accounts Receivable is the amount of the total claims against customers on open account. The credit balance of $3,000 in Allowance for Doubtful Accounts is the amount to be deducted from Accounts Receivable to determine the net realizable value.

Uncollectible accounts expense is normally reported on the income statement as an administrative expense. This classification is used because the credit-granting and collection duties are the responsibilities of departments within the administrative area. At the end of the period, the $3,000 balance in Uncollectible Accounts Expense is closed to Income Summary.

The accounts receivable may be presented as shown below in the Current Assets section of the balance sheet. Alternatively, the accounts receivable may be listed on the balance sheet at the net amount of $102,000, with a notation in parentheses showing the amount of the allowance.

Current assets:		
Cash		$ 21,600
Accounts receivable	$105,000	
Less allowance for doubtful accounts	3,000	102,000

WRITE-OFFS TO THE ALLOWANCE ACCOUNT

When an account is believed to be uncollectible, it is written off against the allowance account as follows:

Jan. 21	Allowance for Doubtful Accounts	610	
	Accounts Receivable—John Parker		610
	To write off the uncollectible account.		

Authorization for write-offs should originate with the credit manager or other designated officer. The authorizations, which should be written, serve as support for the accounting entry.

The total amount written off against the allowance account during a period will rarely be equal to the amount in the account at the beginning of the period. The allowance account will have a credit balance at the end of the period if the write-offs during the period are less than the beginning balance. It will have a debit balance if the write-offs exceed the beginning balance. After the year-end adjusting entry is recorded, the allowance account will have a credit balance.

An account receivable that has been written off against the allowance account may later be collected. In such cases, the account should be reinstated by an entry that is the exact reverse of the write-off entry. For example, assume that the account of $610 written off in the preceding entry is later collected. The entry to reinstate the account would be as follows:

June 10	Accounts Receivable—John Parker	610	
	Allowance for Doubtful Accounts		610
	To reinstate account written off on January 21.		

The cash received in payment would be recorded as a receipt on account as follows:

June 10	Cash	610	
	Accounts Receivable—John Parker		610

The two preceding entries can be combined. However, recording two separate entries in the customer's account, with proper notation, provides useful credit information.

ESTIMATING UNCOLLECTIBLES

How is the amount of uncollectible accounts estimated? The estimate of uncollectibles at the end of a fiscal period is based on past experience and forecasts of future business activity. When the general economic environment is favorable, the amount of the expense should normally be less than when the trend is in the opposite direction. The estimate of uncollectibles is usually based on either (1) the amount of sales for the period or (2) the amount and the age of the receivable accounts at the end of the period.

Estimate Based on Sales

Accounts receivable are acquired as a result of sales on account. The amount of such sales during the year may therefore be used to estimate the amount of uncollectible accounts. The amount of this estimate is added to whatever balance exists in Allowance for Doubtful Accounts. For example, assume that the allowance account has a credit balance of $700 before adjustment. It is estimated from past experience that 1% of credit sales will be uncollectible. If credit sales for the period are $300,000, the adjusting entry for uncollectible accounts at the end of the period is as follows:

Dec. 31	Uncollectible Accounts Expense	3,000	
	Allowance for Doubtful Accounts		3,000

After the adjusting entry has been posted, the balance in the allowance account is $3,700. If there had been a debit balance of $200 in the allowance account before the year-end adjustment, the amount of the adjustment would still have been $3,000. The balance in the allowance account, after the adjusting entry has been posted, would be $2,800 ($3,000 – $200).

Instead of credit sales, total sales (including those made for cash) may be used in estimating the percentage of uncollectible accounts. Using total sales is less costly, since total sales is available in the sales account in the ledger. In contrast, a separate analysis may be required to determine credit sales. If the ratio of credit sales to cash sales does not change very much from year to year, estimates using total sales will be acceptable. In the above example, if 3/4 of 1% is used to estimate uncollectibles, based upon total sales of $400,000, the same estimate of $3,000 would result.

The estimate-based-on-sales method is widely used. Its advantages are that it is simple and it emphasizes the matching of uncollectible accounts expense with the related sales of the period.

Estimate Based on Analysis of Receivables

The longer an account receivable remains outstanding, the less likely that it will be collected. For example, the *Annual Collectibility Survey* conducted by the Commercial Collection Agency Section of the Commercial Law League of America reported the following statistics on collection rates:[4]

[4] *Boardroom Reports,* May 1994, p. 12.

Number of Months Past Due	*Collection Rate*
1	93.4%
2	84.6
3	72.9
6	57.0
9	41.9
12	25.4
24	12.5

We can base the estimate of uncollectible accounts on how long the accounts have been outstanding. For this purpose, we can use a process called **aging the receivables.**

The beginning point for determining the age of a receivable is its due date. Exhibit 1 shows an example of a typical aging of accounts receivable.

Exhibit 1
Aging of Accounts Receivable

			Days Past Due					
Customer	*Balance*	*Not Due*	*1-30*	*31-60*	*61-90*	*91-180*	*181-365*	*over 365*
Ashby & Co.	$ 150			$ 150				
B.T. Barr	610					$ 350	$260	
Brock Co.	470	$ 470						
J. Zimmer Co.	160							160
Total	$86,300	$75,000	$4,000	$3,100	$1,900	$1,200	$800	$300

The aging schedule is completed by adding the columns to determine the total amount of receivables in each age group. A sliding scale of percentages, based on industry or company experience, is used to estimate the amount of uncollectibles in each group. The manner in which the data may be presented is shown in Exhibit 2.

Exhibit 2
Estimate of Uncollectible Accounts

		Estimated Uncollectible Accounts	
Age Interval	*Balance*	*Percent*	*Amount*
Not due	$75,000	2%	$1,500
1-30 days past due	4,000	5	200
31-60 days past due	3,100	10	310
61-90 days past due	1,900	20	380
91-180 days past due	1,200	30	360
181-365 days past due	800	50	400
Over 365 days past due	300	80	240
Total	$86,300		$3,390

The estimate of uncollectible accounts is $3,390 in Exhibit 2. This amount is deducted from accounts receivable to yield the accounts receivable net realizable value. It is also the amount of the desired balance of the allowance account at the end of the period. The excess of this amount over the balance of the allowance account before adjustment is the amount of the uncollectible accounts expense for the period.

To continue the example, assume that the allowance account has a credit balance of $510 before adjustment. The amount to be added to this balance is therefore $2,880 ($3,390 – $510). The adjusting entry is as follows:

Dec. 31	Uncollectible Accounts Expense	2,880	
	Allowance for Doubtful Accounts		2,880

After the adjusting entry has been posted, the credit balance in the allowance account is $3,390, the desired amount. If there had been a debit balance of $300 in the allowance account before the year-end adjustment, the amount of the adjustment would have been $3,690 ($3,390 desired balance + $300 debit balance).

Estimates of uncollectible accounts expense based on analyzing receivables are less common than estimates based on sales volume. The primary advantage of analyzing receivables is that it emphasizes the current net realizable value of the receivables.

Direct Write-Off Method of Accounting for Uncollectibles

Objective 5
Journalize the entries for the direct write-off of uncollectible receivables.

The allowance method emphasizes reporting uncollectible accounts expense in the period in which the sales occur. This emphasis on matching expenses with related revenue is the preferred method of accounting for uncollectible receivables. However, there are situations in which it is impossible to estimate, with reasonable accuracy, the uncollectibles at the end of the period. Also, if a business sells most of its goods or services on a cash basis, the amount of its expense from uncollectible accounts is usually small in relation to its revenue. The amount of its receivables at any time is also likely to represent a relatively small part of its total current assets. Examples of such a business are a physician's office, an attorney's office, and a small retail store such as a hardware store. In such cases, it is acceptable to delay recognizing uncollectible expense until the accounts are determined to be worthless. Thus, under the direct write-off method, an allowance account and an adjusting entry are not needed at the end of the period. The entry to write off an account when it is determined to be uncollectible is as follows:

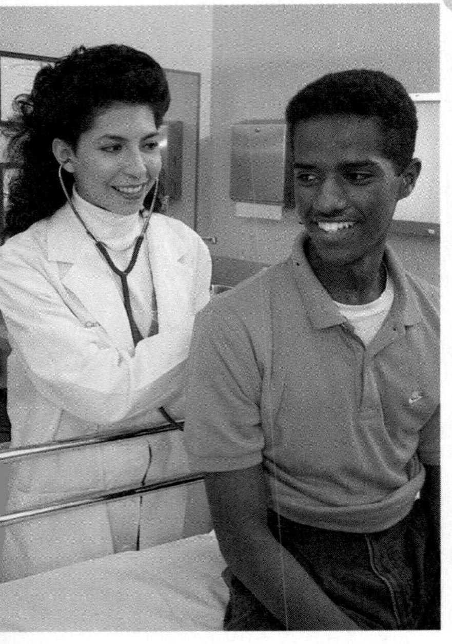

For physicians, the amount of receivables is typically small in relation to the total current assets of the business.

May 10	Uncollectible Accounts Expense	420	
	Accounts Receivable—D. L. Ross		420
	To write off uncollectible account.		

What if a customer later pays on an account that has been written off? If this happens, the account should be reinstated. If the recovery is in the same period as the write-off, the earlier entry should be reversed to reinstate the account. For example, assume that the account written off in the May 10 entry is collected in November of the same fiscal year. The entry to reinstate the account is as follows:

Nov. 21	Accounts Receivable—D. L. Ross	420	
	Uncollectible Accounts Expense		420
	To reinstate account written off on May 10.		

The receipt of cash in payment of the reinstated amount is recorded in the usual manner. That is, Cash is debited and Accounts Receivable is credited.

When an account that has been written off is collected in a later fiscal year, it may be reinstated by debiting Accounts Receivable and crediting Uncollectible Accounts Expense. An alternative is to credit some other appropriately titled account, such as Recovery of Uncollectible Accounts Written Off. The credit balance in such an account at the end of the period may then be reported on the income statement as a deduction from Uncollectible Accounts Expense. In either case, only the net uncollectible expense is reported.

Characteristics of Notes Receivable

Objective 6
State the accounting implications of promissory notes.

The typical retail business makes most of its sales for cash or on credit. If the account of a customer is past due, the business may insist that the account receivable be converted into a note receivable.

A claim supported by a note has some advantages over a claim in the form of an account receivable. By signing a note, the debtor recognizes the debt and agrees to pay it according to the terms listed. A note is therefore a stronger legal claim if there is a court action. A note is also normally more liquid than an open account. That is, if the business needs cash, it is usually easier to convert a note receivable to cash than an account receivable.

Notes may also be received by retail firms that sell merchandise on long-term credit. For example, a dealer in automobiles or furniture may require a down payment at the time of sale and accept a note or a series of notes for the remainder. Such arrangements usually provide for monthly payments.

As we stated earlier in the chapter, a note is a written promise to pay a sum of money on demand or at a definite time. It must be payable to the order of a certain person or firm or to the bearer. It must be signed by the person or firm that makes the promise. The one to whose order the note is payable is called the **payee,** and the one making the promise is called the **maker.** In the example in Exhibit 3, Pearland Company is the payee and Selig Company is the maker.

Exhibit 3
Promissory Note

$ 2,500.00 Fresno, California March 16 19 97

Ninety days AFTER DATE We PROMISE TO PAY TO

THE ORDER OF Pearland Company

Two thousand five hundred 00/100---------------------- DOLLARS

PAYABLE AT First National Bank

VALUE RECEIVED WITH INTEREST AT 10%

NO. 14 DUE June 14, 1997 H.B. Lane

TREASURER, *SELIG COMPANY*

Notes have several characteristics that have accounting implications. We describe these characteristics in the following paragraphs.

DUE DATE

The date a note is to be paid is called the due date or maturity date. The period of time between the issuance date and the due date of a short-term note may be stated in either days or months. When the term of a note is stated in days, the due date is the specified number of days after its issuance. To illustrate, the due date of the 90-day note in Exhibit 3 is determined as follows:

Term of the note		90
March (days)	31	
Date of note	16	15
Number of days remaining		75
April (days)		30
		45
May (days)		31
Due date, June		14

When the term of a note is stated as a certain number of months after the issuance date, the due date is determined by counting the number of months from the issuance date. For example, a three-month note dated June 5 would be due on September 5. In those cases in which there is no date in the month of maturity that corresponds to the issuance date, the due date becomes the last day of the month. For example, a two-month note dated July 31 would be due on September 30.

INTEREST

A note normally specifies that interest be paid for the period between the issuance date and the due date.[5] Notes covering a period of time longer than one year normally provide that the interest be paid semiannually, quarterly, or at some other stated interval. The time involved in business credit transactions is usually less than one year, and the interest provided for by a note is payable at the time the note is paid.

The interest rate on such notes is normally stated in terms of a year, regardless of the actual period of time involved. Thus, the interest on $2,000 for one year at 12% is $240 (12% of $2,000). The interest on $2,000 for one-fourth of one year at 12% is $60 (1/4 of $240).

The basic formula for computing interest is as follows:

Face Amount (or Principal) × Rate × Time = Interest

To illustrate the formula, the $62.50 interest for the $2,500, 10%, 90-day note in Exhibit 3 is computed as follows:

$$\$2{,}500 \times 10\% \times \frac{90}{360} = \$62.50 \text{ interest}$$

It is important for consumers to understand how interest is computed on credit or installment purchases because slight variations in interest rates can mean significant savings.

In computing interest for a period of less than one year, agencies of the federal government and many financial institutions use the actual number of days in the year. For example, 90 days is 90/365 of one year. However, some businesses use 360 days rather than 365. To simplify computations, we will use 360 days. Thus, 90 days is considered to be 90/360, or one-fourth of a year.

When the term of a note is stated in months instead of in days, each month may be considered 1/12 of a year. Alternatively, the actual number of days in the term may be counted. For example, the interest on a three-month note dated June 1 could be computed on the basis of 3/12 of a year or on the basis of 92/360 of a year. To simplify, we will treat a month as 1/12 of a year.

Understanding interest is also useful to you. For example, credit card balances that remain unpaid at the end of the month incur an interest charge expressed in terms of a percent per month. Interest charges of 1 1/2% per month are common. Such charges approximate an annual interest rate of 18% per year (1 1/2% × 12). Thus, if you can borrow money at less than 18%, you are better off borrowing the money and paying off the credit card balance than incurring the monthly interest charges on the unpaid balance. Likewise, many companies charge penalties for

[5] You may occasionally see references to non-interest-bearing notes receivable. Such notes are not widely issued and normally include an implicit interest rate.

USING ACCOUNTING TO UNDERSTAND BUSINESS

Whenever a business borrows money or enters into a credit agreement that requires the payment of interest, it is important for the business to understand how the interest will be computed. For example, the difference in 180 days' interest computed on the basis of a 365-day year versus a 360-day year is shown below for a loan of $40,000 at an interest rate of 12%:

$40,000 × 12% × 180/365 = $2,367.12
$40,000 × 12% × 180/360 = $2,400.00

The difference of $32.88 may seem relatively small, but for a business that might enter into thousands of such transactions for millions of dollars, the difference between computing interest on a 360-day year versus a 365-day year can be significant.

late payment of bills. For example, a utility bill might be due on the 15th of the month, with a late charge of 5% if paid after the 15th. If the bill remains unpaid after 30 days, the utility stops services. If you pay late and incur the 5% late charge, you are, in effect, borrowing the amount of the bill for an extra 15 days. But the extra 15 days cost you 5%, which approximates an annual rate of 120% [(360 days ÷ 15 days) × 5%]. Again, you would be better off borrowing to avoid the late charge.

MATURITY VALUE

The amount that is due at the maturity or due date is called the **maturity value**. The maturity value of a note is the sum of the face amount and the interest. In the note in Exhibit 3, the maturity value is $2,562.50 ($2,500 face amount plus $62.50 interest).

Accounting for Notes Receivable

Objective 7
Journalize the entries for notes receivable transactions, including discounted notes receivable and dishonored notes receivable.

When a note is received from a customer to apply on account, the facts are recorded by debiting the notes receivable account and crediting Accounts Receivable and the account of the customer from whom the note is received. To illustrate, assume that a 30-day, 12% note dated November 21, 1997, is accepted in settlement of the account of W. A. Bunn Co., which is past due and has a balance of $6,000. The entry to record the transaction is as follows:

Nov. 21	Notes Receivable	6,000	
	Accounts Receivable—W. A. Bunn Co.		6,000
	Received 30-day, 12% note dated November 21, 1997.		

At the time the note matures, the entry to record the receipt of $6,060 ($6,000 principal plus $60 interest) is as follows:

Dec. 21	Cash	6,060	
	Notes Receivable		6,000
	Interest Income		60

If a note matures in a later fiscal period, the interest accrued in the period in which the note is received must be recorded. For example, assume that a 90-day, 12% note dated December 1 is received from Crawford Company to settle its account, which has a balance of $4,000. The entry to record the receipt of the note is similar to the November 21 entry above. On December 31, the following adjusting entry is necessary to record the $40 interest earned for 30 days in December ($4,000 × 12% × 30/360):

Dec. 31	Interest Receivable	40	
	Interest Income		40

The interest income account is closed at December 31. The amount of interest income is reported in the Other Income section of the income statement for the year ended December 31, 1997.

DISCOUNTING NOTES RECEIVABLE

Although it is not a common transaction, a company in need of cash may transfer its notes receivable to a bank by endorsement. The discount (interest) charged by the bank is computed on the maturity value of the note for the period that the bank must hold the note. This period, called the **discount period,** is the time that will pass between the date of the transfer and the due date of the note. The amount of the proceeds paid to the endorser is the excess of the maturity value over the discount.

For example, assume that a 90-day, 12%, $1,800 note receivable from Pryor & Co., dated April 8, is discounted at the payee's bank on May 3 at the rate of 14%. The data used in determining the effect of the transaction are as follows:

Face value of note dated April 8	$1,800.00
Interest on note (90 days at 12%)	54.00
Maturity value of note due July 7	$1,854.00
Discount on maturity value (65 days from May 3 to July 7, at 14%)	46.87
Proceeds	$1,807.13

The excess of the proceeds from discounting the note, $1,807.13, over its face value, $1,800, is recorded as interest income. The entry for the transaction is as follows:

May 3	Cash	1,807.13	
	Notes Receivable		1,800.00
	Interest Income		7.13

What if the proceeds from discounting a note receivable are less than the face value? When this situation occurs, the excess of the face value over the proceeds is recorded as interest expense. The length of the discount period and the difference between the interest rate and the discount rate determines whether interest expense or interest income will result from discounting.

Without a statement limiting responsibility, the endorser of a note is committed to paying the note if the maker defaults. Such potential obligations will become actual liabilities only if certain events occur in the future. These potential obligations are called contingent liabilities. Thus, the endorser of a note that has been discounted has a contingent liability until the due date. If the maker pays the promised amount at maturity, the contingent liability is removed without any action on the part of the endorser. If, on the other hand, the maker defaults and the endorser is notified according to legal requirements, the liability becomes an actual one.

Significant contingent liabilities should be disclosed on the balance sheet or in an accompanying note. In a later chapter, we will discuss disclosure requirements for contingent liabilities.

DISHONORED NOTES RECEIVABLE

If the maker of a note fails to pay the debt on the due date, the note is said to be dishonored. A **dishonored note receivable** is no longer negotiable. For this reason, the holder usually transfers the claim, including any interest due, to the accounts receivable account. For example, assume that the $6,000, 30-day, 12% note received from W. A. Bunn Co. and recorded on November 21 is dishonored at maturity. The entry to charge the note, including the interest, back to the customer's account is as follows:

Dec. 21	Accounts Receivable—W. A. Bunn Co.	6,060	
	Notes Receivable		6,000
	Interest Income		60
	Dishonored note and interest.		

When a discounted note receivable is dishonored, the holder usually notifies the endorser of that fact and asks for payment. If the request for payment and notification of dishonor are timely, the endorser is legally obligated to pay the amount due on the note. The entire amount paid to the holder by the endorser, including the interest, should be debited to the account receivable of the maker. For example, assume that the $1,800, 90-day, 12% note discounted on May 3 is dishonored at maturity by the maker, Pryor & Co. The entry to record the payment by the endorser is as follows:

July 7	Accounts Receivable—Pryor & Co.	1,854	
	Cash		1,854

In some cases, the holder of a dishonored note gives the endorser a notarized statement of the facts of the dishonor. The fee for this statement, known as a protest fee, is charged to the endorser, who in turn charges it to the maker of the note. For example, if the bank charges a protest fee of $12 in connection with the dishonored Pryor & Co. note, the entry to record the payment by the endorser is as follows:

July 7	Accounts Receivable—Pryor & Co.	1,866	
	Cash		1,866

Temporary Investments

Objective 8
Define temporary investments.

A business may have excess cash that it does not need immediately for operations. Rather than allow this excess cash to be idle until it is needed, a business may invest all or a part of it in income-yielding securities. Since these investments can be quickly sold and converted to cash as needed, they are called **temporary investments** or **marketable securities**. Although such investments may be retained for a number of years, they continue to be classified as temporary, provided they meet two conditions. First, the securities are readily marketable and can be sold for cash at any time. Second, management intends to sell the securities when the business needs more cash for operations.

Temporary investments are either debt securities or equity securities.[6] A **debt security** represents a creditor relationship between the entity issuing the security and the individuals or entities holding the security. Debt securities are issued by corporations and government agencies. Examples of such securities include bonds issued by corporations and U.S. Treasury Notes. An **equity security** represents ownership in a business. The most common example of an equity security is stock in a corporation.

[6] *Statement of Financial Accounting Standards, No. 115,* "Accounting for Certain Investments in Debt and Equity Securities," Norwalk, Conn., 1993, par. 1.

The accounting for temporary investments in debt and equity securities depends upon whether the particular security is classified as (1) a held-to-maturity security, (2) a trading security, or (3) an available-for-sale security.[7] A held-to-maturity security is a debt security that management intends to hold to its maturity. Such securities that will mature within one year are recorded at their cost and reported as temporary investments on the balance sheet.

A trading security can be either a debt security or an equity security that management intends to actively trade for profit. Thus, businesses holding trading securities are those whose normal operations involve buying and selling securities. Examples of such businesses include banks and insurance companies.[8]

An available-for-sale security may be a debt or equity security that is not classified as either a held-to-maturity or trading security.[9] Available-for-sale securities that are expected to be sold within one year are reported as temporary investments on the balance sheet. Such securities should be reported at their total fair market value as of the balance sheet date. Any difference between the fair market value of the securities and their cost is an **unrealized holding gain or loss.** This gain or loss is termed "unrealized" because a transaction (the sale of the securities) to verify the gain or loss has not occurred.[10]

To illustrate, assume that Crabtree Co. owns the following portfolio of available-for-sale equity securities:

Temporary Investment Portfolio	*Cost*	*Market*	*Unrealized Gain (Loss)*
Equity Security A	$150,000	$100,000	$(50,000)
Equity Security B	200,000	200,000	—
Equity Security C	180,000	210,000	30,000
Equity Security D	160,000	150,000	(10,000)
Total	$690,000	$660,000	$(30,000)

These temporary investments are reported at their cost of $690,000 less the unrealized loss of $30,000. The unrealized loss of $30,000 would also reduce the owner's equity. If the total market value of the portfolio had been $725,000, an unrealized gain of $35,000 ($725,000 – $690,000) would be reported as an increase in owner's equity. The temporary investments would be reported at $725,000—their cost of $690,000 plus the unrealized gain of $35,000.

Unrealized holding gains or losses are not reported on the income statement. When temporary investments are sold, however, the difference between their cost and the proceeds from the sale is reported on the income statement as a **realized gain or loss.**

Temporary Investments and Receivables in the Balance Sheet

Objective 9
Prepare the Current Assets section of the balance sheet that includes temporary investments and receivables.

Temporary investments and all receivables that are expected to be realized in cash within a year are presented in the Current Assets section of the balance sheet. It is normal to list the assets in the order of their liquidity. This is the order in which they are expected to be converted to cash during normal operations. An example of the

[7] *Ibid.*, pars. 7 and 12.
[8] The accounting for trading securities is further described and illustrated in advanced accounting texts.
[9] For purposes of illustration, we will assume that available-for-sale securities consist of corporate stocks.
[10] The discussion of temporary investments in this chapter focuses on the concepts applicable to their presentations on the financial statements. Other aspects of accounting for investments, such as dividend income and interest income, are discussed in a later chapter.

presentation of temporary investments and receivables is shown in the partial balance sheet for Crabtree Co. in Exhibit 4.

Exhibit 4
Temporary Investments and Receivables in Balance Sheet

Crabtree Co.
Balance Sheet
December 31, 19—

Assets		
Current assets:		
Cash		$119 5 0 0 00
Temporary investments in		
marketable equity securities	$690 0 0 0 00	
Less unrealized loss	30 0 0 0 00	660 0 0 0 00
Notes receivable		250 0 0 0 00
Accounts receivable	$445 0 0 0 00	
Less allowance for doubtful accounts	15 0 0 0 00	430 0 0 0 00
Interest receivable		14 5 0 0 00

The balances of Crabtree's notes receivable, accounts receivable, and interest receivable accounts are reported in Exhibit 4. The allowance for doubtful accounts is subtracted from the accounts receivable. When the allowance account includes provision for doubtful notes as well as accounts, it should be deducted from the total of Notes Receivable and Accounts Receivable.

Other disclosures related to receivables are presented either on the face of the financial statements or in the accompanying notes. Such disclosures include the market (fair) value of the receivables.[11] Generally, the market value of receivables approximates their carrying value. In addition, if unusual credit risks exist within the receivables, the nature of the risks should be disclosed. For example, if the majority of the receivables are due from one customer or are due from customers located in one area of the country or one industry, these facts should be disclosed.[12] An illustration of a credit risk disclosure taken from the 1994 financial statements of Deere & Company is shown below.

Credit receivables at October 31 consisted of the following in millions of dollars:

	1994	*1993*
Retail notes:		
John Deere equipment:		
Agricultural	*$2,798*	*$2,242*
Industrial	*535*	*351*
Lawn and grounds care	*204*	*213*
Recreational products	*1,359*	*1,361*
Total	*4,896*	*4,167*

Credit receivables have significant concentrations of credit risk in the agricultural, industrial, lawn and grounds care, and recreational product business sectors as shown in the previous table. On a geographic basis, there is not a disproportionate concentration of credit risk in any area. . . .

[11] *Statement of Financial Accounting Standards, No. 107,* "Disclosures about Fair Value of Financial Instruments," Financial Accounting Standards Board, Norwalk, 1991, pars. 10 and 19.

[12] *Statement of Financial Accounting Standards, No. 105,* "Disclosure of Information about Financial Instruments with Off-Balance Sheet Risk and Financial Instruments with Concentrations of Credit Risk," Financial Accounting Standards Board, Norwalk, 1990, par. 20, and *Statement of Financial Accounting Standards, No. 107, op.cit.,* par. 13.

KEY POINTS

Objective 1. List the common classifications of receivables.

The term receivables includes all money claims against other entities, including people, business firms, and other organizations. They are normally classified as accounts receivable, notes receivable, or other receivables.

Objective 2. Summarize and provide examples of internal control procedures that apply to receivables.

The internal controls that apply to receivables include the separation of responsibilities for related functions. In this way, the work of one employee can serve as a check on the work of another employee. Other controls are the use of subsidiary ledgers and authorization procedures for credit approval and adjustments of accounts.

Objective 3. Describe the nature of and the accounting for uncollectible receivables.

Regardless of controls in granting credit and in collection procedures, some sales to customers on account will not be collected. The two methods of accounting for uncollectible receivables are the allowance method and the direct write-off method. The allowance method provides in advance for uncollectible receivables. The direct write-off method recognizes the expense only when the account is judged to be uncollectible.

Objective 4. Journalize the entries for the allowance method of accounting for uncollectibles, and estimate uncollectible receivables based on sales and on an analysis of receivables.

An adjusting entry made at the end of the fiscal period provides for (1) the reduction of the value of the receivables to the amount of cash expected to be realized from them in the future and (2) the allocation to the current period of the expected expense resulting from such reduction. The adjusting entry debits Uncollectible Accounts Expense and credits Allowance for Doubtful Accounts. When an account is believed to be uncollectible, it is written off against the allowance account.

When the estimate of uncollectibles is based upon the amount of sales for the fiscal period, the adjusting entry at the end of the period is made without regard to the balance of the allowance account. When the estimate of uncollectibles is based upon the amount and the age of the receivable accounts at the end of the period, the adjusting entry is recorded so that the balance of the allowance account will equal the estimated uncollectibles at the end of the period.

The allowance account, which will have a credit balance after the adjusting entry has been posted, is a contra asset account. The uncollectible accounts expense is generally reported on the income statement as an administrative expense.

Objective 5. Journalize the entries for the direct write-off of uncollectible receivables.

Under the direct write-off method, the entry to write off an account debits Uncollectible Accounts Expense and credits Accounts Receivable. Neither an allowance account nor an adjusting entry is needed at the end of the period.

Objective 6. State the accounting implications of promissory notes.

The accounting implications of a promissory note include recognizing interest and determining the due date and the maturity value of the note. The basic formula for computing interest on a note is: Principal × Rate × Time = Interest. The due date is the date a note is to be paid, and the period of time between the issuance date and the due date is normally stated in either days or months. The maturity value of a note is the sum of the face amount and the interest.

Objective 7. Journalize the entries for notes receivable transactions, including discounted notes receivable and dishonored notes receivable.

A note received in settlement of an account receivable is recorded as a debit to Notes Receivable and a credit to Accounts Receivable. When a note matures, Cash is debited, Notes Receivable is credited, and Interest Income is credited. A note receivable may be discounted at a bank. In this case, Cash is debited for the proceeds, Notes Receivable is credited, and any interest income or interest expense is recorded.

If the maker of a note fails to pay the debt on the due date, the note is said to be dishonored. When the holder of a dishonored note has been paid by the endorser, the amount of the endorser's claim against the maker of the note is debited to an accounts receivable account.

Objective 8. Define temporary investments.

Temporary investments or marketable securities are either debt securities or equity securities. A debt security is an obligation between a creditor and a business issuing the obligation. Equity securities represent ownership in a business, such as stock in a corporation.

The accounting for temporary investments in debt and equity securities depends upon whether the particular security is (1) a held-to-maturity security, (2) a trading security, or (3) an available-for-sale security. A held-to-maturity security is a debt security that management intends to hold to its maturity. Such securities maturing within one year are recorded at their cost. A trading security is a debt or equity security that management intends to actively trade for profit.

An available-for-sale security is a debt or equity security that is not classified as either a held-to-maturity or trading security. Such securities are reported at their total fair market value at the balance sheet date. Any difference between the fair market value of the securities and their cost is an unrealized holding gain or loss. When such securities are sold, the realized gain or loss is reported on the income statement.

Objective 9. Prepare the current assets section of the balance sheet that includes temporary investments and receivables.

Temporary investments and all receivables that are expected to be realized in cash within a year are presented in the current assets section of the balance sheet. It is normal to list the assets in the order of their liquidity, which is the order in which they can be converted to cash in normal operations.

GLOSSARY OF KEY TERMS

Aging the receivables. The process of analyzing the accounts receivable and classifying them according to various age groupings, with the due date being the base point for determining age. *Objective 4*

Allowance method. A method of accounting for uncollectible receivables, whereby advance provision for the uncollectibles is made. *Objective 3*

Available-for-sale security. A debt or equity security that is not classified as either a held-to-maturity or a trading security. *Objective 8*

Contingent liabilities. Potential obligations that will materialize only if certain events occur in the future. *Objective 7*

Debt security. A security that represents an obligation between a creditor and the business issuing the obligation. *Objective 8*

Direct write-off method. A method of accounting for uncollectible receivables, whereby an expense is recognized only when specific accounts are judged to be uncollectible. *Objective 3*

Discount. The interest deducted from the maturity value of a note receivable. *Objective 7*

Dishonored note receivable. A note that the maker fails to pay on its due date. *Objective 7*

Equity security. A security that represents ownership in a business, such as stock in a corporation. *Objective 8*

Held-to-maturity security. A debt security that management intends to hold until its maturity. *Objective 8*

Marketable securities. Investments in securities that can be readily sold when cash is needed. *Objective 8*

Maturity value. The amount due (face value plus interest) at the maturity or due date of a note. *Objective 6*

Note receivable. A written promise to pay, representing an amount to be received by a business. *Objective 1*

Proceeds. The net amount available from discounting a note. *Objective 7*

Promissory note. A written promise to pay a sum in money on demand or at a definite time. *Objective 1*

Temporary investments. Investments in securities that can be readily sold when cash is needed. *Objective 8*

Trading security. A debt or equity security that management intends to actively trade for profit. *Objective 8*

ILLUSTRATIVE PROBLEM

Ditzler Company, a construction supply company, uses the allowance method of accounting for uncollectible accounts receivable. Selected transactions completed by Ditzler Company are as follows:

Feb. 1. Sold merchandise on account to Ames Co., $8,000.
Mar. 15. Accepted a 60-day, 12% note for $8,000 from Ames Co. on account.
Apr. 9. Wrote off a $2,500 account from Dorset Co. as uncollectible.
21. Loaned $7,500 cash to Jill Klein, receiving a 90-day, 14% note.
May 14. Received the interest due from Ames Co. and a new 90-day, 14% note as a renewal of the loan. (Record both the debit and the credit to the notes receivable account.)
21. Discounted the note from Jill Klein at the City National Bank at 12%.
June 13. Reinstated the account of Dorset Co., written off on April 9, and received $2,500 in full payment.
July 20. Received notice from City National Bank that Jill Klein dishonored her note. Paid the bank the maturity value of the note plus a $25 protest fee.
Aug. 12. Received from Ames Co. the amount due on its note of May 14.
19. Received from Jill Klein the amount owed on the dishonored note, plus interest for 30 days at 15%, computed on the maturity value of the note and the protest fee.
Dec. 16. Accepted a 60-day, 12% note for $12,000 from Global Company on account.
31. It is estimated that 3% of the credit sales of $1,375,000 for the year ended December 31 will be uncollectible.

Instructions

1. Journalize the transactions.
2. Journalize the adjusting entry to record the accrued interest on December 31 on the Global Company note.

Solution

1.

Feb. 1	Accounts Receivable—Ames Co.	8,000.00	
	Sales		8,000.00
Mar. 15	Notes Receivable—Ames Co.	8,000.00	
	Accounts Receivable—Ames Co.		8,000.00

			Debit	Credit
Apr. 9	Allowance for Doubtful Accounts		2,500.00	
	Accounts Receivable—Dorset Co.			2,500.00
21	Notes Receivable—Jill Klein		7,500.00	
	Cash			7,500.00
May 14	Notes Receivable—Ames Co.		8,000.00	
	Cash		160.00	
	Notes Receivable—Ames Co.			8,000.00
	Interest Income			160.00
21	Cash		7,607.25	
	Notes Receivable—Jill Klein			7,500.00
	Interest Income			107.25
	Face value	$7,500.00		
	Interest on note (90 days at 14%)	262.50		
	Maturity value	$7,762.50		
	Discount on maturity value (60 days at 12%)	155.25		
	Proceeds	$7,607.25		
June 13	Accounts Receivable—Dorset Co.		2,500.00	
	Allowance for Doubtful Accounts			2,500.00
13	Cash		2,500.00	
	Accounts Receivable—Dorset Co.			2,500.00
July 20	Accounts Receivable—Jill Klein		7,787.50	
	Cash			7,787.50
	($7,500 + $262.50 + $25)			
Aug. 12	Cash		8,280.00	
	Notes Receivable—Ames Co.			8,000.00
	Interest Income			280.00
19	Cash		7,884.84	
	Accounts Receivable—Jill Klein			7,787.50
	Interest Income			97.34
	($7,787.50 × 15% × 30/360)			
Dec. 16	Notes Receivable—Global Company		12,000.00	
	Accounts Receivable—Global Company			12,000.00
31	Uncollectible Accounts Expense		41,250.00	
	Allowance for Doubtful Accounts			41,250.00

2.

Dec. 31	Interest Receivable	60.00	
	Interest Income		60.00
	($12,000 × 12% × 15/360)		

SELF-EXAMINATION QUESTIONS (ANSWERS AT END OF CHAPTER)

1. At the end of the fiscal year, before the accounts are adjusted, Accounts Receivable has a balance of $200,000 and Allowance for Doubtful Accounts has a credit balance of $2,500. If the estimate of uncollectible accounts determined by aging the receivables is $8,500, the current provision to be made for uncollectible accounts expense is:
   A. $2,500 C. $8,500
   B. $6,000 D. $11,000

2. At the end of the fiscal year, Accounts Receivable has a balance of $100,000 and Allowance for Doubtful Accounts has a balance of $7,000. The expected net realizable value of the accounts receivable is:
   A. $7,000 C. $100,000
   B. $93,000 D. $107,000

3. What is the maturity value of a 90-day, 12% note for $10,000?
   A. $8,800 C. $10,300
   B. $10,000 D. $11,200

4. On June 16, an enterprise discounts a 60-day, 10% note receivable for $15,000, dated June 1, at the rate of 12%. The proceeds are:
   A. $15,000.00 C. $15,250.00
   B. $15,021.25 D. $15,478.75

5. Under what caption would a temporary investment in stock be reported in the balance sheet?
   A. Current assets C. Investments
   B. Plant assets D. Current liabilities

DISCUSSION QUESTIONS

1. What are the three classifications of receivables?
2. What types of transactions give rise to accounts receivable?
3. Describe the nature of a promissory note.
4. In what section of the balance sheet should a note receivable be listed if its term is (a) 90 days, (b) 5 years?
5. Give two examples of other receivables.
6. The accounts receivable clerk is also responsible for handling cash receipts. Which principle of internal control is violated in this situation?
7. Which of the two methods of accounting for uncollectible accounts provides for the recognition of the expense at the earlier date?
8. What kind of an account (asset, liability, etc.) is Allowance for Doubtful Accounts, and is its normal balance a debit or a credit?
9. After the accounts are adjusted and closed at the end of the fiscal year, Accounts Receivable has a balance of $201,250 and Allowance for Doubtful Accounts has a balance of $12,250. Describe how the accounts receivable and the allowance for doubtful accounts are reported on the balance sheet.
10. A firm has consistently adjusted its allowance account at the end of the fiscal year by adding a fixed percent of the period's net sales on account. After five years, the balance in Allowance for Doubtful Accounts has become disproportionately large in relationship to the balance in Accounts Receivable. Give two possible explanations.
11. Which of the two methods of estimating uncollectibles, when advance provision for uncollectible receivables is made, provides for the most accurate estimate of the current net realizable value of the receivables?
12. For a business, what are the advantages of a note receivable in comparison to an account receivable?
13. Fess Company issued a promissory note to Hubble Company. (a) Who is the payee? (b) What is the title of the account used by Hubble Company in recording the note?
14. If a note provides for payment of principal of $10,000 and interest at the rate of 10%, will the interest amount to $1,000? Explain.
15. Collins Co. accepted a 60-day, 9% note for $5,000, dated June 1, from one of its customers. (a) What is the face value of the note? (b) What is the due date of the note?
16. Lemke Co. accepted a 60-day, 9% note for $5,000, dated April 20, from one of its customers. Instead of waiting for receipt of the maturity value of $5,075.00 on June 19, Lemke Co. endorses it to a bank on May 10. The bank discounts the note at 10% and pays Lemke Co. $5,018.61. Why would Lemke Co. be willing to accept less from the bank than from the customer?
17. DeLong Co. received a 90-day note dated August 7 from a customer on account. DeLong Co. discounted the note at the bank August 22. (a) Did DeLong Co. have a contingent liability on August 22 after the note was discounted? (b) If the answer in (a) is "yes," when does the contingent liability expire?
18. During the year, a business discounted notes receivable of $160,000 at a bank. By the end of the year, $112,500 of these notes have matured. How should the business report the contingent liability for notes discounted at the end of the year?
19. The maker of a $6,000, 8%, 90-day note receivable failed to pay the note on the due date. What accounts should be debited and credited by the payee to record the dishonored note receivable?
20. A discounted note receivable is dishonored by the maker, and the endorser pays the bank the face of the note, $10,000, the interest, $500, and a protest fee of $150. What entry should be made in the accounts of the endorser to record the payment?
21. Under what caption should securities held as a temporary investment be reported on the balance sheet?
22. Describe how held-to-maturity securities and available-for-sale securities are reported on the balance sheet.
23. A company has two available-for-sale securities that it holds as a temporary investment. If they have a total cost of $210,000 and a fair market value of $202,750, at what amount should these securities be reported in the Current Assets section of the company's balance sheet?
24. If the market value of the securities in Question 23 rises in the following year to $225,000, how should the securities be reported in the Current Assets section of the company's balance sheet?

EXERCISES

EXERCISE 8–1
Internal control procedures
Objective 2

Omar Carpet Company sells carpeting. Over 85% of all carpet sales are on credit. The following procedures are used by Omar to process this large number of credit sales and the subsequent collections.

a. All credit sales to a first-time customer must be approved by the Credit Department. Salespersons will assist the customer in filling out a credit application, but an employee in the Credit Department is responsible for verifying employment and checking the customer's credit history before granting credit.
b. Omar's standard credit period is 45 days. The Credit Department may approve an extension of this repayment period of up to one year. Whenever an extension is granted, the customer signs a promissory note. Up to 30% of the credit sales in any one year are for repayment periods exceeding 45 days.
c. A formal ledger is not maintained for customers who sign promissory notes. Omar simply keeps a copy of each signed note in a file cabinet. These unpaid notes are filed by due date.
d. Omar employs an accounts receivable clerk. The clerk is responsible for recording customer credit sales (based on sales tickets), receiving cash from customers, giving customers credit for their payments, and handling all customer billing complaints.
e. The general ledger control account for Accounts Receivable is maintained by the General Accounting Department at Omar. This department records total credit sales, based on credit sale information from the store's electronic cash register, and total customer receipts, based on the bank deposit slip.

State whether each of these procedures is appropriate or inappropriate, considering the principles of internal control. If inappropriate, state which internal control procedure is violated.

EXERCISE 8–2
Nature of uncollectible accounts
Objective 3

Hilton Hotels Corporation owns and operates casinos at several of its hotels, located primarily in Nevada. At the end of a recent fiscal year, the following accounts and notes receivable were reported (in thousands):

Hotel accounts and notes receivable	$75,796	
Less: Allowance for doubtful accounts	3,256	
		$72,540
Casino accounts receivable	$26,334	
Less: Allowance for doubtful accounts	6,654	
		19,680

a. Compute the percentage of allowance for doubtful accounts to the gross hotel accounts and notes receivable for the end of the fiscal year.
b. Compute the percentage of the allowance for doubtful accounts to the gross casino accounts receivable for the end of the fiscal year.
c. Discuss possible reasons for the difference in the two ratios computed in (a) and (b).

EXERCISE 8–3
Estimating doubtful accounts
Objective 4

The aging of accounts receivable for Wyckoff Co., a wholesaler of office supplies, revealed the following balances on December 31, 1997:

Age Interval	*Balance*
Not due	$215,500
1-30 days past due	86,000
31-60 days past due	17,000
61-90 days past due	12,000
91-180 days past due	8,400
Over 180 days past due	3,500
	$342,400

A historical analysis indicates the following percentage of uncollectible accounts in each age category:

Age Interval	*Percent Uncollectible*
Not due	2%
1-30 days past due	4
31-60 days past due	9
61-90 days past due	15
91-180 days past due	60
Over 180 days past due	90

Estimate what the proper balance of the allowance for doubtful accounts should be as of December 31, 1997.

EXERCISE 8–4
Entry for uncollectible accounts
Objective 4

Using the data in Exercise 8–3, assume that the allowance for doubtful accounts for Wyckoff Co. had a debit balance of $1,280 as of December 31, 1997.

Journalize the adjusting entry for uncollectible accounts as of December 31, 1997.

EXERCISE 8–5
Provision for doubtful accounts
Objective 4

At the end of the current year, the accounts receivable account has a debit balance of $450,000, and net sales for the year total $4,100,000. Determine the amount of the adjusting entry to record the provision for doubtful accounts under each of the following assumptions:

a. The allowance account before adjustment has a credit balance of $2,750. Uncollectible accounts expense is estimated at 1/4 of 1% of net sales.
b. The allowance account before adjustment has a credit balance of $2,750. Analysis of the accounts in the customer's ledger indicates doubtful accounts of $18,350.
c. The allowance account before adjustment has a debit balance of $1,050. Uncollectible accounts expense is estimated at 1/2 of 1% of net sales.
d. The allowance account before adjustment has a debit balance of $1,050. Analysis of the accounts in the customer's ledger indicates doubtful accounts of $21,400.

EXERCISE 8–6
Entries for write-off of accounts receivable
Objectives 4, 5

Martin Company, a computer consulting firm, has decided to write off the $1,050 balance of an account owed by a customer. Journalize the entry to record the write-off in the general ledger, (a) assuming that the allowance method is used, and (b) assuming that the direct write-off method is used.

EXERCISE 8–7
Entries for uncollectible receivables using allowance method
Objective 4

Journalize the following transactions in the accounts of Bella Company, a restaurant supply company that uses the allowance method of accounting for uncollectible receivables:

Feb. 20. Sold merchandise on account to J. Harrey, $3,500. The cost of the merchandise sold was $1,400.
May 19. Received $1,000 from J. Harrey and wrote off the remainder owed on the sale of February 20 as uncollectible.
Sept. 30. Reinstated the account of J. Harrey that had been written off on May 19 and received $2,500 cash in full payment.

EXERCISE 8–8
Entries for uncollectible accounts using direct write-off method
Objective 5

Journalize the following transactions in the accounts of Webster Co., a hospital supply company that uses the direct write-off method of accounting for uncollectible receivables:

Mar. 11. Sold merchandise on account to E. Dodge, $3,200. The cost of the merchandise sold was $1,250.
May 1. Received $1,800 from E. Dodge and wrote off the remainder owed on the sale of March 11 as uncollectible.
Nov. 15. Reinstated the account of E. Dodge that had been written off on May 1 and received $1,400 cash in full payment.

EXERCISE 8–9
Effect of doubtful accounts on net income
Objectives 4, 5

During its first year of operations, Waterloo Automotive Supply Co. had net sales of $1,250,000, wrote off $12,800 of accounts as uncollectible, using the direct write-off method, and reported net income of $72,600. If the allowance method of accounting for uncollectibles had been used, 1.5% of net sales would have been estimated as uncollectible. Determine what the net income would have been if the allowance method had been used.

EXERCISE 8–10
Effect of doubtful accounts on net income
Objectives 4, 5

Using the data in Exercise 8–9, assume that during the second year of operations Waterloo Automotive Supply Co. had net sales of $1,800,000, wrote off $24,500 of accounts as uncollectible, using the direct write-off method, and reported net income of $112,300.

a. Determine what net income would have been in the second year if the allowance method (using 1.5% of net sales) had been used in both the first and second years.
b. Determine what the balance of the allowance for doubtful accounts would have been at the end of the second year if the allowance method had been used in both the first and second years.

EXERCISE 8–11
Determining due date and interest on notes
Objective 6

Determine the due date and the amount of interest due at maturity on the following notes:

	Date of Note	*Face Amount*	*Term of Note*	*Interest Rate*
a.	March 3	$ 5,000	45 days	8%
b.	May 20	6,000	60 days	10%
c.	May 31	10,000	75 days	14%
d.	June 9	15,000	90 days	10%
e.	July 1	17,500	120 days	12%

EXERCISE 8–12
Estimating the rate of interest on notes
Objective 6

Muscatine Co. borrowed $100,000 from Fairfield National Bank, signing a 90-day note. Fairfield National Bank deducted interest of $2,900 and deposited the proceeds of $97,100 in Muscatine Co.'s account. Estimate (to the nearest whole percent) the interest rate that Fairfield National Bank charged Muscatine Co. on the note.

EXERCISE 8–13
Entries for notes receivable
Objectives 6, 7

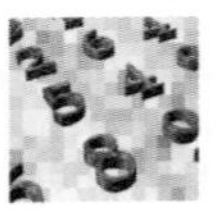

Burke Interior Decorators issued a 60-day, 9% note for $15,000, dated March 3, to Loree Furniture Company on account.

a. Determine the due date of the note.
b. Determine the maturity value of the note.
c. Journalize the entries to record the following: (1) receipt of the note by the payee, and (2) receipt by the payee of payment of the note at maturity.

EXERCISE 8–14
Entries for notes receivable
Objective 7

The series of six transactions recorded in the following T accounts were related to a sale to a customer on account and the receipt of the amount owed. Briefly describe each transaction.

Cash			
(4)	27,305	(5)	28,000
(6)	28,300		

Sales			
(2)	2,500	(1)	30,000

Notes Receivable			
(3)	27,500	(4)	27,500

Interest Income			
		(6)	300

Accounts Receivable			
(1)	30,000	(2)	2,500
(5)	28,000	(3)	27,500
		(6)	28,000

Interest Expense			
(4)	195		

EXERCISE 8–15
Entries for notes receivable, including year-end entries
Objective 7

The following selected transactions were completed during the current year by Elastic Co., a supplier of elastic bands for clothing:

Dec. 15. Received from Dino Co., on account, an $18,000, 90-day, 10% note dated December 15.
31. Recorded an adjusting entry for accrued interest on the note of December 15.
31. Closed the interest income account. The only entry in this account originated from the December 31 adjustment.

Journalize the transactions.

EXERCISE 8–16
Discounting notes receivable
Objective 7

Woodbridge Co., a building construction company, holds a 90-day, 8% note for $25,000, dated July 18, which was received from a customer on account. On August 21, the note is discounted at the bank at the rate of 12%.

a. Determine the maturity value of the note.
b. Determine the number of days in the discount period.
c. Determine the amount of the discount.
d. Determine the amount of the proceeds.
e. Journalize the entry to record the discounting of the note on August 21.

EXERCISE 8–17
Entries for receipt and discounting of note receivable and dishonored notes
Objective 7

Journalize the following transactions in the accounts of Les Mis Theater Productions:

Aug. 1. Received a $50,000, 90-day, 10% note dated August 1 from Revolt Company on account.
16. Discounted the note at Choice National Bank at 11%.
Oct. 30. The note is dishonored by Revolt Company; paid the bank the amount due on the note, plus a protest fee of $100.
Nov. 29. Received the amount due on the dishonored note plus interest for 30 days at 15% on the total amount charged to Revolt Company on October 30.

EXERCISE 8–18
Entries for receipt and dishonor of notes receivable
Objectives 4, 7

Journalize the following transactions in the accounts of Davenport Co., which operates a riverboat casino:

Mar. 1. Received a $10,000, 30-day, 12% note dated March 1 from Moline Co. on account.
21. Received a $15,000, 60-day, 10% note dated March 10 from Walcott Co. on account.
31. The note dated March 1 from Moline Co. is dishonored, and the customer's account is charged for the note, including interest.
May 20. The note dated March 21 from Walcott Co. is dishonored, and the customer's account is charged for the note, including interest.
June 29. Cash is received for the amount due on the dishonored note dated March 1 plus interest for 90 days at 12% on the total amount debited to Moline Co. on March 31.
Aug. 31. Wrote off against the allowance account the amount charged to Walcott Co. on May 20 for the dishonored note dated March 21.

EXERCISE 8–19
Temporary investments in financial statements
Objective 9

As of December 31, 1997, the end of its first year of operations, Mason Oil Supply Company has the following portfolio of available-for-sale marketable securities:

	Cost	*Market*
Security A	$65,500	$68,000
Security B	21,000	18,100
Security C	39,250	35,000
Security D	40,250	41,300

Describe how the portfolio of securities would be reported on the December 31, 1997 balance sheet and the income statement for the year ended December 31, 1997.

EXERCISE 8–20
Temporary investments in financial statements
Objective 9

Using the data from Exercise 8–19, assume that as of December 31, 1998, Mason Oil Supply Company has the following portfolio of available-for-sale securities:

	Cost	*Market*
Security A	$65,500	$71,000
Security B	21,000	17,100
Security D	40,250	44,000
Security E	18,000	19,500
Security F	7,500	7,200

During 1998, Mason Oil Supply Company sold Security C for $36,000.

Describe how the selling of Security C and how the remaining portfolio of securities would be reported on the December 31, 1998 balance sheet and the income statement for the year ended December 31, 1998.

EXERCISE 8–21
Receivables and temporary investments in the balance sheet
Objective 9

List any errors you can find in the following partial balance sheet.

Thomas Company
Balance Sheet
December 31, 19—

Assets		
Current assets:		
Cash		$ 95,000
Marketable equity securities (cost)	$460,000	
Deduct unrealized gain	30,000	430,000
Notes receivable		250,000
Accounts receivable	$445,000	
Plus allowance for doubtful accounts	15,000	460,000
Interest receivable		9,000

PROBLEMS SERIES A

PROBLEM 8–1A
Entries related to uncollectible accounts
Objective 4

The following transactions, adjusting entries, and closing entries were completed by The Etching Art Gallery during the current fiscal year ended December 31:

Jan. 21. Reinstated the account of Jon Hillis, which had been written off in the preceding year as uncollectible. Journalized the receipt of $2,025 cash in full payment of Hillis' account.
28. Wrote off the $8,500 balance owed by D'Arrigo Co., which is bankrupt.
June 7. Received 40% of the $8,000 balance owed by Lombard Co., a bankrupt business, and wrote off the remainder as uncollectible.
Aug. 29. Reinstated the account of Louis Estes, which had been written off two years earlier as uncollectible. Recorded the receipt of $900 cash in full payment.
Dec. 30. Wrote off the following accounts as uncollectible (compound entry): Channel Co., $1,050; Engel Co., $1,260; Loach Furniture, $1,775; Briana Parker, $820.
31. Based on an analysis of the $435,500 of accounts receivable, it was estimated that $22,000 will be uncollectible. Journalized the adjusting entry.
31. Journalized the entry to close the appropriate account to Income Summary.

Instructions

1. Record the following January 1 credit balance in the account indicated:

115	Allowance for Doubtful Accounts	$18,955
313	Income Summary	—
718	Uncollectible Accounts Expense	—

2. Journalize the transactions and the adjusting and closing entries described. After it has been journalized, post each entry to the three selected accounts affected and extend the new balances.
3. Determine the expected net realizable value of the accounts receivable as of December 31.
4. Assuming that, instead of basing the provision for uncollectible accounts on an analysis of receivables, the adjusting entry on December 31 had been based on an estimated expense of 3/4 of 1% of the net sales of $3,500,000 for the year, determine the following:
   a. Uncollectible accounts expense for the year.
   b. Balance in the allowance account after the adjustment of December 31.
   c. Expected net realizable value of the accounts receivable as of December 31.

PROBLEM 8–2A
Comparing two methods of accounting for uncollectible receivables
Objectives 4, 5

Ananda Company, which operates a chain of 10 electronics supply stores, has just completed its fourth year of operations. The direct write-off method of recording uncollectible accounts expense has been used during the entire period. Because of substantial increases in sales volume and amount of uncollectible accounts, the firm is considering the possibility of changing to the allowance method. Information is requested as to the effect that an annual provision of 1% of sales would have had on the amount of uncollectible accounts expense reported for each of the past four years. It is also considered desirable to know what the balance of Allowance for Doubtful Accounts would have been at the end of each year. The following data have been obtained from the accounts:

Year	Sales	Uncollectible Accounts Written Off	Year of Origin of Accounts Receivable Written Off as Uncollectible			
			1st	2nd	3rd	4th
1st	$ 650,000	$2,600	$2,600			
2nd	720,000	3,500	1,950	$1,550		
3rd	850,000	8,600	2,200	3,400	$3,000	
4th	1,050,000	9,550		2,300	2,950	$4,300

Instructions

1. Assemble the desired data, using the following columnar captions:

Year	Uncollectible Accounts Expense			Balance of Allowance Account, End of Year
	Expense Actually Reported	Expense Based on Estimate	Increase (Decrease) in Amount of Expense	

2. Experience during the first four years of operations indicated that the receivables were either collected within two years or had to be written off as uncollectible. Does the estimate of 1% of sales appear to be reasonably close to the actual experience with uncollectible accounts originating during the first two years? Explain.

PROBLEM 8–3A
Sales, notes receivable, discounting notes receivable transactions
Objective 7

The following were selected from among the transactions completed during the current year by Nash Co., an appliance wholesale company:

Jan. 11. Sold merchandise on account to Atlas Co., $15,000. The cost of merchandise sold was $10,000.
Mar. 12. Accepted a 60-day, 10% note for $15,000 from Atlas Co. on account.
May 11. Received from Atlas Co. the amount due on the note of March 12.
June 1. Sold merchandise on account to Kohl's for $5,000. The cost of merchandise sold was $3,500.
5. Loaned $7,500 cash to Frank Gary, receiving a 30-day, 12% note.
11. Received from Kohl's the amount due on the invoice of June 1, less 2% discount.
July 5. Received the interest due from Frank Gary and a new 60-day, 14% note as a renewal of the loan of June 5. (Record both the debit and the credit to the notes receivable account.)
Sept. 3. Received from Frank Gary the amount due on his note of July 5.
4. Sold merchandise on account to Hanover Co., $4,000. The cost of merchandise sold was $2,500.
Oct. 4. Accepted a 60-day, 12% note for $4,000 from Hanover Co. on account.
Nov. 3. Discounted the note from Hanover Co. at the Pelican National Bank at 10%.
Dec. 3. Received notice from Pelican National Bank that Hanover Co. had dishonored the note. Paid the bank the maturity value of the note.
18. Received from Hanover Co. the amount owed on the dishonored note, plus interest for 15 days at 10% computed on the maturity value of the note.

Instructions

Journalize the transactions.

PROBLEM 8–4A
Details of notes receivable, including discounting
Objective 7

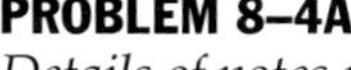

During the last six months of the current fiscal year, Lite-Up Co. received the following notes. Lite-Up Co. produces advertising videos. Notes (3) and (4) were discounted on the dates and at the rates indicated.

	Date	Face Amount	Term	Interest Rate	Date Discounted	Discount Rate
1.	Apr. 1	$20,000	90 days	8%	—	—
2.	June 10	12,000	60 days	12%	—	—
3.	July 11	15,000	90 days	8%	Aug. 10	10%
4.	Sept. 1	20,000	90 days	7%	Oct. 1	12%
5.	Dec. 1	24,000	60 days	9%	—	—
6.	Dec. 16	36,000	30 days	13%	—	—

Instructions

1. Determine for each note (a) the due date and (b) the amount of interest due at maturity, identifying each note by number.
2. Determine for notes (3) and (4) (a) the maturity value, (b) the discount period, (c) the discount, (d) the proceeds, and (e) the interest income or interest expense, identifying each note by number.
3. Journalize entries to record the discounting of notes (3) and (4) at a bank.
4. Journalize the adjusting entry to record the accrued interest on Notes (5) and (6) on December 31.

PROBLEM 8–5A
Notes receivable entries
Objective 7

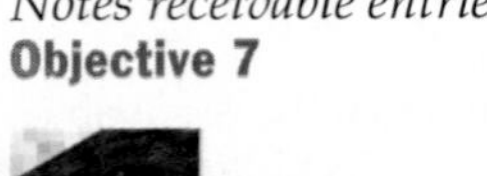

The following data relate to notes receivable and interest for Barth Co., a financial services company. (All notes are dated as of the day they are received.)

Mar. 1. Received a $20,000, 9%, 60-day note on account.
21. Received an $18,000, 9%, 90-day note on account.
Apr. 30. Received $20,300 on note of March 1.
May 16. Received a $12,000, 12%, 90-day note on account.
31. Received a $7,500, 8%, 30-day note on account.
June 19. Received $18,405 on note of March 21.
30. Received $7,550 on note of May 31.
July 1. Received a $10,000, 12%, 30-day note on account.
31. Received $10,100 on note of July 1.
Aug. 14. Received $12,360 on note of May 16.

Instructions
Journalize the entries to record the transactions.

PROBLEMS SERIES B

PROBLEM 8–1B
Entries related to uncollectible accounts
Objective 4

The following transactions, adjusting entries, and closing entries were completed by Johnson Contractors Co. during the current fiscal year ended December 31:

Mar. 10. Received 65% of the $12,000 balance owed by Agnew Co., a bankrupt business, and wrote off the remainder as uncollectible.
June 3. Reinstated the account of B. Bush, which had been written off in the preceding year as uncollectible. Journalized the receipt of $1,050 cash in full payment of Bush's account.
Sept. 19. Wrote off the $7,250 balance owed by Larkin Co., which has no assets.
Oct. 30. Reinstated the account of Giles Co., which had been written off in the preceding year as uncollectible. Journalized the receipt of $3,500 cash in full payment of the account.
Dec. 31. Wrote off the following accounts as uncollectible (compound entry): Huang Co., $2,950; Nance Co., $1,600; Powell Distributors, $9,500; J. J. Stevens, $5,200.
31. Based on an analysis of the $795,000 of accounts receivable, it was estimated that $42,700 will be uncollectible. Journalized the adjusting entry.
31. Journalized the entry to close the appropriate account to Income Summary.

Instructions

1. Record the following January 1 credit balance in the account indicated:

115	Allowance for Doubtful Accounts	$19,050
313	Income Summary	—
718	Uncollectible Accounts Expense	—

2. Journalize the transactions and the adjusting and closing entries described. After it has been journalized, post each entry to the three selected accounts affected and extend the new balances.
3. Determine the expected net realizable value of the accounts receivable as of December 31.
4. Assuming that, instead of basing the provision for uncollectible accounts on an analysis of receivables, the adjusting entry on December 31 had been based on an estimated expense of 3/4 of 1% of the net sales of $6,100,000 for the year, determine the following:
   a. Uncollectible accounts expense for the year.
   b. Balance in the allowance account after the adjustment of December 31.
   c. Expected net realizable value of the accounts receivable as of December 31.

PROBLEM 8–2B
Comparing two methods of accounting for uncollectible receivables
Objectives 4, 5

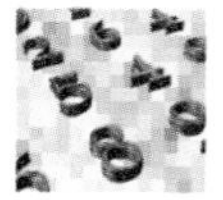

WBC Company, a telephone service and supply company, has just completed its fourth year of operations. The direct write-off method of recording uncollectible accounts expense has been used during the entire period. Because of substantial increases in sales volume and amount of uncollectible accounts, the firm is considering the possibility of changing to the allowance method. Information is requested as to the effect that an annual provision of 1% of sales would have had on the amount of uncollectible accounts expense reported for each of the past four years. It is also considered desirable to know what the balance of Allowance for Doubtful Accounts would have been at the end of each year. The following data have been obtained from the accounts:

			Year of Origin of Accounts Receivable Written Off as Uncollectible			
Year	*Sales*	*Uncollectible Accounts Written Off*	*1st*	*2nd*	*3rd*	*4th*
1st	$ 450,000	$2,500	$2,500			
2nd	660,000	3,950	1,900	$2,050		
3rd	950,000	5,700	700	2,600	$2,400	
4th	1,000,000	6,800		2,200	2,550	$2,050

Instructions

1. Assemble the desired data, using the following columnar captions:

	Uncollectible Accounts Expense			
Year	*Expense Actually Reported*	*Expense Based on Estimate*	*Increase (Decrease) in Amount of Expense*	*Balance of Allowance Account, End of Year*

2. Experience during the first four years of operations indicated that the receivables were either collected within two years or had to be written off as uncollectible. Does the estimate of 1% of sales appear to be reasonably close to the actual experience with uncollectible accounts originating during the first two years? Explain.

PROBLEM 8–3B
Sales, notes receivable, discounting notes receivable transactions
Objective 7

The following were selected from among the transactions completed by Beverly Co. during the current year. Beverly Co. sells and installs home and business security systems.

Jan. 10. Loaned $20,000 cash to Joyce Curtis, receiving a 90-day, 8% note.
Feb. 1. Sold merchandise on account to Peabody and Son, $9,000. The cost of the merchandise sold was $4,800.
20. Sold merchandise on account to C. D. Connors Co., $8,000. The cost of the merchandise sold was $5,000.
Mar. 2. Received from C. D. Connors Co. the amount of the invoice of February 20, less 1% discount.
3. Accepted a 60-day, 10% note for $9,000 from Peabody and Son on account.

Apr. 10. Received the interest due from Joyce Curtis and a new 90-day, 12% note as a renewal of the loan of January 10. (Record both the debit and the credit to the notes receivable account.)
May 2. Received from Peabody and Son the amount due on the note of March 3.
July 9. Received from Joyce Curtis the amount due on her note of April 10.
10. Sold merchandise on account to Song Yu and Co., $30,000. The cost of merchandise sold was $20,000.
Aug. 9. Accepted a 60-day, 12% note for $30,000 from Song Yu and Co. on account.
Sept. 8. Discounted the note from Song Yu and Co. at the American National Bank at 14%.
Oct. 8. Received notice from the American National Bank that Song Yu and Co. had dishonored its note. Paid the bank the maturity value of the note.
28. Received from Song Yu and Co. the amount owed on the dishonored note, plus interest for 20 days at 12% computed on the maturity value of the note.

Instructions
Journalize the transactions.

PROBLEM 8–4B
Details of notes receivable, including discounting
Objective 7

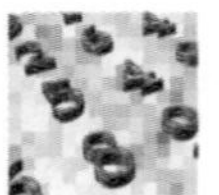

During the current fiscal year, Flushing Co. received the following notes. Flushing Co. wholesales bathroom fixtures. Notes (1) and (2) were discounted on the dates and at the rates indicated.

	Date	*Face Amount*	*Term*	*Interest Rate*	*Date Discounted*	*Discount Rate*
1.	May 1	$18,000	60 days	8%	May 16	12%
2.	June 11	10,000	30 days	12%	June 21	14%
3.	Aug. 20	7,200	90 days	7%		
4.	Oct. 31	12,000	60 days	9%		
5.	Nov. 28	15,000	60 days	8%	—	—
6.	Dec. 26	18,000	30 days	12%	—	—

Instructions

1. Determine for each note (a) the due date and (b) the amount of interest due at maturity, identifying each note by number.
2. Determine for notes (1) and (2) (a) the maturity value, (b) the discount period, (c) the discount, (d) the proceeds, and (e) the interest income or interest expense, identifying each note by number.
3. Journalize the entries to record the discounting of notes (1) and (2) at a bank.
4. Journalize the adjusting entry to record the accrued interest on Notes (5) and (6) on December 31.

PROBLEM 8–5B
Notes receivable entries
Objective 7

The following data relate to notes receivable and interest for Fiber Optic Co., a cable manufacturer and supplier. (All notes are dated as of the day they are received.)

July 1. Received an $8,000, 9%, 60-day note on account.
Aug. 16. Received a $30,000, 10%, 120-day note on account.
30. Received $8,120 on note of July 1.
Sept. 1. Received a $15,000, 8%, 60-day note on account.
Oct. 31. Received $15,200 on note of September 1.
Nov. 8. Received a $24,000, 7%, 30-day note on account.
30. Received a $3,000, 10%, 30-day note on account.
Dec. 8. Received $24,140 on note of November 8.
14. Received $31,000 on note of August 16.
30. Received $3,025 on note of November 30.

Instructions
Journalize entries to record the transactions.

CASES

CASE 8–1
Taos National Bank
Calculating interest

Nataline Smith, vice-president of operations for Taos National Bank, has instructed the bank's computer programmer to program the bank's computers to calculate interest on depository accounts (payables) using a 365-day year. Nataline also instructed the programmer to use a 360-day year to compute interest on loans (receivables).

Discuss whether Nataline is behaving in an ethical manner.

CASE 8–2
Do-Rite Construction Supplies Co.
Collecting accounts receivable

The following is an excerpt from a conversation between the office manager, Valerie Cook, and the president of Do-Rite Construction Supplies Co., Marvin Howard. Do-Rite sells building supplies to local contractors.

Valerie: Marvin, we're going to have to do something about these overdue accounts receivable. One-third of our accounts are over 60 days past due, and I've had accounts that have stayed open for almost a year!

Marvin: I didn't realize it was that bad. Any ideas?

Valerie: Well, we could stop giving credit. Make everyone pay with cash or a credit card. We accept MasterCard and Visa already, but only the walk-in customers use them. Almost all of the contractors put purchases on their bills.

Marvin: Yes, but we've been allowing credit for years. As far as I know, all of our competitors allow contractors credit. If we stopped giving credit, we'd lose many of our contractors. They'd just go elsewhere. You know, some of these guys run up bills as high as $40,000 or $50,000. There's no way they could put that kind of money on a credit card.

Valerie: That's a good point. But we've got to do something.

Marvin: How many of the contractor accounts do you actually end up writing off as uncollectible?

Valerie: Not many. Almost all eventually pay. It's just that they take so long!

Suggest one or more solutions to Do-Rite Construction Supplies Co.'s problem concerning the collection of accounts receivable.

CASE 8–3
La Meriden Company
Reporting marketable securities

The following is an excerpt from a conversation between Pierre LaBoone, president of La Meriden Company, and Jill Klossmyer, the controller for La Meriden.

Pierre: Jill, I have a question about our latest balance sheet.

Jill: Sure, Pierre. What's your question?

Pierre: I see that you've listed our marketable securities at their cost plus a market adjustment of $30,000. Let's see . . . you list this adjustment as an unrealized holding gain.

Jill: That's right. There's a new accounting standard . . . FASB 115 . . . that requires us to list our marketable securities at their fair market value.

Pierre: Okay. But it seems to me that we ought to show this $30,000 gain in our income statement. After all, the securities are worth $30,000 more than we paid. We could cash them in tomorrow if we had to. As a matter of fact, I'll probably sell them in three or four months anyway.

How do you think Jill should respond to Pierre's suggestion that the $30,000 unrealized gain should be reported as part of net income on the income statement? Include in your answer what you believe was the FASB's rationale for NOT including such gains as part of income.

CASE 8–4
Hershey Foods Corporation
Financial analysis

Businesses that grant long credit terms usually have larger accounts receivable balances than those granting short credit terms. In either case, it is desirable to collect receivables as promptly as possible. The cash collected from receivables improves solvency, and prompt collection also lessens the risk of loss from uncollectible accounts.

There are two financial measures that are especially useful in evaluating the efficiency in collecting accounts receivable: (1) accounts receivable turnover and (2) number of days' sales in receivables. The accounts receivable turnover is computed as follows:

$$\text{Accounts receivable turnover} = \frac{\textbf{Net sales on account}}{\textbf{Average accounts receivable}}$$

The average accounts receivable can be determined by adding the beginning and ending accounts receivable balances and dividing by two.

The number of days' sales in receivables is an estimate of the length of time the accounts receivable have been outstanding and is computed as follows:

$$\text{Number of days' sales in receivables} = \frac{\text{Accounts receivable, end of year}}{\text{Average daily sales on account}}$$

Average daily sales on account is determined by dividing net sales on account by 365 days.

An improvement in the efficiency in collecting accounts receivable is indicated by an increase in the accounts receivable turnover and a decrease in the number of days' sales in receivables.

1. For Hershey Foods Corporation, assume that all sales are credit sales and that the accounts receivable were $159,805,000 at December 31, 1991.
   a. Compute the accounts receivable turnover for 1992 and 1993.
   b. Compute the number of days' sales in receivables at December 31, 1992 and 1993.
2. What conclusions can be drawn from these analyses regarding Hershey's efficiency in collecting receivables?

CASE 8–5

Sports Rehab Co.

Estimating uncollectible accounts

For several years, sales have been on a "cash only" basis. On January 1, 1993, however, Sports Rehab Co. began offering credit on terms of n/30. The amount of the adjusting entry to record the estimated uncollectible receivables at the end of each year has been 1/2 of 1% of credit sales, which is the rate reported as the average for the industry. Credit sales and the year-end credit balances in Allowance for Doubtful Accounts for the past four years are as follows:

Year	*Credit Sales*	*Allowance for Doubtful Accounts*
1993	$5,800,000	$ 5,800
1994	6,000,000	8,200
1995	6,100,000	15,400
1996	6,050,000	19,000

Joe Johnson, president of Sports Rehab Co., is concerned that the method used to account for and write off uncollectible receivables is unsatisfactory. He has asked for your advice in the analysis of past operations in this area and for recommendations for change.

1. Determine the amount of (a) the addition to Allowance for Doubtful Accounts and (b) the accounts written off for each of the four years.
2. a. Advise Joe Johnson as to whether the estimate of 1/2 of 1% of credit sales appears reasonable.
   b. Assume that after discussing (a) with Joe Johnson, he asked you what action might be taken to determine what the balance of Allowance for Doubtful Accounts should be at December 31, 1996, and what possible changes, if any, you might recommend in accounting for uncollectible receivables. How would you respond?

ANSWERS TO SELF-EXAMINATION QUESTIONS

1. **B** The estimate of uncollectible accounts, $8,500 (answer C), is the amount of the desired balance of Allowance for Doubtful Accounts after adjustment. The amount of the current provision to be made for uncollectible accounts expense is thus $6,000 (answer B), which is the amount that must be added to the Allowance for Doubtful Accounts credit balance of $2,500 (answer A), so that the account will have the desired balance of $8,500.
2. **B** The amount expected to be realized from accounts receivable is the balance of Accounts Receivable, $100,000, less the balance of Allowance for Doubtful Accounts, $7,000, or $93,000 (answer B).
3. **C** Maturity value is the amount that is due at the maturity or due date. The maturity value of $10,300 (answer C) is determined as follows:

Face amount of note	$10,000
Plus interest ($10,000 × 12% × 90/360)	300
Maturity value of note	$10,300

4. **B** The proceeds of $15,021.25 (answer B) are determined as follows:

Face value of note dated June 1	$15,000.00
Interest on note (60 days at 10%)	250.00
Maturity value of note due July 31	$15,250.00
Discount on maturity value (45 days, from June 16 to July 31, at 12%)	228.75
Proceeds	$15,021.25

5. **A** Securities held as temporary investments are classified on the balance sheet as current assets (answer A).

9 Inventories

YOU AND ACCOUNTING

Assume that you purchased a Compact Disc (CD)/ Receiver in June. You planned on attaching pairs of speakers to the system. Initially, however, you could afford only one pair of speakers, which cost $160. In October, you purchased the second pair of speakers at a cost of $180.

Over the holidays, someone broke into your home and stole one pair of speakers. Luckily, your renters/ homeowners insurance policy will cover the theft, but the insurance company needs to know the cost of the speakers that were stolen.

All of the speakers are identical. To respond to the insurance company, however, you will need to identify which pair of speakers was stolen. Was it the first pair, which cost $160? Or was it the second pair, which cost $180? Whichever assumption you make may determine the amount that you receive from the insurance company.

Merchandising businesses make similar assumptions when identical merchandise is purchased at different costs. At the end of a period, some of the merchandise will be on hand and some will have been sold. But which costs relate to the sold merchandise and which costs relate to the merchandise on hand? The business's assumption can involve large dollar amounts and thus can have a significant impact on the financial statements. For example, The Home Depot, Inc.'s financial statements for the period ending January 30, 1994, report merchandise inventories that are over $1 billion and a cost of merchandise sold of over $6 billion. The company's net income for this same period was just over $450 million.

In this chapter, we will discuss such issues as how to determine the cost of merchandise on hand and the cost of merchandise sold. However, we begin this chapter by discussing internal controls over merchandise inventory.

After studying this chapter, you should be able to:

Objective 1
Summarize and provide examples of internal control procedures that apply to inventories.

Objective 2
List the procedures for determining the actual quantities in inventory.

Objective 3
Compute the cost of inventory under the perpetual inventory system, using the following costing methods:

First-in, first-out
Last-in, first-out
Average cost

Objective 4
Compute the cost of inventory under the periodic inventory system, using the following costing methods:

First-in, first-out
Last-in, first-out
Average cost

Objective 5
Compare the use of the three inventory costing methods.

Objective 6
Compute the proper valuation of inventory at other than cost, using the lower-of-cost-or-market and net realizable value concepts.

Objective 7
Prepare a balance sheet presentation of merchandise inventory.

Objective 8
Estimate the cost of inventory, using the retail method and the gross profit method.

Internal Control of Inventories

Objective 1
Summarize and provide examples of internal control procedures that apply to inventories.

What is included in inventory? The term **inventory** is used to indicate (1) merchandise held for sale in the normal course of business and (2) materials in the process of production or held for production. In this chapter, we focus primarily on inventory of merchandise purchased for resale. We discuss inventories of raw materials and partially processed materials of a manufacturing enterprise in a later chapter.

Merchandise inventory is a significant item in many businesses' financial statements. For example, The Home Depot, Inc.'s merchandise inventory represents over 65% of its current assets and over 25% of its total assets. Likewise, the cost of merchandise sold represents over 70% of its net sales. For companies such as The Home Depot, good internal control over inventory must be maintained.

The objective of internal controls over inventory is to ensure that the inventory is safeguarded and is properly reported in the financial statements. These internal controls can be either preventive or detective in nature, as we discuss in the following paragraphs. A preventive control is designed to prevent errors or misstatements from occurring. A detective control is designed to detect an error or misstatement after it has occurred.

Control over inventory should begin as soon as the inventory is received. Prenumbered receiving reports should be completed by the company's receiving department in order to establish the initial accountability for the inventory. To make sure the inventory received is what was ordered, each receiving report should be reconciled to the company's original purchase order for the merchandise. Likewise, the price at which the inventory was ordered, as shown on the purchase order, should be compared to the price at which the vendor billed the company, as shown on the vendor's invoice. After the receiving report, purchase order, and vendor's invoice have been reconciled, the company should record the inventory and related account payable in the accounting records.

Internal controls for safeguarding inventory include developing and using security measures to prevent inventory damage or employee theft. For example, inventory should be stored in a warehouse or other area to which access is restricted to authorized employees. The removal of merchandise from the warehouse should

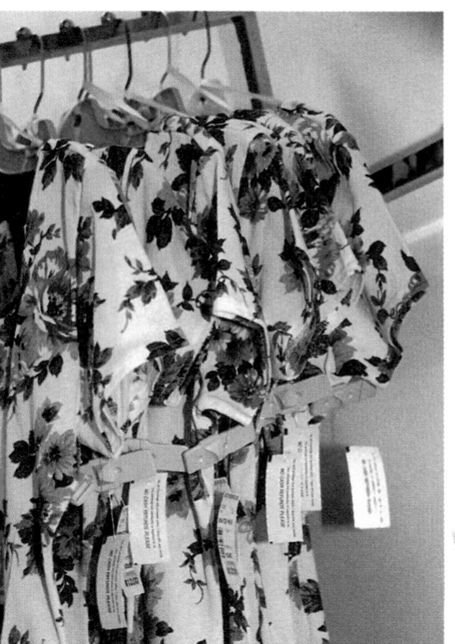

In order to safeguard inventory, retail clothing stores often place plastic alarm tags on merchandise.

be controlled by using requisition forms, which should be properly authorized. The storage area should also be climate controlled to prevent inventory damage from heat or cold. Further, when the business is not operating or is not open, the storage area should be locked.

When you have been shopping, you may have noticed how retail stores protect inventory from customer theft. Retail stores often use such devices as two-way mirrors, cameras, and security guards. High-priced items are often displayed in locked cabinets. For example, notebook computers and jewelry at Sam's Club stores are kept in locked glass cases to prevent theft of these small, portable items. An employee also checks the customer's cash receipts against the items in their possession as they leave the store. Likewise, retail clothing stores often place plastic alarm tags on valuable items such as leather coats. Sensors at the exit doors set off alarms if the tags have not been removed by the cash register clerk. These controls are designed to prevent customers from taking merchandise without paying (shoplifting).

Using a perpetual inventory system for merchandise also provides an effective means of control over inventory. The amount of each type of merchandise on hand is always readily available in a subsidiary **inventory ledger.** In addition, the subsidiary ledger can be an aid in maintaining inventory quantities at optimum levels. Frequently comparing balances with predetermined maximum and minimum levels allows for the timely reordering of merchandise and prevents the ordering of excess inventory.

To ensure the accuracy of the amount of inventory reported in the financial statements, a merchandising business should take a physical inventory (i.e., count the merchandise on hand). In a perpetual inventory system, the physical inventory is compared to the recorded inventory in order to determine the amount of shrinkage or shortage. If the inventory shrinkage is unusually large, management can investigate further and take any necessary corrective action. Knowledge that a physical inventory will be taken also serves to deter (prevent) employee thefts or misuses of inventory.

Determining Actual Quantities in the Inventory

Objective 2
List the procedures for determining the actual quantities in inventory.

In the preceding section, we discussed the importance of taking a physical inventory as part of a company's controls over inventory. In this section, we describe the procedures for taking a physical inventory. We then illustrate how errors in taking a physical inventory affect the financial statements.

PROCEDURES FOR TAKING A PHYSICAL INVENTORY

How do you "take" a physical inventory? The first step in this process is to determine the quantity of each kind of merchandise owned by the business. The specific procedures for determining inventory quantities and assembling the data differ among companies. A common practice is to use teams made up of two persons. One person counts, weighs, or otherwise determines quantity, and the other lists the description and the quantity on inventory count sheets. The quantities indicated for high-cost items may be checked by a second count team during the inventory-taking process. The second count team should also check quantities of other items selected at random from the inventory count sheets.

All the merchandise owned by the business on the inventory date, and only such merchandise, should be included in the inventory. For merchandise in transit, the party (the seller or the buyer) who has title to the merchandise on the inventory date must be determined. To determine who has title, it may be necessary to examine purchases and sales invoices of the last few days of the current period and the first few days of the following period.

As we discussed in a previous chapter, shipping terms are often helpful in determining when title passes. When goods are purchased or sold **FOB shipping point,** title usually passes to the buyer when the goods are shipped. When the terms are **FOB destination,** title usually does not pass to the buyer until the goods are delivered.

To illustrate, assume that merchandise purchased FOB shipping point is shipped by the seller on the last day of the buyer's fiscal period. The merchandise does not arrive until the following period and thus is not available for counting by the inventory crew. However, such merchandise should be included in the buyer's inventory because title has passed. A debit to Merchandise Inventory and a credit to Accounts Payable should be recorded by the buyer as of the end of the current period.

Another example, though less common, further illustrates the importance of carefully examining transactions involving shipments of merchandise. Manufacturers sometimes ship merchandise to retailers who act as the manufacturer's agent when selling the merchandise. The manufacturer retains title until the goods are sold. Such merchandise is said to be shipped *on consignment* to the retailers. The unsold merchandise is a part of the manufacturer's (consignor's) inventory, even though the merchandise is in the hands of the retailers. Likewise, the consigned merchandise should not be included in the retailer's (consignee's) inventory.

EFFECT OF INVENTORY ERRORS ON FINANCIAL STATEMENTS

Any errors in the inventory count will affect both the balance sheet and the income statement. For example, an error in the physical inventory will misstate the ending inventory, current assets, and total assets on the balance sheet. This is because the physical inventory is the basis for recording the adjusting entry for inventory shrinkage. Also, an error in taking the physical inventory misstates the cost of goods sold, gross profit, and net income on the income statement. In addition, because net income is closed to the owner's equity at the end of the period, owner's equity will also be misstated on the balance sheet. This misstatement of owner's equity will equal the misstatement of the ending inventory, current assets, and total assets.

To illustrate, assume that in taking the physical inventory on December 31, 1997, Sapra Company incorrectly recorded its physical inventory as $115,000 instead of the correct amount of $125,000. As a result, the merchandise inventory, current assets, and total assets reported on the December 31, 1997 balance sheet would be understated by $10,000 ($125,000 – $115,000). Because the ending physical inventory is understated, the inventory shrinkage and the cost of merchandise sold will be overstated by $10,000. Thus, the gross profit and the net income for the year will be understated by $10,000. Since the net income is closed to owner's equity at the end of the period, the owner's equity on the December 31, 1997 balance sheet will also be understated by $10,000. The effects on Sapra Company's financial statements are summarized below:

	Balance Sheet
Merchandise inventory	$10,000 understated
Current assets	$10,000 understated
Total assets	$10,000 understated
Owner's equity	$10,000 understated

	Income Statement
Cost of merchandise sold	$10,000 overstated
Gross profit	$10,000 understated
Net income	$10,000 understated

Assume that in the preceding example the physical inventory had been overstated on December 31, 1997, by $10,000. That is, Sapra Company erroneously recorded its inventory as $135,000. In this case, the effects on the balance sheet and income statement would be just the opposite of those indicated.

When a company uses the perpetual inventory system, errors in the physical inventory are infrequent. In addition, when errors such as the one just described do occur, they are normally detected in the following period. In this case, the financial statements of the prior year must be corrected. We will discuss such corrections in a later chapter.

The effect of misstated inventory on the financial statements has been used to defraud investors and others. For example, during the 1980s, Crazy Eddie Inc. reported rapid gains in sales and earnings due to what the company said was expansion of its electronics stores, adept sales-floor techniques, and catchy commercials. However, it now appears that the rapid growth was due to a fraudulent scheme by Crazy Eddie's founder, Eddie Antar, and others. This scheme resulted in the reporting of misstated inventory and income. In part, Crazy Eddie overstated inventory counts at one warehouse by $10 million, drafted phony inventory count sheets, and included $4 million of merchandise in inventory when, in fact, the merchandise was being returned to suppliers. As a result, income was overstated. The apparent purpose of the scheme was to "artificially inflate the net worth of the company" and the value of stock owned by Mr. Antar and others.[1]

Inventory Costing Methods Under a Perpetual Inventory System

Objective 3

Compute the cost of inventory under the perpetual inventory system, using the following costing methods:

First-in, first-out
Last-in, first-out
Average cost

As we described in an earlier chapter, all merchandise increases and decreases in a perpetual system are recorded in a manner similar to the recording of increases and decreases in cash. The merchandise inventory account at the beginning of an accounting period indicates the merchandise on hand on that date. Purchases are recorded by debiting Merchandise Inventory and crediting Cash or Accounts Payable. On the date of each sale, the cost of the merchandise sold is recorded by debiting Cost of Merchandise Sold and crediting Merchandise Inventory. Thus, the merchandise inventory account constantly (perpetually) discloses the balance of merchandise on hand. At the end of the period, the balance in the merchandise inventory account, adjusted for any inventory shrinkage, is reported on the balance sheet. The balance in the cost of merchandise sold account is reported on the income statement.

What costs should be included in inventory? The purchase price of merchandise, less any purchases discounts, is part of the cost of inventory. In addition, costs incurred in acquiring the merchandise, such as transportation, customs duties, and insurance against losses in transit, are normally included in the cost of inventory. However, some costs of acquiring merchandise, such as the salaries of Purchasing Department employees and other administrative costs, are not easily allocated to the inventory. Therefore, these costs are treated as operating expenses of the period.

A major accounting issue arises in using the perpetual system when identical units of a commodity are acquired at different unit costs during a period. In such cases, when an item is sold, it is necessary to determine its unit cost so that the proper accounting entry can be recorded. To illustrate, assume that three identical units of Commodity X are available for sale during the first ten days in January.

[1] Jeffrey A. Tannenbaum, "Filings by Crazy Eddie Suggest Founder Led Scheme to Inflate Company's Value," *The Wall Street Journal*, May 31, 1988, p. 28.

One of these units was in the inventory at the beginning of the year, and the other two were purchased on January 4 and January 9. The costs per unit are as follows:

		Commodity X	*Units*	*Cost*
Jan.	1	Inventory	1	$ 9
	4	Purchase	1	13
	9	Purchase	1	14
Total			3	$36
Average cost per unit				$12

Assume that one unit is sold on January 10. If this unit can be identified with a specific purchase, the **specific identification method** can be used to determine the cost of the unit sold. For example, if the unit sold was purchased on January 4, the cost assigned to the unit is $13.

The specific identification method is not practical unless each unit can be identified accurately. An automobile dealer, for example, may be able to use this method. For businesses that buy and sell units that are identical, however, a cost flow must be assumed. That is, an assumption must be made as to which unit was sold and which units are still on hand. The three most common cost flow assumptions are as follows:

1. Cost flow is in the order in which the costs were incurred—first-in, first-out.
2. Cost flow is in the reverse order in which the costs were incurred—last-in, first-out.
3. Cost flow is an average of the costs.

The cost of the unit of Commodity X sold and the cost of the two remaining units are shown here for each of the cost flow assumptions.

	Cost of Units Available		*Cost of Unit Sold*		*Cost of Units Remaining*
1. In order in which costs were incurred (first-in, first-out)	$36	–	$ 9	=	$27
2. In reverse order in which costs were incurred (last-in, first-out)	36	–	14	=	22
3. In accordance with average costs	36	–	12	=	24

The three most widely used inventory costing methods (which correspond to the three assumptions of cost flows) are:

1. **First-in, first-out (fifo)**
2. **Last-in, first-out (lifo)**
3. **Average cost**

The chart in Exhibit 1 shows the frequency with which fifo, lifo, and the average methods are used in practice.

FIRST-IN, FIRST-OUT METHOD

When the **first-in, first-out (fifo) method** of costing inventory is used, costs are assumed to be charged against revenue in the order in which they were incurred. Hence, the inventory remaining is assumed to be made up of the most recent costs.

Exhibit 1
Inventory Costing Methods

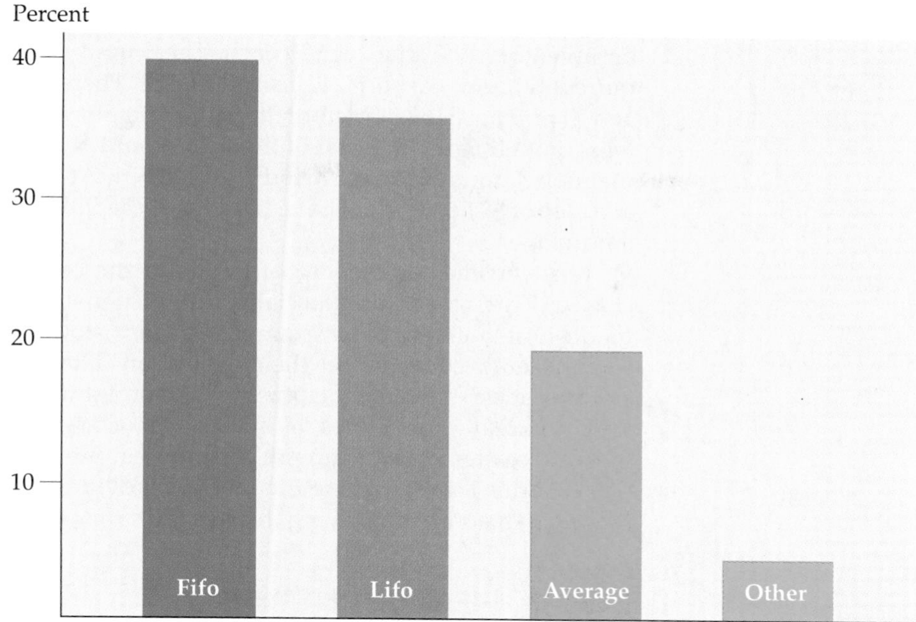

Source: *Accounting Trends & Techniques*, 48th ed., American Institute of Certified Public Accountants, New York, 1994.

We illustrate the fifo method using the following data for merchandise identified as Commodity 127B:

	Commodity 127B	*Units*	*Cost*
Jan. 1	Inventory	10	$20
4	Sale	7	
10	Purchase	8	21
22	Sale	4	
28	Sale	2	
30	Purchase	10	22

To illustrate the fifo method of cost flow in a perpetual inventory system, Exhibit 2 shows the inventory ledger account for Commodity 127B. The number of units on hand after each transaction, together with total costs and unit costs, appear in the inventory section of the account.

Exhibit 2
Perpetual Inventory Account (Fifo)

Commodity 127B

	Purchases			*Cost of Merchandise Sold*			*Inventory*		
Date	*Quantity*	*Unit Cost*	*Total Cost*	*Quantity*	*Unit Cost*	*Total Cost*	*Quantity*	*Unit Cost*	*Total Cost*
Jan. 1							10	20	200
4				7	20	140	3	20	60
10	8	21	168				3 8	20 21	60 168
22				3 1	20 21	60 21	7	21	147
28				2	21	42	5	21	105
30	10	22	220				5 10	21 22	105 220

Note that after the 7 units of the commodity were sold on January 4, there was an inventory of 3 units at $20 each. The 8 units purchased on January 10 were acquired at a unit cost of $21, instead of $20. Therefore, the inventory after the January 10 purchase is reported on two lines, 3 units at $20 each and 8 units at $21 each. Next, note that the $81 cost of the 4 units sold on January 22 is comprised of the remaining 3 units at $20 each and 1 unit at $21. At this point, 7 units are in inventory at a cost of $21 per unit. The remainder of the illustration can be explained in a similar manner.

Most businesses dispose of goods in the order in which the goods are purchased. This would be especially true of perishables and goods whose styles or models often change. For example, grocery stores stock their shelves with goods such as milk products by their expiration dates. Likewise, men's and women's clothing stores stock their clothes by season. At the end of a season, they often have sales to clear their stores of off-season or out-of-style clothing. Thus, the fifo method is often consistent with the physical movement of merchandise. To the extent that this is the case, the fifo method provides results that are about the same as those obtained by identifying the specific costs of each item sold and in inventory.

LAST-IN, FIRST-OUT METHOD

When the **last-in, first-out (lifo) method** is used in a perpetual inventory system, the cost of the units sold is the cost of the most recent purchases. To illustrate, Exhibit 3 shows the ledger account for Commodity 127B, prepared on a lifo basis.

Comparing the ledger accounts for the fifo perpetual system and the lifo perpetual system indicates that the accounts are the same through the January 10 purchase. Using the lifo perpetual system, however, the cost of the 4 units sold on January 22 is the cost of the units from the January 10 purchase ($21 per unit). The cost of the 7 units in inventory after the sale on January 22 is the cost of the 3 units remaining from the beginning inventory and the cost of the 4 units remaining from the January 10 purchase. The remainder of the lifo illustration can be explained in a similar manner.

When the lifo method is used, the inventory ledger is sometimes maintained in units only. The units are converted to dollars when the financial statements are prepared at the end of the period.

The use of the lifo method was originally limited to rare situations in which the units sold were taken from the most recently acquired goods. For tax reasons, its

Exhibit 3
Perpetual Inventory Account (Lifo)

Commodity 127B

	Purchases			*Cost of Merchandise Sold*			*Inventory*		
Date	*Quantity*	*Unit Cost*	*Total Cost*	*Quantity*	*Unit Cost*	*Total Cost*	*Quantity*	*Unit Cost*	*Total Cost*
Jan. 1							10	20	200
4				7	20	140	3	20	60
10	8	21	168				3 8	20 21	60 168
22				4	21	84	3 4	20 21	60 84
28				2	21	42	3 2	20 21	60 42
30	10	22	220				3 2 10	20 21 22	60 42 220

use has greatly increased during the past few decades. Lifo is now often used even when it does not represent the physical flow of goods.

AVERAGE COST METHOD

When the average cost method is used in a perpetual inventory system, an average unit cost for each type of commodity is computed each time a purchase is made. This unit cost is then used to determine the cost of each sale until another purchase is made and a new average is computed. This averaging technique is called a **moving average.** Since the average cost method is not often used in a perpetual inventory system, we do not illustrate it in this chapter.

USING ACCOUNTING TO UNDERSTAND BUSINESS

The fifo, lifo, and average cost flow assumptions also apply to other areas of business. For example, individuals and businesses often purchase marketable securities at different costs per share. When such investments are sold, the investor must either specifically identify which shares are sold or make a cost flow assumption. To illustrate, assume that a business purchased 100 shares of Microsoft Corporation at $52 and 100 shares at $58. If the business later sells 100 shares for $53, which shares did it sell? The business must determine the cost of the shares sold so that it can report a gain or loss on the sale for tax purposes. In addition, it must report the gain or loss on its income statement.

COMPUTERIZED PERPETUAL INVENTORY SYSTEMS

A perpetual inventory system may be maintained using manually kept records. However, such a system is often too costly and too time consuming for businesses with a large number of inventory items or many purchase and sales transactions. In such cases, the record keeping is often computerized.

An example of using computers in maintaining perpetual inventory records for retail stores is described as follows:

1. The relevant details for each inventory item, such as a description, quantity, and unit size, are stored in an inventory record. The individual inventory records make up the computerized inventory file, the total of which agrees with the balance of the inventory ledger account.
2. Each time an item is purchased or returned by a customer, the inventory data are entered into the computer's inventory records and files.
3. Each time an item is sold, a sales clerk scans the item's bar code with an optical scanner. The scanner *reads* the magnetic code and rings up the sale on the cash register. The inventory records and files are then updated.
4. After a physical inventory is taken, the inventory count data are entered into the computer. These data are compared with the current balances, and a listing of the overages and shortages is printed. The inventory balances are then adjusted to the quantities determined by the physical count.

By entering additional data, this system can be extended to aid in maintaining inventory quantities at optimal levels. For example, data on the most economical quantity to be purchased in a single order and the minimum quantity to be maintained for each item can be entered into the computer records. The computer software is then programmed to compare these data with the quantities in the inventory records. As necessary, the computer program begins the purchasing activity by preparing purchase orders.

Retail store managers can use scanned sales data to develop and fine-tune their marketing strategies. For example, such data can determine the effectiveness of advertising campaigns, sales promotions, and sales patterns of products.

The system can also be extended to aid in processing the related accounting transactions. For example, as cash sales are entered on an electronic cash register, the sales data are accumulated and used for the daily accounting entries. These entries debit Cash and credit Sales as well as debit Cost of Merchandise Sold and credit Merchandise Inventory.

Inventory Costing Methods Under a Periodic Inventory System

Objective 4
Compute the cost of inventory under the periodic inventory system, using the following costing methods:

First-in, first-out
Last-in, first-out
Average cost

When the periodic inventory system is used, only revenue is recorded each time a sale is made. No entry is made at the time of the sale to record the cost of the merchandise sold. At the end of the accounting period, a physical inventory is taken to determine the cost of the inventory on hand and the cost of the merchandise sold.

Like the perpetual inventory system, a cost flow assumption must be made when identical units of a commodity are acquired at different unit costs during a period. In such cases, the fifo, lifo, or average cost method is normally used.

FIRST-IN, FIRST-OUT METHOD

To illustrate the use of the first-in, first-out method in a periodic inventory system, we assume the following data for a commodity:

Jan. 1	Inventory:	200 units at	$ 9	$ 1,800
Mar. 10	Purchase:	300 units at	10	3,000
Sept. 21	Purchase:	400 units at	11	4,400
Nov. 18	Purchase:	100 units at	12	1,200
	Available for sale during year	1,000		$10,400

The physical count on December 31 shows that 300 units of the commodity are on hand. Using the fifo method, the cost of these units is determined as follows:

Most recent costs, Nov. 18:	100 units at	$12	$1,200
Next most recent costs, Sept. 21:	200 units at	11	2,200
Inventory, Dec. 31:	300		$3,400

Deducting the inventory of $3,400 from the $10,400 of merchandise available for sale yields $7,000 as the cost of merchandise sold. The $7,000 cost of merchandise sold is made up of the earliest costs incurred for this commodity. Exhibit 4 shows the relationship of the inventory at December 31 and the cost of merchandise sold during the year.

Exhibit 4
First-In, First-Out Flow of Costs

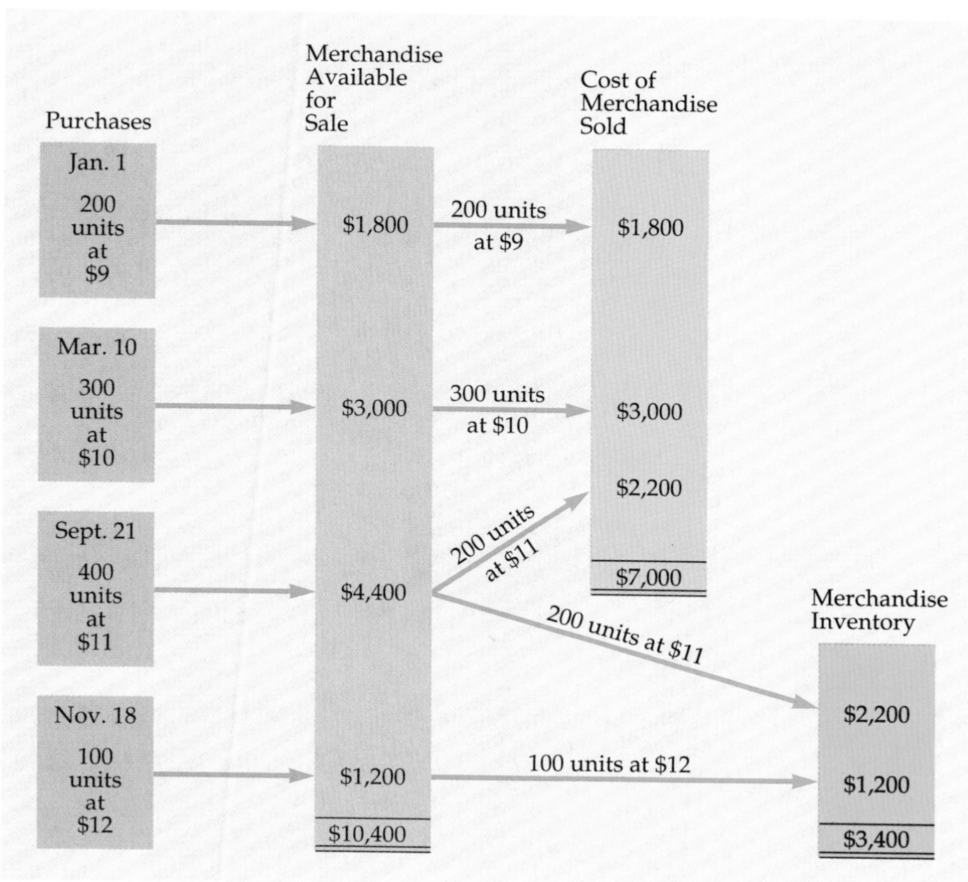

LAST-IN, FIRST-OUT METHOD

When the last-in, first-out method of inventory costing is used, the inventory remaining is assumed to comprise the earliest costs. Based on the data in the fifo example, the cost of the 300 units of inventory is determined as follows:

Earliest costs, Jan. 1:	200 units at $ 9	$1,800
Next earliest costs, Mar. 10:	100 units at 10	1,000
Inventory, Dec. 31:	300	$2,800

Deducting the inventory of $2,800 from the $10,400 of merchandise available for sale yields $7,600 as the cost of merchandise sold. The $7,600 cost of merchandise sold is made up of the most recent costs incurred for this commodity. Exhibit 5 shows the relationship of the inventory at December 31 and the cost of merchandise sold during the year.

AVERAGE COST METHOD

The average cost method is sometimes called the **weighted average method.** When this method is used, costs are assumed to be matched against revenue according to an average of the unit costs of the goods sold. The same weighted average unit costs are used in determining the cost of the merchandise inventory at the end of the period.

The weighted average unit cost is determined by dividing the total cost of the units of each commodity available for sale during the period by the related number

Exhibit 5
Last-In, First-Out Flow of Costs

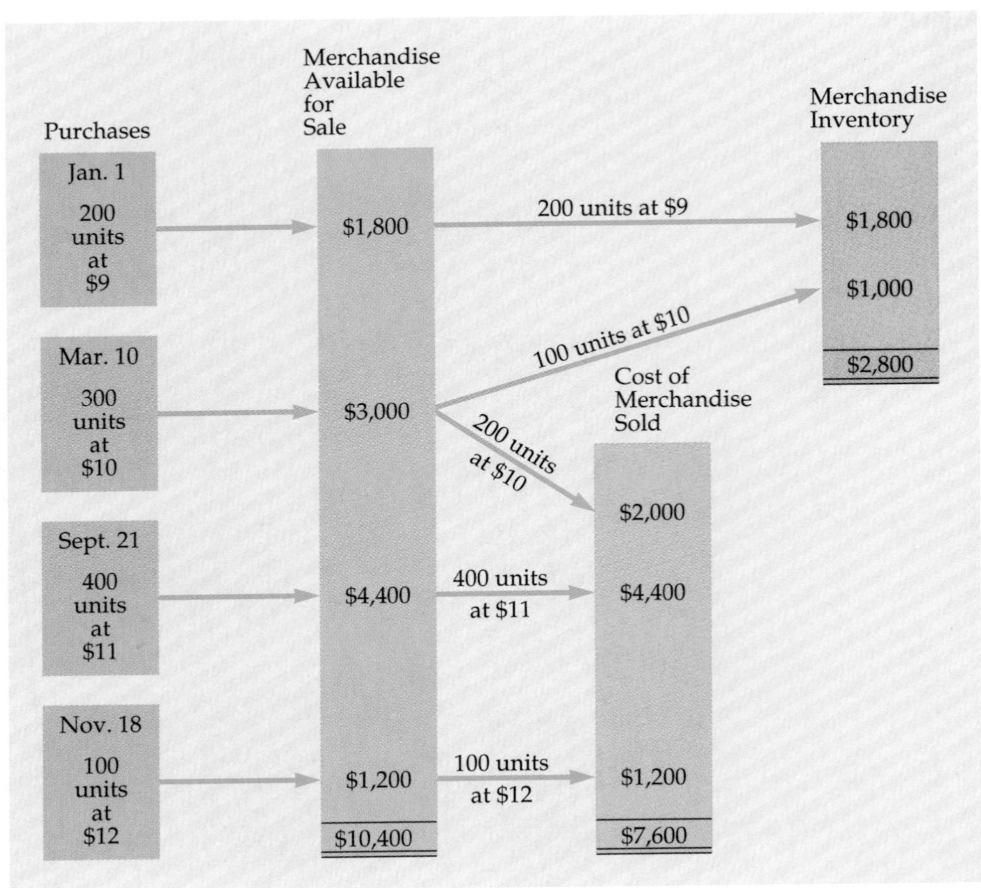

of units of that commodity. Using the same cost data as in the fifo and lifo examples, the average cost of the 1,000 units, $10.40, and the cost of the 300 units in inventory, $3,120, are determined as follows:

Average unit cost: $10,400 ÷ 1,000 units = $10.40
Inventory, Dec. 31: 300 units at $10.40 = $3,120

Deducting the inventory of $3,120 from the $10,400 of merchandise available for sale yields $7,280 (700 units × $10.40) as the cost of merchandise sold.

Comparing Inventory Costing Methods

Objective 5
Compare the use of the three inventory costing methods.

A different cost flow is assumed for each of the three alternative methods of costing inventories. You should note that if the cost of units had remained stable, all three methods would have yielded the same results. Since prices do change, however, the three methods will normally yield different amounts for (1) the ending inventory, (2) the cost of the merchandise sold for the period, and (3) the gross profit (and net income) for the period. Using the preceding examples for the periodic inventory system and assuming that net sales were $15,000, the following partial income statements indicate the effects of each method when prices are rising:[2]

[2] Similar results would also occur when comparing inventory costing methods under a perpetual inventory system.

	First-In, First-Out		Average Cost		Last-In, First-Out	
Net sales		$15,000		$15,000		$15,000
Cost of merchandise sold:						
Beginning inventory	$ 1,800		$ 1,800		$ 1,800	
Purchases	8,600		8,600		8,600	
Merchandise available for sale	$10,400		$10,400		$10,400	
Less ending inventory	3,400		3,120		2,800	
Cost of merchandise sold		7,000		7,280		7,600
Gross profit		$ 8,000		$ 7,720		$ 7,400

As shown in the income statements, the fifo method yielded the lowest amount for the cost of merchandise sold and the highest amount for gross profit (and net income). It also yielded the highest amount for the ending inventory. On the other hand, the lifo method yielded the highest amount for the cost of merchandise sold, the lowest amount for gross profit (and net income), and the lowest amount for ending inventory. The average cost method yielded results that were between those of fifo and lifo.

USE OF THE FIRST-IN, FIRST-OUT METHOD

When the fifo method is used, as we discussed earlier, the costs of the units sold are assumed to be in the order in which they were incurred. During a period of inflation or rising prices, the earlier unit costs are lower than the more recent unit costs, as shown in the preceding fifo example. Much of the benefit of the larger amount of gross profit is lost, however, because the inventory must be replaced at ever higher prices. When the rate of inflation reaches double digits, as it did during the 1970s, the larger gross profits that result from the fifo method are often called *inventory profits* or *illusory profits*.

You should note that in a period of deflation or declining prices, this effect is just the opposite. The fifo method, compared to the other methods, yields the lowest amount of gross profit. A major criticism of the fifo method is its tendency to pass through the effects of inflationary and deflationary trends to gross profit. An advantage of the fifo method, however, is that the balance sheet will report the ending merchandise inventory at an amount that is about the same as its current replacement cost.

USE OF THE LAST-IN, FIRST-OUT METHOD

When the lifo method is used during a period of inflation or rising prices, the results are opposite those of the other two methods. As shown in the preceding example, the lifo method will yield a lower amount of inventory at the end of the period, a higher amount of cost of merchandise sold, and a lower amount of gross profit than the other two methods. The reason for these effects is that the cost of the most recently acquired units most nearly approximates the cost of their replacement. In a period of inflation, the more recent unit costs are higher than the earlier unit costs. Thus, it can be argued that the lifo method more nearly matches current costs with current revenues. This latter point was one reason that Chrysler Corporation changed from the fifo method to the lifo method, as stated in the following footnote that accompanied Chrysler's financial statements:

Chrysler changed its method of accounting from first-in, first-out (fifo) to last-in, first-out (lifo) for substantially all of its domestic productive inventories. The change to lifo was made to more accurately match current costs with current revenues.

During periods of rising prices, using lifo offers an income tax savings. The income tax savings results because lifo reports the lowest amount of net income of the three methods. During the double-digit inflationary period of the 1970s, many businesses changed from fifo to lifo to take advantage of tax savings.

At Walgreen's, inventories are valued using the LIFO costing method.

Again, you should note that in a period of deflation or falling price levels, this effect is just the opposite. The lifo method yields the highest amount of gross profit. The major argument for using lifo is its tendency to minimize the effect of price trends on gross profit. A criticism of using lifo, however, is that the ending merchandise inventory on the balance sheet may be quite different from its current replacement cost. In such cases, however, the financial statements normally include a note that states the estimated difference between the lifo inventory and the inventory if fifo had been used. An example of such a note accompanied the 1994 statements of The Walgreen Co., as shown.

Inventories are valued on a . . . last-in, first-out (LIFO) cost . . . basis. At August 31, 1994 and 1993, inventories would have been greater by $393,568,000 and $388,464,000 respectively, if they had been valued on a . . . first-in, first-out (FIFO) cost . . . basis.

USE OF THE AVERAGE COST METHOD

As you might assume, the average cost method of inventory costing is, in a sense, a compromise between fifo and lifo. The effect of price trends is averaged in determining the cost of merchandise sold and the ending inventory. For a series of purchases, the average cost will be the same, regardless of the direction of price trends. For example, a complete reversal of the sequence of unit costs presented in the preceding illustration would not affect the reported cost of merchandise sold, gross profit, or ending inventory.

SELECTION OF AN INVENTORY COSTING METHOD

The preceding comparisons show the importance attached to the selection of the inventory costing method. Often enterprises apply one method to one class of inventory and a different method to another class. For example, a computer retailer might use the fifo method for its microcomputer inventory and the lifo method for software and other inventory. The method(s) used may also be changed for a valid reason. The effect of any change in method and the reason for the change should be disclosed in the financial statements for the period in which the change occurred.

Valuation of Inventory at Other Than Cost

Objective 6
Compute the proper valuation of inventory at other than cost, using the lower-of-cost-or-market and net realizable value concepts.

As we discussed earlier in the chapter, cost is the primary basis for evaluating inventories. In some cases, however, inventory is valued at other than cost. Two such cases arise when (1) the cost of replacing items in inventory is below the recorded cost and (2) the inventory is not salable at normal sales prices. This latter case may be due to imperfections, shop wear, style changes, or other causes.

VALUATION AT LOWER OF COST OR MARKET

If the cost of replacing an item in inventory is lower than the original purchase cost, the lower-of-cost-or-market method is used to value the inventory. *Market*, as used in the phrase *lower of cost or market*, is the cost to replace the merchandise on the inventory date. This market value is based on quantities normally purchased from the usual source of supply. In businesses where inflation is the norm, market prices rarely decline. In businesses where technological improvements are the norm (e.g., video recorders), market declines are not uncommon.

The lower-of-cost-or-market method provides two advantages. First, the gross profit (and net income) is reduced in the period in which the decline occurred. Second, an approximately normal gross profit will be realized during the period in which the item is later sold.

To illustrate, assume that merchandise with a unit cost of $70 has sold at $100 during the period, yielding a gross profit of $30 a unit, or 30% of sales. Assume also that at the end of the year, there is a single unit in the inventory and that its replacement cost has declined to $63. In such a case, it would be expected that the selling price would also decline, if it has not already done so. Assuming a reduction in the selling price to $90, the gross profit based on the replacement cost of $63 would be $27, which is also 30% of the selling price.

The valuation of the unit in the inventory at $63 reduces gross profit of the prior period by $7 and permits a normal gross profit of $27 to be realized on its sale in the following period. If the unit had been valued at its original cost of $70, the gross profit determined for the past year would have been $7 greater. Likewise, the gross profit for the sale of the item in the following period would have been $7 less.

To apply the lower-of-cost-or-market method, the cost and the replacement cost can be determined for (1) each item in the inventory, (2) major classes or categories, or (3) the inventory as a whole. In practice, the cost and replacement cost of each item are usually determined. To illustrate, assume that there are 400 identical units of Commodity A in the inventory, each acquired at a unit cost of $10.25. If at the inventory date the item would cost $10.50 to replace, the cost price of $10.25 would be multiplied by 400 to determine the inventory value. On the other hand, if the item could be replaced at $9.50 a unit, the replacement cost of $9.50 would be used for valuation purposes. The table in Exhibit 6 illustrates the most common method of organizing inventory data and applying the lower-of-cost-or-market method to each inventory item.

Exhibit 6
Determining Inventory at Lower of Cost or Market

Commodity	*Inventory Quantity*	*Unit Cost Price*	*Unit Market Price*	*Total*		
				Cost	*Market*	*Lower of C or M*
A	400	$10.25	$ 9.50	$ 4,100	$ 3,800	$ 3,800
B	120	22.50	24.10	2,700	2,892	2,700
C	600	8.00	7.75	4,800	4,650	4,650
D	280	14.00	14.75	3,920	4,130	3,920
Total				$15,520	$15,472	$15,070

Although accumulating the data for total cost is not necessary, as shown in Exhibit 6, it provides management with the amount of the reduction in inventory value caused by the decline in market prices. The amount of the market decline, $450 ($15,520 – $15,070), may be reported as a separate item on the income statement. Otherwise, the market decline will be included in the cost of merchandise sold. Regardless, net income will be reduced by the amount of the market decline.

VALUATION AT NET REALIZABLE VALUE

As you would probably expect, obsolete, spoiled, or damaged merchandise and other merchandise that can be sold only at prices below cost should be written down. Such merchandise should be valued at net realizable value. **Net realizable value** is the estimated selling price less any direct cost of disposal, such as sales commissions. For example, assume that damaged merchandise costing $1,000 can be sold for only $800, and direct selling expenses are estimated to be $150. This inventory should be valued at $650 ($800 – $150), which is its net realizable value.

Presentation of Merchandise Inventory on the Balance Sheet

Objective 7
Prepare a balance sheet presentation of merchandise inventory.

As we discussed in an earlier chapter, merchandise inventory is usually presented in the Current Assets section of the balance sheet, following receivables. Both the method of determining the cost of the inventory (fifo, lifo, or average) and the method of valuing the inventory (cost or the lower of cost or market) should be shown. These details may be disclosed in parentheses on the balance sheet or in a footnote to the financial statements. Exhibit 7 shows how parentheses may be used.

Exhibit 7
Merchandise Inventory on the Balance Sheet

Afro-Arts
Balance Sheet
December 31, 1998

Assets		
Current assets:		
Cash		$ 19 4 0 0 00
Accounts receivable	$80 0 0 0 00	
Less allowance for doubtful accounts	3 0 0 0 00	77 0 0 0 00
Merchandise inventory—at lower of cost (first-in, first-out method) or market		216 3 0 0 00

As we noted previously, it is not unusual for large businesses with varied activities to use different costing methods for different segments of their inventories. The following note taken from the financial statements of Sears illustrates how this information may be disclosed:

Inventories of domestic operations are valued primarily at the lower of cost (using the last-in, first-out or LIFO method) or market . . . Inventories of international operations, Western Auto and Puerto Rico, which represent approximately 19% of inventories, are stated at the lower of cost (using the first-in, first-out or FIFO basis) or market.

Estimating Inventory Cost

Objective 8
Estimate the cost of inventory, using the retail method and the gross profit method.

In practice, it may be necessary to know the amount of inventory when perpetual inventory records are not maintained and it is impractical to take a physical inventory. For example, a business that uses a periodic inventory system may need monthly income statements, but taking a physical inventory each month may be too costly. Moreover, when a disaster such as a fire has destroyed the inventory, the amount of the loss must be determined. In this case, taking a physical inventory is impossible, and even if perpetual inventory records have been kept, these records may also have been destroyed. In such cases, the inventory cost can be estimated by using (1) the retail method or (2) the gross profit method.

RETAIL METHOD OF INVENTORY COSTING

When a disaster such as a fire has destroyed the inventory, its cost can be estimated using either the retail or the gross profit method.

The retail inventory method of estimating inventory cost is based on the relationship of the cost of merchandise available for sale to the retail price of the same merchandise. To use this method, the retail prices of all merchandise acquired are accumulated. Next, the inventory at retail is determined by deducting sales for the period from the retail price of the goods that were available for sale during the period. The estimated inventory cost is then calculated by multiplying the inventory at retail by the ratio of cost to selling (retail) price for the merchandise available for sale, as we illustrate in Exhibit 8.

When the inventory is estimated as the percent of cost to selling price, we assume that the *mix* of the items in the ending inventory is the same as the entire stock of merchandise available for sale. In Exhibit 8, for example, it is unlikely that the retail price of every item comprised exactly 62% cost and 38% gross profit. We assume, however, that the weighted average of the cost percentages of the merchandise in the inventory ($30,000) is the same as in the merchandise available for sale ($100,000). When the inventory is made up of different classes of merchandise with very different gross profit rates, the cost percentages and the inventory should be developed for each class of inventory.

One of the major advantages of the retail method is that it provides inventory figures for use in preparing monthly or quarterly statements when the periodic system is used. Department stores and similar merchandisers like to determine gross profit and operating income each month but take a physical inventory only once a year. In addition, comparing the estimated ending inventory with the physical ending inventory, both at retail prices, will help identify inventory shortages resulting from shoplifting and other causes. Management can then take appropriate actions.

The retail method may also be used to facilitate taking a physical inventory at the end of the year. In this case, the items counted are recorded on the inventory sheets at their retail (selling) prices instead of their cost prices. The physical inventory at selling price is then converted to cost by applying the ratio of cost to selling (retail) price for the merchandise available for sale.

To illustrate, assume that the data in Exhibit 8 are for an entire fiscal year rather than for only January. If the physical inventory taken at the end of the year totaled $29,000, priced at retail, this amount rather than the $30,000 would be converted to cost. Thus, the inventory at cost would be $17,980 ($29,000 × 62%) instead of $18,600 ($30,000 × 62%). The $17,980 would be used for the year-end financial statements and for income tax purposes.

Exhibit 8
Determining Inventory by the Retail Method

	Cost	*Retail*
Merchandise inventory, January 1	$ 19,400	$ 36,000
Purchases in January (net)	42,600	64,000
Merchandise available for sale	$ 62,000	$100,000

Ratio of cost to retail price: $\frac{\$\ 62{,}000}{\$100{,}000} = 62\%$

Sales for January (net)		70,000
Merchandise inventory, January 31, at retail		$ 30,000
Merchandise inventory, January 31, at estimated cost ($30,000 × 62%)		$ 18,600

GROSS PROFIT METHOD OF ESTIMATING INVENTORIES

The gross profit method uses the gross profit estimated for the period to estimate the inventory at the end of the period. The gross profit is usually estimated from the actual rate for the preceding year, adjusted for any changes made in the cost and sales prices during the current period. By using the gross profit rate, the dollar amount of sales for a period can be divided into its two components: (1) gross profit and (2) cost of merchandise sold. The latter amount may then be deducted from the cost of merchandise available for sale to yield the estimated cost of merchandise on hand.

Exhibit 9 illustrates the gross profit method for estimating a company's inventory on January 31. In this example, the inventory on January 1 is assumed to be $57,000, the net purchases during the month are $180,000, and the net sales during the month are $250,000. In addition, the historical gross profit was 30% of net sales.

Exhibit 9
Estimating Inventory by Gross Profit Method

Merchandise inventory, January 1		$ 57,000
Purchases in January (net)		180,000
Merchandise available for sale		$237,000
Sales in January (net)	$250,000	
Less estimated gross profit ($250,000 × 30%)	75,000	
Estimated cost of merchandise sold		175,000
Estimated merchandise inventory, January 31		$ 62,000

The gross profit method is useful for estimating inventories for monthly or quarterly financial statements in a periodic inventory system. It is also useful in estimating the cost of merchandise destroyed by fire or other disaster.

KEY POINTS

Objective 1. Summarize and provide examples of internal control procedures that apply to inventories.

Internal control procedures for inventories include those developed to protect the inventories from damage, employee theft, and customer theft. In addition, a physical inventory count should be taken periodically to detect shortages as well as to deter employee thefts.

Objective 2. List the procedures for determining the actual quantities in inventory.

The first step in "taking" a physical inventory is to count the merchandise on hand. Count teams are often made up of two persons—one who counts and the other who records the quantities and descriptions on inventory count sheets. Care must be used to include all merchandise in transit that is owned. Consigned merchandise should not be included in the consignee's inventory.

Any errors in reporting inventory based upon the physical inventory will misstate the ending inventory, current assets, total assets, and owner's equity on the balance sheet. In addition, the cost of goods sold, gross profit, and net income will be misstated on the income statement.

Objective 3. Compute the cost of inventory under the perpetual inventory system, using the following costing methods:

First-in, first-out
Last-in, first-out
Average cost

In a perpetual inventory system, the number of units and the cost of each type of merchandise are recorded in a subsidiary inventory ledger, with a separate account for each type of merchandise. Inventory costs and the amounts charged against revenue are illustrated using the fifo and lifo methods.

Objective 4. Compute the cost of inventory under the periodic inventory system, using the following costing methods:

First-in, first-out
Last-in, first-out
Average cost

In a periodic inventory system, a physical inventory is taken to determine the cost of the inventory and the cost of merchandise sold. Inventory costs and the amounts charged against revenue are illustrated using fifo, lifo, and average cost methods.

Objective 5. Compare the use of the three inventory costing methods.
The three inventory costing methods will normally yield different amounts for (1) the ending inventory, (2) the cost of the merchandise sold for the period, and (3) the gross profit (and net income) for the period. During periods of inflation, the fifo method yields the lowest amount for the cost of merchandise sold, the highest amount for gross profit (and net income), and the highest amount for the ending inventory. The lifo method yields the opposite results. During periods of deflation, the preceding effects are reversed. The average cost method yields results that are between those of fifo and lifo.

Objective 6. Compute the proper valuation of inventory at other than cost, using the lower-of-cost-or-market and net realizable value concepts.
If the market price of an item of inventory is lower than its cost, the lower market price is used to compute the value of the item. Market price is the cost to replace the merchandise on the inventory date. It is possible to apply the lower of cost or market to each item in the inventory, to major classes or categories, or to the inventory as a whole.

Merchandise that can be sold only at prices below cost should be valued at net realizable value, which is the estimated selling price less any direct cost of disposal.

Objective 7. Prepare a balance sheet presentation of merchandise inventory.
Merchandise inventory is usually presented in the Current Assets section of the balance sheet, following receivables. Both the method of determining the cost of the inventory (fifo, lifo, or average) and the method of valuing the inventory (cost or the lower of cost or market) should be shown.

Objective 8. Estimate the cost of inventory, using the retail method and the gross profit method.
In using the retail method to estimate inventory, the retail prices of all merchandise acquired are accumulated. The inventory at retail is determined by deducting sales for the period from the retail price of the goods that were available for sale during the period. The inventory at retail is then converted to cost on the basis of the ratio of cost to selling (retail) price for the merchandise available for sale.

In using the gross profit method to estimate inventory, the estimated gross profit is deducted from the sales to determine the estimated cost of merchandise sold. This amount is then deducted from the cost of merchandise available for sale to determine the estimated ending inventory.

GLOSSARY OF KEY TERMS

Average cost method. The method of inventory costing that is based on the assumption that costs should be charged against revenue in accordance with the weighted average unit costs of the items sold. *Objective 3*

First-in, first-out (fifo) method. A method of inventory costing based on the assumption that the costs of merchandise sold should be charged against revenue in the order in which the costs were incurred. *Objective 3*

Gross profit method. A means of estimating inventory based on the relationship of gross profit to sales. *Objective 8*

Last-in, first-out (lifo) method. A method of inventory costing based on the assumption that the most recent merchandise costs incurred should be charged against revenue. *Objective 3*

Lower-of-cost-or-market method. A method of valuing inventory that reports the inventory at the lower of its cost or current market value (replacement cost). *Objective 6*

Net realizable value. The amount at which merchandise that can be sold only at prices below cost should be valued; it is determined as the estimated selling price less any direct cost of disposal. *Objective 6*

Physical inventory. The detailed listing of merchandise on hand. *Objective 1*

Retail inventory method. A means of estimating inventory based on the relationship of the cost and the retail price of merchandise. *Objective 8*

ILLUSTRATIVE PROBLEM

Stewart Co.'s beginning inventory and purchases during the year ended December 31, 1998, were as follows:

		Units	*Unit Cost*	*Total Cost*
January 1	Inventory	1,000	$50.00	$ 50,000
March 10	Purchase	1,200	52.50	63,000
June 25	Sold 800 units			
August 30	Purchase	800	55.00	44,000
October 5	Sold 1,500 units			
November 26	Purchase	2,000	56.00	112,000
December 31	Sold 1,000 units			
Total		5,000		$269,000

Instructions

1. Determine the cost of inventory on December 31, 1998, using the perpetual inventory system and each of the following inventory costing methods:
   a. first-in, first-out
   b. last-in, first-out
2. Determine the cost of inventory on December 31, 1998, using the periodic inventory system and each of the following inventory costing methods:
   a. first-in, first-out
   b. last-in, first-out
   c. average cost
3. Assume that during the fiscal year ended December 31, 1998, sales were $290,000 and the estimated gross profit rate was 40%. Estimate the ending inventory at December 31, 1998, using the gross profit method.

Solution

1. a. First-in, first-out method: $95,200

Date	*Purchases*			*Cost of Merchandise Sold*			*Inventory*		
	Quantity	*Unit Cost*	*Total Cost*	*Quantity*	*Unit Cost*	*Total Cost*	*Quantity*	*Unit Cost*	*Total Cost*
Jan. 1							1,000	50	50,000
Mar. 10	1,200	52.50	63,000				1,000	50	50,000
							1,200	52.50	63,000
June 25				800	50	40,000	200	50	10,000
							1,200	52.50	63,000
Aug. 30	800	55	44,000				200	50	10,000
							1,200	52.50	63,000
							800	55	44,000
Oct. 5				200	50	10,000	700	55	38,500
				1,200	52.50	63,000			
				100	55	5,500			
Nov. 26	2,000	56	112,000				700	55	38,500
							2,000	56	112,000
Dec. 31				700	55	38,500	1,700	56	95,200
				300	56	16,800			

b. Last-in, first-out method: $91,000 ($35,000 + $56,000)

Date	*Purchases*			*Cost of Merchandise Sold*			*Inventory*		
	Quantity	*Unit Cost*	*Total Cost*	*Quantity*	*Unit Cost*	*Total Cost*	*Quantity*	*Unit Cost*	*Total Cost*
Jan. 1							1,000	50	50,000
Mar. 10	1,200	52.50	63,000				1,000	50	50,000
							1,200	52.50	63,000
June 25				800	52.50	42,000	1,000	50	50,000
							400	52.50	21,000
Aug. 30	800	55	44,000				1,000	50	50,000
							400	52.50	21,000
							800	55	44,000
Oct. 5				800	55	44,000	700	50	35,000
				400	52.50	21,000			
				300	50	15,000			
Nov. 26	2,000	56	112,000				700	50	35,000
							2,000	56	112,000
Dec. 31				1,000	56	56,000	700	50	35,000
							1,000	56	56,000

2. a. First-in, first-out method:

1,700 units at $56 = $95,200

b. Last-in, first-out method:

1,000 units at $50	$ 50,000
700 units at $52.50	36,750
1,700 units	$ 86,750

c. Average cost method:

Average cost per unit:	$269,000 ÷ 5,000 units = $53.80
Inventory, December 31, 1998:	1,700 units at $53.80 = $ 91,460

3.

Merchandise inventory, January 1, 1998		$ 50,000
Purchases (net)		219,000
Merchandise available for sale		$269,000
Sales (net)	$290,000	
Less estimated gross profit ($290,000 × 40%)	116,000	
Estimated cost of merchandise sold		174,000
Estimated merchandise inventory, December 31, 1998		$ 95,000

SELF-EXAMINATION QUESTIONS (ANSWERS AT END OF CHAPTER)

1. If the inventory shrinkage at the end of the year is overstated by $7,500, the error will cause an:
   A. understatement of cost of merchandise sold for the year by $7,500.
   B. overstatement of gross profit for the year by $7,500.
   C. overstatement of merchandise inventory for the year by $7,500.
   D. understatement of net income for the year by $7,500.

2. The inventory costing method that is based on the assumption that costs should be charged against revenue in the order in which they were incurred is:
   A. fifo C. average cost
   B. lifo D. perpetual inventory

3. The following units of a particular item were purchased and sold during the period:

Beginning inventory	40 units at $20
First purchase	50 units at $21
Second purchase	50 units at $22
First sale	110 units
Third purchase	50 units at $23
Second sale	45 units

   What is the unit cost of the 35 units on hand at the end of the period as determined under the perpetual inventory system by the lifo costing method?
   A. $20 and $23 C. $20
   B. $20 and $21 D. $23

4. The following units of a particular item were available for sale during the period:

Beginning inventory	40 units at $20
First purchase	50 units at $21
Second purchase	50 units at $22
Third purchase	50 units at $23

   What is the unit cost of the 35 units on hand at the end of the period, as determined under the periodic inventory system by the fifo costing method?
   A. $20 C. $22
   B. $21 D. $23

5. If merchandise inventory is being valued at cost and the price level is steadily rising, the method of costing that will yield the highest net income is:
   A. lifo C. average
   B. fifo D. periodic

DISCUSSION QUESTIONS

1. What security measures may be used by retailers to protect merchandise inventory from customer theft?
2. Which inventory system provides the more effective means of controlling inventories (perpetual or periodic)? Why?
3. Before inventory purchases are recorded, the receiving report should be reconciled to what documents?
4. What document should be presented by an employee requesting inventory items to be released from the company's warehouse?

5. Why is it important to periodically take a physical inventory if the perpetual system is used?
6. The inventory shrinkage at the end of the year was understated by $10,000. (a) Did the error cause an overstatement or an understatement of the gross profit for the year? (b) Which items on the balance sheet at the end of the year were overstated or understated as a result of the error?
7. When does title to merchandise pass from the seller to the buyer if the terms of shipment are (a) FOB shipping point, (b) FOB destination?
8. Bradley Co. sold merchandise to Midland Company on December 31, FOB shipping point. If the merchandise is in transit on December 31, the end of the fiscal year, which company would report it in its financial statements? Explain.
9. A manufacturer shipped merchandise to a retailer on a consignment basis. If the merchandise is unsold at the end of the period, in whose inventory should the merchandise be included?
10. What are the two most widely used inventory costing methods?
11. Which of the three methods of inventory costing—fifo, lifo, or average cost—is based on the assumption that costs should be charged against revenue in the reverse order in which they were incurred?
12. Do the terms *fifo* and *lifo* refer to techniques used in determining quantities of the various classes of merchandise on hand? Explain.
13. Does the term *last-in* in the lifo method mean that the items in the inventory are assumed to be the most recent (last) acquisitions? Explain.
14. Under which method of cost flow are (a) the earliest costs assigned to inventory, (b) the most recent costs assigned to inventory, (c) average costs assigned to inventory?
15. If merchandise inventory is being valued at cost and the price level is steadily rising, which of the three methods of costing—fifo, lifo, or average cost—will yield (a) the highest inventory cost, (b) the lowest inventory cost, (c) the highest gross profit, (d) the lowest gross profit?
16. Which of the three methods of inventory costing—fifo, lifo, or average cost—will in general yield an inventory cost most nearly approximating current replacement cost?
17. If inventory is being valued at cost and the price level is steadily rising, which of the three methods of costing—fifo, lifo, or average cost—will yield the lowest annual income tax expense? Explain.
18. Can a company change its method of costing inventory? Explain.
19. In the phrase *lower of cost or market*, what is meant by *market?*
20. The cost of a particular inventory item is $410, the current replacement cost is $400, and the selling price is $525. At what amount should the item be included in the inventory according to the lower-of-cost-or-market basis?
21. Because of imperfections, an item of merchandise cannot be sold at its normal selling price. How should this item be valued for financial statement purposes?
22. How is the method of determining the cost of the inventory and the method of valuing it disclosed in the financial statements?
23. What uses can be made of the estimate of the cost of inventory determined by the gross profit method?

EXERCISES

EXERCISE 9–1
Internal control of inventories
Objective 1

Easy-Does-It Hardware Store currently uses a periodic inventory system. Phil Strand, the owner, is considering the purchase of a computer system that would make it feasible to switch to a perpetual inventory system.

Phil is unhappy with the periodic inventory system because it does not provide timely information on inventory levels. Phil has noticed on several occasions that the store runs out of good-selling items, while too many poor-selling items are on hand.

Phil is also concerned about lost sales while a physical inventory is being taken. Easy-Does-It Hardware currently takes a physical inventory twice a year. To minimize distractions, the store is closed on the day inventory is taken. Phil believes closing the store is the only way to get an accurate inventory count.

Will switching to a perpetual inventory system strengthen Easy-Does-It Hardware's control over inventory items? Will switching to a perpetual inventory system eliminate the need for a physical inventory count? Explain.

EXERCISE 9–2
Internal control of inventories
Objective 1

Jamaica Luggage Shop is a small retail establishment located in a large shopping mall. This shop has implemented the following procedures regarding inventory items:

a. Since the shop carries mostly high-quality, designer luggage, all inventory items are tagged with a control device that activates an alarm if a tagged item is removed from the store.
b. Since the display area of the store is limited, only a sample of each piece of luggage is kept on the selling floor. Whenever a customer selects a piece of luggage, the sales clerk gets the appropriate piece from the store's stockroom. Since all sales clerks need access to the stockroom, it is not locked. The stockroom is adjacent to the break room used by all mall employees.
c. Whenever Jamaica receives a shipment of new inventory, the items are taken directly to the stockroom. Jamaica's accountant uses the vendor's invoice to record the amount of inventory received.

State whether each of these procedures is appropriate or inappropriate, considering the principles of internal control. If it is inappropriate, state which internal control procedure is violated.

EXERCISE 9–3
Identifying items to be included in inventory
Objective 2

Ednia Co., which is located in Fridley, Minnesota, has identified the following items for possible inclusion in its December 31, 1996 year-end inventory.

a. Ednia has segregated $15,800 of merchandise ordered by one of its customers for shipment on January 3, 1997.
b. Ednia has in its warehouse $21,000 of merchandise on consignment from Minnetonka Co.
c. Merchandise Ednia shipped FOB shipping point on December 31, 1996, was picked up by the freight company at 11:50 p.m.
d. Merchandise Ednia shipped to a customer FOB shipping point was picked up by the freight company on December 26, 1996, but had still not arrived at its destination as of December 31, 1996.
e. Ednia has $35,000 of merchandise on hand, which was sold to customers earlier in the year, but which has been returned by customers to Ednia for various warranty repairs.
f. Ednia has sent $100,000 of merchandise to various retailers on a consignment basis.
g. On December 21, 1996, Ednia ordered $85,000 of merchandise, FOB Fridley. The merchandise was shipped from the supplier on December 28, 1996, but had not been received by December 31, 1996.
h. On December 27, 1996, Ednia ordered $15,000 of merchandise from a supplier in Chicago. The merchandise was shipped FOB Chicago on December 30, 1996, but had not been received by December 31, 1996.
i. On December 31, 1996, Ednia received $28,000 of merchandise that had been returned by customers because the wrong merchandise had been shipped. The replacement order is to be shipped overnight on January 3, 1997.

Indicate which items should be included (I) and which should be excluded (E) from the inventory.

EXERCISE 9–4
Effect of errors in physical inventory
Objective 2

The Rivers Edge sells canoes, kayaks, whitewater rafts, and other boating supplies. During the taking of its physical inventory on December 31, 1997, The Rivers Edge incorrectly counted its inventory as $72,500 instead of the correct amount of $98,300.

a. State the effect of the error on the December 31, 1997 balance sheet of The Rivers Edge.
b. State the effect of the error on the income statement of The Rivers Edge for the year ended December 31, 1997.

EXERCISE 9–5
Effect of errors in physical inventory
Objective 2

Curly's Motorcycle Shop sells motorcycles, jet skis, and other related supplies and accessories. During the taking of its physical inventory on December 31, 1997, Curly's Motorcycle Shop incorrectly counted its inventory as $112,800 instead of the correct amount of $96,900.

a. State the effect of the error on the December 31, 1997 balance sheet of Curly's Motorcycle Shop.
b. State the effect of the error on the income statement of Curly's Motorcycle Shop for the year ended December 31, 1997.

EXERCISE 9–6
Error in inventory shrinkage
Objective 2

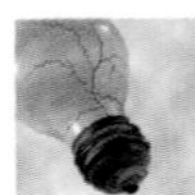

During 1997, it was discovered that the inventory shrinkage at the end of 1996 had been overstated by $60,000. Instead of correcting the error, the accountant decided to understate the inventory shrinkage of 1997 by $60,000. The accountant reasoned that the error in 1996 would be balanced out by the error in 1997.

Are there any flaws in the accountant's reasoning? Explain.

EXERCISE 9–7
Perpetual inventory using fifo
Objective 3

Beginning inventory, purchases, and sales data for Commodity TC19 are as follows:

Mar. 1	Inventory	20 units at $40
7	Sale	15 units
12	Purchase	18 units at $42
20	Sale	12 units
22	Sale	3 units
30	Purchase	10 units at $45

The business maintains a perpetual inventory system, costing by the first-in, first-out method. Determine the cost of the merchandise sold for each sale and the inventory balance after each sale, presenting the data in the form illustrated in Exhibit 2.

EXERCISE 9–8
Perpetual inventory using lifo
Objective 3

Assume that the business in Exercise 9–7 maintains a perpetual inventory system, costing by the last-in, first-out method. Determine the cost of merchandise sold for each sale and the inventory balance after each sale, presenting the data in the form illustrated in Exhibit 3.

EXERCISE 9–9
Perpetual inventory using lifo
Objective 3

Beginning inventory, purchases, and sales data for Commodity M343 for October are as follows:

Inventory:		*Purchases:*		*Sales:*	
Oct. 1	40 units at $15	Oct. 8	10 units at $18	Oct. 11	9 units
		21	15 units at $20	17	25 units
				29	12 units

Assuming that the perpetual inventory system is used, costing by the lifo method, determine the cost of the inventory balance at October 31, presenting data in the form illustrated in Exhibit 3.

EXERCISE 9–10
Perpetual inventory using fifo
Objective 3

Assume that the business in Exercise 9–9 maintains a perpetual inventory system, costing by the first-in, first-out method. Determine the cost of merchandise sold for each sale and the inventory balance after each sale, presenting the data in the form illustrated in Exhibit 2.

EXERCISE 9–11
Fifo, lifo costs under perpetual inventory system
Objective 3

The following units of a particular item were available for sale during the year:

Beginning inventory	20 units at $50
Sale	15 units at $90
First purchase	30 units at $54
Sale	25 units at $93
Second purchase	40 units at $65
Sale	35 units at $98

The firm uses the perpetual system, and there are 15 units of the item on hand at the end of the year. What is the total cost of the ending inventory according to (a) fifo, (b) lifo?

EXERCISE 9–12
Periodic inventory by three methods
Objective 4

The units of an item available for sale during the year were as follows:

Jan. 1	Inventory	35 units at $25
Mar. 4	Purchase	10 units at $24
Aug. 20	Purchase	30 units at $28
Nov. 30	Purchase	25 units at $30

There are 45 units of the item in the physical inventory at December 31. The periodic inventory system is used. Determine the inventory cost by (a) the first-in, first-out method, (b) the last-in, first-out method, and (c) the average cost method.

EXERCISE 9–13
Periodic inventory by three methods; cost of merchandise sold
Objective 4

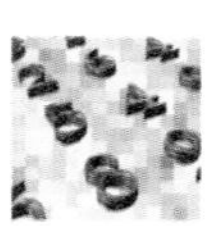

The units of an item available for sale during the year were as follows:

Jan. 1	Inventory	25 units at $60
Feb. 4	Purchase	10 units at $62
July 7	Purchase	30 units at $65
Oct. 15	Purchase	15 units at $70

There are 30 units of the item in the physical inventory at December 31. The periodic inventory system is used. Determine the inventory cost and the cost of merchandise sold by three methods, presenting your answers in the following form:

	Cost	
Inventory Method	*Merchandise Inventory*	*Merchandise Sold*
a. First-in, first-out	$	$
b. Last-in, first-out		
c. Average cost		

EXERCISE 9–14
Lower-of-cost-or-market inventory
Objective 6

On the basis of the following data, determine the value of the inventory at the lower of cost or market. Assemble the data in the form illustrated in Exhibit 6.

Commodity	*Inventory Quantity*	*Unit Cost Price*	*Unit Market Price*
4HU	5	$300	$320
153T	17	110	115
Z10	12	275	260
CW2	30	51	45
SAW1	20	95	100

EXERCISE 9–15
Merchandise inventory on the balance sheet
Objective 7

Based on the data in Exercise 9–14 and assuming that cost was determined by the fifo method, show how the merchandise inventory would appear on the balance sheet.

EXERCISE 9–16
Retail method inventory
Objective 8

A business using the retail method of inventory costing determines that merchandise inventory at retail is $500,000. If the ratio of cost to retail price is 65%, what is the amount of inventory to be reported on the financial statements?

EXERCISE 9–17
Retail inventory method
Objective 8

On the basis of the following data, estimate the cost of the merchandise inventory at April 30 by the retail method:

		Cost	*Retail*
April 1	Merchandise inventory	$444,500	$ 670,500
April 1–30	Purchases (net)	608,500	949,500
April 1–30	Sales (net)		1,140,000

EXERCISE 9–18
Gross profit inventory method
Objective 8

The merchandise inventory was destroyed by fire on July 20. The following data were obtained from the accounting records:

Jan. 1	Merchandise inventory	$ 172,250
Jan. 1–July 20	Purchases (net)	812,250
	Sales (net)	1,080,000
	Estimated gross profit rate	35%

a. Estimate the cost of the merchandise destroyed.
b. Briefly describe the situations in which the gross profit method is useful.

PROBLEMS SERIES A

PROBLEM 9–1A
Fifo perpetual inventory
Objective 3

The beginning inventory of C109 at Red Eye Co. and data on purchases and sales for a three-month period are as follows:

Date	*Transaction*	*Number of Units*	*Per Unit*	*Total*
July 1	Inventory	20,000	$6.10	$122,000
8	Purchase	75,000	6.15	461,250
20	Sale	40,000	7.00	280,000
31	Sale	35,000	7.00	245,000
Aug. 8	Sale	5,000	7.10	35,500
10	Purchase	50,000	6.20	310,000
27	Sale	40,000	7.20	288,000
30	Sale	20,000	7.15	143,000
Sept. 5	Purchase	70,000	6.05	423,500
13	Sale	40,000	7.00	280,000
22	Purchase	30,000	6.00	180,000
30	Sale	55,000	7.00	385,000

Instructions

1. Record the inventory, purchases, and cost of merchandise sold data in a perpetual inventory record similar to the one illustrated in Exhibit 2, using the first-in, first-out method.
2. Determine the total sales and the total cost of C109 sold for the period. Journalize the entries in the sales and cost of merchandise sold accounts. Assume that all sales were on account.
3. Determine the gross profit from sales for the period.

PROBLEM 9–2A
Lifo perpetual inventory
Objective 3

The beginning inventory of C109 at Red Eye Co. and data on purchases and sales for a three-month period are shown in Problem 9–1A.

Instructions

1. Record the inventory, purchases, and cost of merchandise sold data in a perpetual inventory record similar to the one illustrated in Exhibit 3, using the last-in, first-out method.
2. Determine the total sales, the total cost of units sold, and the gross profit from sales for the period.

PROBLEM 9–3A
Periodic inventory by three methods
Objective 4

Color-Tron Television uses the periodic inventory system. Details regarding the inventory of television sets at July 1, 1996, purchases invoices during the year, and the inventory count at June 30, 1997, are summarized as follows:

Model	Inventory, July 1	Purchases Invoices 1st	2nd	3rd	Inventory Count, June 30
A37	6 at $240	4 at $250	8 at $260	10 at $262	12
E15	6 at 80	5 at 82	8 at 89	8 at 90	10
L10	2 at 108	2 at 110	3 at 128	3 at 130	3
O18	8 at 88	4 at 79	3 at 85	6 at 92	8
K72	2 at 250	2 at 260	4 at 271	4 at 272	4
S91	5 at 160	4 at 170	4 at 175	7 at 180	8
V17	—	4 at 150	4 at 200	4 at 202	5

Instructions

1. Determine the cost of the inventory on June 30, 1997, by the first-in, first-out method. Present data in columnar form, using the following headings:

   Model *Quantity* *Unit Cost* *Total Cost*

   If the inventory of a particular model comprises one entire purchase plus a portion of another purchase acquired at a different unit cost, use a separate line for each purchase.
2. Determine the cost of the inventory on June 30, 1997, by the last-in, first-out method, following the procedures indicated in (1).
3. Determine the cost of the inventory on June 30, 1997, by the average cost method, using the columnar headings indicated in (1).
4. Discuss which method (fifo or lifo) would be preferred for income tax purposes in periods of (a) rising prices and (b) declining prices.

PROBLEM 9–4A
Lower-of-cost-or-market inventory
Objective 6

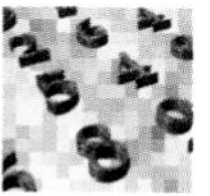

If the working papers correlating with this textbook are not used, omit Problem 9–4A.
Data on the physical inventory of Quatel Company as of December 31, the end of the current fiscal year, are presented in the working papers. The quantity of each commodity on hand has been determined and recorded on the inventory sheet. Unit market prices have also been determined as of December 31 and recorded on the sheet. The inventory is to be determined at cost and also at the lower of cost or market, using the first-in, first-out method. Quantity and cost data from the last purchases invoice of the year and the next-to-the-last purchases invoice are summarized as follows:

	Last Purchases Invoice		Next-to-the-Last Purchases Invoice	
Description	Quantity Purchased	Unit Cost	Quantity Purchased	Unit Cost
F71	20	$ 60	30	$ 58
C22	25	208	20	205
D82	10	145	25	142
E34	150	26	100	24
F17	10	560	10	570
J19	100	15	100	14
K41	10	387	5	384
M21	500	6	500	6
R72	80	17	50	18
T15	5	255	4	260
V55	700	9	500	9
AC2	100	47	50	46
BB7	5	420	5	424
BD1	100	20	75	19
DD1	60	18	40	17
EB2	50	29	25	28
FF7	75	27	60	25
GE4	5	708	5	712

Instructions

Record the appropriate unit costs on the inventory sheet, and complete the pricing of the inventory. When there are two different unit costs applicable to an item, proceed as follows:

1. Draw a line through the quantity, and insert the quantity and unit cost of the last purchase.
2. On the following line, insert the quantity and unit cost of the next-to-the-last purchase. The first item on the inventory sheet has been completed as an example.

PROBLEM 9–5A
Retail method; gross profit method
Objective 8

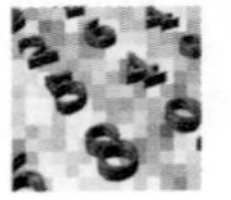

Selected data .on merchandise inventory, purchases, and sales for Cashin Co. and Apex Co. are as follows:

	Cost	*Retail*
Cashin Co.		
Merchandise inventory, August 1	$ 159,800	$270,000
Transactions during August:		
Purchases (net)	658,450	821,000
Sales		890,000
Sales returns and allowances		9,000
Apex Co.		
Merchandise inventory, April 1	$ 117,500	
Transactions during April and May:		
Purchases (net)	725,000	
Sales	1,212,000	
Sales returns and allowances	12,000	
Estimated gross profit rate	40%	

Instructions

1. Determine the estimated cost of the merchandise inventory of Cashin Co. on August 31 by the retail method, presenting details of the computations.
2. a. Estimate the cost of the merchandise inventory of Apex Co. on May 31 by the gross profit method, presenting details of the computations.
   b. Assume that Apex Co. took a physical inventory on May 31 and discovered that $118,000 of merchandise was on hand. What was the estimated loss of inventory due to theft or damage during April and May?

PROBLEMS SERIES B

PROBLEM 9–1B
Fifo perpetual inventory
Objective 3

The beginning inventory of Commodity F3C and data on purchases and sales for a three-month period are as follows:

Date	*Transaction*	*Number of Units*	*Per Unit*	*Total*
April 1	Inventory	10	$220	$2,200
7	Purchase	25	225	5,625
18	Sale	10	300	3,000
22	Sale	8	300	2,400
May 4	Purchase	15	230	3,450
10	Sale	10	310	3,100
21	Sale	5	310	1,550
31	Purchase	20	235	4,700
June 5	Sale	15	315	4,725
13	Sale	10	315	3,150
21	Purchase	15	240	3,600
28	Sale	11	320	3,520

Instructions

1. Record the inventory, purchases, and cost of merchandise sold data in a perpetual inventory record similar to the one illustrated in Exhibit 2, using the first-in, first-out method.
2. Determine the total sales and the total cost of Commodity F3C sold for the period. Journalize the entries in the sales and cost of merchandise sold accounts. Assume that all sales were on account.
3. Determine the gross profit from sales of Commodity F3C for the period.

PROBLEM 9–2B
Lifo perpetual inventory
Objective 3

The beginning inventory of Commodity F3C and data on purchases and sales for a three-month period are shown in Problem 9–1B.

Instructions

1. Record the inventory, purchases, and cost of merchandise sold data in a perpetual inventory record similar to the one illustrated in Exhibit 3, using the last-in, first-out method.
2. Determine the total sales, the total cost of Commodity F3C sold, and the gross profit from sales for the period.

PROBLEM 9–3B
Periodic inventory by three methods
Objective 4

Denny's Television uses the periodic inventory system. Details regarding the inventory of television sets at January 1, purchases invoices during the year, and the inventory count at December 31 are summarized as follows:

Model	*Inventory, January 1*	*Purchases Invoices*			*Inventory Count, December 31*
		1st	*2d*	*3d*	
B91	4 at $149	6 at $151	8 at $157	7 at $156	5
F10	3 at 208	3 at 212	5 at 213	4 at 225	3
H21	2 at 520	2 at 527	2 at 530	2 at 535	3
J39	6 at 520	8 at 531	4 at 549	6 at 542	8
P80	9 at 213	7 at 215	6 at 222	6 at 225	8
T15	6 at 305	3 at 310	3 at 316	4 at 317	5
V11	—	4 at 222	4 at 232	—	2

Instructions

1. Determine the cost of the inventory on December 31 by the first-in, first-out method. Present data in columnar form, using the following headings:

Model	*Quantity*	*Unit Cost*	*Total Cost*

   If the inventory of a particular model comprises one entire purchase plus a portion of another purchase acquired at a different unit cost, use a separate line for each purchase.
2. Determine the cost of the inventory on December 31 by the last-in, first-out method, following the procedures indicated in (1).
3. Determine the cost of the inventory on December 31 by the average cost method, using the columnar headings indicated in (1).
4. Discuss which method (fifo or lifo) would be preferred for income tax purposes in periods of (a) rising prices and (b) declining prices.

PROBLEM 9–4B
Lower-of-cost-or-market inventory
Objective 6

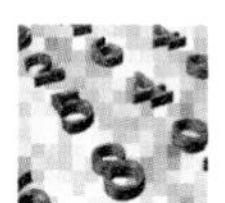

If the working papers correlating with this textbook are not used, omit Problem 9–4B.
Data on the physical inventory of Rozof Co. as of December 31, the end of the current fiscal year, are presented in the working papers. The quantity of each commodity on hand has been determined and recorded on the inventory sheet. Unit market prices have also been determined as of December 31 and recorded on the sheet. The inventory is to be determined at cost and also at the lower of cost or market, using the first-in, first-out method. Quantity and cost data from the last purchases invoice of the year and the next-to-the-last purchases invoice are summarized as follows:

	Last Purchases Invoice		*Next-to-the-Last Purchases Invoice*	
Description	*Quantity Purchased*	*Unit Cost*	*Quantity Purchased*	*Unit Cost*
F71	20	$ 60	40	$ 58
C22	25	190	15	190
D82	15	143	15	142
E34	150	25	100	27
F17	6	550	15	540
J19	75	14	100	13
K41	8	400	5	410
M21	500	6	500	7
R72	70	17	50	16
T15	5	250	4	260
V55	1,000	9	500	10
AC2	100	45	100	46
BB7	5	410	5	400
BD1	100	19	100	18
DD1	50	15	40	16
EB2	40	28	50	27
FF7	55	28	50	28
GE4	6	701	5	700

Instructions

Record the appropriate unit costs on the inventory sheet, and complete the pricing of the inventory. When there are two different unit costs applicable to an item, proceed as follows:

1. Draw a line through the quantity, and insert the quantity and unit cost of the last purchase.
2. On the following line, insert the quantity and unit cost of the next-to-the-last purchase. The first item on the inventory sheet has been completed as an example.

PROBLEM 9–5B
Retail method; gross profit method
Objective 8

Selected data on merchandise inventory, purchases, and sales for Adirondack Co. and Trailways Co. are as follows:

	Cost	*Retail*
Adirondack Co.		
Merchandise inventory, February 1	$ 177,100	$ 227,000
Transactions during February:		
Purchases (net)	986,300	1,435,000
Sales		1,460,000
Sales returns and allowances		43,000
Trailways Co.		
Merchandise inventory, July 1	$ 317,900	
Transactions during July and August:		
Purchases (net)	1,532,100	
Sales	2,330,000	
Sales returns and allowances	57,000	
Estimated gross profit rate	35%	

Instructions

1. Determine the estimated cost of the merchandise inventory of Adirondack Co. on February 28 by the retail method, presenting details of the computations.
2. a. Estimate the cost of the merchandise inventory of Trailways Co. on August 31 by the gross profit method, presenting details of the computations.
   b. Assume that Trailways Co. took a physical inventory on August 31 and discovered that $350,000 of merchandise was on hand. What was the estimated loss of inventory due to theft or damage during July and August?

CASES

CASE 9–1
Hanley Co.
Determining quantities in inventory

Hanley Co. is experiencing a decrease in sales and operating income for the fiscal year ending December 31, 1997. Jill Rizzoli, controller of Hanley Co., has suggested that all orders received before the end of the fiscal year be shipped by midnight, December 31, 1997, even if the shipping department must work overtime. Since Hanley Co. ships all merchandise FOB shipping point, it would record all such shipments as sales for the year ending December 31, 1997, thereby offsetting some of the decreases in sales and operating income.

Discuss whether Jill Rizzoli is behaving in an ethical manner.

CASE 9–2
Walgreen Co.
Fifo vs. lifo

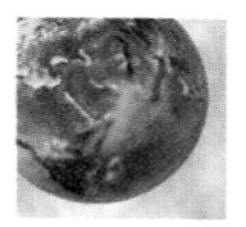

The following footnote was taken from the 1994 financial statements of Walgreen Co.:

Inventories are valued on a . . . last-in, first-out (LIFO) cost . . . basis. At August 31, 1994 and 1993, inventories would have been greater by $393,568,000 and $388,464,000 respectively, if they had been valued on a lower of first-in, first-out (FIFO) cost or market basis.

Additional data are as follows:

Earnings before income taxes, 1994	$ 458,421,000
Total lifo inventories, August 31, 1994	1,263,400,000

Based on the preceding data, determine (a) what the total inventories at August 31, 1994, would have been, using the fifo method, and (b) what the earnings before income taxes for the year ended August 31, 1994, would have been if fifo had been used instead of lifo.

CASE 9–3
Oakey Wholesale Co.
Lifo and inventory flow

The following is an excerpt from a conversation between Leo Kagle, the warehouse manager for Oakey Wholesale Co., and its accountant, Megan Goodman. Oakey Wholesale operates a large regional warehouse that supplies grocery stores in smaller communities with produce and other grocery products.

Leo: Megan, can you explain what's going on here with these monthly statements?

Megan: Sure, Leo. How can I help you?

Leo: I don't understand this last-in, first-out inventory procedure. It just doesn't make sense.

Megan: Well, what it means is that we assume that the last goods we receive are the first ones sold. So the inventory is made up of the items we purchased first.

Leo: Yes, but that's my problem. It doesn't work that way! We always distribute the oldest produce first. Some of that produce is perishable! We can't keep any of it very long or it'll spoil.

Megan: Leo, you don't understand. We only *assume* that the products we distribute are the last ones received. We don't actually have to distribute the goods in this way.

Leo: I always thought that accounting was supposed to show what really happened. It all sounds like "make believe" to me! Why not report what really happens?

Respond to Leo's concerns.

CASE 9–4
Hershey Foods Corporation
Financial analysis

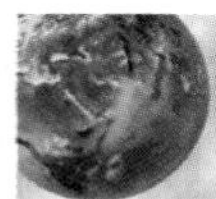

A merchandising business should keep enough inventory on hand to meet the needs of its customers. At the same time, however, too much inventory reduces solvency by tying up funds, and it increases expenses such as storage expense. Moreover, excess inventory increases the risk of losses due to prices declining or the inventory becoming obsolete.

As with many types of financial analyses, it is possible to determine more than one measure to express the relationship between the cost of merchandise sold (cost of sales) and inventory. Two such measures are the inventory turnover and the number of days' sales in inventory. The inventory turnover is computed as follows:

$$\textbf{Inventory turnover} = \frac{\textbf{Cost of merchandise sold}}{\textbf{Average inventory}}$$

The average inventory can be determined by dividing the sum of the inventories at the beginning and end of the year by 2.

Generally, an increase in the turnover indicates an improvement in managing inventory. However, differences in companies and industries are too great to allow a more specific statement as to what is a good inventory turnover. For example, a firm selling food should have a higher turnover than a firm selling furniture. However, for each business, there is a reasonable turnover rate. A turnover lower than this rate could mean that inventory is not being managed properly. In such cases, management should investigate to determine the causes of the lower inventory rate.

The number of days' sales in inventory is computed as follows:

Number of days' sales in inventory = $\frac{\textbf{Inventory, end of year}}{\textbf{Average daily cost of merchandise sold}}$

The average daily cost of merchandise sold is determined by dividing the cost of merchandise sold by 365.

The number of days' sales in inventory is a rough measure of the length of time it takes to acquire, sell, and replace the inventory. Generally, a decrease in the number of days' sales in inventory indicates an improvement in managing the inventory.

a. Hershey Foods Corporation has inventories of $436,917,000 at December 31, 1991. For the years ended December 31, 1993 and 1992, determine: (1) the inventory turnover, and (2) the number of days' sales in inventory.

b. What conclusions can be drawn from these analyses concerning Hershey's efficiency in managing inventory?

CASE 9–5

Gant Company

Costing inventory

Gant Company began operations in 1996 by selling a single product. Data on purchases and sales for the year were as follows:

Purchases:

Date	*Units Purchased*	*Unit Cost*	*Total Cost*
April 8	4,875	$13.20	$ 64,350
May 10	5,125	14.00	71,750
June 4	5,000	14.20	71,000
July 10	5,000	15.00	75,000
August 7	3,400	15.25	51,850
October 5	1,600	15.50	24,800
November 1	1,000	15.75	15,750
December 10	1,000	17.00	17,000
	27,000		$391,500

Sales:

April	2,000 units
May	2,000
June	3,500
July	4,000
August	3,500
September	3,500
October	2,250
November	1,250
December	1,000
Total sales	$434,000

On January 3, 1997, the president of the company, Laura Gant, asked for your advice on costing the 4,000-unit physical inventory that was taken on December 31, 1996. Moreover, since the firm plans to expand its product line, she asked for your advice on the use of a perpetual inventory system in the future.

1. Determine the cost of the December 31, 1996 inventory under the periodic system, using the (a) first-in, first-out method, (b) last-in, first-out method, and (c) average cost method.
2. Determine the gross profit for the year under each of the three methods in (1).
3. a. Explain varying viewpoints why each of the three inventory costing methods may best reflect the results of operations for 1996.
   b. Which of the three inventory costing methods may best reflect the replacement cost of the inventory on the balance sheet as of December 31, 1996?
   c. Which inventory costing method would you choose to use for income tax purposes? Why?
   d. Discuss the advantages and disadvantages of using a perpetual inventory system. From the data presented in this case, is there any indication of the adequacy of inventory levels during the year?

ANSWERS TO SELF-EXAMINATION QUESTIONS

1. **D** The overstatement of inventory shrinkage by $7,500 at the end of the year will cause the cost of merchandise sold for the year to be overstated by $7,500, the gross profit for the year to be understated by $7,500, the merchandise inventory to be understated by $7,500, and the net income for the year to be understated by $7,500 (answer D).
2. **A** The fifo method (answer A) is based on the assumption that costs are charged against revenue in the order in which they were incurred. The lifo method (answer B) charges the most recent costs incurred against revenue, and the average cost method (answer C) charges a weighted average of unit costs of items sold against revenue. The perpetual inventory system (answer D) is a system that continuously discloses the amount of inventory.
3. **A** The lifo method of costing is based on the assumption that costs should be charged against revenue in the

reverse order in which costs were incurred. Thus, the oldest costs are assigned to inventory. Thirty of the 35 units would be assigned a unit cost of $20 (since 10 of the beginning inventory units were sold on the first sale), and the remaining 5 units would be assigned a cost of $23 (answer A).

4. **D** The fifo method of costing is based on the assumption that costs should be charged against revenue in the order in which they were incurred (first-in, first-out). Thus, the most recent costs are assigned to inventory. The 35 units would be assigned a unit cost of $23 (answer D).

5. **B** When the price level is steadily rising, the earlier unit costs are lower than recent unit costs. Under the fifo method (answer B), these earlier costs are matched against revenue to yield the highest possible net income. The periodic inventory system (answer D) is a system and not a method of costing.

10 Plant Assets and Intangible Assets

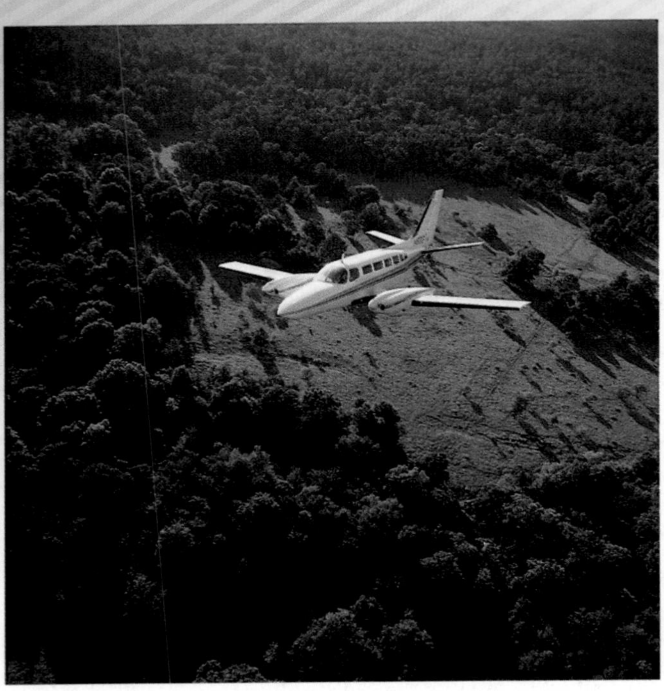

YOU AND ACCOUNTING

Assume that you are a certified flight instructor and you would like to earn a little extra money by teaching people how to fly. Unfortunately, you don't own an airplane. However, one of the pilots at the local airport is willing to let you use her airplane for a fixed fee per year. You will also have to pay your share of the annual operating costs, based on hours flown. The owner will consider your request for upgrading the plane's equipment. At the end of the year, the owner has the right to cancel the agreement.

One of your friends is an airplane mechanic. He is familiar with the plane and has indicated that it needs its annual inspection. There is some structural damage on the right aileron. In addition to this repair, you would like to equip the plane with another radio and a better navigation system.

Since you will not have any ownership in the airplane, it is important for you to distinguish between normal operating costs and costs that add future value or worth to the airplane. These latter costs should be the responsibility of the owner. In this case, you should be willing to pay for part of the cost of the annual inspection. The cost of repairing the structural damage and upgrading the navigation system should be the responsibility of the owner.

Businesses also distinguish between the cost of a plant asset and the cost of operating the asset. In this chapter, we discuss how to determine the portion of a plant asset's cost that becomes an expense over a period of time. We also discuss accounting for the disposal of plant assets and accounting for intangible assets, such as patents and copyrights.

After studying this chapter, you should be able to:

Objective 1
Define plant assets and describe the accounting for their cost.

Objective 2
Compute depreciation, using the following methods: straight-line method, units-of-production method, and declining-balance method.

Objective 3
Classify plant asset costs as either capital expenditures or revenue expenditures.

Objective 4
Journalize entries for the disposal of plant assets.

Objective 5
Define a lease and summarize the accounting rules related to the leasing of plant assets.

Objective 6
Describe internal controls over plant assets and provide examples of such controls.

Objective 7
Compute depletion and journalize the entry for depletion.

Objective 8
Journalize the entries for acquiring and amortizing intangible assets, such as patents, copyrights, and goodwill.

Objective 9
Describe how depreciation expense is reported in an income statement and prepare a balance sheet that includes plant assets and intangible assets.

Nature of Plant Assets

Objective 1
Define plant assets and describe the accounting for their cost.

Plant assets are long-term or relatively permanent tangible assets that are used in the normal business operations. They are owned by the business and are not held for sale in normal operations. Other descriptive titles for such assets are **fixed assets** or **property, plant, and equipment.** These assets may also be described in more specific terms, such as equipment, furniture, tools, machinery, buildings, and land.

There is no standard rule as to the minimum length of life necessary for an asset to be classified as a plant asset. Such assets must be capable of providing repeated use or benefit, and are normally expected to last more than a year. However, an asset need not actually be used on an ongoing basis or even often. For example, items of standby equipment held for use in the event of a breakdown of regular equipment or for use only during peak periods of activity are included in plant assets.

Long-term assets acquired for resale in the normal course of business are not classified as plant assets, regardless of their permanent nature or the length of time they are held. For example, undeveloped land or other real estate acquired as an investment for resale should be listed on the balance sheet in the asset section entitled *Investments*.

The normal costs of using or operating a plant asset are reported as expenses on a company's income statement. The costs of acquiring a plant asset become expenses over a period of time. In the following paragraphs, we discuss these latter costs and the nature of the periodic expense.

COSTS OF ACQUIRING PLANT ASSETS

What is included in the cost of acquiring a plant asset? This cost includes all amounts spent to get an asset in place and ready for use. For example, freight costs and the costs of installing equipment are included as part of the cost of a plant asset. Costs *not necessary* for getting an asset ready for use do not increase the asset's usefulness and should not be included in its cost. For example, costs related to mistakes in installing equipment or to vandalism during installation should be reported as expenses because they do not increase the asset's usefulness. Exhibit 1 summarizes how some of the common costs associated with acquiring such plant assets as equipment should be treated.

Exhibit 1
Costs of Acquiring Plant Assets

The cost of plant assets includes costs of:

Sales taxes	Insurance while asset is in transit
Freight	Assembling
Installation	Modifying for use
Repairs (used assets)	Testing for use
Reconditioning (used assets)	Permits from government agencies

The cost of plant assets excludes costs of:
- Vandalism
- Mistakes in installation
- Uninsured theft
- Damage during unpacking and installing
- Fines for not obtaining proper permits from government agencies

The costs related to acquiring land and buildings often require careful analysis. For example, the cost of land includes not only its negotiated price, but also the broker's commissions, title fees, surveying fees, and other costs of obtaining entitlement to it.[1] If delinquent real estate taxes are paid by the buyer, they are also part of the cost of the land. If unwanted buildings are located on land acquired for a future building site, the cost of their razing or removal, less the proceeds from any salvage, is a cost of the land. The cost of grading, leveling, or otherwise changing the contour of land is also properly included as a cost of the land.

The cost of constructing a building includes the fees paid to architects and engineers for plans and supervision. In addition, insurance incurred during construction and all other necessary costs related to the project should be included in the cost of the building. Generally, interest on money borrowed to finance construction should also be treated as part of the cost of the building.[2]

In some cases, it may be difficult to determine whether costs should be included as part of the land or as part of constructing a building. For instance, a business may be required to pay for the initial cost of paving a public street bordering its land, either by direct payment or by special tax assessment. In this case, the costs related to the paving are normally part of the cost of the land. As another example, the costs incurred in constructing walkways to and around a building are part of the cost of the building, if they are expected to last only as long as the building.

Costs may also be incurred for items that are neither as permanent as land nor directly related to a building. These items are called **land improvements.** Examples of such items include the costs of trees and shrubs, fences, outdoor lighting, and paved parking areas.

NATURE OF DEPRECIATION

As we have discussed in earlier chapters, land has an unlimited life and therefore can provide unlimited services. On the other hand, other plant assets such as equipment, buildings, and land improvements lose their ability, over time, to provide services. As a result, the costs of equipment, buildings, and land improvements

[1] As discussed in this section, land is assumed to be used only as a location or site. Land acquired for its mineral deposits or other natural resources will be considered later in the chapter.

[2] *Statement of Financial Accounting Standards, No. 34,* "Capitalization of Interest Cost," Financial Accounting Standards Board, Stamford, 1979, par. 6.

should be transferred to expense accounts in a systematic manner during their expected useful lives. This periodic cost expiration is called **depreciation.**

Factors that cause a decline in the ability of a plant asset to provide services may be divided into two categories. First, *physical* depreciation caused by wear and tear from use and from the action of the elements decreases usefulness. Second, *functional* depreciation caused by inadequacy and obsolescence decreases usefulness. A plant asset becomes inadequate if its capacity is not able to meet the demands of increased production. A plant asset is obsolete if the item that it produces is no longer in demand or if a newer machine can produce an item of better quality at the same or lower cost. Advances in technology during this century have made obsolescence an increasingly important cause of depreciation.

The meaning of the term *depreciation* as used in accounting is often misunderstood because the same term is also used in business to mean a decline in the market value of an asset. However, the amount of a plant asset's unexpired cost reported in the balance sheet usually does not agree with the amount that could be realized from its sale. Plant assets are held for use in a business rather than for sale. It is assumed that the business will continue as a **going concern.** Thus, a decision to dispose of a plant asset is based mainly on the usefulness of the asset to the business and not on its market value.

Another common misunderstanding is that depreciation accounting provides cash needed to replace plant assets as they wear out. The cash account is neither increased nor decreased by the periodic entries that transfer the cost of plant assets to depreciation expense accounts. The misunderstanding probably occurs because depreciation, unlike most expenses, does not require an outlay of cash in the period in which it is recorded.

USING ACCOUNTING TO UNDERSTAND BUSINESS

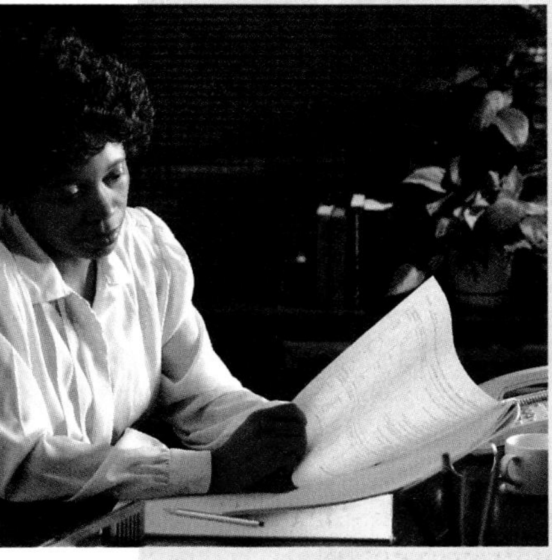

When a plant asset is acquired, it often requires an outlay of cash. This outlay affects the cash flows of the business. Although depreciation is a major expense for many businesses, it does not require a cash outlay. Therefore, in evaluating a business's cash-generating ability, many creditors and investment analysts add back depreciation expense to the reported net income of the business. In this way, the creditors and analysts obtain a rough estimate of cash generated from operations. Thus, in evaluating the earnings and cash flows of a business, depreciation and plant asset replacements are important considerations.

Accounting for Depreciation

Objective 2
Compute depreciation, using the following methods: straight-line method, units-of-production method, and declining-balance method.

Three factors are considered in determining the amount of depreciation expense to be recognized each period. These three factors are (a) the plant asset's initial cost, (b) its expected useful life, and (c) its estimated value at the end of its useful life. This third factor is called the **residual value, scrap value, salvage value,** or **trade-in value.** Exhibit 2 shows the relationship among the three factors and the periodic depreciation expense.

Exhibit 2
Factors that Determine Depreciation Expense

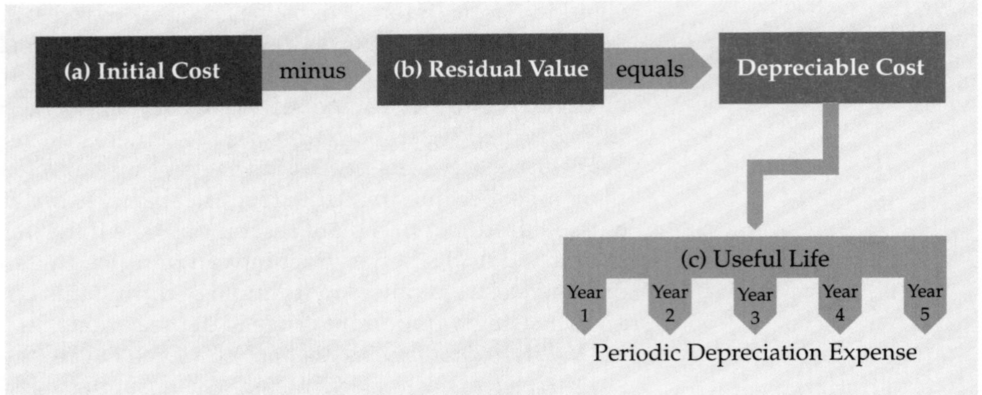

If a plant asset is expected to have no residual value at the time that it is taken out of service, then its initial cost should be spread over its expected useful life as depreciation expense. Also, if a plant asset's estimated residual value at the time it is taken out of service is expected to be very small compared to the cost of the asset, this value may be ignored and the entire cost spread over the asset's expected useful life. If a plant asset is expected to have a significant residual value, the difference between its initial cost and this value is the cost (called **depreciable cost**) that should be spread over the asset's useful life as depreciation expense.

Neither *the period of usefulness* of a plant asset nor its *residual value* at the end of that period can be accurately determined until the asset is taken out of service. However, in determining the amount of the periodic depreciation, these two related factors must be estimated at the time the asset is placed into service. There are no set rules for estimating either factor, and both factors may be affected by management policies. For example, a company that provides its salespersons with a new automobile every year will have different estimates than will a company that keeps its cars for five years. Such variables as climate, use, and maintenance will also affect the estimates.

Where can we find estimates of the useful life of plant assets? Estimates are available from various trade associations and other publications. For federal income tax purposes, the Internal Revenue Service has also established guidelines for useful lives. These guidelines may also be helpful in determining depreciation for financial reporting purposes.

In addition to the many factors that may affect the useful life of an asset, various degrees of accuracy may be used in the computations. A month is normally the smallest unit of time used. When this period of time is used, all assets placed in or taken out of service during the first half of a month are treated as if the event occurred on the first day of that month. Likewise, all plant asset additions and deductions during the second half of a month are treated as if the event occurred on the first day of the next month. In the absence of any statement to the contrary, we will assume this practice throughout this chapter.

It is not necessary that a business use a single method of computing depreciation for all its depreciable assets. The methods used in the accounts and financial statements may also differ from the methods used in determining income taxes and property taxes. The three methods used most often are (1) straight-line, (2) units-of-production, and (3) declining-balance.[3] Exhibit 3 shows the extent of the use of these methods in financial statements.

[3] Another method, called the sum-of-the-years-digits method, is sometimes used. Because it is not often used today, however, it is only described and illustrated in the appendix to this chapter.

Exhibit 3
Use of Depreciation Methods

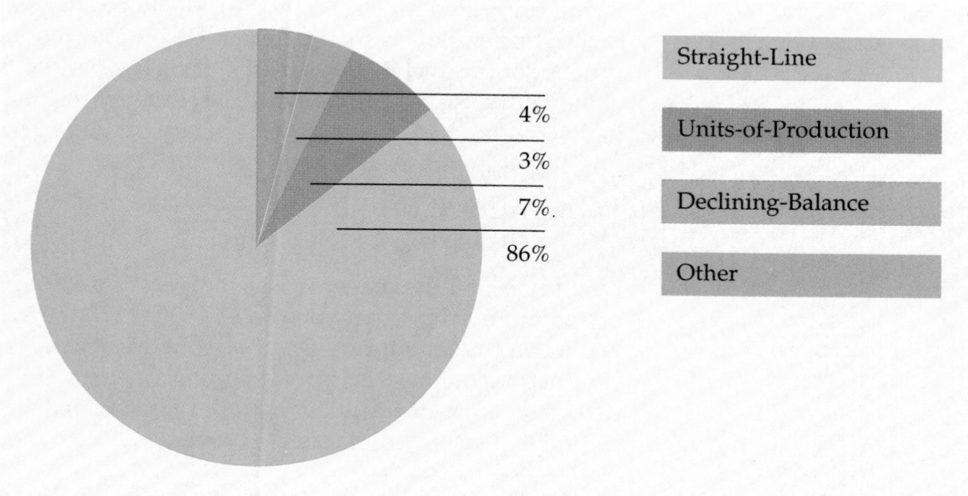

Source: *Accounting Trends & Techniques*, 48th ed., American Institute of Certified Public Accountants, New York, 1994.

STRAIGHT-LINE METHOD

The straight-line depreciation method provides for equal amounts of periodic expense over the estimated useful life of the asset. For example, assume that the cost of a depreciable asset is $16,000, its estimated residual value is $1,000, and its estimated life is 5 years. The annual depreciation is computed as follows:

$$\frac{\$16{,}000 \text{ cost} - \$1{,}000 \text{ estimated residual value}}{5 \text{ years estimated life}} = \$3{,}000 \text{ annual depreciation}$$

When an asset is used for only part of a year, the annual depreciation is prorated. For example, assume that the fiscal year ends on December 31 and that the asset in the above example is first used on October 5. The depreciation for the first fiscal year of use would be $750 ($3,000 × 3/12), computed on the basis of 3 months. If usage had begun in the second half of October, the depreciation for the year would have been $500 ($3,000 × 2/12).

For ease in applying the straight-line method, the annual depreciation may be converted to a percentage of depreciable cost. This percentage is determined by dividing 100% by the number of years of useful life. For example, a useful life of 20 years converts to a 5% (100% ÷ 20) rate, 8 years converts to a 12.5% (100% ÷ 8) rate, and so on.[4] To further illustrate, the straight-line rate in the above example is 20% (100% ÷ 5). The annual depreciation of $3,000 can be computed by multiplying the depreciable cost of $15,000 by this rate.

The straight-line method is simple and is widely used. It provides a reasonable allocation of costs to periodic expense when the usage of the asset and the related revenues from its use are about the same from period to period.

UNITS-OF-PRODUCTION METHOD

The units-of-production depreciation method yields depreciation expense that varies with the asset's usage. In applying this method, the useful life of the asset is expressed in terms of units of productive capacity such as hours or miles. Depreciation

[4] The depreciation rate may also be expressed as a fraction. For example, the annual straight-line rate for an asset with a 3-year useful life is 1/3.

is first computed for each unit of production. The total depreciation expense for each accounting period is then determined by multiplying the unit depreciation by the number of productive units used during the period. For example, assume that a machine with a cost of $16,000 and an estimated residual value of $1,000 is expected to have an estimated life of 10,000 operating hours. The depreciation for a unit of one hour is computed as follows:

$$\frac{\$16{,}000 \text{ cost} - \$1{,}000 \text{ estimated residual value}}{10{,}000 \text{ estimated hours}} = \$1.50 \text{ hourly depreciation}$$

Assuming that the machine was in operation for 2,200 hours during a year, the depreciation for that year would be $3,300 ($1.50 × 2,200 hours).

When the amount of use of a plant asset varies from year to year, the units-of-production method is more appropriate than the straight-line method. In such cases, the units-of-production method better matches the allocation of cost (depreciation expense) with the related revenue.

DECLINING-BALANCE METHOD

The **declining-balance depreciation method** provides for a declining periodic expense over the estimated useful life of the asset. To apply this method, the annual straight-line depreciation rate is doubled. For example, the declining-balance rate for an asset with an estimated life of 5 years is 40%, which is double the straight-line rate of 20% (100% ÷ 5).

This rate is then multiplied by the cost of the asset for the first year of use. After the first year, the rate is multiplied by the declining **book value** (cost minus accumulated depreciation) of the asset. To illustrate, the annual declining-balance depreciation for an asset with an estimated 5-year life and a cost of $16,000 is shown below.

Year	*Cost*	*Accum. Depr. at Beginning of Year*	*Book Value at Beginning of Year*	*Rate*	*Depreciation for Year*	*Book Value at End of Year*
1	$16,000	—	$16,000.00	40%	$6,400.00	$9,600.00
2	16,000	$ 6,400.00	9,600.00	40%	3,840.00	5,760.00
3	16,000	10,240.00	5,760.00	40%	2,304.00	3,456.00
4	16,000	12,544.00	3,456.00	40%	1,382.40	2,073.60
5	16,000	13,926.40	2,073.60	40%	829.44	1,244.16

You should note that when the declining-balance method is used, the estimated residual value is not considered in determining the depreciation rate. It is also ignored in computing the periodic depreciation, except that the asset should not be depreciated below its estimated residual value. In the above example, we assumed that the estimated residual value at the end of the fifth year approximates the book value of $1,244.16. If the estimated residual value were $1,500, the depreciation for the fifth year would have been $573.60 ($2,073.60 – $1,500.00) instead of $829.44.

In the example above, we assumed that the first use of the asset occurred at the beginning of the fiscal year. This is normally not the case in practice, however, and depreciation for the first partial year of use must be computed. For example, assume that the asset above was in service at the end of the *third* month of the fiscal year. In this case, only a portion (9/12) of the first full year's depreciation of $6,400 is allocated to the first fiscal year. Thus, depreciation of $4,800 (9/12 × $6,400) is allocated to the first partial year of use. The method of computing the depreciation for the following years would not be affected. Thus, the depreciation for the second fiscal year would be $4,480 [40% × ($16,000 – $4,800)].

COMPARING DEPRECIATION METHODS

The straight-line method provides for uniform periodic amounts of depreciation expense over the life of the asset. The units-of-production method provides for periodic amounts of depreciation expense that vary, depending upon the amount of usage of the asset.

The declining-balance method provides for a higher depreciation amount in the first year of use of the asset, followed by a gradually declining amount. For this reason, the declining-balance method is often called an **accelerated depreciation method**. It is most appropriate for situations in which the decline in an asset's productivity or earning power is greater in the early years of its use than in later years. Further, using this method is often justified because repairs tend to increase with the age of an asset. The reduced amounts of depreciation in later years are thus offset to some extent by increased repair expenses.

The periodic depreciation amounts for the straight-line method and the declining-balance method are compared in Exhibit 4. This comparison is based on an asset cost of $16,000, an estimated life of 5 years, and an estimated residual value of $1,000.

Exhibit 4
Comparing Depreciation Methods

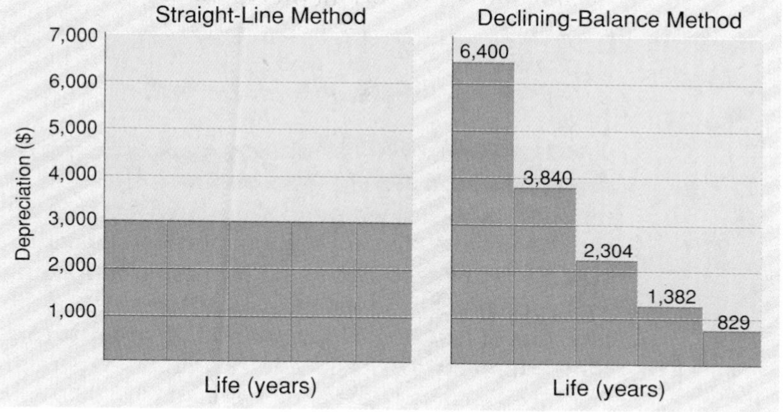

DEPRECIATION FOR FEDERAL INCOME TAX

What depreciation method can a business use for tax purposes? Each of the three methods described can be used to determine depreciation expense for federal income tax purposes for plant assets acquired prior to 1981.[5] For these assets, the declining-balance method has been widely used for tax purposes. This was because accelerating the depreciation expense reduces the income tax liability in the earlier years of an asset's life. This reduces the amount of taxes due and thus increases the amount of cash available to pay for the asset or for other purposes in those earlier years.

For plant assets acquired after 1980 and before 1987, either the straight-line method or the Accelerated Cost Recovery System (ACRS) could be used for federal income tax purposes. ACRS provided for depreciation deductions that were similar to those that would be computed using the 150-percent declining-balance method.[6] For most business property, ACRS provided for three classes of useful life. Each class of useful life was often much shorter than the actual useful life of the asset in that class.

[5] The sum-of-the-years-digits method can also be used for determining depreciation on assets purchased prior to 1981.

[6] The 150-percent declining-balance method uses 150% of the straight-line rate, in contrast to double the straight-line rate (or 200%), as illustrated earlier in this chapter.

For plant assets acquired after 1986, Modified ACRS (MACRS) provides for eight classes of useful life. The two most common classes, other than real estate, are the 5-year class and the 7-year class.[7] The 5-year class includes automobiles and light-duty trucks, and the 7-year class includes most machinery and equipment. The depreciation deduction for these two classes approximates the use of the declining-balance method using twice the straight-line rate.

The Internal Revenue Service has prescribed methods that use annual percentages (rates) in determining depreciation for each class of asset. In using these rates, residual value is ignored, and all plant assets are assumed to be put in service in the middle of the year and taken out of service in the middle of the year. For the 5-year-class assets, depreciation is spread over six years, as shown in the following MACRS schedule of depreciation rates:

Year	*5-Year-Class Depreciation Rates*
1	20.0%
2	32.0
3	19.2
4	11.5
5	11.5
6	5.8
	100.0%

Many companies use one method of depreciation for financial reporting purposes (often the straight-line method) and a different method for tax purposes. To simplify its record keeping, a business will sometimes use the same method for both financial statement and tax purposes, usually an accelerated method such as MACRS. However, David A. Tonneson, a Wakefield, Massachusetts, accountant who specializes in advising small businesses, says this may be a big mistake. In one case, one of his clients lost a $1 million order because the business had used accelerated depreciation for its equipment. Using straight-line depreciation, the equipment would have had a book value of $525,000, which a bank would accept as collateral for a $420,000 loan. However, the book value resulting from the accelerated depreciation was lower ($300,000). So the bank would only loan $240,000. The company needed $400,000.[8]

REVISION OF PERIODIC DEPRECIATION

Earlier in this chapter, we indicated that two of the factors that must be considered in computing the periodic depreciation of a plant asset are (1) its estimated residual value and (2) its estimated useful life. These factors must be estimated at the time the asset is placed into service. Revisions of these estimates are normal and tend to be recurring. When such revisions occur, the revised estimates are used to determine the depreciation expense in future periods.

To illustrate, assume that a plant asset purchased for $130,000 was originally estimated to have a useful life of 30 years and a residual value of $10,000. The asset has been depreciated for 10 years by the straight-line method. At the end of ten years, the asset's book value (undepreciated cost) is $90,000, determined as follows:

Asset cost	$130,000
Less accumulated depreciation ($4,000 per year × 10 years)	40,000
Book value (undepreciated cost), end of tenth year	$ 90,000

[7] Real estate is in 27 1/2-year classes and 31 1/2-year classes and is depreciated by the straight-line method.
[8] Lee Berton, "Do's and Don'ts," *The Wall Street Journal,* June 10, 1988, p. 34R.

During the eleventh year, it is estimated that the remaining useful life is 25 years (instead of 20) and that the residual value is $5,000 (instead of $10,000). The depreciation expense for each of the remaining 25 years is $3,400, computed as follows:

Book value (undepreciated cost), end of tenth year	$90,000
Less revised estimated residual value	5,000
Revised remaining depreciable cost	$85,000
Revised annual depreciation expense ($85,000 ÷ 25)	$ 3,400

You should note that the revisions of the estimates used in determining depreciation do not affect the amounts of depreciation expense recorded in earlier years. Therefore, when revisions are made, only future depreciation expense amounts are affected.[9]

RECORDING DEPRECIATION

An adjusting entry for depreciation may be recorded at the end of each month or at the end of the year. As we discussed in an earlier chapter, the entry to record depreciation is a debit to Depreciation Expense and a credit to a contra asset account entitled Accumulated Depreciation or Allowance for Depreciation. The use of a contra asset account allows the original cost to remain unchanged in the plant asset account.

An exception to recording depreciation only monthly or annually is made when a plant asset is sold, traded in, or scrapped. As we will illustrate, a disposal is recorded by removing from the accounts both the cost of the asset and its related accumulated depreciation as of the date of the disposal. Depreciation for the current period should be recorded before the disposal of the asset is recorded.

SUBSIDIARY LEDGERS FOR PLANT ASSETS

When depreciation is computed on a large number of individual assets, a subsidiary ledger is usually maintained. For example, assume that a business owns 200 items of office equipment with a total cost of $100,000. Unless the business is new, the equipment would have been acquired over a number of years. The individual cost, estimated residual value, and estimated useful life would be different in each case. In addition, the makeup of the assets will continually change because of acquisitions and disposals.

The subsidiary records for depreciable assets may be maintained by a manual system or a computerized system. In either case, a separate ledger account may be maintained for each asset. The subsidiary ledger account shown in Exhibit 5 provides spaces for recording the acquisition and the disposal of the asset, the depreciation charged each period, the accumulated depreciation to date, and the book value. Other relevant data useful to management may also be included.

The number assigned to the account in Exhibit 5 is made up of the number of the controlling account in the general ledger, Office Equipment (123), followed by the number assigned to the specific item of office equipment purchased (215). A tag or plaque with the account number is attached to the asset for control purposes. Depreciation for the year in which the asset was acquired, computed for nine months on a straight-line basis, is $180. Depreciation for the following year is $240. The subsidiary ledger can therefore provide the data for the adjusting entries for depreciation at the end of each year.

[9] The correction of material or large errors made in computing depreciation in prior periods is discussed in a later chapter.

Exhibit 5
An Account in the Office Equipment Ledger

PLANT ASSET RECORD

Account No.: 123–215 **General Ledger Account:** Office Equipment
Item: SF 490 Copier **Depreciation Method:** Straight-Line
Serial No.: AT 47–3926
From Whom Purchased: Hamilton Office Machines Co.
Estimated Useful Life: 10 Years **Estimated Residual Value:** $500 **Depr. per Year:** $240

	Asset			Accumulated Depreciation			Book
Date	Debit	Credit	Balance	Debit	Credit	Balance	Value
04/08/96	2,900		2,900				2,900
12/31/96					180	180	2,720
12/31/97					240	420	2,480

When an asset is disposed of, the asset section of the subsidiary account is credited and the accumulated depreciation section is debited. Thus, the balances of both sections are reduced to zero. The account is then removed from the ledger and filed for future reference.

Subsidiary ledgers for plant assets are useful to accountants in (1) determining periodic depreciation expense, (2) recording the disposal of individual items, (3) preparing tax returns, and (4) preparing insurance claims in the event of insured losses. The subsidiary account forms may also be expanded for accumulating data on the operating efficiency of the asset. Such information as number of breakdowns, length of time out of service, and cost of repairs may be useful to management. For example, when new equipment is to be purchased, these data may be useful in deciding upon size, model, and the best vendor.

DEPRECIATION OF PLANT ASSETS OF LOW UNIT COST

Subsidiary ledgers are not usually maintained for classes of plant assets that are made up of individual items of low unit cost. Examples of such items are hand tools and other small portable equipment, spare parts, and dishes and silverware for a restaurant. Because of hard usage, breakage, and pilferage, such assets may be relatively short-lived and may require frequent replacement.

For plant assets with a low unit cost, the usual depreciation methods are generally not practical. One method of accounting for such assets is to treat them as expenses when they are acquired. Another method of accounting for assets with a low unit cost is to treat them as assets when they are acquired. Then, at the end of the year, an inventory of the items on hand is taken, and their current value is estimated. The difference between this value and the asset's account balance is debited to an expense account and credited to the plant asset account.

COMPOSITE-RATE METHOD

In the preceding examples, we computed depreciation for each individual asset. Another method, called the **composite-rate method,** determines depreciation for groups of assets, using a single rate. The basis for grouping may be estimates of useful lives or other common traits. For example, a group may include all assets within a class, such as office equipment or factory equipment.

The procedures for computing depreciation for groups of assets are similar to those for individual assets. Therefore, we will not illustrate the composite-rate depreciation method.

Capital and Revenue Expenditures

Objective 3
Classify plant asset costs as either capital expenditures or revenue expenditures.

The costs of acquiring plant assets, adding to plant assets, and adding usefulness to plant assets for more than one accounting period are called **capital expenditures.** Such expenditures are either debited to the asset account or debited to the related accumulated depreciation account. Costs that benefit only the current period or costs incurred in order to maintain normal operating efficiency are called **revenue expenditures.** Such expenditures are debited to expense accounts.

It is important for a business to distinguish between capital and revenue expenditures so that its revenues and expenses are properly matched. Capital expenditures will affect the depreciation expense of more than one period, while revenue expenditures will affect the expenses of only the current period.

CAPITAL EXPENDITURES

We discussed accounting for the initial costs of acquiring plant assets earlier in the chapter. In the following paragraphs, we discuss accounting for capital expenditures after a plant asset has been acquired. The three types of expenditures are (a) additions, (b) betterments, and (c) extraordinary repairs.

Additions to Plant Assets

An expenditure for an addition to a plant asset should be debited to the related plant asset account. The cost of an addition should be depreciated over the estimated useful life of the addition. For example, the cost of adding an air conditioning system to a building or of adding a wing to a building should be accounted for as a capital expenditure.

Betterments

An expenditure that increases the operating efficiency or capacity for the remaining useful life of a plant asset is called a **betterment.** Such an expenditure should be debited to the related plant asset account. For example, if the power unit attached to a machine is replaced by one of greater capacity, the cost should be debited to the machine account. Also, the cost and the accumulated depreciation related to the old power unit should be removed from the accounts. The cost of the new power unit is depreciated over its estimated useful life or the remaining useful life of the machine, whichever is shorter.

Extraordinary Repairs

An expenditure that increases the useful life of an asset beyond its original estimate is called an **extraordinary repair.** Such an expenditure should be debited to the related accumulated depreciation account. In such cases, the repairs are said to restore or *make good* a portion of the depreciation accumulated in prior years. The depreciation for future periods should be computed on the basis of the revised book value of the asset and the revised estimate of the remaining useful life.

To illustrate, assume that a machine costing $50,000 has no estimated residual value and an estimated useful life of 10 years. Assume also that the machine has been depreciated for 6 years by the straight-line method ($5,000 annual depreciation). At the beginning of the seventh year, an $11,500 extraordinary repair increases the remaining useful life of the machine to 7 years (instead of 4). The repair

Expenditures for normal maintenance, such as the cost of repainting a building, are debited to expense accounts.

of $11,500 should be debited to Accumulated Depreciation. The annual depreciation for the remaining 7 years of use would be $4,500, computed as follows:

Cost of machine		$50,000
Less Accumulated Depreciation balance:		
Depreciation for first 6 years ($5,000 × 6)	$30,000	
Deduct debit for extraordinary repairs	11,500	
Balance of Accumulated Depreciation		18,500
Revised book value of machine after extraordinary repair		$31,500
Annual depreciation ($31,500 ÷ 7 years remaining useful life)		$ 4,500

REVENUE EXPENDITURES

Expenditures for normal maintenance and repairs are classified as revenue expenditures. For example, the cost of replacing spark plugs in an automobile or the cost of repainting a building should be debited to expense accounts.

Small expenditures that are insignificant in amount are also normally debited to repair expense accounts, even though they may have the qualities of capital expenditures. The saving in time and record-keeping effort justifies the small loss of accuracy. Some businesses establish a minimum dollar amount required to classify an item as a capital expenditure.

SUMMARY OF CAPITAL AND REVENUE EXPENDITURES

Exhibit 6 summarizes the accounting for capital and revenue expenditures related to plant assets.

Exhibit 6
Capital and Revenue Expenditures

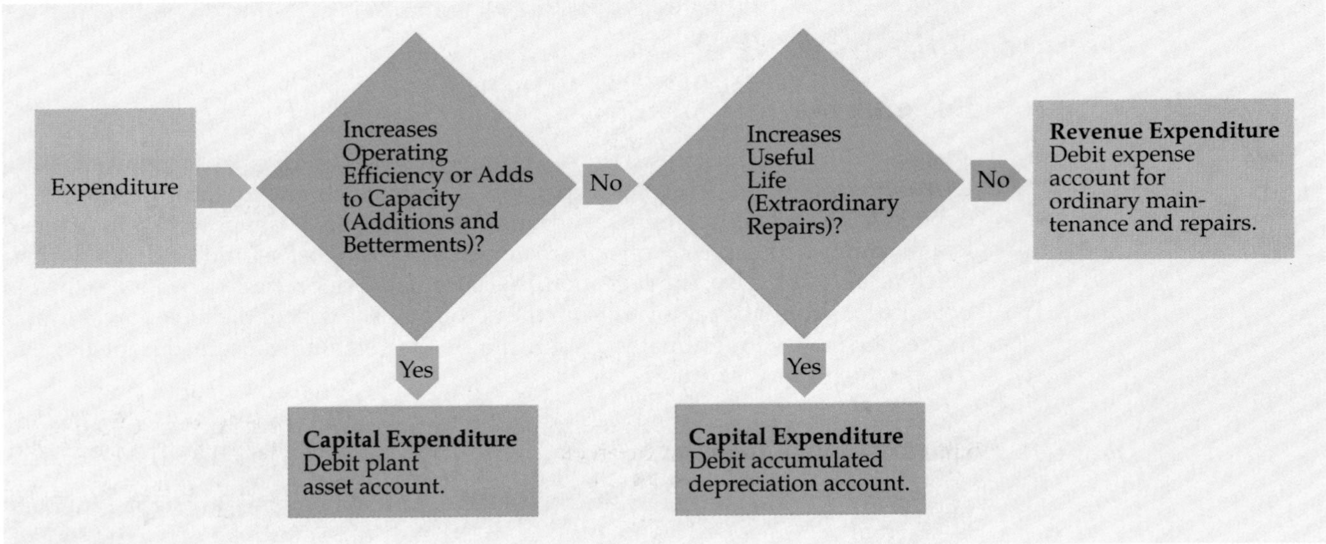

Disposal of Plant Assets

Objective 4
Journalize entries for the disposal of plant assets.

Plant assets that are no longer useful may be discarded, sold, or traded for other plant assets. The details of the entry to record a disposal will vary. In all cases, however, the book value of the asset must be removed from the accounts. The entry for this purpose is a debit to the asset's accumulated depreciation account for its balance on the date of disposal and a credit to the asset account for the cost of the asset.

A plant asset should not be removed from the accounts only because it has been fully depreciated. If the asset is still used by the business, the cost and accumulated depreciation should remain in the ledger. This maintains accountability for the asset in the ledger. If the book value of the asset were removed from the ledger, the accounts would contain no evidence of the continued existence of the asset. In addition, the cost and the accumulated depreciation data on such assets are often needed for property tax and income tax reports.

DISCARDING PLANT ASSETS

When plant assets are no longer useful to the business and have no residual or market value, they are discarded. If the asset has been fully depreciated, no loss is realized. For example, assume that an item of equipment acquired at a cost of $25,000 is fully depreciated at December 31, the end of the preceding fiscal year. On February 14, the equipment is discarded. The entry to record this is as follows:

Feb. 14	Accumulated Depreciation—Equipment	25,000	
	Equipment		25,000
	To write off equipment discarded.		

If an asset has not been fully depreciated, depreciation should be recorded prior to removing it from service and from the accounting records. To illustrate, assume that equipment costing $6,000 is depreciated at an annual straight-line rate of 10%. In addition, assume that on December 31 of the preceding fiscal year, the accumulated depreciation balance, after adjusting entries, is $4,750. Finally, assume that the asset is removed from service on the following March 24. The entry to record the depreciation for the three months of the current period prior to the asset's removal from service is as follows:

Mar. 24	Depreciation Expense—Equipment	150	
	Accumulated Depreciation—Equipment		150
	To record current depreciation on equipment discarded. ($600 × 3/12)		

The discarding of the equipment is then recorded by the following entry:

Mar. 24	Accumulated Depreciation—Equipment	4,900	
	Loss on Disposal of Plant Assets	1,100	
	Equipment		6,000
	To write off equipment discarded.		

In the preceding example, a loss of $1,100 is recorded. This loss occurs because the balance of the accumulated depreciation account ($4,900) is less than the balance in the equipment account ($6,000). Losses on the discarding of plant assets are nonoperating items and are normally reported in the Other expense section of the income statement.

SALE OF PLANT ASSETS

The entry to record the sale of a plant asset is similar to the entries illustrated above, except that the cash or other asset received must also be recorded. If the selling price is more than the book value of the asset, the transaction results in a gain. If the selling price is less than the book value, there is a loss.

To illustrate, assume that equipment is acquired at a cost of $10,000 and is depreciated at an annual straight-line rate of 10%. The equipment is sold for cash on October 12 of the eighth year of its use. The balance of the accumulated depreciation account as of the preceding December 31 is $7,000. The entry to update the depreciation for the nine months of the current year is as follows:

Oct. 12	Depreciation Expense—Equipment	750	
	Accumulated Depreciation—Equipment		750
	To record current depreciation on equipment sold. ($10,000 × 10% × 3/4)		

After the current depreciation is recorded, the book value of the asset is $2,250 ($10,000 – $7,750). The entries to record the sale, assuming three different selling prices, are as follows:

Sold at book value, for $2,250. No gain or loss.

Oct. 12	Cash	2,250	
	Accumulated Depreciation—Equipment	7,750	
	Equipment		10,000

Sold below book value, for $1,000. Loss of $1,250.

Oct. 12	Cash	1,000	
	Accumulated Depreciation—Equipment	7,750	
	Loss on Disposal of Plant Assets	1,250	
	Equipment		10,000

Sold above book value, for $3,000. Gain of $750.

Oct. 12	Cash	3,000	
	Accumulated Depreciation—Equipment	7,750	
	Equipment		10,000
	Gain on Disposal of Plant Assets		750

EXCHANGES OF SIMILAR PLANT ASSETS

Old equipment is often traded in for new equipment having a similar use. In such cases, the seller and the buyer agree to an amount for the old equipment traded in. This amount, which may be either greater or less than the book value of the old equipment, is called the trade-in allowance. The remaining balance that is owed, called boot, is determined by deducting the trade-in allowance from the price of the new equipment. Boot is either paid in cash or a liability is recorded.

Gains on Exchanges

Gains on exchanges of similar plant assets are not recognized for financial reporting purposes. This is based on the theory that revenue occurs from the production and sale of goods produced by plant assets and not from the exchange of similar plant assets.

When the trade-in allowance exceeds the book value of an asset traded in and no gain is recognized, the cost of the new asset is the amount of boot given plus the book value of the old asset. For example, assume the following exchange:

Similar equipment acquired (new):		
Price of new equipment	$5,000	
Trade-in allowance on old equipment	1,100	
Boot given (cash)		$3,900
Equipment traded in (old):		
Cost of old equipment	$4,000	
Accumulated depreciation at date of exchange	3,200	
Book value at June 19, date of exchange		800
Cost of new equipment		$4,700

The entry to record this exchange and the assumed payment of cash is as follows:

June 19	Accumulated Depreciation—Equipment	3,200	
	Equipment	4,700	
	Equipment		4,000
	Cash		3,900

Not recognizing the $300 gain ($1,100 trade-in allowance minus $800 book value) at the time of the exchange reduces future depreciation expense. That is, the depreciation expense for the new asset is based on a cost of $4,700 rather than on the quoted price of $5,000. In effect, the unrecognized gain of $300 reduces the total amount of depreciation taken during the life of the equipment by $300.

In exchanges as described above, gains are also not recognized for federal income tax purposes. Specifically, the Internal Revenue Code (IRC) does not permit gains to be recognized when (1) the asset acquired by the taxpayer is similar in use to the asset given in exchange and (2) any boot involved is given (rather than received) by the taxpayer. Thus, in the above example, the cost of the new equipment for federal income tax purposes is $4,700.

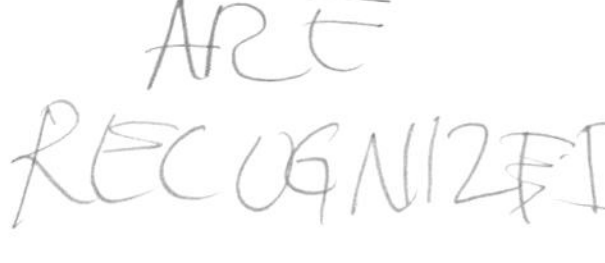

Losses on Exchanges

For financial reporting purposes, losses are recognized on exchanges of similar plant assets if the trade-in allowance is less than the book value of the old equipment. To illustrate, assume the following exchange:

Similar equipment acquired (new):	
Price of new equipment	$10,000
Trade-in allowance on old equipment	2,000
Boot given (cash)	$ 8,000
Equipment traded in (old):	
Cost of old equipment	$ 7,000
Accumulated depreciation at date of exchange	4,600
Book value at September 7, date of exchange	$ 2,400

The amount of the loss recognized on the exchange is the excess of the book value of the equipment traded in ($2,400) over the trade-in allowance ($2,000), or $400. The entry to record the exchange is as follows:

Sept. 7	Accumulated Depreciation—Equipment	4,600	
	Equipment	10,000	
	Loss on Disposal of Plant Assets	400	
	Equipment		7,000
	Cash		8,000

For federal income tax purposes, losses are not recognized when (1) the asset acquired by the taxpayer is similar in use to the asset given in exchange and (2) any boot involved is given (rather than received) by the taxpayer. The cost of the new equipment is determined by adding the boot given to the book value of the equipment traded in. In the above example, the cost of the new equipment for federal income tax purposes is determined as follows:

Book value of equipment traded in	$ 2,400
Boot given (cash)	8,000
Cost of new equipment	$10,400

The unrecognized loss of $400 at the time of the exchange increases the cost of the new equipment. Thus, the total amount of depreciation expense increases by $400 during the useful life of the equipment.

Summary of Accounting for Exchanges

Exhibit 7 summarizes the accounting for exchanges of similar plant assets for financial and income tax reporting, based on the following data:

Quoted price of new equipment acquired	$15,000
Cost of old equipment traded in	$12,500
Accumulated depreciation at date of exchange	10,100
Book value at date of exchange	$ 2,400

Exhibit 7
Summary Illustration—Accounting for Exchanges of Similar Plant Assets

CASE ONE (GAIN): Trade-in allowance is more than book value of asset traded in.
Trade-in allowance, $3,000; boot given, $12,000 ($15,000 – $3,000)

	Financial Reporting			*Income Tax Reporting*		
Cost of new asset	Boot plus book value of asset traded in, $14,400 ($12,000 + $2,400)			Boot plus book value of asset traded in, $14,400 ($12,000 + $2,400)		
Gain recognized	None			None		
Entry	Equipment	14,400		Equipment	14,400	
	Accumulated Depreciation	10,100		Accumulated Depreciation	10,100	
	Equipment		12,500	Equipment		12,500
	Cash		12,000	Cash		12,000

CASE TWO (LOSS): Trade-in allowance is less than book value of asset traded in.
Trade-in allowance, $2,000; boot given, $13,000 ($15,000 – $2,000)

	Financial Reporting			*Income Tax Reporting*		
Cost of new asset	Quoted price of new asset acquired, $15,000			Boot plus book value of asset traded in, $15,400 ($13,000 + $2,400)		
Loss recognized	$400			None		
Entry	Equipment	15,000		Equipment	15,400	
	Accumulated Depreciation	10,100		Accumulated Depreciation	10,100	
	Loss on Disposal	400		Equipment		12,500
	Equipment		12,500	Cash		13,000
	Cash		13,000			

Leasing Plant Assets

Objective 5
Define a lease and summarize the accounting rules related to the leasing of plant assets.

You are probably familiar with leases. A **lease** is a contract for the use of an asset for a stated period of time. The two parties to a lease contract are the lessor and the lessee. The **lessor** is the party who owns the asset. The **lessee** is the party to whom the rights to use the asset are granted by the lessor. The lessee is obligated to make periodic rent payments for the lease term.

All leases are classified by the lessee as either capital leases or operating leases. Capital leases include one or more of the following elements:

1. The lease transfers ownership of the asset to the lessee at the end of the lease term.
2. The lease contains an option for a bargain purchase of the asset by the lessee.
3. The lease term extends over most of the economic life of the asset.
4. The lease requires rental payments that approximate the fair market value of the asset.[10]

[10] *Statement of Financial Accounting Standards, No. 13,* "Accounting for Leases," Financial Accounting Standards Board, Stamford, 1976, par. 7.

A capital lease is accounted for as if the lessee has, in fact, purchased the asset. Thus, under a capital lease, the lessee debits an asset account for the fair market value of the asset and credits a long-term lease liability account. The accounting for capital leases is discussed in detail in more advanced accounting texts.

Leases that do not meet the preceding criteria for a capital lease are classified as **operating leases.** The lease payments under an operating lease are accounted for as rent expense by the lessee. The rentals of assets described in the earlier chapters of this text were accounted for as operating leases. Neither future lease obligations nor the future rights to use the asset are recognized in the accounts. However, the lessee must disclose future lease commitments in footnotes to the financial statements.[11]

Instead of owning a plant asset, a business may acquire the use of a plant asset through a lease. For example, automobiles, computers, medical equipment, buildings, and airplanes are often leased. Of the companies surveyed in the 1994 edition of *Accounting Trends & Techniques*, 91% reported either a capital lease or an operating lease.

Internal Control of Plant Assets

Objective 6
Describe internal controls over plant assets and provide examples of such controls.

Because of the dollar value and the long-term nature of plant assets, it is important to design and implement effective internal controls over plant assets. Such controls should begin with authorization and approval procedures for the purchase of plant assets. Procedures should also exist to ensure that plant assets are acquired at the lowest possible costs. One procedure to achieve this objective is to require competitive bids from preapproved vendors.

Like the assets we discussed in earlier chapters, plant assets should be safeguarded from possible theft, misuse, or other damage. For example, plant assets that are highly marketable and susceptible to theft, such as computers, should be locked or otherwise safeguarded when not in use. For computers, safeguarding includes proper consideration of climate controls and special fire-extinguishing equipment. Procedures should also exist for training employees to properly operate plant assets such as equipment and machinery. Plant assets should also be insured against theft, fire, flooding, or other disasters.

As soon as a plant asset is received, it should be inspected and tagged for control purposes, and an entry should be made in the plant asset subsidiary ledger. A company that maintains a computerized subsidiary ledger may use bar-coded tags, similar to the one on the back of this textbook, so that plant asset data can be directly scanned into computer records.

A physical inventory of plant assets should be taken periodically in order to verify the accuracy of the accounting records. Such an inventory would detect missing, obsolete, or idle plant assets. In addition, plant assets should be inspected periodically in order to determine their state of repair.

Careful control should also be exercised over the disposal of plant assets. All disposals should be properly authorized and approved. Fully depreciated assets should be retained in the accounting records until disposal has been authorized and they are removed from service. In this way, accountability for the asset is maintained throughout the period of ownership.

Depletion

Objective 7
Compute depletion and journalize the entry for depletion.

The periodic allocation of the cost of metal ores and other minerals removed from the earth is called **depletion.** This allocation to expense is based upon a depletion

[11] *Ibid.*, par. 16.

rate that is computed by dividing the cost of the mineral deposit by its estimated size. The amount of periodic depletion is determined by multiplying the quantity extracted during the period by the depletion rate.

To illustrate, assume that a business paid $400,000 for the mining rights to a mineral deposit estimated at 1,000,000 tons of ore. The depletion rate is $0.40 per ton ($400,000 ÷ 1,000,000 tons). If 90,000 tons are mined during the year, the periodic depletion is $36,000 (90,000 tons × $0.40). The entry to record the depletion is shown below.

	Adjusting Entry		
Dec. 31	Depletion Expense	36,000	
	Accumulated Depletion		36,000

Like the accumulated depreciation account, the accumulated depletion account is a contra asset account. It is reported on the balance sheet as a deduction from the cost of the mineral deposit.

In determining income subject to the federal income tax, complex Internal Revenue Code (IRC) rules regarding depletion deductions must be applied. You can find a detailed discussion of the tax law and the regulations regarding depletion in tax textbooks.

Intangible Assets

Objective 8
Journalize the entries for acquiring and amortizing intangible assets, such as patents, copyrights, and goodwill.

Long-term assets that are without physical attributes and not held for sale but are useful in the operations of a business are **intangible assets.** Intangible assets include such items as patents, copyrights, and goodwill.

The basic principles of accounting for intangible assets are like those described earlier for plant assets. The major concerns are (1) determining the initial cost and (2) recognizing the periodic cost expiration, called **amortization.** Amortization results from the passage of time or a decline in the usefulness of the intangible asset.

PATENTS

Manufacturers may acquire exclusive rights to produce and sell goods with one or more unique features. Such rights are granted by **patents,** which the federal government issues to inventors. These rights continue in effect for 17 years. A business may purchase patent rights from others, or it may obtain patents developed by its own research and development efforts.

The initial cost of a purchased patent should be debited to an asset account. This cost should be written off, or amortized, over the years of the patent's expected usefulness. This period of time may be less than the remaining legal life of the patent. The estimated useful life of the patent may also change as technology or consumer tastes change. The straight-line method of amortization is used, unless it can be shown that another method is better.[12]

A separate contra asset account is normally not credited for the write-off or amortization of patents. The credit is normally recorded directly in the patents account. This practice is common for all intangible assets.

To illustrate, assume that at the beginning of its fiscal year a business acquires patent rights for $100,000. The patent had been granted 6 years earlier by the Federal Patent Office. Although the patent will not expire for 11 years, its remaining useful

[12] *Opinions of the Accounting Principles Board, No. 17,* "Intangible Assets," American Institute of Certified Public Accountants, New York, 1970, par. 30.

life is estimated as 5 years. The entry to amortize the patent at the end of the fiscal year is as follows:

	Adjusting Entry		
Dec. 31	Amortization Expense—Patents	20,000	
	Patents		20,000

Assume that after two years of use it appears that this patent will have only two years of remaining usefulness. The cost to be amortized in the third year is $30,000, which is the balance of the asset account, $60,000 ($100,000 – $40,000), divided by two years.

Rather than purchase patent rights, a business may incur significant costs in developing patents through its own research and development efforts. Such costs, called **research and development costs,** are accounted for as current operating expenses in the period in which they are incurred.[13]

Expensing research and development costs in the period they are incurred is justified by two reasons. First, there is a high degree of uncertainty about the future benefits from research and development efforts. In fact, most research and development efforts do not result in patents. Second, even if a patent is granted, it may be difficult to objectively estimate its cost. If many research projects are in process at the same time, for example, it is difficult to separate the costs of one project from another.

Whether patent rights are purchased or developed internally, a business often incurs significant legal fees related to patents. For example, legal fees may be incurred in filing for patents or in defending the legal rights to patents. Such fees should be debited to an asset account and then amortized over the years of usefulness of the patents.

COPYRIGHTS

The exclusive right to publish and sell a literary, artistic, or musical composition is granted by a **copyright.** Copyrights are issued by the federal government and extend for 50 years beyond the author's death. The costs of a copyright include all costs of creating the work plus any administrative or legal costs of obtaining the copyright. A copyright that is purchased from another should be recorded at the price paid for it. Because of the uncertainty regarding the useful life of a copyright, it is normally amortized over a short period of time. For example, the copyright costs of this text are amortized over 3 years.

The exclusive right to sell a creative work like "The Lion King" is granted by a copyright issued by the federal government.

GOODWILL

In business, goodwill refers to an intangible asset of a business that is created from such favorable factors as location, product quality, reputation, and managerial skill. Goodwill allows a business to earn a rate of return on its investment that is often in excess of the normal rate for other firms in the same business.

Generally accepted accounting principles permit the recording of goodwill in the accounts only if it is objectively determined by a transaction. An example of such a transaction is the purchase or sale of a business. In addition, goodwill should be amortized over its estimated useful life, which cannot exceed 40 years.[14] For example, in its 1994 annual report, La-Z-Boy Chair Company reported that it amortizes goodwill from acquired companies over a period of 30 years.

[13]*Statement of Financial Accounting Standards, No. 2,* "Accounting for Research and Development Costs," Financial Accounting Standards Board, Stamford, 1974, par. 12.

[14]*Opinions of the Accounting Principles Board, No. 17,* "Intangible Assets," *op. cit.*, par. 29.

Financial Reporting for Plant Assets and Intangible Assets

Objective 9
Describe how depreciation expense is reported in an income statement and prepare a balance sheet that includes plant assets and intangible assets.

How should plant assets and intangible assets be reported in the financial statements? The amount of depreciation and amortization expense of a period should be reported separately in the income statement or disclosed in a footnote. A general description of the method or methods used in computing depreciation should also be reported.[15]

The amount of each major class of plant assets should be disclosed in the balance sheet or in footnotes. The related accumulated depreciation should also be disclosed, either by major class or in total.[16] If there are too many classes of plant assets, a single amount may be presented in the balance sheet, supported by a separate detailed listing.

The cost of mineral rights or ore deposits is normally shown as part of the plant assets section of the balance sheet. The related accumulated depletion should also be disclosed. In some cases, the mineral rights are shown net of depletion on the face of the balance sheet, accompanied by a footnote that discloses the amount of the accumulated depletion.

Intangible assets are usually reported in the balance sheet in a separate section immediately following plant assets. The balance of each major class of intangible assets should be disclosed at an amount net of amortization taken to date. Exhibit 8 is a partial balance sheet that shows the reporting of plant assets and intangible assets.

Exhibit 8
Plant Assets and Intangible Assets in the Balance Sheet

Discovery Mining Co.
Balance Sheet
December 31, 19—

Assets

Total current assets					$ 462,500
Plant assets:	Cost	Accum. Depr.	Book Value		
Land	$ 30,000	—	$ 30,000		
Buildings	110,000	$ 26,000	84,000		
Factory equipment	650,000	192,000	458,000		
Office equipment	120,000	13,000	107,000		
	$ 910,000	$ 231,000		$679,000	
Mineral deposits:	Cost	Accum. Depletion	Book Value		
Alaska deposit	$1,200,000	$ 800,000	$400,000		
Wyoming deposit	750,000	200,000	550,000		
	$1,950,000	$1,000,000		950,000	
Total plant assets					$1,629,000
Intangible assets:					
Patents				$ 75,000	
Goodwill				50,000	
Total intangible assets					125,000

[15] *Opinions of the Accounting Principles Board, No. 22,* "Disclosure of Accounting Policies," American Institute of Certified Public Accountants, New York, 1972, par. 13.
[16] *Opinions of the Accounting Principles Board, No. 12,* "Omnibus Opinion—1967," American Institute of Certified Public Accountants, New York, 1967, par. 5.

Appendix: Sum-of-the-Years-Digits Depreciation

At one time, the sum-of-the-years-digits method of depreciation was used by many businesses. However, the tax law changes of the 1980s limited its use for tax purposes. As a result, *Accounting Trends & Techniques* reports that less than 2% of the surveyed companies now use this method for financial reporting purposes.[17]

Under the **sum-of-the-years-digits depreciation method,** depreciation expense is determined by multiplying the original cost of the asset less its estimated residual value by a smaller fraction each year. Thus, the sum-of-the-years-digits method is similar to the declining-balance method, in that the depreciation expense declines each year.

The denominator of the fraction used in determining the depreciation expense is the sum of the digits of the years of the asset's useful life. For example, an asset with a useful life of 5 years would have a denominator of 15 (5 + 4 + 3 + 2 + 1).[18] The numerator of the fraction is the number of years of useful life remaining at the beginning of each year for which depreciation is being computed. Thus, the numerator decreases each year by 1. For a useful life of 5 years, the numerator is 5 the first year, 4 the second year, 3 the third year, and so on.

The following depreciation schedule illustrates the sum-of-the-years-digits method for an asset with a cost of $16,000, an estimated residual value of $1,000, and an estimated useful life of 5 years:

Year	*Cost Less Residual Value*	*Rate*	*Depreciation for Year*	*Accum. Depr. at End of Year*	*Book Value at End of Year*
1	$15,000	5/15	$5,000	$ 5,000	$11,000
2	15,000	4/15	4,000	9,000	7,000
3	15,000	3/15	3,000	12,000	4,000
4	15,000	2/15	2,000	14,000	2,000
5	15,000	1/15	1,000	15,000	1,000

What if the plant asset is not placed in service at the beginning of the year? When the date an asset is first put into service is not the beginning of a fiscal year, each full year's depreciation must be allocated between the two fiscal years benefited. To illustrate, assume that the asset in the above example was put into service at the beginning of the fourth month of the first fiscal year. The depreciation for that year would be $3,750 (9/12 × 5/15 × $15,000). The depreciation for the second year would be $4,250, computed as follows:

3/12 × 5/15 × $15,000	$1,250
9/12 × 4/15 × $15,000	3,000
Total depreciation for second fiscal year	$4,250

KEY POINTS

Objective 1. Define plant assets and describe the accounting for their cost.

Plant assets are long-term tangible assets that are owned by the business and are used in the normal operations of the business. Examples of plant assets are equipment, buildings, and land. The initial cost of a plant asset includes all amounts spent to get the asset in place and ready for use. For example, sales tax, freight, insurance in transit, and installation costs are all included in the cost of a plant asset. As time passes, all plant assets except land lose their ability to provide services. As a result, the cost of a plant asset should be transferred to an expense account, in a systematic manner, during the asset's expected useful life. This periodic cost expiration is called depreciation.

[17] *Accounting Trends & Techniques*, 48th Edition, New York, American Institute of Certified Public Accountants, 1994.

[18] The denominator can also be determined from the following formula: S = N[(N + 1)/2], where S = sum of the digits and N = number of years of estimated life.

Objective 2. Compute depreciation, using the following methods: straight-line method, units-of-production method, and declining-balance method.
In computing depreciation, three factors need to be considered: (1) the plant asset's initial cost, (2) the useful life of the asset, and (3) the residual value of the asset.

The straight-line method spreads the initial cost less the residual value equally over the useful life. The units-of-production method spreads the initial cost less the residual value equally over the units expected to be produced by the asset during its useful life. The declining-balance method is applied by multiplying the declining book value of the asset by twice the straight-line rate.

Objective 3. Classify plant asset costs as either capital expenditures or revenue expenditures.
Costs for additions to plant assets and other costs related to improving efficiency or capacity are classified as capital expenditures. Costs for additions to an asset and costs that add to the usefulness of the asset for more than one period (called betterments) are also classified as capital expenditures. Costs that increase the useful life of an asset beyond the original estimate are a capital expenditure and are called extraordinary repairs. Expenditures that benefit only the current period or that maintain normal operating efficiency are debited to expense accounts and are classified as revenue expenditures.

Objective 4. Journalize entries for the disposal of plant assets.
The journal entries to record disposals of plant assets will vary. In all cases, however, any depreciation for the current period should be recorded, and the book value of the asset is then removed from the accounts. The entry to remove the book value from the accounts is a debit to the asset's accumulated depreciation account and a credit to the asset account for the cost of the asset. For assets retired from service, a loss may be recorded for any remaining book value of the asset.

When a plant asset is sold, the book value is removed and the cash or other asset received is also recorded. If the selling price is more than the book value of the asset, the transaction results in a gain. If the selling price is less than the book value, there is a loss.

When a plant asset is exchanged for another of similar nature, no gain is recognized on the exchange. The acquired asset's cost is adjusted for any gains. A loss on an exchange of similar assets is recorded.

Objective 5. Define a lease and summarize the accounting rules related to the leasing of plant assets.
A lease is a contract for the use of an asset for a period of time. A capital lease is accounted for as if the lessee has purchased the asset. The lease payments under an operating lease are accounted for as rent expense for the lessee.

Objective 6. Describe internal controls over plant assets and provide examples of such controls.
Internal controls over plant assets should include procedures for authorizing the purchase of assets. Once acquired, plant assets should be safeguarded from theft, misuse, or damage. A physical inventory of plant assets should be taken periodically.

Objective 7. Compute depletion and journalize the entry for depletion.
The amount of periodic depletion is computed by multiplying the quantity of minerals extracted during the period by a depletion rate. The depletion rate is computed by dividing the cost of the mineral deposit by its estimated size. The entry to record depletion debits a depletion expense account and credits an accumulated depletion account.

Objective 8. Journalize the entries for acquiring and amortizing intangible assets, such as patents, copyrights, and goodwill.
Long-term assets that are without physical attributes but are used in the business are classified as intangible assets. Examples of intangible assets are patents, copyrights, and goodwill. The initial cost of an intangible asset should be debited to an asset account. This cost should be written off, or amortized, over the years of the asset's expected usefulness by debiting an expense account and crediting the intangible asset account.

Objective 9. Describe how depreciation expense is reported in an income statement and prepare a balance sheet that includes plant assets and intangible assets.
The amount of depreciation expense and the method or methods used in computing depreciation should be disclosed in the financial statements. In addition, each major class of plant assets should be disclosed, along with the related accumulated depreciation. Intangible assets are usually presented in the balance sheet in a separate section immediately following plant assets. Each major class of intangible assets should be disclosed at an amount net of the amortization recorded to date.

changing methods needs to be approved
-supplier could go out of business

GLOSSARY OF KEY TERMS

Accelerated depreciation method. A depreciation method that provides for a high depreciation expense in the first year of use of an asset and a gradually declining expense thereafter. *Objective 2*

Amortization. The periodic expense attributed to the decline in usefulness of an intangible asset. *Objective 8*

Betterment. An expenditure that increases operating efficiency or capacity for the remaining useful life of a plant asset. *Objective 3*

Book value. The cost of a plant asset minus the accumulated depreciation on the asset. *Objective 2*

Boot. The balance owed the supplier when an old asset is traded for a new asset. *Objective 4*

Capital expenditures. Costs that add to the usefulness of assets for more than one accounting period. *Objective 3*

Capital leases. Leases that include one or more of four provisions that result in treating the leased assets as purchased assets in the accounts. *Objective 5*

Declining-balance depreciation method. A method of depreciation that provides declining periodic depreciation expense over the estimated life of an asset. *Objective 2*

Depletion. The cost of metal ores and other minerals removed from the earth. *Objective 7*

Depreciation. The periodic cost expiration for the use of all plant assets except land. *Objective 1*

Extraordinary repair. An expenditure that increases the useful life of an asset beyond the original estimate. *Objective 3*

Goodwill. An intangible asset of a business due to such favorable factors as location, product superiority, reputation, and managerial skill. *Objective 8*

Intangible assets. Long-lived assets that are useful in the operations of a business, are not held for sale, and are without physical qualities. *Objective 8*

Operating leases. Leases that do not meet the criteria for capital leases and thus are accounted for as operating expenses. *Objective 5*

Plant assets. Relatively permanent tangible assets used in the operations of a business. *Objective 1*

Residual value. The estimated recoverable cost of a depreciable asset as of the time of its removal from service. *Objective 2*

Revenue expenditures. Expenditures that benefit only the current period. *Objective 3*

Straight-line depreciation method. A method of depreciation that provides for equal periodic depreciation expense over the estimated life of an asset. *Objective 2*

Trade-in allowance. The amount a seller grants a buyer for a plant asset that is traded in for a similar asset. *Objective 4*

Units-of-production depreciation method. A method of depreciation that provides for depreciation expense based on the expected productive capacity of an asset. *Objective 2*

ILLUSTRATIVE PROBLEM

McCollum Company, a furniture wholesaler, acquired new equipment at a cost of $150,000 at the beginning of the fiscal year. The equipment has an estimated life of 5 years and an estimated residual value of $12,000. Ellen McCollum, the president, has requested information regarding alternative depreciation methods.

Instructions

1. Determine the annual depreciation for each of the five years of estimated useful life of the equipment, the accumulated depreciation at the end of each year, and the book value of the equipment at the end of each year by (a) the straight-line method and (b) the declining-balance method (at twice the straight-line rate).
2. Assume that the equipment was depreciated under the declining-balance method. In the first week of the fifth year, the equipment was traded in for similar equipment priced at $175,000. The trade-in allowance on the old equipment was $10,000, and cash was paid for the balance.
   a. Journalize the entry to record the exchange.
   b. What is the cost basis of the new equipment for computing the amount of depreciation allowable for income tax purposes?

Solution

1.

	Year	*Depreciation Expense*	*Accumulated Depreciation, End of Year*	*Book Value, End of Year*
a.	1	$27,600*	$ 27,600	$122,400
	2	27,600	55,200	94,800
	3	27,600	82,800	67,200
	4	27,600	110,400	39,600
	5	27,600	138,000	12,000

*$27,600 = ($150,000 – $12,000) ÷ 5

	Year	*Depreciation Expense*	*Accumulated Depreciation, End of Year*	*Book Value, End of Year*
b.	1	$60,000**	$ 60,000	$ 90,000
	2	36,000	96,000	54,000
	3	21,600	117,600	32,400
	4	12,960	130,560	19,440
	5	7,440***	138,000	12,000

**$60,000 = $150,000 × 40%

***The asset is not depreciated below the estimated residual value of $12,000.

2.

a. Accumulated Depreciation—Equipment	130,560		
Equipment	175,000		
Loss on Disposal of Plant Assets	9,440		
Equipment		150,000	
Cash		165,000	
b. Book value of old equipment			$ 19,440
Boot given (cash)			165,000
Cost basis of new equipment for income tax purposes			$184,440

SELF-EXAMINATION QUESTIONS (ANSWERS AT END OF CHAPTER)

1. Which of the following expenditures incurred in connection with the acquisition of machinery is a proper charge to the asset account?
   A. Freight
   B. Installation costs
   C. Both A and B
   D. Neither A nor B

2. What is the amount of depreciation, using the declining-balance method (twice the straight-line rate) for the second year of use for equipment costing $9,000, with an estimated residual value of $600 and an estimated life of 3 years?
   A. $6,000
   B. $3,000
   C. $2,000
   D. $400

3. An example of an accelerated depreciation method is:
   A. Straight-line
   B. Declining-balance
   C. Units-of-production
   D. Depletion

4. A plant asset priced at $100,000 is acquired by trading in a similar asset that has a book value of $25,000. Assuming that the trade-in allowance is $30,000 and that $70,000 cash is paid for the new asset, what is the cost of the new asset for financial reporting purposes?
   A. $100,000
   B. $95,000
   C. $70,000
   D. $30,000

5. Which of the following is an example of an intangible asset?
   A. Patents
   B. Goodwill
   C. Copyrights
   D. All of the above

DISCUSSION QUESTIONS

1. Which of the following qualities are characteristic of plant assets? (a) tangible, (b) capable of repeated use in the operations of the business, (c) held for sale in the normal course of business, (d) used continuously in the operations of the business, (e) long-lived.
2. Buckner Office Equipment Co. has a fleet of automobiles and trucks for use by salespersons and for delivery of office supplies and equipment. Ellsworth Auto Sales Co. has automobiles and trucks for sale. Under what caption would the automobiles and trucks be reported on the balance sheet of (a) Buckner Office Equipment Co., (b) Ellsworth Auto Sales Co.?
3. T. Camarillo Co. acquired an adjacent vacant lot with the hope of selling it in the future at a gain. The lot is not intended to be used in Camarillo's business operations. Where should such real estate be listed in the balance sheet?
4. Terminix Company solicited bids from several contractors to construct an addition to its office building. The lowest bid received was for $140,000. Terminix Company decided to construct the addition itself at a cost of $125,000. What amount should be recorded in the building account?
5. Are the amounts at which plant assets are reported in the balance sheet their approximate market values as of the balance sheet date? Discuss.
6. a. Does the recognition of depreciation in the accounts provide a special cash fund for the replacement of plant assets? Explain.
   b. Describe the nature of depreciation as the term is used in accounting.
7. Name the three factors that need to be considered in determining the amount of periodic depreciation.
8. Nordhoff Company purchased a machine that has a manufacturer's suggested life of 15 years. The company plans to use the machine on a special project that will last 6 years. At the completion of the project, the machine will be sold. Over how many years should the machine be depreciated?

9. Is it necessary for a business to use the same method of computing depreciation (a) for all classes of its depreciable assets, (b) in the financial statements and in determining income taxes?
10. Of the three common depreciation methods, which is most widely used?
11. a. Under what conditions is the use of an accelerated depreciation method most appropriate?
    b. Why is an accelerated depreciation method often used for income tax purposes?
    c. What is the Modified Accelerated Cost Recovery System (MACRS), and under what conditions is it used?

12. A revision of depreciable plant asset lives resulted in an increase in the remaining lives of certain plant assets. The company would like to include, as income of the current period, the cumulative effect of the changes, which reduce the depreciation expense of past periods. Is this in accordance with generally accepted accounting principles? Discuss.

    Source: "Q's and A's Technical Hotline," *Journal of Accountancy*, December 1991, p. 89.

13. a. Differentiate between capital expenditures and revenue expenditures.
    b. Why are some items that have the characteristics of capital expenditures treated as revenue expenditures?
14. Immediately after a used truck is acquired, a new motor is installed and the tires are replaced at a total cost of $3,950. Is this a capital expenditure or a revenue expenditure?
15. For some of the plant assets of a business, the balance in Accumulated Depreciation is exactly equal to the cost of the asset. (a) Is it permissible to record additional depreciation on the assets if they are still useful to the business? Explain. (b) When should an entry be made to remove the cost and the accumulated depreciation from the accounts?
16. In what sections of the income statement are gains and losses from the disposal of plant assets presented?
17. Differentiate between a capital lease and an operating lease.

18. The financial statements of La-Z-Boy Chair Company contain the following footnote:

    The Company has several long-term leases covering manufacturing facilities. The lease agreements require the Company to insure and maintain the facilities and provide for annual payments, which include interest. These leases give the Company the option to purchase the facilities for nominal amounts, or in some instances to renew the leases for extended periods at nominal annual rentals.

    Would these leases be classified as operating or capital leases? Discuss.
19. Describe the internal controls for acquiring plant assets.
20. Why is a physical count of plant assets necessary?
21. What is the term applied to the periodic charge for (a) ore removed from a mine, (b) the use of an intangible asset?
22. a. Over what period of time should the cost of a patent acquired by purchase be amortized?
    b. In general, what is the required treatment for research and development costs?
23. How should (a) plant assets and (b) intangible assets be reported in the balance sheet?

EXERCISES

EXERCISE 10–1
Costs of acquiring plant assets
Objective 1

Jill Neagle owns and operates Quality Print Co. During July, Quality Print Co. incurred the following costs in acquiring two printing presses. One printing press was new, and the other was used by a business that recently filed for bankruptcy.

Costs related to new printing press:

1. Sales tax on purchase price
2. Freight
3. Insurance while in transit
4. Special foundation
5. New parts to replace those damaged in unloading
6. Fee paid to factory representative for installation

Costs related to secondhand printing press:

7. Freight
8. Installation

9. Repair of vandalism during installation
10. Replacement of worn-out parts
11. Repair of damage incurred in reconditioning the press
12. Fees paid to attorney to review purchase agreement

a. Indicate which costs incurred in acquiring the new printing press should be debited to the asset account.
b. Indicate which costs incurred in acquiring the secondhand printing press should be debited to the asset account.

EXERCISE 10–2
Determining cost of land
Objective 1

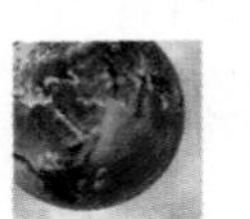

A company has developed a tract of land into a ski resort. The company has cut the trees, cleared and graded the land and hills, and constructed ski lifts. (a) Should the tree cutting, land clearing, and grading costs of constructing the ski slopes be debited to the land account? (b) If such costs are debited to Land, should they be depreciated?

Source: "Technical Issues Feature," *Journal of Accountancy*, December 1987, p. 82.

EXERCISE 10–3
Determining cost of land
Objective 1

Same-Day Delivery Company acquired an adjacent lot to construct a new warehouse, paying $20,000 and giving a short-term note for $80,000. Legal fees paid were $3,500, delinquent taxes assumed were $7,500, and fees paid to remove an old building from the land were $12,100. Materials salvaged from the demolition of the building were sold for $3,000. A contractor was paid $212,500 to construct a new warehouse. Determine the cost of the land to be reported on the balance sheet.

EXERCISE 10–4
Nature of depreciation
Objective 1

Millefleurs Metal Casting Co. reported $425,000 for equipment and $110,000 for accumulated depreciation—equipment on its balance sheet.

Does this mean (a) that the replacement cost of the equipment is $425,000 and (b) that $110,000 is set aside in a special fund for the replacement of the equipment? Explain.

EXERCISE 10–5
Straight-line depreciation rates
Objective 2

Convert each of the following estimates of useful life to a straight-line depreciation rate, stated as a percentage, assuming that the residual value of the plant asset is to be ignored: (a) 4 years, (b) 5 years, (c) 10 years, (d) 20 years, (e) 25 years, (f) 40 years, (g) 50 years.

EXERCISE 10–6
Straight-line depreciation
Objective 2

A refrigerator used by a meat processor has a cost of $113,500, an estimated residual value of $5,500, and an estimated useful life of 8 years. What is the amount of the annual depreciation computed by the straight-line method?

EXERCISE 10–7
Depreciation by units-of-production method
Objective 2

A diesel-powered generator with a cost of $670,000 and estimated residual value of $50,000 is expected to have a useful operating life of 50,000 hours. During August, the generator was operated 1,250 hours. Determine the depreciation for the month.

EXERCISE 10–8
Depreciation by units-of-production method
Objective 2

Prior to adjustment at the end of the year, the balance in Trucks is $139,600, and the balance in Accumulated Depreciation Trucks is $62,800. Details of the subsidiary ledger are as follows:

Truck No.	*Cost*	*Estimated Residual Value*	*Estimated Useful Life*	*Accumulated Depreciation at Beginning of Year*	*Miles Operated During Year*
1	$65,000	$5,000	250,000 miles	$22,500	28,000 miles
2	37,600	3,600	170,000	31,000	20,000
3	18,000	3,000	150,000	9,300	34,500
4	19,000	1,000	200,000	—	12,000

a. Determine the depreciation rates per mile and the amount to be credited to the accumulated depreciation section of each of the subsidiary accounts for the miles operated during the current year.
b. Journalize the entry to record depreciation for the year.

EXERCISE 10–9
Depreciation by two methods
Objective 2

A boiler acquired on January 2 at a cost of $315,000 has an estimated useful life of 20 years. Assuming that it will have no residual value, determine the depreciation for each of the first two years (a) by the straight-line method and (b) by the declining-balance method, using twice the straight-line rate.

EXERCISE 10–10
Depreciation by two methods
Objective 2

A dairy storage tank acquired at the beginning of the fiscal year at a cost of $75,200 has an estimated residual value of $3,200 and an estimated useful life of 8 years. Determine the following: (a) the amount of annual depreciation by the straight-line method and (b) the amount of depreciation for the first and second year computed by the declining-balance method (at twice the straight-line rate).

EXERCISE 10–11
Partial-year depreciation
Objective 2

Sandblasting equipment acquired at a cost of $95,000 has an estimated residual value of $5,000 and an estimated useful life of 5 years. It was placed in service on April 1 of the current fiscal year, which ends on December 31. Determine the depreciation for the current fiscal year and for the following fiscal year by (a) the straight-line method and (b) the declining-balance method, at twice the straight-line rate.

EXERCISE 10–12
Revision of depreciation
Objective 2

X-ray equipment with a cost of $310,000 has an estimated residual value of $10,000, an estimated useful life of 40 years, and is depreciated by the straight-line method. (a) What is the amount of the annual depreciation? (b) What is the book value at the end of the twenty-fifth year of use? (c) If at the start of the twenty-sixth year it is estimated that the remaining life is 15 years and that the residual value is $8,500, what is the depreciation expense for each of the remaining 15 years?

EXERCISE 10–13
Revision of depreciation
Objective 2

Mobile communications equipment acquired on January 5, 1994, at a cost of $92,500, has an estimated residual value of $7,500 and an estimated useful life of 10 years. Depreciation has been recorded for the first four years ended December 31, 1997, by the straight-line method. Determine the amount of depreciation for the current year ended December 31, 1998, if the revised estimated residual value is $3,300 and the revised estimated remaining useful life (including the current year) is 6 years.

EXERCISE 10–14
Capital and revenue expenditures
Objective 3

Baggio Co. incurred the following costs related to trucks and vans used in operating its delivery service:

1. Installed a hydraulic lift to a van.
2. Changed the oil and greased the joints of all the trucks and vans.
3. Removed a two-way radio from one of the trucks and installed a new radio with greater range of communication.
4. Overhauled the engine on one of the trucks that had been purchased four years ago.
5. Replaced the shock absorbers on two of the trucks with new shock absorbers that allow for the delivery of heavier loads.
6. Replaced the brakes and alternator on a truck that had been in service for the past 5 years.
7. Installed security systems on three of the newer trucks.
8. Repaired a flat tire on one of the vans.
9. Tinted the back and side windows of one of the vans to discourage theft of contents.
10. Rebuilt the transmission on one of the vans that had been driven only 25,000 miles. The van was no longer under warranty.

Classify each of the costs as a capital expenditure or a revenue expenditure. For those costs identified as capital expenditures, classify each as an addition, a betterment, or an extraordinary repair.

EXERCISE 10–15
Capital and revenue expenditures
Objective 3

Freddie McGriff Co. owns and operates Home Run Transport Co. During the past year, Freddie incurred the following costs related to his 18-wheel truck.

1. Replaced the hydraulic brake system that had begun to fail during his latest trip through the Smokey Mountains.
2. Replaced a headlight that had burned out.
3. Removed the old CB radio and replaced it with a newer model with greater range.

4. Overhauled the engine.
5. Replaced a shock absorber that had worn out.
6. Installed fog lights.
7. Installed a television in the sleeping compartment of the truck.
8. Replaced the old radar detector with a newer model that detects the KA frequencies now used by many of the state patrol radar guns. The detector is wired directly into the cab, so that it is partially hidden. In addition, Freddie fastened the detector to the truck with a locking device that prevents its removal.
9. Modified the factory-installed turbo charger with a special-order kit designed to add 30 more horsepower to the engine performance.
10. Installed a wind deflector on top of the cab to increase fuel mileage.

Classify each of the costs as a capital expenditure or a revenue expenditure. For those costs identified as capital expenditures, classify each as an addition, a betterment, or an extraordinary repair.

EXERCISE 10–16
Major repair to plant asset
Objective 3

A number of major structural repairs on a building were completed at the beginning of the current fiscal year at a cost of $79,000. The repairs are expected to extend the life of the building 6 years beyond the original estimate. The original cost of the building was $650,000, and it is being depreciated by the straight-line method for 25 years. The residual value is expected to be negligible and has been ignored. The balance of the related accumulated depreciation account after the depreciation adjustment at the end of the preceding year is $286,000.

a. What has the amount of annual depreciation been in past years?
b. To what account should the cost of repairs ($79,000) be debited?
c. What is the book value of the building after the repairs have been recorded?
d. What is the amount of depreciation for the current year, using the straight-line method (assuming that the repairs were completed at the very beginning of the year)?

EXERCISE 10–17
Entries for sale of plant asset
Objective 4

Metal recycling equipment acquired on January 3, 1994, at a cost of $77,500, has an estimated useful life of 6 years, an estimated residual value of $5,500, and is depreciated by the straight-line method.

a. What was the book value of the equipment at December 31, 1997, the end of the fiscal year?
b. Assuming that the equipment was sold on July 1, 1998, for $20,000, journalize the entries to record (1) depreciation for the six months of the current year ending December 31, 1998 and (2) the sale of the equipment.

EXERCISE 10–18
Disposal of plant asset
Objective 4

Millinery equipment acquired on January 3, 1994, at a cost of $42,000, has an estimated useful life of 4 years and an estimated residual value of $2,500.

a. What was the annual amount of depreciation for the years 1994, 1995, and 1996, using the straight-line method of depreciation?
b. What was the book value of the equipment on January 1, 1997?
c. Assuming that the equipment was sold on January 2, 1997, for $10,500, journalize the entry to record the sale.
d. Assuming that the equipment had been sold on January 2, 1997, for $14,500 instead of $10,500, journalize the entry to record the sale.

EXERCISE 10–19
Asset traded for similar asset
Objective 4

A printing press priced at $158,000 is acquired by trading in a similar press and paying cash for the difference between the trade-in allowance and the price of the new press. (a) Assuming that the trade-in allowance is $28,000, what is the amount of boot given? (b) Assuming that the book value of the press traded in is $23,000, what is the cost of the new press for financial reporting purposes? (c) What is the cost of the new press for computing depreciation for federal income tax purposes?

EXERCISE 10–20
Asset traded for similar asset
Objective 4

Assume the same facts as in Exercise 10–19, except that the book value of the press traded in is $35,000. (a) What is the amount of boot given? (b) What is the cost of the new press for financial reporting purposes? (c) What is the cost of the new press for computing depreciation for federal income tax purposes?

EXERCISE 10–21
Entries for trade of plant asset
Objective 4

On April 1, Danavox Co., a water distiller, acquired new bottling equipment with a list price of $235,000. Danavox received a trade-in allowance of $30,000 on the old equipment of a similar type, paid cash of $50,000, and gave a series of five notes payable for the remainder. The following information about the old equipment is obtained from the account in the equipment ledger: cost, $112,500; accumulated depreciation on December 31, the end of the preceding fiscal year, $75,000; annual depreciation, $7,500. Journalize the entries to record (a) the current depreciation of the old equipment to the date of trade-in and (b) the transaction on April 1 for financial reporting purposes.

EXERCISE 10–22
Entries for trade of plant asset
Objective 4

On October 1, Quota Co. acquired a new truck with a list price of $85,000. Quota received a trade-in allowance of $20,000 on an old truck of similar type, paid cash of $10,000, and gave a series of five notes payable for the remainder. The following information about the old truck is obtained from the account in the equipment ledger: cost, $62,500; accumulated depreciation on December 31, the end of the preceding fiscal year, $37,500; annual depreciation, $12,500. Journalize the entries to record (a) the current depreciation of the old truck to the date of trade-in and (b) the transaction on October 1 for financial reporting purposes.

EXERCISE 10–23
Depreciable cost of asset acquired by exchange
Objective 4

On the first day of the fiscal year, a delivery truck with a list price of $45,000 was acquired in exchange for an old delivery truck and $36,000 cash. The old truck had a book value of $10,500 at the date of the exchange.

a. Determine the following:
   1. Depreciable cost for financial reporting purposes.
   2. Depreciable cost for income tax purposes.
b. Assuming that the book value of the old delivery truck was $8,000, determine the following:
   1. Depreciable cost for financial reporting purposes.
   2. Depreciable cost for income tax purposes.

EXERCISE 10–24
Internal control of plant assets
Objective 6

PCNet Co. is a computer software company marketing products in the United States and Canada. While PCNet Co. has over 60 sales offices, all accounting is handled at the company's headquarters in Cincinnati, Ohio.

PCNet Co. keeps all its plant asset records on a computerized system. The computer maintains a subsidiary ledger of all plant assets owned by the company and calculates depreciation automatically. Whenever a manager at one of the sixty sales offices wants to purchase a plant asset, a purchase request is submitted to headquarters for approval. Upon approval, the plant asset is purchased and the invoice is sent back to headquarters so that the asset can be entered into the plant asset system.

A manager who wants to dispose of a plant asset simply sells or disposes of the asset and notifies headquarters to remove the asset from the system. Company cars and personal computers are frequently purchased by employees when they are disposed of. Most pieces of office equipment are traded in when new assets are acquired.

What internal control weakness exists in the procedures used to acquire and dispose of plant assets at PCNet Co.?

EXERCISE 10–25
Depletion entries
Objective 7

Bosch Co. acquired mineral rights for $15,000,000. The mineral deposit is estimated at 60,000,000 tons. During the current year, 11,500,000 tons were mined and sold for $3,500,000.

a. Determine the amount of depletion expense for the current year.
b. Journalize the adjusting entry to recognize the expense.

EXERCISE 10–26
Amortization entries
Objective 8

Cigna Company acquired patent rights on January 3, 1994, for $1,020,000. The patent has a useful life equal to its legal life of 17 years. On January 5, 1997, Cigna successfully defended the patent in a lawsuit at a cost of $105,000.

a. Determine the patent amortization expense for the current year ended December 31, 1997.
b. Journalize the adjusting entry to recognize the amortization.

EXERCISE 10–27
Balance sheet presentation
Objective 9

How many errors can you find in the following partial balance sheet?

Isaacsen Company
Balance Sheet
December 31, 19—

Assets

	Replacement Cost	Accumulated Depreciation	Book Value	
Total current assets:				$297,500
Plant assets:				
Land	$ 65,000	$ 20,000	$ 45,000	
Buildings	160,000	76,000	84,000	
Factory equipment	450,000	192,000	258,000	
Office equipment	120,000	77,000	43,000	
Patents	60,000	—	60,000	
Goodwill	45,000	—	45,000	
Total plant assets	$900,000	$365,000		535,000

APPENDIX EXERCISE 10–28
Sum-of-the-years-digits depreciation

Based on the data in Exercise 10–9, determine the depreciation for the boiler for each of the first two years, using the sum-of-the-years-digits depreciation method.

APPENDIX EXERCISE 10–29
Sum-of-the-years-digits depreciation

Based on the data in Exercise 10–10, determine the depreciation for the dairy storage tank for each of the first two years, using the sum-of-the-years-digits depreciation method.

APPENDIX EXERCISE 10–30
Partial-year depreciation

Based on the data in Exercise 10–11, determine the depreciation for the sandblasting equipment for each of the first two years, using the sum-of-the-years-digits depreciation method.

PROBLEMS SERIES A

PROBLEM 10–1A
Allocating payments and receipts to plant asset accounts
Objective 1

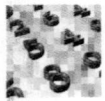

The following payments and receipts are related to land, land improvements, and buildings acquired for use in a ceramic wholesale business. The receipts are identified by an asterisk.

a.	Cost of real estate acquired as a plant site: Land	$250,000
	Building	75,000
b.	Delinquent real estate taxes on property, assumed by purchaser	18,750
c.	Cost of razing and removing building	5,800
d.	Fee paid to attorney for title search	900
e.	Cost of filling and grading land	29,700
f.	Architect's and engineer's fees for plans and supervision	60,000
g.	Premium on 1-year insurance policy during construction	6,600
h.	Payment to building contractor for new building	850,000
i.	Cost of repairing windstorm damage during construction	1,500
j.	Cost of paving parking lot to be used by customers	12,500
k.	Cost of trees and shrubbery planted	15,000
l.	Special assessment paid to city for extension of water main to the property	3,500
m.	Cost of repairing vandalism damage during construction	500
n.	Interest incurred on building loan during construction	48,000
o.	Cost of floodlights installed on parking lot	13,500
p.	Proceeds from sale of salvage materials from old building	2,100*
q.	Money borrowed to pay building contractor	600,000*
r.	Proceeds from insurance company for windstorm damage	4,000*
s.	Refund of premium on insurance policy (g) canceled after 11 months	550*

Instructions

1. Assign each payment and receipt to Land (unlimited life), Land Improvements (limited life), Building, or Other Accounts. Indicate receipts by an asterisk. Identify each item by letter and list the amounts in columnar form, as follows:

Item	*Land*	*Land Improvements*	*Building*	*Other Accounts*

2. The costs assigned to the land, which is used as a plant site, will not be depreciated, while the costs assigned to land improvements will be depreciated. Explain this seemingly contradictory application of the concept of depreciation.

PROBLEM 10–2A
Comparing three depreciation methods
Objective 2

NIFO Company purchased packaging equipment on January 3, 1996, for $315,000. The equipment was expected to have a useful life of 3 years, or 12,000 operating hours, and a residual value of $15,000. The equipment was used for 3,000 hours during 1996, 5,800 hours in 1997, and 3,200 hours in 1998.

Instructions

Determine the amount of depreciation expense for the years ended December 31, 1996, 1997, and 1998 by (a) the straight-line method, (b) the units-of-production method, and (c) the declining-balance method, using twice the straight-line rate. Also determine the total depreciation expense for the three years by each method. The following columnar headings are suggested for recording the depreciation expense amounts:

	Depreciation Expense		
Year	*Straight-Line Method*	*Units-of-Production Method*	*Declining-Balance Method*

PROBLEM 10–3A
Depreciation by three methods; partial years
Objective 2

Gotham Company purchased plastic laminating equipment on July 1, 1996, for $108,000. The equipment was expected to have a useful life of 3 years, or 17,000 operating hours, and a residual value of $6,000. The equipment was used for 2,400 hours during 1996, 7,600 hours in 1997, 4,800 hours in 1998, and 2,200 hours in 1999.

Instructions

Determine the amount of depreciation expense for the years ended December 31, 1996, 1997, 1998, and 1999 by (a) the straight-line method, (b) the units-of-production method, and (c) the declining-balance method, using twice the straight-line rate.

PROBLEM 10–4A
Depreciation by two methods; trade of plant asset
Objectives 2, 4

New lithographic equipment, acquired at a cost of $175,000 at the beginning of a fiscal year, has an estimated useful life of 5 years and an estimated residual value of $15,000. The manager requested information regarding the effect of alternative methods on the amount of depreciation expense each year. On the basis of the data presented to the manager, the declining-balance method was selected.

In the first week of the fifth year, the equipment was traded in for similar equipment priced at $205,000. The trade-in allowance on the old equipment was $26,000, cash of $35,000 was paid, and a note payable was issued for the balance.

Instructions

1. Determine the annual depreciation expense for each of the estimated 5 years of use, the accumulated depreciation at the end of each year, and the book value of the equipment at the end of each year by (a) the straight-line method and (b) the declining-balance method (at twice the straight-line rate). The following columnar headings are suggested for each schedule:

Year	*Depreciation Expense*	*Accumulated Depreciation, End of Year*	*Book Value, End of Year*

2. For financial reporting purposes, determine the cost of the new equipment acquired in the exchange.
3. Journalize the entry to record the exchange.
4. What is the cost of the new equipment for purposes of computing the amount of depreciation allowable for income tax purposes?
5. Journalize the entry to record the exchange, assuming that the trade-in allowance was $15,000 instead of $26,000.
6. What is the cost of the new equipment for purposes of computing the amount of depreciation allowable for income tax purposes, assuming the data presented in (5)?

PROBLEM 10–5A
Correcting entries
Objectives 1, 3, 4

The following recording errors occurred and were discovered during the current year:

a. The $1,050 cost of repairing equipment damaged in the process of installation was charged to Equipment.
b. Store equipment with a book value of $6,700 was traded in for similar equipment with a list price of $50,000. The trade-in allowance on the old equipment was $12,500, and a note payable was given for the balance. A gain on the disposal of plant assets of $5,800 was recorded.
c. Property taxes of $5,000 were paid on real estate acquired during the year and were debited to Property Tax Expense. Of this amount, $3,000 was for taxes that were delinquent at the time the property was acquired.
d. The sale of a computer for $1,750 was recorded by a $1,750 credit to Office Equipment. The original cost of the computer was $7,800, and the related balance in Accumulated Depreciation at the beginning of the current year was $6,000. Depreciation of $800 accrued during the current year, prior to the sale, had not been recorded.
e. The $3,750 cost of a major motor overhaul expected to prolong the life of a truck three years beyond the original estimate was debited to Delivery Expense. The truck was acquired new four years earlier.
f. The $4,500 cost of repainting several interior rooms of a building was debited to Building. The building had been owned and occupied for 20 years.
g. The cost of a razed building, $35,000, was debited to Loss on Disposal of Plant Assets and credited to Building. The building and the land on which it was located had been acquired at a total cost of $110,000 ($75,000 debited to Land, $35,000 debited to Building) as a parking area for the adjacent plant.
h. The fee of $6,100 paid to the wrecking contractor to raze the building in (g) was debited to Miscellaneous Expense.
i. A $350 charge for incoming transportation on an item of store equipment was debited to Transportation In.

$39580

Instructions

Journalize the entries to correct the errors during the current year. Identify each entry by letter.

PROBLEM 10–6A
Transactions for plant assets, including trade
Objectives 1, 3, 4

The following transactions, adjusting entries, and closing entries were completed by Elm Furniture Co. during a 3-year period. All are related to the use of delivery equipment. The declining-balance method (at twice the straight-line rate) of depreciation is used.

1995
Jan. 2. Purchased a used delivery truck for $18,800, paying cash.
7. Paid $1,200 for major repairs to the truck.
Sep. 17. Paid garage $325 for miscellaneous repairs to the truck.
Dec. 31. Recorded depreciation on the truck for the fiscal year. The estimated useful life of the truck is 4 years, with a residual value of $3,000.
31. Closed the appropriate accounts to the income summary account.

1996
June 30. Traded in the used truck for a new truck priced at $35,000, receiving a trade-in allowance of $10,500 and paying the balance in cash. (Record depreciation to date in 1996.) book value 7500
Oct. 9. Paid garage $305 for miscellaneous repairs to the truck.
Dec. 31. Recorded depreciation on the truck. It has an estimated trade-in value of $8,000 and an estimated life of 5 years.
31. Closed the appropriate accounts to the income summary account.

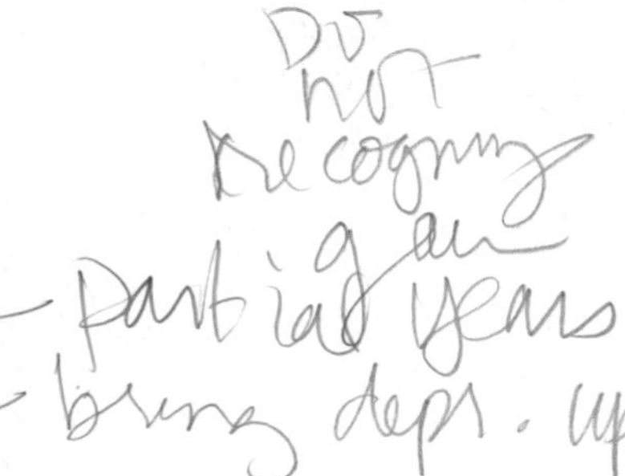

1997
Oct. 1. Purchased a new truck for $42,000, paying cash.
2. Sold the truck purchased June 30, 1996, for $20,000. (Record depreciation for the year.)
Dec. 31. Recorded depreciation on the remaining truck. It has an estimated residual value of $5,000 and an estimated useful life of 8 years.
31. Closed the appropriate accounts to the income summary account.

Instructions

Journalize the transactions and the adjusting and closing entries. Post to the following accounts in the ledger and extend the balances after each posting:

122 Delivery Equipment
123 Accumulated Depreciation—Delivery Equipment
616 Depreciation Expense—Delivery Equipment
617 Truck Repair Expense
812 Gain on Disposal of Plant Assets

PROBLEM 10–7A
Plant asset transactions and subsidiary plant ledger
Objectives 2, 4

If the working papers correlating with this textbook are not used, omit Problem 10–7A.

Key Board Press Co. maintains a subsidiary equipment ledger for the printing equipment and accumulated depreciation accounts in its general ledger. A small portion of the subsidiary ledger, the two controlling accounts, and a journal are presented in the working papers. The company computes depreciation on each individual item of equipment. Transactions and adjusting entries affecting the printing equipment are as follows:

1996
Sep. 1. Purchased a power binder (Model 83X, Serial No. QX31) from Period Manufacturing Co. on account for $180,000. The estimated useful life of the asset is 10 years, it is expected to have no residual value, and the straight-line method of depreciation is to be used. (This is the only transaction of the year that directly affected the printing equipment account.)
Dec. 31. Recorded depreciation for the year in subsidiary accounts 125–30 to 125–32 and inserted the new balances. (An assistant recorded the depreciation and the new balances in accounts 125–1 to 125–29.)
31. Journalized and posted the annual adjusting entry for depreciation on printing equipment. The depreciation for the year, recorded in subsidiary accounts 125–1 to 125–29, totaled $72,500, to which was added the depreciation entered in accounts 125–30 to 125–32.

1997
Mar. 31. Purchased a Model 5T rotary press from Express Press, priced at $80,000, giving the Model G3 flatbed press (Account No. 125–31) in exchange, plus $25,000 cash and a series of six $5,000 notes payable, maturing at 6-month intervals. The estimated useful life of the new press is 10 years, and it is expected to have a residual value of $5,000. (Recorded depreciation to date in 1997 on item traded in.)

Instructions

1. Journalize the transaction of September 1. Post to Printing Equipment in the general ledger and to Account No. 125–32 in the subsidiary ledger.
2. Journalize the adjusting entry on December 31, and post to Accumulated Depreciation Printing Equipment in the general ledger.
3. Journalize the entries required by the purchase of printing equipment on March 31. Post to Printing Equipment and to Accumulated Depreciation Printing Equipment in the general ledger and to Account Nos. 125–31 and 125–33 in the subsidiary ledger.
4. If the rotary press purchased on March 31 had been depreciated by the declining-balance method at twice the straight-line rate, determine the depreciation on this press for the fiscal years ending (a) December 31, 1997 and (b) December 31, 1998.

PROBLEM 10–8A
Amortization and depletion entries
Objectives 7, 8

Data related to the acquisition of timber rights and intangible assets during the current year ended December 31 are as follows:

a. Timber rights on a tract of land were purchased for $180,000 on March 5. The stand of timber is estimated at 900,000 board feet. During the current year, 350,000 board feet of timber were cut.

b. Goodwill in the amount of $500,000 was purchased on January 3. It is decided to amortize over the maximum period allowable.
c. Governmental and legal costs of $75,000 were incurred on July 1 in obtaining a patent with an estimated economic life of 10 years. Amortization is to be for one-half year.

Instructions

1. Determine the amount of the amortization or depletion expense for the current year for each of the foregoing items.
2. Journalize the adjusting entries required to record the amortization or depletion for each item.

APPENDIX PROBLEM 10–9A
Sum-of-the-years-digits depreciation

Use the data in Problem 10–2A in completing the instructions for this problem.

Instructions
Determine the amount of depreciation expense for 1996, 1997, and 1998, using the sum-of-the-years-digits method. Also determine the total depreciation expense for the three years.

APPENDIX PROBLEM 10–10A
Sum-of-the-years-digits depreciation; partial years

Use the data in Problem 10–3A in completing the instructions for this problem.

Instructions
Determine the amount of depreciation expense for the years ended December 31, 1996, 1997, 1998, and 1999, using the sum-of-the-years-digits method.

PROBLEMS SERIES B

PROBLEM 10–1B
Allocating payments and receipts to plant asset accounts
Objective 1

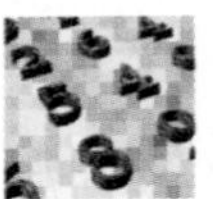

The following payments and receipts are related to land, land improvements, and buildings acquired for use in a wholesale apparel business. The receipts are identified by an asterisk.

a.	Cost of real estate acquired as a plant site: Land	$ 275,000
	Building	30,000
b.	Finder's fee paid to real estate agency	15,000
c.	Fee paid to attorney for title search	1,500
d.	Delinquent real estate taxes on property, assumed by purchaser	18,500
e.	Cost of razing and removing building	21,250
f.	Proceeds from sale of salvage materials from old building	3,500*
g.	Cost of filling and grading land	23,500
h.	Architect's and engineer's fees for plans and supervision	105,000
i.	Premium on 1-year insurance policy during construction	5,700
j.	Cost of paving parking lot to be used by customers	17,500
k.	Cost of trees and shrubbery planted	20,000
l.	Special assessment paid to city for extension of water main to the property	6,500
m.	Cost of repairing windstorm damage during construction	3,500
n.	Cost of repairing vandalism damage during construction	800
o.	Proceeds from insurance company for windstorm and vandalism damage	5,300*
p.	Interest incurred on building loan during construction	85,000
q.	Money borrowed to pay building contractor	1,000,000*
r.	Payment to building contractor for new building	1,250,000
s.	Refund of premium on insurance policy (i) canceled after 10 months	950*

Instructions

1. Assign each payment and receipt to Land (unlimited life), Land Improvements (limited life), Building, or Other Accounts. Indicate receipts by an asterisk. Identify each item by letter and list the amounts in columnar form, as follows:

Item	*Land*	*Land Improvements*	*Building*	*Other Accounts*

2. The costs assigned to the land, which is used as a plant site, will not be depreciated, while the costs assigned to land improvements will be depreciated. Explain this seemingly contradictory application of the concept of depreciation.

PROBLEM 10–2B
Comparing three depreciation methods
Objective 2

Klass Company purchased waterproofing equipment on January 2, 1996, for $130,000. The equipment was expected to have a useful life of 4 years, or 8,000 operating hours, and a residual value of $10,000. The equipment was used for 1,200 hours during 1996, 2,800 hours in 1997, 2,200 hours in 1998, and 1,800 hours in 1999.

Instructions

Determine the amount of depreciation expense for the years ended December 31, 1996, 1997, 1998, and 1999 by (a) the straight-line method, (b) the units-of-production method, and (c) the declining-balance method, using twice the straight-line rate. Also determine the total depreciation expense for the four years by each method. The following columnar headings are suggested for recording the depreciation expense amounts:

	Depreciation Expense		
Year	*Straight-Line Method*	*Units-of-Production Method*	*Declining-Balance Method*

PROBLEM 10–3B
Depreciation by three methods; partial years
Objective 2

Afco Company purchased tool sharpening equipment on July 1, 1996, for $75,000. The equipment was expected to have a useful life of 3 years, or 8,000 operating hours, and a residual value of $3,000. The equipment was used for 1,700 hours during 1996, 3,800 hours in 1997, 1,500 hours in 1998, and 1,000 hours in 1999. The equipment was sold for $3,000 on July 1, 1999.

Instructions

Determine the amount of depreciation expense for the years ended December 31, 1996, 1997, 1998, and 1999 by (a) the straight-line method, (b) the units-of-production method, and (c) the declining-balance method, using twice the straight-line rate.

PROBLEM 10–4B
Depreciation by two methods; trade of plant asset
Objectives 2, 4

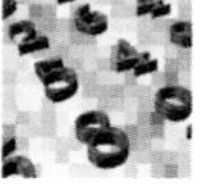

New tire retreading equipment, acquired at a cost of $120,000 at the beginning of a fiscal year, has an estimated useful life of 4 years and an estimated residual value of $10,000. The manager requested information regarding the effect of alternative methods on the amount of depreciation expense each year. On the basis of the data presented to the manager, the declining-balance method was selected.

In the first week of the fourth year, the equipment was traded in for similar equipment priced at $180,000. The trade-in allowance on the old equipment was $25,000, cash of $30,000 was paid, and a note payable was issued for the balance.

Instructions

1. Determine the annual depreciation expense for each of the estimated 4 years of use, the accumulated depreciation at the end of each year, and the book value of the equipment at the end of each year by (a) the straight-line method and (b) the declining-balance method (at twice the straight-line rate). The following columnar headings are suggested for each schedule:

Year	*Depreciation Expense*	*Accumulated Depreciation, End of Year*	*Book Value, End of Year*

2. For financial reporting purposes, determine the cost of the new equipment acquired in the exchange.
3. Journalize the entry to record the exchange.
4. What is the cost of the new equipment for purposes of computing the amount of depreciation allowable for income tax purposes?
5. Journalize the entry to record the exchange, assuming that the trade-in allowance was $5,000 instead of $25,000.
6. What is the cost of the new equipment for purposes of computing the amount of depreciation allowable for income tax purposes, assuming the data presented in (5)?

PROBLEM 10–5B
Correcting entries
Objectives 1, 3, 4

The following recording errors occurred and were discovered during the current year:

a. The $1,850 cost of repairing factory equipment damaged in the process of installation was charged to Factory Equipment.
b. The sale of a personal computer for $575 was recorded by a $575 credit to Office Equipment. The original cost of the computer was $1,850, and the related balance in Accumulated Depreciation at the beginning of the current year was $1,200. Depreciation of $150 accrued during the current year, prior to the sale, had not been recorded.
c. Property taxes of $5,000 were paid on real estate acquired during the year and were debited to Property Tax Expense. Of this amount, $4,000 was for taxes that were delinquent at the time the property was acquired.
d. Office equipment with a book value of $11,200 was traded in for similar equipment with a list price of $60,000. The trade-in allowance on the old equipment was $15,000, and a note payable was given for the balance. A gain on the disposal of plant assets of $3,800 was recorded.
e. The $5,100 cost of a major motor overhaul expected to prolong the life of a truck two years beyond the original estimate was debited to Delivery Expense. The truck was acquired new four years earlier.
f. A $450 charge for incoming transportation on an item of factory equipment was debited to Transportation In.
g. The cost of a razed building, $25,000, was debited to Loss on Disposal of Plant Assets and credited to Building. The building and the land on which it was located had been acquired at a total cost of $150,000 ($125,000 debited to Land, $25,000 debited to Building) as a parking area for the adjacent plant.
h. The fee of $6,500 paid to the wrecking contractor to raze the building in (g) was debited to Miscellaneous Expense.
i. The $7,750 cost of repainting several interior rooms of a building was debited to Building. The building had been owned and occupied for 20 years.

Instructions

Journalize the entries to correct the errors during the current year. Identify each entry by letter.

PROBLEM 10–6B
Transactions for plant assets, including trade
Objectives 1, 3, 4

The following transactions, adjusting entries, and closing entries were completed by Old World Furniture Co. during 3 fiscal years ending on June 30. All are related to the use of delivery equipment. The declining-balance method (at twice the straight-line rate) of depreciation is used.

1994–1995 Fiscal Year

July 2. Purchased a used delivery truck for $21,000, paying cash.
6. Paid $3,000 to replace the automatic transmission and install new brakes on the truck. (Debit Delivery Equipment.)
Dec. 7. Paid garage $275 for changing the oil, replacing the oil filter, and tuning the engine on the delivery truck.
June 30. Recorded depreciation on the truck for the fiscal year. The estimated useful life of the truck is 8 years, with a residual value of $4,000.
30. Closed the appropriate accounts to the income summary account.

1995–1996 Fiscal Year

Sep. 29. Paid garage $310 to tune the engine and make other minor repairs on the truck.
Oct. 31. Traded in the used truck for a new truck priced at $40,000, receiving a trade-in allowance of $17,500 and paying the balance in cash. (Record depreciation to date in 1995.)
June 30. Recorded depreciation on the truck. It has an estimated trade-in value of $3,000 and an estimated life of 10 years.
30. Closed the appropriate accounts to the income summary account.

1996–1997 Fiscal Year

Apr. 1. Purchased a new truck for $45,000, paying cash.
2. Sold the truck purchased October 31, 1995, for $30,000. (Record depreciation for the year.)
June 30. Recorded depreciation on the remaining truck. It has an estimated residual value of $4,500 and an estimated useful life of 10 years.
30. Closed the appropriate accounts to the income summary account.

Instructions

Journalize the transactions and the adjusting and closing entries. Post to the following accounts in the ledger and extend the balances after each posting:

122 Delivery Equipment
123 Accumulated Depreciation—Delivery Equipment
616 Depreciation Expense—Delivery Equipment
617 Truck Repair Expense
812 Gain on Disposal of Plant Assets

PROBLEM 10–7B
Plant asset transactions and subsidiary plant ledger
Objectives 2, 4

If the working papers correlating with this textbook are not used, omit Problem 10–7B.

Keystroke Press Co. maintains a subsidiary equipment ledger for the printing equipment and accumulated depreciation accounts in its general ledger. A small portion of the subsidiary ledger, the two controlling accounts, and a journal are presented in the working papers. The company computes depreciation on each individual item of equipment. Transactions and adjusting entries affecting the printing equipment are as follows:

1996

June 30. Purchased a binder (Model H, Serial No. Q4893) from Typo Manufacturing Co. on account for $222,000. The estimated useful life of the asset is 12 years, it is expected to have no residual value, and the straight-line method of depreciation is to be used. (This is the only transaction of the year that directly affected the printing equipment account.)

Dec. 31. Recorded depreciation for the year in subsidiary accounts 125–30 to 125–32 and inserted the new balances. (An assistant recorded the depreciation and the new balances in accounts 125–1 to 125–29.)

31. Journalized and posted the annual adjusting entry for depreciation on printing equipment. The depreciation for the year, recorded in subsidiary accounts 125–1 to 125–29, totaled $81,200, to which was added the depreciation entered in accounts 125–30 to 125–32.

1997

Sep. 30. Purchased a Model 722 rotary press from Comma Press Co., priced at $75,000, giving the Model G3 flatbed press (Account No. 125–31) in exchange, plus $38,000 cash and a series of ten $2,500 notes payable, maturing at 6-month intervals. The estimated useful life of the new press is 10 years, and it is expected to have a residual value of $7,000. (Recorded depreciation to date in 1997 on item traded in.)

Instructions

1. Journalize the transaction of June 30. Post to Printing Equipment in the general ledger and to Account No. 125–32 in the subsidiary ledger.
2. Journalize the adjusting entry on December 31 and post to Accumulated Depreciation Printing Equipment in the general ledger.
3. Journalize the entries required by the purchase of printing equipment on September 30. Post to Printing Equipment and to Accumulated Depreciation—Printing Equipment in the general ledger and to Account Nos. 125–31 and 125–33 in the subsidiary ledger.
4. If the rotary press purchased on September 30 had been depreciated by the declining-balance method at twice the straight-line rate, determine the depreciation on this press for the fiscal years ending (a) December 31, 1997, and (b) December 31, 1998.

PROBLEM 10–8B
Amortization and depletion entries
Objectives 7, 8

Data related to the acquisition of timber rights and intangible assets during the current year ended December 31 are as follows:

a. Timber rights on a tract of land were purchased for $250,000 on March 3. The stand of timber is estimated at 2,000,000 board feet. During the current year, 750,000 board feet of timber were cut.
b. Goodwill in the amount of $480,000 was purchased on January 4. It is decided to amortize over the maximum period allowable.
c. Governmental and legal costs of $74,800 were incurred on July 10 in obtaining a patent with an estimated economic life of 8 years. Amortization is to be for one-half year.

Instructions

1. Determine the amount of the amortization or depletion expense for the current year for each of the foregoing items.
2. Journalize the adjusting entries to record the amortization or depletion expense for each item.

APPENDIX PROBLEM 10–9B
Sum-of-the-years-digits depreciation

Use the data in Problem 10–2B in completing the instructions for this problem.

Instructions

Determine the amount of depreciation expense for 1996, 1997, 1998, and 1999, using the sum-of-the-years-digits method. Also determine the total depreciation expense for the four years.

APPENDIX PROBLEM 10–10B
Sum-of-the-years-digits depreciation; partial years

Use the data in Problem 10–3B in completing the instructions for this problem.

Instructions

Determine the amount of depreciation expense for the years ended December 31, 1996, 1997, 1998, 1999, using the sum-of-the-years-digits method.

CASES

CASE 10–1
Kaslow Co.
Using plant assets

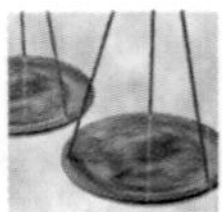

Louetta Westphal, CPA, is an assistant to the controller of Kaslow Co. In her spare time, Louetta also prepares tax returns and performs general accounting services for clients. Frequently, Louetta performs these services after her normal working hours, using Kaslow Co.'s microcomputers and laser printers. Occasionally, Louetta's clients will call her at the office during regular working hours.

Discuss whether Louetta Westphal is performing in an ethical manner.

CASE 10–2
Laminall Co.
Financial vs. tax depreciation

The following is an excerpt from a conversation between two employees of Laminall Co., Wendy Webb and Alan Drexler. Wendy is the accounts payable clerk, and Alan is the cashier.

Wendy: Alan, could I get your opinion on something?
Alan: Sure, Wendy.
Wendy: Do you know Erin, the plant assets clerk?
Alan: I know who she is, but I don't know her real well. Why?
Wendy: Well, I was talking to her at lunch last Monday about how she liked her job, etc. You know, the usual . . . and she mentioned something about having to keep two sets of books . . . one for taxes and one for the financial statements. That can't be good accounting, can it? What do you think?
Alan: Two sets of books? It doesn't sound right.
Wendy: It doesn't seem right to me either. I was always taught that you had to use generally accepted accounting principles. How can there be two sets of books? What can be the difference between the two?

How would you respond to Alan and Wendy if you were Erin?

CASE 10–3
Hershey Foods Corporation
Financial analysis

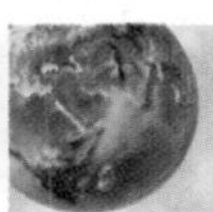

Long-term liabilities (debt) are often secured by mortgages on plant assets. The ratio of total plant assets to long-term liabilities (debt) is a solvency measure that indicates the margin of safety to the creditors. It also indicates the ability of the business to borrow additional funds on a long-term basis. The ratio of plant assets to long-term liabilities (debt) is computed as follows:

$$\textbf{Ratio of plant assets to long-term liabilities (debt)} = \frac{\textbf{Plant assets (net)}}{\textbf{Long-term liabilities (debt)}}$$

a. For Hershey Foods Corporation, compute the ratio of plant assets (property, plant, and equipment) to long-term liabilities (debt) as of December 31, 1993 and 1992.
b. What conclusions can be drawn from these ratios concerning Hershey's ability to borrow additional funds on a long-term basis?

CASE 10–4
Rainbow Construction Co.
Effect of depreciation on net income

Rainbow Construction Co. specializes in building replicas of historic houses. Jill Holland, president of Rainbow, is considering the purchase of various items of equipment on July 1, 1994, for $220,000. The equipment would have a useful life of 5 years and no residual value. In the past, all equipment has been leased. For tax purposes, Jill is considering depreciating the equipment by the straight-line method. She discussed the matter with her CPA and learned that, although the straight-line method could be elected, it was to her advantage to use the modified accelerated cost recovery system (MACRS) for tax purposes. She asked for your advice as to which method to use for tax purposes.

1. Compute depreciation for each of the years (1994, 1995, 1996, 1997, 1998, and 1999) of useful life by (a) the straight-line method and (b) MACRS. In using the straight-line method, one-half year's depreciation should be computed for 1994 and 1999. Use the MACRS rates presented in the chapter.
2. Assuming that income before depreciation and income tax is estimated to be $300,000 uniformly per year and that the income tax rate is 30%, compute the net income for each of the years 1994, 1995, 1996, 1997, 1998, and 1999 if (a) the straight-line method is used and (b) MACRS is used.
3. What factors would you present for Jill's consideration in the selection of a depreciation method?

ANSWERS TO SELF-EXAMINATION QUESTIONS

1. **C** All amounts spent to get a plant asset (such as machinery) in place and ready for use are proper charges to the asset account. In the case of machinery acquired, the freight (answer A) and the installation costs (answer B) are both (answer C) proper charges to the machinery account.
2. **C** The periodic charge for depreciation under the declining-balance method (twice the straight-line rate) for the second year is determined by first computing the depreciation charge for the first year. The depreciation for the first year of $6,000 (answer A) is computed by multiplying the cost of the equipment, $9,000, by 2/3 (the straight-line rate of 1/3 multiplied by 2). The depreciation for the second year of $2,000 (answer C) is then determined by multiplying the book value at the end of the first year, $3,000 (the cost of $9,000 minus the first-year depreciation of $6,000), by 2/3. The third year's depreciation is $400 (answer D). It is determined by multiplying the book value at the end of the second year, $1,000, by 2/3, thus yielding $667. However, the equipment cannot be depreciated below its residual value of $600; thus, the third-year depreciation is $400 ($1,000 – $600).
3. **B** A depreciation method that provides for a higher depreciation amount in the first year of the use of an asset and a gradually declining periodic amount thereafter is called an accelerated depreciation method. The declining-balance method (answer B) is an example of such a method.
4. **B** The acceptable method of accounting for an exchange of similar assets in which the trade-in allowance ($30,000) exceeds the book value of the old asset ($25,000) requires that the cost of the new asset be determined by adding the amount of boot given ($70,000) to the book value of the old asset ($25,000), which totals $95,000.
5. **D** Long-lived assets that are useful in operations, not held for sale, and without physical qualities are called intangible assets. Patents, goodwill, and copyrights are examples of intangible assets (answer D).

11

Payroll, Notes Payable, and Other Current Liabilities

YOU AND ACCOUNTING

If you are employed, you know that your paycheck is normally less than the total amount you earned because your employer deducted amounts for such items as federal income tax and FICA tax. For example, if you worked 20 hours last week at $10 per hour and you are paid weekly, your payroll check could appear as follows:

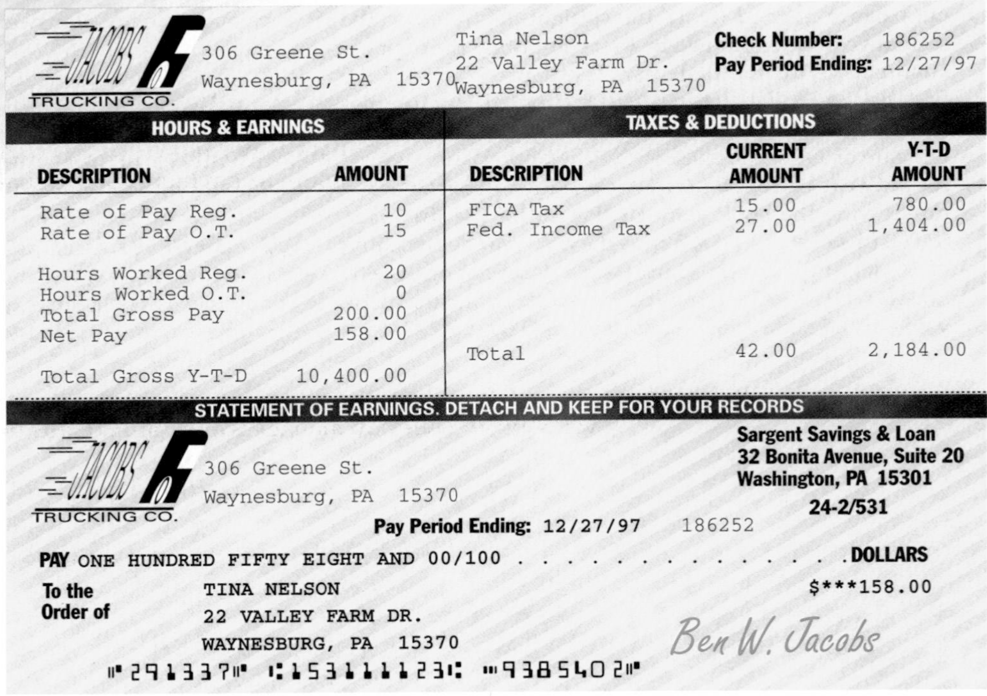

JACOBS TRUCKING CO.
306 Greene St.
Waynesburg, PA 15370

Tina Nelson
22 Valley Farm Dr.
Waynesburg, PA 15370

Check Number: 186252
Pay Period Ending: 12/27/97

HOURS & EARNINGS		TAXES & DEDUCTIONS		
DESCRIPTION	**AMOUNT**	**DESCRIPTION**	**CURRENT AMOUNT**	**Y-T-D AMOUNT**
Rate of Pay Reg.	10	FICA Tax	15.00	780.00
Rate of Pay O.T.	15	Fed. Income Tax	27.00	1,404.00
Hours Worked Reg.	20			
Hours Worked O.T.	0			
Total Gross Pay	200.00			
Net Pay	158.00			
Total Gross Y-T-D	10,400.00	Total	42.00	2,184.00

STATEMENT OF EARNINGS. DETACH AND KEEP FOR YOUR RECORDS

JACOBS TRUCKING CO.
306 Greene St.
Waynesburg, PA 15370

Sargent Savings & Loan
32 Bonita Avenue, Suite 20
Washington, PA 15301
24-2/531

Pay Period Ending: 12/27/97 186252

PAY ONE HUNDRED FIFTY EIGHT AND 00/100 . . . . **.DOLLARS**

$***158.00

To the Order of TINA NELSON
22 VALLEY FARM DR.
WAYNESBURG, PA 15370

Ben W. Jacobs

⑈291337⑈ ⑆153111123⑆ ⑈9385402⑈

Your employer has a liability to you for your earnings until you are paid with cash or a check such as the one above. Your employer also has a liability to deposit the taxes withheld. In this chapter, we will discuss current payroll and tax liabilities. We will also discuss other payroll-related liabilities, such as vacation pay and pensions, and liabilities from notes payable and product warranties.

After studying this chapter, you should be able to:

Objective 1
Determine employer's liabilities for payroll, including liabilities arising from employee earnings and deductions from earnings.

Objective 2
Record payroll and payroll taxes, using a payroll register, employees' earnings records, and a general journal.

Objective 3
Journalize entries for employee fringe benefits, including vacation pay and pensions.

Objective 4
Journalize entries for short-term notes payable.

Objective 5
Journalize entries for product warranties.

Payroll and Payroll Taxes

Objective 1
Determine employer's liabilities for payroll, including liabilities arising from employee earnings and deductions from earnings.

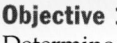

We are all familiar with the term payroll. In accounting, the term payroll refers to the amount paid to employees for services provided during a period. A business's payroll is usually significant for several reasons. First, employees are sensitive to payroll errors and irregularities. Maintaining good employee morale requires that the payroll be paid on a timely, accurate basis. Second, payroll expenditures are subject to various federal and state regulations. Finally, payroll expenditures and related payroll taxes have a significant effect on the net income of most businesses. Although the amount of such expenses varies widely, it is not unusual for a business to expend nearly a third of its revenue for payroll and payroll-related expenses.

LIABILITY FOR EMPLOYEE EARNINGS

The term **salary** usually refers to payment for managerial, administrative, or similar services. The rate of salary is normally expressed in terms of a month or a year. The term **wages** usually refers to payment for manual labor, both skilled and unskilled. The rate of wages is normally stated on an hourly or weekly basis. In practice, the terms salary and wages are often used interchangeably.

The basic salary or wage of an employee may be increased by commissions, profit sharing, or cost-of-living adjustment. Although payment is usually made in cash, it may take such forms as securities, notes, lodging, or other property or services. Generally, the form of payment has no effect on how salaries and wages are treated by either the employer or the employee.

Many businesses pay managers an annual bonus in addition to a regular salary. The amount of the bonus is often based on some measure of productivity, such as income or profit of the business. Therefore, managers have a personal interest in selecting accounting principles and determining accounting estimates. For example, a chief executive officer (CEO) who plans to retire in the near future might select accounting principles that tend to increase reported income, such as straight-line depreciation and the first-in, first-out inventory costing method, so as to increase the bonus. Likewise, such managers might tend to bias accounting estimates, such as uncollectible accounts expense, in favor of reporting more income.

Salary and wage rates are determined by agreement between the employer and the employees. Businesses engaged in interstate commerce must follow the requirements of the Fair Labor Standards Act. Employers covered by this legislation, which is commonly called the Federal Wage and Hour Law, are required to pay a minimum rate of 1 1/2 times the regular rate for all hours worked in excess of 40 hours per week. Exemptions are provided for executive, administrative, and certain supervisory positions. Premium rates for overtime or for working at night, holidays, or other less desirable times are fairly common, even when not required by law. In some cases, the premium rates may be as much as twice the base rate.

To illustrate computing an employee's earnings, assume that John T. McGrath is employed by McDermott Supply Co. at the rate of $25 per hour. Any hours in excess of 40 hours per week are paid at a rate of 1 1/2 times the normal rate, or $37.50 ($25 + $12.50) per hour. For the week ended December 27, McGrath's time card indicates that he worked 44 hours. His earnings for that week are computed as follows:

Earnings at base rate (40 × $25)	$1,000
Earnings at overtime rate (4 × $37.50)	150
Total earnings	$1,150

DEDUCTIONS FROM EMPLOYEE EARNINGS

The total earnings of an employee for a payroll period, including bonuses and overtime pay, are called gross pay. From this amount is subtracted one or more **deductions** to arrive at the net pay. Net pay is the amount the employer must pay the employee. The deductions for federal taxes are usually the largest deduction. Deductions may also be required for state or local income taxes. Other deductions may be made for medical insurance, contributions to pensions, and for items authorized by individual employees.

FICA Tax

Most of us have FICA tax withheld from our payroll checks. Employers are required by the Federal Insurance Contributions Act (FICA) to withhold a portion of the earnings of each of the employees. The amount of FICA tax withheld is the employees' contribution to two federal programs. The first program, called social security, is for old age, survivors, and disability insurance. The second program, called Medicare, is for health insurance.

USING ACCOUNTING TO UNDERSTAND BUSINESS

In many companies, the chief executive officer (CEO) has the highest salary of all employees in the business. There are wide differences in the salaries and bonuses earned by CEOs. The highest paid CEO in 1993 was Michael Eisner, CEO of Walt Disney, whose total compensation (including stock) was $202 million. The following are the salaries and bonuses for CEOs of some familiar companies:

CEO	*Company*	*Salary*	*Bonus*
Robert J. Eaton	Chrysler	$ 929,000	$1,900,000
Louis V. Gerstner	IBM	1,500,000	1,125,000
Roberto C. Goizueta	Coca Cola	1,454,000	2,200,000
Lee R. Raymond	Exxon	1,143,000	500,000
John S. Reed	Citicorp	1,150,000	3,000,000
Jack F. Welch	General Electric	1,750,000	2,200,000

The amount of tax that employers are required to withhold from each employee is normally based on the amount of earnings paid in the calendar year. Although both the schedule of future tax rates and the maximum amount subject to tax are revised often by Congress, such changes have little effect on the basic payroll system.[1] In this text, we will use a combined rate of 7.5% on the first $70,000 of annual earnings and a rate of 1.5% on annual earnings in excess of $70,000.

To illustrate, assume that John T. McGrath's annual earnings prior to the current payroll period total $69,150. Assume also that the current period earnings are $1,150. The FICA tax of $68.25 is determined as follows:[2]

Earnings subject to 7.5% FICA tax		
($70,000 – $69,150)	$ 850	
FICA tax rate	× 7.5%	
FICA tax		$63.75
Earnings subject to 1.5% FICA tax		
($69,150 + $1,150 – $70,000)	$ 300	
FICA tax rate	× 1.5%	
FICA tax		4.50
Total FICA tax		$68.25

YOUR SOCIAL SECURITY TAXES

In its 1936 publication, *Security in Your Old Age*, the Social Security Board set forth the following explanation of how the social security tax would affect a worker's paycheck:

The taxes called for in this law will be paid both by your employer and by you. For the next 3 years you will pay maybe 15 cents a week, maybe 25 cents a week, maybe 30 cents or more, according to what you earn. That is to say, during the next 3 years, beginning January 1, 1937, you will pay 1 cent for every dollar you earn, and at the same time your employer will pay 1 cent for every dollar you earn, up to $3,000 a year. Twenty-six million other workers and their employers will be paying at the same time.

After the first 3 years—that is to say, beginning in 1940—you will pay, and your employer will pay, 1 1/2 cents for each dollar you earn, up to $3,000 a year. This will be the tax for 3 years, and then beginning in 1943, you will pay 2 cents, and so will your employer, for every dollar you earn for the next three years. After that, you and your employer will each pay half a cent more for 3 years, and finally, beginning in 1949, twelve years from now, you and your employer will each pay 3 cents on each dollar you earn, up to $3,000 a year. That is the most you will ever pay.

The rate on January 1, 1995, was 7.65 cents per dollar earned (7.65%). The social security portion was 6.2% on the first $61,200 of earnings. The Medicare portion is 1.45% on all earnings.

Source: Arthur Lodge, "That Is the Most You Will Ever Pay," *Journal of Accountancy*, October 1985, p. 44.

INCOME TAXES

Except for certain types of employment, all employers must withhold a portion of employee earnings for payment of the employees' federal income tax. As a basis for determining the amount to be withheld, each employee completes and submits to the employer an "Employee's Withholding Allowance Certificate," often called a W-4. Exhibit 1 on the next page is an example of a completed W-4 form.

You may recall filling out a W-4 form. On the W-4, an employee indicates marital status, the number of withholding allowances, and whether any additional withholdings are authorized. A single employee may claim one withholding allowance. A married employee may claim an additional allowance for a spouse. An

[1] The FICA rates for 1995 are 7.65% for the first $61,200 of earnings and 1.45% for earnings in excess of $61,200.

[2] Tables are available from the Internal Revenue Service for determining FICA withholding.

Exhibit 1
W-4 Form

Cut here and give the certificate to your employer. Keep the top portion for your records.

Form **W-4** Department of the Treasury Internal Revenue Service

Employee's Withholding Allowance Certificate

▶ For Privacy Act and Paperwork Reduction Act Notice, see reverse.

OMB No. 1545-0010 **1994**

1 Type or print your first name and middle initial: John T. — Last name: McGrath — 2 Your social security number: 381-48-9120

Home address (number and street or rural route): 1830 4th Street — 3 ☒ Single ☐ Married ☐ Married, but withhold at higher Single rate. Note: If married, but legally separated, or spouse is a nonresident alien, check the Single box

City or town, state, and ZIP code: Clinton, Iowa 52732-6142 — 4 If your last name differs from that on your social security card, check here and call 1-800-772-1213 for more information . . . . ▶ ☐

5 Total number of allowances you are claiming (from line G above or from the worksheets on page 2 if they apply) . — 5 — 1

6 Additional amount, if any, you want withheld from each paycheck . . . . — 6 — $

7 I claim exemption from withholding for 1994 and I certify that I meet **BOTH** of the following conditions for exemption:

- Last year I had a right to a refund of **ALL** Federal income tax withheld because I had **NO** tax liability; **AND**
- This year I expect a refund of **ALL** Federal income tax withheld because I expect to have **NO** tax liability.

If you meet both conditions, enter "EXEMPT" here . . . . ▶ 7

Under penalties of perjury, I certify that I am entitled to the number of withholding allowances claimed on this certificate or entitled to claim exempt status.

Employee's signature ▶ *John T. McGrath* — Date ▶ June 2, 1994

8 Employer's name and address (Employer: Complete 8 and 10 only if sending to the IRS) — 9 Office code (optional) — 10 Employer identification number

Cat. No. 10220Q

employee may also claim an allowance for each dependent other than a spouse. Each allowance claimed reduces the amount of federal income tax withheld from the employee's check.

The amount that must be withheld for income tax differs, depending upon each employee's gross pay and completed W-4. Most employers use wage bracket withholding tables furnished by the Internal Revenue Service to determine the amount to be withheld.[3]

Exhibit 2 is an example of a wage bracket withholding table. This table is for a single employee who is paid weekly. Other tables are used for employees who are married or who are paid biweekly, semimonthly, monthly, or at other time periods. Unlike FICA tax, there is no ceiling on the amount of employee earnings subject to federal income tax withholding.

In using the withholding table, you would first locate the employee's wage bracket in the left-hand column. Then locate the number of withholding allowances across the horizontal columns. The intersection of the employee's wage bracket with the appropriate withholding allowance column indicates the federal withholding. For example, assume that John T. McGrath, who is single and has declared one withholding allowance, made $1,150 for the week ended December 27. Using the withholding table in Exhibit 2, the amount of federal income tax withheld is $247.

In addition to the federal income tax, employees may also be required to pay a state income tax and a city income tax. State and city taxes are withheld from employees' earnings and paid to state and city governments. We will not illustrate state and city tax withholding in our examples, since these taxes are very similar to federal tax withholding.

Other Deductions

Neither the employer nor the employee has any choice in deducting taxes from gross earnings. However, employees may choose to have additional amounts deducted for other purposes. For example, you as an employee may authorize deductions for the purchase of U.S. savings bonds, for contributions to charitable organizations, for premiums on employee insurance, or for retirement annuities. A union contract may also require the deduction of union dues.

[3] Current federal income tax withholding tables are available from the Internal Revenue Service as part of *Circular E*, "Employer's Tax Guide."

Exhibit 2
Wage Bracket Withholding Table

SINGLE Persons—**WEEKLY** Payroll Period

If the wages are–		And the number of withholding allowances claimed is—										
At least	But less than	0	1	2	3	4	5	6	7	8	9	10
		The amount of income tax to be withheld is—										
900	**910**	186	173	159	146	133	120	107	93	80	67	58
910	**920**	189	175	162	149	136	123	109	96	83	70	59
920	**930**	191	178	165	152	139	125	112	99	86	73	61
930	**940**	194	181	168	155	141	128	115	102	89	75	62
940	**950**	197	184	171	157	144	131	118	105	91	78	65
950	**960**	200	187	173	160	147	134	121	107	94	81	68
960	**970**	203	189	176	163	150	137	123	110	97	84	71
970	**980**	206	192	179	166	153	139	126	113	100	87	73
980	**990**	209	195	182	169	155	142	129	116	103	89	76
990	**1,000**	212	198	185	171	158	145	132	119	105	92	79
1,000	**1,010**	215	201	187	174	161	148	135	121	108	95	82
1,010	**1,020**	218	203	190	177	164	151	137	124	111	98	85
1,020	**1,030**	221	206	193	180	167	153	140	127	114	101	87
1,030	**1,040**	224	210	196	183	169	156	143	130	117	103	90
1,040	**1,050**	227	213	199	185	172	159	146	133	119	106	93
1,050	**1,060**	230	216	201	188	175	162	149	135	122	109	96
1,060	**1,070**	233	219	204	191	178	165	151	138	125	112	99
1,070	**1,080**	237	222	207	194	181	167	154	141	128	115	101
1,080	**1,090**	240	225	210	197	183	170	157	144	131	117	104
1,090	**1,100**	243	228	214	199	186	173	160	147	133	120	107
1,100	**1,110**	246	231	217	202	189	176	163	149	136	123	110
1,110	**1,120**	249	234	220	205	192	179	165	152	139	126	113
1,120	**1,130**	252	237	223	208	195	181	168	155	142	129	115
1,130	**1,140**	255	241	226	211	197	184	171	158	145	131	118
1,140	**1,150**	258	244	229	214	200	187	174	161	147	134	121
1,150	**1,160**	261	247	232	218	203	190	177	163	150	137	124
1,160	**1,170**	264	250	235	221	206	193	179	166	153	140	127
1,170	**1,180**	268	253	238	224	209	195	182	169	156	143	129
1,180	**1,190**	271	256	241	227	212	198	185	172	159	145	132
1,190	**1,200**	274	259	245	230	215	201	188	175	161	148	135
1,200	**1,210**	277	262	248	233	218	204	191	177	164	151	138
1,210	**1,220**	280	265	251	236	222	207	193	180	167	154	141
1,220	**1,230**	283	268	254	239	225	210	196	183	170	157	143
1,230	**1,240**	286	272	257	242	228	213	199	186	173	159	146
1,240	**1,250**	289	275	260	245	231	216	202	189	175	162	149
$1,250 and over		Use Table 1(a) for a **SINGLE person** on page 29. Also see the instructions on page 27.										

COMPUTING EMPLOYEE NET PAY

Gross earnings less payroll deductions equals the amount to be paid to an employee for the payroll period. This amount is the *net pay*, which is often called the *take-home pay*. The amount to be paid John T. McGrath for the week ended December 27 is $809.75, as shown below.

Gross earnings for the week		$1,150.00
Deductions:		
FICA tax	$ 68.25	
Federal income tax	247.00	
U.S. savings bonds	20.00	
United Fund	5.00	
Total deductions		340.25
Net pay		$ 809.75

We illustrated determining the gross earnings and the FICA tax and federal income tax withheld for McGrath earlier in the chapter. We assumed that the deductions for the purchase of bonds and for the United Fund contribution were authorized by McGrath.

LIABILITY FOR EMPLOYER'S PAYROLL TAXES

So far, we have discussed payroll taxes from the employees' point of view. These taxes are assessed against employees and are withheld by employers. Most employers are also subject to federal and state payroll taxes based on the amount paid their employees. Such taxes are an operating expense of the business.

FICA Tax

Employers are required to contribute to the Federal Insurance Contributions Act (FICA) program for each employee. The tax rates are the same as those we discussed earlier for employees.

Federal Unemployment Compensation Tax

Unemployment insurance provides temporary payments to those who become unemployed as a result of layoffs due to economic causes beyond their control. Types of employment subject to the unemployment insurance program are similar to those covered by the FICA tax. The tax of 0.8% is levied on employers only, rather than on both employers and employees.[4] It is applied to only the first $7,000 of the earnings of each covered employee during a calendar year. The rate and maximum earnings subject to federal unemployment compensation tax are often revised by Congress. The funds collected by the federal government are not paid directly to the unemployed, but are allocated among the states for use in state programs.

State Unemployment Compensation Tax

The amounts paid as benefits to unemployed persons are obtained, for the most part, by taxes levied upon employers only. A few states require employee contributions also. The rates of tax and the tax bases vary. In most states, employers who provide stable employment for their employees are granted reduced rates. The employment experience and the status of each employer's tax account are reviewed annually, and the tax rates are adjusted accordingly.[5]

Accounting Systems for Payroll and Payroll Taxes

Objective 2
Record payroll and payroll taxes, using a payroll register, employees' earnings records, and a general journal.

As an employee, you expect and are entitled to be paid at regular intervals at the end of each payroll period. Regardless of the number of employees, the payroll system must be designed to process payroll data quickly and accurately.

In designing payroll systems, the requirements of various federal, state, and local agencies for payroll data are considered. Payroll data must not only be maintained for each payroll period, but also for each employee. Periodic reports using payroll data must be submitted to governmental agencies. The payroll data itself must be retained for possible inspection by the various agencies.

Payroll systems should also be designed to provide useful data for management decision-making needs. Such needs might include settling employee grievances and negotiating retirement or other benefits with employees.

Although payroll systems differ among businesses, the major components common to most payroll systems are the payroll register, employee's earnings record, and payroll checks. We discuss and illustrate each of these major components below. We have kept the illustrations relatively simple, and they may be modified in practice to meet the needs of each individual business.

PAYROLL REGISTER

The **payroll register** is a multicolumn form used in assembling and summarizing the data needed for each payroll period. Its design varies according to the number

[4] The rate on January 1, 1995, was 6.2%, which may be reduced to 0.8% for credits for state unemployment compensation tax.

[5] As of January 1, 1995, the maximum state rate recognized by the federal unemployment system was 5.4% of the first $7,000 of each employee's earnings during a calendar year.

and classes of employees and the extent to which computers are used. Exhibit 3 shows a form suitable for a small number of employees.

The nature of the data appearing in the payroll register is evident from the column headings. The number of hours worked and the earnings and deduction data are inserted in their proper columns. The sum of the deductions for each employee is then subtracted from the total earnings to yield the amount to be paid. The check numbers are recorded in the payroll register as evidence of payment.

The last two columns of the payroll register are used to accumulate the total wages or salaries to be debited to the various expense accounts. This process is usually called **payroll distribution.** If a large number of accounts are to be debited, the data may be accumulated on a separate payroll distribution sheet.

The format of the payroll register in Exhibit 3 aids in determining the mathematical accuracy of the payroll before checks are issued to employees. All column totals should be cross-verified, as shown below.

Earnings:		
Regular	$13,328.00	
Overtime	574.00	
Total		$13,902.00
Deductions:		
FICA tax	$ 851.60	
Federal income tax	3,332.00	
U.S. savings bonds	680.00	
United Fund	470.00	
Accounts receivable	50.00	
Total		5,383.60
Paid—net amount		$ 8,518.40
Accounts debited:		
Sales Salaries Expense		$11,122.00
Office Salaries Expense		2,780.00
Total (as above)		$13,902.00

Recording Employees' Earnings

Amounts in the payroll register may be posted directly to the accounts. An alternative is to use the payroll register as a supporting record for a journal entry. The entry based on the payroll register in Exhibit 3 follows.

Dec. 27	Sales Salaries Expense	11,122.00	
	Office Salaries Expense	2,780.00	
	FICA Tax Payable		851.60
	Employees Federal Income Tax Payable		3,332.00
	Bond Deductions Payable		680.00
	United Fund Deductions Payable		470.00
	Accounts Receivable—Fred G. Elrod		50.00
	Salaries Payable		8,518.40
	Payroll for week ended December 27.		

The total expense incurred for the services of employees is recorded by the debits to the salary expense accounts. Amounts withheld from employees' earnings have no effect on the debits to these accounts. Five of the credits in the preceding entry increase liability accounts and one credit decreases the accounts receivable account.

Recording and Paying Payroll Taxes

It is important for you to note that all employer's payroll taxes become liabilities when the related payroll is *paid* to employees. In addition, employers are required

Exhibit 3
Payroll Register

		EARNINGS		
Employee Name	*Total Hours*	*Regular*	*Overtime*	*Total*
Abrams, Julie S.	40	500.00		500.00
Elrod, Fred G.	44	392.00	58.80	450.80
Gomez, Jose C.		840.00		840.00
McGrath, John T.	**44**	**1,000.00**	**150.00**	**1,150.00**
Wilkes, Glenn K.	40	480.00		480.00
Zumpano, Michael W.		600.00		600.00
Total		13,328.00	574.00	13,902.00

to compute and report payroll taxes on a *calendar-year* basis. The calendar year must be used for payroll taxes, even if a different fiscal year is used for financial reporting and income tax purposes.

To illustrate the accounting implications of the preceding requirement, assume that Everson Company's fiscal year ends on April 30. Also, assume that Everson Company owes its employees $26,000 of wages on December 31. The following portions of the $26,000 of wages are subject to payroll taxes on December 31:

	Earnings Subject to Payroll Taxes
FICA—Social Security and Medicare (7.5%)	$18,000
FICA—Medicare only (1.5%)	8,000
State and Federal Unemployment Compensation	1,000

If the payroll is paid on December 31, the payroll taxes will be based on the preceding amounts. If the payroll is paid on January 2, however, the *entire* $26,000 will be subject to payroll taxes.

Each time the payroll is prepared, the amount of employer payroll taxes should be determined. The payroll tax expense accounts are then debited and the related liability accounts credited.

To illustrate, the payroll register in Exhibit 3 indicates that the amount of FICA tax withheld is $851.60. Since the employer must match the employees' FICA contributions, the employer's FICA payroll tax will also be $851.60. Further, assume that the earnings subject to state and federal unemployment compensation taxes are $2,710. Multiplying this amount by the state (5.4%) and federal (0.8%) unemployment tax rates yields the unemployment compensation taxes shown below.

FICA tax	$ 851.60
State unemployment compensation tax (5.4% × $2,710)	146.34
Federal unemployment compensation tax (0.8% × $2,710)	21.68
Total payroll tax expense	$1,019.62

The entry to journalize the payroll tax expense for the week and the liability for the taxes accrued is shown below. Payment of the liabilities for payroll taxes is recorded in the same manner as the payment of other liabilities.

DEDUCTIONS					*PAID*		*ACCOUNTS DEBITED*	
FICA Tax	*Federal Income Tax*	*U.S. Savings Bonds*	*Miscel- laneous*	*Total*	*Net Amount*	*Check No.*	*Sales Salaries Expense*	*Office Salaries Expense*
37.50	74.00	20.00	UF 10.00	141.50	358.50	6857	500.00	
33.81	62.00		AR 50.00	145.81	304.99	6858		450.80
12.60	173.00	25.00	UF 10.00	220.60	619.40	6859	840.00	
68.25	**247.00**	**20.00**	**UF 5.00**	**340.25**	**809.75**	**6860**	**1,150.00**	
36.00	69.00	10.00		115.00	365.00	6880	480.00	
45.00	71.00	5.00	UF 2.00	123.00	477.00	6881		600.00
851.60	3,332.00	680.00	UF 470.00 AR 50.00	5,383.60	8,518.40		11,122.00	2,780.00

Miscellaneous Deductions UF—United Fund; AR—Accounts Receivable

Exhibit 3 *(concluded)*

Dec. 27	Payroll Tax Expense	1,019.62	
	FICA Tax Payable		851.60
	State Unemployment Tax Payable		146.34
	Federal Unemployment Tax Payable		21.68
	Payroll taxes for week ended December 27.		

FICA contributions (both the employees' and employer's amounts) and federal income taxes must be deposited quarterly in a federal depository bank. In addition, an "Employer's Quarterly Federal Tax Return" (Form 941) must be filed.

Unemployment compensation tax returns and payments are required by the federal government on an annual basis. Earlier payments are required when the tax exceeds a certain minimum. Unemployment compensation tax returns and payments are required by most states on a basis similar to that required by the federal government.

EMPLOYEE'S EARNINGS RECORD

The amount of each employee's earnings to date must be readily available at the end of each payroll period. This cumulative amount is required in order to compute each employee's earnings subject to FICA tax and federal and state unemployment taxes. Without this cumulative amount, there would be no means of determining the employee's FICA tax withholding and employer's payroll taxes. It is essential, therefore, that a detailed payroll record be maintained for each employee. This record is called an **employee's earnings record.**

Exhibit 4 shows a portion of the employee's earnings record for John T. McGrath. The relationship between this record and the payroll register can be seen by tracing the amounts entered on McGrath's earnings record for December 27 back to its source—the fourth line of the payroll register in Exhibit 3.

In addition to spaces for recording data for each payroll period and the cumulative total of earnings, the employee's earnings record has spaces for quarterly totals and the yearly total. These totals are used in various reports for tax, insurance, and other purposes. One such report is the Wage and Tax Statement, commonly called a Form W-2. You may recall receiving a W-2 form for use in preparing your individual tax return. This form must be provided annually to each employee as well as to the Social Security Administration. The amounts reported

Exhibit 4
Employee's Earnings Record

John T. McGrath
1830 4th Street
Clinton, IA 52732–6142 PHONE: 555-3148

MARRIED | NUMBER OF WITHHOLDING ALLOWANCES: 1 | PAY RATE: $1,000.00 Per Week

OCCUPATION: Salesperson | EQUIVALENT HOURLY RATE: $25

Period Ending	*Total Hours*	*EARNINGS* *Regular Earnings*	*Overtime*	*Total Earnings*	*Cumulative Total*
SEP. 27	51	1,000.00	412.50	1,412.50	52,800.00
THIRD QUARTER		13,000.00	4,800.00	17,800.00	
OCT. 4	50	1,000.00	375.00	1,375.00	54,175.00
NOV. 15	48	1,000.00	300.00	1,300.00	62,200.00
NOV. 22	50	1,000.00	375.00	1,375.00	63,575.00
NOV. 29	52	1,000.00	450.00	1,450.00	65,025.00
DEC. 6	50	1,000.00	375.00	1,375.00	66,400.00
DEC. 13	48	1,000.00	300.00	1,300.00	67,700.00
DEC. 20	52	1,000.00	450.00	1,450.00	69,150.00
DEC. 27	44	1,000.00	150.00	1,150.00	70,300.00
FOURTH QUARTER		13,000.00	4,500.00	17,500.00	
YEARLY TOTAL		52,000.00	18,300.00	70,300.00	

in the example of a Form W-2 shown below were taken from John T. McGrath's employee's earnings record.

a. Employer's identification number 61-8436524	1. Wages, tips, other compensation 70,300.00	2. Federal income tax withheld 16,772.00
b. Employer's name, address, and ZIP code McDermott Supply Co. 415 5th Ave. So. Dubuque, IA 52736-0142	3. FICA wages 70,300.00	4. FICA taxes withheld 5,254.50
	5. Social security tips	6. Benefits
	7. Other	
c. Employee's social security number 381-48-9120	8. Name of State IA	9. State wages / 10. State taxes withheld
d. Employee's name, address, and ZIP code John T. McGrath 1830 4th St. Clinton, IA 52732-6142	11. Name of Locality Dubuque	12. Local wages / 13. Local taxes withheld
	14. Statutory employee ☐ Deceased ☐ Pension plan ☐ Legal rep. ☐ 942 emp. ☐ Subtotal ☐ Deferred compensation ☐	

PAYROLL CHECKS

At the end of each pay period, one of the major outputs of the payroll system is a series of **payroll checks.** These checks are prepared from the payroll register, in which each line applies to an employee. Normally, the payroll check includes a detachable statement showing the details of how the net pay was computed. Exhibit 5 is a payroll check for John T. McGrath.

SOC. SEC. NO.: 381-48-9120 **EMPLOYEE NO.: 814**

DATE OF BIRTH: February 15, 1974

DATE EMPLOYMENT TERMINATED:

DEDUCTIONS					*PAID*	
FICA Tax	*Federal Income Tax*	*U.S. Bonds*	*Other*	*Total*	*Net Amount*	*Check No.*
105.94	339.00	20.00		464.94	947.56	6175
1,342.50	4,296.00	260.00	UF 40	5,938.50	11,861.50	
103.13	330.00	20.00		453.13	921.88	6225
97.50	312.00	20.00		429.50	870.50	6530
103.13	330.00	20.00		453.13	921.88	6582
108.75	348.00	20.00		476.75	973.25	6640
103.13	330.00	20.00	UF 5	458.13	916.88	6688
97.50	312.00	20.00		429.50	870.50	6743
108.75	348.00	20.00		476.75	973.25	6801
68.25	247.00	20.00	UF 5	340.25	809.75	6860
1,294.50	4,100.00	260.00	UF 15	5,669.50	11,830.50	
5,254.50	16,772.00	1,040.00	UF 100	23,166.50	47,133.50	

Exhibit 4 *(concluded)*

When the voucher system is used, it is necessary to prepare a voucher for the net amount to be paid the employees. The voucher is then recorded as a debit to Salaries Payable and a credit to Accounts Payable. The payment of the voucher is recorded in the usual manner. If the voucher system is not used, the payment is recorded by a debit to Salaries Payable and a credit to Cash.

The amount paid to employees is normally recorded as a single amount, regardless of the number of employees. There is no need to record each payroll check separately in the journal, since all of the details are available in the payroll register.

For paying their payroll, most employers use payroll checks drawn on a special bank account. After the data for the payroll period have been recorded and summarized in the payroll register, a single check for the total amount to be paid is written on the firm's regular bank account. This check is then deposited in the special payroll bank account. Individual payroll checks are written from the payroll account, and the numbers of the payroll checks are inserted in the payroll register.

An advantage of using a separate payroll bank account is that the task of reconciling the bank statements is simplified. The paid payroll checks are returned by the bank with a bank statement for the payroll account. If all the payroll checks have been cashed by employees, the balance of the payroll account should be zero or the amount initially required by the bank to open the account. This is because the amount of each deposit is equal to the total amount of payroll checks written. Any payroll checks not cashed by employees will appear as outstanding checks on the bank reconciliation. After a period of time, funds for payroll checks that have not been cashed are transferred to the regular bank account. This establishes control over these items and prevents the theft or misuse of uncashed payroll checks.

Exhibit 5
Payroll Check

McDermott Supply Co.
415 5th Ave. So.
Dubuque, IA 52736-0142

John T. McGrath
1830 4th St.
Clinton, IA 52732-6142

Check Number: 6860
Pay Period Ending: 12/27/96

HOURS & EARNINGS		TAXES & DEDUCTIONS		
DESCRIPTION	**AMOUNT**	**DESCRIPTION**	**CURRENT AMOUNT**	**Y-T-D AMOUNT**
Rate of Pay Reg.	25	FICA Tax	68.25	5,254.50
Rate of Pay O.T.	37.50	Fed. Income Tax	247.00	16,772.00
Hours Worked Reg.	40	U.S. Savings Bonds	20.00	1,040.00
Hours Worked O.T.	4	United Fund	5.00	100.00
Net Pay	809.75			
Total Gross Pay	1,150.00	Total	340.25	23,166.50
Total Gross Y-T-D	70,300.00			

STATEMENT OF EARNINGS. DETACH AND KEEP FOR YOUR RECORDS

McDermott Supply Co.
415 5th Ave. So.
Dubuque, IA 52736-0142

LaGesse Savings & Loan
33 Katie Avenue, Suite 33
Clinton, IA 52736-3581
24-2/531

Pay Period Ending: 12/27/96 6860

PAY EIGHT HUNDRED NINE AND 75/100. . . . . **DOLLARS**

$***809.75

To the Order of JOHN T. MCGRATH
1830 4TH ST.
CLINTON, IA 52732-6142

Franklin D. McDermott

⑈6860⑈ ⑆153111123⑆ ⑈938540 2⑈

Currency may be used to pay payroll. For example, currency is often used for paying part-time workers or for employees, such as construction workers, who are paid at remote locations where cashing checks is difficult. In such cases, a single check, payable to Payroll, is written for the entire amount to be paid. The check is then cashed at the bank and the money is inserted in individual pay envelopes. The employees should be asked for identification and should be required to sign a receipt when picking up their pay envelopes. Journalizing the payroll is the same as if payroll checks were used.

Many employees have their net pay deposited directly in a bank. In these cases, funds are transferred electronically.

PAYROLL SYSTEM DIAGRAM

You may find Exhibit 6 useful in following the flow of data within the payroll segment of an accounting system. The diagram indicates the relationships among the primary components of the payroll system we described in this chapter. The need to update the employee's earnings record is indicated by the dotted line.

Our focus in the preceding discussion has been on the outputs of a payroll system: the payroll register, payroll checks, the employee's earnings record, and tax and other reports. As shown in the diagram in Exhibit 6, the inputs into a payroll system may be classified as either constants or variables.

Constants are data that remain unchanged from payroll to payroll and thus do not need to be inputted into the system each pay period. Examples of constants include such data as each employee's name and social security number, marital status, number of income tax withholding allowances, rate of pay, payroll category (office, sales, etc.), and department where employed. The FICA tax rates and various tax tables are also constants that apply to all employees. In a computerized accounting system, constants are stored within a business's database.

Variables are data that change from payroll to payroll and thus must be inputted into the system each pay period. Examples of variables include such data as

Exhibit 6
Flow of Data in a Payroll System

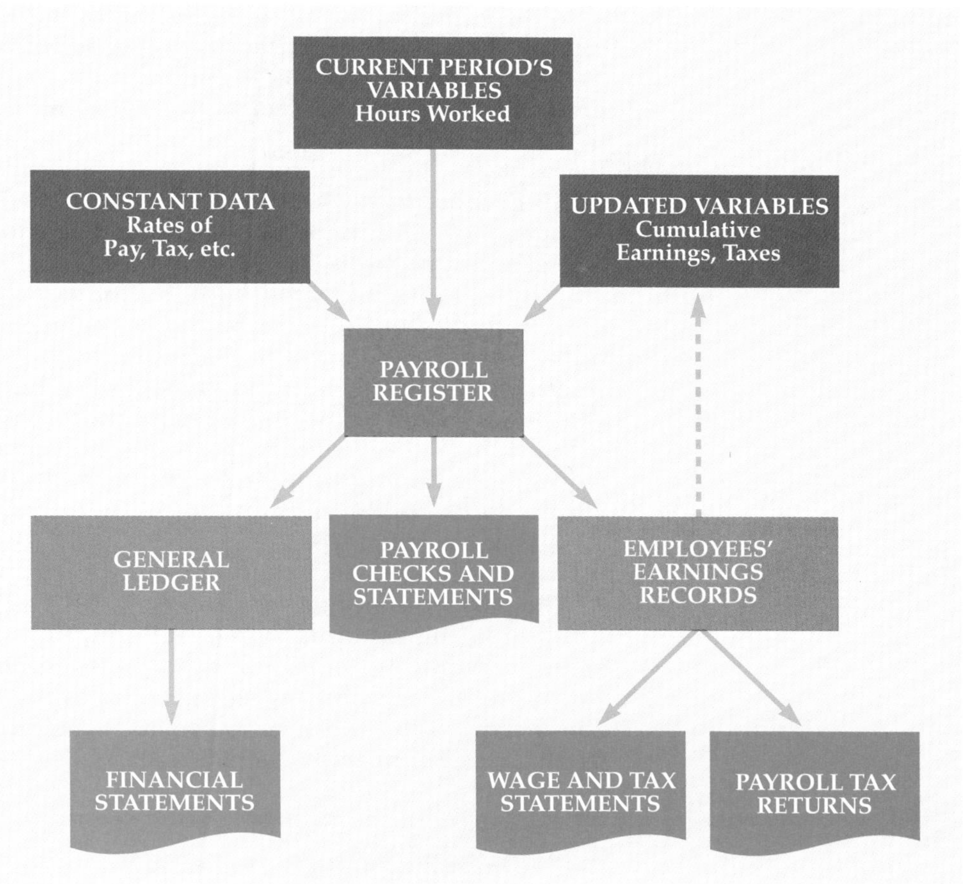

Internal controls for payroll systems will help avert schemes to misuse funds like that portrayed in "Superman III."

the number of hours or days worked for each employee during the payroll period, days of sick leave with pay, vacation credits, and cumulative earnings and taxes withheld. If salespersons are paid commissions, the amount of their sales would also vary from period to period.

INTERNAL CONTROLS FOR PAYROLL SYSTEMS

Payroll processing, as we discussed above, requires the input of a large amount of data, along with numerous and sometimes complex computations. These factors, combined with the large dollar amounts involved, require controls to ensure that payroll payments are timely and accurate. In addition, the system must also provide adequate safeguards against theft or other misuse of funds.

One scheme to misuse payroll funds was portrayed in the movie *Superman III.* In this movie, actor Richard Pryor played a computer programmer, Gus Gorman, who embezzled payroll funds. Gus programmed the computer to round down each employee's payroll amount to the nearest penny. The amount "rounded out" was then added to Gus's payroll check. For example, if an employee's total payroll was $458.533, the payroll program would pay the employee $458.53 and add the $.003 to a special account. The total in this special account would be transferred to Gus's paycheck at the end of the processing of the payroll. In this way, Gus's check increased from $143.80 to $85,000 in one pay period.

The cash payment controls we discussed in the cash chapter also apply to payrolls. Thus, it is normally desirable to use a voucher system that includes procedures for proper authorization and approval of payroll. When a check-signing machine is used, it is important that blank payroll checks and access to the machine be carefully controlled to prevent the theft or misuse of payroll funds.

It is especially important to authorize and approve in writing employee additions and deletions and changes in pay rates. For example, numerous payroll frauds have occurred where fictitious employees have been added to the payroll by a supervisor. The supervisor then cashes the fictitious employees' checks. Similar frauds have occurred where employees have been fired but the Payroll Department is not notified. As a result, payroll checks to the fired employees are prepared and cashed by a supervisor.

To prevent or detect frauds such as those we described above, employees' attendance records should be controlled. For example, you may have used an "In and Out" card on which your time of arrival to and departure from work was recorded when you inserted the card into a time clock. A Payroll Department employee may be stationed near the time clock during normal arrival and departure times in order to verify that employees only "clock in" once and only for themselves. Employee identification cards or badges may also be used to verify that only authorized employees are clocking in and are permitted to enter work areas. When payroll checks are distributed, employee identification cards may be used to deter one employee from picking up another's check.

Other controls include verifying and approving all payroll rate changes. In addition, in a computerized system, all program changes should be properly approved and tested by employees who are independent of the payroll system. This would prevent or detect any changes such as those portrayed in the movie mentioned above. The use of a special payroll bank account, as we discussed earlier in the chapter, also enhances control over payroll.

Employees' Fringe Benefits

Objective 3
Journalize entries for employee fringe benefits, including vacation pay and pensions.

Many companies provide their employees a variety of benefits in addition to salary and wages earned. These benefits are often called **fringe benefits.** Such benefits may take many forms, including vacations, pension plans, and health, life, and disability insurance. When the employer pays part or all of the cost of the fringe benefits, these costs must be recognized as expenses. To properly match revenues and expenses, the estimated cost of these benefits should be recorded as an expense during the period in which the employee earns the benefit. In the following paragraphs, we discuss applying this matching concept to vacation pay and pension costs.

VACATION PAY

Most employers grant vacation rights, sometimes called compensated absences, to their employees. To properly match revenues and expense, employees' vacation pay should be accrued as a liability as the vacation rights are earned.[6] The entry to accrue vacation pay may be recorded in total at the end of each fiscal year, or it may be recorded at the end of each pay period. To illustrate this latter case, assume that employees earn one day of vacation for each month worked during the year. Assume also that the estimated vacation pay for the payroll period ending May 5 is $2,000. The entry to record the accrued vacation pay for this pay period is shown below.

May 5	Vacation Pay Expense	2,000	
	Vacation Pay Payable		2,000
	Vacation pay for week ended May 5.		

[6] *Statement of Financial Accounting Standards, No. 43,* "Accounting for Compensated Absences," Financial Accounting Standards Board, Stamford, 1980, par 6.

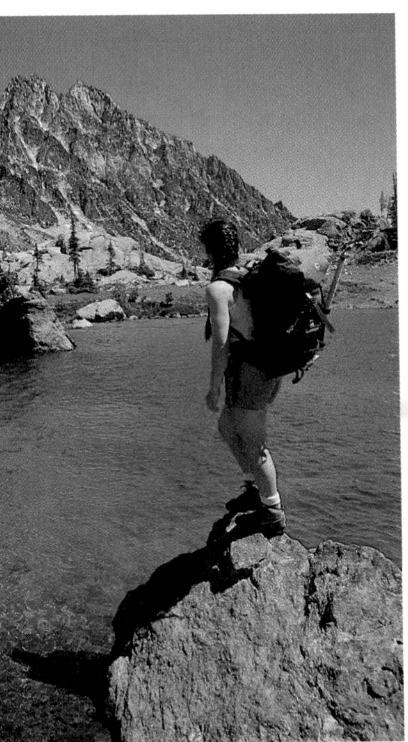

Employee vacations and the cost of other fringe benefits are recorded as expenses.

If employees are required to take all their vacation time within one year, the vacation pay payable is reported on the balance sheet as a current liability. If employees are allowed to accumulate their vacation time, the estimated portion of vacation pay payable that is applicable to time that will not be taken within one year is a long-term liability.

When payroll is prepared for the period in which employees have taken vacations, the vacation pay payable is reduced. The entry debits Vacation Pay Payable and credits Salaries Payable and the other related accounts for taxes and withholdings.

PENSIONS

A **pension** represents a cash payment to retired employees. Rights to pension payments are earned by employees during their working years, based on the pension plan established by the employer. One of the fundamental characteristics of such a plan is whether it is a defined contribution plan or a defined benefit plan.

Defined Contribution Plan

A defined contribution plan requires that a fixed amount of money be invested for the employee's behalf during the employee's working years. The most popular type of defined contribution plan is a **401K plan,** named after the Internal Revenue Service Code section that regulates its tax status.

In a defined contribution plan, the employer is required to make annual pension contributions, but there is no promise with regard to future pension payments. Thus, the employee bears the investment risk in a defined contribution plan. The employer's cost of an employee's pension plan in a given period is called the **net periodic pension cost.** This cost is debited to Pension Expense.[7] Cash is credited for the same amount. To illustrate, assume that the pension plan of Flossmoor Industries requires a contribution equal to 10% of employee annual salaries to the pension fund trustee, Equity Insurance Company. The entry to record the transaction, assuming $500,000 of annual salaries, is as follows:

Pension Expense	50,000	
Cash		50,000

After Flossmoor makes the annual contribution to the pension plan trustee, Flossmoor's obligation is completed. The employee's final pension will depend on the investment results earned by Equity Insurance on the contributed balances.

Defined Benefit Plan

A defined benefit plan promises employees a fixed annual pension benefit at retirement, based on years of service and compensation levels. An example of a defined benefit plan would be one that promises a benefit based on a formula, such as the following: 1.5% × years of service × average salary for most recent 3 years prior to retirement. Unlike a defined contribution plan, the employer bears the investment risk in funding a future retirement income benefit. As a result, many companies are replacing their defined benefit plans with defined contribution plans.

The accounting for defined benefit plans is usually very complex due to the uncertainties of projecting future pension obligations. These obligations depend upon such factors as employee life expectancies, employee turnover, expected employee

[7] *Statement of Financial Accounting Standards, No. 87,* "Employers' Accounting for Pensions," Financial Accounting Standards Board, Stamford, 1985, par. 64.

USING ACCOUNTING TO UNDERSTAND BUSINESS

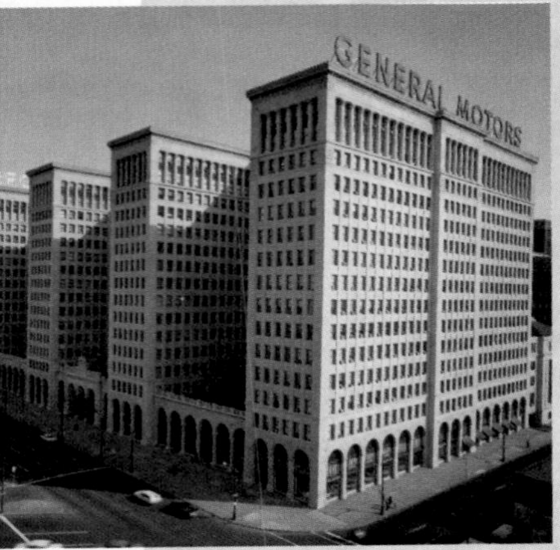

Many companies have underfunded defined benefit pension plans. Below is a list of major companies and the size of their unfunded pension liability.

Company	*Unfunded Pension Liability (millions)*
Aluminum Company of America	$ 197
Caterpillar	110
Chrysler	3,996
Exxon	1,567
Ford	1,897
General Motors	14,000
Mobil	449
United Technologies	238
Westinghouse	303
Woolworth	123

Source: *Wall Street Journal*, September 2, 1993, p. A6.

compensation levels, and investment income on pension contributions. Pension funding obligations are estimated by using sophisticated mathematical and statistical models.

The net periodic pension cost of a defined benefit plan is debited to Pension Expense. The amount funded is credited to Cash. Any unfunded amount is credited to Unfunded Pension Liability. For example, assume that the pension plan of Hinkle Co. requires an annual pension cost of $80,000, based on a mathematical estimate of the future benefit obligation. Further assume that Hinkle Co. pays $60,000 to the fund trustee, Equity Insurance Company. The entry to record the transaction is as follows:

Pension Expense	80,000	
Cash		60,000
Unfunded Pension Liability		20,000

If the unfunded pension liability is to be paid within one year, it will be classified as a current liability. That portion of the liability to be paid beyond one year is a long-term liability.

POSTRETIREMENT BENEFITS OTHER THAN PENSIONS

In addition to the pension benefits described above, employees may earn rights to other **postretirement benefits** from their employer after they retire. Such benefits may include dental care, eye care, medical care, life insurance, tuition assistance, tax services, and legal services for employees or their dependents.

Generally accepted accounting principles require postretirement benefit expenses to be recognized in the financial statements as employees earn the rights to the benefits.[8] The amount of the annual expense is based upon health and longevity statistics of the workforce. The entry to recognize benefits earned in the current year debits Postretirement Benefits Expense. Cash is credited for the same amount if the benefits are fully funded. If the benefits are not fully funded, a postretirement

[8] *Statement of Financial Accounting Standards, No. 106,* "Employer's Accounting for Postretirement Benefits Other Than Pensions," Financial Accounting Standards Board, Norwalk, 1990, par. 6.

benefits plan liability account is credited. Thus, the accounting for postretirement health benefits is very similar to that of defined benefit pension plans.

An entity's financial statements should fully disclose the nature of its postretirement benefit obligations. These disclosures are usually included as footnotes to the financial statements. The complex nature of accounting for postretirement benefits is described in more advanced accounting courses.

Short-Term Notes Payable

Objective 4
Journalize entries for short-term notes payable.

Notes may be issued to creditors to temporarily satisfy an account payable created earlier. They may also be issued at the time merchandise or other assets are purchased. For example, assume that a business issues a 90-day, 12% note for $1,000, dated August 1, 1997, to Murray Co. for a $1,000 overdue account. The entry to record the issuance of the note is as follows:

Aug. 1	Accounts Payable—Murray Co.	1,000	
	Notes Payable		1,000
	Issued a 90-day, 12% note on account.		

At the time the note matures, the entry to record the payment of $1,030 ($1,000 principal plus $30 interest) is as follows:

Oct. 30	Notes Payable	1,000	
	Interest Expense	30	
	Cash		1,030

The interest expense account is reported in the Other Expense section of the income statement for the year ended December 31, 1997.

The preceding entries for notes payable are similar to those we discussed in an earlier chapter for notes receivable. Notes payable entries are presented from the viewpoint of the borrower, while notes receivable entries are presented from the viewpoint of the creditor or lender. To illustrate, the following entries are journalized for a borrower (Bowden Co.), who issues a note payable to a creditor (Coker Co.):

	Bowden Co. (Borrower)			*Coker Co. (Creditor)*		
May 1. Bowden Co. purchased merchandise on account from Coker Co., $10,000, n/30.	Merchandise Inventory Accounts Payable	10,000	 10,000	Accounts Receivable Sales Cost of Merchandise Sold Merchandise Inventory	10,000 7,500	 10,000 7,500
May 31. Bowden Co. issued a 60-day, 12% note for $10,000 to Coker Co. on account.	Accounts Payable Notes Payable	10,000	 10,000	Notes Receivable Accounts Receivable	10,000	 10,000
July 30. Bowden Co. paid Coker Co. the amount due on the note of May 31. Interest: $\$10,000 \times 12\% \times 60/360$	Notes Payable Interest Expense Cash	10,000 200	 10,200	Cash Interest Income Notes Receivable	10,200	 200 10,000

Notes may also be issued when money is borrowed from banks. Although the terms may vary, many banks would accept from the borrower an interest-bearing note for the amount of the loan. For example, assume that on September 19 a firm borrows $4,000 from the First National Bank by giving the bank a 90-day, 15% note. The entry to record the receipt of cash and the issuance of the note is as follows:

Sep. 19	Cash	4,000	
	Notes Payable		4,000

On the due date of the note (December 18), the borrower owes $4,000, the principal of the note, plus interest of $150. The entry to record the payment of the note is as follows:

Dec. 18	Notes Payable	4,000	
	Interest Expense	150	
	Cash		4,150

Sometimes a borrower will issue a non-interest-bearing note to the bank rather than an interest-bearing note. The face amount of the note is the amount that is to be paid at maturity. Although such a note does not specify an interest rate, the bank sets a rate of interest and deducts the interest from the maturity value of the note. The borrower is given the remainder. This deduction of interest from the maturity value is called discounting. The rate used in computing the amount deducted is called the **discount rate,** and the deduction is called the **discount.** The net amount received by the borrower is called the **proceeds.**

To illustrate, assume that on August 10 a business issues to a bank a $4,000, 90-day, non-interest-bearing note, which the bank discounts at a rate of 15%. The amount of the discount is $150, and the proceeds are $3,850. The entry to record the note is as follows:

Aug. 10	Cash	3,850	
	Interest Expense	150	
	Notes Payable		4,000

Cash is debited for the proceeds received from the bank from issuing the note. Notes Payable is credited for the face amount of the note, which is also its maturity value. Since most discounted notes mature within a short period of time, the amount of the discount is normally debited to Interest Expense. If the accounting period ends before the maturity date of the note, an adjusting entry should be prepared, allocating the interest expense between accounting periods.

When the note in the preceding illustration is paid, the following entry is recorded:

Nov. 8	Notes Payable	4,000	
	Cash		4,000

Short-term notes payable are presented in the Current Liabilities section of the balance sheet. If the market (fair) value of short-term notes payable differs from the carrying (book) value, the market value of the notes should be disclosed in notes to the financial statements.[9] In most cases, however, the carrying value of short-term notes payable approximates the market value, and such disclosures are unnecessary.

Product Warranty Liability

Objective 5
Journalize entries for product warranties.

At the time of sale, a company may grant a warranty on a product. You may be familiar with warranties on electronic equipment and automobiles. To match revenues and expenses properly, warranty costs should be recognized as expenses in the same

[9] *Statement of Financial Accounting Standards, No. 107,* "Disclosures about Fair Value of Financial Instruments," Financial Accounting Standards Board, Norwalk, 1991, pars. 10 and 13.

period in which the revenues to which they relate are recorded. In other words, estimated warranty costs should be recognized as expenses in the period in which the sale is recorded.[10] Later, when the product is repaired or replaced, the liability will be reduced.

To illustrate, assume that during June a company sells $60,000 of a product, on which there is a 36-month warranty for repairing defects in the product. Past experience indicates that the average cost to repair defects is 5% of the sales price. The entry to record the estimated warranty expense for June is as follows:

June 30	Product Warranty Expense	3,000	
	Product Warranty Payable		3,000
	Product warranty for June, 5% × $60,000.		

When the defective product is repaired, the repair costs are recorded by debiting Product Warranty Payable and crediting Cash, Supplies, or other appropriate accounts.

KEY POINTS

Objective 1. Determine employer's liabilities for payroll, including liabilities arising from employee earnings and deductions from earnings.
An employer's liability for payroll is calculated by determining employees' total earnings for a payroll period, including overtime pay. From this amount is subtracted employee deductions to arrive at the net pay to be paid each employee. Employer's liabilities for employee deductions are recognized at the time the payroll is recorded. Most employers also incur liabilities for payroll taxes, such as FICA tax, federal unemployment compensation tax, and state unemployment compensation tax.

Objective 2. Record payroll and payroll tax, using a payroll register, employees' earnings records, and a general journal.
The payroll register is a multicolumn form used in assembling and summarizing the data needed for each payroll period. The data recorded in the payroll register include the number of hours worked and the earning and deduction data for each employee. The sum of the deductions for each employee is subtracted from the total earnings to yield the amount to be paid. Check numbers are recorded in the payroll register as evidence of payment to each employee. The payroll register also includes columns for accumulating total wages or salaries to be debited to the various expense accounts.

Amounts in the payroll register may be posted directly to the accounts. Alternatively, the payroll register may be used as a supporting record for recording the payroll for the period in the general journal. The payroll register is supported by a detailed payroll record for each employee, called an employee's earnings record.

Objective 3. Journalize entries for employee fringe benefits, including vacation pay and pensions.
Fringe benefits should be recognized as expenses of the period in which the employees earn the benefits. Fringe benefits are recorded by debiting an expense account and crediting a liability account. For example, the entry to record accrued vacation pay debits Vacation Pay Expense and credits Vacation Pay Payable.

Objective 4. Journalize entries for short-term notes payable.
A note issued to a creditor to temporarily satisfy an account payable is recorded as a debit to Accounts Payable and a credit to Notes Payable. At the time the note is paid, Notes Payable and Interest Expense are debited and Cash is credited. Notes may also be issued to purchase merchandise or other assets or to borrow money from a bank. When a non-interest-bearing note is issued to a bank, Interest (discount) Expense is debited for the interest deduction at the time of issuance, Cash is debited for the proceeds, and Notes Payable is credited for the face value of the note. The face value and the maturity value of a non-interest-bearing note are equal.

Objective 5. Journalize entries for product warranties.
If a company grants a warranty on a product, an estimated warranty expense and liability should be recorded in the period of the sale. The expense and the liability are recorded by debiting Product Warranty Expense and crediting Product Warranty Payable.

[10] *Statement of Financial Accounting Standards, No. 5,* "Accounting for Contingencies," Financial Accounting Standards Board, Stamford, 1975, pars. 8 and 24.

GLOSSARY OF KEY TERMS

Defined benefit plan. A pension plan that promises employees a fixed annual pension benefit at retirement, based on years of service and compensation levels. *Objective 3*

Defined contribution plan. A pension plan that requires a fixed amount of money to be invested for the employee's behalf during the employee's working years. *Objective 3*

Discount. The interest deducted from the maturity value of a note. *Objective 4*

Discount rate. The rate used in computing the interest to be deducted from the maturity value of a note. *Objective 4*

Employee's earnings record. A detailed record of each employee's earnings. *Objective 2*

FICA tax. Federal Insurance Contributions Act tax used to finance federal programs for old-age and disability benefits (social security) and health insurance for the aged (Medicare). *Objective 1*

Gross pay. The total earnings of an employee for a payroll period. *Objective 1*

Net pay. Gross pay less payroll deductions; the amount the employer is obligated to pay the employee. *Objective 1*

Payroll. The total amount paid to employees for a certain period. *Objective 1*

Payroll register. A multicolumn form used to assemble and summarize payroll data at the end of each payroll period. *Objective 2*

Postretirement benefits. Rights to benefits that employees earn during their term of employment for themselves and their dependents after they retire. *Objective 3*

Proceeds. The net amount available from discounting a note. *Objective 4*

ILLUSTRATIVE PROBLEM

Selected transactions of Taylor Company, completed during the fiscal year ended December 31, are as follows:

Mar. 1. Purchased merchandise on account from Kelvin Co., $20,000.
Apr. 10. Issued a 60-day, 12% note for $20,000 to Kelvin Co. on account.
June 9. Paid Kelvin Co. the amount owed on the note of April 10.
Aug. 1. Issued a 90-day, non-interest-bearing note for $50,000 to Capital City National Bank. The bank discounted the note at 15%.
Oct. 30. Paid Capital City National Bank the amount due on the note of August 1.
Dec. 27. Journalized the entry to record the biweekly payroll. A summary of the payroll record follows:

Salary distribution:		
Sales	$63,400	
Officers	36,600	
Office	10,000	$110,000
Deductions:		
FICA tax	$ 6,700	
Federal income tax withheld	17,600	
State income tax withheld	4,950	
Savings bond deductions	850	
Medical insurance deductions	1,120	31,220
Net amount		$ 78,780

30. Issued a check in payment of employees' federal income tax of $17,600 and FICA tax of $13,400 due.
31. Issued a check for $9,500 to the pension fund trustee to fully fund the pension cost for December.
31. Journalized an entry to record the employees' accrued vacation pay, $36,100.
31. Journalized an entry to record the estimated accrued product warranty liability, $37,240.

Instructions

Journalize the preceding transaction.

Solution

Mar. 1	Merchandise Inventory	20,000	
	Accounts Payable—Kelvin Co.		20,000

Apr. 10	Accounts Payable—Kelvin Co.	20,000	
	Notes Payable		20,000
June 9	Notes Payable	20,000	
	Interest Expense	400	
	Cash		20,400
Aug. 1	Cash	48,125	
	Interest Expense	1,875	
	Notes Payable		50,000
Oct. 30	Notes Payable	50,000	
	Cash		50,000
Dec. 27	Sales Salaries Expense	63,400	
	Officers Salaries Expense	36,600	
	Office Salaries Expense	10,000	
	FICA Tax Payable		6,700
	Employees Federal Income Tax Payable		17,600
	Employees State Income Tax Payable		4,950
	Bond Deductions Payable		850
	Medical Insurance Payable		1,120
	Salaries Payable		78,780
30	Employees Federal Income Tax Payable	17,600	
	FICA Tax Payable	13,400	
	Cash		31,000
31	Pension Expense	9,500	
	Cash		9,500
31	Vacation Pay Expense	36,100	
	Vacation Pay Payable		36,100
31	Product Warranty Expense	37,240	
	Product Warranty Payable		37,240

SELF-EXAMINATION QUESTIONS (ANSWERS AT END OF CHAPTER)

1. An employee's rate of pay is $20 per hour, with time and a half for all hours worked in excess of 40 during a week. The FICA rate is 7.5% on the first $70,000 of annual earnings and 1.5% on earnings in excess of $70,000. The following additional data are available:

Hours worked during current week	45
Year's cumulative earnings prior to current week	$69,400
Federal income tax withheld	212

   Based on these data, the amount of the employee's net pay for the current week is:
   A. $620.50 C. $666.75
   B. $641.50 D. $687.75

2. Which of the following taxes are employers usually not required to withhold from employees?
   A. Federal income tax C. FICA tax
   B. Federal unemployment compensation tax D. State and local income tax

3. With limitations on the maximum earnings subject to the tax, employers do not incur operating costs for which of the following payroll taxes?
   A. FICA tax C. State unemployment compensation tax
   B. Federal unemployment compensation tax D. Employees' federal income tax

4. A business issued a $5,000, 60-day, 12% note to the bank. The amount due at maturity is:
   A. $4,900 C. $5,100
   B. $5,000 D. $5,600

5. A business issued a $5,000, 60-day, non-interest-bearing note to the bank, and the bank discounts the note at 12%. The proceeds are:
   A. $4,400 C. $5,000
   B. $4,900 D. $5,100

DISCUSSION QUESTIONS

1. What term is frequently used to refer to the total amount paid to employees for a certain period?
2. What is (a) gross pay? (b) net, or take-home, pay?
3. What programs are funded by the FICA (Federal Insurance Contributions Act) tax?

4. a. Identify the federal taxes that most employers are required to withhold from employees.
   b. Give the titles of the accounts to which the amounts withheld are credited.
5. For each of the following payroll-related taxes, indicate whether there is a ceiling on the annual earnings subject to the tax: (a) FICA tax, (b) federal income tax, (c) federal unemployment compensation tax.
6. Identify the payroll taxes levied against employers.
7. Why are deductions from employees' earnings classified as liabilities for the employer?
8. Do payroll taxes levied against employers become liabilities at the time the liabilities for wages are incurred or at the time the wages are paid?
9. Taylor Company, with 20 employees, is expanding operations. It is trying to decide whether to hire one employee full-time for $25,000 or two employees part-time for a total of $25,000. Would any of the employer's payroll taxes discussed in this chapter have a bearing on this decision? Explain.
10. For each of the following payroll-related taxes, indicate whether they generally apply to (a) employees only, (b) employers only, (c) both employees and employers:
    1. FICA tax
    2. Federal income tax
    3. Federal unemployment compensation tax
    4. State unemployment compensation tax
11. What type of information is recorded in the employee's earnings record, and for what purpose is this information used?
12. An employer pays the employees in currency, and the pay envelopes are prepared by an employee rather than by the bank. (a) Why would it be advisable to obtain from the bank the exact amount of money needed for a payroll? (b) How could the exact number of each bill and coin denomination needed be determined efficiently in advance?
13. What are the principal reasons for using a special payroll checking account?
14. A company uses a weekly payroll period and a special bank account for payroll. (a) When should deposits be made in the account? (b) How is the amount of the deposit calculated? (c) Is it necessary to have in the general ledger an account entitled "Cash—Special Payroll Account?" Explain. (d) The bank statement for the payroll bank account for the month ended June 30 indicates a bank balance of $7,127.50. Assuming that the bank has made no errors, what does this amount represent?
15. In a payroll system, what type of input data are referred to as (a) constants, (b) variables?
16. To strengthen internal controls, what department should provide written authorizations for the addition of names to the payroll?
17. Explain how a payroll system that is properly designed and operated tends to ensure that (a) wages paid are based upon hours actually worked and (b) payroll checks are not issued to fictitious employees.
18. What are employee fringe benefits? Give three examples of such fringe benefits.
19. To match revenues and expenses properly, should the expense for employee vacation pay be recorded in the period during which the vacation privilege is earned or during the period in which the vacation is taken? Discuss.
20. Differentiate between a defined contribution plan and a defined benefit pension plan.
21. Identify several factors that influence the future pension obligation of an employer under a defined benefit pension plan.
22. Where should the unfunded pension liability from a defined benefit pension plan be reported on the balance sheet?
23. What are some examples of postretirement benefits other than pensions that employees may earn for themselves and their dependents?
24. In borrowing money from a bank, a business issued a $50,000, 60-day, non-interest-bearing note, which the bank discounted at 12%. Are the proceeds $50,000? Explain.
25. When should the liability associated with a product warranty be recorded? Discuss.

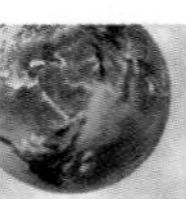

26. The 1993 annual report for **Compaq Computer Corporation** reported $166 million of product warranties in the current liability section of its December 31, 1993 balance sheet. How would costs of repairing a defective product be recorded?
27. The "Questions and Answers Technical Hotline" in the *Journal of Accountancy* included the following question:

    Several years ago, Company B instituted legal action against Company A. Under a memorandum of settlement and agreement, Company A agreed to pay Company B a total of $17,500 in three installments—$5,000 on March 1, $7,500 on July 1, and the remaining $5,000 on December 31.

Company A paid the first two installments during its fiscal year ended September 30. Should the unpaid amount of $5,000 be presented as a current liability at September 30?

How would you answer this question?

EXERCISES

EXERCISE 11–1
Calculating payroll
Objective 1

An employee earns $18 per hour and 1 1/2 times that rate for all hours in excess of 40 hours per week. Assume that the employee worked 50 hours during the week, and that the gross pay prior to the current week totaled $59,760. Assume further that the FICA tax rate was 7.5% (with earnings up to $70,000 subject to the 7.5% rate), and federal income tax to be withheld was $198.

a. Determine the gross pay for the week.
b. Determine the net pay for the week.

EXERCISE 11–2
Calculating payroll
Objective 1

Spectrum Business Consultants has three employees—a consultant, a computer programmer, and an administrator. The following payroll information is available for each employee:

	Consultant	*Computer Programmer*	*Administrator*
Regular earnings rate	$1,800 per week	$24 per hour	$16 per hour
Overtime earnings rate	Not applicable	1 1/2 times hourly rate	1 1/2 times hourly rate
Accumulated gross pay prior to current pay period	$91,800	$69,200	$41,100
Number of withholding allowances	1	4	3

For the current pay period, the computer programmer worked 43 hours and the administrator worked 52 hours. For the current pay period, the federal income tax withheld for the consultant was $428. The federal income tax withheld for the computer programmer and the administrator can be determined from the wage bracket withholding table in Exhibit 2 in the chapter. Assume further that the FICA tax rate was 7.5% on the first $70,000 of annual earnings and 1.5% on annual earnings in excess of $70,000.

Determine the gross pay and the net pay for each of the three employees for the current pay period.

EXERCISE 11–3
Summary payroll data
Objectives 1, 2

In the following summary of data for a payroll period, some amounts have been intentionally omitted:

Earnings:	
1. At regular rate	?
2. At overtime rate	$ 6,100
3. Total earnings	?
Deductions:	
4. FICA tax	8,600
5. Income tax withheld	15,500
6. Medical insurance	1,050
7. Union dues	?
8. Total deductions	26,300
9. Net amount paid	92,620
Accounts debited:	
10. Factory Wages	86,250
11. Sales Salaries	?
12. Office Salaries	7,500

a. Calculate the amounts omitted in lines (1), (3), (7), and (11).
b. Journalize the entry to record the payroll.
c. Journalize the entry to record the voucher for the payroll.
d. Journalize the entry to record the payment of the voucher.
e. From the data given in this exercise and your answer to (a), would you conclude that this payroll was paid sometime during the first few weeks of the calendar year? Explain.

EXERCISE 11–4
Internal control procedures
Objective 2

Memphis Sounds is a retail store specializing in the sale of jazz compact discs and cassettes. The store employs 3 full-time and 10 part-time workers. The store's weekly payroll averages $1,800 for all 13 workers.

Memphis Sounds uses a personal computer to assist in preparing paychecks. Each week, the store's accountant collects employee time cards and enters the hours worked into the payroll program. The payroll program calculates each employee's pay and prints a paycheck. The accountant uses a check-signing machine to sign the paychecks. Next, a voucher is prepared to transfer funds from the store's regular bank account to the payroll account. This voucher is authorized by the store's owner.

For the week of May 10, the accountant accidentally recorded 400 hours worked instead of 40 hours for one of the full-time employees. Does Memphis Sounds have internal controls in place to catch this error? If so, how will this error be detected?

EXERCISE 11–5
Internal control procedures
Objective 2

Taylor Tools is a small manufacturer of home workshop power tools. The company employs 30 production workers and 10 administrative persons. The following procedures are used to process the company's weekly payroll:

a. Whenever a salaried employee is terminated, Personnel authorizes Payroll to remove the employee from the payroll system. However, this procedure is not required when an hourly worker is terminated. Hourly employees only receive a paycheck if their time card shows hours worked. The computer automatically drops an employee from the payroll system when that employee has six consecutive weeks with no hours worked.
b. Whenever an employee receives a pay raise, the supervisor must fill out a wage adjustment form, which is signed by the company president. This form is used to change the employee's wage rate in the payroll system.
c. All employees are required to record their hours worked by clocking in and out on a time clock. Employees must clock out for lunch break. Due to congestion around the time clock area at lunch time, management has not objected to having one employee clock in and out for an entire department.
d. Paychecks are signed by using a check-signing machine. This machine is located in the main office, so that it can be easily accessed by anyone needing a check signed.
e. Taylor maintains a separate checking account for payroll checks. Each week, the total net pay for all employees is transferred from the company's regular bank account to the payroll account.

State whether each of the procedures is appropriate or inappropriate after considering the principles of internal control. If a procedure is inappropriate, state what action must be taken to correct it.

EXERCISE 11–6
Payroll tax entries
Objective 2

According to a summary of the payroll of Classic Publishing Co., the amount of earnings for the payroll paid on November 30 of the current year was $680,000. Of this amount, $650,000 was subject to the 7.5% FICA tax rate and $30,000 was subject to the 1.5% FICA tax rate. Also, $15,000 was subject to state and federal unemployment taxes.

a. Calculate the employer's payroll taxes expense on the payroll, using the following rates: state unemployment, 4.3%; federal unemployment, 0.8%.
b. Journalize the entry to record the accrual of payroll taxes.

EXERCISE 11–7
Payroll procedures
Objective 2

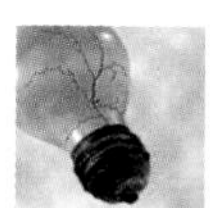

The fiscal year for Crestwood Co. ends on June 30. However, the company computes and reports payroll taxes on the calendar-year basis.

What is wrong with these procedures for accounting for payroll taxes?

EXERCISE 11–8
Accrued vacation pay
Objective 3

A business provides its employees with varying amounts of vacation per year, depending on the length of employment. The estimated amount of the current year's vacation pay is $318,000. Journalize the adjusting entry required on January 31, the end of the first month of the current year, to record the accrued vacation pay.

EXERCISE 11–9
Pension plan entries
Objective 3

Tice Company maintains a defined benefit pension plan for its employees. The plan requires quarterly installments to be paid to the funding agent, Interstate Insurance Company, by the fifteenth of the month following the end of each quarter. Assuming that the pension cost is $125,000 for the quarter ended December 31, journalize entries to record (a) the accrued pension liability on December 31 and (b) the payment to the funding agent on January 15.

EXERCISE 11–10
Entries for discounting notes
Objective 4

Zelda Co. issues a 60-day, non-interest-bearing note for $200,000 to First National Bank and Trust Co., and the bank discounts the note at 12%.

a. Journalize the borrower's entries to record:
   1. the issuance of the note.
   2. the payment of the note at maturity.
b. Journalize the creditor's entries to record:
   1. the receipt of the note.
   2. the receipt of payment of the note at maturity.

EXERCISE 11–11
Evaluating alternative note receivables
Objective 4

A bank has two alternatives in making a $60,000 loan: (1) accepting a $60,000, 60-day, 10% note or (2) discounting a 60-day, $60,000 non-interest-bearing note at 10%.

a. Determine the amount of money loaned in each situation.
b. Which alternative is more favorable to the bank? Explain.

EXERCISE 11–12
Entries for notes payable
Objective 4

A business issued a 90-day, 10% note for $15,000 to a creditor on account. Journalize the entries to record (a) the issuance of the note and (b) the payment of the note at maturity, including interest.

EXERCISE 11–13
Calculating interest on notes issued
Objective 4

In negotiating a 90-day loan, a business has the option of either (1) issuing a $500,000, non-interest-bearing note that will be discounted at the rate of 10% or (2) issuing a $500,000 note that bears interest at the rate of 10% and that will be accepted at face value.

a. Calculate the amount of the interest expense for each option.
b. Calculate the amount of the proceeds for each option.
c. Which option is more favorable to the borrower? Explain.

EXERCISE 11–14
Plant asset purchases with note
Objective 4

On June 30, Valdez Company purchased land for $200,000 and a building for $670,000, paying $150,000 cash and issuing an 8% note for the balance, secured by a mortgage on the property. The terms of the note provide for 18 semiannual payments of $40,000 on the principal plus the interest accrued from the date of the preceding payment. Journalize the entry to record (a) the transaction on June 30, (b) the payment of the first installment on December 31, and (c) the payment of the second installment the following June 30.

EXERCISE 11–15
Accrued product warranty
Objective 5

Park Company warrants its products for one year. The estimated product warranty is 2% of sales. Assuming that sales were $500,000 for January, journalize the adjusting entry required at January 31, the end of the first month of the current year, to record the accrued product warranty.

PROBLEMS SERIES A

PROBLEM 11–1A
Entries for payroll and payroll taxes
Objectives 1, 2

The following information relative to the payroll for the week ended December 30 was obtained from the records of Giles Co.:

Salaries:		Deductions:	
Sales salaries	$ 98,700	Income tax withheld	$25,300
Warehouse salaries	21,280	FICA tax withheld	9,850
Office salaries	16,020	U.S. savings bonds	4,400
	$136,000	Group insurance	2,800

Tax rates assumed:
FICA, 7.5% on first $70,000 and 1.5% on excess of $70,000 of employee annual earnings
State unemployment (employer only), 3.8%
Federal unemployment, 0.8%

Instructions

1. Assuming that the payroll for the last week of the year is to be paid on December 31, journalize the following entries:
   a. December 30, to record the payroll.
   b. December 30, to record the employer's payroll taxes on the payroll to be paid on December 31. Of the total payroll for the last week of the year, $15,000 is subject to unemployment compensation taxes.
2. Assuming that the payroll for the last week of the year is to be paid on January 4 of the following fiscal year, journalize the following entries:
   a. December 30, to record the payroll.
   b. January 4, to record the employer's payroll taxes on the payroll to be paid on January 4.

If the working papers correlating with this textbook are not used, omit Problem 11–2A.

PROBLEM 11–2A
Payroll register
Objectives 1,2

The payroll register for N. B. Sullivan Co. for the week ended December 12 of the current fiscal year is presented in the working papers.

Instructions

1. Journalize the entry to record the payroll for the week.
2. Assuming the use of a voucher system and payment by regular check, journalize the entries to record the payroll voucher and the issuance of the checks to employees.
3. Journalize the entry to record the employer's payroll taxes for the week. Assume the following tax rates: state unemployment, 3.8%; federal unemployment, 0.8%. Of the earnings, $1,020 is subject to unemployment taxes.
4. Journalize the entries to record the following selected transactions:

Dec. 15. Prepared a voucher, payable to Second National Bank, for employees' income taxes, $1,294.00, and FICA taxes, $1,163.40.
15. Issued a check to Second National Bank in payment of the voucher.

PROBLEM 11–3A
Wage and tax statement data and employer FICA tax
Objectives 1, 2

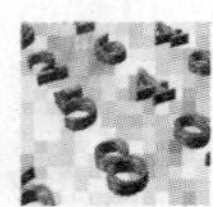

Jerico Company began business on January 2 of last year. Salaries were paid to employees on the last day of each month, and both FICA tax and federal income tax were withheld in the required amounts. An employee who is hired in the middle of the month receives half the monthly salary for that month. All required payroll tax reports were filed, and the correct amount of payroll taxes was remitted by the company for the calendar year. Before the Wage and Tax Statements (Form W-2) could be prepared for distribution to employees and for filing with the Social Security Administration, the employees' earnings records were inadvertently destroyed.

None of the employees resigned or were discharged during the year, and there were no changes in salary rates. The FICA tax was withheld at the rate of 7.5% on the first $70,000 of salary and at the rate of 1.5% on salary in excess of $70,000. Data on dates of employment, salary rates, and employees' income taxes withheld, which are summarized as follows, were obtained from personnel records and payroll records.

Employee	*Date First Employed*	*Monthly Salary*	*Monthly Income Tax Withheld*
Albright	June 2	$3,000	$ 500
Charles	Jan. 2	7,000	1,960
Given	Mar. 1	3,200	624
Nelson	Jan. 2	4,000	810
Quinn	Nov. 15	3,600	652
Ramsey	Apr. 15	2,800	461
Wu	Jan. 16	6,400	1,610

Instructions

1. Calculate the amounts to be reported on each employee's Wage and Tax Statement (Form W-2) for the year, arranging the data in the following form:

Employee	*Gross Earnings*	*Federal Income Tax Withheld*	*FICA Tax Withheld*

2. Calculate the following employer payroll taxes for the year: (a) FICA; (b) state unemployment compensation at 3.8% on the first $7,000 of each employee's earnings; (c) federal unemployment compensation at 0.8% on the first $7,000 of each employee's earnings; (d) total.

PROBLEM 11–4A
Payroll register
Objectives 1, 2

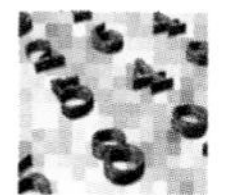

The following data for Wang Co. relate to the payroll for the week ended December 7, 1997:

Employee	*Hours Worked*	*Hourly Rate*	*Weekly Salary*	*Federal Income Tax*	*U.S. Savings Bonds*	*Accumulated Earnings, Nov. 30*
A	44	$24.00		$336	$37.50	$51,640
B	40	20.00		166	25.00	38,880
C			$1,425	356	50.00	69,825
D	40	18.00		97		36,000
E	40	15.00		115	25.00	30,000
F	48	12.75		125		15,300
G	40	12.00		80	25.00	24,000
H			400	40		3,200
I	20	11.00		15		2,700
J	40	11.00		68		22,000

Employees C and H are office staff, and all of the other employees are sales personnel. All sales personnel are paid 1 1/2 times the regular rate for all hours in excess of 40 hours per week. The FICA tax rate is 7.5% on the first $70,000 of annual earnings and 1.5% of annual earnings in excess of $70,000 for each employee. The next payroll check to be used is No. 981.

Instructions

1. Prepare a payroll register for Wang Co. for the week ended December 7, 1997.
2. Journalize the entry to record the payroll for the week.

PROBLEM 11–5A
Payroll accounts and year-end entries
Objectives 1, 2

The following accounts, with the balances indicated, appear in the ledger of B & B Co. on December 1 of the current year:

212	Salaries Payable	—
213	FICA Tax Payable	$ 7,550
214	Employees Federal Income Tax Payable	8,820
215	Employees State Income Tax Payable	14,586
216	State Unemployment Tax Payable	1,881

217	Federal Unemployment Tax Payable	$ 396
218	Bond Deductions Payable	850
219	Medical Insurance Payable	3,200
611	Sales Salaries Expense	694,430
711	Officers Salaries Expense	342,980
712	Office Salaries Expense	94,050
719	Payroll Taxes Expense	101,673

The following transactions relating to payroll, payroll deductions, and payroll taxes occurred during December:

Dec. 2. Prepared Voucher No. 745 for $850, payable to First National Bank, to purchase U.S. savings bonds for employees.
2. Issued Check No. 728 in payment of Voucher No. 745.
3. Prepared Voucher No. 746 for $16,370, payable to First National Bank for $7,550 of FICA tax and $8,820 of employees' federal income tax due.
3. Issued Check No. 729 in payment of Voucher No. 746.
14. Journalized the entry to record the biweekly payroll. A summary of the payroll record follows:

Salary distribution:		
Sales	$36,230	
Officers	16,720	
Office	4,180	$57,130
Deductions:		
FICA tax	$ 4,165	
Federal income tax withheld	10,060	
State income tax withheld	2,112	
Savings bond deductions	375	
Medical insurance deductions	528	17,240
Net amount		$39,890

14. Prepared Voucher No. 757, payable to Payroll Bank Account, for the net amount of the biweekly payroll.
14. Issued Check No. 738 in payment of Voucher No. 757.
14. Journalized the entry to record payroll taxes on employees' earnings of December 14: FICA, $4,165; state unemployment tax, $162; federal unemployment tax, $35.
17. Prepared Voucher No. 758 for $18,390, payable to First National Bank for $8,330 of FICA tax and $10,060 of employees' federal income tax due.
17. Issued Check No. 744 in payment of Voucher No. 758.
18. Prepared Voucher No. 760 for $3,200, payable to Pico Insurance Company, for the semiannual premium on the group medical insurance policy.
19. Issued Check No. 750 in payment of Voucher No. 760.
28. Journalized the entry to record the biweekly payroll. A summary of the payroll record follows:

Salary distribution:		
Sales	$31,350	
Officers	16,720	
Office	4,180	$52,250
Deductions:		
FICA tax	$ 3,311	
Federal income tax withheld	8,322	
State income tax withheld	2,029	
Savings bond deduction	375	14,037
Net amount		$38,213

28. Prepared Voucher No. 795, payable to Payroll Bank Account, for the net amount of the biweekly payroll.
28. Issued Check No. 782 in payment of Voucher No. 795.
28. Journalized the entry to record payroll taxes on employees' earnings of December 28: FICA, $3,311; state unemployment tax, $161; federal unemployment tax, $33.

Dec. 30. Prepared Voucher No. 801 for $750, payable to First National Bank, to purchase U.S. savings bonds for employees.
30. Issued Check No. 791 in payment of Voucher No. 801.
30. Prepared Voucher No. 802 for $14,586, payable to First National Bank, for employees' state income tax due on December 31.
30. Issued Check No. 792 in payment of Voucher No. 802.

Instructions

1. Journalize the transactions.
2. Journalize the adjusting entry on December 31 to record salaries for the incomplete payroll period. Salaries accrued are as follows: sales salaries, $3,245; officers salaries, $1,800; office salaries, $450. The payroll taxes are immaterial and are not accrued.

PROBLEM 11–6A
Liability transactions
Objectives 3, 4, 5

The following items were selected from among the transactions completed by Diego Co. during the current year:

Mar. 2. Purchased merchandise on account from Chavez Co., $6,000, terms 2/10, n/30.
8. Purchased merchandise on account from Mautz Co., $10,000, terms 2/10, n/30.
12. Paid Chavez Co. for the invoice of March 2.
Apr. 7. Issued a 60-day, 12% note for $10,000 to Mautz Co., on account.
May 10. Issued a 120-day, non-interest-bearing note for $90,000 to Hope City Bank. The bank discounted the note at the rate of 14%.
June 5. Paid Mautz Co. the amount owed on the note of April 7.
Aug. 5. Borrowed $7,500 from First Financial Corporation, issuing a 60-day, 14% note for that amount.
Sep. 7. Paid Hope City Bank the amount due on the note of May 10.
Oct. 4. Paid First Financial Corporation the interest due on the note of August 5 and renewed the loan by issuing a new 30-day, 16% note for $7,500. (Record both the debit and credit to the notes payable account.)
Nov. 3. Paid First Financial Corporation the amount due on the note of October 4.
15. Purchased store equipment from Singer Equipment Co. for $100,000, paying $16,000 and issuing a series of seven 12% notes for $12,000 each, coming due at 30-day intervals.
Dec. 15. Paid the amount due Singer Equipment Co. on the first note in the series issued on November 15.
31. Paid $36,200 of the annual pension cost of $45,000. (Record both the payment and the unfunded pension liability.)

Instructions

1. Journalize the transactions.
2. Journalize the adjusting entries for the following accrued expenses for the current year:
   a. Vacation pay, $18,300.
   b. Product warranty cost, $14,000.
3. Journalize the adjusting entry for the accrued interest at December 31 on the six notes owed to Singer Equipment Co.
4. Assume that a single note for $84,000 had been issued on November 15 instead of the series of seven notes and that its terms required principal payments of $12,000 each 30 days, with interest at 12% on the principal balance before applying the $12,000 payment. Calculate the amount that would have been due and payable on December 15.

PROBLEMS SERIES B

PROBLEM 11–1B
Entries for payroll and payroll taxes
Objectives 1, 2

The following information relative to the payroll for the week ended December 30 was obtained from the records of Winck Co.:

Salaries:		Deductions:	
Sales salaries	$121,000	Income tax withheld	$25,100
Warehouse salaries	28,980	FICA tax withheld	11,250
Office salaries	10,020	Group insurance	1,350
	$160,000	U.S. savings bonds	1,200

Tax rates assumed:
FICA, 7.5% on first $70,000 and 1.5% on excess of $70,000 of employee annual earnings;
State unemployment (employer only), 4.2%;
Federal unemployment, 0.8%

Instructions

1. Assuming that the payroll for the last week of the year is to be paid on December 31, journalize the following entries:
   a. December 30, to record the payroll.
   b. December 30, to record the employer's payroll taxes on the payroll to be paid on December 31. Of the total payroll for the last week of the year, $9,000 is subject to unemployment compensation taxes.
2. Assuming that the payroll for the last week of the year is to be paid on January 5 of the following year, journalize the following entries:
   a. December 30, to record the payroll.
   b. January 5, to record the employer's payroll taxes on the payroll to be paid on January 5.

PROBLEM 11–2B
Payroll register
Objectives 1, 2

If the working papers correlating with this textbook are not used, omit Problem 11–2B.

The payroll register for J. McCune Co. for the week ended December 12 of the current fiscal year is presented in the working papers.

Instructions

1. Journalize the entry to record the payroll for the week.
2. Assuming the use of a voucher system and payment by regular check, journalize the entries to record the payroll voucher and the issuance of the checks to employees.
3. Journalize the entry to record the employer's payroll taxes for the week. Assume the following tax rates: state unemployment, 3.1%; federal unemployment, 0.8%. Of the earnings, $1,020 is subject to unemployment taxes.
4. Journalize the entries to record the following selected transactions:

Dec. 16. Prepared a voucher, payable to Burbank National Bank, for employees' income taxes, $1,294.00, and FICA taxes, $1,163.40.
16. Issued a check to Burbank National Bank in payment of the voucher.

PROBLEM 11–3B
Wage and tax statement data on employer FICA tax
Objectives 1, 2

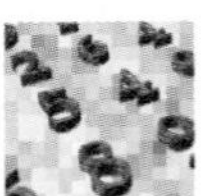

Kato Company began business on January 2 of last year. Salaries were paid to employees on the last day of each month, and both FICA tax and federal income tax were withheld in the required amounts. An employee who is hired in the middle of the month receives half the monthly salary for that month. All required payroll tax reports were filed, and the correct amount of payroll taxes was remitted by the company for the calendar year. Before the Wage and Tax Statements (Form W-2) could be prepared for distribution to employees and for filing with the Social Security Administration, the employees' earnings records were inadvertently destroyed.

None of the employees resigned or were discharged during the year, and there were no changes in salary rates. The FICA tax was withheld at the rate of 7.5% on the first $70,000 of salary and at the rate of 1.5% on salary in excess of $70,000. Data on dates of employment, salary rates, and employees' income taxes withheld, which are summarized as follows, were obtained from personnel records and payroll records.

Employee	*Date First Employed*	*Monthly Salary*	*Monthly Income Tax Withheld*
Alvarez	Jan. 16	$3,800	$ 692
Conrad	Nov. 1	2,500	394
Felix	Jan. 2	6,000	1,505
Lydall	July 16	3,400	636
Porter	Jan. 2	6,300	1,603
Soong	May 1	3,600	652
Walker	Feb. 16	4,000	864

Instructions

1. Calculate the amounts to be reported on each employee's Wage and Tax Statement (Form W-2) for the year, arranging the data in the following form:

Employee	*Gross Earnings*	*Federal Income Tax Withheld*	*FICA Tax Withheld*

2. Calculate the following employer payroll taxes for the year: (a) FICA; (b) state unemployment compensation at 4.2% on the first $7,000 of each employee's earnings; (c) federal unemployment compensation at 0.8% on the first $7,000 of each employee's earnings; (d) total.

PROBLEM 11–4B
Payroll register
Objectives 1, 2

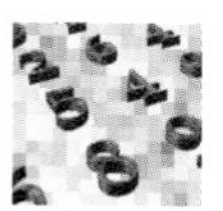

The following data for Bonito Co. relate to the payroll for the week ended December 7, 1997:

Employee	*Hours Worked*	*Hourly Rate*	*Weekly Salary*	*Federal Income Tax*	*U.S. Savings Bonds*	*Accumulated Earnings, Nov. 30*
A	40	$25.00		$208	$25.00	$48,600
B	42	20.00		265	37.50	40,500
C			$1,450	365	50.00	71,050
D	40	11.00		68		22,000
E	40	18.00		138	25.00	36,000
F	48	12.75		125		15,300
G	40	16.00		106	25.00	32,000
H			350	35		2,100
I	20	11.00		15		2,700
J	40	15.00		81		30,000

Employees C and H are office staff, and all of the other employees are sales personnel. All sales personnel are paid 1 1/2 times the regular rate for all hours in excess of 40 hours per week. The FICA tax rate is 7.5% on the first $70,000 of annual earnings and 1.5% of annual earnings in excess of $70,000 for each employee. The next payroll check to be used is No. 818.

Instructions

1. Prepare a payroll register for Bonito Co., for the week ended December 7, 1997.
2. Journalize the entry to record the payroll for the week.

PROBLEM 11–5B
Payroll accounts and year-end entries
Objectives 1, 2

The following accounts, with the balances indicated, appear in the ledger of Hamm Company on December 1 of the current year:

212	Salaries Payable	—
213	FICA Tax Payable	$ 6,500
214	Employees Federal Income Tax Payable	7,500
215	Employees State Income Tax Payable	13,260
216	State Unemployment Tax Payable	1,710
217	Federal Unemployment Tax Payable	360
218	Bond Deductions Payable	655
219	Medical Insurance Payable	3,875
611	Sales Salaries Expense	631,300
711	Officers Salaries Expense	311,800
712	Office Salaries Expense	85,500
719	Payroll Taxes Expense	92,430

The following transactions relating to payroll, payroll deductions, and payroll taxes occurred during December:

Dec. 2. Prepared Voucher No. 637 for $655, payable to Marine National Bank, to purchase U.S. savings bonds for employees.

Dec. 2. Issued Check No. 620 in payment of Voucher No. 637.
3. Prepared Voucher No. 638 for $14,000, payable to Marine National Bank for $6,500 of FICA tax and $7,500 of employees' federal income tax due.
3. Issued Check No. 621 in payment of Voucher No. 638.
14. Journalized the entry to record the biweekly payroll. A summary of the payroll record follows:

Salary distribution:		
Sales	$32,400	
Officers	15,200	
Office	3,800	$51,400
Deductions:		
FICA tax	$ 3,450	
Federal income tax withheld	8,224	
State income tax withheld	1,920	
Savings bond deductions	315	
Medical insurance deductions	480	14,389
Net amount		$37,011

14. Prepared Voucher No. 646, payable to Payroll Bank Account, for the net amount of the biweekly payroll.
14. Issued Check No. 627 in payment of Voucher No. 646.
14. Journalized the entry to record payroll taxes on employees' earnings of December 14: FICA, $3,450; state unemployment tax, $163; federal unemployment tax, $35.
17. Prepared Voucher No. 647 for $15,124 payable to Marine National Bank for $6,900 of FICA tax and $8,224 of employees' federal income tax due.
17. Issued Check No. 633 in payment of Voucher No. 647.
18. Prepared Voucher No. 650 for $3,875, payable to Wilson Insurance Company, for the semiannual premium on the group medical insurance policy.
19. Issued Check No. 639 in payment of Voucher No. 650.
28. Journalized the entry to record the biweekly payroll. A summary of the payroll record follows:

Salary distribution:		
Sales	$28,500	
Officers	15,200	
Office	3,800	$47,500
Deductions:		
FICA tax	$ 3,010	
Federal income tax withheld	7,565	
State income tax withheld	1,845	
Savings bond deductions	315	12,735
		$34,765

28. Prepared Voucher No. 684, payable to Payroll Bank Account, for the net amount of the biweekly payroll.
28. Issued check No. 671 in payment of Voucher No. 684.
28. Journalized the entry to record payroll taxes on employees' earnings of December 28: FICA, $3,010; state unemployment tax, $160; federal unemployment tax, $33.
30. Prepared Voucher No. 690 for $630, payable to Marine National Bank, to purchase U.S. savings bonds for employees.
30. Issued Check No. 680 in payment of Voucher No. 690.
30. Prepared Voucher No. 691 for $13,260, payable to Marine National Bank, for employees' state income tax due on December 31.
30. Issued Check No. 681 in payment of Voucher No. 691.

Instructions

1. Journalize the transactions.
2. Journalize the adjusting entry on December 31 to record salaries for the incomplete payroll period. Salaries accrued are as follows: sales salaries, $2,950; officers salaries, $1,640; office salaries, $410. The payroll taxes are immaterial and are not accrued.

PROBLEM 11–6B
Liability transactions
Objectives 3, 4, 5

The following items were selected from among the transactions completed by Lucas Co. during the current year:

Feb. 15. Purchased merchandise on account from Rollins Co., $8,600, terms 1/10, n/30.
Mar. 1. Purchased merchandise on account from Estavez Co., $9,600, terms 1/10, n/30.
11. Paid Estavez Co. for the invoice of March 1.
17. Issued a 30-day, 12% note for $8,600 to Rollins Co., on account.
Apr. 16. Paid Rollins Co. the amount owed on the note on March 17.
July 15. Borrowed $8,000 from Security Bank, issuing a 90-day, 13% note.
25. Issued a 120-day, non-interest-bearing note for $40,000 to Sun State Bank. The bank discounted the note at the rate of 15%.
Oct. 13. Paid Security Bank the interest due on the note of July 15 and renewed the loan by issuing a new 30-day, 15% note for $8,000. (Journalize both the debit and credit to the notes payable account.)
Nov.12. Paid Security Bank the amount due on the note of October 13.
22. Paid Sun State Bank the amount due on the note of July 25.
Dec. 1. Purchased office equipment from Young Equipment Co. for $107,500, paying $7,500 and issuing a series of ten 12% notes for $10,000 each, coming due at 30-day intervals.
31. Paid the amount due Young Equipment Co. on the first note in the series issued on December 1.
31. Paid $32,500 of the annual pension cost of $40,000. (Record both the payment and unfunded pension liability.)

Instructions

1. Journalize the transactions.
2. Journalize the adjusting entries for each of the following accrued expenses for the current year:
   a. Vacation pay, $17,000.
   b. Product warranty cost, $11,450.
3. Journalize the adjusting entry for the accrued interest at December 31 on the nine notes owed to Young Equipment Co.
4. Assume that a single note for $100,000 had been issued on December 1 instead of the series of ten notes and that its terms required principal payments of $10,000 each 30 days, with interest at 12% on the principal balance before applying the $10,000 payment. Calculate the amount that would have been due and payable on December 31.

COMPREHENSIVE PROBLEM 3

Selected transactions completed by Gold Co. during its first fiscal year ending December 31 were as follows:

a. Prepared a voucher to establish a petty cash fund of $200 and issued a check in payment of the voucher. (Journalize two entries.)
b. Prepared a voucher to replenish the petty cash fund, based on the following summary of petty cash receipts: office supplies, $46; miscellaneous selling expense, $54; miscellaneous administrative expense, $64.
c. Prepared a voucher for the purchase of $5,000 of merchandise, 1/10, n/30. Purchase invoices are recorded at the net amount using a perpetual inventory system.
d. Paid the invoice in (c) after the discount period had passed.
e. Received cash from daily cash sales for $9,460. The amount indicated by the cash register was $9,500.
f. Received a 60-day, 10% note for $60,000 on account.
g. Discounted note received in (f) at the bank, 30 days prior to maturity, at 12%.
h. Received notice from the bank that the note discounted in (g) had been dishonored. Paid the bank the maturity value of the note.
i. Received amount owed on dishonored note in (h) plus interest for 45 days at 12% computed on the maturity value of the note.

j. Received $800 on account and wrote off the remainder owed on a $1,400 accounts receivable balance. (The allowance method is used in accounting for uncollectible receivables.)
k. Reinstated the account written off in (j) and received $600 cash in full payment.
l. Traded office equipment on May 31 for new equipment with a list price of $120,000. A trade-in allowance of $25,000 was received on the old equipment that had cost $100,000 and had accumulated depreciation of $65,000 as of May 31. A voucher was prepared for the amount owed of $95,000.
m. Journalized the monthly payroll for November, based on the following data:

Salaries:		Deductions:	
Sales salaries	$13,500	Income tax withheld	$3,960
Office salaries	4,500	FICA tax withheld	1,300
	$18,000		

Unemployment tax rates assumed:
State unemployment, 3.8%
Federal unemployment, .8%
Amount subject to unemployment taxes:
State unemployment $2,000
Federal unemployment 2,000

n. Journalized the employer's payroll taxes on the payroll in (m).
o. Issued a 90-day, non-interest-bearing note for $25,000 to the bank, which discounted it at 12%.
p. Journalized voucher for payment of the note in (o) at maturity.
q. The pension cost for the year was $34,000, and a voucher was prepared for $28,000, payable to the trustee for the funded portion.

Instructions

1. Journalize the selected transactions.
2. Based on the following data, prepare a bank reconciliation for November of the current year:
   a. Balance according to the bank statement at November 30, $94,240.
   b. Balance according to the ledger at November 30, $74,390.
   c. Checks outstanding at November 30, $42,350.
   d. Deposit in transit, not recorded by bank, $22,300.
   e. Bank debit memorandum for service charges, $65.
   f. A check for $150 in payment of a voucher was erroneously recorded in the accounts as $15.
3. Based on the bank reconciliation prepared in (2), journalize the entry or entries to be made by Gold Co.
4. Based on the following selected data, journalize the adjusting entries as of December 31 of the current year:
   a. Estimated uncollectible accounts from aging the accounts receivable at December 31, $5,510. The balance of Allowance for Doubtful Accounts at December 31 was $900 (debit).
   b. Gold Co. uses a perpetual inventory system. The physical inventory on December 31 indicated an inventory shrinkage of $2,000.
   c. Prepaid insurance expired during the year, $16,200.
   d. Office supplies used during the year, $4,800.
   e. Depreciation is computed as follows:

Asset	*Cost*	*Residual Value*	*Acquisition Date*	*Useful Life in Years*	*Depreciation Method Used*
Buildings	$275,000	$ 0	January 2	50	Straight-line
Office Equip.	120,000	12,000	July 1	5	Straight-line
Store Equip.	60,000	10,000	January 3	8	Declining-balance (at twice the straight-line rate)

f. A patent costing $24,000 when acquired on January 2 has a remaining legal life of 9 years, and was expected to have value for 6 years.
g. The cost of mineral rights was $50,000. Of the estimated deposit of 25,000 tons of ore, 4,000 tons were mined during the year.
h. Total vacation pay expense for the year, $5,000.
i. A product warranty was granted beginning December 1 and covering a one-year period. The estimated cost is 3% of sales, which totaled $180,000 in December.

5. Based on the following post-closing trial balance and other data, prepare a balance sheet in report form at December 31 of the current year:

Gold Co.
Post-Closing Trial Balance
December 31, 19—

Petty Cash	200	
Cash	39,250	
Marketable Equity Securities	40,000	
Unrealized Loss on Marketable Securities		5,210
Notes Receivable	50,000	
Accounts Receivable	152,300	
Allowance for Doubtful Accounts		5,510
Merchandise Inventory	220,250	
Prepaid Insurance	12,950	
Office Supplies	2,300	
Land	50,000	
Buildings	275,000	
Accumulated Depreciation—Buildings		5,500
Office Equipment	120,000	
Accumulated Depreciation—Office Equipment		10,800
Store Equipment	60,000	
Accumulated Depreciation—Store Equipment		15,000
Mineral Rights	50,000	
Accumulated Depletion		8,000
Patents	20,000	
FICA Tax Payable		3,000
Employees Federal Income Tax Payable		3,960
State Unemployment Tax Payable		1,550
Federal Unemployment Tax Payable		320
Salaries Payable		14,000
Accounts Payable		88,000
Product Warranty Payable		5,400
Vacation Pay Payable		5,000
Unfunded Pension Liability		6,000
Notes Payable		450,000
J. Gold, Capital		465,000
	1,092,250	1,092,250

The following information relating to the balance sheet accounts at December 31 is obtained from supplementary records:

Notes receivable is a current asset.
The merchandise inventory is stated at cost by the lifo method.
The product warranty payable is a current liability.
Vacation pay payable:

Current liability	$ 3,000
Long-term liability	2,000

The unfunded pension liability is a long-term liability.
Notes payable:

Current liability	$ 50,000
Long-term liability	400,000

6. On February 7 of the following year, the merchandise inventory was destroyed by fire. Based on the following data obtained from the accounting records, estimate the cost of the merchandise destroyed:

Jan. 1 Merchandise inventory	$220,250
Jan. 1–Feb. 7 Purchases (net)	194,250
Sales (net)	340,000
Estimated gross profit rate	40%

CASES

CASE 11–1
Cranfield, CPA
Payroll ethical issues

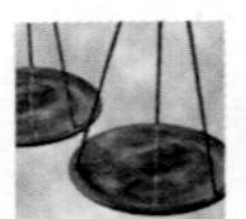

Ellen Burks is a certified public accountant (CPA) and staff assistant for Cranfield, CPAs, a local CPA firm. It had been the policy of the firm to provide a holiday bonus equal to two weeks' salary to all employees. The firm's new management team announced on November 25 that a bonus equal to only one week's salary would be made available to employees this year. Ellen thought that this policy was unfair because she and her co-workers planned on the full two-week bonus. The two-week bonus had been given for ten straight years, so it seemed as though the firm had breached an implied commitment. Thus, Ellen decided that she would make up the lost bonus week by working an extra six hours of overtime per week over the next five weeks until the end of the year. Cranfield's policy is to pay overtime at 150% of straight time.

Ellen's supervisor was surprised to see overtime being reported, since there is generally very little additional or unusual client service demands at the end of the calendar year. However, the overtime was not questioned, since firm employees are on the "honor system" in reporting their overtime.

Discuss whether Ellen is behaving in an ethical manner. Is the firm acting in an ethical manner?

CASE 11–2
Tango Company
Recognizing pension expense

The annual examination of Tango Company's financial statements by its external public accounting firm (auditors) is nearing completion. The following conversation took place between the controller of Tango Company (Donald) and the audit manager from the public accounting firm (Cathy).

Cathy: You know, Donald, we are about to wrap up our audit for this fiscal year. Yet, there is one item still to be resolved.

Donald: What's that?

Cathy: Well, as you know, at the beginning of the year, Tango began a defined benefit pension plan. This plan promises your employees an annual payment when they retire, based upon their salaries at retirement and years of service. I believe that a pension expense should be recognized this year equal to the amount of pension earned by your employees.

Donald: Wait a minute. I think you have it all wrong. The company doesn't have a pension expense until it actually pays the pension in cash when the employee retires. After all, some of these employees may not reach retirement, and if they don't, the company doesn't owe them anything.

Cathy: You're not really seeing this the right way. The pension is earned by your employees during their working years. You actually make the payment much later—when they retire. It's like one long accrual—much like incurring wages in one period and paying them in the next. Thus, I think that you should recognize the expense in the period the pension is earned by the employees.

Donald: Let me see if I've got this straight. I should recognize an expense this period for something that may not be paid to the employees in 20 or 30 years, when they finally retire—if at all. How am I supposed to determine what the expense is for the current year? The amount of the final retirement depends on many uncertainties: salary levels, employee longevity, mortality rates, and interest earned on investments to fund the pension. I don't think that an amount can be determined, even if I accepted your arguments.

Evaluate Cathy's position. Is she right or is Donald correct?

CASE 11–3
Stevens' Trucking Company
Executive bonuses and accounting methods

Bill Stevens, the owner of Stevens' Trucking Company, initiated an executive bonus plan for his chief executive officer (CEO). The new plan provides a bonus to the CEO equal to 3% of the income before taxes. Upon learning of the new bonus arrangement, the CEO issued instructions to change the company's accounting for trucks. The CEO has asked the controller to make the following two changes:

a. Change from the double-declining-balance method to the straight-line method of depreciation.
b. Add 50% to the useful lives of all trucks.

Why would these changes favor the CEO? How would you respond to the CEO's request?

CASE 11–4
Hershey Foods Corporation
Financial analysis

Several measures can be used to assess the ability of a business to pay its current liabilities. Two such analyses that are of special interest to short-term creditors are the current ratio and the acid-test ratio.

The current ratio is computed by dividing current assets by current liabilities, as indicated below:

$$\text{Current ratio} = \frac{\text{Current assets}}{\text{Current liabilities}}$$

The acid-test ratio, or quick ratio, is the ratio of the total quick assets to the total current liabilities. Quick assets are cash and other current assets that can be quickly converted to cash. Quick assets normally include cash, marketable securities, and receivables. The ratio is computed as follows:

$$\text{Acid-test ratio} = \frac{\text{Quick assets}}{\text{Current liabilities}}$$

The current ratio does not consider the makeup of the current assets. The acid-test ratio measures the "instant" debt-paying ability of the company and focuses on the assets that can generally be converted to cash rather quickly to meet current liabilities.

a. For Hershey Foods Corporation, compute as of December 31, 1993 and 1992:
   1. the current ratio, and
   2. the acid-test ratio. (In computing the acid-test ratio, consider the "investment interest" to be a short-term receivable.)
b. What conclusions can be drawn from these data as to Hershey's ability to meet its current liabilities?

CASE 11–5
Royal Co.
Income adjustment for expense accruals

In 1996, your mother retired as president of the family-owned business, Royal Co., and a new president was recruited by an executive search firm. The new president's contract called for an annual base salary of $80,000 plus a bonus of 12% of income before deducting the bonus and income taxes.

In 1997, the first full year under the new president, Royal Co. reported income of $630,000 before deducting the bonus and income taxes. After being fired on January 3, 1998, the new president demanded immediate payment of a $75,600 bonus for 1997.

Your mother was concerned about the accounting practices used during 1997, and she has asked you to help her in reviewing the accounting records before the bonus is paid. Upon investigation, you have discovered the following facts:

1. The payroll for December 27–31, 1997, was not accrued at the end of the year. The salaries for the five-day period and the applicable payroll taxes are as follows:

Sales salaries	$9,000
Office salaries	3,000
FICA tax	7.5%
State unemployment tax (employer only)	3.2%
Federal unemployment tax	.8%

   The payroll was paid on January 9, 1998, for the period December 27, 1997, through January 7, 1998.

2. The semiannual pension cost of $56,200 was not accrued for the last half of 1997. The pension cost was paid to Reliance Insurance Company on January 12, 1998, and was journalized by a debit to Pension Expense and a credit to Cash for $56,200.
3. The estimated product warranty liability of $12,000 for products sold during the year ended December 31, 1997, was not journalized.
4. On July 1, 1997, a one-year insurance policy was purchased for $10,640, debiting the cost to Prepaid Insurance. No adjusting entry was made for insurance expired at December 31, 1997.
5. The vacation pay liability of $12,000 for the year ended December 31, 1997, was not journalized.

a. What accounting errors were made in 1997 that would affect the amount of the president's bonus?
b. Based on the employment contract and your answer to (a), what is the correct amount of the president's bonus for 1997?
c. How much did the president's demand for a $75,600 bonus exceed the correct amount of the bonus under the employment contract?
d. Describe the major advantage and disadvantage of using income-sharing bonuses in employment contracts.

ANSWERS TO SELF-EXAMINATION QUESTIONS

1. **D** The amount of net pay of $687.75 (answer D) is determined as follows:

Gross pay:			
40 hours at $20		$800.00	
5 hours at $30		150.00	$950.00
Deductions:			
Federal income tax withheld		$212.00	
FICA:			
$600 × .075	$45.00		
$350 × .015	5.25	50.25	262.25
Net pay			$687.75

2. **B** Employers are usually required to withhold a portion of the earnings of their employees for payment of federal income taxes (answer A), FICA tax (answer C), and state and local income taxes (answer D). Generally, federal unemployment compensation taxes (answer B) are levied against the employer only and thus are not deducted from employee earnings.

3. **D** The employer incurs operating costs for FICA tax (answer A), federal unemployment compensation tax (answer B), and state unemployment compensation tax (answer C). The employees' federal income tax (answer D) is not an operating cost of the employer. It is withheld from the employees' earnings.

4. **C** The maturity value is $5,100, determined as follows:

Face amount of note	$5,000
Plus interest ($5,000 × 12% × 60/360)	100
Maturity value	$5,100

5. **B** The net amount available to a borrower from discounting a note payable is called the proceeds. The proceeds of $4,900 (answer B) is determined as follows:

Face amount of note	$5,000
Less discount ($5,000 × 12% × 60/360)	100
Proceeds	$4,900

PART FOUR

Accounting Principles

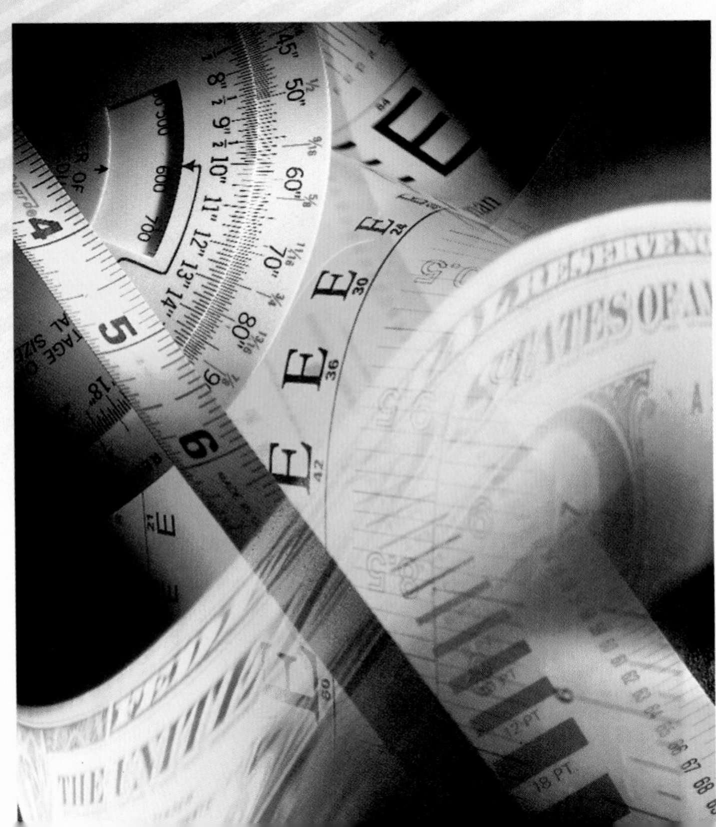

12 Concepts and Principles

YOU AND ACCOUNTING

Can you determine how many triangles there are in the figure below?[1]

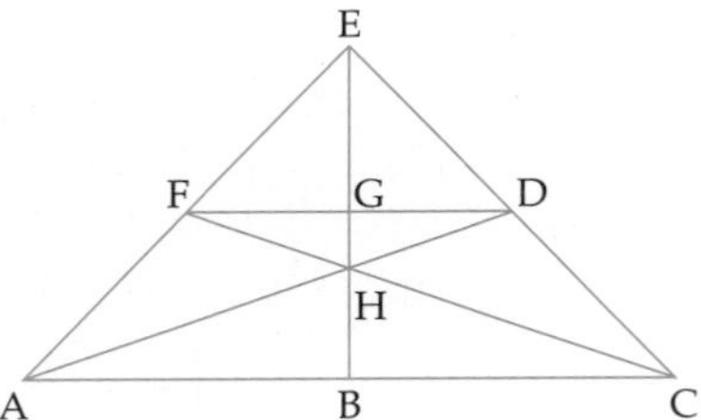

The answer to this puzzle is at the end of this chapter, following the answers to the self-examination questions. Given the physical principles and concepts of geometry, there is only one correct answer to this puzzle.

Unlike geometry, however, concepts and principles of accounting are developed through consensus and general acceptance. In many cases, there are equally acceptable methods of recording transactions. In this chapter, we discuss the development of accounting principles and concepts. We then describe and apply ten of the most important concepts underlying accounting practice. You will already be familiar with some of these concepts, such as the business entity and matching concepts, which we introduced in previous chapters.

[1] Pat Battaglia, *So You Think You're Smart,* "150 Fun and Challenging Brain Teasers," Tab Books, Blue Ridge Summit, Pa., 1988, p. 34.

After studying this chapter, you should be able to:

Objective 1
Describe the nature of accounting concepts and principles.

Objective 2
Describe the *Statements of Financial Accounting Concepts.*

Objective 3
Describe and apply ten basic accounting concepts and principles:
a. Business entity
b. Going concern
c. Objectivity
d. Unit of measurement
e. Accounting period
f. Matching
g. Adequate disclosure
h. Consistency
i. Materiality
j. Conservatism

Objective 4
Describe the role of auditing in attesting to the fairness of financial statements.

Nature of Concepts and Principles

Objective 1
Describe the nature of accounting concepts and principles.

Accounting concepts and principles provide the framework for the practice of accounting.[2] They are based on reason and observation. As such, they do not have the same universal authority as concepts and principles that you might be familiar with in the natural sciences, such as physics or chemistry.

The primary criterion for the establishment of an accounting concept or principle is its general acceptance among users of financial statements and members of the accounting profession. In some areas, alternative concepts and principles exist because a clear consensus and acceptance is lacking. In addition, accounting concepts and principles must be continually reexamined and revised in order to keep pace with the changing business environment.

DEVELOPMENT OF CONCEPTS AND PRINCIPLES

The responsibility for developing accounting concepts and principles has rested primarily on practicing accountants and accounting educators. These individuals, working independently or under the sponsorship of various organizations, strive to develop sound accounting concepts and principles to meet user needs. Accounting concepts and principles are influenced by business practices, governmental agencies, stock exchanges, and other groups that use accounting information. In the following paragraphs, we briefly describe the organizations that have most influenced the development of accounting concepts and principles.

Financial Accounting Standards Board

As we discussed in an earlier chapter, the **Financial Accounting Standards Board (FASB)** is currently the primary body developing accounting concepts and principles in the United States. The FASB often directs research to identify financial accounting issues and possible solutions. Normally, the FASB will solicit comments on discussion memoranda that describe its preliminary proposals for resolving the issues. After evaluating these comments, the Board issues *Statements of Financial Accounting Standards*. These *Standards* become part of generally accepted accounting principles. To explain, clarify, or elaborate on existing standards, the Board may also issue *Interpretations*, which have the same authority as the *Standards*.

[2] For our purposes, it is not necessary to distinguish between concepts and principles. Such distinctions are addressed in advanced courses in accounting theory.

THE IMPORTANCE OF ACCOUNTING STANDARDS

No amount of policing by the public accounting profession or regulatory agencies to prevent abuses in financial reporting can satisfy the public need for comparable information from all companies. Only financial accounting and reporting standards can satisfy that need. The challenge to the FASB is to strike a reasonable balance between the prevention of abuses and the portrayal of economic reality. As standard setters, we must try to avoid the concern about potential abuses leading to standards that make significantly different situations look the same—in other words, forcing square pegs into round holes.

Donald J. Kirk is the former chairman of the FASB, which determines standards for financial accounting.

Source: Donald J. Kirk, former FASB chairman (from a speech before the National Association of Accountants Second Annual International-European Conference, Paris, April 19, 1985).

As an ongoing project, the FASB is developing a broad conceptual framework for financial accounting. This framework will be used to evaluate current standards and to develop future standards. The outcome of this project has been six *Statements of Financial Accounting Concepts*. We discuss these *Statements* in more detail later in this chapter.

Governmental Accounting Standards Board

The **Governmental Accounting Standards Board (GASB)** was formed in 1984 as an extension of the Financial Accounting Foundation. The GASB has a full-time chairperson and four part-time members who are responsible for establishing accounting principles to be followed by state and municipal governments. The GASB employs a full-time research staff and administrative staff.

Accounting Organizations

National accounting organizations, as well as many state societies and local chapters of the national and state organizations, provide forums for the discussion of accounting concepts and principles. Among the largest and most influential of these organizations are the **American Institute of Certified Public Accountants (AICPA),** the **Institute of Management Accountants (IMA),** and the **American Accounting Association (AAA).** Each organization publishes monthly or quarterly periodicals and often publishes research studies, technical opinions, and monographs.

The AICPA is comprised of CPAs, many of whom are in practice. The IMA is comprised mostly of management accountants, many of whom hold the CMA certificate. The AAA is comprised mostly of college and university accounting teachers. The AICPA has over 300,000 members, the IMA has over 80,000 members, and the AAA has over 10,000 members.

Government Organizations

Of the various governmental agencies, the **Securities and Exchange Commission (SEC)** is one of the most influential. Established by an act of Congress in 1934, the SEC regulates securities traded on the public stock exchanges and over the counter. The SEC's rules and regulations must be used in preparing financial statements and other reports filed with the Commission.

The **Internal Revenue Service (IRS)** oversees the laws and regulations for preparing federal tax returns. These laws and regulations determine how income is reported for federal income tax purposes. These rules sometimes conflict with generally accepted accounting principles for preparing financial statements.

Other regulatory agencies exercise a major influence over the accounting principles of the industries under their jurisdiction. For example, the Controller of the Currency and the Federal Deposit Insurance Corporation greatly influence generally accepted accounting principles used by banks. In rare situations, Congress may also enact special laws that require firms to use specific accounting methods.

International Accounting Standards

The need for developing uniform international accounting standards arose from the increase in global business activities in nations throughout the world.

The United States economy, as well as the economies of other nations throughout the world, is becoming more global in nature. For example, more and more investors are investing in companies outside the United States. Likewise, banks and other financial institutions frequently loan monies on an international scale. Also, many companies are involved in international transactions with customers and suppliers.

Currently, accounting concepts and principles differ greatly among countries. These differences exist because of differences in cultures, legal systems, political systems, economies, and the processes by which concepts and principles are developed.

As a result of the increasing global business activity, attention has been focused on developing uniform international accounting standards. The primary group involved in this effort is the **International Accounting Standards Committee (IASC).** The IASC was formed in 1973 by the leading professional accounting bodies of nine nations: Australia, Canada, France, Germany, Japan, Mexico, the Netherlands, the United Kingdom, and Ireland.[3] At the present time, over 101 accounting organizations from 77 different countries make up the IASC.

The IASC functions very similarly to the FASB, which we described earlier. For example, after studying an issue, the IASC prepares a preliminary draft of a new standard, which is exposed among its members for comments. After revising the proposed standard for any comments, the IASC votes for or against its release as an *International Accounting Standard.* Currently, over thirty Standards have been issued.

The IASC has no enforcement powers. Instead, the members pledge to use their best efforts to advocate the adoption of the *Standards* in their own countries. As a result, accounting concepts and principles still differ significantly among countries. For example, in the United States and Germany, research and development costs are treated as expenses when incurred. In Japan and the United Kingdom, they are treated as assets when incurred and then amortized as expenses in future periods. Over time, however, as the economies throughout the world become more and more interdependent, the trend towards more uniformity will continue.

Statements of Financial Accounting Concepts

Objective 2
Describe the *Statements of Financial Accounting Concepts.*

As we mentioned in the preceding section, the FASB's *Statements of Financial Accounting Concepts* are the framework for financial accounting. Four of these *Statements* are relevant to our discussions of accounting for business and are summarized in Exhibit 1.[4]

[3] The United States was represented by the AICPA.

[4] Of the six *Statements* that have been issued to date, one has been superseded and the other focuses on accounting for nonbusiness organizations.

Throughout the earlier chapters of this text, we have integrated the substance of the *Statements of Concepts* described in Exhibit 1. For example, we have discussed the objectives of financial statements. The primary objective is to provide useful information to investors, managers, creditors, and others. We have described and illustrated the basic financial statements for businesses, including the income statement, statement of owner's equity, balance sheet, and statement of cash flows. Each of these statements provides useful information for predicting future results of operations and cash flows. We have defined and used the basic elements of the financial statements, including assets, liabilities, owner's equity, revenue, and expenses.

Exhibit 1
Statements of Financial Accounting Concepts

Objectives of Financial Reporting by Business Enterprises (Statement No. 1)

Sets forth three broad objectives of financial reporting:

1. To provide financial information that is useful in making rational investment, credit, and similar decisions.
2. To provide financial information to enable users to predict cash flows to the business and subsequently to themselves.
3. To provide financial information about business resources (assets), claims to these resources (liabilities and owner's equity), and changes in these resources and claims.

Qualitative Characteristics of Accounting Information (Statement No. 2)

Identifies the essential qualities of the accounting information included in financial reports as follows: usefulness, understandability, relevance, reliability, verifiability, timeliness, neutrality, completeness, and comparability.

Recognition and Measurement in Financial Statements of Business Enterprises (Statement No. 5)

Identifies the financial statements that should be prepared to meet the objectives of financial reporting for businesses.

Elements of Financial Statements (Statement No. 6)

Defines the interrelated elements of financial statements that are directly related to measuring the performance and status of businesses and nonprofit organizations.

Statement of Concepts No. 2 identifies characteristics of accounting information. As we indicated above, the most important characteristic of financial statements is **usefulness.** To be useful, financial statements must be **understandable** and clear in their presentation. They must also be **relevant** to the decision-making needs of users such as investors and creditors. Financial statements should be objective in nature so that they can be **verified** by others. Objectivity also implies that the statements should not be biased towards any one purpose or user. That is, the statements should be **neutral** in content and presentation. To be most useful, statements should also be prepared for an accounting period that is **timely** to user needs. Finally, the statements should be **complete,** with full disclosure, and should be **comparable** or consistent so that the statements can be compared over time.

In the next section, we will apply the broad framework of the **Statements of Concepts** to the practice of accounting. To do this, we will focus on the ten concepts listed below:

- Business entity
- Going concern
- Objectivity
- Unit of measurement
- Accounting period
- Matching
- Adequate disclosure
- Consistency
- Materiality
- Conservatism

Business Entity Concept

Objective 3a
Describe and apply the business entity concept.

Under the business entity concept, a business is assumed to be separate from the persons who supply its assets. For example, in Chapter 1 we noted that Pat King and Computer King were separate entities for accounting purposes. This separation exists regardless of the legal form of the business organization. The business entity concept is implied by the accounting equation, Assets = Liabilities + Owner's Equity. That is, the business owns the assets and must account for the use of the assets to the owner(s) and creditors. Thus, accounting is mainly concerned with the enterprise as an economic (business) entity and with reporting changes in its assets and related obligations.

The business entity concept used in accounting for a sole proprietorship is different from the legal concept of a sole proprietorship. In accounting for a sole proprietorship, the nonbusiness assets, liabilities, revenues, and expenses are excluded from the business accounts. If a sole proprietor owns two or more businesses, each one is treated as a separate entity for accounting purposes. Legally, however, a sole proprietor is personally liable for all business debts and may be required to use nonbusiness assets to satisfy the business creditors. Likewise, business assets may be required under law to be used to satisfy the claims of the proprietor's personal creditors.

In later chapters, we will consider differences between the business entity concept and the legal nature of other forms of business organization. Under generally accepted accounting principles, however, the revenue and expenses of a business are viewed as affecting the business's assets and liabilities, not the individual investor's assets and liabilities.

Going Concern Concept

Objective 3b
Describe and apply the going concern concept.

Only in rare cases is a business organized with the expectation of operating for only a certain period of time. In most cases, the amount of time it will operate is not known, so an assumption must be made. The assumption will affect the recording of the business transactions, which, in turn, will affect the financial statements.

We normally assume that a business entity expects to continue operating at a profit for an indefinite period of time. This going concern concept justifies our

The "going concern concept" justifies depreciating plant assets like a printing press without reference to market value.

recording plant assets at cost and depreciating them without reference to their current realizable (market) values. Under the going concern concept, we assume that plant assets will be used in the normal operations of the entity to generate revenues. If the plant assets are not expected to be sold, there is little reason to report them on the balance sheet at their market values. This is true regardless of whether the market values are less or more than the book values. Changes in market values do not affect the usefulness of the assets.

The going concern assumption also supports the recording of prepaid expenses as assets, even though in many cases they cannot be sold. For example, assume that on the last day of its fiscal year, a retail firm receives from a printer a $20,000 order of special sales catalogs. Without assuming a going concern, the catalogs would be worthless scrap paper with little value. In contrast, the going concern concept allows for the recording of the catalogs as a prepaid expense at a cost of $20,000. As the catalogs are distributed and generate revenues, the cost will be charged to expense.

When the ability of a business to continue as a going concern is doubtful, this fact should be disclosed in a note to the financial statements. An example of such a note taken from the financial statements of The Wurlitzer Company is shown in Exhibit 2.

What do we do if there is strong evidence that a business entity has a limited life? In such cases, the accounting methods used should reflect the expected terminal date of the entity. For example, changes in normal accounting methods may be needed for businesses in receivership or bankruptcy. These changes should be disclosed in the financial statements. In addition, the statements should be prepared from the *quitting concern* or liquidation point of view, rather than from a *going concern* point of view.

Exhibit 2
Disclosure of Doubt About Going Concern

The Company's . . . financial statements have been presented on the basis that it is a going concern, which contemplates the realization of assets and the satisfaction of liabilities in the normal course of business. . . .

The Company's continued existence is dependent upon its ability to resolve its liquidity problems, principally by obtaining additional debt financing and equity capital. While pursuing additional debt and equity funding, the Company must continue to operate on limited cash flow generated internally. The Company has experienced a net loss from continuing operations for the quarter ended June 30 . . . of $926,000 (unaudited) compared to a net loss from continuing operations for the [comparable quarter last year]. . . of $1,580,000 (unaudited).

Objectivity Concept

Objective 3c
Describe and apply the objectivity concept.

The objectivity concept requires that entries in the accounting records and data reported on financial statements be based on objective evidence. If this concept is ignored, the confidence of users of the financial statements could not be maintained. For example, such evidence as invoices and vouchers for purchases, bank statements for the amount of cash in the bank, and physical counts of merchandise on hand supports the accounting entries and records. Such evidence is objective and can be verified.

In some cases, judgments, estimates, and other subjective factors must be used in preparing financial statements. In such situations, the most objective evidence available should be used. For example, the provision for doubtful accounts is an estimate of the losses expected from failure to collect credit sales. This estimate should be based as much as possible on objective factors, such as the business's past experience with bad debts and economic forecasts of future business conditions.

Unit of Measurement Concept

Objective 3d
Describe and apply the unit of measurement concept.

In the United States, all business transactions are recorded in dollars. Other relevant, nonfinancial data may also be recorded, such as terms of contracts and the purpose, amount, and term of insurance policies. However, it is only through the use of dollar amounts that the various transactions and activities of a business may be measured, summarized, reported, and compared. Money is common to all business transactions and thus is a unit of measurement that allows for the reporting of uniform financial data.

The use of the monetary unit for recording and reporting the activities of a business has two major limitations. First, it limits the scope of accounting reports; secondly, it assumes a stable unit of measure.

SCOPE OF ACCOUNTING REPORTS

Many factors affecting the activities and the future prospects of a business cannot be expressed in monetary terms. In general, accounting does not attempt to report such factors. For example, information regarding the abilities of management, the fairness of an employee health program, and the strengths and weaknesses of competitors cannot be expressed in monetary terms. Although such matters may be important to investors or other interested parties, accounting does not report such data in the financial statements.

CHANGES IN THE VALUE OF THE DOLLAR

As a unit of measure, the dollar differs from such measures as the kilogram, liter, or meter, which have not changed for centuries. It is a well-known fact that the value of the dollar, sometimes called its purchasing power, continually changes. Accountants are also aware of the potential impact of the changing value of the dollar on the financial condition of a business. In the past, however, this impact was not recognized in the accounts or in the financial statements.

To indicate the potential impact of the changing value of the dollar, assume that the plant assets acquired for $100,000 twenty years ago are now to be replaced with similar assets. The cost of similar plant assets at current price levels is $200,000. Assume also that during the twenty-year period, the plant assets were fully depreciated and the net income of the business was $300,000. The plant assets generated revenue through their use, which in turn contributed to the total net income of $300,000. During this same time, depreciation expense of $100,000 was recognized. However, the depreciation expense of $100,000 amounts to only half of the cost of replacing the plant assets. Because of the increase in the cost of replacing the plant assets, the business has suffered a loss of purchasing power. Taking into consideration the cost of replacing the plant assets, the business has, in effect, earned only $200,000 of net income ($300,000 less the $100,000 increase in the price of the plant assets) during the twenty-year period.

What is the primary advantage of assuming a stable dollar? It allows for greater objectivity in preparing financial statements. This is because changes in price levels can be difficult to measure across a wide variety of assets. Thus, historical-dollar financial statements are still considered more useful than statements based on changing price levels. There are, however, two widely discussed methods for supplementing historical-dollar statements with disclosures on the impact of changing price levels. The first method discloses supplemental financial data based on current costs. The second method discloses supplemental financial data based on constant dollars.

Current Cost Data

Current cost is the amount that would have to be paid currently to acquire assets of the same age and in the same condition as existing assets. When current costs are used as the basis for financial reporting, assets, liabilities, and owner's equity are stated at current values. Likewise, expenses are stated at the current cost of doing business. The use of current costs identifies gains and losses resulting from holding assets during periods of changes in price levels. For example, assume that a firm acquired land at the beginning of the fiscal year for $50,000, and that at the end of the year, its current cost (value) is $60,000. The land could be reported at its current cost of $60,000, and the $10,000 increase in value could be reported as an unrealized gain from holding the land.

The major disadvantage in the use of current costs is the lack of standards for determining such costs. However, many accountants believe that adequate standards will evolve over time through experimenting with actual applications.

Constant Dollar Data

Constant dollar data, also known as general price-level data, are historical costs that have been restated to constant dollars through the use of a price-level index. In this manner, financial statement elements are reported in dollars, which have the same (that is, constant) purchasing power.

A price-level index is the ratio of the total cost of a group of goods at a specific time to the total cost of the same group of goods at an earlier base time. The total cost of the goods at the base time is assigned a value of 100. The price-level indexes for all later times are expressed as a ratio to 100. For example, assume that the cost of a group of goods is $12,000 at the base time and $13,200 today. The price index for the earlier, or base, time becomes 100, and the current price index is 110 [(13,200 ÷ 12,000) × 100].

A general price-level index may be used to restate financial statement items to **constant dollar equivalents.** For example, assume a price index of 120 at the time of purchasing land for $10,000. The current price index is 150. The constant dollar equivalent of the original cost of $10,000 is computed as follows:

$$\frac{\textbf{Current Price Index}}{\textbf{Price Index at Date of Purchase}} \times \textbf{Original Cost} = \textbf{Constant Dollar Equivalent}$$

$$\frac{150}{120} \times \$10{,}000 = \$12{,}500 \text{ Constant Dollar Equivalent}$$

Reporting Price-Level Changes

The FASB encourages companies to disclose voluntarily the effects of changing prices.[5] An example of such a disclosure is the footnote from an annual report of The Pillsbury Company, shown in Exhibit 3.

[5] *Statement of Financial Accounting Standards*, No. 89, "Financial Reporting and Changing Prices," Financial Accounting Standards Board, Stamford, 1986.

Exhibit 3
Disclosure of Effects of Changing Prices

Financial statements, prepared using historical costs as required by generally accepted accounting principles, may not reflect the full impact of current costs and general inflation.

The following supplementary disclosures attempt to remeasure certain historical financial information to recognize the effects of changes in current costs using specific price indices. The current cost information is then expressed in average . . . dollars to reflect the effects of general inflation, based on the U.S. Consumer Price Index. . . .

Accounting Period Concept

Objective 3e
Describe and apply the accounting period concept.

We cannot determine a complete and accurate reporting of a business's success or failure until it discontinues operations, converts its assets into cash, and pays off its debts. Then, and only then, can we determine its net income. But many decisions regarding the business must be made by management and interested outsiders during its existence. We must therefore prepare periodic reports on operations, financial position, and cash flows.

We may prepare reports when a certain job or project is completed, but more often we prepare reports at specified time intervals. For a number of reasons, including custom and various legal requirements, the longest interval between reports is normally one year.

The accounting period concept creates many areas of difficulty. The basic difficulty is determining periodic net income. For example, adjusting entries, as discussed in earlier chapters, are needed to report net income for a period of time. The difficulties of inventory costing, estimating uncollectible receivables, and selecting depreciation methods are also directly related to measuring periodic income. In addition, the amounts of the assets and the rights to the assets reported on the balance sheet are also affected by the methods used in determining net income.

Matching Concept

Objective 3f
Describe and apply the matching concept.

The balance sheet was once viewed as the primary financial statement. Over the years, the emphasis has shifted to the income statement and cash flow statement, as users of financial statements have become more concerned with the results of business operations than with financial position.

Determining periodic net income is a two-fold process of **matching** revenue for the period with expenses incurred in generating revenues.

REVENUE RECOGNITION

Revenue is the amount of assets received by rendering services to customers or selling merchandise to them. Preparing periodic financial statements creates an issue of timing; that is, at what point is the revenue recorded? When revenue is recorded, it is said to be recognized. For a given accounting period, the question is whether revenue items should be recognized and reported in the current period or whether they should be recognized and reported in a future period.

Various criteria exist for determining when revenue is recognized. Generally, the criteria used should agree with any contractual terms with the customer and should be based on objective evidence.

In the following paragraphs, we describe the point-of-sale, receipt-of-payment, installment, completed-contract, and percentage-of-completion methods of recognizing revenue. You should note that for a given set of facts, these methods should not be viewed as alternatives. That is, each method is appropriate for a specific situation.

Point-of-Sale Method

Revenue from the sale of merchandise is usually determined using the **point-of-sale method.** Under this method, revenue is recognized at the time title passes to the buyer. At the point of sale, the sale price has been agreed upon, the buyer acquires the right of ownership of the merchandise, and the seller has a legal claim against the buyer.

For example, **General Motors Corporation** recognizes revenue on sales of its automobiles to dealers when the cars are shipped to the dealers. Revenue from the sale of services is normally recognized in the same manner. That is, revenue is recognized when the services have been performed. For example, assume that a contract for repair services has been signed. The price agreed to in the contract does not become revenue until the work has been performed.

In theory, revenue from producing and selling goods and rendering services is earned as the effort is expended. As a practical matter, however, it is usually not possible to objectively determine the amount of revenue earned until (1) a contract has been signed and (2) the seller's portion of the contract has been completed.

Receipt-of-Payment Method

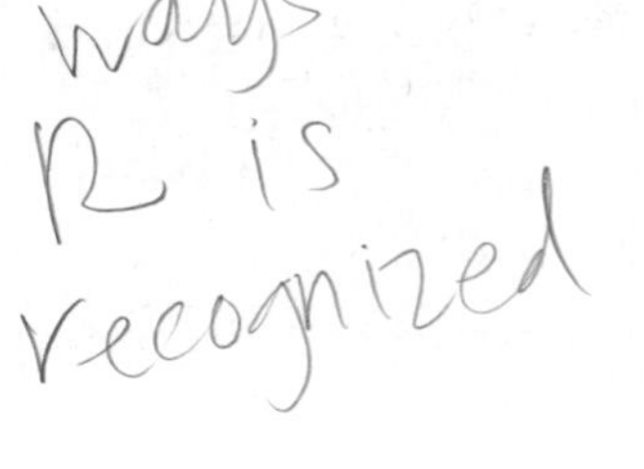

In some cases, the recognition of revenue may be delayed until payment is received. That is, revenue is realized at the time the cash is collected, regardless of when the sale was made. This method of recognizing revenue is referred to as the cash basis. The cash basis is widely used by physicians, attorneys, and other businesses in which professional services are rendered. In theory, this method has little justification. However, it is simple, and it may be used where no significant differences would arise if the point-of-sale method had been used. Its use in practice is influenced by the fact that it may be used in determining federal income tax. It is not, however, a proper method of recognizing revenue from the sale of merchandise.

Installment Method

In some businesses, especially in the retail field, it is common to make sales on the installment plan. In a typical installment sale, the buyer makes a down payment and agrees to pay the remainder over a period of time. The seller may retain title to the goods or may use other contractual means to make repossession of the goods easier if the buyer does not make the payments. Despite such provisions, installment sales should normally be recorded in the same manner as any other sale on account. That is, the revenue is considered to be recognized at the point of sale.

In rare cases, the collection of receivables from installment sales may not be reasonably assured. In these cases, the **installment method** of recognizing revenue may be used.[6] Under this method, revenue is recognized upon the receipt of cash. Each cash receipt is considered to be (1) part cost of merchandise sold and (2) part gross profit on the sale.

To illustrate, assume that in the first year of operations, a dealer in household appliances had total installment sales of $300,000, with a related cost of $180,000 of merchandise sold. Assume also that collections of the installment accounts receivable are

[6] *Opinions of the Accounting Principles Board, No. 10,* "Omnibus Opinion—1966," American Institute of Certified Public Accountants, New York, 1966, par. 12.

spread over three years as follows: first year, $140,000; second year, $100,000; third year, $60,000. Under the point-of-sale method, all of the revenue would be recognized in the first year, and the gross profit recognized in that year would be as follows:

Point-of-sale method:	
Installment sales	$300,000
Cost of merchandise sold	180,000
Gross profit	$120,000

Under the installment method, gross profit is allocated according to the amount of receivables collected in each year. This allocation is based on the percent of gross profit to sales. The rate of gross profit to sales is determined as follows:

$$\frac{\textbf{Gross profit}}{\textbf{Installment sales}} = \frac{\$120{,}000}{\$300{,}000} = 40\%$$

The amounts reported as gross profit for each of the three years in the illustration, based on collections of installment accounts receivable, are as follows:

Installment method:		
1st year collections:	$140,000 × 40%	$ 56,000
2nd year collections:	100,000 × 40%	40,000
3rd year collections:	60,000 × 40%	24,000
Total	$300,000	$120,000

Businesses engaged in large construction projects which may take years to complete often use the percentage-of-completion method of revenue recognition.

Completed-Contract Method

Businesses engaged in large construction projects may take years to complete a contract. For example, assume that a contractor begins a project that will require three years to complete at a total contract price of $50,000,000. Also assume that the total estimated cost to be incurred over the three-year period is $44,000,000. Using the point-of-sale method, no revenue or expense would be recognized until the project is completed. Thus, the entire net income from the contract would be reported in the third year. This method of recognizing revenue from long-term contracts is called the **completed-contract method.**

Percentage-of-Completion Method

Whenever the total cost of a long-term contract and the project's progress can be reasonably estimated, revenue is often recognized over the entire life of the contract by the **percentage-of-completion method.**[7] The amount of revenue recognized in a period is determined by estimating the percentage of the contract that has been completed during the period. One method of estimating the percentage of completion is by comparing the amount of incurred costs with the estimated total costs. Other methods of estimating the percentage of completion include using estimates developed by engineers, architects, or other qualified personnel.

Continuing with the preceding example, assume that by the end of the first fiscal year, the contract is estimated to be one-fourth completed. The costs incurred during the first year were $11,200,000. Using the percentage-of-completion method, the revenue recognized and the income for the year are as follows:

Revenue recognized ($50,000,000 × 25%)	$12,500,000
Costs incurred	11,200,000
Income (Year 1)	$ 1,300,000

[7] *Accounting Research and Terminology Bulletins—Final Edition,* "No. 45, Long-term Construction-type Contracts," American Institute of Certified Public Accountants, New York, 1961, par. 15.

The 1994 edition of *Accounting Trends & Techniques* indicated that 74% of the surveyed companies with long-term contracts used the percentage-of-completion method. This method involves estimates and hence possible inaccuracies in determining and reporting revenue. However, the financial statements are often considered more informative and more useful than if the completed-contract method is used.

Whichever method is used to recognize revenue on a long-term contract, it should be disclosed in the financial statements. Exhibit 4 is an excerpt taken from a note to the financial statements of Lockheed Martin Corporation.

Exhibit 4
Disclosure of Revenue Recognition Methods

Sales under long-term contracts generally are recognized under the percentage-of-completion method, and include a proportion of the earnings expected to be realized on the contract. . . . Other sales are recorded upon shipment of products or performance of services.

EXPENSE RECOGNITION

As we discussed in earlier chapters, an expense is the using up of an asset to generate revenues. The amount of an asset's cost that is used up is a measure of the expense. Each expense must be matched against its related revenue in order to properly determine the amount of net income or net loss for the period.

We have discussed the concepts and methods used to record expenses. For example, we discussed the recording of salaries in the period in which they helped generate revenue. This often involved the use of adjusting entries at the end of the period to properly match revenues and expenses. Also, we discussed the allocation of the cost of plant assets to expense. This required the use of adjusting entries for depreciation expense at the end of the period to properly match expenses with related revenues.

Adequate Disclosure Concept

Objective 3g
Describe and apply the adequate disclosure concept.

Financial statements, including all their related footnotes and other disclosures, should contain all of the relevant data essential to a user's understanding of the entity's financial status. The decision as to whether adequate disclosure, or **full disclosure,** has been achieved is often more subjective than objective.

Although all essential data should be disclosed within the financial statements or in notes attached to those statements, nonessential data should be excluded to avoid clutter. For example, the balance of each cash account is usually not reported separately. Instead, the balances are normally grouped together and reported as one total. In some cases, the investments in temporary marketable securities are also included with cash and reported as *cash and cash equivalents*.

In most cases, all relevant data needed by users cannot be presented in the financial statements. Therefore, the statements normally include explanatory data in accompanying notes. For example, a note used to present supplemental information related to the effects of price-level changes on the financial statements of The Pillsbury Company was shown in Exhibit 3.

In the following paragraphs, we describe and illustrate some of the most important disclosures that appear in the notes to the financial statements. These disclosures include the accounting methods used, changes in estimates, contingent liabilities, financial instruments, segments of a business, and subsequent events. We illustrate these disclosures by using excerpts from notes taken from companies' annual reports. Such notes are normally presented in annual reports in a section entitled "Notes to Financial Statements."

ACCOUNTING METHODS USED

Many times there are several acceptable accounting methods that can be used in preparing the financial statements. The method used should be disclosed if its use has a significant effect on the statements. In the 1994 Edition of *Accounting Trends & Techniques,* depreciation methods were disclosed by 97% of the companies, and inventory cost flow methods were disclosed by 93% of the companies surveyed.

There is wide variation in the format for disclosing accounting methods in the financial statements. One form of disclosure is to present "Significant Accounting Policies" as the first note. Some examples of such notes are shown in Exhibit 5.

Exhibit 5
Disclosure of Accounting Methods Used

Digital Equipment Corporation

Note A—Significant Accounting Policies

Inventories—Inventories are stated at the lower of cost (first-in, first-out) or market.

Property, Plant and Equipment—Depreciation expense is computed principally on the following bases:

Classification	*Depreciation Lives and Methods*
Buildings	*33 years (straight-line)*
Machinery and equipment	*4 and 5 years (double-declining-balance)*

Atico Financial Corporation

Sales of home sites are recorded under the installment method of accounting. All depreciable assets are recorded at cost; depreciation is calculated using the straight-line method.

CHANGES IN ACCOUNTING ESTIMATES

There are many cases in accounting in which the use of estimates is necessary. These estimates should be revised when additional data or later developments allow for better, more accurate estimates. If the effect of such a change on net income is significant, it should be disclosed in the financial statements for the year in which the change is made.[8] The example in Exhibit 6 appeared in an annual report of Time Incorporated.

Exhibit 6
Disclosure of Change in Estimate

. . . The Company changed the rate of amortization of its pay-TV programming costs to more closely reflect audience viewing patterns. The effect of this change was to reduce programming costs by $58 million . . . , resulting in increased net income of $35 million . . . , or $.58 per share. . . .

[8] *Opinions of the Accounting Principles Board, No. 20,* "Accounting Changes," American Institute of Certified Public Accountants, New York, 1971, pars. 31–33.

CONTINGENT LIABILITIES

Contingent liabilities are potential obligations that will become liabilities only if certain events occur in the future. If the liability is probable and the amount of the liability can be reasonably estimated, it should be recorded in the accounts. Examples of such liabilities include vacation pay payable and product warranty payable. Although the vacation pay liability depends upon employees taking vacations, the liability is probable and is reasonably estimated. Likewise, although the product warranty liability depends upon customers presenting products for repair, the liability is probable and is reasonably estimated.

If the amount of the potential obligation cannot be reasonably estimated, the facts of the contingency should be disclosed.[9] For example, the footnote in Exhibit 7, taken from an annual report of Harley-Davidson, Inc., describes a potential liability for environmental contamination:

Exhibit 7
Disclosure of Contingency

The Company is involved in various environmental matters, including soil contamination at its York, Pennsylvania facility (the Facility), with various governmental and environmental agencies. During the third quarter of 1991, the Company discovered additional soil contamination at the Facility in an area formerly owned and used by the U.S. Navy and AMF (the predecessor corporation of Minstar), from whom the Company was purchased in 1981. Based on the preliminary information available to the Company, the Company is unable to determine what remediation will be necessary, what the costs of such remediation will be and what the Company's share of such costs might be, relative to either the Navy's share or other former owner's share. The Company is therefore unable to determine at this time whether the potential liability relating to this matter will have a material effect on the Company's financial condition. Based on preliminary information available to the Company and admission by the Navy in the pending . . . action, the Company believes that the Navy should be liable for a substantial portion of the on-going investigation and future cleanup of the Facility.

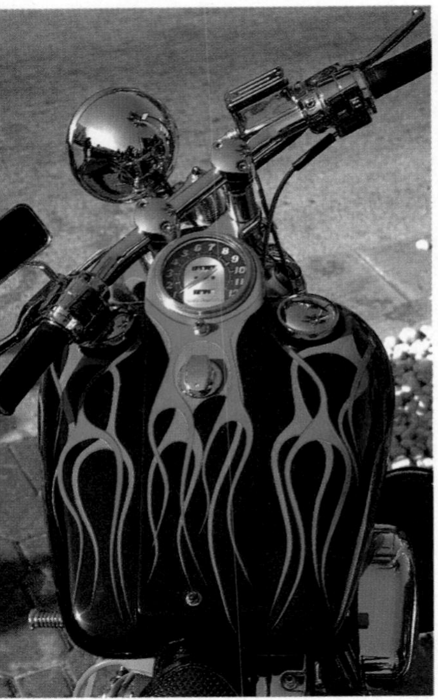

Harley-Davidson, Inc. disclosed the facts of a contingent liability for environmental contamination in one of its annual reports.

Common examples of contingent liabilities disclosed in notes to the financial statements are litigation, guarantees, and discounting receivables. The 1994 edition of *Accounting Trends & Techniques* indicated that 64% of the surveyed companies disclosed contingencies for litigations, 35% for guarantees, and 9% for discounting receivables. These contingent liabilities are briefly discussed below.

Litigation

Most companies have lawsuits filed against them at one time or another. In many cases, litigation takes many months or years to complete. Although it is often difficult to estimate the amount of the liability, if any, the litigation should be disclosed. An example of a note in the financial statements of Pier 1 Imports, Inc., disclosing a contingent liability arising from litigation, is shown in Exhibit 8.

Exhibit 8
Disclosure of Contingency from Litigation

In August 1988, a suit was filed in the 113th District Court of Harris County, Texas against Wolfe Nursery, Inc. (a wholly owned subsidiary of the Company), an apartment complex owner, a chemical distributor, a chemical manufacturer, and others, alleging that the improper use of chemicals and a failure to warn resulted in personal injury, and in certain cases, wrongful death. The plaintiffs seek $90 million. One defendant, a chemical manufacturer, has settled with the plaintiffs and has been dismissed from the lawsuit. The Company continues to deny liability in this action and intends to vigorously pursue all available defenses. The Company believes that its ultimate liability, if any, will not have a material adverse effect on the Company.

[9] *Statement of Financial Accounting Standards, No. 5,* "Accounting for Contingencies," Financial Accounting Standards Board, Stamford, 1975, pars. 8, 10, 12.

Guarantees

Companies sometimes guarantee a loan for another company, often an affiliate, supplier, or major customer. In such cases, the company is obligated to pay the loan if the borrower fails to make payment. Such a contingency may be disclosed in a note to the financial statements, such as that shown in Exhibit 9 for PepsiCo, Inc.

Exhibit 9
Disclosure of Contingency from Guarantees

At year-end . . . , PepsiCo was contingently liable under direct and indirect guarantees aggregating $86 million and $97 million, respectively. The guarantees are primarily issued to support financial arrangements of certain restaurant and bottling franchisees and PepsiCo joint ventures. PepsiCo manages the risk associated with these guarantees by performing appropriate credit reviews in addition to retaining certain rights as a franchisor or joint venture partner.

Discounted Receivables

The contingent liability arising from discounting a note receivable was discussed in a previous chapter. A similar obligation may also arise from the sale of receivables. The contingent liability exists until the due date for discounted receivables. An example of a note disclosing such an obligation is shown below in Exhibit 10 for The Wurlitzer Company.

Exhibit 10
Disclosure of Contingency from Discounted Receivables

During the year ended March 31, . . . the Company negotiated an agreement to sell at face value approximately $6,100,000 of accounts receivable to an outside finance company. Cash proceeds of the sale were approximately $6,000,000: the remaining $100,000 is held by the outside finance company as security for the uncollected recourse receivables. At March 31, . . . the Company remained contingently liable on approximately $1,900,000 of the sold receivables; however, management believes that the allowance for doubtful accounts will be adequate for any such uncollectible receivables.

FINANCIAL INSTRUMENTS

In the past decade there has been a widespread growth in the variety and types of financial instruments issued by businesses. A **financial instrument** is cash, a security that evidences ownership interest in an entity, or a contract that imposes certain obligations and rights upon another entity.[10] Examples of financial instruments include such items as cash, accounts receivable, notes receivable, accounts payable, notes payable, bonds payable, and other securities traded in the marketplace.

Generally accepted accounting principles require specific disclosures related to financial instruments. These disclosures include the market (fair) value of the financial instruments.[11] In addition, any unusual risks related to the financial instruments in excess of the amounts reported in the financial statements must also be disclosed. Finally, any unusual credit risks must also be reported.[12] For example, a retailer whose receivables are concentrated in one geographical area should disclose this fact in the notes to the financial statements.

[10] *Statement of Financial Accounting Standards, No. 107,* "Disclosures about Fair Value of Financial Instruments," Financial Accounting Standards Board, Norwalk, 1991, par. 3.
[11] *Ibid.*, par. 10.
[12] *Statement of Financial Accounting Standards, No. 105,* "Disclosure of Information about Financial Instruments with Off-Balance Sheet Risk and Financial Instruments with Concentrations of Credit Risk," Financial Accounting Standards Board, Norwalk, 1990, pars. 18 and 20.

SEGMENTS OF A BUSINESS

Many companies are involved in more than one type of business activity or market. For example, a company may operate both radio and television stations in both domestic and foreign markets. The individual segments of such companies normally experience differing rates of profit, degrees of risk, and growth. To help financial statement users assess operating results, the financial statements should disclose segment information. The information reported for each major segment includes revenue, income from operations, and identifiable assets related to the segment.[13] In the 1994 Edition of *Accounting Trends & Techniques*, 59% of the 600 companies surveyed reported segment revenues. An example of financial reporting for segments is shown in Exhibit 11 in the note adapted from financial statements of The Gillette Company.

Exhibit 11
Disclosure of Segment Information

Financial Information by Business Segment
(Millions of Dollars)

	Blades & Razors	*Toiletries & Cosmetics*	*Stationery Products*	*Braun Products*	*Oral-B Products*	*Other*	*Corporate*	*Total*
Net sales	$1,750.1	$946.9	$460.3	$1,215.8	$308.1	$2.7	$ —	$4,683.9
Profit from operations	555.6	114.1	48.8	145.3	38.8	(.1)	(40.9)	861.6
Identifiable assets	1,477.9	486.9	423.2	883.2	248.4	2.3	364.8	3,886.7
Capital expenditures	126.5	37.6	27.8	78.0	11.1	—	5.0	286.0
Depreciation	71.6	19.1	11.9	56.3	7.8	.3	5.4	172.4

EVENTS SUBSEQUENT TO DATE OF STATEMENTS

Events that have a significant effect on the financial statements may occur or become known after the close of the fiscal period. Such events should be disclosed in the financial statements.[14] For example, a business might suffer a loss from a fire, flood, or other natural disaster between the end of its fiscal year and the issuance of statements for that year. In such a case, the facts of the event should be disclosed, even though the event occurred after the end of the fiscal year. Likewise, the issuance of long-term debt or the purchase of another business after the close of the period should be disclosed.

In the 1994 Edition of *Accounting Trends & Techniques*, 284 subsequent events were disclosed by the 600 companies surveyed. Delta Air Lines Inc. reported a subsequent event in a note to its financial statements, as shown in Exhibit 12.

Exhibit 12
Disclosure of Subsequent Event

On July 27, . . . Delta entered into an asset purchase agreement, as amended, with Pan Am Corporation and certain of its subsidiaries (Pan Am's), providing for Delta's purchase of a package of Pan Am assets, including Pan Am's New York to Europe routes, its Frankfurt hub operation, its Miami-London and Detroit-London routes, its Boston-New York-Washington, D.C. Shuttle, Pan Am's leasehold or other interests in up to 45 aircraft, and various related assets and facilities. Delta's purchase price for the asset acquisition is $416 million. In addition, Delta has agreed to assume certain liabilities, including approximately $70 million in mortgages on assets to be acquired by Delta and up to $100 million of Pan Am passenger tickets under certain circumstances. As part of the asset purchases, Delta has also agreed to offer employment to 6,600 Pan Am personnel.

[13] *Statement of Financial Accounting Standards, No. 14*, "Financial Reporting for Segments of a Business Enterprise," Financial Accounting Standards Board, Stamford, 1976. Nonpublic corporations are exempted from this requirement by *Statement of Financial Accounting Standards, No. 21*, "Suspension of the Reporting of Earnings per Share and Segment Information by Nonpublic Enterprises," Financial Accounting Standards Board, Stamford, 1978.
[14] *Statement on Auditing Standards, No. 1*, "Codification of Auditing Standards and Procedures," American Institute of Certified Public Accountants, New York, 1988, section 560.

Consistency Concept

Objective 3h
Describe and apply the consistency concept.

The amount and direction of change in net income and financial position from period to period may influence readers' judgments and decisions. Readers of financial statements should be able to assume that the financial statements of a business are based on the same principles from period to period. Otherwise, the changes and trends reported in the statements could be the result of changes in principles rather than changes in operations.

We have discussed a number of alternative generally accepted accounting principles in this text. These principles may significantly affect the financial statements. Because of these potential effects, consistency is needed to ensure that financial statements can be compared across fiscal periods.

The **consistency** concept does not prohibit changes in the accounting principles used. Changes are allowed if the change will more fairly report net income and financial position. Examples of changes in accounting principles include changes in inventory cost flow assumptions, changes in depreciation methods, and changes in recognizing revenue from long-term construction contracts. Changes in accounting principles must meet the following general rule for disclosure of such changes:

The nature of and justification for a change in accounting principle and its effect on income should be disclosed in the financial statements of the period in which the change is made. The justification for the change should explain clearly why the newly adopted accounting principle is preferable.[15]

An example of a disclosure of a change in an accounting method, taken from an annual report of General Motors Corporation, is shown in Exhibit 13.

Exhibit 13
Disclosure of Accounting Change

Effective January 1, . . . accounting procedures were changed to include in inventory general purpose spare parts previously charged directly to expense. The Corporation believes this change is preferable because it provides a better matching of costs with related revenues. The effect of this change on . . . earnings was a favorable adjustment of $306.5 million . . .

There are various ways of reporting the effect of a change in an accounting principle on net income. The cumulative effect of the change on net income may be reported on the income statement of the period in which the change is made. In some cases, the effect of the change could be applied to past periods by reporting revised income statements for the earlier years. Methods of disclosure of such effects are discussed in more detail in a later chapter.

The consistency concept does not require that an accounting method be used throughout a business. For example, it is not unusual for businesses to use different costing and pricing methods for different segments of their inventories. This is illustrated by the note from the financial statements of Hartmarx Corporation, shown in Exhibit 14.

Exhibit 14
Disclosure of Accounting Methods Used

. . . Approximately 23% . . . of the Company's inventories at November 30, . . . primarily work in process and finished goods, are valued using the last-in, first-out (LIFO) method. The first-in, first-out (FIFO) method is used for substantially all raw materials and the remaining manufacturing and retail inventories.

[15]*Opinions of the Accounting Principles Board, No. 20,* "Accounting Changes," American Institute of Certified Public Accountants, New York, 1971, par. 17.

Materiality Concept

Objective 3i
Describe and apply the materiality concept.

Generally accepted accounting principles should be applied to all significant items in preparing the financial statements. Insignificant items may be treated in the easiest manner. Determining what is and what is not significant or material requires judgment. Precise criteria cannot be developed.

Statement of Financial Accounting Concepts, No. 2 defines **materiality** as follows:

The omission or misstatement of an item in a financial report is material if, in light of the surrounding circumstances, the magnitude of the item is such that it is probable that the judgment of a reasonable person relying upon the report would have been changed or influenced by the inclusion or correction of the item.[16]

USING ACCOUNTING TO UNDERSTAND BUSINESS

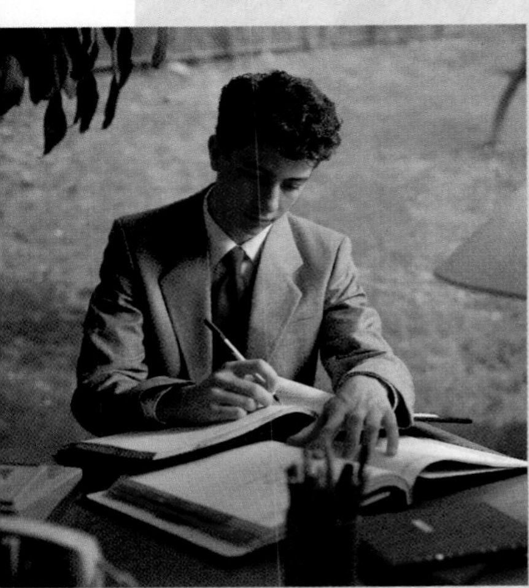

This is the story as it comes to us: An accountant . . . was [asked] to check the cash of a concern, which may be called the XYZ Corporation. This concern among its activities included a selling department where goods of small value were sold in fairly large quantities. When the cash of the selling department was counted, it was found that the amount on hand was, let us say, $2.04—a fictitious amount greater than the actual sum—more than it should have been. Now this incident happened in the city of New York where, as all citizens know to their sorrow, there is a two percent tax on sales. Evidently, therefore, this excessive sum of $2.04 represented the sale of some article for $2, plus a tax of four cents. . . . Apparently, a careless member of the staff had sold such an article, placed the proceeds in the till and forgot to make the proper record of the whole stupendous transaction. The carelessness was unpardonable, of course. No member of any staff anywhere should forget anything. However, the error occurred and the perspicacious young [accountant] discovered it, as he could not very well avoid doing. He found the unaccountable excess and, like a well-trained man, conscious of his complete efficiency, he set to work to trace the mistake and to expose the guilty person. Here was a chance for him to demonstrate his incalculable value to his firm. . . . Such wrongdoing must not escape unchallenged. Relying upon his supposed authority, he began a search, a veritable inquisition, and after two or three days of earnest effort, during which he had interrupted the work of the entire . . . office and had . . . considerable . . . time expended, he was compelled to admit that he could not find a shortage in the inventory to account for the surplus cash, nor could he rightfully determine who had committed the crime. At last he regretfully reported the matter to his superior and confessed himself defeated. What the superior had to say about the matter is not recorded; but one can imagine the attitude of the [superior] and can form a reasonably accurate notion of the comments which were made. . . .

This little story bears a moral which every accountant may well take to heart. It might be unwise to say that errors should be overlooked or that carelessness should be condoned. But surely there is no sense whatever in a ridiculous adherence to meticulous detail when the sole purpose is to trace something which is not worth tracing.

. . . What the [accountant] should have done in the present case is clear. He should have made a note of the excess, and, after spending a few minutes in trying to trace it to its source, he should have gone on to weightier things. It is a great pity that this sort of incident ever occurs; but we are told that the case before us is not unique. There are many little fellows who revel in the most microscopic minutiae. They can't help it. They probably were born that way, but they should never, never, be employed in the work of accountancy, which, after all, is a matter of principles, not of pin points.

Source: A. P. Richardson, *The Journal of Accountancy,* October 1936, pp. 233–235.

[16] *Statement of Financial Accounting Concepts, No. 2,* "Qualitative Characteristics of Accounting Information," Financial Accounting Standards Board, Stamford, 1980, par. 132.

In assessing the materiality of an item, you should consider the size of the item, its nature, and relationship to other items in the financial statements. For example, an error in classifying a $10,000 asset on a balance sheet with total assets of $10,000,000 would probably be immaterial. If the assets totaled only $100,000, however, the error would be material. If the $10,000 were a note receivable from an officer of the company, it might well be material even in the first case. Assume further that the loan increased to $100,000 between the end of the fiscal period and the issuance of the financial statements. In this case, the nature of the item, its amount at the balance sheet date, and its subsequent increase in amount should be disclosed in the statements.

The materiality concept may also be applied to the recording of transactions. For example, as we mentioned in a previous chapter, many companies record small expenditures for plant assets as an expense of the period rather than as an asset. In setting the dollar cutoff between revenue and capital expenditures, factors such as the following should be considered: (1) the amount of plant assets, (2) the amount of other assets, (3) the number of such expenditures, (4) the nature and expected life of the plant assets, and (5) the effect on reported net income.

A common use of the materiality concept is the practice of omitting cents in preparing financial statements. Many large companies round financial statement items to thousands or even millions of dollars for reporting purposes. For example, the 1994 edition of *Accounting Trends & Techniques* indicated that 8 of 600 companies reported amounts to the nearest dollar, 376 to the nearest thousand dollars, and 176 to the nearest million dollars.

Some companies use "whole-dollar" accounting in which the cents amounts are eliminated from accounting records at the earliest possible point in the accounting process. Any differences introduced into the accounts by rounding tend to balance out, and any final difference is usually not material. There may be some accounts, however, such as those with customers and creditors, for which it may not be feasible to use "whole-dollar" accounting.

Conservatism Concept

Objective 3j
Describe and apply the conservatism concept.

The financial statements are significantly affected by the selection of accounting principles and other value judgments. In accounting, there has been a tendency for accountants to be conservative in selecting among principles and in making estimates. The method that yielded the lesser amount of net income or of asset value was often selected. This attitude of **conservatism** was often expressed in the statement to "anticipate no profits and provide for all losses."

Examples of the conservatism concept still exist today. Generally accepted accounting principles require that merchandise inventory be reported at the lower of cost or market. If market price is higher than cost, the higher amount is ignored in the accounts.

Much of current accounting thought has shifted away from the conservatism concept. Conservatism is no longer considered to be the dominant factor in selecting among alternatives. The objectivity and matching principles and the concepts of consistency, disclosure, and materiality are more important than the conservatism concept. The latter concept is only a factor when the others do not play a significant role.

Role of Auditing of Financial Statements

Objective 4
Describe the role of auditing in attesting to the fairness of financial statements.

As you might expect, the accounting concepts we have discussed in the preceding paragraphs often allow companies significant latitude in applying and choosing among alternative generally accepted accounting principles and methods. Such choices often involve subjective judgments. For example, recording a contingent liability depends on estimating it and judging the likelihood of its becoming a liability. Likewise, as we mentioned earlier, use of the percentage-of-completion method by a construction company requires that the project's progress be reasonably estimated. The role of auditing is to add credibility to the financial statements by having an independent, outside party attest to the fairness of the selection and use of accounting concepts in preparing the financial statements. Such audits are conducted by certified public accountants (CPAs).

All public corporations are required to have an annual, independent audit of their financial statements. Other companies that have loans outstanding with banks or other financial institutions may be required to have their financial statements audited. Some companies may choose to have an independent audit.

Independent auditors use generally accepted accounting principles and the concepts we have discussed in this chapter in assessing the fairness of a company's financial statements. For example, in our preceding illustration, the independent auditor would assess whether the progress of a construction project can be reasonably estimated. Using this assessment, the auditor could then decide whether the percentage-of-completion method is an appropriate method of recognizing revenue for the client.

Upon completing an audit, which may take several weeks or longer, the auditor issues an Independent Auditors' Report. This report accompanies the financial statements when they are distributed to outside users. The normal audit report includes the following three paragraphs:

1. An introductory paragraph identifying the financial statements audited.
2. A scope paragraph describing the nature of the audit.
3. An opinion paragraph presenting the auditor's opinion as to the fairness of the statements.

The audit report for Intel Corporation shown in Exhibit 15 uses standard language. For the financial statements of most companies, the auditor renders an **unqualified** or **clean opinion,** such as the one in Exhibit 15.

Exhibit 15
Independent Auditors' Report

Report of Ernst & Young,
Independent Auditors
The Board of Directors and Stockholders, Intel Corporation

We have audited the accompanying consolidated balance sheets of Intel Corporation as of December 25, 1993 and December 26, 1992, and the related consolidated statements of income, stockholders' equity, and cash flows for each of the three years in the period ended December 25, 1993. These financial statements are the responsibility of the Company's management. Our responsibility is to express an opinion on these financial statements based on our audits.

We conducted our audits in accordance with generally accepted auditing standards. Those standards require that we plan and perform the audit to obtain reasonable assurance about whether the financial statements are free of material misstatement. An audit includes examining, on a test basis, evidence supporting the amounts and disclosures in the financial statements. An audit also includes assessing the accounting principles used and significant estimates made by management, as well as evaluating the overall financial statement presentation. We believe that our audits provide a reasonable basis for our opinion.

In our opinion, the financial statements referred to above present fairly, in all material respects, the consolidated financial position of Intel Corporation at December 25, 1993 and December 26, 1992, and the consolidated results of its operations and its cash flows for each of the three years in the period ended December 25, 1993, in conformity with generally accepted accounting principles.

Ernst & Young
San Jose, California
January 17, 1994

Auditors may add a paragraph to the unqualified or clean opinion to call attention to an important event or fact. For example, if the auditor has "substantial doubt" about the ability of the company to continue operating as a going concern, the auditor will add a paragraph to the audit report calling the reader's attention to this possibility. Likewise, if a company changes accounting methods, the auditor will add a paragraph to the audit report, calling the reader's attention to the change. An example of such an audit report for Circuit City Stores, Inc. is shown in Exhibit 16.

Exhibit 16
Independent Auditors' Report—Modified for Consistency

The Board of Directors and Stockholders of Circuit City Stores, Inc.:

We have audited the accompanying consolidated balance sheets of Circuit City Stores, Inc. and subsidiaries as of February 28, 1994 and 1993, and the related consolidated statements of earnings, stockholders' equity, and cash flows for each of the fiscal years in the three-year period ended February 28, 1994. These consolidated financial statements are the responsibility of the Company's management. Our responsibility is to express an opinion on these consolidated financial statements based on our audits.

We conducted our audits in accordance with generally accepted auditing standards. Those standards require that we plan and perform the audit to obtain reasonable assurance about whether the financial statements are free of material misstatement. An audit includes examining, on a test basis, evidence supporting the amounts and disclosures in the financial statements. An audit also includes assessing the accounting principles used and significant estimates made by management, as well as evaluating the overall financial statement presentation. We believe that our audits provide a reasonable basis for our opinion.

In our opinion, the consolidated financial statements referred to above present fairly, in all material respects, the financial position of Circuit City Stores, Inc. and subsidiaries as of February 28, 1994 and 1993, and the results of their operations and their cash flows for each of the fiscal years in the three-year period ended February 28, 1994, in conformity with generally accepted accounting principles.

As discussed in Note 1 (G) to the consolidated financial statements, the Company changed its method of accounting for income taxes in fiscal 1993.

KPMG Peat Marwick
Richmond, Virginia
April 4, 1994

It is possible that accounting methods used by a company do not conform to generally accepted accounting principles. In such cases, a **qualified opinion** is issued, and the reason for it is briefly described. If the departure from accepted principles is extreme, an **adverse** or **negative opinion** is issued and the reason for the opinion described. In rare cases, the auditors may be unable to reach an opinion on the financial statements. The auditors then issues a **disclaimer** and briefly describe why an opinion could not be reached.

KEY POINTS

Objective 1. Describe the nature of accounting concepts and principles.

Accounting concepts and principles provide guidance on how to practice accounting. The FASB, which issues *Statements of Financial Accounting Standards, Interpretations, and Statements of Financial Accounting Concepts,* is the primary accounting concept-setting body. Other organizations that impact the development of accounting concepts include the Governmental Accounting Standards Board, American Institute of Certified Public Accountants, the Institute of Management Accountants, the American Accounting Association, the Securities and Exchange Commission, and the Internal Revenue Service.

The primary effort in developing uniform international accounting standards is being led by the International Accounting Standards Committee (IASC). The IASC has issued over thirty International Accounting Standards.

Objective 2. Describe the *Statements of Financial Accounting Concepts.*

The four *Statements of Concepts* that are relevant to our discussion of accounting for business are summarized in Exhibit 1. The essence of the *Statements of Concepts* have been integrated throughout this chapter and the earlier chapters of this text.

Objective 3a. Describe and apply the business entity concept.

Under the business entity concept, it is assumed that a business is separate from the persons who supply its assets. This separation exists regardless of the legal form of the organization. The application of the business entity concept justifies the recording of transactions affecting a business's assets separately from the owner's assets.

Objective 3b. Describe and apply the going concern concept.

Under the going concern concept, it is assumed that a business entity will continue in business at a profit for an indefinite period of time. The application of the going concern concept justifies recording plant assets at cost and depreciating them without reference to their current realizable (market) values.

Objective 3c. Describe and apply the objectivity concept.

The objectivity concept requires that entries in the accounting records and data reported on financial statements be based on objectively determined evidence. Examples of such evidence include invoices and vouchers for purchases, bank statements for the amount of cash in the bank, and physical counts for merchandise on hand.

Objective 3d. Describe and apply the unit of measurement concept.

The unit of measurement concept requires that all business transactions be recorded in terms of money. The monetary unit is also assumed to be stable. The financial statements may, however, be supplemented to disclose changes in price levels through using current costs or constant dollars.

Objective 3e. Describe and apply the accounting period concept.

The accounting period concept requires that periodic reports on operations, financial position, and cash flows of a business be prepared so that management and others can make informed decisions regarding the business.

Objective 3f. Describe and apply the matching concept.

The matching concept requires that expenses be properly matched and reported with their related revenues in determining net income. Thus, periodic net income is determined by a two-fold process of (1) recognizing revenues during the period and (2) matching the related expenses with the revenues.

Revenues may be recognized at the point of sale, upon receipt of payment, or under the installment method. Revenues for long-term projects may be recognized using the completed-contract or percentage-of-completion method.

An expense is the using up of an asset to generate revenues. The amount of an asset's cost that is used up is a measure of the expense. The proper matching of each expense with its related revenue often requires the use of adjusting entries at the end of the period for such items as depreciation and accrued salaries.

Objective 3g. Describe and apply the adequate disclosure concept.

The adequate disclosure concept requires that financial statements and their accompanying footnotes or other explanatory materials contain all of the relevant data essential to the user's understanding of the business's financial status. Applying this concept requires such disclosures as the accounting methods used, changes in accounting estimates, contingent liabilities, financial instruments, segment data, and subsequent events.

Objective 3h. Describe and apply the consistency concept.

The consistency concept implies that the financial statements should be prepared by applying the same principles year after year. If changes in principles do occur, their effect on the financial statements should be disclosed.

Objective 3i. Describe and apply the materiality concept.

The materiality concept requires accountants to consider the relative importance of any event, accounting procedure, or change in procedure that affects the financial statements. Generally accepted accounting principles should be applied to all material items in preparing the financial statements. Immaterial items may be treated in the easiest manner.

Objective 3j. Describe and apply the conservatism concept.

The conservatism concept implies that, in selecting among alternative accounting principles, the principle that yields the lesser amount of net income or asset value is chosen. An example of applying the conservatism concept is the reporting of merchandise inventory at the lower of cost or market. If market price is higher than cost, the higher amount is ignored in the accounts. The conservatism concept is no longer considered to be a dominant factor in selecting among alternatives.

Objective 4. Describe the role of auditing in attesting to the fairness of financial statements.

The role of auditing is to add credibility to the financial statements by having an independent auditor attest to the fairness of the financial statements. Certified public accountants use generally accepted accounting principles and the concepts we have discussed in this chapter in assessing the fairness of a company's financial statements. At the completion of the audit, an Independent Auditors' Report is issued.

GLOSSARY OF KEY TERMS

Adequate disclosure. The concept that financial statements and their accompanying footnotes should contain all of the pertinent data believed essential to the reader's understanding of a business's financial status. *Objective 3g*

Business entity concept. The concept that assumes that accounting applies to individual economic units and that each unit is separate and distinct from the persons who supply its assets. *Objective 3a*

Completed-contract method. The method that recognizes revenue from long-term construction contracts when the project is completed. *Objective 3f*

Conservatism. The concept that dictates that in selecting among alternatives, the method or procedure that yields the lesser amount of net income or asset value should be selected. *Objective 3j*

Consistency. The concept that assumes that the same generally accepted accounting principles have been applied in preparing successive financial statements. *Objective 3h*

Constant dollar data. Historical costs that have been converted into dollars of constant value through the use of a price-level index. *Objective 3d*

Current cost. The amount of cash that would have to be paid currently to acquire assets of the same age and in the same condition as existing assets. *Objective 3d*

Financial Accounting Standards Board (FASB). The current authoritative body for the development of accounting principles for all entities except state and municipal governments. *Objective 1*

Going concern concept. The concept that assumes that a business entity has a reasonable expectation of continuing in business at a profit for an indefinite period of time. *Objective 3b*

Installment method. The method of recognizing revenue, whereby each receipt of cash from installment sales is considered to be part cost of merchandise sold and part gross profit. *Objective 3f*

International Accounting Standards Committee (IASC). The primary body leading the effort in developing uniform international accounting standards. *Objective 1*

Matching. The concept of accounting that all expenses incurred in earning revenues during a period of time should be matched with those revenues. *Objective 3f*

Materiality. The concept that recognizes that small or insignificant deviations from generally accepted accounting principles can be treated in the easiest manner. *Objective 3i*

Percentage-of-completion method. The method of recognizing revenue from long-term contracts over the entire life of the contract. *Objective 3f*

Point-of-sale method. The method of recognizing revenue, whereby the revenue is determined to be realized at the time that title passes to the buyer. *Objective 3f*

Price-level index. The ratio of the total cost of a group of commodities prevailing at a particular time to the total cost of the same group of commodities at an earlier base time. *Objective 3d*

ILLUSTRATIVE PROBLEM

Showcase Furniture Company makes all sales on the installment basis and recognizes revenue at the point of sale. Condensed income statements and the amounts collected from customers for each of the first three years of operations are as follows:

	1996	*1997*	*1998*
Sales	$200,000	$240,000	$180,000
Cost of merchandise sold	140,000	163,200	129,600
Gross profit	$ 60,000	$ 76,800	$ 50,400
Operating expenses	33,900	41,500	30,000
Net income	$ 26,100	$ 35,300	$ 20,400
Collected from sales of first year	$ 60,000	$110,000	$ 30,000
Collected from sales of second year		80,000	120,000
Collected from sales of third year			45,000

Instructions

1. Determine the gross profit percentages for each year.
2. Using the installment method, determine the amount of net income or loss that would have been reported in each year.

Solution

1. Gross profit percentages:

 1996: $60,000 ÷ $200,000 = 30%
 1997: $76,800 ÷ $240,000 = 32%
 1998: $50,400 ÷ $180,000 = 28%

2.

	1996	*1997*	*1998*
Gross profit recognized on collections from sales of:			
1996: 30% × $ 60,000	$ 18,000		
30% × $110,000		$33,000	
30% × $ 30,000			$ 9,000
1997: 32% × $ 80,000		25,600	
32% × $120,000			38,400
1998: 28% × $ 45,000			12,600
Total gross profit realized	$ 18,000	$58,600	$60,000
Operating expenses	33,900	41,500	30,000
Net income (loss)	$(15,900)	$17,100	$30,000

SELF-EXAMINATION QUESTIONS (ANSWERS AT END OF CHAPTER)

1. Equipment that was acquired for $250,000 has a current book value of $100,000 and an estimated market value of $120,000. If the replacement cost of the equipment is $350,000, at what amount should the equipment be reported in the balance sheet?
 A. $100,000 C. $150,000
 B. $120,000 D. $350,000

2. Merchandise costing $140,000 was sold on the installment plan for $200,000 during the current year. Down payments of $40,000 and installment payments of $35,000 were received during the current year. If the installment method of accounting is used, what is the amount of gross profit to be realized in the current year?
 A. $22,500 C. $ 75,000
 B. $60,000 D. $140,000

3. The total contract price for the construction of an ocean liner was $20,000,000, and the estimated construction costs were $17,000,000. During the current year, the project was estimated to be 40% completed and the costs incurred totaled $7,050,000. Under the percentage-of-completion method of accounting, what amount of income would be recognized for the current year?
 A. $ 950,000 C. $2,820,000
 B. $1,200,000 D. $3,000,000

4. The consistency concept requires that the nature of and justification for a change in an accounting principle and its effect on income be disclosed in the financial statements of the period in which the change is made. An example of a change that is not a change in an accounting principle is a:
 A. change in method of inventory pricing.
 B. change in depreciation method for previously recorded plant assets.
 C. change in method of accounting for installment sales.
 D. change in method of reporting cents in the financial statements.

5. A corporation's financial statements do not report cents amounts. This is an example of the application of which of the following concepts?
 A. Business entity C. Consistency
 B. Going concern D. Materiality

DISCUSSION QUESTIONS

1. Accounting principles are broad guides to accounting practice. (a) How do these principles differ from the principles relating to the physical sciences? (b) Of what significance is acceptability in the development of accounting principles? (c) Why must accounting principles be continually reexamined and revised?
2. What body is currently dominant in the development of (a) generally accepted accounting principles for business enterprises and (b) principles for state and municipal governments?
3. Briefly discuss the process by which the Financial Accounting Standards Board (FASB) develops *Statements of Financial Accounting Standards.*

4. Organizations that have an interest in the development of generally accepted accounting principles are represented by the following abbreviations. What is the name of each organization?
   a. FASB d. AAA
   b. GASB e. SEC
   c. AICPA f. IRS
5. Which body is most influential in developing uniform international accounting standards?
6. What accounting concept assumes that a business is separate and distinct from the persons who supply its assets?
7. For accounting purposes, what is the nature of the assumption as to the length of life of a business?
8. Assume that a business is in receivership and the receiver expects to dissolve it. Should the going concern concept be used as the basis for preparing the current financial statements? Discuss.
9. Why should the most objective evidence available be used as the basis for data reported on financial statements?
10. Plant assets are reported on the balance sheet at a total cost of $500,000 less accumulated depreciation of $300,000. (a) Is it possible that the assets might realize considerably more or considerably less than $200,000 if the business was discontinued and the assets were sold separately? (b) Why aren't plant assets reported on the balance sheet at their estimated market values?
11. During the current year, a note payable for $1,000,000, issued by Pendleton Company 8 years ago, became due and was paid. Assuming that the general price level had increased by 50% during the 8-year period, did the loan result in an increase or a decrease in Pendleton Company's purchasing power? Explain.
12. Conventional financial statements do not give recognition to the instability of the purchasing power of the dollar. How can the effect of the fluctuating dollar on business operations be presented to the users of the financial statements?
13. What is the current cost of an asset?
14. Land was purchased for $120,000 when the general price-level index was 180, and the general price-level index has risen to 210. Is the constant dollar equivalent of the original cost of the land more than $120,000 or less than $120,000?
15. When can a complete and accurate picture of a business's success or failure be obtained?
16. Is revenue from sales of merchandise on account more commonly recognized at the time of sale or at the time of cash receipt?
17. Under the installment method, when is revenue recognized?
18. Under which method—(a) the percentage-of-completion method or (b) the completed-contract method—is revenue recorded (recognized) earlier? Explain.
19. On January 12 of the current year, Ideal Realty Company acquired a 10-acre tract of land for $500,000. Before the end of the year, $125,000 was spent on subdividing the tract and paving streets. The market value of the land at the end of the year was estimated at $700,000. Although no lots were sold during the year, the income statement for the year reported revenue of $200,000, expenses of $125,000, and net income of $75,000 from the project. Were generally accepted accounting principles followed? Discuss.
20. Maxi-Storage Company constructed a warehouse at a cost of $135,000 after a local contractor had submitted a bid of $180,000. The building was recorded at $180,000, and income of $45,000 was recognized. Were generally accepted accounting principles followed? Discuss.
21. Lapin Company purchased equipment for $150,000 at the beginning of a fiscal year. The equipment could be sold for $170,000 at the end of the fiscal year. It was proposed that since the equipment was worth more at the end of the year than at the beginning of the year, (a) no depreciation should be recorded for the current year, and (b) the gain of $20,000 should be recorded. Discuss the propriety of the proposals.
22. When there are several acceptable alternative accounting methods that could be used, the method used by a business should be disclosed in the financial statements. Give examples of accounting methods that fall in this category.
23. If significant changes are made in the accounting principles applied from one period to the next, why should the effect of these changes be disclosed in the financial statements?
24. You have just been employed by a relatively small merchandising business that records its revenues only when cash is received and its expenses only when cash is paid. You are

aware of the fact that the business should record its revenues and expenses on the accrual basis. Would changing to the accrual basis violate the principle of consistency? Discuss.

25. The accountant for a large department store charged the acquisition of various office items, such as a pencil sharpener, to an expense account, even though the assets had estimated useful lives of 10 years. Which accounting concept supports this treatment of the expenditure?
26. (a) What is a subsequent event? (b) Give two examples of subsequent events that should be disclosed in notes to financial statements.
27. How does an independent audit add credibility to financial statements?
28. Describe an independent auditor's normal report.
29. If an auditor has "substantial doubt" about the ability of the client to continue operating, how is the independent audit report modified?

EXERCISES

EXERCISE 12–1
Accounting concepts
Objective 3

Indicate the letter of the concept that best justifies each of the accounting practices described below. Use a concept only once.

Concept

A. Accounting period	F. Going concern
B. Adequate disclosure	G. Matching
C. Business entity	H. Materiality
D. Conservatism	I. Objectivity
E. Consistency	J. Unit of measurement

Accounting Practice

1. The amounts on the financial statements are rounded to the nearest thousand.
2. A liability for future warranty costs related to the current year's sales is recorded at the end of the fiscal year.
3. A business prepares monthly financial statements for distribution to owners.
4. The cost of printing sales coupons to be distributed in the next year is reported as an asset at the end of the current year.
5. Plant assets are reported in the balance sheet at their historical cost rather than at their constant dollar equivalent.
6. A business changes its method of depreciation from the straight-line method to the double-declining method for plant assets acquired in the current year and for plant assets to be acquired in future years.
7. A business indicates in a footnote to its financial statements that it uses the percentage-of-completion method of recognizing revenue on long-term construction contracts.
8. The transactions for a sole proprietorship are recorded separately from the personal transactions of the owner.
9. In recording a probable liability for litigation involving a violation of environmental laws and regulations, a business obtains an estimate from an independent, environmental attorney.
10. Because of the uncertainty of the collectibility of receivables, a business decides to use the installment method of accounting for installment sales.

EXERCISE 12–2
Accounting concepts
Objective 3

Fabri-Kate Co. is a wholesaler of prefabricated buildings for use by businesses. Indicate the letter of the concept that is violated by each of the accounting practices of Fabri-Kate Co. described below. Use a concept only once.

Concept

A. Accounting period	F. Going concern
B. Adequate disclosure	G. Matching
C. Business entity	H. Materiality
D. Conservatism	I. Objectivity
E. Consistency	J. Unit of measurement

Accounting Practice

1. The notes section of the published financial statements of Fabri-Kate Co. do not include a listing of "significant accounting policies."
2. Cash advances on sales to be made in future years have been recorded as revenues of the current period.
3. Fabri-Kate Co. changed its method of costing merchandise inventory from last-in, first-out to first-in, first-out.
4. Cash received by the owner of Fabri-Kate for the sale of a personal automobile was recorded by Fabri-Kate as a cash sale.
5. The last three sets of financial statements prepared by Fabri-Kate covered 9 months, 8 1/2 months, and 14 months.
6. The plant assets of Fabri-Kate have been reported at their liquidation values on the balance sheet.
7. Some of the inventory of Fabri-Kate is recorded at its current costs, which exceeds the cost of the inventory.
8. In estimating the allowance for doubtful accounts, Fabri-Kate selected the estimation method that resulted in the lowest balance for the allowance account.
9. Rather than using the estimate of an independent, outside professional for the amount of Fabri-Kate's employees' health benefits liability, Fabri-Kate used the estimate of its personnel manager.
10. Fabri-Kate recorded $5,500 of office equipment as office supplies expense because it was not a significant amount. Fabri-Kate's reported net income was $25,300.

EXERCISE 12–3
Accounting concepts
Objective 3

Match each of the following accounting concepts with the related accounting practice that they justify. Use a concept only once.

A. Going concern
B. Unit of measurement
C. Matching
D. Adequate disclosure
E. Materiality
F. Conservatism

1. Reporting the cost of producing a television commercial to be aired in the following period as prepaid advertising.
2. Publishing financial statements with amounts rounded to the nearest million dollars.
3. Reporting inventory at the lower of cost or market.
4. Preparing and posting adjusting journal entries at the end of the fiscal year.
5. Reporting plant assets at their historical cost rather than at their fair market value.
6. Reporting future lease commitments in the footnotes to the financial statements.

EXERCISE 12–4
Business entity concept
Objective 3a

Bag-One Sports Co. sells hunting and fishing equipment and provides guided hunting and fishing trips. Bag-One Sports Co. is owned and operated by Marc Trailer, a well-known sports enthusiast and hunter. Marc's wife, Robin, owns and operates Red Bird Boutique, a women's clothing store. Marc and Robin have established a trust fund to finance their children's college education. The trust fund is maintained by First Wyoming Bank in the name of the children, Sparrow and Trout.

For each of the following transactions, identify which of the entities listed should record the transaction in its records.

Entities

B Bag-One Sports Co.
F First Wyoming Bank
R Red Bird Boutique
X None of the above

1. Marc received a cash advance from customers for a guided hunting trip.
2. Robin deposited a $5,000 personal check in the trust fund at First Wyoming Bank.
3. Robin ordered three dozen spring dresses from a Denver designer for a special spring sale.
4. Marc paid a local doctor for his annual physical, which was required by the workmen's compensation insurance policy carried by Bag-One Sports Co.
5. Marc paid for an advertisement in a hunters' magazine.
6. Robin purchased mutual fund shares as an investment for the children's trust.
7. Marc paid for dinner and a movie to celebrate their tenth wedding anniversary.

8. Robin donated several dresses from inventory for a local charity auction for the benefit of a women's abuse shelter.
9. Marc paid a breeder's fee for an English springer spaniel to be used as a hunting guide dog.
10. Robin paid her dues to the Young Republican's Club.

EXERCISE 12–5
Reporting machine on balance sheet
Objective 3d

A machine with a cost of $75,000 and accumulated depreciation of $65,000 will soon need to be replaced by a similar machine that will cost $120,000. (a) At what amount should the machine presently owned be reported on the balance sheet? (b) What amount should management use in planning for the cash required to replace the machine?

EXERCISE 12–6
Effect of changes in purchasing power of dollar
Objective 3d

During May, merchandise costing $125,000 was sold for $175,000 in cash. Because the purchasing power of the dollar has declined, it will cost $130,000 to replace the merchandise. (a) What is the amount of gross profit in May? (b) Assuming that all operating expenses for the month are paid in cash and that the owner withdraws cash in the amount of the net income, would there be enough cash remaining from the $175,000 of sales to replace the merchandise sold? Discuss.

EXERCISE 12–7
Effect of price-level change on investment in land
Objective 3d

Several years ago, Repo Real Estate Investment Company purchased land as a future building site for $125,000. The price-level index at that time was 160. On February 25 of the current year, when the price-level index was 192, the land was sold for $168,000.

a. Determine the amount of the gain that would be recognized according to conventional accounting.
b. Indicate the amount of the gain that may be (1) attributed to the change in purchasing power and (2) considered a true gain in terms of current dollars.

EXERCISE 12–8
Effect of current costs on income
Objective 3d

The following footnote was taken from the 1993 annual report of Maytag Corporation:

INVENTORIES

In thousands	*1993*	*1992*
Finished products	$282,841	$249,289
Work in process, raw materials and supplies	146,313	151,794
	$429,154	$401,083

If . . . [current costs had] been used for all inventories, they would have been $76.3 million and $78.1 million higher than reported at December 31, 1993 and 1992.

Maytag Corporation reported operating income before income taxes of $158,878,000 for the year ended December 31, 1993. Based upon the preceding data, determine the income before income taxes that would have been reported in 1993 if inventories had been valued using current costs.

EXERCISE 12–9
Change in accounting method
Objective 3g

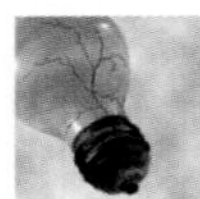

Ari Department Stores has been reporting merchandise inventory by the lower-of-cost-or-market method. However, the replacement cost of its inventory has risen significantly during the current year. Therefore, Ari Department Stores elected to report the merchandise inventory at the end of the current year at current market prices. The change in method was disclosed in a note to the financial statements that fully reported the effect of the use of market prices on the balance sheet and income statement.

Is there anything wrong with the reporting? Discuss.

EXERCISE 12–10
Recognizing revenue
Objective 3f

Each of the following items involves revenue for a different company:

a. Merchandise on hand at the end of the current fiscal year, costing $217,500, is expected to be sold in the following year for $325,000.
b. Season tickets for a series of eight concerts were sold for $150,000. Six concerts were played during the current year.
c. Forty-five days before the end of the current fiscal year, $120,000 was loaned at 8% for 120 days.
d. Sales of merchandise on terms of n/45 and delivered during the current year totaled $315,000. No cash was received on these credit sales during the current year.

e. The contract price for building a bridge is $18,000,000. During the current year, the first year of construction, the bridge is estimated to be 30% completed and the costs incurred totaled $3,950,000. Revenue is recognized by the percentage-of-completion method.
f. Salespersons submitted orders in the current year for merchandise to be delivered in the following year. The merchandise had a cost of $25,000 and a selling price of $39,250.
g. A tract of land was leased on the first day of the tenth month of the current year, and one year's rent of $48,000 was received.

h. Cash of $18,000 was received in the current year on the sale of gift certificates to be redeemed in merchandise in the following year.
i. Thirty days before the end of the current fiscal year, a $60,000, 90-day note was accepted at a discount of 9%. Proceeds in the amount of $58,650 were given to the maker of the note.

Indicate for each of the above items the amount of revenue that should be reported for the current year and the amount of revenue that should be postponed to a future period. Give a reason for your answer.

EXERCISE 12–11
Gross profit by point-of-sale and installment methods
Objective 3f

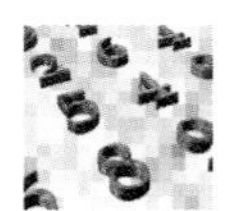

Genre Company, an appliance retailer, makes all sales on the installment plan. Data related to merchandise sold during the current fiscal year are as follows:

Sales	$1,200,000
Cash received on the $1,200,000 of installment contracts	480,000
Cost of merchandise sold	744,000

Determine the amount of gross profit that would be recognized for the current fiscal year according to (a) the point-of-sale method and (b) the installment method.

EXERCISE 12–12
Determining cost of products and services acquired
Objective 3f

Properties and services acquired by a business are generally recorded at cost. For each of the following, determine the cost.

a. Materials and supplies costing $5,500 were purchased for the construction of a display case. An additional $2,500 was paid to hire a carpenter to build the display case. A similar case would cost $10,000 if purchased from a manufacturer.
b. An adjacent tract of land was acquired for $60,000 to provide additional parking for customers. The structures on the land were removed at a cost of $10,500. The salvaged material from the structures was sold for $1,200. The cost of grading the land was $1,750.
c. Equipment was purchased for $50,000 under terms of n/30, FOB shipping point. The freight charge amounted to $815, and installation costs totaled $1,050.

EXERCISE 12–13
Effects on financial statements of failure to accrue commissions
Objective 3f

Salespersons for Select Realty receive a commission of 5% of sales, the amount of commissions due on sales of one month being paid in the middle of the following month. At the end of each of the first three years of operations, the accountant failed to record accrued sales commissions expense as follows: first year, $30,000; second year, $47,500; third year, $33,500. In each case, the commissions were paid during the first month of the succeeding year and were charged as an expense of that year. Accrued sales commissions expense was properly recorded at the end of the fourth year.

a. Determine the amount by which net income was overstated or understated for each of the four years.
b. Determine the items on the balance sheet that would have been overstated or understated at the end of each of the four years and the amount of overstatement or understatement.

EXERCISE 12–14
Effect on financial statements of failure to record sales
Objective 3f

TriBall Company, a locally-owned hardware store, sells most of its products on a cash basis, but extends short-term credit to a few of its customers. Invoices for sales on account are placed in a file and are not recorded until cash is received, at which time the sale is recorded in the same manner as a cash sale. The net income reported for the first three years of operations was $121,500, $150,000, and $202,000, respectively. The total amount of the uncollected sales invoices in the file at the end of each of the three years was $6,500, $12,500, and $9,100, respectively. In each case, the entire amount was collected during the first month of the succeeding year.

a. Determine the amount by which net income was overstated or understated for each of the three years.
b. Determine the items on the balance sheet that were overstated or understated, and the amount of overstatement or understatement, as of the end of each year.

EXERCISE 12–15
Materiality
Objectives 3g, 3i

Of the following matters, considered individually, indicate those that are material and that should be disclosed in the financial statements or in accompanying explanatory notes.

a. A change in the estimate of the remaining usefulness of computer equipment decreased the amount of net income that would otherwise have been reported from $900,000 to $750,000.
b. A change in accounting for depreciation of plant assets was adopted in the current year. The amount of net income that would otherwise have been reported decreased from $990,000 to $975,000.
c. A merchandising company uses the first-in, first-out cost flow assumption and prices its inventory at the lower of cost or market.
d. A company is facing litigation involving restraint of trade. Damages might amount to $6,000,000. Annual net income reported in the past few years has ranged from $10,000,000 to $13,500,000.
e. Between the end of the fiscal year and the date of publication of the annual report, a fire completely destroyed one of three principal plants. The loss was estimated at $5,000,000 and was fully covered by insurance. The net income for the fiscal year was $1,125,000.

EXERCISE 12–16
Effect of different inventory cost methods on net income
Objectives 3g, 3i

The cost of merchandise inventory at the end of the first fiscal year of operations, according to three different methods, is as follows: fifo, $90,000; average, $76,500; lifo, $68,000. If the average cost method is used, the net income reported will be $125,000.

a. What will be the amount of net income reported if the lifo method is adopted?
b. What will be the amount of net income reported if the fifo method is adopted?
c. Which of the three methods is the most conservative in terms of net income?
d. Is the particular method adopted of sufficient materiality to require disclosure in the financial statements?

EXERCISE 12–17
Effect of change in depreciation methods
Objectives 3h, 3i

For many years, Douglas Transportation Company has used the declining-balance method of computing depreciation. For the current year, the straight-line method was used, depreciation expense amounted to $175,000, and net income amounted to $80,000. Depreciation computed by the declining-balance method would have been $205,000.

a. What is the quantitative effect of the change in method on the net income for the current year?
b. Is the effect of the change material? Discuss.
c. Should the effect of the change in method be disclosed in the financial statements? Discuss.

EXERCISE 12–18
Generally accepted accounting principles
Objective 3

State whether or not you agree with the decision in each of the following statements. Support your answer with reference to generally accepted accounting principles that are applicable in the circumstances.

a. All minor expenditures for office equipment are charged to an expense account.
b. Merchandise transferred to other parties on a consignment basis and not sold was included in merchandise inventory.
c. In preparing the balance sheet, detailed information as to each amount due to dozens of creditors was omitted. The total amount was presented under the caption *Accounts Payable*.
d. Land, used as a parking lot, was purchased 20 years ago for $50,000. Since its market value is now $350,000, the land account is debited for $300,000 and a gain account is credited for a like amount. The gain is presented as an *Other income* item in the income statement.
e. Used computer equipment, with an estimated useful life of 5 years and no salvage value, was purchased early in the current fiscal year for $150,000. Since the company planned to purchase new equipment, costing $200,000, to replace this equipment at the end of five years, depreciation expense of $40,000 was recorded for the current year. The depreciation expense thus provided for one-fifth of the cost of the replacement.

f. Merchandise inventory at the end of the current year was estimated by the general manager, who "eye-balled" the inventory on hand and then determined its cost, based on an estimate of current costs. The accountant used the general manager's estimate for recording the cost of the inventory in the accounts.
g. Net income for the current year is expected to be larger than normal. Therefore, the accountant used the declining-balance method for determining depreciation for the current year to reduce the net income to a more normal amount. The accountant plans to use the straight-line method in future years. The straight-line method has been used in all past years for determining income.
h. Thirty days before the end of the current year, sales catalogs were acquired for $35,000. Although the catalogs are not salable, the unused portion is included as an asset in the balance sheet at the end of the year.
i. Financial statements adjusted to eliminate the effects of inflation (using the current cost method) were presented as supplementary financial data.

PROBLEMS SERIES A

PROBLEM 12–1A
Installment sales
Objective 3f

Ibex Co. sells and installs elevators. Ibex Co. makes all sales on the installment basis and recognizes revenue at the point of sale. Condensed income statements and the amounts collected from customers for each of the first three years of operations are as follows:

	First Year	*Second Year*	*Third Year*
Sales	$285,000	$340,000	$400,000
Cost of merchandise sold	190,950	224,400	260,000
Gross profit	$ 94,050	$115,600	$140,000
Operating expenses	62,500	68,500	98,400
Net income	$ 31,550	$ 47,100	$ 41,600
Collected from sales of first year	$100,000	$125,000	$ 60,000
Collected from sales of second year		110,000	180,000
Collected from sales of third year			150,000

Instructions

1. Determine the gross profit percentage for each year.
2. Determine the amount of net income or loss that would have been reported in each year if the installment method of recognizing revenue had been used, ignoring the possible effects of uncollectible accounts on the computation.

PROBLEM 12–2A
Installment sale and repossession
Objective 3f

Metromedia Co. sells home appliances ranging from televisions and VCRs to washers and dryers. Metromedia Co. uses the installment method of recognizing gross profit for sales made on the installment plan. Details of a particular installment sale, amounts collected from the buyer, and the repossession of the item sold are as follows:

First year:
Sold for $850 a television set having a cost of $510; received a down payment of $130.
Second year:
Received 12 monthly payments of $20 each.
Third year:
The buyer defaulted on the monthly payments, the set was repossessed, and the remaining 24 installments were canceled. The set was sold for $320.

Instructions

1. Determine the gross profit to be recognized in the first year.
2. Determine the gross profit to be recognized in the second year.
3. Determine the gain or loss to be recognized from the repossession and sale of the set in the third year. (*Suggestion:* First determine the amount of the unrecovered cost in the canceled installments. The gain or loss will then be the difference between this unrecovered cost and the sales price of the repossessed set.)

PROBLEM 12–3A
Percentage-of-completion method
Objective 3f

Brownstone Company began construction on a hospital and two office buildings during 1996. The three contract prices and construction activities for 1996, 1997, and 1998 were as follows:

		1996		*1997*		*1998*	
Contract	*Contract Price*	*Costs Incurred*	*Percent Completed*	*Costs Incurred*	*Percent Completed*	*Costs Incurred*	*Percent Completed*
1	$6,500,000	$3,175,000	50%	$2,250,000	50%		
2	4,000,000	600,000	20	1,375,000	40	$1,500,000	40%
3	3,000,000	655,000	30	1,050,000	40	775,000	30

Instructions
Determine the amount of revenue and the income to be recognized for each of the years, 1996, 1997, and 1998. Revenue is to be recognized by the percentage-of-completion method.

PROBLEM 12–4A
Changes in accounting principles
Objective 3f

Rebound Co., organized on January 3, 1996, sells basketball equipment ranging from shoes to portable basketball goals. During its first three years of operations, the company calculated uncollectible accounts expense by the direct write-off method, the cost of the merchandise inventory at the end of the period by the last-in, first-out method, and depreciation expense by the straight-line method. The amount of net income reported and the amounts of the foregoing items for each of the three years were as follows:

	First Year	*Second Year*	*Third Year*
Net income reported	$60,200	$70,750	$89,900
Uncollectible accounts expense	900	1,350	3,250
Ending merchandise inventory	49,750	54,000	58,150
Depreciation expense	15,000	15,000	15,000

The firm is considering the possibility of changing to the following methods in determining net income for the fourth and subsequent years: provision for doubtful accounts through the use of an allowance account, first-in, first-out inventory, and declining-balance depreciation at twice the straight-line rate. To consider the probable future effect of these changes on net income, the management requests that net income of the past three years be recomputed on the basis of the proposed methods. The uncollectible accounts expense, inventory, and depreciation expense for the past three years, computed in accordance with the proposed methods, are as follows:

	First Year	*Second Year*	*Third Year*
Uncollectible accounts expense	$ 1,225	$ 2,800	$ 3,000
Ending merchandise inventory	53,000	52,900	59,650
Depreciation expense	28,000	22,000	11,520

Instructions
Recompute the net income for each of the three years, presenting the figures in the following format:

	First Year	*Second Year*	*Third Year*
Net income reported			
Increase (decrease) in net income attributable to change in method of determining:			
Uncollectible accounts expense			
Ending merchandise inventory			
Depreciation expense			
Total			
Net income as recomputed			

PROBLEM 12–5A
Adjusting and correcting entries
Objective 3

You are asked to review the accounting records of Syn-Comm Company prior to the closing of the revenue and expense accounts as of June 30, the end of the current fiscal year. Syn-Comm Company is a retailer of communications equipment. The following information comes to your attention during the review:

a. No interest has been accrued on a $120,000, 8%, 90-day note payable, dated May 31 of the current year.
b. Since net income for the current year is expected to be considerably less than it was for the preceding year, depreciation on equipment has not been recorded. Depreciation for the year, determined in a manner consistent with the preceding year, amounts to $39,600.
c. Land recorded in the accounts at a cost of $60,000 was appraised at $95,000 by two expert appraisers.
d. The office supplies account has a balance of $6,250. The cost of the office supplies at June 30, as determined by a physical count, was $1,300.
e. Merchandise inventory at June 30 of the current year has been recorded in the accounts at cost, $115,200. Current market price of the inventory is $128,500.
f. Accounts receivable includes $24,625 owed by Taft Co., a bankrupt company. Syn-Comm Company expects to receive twenty cents on each dollar owed. The allowance method of accounting for receivables is used.
g. The company received a debit memorandum with the bank statement from Trust Company Bank, indicating that a customer note discounted at the bank has been dishonored. The 10%, 90-day note is from Sattler Co. and has a $50,000 face value. Syn-Comm Company has not recorded the memorandum, which included a protest fee of $200.
h. The company is being sued for $4,500,000 by a customer who claims damages for personal injury allegedly caused by a defective product. Company attorneys and outside legal counsel feel extremely confident that the company will have no liability for damages resulting from this case.

Instructions

Journalize any entries required to adjust or correct the accounts, identifying each entry by letter. For those items for which no entry is necessary, explain why an entry should not be made.

PROBLEMS SERIES B

PROBLEM 12–1B
Installment sales
Objective 3f

Stucco Co. sells dairy equipment to farmers throughout the Midwest. Stucco Co. makes all sales on the installment basis and recognizes revenue at the point of sale. Condensed income statements and the amounts collected from customers for each of the first three years of operations are as follows:

	First Year	*Second Year*	*Third Year*
Sales	$425,000	$340,000	$382,000
Cost of merchandise sold	293,250	227,800	229,200
Gross profit	$131,750	$112,200	$152,800
Operating expenses	60,000	51,500	62,250
Net income	$ 71,750	$ 60,700	$ 90,550
Collected from sales of first year	$146,500	$157,500	$121,000
Collected from sales of second year		95,000	145,000
Collected from sales of third year			181,000

Instructions

1. Determine the gross profit percentage for each year.
2. Determine the amount of net income or loss that would have been reported in each year if the installment method of recognizing revenue had been used, ignoring the possible effects of uncollectible accounts on the computation.

PROBLEM 12–2B
Installment sale and repossession
Objective 3f

Sofa Furniture Co. sells sofas for the home and office. Sofa Furniture Co. uses the installment method of recognizing gross profit for sales made on the installment plan. Details of a particular installment sale, amounts collected from the buyer, and the repossession of the item sold are as follows:

First year:
Sold for $1,800 a sofa set having a cost of $1,170; received a down payment of $360.
Second year:
Received 12 monthly payments of $40 each.
Third year:
The buyer defaulted on the monthly payments, the sofa was repossessed, and the remaining 24 installments were canceled. The set was sold for $400.

Instructions

1. Determine the gross profit to be recognized in the first year.
2. Determine the gross profit to be recognized in the second year.
3. Determine the gain or loss to be recognized from the repossession and sale of the sofa in the third year. (*Suggestion:* First determine the amount of the unrecovered cost in the canceled installments. The gain or loss will then be the difference between this unrecovered cost and the sales price of the repossessed sofa.)

PROBLEM 12–3B
Percentage-of-completion method
Objective 3f

Renotex Company began construction on a warehouse, an office building, and a school building during 1996. The three contract prices and construction activities for 1996, 1997, and 1998 were as follows:

		1996		*1997*		*1998*	
Contract	*Contract Price*	*Costs Incurred*	*Percent Completed*	*Costs Incurred*	*Percent Completed*	*Costs Incurred*	*Percent Completed*
1	$ 6,000,000	$1,810,000	45%	$1,575,000	35%	$1,390,000	20%
2	10,000,000	2,550,000	30	2,625,000	30	2,695,000	30
3	7,500,000	3,710,000	60	2,815,000	40	—	—

Instructions
Determine the amount of revenue and the income to be recognized for each of the years, 1996, 1997, and 1998. Revenue is to be recognized by the percentage-of-completion method.

PROBLEM 12–4B
Changes in accounting principles
Objective 3f

Spring Creek Co., organized on January 3, 1996, bottles spring water and sells it throughout the Northwest. During its first three years of operations, the company calculated uncollectible accounts expense by the direct write-off method, the cost of the merchandise inventory at the end of the period by the first-in, first-out method, and depreciation expense by the straight-line method. The amount of net income reported and the amounts of the foregoing items for each of the three years were as follows:

	First Year	*Second Year*	*Third Year*
Net income reported	$95,000	$142,000	$185,000
Uncollectible accounts expense	2,125	3,800	6,950
Ending merchandise inventory	60,750	82,000	112,000
Depreciation expense	20,000	20,000	20,000

The firm is considering the possibility of changing to the following methods in determining net income for the fourth and subsequent years: provision for doubtful accounts through the use of an allowance account, last-in, first-out inventory, and declining-balance depreciation at twice the straight-line rate. To consider the probable future effect of these changes on the determination of net income, the management requests that net income of the past three years be recomputed on the basis of the proposed methods. The uncollectible accounts expense, inventory, and depreciation expense for the past three years, computed in accordance with the proposed methods, are as follows:

	First Year	Second Year	Third Year
Uncollectible accounts expense	$ 3,625	$ 5,500	$ 6,250
Ending merchandise inventory	59,000	70,100	92,750
Depreciation expense	40,000	28,840	14,100

Instructions

Recompute the net income for each of the three years, presenting the figures in the following format:

	First Year	Second Year	Third Year
Net income reported			
Increase (decrease) in net income attributable to change in method of determining:			
Uncollectible accounts expense			
Ending merchandise inventory			
Depreciation expense			
Total			
Net income as recomputed			

PROBLEM 12–5B
Adjusting and correcting entries
Objective 3

You are asked to review the accounting records of Innovax Company prior to the closing of the revenue and expense accounts as of December 31, the end of the current fiscal year. Innovax Company wholesales discontinued office equipment. The following information comes to your attention during the review:

a. The company is being sued for $3,000,000 by a customer who claims damages for personal injury allegedly caused by a defective product. Company attorneys and outside legal counsel feel extremely confident that the company will have no liability for damages resulting from this case.
b. The prepaid insurance account has a balance of $11,175. At December 31, the unexpired premiums were $7,200.
c. Accounts receivable include $5,650 owed by J. Ryder Co., a bankrupt company. There is no prospect of collecting any of the receivable. The allowance method of accounting for receivables is used.
d. Land recorded in the accounts at a cost of $115,000 was appraised at $132,500 by two expert appraisers.
e. Since net income for the current year is expected to be considerably less than it was for the preceding year, depreciation on buildings has not been recorded. Depreciation for the year, determined in a manner consistent with the preceding year, amounts to $42,100.
f. No interest has been accrued on a $150,000, 10%, 90-day note receivable, dated November 1 of the current year.
g. Merchandise inventory at December 31 of the current year has been recorded in the accounts at cost, $177,150. Current market price of the inventory is $186,500.

Instructions

Journalize any entries required to adjust or correct the accounts, identifying each entry by letter. For those items for which no entry is necessary, explain why an entry should not be made.

CASES

CASE 12–1
Baird & Associates
Financial disclosures

John Baird is negotiating the sale of his law practice, Baird & Associates, to Lavoir Terry. As part of the negotiations, John has prepared a list of his clients, with an estimate of fees expected to be earned from each. In some cases, the estimated fees differ from the amounts earned from clients and that have been included in the preceding year's financial statements. In other cases, an amount has been listed as an expected fee from a client for whom no services have been rendered in the past.

Discuss whether John Baird is behaving in an ethical manner.

CASE 12–2

Neptune Software Co.

Recognizing revenue

Neptune Software Co. creates and produces computer software for various office applications. The majority of the software is designed to run on a networked system of personal computers.

Neptune Software licenses its software to its customers under an agreement that requires a fee payment within 30 days. Neptune has designed authorization codes into all its software. These authorization codes allow the user to run the software only if the proper code is entered. When a customer initially enters into the licensing agreement for software, Neptune provides the customer with a temporary authorization code that will expire in 30 days. Thus, if the customer has not paid within 30 days, Neptune can deny use of the software by not providing the customer a permanent authorization code. In some cases, Neptune will provide an additional temporary authorization code if the customer has made partial payment within 30 days and has agreed to a payment plan. A permanent authorization code is provided only when full payment has been received.

The controller for Neptune Software is uncertain as to when to recognize revenue associated with the licensing of the software, specifically, the following three times for recognizing revenue are being considered:

(1) Record the revenue when the software is delivered to the customer.
(2) Record the revenue as payments from customers are received.
(3) Record the revenue only when the permanent authorization code has been provided the customer and full payment has been received.

When would you suggest the controller of Neptune recognize revenue from the licensing agreements? Explain your answer.

CASE 12–3

Platinum Co.

Disclosing market values

The following is an excerpt from a telephone conversation between Stella Regis, a new commercial loan officer for Park Avenue Bank & Trust Co., and Jeffrey Jarvis, the controller for Platinum Co. Platinum Co. has a $500,000 loan from Park Avenue Bank & Trust Co. that requires it to submit audited financial statements to the bank each year.

Stella: Jeff, thanks for returning my call.

Jeffrey: Sure, what can I help you with?

Stella: Well, I was reviewing your financial statements for this past year and I have a question concerning the value of your building and equipment.

Jeffrey: What's the question?

Stella: As you know, the building and equipment are collateral for your loan, and I can't find the market value of these assets anywhere in the financial statements. All I can find is a note that indicates that the assets are pledged as collateral on the loan.

Jeffrey: That's right. Generally accepted accounting principles require that plant assets be reported at their cost, not at their market values. We had an appraisal on the building and equipment three years ago when we negotiated the loan. At that time, the market value was approximately $800,000—well in excess of the face value of the loan.

Stella: I'm sure the appraised value has changed. We'd like you to get a new appraisal for our files.

Jeffrey: I don't know. I'll have to discuss this with our president, Joan Golden. I'll get back to you some time tomorrow.

a. Discuss the accounting principles that justify recording plant assets at their historical cost rather than at their market values.
b. What is the primary risk to Park Avenue Bank & Trust Co. concerning the loan of $500,000?
c. Assume that although Platinum Co. reported only a small net loss for the past year, Platinum is suffering financial distress and is likely to file for bankruptcy within a year. Should the financial statements of Platinum disclose this possibility?
d. Does Platinum Co. have to comply with Stella's request for a new appraisal on the building and equipment?

CASE 12–4

Hershey Foods Corporation

Financial analysis

Financial statements, including their related notes and other disclosures, should contain all of the data essential to a user's understanding of the company's financial status and operations. Matters that are normally disclosed in notes are the accounting methods used in preparing the financial statements. If a company is involved in more than one type of business activity or market, the disclosures generally include segment information by type of activity or market.

a. Identify the accounting methods used by Hershey Foods Corporation in:
   1. valuing inventories
   2. depreciating plant assets
b. What segments are used by Hershey in reporting segment information?

CASE 12–5

Carquest Co.

Accounting concepts

Carquest Co. operates ten cash-and-carry auto parts stores in the Southeast. In an effort to expand sales, the company has decided to offer two additional sales plans:

1. Credit sales to commercial businesses, such as body and repair shops, with free 24-hour delivery.
2. Installment sales of major dollar items, with payments spread over 24 months.

The company president has asked you when the revenue from each of the two new plans would be recognized in the accounting records and statements.

a. Indicate to the president when the revenue from each type of sale should be journalized in the accounting records.

b. While discussing the concepts in (a), the president raised the following questions related to various accounting concepts. How would you respond to each?

1. "Many businesses cease operating each year; so why do accountants assume a going concern concept when preparing the financial statements?"
2. "To assume that the value of the dollar does not change and that we don't have inflation is wrong! An automatic transmission that cost $600 five years ago costs $900 today. Why wouldn't it be better to use current dollars, at least for the inventory?"
3. "With so many different accounting methods that can be used, why can't I switch methods to improve net income this year?"
4. "Our annual bonuses to store managers are based on store profits. It's not fair to 'anticipate no profits and provide for all losses.'"

ANSWERS TO SELF-EXAMINATION QUESTIONS

1. **A** In the balance sheet, the equipment should be reported at its cost less accumulated depreciation, $100,000 (answer A). The effect of the declining value of the dollar on plant assets, the market value of plant assets, and the replacement cost of plant assets are not recognized in the basic historical cost statements.
2. **A** Under the installment method of accounting, gross profit is recognized according to the amount of cash collected in each year, based on the percent of gross profit to sales. For this question, the amount of gross profit to be realized for the current year is $22,500 (answer A), determined as follows:

   Percent of gross profit to sales:
   $60,000 ÷ $200,000 = 30%
   Gross profit realized:
   $75,000 × 30% = $22,500

3. **A** Under the percentage-of-completion method of accounting, the amount of revenue to be recognized during a period is determined on the basis of the estimated percentage of the contract that has been completed during the period. The costs incurred during the period are deducted from this revenue to yield the income from the contract. The $950,000 of income (answer A) is determined as follows:

Revenue realized (40% × $20,000,000)	$8,000,000
Costs incurred	7,050,000
Income	$ 950,000

4. **D** In some situations, there are a number of accepted alternative principles that can be used. To ensure a high degree of comparability of the financial statements between periods, a change from one accepted principle to another should be disclosed. A change in method of inventory pricing (answer A), a change in depreciation method for previously recorded plant assets (answer B), and a change in method of accounting for installment sales (answer C) are examples of changes in accepted alternative principles that should be appropriately disclosed. A change in the method of reporting cents in the financial statements (answer D) is not a change in a principle.
5. **D** The concept of materiality (answer D) relates to the acceptance of a procedure that deviates from absolute accuracy for insignificant or immaterial items, such as reporting cents in financial statements.

Answer to Triangle Puzzle

Twenty-four triangles are in the figure, as follows: ABE, ABH, ACD, ACE, ACF, ACH, ADE, ADF, AEH, AFH, BCE, BCH, CDF, CDH, CEF, CEH, DEF, DEG, DEH, DFH, DGH, EFG, EFH, FGH

PART FIVE

Partnerships

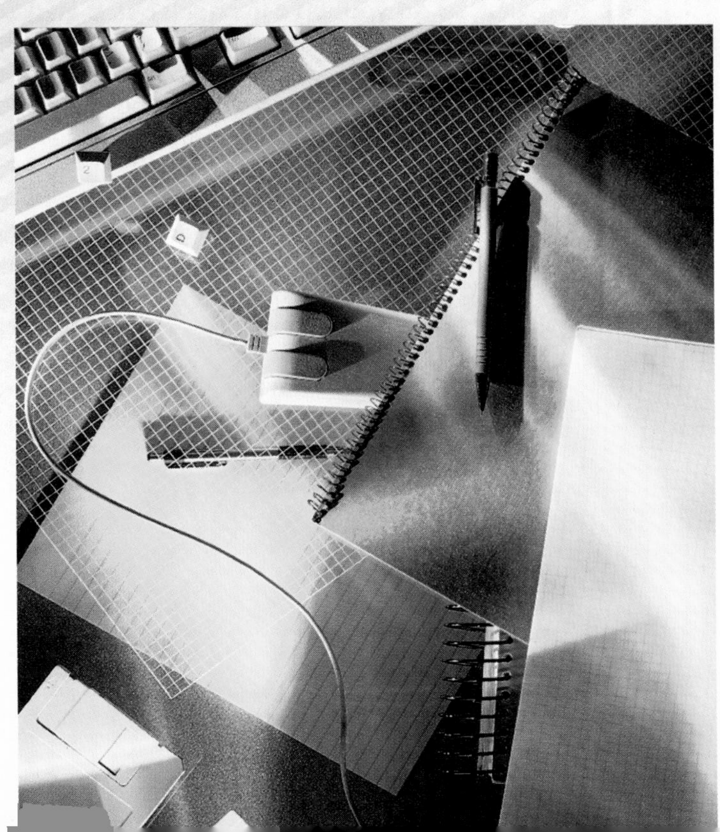

13

Partnership Formation, Income Division, and Liquidation

YOU AND ACCOUNTING

Assume that you and a friend have an idea for starting a part-time business to earn some extra money.

What does it take to start a business operated by two or more individuals? How much money should each individual (you and your friend) contribute to start the business? How will the profits be divided? Can you withdraw money from the business whenever you want, or do you have to have your friend's (partner's) approval? Can your friend bring someone else into the business as a partner without your approval? Could you or your friend quit the business at any time? Will you be liable for commitments made by your partner, even if they were made without your knowledge? Is the amount you can lose in the business, if it's not successful, limited to the amount you initially invested?

The partnership form of business organization allows two or more persons to combine capital, managerial talent, and experience with a minimum of effort. This form is widely used by small businesses. In many cases, the only alternative to the partnership form of organization is the corporate form. Some states, however, do not permit the corporate form for certain types of businesses. For example, physicians, attorneys, and certified public accountants often organize as partnerships. Medical and legal partnerships made up of 20 or more partners are not unusual, and the number of partners in some national CPA firms exceeds 1,000.

The preceding chapters focused on the accounting for sole proprietorships. This chapter describes and illustrates the accounting for the partnership form of organization, which is the form you and your friend would be using in operating your business. The answers to the questions above and the accounting for partnerships will be addressed throughout this discussion.

After studying this chapter, you should be able to:

Objective 1
Identify and list the basic characteristics of the partnership form of organization.

Objective 2
Journalize the entries for the formation of partnerships.

Objective 3
Journalize the entries for dividing partnership net income and net loss.

Objective 4
Journalize the entries for partnership dissolution, including admission of new partners and the withdrawal or death of partners.

Objective 5
Journalize the entries for liquidating partnerships.

Characteristics of Partnerships

Objective 1
Identify and list the basic characteristics of the partnership form of organization.

A **partnership** is "an association of two or more persons to carry on as co-owners a business for profit."[1] Partnerships have several characteristics with accounting implications. These characteristics are described in the following paragraphs.

A partnership has a **limited life.** Dissolving of a partnership occurs whenever a partner ceases to be a member of the firm. For example, a partnership is dissolved if a partner withdraws due to bankruptcy, incapacity, or death. Likewise, admitting a new partner dissolves the old partnership. When a partnership is dissolved, a new partnership must be formed if operations of the business are to continue. This situation often occurs in professional partnerships, such as medical, legal, and accounting firms. Their membership changes as new partners join the firm and others retire.

Most partnerships are *general partnerships,* in which the partners have **unlimited liability.** Each partner is individually liable to creditors for debts incurred by the partnership. Thus, if a partnership becomes insolvent, the partners must contribute sufficient personal assets to settle the debts of the partnership. In some states, a *limited partnership* may be formed. In a limited partnership, the liability of some partners may be limited to the amount of their capital investment. However, a limited partnership must have at least one general partner who has unlimited liability. In this chapter, the discussion focuses on the general partnership.

Partners have **co-ownership of partnership property.** The property invested in a partnership by a partner becomes the property of all the partners jointly. When a partnership is dissolved, the partners' claims against the assets are measured by the amount of the balances in their capital accounts.

Another characteristic of a partnership is **mutual agency.** This means that each partner is an agent of the partnership. Thus, each partner has the authority to enter into contracts for the partnership. The acts of each partner bind the entire partnership and become the obligations of all partners.

An important right of partners is **participation in income** of the partnership. Net income and net loss are distributed among the partners according to their agreement. In the absence of any agreement, all partners share equally. If the agreement indicates a profit distribution but is silent as to losses, the losses are shared in the same manner as profits.

A partnership, like a sole proprietorship, is a **nontaxable entity** and thus does not pay federal income taxes. However, revenue and expense and other results of partnership operations must be reported annually to the Internal Revenue Service.

[1] This definition of a partnership is included in the Uniform Partnership Act, which has been adopted by over ninety percent of the states.

USING ACCOUNTING TO UNDERSTAND BUSINESS

The eight largest partnerships in the United States, as ranked by revenues, are listed below. Six of these partnerships are accounting firms.

Largest Partnerships in the United States

Name	*Business*	*Revenues ($000,000)*	*Number of employees*
Goldman, Sachs, & Co.	Securities brokerage, investment banking	12,450	7,000
KPMG Peat Marwick	Accounting	6,375	76,000
Arthur Andersen & Co.	Accounting	6,017	68,078
Ernst & Young	Accounting	5,900	63,558
Coopers & Lybrand	Accounting	5,602	67,064
Deloitte & Touche	Accounting	5,000	56,000
Price Waterhouse	Accounting	3,887	49,000
McKinsey & Co.	Management consulting	1,230	5,560

Source: *Forbes*, December 6, 1993, pp. 170–200.

This reporting is done on information returns. The partners must, in turn, report their share of partnership income on their personal tax returns.

A partnership is created by a contract. It is not necessary that the contract be in writing, nor even that its terms be specifically expressed. However, good business practice requires that the contract be in writing and that it clearly expresses the intentions of the partners. The contract is known as the **partnership agreement** or **articles of partnership.** It should include statements regarding such matters as amounts to be invested, limits on withdrawals, distributions of income and losses, and admission and withdrawal of partners.

ADVANTAGES AND DISADVANTAGES OF PARTNERSHIPS

The partnership form of business organization is less widely used than are the sole proprietorship and corporate forms. For many business purposes, however, the advantages of the partnership form are greater than its disadvantages.

A partnership is relatively easy and inexpensive to organize, requiring only an agreement between two or more persons. A partnership has the advantage of bringing together more capital, managerial skills, and experience than does a sole proprietorship. Since a partnership is a nontaxable entity, the combined income taxes paid by the individual partners may be lower than the income taxes that would be paid by a corporation, which is a taxable entity.

A major disadvantage of the partnership form of business organization is the unlimited liability feature for partners. In May 1992, for example, an Arizona state court ordered Price Waterhouse to pay $338 million in damages for negligence. This amount was about 3 times the firm's insurance coverage. If an appeals court upholds the original order, the accounting firm's 950 partners will pay approximately $200 million in total out of their own pockets.

Other disadvantages of a partnership are that its life is limited, and one partner can bind the partnership to contracts. Also, raising large amounts of capital is more difficult for a partnership than for a corporation.

USING ACCOUNTING TO UNDERSTAND BUSINESS

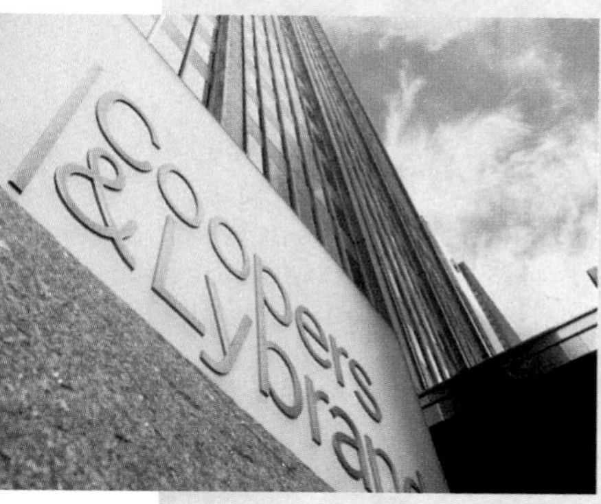

Four of the largest public accounting firms, Coopers & Lybrand, Ernst & Young, Price Waterhouse, and Arthur Andersen & Co. indicate that they will soon adopt a "limited liability partnership." This new type of partnership, which is recognized by the state of New York, can be used to shield partners' personal assets from lawsuits and other claims against the partnership.

ACCOUNTING FOR PARTNERSHIPS

Most of the day-to-day accounting for a partnership is the same as the accounting for any other form of business organization. The accounting system described in previous chapters may, with little change, be used by a partnership. The chart of accounts, with the exception of drawing and capital accounts for each partner, does not differ from the chart of accounts of a similar business conducted by a single owner. However, the formation, income distribution, dissolution, and liquidation of partnerships give rise to unique transactions. In the remainder of this chapter, we discuss accounting principles related to these areas.

Formation of a Partnership

Objective 2
Journalize the entries for the formation of partnerships.

A separate entry is made for the investment of each partner in a partnership. The assets contributed by a partner are debited to the partnership asset accounts. If liabilities are assumed by the partnership, the partnership liability accounts are credited. The partner's capital account is credited for the net amount.

To illustrate, assume that Joseph A. Stevens and Earl S. Foster, sole owners of competing hardware stores, agree to combine their businesses in a partnership. Each is to contribute certain amounts of cash and other assets. It is also agreed that the partnership is to assume the liabilities of the separate businesses. The entry to record the assets contributed and the liabilities transferred by Stevens is as follows:

Apr. 1	Cash	7,200	
	Accounts Receivable	16,300	
	Merchandise Inventory	28,700	
	Store Equipment	5,400	
	Office Equipment	1,500	
	Allowance for Doubtful Accounts		1,500
	Accounts Payable		2,600
	Joseph A. Stevens, Capital		55,000

A similar entry would record the assets contributed and the liabilities transferred by Foster. In each entry, the noncash assets are recorded at values agreed upon by the partners. These values represent the acquisition cost to the new partnership. The agreed-upon values normally represent current market values and therefore usually differ from the book values of the assets in the records of the separate businesses. For example, the store equipment recorded at $5,400 in the preceding entry may have had a book value of $3,500 in Stevens's ledger (cost of $10,000 less accumulated depreciation of $6,500).

Receivables contributed to the partnership are recorded at their face amount. Future bad debts are provided for by crediting a contra account. Only accounts that are likely to be collected are normally transferred to the partnership. For example, assume that in the prior example the accounts receivable ledger of Stevens totaled $17,600. Of this total, accounts of $1,300 are considered worthless. The remaining receivables of $16,300 were transferred to the partnership accounts by a debit to the accounts receivable account in the general ledger. A subsidiary ledger is set up by debiting each customer's individual account. Finally, an allowance for possible uncollectible accounts is recorded by crediting Allowance for Doubtful Accounts for $1,500.

Dividing Net Income or Net Loss

Objective 3
Journalize the entries for dividing partnership net income and net loss.

Many partnerships have been dissolved because partners could not agree on an equitable distribution of income. Therefore, the method of dividing partnership income should be stated in the partnership agreement. In the absence of an agreement or if the agreement is silent on dividing net income or net losses, all partners share equally. However, if one partner contributes a larger portion of capital than the others, then net income should be divided to reflect the unequal capital contributions. Likewise, if the services rendered by one partner are more important than those of the others, net income should be divided to reflect the unequal service contributions. In the following paragraphs, we illustrate partnership agreements that recognize these differences.

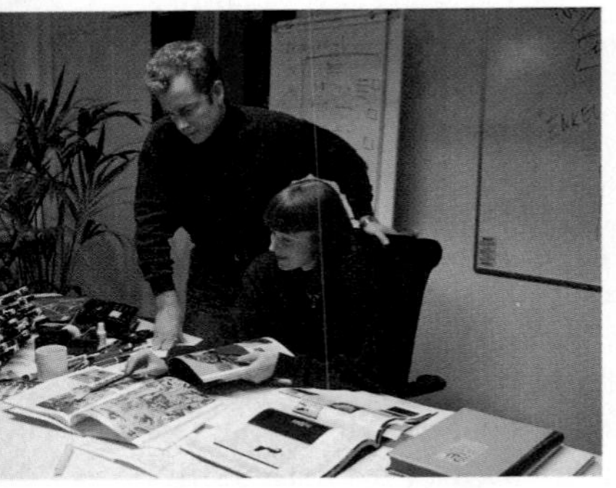

An equitable distribution of income among partners is vital to the success of the business. Therefore, a method of dividing partnership income should be stated in the partnership agreement.

INCOME DIVISION—SERVICES OF PARTNERS

One method of recognizing differences in partners' abilities and amount of time devoted to the business is to provide salary allowances to partners. Since partners are legally not employees of the partnership, such allowances are treated as divisions of the net income and are credited to the partners' capital accounts.

To illustrate, assume that the partnership agreement of Jennifer L. Stone and Crystal R. Mills provides for monthly salary allowances. Jennifer Stone is to receive a monthly allowance of $2,500, and Crystal Mills is to receive $2,000 a month. Any net income remaining after the salary allowances is to be divided equally. Assume also that the net income for the year is $75,000.

A report of the division of net income may be presented as a separate statement to accompany the balance sheet and the income statement. Another format is to add the division to the bottom of the income statement. If the latter format is used, the lower part of the income statement would appear as follows:

Net income			$75,000
Division of net income:			

	J. L. Stone	*C. R. Mills*	*Total*
Salary allowance	$30,000	$24,000	$54,000
Remaining income	10,500	10,500	21,000
Net income	$40,500	$34,500	$75,000

Net income division is recorded as a closing entry, even if the partners do not actually withdraw the amounts of their salary allowances. The entry for dividing net income is as follows:

Dec. 31	Income Summary	75,000	
	Jennifer L. Stone, Capital		40,500
	Crystal R. Mills, Capital		34,500

If Stone and Mills had withdrawn their salary allowances monthly, the withdrawals would have been debited to their drawing accounts during the year. At the end of the year, the debit balances of $30,000 and $24,000 in their drawing accounts would be transferred as reductions to their capital accounts.

Accountants should be careful to distinguish between salary allowances and partner withdrawals. The amount of net income distributed to each partner's capital account at the end of the year may differ from the amount the partner withdraws during the year. In some cases, the partnership agreement may limit the amount of withdrawals a partner may make during a period.

INCOME DIVISION—SERVICES OF PARTNERS AND INVESTMENT

Partners may agree that the most equitable plan of dividing income is to provide for (1) salary allowances and (2) interest on capital investments. Any remaining net income is then divided as agreed. For example, assume that the partnership agreement for Stone and Mills divides income as follows:

1. Monthly salary allowances of $2,500 for Stone and $2,000 for Mills.
2. Interest of 12% on each partner's capital balance on January 1.
3. Any remaining net income divided equally between the partners.

Stone had a credit balance of $80,000 in her capital account on January 1 of the current fiscal year, and Mills had a credit balance of $60,000 in her capital account. The $75,000 net income for the year is divided in the schedule below.

Net income			$75,000
Division of net income:			

	J. L. Stone	*C. R. Mills*	*Total*
Salary allowance	$30,000	$24,000	$54,000
Interest allowance	9,600	7,200	16,800
Remaining income	2,100	2,100	4,200
Net income	$41,700	$33,300	$75,000

For the above example, the entry to close the income summary account is shown below.

Dec. 31	Income Summary	75,000	
	Jennifer L. Stone, Capital		41,700
	Crystal R. Mills, Capital		33,300

INCOME DIVISION—ALLOWANCES EXCEED NET INCOME

In the examples so far, the net income has exceeded the total of the salary and interest allowances. If the net income is less than the total of the allowances, the **remaining balance** will be a negative amount. This amount must be divided among the partners as though it were a net loss.

To illustrate, assume the same salary and interest allowances as in the above example, but assume that the net income is $50,000. The salary and interest allowances total $39,600 for Stone and $31,200 for Mills. The sum of these amounts, $70,800, exceeds the net income of $50,000 by $20,800. It is necessary to divide the $20,800 excess between Stone and Mills. Under the partnership agreement, any net income or net loss remaining after deducting the allowances is divided equally between Stone and Mills. Thus, each partner is allocated one-half of the $20,800, and $10,400 is deducted from each partner's share of the allowances. The final division of net income between Stone and Mills is shown below.

Net income			$50,000
Division of net income:			
	J. L. Stone	*C. R. Mills*	*Total*
Salary allowance	$30,000	$24,000	$54,000
Interest allowance	9,600	7,200	16,800
Total	$39,600	$31,200	$70,800
Excess of allowances over income	10,400	10,400	20,800
Net income	$29,200	$20,800	$50,000

In closing Income Summary at the end of the year, $29,200 would be credited to Jennifer L. Stone, Capital, and $20,800 would be credited to Crystal R. Mills, Capital.

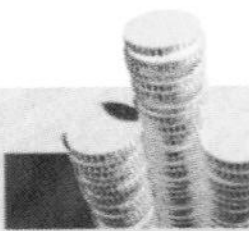

EXECUTIVE COMPENSATION—A PARTNERSHIP VS. A CORPORATION

In a report prepared for a Congressional subcommittee, Deloitte, Haskins & Sells (now Deloitte & Touche, a public accounting partnership) described its view of partner compensation and the division of the firm's income. Excerpts from that report are as follows:

. . . As a general rule, compensation in major mid-sized corporations (to which we might be compared based on revenue size, number of personnel, etc.) consists of current cash, deferred payments, payments made on behalf of an individual for retirement benefits, and perquisites. In addition, options to purchase stock at potentially favorable prices may also be an attractive compensation component. Unlike a corporation, partners . . . must provide from their own earnings for their own retirement benefits, as well as paying for self-employment taxes, group insurance, and other benefit programs. . . .

Each year the majority of the firm's earnings are distributed to the partners. Some small percentage is usually retained for working capital needs. No amounts are guaranteed, like a "preset" annual salary. If earnings decline, partners'. . . individual earnings also decline. Partners . . . are also required to invest capital in the firm. As such, part of their earnings represent a return on their investment. . . .

The factors mentioned above must be considered in making meaningful comparisons of partners' compensation with other business executives. To simply compare amounts would be misleading.

The average earnings of all of our partners for fiscal year 1985 was approximately $143,000. As to our five most highly compensated partners, their individual earnings ranged from $385,000 to $725,000, and their average was $500,000. . . .

Source : Deloitte, Haskins & Sells, *A Report for Congress and the Public,* September 1985.

REPORTING CHANGES IN PARTNERS' EQUITIES

The balance of the capital account of each partner is usually reported on the partnership balance sheet. In addition, the changes in the owner's equity of a partnership during the period should be reported. These changes are normally reported in a statement of owner's equity. The purpose of this statement is similar to that of the statement of owner's equity for a sole proprietorship.

There are a number of different forms of the partnership statement of owner's equity. One such format is shown below for the Stone and Mills partnership.

Stone and Mills
Statement of Owner's Equity
For the Year Ended December 31, 19—

	Jennifer L. Stone	*Crystal R. Mills*	*Total*
Capital, January 1, 19—	$ 80,000	$60,000	$140,000
Additional investment during the year		5,000	5,000
	$ 80,000	$65,000	$145,000
Net income for the year	41,700	33,300	75,000
	$121,700	$98,300	$220,000
Withdrawals during the year	30,000	24,000	54,000
Capital, December 31, 19—	$ 91,700	$74,300	$166,000

Partnership Dissolution

Objective 4
Journalize the entries for partnership dissolution, including admission of new partners and the withdrawal or death of partners.

One of the basic characteristics of the partnership form of organization is its limited life. Any change in the ownership dissolves the partnership. Thus, admission of a new partner dissolves the old firm. Likewise, death, bankruptcy, or withdrawal of a partner dissolves the partnership.

When a partnership dissolves, its affairs are not necessarily wound up. For example, a partnership of two partners may admit a third partner. Or if one of the partners in a business withdraws, the remaining partners may continue to operate the business. In such cases a new partnership is formed and a new partnership agreement should be prepared. Many partnerships provide for the admission of new partners and partner withdrawals in the partnership agreement so that the partnership may continue operations without executing a new agreement.

ADMISSION OF A PARTNER

A person may be admitted to a partnership only with the consent of all the current partners, through either of two methods:[2]

1. Purchasing an interest from one or more of the current partners.
2. Contributing assets to the partnership.

[2] Although an individual cannot become a partner without the consent of the other partners, the rights of a partner, such as the right to share in the income of a partnership, may be assigned to others without the consent of the other partners. Such issues are discussed in business law textbooks.

When the first method is used, the capital interest of the incoming partner is obtained from current partners, and *neither the total assets nor the total owner's equity of the business is affected*. When the second method is used, *both the total assets and the total owner's equity of the business are increased*. In the following paragraphs, we discuss each of these methods.

Purchasing an Interest in a Partnership

A person may be admitted to a partnership by buying an interest from one or more of the existing partners. The purchase and sale of the partnership interest occurs between the new partner and the existing partners acting as individuals. Thus, the purchase price is paid directly to the selling partners. Neither the total assets nor the total owner's equity of the business are affected. The only entry needed is to transfer owner's equity amounts from the capital accounts of the selling partners to the capital account established for the incoming partner.

As an example, assume that partners Tom Andrews and Nathan Bell have capital balances of $50,000 each. On June 1, each sells one-fifth of his equity to Joe Canter for $10,000 in cash. The exchange of cash is not a partnership transaction and thus is not recorded by the partnership. The only entry required in the partnership accounts is as follows:

June 1	Tom Andrews, Capital	10,000	
	Nathan Bell, Capital	10,000	
	Joe Canter, Capital		20,000

The effect of the transaction on the partnership accounts is presented in the following diagram:

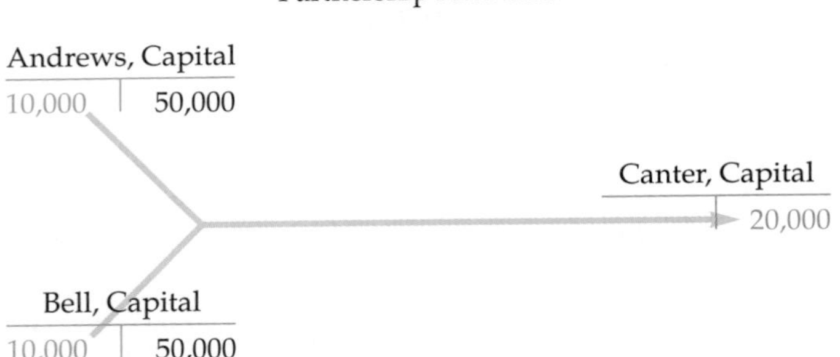

The preceding entry is not affected by the amount paid by Canter for the one-fifth interest. If the firm had been earning a high rate of return on the investment, Canter might have paid more than $20,000. If the existing partners had been eager to sell, he might have acquired the one-fifth interest for less than $20,000. In either case, the entry to transfer the capital interests is the same as shown above.

After Canter is admitted to the partnership, the total owner's equity of the firm is still $100,000. Canter now has a one-fifth interest, or a $20,000 capital balance. However, Canter may not be entitled to a one-fifth share of the partnership net income. Division of net income or net loss will be made according to the new partnership agreement.

Contributing Assets to a Partnership

Instead of buying an interest from the current partners, the incoming partner may contribute assets to the partnership. In this case, both the assets and the owner's equity of the firm increase. For example, assume that Donald Lewis and Gerald

Morton are partners with capital accounts of $35,000 and $25,000. On June 1, Sharon Nelson invests $20,000 cash in the business for an ownership equity of $20,000. The entry to record this transaction is as follows:

June 1	Cash	20,000	
	Sharon Nelson, Capital		20,000

The major difference between the admission of Nelson and the admission of Canter in the preceding examples may be observed by comparing the following diagram with the preceding diagram.

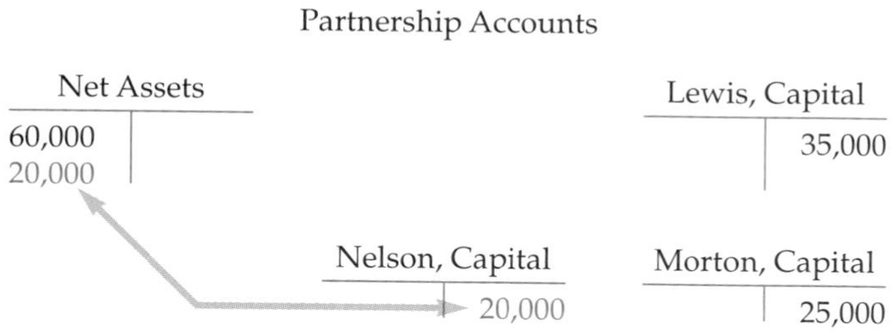

Partnership Accounts

Net Assets	
60,000	
20,000	

Lewis, Capital	
	35,000

Nelson, Capital	
	20,000

Morton, Capital	
	25,000

By admitting Nelson, the total owners' equity of the new partnership becomes $80,000, of which Nelson has a one-fourth interest, or $20,000. The extent of Nelson's share in partnership net income will be determined by the partnership agreement.

Revaluation of Assets

A partnership's asset account balances should be stated at current values when a new partner is admitted. If the accounts do not approximate current market values, the accounts should be adjusted. The net adjustment (increase or decrease) in asset values is divided among the capital accounts of the existing partners according to their income-sharing ratio. Failure to adjust the accounts for current values may result in the new partner sharing in asset gains or losses that arose in prior periods.

To illustrate, assume that in the preceding example for the Lewis and Morton partnership, the balance of the merchandise inventory account is $14,000 and the current replacement value is $17,000. Assuming that Lewis and Morton share net income equally, the revaluation is recorded as follows:

June 1	Merchandise Inventory	3,000	
	Donald Lewis, Capital		1,500
	Gerald Morton, Capital		1,500

If a number of assets are revalued, the adjustments may be debited or credited to a temporary account entitled Asset Revaluations. After all adjustments are made, this account is closed to the partner capital accounts.

Partner Bonuses

When a new partner is admitted to a partnership, the incoming partner may pay a bonus to the existing partners for the privilege of joining the partnership. Such a bonus is usually paid in expectation of high partnership profits in the future due to the contributions of the existing partners. Alternatively, the existing partners may pay the incoming partner a bonus to join the partnership. In this case, the bonus is usually paid in recognition of special qualities or skills that the incoming partner is bringing to the partnership. For example, celebrities such as actors, musicians, or sports figures often provide name recognition that is expected to increase partnership profits in the future. The amount of any bonus paid to the partnership is distributed among the partner capital accounts.[3]

To illustrate, assume that on March 1 the partnership of Marsha Jenkins and Helen Kramer is considering admitting a new partner, William Larson. After the assets of the partnership have been adjusted to current market values, the capital balance of Jenkins is $20,000 and the capital balance of Kramer is $24,000. Jenkins and Kramer agree to admit Larson to the partnership for $31,000. In return, Larson will receive a one-third equity in the partnership and will share equally with Jenkins and Kramer in partnership income or losses.

In this case Larson is paying Jenkins and Kramer a $6,000 bonus to join the partnership. This bonus is computed as follows:

Equity of Jenkins	$20,000
Equity of Kramer	24,000
Contribution of Larson	31,000
Total equity after admission of Larson	$75,000
Larson's equity interest after admission	× 1/3
Larson's equity after admission	$25,000
Contribution of Larson	$31,000
Larson's equity after admission	25,000
Bonus paid to Jenkins and Kramer	$ 6,000

The bonus is distributed to Jenkins and Kramer according to their income-sharing ratio. Assuming that Jenkins and Kramer share profits and losses equally, the entry to record the admission of Larson to the partnership is as follows:

Mar. 1	Cash	31,000	
	William Larson, Capital		25,000
	Marsha Jenkins, Capital		3,000
	Helen Kramer, Capital		3,000

If a new partner possesses unique qualities or skills, the existing partners may agree to pay the new partner a bonus to join the partnership. To illustrate, assume that after adjustment to market values the capital balance of Janice Cowen is $80,000 and the capital balance of Steve Dodd is $40,000. Cowen and Dodd agree to admit Sandra Ellis to the partnership on June 1 for an investment of $30,000. In return, Ellis will receive a one-fourth equity interest in the partnership and will share in one-fourth of the profits and losses.

In this case Cowen and Dodd are paying Ellis a $7,500 bonus to join the partnership. This bonus is computed as follows:

Equity of Cowen	$ 80,000
Equity of Dodd	40,000
Contribution of Ellis	30,000
Total equity after admission of Ellis	$150,000
Ellis's equity interest after admission	× 25%
Ellis's equity after admission	$ 37,500
Contribution of Ellis	30,000
Bonus paid to Ellis	$ 7,500

Assuming that the income-sharing ratio of Cowen and Dodd was 2:1 before the admission of Ellis, the entry to record the bonus and admission of Ellis to the partnership is as follows:

[3] Another method is sometimes used to record the admission of partners in situations such as that described in this paragraph. This method attributes goodwill rather than a bonus to the partners. This method is discussed in advanced accounting textbooks.

June 1	Cash	30,000	
	Janice Cowen, Capital	5,000	
	Steve Dodd, Capital	2,500	
	Sandra Ellis, Capital		37,500

WITHDRAWAL OF A PARTNER

When a partner retires or withdraws from a partnership, one or more of the remaining partners may buy the withdrawing partner's interest. The firm may then continue its operations uninterrupted. In such cases the purchase and sale of the partnership interest is between the partners as individuals. The only entry on the partnership's records is to debit the capital account of the partner withdrawing and to credit the capital account of the partner or partners buying the additional interest.

If the withdrawing partner sells the interest directly to the partnership, both the assets and the owner's equity of the partnership are reduced. Before the sale, the asset accounts should be adjusted to current values, so that the withdrawing partner's equity may be accurately determined. The net amount of the adjustment should be divided among the capital accounts of the partners according to their income-sharing ratio. If not enough partnership cash or other assets are available to pay the withdrawing partner, a liability may be created (credited) for the amount owed the withdrawing partner.

DEATH OF A PARTNER

The death of a partner dissolves the partnership. In the absence of an agreement, the accounts should be closed as of the date of death. The net income for this part of the current year should be determined and divided among the partners' capital accounts. It is not unusual, however, for the partnership agreement to indicate that the accounts should remain open until the end of the current fiscal year. At that time, the net income of the entire period is divided, as provided by the agreement, between the periods before and after the partner's death.

The balance in the capital account of the deceased partner is then transferred to a liability account with the deceased's estate. The remaining partner or partners may continue the business, or the affairs may be terminated. If the partnership continues in business, the procedures for settling with the estate are the same as those discussed for the withdrawal of a partner.

Liquidating Partnerships

Objective 5
Journalize the entries for liquidating partnerships.

When a partnership goes out of business, it usually sells the assets, pays the creditors, and distributes the remaining cash or other assets to the partners. This winding-up process is called the **liquidation** of the partnership. Although liquidating refers to the payment of liabilities, it is often used to include the entire winding-up process.

When the partnership goes out of business and the normal operations are discontinued, the accounts should be adjusted and closed. The only accounts remaining open will be the asset, contra asset, liability, and owner's equity accounts.

The sale of the assets is called **realization.** As cash is realized, it is used to pay the claims of creditors. After all liabilities have been paid, the remaining cash is distributed to the partners based on the balances in their capital accounts.

The liquidating process may extend over a long period of time as individual assets are sold. This delays the distribution of cash to partners, but does not affect the amount each partner will receive.

As a basis for illustration, assume that Farley, Greene, and Hall share income and losses in a ratio of 5:3:2 (5/10, 3/10, 2/10). On April 9, after discontinuing business operations of the partnership and closing the accounts, the following trial balance in summary form was prepared:

Cash	11,000	
Noncash Assets	64,000	
Liabilities		9,000
Jean Farley, Capital		22,000
Brad Greene, Capital		22,000
Alice Hall, Capital		22,000
Total	75,000	75,000

Based on these facts, we will show the accounting for liquidating the partnership by using three different selling prices for the noncash assets. To simplify, we assume that all noncash assets are sold in a single transaction and that all liabilities are paid at one time. In addition, Noncash Assets and Liabilities will be used as account titles in place of the various asset, contra asset, and liability accounts.

GAIN ON REALIZATION

Between April 10 and April 30 of the current year, Farley, Greene, and Hall sell all noncash assets for $72,000. Thus, a gain of $8,000 ($72,000 – $64,000) is realized. The gain is divided among the capital accounts in the income-sharing ratio of 5:3:2. The liabilities are paid, and the remaining cash is distributed to the partners. *The cash is distributed to the partners based on the balances in their capital accounts.* A statement of partnership liquidation, which summarizes the liquidation process, is shown in Exhibit 1.

Exhibit 1
Gain on Realization

Farley, Greene, and Hall
Statement of Partnership Liquidation
For Period April 10–30, 19—

							Capital				
	Cash	+	*Noncash Assets*	=	*Liabilities*	+	*Farley (50%)*	+	*Greene (30%)*	+	*Hall (20%)*
Balances before realization	$11,000		$64,000		$9,000		$22,000		$22,000		$22,000
Sale of assets and division of gain	+72,000		–64,000		—		+ 4,000		+ 2,400		+ 1,600
Balances after realization	$83,000		$ 0		$9,000		$26,000		$24,400		$23,600
Payment of liabilities	– 9,000		—		–9,000		—		—		—
Balances after payment of liabilities	$74,000		$ 0		$ 0		$26,000		$24,400		$23,600
Cash distributed to partners	–74,000		—		—		–26,000		–24,400		–23,600
Final balances	$ 0		$ 0		$ 0		$ 0		$ 0		$ 0

The entries to record the steps in the liquidating process are as follows:

Sale of assets:	Cash	72,000	
	Noncash Assets		64,000
	Gain on Realization		8,000
Division of gain:	Gain on Realization	8,000	
	Jean Farley, Capital		4,000
	Brad Greene, Capital		2,400
	Alice Hall, Capital		1,600

Payment of liabilities:	Liabilities	9,000	
	Cash		9,000
Distribution of cash to partners:	Jean Farley, Capital	26,000	
	Brad Greene, Capital	24,400	
	Alice Hall, Capital	23,600	
	Cash		74,000

As shown in Exhibit 1, the cash is distributed to the partners based on the balances of their capital accounts. These balances are determined after the gain on realization has been divided among the partners. *The income-sharing ratio should not be used as a basis for distributing the cash to partners.*

LOSS ON REALIZATION

Assume that in the preceding example, Farley, Greene, and Hall dispose of all noncash assets for $44,000. A loss of $20,000 ($64,000 – $44,000) is realized. The steps in liquidating the partnership are summarized in Exhibit 2.

Exhibit 2
Loss on Realization

Farley, Greene, and Hall
Statement of Partnership Liquidation
For Period April 10–30, 19—

	Cash	+	*Noncash Assets*	=	*Liabilities*	+	*Capital Farley (50%)*	+	*Greene (30%)*	+	*Hall (20%)*
Balances before realization	$11,000		$64,000		$9,000		$22,000		$22,000		$22,000
Sale of assets and division of loss	+44,000		–64,000		—		–10,000		– 6,000		– 4,000
Balances after realization	$55,000		$ 0		$9,000		$12,000		$16,000		$18,000
Payment of liabilities	– 9,000		—		–9,000		—		—		—
Balances after payment of liabilities	$46,000		$ 0		$ 0		$12,000		$16,000		$18,000
Cash distributed to partners	–46,000		—		—		–12,000		–16,000		–18,000
Final balances	$ 0		$ 0		$ 0		$ 0		$ 0		$ 0

The entries to liquidate the partnership are as follows:

Sale of assets:	Cash	44,000	
	Loss on Realization	20,000	
	Noncash Assets		64,000
Division of loss:	Jean Farley, Capital	10,000	
	Brad Greene, Capital	6,000	
	Alice Hall, Capital	4,000	
	Loss on Realization		20,000
Payment of liabilities:	Liabilities	9,000	
	Cash		9,000
Distribution of cash to partners:	Jean Farley, Capital	12,000	
	Brad Greene, Capital	16,000	
	Alice Hall, Capital	18,000	
	Cash		46,000

LOSS ON REALIZATION—CAPITAL DEFICIENCY

In the preceding example the capital account of each partner was large enough to absorb the partner's share of the loss from realization. The partners received cash to the extent of the remaining balances in their capital accounts. The share of loss on realization may exceed, however, the balance in the partner's capital account. The resulting debit balance in the capital account is called a **deficiency**. It represents a claim of the partnership against the partner.

To illustrate, assume that Farley, Greene, and Hall sell all of the noncash assets for $10,000. A loss of $54,000 ($64,000 – $10,000) is realized. The share of the loss allocated to Farley, $27,000 (50% of $54,000), exceeds the $22,000 balance in her capital account. This $5,000 deficiency represents an amount that Farley owes the partnership. Assuming that Farley pays the entire deficiency to the partnership, sufficient cash is available to distribute to the remaining partners according to their capital balances. The steps in liquidating the partnership in this case are summarized in Exhibit 3.

Exhibit 3
Loss on Realization—Capital Deficiency

Farley, Greene, and Hall
Statement of Partnership Liquidation
For Period April 10–30, 19—

							Capital				
	Cash	+	*Noncash Assets*	=	*Liabilities*	+	*Farley (50%)*	+	*Greene (30%)*	+	*Hall (20%)*
Balances before realization	$11,000		$64,000		$9,000		$22,000		$22,000		$22,000
Sale of assets and division of loss	+10,000		–64,000		—		–27,000		–16,200		–10,800
Balances after realization	$21,000		$ 0		$9,000		$ 5,000(Dr.)		$ 5,800		$11,200
Payment of liabilities	– 9,000		—		–9,000		—		—		—
Balances after payment of liabilities	$12,000		$ 0		$ 0		$ 5,000(Dr.)		$ 5,800		$11,200
Receipt of deficiency	+ 5,000		—		—		+ 5,000		—		—
Balances	$17,000		$ 0		$ 0		$ 0		$ 5,800		$11,200
Cash distributed to partners	–17,000		—		—		—		– 5,800		–11,200
Final balances	$ 0		$ 0		$ 0		$ 0		$ 0		$ 0

The entries to record the liquidation are as follows:

Sale of assets:	Cash	10,000	
	Loss on Realization	54,000	
	Noncash Assets		64,000
Division of loss:	Jean Farley, Capital	27,000	
	Brad Greene, Capital	16,200	
	Alice Hall, Capital	10,800	
	Loss on Realization		54,000
Payment of liabilities:	Liabilities	9,000	
	Cash		9,000
Receipt of deficiency:	Cash	5,000	
	Jean Farley, Capital		5,000
Distribution of cash to partners:	Brad Greene, Capital	5,800	
	Alice Hall, Capital	11,200	
	Cash		17,000

If cash is not collected from a deficient partner, the partnership cash will not be large enough to pay the other partners in full. Any uncollected deficiency becomes a loss to the partnership and is divided among the remaining partners' capital balances, based on their income-sharing ratio. The cash balance will then equal the sum of the capital account balances. Cash is then distributed to the remaining partners, based on the balances of their capital accounts.[4]

ERRORS IN LIQUIDATION

The type of error that occurs most often in liquidating a partnership is an improper distribution of cash to the partners. Such errors usually occur because the distribution of cash to partners in liquidation is confused with the division of gains and losses on realization.

Gains and losses on realization result from the disposal of assets to outsiders. *Realization gains and losses should be divided among the partner capital accounts in the same manner as net income or net loss from normal business operations—using the income-sharing ratio.* On the other hand, the distribution of cash (or other assets) to the partners in liquidation is not directly related to the income-sharing ratio. The distribution of assets to the partners in liquidation is the exact reverse of the contribution of assets by the partners at the time the partnership was established. *The distribution of assets to partners in liquidation is equal to the credit balances in their capital accounts after all gains and losses on realization have been divided and allowances have been made for any partner deficiencies.*

KEY POINTS

Objective 1. Identify and list the basic characteristics of the partnership form of organization.

A partnership is "an association of two or more persons to carry on as co-owners a business for profit." Partnership characteristics that have accounting implications are limited life, unlimited liability, co-ownership of property, mutual agency, and participation in income.

The principal advantages of a partnership include the ease with which it can be organized, bringing together capital of one or more individuals, and the fact that it is a nontaxable entity. The major disadvantages of a partnership are its limited life, its unlimited liability, and its limitations for raising large amounts of capital.

Objective 2. Journalize the entries for the formation of partnerships.

When a partnership is formed, accounts are debited for the assets contributed, accounts are credited for the liabilities assumed, and the partners' capital accounts are credited for their respective net amounts. Noncash assets are recorded at amounts agreed upon by the partners.

Objective 3. Journalize the entries for dividing partnership net income and net loss.

The net income (net loss) of a partnership is divided among the partners by debiting (crediting) Income Summary and crediting (debiting) the partners' capital accounts. The net income or net loss may be divided on the basis of services rendered by individual partners and/or on the basis of the investments of the individual partners. In the absence of any agreement, net income is divided equally among the partners.

The division of partnership net income should be disclosed in the partnership financial statements. In addition, changes in the owner's equity during the period should be reported in the statement of owner's equity.

Objective 4. Journalize the entries for partnership dissolution, including admission of new partners and the withdrawal or death of partners.

Any change in the personnel or ownership dissolves the partnership. A partnership may be dissolved by admission of a new partner, withdrawal of a partner, or death of a partner. A partnership's asset account balances should be stated at current values at the time of dissolution of the partnership.

A new partner may be admitted to a partnership by buying an interest from one or more of the existing partners. The admission of the new partner is recorded by debiting the capital accounts of the selling partners and crediting the capital account of the new partner.

A new partner may be admitted to a partnership by contributing assets to the partnership. The admission of the new

[4] The accounting for uncollectible deficiencies of partners is discussed and illustrated in advanced accounting texts.

partner is recorded by debiting asset accounts for the fair market value of the assets contributed and crediting the capital account of the new partner.

When a new partner is admitted to a partnership, the incoming partner may pay a bonus to the existing partners. Alternatively, the existing partners may pay a bonus to the new partner to join the partnership.

When a partner retires, dies, or withdraws from a partnership, one or more of the remaining partners may buy the withdrawing partner's interest. The only entry for the partnership is to debit the capital account of the withdrawing partner and to credit the capital account of the partner or partners purchasing the additional interest.

Objective 5. Journalize the entries for liquidating partnerships.
When a partnership liquidates, it sells its noncash assets, pays the creditors, and distributes the remaining cash or other assets to the partners. The journal entries for the sale of noncash assets and the payment of liabilities are similar to those illustrated in earlier chapters. Any gain or loss on the sale of the noncash assets should be divided among the partners according to their income-sharing ratio. The final asset distribution to partners is based on the balances of the partners' capital accounts after all noncash assets have been sold and liabilities paid. The journal entry for the final distribution of assets debits the partners' capital accounts and credits the asset accounts.

GLOSSARY OF KEY TERMS

Deficiency. The debit balance in the owner's equity account of a partner. *Objective 5*

Liquidation. The winding-up process when a partnership goes out of business. *Objective 5*

Partnership. An unincorporated business of two or more persons to carry on as co-owners a business for profit. *Objective 1*

Partnership agreement. The formal written contract creating a partnership. *Objective 1*

Realization. The sale of assets when a partnership is being liquidated. *Objective 5*

ILLUSTRATIVE PROBLEM

Radcliffe, Sonders, and Towers, who share in income and losses in the ratio of 2:3:5, decided to discontinue operations as of April 30 and liquidate their partnership. After the accounts were closed on April 30, the following trial balance was prepared:

Cash	5,900	
Noncash Assets	109,900	
Liabilities		26,800
Radcliffe, Capital		14,600
Sonders, Capital		27,900
Towers, Capital		46,500
Total	115,800	115,800

Between May 1 and May 18, the noncash assets were sold for $27,400, and the liabilities were paid.

Instructions

1. Assuming that the partner with the capital deficiency pays the entire amount owed to the partnership, prepare a statement of partnership liquidation.
2. Journalize the entries to record (a) the sale of the assets, (b) the division of loss on the sale of the assets, (c) the payment of the liabilities, (d) the receipt of the deficiency, and (e) the distribution of cash to the partners.

Solution

1.

Radcliff, Sonders, and Towers
Statement of Partnership Liquidation
For Period May 1–18, 19—

	Cash	+	Noncash Assets	=	Liabilities	+	Capital Radcliffe (20%)	+	Sonders (30%)	+	Towers (50%)
Balances before realization	$ 5,900		$109,900		$26,800		$14,600		$27,900		$46,500
Sale of assets and division of loss	+27,400		−109,900		—		−16,500		−24,750		−41,250
Balances after realization	$33,300		$ 0		$26,800		$ 1,900 (Dr.)		$ 3,150		$ 5,250
Payment of liabilities	−26,800		—		−26,800		—		—		—
Balances after payment of liabilities	$ 6,500		$ 0		$ 0		$ 1,900 (Dr.)		$ 3,150		$ 5,250
Receipt of deficiency	+ 1,900		—		—		+ 1,900		—		—
Balances	$ 8,400		$ 0		$ 0		$ 0		$ 3,150		$ 5,250
Cash distributed to partners	− 8,400		—		—		—		− 3,150		− 5,250
Final balances	$ 0		$ 0		$ 0		$ 0		$ 0		$ 0

2.

		Debit	Credit
a.	Cash	27,400	
	Loss on Realization	82,500	
	Noncash Assets		109,900
b.	Radcliffe, Capital	16,500	
	Sonders, Capital	24,750	
	Towers, Capital	41,250	
	Loss on Realization		82,500
c.	Liabilities	26,800	
	Cash		26,800
d.	Cash	1,900	
	Radcliffe, Capital		1,900
e.	Sonders, Capital	3,150	
	Towers, Capital	5,250	
	Cash		8,400

SELF-EXAMINATION QUESTIONS (ANSWERS AT END OF CHAPTER)

1. As part of the initial investment, a partner contributes office equipment that had cost $20,000 and on which accumulated depreciation of $12,500 had been recorded. If the partners agree on a valuation of $9,000 for the equipment, what amount should be debited to the office equipment account?
   A. $7,500 C. $12,500
   B. $9,000 D. $20,000

2. X and Y agree to form a partnership. X is to contribute $50,000 in assets and to devote one-half time to the partnership. Y is to contribute $20,000 and to devote full time to the partnership. How will X and Y share in the division of net income or net loss?
   A. 5:2 C. 1:1
   B. 1:2 D. 2.5:1

3. X and Y invest $100,000 and $50,000 respectively in a partnership and agree to a division of net income that provides for an allowance of interest at 10% on original investments, salary allowances of $12,000 and $24,000 respectively, with the remainder divided equally. What would be X's share of a periodic net income of $45,000?
   A. $22,500 C. $19,000
   B. $22,000 D. $10,000

4. X and Y are partners who share income in the ratio of 2:1 and who have capital balances of $65,000 and $35,000 respectively. If P, with the consent of Y, acquired one-half of X's interest for $40,000, for what amount would P's capital account be credited?
   A. $32,500 C. $50,000
   B. $40,000 D. $72,500

5. X and Y share gains and losses in the ratio of 2:1. After selling all assets for cash, dividing the losses on realization, and paying liabilities, the balances in the capital accounts were as follows: X, $10,000 Cr.; Y, $2,000 Cr. How much of the cash of $12,000 would be distributed to X?
   A. $2,000 C. $10,000
   B. $8,000 D. $12,000

DISCUSSION QUESTIONS

1. In a *general* partnership, what is the liability of the partners?
2. In a *limited* partnership, what is the liability of the partners?
3. Alan Biles and Joan Crandall joined together to form a partnership. Is it possible for them to lose a greater amount than the amount of their investment in the partnership? Explain.
4. Must a partnership (a) file a federal income tax return or (b) pay federal income taxes? Explain.
5. The partnership agreement between Roberta Baker and Jose Cruz provides for the sharing of partnership net income in the ratio of 3:2. Since the agreement is silent concerning the sharing of net losses, in what ratio will they be shared?
6. In the absence of an agreement, how will the net income be distributed between Michael Evans and Janice Farr, partners in the firm of E and F Environmental Consultants?
7. Paul Boyer, Fran Carrick, and Ed DiPano are contemplating the formation of a partnership. According to the partnership agreement, Boyer is to invest $60,000 and devote one-half time, Carrick is to invest $40,000 and devote three-fourths time, and DiPano is to make no investment and devote full time. Would DiPano be correct in assuming that, since he is not contributing any assets to the firm, he is risking nothing? Explain.
8. What are the disadvantages of the partnership over the corporation as a form of organization for a profit-making business?
9. As a part of the initial investment, a partner contributes delivery equipment that had originally cost $50,000 and on which accumulated depreciation of $37,500 had been recorded. The partners agree on a valuation of $15,000. How should the delivery equipment be recorded in the accounts of the partnership?
10. All partners agree that $200,000 of accounts receivable invested by a partner will be collectible to the extent of 90%. How should the accounts receivable be recorded in the general ledger of the partnership?
11. Ramon Flores and Joel Garcia are contemplating the formation of a partnership in which Flores is to devote full time and Garcia is to devote one-half time. In the absence of any agreement, will the partners share in net income or net loss in the ratio of 2:1? Explain.
12. During the current year, Helen Bray withdrew $3,000 monthly from the partnership of Bray and Cox Water Management Consultants. Is it possible that her share of partnership net income for the current year might be more or less than $36,000? Explain.
13. a. What accounts are debited and credited to record a partner's cash withdrawal in lieu of salary?
    b. At the end of the fiscal year, what accounts are debited and credited to record the division of net income among partners?
    c. The articles of partnership provide for a salary allowance of $5,000 per month to partner C. If C withdrew only $4,000 per month, would this affect the division of the partnership net income?
14. How can the division of net income be disclosed in the financial statements of a partnership?
15. Harry Imes, a partner in the firm of Greene, Herbert, and Imes, sells his investment (capital balance of $75,000) to Agnes Smith. (a) Does the withdrawal of Imes dissolve the partnership? (b) Are Greene and Herbert required to admit Smith as a partner?
16. Explain the difference between the admission of a new partner to a partnership (a) by purchase of an interest from another partner and (b) by contribution of assets to the partnership.
17. Why is it important to state all partnership assets in terms of current prices at the time of the admission of a new partner?
18. When a new partner is admitted to a partnership and agrees to pay a bonus to the original partners, how should the amount of the bonus be allocated to the capital accounts of the original partners?
19. Why might a partnership pay a bonus to a newly admitted partner?
20. a. Differentiate between *dissolution* and *liquidation* of a partnership.
    b. What does *realization* mean when used in connection with liquidation of a partnership?
21. In the liquidation process, (a) how are losses and gains on realization divided among the partners, and (b) how is cash distributed among the partners?

EXERCISES

EXERCISE 13–1
Entry for partner's original investment
Objective 2

Todd Jost and D. Caldwell decide to form a partnership by combining the assets of their separate businesses. Jost contributes the following assets to the partnership: cash, $6,000; accounts receivable with a face amount of $96,000 and an allowance for doubtful accounts of $6,600; merchandise inventory with a cost of $85,000; and equipment with a cost of $140,000 and accumulated depreciation of $90,000.

The partners agree that $5,000 of the accounts receivable are completely worthless and are not to be accepted by the partnership, that $8,000 is a reasonable allowance for the uncollectibility of the remaining accounts, that the merchandise inventory is to be recorded at the current market price of $76,500, and that the equipment is to be valued at $90,000.

Journalize the partnership's entry to record Jost's investment.

EXERCISE 13–2
Dividing partnership income
Objective 3

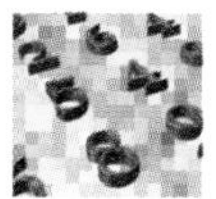

Dan Moore and T. J. Knell formed a partnership, investing $240,000 and $120,000 respectively. Determine their participation in the year's net income of $120,000 under each of the following independent assumptions: (a) no agreement concerning division of net income; (b) divided in the ratio of original capital investment; (c) interest at the rate of 10% allowed on original investments and the remainder divided in the ratio of 2:3; (d) salary allowances of $40,000 and $50,000 respectively, and the balance divided equally; (e) allowance of interest at the rate of 10% on original investments, salary allowances of $40,000 and $50,000 respectively, and the remainder divided equally.

EXERCISE 13–3
Dividing partnership income
Objective 3

Determine the participation of Moore and Knell in the year's net income of $180,000, according to each of the five assumptions as to income division listed in Exercise 13–2.

EXERCISE 13–4
Dividing partnership net loss
Objective 3

Jane Williams and Y. Osaka formed a partnership in which the partnership agreement provided for salary allowances of $40,000 and $60,000 respectively. Determine the division of a $20,000 net loss for the current year.

EXERCISE 13–5
Negotiating income-sharing ratio
Objective 3

Sixty-year-old Jim Ebers retired from his computer consulting business in Boston and moved to Florida. There he met 27-year-old Ann Bowers, who had just graduated from Eldon Community College with an associate degree in computer science. Jim and Ann formed a partnership called E&B Computer Consultants. Jim contributed $15,000 for startup costs and devoted one-half time to the business. Ann devoted full time to the business. The monthly drawings were $1,500 for Jim and $3,000 for Ann.

At the end of the first year of operations, the two partners disagreed on the division of net income. Jim reasoned that the division should be equal. Although he devoted only one-half time to the business, he contributed all of the startup funds. Ann reasoned that the income-sharing ratio should be 2:1 in her favor because she devoted full-time to the business and her monthly drawings were twice those of Jim.

Can you identify any flaws in the partners' reasoning regarding the income-sharing ratio?

EXERCISE 13–6
Partnership entries and statement of owner's equity
Objective 3

The capital accounts of Walt Bigney and Dan Harris have balances of $80,000 and $95,000 respectively on January 1, the beginning of the current fiscal year. On April 10, Bigney invested an additional $10,000. During the year, Bigney and Harris withdrew $72,000 and $84,000 respectively, and net income for the year was $160,000. The articles of partnership make no reference to the division of net income.

a. Journalize the entries to close (1) the income summary account and (2) the drawing accounts.
b. Prepare a statement of owner's equity for the current year for the partnership of Bigney and Harris.

EXERCISE 13–7
Admitting new partners
Objective 4

Jenny Kirk and Harold Spock are partners who share in the income equally and have capital balances of $90,000 and $62,500, respectively. Kirk, with the consent of Spock, sells one-third of her interest to Benjamin McCoy. What entry is required by the partnership if the sale price is (a) $20,000? (b) $40,000?

EXERCISE 13–8
Admitting new partners
Objective 4

The international public accounting partnership of Arthur Andersen & Co. disclosed worldwide revenues of $6,738,400,000 for 1994. The revenues were attributable to 2,517 active partners.

a. What was the average revenue per active partner for 1994? Round to nearest $1,000.
b. Assuming that the total partners' capital is $800,000,000 and that it approximates the fair market value of the firm's net assets, what would be considered a minimum contribution for admitting a new partner to the firm? Round to nearest $10,000.
c. Why might the amount to be contributed by a new partner for admission to the firm exceed the amount determined in (b)?

EXERCISE 13–9
Admitting new partners who buy an interest and contribute assets
Objective 4

The capital accounts of Susan Yu and Ben Hardy have balances of $100,000 and $90,000 respectively. Ken Mahl and Jeff Wood are to be admitted to the partnership. Mahl buys one-fourth of Yu's interest for $27,500 and one-fifth of Hardy's interest for $20,000. Wood contributes $35,000 cash to the partnership, for which he is to receive an ownership equity of $35,000.

a. Journalize the entries to record the admission of (1) Mahl and (2) Wood.
b. What are the capital balances of each partner after the admission of the new partners?

EXERCISE 13–10
Admitting new partner who contributes assets
Objective 4

After the tangible assets have been adjusted to current market prices, the capital accounts of Cecil Jacobs and Maria Estaban have balances of $61,000 and $59,000 respectively. Lee White is to be admitted to the partnership, contributing $45,000 cash to the partnership, for which she is to receive an ownership equity of $55,000. All partners share equally in income.

a. Journalize the admission of White, who is to receive a bonus of $10,000.
b. What are the capital balances of each partner after the admission of the new partner?

EXERCISE 13–11
Withdrawal of partner
Objective 4

Glenn Otis is to retire from the partnership of Otis and Associates as of March 31, the end of the current fiscal year. After closing the accounts, the capital balances of the partners are as follows: Glenn Otis, $200,000; Tammie Sawyer, $125,000; and Joe Parrott, $140,000. They have shared net income and net losses in the ratio of 3:2:2. The partners agree that the merchandise inventory should be increased by $15,000, and the allowance for doubtful accounts should be increased by $3,100. Otis agrees to accept a note for $150,000 in partial settlement of his ownership equity. The remainder of his claim is to be paid in cash. Sawyer and Parrott are to share equally in the net income or net loss of the new partnership.

Journalize the entries to record (a) the adjustment of the assets to bring them into agreement with current market prices and (b) the withdrawal of Otis from the partnership.

EXERCISE 13–12
Distribution of cash upon liquidation
Objective 5

Hires and Bellman are partners, sharing gains and losses equally. At the time they decide to terminate their partnership, their capital balances are $5,000 and $20,000 respectively. After all noncash assets are sold and all liabilities are paid, there is a cash balance of $20,000.

a. What is the amount of a gain or loss on realization?
b. How should the gain or loss be divided between Hires and Bellman?
c. How should the cash be divided between Hires and Bellman?

EXERCISE 13–13
Distribution of cash upon liquidation
Objective 5

Jacob Goldburg and Harlan Luce, with capital balances of $57,000 and $40,000 respectively, decide to liquidate their partnership. After selling the noncash assets and paying the liabilities, there is $67,000 of cash remaining. If the partners share income and losses equally, how should the cash be distributed?

EXERCISE 13–14
Liquidating partnerships—capital deficiency
Objective 5

Bakki, Towers, and Nell share equally in net income and net losses. After the partnership sells all assets for cash, divides the losses on realization, and pays the liabilities, the balances in the capital accounts are as follows: Bakki, $20,000 Cr.; Towers, $57,500 Cr.; Nell, $17,500 Dr.

a. What term is applied to the debit balance in Nell's capital account?
b. What is the amount of cash on hand?
c. Journalize the transaction that must take place for Bakki and Towers to receive cash in the liquidation process equal to their capital account balances.

EXERCISE 13–15
Distribution of cash upon liquidation
Objective 5

Allyn Meyer, Jim Ball, and Laura David arranged to import and sell orchid corsages for a university dance. They agreed to share equally the net income or net loss of the venture. Meyer and Ball advanced $175 and $125 of their own respective funds to pay for advertising and other expenses. After collecting for all sales and paying creditors, the partnership has $600 in cash.

a. How should the money be distributed?
b. Assuming that the partnership has only $120 instead of $600, do any of the three partners have a capital deficiency? If so, how much?

EXERCISE 13–16
Liquidating partnerships—capital deficiency
Objective 5

Duncan, Tribe, and Ho are partners sharing income 3:2:1. After the firm's loss from liquidation is distributed, the capital account balances were: Duncan, $15,000 Dr.; Tribe, $50,000 Cr.; and Ho, $40,000 Cr. If Duncan is personally bankrupt and unable to pay any of the $15,000, what will be the amount of cash received by Tribe and Ho upon liquidation?

EXERCISE 13–17
Statement of partnership liquidation
Objective 5

After closing the accounts on July 1, prior to liquidating the partnership, the capital account balances of Gibbs, Hill, and Manson are $24,000, $28,000, and $14,000 respectively. Cash, noncash assets, and liabilities total $11,000, $85,000, and $30,000 respectively. Between July 1 and July 29, the noncash assets are sold for $61,000, the liabilities are paid, and the remaining cash is distributed to the partners. The partners share net income and loss in the ratio of 3:2:1. Prepare a statement of partnership liquidation for the period July 1–29.

PROBLEMS SERIES A

PROBLEM 13–1A
Entries and balance sheet for partnership
Objectives 2, 3

On November 1 of the current year, E. Tsao and Mark Ivens form a partnership. Tsao agrees to invest $15,000 cash and merchandise inventory valued at $55,000. Ivens invests certain business assets at valuations agreed upon, transfers business liabilities, and contributes sufficient cash to bring his total capital to $85,000. Details regarding the book values of the business assets and liabilities, and the agreed valuations, follow:

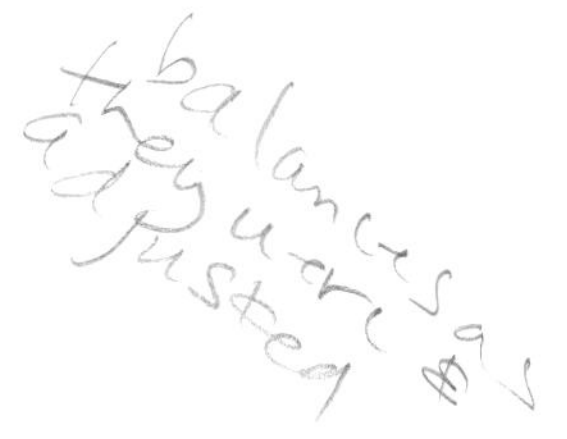

	Ivens' Ledger Balance	*Agreed-Upon Valuation*
Accounts Receivable	$33,250	$31,500
Allowance for Doubtful Accounts	500	800
Merchandise Inventory	42,500	42,900
Equipment	50,000	25,000
Accumulated Depreciation	29,700	
Accounts Payable	9,700	9,700
Notes Payable	10,000	10,000

The partnership agreement includes the following provisions regarding the division of net income: interest of 10% on original investments, salary allowances of $24,000 and $18,000 respectively, and the remainder equally.

Instructions

1. Journalize the entries to record the investments of Tsao and Ivens in the partnership accounts.
2. Prepare a balance sheet as of November 1, the date of formation of the partnership of Tsao and Ivens.
3. After adjustments and the closing of revenue and expense accounts at October 31, the end of the first full year of operations, the income summary account has a credit balance of $75,500, and the drawing accounts have debit balances of $26,000 (Tsao) and $17,500 (Ivens). Journalize the entries to close the income summary account and the drawing accounts at October 31.

PROBLEM 13–2A
Dividing partnership income
Objective 3

Phil Haddox and Russ French have decided to form a partnership. They have agreed that Haddox is to invest $120,000 and that French is to invest $180,000. Haddox is to devote full time to the business, and French is to devote one-half time. The following plans for the division of income are being considered:

a. Equal division.
b. In the ratio of original investments.

c. In the ratio of time devoted to the business.
d. Interest of 10% on original investments and the remainder in the ratio of 3:2.
e. Interest of 10% on original investments, salary allowances of $60,000 to Haddox and $30,000 to French, and the remainder equally.
f. Plan (e), except that Haddox is also to be allowed a bonus equal to 20% of the amount by which net income exceeds the salary allowances.

Instructions

For each plan, determine the division of the net income under each of the following assumptions: (1) net income of $150,000 and (2) net income of $90,000. Present the data in tabular form, using the following columnar headings:

	$150,000		*$90,000*	
Plan	*Haddox*	*French*	*Haddox*	*French*

PROBLEM 13–3A
Financial statements for partnerships
Objective 3

The ledger of Dan Reeves and Ron Strange, attorneys-at-law, contains the following accounts and balances after adjustments have been recorded on December 31, the end of the current fiscal year:

Cash	$ 24,500
Accounts Receivable	40,500
Supplies	2,400
Land	50,000
Building	150,000
Accumulated Depreciation—Building	77,500
Office Equipment	40,000
Accumulated Depreciation—Office Equipment	22,400
Accounts Payable	1,000
Salaries Payable	1,500
Dan Reeves, Capital	75,000
Dan Reeves, Drawing	50,000
Ron Strange, Capital	55,000
Ron Strange, Drawing	60,000
Professional Fees	316,750
Salary Expense	84,500
Depreciation Expense—Building	10,500
Property Tax Expense	10,000
Heating and Lighting Expense	9,900
Supplies Expense	5,750
Depreciation Expense—Office Equipment	5,000
Miscellaneous Expense	6,100

The balance in Strange's capital account includes an additional investment of $5,000 made on April 5 of the current year.

Instructions

1. Prepare an income statement for the current fiscal year, indicating the division of net income. The articles of partnership provide for salary allowances of $25,000 to Reeves and $35,000 to Strange, allowances of 12% on each partner's capital balance at the beginning of the fiscal year, and equal division of the remaining net income or net loss.
2. Prepare a statement of owner's equity for the current fiscal year.
3. Prepare a balance sheet in report form as of the end of the current fiscal year.

PROBLEM 13–4A
Admitting new partner
Objective 4

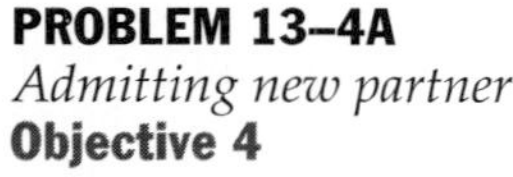

Adrian Capps and Lisa Knight have operated a successful firm for many years, sharing net income and net losses equally. Todd Aguero is to be admitted to the partnership on June 1 of the current year, in accordance with the following agreement:

a. Assets and liabilities of the old partnership are to be valued at their book values as of May 31, except for the following:

- Accounts receivable amounting to $3,250 are to be written off, and the allowance for doubtful accounts is to be increased to 5% of the remaining accounts.
- Merchandise inventory is to be valued at $63,400.
- Equipment is to be valued at $108,000.

b. Aguero is to purchase $25,000 of the ownership interest of Capps for $37,500 cash and to contribute $25,000 cash to the partnership for a total ownership equity of $50,000.
c. The income-sharing ratio of Capps, Knight, and Aguero is to be 2:1:1.

The post-closing trial balance of Capps and Knight as of May 31 is as follows:

Capps and Knight
Post-Closing Trial Balance
May 31, 19—

Cash	9,500	
Accounts Receivable	29,250	
Allowance for Doubtful Accounts		500
Merchandise Inventory	60,100	
Prepaid Insurance	2,000	
Equipment	162,000	
Accumulated Depreciation—Equipment		72,500
Accounts Payable		9,850
Notes Payable		20,000
Adrian Capps, Capital		120,000
Lisa Knight, Capital		40,000
	262,850	262,850

Instructions

1. Journalize the entries as of May 31 to record the revaluations, using a temporary account entitled Asset Revaluations. The balance in the accumulated depreciation account is to be eliminated.
2. Journalize the additional entries to record the remaining transactions relating to the formation of the new partnership. Assume that all transactions occur on June 1.
3. Present a balance sheet for the new partnership as of June 1.

PROBLEM 13–5A
Statement of partnership liquidation
Objective 5

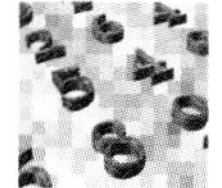

After the accounts are closed on May 10, prior to liquidating the partnership, the capital accounts of Mark Wilson, Donna Crowder, and Janice Patel are $27,800, $8,300, and $13,900 respectively. Cash and noncash assets total $6,500 and $89,100 respectively. Amounts owed to creditors total $45,600. The partners share income and losses in the ratio of 2:1:1. Between May 10 and May 30, the noncash assets are sold for $37,500, the partner with the capital deficiency pays his or her deficiency to the partnership, and the liabilities are paid.

Instructions

1. Prepare a statement of partnership liquidation, indicating (a) the sale of assets and division of loss, (b) the receipt of the deficiency (from the appropriate partner), (c) the payment of liabilities, and (d) the distribution of cash.
2. If the partner with the capital deficiency declares bankruptcy and is unable to pay the deficiency, explain how the deficiency would be divided between the partners.

PROBLEM 13–6A
Partnership liquidation
Objective 5

If the working papers correlating with this textbook are not used, omit Problem 13–6A.

Bill Mentzer, Ted Holder, and Dan Wong decided to discontinue business operations and liquidate their partnership. A summary of the various transactions that have occurred thus far is presented in the working papers in a partial statement of liquidation.

Instructions

1. Prepare a statement of partnership liquidation. Assume that the partner with the capital deficiency is bankrupt and the deficiency is divided between the remaining partners. Allocate $3,000 of the deficiency to Mentzer and $1,200 to Wong.
2. Journalize the entries to record (a) the sale of assets, (b) the division of loss on the sale of assets, (c) the payment of liabilities, (d) the division of the partner's deficiency, and (e) the distribution of cash to partners.

PROBLEM 13–7A
Statement of partnership liquidation
Objective 5

On May 3, the firm of Imhoff, Baxter, and Wise decided to liquidate their partnership. The partners have capital balances of $30,000, $90,000, and $120,000 respectively. The cash balance is $10,000, the book values of noncash assets total $285,000, and liabilities total $55,000. The partners share income and losses in the ratio of 1:2:2.

Instructions

Prepare a statement of partnership liquidation, covering the period May 3 through May 29 for each of the following independent assumptions:

1. All of the noncash assets are sold for $345,000 in cash, the creditors are paid, and the remaining cash is distributed to the partners.
2. All of the noncash assets are sold for $175,000 in cash, the creditors are paid, and the remaining cash is distributed to the partners.
3. All of the noncash assets are sold for $105,000 in cash, the creditors are paid, the partner with the debit capital balance pays the amount owed to the firm, and the remaining cash is distributed to the partners.

PROBLEMS SERIES B

PROBLEM 13–1B
Entries and balance sheet for partnership
Objectives 2, 3

On May 1 of the current year, Crystal Hall and Doug Tucker form a partnership. Hall agrees to invest $10,500 in cash and merchandise inventory valued at $36,500. Tucker invests certain business assets at valuations agreed upon, transfers business liabilities, and contributes sufficient cash to bring his total capital to $40,000. Details regarding the book values of the business assets and liabilities, and the agreed valuations, follow:

	Tucker's Ledger Balance	*Agreed-Upon Valuation*
Accounts Receivable	$20,750	$18,000
Allowance for Doubtful Accounts	950	1,000
Equipment	79,100	40,000
Accumulated Depreciation	35,200	
Accounts Payable	14,000	14,000
Notes Payable	15,000	15,000

The partnership agreement includes the following provisions regarding the division of net income: interest on original investments at 10%, salary allowances of $18,000 and $21,000 respectively, and the remainder equally.

Instructions

1. Journalize the entries to record the investments of Hall and Tucker in the partnership accounts.
2. Prepare a balance sheet as of May 1, the date of formation of the partnership of Hall and Tucker.
3. After adjustments and the closing of revenue and expense accounts at April 30, the end of the first full year of operations, the income summary account has a credit balance of $72,700, and the drawing accounts have debit balances of $20,000 (Hall) and $26,000 (Tucker). Journalize the entries to close the income summary account and the drawing accounts at April 30.

PROBLEM 13–2B
Dividing partnership income
Objective 3

Garland and Driscoe have decided to form a partnership. They have agreed that Garland is to invest $200,000 and that Driscoe is to invest $100,000. Garland is to devote one-half time to the business and Driscoe is to devote full time. The following plans for the division of income are being considered:

a. Equal division.
b. In the ratio of original investments.
c. In the ratio of time devoted to the business.
d. Interest of 12% on original investments and the remainder equally.

e. Interest of 12% on original investments, salary allowances of $30,000 to Garland and $60,000 to Driscoe, and the remainder equally.

f. Plan (e), except that Driscoe is also to be allowed a bonus equal to 20% of the amount by which net income exceeds the salary allowances.

Instructions

For each plan, determine the division of the net income under each of the following assumptions: (1) net income of $90,000 and (2) net income of $240,000. Present the data in tabular form, using the following columnar headings:

	$90,000		*$240,000*	
Plan	*Garland*	*Driscoe*	*Garland*	*Driscoe*

PROBLEM 13–3B
Financial statements for partnership
Objective 3

The ledger of Peter Tracy and May Hepburn, attorneys-at-law, contains the following accounts and balances after adjustments have been recorded on December 31, the end of the current fiscal year:

Cash	$ 22,000
Accounts Receivable	38,900
Supplies	1,900
Land	25,000
Building	130,000
Accumulated Depreciation—Building	69,200
Office Equipment	39,000
Accumulated Depreciation—Office Equipment	21,500
Accounts Payable	2,100
Salaries Payable	2,000
Peter Tracy, Capital	75,000
Peter Tracy, Drawing	60,000
May Hepburn, Capital	55,000
May Hepburn, Drawing	75,000
Professional Fees	285,650
Salary Expense	80,500
Depreciation Expense—Building	10,500
Property Tax Expense	8,000
Heating and Lighting Expense	7,900
Supplies Expense	2,850
Depreciation Expense—Office Equipment	2,800
Miscellaneous Expense	6,100

The balance in Hepburn's capital account includes an additional investment of $5,000 made on August 10 of the current year.

Instructions

1. Prepare an income statement for the current fiscal year, indicating the division of net income. The articles of partnership provide for salary allowances of $30,000 to Tracy and $40,000 to Hepburn, allowances of 12% on each partner's capital balance at the beginning of the fiscal year, and equal division of the remaining net income or net loss.
2. Prepare a statement of owner's equity for the current fiscal year.
3. Prepare a balance sheet in report form as of the end of the current fiscal year.

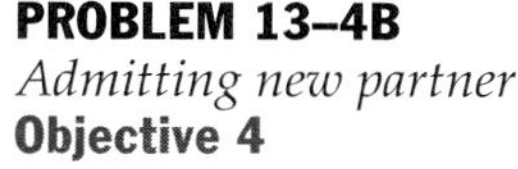

PROBLEM 13–4B
Admitting new partner
Objective 4

Tom Denney and Cheryl Burks have operated a successful firm for many years, sharing net income and net losses equally. Sara Wold is to be admitted to the partnership on May 1 of the current year, in accordance with the following agreement:

a. Assets and liabilities of the old partnership are to be valued at their book values as of April 30, except for the following:
   - Accounts receivable amounting to $1,900 are to be written off, and the allowance for doubtful accounts is to be increased to 5% of the remaining accounts.

- Merchandise inventory is to be valued at $53,100.
- Equipment is to be valued at $100,000.

b. Wold is to purchase $20,000 of the ownership interest of Burks for $25,000 cash and to contribute $20,000 cash to the partnership for a total ownership equity of $40,000.
c. The income-sharing ratio of Denney, Burks, and Wold is to be 2:1:1.

The post-closing trial balance of Denney and Burks as of April 30 is as follows:

Denney and Burks
Post-Closing Trial Balance
April 30, 19—

Cash	7,900	
Accounts Receivable	22,500	
Allowance for Doubtful Accounts		550
Merchandise Inventory	50,600	
Prepaid Insurance	1,650	
Equipment	145,000	
Accumulated Depreciation—Equipment		65,000
Accounts Payable		12,100
Notes Payable		10,000
Tom Denney, Capital		80,000
Cheryl Burks, Capital		60,000
	227,650	227,650

Instructions

1. Journalize the entries as of April 30 to record the revaluations, using a temporary account entitled Asset Revaluations. The balance in the accumulated depreciation account is to be eliminated.
2. Journalize the additional entries to record the remaining transactions relating to the formation of the new partnership. Assume that all transactions occur on May 1.
3. Present a balance sheet for the new partnership as of May 1.

PROBLEM 13–5B
Statement of partnership liquidation
Objective 5

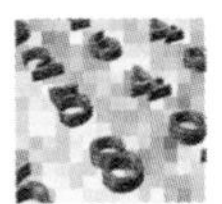

After the accounts are closed on May 3, prior to liquidating the partnership, the capital accounts of Ann Booth, Harold Owen, and Carla Ramariz are $20,000, $3,900, and $10,000 respectively. Cash and noncash assets total $1,900 and $62,000 respectively. Amounts owed to creditors total $30,000. The partners share income and losses in the ratio of 2:1:1. Between May 3 and May 29, the noncash assets are sold for $26,000, the partner with the capital deficiency pays her deficiency to the partnership, and the liabilities are paid.

Instructions

1. Prepare a statement of partnership liquidation, indicating (a) the sale of assets and division of loss, (b) the receipt of the deficiency (from the appropriate partner), (c) the payment of liabilities, and (d) the distribution of cash.
2. If the partner with the capital deficiency declares bankruptcy and is unable to pay the deficiency, explain how the deficiency would be divided between the partners.

PROBLEM 13–6B
Partnership liquidation
Objective 5

If the working papers correlating with this textbook are not used, omit Problem 13–6B.
Bill Mentzer, Ted Holder, and Dan Wong decided to discontinue business operations and liquidate their partnership. A summary of the various transactions that have occurred thus far is presented in the working papers in a partial statement of liquidation.

Instructions

1. Assuming that the partner with the capital deficiency pays the entire amount owed to the partnership, prepare a statement of partnership liquidation.
2. Journalize the entries to record (a) the sale of assets, (b) the division of loss on the sale of assets, (c) the payment of liabilities, (d) the receipt of the deficiency, and (e) the distribution of cash to partners.

PROBLEM 13–7B
Statement of partnership liquidation
Objective 5

On October 1, the firm of Ewing, Johnson, and Landry, decided to liquidate their partnership. The partners have capital balances of $100,000, $90,000, and $30,000 respectively. The cash balance is $20,000, the book values of noncash assets total $250,000, and liabilities total $50,000. The partners share income and losses in the ratio of 2:2:1.

Instructions
Prepare a statement of partnership liquidation, covering the period October 1 through October 30 for each of the following independent assumptions:

1. All of the noncash assets are sold for $330,000 in cash, the creditors are paid, and the remaining cash is distributed to the partners.
2. All of the noncash assets are sold for $120,000 in cash, the creditors are paid, and the remaining cash is distributed to the partners.
3. All of the noncash assets are sold for $50,000 in cash, the creditors are paid, the partner with the debit capital balance pays the amount owed to the firm, and the remaining cash is distributed to the partners.

CASES

CASE 13–1
Miller and Harrison
Partnership agreement

Ted Miller, M.D., and Glen Harrison, M.D., are sole owners of two medical practices that operate in the same medical building. The two doctors agree to combine assets and liabilities of the two businesses to form a partnership. The partnership agreement calls for dividing income equally between the two doctors. After several months, the following conversation takes place between the two doctors:

Miller: I've noticed that your patient load has dropped over the last couple of months. When we formed our partnership, we were seeing about the same number of patients per week. However, now our patient records show that you have been seeing about half as many patients as I have. Are there any issues that I should be aware of?

Harrison: There's nothing going on. When I was working on my own, I was really putting in the hours. One of the reasons I formed this partnership was to enjoy life a little more and scale back a little bit.

Miller: I see. Well, I find that I'm working as hard as I did when I was on my own, yet making less than I did previously. Essentially, you're sharing in half of my billings and I'm sharing in half of yours. Since you are working much less than I am, I end up on the short end of the bargain.

Harrison: Well, I don't know what to say. An agreement is an agreement. The partnership is based on a 50/50 split. That's what a partnership is all about.

Miller: If that's so, then it applies equally well to the effort end of the equation as to the income end.

Discuss whether Harrison is acting in an ethical manner. How could Miller rewrite the partnership agreement to avoid this dispute?

CASE 13–2
Adair and Fontana
Dividing partnership income

John Adair and Raul Fontana decide to form a partnership. Adair will contribute $300,000 to the partnership, while Fontana will contribute only $30,000. However, Fontana will be responsible for running the day-to-day operations of the partnership, which are anticipated to require about 50 hours per week. In contrast, Adair will only work 5 hours per week for the partnership. The two partners are attempting to determine a formula for dividing partnership net income. Adair believes the partners should divide income in the ratio of 7:3, favoring Adair, since Adair provides the majority of the capital. Fontana believes the income should be divided 7:3, favoring Fontana, since Fontana provides the majority of effort in running the partnership business.

How would you advise the partners in developing a method for dividing income?

CASE 13–3
Big Six CPA Firms
Unlimited liability

The table at the right shows the gross accounting and audit revenues and litigation-related judgments for the "Big Six" CPA firms.

a. Determine the litigation-related judgments as a percent of gross accounting and audit revenues for each year.
b. Interpret this information.

Revenues and Litigation Judgments
Big Six CPA Firms
($ million)

	1990	*1991*	*1992*	*1993*
Gross accounting and audit revenues	$5,257	$5,319	$5,470	$5,588
Litigation-related judgments	367	485	783	1,082

Source: *Public Accounting Report*, June 30, 1994.

CASE 13–4
Ellen, Cook, and Cierra
Admitting new partner

Ted Cierra wishes to join the Ellen and Cook partnership. Ellen and Cook share all partnership income equally. Cierra would be admitted as an equal partner. The capital accounts are $50,000 each for Ellen and Cook prior to admitting Cierra. The fair market value of the net assets is $160,000. The following exchange took place during the final negotiations between the partners and Cierra:

Cierra: I'm looking forward to joining the partnership. I've drawn a check for my share, which I believe is $50,000.

Ellen: Well, Ted, we're also looking forward to you joining us. How did you arrive at the $50,000 number?

Cierra: Easy. Just look at the partnership books. You each have a capital account of $50,000, which yields a total partnership value of $100,000. If I'm to be an equal partner, I should contribute as much as each of you did—namely, $50,000. That will bring the total capital to $150,000, with each of us having a 1/3 investment in the partnership. What could be more fair?

Cook: Ted, I'm not very comfortable with that number. We believe you should give us a check for $80,000.

Cierra: What? We never talked about any kind of partner bonuses upon my entry into the firm. We all previously agreed that you need me and I need you. That was that. Now you're bringing up some partner bonus scheme at the last minute of negotiations. I'm not too sure I want to be part of a partnership that deals in this way.

Discuss whether Ellen and Cook behaved in an ethical manner.

CASE 13–5
Felix and Diaz
Financial analysis

The partnership of Felix and Diaz, CPAs, has 200 partners and 1,500 staff professionals. Each partner shares equally in partnership income. Assume that the average income for partners in CPA firms across the country is $132,000 per year, and the average income for staff professionals is $38,000 per year. In addition, assume that the prevailing interest rate is 12% per year. The partnership income statement for the year is as follows:

Revenues		$94,000,000
Staff professional salaries	$60,000,000	
Nonprofessional salaries	6,000,000	
Supplies	1,000,000	
Travel	2,000,000	
Litigation losses	18,000,000	87,000,000
Net income		$ 7,000,000

The total partnership capital balance is $20,000,000 for 200 partners or $100,000 per partner.

a. Evaluate the financial performance of the partnership from a partner's perspective. In other words, if you were a partner in this firm, would you be satisfied or dissatisfied with partnership performance? Support your answer.
b. What are some explanations for the partnership's performance?

CASE 13–6
Abbott and Martin
Dividing partnership income

Twelve years ago, Chet Abbott and Alicia Martin formed a partnership by each contributing $100,000 in capital. The partnership agreement indicated the following division of net income: salary allowances of $20,000 and $30,000 to Abbott and Martin respectively, and all remaining net income divided equally.

Martin recently expressed concern with the manner in which profits are being divided. Specifically, the income-sharing agreement did not consider changes in the amounts invested by each partner as reflected in the balances of their capital accounts. Over the years, Abbott has consistently withdrawn more from the partnership than Martin, with the result that the capital balances as of January 1, 1997, indicated an investment of $200,000 by Abbott and $362,500 by Martin.

Abbott agreed with Martin that a change in the income-sharing agreement was warranted and accordingly proposed the following two alternatives:

Proposal I:

a. The salary allowances of Abbott and Martin would be increased to $30,000 and $45,000 respectively.
b. Interest of 8% would be allowed on the January 1 balances of the capital accounts.
c. All remaining income would be divided equally.

Proposal II:

a. The salary allowances of Abbott and Martin would not be changed.
b. No interest would be allowed on the capital balances.
c. Martin would be allowed a bonus of 20% of the amount by which net income exceeds salary allowances, and the remainder would be divided equally.

Martin has asked for your advice on which of the two proposals she should accept.

1. For each proposal, prepare an analysis of the distribution of net income between Abbott and Martin for 1997 for net income levels of $90,000, $130,000, and $190,000.
2. Which proposal would you recommend that Martin accept?
3. Elizabeth Sanford has offered to purchase for $250,000 a one-fourth interest in the partnership capital and net income. Assuming that the net tangible assets of the partnership approximate their fair market values at January 1, 1997, how much bonus is Sanford paying to the partnership?

ANSWERS TO SELF-EXAMINATION QUESTIONS

1. **B** Noncash assets contributed to a partnership should be recorded at the amounts agreed upon by the partners. The preferred practice is to record the office equipment at $9,000 (answer B).
2. **C** Net income and net loss are divided among the partners in accordance with their agreement. In the absence of any agreement, all partners share equally (answer C).
3. **C** X's share of the $45,000 of net income is $19,000 (answer C), determined as follows:

	X	*Y*	*Total*
Interest allowance	$10,000	$ 5,000	$15,000
Salary allowance	12,000	24,000	36,000
Total	$22,000	$29,000	$51,000
Excess of allowances over income	3,000	3,000	6,000
Net income distribution	$19,000	$26,000	$45,000

4. **A** When an additional person is admitted to a partnership by purchasing an interest from one or more of the partners, the purchase price is paid directly to the selling partner(s). The amount of capital transferred from the capital account(s) of the selling partner(s) to the capital account of the incoming partner is the capital interest acquired from the selling partner(s). In the question, the amount is $32,500 (answer A), which is one-half of X's capital balance of $65,000.
5. **C** Partnership cash would be distributed in accordance with the credit balances in the partners' capital accounts. Therefore, $10,000 (answer C) would be distributed to X (X's $10,000 capital balance).

PART SIX

Corporations

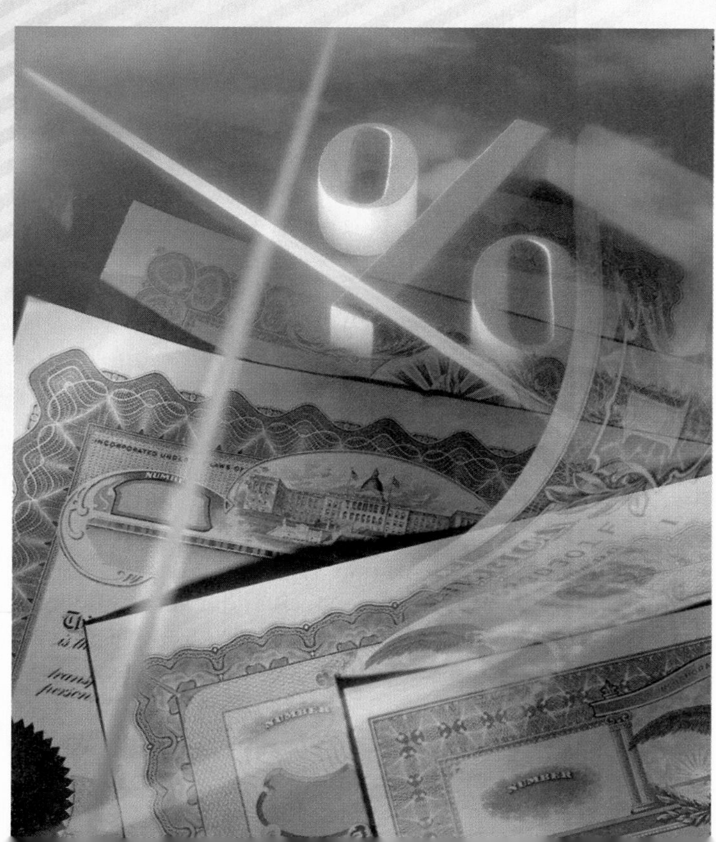

14 Corporations: Organization and Equity Rights

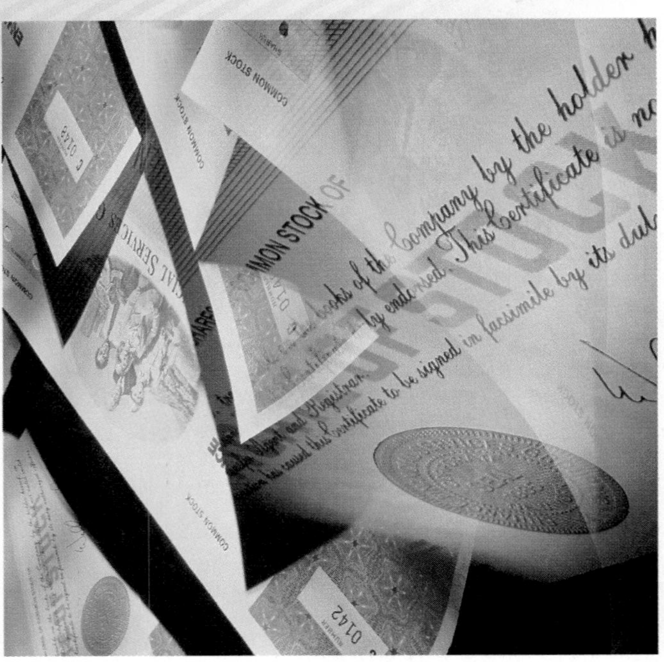

YOU AND ACCOUNTING

If you own stock in a corporation, you are interested in how the stock is performing in the market. If you are considering buying stocks, you are interested in what your rights are as a stockholder and what kind of returns you might expect from the stock. In either case, you should be able to interpret stock market quotations, such as the following:

30½	22⅜	WalMart	WMT	.17	.7	24	15738	25½	25	25	– ¼
22⅝	19⅛	WaldnResdntl	WDN	.67e	3.3	...	63	20⅜	20¼	20⅜	...
43⅝	33¾	Walgreen	WAG	.68	1.9	17	2810	37⅛	36¼	36¼	– ⅞
36¼	22⅞	WallaceCS	WCS	.64	2.0	16	289	32¼	31⅝	32	+ ¼
35⅝	26¼	Warnaco	WAC		...	11	1341	34⅜	33¾	34⅜	+ ⅝
7⅞	2¼	WarnerIns	WCP	.04	1.6	dd	220	2½	2⅜	2½	...
72½	60	WarnerLamb	WLA	2.44	3.6	26	6625	68½	64	68½	+4⅜
22⅝	14⅜	WashnEngy	WEG	1.00	6.7	dd	283	15⅛	14⅝	14⅞	...
45⅝	36¼	WashGasLt	WGL	2.22	5.8	14	122	38¾	38⅛	38¼	+ ⅜
10⅜	5	WashHomes	WHI	.20	3.6	7	62	5⅝	5⅝	5⅝	...

Although you may not own any stocks, you probably buy services or products from corporations, and you may work for a corporation. Understanding the corporate form of organization will help you in your role as a stockholder, a consumer, or an employee. In this chapter, we discuss the characteristics of corporations, as well as how corporations account for stocks.

After studying this chapter, you should be able to:

Objective 1
Describe the nature of the corporate form of organization.

Objective 2
List the two main sources of stockholders' equity.

Objective 3
List the major sources of paid-in capital, including the various classes of stock.

Objective 4
Journalize the entries for issuing stock.

Objective 5
Journalize the entries for treasury stock transactions.

Objective 6
Prepare the Paid-In Capital section of a corporate balance sheet.

Objective 7
State the effect of stock splits on corporate financial statements.

Objective 8
Journalize the entries for cash dividends and stock dividends.

Objective 9
Journalize appropriations of retained earnings.

Objective 10
Prepare a retained earnings statement.

Objective 11
Prepare a statement of stockholders' equity.

Nature of a Corporation

Objective 1
Describe the nature of the corporate form of organization.

What is a corporation? In the Dartmount College case in 1819, Chief Justice Marshall of the United States Supreme Court stated: "A corporation is an artificial being, invisible, intangible, and existing only in contemplation of the law."

The concept underlying this definition is the basis for recognizing a corporation as a legal entity, distinct and separate from the individuals who create and operate it. Almost all large businesses in the United States are organized as corporations.

CHARACTERISTICS OF CORPORATIONS

As a separate legal entity, a corporation may acquire, own, and dispose of property in its own name. It may also incur liabilities and enter into other types of contracts.

The ownership of a corporation is divided into units called shares of **stock.** A corporation may have several classes of stock, and each share within a class has the same rights as every other share of stock in its class. The owners of the shares of stock own the corporation and are called **stockholders** or **shareholders.**

Because a corporation has a separate legal existence, shares of stock may be bought and sold without affecting the operations or continued existence of the corporation. This is in contrast to the partnership form of organization, in which changes in the ownership dissolve the partnership. Corporations whose shares of stock are traded in public markets are called **public corporations.** Corporations whose shares are not traded publicly are usually owned by a small group of investors and are called **nonpublic** or **private corporations.** The Mars Candy Company is a private corporation that is well-known.

The stockholders of a corporation have **limited liability.** A corporation is responsible for its own acts and obligations under law. Therefore, a corporation's creditors usually may not go beyond the assets of the corporation to satisfy their claims. Thus, the financial loss that a stockholder may suffer is limited to the amount invested. This limited liability feature contributed to the rapid growth of the corporate form of organization.

Stockholders exercise control over the management of a corporation's operations and activities by electing a **board of directors.** The board of directors meets periodically to establish corporate policies. The board selects the chief executive officer (CEO) and other major officers to manage the day-to-day affairs of the corporation. The board also has responsibility for deciding when and how much corporate income to distribute to stockholders in the form of **dividends.**

Exhibit 1 shows the organizational structure of a corporation.

Exhibit 1
Organizational Structure of a Corporate Enterprise

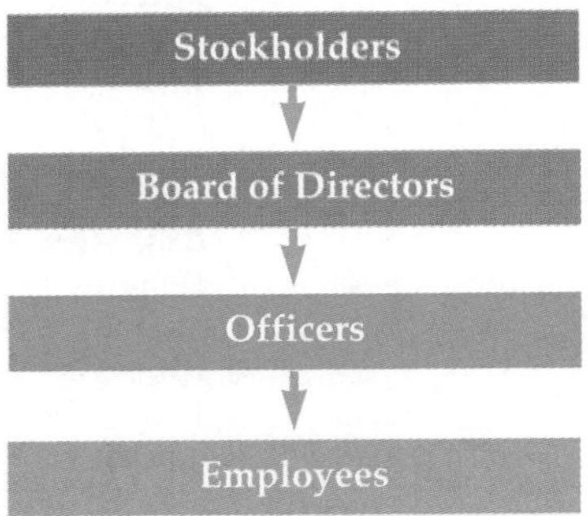

As separate entities, corporations are subject to **taxes.** Thus, unlike the sole proprietorship and partnership forms of organization, corporations must pay federal income taxes. Some states also require corporations to pay income taxes. Stockholders must also pay income taxes on any dividends distributed to them. This *double taxation* of corporate earnings is a major disadvantage of the corporate form of organization.[1]

Corporations may be organized for nonprofit reasons, such as recreational, educational, charitable, or humanitarian purposes. However, most corporations are organized to earn a profit and a fair rate of return for their stockholders. Throughout this chapter, we focus on corporations organized for profit.

FORMING A CORPORATION

The first step in forming a corporation is to file an **application of incorporation** with the state. State incorporation laws differ, and corporations often organize in those states with the more favorable laws. For example, more than half of the largest companies are incorporated in Delaware. Exhibit 2 lists some corporations that you may be familiar with, their states of incorporation, and the location of their headquarters.

After the application of incorporation has been approved, the state grants a **charter** or **articles of incorporation.**[2] The articles of incorporation formally create the corporation. Shortly after the granting of the articles of incorporation, the corporate management and board of directors prepare a set of **bylaws,** which are the rules and procedures for conducting the affairs of the corporation.

Significant costs are often incurred in organizing a corporation. These costs include legal fees, taxes, state incorporation fees, license fees, and promotional costs. Such costs are debited to an intangible asset account entitled *Organization Costs*. Although such costs have no value upon liquidation, they are accounted for as an asset, since the corporation could not have been created without them.

The organizers of a corporation normally assume that it will continue in existence indefinitely. Thus, we could argue that organization costs should be carried in

[1] Under the *Internal Revenue Code,* a corporation with a few stockholders may elect to be treated like a partnership for income tax purposes. Such corporations are known as Subchapter S corporations.

[2] The articles of incorporation may restrict a corporation's activities in certain areas, such as owning certain types of real estate, conducting certain types of business activities, or purchasing its own stock.

Exhibit 2
Examples of Corporations and their States of Incorporation

Corporation	*State of Incorporation*	*Headquarters*
Bethlehem Steel Corporation	Delaware	Bethlehem, Pa.
Borden, Inc.	New Jersey	New York, N.Y.
Caterpillar, Inc.	Delaware	Peoria, Ill.
Delta Air Lines, Inc.	Delaware	Atlanta, Ga.
Dow Chemical Company	Delaware	Midland, Mich.
General Electric Company	New York	Fairfield, Conn.
The Home Depot	Delaware	Atlanta, Ga.
Honeywell Inc.	Delaware	Minneapolis, Minn.
Kellogg Company	Delaware	Battle Creek, Mich.
3M	Delaware	St. Paul, Minn.
McDonnell Douglas Corporation	Maryland	St. Louis, Mo.
May Department Stores	New York	St. Louis, Mo.
RJR Nabisco	Delaware	New York, N.Y.
Tandy Corporation	Delaware	Ft. Worth, Tex.
The Washington Post Company	Delaware	Washington, D.C.
Whirlpool Corporation	Delaware	Benton Harbor, Mich.
Zenith Electronics Corporation	Delaware	Glenview, Ill.

the accounts as an asset until the corporation ceases its operations and liquidates. As a practical matter, however, organization costs are written off, or amortized.

The *Internal Revenue Code* allows the amortization of organization costs equally over a period of not less than sixty months (5 years), beginning with the month the corporation begins business. Since the effect of organization costs on the financial statements is generally small, such costs are normally amortized over five years.

The following entries illustrate the recording of organization costs of $8,500 on January 5 and the subsequent amortization on December 31, the end of the first year of operations:

Jan. 5	Organization Costs	8,500	
	Cash		8,500
Dec. 31	Amortization Expense—Organization Costs	1,700	
	Organization Costs		1,700
	($8,500 ÷ 5 years = $1,700)		

Stockholders' Equity

Objective 2
List the two main sources of stockholders' equity.

The owners' equity in a corporation is commonly called **stockholders' equity, shareholders' equity, shareholders' investment,** or **capital.** In a corporation balance sheet, the owners' equity section is called the Stockholders' Equity section. This section reports the amount of each of the two main sources of stockholders' equity. The first source is capital contributed to the corporation by the stockholders and others, called **paid-in capital** or **contributed capital.** The second source is net income retained in the business, called **retained earnings.** An example of a Stockholders' Equity section of a corporation balance sheet is shown below.

Stockholders' Equity		
Paid-in capital:		
Common stock	$330,000	
Retained earnings	80,000	
Total stockholders' equity		$410,000

The paid-in capital contributed by the stockholders is recorded in separate accounts for each class of stock. If there is only one class of stock, the account is entitled *Common Stock* or *Capital Stock.*

Retained earnings results from transferring the balance in the income summary account (the net income or net loss) to the retained earnings account at the end of each fiscal year. As a result of net losses, a debit balance in Retained Earnings may occur. Such a balance is called a **deficit**. In the Stockholders' Equity section of the balance sheet, a deficit is deducted from paid-in capital in determining total stockholders' equity. The dividends account, which is similar to the drawings account for a sole proprietorship or partnership, is also closed to Retained Earnings. Thus, the balance of Retained Earnings represents the corporation's accumulated net income that has not been distributed to stockholders as dividends.

There are a number of alternative terms used for retained earnings, including *earnings retained for use in the business* and *earnings reinvested in the business.* These terms refer to the *use* of retained earnings and not to an amount of *surplus cash* or *cash left over for dividends*. Earnings retained in the business normally are used by management to improve or expand operations. Over time, as the amount of retained earnings from profitable operations increases, it will have less and less of a relationship to the amount of cash on hand.

Sources of Paid-in Capital

Objective 3
List the major sources of paid-in capital, including the various classes of stock.

As we mentioned in the preceding section, the two main sources of stockholders' equity are **paid-in capital** (or contributed capital) and retained earnings. The main source of paid-in capital is from issuing stock. In the following paragraphs, we discuss the characteristics of the various classes of stock. We conclude this section with a brief discussion of other sources of paid-in capital.

STOCK

The number of shares of stock that a corporation is authorized to issue is stated in its charter. The term *issued* refers to the shares issued to the stockholders. A corporation may, under circumstances we discuss later in this chapter, reacquire some of the stock that it has issued. The stock remaining in the hands of stockholders is then called **outstanding stock.**

Shares of stock are often assigned a monetary amount, known as **par**. As a written representation of ownership, corporations may issue **stock certificates** to stockholders.[3] Printed on a stock certificate is the par value of the stock, the name of the stockholder, and the number of shares owned. Stock may also be issued without par, in which case it is called **no-par stock.** Some states require the board of directors to assign a **stated value** to no-par stock.

Because of the limited liability feature of corporations, creditors have no claim against the personal assets of stockholders. However, some state laws require that corporations maintain a minimum contribution by the stockholders as protection for creditors. This minimum amount is called **legal capital.** The amount of required legal capital varies among the states, but it usually includes the amount of par or stated value of the shares of stock issued.

The major rights that accompany ownership of a share of stock are as follows:

1. The right to vote in matters concerning the corporation.
2. The right to share in distributions of earnings.

[3] Some corporations have stopped issuing stock certificates except on special request. In these cases, the corporation maintains records of ownership by using electronic media.

3. The preemptive right, which is the right to maintain the same fractional interest in the corporation by purchasing shares of any additional issuances of stock.[4]
4. The right to share in assets on liquidation.

When only one class of stock is issued, it is called common stock. In this case, each share of common stock has equal rights. To appeal to a broader investment market, a corporation may issue one or more classes of stock with various preference rights. An example of such a right is the preference to share in distributions of earnings. Such stock is generally called preferred stock.

The board of directors has the sole authority to distribute dividends to the stockholders. When such action is taken, the directors are said to *declare* a dividend. Since dividends are normally based on earnings, a corporation cannot guarantee dividends to its stockholders.

A corporation with both preferred stock and common stock is permitted to declare dividends on the common only after it meets the dividend preference of the preferred stock. The dividend preference of the preferred stock may be stated in monetary terms or as a percent of par. For example, $4 preferred stock has a prior claim to an annual $4 per share dividend. If the par value of the preferred stock were $50, the same claim on dividends could be stated as 8% preferred stock.

Nonparticipating and Participating Preferred Stock

The preferred stockholders' dividend preference is usually limited to a certain amount. Such stock is said to be nonparticipating preferred stock. To continue the preceding example, assume that a corporation has 1,000 shares of $4 nonparticipating preferred stock and 4,000 shares of common stock outstanding. Also assume that the net income, amount of earnings retained, and the amount of earnings distributed by the board of directors for the first three years of operations are as follows:

	First Year	*Second Year*	*Third Year*
Net income	$20,000	$55,000	$100,000
Amount retained	10,000	20,000	40,000
Amount distributed	$10,000	$35,000	$ 60,000

Exhibit 3 shows the distribution of the earnings between the preferred stock and the common stock for each year.

Exhibit 3
Dividends to Nonparticipating Preferred Stock

	First Year	*Second Year*	*Third Year*
Amount distributed	$10,000	$35,000	$60,000
Preferred dividend (1,000 shares)	4,000	4,000	4,000
Common dividend (4,000 shares)	$ 6,000	$31,000	$56,000
Dividends per share:			
Preferred	$ 4.00	$ 4.00	$ 4.00
Common	$ 1.50	$ 7.75	$ 14.00

In this example, the preferred stockholders received an annual dividend of $4 per share, compared to the common stockholders' dividends of $1.50, $7.75, and $14.00 per share. The preferred stockholders have a greater chance of receiving

[4] In recent years, stockholders of a number of corporations have, by formal action, given up their preemptive rights.

regular dividends than do the common stockholders. On the other hand, common stockholders have a greater chance of receiving larger dividends than do the preferred stockholders.

Preferred stock may provide for the possibility of receiving additional dividends if certain conditions are met. These conditions often include reaching a certain level of earnings and distributing a certain amount of dividends to common stockholders. Such stock is called **participating preferred stock.** It is rarely used in today's financial markets.

Cumulative and Noncumulative Preferred Stock

Preferred stock may contain special provisions if regular preferred dividends are passed (not declared) by the board of directors. These provisions normally prohibit the payment of any common stock dividends if any preferred dividends have been passed in prior years. Such preferred stock is said to be **cumulative preferred stock,** and any preferred dividends that have been passed are said to be *in arrears*. Preferred stock not having this cumulative right is called **noncumulative preferred stock.**

To illustrate, assume that a corporation has outstanding 1,000 shares of $4 cumulative preferred stock and 4,000 shares of common stock. Also assume that no dividends have been paid in the preceding two years. In the third (current) year, dividends of $22,000 are declared. Exhibit 4 shows the distribution of these dividends between the preferred and common stock.

Exhibit 4
Dividends to Cumulative Preferred Stock

Amount distributed		$22,000
Preferred dividend (1,000 shares):		
First-year dividend in arrears	$4,000	
Second-year dividend in arrears	4,000	
Third-year current dividend	4,000	12,000
Common dividend (4,000 shares)		$10,000
Dividends per share:		
Preferred		$ 12.00
Common		$ 2.50

Other Preferential Rights

In addition to the preference rights in dividend distributions, preferred stock may be given preference rights on assets in liquidation of the corporation. However, claims of creditors must be satisfied first before any assets are distributed to stockholders. Any assets remaining after the creditors have been paid are first distributed to preferred stockholders. Any remaining assets are then distributed to common stockholders. Common stockholders of corporations that liquidate rarely get back their full investment value.

OTHER SOURCES OF PAID-IN CAPITAL

In addition to the issuance of stock, paid-in capital may arise from donations of real estate or other properties to a corporation. Civic groups and municipalities sometimes give land or buildings to a corporation as an incentive to locate or remain in a community. In such cases, the corporation debits the assets for their fair market value and credits *Donated Capital*.

PREFERRED STOCK—RISKS VS. REWARDS

Preferred stocks shield shareholders somewhat from the lows of corporate fortunes. If dividend payments must be reduced, preferred stockholders receive dividends before common shareholders. However, preferred stockholders often miss out on the highs of corporate fortunes. Because preferred shareholders receive a fixed dividend, and the bulk of any large dividends goes to common shareholders, most preferred stock is nonparticipating. These "safe-but-stodgy" equities can offer dramatic profits, however, as described in the following excerpt from an article in *Business Week:*

. . . In times of grave financial trouble, dividends on preferreds are often suspended and placed in arrears. . . . If and when the company reinstates dividends, current shareholders are entitled to all the back payments, whether or not they owned stock during the arrearage period—if the preferred is cumulative. . . .

The gains [from purchasing preferred stock with dividends in arrears] can be impressive. Bethlehem Steel announced in April that it would pay $22.5 million in arrears and resume the regular quarterly dividend on its two classes of preferred stock. Because Bethlehem had missed four payments, investors receive an extra year's worth of dividends: One class that usually pays $1.25 quarterly will return $6.25—not bad on a stock that traded in the low 30s just a few months ago.

Playing preferreds in arrears requires patience. Long Island Lighting, for instance, recently announced that it would try to resume paying dividends next year after a four-year hiatus. But the larger concern lies in the fact that you're betting on a turnaround. And all bets are off if the company goes bankrupt: You not only lose arrearages but you're also sure to see the share price plummet. On the repayment totem pole, preferreds occupy the second-lowest notch—before the common shareholders but after the creditors and bondholders. . . .

Source: Troy Segal, "Preferred Stock: The Risky Hunt for Hidden Rewards," *Business Week,* June 13, 1988, p. 114.

Paid-in capital may also arise when a corporation buys and sells its own stock in the marketplace. Such stock is called **treasury stock.** Later in this chapter, we will discuss the recording of treasury stock transactions, including the recording of paid-in capital from such transactions.

Issuing Stock

Objective 4
Journalize the entries for issuing stock.

A separate account is used for recording the amount of each class of stock issued to investors in a corporation. For example, assume that a corporation is authorized to issue 10,000 shares of preferred stock, $100 par, and 100,000 shares of common stock, $20 par. One-half of each class of authorized shares is issued at par for cash. The entry to record the stockholders' investment and the receipt of the cash is as follows:[5]

Cash	1,500,000	
Preferred Stock		500,000
Common Stock		1,000,000

The stock accounts (Preferred Stock, Common Stock) are controlling accounts. A record of each stockholder's name, address, and number of shares held is normally kept in a subsidiary ledger. This subsidiary ledger is called the **stockholders**

[5] The accounting for long-term investments in stocks from the point of view of the investor is discussed in a later chapter.

ledger. It provides the information for issuing dividend checks, annual meeting notices, and financial reports to individual stockholders.[6]

Stock is often issued by a corporation at a price other than its par. This is because the par value of a stock is simply a way of dividing owners' equity into units of ownership. The price at which stock can be sold by a corporation depends on a variety of factors, such as:

1. The financial condition, earnings record, and dividend record of the corporation.
2. Investor expectations of the corporation's potential earning power.
3. General business and economic conditions and prospects.

When stock is issued for a price that is more than its par, the stock has sold at a **premium.** When stock is issued for a price that is less than its par, the stock has sold at a **discount.** Thus, if stock with a par of $50 is issued for a price of $60, the stock has sold at a premium of $10. If the same stock is issued for a price of $45, the stock has sold at a discount of $5.

Many states do not permit the issuance of stock at a discount. In others, it may be done only under unusual conditions. Since issuing stock at a discount is rare, we will not illustrate it.

PREMIUM ON STOCK

When stock is issued at a premium, Cash or other asset accounts are debited for the amount received. The stock account is then credited for the par amount. The excess of the amount paid over par is a part of the total investment of the stockholders in

INTERPRETING STOCK QUOTATIONS

The following stock quotation for Wal-Mart Corporation is taken from the August 5, 1994 *Wall Street Journal:*

NEW YORK STOCK EXCHANGE

52 Weeks Hi	Lo	Stock	Sym	Div	Yld %	PE	Vol 100s	Hi	Lo	Close	Net Chg
30½	22⅝	WalMart	WMT	.17	.7	24	15738	25½	25	25	– ¼

The preceding quotation is interpreted as follows:

Hi	Highest price during the past 52 weeks
Lo	Lowest price during the past 52 weeks
Stock	Name of the company
Sym	Stock exchange symbol (WMT for Wal-Mart)
Div	Dividends paid per share during the past year
Yld %	Annual dividend yield per share based on the closing price (Wal-Mart's .7% yield on common stock is computed as $.17 ÷ $25)
PE	Price-earnings ratio on common stock (discussed in a later chapter)
Vol	The volume of stock traded in 100s
Hi	Highest price for the day
Lo	Lowest price for the day
Close	Closing price for the day
Net Chg	The net change in price from the previous day

[6] Large public corporations often use a financial institution, such as a bank, as transfer agent or registrar for maintaining stockholder records.

the corporation. Therefore, such an amount in excess of par should be classified as a part of the paid-in capital. An account entitled Paid-In Capital in Excess of Par is usually credited for this amount.

To illustrate, if Caldwell Company issues 2,000 shares of $50 par preferred stock for cash at $55, the entry to record the transaction is as follows:

Cash	110,000	
Preferred Stock		100,000
Paid-In Capital in Excess of Par—Preferred Stock		10,000

Although the $10,000 in excess of par is a part of the paid-in capital, it is recorded in an account separate from the stock account to which it relates. This is because, in some states, the amount received in excess of par may not be considered a part of legal capital. If so, this amount may be used for dividends to stockholders. However, if this amount is used for dividends, stockholders should be clearly notified that the dividend is a return of paid-in capital rather than a distribution of earnings.

When stock is issued in exchange for assets other than cash, such as land, buildings, and equipment, the assets acquired should be recorded at their fair market value. If the fair market value of the assets cannot be objectively determined, the fair market price of the stock issued may be used.

To illustrate, assume that a corporation acquired land for which the fair market value cannot be determined. In exchange, the corporation issued 10,000 shares of its $10 par common. Assuming the stock has a current market price of $12 per share, the transaction is recorded as follows:

Land	120,000	
Common Stock		100,000
Paid-In Capital in Excess of Par		20,000

NO-PAR STOCK

In most states, both preferred and common stock may be issued without a par value. Preferred stock, however, is normally assigned a par value. When no-par stock is issued, the entire proceeds are credited to the stock account. This is true even though the issuance price varies from time to time. For example, assume that at the time of organization a corporation issues 10,000 shares of no-par common stock at $40 a share and at a later date issues 1,000 additional shares at $36. The entries to record the issuances of the no-par stock are as follows:

Original issuance of 10,000 shares of no-par common at $40.

Cash	400,000	
Common Stock		400,000

Subsequent issuance of 1,000 shares of no-par common at $36.

Cash	36,000	
Common Stock		36,000

The laws of some states require that the entire proceeds from the issuance of no-par stock be regarded as legal capital. The preceding entries follow this principle. In other states, no-par stock may be assigned a stated value per share. The stated value is treated similarly to par value, and the excess of the proceeds over the stated value is credited to *Paid-In Capital in Excess of Stated Value*. If we assume that in the preceding example the stated value is $25, the issuance of the no-par stock is recorded as follows:

Original issuance of 10,000 shares of no-par common at $40, stated value $25.	Cash	400,000	
	Common Stock		250,000
	Paid-In Capital in Excess of Stated Value		150,000
Subsequent issuance of 1,000 shares of no-par common at $36, stated value $25.	Cash	36,000	
	Common Stock		25,000
	Paid-In Capital in Excess of Stated Value		11,000

Treasury Stock Transactions

Objective 5
Journalize the entries for treasury stock transactions.

The 1994 edition of *Accounting Trends & Techniques* indicated that over 63% of the companies surveyed reported treasury stock. Although some state laws restrict the practice, a corporation may buy its own stock in order to provide shares for resale to employees, for reissuance as a bonus to employees, or for supporting the market price of the stock. For example, General Motors bought back some of its common stock and stated that two primary uses of the treasury stock would be for incentive compensation plans and employee savings plans.

Treasury stock is stock that:

1. Has been issued as fully paid
2. Has been reacquired by the corporation
3. Has not been canceled or reissued

A commonly used method of accounting for the purchase and the resale of treasury stock is the **cost method.**[7] When the stock is purchased by the corporation, the account *Treasury Stock* is debited for its cost (the price paid for it). The par value and the price at which the stock was originally issued are ignored. When the stock is resold, Treasury Stock is credited for its cost, and any difference between the cost and the selling price is normally debited or credited to a paid-in capital account. This latter account is entitled *Paid-In Capital from Sale of Treasury Stock.*

To illustrate the cost method, assume that the paid-in capital of a corporation is as follows:

Common stock, $25 par (20,000 shares authorized and issued)	$500,000	
Excess of issue price over par	150,000	$650,000

The transactions involving treasury stock and the related entries are as follows:

Purchased 1,000 shares of treasury stock at $45.	Treasury Stock	45,000	
	Cash		45,000
Sold 200 shares of treasury stock at $60.	Cash	12,000	
	Treasury Stock		9,000
	Paid-In Capital from Sale of Treasury Stock		3,000
Sold 200 shares of treasury stock at $40.	Cash	8,000	
	Paid-In Capital from Sale of Treasury Stock	1,000	
	Treasury Stock		9,000

[7] Another method that is infrequently used, called the *par value method,* is discussed in advanced accounting texts.

As we illustrated, a sale of treasury stock may result in a decrease in paid-in capital. To the extent that Paid-In Capital from Sale of Treasury Stock has a credit balance, it should be debited for any decrease. Any remaining decrease should then be debited to the retained earnings account.

Reporting Paid-In Capital

Objective 6
Prepare the Paid-In Capital section of a corporate balance sheet.

As with other sections of the balance sheet, alternative terms and formats may be used in reporting paid-in capital. Exhibit 5 illustrates some examples of these alternatives.

Exhibit 5
Paid-In Capital Section of Stockholders' Equity

Stockholders' Equity			
Paid-in capital:			
Preferred $5 stock, cumulative, $50 par (2,000 shares authorized and issued)	$100,000		
Excess of issue price over par	10,000	$ 110,000	
Common stock, $20 par (50,000 shares authorized, 45,000 shares issued)	$900,000		
Excess of issue price over par	132,000	1,032,000	
From donated land		60,000	
Total paid-in capital			$1,202,000
Shareholders' Equity			
Contributed capital:			
Preferred 10% stock, cumulative, $50 par (2,000 shares authorized and issued)		$100,000	
Common stock, $20 par (50,000 shares authorized, 45,000 shares issued)		900,000	
Additional paid-in capital		202,000	
Total contributed capital			$1,202,000

In the first example in Exhibit 5, each class of stock is listed, followed by its related paid-in capital accounts. In the second example, the stock accounts are listed first. The other paid-in capital accounts are listed as a single item described as *Additional paid-in capital.* These combined accounts could also be described as *Capital in excess of par (or stated value) of shares* or another similar title.

How are treasury stock and paid-in capital from the sale of treasury stock reported in the balance sheet? Paid-In Capital from Sale of Treasury Stock is reported in the Paid-In Capital section. Treasury Stock is deducted from the total of the paid-in capital and retained earnings. To illustrate, Exhibit 6 shows a Stockholders' Equity section with treasury stock.

The Stockholders' Equity section of the balance sheet indicates that 20,000 shares of stock were issued, of which 600 are held as treasury stock. The number of shares outstanding is therefore 19,400. Owners of 19,400 shares would have the right to vote at a stockholders' meeting.

Exhibit 6
Stockholders' Equity Section with Treasury Stock

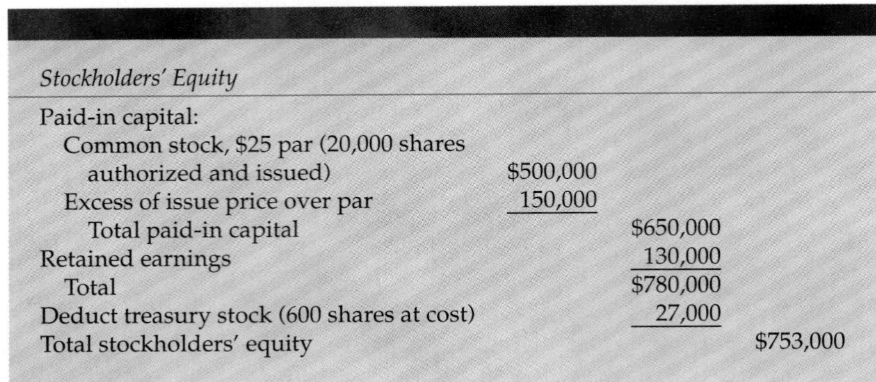

Stockholders' Equity			
Paid-in capital:			
Common stock, $25 par (20,000 shares authorized and issued)	$500,000		
Excess of issue price over par	150,000		
Total paid-in capital		$650,000	
Retained earnings		130,000	
Total		$780,000	
Deduct treasury stock (600 shares at cost)		27,000	
Total stockholders' equity			$753,000

Significant changes in paid-in capital during a period should also be disclosed. Such disclosures may be presented either in a *statement of stockholders' equity* or in notes to the financial statements. We describe and illustrate the statement of stockholders' equity later in this chapter.

Stock Splits

Objective 7
State the effect of stock splits on corporate financial statements.

Corporations sometimes reduce the par or stated value of their common stock and issue a proportionate number of additional shares. When this is done, a corporation is said to have *split its stock,* and the process is a **stock split** or **stock split-up.**

When stock is split, the reduction in par or stated value applies to all shares, including the unissued, issued, and treasury shares. A major objective of a stock split is to reduce the market price per share of the corporation's stock. The lower stock price encourages more investors to enter the market for the stock. This, in turn, tends to increase or broaden the types and numbers of a corporation's stockholders. For example, when **Nature's Sunshine Products Inc.** declared a two-for-one stock split, the company president said:

We believe the split will place our stock price in a range attractive to both individual and institutional investors, broadening the market for the stock.

To illustrate a stock split, assume that the board of directors of Rojek Corporation, which has 10,000 shares of $100 par common stock outstanding, reduces the par to $20 and increases the number of shares to 50,000 (5-for-1 split). The amount of common stock outstanding is $1,000,000 both before and after the stock split. Only the number of shares and the par per share are changed. Since there are no changes in the balances of any of the corporation's accounts, no entry to record a stock split is required. However, the details of stock splits are normally disclosed within notes to the financial statements because they significantly change the make-up of the paid-in capital.

Each shareholder in a corporation whose stock is split owns the same total par amount of stock before and after the stock split. For example, a Rojek Corporation stockholder who owned 100 shares of $100 par stock before the split (total par of $10,000) would own 500 shares of $20 par stock after the split (total par of $10,000).

Accounting for Dividends

Objective 8
Journalize the entries for cash dividends and stock dividends.

A dividend usually represents a distribution of retained earnings. Dividends may be paid in cash, in stock of the company, or in other property. In rare cases, a dividend may also represent a distribution of paid-in capital.

CASH DIVIDENDS

A cash distribution of earnings by a corporation to its shareholders is called a cash dividend. Cash dividends are the most common form of dividend.

Can a corporation pay a cash dividend at any time? There are usually three conditions that a corporation must meet to pay a cash dividend:

1. Sufficient retained earnings
2. Sufficient cash
3. Formal action by the board of directors

A large amount of retained earnings does not always mean that a corporation is able to pay dividends. There must also be enough cash in excess of normal operating needs. A corporation's board of directors is not required by law to declare dividends. This is true even if both retained earnings and cash are large enough to justify a dividend. When a dividend has been *declared*, however, it becomes a liability of the corporation.

Most corporations try to maintain a stable dividend record in order to make their stock attractive to investors. Dividends may be paid once a year or semiannually or quarterly. The general tendency is to pay quarterly dividends on both common and preferred stock. In periods of high profitability, the board of directors may declare an *extra* dividend on common stock. It may be paid at one of the usual dividend dates or at some other date.

You may have seen corporate announcements of dividend declarations in newspapers. Dividend declarations are usually announced and reported in financial newspapers and investor services. Three dates are important in a dividend announcement:

1. The date of declaration
2. The date of record
3. The date of payment

The date of declaration is the date the board of directors takes formal action to declare the dividend. The date of record is the date on which ownership of shares is to be determined. The date of payment is the date on which the dividend is to be paid. For example, a dividend announcement might read:

On June 26, the board of directors of Campbell Soup Co. declared a quarterly cash dividend of $.33 per common share to stockholders of record as of the close of business on July 8, payable on July 31.

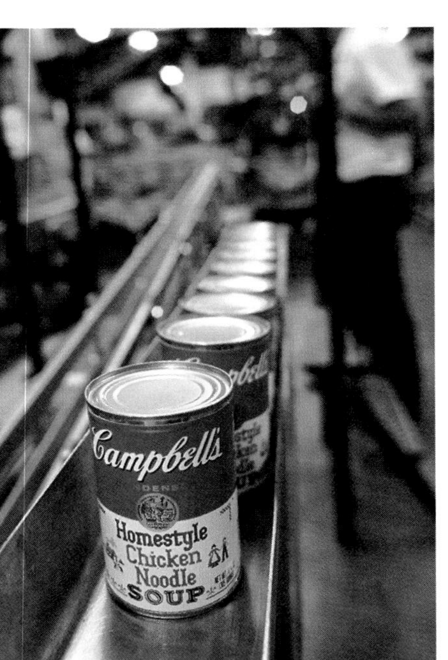

Corporations such as Campbell Soup Co. include the important dates of declaration, record, and payment in their dividend announcements.

The liability for a dividend is recorded on the declaration date. No entry is required on the date of record. This date merely sets the date for determining the identity of the stockholders who will receive the dividend. The period of time between the record date and the payment date allows for the preparation of the dividend checks. During this period, a stock's price is usually quoted as selling *ex-dividends.* This means that since the date of record has passed, a new investor will not receive the unpaid dividends. On the date of payment, the corporation's dividend liability is paid by mailing the dividend checks.

To illustrate, assume that on December 1 the board of directors of Hiber Corporation declares both a preferred stock and a common stock dividend. The preferred stock dividend is a regular quarterly dividend of $2.50 on the 5,000 shares of $100 par, 10% preferred stock outstanding (total dividend of $12,500). The common stock dividend is a quarterly dividend of $0.30 on the 100,000 shares of $10 par common stock outstanding (total dividend of $30,000). The record date is December 10, and checks are to be issued to stockholders on January 2. The entry to record the declaration of the dividends is as follows:

Dec.	1	Cash Dividends	42,500	
		Cash Dividends Payable		42,500

The balance in Cash Dividends will be transferred to Retained Earnings as a part of the closing process by debiting Retained Earnings and crediting Cash Dividends. Cash Dividends Payable will be listed on the December 31 balance sheet as a current liability. The entry to record the payment of the dividends on January 2 is as follows:

Jan.	2	Cash Dividends Payable	42,500	
		Cash		42,500

If a corporation that holds treasury stock declares a cash dividend, the dividends are not paid on the treasury shares. To do so would place the corporation in the position of earning income through dealing with itself. For example, if Hiber Corporation in the preceding illustration had held 5,000 shares of its own common stock, the cash dividends on the common stock would have been $28,500 [(100,000 – 5,000) × $.30] instead of $30,000.

Dividends on cumulative preferred stock do not become a liability of the corporation until formal action is taken by the board of directors. However, dividends in arrears at a balance sheet date should be disclosed. This disclosure may be made by a footnote or a parenthetical note.

STOCK DIVIDENDS

A **stock dividend** is a pro rata distribution of shares of stock to stockholders through a transfer of retained earnings to paid-in capital. Such distributions are usually in common stock and are issued to holders of common stock. It is possible to issue common stock to preferred stockholders or vice versa, but such stock dividends are rare.

Stock dividends are different from cash dividends in that there is no distribution of cash or other assets to stockholders. Stock dividends are often issued by corporations that are experiencing rapid growth. Such corporations use most of the cash generated from operations to acquire new facilities or to expand their operations and thus do not wish to use cash to pay dividends.

When a corporation holding treasury stock declares a stock dividend, the number of shares to be issued may be based on either (1) the number of shares outstanding or (2) the number of shares issued. In practice, the number of shares held as

USING ACCOUNTING TO UNDERSTAND BUSINESS

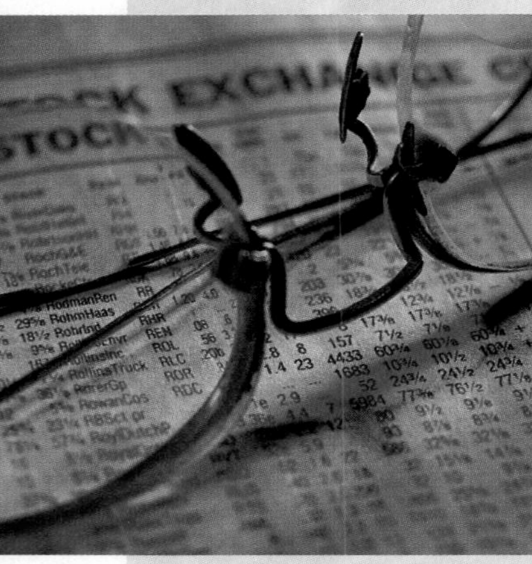

Potential investors in a corporation often rely on accounting information in assessing the attractiveness of stocks. For example, the existence of dividends in arrears on cumulative preferred stock can serve as a warning that the corporation does not pay dividends every year. Such dividends in arrears must be paid before any dividends are available to common stockholders. Likewise, any liquidation preference of preferred stock ranks ahead of the common stock if the corporation goes out of business. If the ability to earn dividends from investing in the stock is a primary concern, then the size of retained earnings, the dividend history of the corporation, and the amount of cash and cash equivalents as well as cash flows are important pieces of information.

treasury stock usually is a small percent of the number of shares issued. Further, the rate of dividend is normally small, so the difference between the methods is usually not significant.

The effect of a stock dividend on the stockholders' equity of the issuing corporation is to transfer retained earnings to paid-in capital. The amount of this transfer, however, has been subject to some debate in the accounting profession. The laws of most states require that a minimum amount equal to the par or stated value of a stock dividend be transferred from retained earnings to paid-in capital. For large public corporations, the *fair value* (market price) of the shares issued in a stock dividend is the amount transferred from retained earnings to paid-in capital. The justification for the transfer of *fair value* for public corporations is expressed as follows:

. . . Many recipients of stock dividends look upon them as distributions of corporate earnings and usually in an amount equivalent to the fair value of the additional shares received. . . . [Such] views . . . are . . . strengthened in those instances, which by far are the most numerous where the [stock dividends] are so small in comparison with the shares previously outstanding that they do not have any apparent effect upon the share market price and, consequently, the market value of the shares previously held remains substantially unchanged.[8]

To illustrate a stock dividend for a public corporation, assume that the stockholders' equity accounts of Hendrix Corporation as of December 15 are as follows:

Common Stock, $20 par (2,000,000 shares issued)	$40,000,000
Paid-In Capital in Excess of Par—Common Stock	9,000,000
Retained Earnings	26,600,000

On December 15, the board of directors declares a stock dividend of 5% or 100,000 shares (2,000,000 shares × 5%), to be issued on January 10. The market price of the stock on the declaration date is $31 a share. The entry to record the declaration is as follows:

Dec. 15	Stock Dividends (100,000 × $31 market price)	3,100,000	
	Stock Dividends Distributable (100,000 × $20 Par)		2,000,000
	Paid-In Capital in Excess of Par—Common Stock		1,100,000

The following entry records the issuance of the stock on January 10:

Jan. 10	Stock Dividends Distributable	2,000,000	
	Common Stock		2,000,000

The $3,100,000 debit to Stock Dividends is closed to Retained Earnings at the end of the period. The effect of the stock dividend is to transfer $3,100,000 of retained earnings to paid-in capital and to increase by 100,000 the number of shares outstanding. There is no change in the assets, liabilities, or total stockholders' equity of the corporation. If financial statements are prepared between the date of declaration and the date of issuance, the stock dividends distributable account is listed in the Paid-In Capital section of the balance sheet.

The issuance of the additional stock dividend shares does not affect the total amount of a stockholder's equity. A stock dividend also does not affect a stockholder's proportionate interest (equity) in the corporation. We illustrate this for a stockholder who is assumed to own 1,000 shares.

[8] *Accounting Research and Terminology Bulletins—Final Edition,* "No. 43, Restatement and Revision of Accounting Research Bulletins," American Institute of Certified Public Accountants, New York, 1961, Ch. 7, Sec. B, par. 10.

The Corporation	*Before Stock Dividend*	*After Stock Dividend*
Common stock	$40,000,000	$42,000,000
Excess of issue price over par	9,000,000	10,100,000
Retained earnings	26,600,000	23,500,000
Total stockholders' equity	$75,600,000	$75,600,000
Number of shares outstanding	2,000,000	2,100,000
Equity per share	$37.80	$36.00
A Stockholder		
Number of shares owned	1,000	1,050
Total equity	$37,800	$37,800
Portion of corporation owned	.05%	.05%

LIQUIDATING DIVIDENDS

A **liquidating dividend** is a distribution to stockholders from paid-in capital. Such dividends are rare and are usually paid when a corporation is permanently reducing its operations or winding up its affairs completely. Since dividends are normally paid from retained earnings, dividends that reduce paid-in capital should be identified as liquidating dividends when paid.

Appropriations of Retained Earnings

Objective 9
Journalize appropriations of retained earnings.

A corporation's retained earnings available for use as dividends may be limited (restricted) by action of its board of directors. The amount restricted is called an **appropriation** or a **reserve.** This amount remains a part of retained earnings and is reported as such in the financial statements.

An appropriation is usually reflected in the accounts by transferring the amount from the retained earnings account to a special account. This special account is identified as an appropriation with a description of its purpose. An example of such an account would be *Appropriation for Plant Expansion.*

Appropriations may be required by law for the amounts paid for treasury stock. To illustrate, assume that a corporation with retained earnings of $200,000 buys treasury stock for $50,000. An appropriation of $50,000 would be transferred to the account Appropriation for Treasury Stock. This appropriation would restrict the payment of dividends to not more than $150,000. In this way, the corporation's legal capital will not be used for dividends. The entry to record the appropriation is as follows:

Apr. 24	Retained Earnings	50,000	
	Appropriation for Treasury Stock		50,000

When a part or all of an appropriation is no longer needed, it is transferred back to the retained earnings account. In the preceding example, when the corporation sells the treasury stock, the following entry is made:

Nov. 10	Appropriation for Treasury Stock	50,000	
	Retained Earnings		50,000

Appropriations may also be required by contract, such as a bank loan or the corporation's cumulative preferred stock with dividends in arrears. For example, when a corporation borrows a large amount of money, the lender may require restrictions on dividends until the debt is paid. The amount restricted is usually equal to the amount of the debt outstanding. The appropriation of retained earnings may be made in total, or an annual buildup of appropriations may be required. Even if the lender does not require the appropriation of retained earnings, the corporation's board of directors might make such an appropriation. In this case, the appropriation is said to be **discretionary** rather than **contractual.**

The board of directors may establish appropriations for other discretionary purposes. For example, a board of directors may appropriate retained earnings for contingencies, such as inventory price declines, a possible settlement of a pending lawsuit, or possible losses from self-insurance.

You should note that an appropriation of retained earnings is not related to any specific assets. Thus, an appropriation does not mean that there is an equivalent amount of cash or other assets set aside in a special fund. *The only purpose of an appropriation is to restrict dividend distributions to stockholders.* The cash that otherwise might be distributed as dividends could be invested in other assets, such as plant and equipment, or used to reduce liabilities.

The board of directors of a corporation may as a separate action set aside assets such as cash or marketable securities for a specific purpose. This setting aside of assets may also be accompanied by an appropriation of retained earnings. In this case, the appropriation is said to be **funded.**

Reporting Retained Earnings

Objective 10
Prepare a retained earnings statement.

As we discussed earlier, retained earnings is reported in the balance sheet. Changes in retained earnings may be reported in a separate retained earnings statement. In the following paragraphs, we illustrate the reporting of retained earnings and the combining of the retained earnings statement and the income statement.

REPORTING RETAINED EARNINGS IN THE BALANCE SHEET

In the balance sheet, retained earnings should be reported so that readers of the statement can clearly distinguish between the *appropriated* and *unappropriated* portions. An example of such a presentation is shown below.

Retained earnings:		
Appropriated:		
For plant expansion	$ 250,000	
Unappropriated	1,800,000	
Total retained earnings		$2,050,000

Presentations, other than the above, could be used to report retained earnings in the balance sheet. For example, the preceding data could be presented in a note accompanying the balance sheet. Such a presentation, including the note, might appear as follows:

Retained earnings (see note) $2,050,000

Note:
Retained earnings in the amount of $250,000 are appropriated for expansion of plant facilities; the remaining $1,800,000 is unappropriated.

RETAINED EARNINGS STATEMENT

When a separate retained earnings statement is prepared, it is normal to divide the statement into two major sections: (1) appropriated and (2) unappropriated. The first section presents for each appropriation account its beginning balance, any additions or deductions during the period, and its ending balance. The second section presents for the unappropriated retained earnings account its beginning balance, net income or net loss for the period, dividends, transfers to and from the appropriation accounts, and the ending balance. The final figure on the statement is the total retained earnings as of the end of the period. An example of this form of retained earnings statement is shown in Exhibit 7 for Lester Corporation.

Exhibit 7
Retained Earnings Statement with Appropriations

Lester Corporation
Retained Earnings Statement
For the Year Ended December 31, 1997

Appropriated:			
Appropriation for plant expansion, January 1, 1997		$ 180,000	
Additional appropriation (see below)		100,000	
Retained earnings appropriated, December 31, 1997			$ 280,000
Unappropriated:			
Balance, January 1, 1997	$1,414,500		
Net income for the year	580,000	$1,994,500	
Cash dividends declared	$ 125,000		
Transfer to approp. for plant expansion	100,000	225,000	
Retained earnings unappropriated, December 31, 1997			1,769,500
Total retained earnings, December 31, 1997			$2,049,500

COMBINED INCOME AND RETAINED EARNINGS STATEMENT

An alternative format for presenting the retained earnings statement is to combine it with the income statement. This combined form was used by 24 of the 600 industrial and merchandising companies surveyed in the 1994 edition of *Accounting Trends & Techniques*. An example of the combined income and retained earnings statement is shown in Exhibit 8 for Wm. Wrigley Jr. Company.

Exhibit 8
Combined Income and Retained Earnings Statement

Wm. Wrigley Jr. Company
Combined Income and Retained Earnings Statement
For the Year Ended December 31, 1993

EARNINGS	*In thousands of dollars*
Revenues:	
Net sales	$1,428,504
Investment and other interest income	11,938
Total revenues	$1,440,442
Costs and expenses:	
Cost of sales	$ 617,156
Selling, distribution, and general administrative	542,944
Interest	1,507
Total costs and expenses	$1,161,607
Earnings before income taxes	$ 278,835
Income taxes	103,944
Net income	$ 174,891
RETAINED EARNINGS	
Retained earnings at beginning of the year	491,481
Dividends declared	(87,301)
Treasury stock retirement	(14,431)
Retained earnings at end of the year	$ 564,640

An advantage of the combined format is that it emphasizes net income as the connecting link between the income statement and the retained earnings portion of stockholders' equity. A disadvantage of the combined form is that the net income figure is buried in the body of the statement.

Statement of Stockholders' Equity

Objective 11
Prepare a statement of stockholders' equity.

Significant changes in stockholders' equity should be reported for the period in which they occur. Although these changes may be reported in the retained earnings statement or the balance sheet, they are often reported in a statement of stockholders' equity.

The statement of stockholders' equity may be prepared in a columnar format, where each column represents a major stockholders' equity classification. Changes in each classification are then described in the left-hand column. Exhibit 9 is a statement of stockholders' equity for Telex Inc.

Exhibit 9
Statement of Stockholders' Equity

Telex Inc.
Statement of Stockholders' Equity
For the Year Ended December 31, 1997

	Preferred Stock	*Common Stock*	*Paid-In Capital in Excess of Par—Common Stock*	*Unappropriated Retained Earnings*	*Retained Earnings Appropriated for Treasury Stock*	*Treasury (Common) Stock*	*Total*
Balance, Jan. 1	$5,000,000	$10,000,000	$3,000,000	$1,500,000	$500,000	$(500,000)	$19,500,000
Net income				850,000			850,000
Dividends on preferred stock				(250,000)			(250,000)
Dividends on common stock				(400,000)			(400,000)
Issuance of additional common stock		500,000	50,000				550,000
Purchase of treasury stock						(30,000)	(30,000)
Increase in appropriation for treasury stock				(30,000)	30,000		
Balance, Dec. 31	$5,000,000	$10,500,000	$3,050,000	$1,670,000	$530,000	$(530,000)	$20,220,000

KEY POINTS

Objective 1. Describe the nature of the corporate form of organization.
Characteristics of corporations that have accounting implications are separate legal existence, transferable units of stock, and limited liability. Corporations may be either public or private corporations, and they are subject to federal income taxes.

The documents included in forming a corporation include an application of incorporation, articles of incorporation, and bylaws. Costs often incurred in organizing a corporation include legal fees, taxes, state incorporation fees, and promotional costs. Such costs are debited to an asset account entitled Organization Costs. They are normally amortized to expense over five years.

Objective 2. List the two main sources of stockholders' equity.
The two main sources of stockholders' equity are (1) capital contributed by the stockholders and others, called paid-in capital, and (2) net income retained in the business, called retained earnings. Stockholders' equity is reported in a corporation balance sheet according to these two sources.

Objective 3. List the major sources of paid-in capital, including the various classes of stock.
The main source of paid-in capital is from the issuance of stock. The two primary classes of stock are common stock and preferred stock. Preferred stock is normally nonparticipating and may be cumulative or noncumulative. In addition to the issuance of stock, paid-in capital may arise from donations of assets and from treasury stock transactions.

Objective 4. Journalize the entries for issuing stock.
When a corporation issues stock at par for cash, the cash account is debited, and the class of stock issued is credited for its par amount. When a corporation issues stock at more than par, Paid-In Capital in Excess of Par is credited for the difference between the cash received and the par value of the stock. When stock is issued in exchange for assets other than cash, the assets acquired should be recorded at their fair market price.

When no-par stock is issued, the entire proceeds are credited to the stock account. No-par stock may be assigned a stated value per share, and the excess of the proceeds over the stated value may be credited to Paid-In Capital in Excess of Stated Value.

Objective 5. Journalize the entries for treasury stock transactions.
When a corporation purchases its own stock, the cost method of accounting is normally used. Treasury Stock is debited for its cost, and Cash is credited. If the stock is resold, Treasury Stock is credited for its cost and any difference between the cost and the selling price is normally debited or credited to Paid-In Capital from Sale of Treasury Stock.

Objective 6. Prepare the Paid-In Capital section of a corporate balance sheet.
Alternative terms and formats may be used in reporting paid-in capital. Using one format, each class of stock is listed, followed by its related paid-in capital accounts. Other paid-in capital, such as Paid-In Capital from Sale of Treasury Stock, is then listed. Treasury Stock is deducted from the total of the paid-in capital and retained earnings.

Objective 7. State the effect of stock splits on corporate financial statements.
When a corporation reduces the par or stated value of its common stock and issues a proportionate number of additional shares, a stock split or stock split-up has occurred. There are no changes in the balances of any corporation accounts, and no entry is required for a stock split.

Objective 8. Journalize the entries for cash dividends and stock dividends.
The entry to record a declaration of cash dividends is to debit Dividends and credit Dividends Payable for each class of stock. The payment of dividends is recorded in the normal manner. When a stock dividend is declared, Stock Dividends is debited for the fair value of the stock to be issued. Stock Dividends Distributable is credited for the par or stated value of the common stock to be issued. The difference between the fair value of the stock and its par or stated value is credited to Paid-In Capital in Excess of Par—Common Stock. When the stock is issued on the date of payment, Stock Dividends Distributable is debited and Common Stock is credited for the par or stated value of the stock issued.

Objective 9. Journalize appropriations of retained earnings.
The retained earnings available for distribution to stockholders may be limited by action of the board of directors or by law or contract. An appropriation is recorded by debiting the retained earnings account and crediting a special appropriation of retained earnings account. The appropriation account is normally identified according to its purpose, such as "for plant expansion." When a part or all of an appropriation is no longer needed, it is transferred back to the retained earnings account by reversing the entry.

Objective 10. Prepare a retained earnings statement.
A retained earnings statement is normally divided into two major sections: (1) appropriated and (2) unappropriated. The first section presents the beginning balances of any appropriations, any additions or deductions during the period, and an ending balance. The second section presents for the unappropriated retained earnings account its beginning balance, net income or net loss for the period, dividends, transfers to and from the appropriation accounts, and the ending balance. The statement concludes with the total retained earnings as of the end of the period. An alternative format for reporting retained earnings is to combine the retained earnings statement and the income statement.

Objective 11. Prepare a statement of stockholders' equity.
Significant changes in stockholders' equity should be reported for the period in which they occur. These changes may be reported in a statement of stockholders' equity in a columnar format, where each column represents a major stockholders' equity classification.

GLOSSARY OF KEY TERMS

Appropriation. The amount of a corporation's retained earnings that has been restricted and therefore is not available for distribution to shareholders as dividends. *Objective 9*

Cash dividend. A cash distribution of earnings by a corporation to its shareholders. *Objective 8*

Common stock. The basic ownership class of corporate stock. *Objective 3*

Cumulative preferred stock. Preferred stock that is entitled to current and past dividends before dividends may be paid on common stock. *Objective 3*

Deficit. A debit balance in the retained earnings account. *Objective 2*

Discount. The excess of par value of stock over its sales price. *Objective 4*

Funded. An appropriation of retained earnings accompanied by a segregation of cash or marketable securities. *Objective 9*

Liquidating dividend. A distribution out of paid-in capital when a corporation permanently reduces its operations or winds up its affairs completely. *Objective 8*

Nonparticipating preferred stock. Preferred stock with a limited dividend preference. *Objective 3*

Outstanding stock. The stock that is in the hands of stockholders. *Objective 3*

Paid-in capital. The capital acquired from stockholders. *Objective 3*

Par. The monetary amount printed on a stock certificate. *Objective 3*

Preemptive right. The right of each shareholder to maintain the same fractional interest in the corporation by purchasing shares of any additional issuances of stock. *Objective 3*

Preferred stock. A class of stock with preferential rights over common stock. *Objective 3*

Premium. The excess of the sales price of stock over its par amount. *Objective 4*

Retained earnings. Net income retained in a corporation. *Objective 2*

Stated value. A value approved by the board of directors of a corporation for no-par stock. Similar to par value. *Objective 3*

Statement of stockholders' equity. A summary of the changes in the stockholders' equity of a corporation that have occurred during a specific period of time. *Objective 11*

Stock. Shares of ownership of a corporation. *Objective 1*

Stock dividend. Distribution of a company's own stock to its shareholders. *Objective 8*

Stock split. A reduction in the par or stated value of a share of common stock and the issuance of a proportionate number of additional shares. *Objective 7*

Stockholders. The owners of a corporation. *Objective 1*

Stockholders' equity. The equity of the shareholders in a corporation. *Objective 2*

Treasury stock. A corporation's issued stock that has been reacquired. *Objective 3*

ILLUSTRATIVE PROBLEM

Altenburg Inc. is a lighting fixture wholesaler located in Arizona. During its current fiscal year, ended December 31, 1997, Altenburg Inc. completed the following selected transactions:

Feb. 3. Purchased 2,500 shares of its own common stock at $26, recording the stock at cost. (Prior to the purchase, there were 40,000 shares of $20 par common stock outstanding.)

May 1. Declared a semiannual dividend of $1 on the 10,000 shares of preferred stock and a 30¢ dividend on the common stock to stockholders of record on May 31, payable on June 15.

June 15. Paid the cash dividends.

Sept. 23. Sold 1,000 shares of treasury stock at $28, receiving cash.

Nov. 1. Declared semiannual dividends of $1 on the preferred stock and 30¢ on the common stock. In addition, a 5% common stock dividend was declared on the common stock outstanding, to be capitalized at the fair market value of the common stock, which is estimated at $30.

Dec. 1. Paid the cash dividends and issued the certificates for the common stock dividend.

31. The board of directors authorized the appropriation necessitated by the holding of treasury stock.

Instructions

Journalize the entries to record the transactions for Altenburg Inc.

Solution

Date	Account	Debit	Credit
1997			
Feb. 3	Treasury Stock	65,000	
	Cash		65,000
May 1	Cash Dividends	21,250	
	Cash Dividends Payable		21,250*
	*(10,000 × $1) + [(40,000 – 2,500) × $.30]		
June 15	Cash Dividends Payable	21,250	
	Cash		21,250

Sept. 23	Cash	28,000	
	Treasury Stock		26,000
	Paid-In Capital from Sale of Treasury Stock		2,000
Nov. 1	Cash Dividends	21,550*	
	Cash Dividends Payable		21,550
	*(10,000 × $1) + [(40,000 – 1,500) × $.30]		
1	Stock Dividends	57,750*	
	Stock Dividends Distributable		38,500
	Paid-In Capital in Excess of Par—Common Stock		19,250
	*(40,000 – 1,500) × 5% × $30		
Dec. 1	Cash Dividends Payable	21,550	
	Stock Dividends Distributable	38,500	
	Cash		21,550
	Common Stock		38,500
31	Retained Earnings	39,000	
	Appropriation for Treasury Stock		39,000*
	*(1,500 × $26)		

SELF-EXAMINATION QUESTIONS (ANSWERS AT END OF CHAPTER)

1. If a corporation has outstanding 1,000 shares of $9 cumulative preferred stock of $100 par, and dividends have been passed for the preceding three years, what is the amount of preferred dividends that must be declared in the current year before a dividend can be declared on common stock?
   A. $ 9,000
   B. $27,000
   C. $36,000
   D. $45,000

2. Paid-in capital for a corporation may arise from which of the following sources?
   A. Issuing cumulative preferred stock
   B. Receiving donations of real estate
   C. Selling the corporation's treasury stock
   D. All of the above

3. The Stockholders' Equity section of the balance sheet may include:
   A. Common Stock
   B. Donated Capital
   C. Preferred Stock
   D. All of the above

4. If a corporation reacquires its own stock, the stock is listed on the balance sheet in the:
   A. Current Assets section
   B. Long-Term Liabilities section
   C. Stockholders' Equity section
   D. Investments section

5. An appropriation for plant expansion would be reported on the balance sheet in the:
   A. Plant Assets section
   B. Long-Term Liabilities section
   C. Stockholders' Equity section
   D. Current Liabilities section

DISCUSSION QUESTIONS

1. Contrast the owners' liability to creditors of (a) a partnership (partners) and (b) a corporation (stockholders).
2. Why is it said that the earnings of a corporation are subject to *double taxation?* Discuss.
3. Why are most large businesses organized as corporations?
4. (a) What type of expenditure is charged to the organization costs account?
   (b) Give examples of such expenditures.
   (c) In what section of the balance sheet is the balance of Organization Costs listed?
5. What are the titles of the two principal subdivisions of the Stockholders' Equity section of a corporate balance sheet?
6. Distinguish between paid-in capital and retained earnings of a corporation.
7. The retained earnings account of a corporation at the beginning of the year had a credit balance of $125,000. The only other entry in the account during the year was a debit of $170,000 transferred from the income summary account at the end of the year. (a) What is the term applied to the $170,000 debit? (b) What is the term applied to the debit balance of retained earnings at the end of the year, after all closing entries have been posted?

8. Of two corporations organized at approximately the same time and engaged in competing businesses, one issued $25 par common stock, and the other issued $10 par common stock. Do the par designations provide any indication as to which stock is preferable as an investment? Explain.
9. What are the four basic rights that accompany ownership of a share of common stock?
10. a. Differentiate between common stock and preferred stock.
    b. Describe briefly (1) nonparticipating preferred stock and (2) cumulative preferred stock.
11. A stockbroker advises a client to "buy cumulative preferred stock. . . . With that type of stock, . . .[you] will never have to worry about losing the dividends." Is the broker right?
12. What are some sources of paid-in capital other than the issuance of stock?
13. If a corporation is given land as an inducement to locate in a particular community, (a) how should the amount of the debit to the land account be determined, and (b) what is the title of the account that should be credited for the same amount?
14. If common stock of $20 par is sold for $30, what is the $10 difference between the issue price and par called?
15. What are some of the factors that influence the market price of a corporation's stock?
16. When a corporation issues stock at a premium, is the premium income? Explain.
17. Land is acquired by a corporation for 5,000 shares of its $25 par common stock, which is currently selling for $35 per share on a national stock exchange. What accounts should be credited to record the transaction?
18. a. In what respect does treasury stock differ from unissued stock?
    b. How should treasury stock be presented on the balance sheet?
19. A corporation reacquires 2,000 shares of its own $40 par common stock for $95,000, recording it at cost. (a) What effect does this transaction have on revenue or expense of the period? (b) What effect does it have on stockholders' equity?
20. The treasury stock in Question 19 is resold for $125,000. (a) What is the effect on the corporation's revenue of the period? (b) What is the effect on stockholders' equity?
21. In which section of the corporation balance sheet would Paid-In Capital in Excess of Par—Preferred Stock appear?
22. Indicate which of the following accounts would be reported as part of paid-in capital on the balance sheet:
    a. Retained Earnings
    b. Common Stock
    c. Donated Capital
    d. Preferred Stock
23. a. What is a stock split?
    b. What is the primary purpose of a stock split?
24. What are the three conditions for the declaration and the payment of a cash dividend?
25. The dates in connection with the declaration of a cash dividend are April 1, May 15, and May 30. Identify each date.
26. A corporation with both cumulative preferred stock and common stock outstanding has a substantial credit balance in its retained earnings account at the beginning of the current fiscal year. Although net income for the current year is sufficient to pay the preferred dividend of $50,000 each quarter and a common dividend of $200,000 each quarter, the board of directors declares dividends only on the preferred stock. Suggest possible reasons for passing the dividends on the common stock.
27. An owner of 200 shares of Dunston Company common stock receives a stock dividend of 4 shares. (a) What is the effect of the stock dividend on the equity per share of the stock? (b) How does the total equity of 204 shares compare with the total equity of 200 shares before the stock dividend?
28. a. Where should a declared but unpaid cash dividend be reported on the balance sheet?
    b. Where should a declared but unissued stock dividend be reported on the balance sheet?
29. What term is used to identify a distribution to stockholders from paid-in capital?
30. Appropriations of retained earnings may be (a) required by law, (b) required by contract, or (c) made at the discretion of the board of directors. Give an illustration of each type of appropriation.
31. A credit balance in Retained Earnings does not represent cash. Explain.
32. The board of directors votes to appropriate $250,000 of retained earnings for self-insurance. What is the effect of this action on (a) cash, (b) total retained earnings, and (c) retained earnings available for dividends?

33. a. What two financial statements are frequently combined and presented as a single statement?
    b. What is the major disadvantage of the combined statement?
34. Why do some corporations report a statement of stockholders' equity? Describe the normal format of the statement of stockholders' equity.

EXERCISES

EXERCISE 14–1
Dividends per share
Objective 3

Meek Inc., a computer software development firm, has stock outstanding as follows: 20,000 shares of $4 (4%) cumulative, nonparticipating preferred stock of $100 par, and 100,000 shares of $50 par common. During its first five years of operations, the following amounts were distributed as dividends: first year, none; second year, $20,000; third year, $80,000; fourth year, $220,000; fifth year, $240,000. Calculate the dividends per share on each class of stock for each of the five years.

EXERCISE 14–2
Entries for issuing par stock
Objective 4

On June 5, Goulet Inc., a marble contractor, issued for cash 10,000 shares of $20 par common stock at $24, and on August 7, it issued for cash 5,000 shares of $10 par preferred stock at $14.

a. Journalize the entries for June 5 and August 7.
b. What is the total amount invested (total paid-in capital) by all stockholders as of August 7?

EXERCISE 14–3
Entries for issuing no-par stock
Objective 4

On January 3, Rug Corp., a carpet wholesaler, issued for cash 1,000 shares of no-par common stock (with a stated value of $100) at $110, and on May 15, it issued for cash 2,000 shares of $20 par preferred stock at $22.

a. Journalize the entries for January 3 and May 15, assuming that the common stock is to be credited with the stated value.
b. What is the total amount invested (total paid-in capital) by all stockholders as of May 15?

EXERCISE 14–4
Issuing stock for assets other than cash
Objective 4

On April 10, Universal Corporation, a wholesaler of hydraulic lifts, acquired land in exchange for 1,000 shares of $50 par common stock with a current market price of $60. Journalize the entry to record the transaction.

EXERCISE 14–5
Selected stock transactions
Objective 4

Mojo Guitar Corp., an electric guitar retailer, was organized by Mike Giardinelli, Susan Mirken, and Scott Wooster. The charter authorized 20,000 shares of common stock with a par of $10. The following transactions affecting stockholders' equity were completed during the first year of operations:

a. Issued 1,000 shares of stock at par to Wooster for cash.
b. Issued 500 shares of stock at par to Giardinelli for promotional services rendered in connection with the organization of the corporation, and issued 1,500 shares of stock at par to Giardinelli for cash.
c. Purchased land and a building from Mirken. The building is mortgaged for $125,000 for 22 years at 12%, and there is accrued interest of $4,000 on the mortgage note at the time of the purchase. It is agreed that the land is to be priced at $49,000 and the building at $130,000, and that Mirken's equity will be exchanged for stock at par. The corporation agreed to assume responsibility for paying the mortgage note and the accrued interest.

Journalize the entries to record the transactions.

EXERCISE 14–6
Treasury stock transactions
Objective 5

Twist Inc. bottles and distributes spring water. On July 1 of the current year, Twist Inc. reacquired 2,000 shares of its common stock at $32 per share. On August 10, Twist Inc. sold 500 of the reacquired shares at $41 per share. The remaining 1,500 shares were sold at $30 per share on December 19.

a. Journalize the transactions of July 1, August 10, and December 19.
b. What is the balance in Paid-In Capital from Sale of Treasury Stock on December 31 of the current year?
c. Where will the balance in Paid-In Capital from Sale of Treasury Stock be reported on the balance sheet?
d. For what reasons might Twist Inc. have purchased the treasury stock?

EXERCISE 14–7
Issuing stock; reporting paid-in capital
Objectives 4, 6

Embryology Inc., with an authorization of 10,000 shares of preferred stock and 100,000 shares of common stock, completed several transactions involving its stock on July 1, the first day of operations. The trial balance at the close of the day follows:

Cash	550,000	
Land	110,000	
Buildings	250,000	
Preferred $5 Stock, $100 par		300,000
Paid-In Capital in Excess of Par—Preferred Stock		60,000
Common Stock, $50 par		500,000
Paid-In Capital in Excess of Par—Common Stock		50,000
	910,000	910,000

All shares within each class of stock were sold at the same price. The preferred stock was issued in exchange for the land and buildings.

a. Journalize the two entries to record the transactions summarized in the trial balance.
b. Prepare the Stockholders' Equity section of the balance sheet as of July 1.

EXERCISE 14–8
Corporate organization; stockholders' equity section of balance sheet
Objectives 1, 6

Progressive Products Inc., a wholesaler of office products, was organized on January 7 of the current year, with an authorization of 20,000 shares of $3 noncumulative preferred stock, $100 par, and 100,000 shares of $20 par common stock.

The following selected transactions were completed during the first year of operations:

Jan. 7. Issued 15,000 shares of common stock at par for cash.
9. Issued 1,000 shares of common stock at par to an attorney in payment of legal fees for organizing the corporation.
Feb. 4. Issued 10,000 shares of common stock in exchange for land, buildings, and equipment with fair market prices of $80,000, $120,000, and $25,000 respectively.
Mar. 15. Issued 1,000 shares of preferred stock at $101 for cash.

a. Journalize the transactions.
b. Prepare the Stockholders' Equity section of the balance sheet as of December 31, the end of the current year. The net income for the year amounted to $47,500.

EXERCISE 14–9
Reporting paid-in capital
Objective 6

The following accounts and their balances appear in the ledger of HWY Inc. on April 30 of the current year:

Common Stock, $10 par	$200,000
Paid-In Capital in Excess of Par	40,000
Paid-In Capital from Sale of Treasury Stock	3,000
Retained Earnings	215,000
Treasury Stock	18,000

Prepare the Stockholders' Equity section of the balance sheet as of June 30. Twenty-five thousand shares of common stock are authorized, and 2,000 shares have been reacquired.

EXERCISE 14–10
Stockholders' equity section of balance sheet
Objective 6

Racorp Inc. retails racing products for BMWs, Porsches, and Ferraris. The following accounts and their balances appear in the ledger of Racorp Inc. on December 31, the end of the current year:

Common Stock, $10 par	$750,000
Paid-In Capital in Excess of Par—Common Stock	127,500
Paid-In Capital in Excess of Par—Preferred Stock	37,500
Paid-In Capital from Sale of Treasury Stock—Common	13,875
Preferred $2 Stock, $100 par	500,000
Retained Earnings	617,000
Treasury Stock—Common	17,500

Ten thousand shares of preferred and 150,000 shares of common stock are authorized. There are 2,050 shares of common stock held as treasury stock.

Prepare the Stockholders' Equity section of the balance sheet as of December 31, the end of the current year.

EXERCISE 14–11
Reporting paid-in capital
Objective 6

The following accounts and their balances were selected from the unadjusted trial balance of Express Inc., a freight forwarder, at December 31, the end of the current fiscal year:

Preferred $1 Stock, $50 par	$500,000
Paid-In Capital in Excess of Par—Preferred Stock	75,000
Common Stock, no par, $10 stated value	800,000
Paid-In Capital in Excess of Par—Common Stock	140,000
Paid-In Capital from Sale of Treasury Stock	7,500
Donated Capital	150,000
Retained Earnings	550,000

Prepare the Paid-In Capital portion of the Stockholders' Equity section of the balance sheet. There are 100,000 shares of common stock authorized and 50,000 shares of preferred stock authorized.

EXERCISE 14–12
Reporting paid-in capital
Objective 6

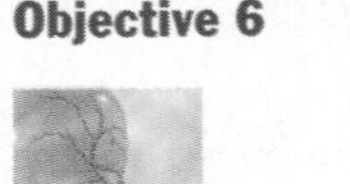

How many errors can you find in the following Stockholders' Equity section of the balance sheet prepared as of the end of the current year?

Stockholders' Equity

Paid-in capital:		
Preferred $2 stock, cumulative, $100 par (2,500 shares authorized and issued)	$250,000	
Excess of issue price over par	60,000	$ 310,000
Unappropriated retained earnings		140,000
Treasury stock (4,000 shares at cost)		75,000
Dividends payable		60,000
Total paid-in capital		$ 585,000
Common stock, $15 par (50,000 shares authorized, 40,000 shares issued)	$810,000	
Appropriated retained earnings for plant expansion	200,000	
Donated capital	100,000	
Organization costs	50,000	1,160,000
Total stockholders' equity		$1,745,000

EXERCISE 14–13
Effect of stock split
Objective 7

Patek Corporation wholesales ovens and ranges to restaurants throughout the Northwest. Patek Corporation, which had 10,000 shares of common stock outstanding, declared a 5-for-1 stock split (4 additional shares for each share issued).

a. What will be the number of shares outstanding after the split?
b. If the common stock had a market price of $125 per share before the stock split, what would be an approximate market price per share after the split?

EXERCISE 14–14
Effect of cash dividend
Objective 8

Indicate whether the following actions would (+) increase, (–) decrease, or (0) not affect Webster Inc.'s total assets, liabilities, and stockholders' equity:

	Assets	Liabilities	Stockholders' Equity
(1) Declaring a cash dividend	______	______	______
(2) Paying the cash dividend declared in (1)	______	______	______
(3) Declaring a stock dividend	______	______	______
(4) Issuing stock certificates for the stock dividend declared in (3)	______	______	______
(5) Authorizing and issuing stock certificates in a stock split	______	______	______

EXERCISE 14–15
Entries for cash dividends
Objective 8

The dates of importance in connection with a cash dividend of $35,000 on a corporation's common stock are January 2, January 22, and February 1. Journalize the entries required on each date.

EXERCISE 14–16
Entries for stock dividends
Objective 8

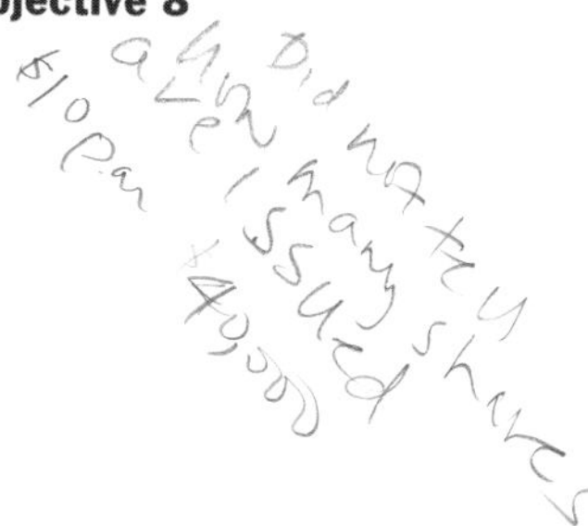

Med-Care Inc. is an HMO for twelve businesses in the Pittsburgh area. The following account balances appear on the balance sheet of Med-Care Inc.: Common stock (50,000 shares authorized), $10 par, $400,000; Paid-in capital in excess of par—common stock, $42,500; and Retained earnings, $299,500. The board of directors declared a 4% stock dividend when the market price of the stock was $15 a share. Med-Care Inc. reported no income or loss for the current year.

a. Journalize the entries to record (1) the declaration of the dividend, capitalizing an amount equal to market value, and (2) the issuance of the stock certificates.
b. Determine the following amounts before the stock dividend was declared: (1) total paid-in capital, (2) total retained earnings, and (3) total stockholders' equity.
c. Determine the following amounts after the stock dividend was declared and closing entries were recorded at the end of the year: (1) total paid-in capital, (2) total retained earnings, and (3) total stockholders' equity.

EXERCISE 14–17
Entries for treasury stock and appropriation
Objectives 5, 9

A corporation purchased for cash 3,500 shares of its own $10 par common stock at $18 a share. In the following year, it sold 2,000 of the treasury shares at $21 a share for cash.

a. Journalize the entries (1) to record the purchase (treasury stock is recorded at cost) and (2) to provide for the appropriation of retained earnings.
b. Journalize the entries (1) to record the sale of the stock and (2) to reduce the appropriation.

EXERCISE 14–18
Retained earnings statement with appropriations
Objective 10

Dorite Corporation, a manufacturer of industrial pumps, reports the following results of transactions affecting net income and retained earnings for its first fiscal year of operations ended on December 31:

Appropriation for plant expansion	$ 50,000
Cash dividends declared	20,000
Net income	218,000

Prepare a retained earnings statement for the fiscal year ended December 31.

EXERCISE 14–19
Combined income and retained earnings statement
Objective 10

Rozier Inc. is a wholesaler of surgical equipment to hospitals. Summary operating data for Rozier Inc. during the current year ended August 31, 1997, are as follows: administrative expenses, $125,000; cost of merchandise sold, $750,000; income tax, $55,000; interest expense, $25,000; net sales, $1,500,000; and selling expenses, $350,000. Assume that the balance of Retained Earnings was $715,000 on September 1, 1996, and that $90,000 of dividends was paid during the year.

a. Prepare a combined income and retained earnings statement for Rozier Inc. (Use the single-step form for the income statement portion.)
b. Prepare the entries to close the income summary account and dividends account to retained earnings.

EXERCISE 14–20
Statement of stockholders' equity
Objective 11

The stockholders' equity accounts of Reese Corporation for the current fiscal year ended December 31 are as follows.

COMMON STOCK, $1 PAR

Date		Item	Debit	Credit	Balance Debit	Balance Credit
19—						
Jan.	1	Balance				100,000
May	20	Issued 50,000 shares		50,000		150,000

PAID-IN CAPITAL IN EXCESS OF PAR

Date		Item	Debit	Credit	Balance Debit	Balance Credit
19—						
Jan.	1	Balance				400,000
May	20	Issued 50,000 shares		25,000		425,000

TREASURY STOCK

Date		Item	Debit	Credit	Balance Debit	Balance Credit
19—						
Nov.	30	Purchased 5,000 shares	8,000		8,000	

APPROPRIATION FOR TREASURY STOCK

Date		Item	Debit	Credit	Balance Debit	Balance Credit
19—						
Dec.	31	Retained earnings		8,000		8,000

RETAINED EARNINGS

Date		Item	Debit	Credit	Balance Debit	Balance Credit
19—						
Jan.	1	Balance				925,000
Dec.	31	Income summary		320,000		1,245,000
	31	Appropriation for treasury stock	8,000			1,237,000
	31	Cash dividends	15,000			1,222,000

CASH DIVIDENDS

Date		Item	Debit	Credit	Balance Debit	Balance Credit
19—						
Mar.	12		10,000		10,000	
June	17		5,000		15,000	
Dec.	31	Closing		15,000	—	—

Prepare a statement of stockholders' equity for the fiscal year ended December 31.

PROBLEMS SERIES A

PROBLEM 14–1A
Dividends on preferred and common stock
Objective 3

Omni Inc. owns and operates movie theaters throughout California and Arizona. Omni Inc. has declared the following annual dividends over a six-year period: 1993, $26,000; 1994, $40,000; 1995, $84,000; 1996, $60,000; 1997, $72,000; and 1998, $90,000. During the entire period, the outstanding stock of the company was composed of 5,000 shares of cumulative nonparticipating, $10 preferred stock, $100 par, and 10,000 shares of common stock, $75 par.

Instructions

1. Calculate the total dividends and the per-share dividends declared on each class of stock for each of the six years. There were no dividends in arrears on January 1, 1993. Summarize the data in tabular form, using the following column headings:

Year	*Total Dividends*	*Preferred Dividends*		*Common Dividends*	
		Total	*Per Share*	*Total*	*Per Share*
1993	$26,000				
1994	40,000				
1995	84,000				
1996	60,000				
1997	72,000				
1998	90,000				

2. Calculate the average annual dividend per share for each class of stock for the six-year period.
3. Assuming that the preferred stock was sold at par and common stock was sold at $80 at the beginning of the six-year period, calculate the percentage return on initial shareholders' investment, based on the average annual dividend per share (a) for preferred stock and (b) for common stock.

PROBLEM 14–2A
Corporate expansion; stockholders' equity section of balance sheet
Objectives 3, 6

On January 1 of the current year, the following accounts and their balances appear in the ledger of Medallion Corp., a meat processor:

Preferred $9 Stock, $100 par (10,000 shares authorized, 5,000 shares issued)	$ 500,000
Paid-In Capital in Excess of Par—Preferred Stock	80,000
Common Stock, $20 par (100,000 shares authorized, 75,000 shares issued)	1,500,000
Paid-In Capital in Excess of Par—Common Stock	125,000
Retained Earnings	505,000

At the annual stockholders' meeting on February 11, the board of directors presented a plan for modernizing and expanding plant operations at a cost of approximately $600,000. The plan provided (a) that the corporation borrow $175,000, (b) that 1,000 shares of the unissued preferred stock be issued through an underwriter, and (c) that a building, valued at $280,000, and the land on which it is located, valued at $50,000, be acquired in accordance with preliminary negotiations by the issuance of 15,000 shares of common stock. The plan was approved by the stockholders and accomplished by the following transactions:

Mar. 3. Issued 15,000 shares of common stock in exchange for land and a building, according to the plan.
15. Issued 1,000 shares of preferred stock, receiving $105 per share in cash from the underwriter.
31. Borrowed $175,000 from Highland National Bank, giving a 12% mortgage note.

No other transactions occurred during March.

Instructions

1. Journalize the entries to record the foregoing transactions.
2. Prepare the Stockholders' Equity section of the balance sheet as of March 31.

PROBLEM 14–3A
Stock transactions; stockholders' equity section of balance sheet
Objectives 4, 5, 6, 8, 9, 11

The following selected accounts appear in the ledger of Commack Environmental Corporation on July 1, 1996, the beginning of the current fiscal year:

Preferred 4% Stock, $50 par (10,000 shares authorized, 7,000 shares issued)	$350,000
Paid-In Capital in Excess of Par—Preferred Stock	28,000
Common Stock, $20 par (50,000 shares authorized, 25,000 shares issued)	500,000
Paid-In Capital in Excess of Par—Common Stock	90,000
Retained Earnings	537,000

During the year, the corporation completed a number of transactions affecting the stockholders' equity. They are summarized as follows:

a. Purchased 2,000 shares of treasury common for $55,000.
b. Sold 500 shares of treasury common for $16,000.
c. Issued 5,000 shares of common stock at $30, receiving cash.
d. Sold 1,000 shares of preferred 4% stock at $52.50.
e. Sold 600 shares of treasury common for $15,600.
f. Declared cash dividends of $2 per share on preferred stock and $1 per share on common stock.
g. Paid the cash dividends.
h. The board of directors authorized the appropriation necessitated by the holding of treasury stock.

Instructions

1. Journalize the entries to record the transactions. Identify each entry by letter.
2. Prepare a statement of stockholders' equity for the year ended June 30, 1997, the end of the current fiscal year. The net income for the year was $165,000.
3. Prepare the Stockholders' Equity section of the balance sheet as of June 30, 1997.

PROBLEM 14–4A
Entries for selected corporate transactions
Objectives 4, 5, 6, 8, 9

Schulman Enterprises Inc. manufactures bathroom fixtures. The stockholders' equity accounts of Schulman Enterprises Inc., with balances on January 1 of the current fiscal year, are as follows:

Common Stock, $25 stated value (100,000 shares authorized, 50,000 shares issued)	$1,250,000
Paid-In Capital in Excess of Stated Value	250,000
Appropriation for Plant Expansion	150,000
Appropriation for Treasury Stock	80,000
Retained Earnings	725,000
Treasury Stock (2,500 shares, at cost)	80,000

The following selected transactions occurred during the year:

Jan. 20. Received land from the city as a donation. The land had an estimated fair market value of $100,000.
29. Paid cash dividends of $1 per share on the common stock. The dividend had been properly recorded when declared on December 30 of the preceding fiscal year for $47,500.
Mar. 3. Sold all of the treasury stock for $95,000.
Apr. 1. Issued 6,000 shares of common stock for $240,000.
July 1. Declared a 2% stock dividend on common stock, to be capitalized at the market price of the stock, which is $40 a share.
Aug. 11. Issued the certificates for the dividend declared on July 1.
Nov. 20. Purchased 2,000 shares of treasury stock for $72,000.
Dec. 21. The board of directors authorized an increase of the appropriation for plant expansion by $50,000.
21. Declared a $0.50-per-share dividend on common stock.
21. Decreased the appropriation for treasury stock to $72,000.
31. Closed the credit balance of the income summary account, $169,400.
31. Closed the two dividends accounts to Retained Earnings.

Instructions

1. Enter the January 1 balances in T accounts for the stockholders' equity accounts listed. Also prepare T accounts for the following: Paid-In Capital from Sale of Treasury Stock; Donated Capital; Stock Dividends Distributable; Stock Dividends; Cash Dividends.
2. Journalize the entries to record the transactions, and post to the eleven selected accounts.
3. Prepare the Stockholders' Equity section of the balance sheet as of December 31 of the current fiscal year.

PROBLEM 14–5A
Entries for selected corporate transactions
Objectives 5, 7, 8, 9

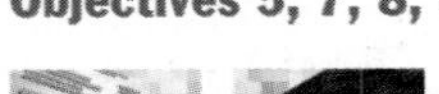

Selected transactions completed by Chempar Boating Supply Corporation during the current fiscal year are as follows:

Jan. 9. Split the common stock 4 for 1 and reduced the par from $100 to $25 per share. After the split, there were 100,000 common shares outstanding.
Feb. 10. Purchased 5,000 shares of the corporation's own common stock at $42, recording the stock at cost.
May 1. Declared semiannual dividends of $3 on 5,000 shares of preferred stock and $1 on the common stock to stockholders of record on May 20, payable on July 15.
July 15. Paid the cash dividends.
Aug. 22. Sold 2,500 shares of treasury stock at $50, receiving cash.
Nov. 30. Declared semiannual dividends of $3 on the preferred stock and $0.80 on the common stock. In addition, a 2% common stock dividend was declared on the common stock outstanding. The fair market value of the common stock is estimated at $51.

Dec. 30. Paid the cash dividends and issued the certificates for the common stock dividend.
30. The board of directors authorized the appropriation necessitated by the holding of treasury stock.

Instructions

Journalize the transactions.

PROBLEM 14–6A
Retained earnings statement
Objective 10

For the current fiscal year ended December 31, the retained earnings accounts of Dermo Corporation, a pharmaceutical company specializing in skin ointments, are as follows:

APPROPRIATION FOR PLANT EXPANSION

Date		Item	Debit	Credit	Balance	
					Debit	Credit
19—						
Jan.	1	Balance				250,000
Dec.	31	Retained earnings		75,000		325,000

APPROPRIATION FOR TREASURY STOCK

Date		Item	Debit	Credit	Balance	
					Debit	Credit
19—						
Jan.	1	Balance				375,000
Dec.	31	Retained earnings	175,000			200,000

RETAINED EARNINGS

Date		Item	Debit	Credit	Balance	
					Debit	Credit
19—						
Jan.	1	Balance				715,000
Dec.	31	Income summary		185,000		900,000
	31	Appropriation for plant expansion	75,000			825,000
	31	Appropriation for treasury stock		175,000		1,000,000
	31	Cash dividends	100,000			900,000
	31	Stock dividends	150,000			750,000

CASH DIVIDENDS

Date		Item	Debit	Credit	Balance	
					Debit	Credit
19—						
July	27		100,000		100,000	
Dec.	31	Retained earnings		100,000	—	—

STOCK DIVIDENDS

Date		Item	Debit	Credit	Balance	
					Debit	Credit
19—						
July	27		150,000		150,000	
Dec.	31	Retained earnings		150,000	—	—

Instructions

Prepare a retained earnings statement for the fiscal year ended December 31.

PROBLEMS SERIES B

PROBLEM 14–1B
Dividends on preferred and common stock
Objective 3

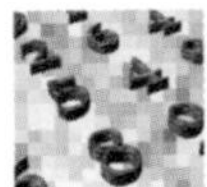

Canyon Corp. manufactures mountain bikes and distributes them through retail outlets in Colorado and Utah. Canyon Corp. has declared the following annual dividends over a six-year period: 1993, $30,000; 1994, $15,000; 1995, $10,000; 1996, $4,000; 1997, $50,000; and 1998, $75,000. During the entire period, the outstanding stock of the company was composed of 10,000 shares of cumulative, nonparticipating, $2 preferred stock, $50 par, and 25,000 shares of common stock, $10 par.

Instructions

1. Calculate the total dividends and the per-share dividends declared on each class of stock for each of the six years. There were no dividends in arrears on January 1, 1993. Summarize the data in tabular form, using the following column headings:

Year	*Total Dividends*	*Preferred Dividends*		*Common Dividends*	
		Total	*Per Share*	*Total*	*Per Share*
1993	$30,000				
1994	15,000				
1995	10,000				
1996	4,000				
1997	50,000				
1998	75,000				

2. Calculate the average annual dividend per share for each class of stock for the six-year period.
3. Assuming that the preferred stock was sold at par and common stock was sold at $15 at the beginning of the six-year period, calculate the percentage return on initial shareholders' investment, based on the average annual dividend per share (a) for preferred stock and (b) for common stock.

PROBLEM 14–2B
Corporate expansion; stockholders' equity section of balance sheet
Objectives 3, 6

Sangean Corp. produces medical lasers for use in hospitals. The following accounts and their balances appear in the ledger of Sangean Corp. on April 30 of the current year:

Preferred $9 Stock, $100 par (10,000 shares authorized, 8,000 shares issued)	$ 800,000
Paid-In Capital in Excess of Par—Preferred Stock	86,000
Common Stock, $20 par (100,000 shares authorized, 75,000 shares issued)	1,500,000
Paid-In Capital in Excess of Par—Common Stock	210,000
Retained Earnings	715,000

At the annual stockholders' meeting on May 12, the board of directors presented a plan for modernizing and expanding plant operations at a cost of approximately $750,000. The plan provided (a) that the corporation borrow $200,000, (b) that 1,000 shares of the unissued preferred stock be issued through an underwriter, and (c) that a building, valued at $355,000, and the land on which it is located, valued at $100,000, be acquired in accordance with preliminary negotiations by the issuance of 18,000 shares of common stock. The plan was approved by the stockholders and accomplished by the following transactions:

June 2. Issued 18,000 shares of common stock in exchange for land and a building, according to the plan.
10. Issued 1,000 shares of preferred stock, receiving $105 per share in cash from the underwriter.
30. Borrowed $200,000 from Palmer National Bank, giving a 14% mortgage note.

No other transactions occurred during June.

Instructions

1. Journalize the entries to record the foregoing transactions.
2. Prepare the Stockholders' Equity section of the balance sheet as of June 30.

PROBLEM 14–3B
Stock transactions; stockholders' equity section of balance sheet
Objectives 4, 5, 6, 8, 9, 11

Cardinal Corporation sells and services pipe welding equipment in Missouri. The following selected accounts appear in the ledger of Cardinal Corporation on January 1, 1997, the beginning of the current fiscal year:

Preferred 3% Stock, $100 par (20,000 shares authorized, 12,500 shares issued)	$1,250,000
Paid-In Capital in Excess of Par—Preferred Stock	112,500
Common Stock, $10 par (600,000 shares authorized, 400,000 shares issued)	4,000,000
Paid-In Capital in Excess of Par—Common Stock	600,000
Retained Earnings	1,450,000

During the year, the corporation completed a number of transactions affecting the stockholders' equity. They are summarized as follows:

a. Purchased 15,000 shares of treasury common for $180,000.
b. Sold 3,000 shares of treasury common for $45,000.
c. Sold 2,000 shares of preferred 3% stock at $105.
d. Issued 50,000 shares of common stock at $15, receiving cash.
e. Sold 10,000 shares of treasury common for $140,000.
f. Declared cash dividends of $3 per share on preferred stock and $.25 per share on common stock.
g. Paid the cash dividends.
h. The board of directors authorized the appropriation necessitated by the holding of treasury stock.

Instructions

1. Journalize the entries to record the transactions. Identify each entry by letter.
2. Prepare a statement of stockholders' equity for the year ended December 31, 1997. The net income for the year was $750,000.
3. Prepare the Stockholders' Equity section of the balance sheet as of December 31, 1997.

PROBLEM 14–4B
Entries for selected corporate transactions
Objectives 4, 5, 6, 8, 9

Kahn Enterprises Inc. produces aeronautical navigation equipment. The stockholders' equity accounts of Kahn Enterprises Inc., with balances on January 1 of the current fiscal year, are as follows:

Common Stock, $10 stated value (100,000 shares authorized, 80,000 shares issued)	$800,000
Paid-In Capital in Excess of Stated Value	110,000
Appropriation for Plant Expansion	175,000
Appropriation for Treasury Stock	60,000
Retained Earnings	497,750
Treasury Stock (4,000 shares, at cost)	60,000

The following selected transactions occurred during the year:

Jan. 31. Paid cash dividends of $1 per share on the common stock. The dividend had been properly recorded when declared on December 28 of the preceding fiscal year for $76,000.
Mar. 7. Sold all of the treasury stock for $72,000.
May 5. Issued 10,000 shares of common stock for $155,000.
June 11. Received land from the Olinville City Council as a donation. The land had an estimated fair market value of $150,000.
July 30. Declared a 4% stock dividend on common stock, to be capitalized at the market price of the stock, which is $16 a share.
Aug. 27. Issued the certificates for the dividend declared on July 30.

Oct. 8. Purchased 2,500 shares of treasury stock for $42,500.
Dec. 20. Declared an $0.80-per-share dividend on common stock.
20. The board of directors authorized an increase of the appropriation for plant expansion by $75,000.
20. Decreased the appropriation for treasury stock by $17,500.
31. Closed the credit balance of the income summary account, $182,500.
31. Closed the two dividends accounts to Retained Earnings.

Instructions

1. Enter the January 1 balances in T accounts for the stockholders' equity accounts listed. Also prepare T accounts for the following: Paid-In Capital from Sale of Treasury Stock; Donated Capital; Stock Dividends Distributable; Stock Dividends; Cash Dividends.
2. Journalize the entries to record the transactions, and post to the eleven selected accounts.
3. Prepare the Stockholders' Equity section of the balance sheet as of December 31 of the current fiscal year.

PROBLEM 14–5B
Entries for selected corporate transactions
Objectives 5, 7, 8, 9

Malibu Corporation manufactures and distributes leisure clothing. Selected transactions completed by Malibu Corporation during the current fiscal year are as follows:

Jan. 2. Split the common stock 5 for 1 and reduced the par from $50 to $10 per share. After the split, there were 75,000 common shares outstanding.
Mar. 3. Declared semiannual dividends of $3 on 10,000 shares of preferred stock and $0.40 on the 75,000 shares of $10 par common stock to stockholders of record on March 28, payable on April 15.
Apr. 15. Paid the cash dividends.
30. Purchased 8,000 shares of the corporation's own common stock at $18, recording the stock at cost.
July 10. Sold 3,000 shares of treasury stock at $20, receiving cash.
23. Declared semiannual dividends of $3 on the preferred stock and $0.40 on the common stock. In addition, a 2% common stock dividend was declared on the common stock outstanding, to be capitalized at the fair market value of the common stock, which is estimated at $21.
Aug. 25. Paid the cash dividends and issued the certificates for the common stock dividend.
Dec. 31. The board of directors authorized the appropriation necessitated by the holding of treasury stock.

Instructions
Journalize the transactions.

PROBLEM 14–6B
Retained earnings statement
Objective 10

Nederland Corporation produces and sells playground equipment. The retained earnings accounts of Nederland Corporation for the current fiscal year ended December 31 are as follows:

APPROPRIATION FOR PLANT EXPANSION

Date		Item	Debit	Credit	Balance Debit	Balance Credit
19—						
Jan.	1	Balance				200,000
Dec.	31	Retained earnings		100,000		300,000

APPROPRIATION FOR TREASURY STOCK

Date		Item	Debit	Credit	Balance Debit	Balance Credit
19—						
Jan.	1	Balance				125,000
Dec.	31	Retained earnings	30,000			95,000

RETAINED EARNINGS

Date		Item	Debit	Credit	Balance	
					Debit	Credit
19—						
Jan.	1	Balance				515,000
Dec.	31	Income summary		190,000		705,000
	31	Appropriation for plant expansion	100,000			605,000
	31	Appropriation for treasury stock		30,000		635,000
	31	Cash dividends	50,000			585,000
	31	Stock dividends	120,000			465,000

CASH DIVIDENDS

Date		Item	Debit	Credit	Balance	
					Debit	Credit
19—						
Apr.	10		25,000		25,000	
Oct.	13		25,000		50,000	
Dec.	31	Retained earnings		50,000	—	—

STOCK DIVIDENDS

Date		Item	Debit	Credit	Balance	
					Debit	Credit
19—						
Oct.	13		120,000		120,000	
Dec.	31	Retained earnings		120,000	—	—

Instructions

Prepare a retained earnings statement for the fiscal year ended December 31.

CASES

CASE 14–1

Mines Unlimited Inc.

Par value of stock

Ignacio Maglie and Don Tomlin are organizing Mines Unlimited Inc. to undertake a high-risk gold-mining venture in Mexico. Ignacio and Don tentatively plan to request authorization for 100,000,000 shares of common stock to be sold to the general public. Ignacio and Don have decided to establish par of $0.10 per share in order to appeal to a wide variety of potential investors. Ignacio and Don feel that investors would be more willing to invest in the company if they received a large quantity of shares for what might appear to be a "bargain" price.

Discuss whether Ignacio and Don are behaving in an ethical manner.

CASE 14–2

Protection-Plus Inc.

Issuing stock

Protection-Plus Inc. began operations on January 3, 1997, with the issuance of 25,000 shares of $100 par common stock. The sole stockholders of Protection-Plus Inc. are Judi Barnett and Dr. Herman Elfand, who organized Protection-Plus Inc. with the objective of developing a new flu vaccine. Dr. Elfand claims that the flu vaccine, which is nearing the final development stage, will protect individuals against 99% of the flu types that have been medically identified. To complete the project, Protection-Plus Inc. needs $1,500,000 of additional funds. The local banks have been unwilling to loan the funds because of the lack of sufficient collateral and the riskiness of the business.

The following is a conversation between Judi Barnett, the chief executive officer of Protection-Plus Inc., and Dr. Herman Elfand, the leading researcher.

Barnett: What are we going to do? The banks won't loan us any more money, and we've got to have $1.5 million to complete the project. We are so close! It would be a disaster to quit now. The only thing I can think of is to issue additional stock. Do you have any suggestions?

Elfand: I guess you're right. But if the banks won't loan us any more money, how do you think we can find any investors to buy stock?

Barnett: I've been thinking about that. What if we promise the investors that we will pay them 2% of net sales until they have received an amount equal to what they paid for the stock?

Elfand: What happens when we pay back the $1.5 million? Do the investors get to keep the stock? If they do, it'll dilute our ownership.

Barnett: How about, if after we pay back the $1.5 million, we make them turn in their stock for $200 per share? That's twice what they paid for it, plus they would have already gotten all their money back. That's a $200 profit per share for the investors.

Elfand: It could work. We get our money, but don't have to pay any interest, dividends, or the $200 until we start generating net sales. At the same time, the investors could get their money back plus $200 per share.

Barnett: We'll need current financial statements for the new investors. I'll get our accountant working on them and contact our attorney to draw up a legally binding contract for the new investors. Yes, this could work.

In late 1997, the attorney and the various regulatory authorities approved the new stock offering, and 15,000 shares of common stock were privately sold to new investors at the stock's par of $100.

In preparing financial statements for 1997, Judi Barnett and Ed Thaxton, the controller for Protection-Plus Inc., have the following conversation.

Thaxton: Judi, I've got a problem.

Barnett: What's that, Ed?

Thaxton: Issuing common stock to raise that additional $1.5 million was a great idea. But. . .

Barnett: But what?

Thaxton: I've got to prepare the 1997 annual financial statements, and I am not sure how to classify the common stock.

Barnett: What do you mean? It's common stock.

Thaxton: I'm not so sure. I called the auditor and explained how we are contractually obligated to pay the new stockholders 2% of net sales until $100 per share is paid. Then, we may be obligated to pay them $200 per share.

Barnett: So. . .

Thaxton: So the auditor thinks that we should classify the additional issuance of $1.5 million as debt, not stock! And, if we put the $1.5 million on the balance sheet as debt, we will violate our other loan agreements with the banks. And, if these agreements are violated, the banks may call in all our debt immediately. If they do that, we are in deep trouble. We'll probably have to file for bankruptcy. We just don't have the cash to pay off the banks.

1. Discuss the arguments for and against classifying the issuance of the $1.5 million of stock as debt.
2. What do you think might be a practical solution to this classification problem?

CASE 14–3
Hershey Foods Corporation
Financial analysis

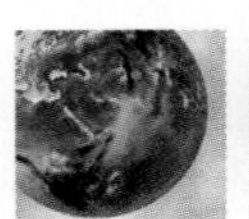

Two profitability measures included in the stock quotations that appear daily in *The Wall Street Journal* and similar publications are the price-earnings ratio and the dividend yield per share of common stock. The price-earnings (P/E) ratio is an indication of a firm's future earnings prospects and is computed as follows:

$$\text{Price-Earnings Ratio} = \frac{\text{Market Price per Share of Common Stock}}{\text{Earnings per Share of Common Stock}}$$

The market price per common share is the price at a specific date, and the earnings are the annual earnings per common share. A high P/E ratio indicates that investors expect the company's earnings to be above average for comparable companies.

The dividend yield is a profitability measure that shows the rate of return to common stockholders in terms of cash dividends. It is computed as follows:

$$\text{Dividend Yield} = \frac{\text{Dividends per Share of Common Stock}}{\text{Market Price per Share of Common Stock}}$$

The dividends per common share are the annual dividends per share, and the market price per common share is the price at a specific date. Dividend yield is of special interest to investors who look for a current return (dividend) from their investment.

a. Determine Hershey Foods Corporation's price-earnings ratio on December 31, 1993 and 1992.
b. Determine Hershey's dividend yield as of December 31, 1993 and 1992 on common stock (exclude Class B Common Stock).
   Note: Hershey's common stock price was $49 and $47 on December 31, 1993 and 1992, respectively.
c. What conclusions can you reach from an analysis of these data?

CASE 14–4

Digital Corp.

Dividends

Digital Corp. has paid quarterly cash dividends since 1987. These dividends have steadily increased from $0.20 per share to the latest dividend declaration of $0.50 per share. The board of directors would like to continue this trend and is hesitant to suspend or decrease the amount of quarterly dividends. Unfortunately, sales dropped sharply in the fourth quarter of 1997 because of worsening economic conditions and increased competition. As a result, the board is uncertain as to whether it should declare a dividend for the last quarter of 1997.

On November 1, 1997, Digital Corp. borrowed $500,000 from Second National Bank to use in modernizing its retail stores and to expand its product line in reaction to its competition. The terms of the 10-year, 12% loan require Digital Corp. to:

a. Pay monthly interest on last day of month.
b. Pay $50,000 of the principal each November 1, beginning in 1998.
c. Maintain a current ratio (current assets ÷ current liabilities) of 2:1.
d. Appropriate $500,000 of retained earnings until the loan is fully paid.
e. Maintain a minimum balance (a compensating balance) of $25,000 in its Second National Bank account.

On December 31, 1997, 25% of the $500,000 loan had been disbursed in modernization of the retail stores and in expansion of the product line, and the remainder is temporarily invested in U.S. Treasury Notes. Digital Corp.'s balance sheet as of December 31, 1997, is as follows:

Digital Corp.
Balance Sheet
December 31, 1997

Assets			
Current assets:			
Cash		$ 40,000	
Marketable securities	$375,000		
Add unrealized gain	4,500	379,500	
Accounts receivable	$ 91,500		
Less allowance for doubtful accounts	6,500	85,000	
Merchandise inventory		120,500	
Prepaid expenses		4,500	
Total current assets			$ 629,500
Plant assets:			
Land		$150,000	
Buildings	$950,000		
Less accumulated depreciation	215,000	735,000	
Equipment	$460,000		
Less accumulated depreciation	110,000	350,000	
Total plant assets			1,235,000
Total assets			$1,864,500
Liabilities			
Current liabilities:			
Accounts payable	$ 71,800		
Notes payable (Second National Bank)	50,000		
Salaries payable	3,200		
Total current liabilities		$125,000	
Long-term liabilities:			
Notes payable (Second National Bank)		450,000	
Total liabilities			$ 575,000
Stockholders' Equity			
Paid-in capital:			
Common stock, $20 par (50,000 shares authorized, 25,000 shares issued)	$500,000		
Excess of issue price over par	40,000		
Total paid-in capital		$540,000	
Retained earnings:			
Appropriated for provision of Second National Bank loan	$500,000		
Unappropriated	249,500		
Total retained earnings		749,500	
Total stockholders' equity			1,289,500
Total liabilities and stockholders' equity			$1,864,500

The board of directors is scheduled to meet January 10, 1998, to discuss the results of operations for 1997 and to consider the declaration of dividends for the fourth quarter of 1997. The chairman of the board has asked for your advice on the declaration of dividends.

1. What factors should the board consider in deciding whether to declare a cash dividend?
2. The board is considering the declaration of a stock dividend instead of a cash dividend. Discuss the issuance of a stock dividend from the point of view of (a) a stockholder and (b) the board of directors.

ANSWERS TO SELF-EXAMINATION QUESTIONS

1. **C** If a corporation has cumulative preferred stock outstanding, dividends that have been passed for prior years plus the dividend for the current year must be paid before dividends may be declared on common stock. In this case, dividends of $27,000 ($9,000 × 3) have been passed for the preceding three years, and the current year's dividends are $9,000, making a total of $36,000 (answer C) that must be paid to preferred stockholders before dividends can be declared on common stock.
2. **D** Paid-in capital is one of the two major subdivisions of the stockholders' equity of a corporation. It may result from many sources, including the issuance of cumulative preferred stock (answer A), the receipt of donated real estate (answer B), or the sale of a corporation's treasury stock (answer C).
3. **D** The Stockholders' Equity section of corporate balance sheets is divided into two principal subsections: (1) investments contributed by the stockholders and others and (2) net income retained in the business. Included as part of the investments by stockholders and others is the par of common stock (answer A), donated capital (answer B), and the par of preferred stock (answer C).
4. **C** Reacquired stock, known as treasury stock, should be listed in the Stockholders' Equity section (answer C) of the balance sheet. The price paid for the treasury stock is deducted from the total of all the stockholders' equity accounts.
5. **C** An appropriation for plant expansion is a portion of total retained earnings and would be reported in the Stockholders' Equity section of the balance sheet (answer C).

15 Corporate Earnings, International Transactions, and Investments in Stocks

YOU AND ACCOUNTING

You are planning a trip to Germany, and before you leave, you plan to convert some U.S. dollars to German deutsche marks (DM). You've contacted the foreign exchange office at the airport, and they have told you that the U.S. dollar is worth 1.6579 deutsche marks.

If you decide to convert $1,000 to German deutsche marks, how much foreign currency should you expect to receive? In this case, you should receive DM 1,657.90. This amount is determined by multiplying $1,000 by the exchange rate of 1.6579.

During your trip to Germany, you find several items of merchandise in a small antique shop in Berlin. The total price of the items is DM 568. However, you have depleted your supply of deutsche marks, and the store is about to close for the weekend. The owner has agreed to take your U.S. dollars at the exchange rate of 1.6579. How much in U.S. currency should you give the shop owner for the merchandise? In this case, you should give the owner $342.60. This amount is determined by dividing the price of the merchandise in deutsche marks, DM 568, by the exchange rate of 1.6579.

Many businesses enter into transactions with foreign companies. Computations such as those above determine the amounts to be received and paid. In this chapter, we discuss the accounting for international transactions. In addition, we discuss a variety of topics related to corporate earnings. We conclude the chapter with a brief discussion of accounting for long-term investments in stocks, business combinations, and prior-period adjustments.

After studying this chapter, you should be able to:

Objective 1
Journalize the entries for corporate income taxes, including deferred income taxes.

Objective 2
Prepare an income statement reporting the following unusual items: discontinued operations, extraordinary items, and changes in accounting principles.

Objective 3
Prepare an income statement reporting earnings per share data.

Objective 4
Journalize entries for international transactions involving foreign currency exchange gains and losses.

Objective 5
Prepare a retained earnings statement reporting a prior-period adjustment.

Objective 6
Compute the price-earnings ratio and equity per share.

Objective 7
Journalize entries for long-term investments in stocks, using the cost method and the equity method.

Objective 8
Describe alternative methods of combining businesses and the preparation of consolidated financial statements.

Corporate Income Taxes

Objective 1
Journalize the entries for corporate income taxes, including deferred income taxes.

As we mentioned in an earlier chapter, corporations are taxable entities that must pay income taxes. Some corporations pay not only federal income taxes but also state and local income taxes. Although we limit the following discussion to federal income taxes, the basic concepts also apply to state and local income taxes.

PAYMENT OF INCOME TAXES

Most corporations are required to pay estimated federal income taxes in four installments throughout the year. For example, assume that a corporation with a calendar-year accounting period estimates its income tax expense for the year as $84,000. The entry to record each of the four estimated tax payments of $21,000 (1/4 of $84,000) is as follows:

Income Tax	21,000	
Cash		21,000

At year end, the actual taxable income and the actual tax are determined. If additional taxes are owed, the additional liability is recorded.[1] If the total estimated tax payments are greater than the tax liability based on actual income, the overpayment should be debited to a receivable account and credited to Income Tax.

Because income tax is often a significant amount, it is normally reported on the income statement as a special deduction, as shown below in an excerpt from the 1994 income statement for **Microsoft Corporation.**

[1] A corporation's income tax returns and supporting records are subject to audits by taxing authorities, who may assess additional taxes. Because of this possibility, the liability for income taxes is sometimes described in the balance sheet as *Estimated income tax payable.*

Microsoft Corporation
Income Statement (In Millions)
For the Year Ended June 30, 1994

Net revenues	$4,649
...	
Income before income taxes	$1,722
Income taxes	576
Net income	$1,146

ALLOCATION OF INCOME TAXES

The taxable income of a corporation must be determined according to the tax laws. It is often different from the income before income tax determined and reported according to generally accepted accounting principles. As a result, the income tax based on taxable income usually differs from the income tax based on income before taxes in the income statement. This difference may need to be allocated between various financial statement periods, depending on the nature of the items causing the differences.

Some differences between taxable income and income before income tax are created because items are recognized in one period for tax purposes and in another period for income statement purposes. Such differences, called temporary differences, reverse or turn around in later years. Some examples of items that create temporary differences are listed below.[2]

1. Revenues or gains are taxed after they are reported in the income statement. Example: The point-of-sale method of recognizing revenue is used for financial statement reporting, and the installment method of recognizing revenue is used for tax reporting.
2. Expenses or losses are deducted in determining taxable income after they are reported in the income statement. Example: Product warranty expense estimated and reported in the year of the sale for financial statement reporting is deducted for tax reporting when paid.
3. Revenues or gains are taxed before they are reported in the income statement. Example: Cash received in advance for magazine subscriptions is included in taxable income when received but included in the income statement only when earned in a future period.
4. Expenses or losses are deducted in determining taxable income before they are reported in the income statement. Example: MACRS depreciation is used for tax purposes, and the straight-line method is used for financial reporting purposes.

Over the life of a business, temporary differences do not change or reduce the total amount of tax paid. Temporary differences affect only the timing of when the taxes are paid. In most cases, managers use tax-planning techniques so that temporary differences will delay or defer the payment of taxes to later years. As a result, at the end of each year, the amount of the current tax liability and the postponed (deferred) liability must be recorded.

To illustrate, assume that at the end of the first year of operations a corporation reports $300,000 income before income taxes on its income statement. If we assume an income tax rate of 40%, the income tax reported on the income statement is $120,000 ($300,000 × 40%).[3] However, to reduce the amount owed for current income taxes, the corporation uses tax planning to reduce the taxable income to $100,000. Thus, the income tax actually due for the year is only $40,000 ($100,000 × 40%). The $80,000 ($120,000 – $40,000) difference between the two tax amounts is

[2] *Statement of Financial Accounting Standards, No. 109,* "Accounting for Income Taxes," Financial Accounting Standards Board, Norwalk, 1992, par. 11.

[3] For purposes of illustration, the 40% tax rate is assumed to include all federal, state, and local income taxes.

created by timing differences in recognizing revenue. It represents a deferment of $80,000 of income tax to future years. The example is summarized below.

Income tax based on $300,000 reported income at 40%	$120,000
Income tax based on $100,000 taxable income at 40%	40,000
Income tax deferred to future years	$ 80,000

The income tax reported on the income statement is the total tax, $120,000, expected to be paid on the income for the year. This income tax includes the $80,000 that relates to this year's income but that will be paid in future years. In this way, the current year's expenses (including income tax) are matched against the current year's revenue. To achieve this matching on the income statement, income tax is allocated between periods, using the following journal entry:

Income Tax	120,000	
Income Tax Payable		40,000
Deferred Income Tax Payable		80,000

In future years, the $80,000 in Deferred Income Tax Payable will be transferred to Income Tax Payable as the timing differences reverse and the taxes become due. For example, if $48,000 of the deferred tax reverses and becomes due in the second year, the following journal entry would be made in the second year:

Deferred Income Tax Payable	48,000	
Income Tax Payable		48,000

The balance of Deferred Income Tax Payable at the end of a year is reported as a liability. The amount due within one year is classified as a current liability. The remainder is classified as a long-term liability or reported in a Deferred Credits section following the Long-Term Liabilities section.[4]

Differences between taxable income and income (before taxes) reported on the income statement may also arise because certain revenues are exempt from tax and certain expenses are not deductible in determining taxable income.[5] For example, interest income on municipal bonds may be exempt from taxation. Such differences create no special financial reporting problems, since the amount of income tax determined according to the tax laws is the same amount reported on the income statement.

Unusual Items that Affect the Income Statement

Objective 2

Prepare an income statement reporting the following unusual items:

Discontinued operations
Extraordinary items
Changes in accounting principles

Three types of unusual items that may affect the current year's net income are:

1. The results of discontinued operations.
2. Extraordinary items of gain or loss.
3. A change from one generally accepted accounting principle to another.

These items and the related tax effects are reported separately in the income statement, as shown in the partial income statement for Jones Corporation in Exhibit 1. Many different terms and formats may be used. For example, the related tax effects of unusual items may be reported with the item with which they are associated or in the notes to the statement.

[4] In some cases, a deferred tax asset may arise for tax benefits to be received in the future. Such deferred tax assets are reported as either a current or long-term asset, depending on when the expected benefits are expected to be realized.

[5] Such differences, which will not reverse with the passage of time, are sometimes called *permanent differences*.

Exhibit 1
Unusual Items in Income Statement

Jones Corporation
Income Statement
For the Year Ended December 31, 1997

Net sales	$9,600,000
Income from continuing operations before income tax	$1,310,000
Income tax	620,000
Income from continuing operations	$ 690,000
Loss on discontinued operations (Note A)	100,000
Income before extraordinary items and cumulative effect of a change in accounting principle	$ 590,000
Extraordinary item:	
Gain on condemnation of land, net of applicable income tax of $65,000	150,000
Cumulative effect on prior years of changing to a different depreciation method (Note B)	92,000
Net income	$ 832,000

Note A.

On July 1 of the current year, the electrical products division of the corporation was sold at a loss of $100,000, net of applicable income tax of $50,000. The net sales of the division for the current year were $2,900,000. The assets sold were composed of inventories, equipment, and plant totaling $2,100,000. The purchaser assumed liabilities of $600,000.

Note B.

Depreciation of all property, plant, and equipment has been computed by the straight-line method in 1997. Prior to 1997, depreciation of equipment for one of the divisions had been computed on the double-declining-balance method. In 1997, the straight-line method was adopted for this division in order to achieve uniformity and to better match depreciation charges with the estimated economic utility of such assets. Consistent with APB Opinion No. 20, this change in depreciation has been applied to prior years. The effect of the change was to increase income by $30,000 before extraordinary items for 1997. The adjustment of $92,000 (after reduction for income tax of $88,000) to apply the new method to prior years is also included in income for 1997.

In the following paragraphs, we briefly discuss each of the three types of unusual items. We assume that the items illustrated are material to the financial statements. Immaterial items would not affect the normal financial statement presentation.

DISCONTINUED OPERATIONS

A gain or loss resulting from disposing of a business segment is reported on the income statement as a gain or loss from discontinued operations. The term *discontinued* refers to "the operations of a segment of a business . . . that has been sold, abandoned, spun off, or otherwise disposed of or . . . is the subject of a formal plan for disposal."[6]

The term *business segment* refers to a major line of business for a company, such as a division or department or a certain class of customer. For example, assume that a company owns newspapers, television stations, and radio stations. If it were to sell its radio stations, any gain or loss on the discontinued operations should be reported. The results from *continuing operations* should also be reported. The results

[6] *Opinions of the Accounting Principles Board, No. 30,* "Reporting the Results of Operations," American Institute of Certified Public Accountants, New York, 1973, par. 8.

from continuing operations are presented first, followed by the gain or loss from discontinued operations, as shown in Exhibit 1. In addition, the identity of the segment, the disposal date, a description of the segment's assets and liabilities, and the manner of disposal should be presented. These data are often disclosed in a note to the financial statements.

EXTRAORDINARY ITEMS

Extraordinary gains and losses result from "events and transactions that are unusual in nature and infrequent in occurrence."[7] Such gains and losses, other than those from disposing of a business segment, should be reported in the income statement as **extraordinary items**, as shown in Exhibit 1. To be classified as an extraordinary item, an event must meet both of the following requirements:

1. Unusual nature—the event should be significantly different from the typical or the normal operating activities of the entity.
2. Infrequent occurrence—the event should not be expected to recur often.

Events that meet both of the preceding requirements are uncommon. For example, the 1994 edition of *Accounting Trends & Techniques* indicated that only 91 of the 600 industrial and merchandising companies surveyed reported extraordinary items on their income statements. Usually, extraordinary items result from natural disasters, such as floods, earthquakes, and fires, which are not expected to recur. Gains or losses from condemning land or buildings for public use are also considered extraordinary.

Sometimes extraordinary events result in unusual financial results. For example, in its 1989 income statement, **Delta Air Lines** reported an extraordinary gain of over $5.5 million as the result of the crash of one of its 727 airplanes earlier in the fiscal year. The plane that crashed was insured for $6.5 million, but its book value in Delta's accounting records was $962,000.

Gains and losses on the disposal of plant assets are not extraordinary items. This is because (1) they are not unusual and (2) they recur from time to time in the normal operations of a business. Likewise, gains and losses from the sale of investments are usual and recurring for most businesses. However, if a company has owned only one type of investment during its entire existence, a gain or loss on its sale might qualify as an extraordinary item, provided there was no intention of acquiring other similar investments in the future.

CHANGES IN ACCOUNTING PRINCIPLES

A change in accounting principle "results from adoption of a generally accepted accounting principle different from the one used previously for reporting purposes."[8] The issuance of a new FASB accounting standard often results in an accounting change. We discussed the consistency concept as it relates to changes in accounting methods in a prior chapter.

A change in generally accepted accounting principles or methods should be disclosed in the financial statements (or in notes to the statements) of the period in which the change is made. This disclosure should include the nature of the change and its justification. In addition, the effects of the change should be disclosed as follows:

1. The effect on the current year's net income should be disclosed.
2. The cumulative effect of the change on the net income of prior periods should be reported in a special section of the income statement.

[7] *Ibid.*, par. 20.

[8] *Opinions of the Accounting Principles Board, No. 20,* "Accounting Changes," American Institute of Certified Public Accountants, New York, 1971, par. 7.

USING ACCOUNTING TO UNDERSTAND BUSINESS

Reporting unusual items separately on the income statement allows investors to isolate the effects of these items on income and cash flows. By reporting such items, potential investors and other users of the financial statements can consider such factors in evaluating past performance and in predicting a business's future income and cash flows.

For example, McDonnell Douglas Corporation reported income from continuing operations of $359 million in 1993 and $1,086 million in 1992. However, after including the effects of discontinued operations (a $57 million gain) and a change in accounting principles (a $1,536 million reduction of income), McDonnell Douglas reported a net loss of $781 million for 1992. Obviously, without adequate disclosure and reporting of these unusual items, a reasonable prediction of future earnings and cash flows based on the 1993 and 1992 results would have been impossible.

The special section in which the cumulative effect is reported should follow any extraordinary items and immediately precede the net income, as shown in Exhibit 1.[9] If financial statements of prior periods are presented on a comparative basis with the current period's statements, the following additional disclosures should be made:

1. The financial statements of the prior periods should be restated as if the change had been made in the prior periods.
2. The effect of the restatement of the prior periods' statements should be reported either on the face of the statements or in a note to the statements.

Earnings Per Common Share

Objective 3
Prepare an income statement reporting earnings per share data.

The amount of net income is often used by investors and creditors in evaluating a company's profitability. However, net income by itself is difficult to use in comparing companies of different sizes. For example, a net income of $750,000 may be acceptable for a small computer software company, but it would be unacceptable for Apple Computer Inc. Moreover, trends in net income may be difficult to evaluate, using only net income, when there have been significant changes in a company's stockholders' equity.

In addressing these concerns, the profitability of companies is often expressed as earnings per share. Earnings per share (EPS) is the net income per share of common stock outstanding during a period. Public corporations must report earnings per share on their income statements.[10]

[9] Two exceptions to these disclosures are made for a change from the last-in, first-out inventory method or for a change in the method of accounting for long-term construction contracts. The disclosures for these changes are discussed in advanced accounting texts.

[10] Nonpublic corporations are exempt from reporting earnings per share under *Statement of Financial Accounting Standards, No. 21,* "Suspension of the Reporting of Earnings per Share and Segment Information by Nonpublic Enterprises," Financial Accounting Standards Board, Stamford, 1978.

USING ACCOUNTING TO UNDERSTAND BUSINESS

Because of its importance, earnings per share is reported in the financial press and by various investor services, such as Moody's and Standard & Poors. Changes in earnings per share can lead to significant changes in the price of a corporation's stock in the marketplace. For example, Ben & Jerry's Homemade Inc. stock dropped to its lowest point in three years ($13.375 per share) in August 1994, after the company announced earnings per share of 10 cents. The premium ice cream company had earned 34 cents per share a year earlier, and Wall Street stock analysts had been expecting earnings of 27 cents per share. In contrast, during the same time, the stock of Scientific-Atlanta Inc. surged by over 13 percent to $39 per share, after it announced earnings per share of 53 cents as compared to 25 cents per share a year ago. Wall Street stock analysts had been expecting earnings per share of 41 cents.

Source: *The New York Times*, August 6, 1994.

If a company has only common stock outstanding, the earnings per share of common stock is determined by dividing net income by the number of common shares outstanding. If preferred stock is outstanding, the net income must be reduced by the amount of any preferred dividend requirements before dividing by the number of common shares outstanding.

The effect of unusual items should be considered in computing earnings per share. Otherwise, a single earnings per share amount based on net income could be misleading. For example, assume that Jones Corporation, whose partial income statement was presented in Exhibit 1, reported net income of $700,000 for 1996. Also assume that no extraordinary or other special items were reported in 1996. The corporation had 200,000 common shares outstanding during 1996 and 1997. The earnings per share is $3.50 ($700,000 ÷ 200,000) for 1996 and $4.16 ($832,000 ÷ 200,000) for 1997. Comparing the two earnings per share amounts for 1996 and 1997 suggests that operations had significantly improved. However, the current year's per share amount that is comparable to $3.50 is $3.45, which is the income from continuing operations of $690,000 divided by 200,000 shares of common stock outstanding. This latter amount indicates a slight downward trend in normal operations.

When unusual items exist, earnings per share should be reported for the following items:

1. Income from continuing operations.
2. Income before extraordinary items and the cumulative effect of a change in accounting principle.
3. The cumulative effect of a change in accounting principle.
4. Net income.

The reporting of earnings per share for the gain or loss on discontinued operations and for extraordinary items is optional. Earnings per share data may be shown in parentheses or added at the bottom of the statement, as shown in Exhibit 2 for Jones Corporation.

In computing the earnings per share of common stock, all factors that could affect the number of common shares outstanding should be considered. For example, an issue of preferred stock or bonds (debt) with the right to convert to common stock may be outstanding. Such securities that are convertible to common stock may be classified as common stock equivalents.[11]

[11] To be classified as a common stock equivalent, a security must satisfy certain requirements set forth in *Opinions of the Accounting Principles Board, No. 15,* "Earnings per Share," American Institute of Certified Public Accountants, New York, 1969.

Exhibit 2
Income Statement with Earnings per Share

Jones Corporation
Income Statement
For the Year Ended December 31, 1997

Income from continuing operations	$690,000
Net income	$832,000
Earnings per common share:	
Income from continuing operations	$ 3.45
Loss on discontinued operations	.50
Income before extraordinary item and cumulative effect of a change in accounting principle	$ 2.95
Extraordinary item	.75
Cumulative effect on prior years of changing to a different depreciation method	.46
Net income	$ 4.16

When common stock equivalents exist, two amounts for earnings per share are normally reported. One amount is computed without regard for the conversion privilege. This amount is called basic (primary) earnings per share. The second amount is based on the assumption that the preferred stock or bonds are converted to common stock, thus reducing the earnings per share. This amount is called *fully diluted earnings per share*.[12]

A note accompanying the financial statements normally explains how the earnings per share were computed. An example of such a note, taken from the financial statements of The Pillsbury Company, follows:

Net earnings per share are computed using the weighted average number of common shares, including common share equivalents of stock options, outstanding during each year. Net earnings per share assuming full dilution would be substantially the same.

Foreign Currency Exchange Gains and Losses

Objective 4
Journalize entries for international transactions involving foreign currency exchange gains and losses.

In the preceding section, we described and illustrated unusual items reported on the income statement. In the following paragraphs, we extend this discussion to include gains and losses that may arise when a U.S. company enters into transactions with foreign businesses. In these transactions, the U.S. company sells products or services to foreign companies or buys foreign products or services.

If transactions with foreign companies require payment or receipt in U.S. dollars, no special accounting problems arise.[13] Such transactions are recorded as we described and illustrated earlier in this text. For example, the sale of merchandise to a Japanese company that is billed in and paid for in dollars would be recorded by the U.S. company in the normal manner. However, if the transaction is billed and payment is to be received in Japanese yen, the U.S. company may incur an exchange gain or loss. Some foreign manufacturers have begun building manufacturing plants in the U.S., which avoids such gains and losses. For example, BMW is constructing its first U.S. plant.

[12]Additional issues related to computing earnings per share are discussed in advanced accounting texts.
[13]This discussion is from the point of view of a U.S. company. Unless otherwise indicated, the reference to the dollar refers to the U.S. dollar rather than a dollar of another country, such as Canada.

REALIZED CURRENCY EXCHANGE GAINS AND LOSSES

Some foreign companies like BMW have begun to build manufacturing plants in the U.S. to, in part, avoid currency exchange gains and losses.

When a U.S. company receives foreign currency, the amount must be converted to its equivalent in U.S. dollars for recording in the accounts. When payment is to be made in a foreign currency, U.S. dollars must be exchanged for the foreign currency for payment. To illustrate, assume that a U.S. company purchases merchandise from a British company that requires payment in British pounds. In this case, U.S. dollars ($) must be exchanged for British pounds (£) to pay for the merchandise. This exchange of one currency for another involves using an exchange rate. The **exchange rate** is the rate at which one unit of currency (the dollar, for example) can be converted into another currency (the British pound, for example).

To continue the example, assume that the U.S. company had purchased merchandise for £1,000 from a British company on June 1, when the exchange rate was $1.40 per British pound. Thus, $1,400 must be exchanged for £1,000 to make the purchase.[14] The U.S. company records the transaction in dollars, as follows:

June 1	Merchandise Inventory	1,400	
	Cash		1,400
	Payment of Invoice No. 1725 from W. A. Sterling Co., £1,000; exchange rate, $1.40 per British pound.		

Instead of a cash purchase, the purchase may be made on account. In this case, the exchange rate may change between the date of purchase and the date of payment of the account payable in the foreign currency. In practice, exchange rates vary daily.

To illustrate, assume that the preceding purchase was made on account. The entry to record it is as follows:

June 1	Merchandise Inventory	1,400	
	Accounts Payable—W. A. Sterling Co.		1,400
	Purchase on account; Invoice No. 1725 from W. A. Sterling Co., £1,000; exchange rate, $1.40 per British pound.		

Assume that on the date of payment, June 15, the exchange rate was $1.45 per pound. The £1,000 account payable must be settled by exchanging $1,450 (£1,000 × $1.45) for £1,000. In this case, the U.S. company incurs an exchange loss of $50 because $1,450 was needed to settle a $1,400 account payable. The cash payment is recorded as follows:

June 15	Accounts Payable—W. A. Sterling Co.	1,400	
	Exchange Loss	50	
	Cash		1,450
	Cash paid on Invoice No. 1725, for £1,000, or $1,400, when exchange rate was $1.45 per pound.		

We can analyze all transactions with foreign companies in the manner described. For example, assume that a sale on account for $1,000 to a Swiss company on May 1 was billed in Swiss francs. The cost of the merchandise sold was $600, and the selling company uses a perpetual inventory system. If the exchange rate was $0.25 per Swiss franc (F) on May 1, the transaction is recorded as follows:

[14] Foreign exchange rates are quoted in major financial reporting services. Because the exchange rates are quite volatile, those used in this chapter are assumed rates.

May 1	Accounts Receivable—D. W. Robinson Co.	1,000	
	Sales		1,000
	Invoice No. 9772, F4,000; exchange rate, $0.25 per Swiss franc.		
1	Cost of Merchandise Sold	600	
	Merchandise Inventory		600

Assume that the exchange rate increases to $0.30 per Swiss franc on May 31 when cash is received. In this case, the U.S. company realizes an exchange gain of $200. This gain is realized because the F4,000, which had a value of $1,000 on the date of sale, has increased in value to $1,200 (F4,000 × $0.30) on May 31 when the payment is received. The receipt of the cash is recorded as follows:

May 31	Cash	1,200	
	Accounts Receivable—D. W. Robinson Co.		1,000
	Exchange Gain		200
	Cash received on Invoice No. 9772, for F4,000, or $1,000, when exchange rate was $0.30 per Swiss franc.		

UNREALIZED CURRENCY EXCHANGE GAINS AND LOSSES

In the previous examples, the transactions were completed by either the receipt or the payment of cash. On the date the cash was received or paid, any related exchange gain or loss was realized and was recorded in the accounts. However, financial statements may be prepared between the date of the sale or purchase on account and the date the cash is received or paid. In this case, any exchange gain or loss created by a change in exchange rates between the date of the original transaction and the balance sheet date must be recorded. Such an exchange gain or loss is reported in the financial statements as an unrealized exchange gain or loss.

To illustrate, assume that a sale on account for $1,000 had been made to a German company on December 20 and had been billed in deutsche marks (DM). The cost of merchandise sold was $700. On this date, the exchange rate was $0.50 per deutsche mark. The transaction is recorded as follows:

Dec. 20	Accounts Receivable—T. A. Mueller Inc.	1,000	
	Sales		1,000
	Invoice No. 1793, DM2,000; exchange rate, $0.50 per deutsche mark.		
20	Cost of Merchandise Sold	700	
	Merchandise Inventory		700

Assume that the exchange rate decreases to $0.45 per deutsche mark on December 31, the date of the balance sheet. Thus, the $1,000 account receivable on December 31 has a value of only $900 (DM2,000 × $0.45). This unrealized loss of $100 ($1,000 – $900) is recorded as follows:

Dec. 31	Exchange Loss	100	
	Accounts Receivable—T. A. Mueller Inc.		100
	Invoice No. 1793, DM2,000 × $0.05 decrease in exchange rate.		

Any additional change in the exchange rate during the following period is recorded when the cash is received. To continue the illustration, assume that the exchange rate declines from $0.45 to $0.42 per deutsche mark by January 19, when the DM2,000 is received. The receipt of the cash on January 19 is recorded as follows:

		Dr.	Cr.
Jan. 19	Cash (DM2,000 × $0.42)	840	
	Exchange Loss (DM2,000 × $0.03)	60	
	Accounts Receivable—T. A. Mueller Inc.		900
	Cash received on Invoice No. 1793, for DM2,000, or $900, when exchange rate was $0.42 per deutsche mark.		

In contrast, assume that in the preceding example the exchange rate increases between December 31 and January 19. In this case, an exchange gain would be recorded on January 19. For example, if the exchange rate increases from $0.45 to $0.47 per deutsche mark during this period, Exchange Gain would be credited for $40 (DM2,000 × $0.02).

A balance in the exchange loss account at the end of the fiscal period is reported in the Other Expense section of the income statement. A balance in the exchange gain account is reported in the Other Income section.

Prior-Period Adjustments

Objective 5
Prepare a retained earnings statement reporting a prior-period adjustment.

Material errors in a prior period's net income may arise from mathematical mistakes and from mistakes in applying accounting principles. The effect of material errors that are not discovered within the same fiscal period in which they occurred should not be included in determining net income for the current period.[15] Corrections of such errors are called **prior-period adjustments.** These errors are reported as an adjustment of the retained earnings balance at the beginning of the period in which the error is discovered and corrected. For example, correcting a material error in computing a prior period's depreciation expense is a prior-period adjustment. In addition, a change from an unacceptable accounting principle to an acceptable accounting principle is considered a correction of a material error and is reported as a prior-period adjustment. For example, a change from reporting plant assets at market values to historical costs would be a prior-period adjustment.

Differences between estimated and actual amounts are not errors or prior-period adjustments. Estimates must be used throughout the accounting process. For example, uncollectible accounts receivable must be estimated. Any differences between the estimated and the actual uncollectibles are included in determining the current period's net income.

Exhibit 3 illustrates the reporting of a prior-period adjustment in the retained earnings statement.

Exhibit 3
Retained Earnings Statement with Prior-Period Adjustment

Casper Inc.
Retained Earnings Statement
For the Year Ended December 31, 1998

Retained earnings, January 1, 1998		$310,500
Less prior-period adjustment:		
Correction of error in depreciation expense in 1997, net of applicable income tax of $13,000		29,200
Corrected retained earnings, January 1, 1998		$281,300
Net income for year	$77,350	
Less dividends	40,000	
Increase in retained earnings		37,350
Retained earnings, December 31, 1998		$318,650

[15] Corrections of errors that are discovered in the same period in which they occur were discussed in a previous chapter.

Prior-period adjustments are reported net of any related income tax. If only the current period's financial statements are presented, the effect of the adjustment on the net income of the preceding period should also be disclosed. If financial statements for prior periods are presented on a comparative basis, the prior periods' statements should be restated and the amount of the adjustment disclosed.

Prior-period adjustments are rare in financial reporting. For example, the 1994 edition of *Accounting Trends & Techniques* reported no prior-period adjustments. Annual audits by independent public accountants, combined with good internal control policies and procedures, reduce the chance of errors.

Analyzing Investments in Stocks

Objective 6
Compute the price-earnings ratio and equity per share.

In the preceding paragraphs, we have described and illustrated a variety of items that are reported in the financial statements. Such information may be important for businesses that desire to invest in another company's stock.

In the following paragraphs, we discuss two financial measures that are useful in analyzing possible stock investments. Before we look at these measures—the price-earnings ratio and equity per share—we should answer the question: Why do businesses invest in stocks? Like individuals, businesses invest in other companies for a variety of reasons. A business may purchase the stock of another company, called an equity security, as a means of developing or maintaining business relationships with the other company. In other cases, a business may purchase common stock as a means of gaining control of another company's operations. In still other cases, a business may invest in equity securities as a means of earning a short-term return on excess cash that it does not need for its normal operations.[16]

PRICE-EARNINGS RATIO

The price-earnings ratio, or P/E ratio, is commonly quoted by the financial press.[17] The price-earnings ratio represents how much the market is willing to pay per dollar of a company's earnings. Generally, the price-earnings ratio indicates the market's assessment of a firm's growth potential and future earnings prospects. A high price-earnings ratio indicates that the market expects high growth and earnings in the future. Likewise, a low P/E ratio indicates lower growth and earnings expectations.

The price-earnings ratio on common stock is computed by dividing the market price per share of common stock at a specific date by the company's annual earnings per share on common stock. To illustrate, assume that Harper Inc. reported earnings per share of $1.64 in 1997 and $1.35 in 1996. The market prices per common share are 20 1/2 at the end of 1997 and 13 1/2 at the end of 1996. The price-earnings ratio on this stock is computed as follows:

	1997	*1996*
Market price per share	$ 20.50	$ 13.50
Earnings per share	÷ $1.64	÷ $1.35
Price-earnings ratio	12.5	10.0

The price-earnings ratio indicates that a share of Harper Inc.'s common stock was selling for 10 times the amount of earnings per share at the end of 1996. At the end of 1997, the common stock was selling for 12.5 times the amount of earnings

[16] Accounting for temporary investments in equity securities was discussed in a prior chapter.
[17] The P/E ratio is included in *The Wall Street Journal's* stock market quotations.

per share. These results would indicate a generally improving expectation of growth and earnings for Harper Inc.

EQUITY PER SHARE

Equity per share, or **book value per share,** is also quoted in the financial press. It represents the stockholders' equity per share of stock outstanding. If there is only one class of stock, equity per share is determined by dividing the total stockholders' equity by the number of shares outstanding.

If a corporation has both preferred and common stock, the equity per share for both classes of stock is determined. First, the total stockholders' equity must be allocated between the two classes, considering the liquidation rights and cumulative dividend features of the preferred stock. Then, the allocated stockholders' equity is divided by the outstanding shares of each class.

To illustrate, assume that as of the end of the current fiscal year, a corporation has preferred and common shares outstanding, no preferred dividends are in arrears, and preferred stock is entitled to $105 per share upon liquidation. The stockholders' equity and the computation of the equity per share are shown below.

Stockholders' Equity	
Preferred $9 stock, cumulative, $100 par (1,000 shares outstanding)	$100,000
Excess of issue price over par—preferred stock	2,000
Common stock, $10 par (50,000 shares outstanding)	500,000
Excess of issue price over par—common stock	50,000
Retained earnings	253,000
Total stockholders' equity	$905,000

Allocation of Total Equity to Preferred and Common Stock	
Total stockholders' equity	$905,000
Allocated to preferred stock:	
Liquidation price	105,000
Allocated to common stock	$800,000

Equity per Share

$$\textbf{Equity per share of preferred stock} = \frac{\textbf{Total equity of preferred stock}}{\textbf{Number of shares of preferred stock outstanding}}$$

$$\textbf{Equity per share of preferred stock} = \frac{\textbf{\$105,000}}{\textbf{1,000 shares}} = \textbf{\$105 per share}$$

$$\textbf{Equity per share of common stock} = \frac{\textbf{Total equity of common stock}}{\textbf{Number of shares of common stock outstanding}}$$

$$\textbf{Equity per share of common stock} = \frac{\textbf{\$800,000}}{\textbf{50,000 shares}} = \textbf{\$16 per share}$$

Assume that the preferred stock is entitled to dividends in arrears upon liquidation and dividends are in arrears for two years. The equity per share in the preceding example would then be determined as follows:

Total stockholders' equity		$905,000
Allocated to preferred stock:		
Liquidation price	$105,000	
Dividends in arrears	18,000	123,000
Allocated to common stock		$782,000

$$\text{Equity per share of preferred stock} = \frac{\$123{,}000}{1{,}000\ \text{shares}} = \$123\ \text{per share}$$

$$\text{Equity per share of common stock} = \frac{\$782{,}000}{50{,}000\ \text{shares}} = \$15.64\ \text{per share}$$

Since the book values of assets are based on historical costs, the market value of a corporation's stock is normally higher than its equity per share. In some cases, so-called "hot" stocks may sell at multiples of more than ten times their equity per share. On the other hand, some stocks may sell near to or less than their equity per share. This may be because a corporation has reported losses or unfavorable earnings trends and that future earnings prospects are not very favorable. Many investors search for such stocks that may be undervalued as long-term investments.

Accounting for Long-Term Investments in Stocks

Objective 7
Journalize entries for long-term investments in stocks, using the cost method and the equity method.

We discussed the accounting for short-term (temporary) investments in stocks in an earlier chapter. In the following paragraphs, we focus our attention on long-term investments in stocks. Such investments are not intended as a source of cash in the normal operations of the business. They are reported in the balance sheet under the caption *Investments*.

There are two methods of accounting for long-term investments in stock: (1) the cost method and (2) the equity method. The method used depends on whether the investor (buyer of the stock) has a significant influence over the operating and financing activities of the company (the investee) whose stock is owned. If the investor does not have a significant influence, the cost method is used. If the investor has a significant influence, the equity method is used. Evidence of such influence includes the percentage of ownership, the existence of intercompany transactions, and the interchange of managerial personnel. Generally, if the investor owns 20% or more of the voting stock of the investee, it is assumed that the investor has significant influence over the investee.

COST METHOD

As with the purchase of other assets, the cost of stocks purchased includes all expenditures necessary to acquire the stocks. For example, the cost of stocks includes not only the amount paid to the seller but also such costs as a broker's commission. The total cost of a stock purchased is debited to an investment account.

Cash dividends may be received on stock held as an investment. When the **cost method** is used, such dividends are recorded as an increase (debit) to an asset account and an increase (credit) to a dividend income account.

To illustrate, assume that on March 1, Makowski Corporation purchases 100 shares of Compton Corporation common stock at 59 plus a brokerage fee of $40. On April 30, Compton Corporation declares a $2-per-share cash dividend payable on June 15 to stockholders of record on May 15. The entries in the accounts of Makowski Corporation to record the purchase of the stock and the receipt of the dividend are as follows:

Purchase of Compton Corp. common stock

Mar.	1	Investment in Compton Corp. Stock	5,940	
		Cash		5,940

Receipt of cash dividends on Compton Corp. common stock

June 15	Cash	200	
	Dividend Income		200

Under the cost method, long-term investments in stocks whose value can be readily determined are reported in the balance sheet at their market (fair) value.[18] Such securities are described as **available-for-sale securities.**[19] Their market value is normally available from stock quotations in financial newspapers, such as *The Wall Street Journal*.

The market value of available-for-sale securities is determined on the balance sheet date for stock investments as a whole. If the total market value of the investments is higher than the total cost, an unrealized gain is reported. If the total market value is lower, an unrealized loss is reported. The securities are normally presented on the balance sheet at their total cost plus or minus the amount of the total unrealized gain or loss. Unrealized gains and losses are not reported on the income statement. Instead, they are reported as a separate component of the Stockholders' Equity section of the balance sheet. The amount of the unrealized gains or losses will change each year as the market values of the securities change. When a security is sold, the gain or loss is recognized.[20] We illustrate the recording of these gains and losses later in this chapter.

An exception to reporting unrealized gains and losses is made if the decrease in the market value for a stock is considered permanent. This might be the case, for example, if a corporation has filed for bankruptcy. In this case, the cost of the individual stock is written down (decreased), and the amount of the write-down is reported as a loss on the income statement. After the write-down, the revised carrying value (book value) of the stock is treated as the cost.[21]

EQUITY METHOD

Under the equity method, a stock purchase is recorded in the same manner as if the cost method were used. The equity method, however, is different from the cost method in the way in which net income and cash dividends of the investee are recorded. The equity method of recording these items is summarized as follows:

1. The investor's share of the periodic net income of the investee is recorded as an increase in the investment account on the balance sheet. This increase is also recorded on the income statement as revenue for the period. Likewise, the investor's share of an investee's net loss is recorded as a decrease in the investment and as a loss for the period.
2. The investor's share of cash dividends is recorded as an increase in the cash account and a decrease in the investment account.

To illustrate, assume that on January 2, Hally Inc. pays cash of $350,000 for 40% of the common (voting) stock of Brock Corporation. Assume also that, for the year ending December 31, Brock Corporation reports net income of $105,000 and declares and pays $45,000 in dividends. Using the equity method, Hally Inc. (the investor) records these transactions as follows:

Purchase of 40% of Brock Corp. common stock

Jan. 2	Investment in Brock Corp. Stock	350,000	
	Cash		350,000

Share (40%) of Brock Corp. net income of $105,000

Dec. 31	Investment in Brock Corp. Stock	42,000	
	Income of Brock Corp.		42,000

[18] *Statement of Financial Accounting Standards No. 115,* "Accounting for Certain Investments in Debt and Equity Securities," Financial Accounting Standards Board, Norwalk, Conn., 1993.
[19] *Ibid.*, par. 12.
[20] *Ibid.*, pars. 13–14.
[21] *Ibid.*, par. 16.

Share (40%) of cash dividends of $45,000 paid by Brock Corp.

Dec. 31	Cash	18,000	
	Investment in Brock Corp. Stock		18,000

The combined effect of recording 40% of Brock Corporation's net income and dividends is to increase Cash by $18,000, Investment in Brock Corp. Stock by $24,000, and Income of Brock Corp. by $42,000.

SALE OF LONG-TERM INVESTMENTS IN STOCKS

When shares of stock are sold, the investment account is credited for the carrying value (book value) of the shares sold. The cash or receivable account is debited for the proceeds (sales price less commission and other selling costs). Any difference between the proceeds and the carrying value is recorded as a gain or loss on the sale.

To illustrate, assume that an investment in Drey Inc. stock has a carrying value of $15,700. If the proceeds from the sale of the stock are $17,500, the entry to record the transaction is as follows:

Cash	17,500	
Investment in Drey Inc. Stock		15,700
Gain on Sale of Investments		1,800

Business Combinations

Objective 8
Describe alternative methods of combining businesses and the preparation of consolidated financial statements.

Each year, many businesses combine in order to produce more efficiently or to diversify product lines. Business combinations often involve complex accounting principles and terminology. Our objective in the following paragraphs is to introduce you to some of the unique terminology and concepts related to business combinations. We also briefly describe the use and preparation of consolidated statements.

MERGERS AND CONSOLIDATIONS

A **merger** is the joining of two corporations by one acquiring the properties of another that is then dissolved. Usually, all the assets and liabilities of the acquired company are taken over by the acquiring company. The acquiring company may use cash, debt obligations, or its own stock as the form of payment. Whatever the form of payment, the amount received by the dissolving corporation is distributed to its stockholders in final liquidation.

A **consolidation** is the creation of a new corporation, to which is transferred the assets and liabilities of two or more existing corporations. The new corporation usually issues its own stock in exchange for the net assets acquired. The original corporations are then dissolved.

PARENT AND SUBSIDIARY CORPORATIONS

Business combinations may also occur when one corporation buys a controlling share of the outstanding voting stock of one or more other corporations. In this case, none of the participating corporations dissolve. The corporations continue as separate legal entities in a parent-subsidiary relationship. The corporation owning all or a majority of the voting stock of the other corporation is called the **parent company**. The corporation that is controlled is called the **subsidiary company**. Two or more corporations closely related through stock ownership are sometimes called

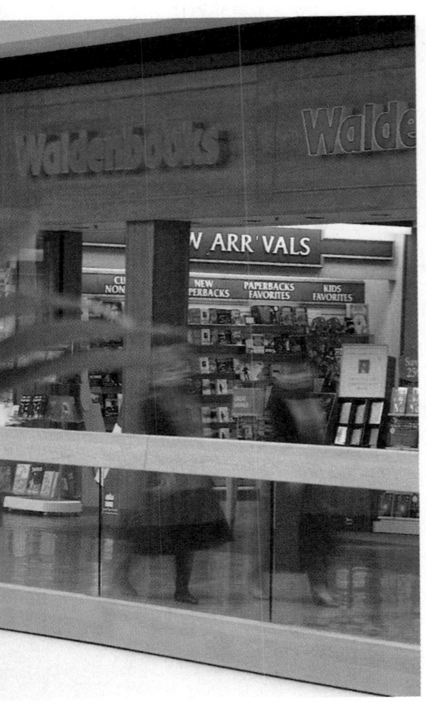

K Mart and Waldenbooks, a subsidiary, are affiliated companies.

affiliated or associated companies. Examples of affiliated companies include **Waldenbooks,** a subsidiary of **K Mart,** and **NBC,** a subsidiary of **General Electric.**

In accounting terms, parent and subsidiary relationships are created by either a *purchase* or a *pooling of interests*. A corporation may acquire the controlling share of the voting common stock of another corporation by paying cash, exchanging other assets, issuing debt, or some combination of these methods. The stockholders of the acquired company, in turn, transfer their stock to the parent corporation. In such cases, the transaction is recorded like a normal purchase of assets, and the combination is accounted for by the **purchase method.**

A parent-subsidiary relationship may be created by exchanging the voting common stock of the acquiring corporation (the parent) for the common stock of the acquired corporation (the subsidiary). If at least 90% of the stock of the subsidiary is acquired in this way, the transaction is a pooling of interests, and the combination is accounted for by the **pooling-of-interests method.** In a pooling of interests, the stockholders of the acquired company (the subsidiary) become stockholders of the acquiring company (the parent).

The accounting for a purchase and a pooling of interests are significantly different. A purchase is accounted for as a sale-purchase transaction, whereas a pooling of interests is accounted for as a *joining of ownership interests*.

Generally accepted accounting principles set forth very strict criteria that must be met before the pooling-of-interests method can be used. As a result, only a few business combinations are accounted for by the pooling-of-interests method. The 1994 edition of *Accounting Trends & Techniques* reported that 90% of the business combinations surveyed were accounted for by the purchase method.

CONSOLIDATED FINANCIAL STATEMENTS

Although the corporations that make up a parent-subsidiary affiliation may operate as a single economic unit, they continue to maintain separate accounting records and prepare their own periodic financial statements. At the end of the year, the financial statements of the parent and subsidiary are combined and reported as a single company. These combined financial statements of the parent and subsidiary are called **consolidated statements.** Such statements are usually identified by adding "and subsidiary(ies)" to the name of the parent corporation or by adding "consolidated" to the statement title.

Consolidated financial statements are considered more meaningful to stockholders of the parent company than separate statements for each corporation. This is because the parent company, *in substance*, controls the subsidiaries even though the parent and its subsidiaries are separate entities.

When the data on the financial statements of the parent corporation and its subsidiaries are combined to form the consolidated statements, special attention should be given to intercompany transactions. For example, the parent may purchase goods from the subsidiary, or the subsidiary may loan money to the parent.

Intercompany transactions affect the individual accounts of the parent and subsidiary and thus the financial statements of both companies.[22] For example, assume that P Inc. (the parent) sold merchandise to S Inc. (the subsidiary) for $90,000. In turn, S Inc. sold the merchandise to nonaffiliated companies for $120,000. The income statements of P Inc. and S Inc. are shown in Exhibit 4.

The consolidated income statement for P Inc. and S Inc. is shown in Exhibit 5. This statement presents the income statements of the parent and the subsidiary as if they were one operating entity. Thus, P's $90,000 sale and S's $90,000 cost of merchandise sold are eliminated. This is because the consolidated entity cannot sell to itself or buy from itself.

[22]Examples of accounts often affected by intercompany transactions include Accounts Receivable and Accounts Payable, Interest Receivable and Interest Payable, and Interest Expense and Interest Income.

Exhibit 4
Income Statements for P Inc. and S Inc.

	P Inc.		S Inc.	
Sales		$950,000		$400,000
Cost of merchandise sold		625,000		240,000
Gross profit		$325,000		$160,000
Operating expenses:				
Selling expenses	$155,000		$55,000	
Administrative expenses	85,000	240,000	35,000	90,000
Net income		$ 85,000		$ 70,000

Exhibit 5
Consolidated Income Statement for P Inc. and S Inc.

Sales		$1,260,000*
Cost of merchandise sold		775,000**
Gross profit		$ 485,000
Operating expenses:		
Selling expenses	$210,000	
Administrative expenses	120,000	330,000
Net income		$ 155,000

*$950,000 – $90,000 + $400,000
**$625,000 + $240,000 – $90,000

In addition to intercompany transactions, the ownership interest of the parent in the subsidiary's stock, which is represented by the balance in the parent's investment in subsidiary account, must also be eliminated. This is done by eliminating the parent's investment in subsidiary account against the balances of the subsidiary's stockholders' equity accounts.

If the parent owns less than 100% of the subsidiary stock, the subsidiary stock owned by outsiders is called the **minority interest**. The minority interest is not eliminated but is normally reported on the consolidated balance sheet immediately preceding the consolidated stockholders' equity. The 1994 edition of *Accounting Trends & Techniques* indicates that most of the companies surveyed reported minority interest in the Long-Term Liabilities (noncurrent) section of the consolidated balance sheet.

When a business combination is accounted for as a purchase, the subsidiary's net assets are reported in the consolidated balance sheet at their fair market value at the time of the purchase. In some cases, a parent may pay more than the fair market value of a subsidiary's net assets because the subsidiary has prospects for high future earnings. The difference between the amount paid by the parent and the fair market value of the subsidiary's net assets is reported on the consolidated balance sheet as an intangible asset. This asset is identified as **Goodwill** or **Excess of cost of business acquired over related net assets.**

Many U.S. corporations own subsidiaries in foreign countries. Such corporations are often called multinational corporations. The financial statements of the foreign subsidiary are usually prepared in foreign currency. Before the financial statements of foreign subsidiaries are consolidated with their domestic parent's financial statements, the amounts shown on the statements for the foreign companies must be converted to U.S. dollars.[23]

[23] Additional discussion of business combinations and multinational corporations can be found in advanced accounting texts.

KEY POINTS

Objective 1. Journalize the entries for corporate income taxes, including deferred income taxes.

Corporations are subject to federal income tax and are required to make estimated payments throughout the year. To record the payment of estimated tax, Income Tax is debited and Cash is credited. If additional taxes are owed at the end of the year, Income Tax is debited and Income Tax Payable is credited for the amount owed. If the estimated tax payments are greater than the actual tax liability, a receivable account is debited and Income Tax is credited.

The tax effects of temporary differences between taxable income and income before income tax must be allocated between periods. The journal entry for such allocations normally debits Income Tax and credits Income Tax Payable and Deferred Income Tax Payable.

Objective 2. Prepare an income statement reporting the following unusual items: discontinued operations, extraordinary items, and changes in accounting principles.

Discontinued operations: A gain or loss resulting from the disposal of a segment of a business should be identified on the income statement, net of related income tax. The results of continuing operations should also be identified.

Extraordinary items: Gains and losses may result from events and transactions that are unusual in nature and infrequent in occurrence. Such items, net of related income tax, should be identified on the income statement.

Changes in accounting principles: A change in an accounting principle results from the adoption of a generally accepted accounting principle different from the one used previously for reporting purposes. The effect of the change in principle on net income in the current period, as well as the cumulative effect on income of prior periods, should be disclosed in the financial statements. The effects of a change in an accounting principle should be reported net of related income tax.

Objective 3. Prepare an income statement reporting earnings per share data.

Earnings per share data are reported on the income statements of public corporations. If there are nonrecurring items on the income statement, the per share amount should be presented for (1) income from continuing operations, (2) income before extraordinary items and the cumulative effect of a change in accounting principle, (3) the cumulative effect of a change in accounting principle, and (4) net income.

Objective 4. Journalize entries for international transactions involving foreign currency exchange gains and losses.

When a U.S. company enters into a transaction with a company in a foreign country using a currency other than the dollar, an exchange rate is used to convert the foreign currency into dollars. The transaction is then recorded in dollars, similar to other transactions.

When foreign currency is received in payment of a receivable or when foreign currency is paid in payment of a payable, an exchange gain or loss may be realized. Such a gain or loss will be realized if the foreign exchange rate changes between the initial recording of the transaction and the receipt or payment of the foreign currency. If a foreign transaction has not been completed by the end of the year, an adjusting entry to record any unrealized currency exchange gains or losses may need to be recorded.

Objective 5. Prepare a retained earnings statement reporting a prior-period adjustment.

Material errors related to a prior period are called prior-period adjustments. Prior-period adjustments are reported as an adjustment to the retained earnings balance at the beginning of the period in which the correction is made.

Objective 6. Compute the price-earnings ratio and equity per share.

The price-earnings ratio, or P/E ratio, is computed by dividing the market price per share of common stock at a specific date by the company's earnings per share on common stock. It indicates the market's assessment of a firm's growth potential and future earnings prospects. Equity per share, or book value per share, represents the stockholders' equity per share of each class of stock outstanding. If there is only one class of stock outstanding, it is computed by dividing the total stockholders' equity by the number of shares outstanding. If a corporation has both preferred and common stock, the total stockholders' equity must be allocated between the two classes of stock. This allocation should consider any liquidation rights and any cumulative dividend features of the preferred stock.

Objective 7. Journalize entries for long-term investments in stocks, using the cost method and the equity method.

The cost of purchasing a long-term investment in a stock includes all expenditures necessary to acquire the stock. The total cost of a stock purchased is debited to an investment account.

When the cost method is used, cash dividends are recorded as an increase in the cash account (debit) and an increase in the dividend income account (credit). Under the cost method, long-term investments in stocks whose value can be readily determined are reported in the balance sheet at their fair value. If the total market value of the investments is higher than the total cost, an unrealized gain is reported. If the total market value is lower, an unrealized loss is reported. The securities are normally presented on the balance sheet at their total cost plus or minus the amount of the total unrealized gain or loss. Unrealized gains and losses are reported as a separate component of the Stockholders' Equity section of the balance sheet.

Under the equity method, the investor records its share of the periodic net income of the investee as an increase in the investment account (debit) and as an increase in an income account (credit). The investor's share of the investee's periodic net loss is recorded in a loss account (debit) and as a decrease in the investment account (credit). The investor records its share of cash dividends as an increase in the cash account (debit) and as a decrease in the investment account (credit).

When shares of stock held as a long-term investment are sold, cash or a receivable account is debited for the proceeds and the investment account is credited for the carrying amount of the shares sold. Any difference between the proceeds and the carrying amount is recorded as a gain or loss on the sale.

Objective 8. Describe alternative methods of combining businesses and the preparation of consolidated financial statements.

Businesses may combine in a merger or a consolidation. Business combinations may also occur when one corporation acquires a controlling share of the outstanding voting stock of another corporation. In this case, a parent-subsidiary relationship exists, and the companies are called affiliated or associated companies.

Although the corporations that make up a parent-subsidiary affiliation may operate as a single economic unit, they usually continue to maintain separate accounting records and prepare their own periodic financial statements. The financial statements prepared by combining the parent and subsidiary statements are called consolidated statements.

Under the purchase method, the parent's investment account at the date of acquisition is reciprocal to the parent's share of the subsidiary's stockholders' equity accounts. When a parent corporation purchases less than 100% of the subsidiary's stock, the remaining stockholders' equity is identified as minority interest. The minority interest is reported on the consolidated balance sheet, usually preceding stockholders' equity.

In preparing consolidated income statements for a parent and its subsidiary, all amounts from intercompany transactions, such as management fees, are eliminated. Any intercompany sales of merchandise and cost of merchandise sold are also eliminated.

GLOSSARY OF KEY TERMS

Consolidated statements. Financial statements resulting from combining parent and subsidiary company statements. *Objective 8*

Consolidation. The creation of a new corporation by the transfer of assets and liabilities from two or more existing corporations. *Objective 8*

Cost method. A method of accounting for an investment in common stock, by which the investor recognizes as income its share of cash dividends of the investee. *Objective 7*

Discontinued operations. The operations of a business segment that has been disposed of. *Objective 2*

Earnings per share (EPS). The profitability ratio of net income available to common shareholders to the number of common shares outstanding. *Objective 3*

Equity method. A method of accounting for investments in common stock, by which the investment account is adjusted for the investor's share of periodic net income and property dividends of the investee. *Objective 7*

Equity per share. The ratio of stockholders' equity to the related number of shares of stock outstanding. *Objective 6*

Equity security. Preferred or common stock. *Objective 6*

Exchange rate. The rate at which one currency can be converted into another currency. *Objective 4*

Extraordinary items. Events or transactions that are unusual and infrequent. *Objective 2*

Merger. The combining of two corporations by the acquisition of the properties of one corporation by another, with the dissolution of one of the corporations. *Objective 8*

Minority interest. The portion of a subsidiary corporation's stock that is not owned by the parent corporation. *Objective 8*

Parent company. The company owning a majority of the voting stock of another corporation. *Objective 8*

Pooling-of-interests method. A method of accounting for an affiliation of two corporations resulting from an exchange of voting stock of one corporation for substantially all the voting stock of the other corporation. *Objective 8*

Price-earnings ratio. The ratio, often called the P/E ratio, computed by dividing the market price per share of common stock at a specific date by the company's earnings per share on common stock. *Objective 6*

Prior-period adjustments. Corrections of material errors related to a prior period or periods, excluded from the determination of net income. *Objective 5*

Purchase method. The accounting method employed when a parent company acquires a controlling share of the voting stock of a subsidiary other than by the exchange of voting common stock. *Objective 8*

Subsidiary company. The corporation that is controlled by a parent company. *Objective 8*

Taxable income. The base on which the amount of income tax is determined. *Objective 1*

Temporary differences. Differences between income before income tax and taxable income created by items that are recognized in one period for income statement purposes and in another period for tax purposes. Such differences reverse, or turn around, in later years. *Objective 1*

ILLUSTRATIVE PROBLEM

Selected data from the balance sheets of five corporations, identified by letter, are as follows:

A.	Common stock, $20 par	$ 1,600,000
	Paid-in capital in excess of par—common stock	300,000
	Retained earnings	200,000

B.	Preferred $8 stock, $100 par	$ 1,000,000
	Paid-in capital in excess of par—preferred stock	250,000
	Common stock, no par, 50,000 shares outstanding	1,250,000
	Deficit	150,000
	Preferred stock has prior claim to assets on liquidation to the extent of par.	
C.	Preferred 8% stock, $20 par	$ 4,000,000
	Paid-in capital in excess of par—preferred stock	480,000
	Common stock, $15 par	3,750,000
	Retained earnings	750,000
	Preferred stock has prior claim to assets on liquidation to the extent of 110% of par.	
D.	Preferred 6% stock, $1,000 par	$25,000,000
	Common stock, $50 par	4,000,000
	Paid-in capital in excess of par—common stock	260,000
	Retained earnings	1,800,000
	Dividends on preferred stock are in arrears for 2 years, including the dividend passed during the current year. Preferred stock is entitled to par plus unpaid cumulative dividends on liquidation to the extent of retained earnings.	
E.	Preferred $1 stock, $25 par	$ 500,000
	Common stock, $8 par	2,000,000
	Deficit	220,000
	Dividends on preferred stock are in arrears for 3 years, including the dividend passed during the current year. Preferred stock is entitled to par plus unpaid cumulative dividends on liquidation, regardless of the availability of retained earnings.	

Instructions

Calculate for each corporation the equity per share of each class of stock, presenting the total shareholders' equity allocated to each class and the number of shares outstanding.

Solution

Class of Stock		*Total Equity Allocated*	÷	*Number of Shares*	=	*Equity per Share*
A.	Common	$2,100,000		80,000		$ 26.25
B.	Preferred	1,000,000		10,000		100.00
	Common	1,350,000*		50,000		27.00
	*(250,000 + 1,250,000 – $150,000)					
C.	Preferred	4,400,000**		200,000		22.00
	Common	4,580,000		250,000		18.32
	**(4,000,000 × 1.10)					
D.	Preferred	26,800,000***		25,000		1,072.00
	Common	4,260,000		80,000		53.25
	***(25,000,000 + 1,800,000)					
E.	Preferred	560,000		20,000		28.00
	Common	1,720,000****		250,000		6.88
	****[2,000,000 – 220,000 – 3(20,000)]					

SELF-EXAMINATION QUESTIONS (ANSWERS AT END OF CHAPTER)

1. During its first year of operations, a corporation elected to use the straight-line method of depreciation for financial reporting purposes and MACRS in determining taxable income. If the income tax is 40% and the amount of depreciation expense is $60,000 under the straight-line method and $100,000 under MACRS, what is the amount of income tax deferred to future years?
   A. $16,000 C. $40,000
   B. $24,000 D. $60,000

2. A material gain resulting from condemning land for public use would be reported on the income statement as:
   A. an extraordinary item. C. revenue from sales.
   B. an other income item. D. a change in estimate.

3. On July 9, 1998, a sale on account for $10,000 to a Mexican company was billed for 25,000,000 pesos. The exchange rate was $.0004 per peso on July 9 and $.0005 per peso on August 8, 1998, when the cash was received on account.

Which of the following statements identifies the exchange gain or loss for the fiscal year ended December 31, 1998?

A. Realized exchange loss, $2,500.
B. Realized exchange gain, $2,500.
C. Unrealized exchange loss, $2,500.
D. Unrealized exchange gain, $2,500.

4. An item treated as a prior-period adjustment should be reported in the financial statements as:
   A. an extraordinary item.
   B. an other expense item.
   C. an adjustment of the beginning balance of Retained Earnings.
   D. a change in estimate.

5. A corporation's balance sheet includes 10,000 outstanding shares of $8 cumulative preferred stock of $100 par; 100,000 outstanding shares of $20 par common stock; paid-in capital in excess of par—common stock of $100,000; and retained earnings of $540,000. If preferred dividends are three years in arrears, including the current dividend, and the preferred stock is entitled to dividends in arrears plus $110 per share in the event of liquidation, what is the equity per common share?
   A. $20.00
   B. $22.20
   C. $23.00
   D. $25.40

DISCUSSION QUESTIONS

1. A corporation has paid estimated federal income tax during the year on the basis of its estimated income. Indicate the accounts that would be debited and credited at the end of the year if the corporation (a) owes an additional tax; (b) overpaid its tax.
2. How would the amount of deferred income tax payable be reported in the balance sheet if (a) it is payable within one year and (b) it is payable beyond one year?
3. What two criteria must be met to classify an item as an extraordinary item on the income statement?
4. During the current year, 20 acres of land that cost $100,000 were condemned for construction of an interstate highway. Assuming that an award of $140,000 in cash was received and that the applicable income tax on this transaction is 30%, how would this information be presented in the income statement?
5. Corporation X realized a material gain when its facilities at a designated floodway were acquired by the urban renewal agency. How should the gain be reported in the income statement?

   Source: "Technical Hotline," *Journal of Accountancy*, June 1989, p. 32.

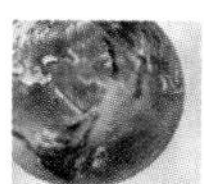

6. The 1993 annual report of Sears, Roebuck and Co. disclosed the discontinuance of several business segments, including Coldwell Banker Residential Services. The estimated loss on disposal of these operations was $64 million, including $22 million of tax expense. Indicate how the loss from discontinued operations should be reported by Sears, Roebuck and Co. on its income statement for the year ended December 31, 1993.
7. If significant changes are made in the accounting principles applied from one period to the next, why should the effect of these changes be disclosed in the financial statements?
8. A corporation reports earnings per share of $9.50 for the most recent year and $7.00 for the preceding year. The $9.50 includes a $3.00-per-share gain from a sale of the only investment owned since the business was organized in 1940. (a) Should the composition of the $9.50 be disclosed in the financial reports? (b) On the basis of the limited information presented, would you conclude that operations had improved or declined?
9. Can a U.S. company incur an exchange gain or loss because of fluctuations in the exchange rate if its receivables or payables transactions with foreign countries are executed in (a) dollars, (b) the foreign currency?
10. A U.S. company purchased merchandise for 20,000 francs on account from a French company. If the exchange rate was $0.19 per franc on the date of purchase and $0.18 per franc on the date of payment of the account, was there an exchange gain or loss realized by the U.S. company?
11. What two conditions give rise to unrealized currency exchange gains and losses from sales and purchases on account that are to be settled in the foreign currency?
12. Indicate how prior-period adjustments would be reported on the financial statements presented only for the current period.
13. How is the price-earnings ratio computed?
14. What does the price-earnings ratio indicate about the market's assessment of the future prospects of a company?
15. Describe how equity per share is computed (a) when there is only one class of stock outstanding and (b) when there is both preferred stock and common stock outstanding.

16. Differentiate between equity per share and market price per share of stock.
17. Common stock has a par of $10 per share, the current equity per share is $22.50, and the market price per share is $55. Suggest reasons for the comparatively high market price in relation to par and equity per share.
18. a. What are two methods of accounting for long-term investments in stock?
    b. Under what caption are long-term investments in stock reported on the balance sheet?
19. Avery Inc. received a $0.30-per-share cash dividend on 15,000 shares of CMI Corporation common stock, which Avery Inc. carries as a long-term investment. (a) Assuming that Avery Inc. uses the cost method of accounting for its investment in CMI Corporation, what account would be credited for the receipt of the $4,500 dividend? (b) Assuming that Avery Inc. uses the equity method of accounting for its investment in CMI Corporation, what account would be credited for the receipt of the $4,500 dividend?
20. What terms are applied to the following: (a) a corporation that is controlled by another corporation through ownership of a controlling interest in its stock; (b) a corporation that owns a controlling interest in the voting stock of another corporation; (c) a group of corporations related through stock ownership?
21. Which method of accounting for long-term investments in stock (cost or equity) should be used by the parent company in accounting for its investments in stock of subsidiaries?
22. What are the two methods by which a parent-subsidiary relationship may be established?
23. What are consolidated (financial) statements?
24. P Company purchases the entire common stock of S Corporation for $25,000,000. What accounts on S's balance sheet are represented in the investment account on P's balance sheet?
25. Parent Corporation owns 90% of the outstanding common stock of Subsidiary Corporation, which has no preferred stock. (a) What is the term applied to the remaining 10% interest? (b) Where is the amount of Subsidiary's book equity allocable to outsiders reported on the consolidated balance sheet?

26. An annual report of The Campbell Soup Company reported on its income statement $2.4 million as "equity in earnings of affiliates." Journalize the entry that Campbell would have made to record this equity in earnings of affiliates.

EXERCISES

EXERCISE 15–1
Income tax entries
Objective 1

Journalize the entries to record the following selected transactions of Zasky Grave Markers Inc.:

Apr. 15. Paid the first installment of the estimated income tax for the current fiscal year ending December 31, $80,000. No entry had been made to record the liability.
June 15. Paid the second installment of $80,000.
Sep. 15. Paid the third installment of $80,000.
Dec. 31. Recorded the estimated income tax liability for the year just ended and the deferred income tax liability, based on the transactions above and the following data:

Income tax rate	40%
Income before income tax	$1,000,000
Taxable income according to tax return	900,000

Jan. 15. Paid the fourth installment of $120,000.

EXERCISE 15–2
Extraordinary item
Objective 2

A company received life insurance proceeds on the death of its president before the end of its fiscal year. It intends to report the amount in its income statement as an extraordinary item.
Would this be in conformity with generally accepted accounting principles? Discuss.
Source: "Technical Hotline," *Journal of Accountancy*, June 1989, p. 31.

EXERCISE 15–3
Identifying extraordinary items
Objective 2

Assume that the amount of each of the following items is material to the financial statements. Classify each item as either normally recurring (NR) or extraordinary (E).

a. Loss on disposal of equipment considered to be obsolete because of development of new technology.

b. Uninsured loss on building due to hurricane damage. The firm was organized in 1920 and had not previously incurred hurricane damage.
c. Loss on sale of plant assets.
d. Interest income on notes receivable.
e. Uninsured flood loss. (Flood insurance is unavailable because of periodic flooding in the area.)
f. Salaries of corporate officers.
g. Gain on sale of land condemned for public use.
h. Uncollectible accounts expense.

EXERCISE 15–4
Income statement
Objective 2

Nautical Inc. produces and distributes equipment for sailboats. On the basis of the following data for the current fiscal year ended June 30, prepare a multiple-step income statement for Nautical Inc., including an analysis of earnings per share in the form illustrated in this chapter. There were 10,000 shares of $25 par common stock outstanding throughout the year.

Administrative expenses	$ 36,250
Cost of merchandise sold	722,500
Cumulative effect on prior years of changing to a different depreciation method (decrease in income)	50,000
Gain on condemnation of land (extraordinary item)	37,750
Income tax reduction applicable to change in depreciation method	20,000
Income tax applicable to gain on condemnation of land	6,750
Income tax reduction applicable to loss from discontinued operations	45,500
Income tax applicable to ordinary income	107,200
Loss on discontinued operations	114,500
Sales	1,092,500
Selling expenses	65,750

EXERCISE 15–5
Income statement
Objectives 2, 3

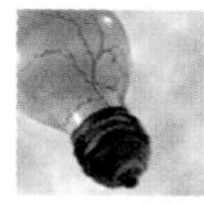

Collegium Sound Inc. sells automotive and home stereo equipment. It has 25,000 shares of $50 par common stock and 10,000 shares of $2, $100 par cumulative preferred stock outstanding as of December 31, 1997. It also holds 5,000 shares of common stock as treasury stock as of December 31, 1997. How many errors can you find in the following income statement for the year ended December 31, 1997?

Collegium Sound Inc.
Income Statement
For the Year Ended December 31, 1997

Net sales		$7,650,000
Cost of merchandise sold		6,100,000
Gross profit		$1,550,000
Operating expenses:		
Selling expenses	$720,000	
Administrative expenses	280,000	1,000,000
Income from continuing operations before income tax		$ 550,000
Income tax		220,000
Income from continuing operations		$ 230,000
Cumulative effect on prior years' income (decrease) of changing to a different depreciation method (net of applicable income tax of $36,000)		(92,000)
Correction of error (understatement) in December 31, 1996 physical inventory (net of applicable income tax of $20,000)		30,000
Income before condemnation of land and discontinued operations		$ 168,000
Extraordinary item:		
Gain on condemnation of land, net of applicable income tax of $65,000		150,000
Loss on discontinued operations (net of applicable income tax of $64,000)		(96,000)
Net income		$ 222,000

Earnings per common share:	
Income from continuing operations	$ 9.20
Cumulative effect on prior years' income (decrease) of changing to a different depreciation method	(3.68)
Correction of error (understatement) in December 31, 1996 physical inventory	1.20
Income before extraordinary item and discontinued operations	$ 6.72
Extraordinary item	6.00
Loss on discontinued operations	(3.84)
Net income	$ 8.88

EXERCISE 15–6
Entries for sales made in foreign currency
Objective 4

Acutone Electric Guitar Company makes sales on account to several Swedish companies that it bills in kronas. Journalize the entries for the following selected transactions completed during the current year, assuming that Acutone uses the perpetual inventory system:

June 2. Sold merchandise on account, 10,000 kronas; exchange rate, $0.13 per krona. The cost of merchandise sold was $1,100.
July 3. Received cash from sale of June 2, 10,000 kronas; exchange rate, $0.14 per krona.
Aug. 30. Sold merchandise on account, 12,000 kronas; exchange rate, $0.14 per krona. The cost of merchandise sold was $1,250.
Sep. 30. Received cash from sale of August 30, 12,000 kronas; exchange rate, $0.12 per krona.

EXERCISE 15–7
Entries for purchases made in foreign currency
Objective 4

Prosthetic Inc. sells artificial arms and legs to hospitals and physicians. It purchases merchandise from a German company that requires payment in deutsche marks. Journalize the entries for the following selected transactions completed during the current year, assuming that Prosthetic Inc. uses the perpetual inventory system:

Feb. 10. Purchased merchandise on account, net 30, 6,000 deutsche marks; exchange rate, $0.58 per deutsche mark.
Mar. 9. Paid invoice of Feb. 10; exchange rate, $0.59 per deutsche mark.
Apr. 1. Purchased merchandise on account, net 30, 5,000 deutsche marks; exchange rate, $0.59 per deutsche mark.
May 1. Paid invoice of April 1; exchange rate, $0.57 per deutsche mark.

EXERCISE 15–8
Prior-period adjustment
Objective 5

Orthotics Company sells supplies to dentists in Texas and Oklahoma. It reported the following results of transactions affecting retained earnings for the current year ended December 31, 1997:

Net income	$132,500
Dividends	40,000
Prior-period adjustment for understatement of merchandise inventory on December 31, 1996, net of applicable income tax of $12,000	18,000

Assuming that the retained earnings balance reported on the retained earnings statement as of December 31, 1996, was $292,500, prepare a retained earnings statement for the year ended December 31, 1997.

EXERCISE 15–9
Earnings per share, price-earnings ratio, and equity per share
Objectives 3, 6

Sports Mart Inc., a sporting goods wholesaler, has the following stockholders' equity accounts at the end of the current fiscal year, after all closing entries have been posted: Common Stock, $15 par, $1,500,000; Paid-In Capital in Excess of Par—Common Stock, $300,000; Paid-In Capital from Treasury Stock, $18,000; Retained Earnings, $1,860,000. The earnings for the current year, during which there were no unusual items, were $350,000.

a. Compute the earnings per share of common stock.
b. Assuming that the market price of the common stock at the end of the current fiscal year was $63, compute the price-earnings ratio.
c. Compute the equity per share of common stock as of the end of the current fiscal year.
d. Why would the equity per share of common stock normally differ from the market price of the common stock?

EXERCISE 15–10
Equity per share
Objective 6

Apothecary Inc. produces and distributes over-the-counter medicines and drugs. The stockholders' equity accounts of Apothecary Inc. at the end of the current fiscal year are as follows: Preferred $2 Stock, $100 par, $1,000,000; Common Stock, $15 par, $15,000,000; Paid-In Capital in Excess of Par—Common Stock, $300,000; Paid-In Capital in Excess of Par—Preferred Stock, $40,000; Retained Earnings, $1,060,000.

a. Calculate the equity per share of each class of stock, assuming that the preferred stock is entitled to receive $110 on liquidation.
b. Calculate the equity per share of each class of stock, assuming that the preferred stock is to receive $110 per share plus the dividends in arrears in the event of liquidation and that only the dividends for the current year are in arrears.

EXERCISE 15–11
Equity per share; liquidation amounts
Objective 6

The following items were listed in the Stockholders' Equity section of the balance sheet on April 30: Preferred stock, $75 par, $300,000; Common stock, $10 par, $2,500,000; Paid-in capital in excess of par—common stock, $250,000; Deficit, $150,000. On May 1, the board of directors voted to dissolve the corporation immediately. A short time later, after all noncash assets were sold and liabilities were paid, cash of $1,825,000 remained for distribution to stockholders.

a. Assuming that preferred stock is entitled to preference in liquidation of $80 per share, calculate the equity per share on April 30 of (1) preferred stock and (2) common stock.
b. Calculate the amount of the $1,825,000 that will be distributed for each share of (1) preferred stock and (2) common stock.
c. Explain the reason for the difference between the common stock equity per share on April 30 and the amount of the cash distribution per common share.

EXERCISE 15–12
Treasury stock and equity per share
Objective 6

The following items were listed in the Stockholders' Equity section of the balance sheet of June 30: Common stock, $25 par (10,000 shares outstanding), $250,000; Paid-in capital in excess of par—common stock, $15,000; Retained earnings, $290,000. On July 1, the corporation purchased 1,000 shares of its stock for $31,200.

a. Calculate the equity per share of stock on June 30.
b. Calculate the equity per share on July 1.

EXERCISE 15–13
Equity method
Objective 7

The following note to the consolidated financial statements for The Goodyear Tire and Rubber Co. related to the principles of consolidation used in preparing the financial statements:

The Company's investments in 20% to 50% owned companies in which it has the ability to exercise significant influence over operating and financial policies are accounted for by the equity method. Accordingly, the Company's share of the earnings of these companies is included in consolidated net income.

Is it a requirement that Goodyear use the equity method in this situation? Explain.

EXERCISE 15–14
Entries for investment in stock, receipt of dividends, and sale of shares
Objective 7

On February 3, Vascular Corporation acquired 1,000 shares of the 40,000 outstanding shares of Surgery Co. common stock at 52 1/2 plus commission charges of $540. On August 13, a cash dividend of $1 per share and a 4% stock dividend were received. On November 15, 400 shares were sold at 53 1/4, less commission charges of $275. Journalize the entries to record (a) the purchase of the stock, (b) the receipt of dividends, and (c) the sale of the 400 shares.

EXERCISE 15–15
Entries using equity method for stock investment
Objective 7

At a total cost of $8,000,000, Poko Corporation acquired 75,000 shares of Paragon Corp. common stock as a long-term investment. Poko Corporation uses the equity method of accounting for this investment. Paragon Corp. has 250,000 shares of common stock outstanding, including the shares acquired by Poko Corporation. Journalize the entries by Poko Corporation to record the following information:

a. Paragon Corp. reports net income of $600,000 for the current period.
b. A cash dividend of $1.20 per common share is paid by Paragon Corp. during the current period.

EXERCISE 15–16
Eliminations for consolidated income statement
Objective 8

For the current year ended April 30, the results of operations of Park Corporation and its wholly owned subsidiary, Starbuck Enterprises, are as follows:

	Park Corporation		Starbuck Enterprises	
Sales		$1,150,000		$500,000
Cost of merchandise sold	$725,000		$340,000	
Selling expenses	255,000		75,000	
Administrative expenses	85,000		35,000	
Interest expense (income)	(12,000)	1,053,000	12,000	462,000
Net income		$ 97,000		$ 38,000

During the year, Park sold merchandise to Starbuck for $120,000. The merchandise was sold by Starbuck to nonaffiliated companies for $150,000. Park's interest income was realized from a long-term loan to Starbuck.

Determine: (1) the amounts to be eliminated from the following items in preparing a consolidated income statement for the current year: (a) sales and (b) cost of merchandise sold and (2) the consolidated net income.

PROBLEMS SERIES A

PROBLEM 15–1A
Income tax allocation
Objective 1

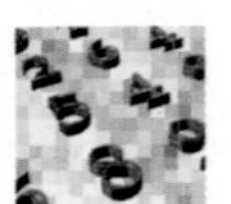

Differences between the accounting methods applied to accounts and financial reports and those used in determining taxable income yielded the following amounts for the first four years of a corporation's operations:

	First Year	*Second Year*	*Third Year*	*Fourth Year*
Income before income tax	$318,000	$337,500	$406,250	$649,000
Taxable income	250,000	292,500	383,750	678,750

The income tax rate for each of the four years was 40% of taxable income, and each year's taxes were promptly paid.

Instructions

1. Determine for each year the amounts described by the following captions, presenting the information in the form indicated:

			Deferred Income Tax Payable	
Year	*Income Tax Deducted on Income Statement*	*Income Tax Payments for the Year*	*Year's Addition (Deduction)*	*Year-End Balance*

2. Total the first three amount columns.

PROBLEM 15–2A
Income tax; income statement
Objectives 1, 2

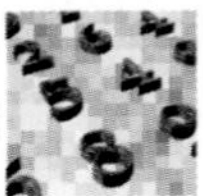

The following data were selected from the records of Botanica Greenhouses Inc. for the current fiscal year ended August 31:

Advertising expense	$ 37,250
Cost of merchandise sold	750,000
Delivery expense	19,750
Depreciation expense—office equipment	5,200
Depreciation expense—store equipment	19,000
Gain on condemnation of land	25,000
Income tax:	
Applicable to continuing operations	27,200
Applicable to loss from disposal of a segment of the business (reduction)	24,000
Applicable to gain on condemnation of land	10,000
Insurance expense	8,000
Interest expense	15,200

Loss from disposal of a segment of the business	$ 60,200
Miscellaneous administrative expense	3,550
Miscellaneous selling expense	5,600
Office salaries expense	42,750
Office supplies expense	1,700
Rent expense	21,000
Sales	1,097,500
Sales commissions expense	53,500
Sales salaries expense	42,500
Store supplies expense	4,500

Instructions

Prepare a multiple-step income statement, concluding with a section for earnings per share in the form illustrated in this chapter. There were 10,000 shares of common stock (no preferred) outstanding throughout the year. Assume that the gain on condemnation of land is an extraordinary item.

PROBLEM 15–3A
Foreign currency transactions
Objective 4

Crosstown Inc. is a wholesaler of sports equipment, including golf clubs and gym sets. It sells to and purchases from companies in Canada and the Philippines. These transactions are settled in the foreign currency. The following selected transactions were completed during the current fiscal year:

June 10. Sold merchandise on account to Salas Company, net 30, 400,000 pesos; exchange rate, $0.038 per Philippines peso. The cost of merchandise sold was $8,500.
July 10. Received cash from Salas Company; exchange rate, $0.037 per Philippines peso.
15. Purchased merchandise on account from LeRa Inc., net 30, $5,000 Canadian; exchange rate, $0.76 per Canadian dollar.
Aug. 14. Issued check for amount owed to LeRa Inc.; exchange rate, $0.75 per Canadian dollar.
31. Sold merchandise on account to Kaspar Company, net 30, 200,000 pesos; exchange rate, $0.034 per Philippines peso. The cost of merchandise sold was $3,800.
Sep. 30. Received cash from Kaspar Company; exchange rate, $0.036 per Philippines peso.
Oct. 8. Purchased merchandise on account from Chevalier Company, net 30, $50,000 Canadian; exchange rate, $0.73 per Canadian dollar.
Nov. 7. Issued check for amount owed to Chevalier Company; exchange rate, $0.74 per Canadian dollar.
Dec. 15. Sold merchandise on account to Jason Company, net 30, $80,000 Canadian; exchange rate, $0.75 per Canadian dollar. The cost of merchandise sold was $32,500.
16. Purchased merchandise on account from Santos Company, net 30, 450,000 pesos; exchange rate, $0.037 per Philippines peso.
31. Recorded unrealized currency exchange gain and/or loss on transactions of December 15 and 16. Exchange rates on December 31: $0.76 per Canadian dollar; $0.038 per Philippines peso.

Instructions

1. Journalize the entries to record the transactions and adjusting entries for the year, assuming that Crosstown uses the perpetual inventory system.
2. Journalize the entries to record the payment of the December 16 purchase, on January 15, when the exchange rate was $0.036 per Philippines peso, and the receipt of cash from the December 15 sale, on January 17, when the exchange rate was $0.77 per Canadian dollar.

PROBLEM 15–4A
Equity per share
Objective 6

Selected data from the balance sheets of six corporations, identified by letter, are as follows:

A.	Common stock, $10 par	$ 750,000
	Paid-in capital in excess of par—common stock	125,000
	Deficit	50,000
B.	Preferred $1 stock, $50 par	$ 500,000
	Common stock, $100 par	2,500,000
	Paid-in capital in excess of par—common stock	130,000
	Retained earnings	350,000
	Preferred stock has prior claim to assets on liquidation to the extent of par.	

C.

Preferred $3 stock, $150 par	$3,000,000
Paid-in capital in excess of par—preferred stock	150,000
Common stock, no par, 50,000 shares outstanding	4,250,000
Deficit	300,000

Preferred stock has prior claim to assets on liquidation to the extent of par.

D.

Preferred 11% stock, $50 par	$2,000,000
Paid-in capital in excess of par—preferred stock	275,000
Common stock, $25 par	3,750,000
Retained earnings	450,000

Preferred stock has prior claim to assets on liquidation to the extent of 110% of par.

E.

Preferred 3% stock, $100 par	$1,000,000
Common stock, $50 par	2,000,000
Paid-in capital in excess of par—common stock	140,000
Retained earnings	208,000

Dividends on preferred stock are in arrears for 2 years, including the dividend passed during the current year. Preferred stock is entitled to par plus unpaid cumulative dividends on liquidation to the extent of retained earnings.

F.

Preferred $2 stock, $25 par	$ 500,000
Common stock, $10 par	2,000,000
Deficit	170,000

Dividends on preferred stock are in arrears for 3 years, including the dividend passed during the current year. Preferred stock is entitled to par plus unpaid cumulative dividends on liquidation, regardless of the availability of retained earnings.

Instructions

Calculate for each corporation the equity per share of each class of stock, presenting the total shareholders' equity allocated to each class and the number of shares outstanding.

PROBLEM 15–5A
Entries for investments in stock
Objective 7

Garibaldi Company is a wholesaler of men's hair products. The following transactions relate to certain securities acquired by Garibaldi Company, whose fiscal year ends on December 31:

1994

Jan. 11. Purchased 1,500 shares of the 40,000 outstanding common shares of Cuisine Corporation at 20 plus commission and other costs of $264.

July 5. Received the regular cash dividend of $1 a share on Cuisine Corporation stock.

Dec. 5. Received the regular cash dividend of $1 a share plus an extra dividend of $0.20 a share on Cuisine Corporation stock.
(Assume that all intervening transactions have been recorded properly and that the number of shares of stock owned have not changed from December 31, 1994, to December 31, 1997.)

1998

July 7. Received the regular cash dividend of $1 a share and a 4% stock dividend on the Cuisine Corporation stock.

Aug. 20. Sold 500 shares of Cuisine Corporation stock at 22. The broker deducted commission and other costs of $125, remitting the balance.

Dec. 9. Received a cash dividend at the new rate of $1.05 a share on the Cuisine Corporation stock.

Instructions

Journalize the entries for the preceding transactions.

PROBLEMS SERIES B

PROBLEM 15–1B
Income tax allocation
Objective 1

Differences between the accounting methods applied to accounts and financial reports and those used in determining taxable income yielded the following amounts for the first four years of a corporation's operations:

	First Year	*Second Year*	*Third Year*	*Fourth Year*
Income before income tax	$226,250	$316,250	$417,500	$495,000
Taxable income	170,000	282,500	428,750	510,000

The income tax rate for each of the four years was 40% of taxable income, and each year's taxes were promptly paid.

Instructions

1. Determine for each year the amounts described by the following captions, presenting the information in the form indicated:

			Deferred Income Tax Payable	
Year	*Income Tax Deducted on Income Statement*	*Income Tax Payments for the Year*	*Year's Addition (Deduction)*	*Year-End Balance*

2. Total the first three amount columns.

PROBLEM 15–2B
Income tax; income statement
Objectives 1, 2

Ejector Inc. produces and sells off-road motorcycles and jeeps. The following data were selected from the records of Ejector Inc. for the current fiscal year ended March 31:

Advertising expense	$ 32,500
Cost of merchandise sold	395,000
Delivery expense	10,400
Depreciation expense—office equipment	4,250
Depreciation expense—store equipment	21,500
Gain on condemnation of land	40,000
Income tax:	
Applicable to continuing operations	56,000
Applicable to loss from disposal of a segment of the business (reduction)	5,000
Applicable to gain on condemnation of land	16,000
Insurance expense	7,100
Interest income	13,700
Loss from disposal of a segment of the business	25,000
Miscellaneous administrative expense	2,800
Miscellaneous selling expense	3,500
Office salaries expense	46,000
Office supplies expense	1,750
Rent expense	20,000
Sales	787,500
Sales commissions expense	44,900
Sales salaries expense	66,900
Store supplies expense	2,600

Instructions

Prepare a multiple-step income statement, concluding with a section for earnings per share in the form illustrated in this chapter. There were 25,000 shares of common stock (no preferred) outstanding throughout the year. Assume that the gain on condemnation of land is an extraordinary item.

PROBLEM 15–3B
Foreign currency transactions
Objective 4

Rheumatic Company is a wholesaler of medicine and drugs for relieving rheumatism pain. It sells to and purchases from Canadian and Japanese companies. These transactions are settled in the foreign currency. The following selected transactions were completed during the current fiscal year:

Jan. 20. Purchased merchandise on account from Robert Company, net 30, $70,000 Canadian; exchange rate, $0.74 per Canadian dollar.
Feb. 19. Issued check for amount owed to Robert Company; exchange rate, $0.76 per Canadian dollar.
Mar. 3. Sold merchandise on account to Niko Company, net 30, 600,000 yen; exchange rate, $0.008 per Japanese yen. The cost of merchandise sold was $1,900.
Apr. 2. Received cash from Niko Company; exchange rate, $0.009 per Japanese yen.
May 30. Purchased merchandise on account from Bernes Company, net 30, $50,000 Canadian; exchange rate, $0.77 per Canadian dollar.
June 29. Issued check for amount owed to Bernes Company; exchange rate, $0.76 per Canadian dollar.
July 3. Sold merchandise on account to Kim Company, net 30, 3,000,000 yen; exchange rate, $0.0075 per Japanese yen. The cost of merchandise sold was $9,000.
Aug. 2. Received cash from Kim Company; exchange rate, $0.0065 per Japanese yen.
Dec. 16. Sold merchandise on account to Claude Company, net 45, $12,000 Canadian; exchange rate, $0.75 per Canadian dollar. The cost of merchandise sold was $3,600.
20. Purchased merchandise on account from Fuji Company, net 30, 5,000,000 yen; exchange rate, $0.007 per Japanese yen.
31. Recorded unrealized currency exchange gain and/or loss on transactions of December 16 and 20. Exchange rates on December 31: $0.73 per Canadian dollar; $0.0065 per Japanese yen.

Instructions

1. Journalize the entries to record the transactions and adjusting entries for the year, assuming that Rheumatic uses the perpetual inventory system.
2. Journalize the entries to record the payment of the December 20 purchase, on January 19, when the exchange rate was $0.0071 per Japanese yen, and the receipt of cash from the December 16 sale, on January 30, when the exchange rate was $0.72 per Canadian dollar.

PROBLEM 15–4B
Equity per share
Objective 6

Selected data from the balance sheets of six corporations, identified by letter, are as follows:

A.	Common stock, no par, 125,000 shares outstanding	$1,050,000
	Deficit	280,000
B.	Preferred $1 stock, $25 par	$ 500,000
	Common stock, $10 par	2,500,000
	Paid-in capital in excess of par—common stock	250,000
	Retained earnings	750,000
	Preferred stock has prior claim to assets on liquidation to the extent of par.	
C.	Preferred $2 stock, $100 par	$ 400,000
	Paid-in capital in excess of par—preferred stock	30,000
	Common stock, $5 par	1,000,000
	Paid-in capital in excess of par—common stock	155,000
	Deficit	275,000
	Preferred stock has prior claim to assets on liquidation to the extent of par.	
D.	Preferred 4% stock, $50 par	$ 800,000
	Paid-in capital in excess of par—preferred stock	100,000
	Common stock, $25 par	1,500,000
	Deficit	300,000
	Preferred stock has prior claim to assets on liquidation to the extent of 115% of par.	
E.	Preferred 11% stock, $100 par	$ 800,000
	Common stock, $5 par	2,000,000
	Paid-in capital in excess of par—common stock	300,000
	Retained earnings	104,000
	Dividends on preferred stock are in arrears for 2 years, including the dividend passed during the current year. Preferred stock is entitled to par plus unpaid cumulative dividends on liquidation to the extent of retained earnings.	

F.

Preferred $1 stock, $25 par	$ 500,000
Paid-in capital in excess of par—preferred stock	10,000
Common stock, $10 par	1,500,000
Deficit	55,000

Dividends on preferred stock are in arrears for 3 years, including the dividend passed during the current year. Preferred stock is entitled to par plus unpaid cumulative dividends on liquidation, regardless of the availability of retained earnings.

Instructions
Calculate for each corporation the equity per share of each class of stock, presenting the total shareholders' equity allocated to each class and the number of shares outstanding.

PROBLEM 15–5B
Entries for investments in stock
Objective 7

Harlequin Company produces and sells theater costumes. The following transactions relate to certain securities acquired by Harlequin Company, whose fiscal year ends on December 31:

1994

Mar. 20. Purchased 2,000 shares of the 25,000 outstanding common shares of Neopolitan Corporation at 30 plus commission and other costs of $270.

June 15. Received the regular cash dividend of $1 a share on Neopolitan Corporation stock.

Dec. 15. Received the regular cash dividend of $1 a share plus an extra dividend of $0.25 a share on Neopolitan Corporation stock.
(Assume that all intervening transactions have been recorded properly and that the number of shares of stock owned have not changed from December 31, 1994, to December 31, 1997.)

1998

Mar. 20. Received the regular cash dividend of $1 a share and a 5% stock dividend on the Neopolitan Corporation stock.

July 20. Sold 750 shares of Neopolitan Corporation stock at 32. The broker deducted commission and other costs of $125, remitting the balance.

Dec. 18. Received a cash dividend at the new rate of $1.10 a share on the Neopolitan Corporation stock.

Instructions
Journalize the entries for the preceding transactions.

CASES

CASE 15–1
Mennella Company
Foreign transactions

Mennella Company has recently begun selling merchandise to foreign customers. Chong Wah, the controller, has implemented a policy that requires all foreign transactions to be executed in U.S. dollars. In this way, Wah transfers to the customers all risks of foreign transactions on sales to foreign markets.

Discuss whether Chong Wah's policy is ethical.

CASE 15–2
Domingo's Oranges Inc.
Reporting extraordinary item

Domingo's Oranges Inc. is in the process of preparing its annual financial statements. Domingo's is a large citrus grower located in central Florida. The following is a discussion between Gene Hoy, the controller, and Judith Domingo, the chief executive officer and president of Domingo's.

Judith: Gene, I've got a question about your rough draft of this year's income statement.

Gene: Sure, Judith. What's your question?

Judith: Well, your draft shows a net loss of $1.5 million.

Gene: That's right. We'd have had a profit, except for this year's frost damage. I figured that the frost destroyed over 25 percent of our crop. We had a good year otherwise.

Judith: That's my concern. I estimated that if we eliminate the frost damage, we'd show a profit of . . . let's see . . . about $500,000.

Gene: That sounds about right.

Judith: This income statement seems misleading. Why can't we show the loss on the frost damage separately? That way the bank and our outside investors will be able to see that this year's loss is just temporary. I'd hate to get them upset over nothing.

Gene: Maybe we can do something. I recall from my accounting courses something about showing unusual items separately. Let's see . . . yes, I remember. They're called extraordinary items.

Judith: Well, we haven't had any frost damage in over five years. This year's damage is certainly extraordinary. Let's do it!

Discuss the appropriateness of revising Domingo's income statement to report the frost damage separately as an extraordinary item.

CASE 15–3
Hershey Foods Corporation
Financial analysis

Hershey Foods Corporation prepares consolidated financial statements that include foreign affiliates. Translation gains or losses related to the consolidation of net assets of foreign affiliates are reported in the Stockholders' Equity section of the balance sheet.

1. Determine Hershey Foods Corporation's basis for carrying investments in affiliate companies.
2. Determine the amount of intangibles (goodwill) resulting from business acquisitions as of December 31, 1993.
3. Determine the amount of the foreign currency translation adjustments for the year ended December 31, 1993. (Note: See the Consolidated Statements of Stockholders' Equity.)

CASE 15–4
Patsy Sapporo
Consolidated financial statements

Your grandmother recently retired, sold her home in Chicago, and moved to a retirement community in Sarasota. With some of the proceeds from the sale of her home, she is considering investing $150,000 in the stock market.

In the process of selecting among alternative stock investments, your grandmother collected annual reports from twenty different companies. In reviewing these reports, however, she has become confused and has questions concerning several items that appear in the financial reports. She has asked for your help and has written down the following questions for you to answer:

a. *In reviewing the annual reports, I noticed many references to "consolidated financial statements." What are consolidated financial statements?*

b. *"Excess of cost of business acquired over related net assets" appears on the consolidated balance sheets in several annual reports. What does this mean? Is it an asset (it appears with other assets)?*

c. *What is minority interest?*

d. *A footnote to one of the consolidated statements indicated interest and the amount of a loan from one company to another had been eliminated. Is this good accounting? A loan is a loan. How can a company just eliminate a loan that hasn't been paid off?*

e. *How can financial statements for an American company (in dollars) be combined with a British subsidiary (in pounds)?*

1. Briefly respond to each of your grandmother's questions.
2. While discussing the items in (1) with your grandmother, she asked for your advice on whether she should limit her investment to one stock. What would you advise?

ANSWERS TO SELF-EXAMINATION QUESTIONS

1. **A** The amount of income tax deferred to future years is $16,000 (answer A), determined as follows:

Depreciation expense, MACRS	$100,000
Depreciation expense, straight-line method	60,000
Excess expense in determining taxable income	$ 40,000
Income tax rate	× 40%
Income tax deferred to future years	$ 16,000

2. **A** Events and transactions that are distinguished by their unusual nature and by the infrequency of their occurrence, such as a gain on condemning land for public use, are reported in the income statement as extraordinary items (answer A).

3. **B** The 25,000,000 pesos billed, which had a value of $10,000 (25,000,000 pesos × $.0004) on July 9, 1998, had increased in value to $12,500 (25,000,000 pesos × $.0005) on

August 8, 1998, when payment was received. The gain, which was realized because the transaction was completed by the receipt of cash, was $2,500 (answer B).

4. **C** The correction of a material error related to a prior period should be excluded from the determination of net income of the current period and reported as an adjustment of the balance of retained earnings at the beginning of the current period (answer C).

5. **C** The total stockholders' equity is determined as follows:

Preferred stock	$1,000,000
Common stock	2,000,000
Excess of issue price over par—common stock	100,000
Retained earnings	540,000
Total equity	$3,640,000

The amount allocated to common stock is determined as follows:

Total equity		$3,640,000
Allocated to preferred stock:		
Liquidation price	$1,100,000	
Dividends in arrears	240,000	1,340,000
Allocated to common stock		$2,300,000

The equity per common share is determined as follows:
$2,300,000 ÷ 100,000 shares = $23 per share

16 Bonds Payable and Investments in Bonds

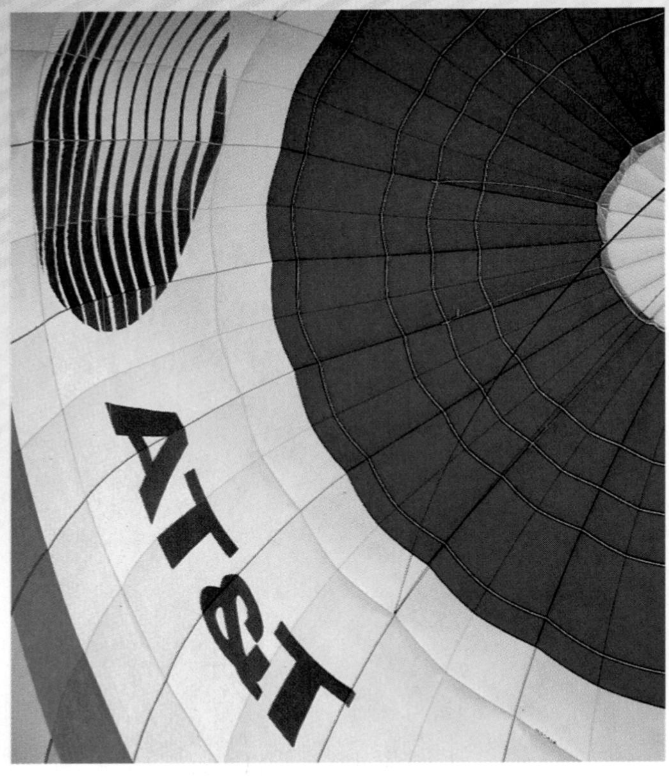

YOU AND ACCOUNTING

You have just inherited $50,000 from a distant relative, and you are considering some options for investing the money. Some of your friends have suggested that you invest it in long-term bonds. As a result, you have scanned *The Wall Street Journal's* August 18, 1994 listing of New York Exchange Bonds. You've identified the following two listings as possible bond investments, both of which mature in the year 2006:

ATT (American Telephone & Telegraph) 7 ½% Bonds
Alsk Ar (Alaska Airlines) Zero

The AT&T bonds are selling for 99¼, while the Alaska Airlines bonds are selling for only 41¼. The AT&T bonds are selling for over twice the price of the Alaska Airlines bonds. Does this mean that the Alaska Airlines bonds are a better buy? Does the 7½% mean that if you buy the AT&T bonds you can actually earn 7½% interest? What does the "zero" mean? Does it have anything to do with the fact that the Alaska Airlines bonds are only selling for 41¼?

In this chapter, we will answer each of these questions. We first discuss the advantages and disadvantages of financing a corporation's operations by issuing debt rather than equity. We then discuss the accounting principles related to issuing long-term debt. Finally, we discuss the accounting for investments in bonds.

After studying this chapter, you should be able to:

Objective 1
Compute the potential impact of long-term borrowing on the earnings per share of a corporation.

Objective 2
Describe the characteristics of bonds.

Objective 3
Compute the present value of bonds payable.

Objective 4
Journalize entries for bonds payable.

Objective 5
Describe bond sinking funds.

Objective 6
Journalize entries for bond redemptions.

Objective 7
Journalize entries for the purchase, interest, discount and premium amortization, and sale of bond investments.

Objective 8
Prepare a corporation balance sheet.

Financing Corporations

Objective 1
Compute the potential impact of long-term borrowing on the earnings per share of a corporation.

Corporations often finance their operations by issuing long-term notes or bonds. We have discussed notes receivable and notes payable in earlier chapters. A bond is simply a form of interest-bearing note. Like a note, a bond requires periodic interest payments and repayment of its principal at a maturity date. Thus, bondholders are creditors of the issuing corporation, and their claims on the assets of the corporation rank ahead of stockholders.

One of the many factors that influence the decision to issue debt or equity is the effect of each alternative on earnings per share. To illustrate the possible effects, assume that a corporation's board of directors is considering three alternative plans for financing a $4,000,000 company. In each case, the securities would be issued at their par or face amount. The corporation is expecting to earn $800,000 annually, before deducting interest on the bonds and income tax estimated at 40% of income. Exhibit 1 shows the effect of the three plans on the income of the corporation and its common stockholders.

Exhibit 1
Effect of Alternative Financing Plans—$800,000 Earnings

	Plan 1	*Plan 2*	*Plan 3*
12% bonds	—	—	$2,000,000
Preferred 9% stock, $50 par	—	$2,000,000	1,000,000
Common stock, $10 par	$4,000,000	2,000,000	1,000,000
Total	$4,000,000	$4,000,000	$4,000,000
Earnings before interest and income tax	$ 800,000	$ 800,000	$ 800,000
Deduct interest on bonds	—	—	240,000
Income before income tax	$ 800,000	$ 800,000	$ 560,000
Deduct income tax	320,000	320,000	224,000
Net income	$ 480,000	$ 480,000	$ 336,000
Dividends on preferred stock	—	180,000	90,000
Available for dividends on common stock	$ 480,000	$ 300,000	$ 246,000
Shares of common stock outstanding	400,000	200,000	100,000
Earnings per share on common stock	$1.20	$1.50	$2.46

Under Plan 1, all the financing is from issuing common stock. In this case, the earnings per share on the common stock is $1.20 per share. Under Plan 2, one-half of the financing is from issuing 9% preferred stock, and one-half is from issuing common stock. In this case, earnings per common share is $1.50. Under Plan 3, one-half of the financing is from issuing 12% bonds, and the remaining one-half is equally split between issuing 9% preferred stock and common stock. In this case, earnings per common share is $2.46.

In Exhibit 1, Plan 3 is the most attractive for common stockholders. If the estimated earnings are more than $800,000, the difference between the earnings per share to common stockholders under Plan 1 and Plan 3 is even greater. However, if smaller earnings occur, Plans 2 and 3 become less attractive. The effect of earnings of $440,000 rather than $800,000 is shown in Exhibit 2.

Exhibit 2
Effect of Alternative Financing Plans—$440,000 Earnings

	Plan 1	*Plan 2*	*Plan 3*
12% bonds	—	—	$2,000,000
Preferred 9% stock, $50 par	—	$2,000,000	1,000,000
Common stock, $10 par	$4,000,000	2,000,000	1,000,000
Total	$4,000,000	$4,000,000	$4,000,000
Earnings before interest and income tax	$ 440,000	$ 440,000	$ 440,000
Deduct interest on bonds	—	—	240,000
Income before income tax	$ 440,000	$ 440,000	$ 200,000
Deduct income tax	176,000	176,000	80,000
Net income	$ 264,000	$ 264,000	$ 120,000
Dividends on preferred stock	—	180,000	90,000
Available for dividends on common stock	$ 264,000	$ 84,000	$ 30,000
Shares of common stock outstanding	400,000	200,000	100,000
Earnings per share on common stock	$0.66	$0.42	$0.30

In addition to the effect on earnings per share, the board should consider other factors in deciding whether to issue debt or equity. For example, once bonds are issued, periodic interest payments and repayment of principal are beyond the control of the corporation. That is, if these payments are not made, the bondholders could seek court action and potentially force the company into bankruptcy. In contrast, a corporation is not legally obligated to pay dividends.

When interest rates are low, corporations usually finance their operations with debt. For example, as interest rates fell in the early 1990s, corporations rushed to issue new debt. In one day alone, more than $4.5 billion of debt was issued.[1]

Characteristics of Bonds Payable

Objective 2
Describe the characteristics of bonds.

A corporation that issues bonds enters into a contract, called a **bond indenture** or trust indenture, with the bondholders. A bond issue is normally divided into a number of individual bonds, which may be of varying denominations. Usually the principal of each bond, called the face value, is $1,000 or a multiple of $1,000. The interest on bonds may be payable annually, semiannually, or quarterly. Most bonds pay interest semiannually.

The prices of bonds are quoted on bond exchanges as a percentage of the bonds' face value. Thus, investors could purchase or sell **Whirlpool** bonds quoted at 106¼ for $1,062.50. Likewise, bonds quoted at 109 could be purchased or sold for $1,090.

When all bonds of an issue mature at the same time, they are called term bonds. If the maturities are spread over several dates, they are called serial bonds. For

[1] Kenneth N. Gilpin, "More Corporate Issues Are Offered," *The Wall Street Journal*, January 9, 1992, p. C16.

USING ACCOUNTING TO UNDERSTAND BUSINESS

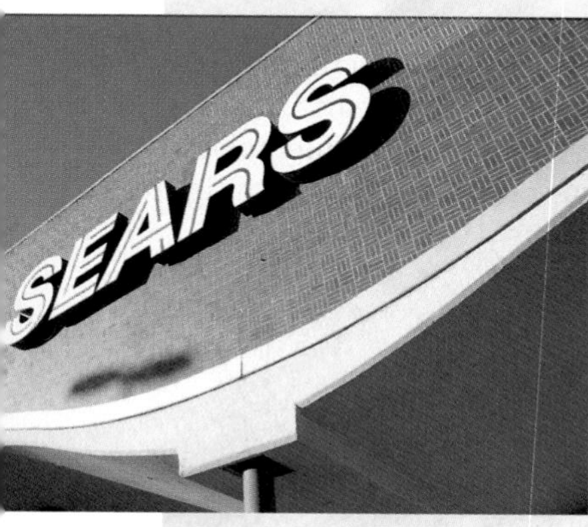

Some of the same factors that influence a corporation's decision on financing are also considered when a company refinances, or changes the structure of its debt and stockholders' equity. These concerns are described in the following excerpt from an article in *USA TODAY.*

When a major company like Allegis Corp. announces that it is "recapitalizing" [refinancing], many shareholders may be baffled. . . . Recapitalization plans aren't as complicated as they seem, however. . . .

How companies balance equity and debt is up to them. At IBM Corp., only 11% of total capital is debt. Sears, Roebuck and Co. has 46% debt. The level of debt a company keeps depends on the risk its managers are willing to assume.

What does risk have to do with it?

It's no different for a company than for an individual. The more debt you have, the greater the risk. Reason: Any profit you earn first must go to meet interest payments. If earnings aren't sufficient to cover the interest owed, you'll have to deplete your savings—or sell something—to raise the needed cash.

What happens in a recapitalization?

A company decides to borrow heavily to raise cash for a large, one-time cash . . . payment to shareholders. . . . [In addition,] . . . shareholders also receive new shares to replace their old shares in the company. . . . [In] the process, the company generally [reduces its equity]. It's replaced with debt.

How can the company afford the debt load?

The company is forced to operate more efficiently than ever. It will have to slash expenses to keep earnings up in the face of higher interest expenses. Owens-Corning Fiberglas Corp., for example, pared its research costs significantly after its recapitalization last year. . . .

Is there any advantage in being so heavily in debt?

Debt does have a good side. By borrowing, you gain "leverage"—the ability to control more assets by using someone else's money. That can magnify the return to shareholders, if business is good and the firm operates efficiently. . . .

Source: Neil Budde, "How Company Recapitalization Plans Work," *USA TODAY*, June 8, 1987.

example, one-tenth of an issue of $1,000,000 bonds, or $100,000, may mature 16 years from the issuance date, another $100,000 in the 17th year, and so on until the final $100,000 matures in the 25th year.

Bonds that may be exchanged for other securities under certain conditions are called convertible bonds. Bonds issued by a corporation that reserves the right to redeem bonds before maturity are called callable bonds. Bonds issued on the basis of the general credit of the corporation are called debenture bonds.

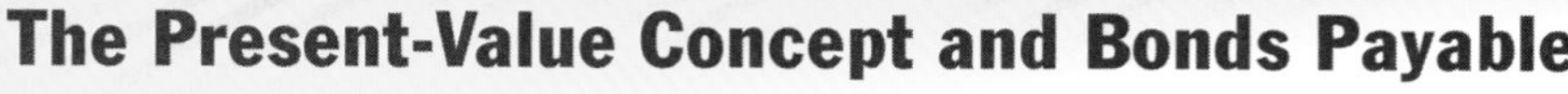

The Present-Value Concept and Bonds Payable

Objective 3
Compute the present value of bonds payable.

The concept of present value plays an important role in many accounting analyses and business decisions. For example, accounting analyses based on the present-value concept are useful for evaluating proposals for long-term investments in plant and equipment. In this chapter, we discuss the concept of present value as it relates to bonds.

The concept of present value is based on the time value of money. What is the time value of money? An amount of cash to be received at some date in the future is not the equivalent of the same amount of cash held at an earlier date. In other words, a sum of cash to be received in the future is not as valuable as the same sum on hand today. This is because cash on hand today can be invested to earn income. For example, $100 on hand today would be more valuable than $100 received a year from today. In this case, if the $100 cash on hand today can be invested to earn

10% per year, the $100 will accumulate to $110 ($100 plus $10 earnings) in one year. The $100 on hand today is the present-value amount that is equivalent to $110 to be received a year from today.

A related concept to present value is future value. In the preceding illustration, the $110 to be received a year from today is the future value of $100 today, assuming an interest rate of 10%.

When a corporation issues bonds, the price that a buyer is willing to pay for the bonds is the sum of the present values of the following amounts:

1. The face amount of the bonds at a maturity date.
2. Periodic interest at a specified percentage of the face amount.

PRESENT VALUE OF THE FACE AMOUNT OF BONDS

The **present value** of the face amount of bonds is the value today of the amount to be received at the maturity date. For example, assume you are to receive $1,000 in one year and that the rate of interest is 12%. The present value of the $1,000 is $892.86 ($1,000 ÷ 1.12). If you are to receive the $1,000 one year later (two years in all), with the interest compounded at the end of the first year, the present value is $797.20 ($892.86 ÷ 1.12).[2]

You can determine the present value of a cash sum to be received in the future by a series of divisions as illustrated above. In practice, however, it is normal to use a table of present values for this purpose. The present value of $1 table can be used to find the present-value factor for $1 to be received for the appropriate number of periods in the future. The amount of the future cash sum is then multiplied by this factor to determine its present value. Exhibit 3 is a partial table of the present value of $1.[3]

Exhibit 3
Present Value of $1 at Compound Interest

Periods	5%	5½%	6%	6½%	7%	10%	11%	12%	13%	14%
1	0.9524	0.9479	0.9434	0.9390	0.9346	0.9091	0.9009	0.8929	0.8850	0.8772
2	0.9070	0.8985	0.8900	0.8817	0.8734	0.8264	0.8116	0.7972	0.7832	0.7695
3	0.8638	0.8516	0.8396	0.8278	0.8163	0.7513	0.7312	0.7118	0.6931	0.6750
4	0.8227	0.8072	0.7921	0.7773	0.7629	0.6830	0.6587	0.6355	0.6133	0.5921
5	0.7835	0.7651	0.7473	0.7299	0.7130	0.6209	0.5935	0.5674	0.5428	0.5194
6	0.7462	0.7252	0.7050	0.6853	0.6663	0.5645	0.5346	0.5066	0.4803	0.4556
7	0.7107	0.6874	0.6651	0.6435	0.6228	0.5132	0.4817	0.4523	0.4251	0.3996
8	0.6768	0.6516	0.6274	0.6042	0.5820	0.4665	0.4339	0.4039	0.3762	0.3506
9	0.6446	0.6176	0.5919	0.5674	0.5439	0.4241	0.3909	0.3606	0.3329	0.3075
10	0.6139	0.5854	0.5584	0.5327	0.5083	0.3855	0.3522	0.3220	0.2946	0.2697

For the preceding example, Exhibit 3 indicates that the present value of $1 to be received in two years with interest of 12% a year is 0.7972. Multiplying $1,000 by 0.7972 yields $797.20. This is the same amount that we determined previously by two consecutive divisions. In Exhibit 3, the Periods column represents the number of compounding periods and the Percentage columns represent the compound interest rate per period. For example, 12% for two years compounded annually, as in the preceding example, is 12% for two periods. Likewise, 12% for two years

[2] Note that the future value of $797.20 in two years, at an interest rate of 12% compounded annually, is $1,000.

[3] To simplify the illustrations and homework assignments, the tables presented in this chapter are limited to 10 periods for a small number of interest rates, and the amounts are carried to only four decimal places. Computer programs are available for determining present value factors for any number of interest rates, decimal places, or periods. More complete interest tables, including future value tables, are presented in Appendix A.

compounded semiannually would be 6% (12% per year ÷ 2 semiannual periods) for four periods (2 years × 2 semiannual periods). Similarly, 12% for three years compounded semiannually would be 6% (12% ÷ 2) for six periods (3 years × 2 semiannual periods).

PRESENT VALUE OF THE PERIODIC BOND INTEREST PAYMENTS

The present value of the periodic bond interest payments is the value today of the amount of interest to be received at the end of each interest period. Such a series of fixed payments at fixed intervals is called an annuity.

Exhibit 4 is a partial table of the present value of an annuity of $1 at compound interest. Exhibit 4 indicates the present value of $1 to be received at the end of each period for various compound rates of interest. For example, the present value of $1,000 to be received at the end of each of the next five periods at 10% compound interest per period is $3,790.80 ($1,000 × 3.7908).

Exhibit 4
Present Value of Annuity of $1 at Compound Interest

Periods	5%	5½%	6%	6½%	7%	10%	11%	12%	13%	14%
1	0.9524	0.9479	0.9434	0.9390	0.9346	0.9091	0.9009	0.8929	0.8850	0.8772
2	1.8594	1.8463	1.8334	1.8206	1.8080	1.7355	1.7125	1.6901	1.6681	1.6467
3	2.7232	2.6979	2.6730	2.6485	2.6243	2.4869	2.4437	2.4018	2.3612	2.3216
4	3.5460	3.5052	3.4651	3.4258	3.3872	3.1699	3.1024	3.0373	2.9745	2.9137
5	4.3295	4.2703	4.2124	4.1557	4.1002	3.7908	3.6959	3.6048	3.5172	3.4331
6	5.0757	4.9955	4.9173	4.8410	4.7665	4.3553	4.2305	4.1114	3.9976	3.8887
7	5.7864	5.6830	5.5824	5.4845	5.3893	4.8684	4.7122	4.5638	4.4226	4.2883
8	6.4632	6.3346	6.2098	6.0888	5.9713	5.3349	5.1461	4.9676	4.7988	4.6389
9	7.1078	6.9522	6.8017	6.6561	6.5152	5.7590	5.5370	5.3283	5.1317	4.9464
10	7.7217	7.5376	7.3601	7.1888	7.0236	6.1446	5.8892	5.6502	5.4262	5.2161

Accounting for Bonds Payable

Objective 4
Journalize entries for bonds payable.

The interest rate specified in the bond indenture is called the contract rate or coupon rate. This rate may differ from the market rate of interest at the time the bonds are issued. If the market or effective rate is higher than the contract rate, the bonds will sell at a discount, or less than their face amount. Why is this the case? Buyers are not willing to pay the face amount for bonds whose contract rate is lower than the market rate. The discount, in effect, represents the amount necessary to make up for the difference in the market and the contract interest rates. In contrast, if the market rate is lower than the contract rate, the bonds will sell at a premium, or more than their face amount. In this case, buyers are willing to pay more than the face amount for bonds whose contract rate is higher than the market rate. Exhibit 5 summarizes the relationship between the contract and market rates of interest and issuing bonds at face value, a discount, or a premium.

Exhibit 5
Relationship of Market Rate and Contract Rate to Discounts and Premiums

Market rate = Contract rate → Bonds sell at face value
Market rate > Contract rate → Bonds sell at discount
Market rate < Contract rate → Bonds sell at premium

BONDS ISSUED AT FACE AMOUNT

To illustrate the journal entries for issuing bonds, assume that on January 1 a corporation issues for cash $100,000 of 12%, five-year bonds, with interest of $6,000 payable semiannually. The market rate of interest at the time the bonds are issued is 12%. Since the contract rate and the market rate of interest are the same, the bonds will sell at their face amount. This amount is the sum of (1) the present value of the face amount of $100,000 to be repaid in five years and (2) the present value of ten semiannual interest payments of $6,000 each. This computation is shown below.[4]

Present value of face amount of $100,000 due in 5 years, at 12% compounded semiannually: $100,000 × 0.5584 (present value of $1 for 10 periods at 6%)	$ 55,840
Present value of 10 semiannual interest payments of $6,000, at 12% compounded semiannually: $6,000 × 7.3601 (present value of annuity of $1 for 10 periods at 6%)	44,160
Total present value of bonds	$100,000

The basic data for computing the above amounts were obtained from the present-value tables in Exhibits 3 and 4. The first of the two amounts, $55,840, is the present value of the $100,000 that is to be repaid in five years. To determine the $55,840:

1. In Exhibit 3, locate the present value of $1 for ten periods (five years of semiannual payments) at 6% semiannually (12% annual rate).
2. Multiply the present-value factor in (1) by $100,000.

If the bond indenture provided that no interest would be paid during the entire five-year period, the bonds would be worth only $55,840 at the time of their issuance. To express the concept of present value from a different viewpoint, if $55,840 were invested today, with interest at 12% compounded semiannually, the sum accumulated at the end of ten semiannual periods would be $100,000.

The second of the two amounts, $44,160, is the present value of the series of ten $6,000 interest payments. To determine the $44,160:

1. In Exhibit 4, locate the present value of an annuity of $1 for ten periods (five years of semiannual payments) at 6% semiannually (12% annual rate).
2. Multiply the present-value factor in (1) by $6,000.

You can also view the present value of $44,160 as the amount that must be deposited today at an interest rate of 12% compounded semiannually to provide ten semiannual withdrawals of $6,000 each. At the end of the tenth withdrawal, the original deposit will be reduced to zero.

The entry to record the issuing of the $100,000 bonds at their face amount is shown below.

Jan.	1	Cash	100,000	
		Bonds Payable		100,000

At six-month intervals following the issuing of the 12% bonds, interest payments of $6,000 are made. The interest payment is recorded in the usual manner by a debit to Interest Expense and a credit to Cash. At the maturity date, the payment of the principal sum of $100,000 is recorded by a debit to Bonds Payable and a credit to Cash.

[4] Because the present-value tables are rounded to four decimal places, minor rounding differences may appear in the illustrations.

BONDS ISSUED AT A DISCOUNT

What if the market rate of interest is higher than the contract rate of interest? If the market rate of interest is 13% and the contract rate is 12%, for example, the bonds will sell at a discount. The present value of the five-year, $100,000 bonds is computed as follows:

Present value of face amount of $100,000 due in 5 years, at 13% compounded semiannually: $100,000 × 0.5327 (present value of $1 for 10 periods at 6½%)	$53,270
Present value of 10 semiannual interest payments of $6,000, at 13% compounded semiannually: $6,000 × 7.1888 (present value of an annuity of $1 for 10 periods at 6½%)	43,133
Total present value of bonds	$96,403

The two present values that make up the total are both less than the comparable amounts in the preceding example. This is because the market rate of interest was 12% in the first example, while the market rate of interest was 13% in the above example. The present value of a future amount becomes less and less as the interest rate used to compute the present value increases. Stated in another way, the amount that has to be invested today to equal a future amount becomes less and less as the interest rate that is assumed to be earned on the investment increases.

The entry to record the issuing of the preceding 12% bonds is shown below.

Jan.	1	Cash	96,403	
		Discount on Bonds Payable	3,597	
		Bonds Payable		100,000

When bonds payable are issued at a discount, the amount of the discount is recorded in a separate contra account. The $3,597 discount may be viewed as the amount that is needed to entice investors to accept a contract rate of interest that is below the market rate. In other words, the discount is the market's way of adjusting a bond's contract rate of interest to the higher market rate of interest. In this sense, the discount represents an additional interest expense beyond the amounts paid as periodic interest based on the contract rate of interest. The discount is paid to the bondholders at the maturity date. That is, in the above example, the issuer must pay the bondholders $100,000 at maturity, even though only $96,403 was initially received when the bonds were issued. Because of this, generally accepted accounting principles require the amortization of discounts to increase the interest expense over the life of a bond issue.

AMORTIZATION OF A BOND DISCOUNT

There are two methods of amortizing discount to interest expense over the life of a bond issue: (1) the **straight-line method** and (2) the **effective interest rate method,** often called the **interest method.** Both methods amortize the same total amount of discount over the life of the bonds. The interest method is required by generally accepted accounting principles. However, the straight-line method is acceptable if the results obtained do not materially differ from the results that would be obtained by using the interest method.[5] Because the straight-line method illustrates the basic concept of amortizing discounts and is simpler, we will illustrate it in this chapter. We illustrate the interest method in an appendix to this chapter.

[5] *Opinions of the Accounting Principles Board, No. 21,* "Interest on Receivables and Payables," American Institute of Certified Public Accountants, New York, 1971, par. 14.

The straight-line method of amortizing bond discount provides for amortization in equal periodic amounts. Applying this method to the preceding example yields amortization of 1/10 of $3,597, or $359.70, each half year. The amount of the interest expense on the bonds remains constant for each half year at $6,000 plus $359.70, or $6,359.70. The entry to record the first interest payment and the amortization of the related amount of discount is shown below.

June 30	Interest Expense	6,359.70	
	Discount on Bonds Payable		359.70
	Cash		6,000.00

Instead of recording the amortization each time the interest is paid, it may be recorded only at the end of the year. When this procedure is used, each interest payment is recorded on the periodic payment date as shown below.

	Interest Expense	6,000.00	
	Cash		6,000.00

The entry to amortize the discount at the end of the first year is shown below. The amount of the discount amortized, $719.40, is made up of the two semiannual amortization amounts of $359.70.

Dec. 31	Interest Expense	719.40	
	Discount on Bonds Payable		719.40

BONDS ISSUED AT A PREMIUM

If the market rate of interest is 11% and the contract rate is 12% on the five-year, $100,000 bonds, the bonds will sell at a **premium.** The present value of these bonds is computed as follows:

Present value of face amount of $100,000 due in 5 years, at 11% compounded semiannually: $100,000 × 0.5854 (present value of $1 for 10 periods at 5½%)	$ 58,540
Present value of 10 semiannual interest payments of $6,000, at 11% compounded semiannually: $6,000 × 7.5376 (present value of an annuity of $1 for 10 periods at 5½%)	45,226
Total present value of bonds	$103,766

The entry to record the issuing of the bonds is as follows:

Jan. 1	Cash	103,766	
	Bonds Payable		100,000
	Premium on Bonds Payable		3,766

AMORTIZATION OF A BOND PREMIUM

The amortization of bond premiums is basically the same as that for bond discounts, except that interest expense is decreased. In the above example, the straight-line method yields amortization of 1/10 of $3,766, or $376.60, each half year. The entry to record the first interest payment and the amortization of the related premium is as follows:

Some corporations, such as Whirlpool, sell zero-coupon bonds at a large discount because these bonds do not pay interest.

June 30	Interest Expense	5,623.40	
	Premium on Bonds Payable	376.60	
	Cash		6,000.00

If the amortization of the premium is recorded only at the end of the year, each interest payment is recorded by debiting Interest Expense and crediting Cash. The amortization of the premium at the end of the first year is then recorded as shown below. The amount of the premium amortized, $753.20, is the sum of the two semiannual amounts of $376.60.

Dec. 31	Premium on Bonds Payable	753.20	
	Interest Expense		753.20

ZERO-COUPON BONDS

Some corporations issue bonds that do not provide for interest payments. Such bonds are called zero-coupon bonds.

Zero-coupon bonds provide for only the payment of the face amount of the bonds at the maturity date. Because the bonds do not provide for interest payments, they sell at a large discount. For example, Whirlpool Corporation's zero-coupon bonds maturing in 2011 were selling for 40 on March 1, 1995.

To further illustrate, if the market rate of interest for five-year bonds that pay interest semiannually is 13%, the present value of $100,000 zero-coupon, five-year bonds is as follows:

Present value of $100,000 due in 5 years, at 13% compounded semiannually: $100,000 × 0.5327 (present value of $1 for 10 periods at 6½%)	$53,270

The accounting for zero-coupon bonds is similar to that for interest-bearing bonds that have been sold at a discount. The discount is amortized as interest expense over the life of the bonds. The entry to record the issuing of the bonds is as follows:

Cash	53,270	
Discount on Bonds Payable	46,730	
Bonds Payable		100,000

USING ACCOUNTING TO UNDERSTAND BUSINESS

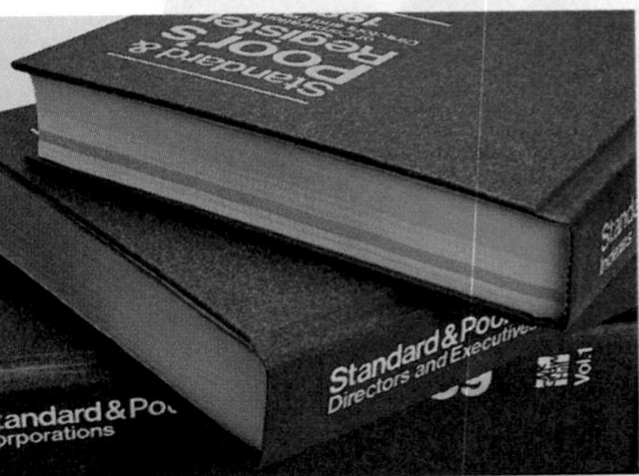

The bonds issued by companies are rated as to their riskiness as investments by such independent financial reporting services as Moody's and Standard and Poors. These services rely heavily upon financial statements and the terms of the bond indenture (for example, whether the bonds are secured) in setting the credit rating. These credit ratings, in turn, influence how much the bonds will sell for in the marketplace.

Bond Sinking Funds

Objective 5
Describe bond sinking funds.

A bond indenture may restrict dividend payments by a corporation as a means of increasing the assurance that the bonds will be paid at maturity.[6] In addition to or instead of this restriction, the bond indenture may require that funds for the payment of the face value of the bonds at maturity be set aside over the life of the bond issue. The amounts set aside are kept separate from other assets in a special fund called a sinking fund.

When cash is transferred to the sinking fund, it is recorded in an account called Sinking Fund Cash. When investments are purchased with the sinking fund cash, they are recorded in an account called **Sinking Fund Investments.** As income (interest or dividends) is received, it is recorded in an account called **Sinking Fund Income.**

Sinking fund income represents earnings of the corporation and is reported in the income statement as *Other income.* The cash and the securities making up the sinking fund are reported in the balance sheet as *Investments,* immediately below the Current Assets section.

Today, to avoid the risks associated with owning other securities, periodic deposits may be made to the sinking fund trustee, who then acquires the corporation's bonds. When such is the case, the accounting is similar to that discussed in the following section for the redemption of bonds.

Bond Redemption

Objective 6
Journalize entries for bond redemptions.

A corporation may call or redeem its bonds before they mature. This is often done if the market rate of interest declines significantly before the bonds' maturity date. In this situation, the corporation may sell new bonds at a lower interest rate and use the funds to redeem the original bond issue. The corporation can thus save on future interest expenses.

A corporation often issues callable bonds to protect itself against significant declines in future interest rates. However, callable bonds are more risky for investors, who may not be able to replace the called bonds with investments paying an equal amount of interest.

Callable bonds can be redeemed by the issuing corporation within the period of time and at the price stated in the bond indenture. Normally, the call price is above the face value. A corporation may also redeem its bonds by purchasing them on the open market.

A corporation usually redeems its bonds at a price different from that of the carrying value (or book value) of the bonds. The carrying value of bonds payable is the balance of the bonds payable account (face amount of the bonds), less any unamortized discount or plus any unamortized premium. If the price paid for redemption is below the bond carrying value, the difference in these two amounts is recorded as a gain. If the price paid for the redemption is above the carrying amount, a loss is recorded. Gains and losses on redemption of bonds are reported as an extraordinary item on the income statement.[7]

To illustrate, assume that on June 30 a corporation has a bond issue of $100,000 outstanding, on which there is an unamortized premium of $4,000. Assuming that the corporation purchases one-fourth ($25,000) of the bonds for $24,000 on June 30, the entry to record the redemption is as follows:

[6] As discussed in an earlier chapter, retained earnings may be appropriated to restrict the payment of dividends.
[7] In an earlier chapter, we discussed the reporting of extraordinary items on the income statement.

June 30	Bonds Payable	25,000	
	Premium on Bonds Payable	1,000	
	Cash		24,000
	Gain on Redemption of Bonds		2,000

In the preceding entry, only a portion of the premium relating to the redeemed bonds is written off. The difference between the carrying value of the bonds purchased, $26,000 ($25,000 + $1,000), and the price paid for the redemption, $24,000, is recorded as a gain.

If the corporation had called the entire bond issue for $105,000 on June 30, the entry to record the redemption is as follows:

June 30	Bonds Payable	100,000	
	Premium on Bonds Payable	4,000	
	Loss on Redemption of Bonds	1,000	
	Cash		105,000

Investments in Bonds

Objective 7
Journalize entries for the purchase, interest, discount and premium amortization, and sale of bond investments.

Throughout this chapter, we have discussed bonds and the related transactions of the issuing corporation (the debtor). However, these transactions also affect investors. In this section, we discuss the accounting for bonds from the point of view of investors.

ACCOUNTING FOR BOND INVESTMENTS—PURCHASE, INTEREST, AND AMORTIZATION

Bonds may be purchased either directly from the issuing corporation or through an organized bond exchange. Bond exchanges, such as the New York Bond Exchange, publish daily bond quotations. These quotations normally include the bond interest rate, maturity date, volume of sales, and the high, low, and closing prices for each corporation's bonds traded during the day. Prices for bonds are quoted as a percentage of the face amount. Thus, the price of a $1,000 bond quoted at 99½ would be $995, while the price of a bond quoted at 104¼ would be $1,042.50.

As with other assets, the cost of a bond investment includes all costs related to the purchase. For example, for bonds purchased through an exchange, the amount paid as a broker's commission should be included as part of the cost of the investment.

When bonds are purchased between interest dates, the buyer normally pays the seller the interest accrued from the last interest payment date to the date of purchase. The amount of the interest paid is normally debited to Interest Income, since it is an offset against the amount that will be received at the next interest date.

To illustrate, assume that an investor purchases a $1,000 bond at 102 plus a brokerage fee of $5.30 and accrued interest of $10.20. The investor records the transaction as follows:

Apr. 2	Investment in Lewis Co. Bonds	1,025.30	
	Interest Income	10.20	
	Cash		1,035.50

The cost of the bond is recorded in a single investment account. The face amount of the bond and the premium (or discount) are normally not recorded in separate accounts. This is different from the accounting for bonds payable. Separate premium and discount accounts are usually not maintained by investors, since bond investments are often not held by businesses until their maturity dates.

When bonds held as long-term investments are purchased at a price other than the face amount, the premium or discount should be amortized over the remaining life of the bonds. The amortization of premium decreases the amount of the investment in bonds account and interest income. The amortization of discount increases the amount of the investment in bonds account and interest income. The amortization of the premium or discount can be determined using either the straight-line or interest methods. Unlike bonds payable, the amortization of premiums and discounts on bond investments are usually recorded at the end of the period, rather than when interest is received.

Interest received on bond investments is recorded by a debit to Cash and a credit to Interest Income. At the end of a period, the interest accrued should be recorded by a debit to Interest Receivable and a credit to Interest Income.

To illustrate, assume that on July 1, Crenshaw Inc. purchases $50,000 of 8% bonds of Deitz Corporation, due in 8¾ years. Crenshaw Inc. purchases the bonds directly from Deitz Corporation to yield an effective interest rate of 11%. The purchase price is $41,706 plus interest of $1,000 ($50,000 × 8% × 3/12) accrued from April 1, the date of the last semiannual interest payment. Entries in the accounts of Crenshaw Inc. at the time of purchase and for the remainder of the fiscal period ending December 31 are as follows:

Payment for investment in bonds and accrued interest

July	1	Investment in Deitz Corp. Bonds	41,706	
		Interest Income	1,000	
		Cash		42,706

Cost of $50,000 of Deitz Corp. bonds	$41,706
Interest accrued ($50,000 × 8% × 3/12)	1,000
Total	$42,706

Receipt of semiannual interest for April 1–October 1 ($50,000 × 8% × 6/12)

Oct.	1	Cash	2,000	
		Interest Income		2,000

Adjusting entry for accrued interest from October 1–December 31 ($50,000 × 8% × 3/12)

Dec.	31	Interest Receivable	1,000	
		Interest Income		1,000

Adjusting entry for amortization of discount by straight-line method for July 1–December 31

Dec.	31	Investment in Deitz Corp. Bonds	474	
		Interest Income		474

Face value of bonds	$50,000
Cost of bond investment	41,706
Discount on bond investment	$ 8,294

Number of months to maturity (8¾ years × 12)	105 months
Monthly amortization (rounded to nearest dollar) ($8,294 ÷ 105 months)	$79 per month
Amortization for 6 months ($79 × 6)	$474

The entries in the interest income account in the above illustration are summarized below.

July	1	Paid accrued interest—3 months	$(1,000)
Oct.	1	Received interest payment—6 months	2,000
Dec.	31	Recorded accrued interest—3 months	1,000
	31	Recorded amortization of discount—6 months	474
		Interest earned—6 months	$ 2,474

ACCOUNTING FOR BOND INVESTMENTS—SALE

Many long-term investments in bonds are sold before their maturity date. When this occurs, the seller receives the sales price (less commissions and other selling costs) plus any accrued interest since the last interest payment date. Before recording the cash proceeds, the seller should amortize any discount or premium for the current period up to the date of sale. Any gain or loss on the sale can then be recorded when the cash proceeds are recorded. Such gains and losses are normally reported in the Other Income section of the income statement.

To illustrate, assume that the Deitz Corporation bonds in the above example are sold for $47,350 plus accrued interest on June 30, seven years after their purchase. The carrying *amount* of the bonds (cost plus amortized discount) as of *January 1* of the year of sale (78 months after their purchase) is $47,868 [$41,706 + ($79 per mo. × 78 months)]. The entries to amortize the discount for the current year and to record the sale of the bonds are as follows:

Amortization of $474 of discount for current year ($79 × 6 months)

June 30	Investment in Deitz Corp. Bonds	474	
	Interest Income		474

Receipt of interest and proceeds from sale of bonds and recognition of loss on sale of bonds

June 30	Cash	48,350	
	Loss on Sale of Investments	992	
	Interest Income		1,000
	Investment in Deitz Corp. Bonds		48,342

Interest for April 1–June 30 ($50,000 × 8% × 3/12)	$ 1,000
Carrying value of bonds on January 1	$47,868
Discount amortized, Jan. 1–June 30	474
Carrying value of bonds on June 30	$48,342
Proceeds of sale	47,350
Loss on sale	$ 992

Corporation Balance Sheet

Objective 8
Prepare a corporation balance sheet.

In previous chapters, we illustrated the income statement and retained earnings statement for a corporation. The consolidated balance sheet in Exhibit 6 illustrates the presentation of many of the items discussed in this and preceding chapters. These items include bond sinking funds, investments in bonds, goodwill, deferred income taxes, bonds payable and unamortized discount, minority interest in subsidiaries, and appropriation of retained earnings.

BALANCE SHEET PRESENTATION OF BONDS PAYABLE

In Exhibit 6, Escoe Corporation's bonds payable are reported as long-term liabilities. If there were two or more bond issues, the details of each would be reported on the balance sheet or in a supporting schedule or note. Separate accounts are normally maintained for each bond issue.

When the balance sheet date is within one year of the maturity date of the bonds, the bonds may require classification as a current liability. This would be the case if the bonds are to be paid out of current assets. If the bonds are to be paid from a sinking fund or if they are to be refinanced with another bond issue, they should remain in the noncurrent category. In this case, the details of the retirement of the bonds are normally disclosed in a note to the financial statements.

Exhibit 6 *Balance Sheet of a Corporation*

Escoe Corporation and Subsidiaries
Consolidated Balance Sheet
December 31, 19—

Assets				
Current assets:				
Cash			$ 255,000	
Marketable securities		$ 160,000		
Less unrealized loss		7,500	152,500	
Accounts and notes receivable		$ 722,000		
Less allowance for doubtful receivables		37,000	685,000	
Inventories, at lower of cost (first-in, first-out) or market			917,500	
Prepaid expenses			70,000	
Total current assets				$2,080,000
Investments:				
Bond sinking fund (market value, $473,000)			$ 422,500	
Investment in bonds of Dalton Company (market value, $231,000)			240,000	
Total investments				662,500
	Cost	*Accumulated Depreciation*	*Book Value*	
Plant assets (depreciated by the straight-line method):				
Land	$ 250,000	—	$ 250,000	
Buildings	920,000	$ 379,955	540,045	
Machinery and equipment	2,764,400	766,200	1,998,200	
Total plant assets	$3,934,400	$1,146,155		2,788,245
Intangible assets:				
Goodwill			$ 300,000	
Organization costs			50,000	
Total intangible assets				350,000
Total assets				$5,880,745
Liabilities				
Current liabilities:				
Accounts payable			$ 508,810	
Income tax payable			120,500	
Dividends payable			94,000	
Accrued liabilities			81,400	
Deferred income tax payable			10,000	
Total current liabilities				$ 814,710
Long-term liabilities:				
Debenture 8% bonds payable, due December 31, 19— (market value, $950,000)		$1,000,000		
Less unamortized discount		60,000	$ 940,000	
Minority interest in subsidiaries			115,000	
Total long-term liabilities				1,055,000
Deferred credits:				
Deferred income tax payable				85,500
Total liabilities				$1,955,210
Stockholders' Equity				
Paid-in capital:				
Common stock, $20 par (250,000 shares authorized, 100,000 shares issued)		$2,000,000		
Excess of issue price over par		320,000		
Total paid-in capital			$2,320,000	
Retained earnings:				
Appropriated for bonded indebtedness		$ 250,000		
Unappropriated		1,355,535		
Total retained earnings			1,605,535	
Total stockholders' equity				3,925,535
Total liabilities and stockholders' equity				$5,880,745

The balance in Escoe's discount on bonds payable account is reported as a deduction from the bonds payable. Conversely, the balance in a bond premium account would be reported as an addition to the related bonds payable. Either on the face of the financial statements or in accompanying notes, a description of the bonds (terms, due date, and effective interest rate) should also be disclosed. In addition, the maturities and sinking fund requirements should be disclosed for each of the next five years.[8] Finally, the market (fair) value of the bonds payable should also be disclosed.[9]

BALANCE SHEET PRESENTATION OF BOND INVESTMENTS

Investments in bonds or other debt securities that management intends to hold to their maturity are called held-to-maturity securities.[10] Such securities are classified as long-term investments under the caption **Investments.** These investments are reported at their cost less any amortized premium or plus any amortized discount. In addition, the market (fair) value of the bond investments should be disclosed, either on the face of the balance sheet or in an accompanying note.[11]

Appendix—Effective Interest Rate Method of Amortization

The effective interest rate method of amortizing discounts and premiums provides for a constant *rate* of interest on the carrying amount of the bonds at the beginning of each period. This is in contrast to the straight-line method, which provides for a constant *amount* of interest expense.

The interest rate used in the interest method of amortization is the market rate on the date the bonds are issued. The carrying amount of the bonds to which the interest rate is applied is the face amount of the bonds minus any unamortized discount or plus any unamortized premium. Under the interest method, the interest expense to be reported on the income statement is computed by multiplying the effective interest rate by the carrying amount of the bonds. The difference between the interest expense computed in this way and the periodic interest payment is the amount of discount or premium to be amortized for the period.

AMORTIZATION OF DISCOUNT BY THE INTEREST METHOD

To illustrate the interest method for amortizing bond discounts, we assume the following data from the chapter illustration of issuing $100,000 bonds at a discount:

Face value of 12%, 5-year bonds, interest compounded semiannually	$100,000
Present value of bonds at effective (market) rate of interest of 13%	96,403
Discount on bonds payable	$ 3,597

Applying the interest method to these data yields the amortization table in Exhibit 7. You should note the following items in this table:

1. The interest paid (Column A) remains constant at 6% of $100,000, the face amount of the bonds.

[8] *Statement of Financial Accounting Standards, No. 47,* "Disclosure of Long-Term Obligations," Financial Accounting Standards Board, Stamford, 1981, par. 10.
[9] *Statement of Financial Accounting Standards, No. 107,* "Disclosures about Fair Value of Financial Instruments," Financial Accounting Standards Board, Norwalk, 1991, par. 10.
[10] *Statement of Financial Accounting Standards, No. 115,* "Accounting for Certain Investments in Debt and Equity Securities," Norwalk, Conn., 1993, par. 1.
[11] *Statement of Financial Accounting Standards, No. 107,* op. cit., par. 10.

2. The interest expense (Column B) is computed at 6½% of the bond carrying value at the beginning of each period. This results in an increasing interest expense each period.
3. The excess of the interest expense over the interest payment of $6,000 is the amount of discount to be amortized (Column C).
4. The unamortized discount (Column D) decreases from the initial balance, $3,597, to a zero balance at the maturity date of the bonds.
5. The carrying value (Column E) increases from $96,403, the amount received for the bonds, to $100,000 at maturity.

Exhibit 7
Amortization of Discount on Bonds Payable

Interest Payment	A *Interest Paid (6% of Face Amount)*	B *Interest Expense (6½% of Bond Carrying Value)*	C *Discount Amortization (B – A)*	D *Unamortized Discount (D – C)*	E *Bond Carrying Value ($100,000 – D)*
				$3,597	$ 96,403
1	$6,000	$6,266 (6½% of $96,403)	$266	3,331	96,669
2	6,000	6,284 (6½% of $96,669)	284	3,047	96,953
3	6,000	6,302 (6½% of $96,953)	302	2,745	97,255
4	6,000	6,322 (6½% of $97,255)	322	2,423	97,577
5	6,000	6,343 (6½% of $97,577)	343	2,080	97,920
6	6,000	6,365 (6½% of $97,920)	365	1,715	98,285
7	6,000	6,389 (6½% of $98,285)	389	1,326	98,674
8	6,000	6,415 (6½% of $98,674)	415	911	99,089
9	6,000	6,441 (6½% of $99,089)	441	470	99,530
10	6,000	6,470 (6½% of $99,530)	470	—	100,000

The entry to record the first interest payment on June 30 and the related discount amortization is as follows:

June 30	Interest Expense	6,266	
	Discount on Bonds Payable		266
	Cash		6,000

If the amortization is recorded only at the end of the year, the amount of the discount amortized on December 31 would be $550. This is the sum of the first two semiannual amortization amounts ($266 and $284) from Exhibit 7.

AMORTIZATION OF PREMIUM BY THE INTEREST METHOD

To illustrate the interest method for amortizing bond premiums, we assume the following data from the chapter illustration of issuing $100,000 bonds at a premium:

Present value of bonds at effective (market) rate of interest of 11%	$103,766
Face value of 12%, 5-year bonds, interest compounded semiannually	100,000
Premium on bonds payable	$ 3,766

Using the interest method to amortize the above premium yields the amortization table in Exhibit 8. You should note the following items in this table:

1. The interest paid (Column A) remains constant at 6% of $100,000, the face amount of the bonds.
2. The interest expense (Column B) is computed at 5½% of the bond carrying value at the beginning of each period. This results in a decreasing interest expense each period.

3. The excess of the periodic interest payment of $6,000 over the interest expense is the amount of premium to be amortized (Column C).
4. The unamortized premium (Column D) decreases from the initial balance, $3,766, to a zero balance at the maturity date of the bonds.
5. The carrying value (Column E) decreases from $103,766, the amount received for the bonds, to $100,000 at maturity.

Exhibit 8
Amortization of Premium on Bonds Payable

Interest Payment	A *Interest Paid (6% of Face Amount)*	B *Interest Expense (5½% of Bond Carrying Value)*	C *Premium Amortization (A – B)*	D *Unamortized Premium (D – C)*	E *Bond Carrying Value ($100,000 + D)*
				$3,766	$103,766
1	$6,000	$5,707 (5½% of $103,766)	$293	3,473	103,473
2	6,000	5,691 (5½% of $103,473)	309	3,164	103,164
3	6,000	5,674 (5½% of $103,164)	326	2,838	102,838
4	6,000	5,657 (5½% of $102,838)	343	2,495	102,495
5	6,000	5,638 (5½% of $102,495)	362	2,133	102,133
6	6,000	5,618 (5½% of $102,133)	382	1,751	101,751
7	6,000	5,597 (5½% of $101,751)	403	1,348	101,348
8	6,000	5,575 (5½% of $101,348)	425	923	100,923
9	6,000	5,551 (5½% of $100,923)	449	474	100,474
10	6,000	5,526 (5½% of $100,474)	474	—	100,000

The entry to record the first interest payment on June 30 and the related premium amortization is as follows:

June 30	Interest Expense	5,707	
	Premium on Bonds Payable	293	
	Cash		6,000

If the amortization is recorded only at the end of the year, the amount of the premium amortized on December 31 would be $602. This is the sum of the first two semiannual amortization amounts ($293 and $309) from Exhibit 8.

KEY POINTS

Objective 1. Compute the potential impact of long-term borrowing on the earnings per share of a corporation.
Three alternative plans for financing a corporation by issuing common stock, preferred stock, or bonds are illustrated in Exhibits 1 and 2. The effects of alternative financing on the earnings per share vary significantly, depending upon the level of earnings.

Objective 2. Describe the characteristics of bonds.
The characteristics of bonds depend upon the type of bonds issued by a corporation. Bonds that may be issued include term bonds, serial bonds, convertible bonds, callable bonds, and debenture bonds.

Objective 3. Compute the present value of bonds payable.
The concept of present value is based on the time value of money. That is, an amount of cash to be received at some date in the future is not the equivalent of the same amount of cash held at an earlier date. For example, if $100 cash today can be invested to earn 10% per year, the $100 today is referred to as the present value amount that is equivalent to $110 to be received a year from today.

A price that a buyer is willing to pay for a bond is the sum of (1) the present value of the face amount of the bonds at the maturity date and (2) the present value of the periodic interest payments.

Objective 4. Journalize entries for bonds payable.
The journal entry for issuing bonds payable debits Cash for the proceeds received and credits Bonds Payable for the face value of the bonds. Any difference between the face value of the bonds and the proceeds is debited to Discount on Bonds Payable or credited to Premium on Bonds Payable.

A discount or premium on bonds payable is amortized to interest expense over the life of the bonds. The entry to amortize a discount debits Interest Expense and credits Discount on Bonds Payable. The entry to amortize a premium debits Premium on Bonds Payable and credits Interest Expense.

Objective 5. Describe bond sinking funds.
A bond indenture may require that funds for the payment of the bonds at maturity be set aside over the life of the bonds. The amounts set aside are kept separate from other assets in a special fund called a sinking fund. A sinking fund is reported as an Investment on the balance sheet. Income from a sinking fund is reported as Other Income on the income statement.

Objective 6. Journalize entries for bond redemptions.
When a corporation redeems bonds, Bonds Payable is debited for the face value of the bonds, the premium (discount) on bonds account is debited (credited) for its balance, Cash is credited, and any gain or loss on the redemption is recorded.

Objective 7. Journalize entries for the purchase, interest, discount and premium amortization, and sale of bond investments.
A long-term investment in bonds is recorded by debiting Investment in Bonds. When bonds are purchased between interest dates, the amount of the interest paid should be debited to Interest Income. Any discount or premium on bond investments should be amortized, using the straight-line or effective interest rate methods. The amortization of a discount is recorded by debiting Investment in Bonds and crediting Interest Income. The amortization of a premium is recorded by debiting Interest Income and crediting Investment in Bonds.

When bonds held as long-term investments are sold, any discount or premium for the current period should first be amortized. Cash is then debited for the proceeds of the sale, Investment in Bonds is credited for its balance, and any gain or loss is recorded.

Objective 8. Prepare a corporation balance sheet.
The corporation balance sheet may include bond sinking funds, investments in bonds, goodwill, deferred income taxes, bonds payable and unamortized premium or discount, minority interest in subsidiaries, and appropriation of retained earnings.

Bonds payable are usually reported as long-term liabilities. A discount on bonds should be reported as a deduction from the related bonds payable. A premium on bonds should be reported as an addition to the related bonds payable. Investments in bonds that are held-to-maturity securities are reported as Investments at cost less any amortized premium or plus any amortized discount.

GLOSSARY OF KEY TERMS

Annuity. A series of equal cash flows at fixed intervals. *Objective 3*

Bond. A form of interest-bearing note employed by corporations to borrow on a long-term basis. *Objective 1*

Bond indenture. The contract between a corporation issuing bonds and the bondholders. *Objective 2*

Carrying value. The amount at which a long-term investment or a long-term liability is reported on the balance sheet; also called basis or book value. *Objective 6*

Contract rate. The interest rate specified on a bond; sometimes called the coupon rate of interest. *Objective 4*

Discount. The excess of the face amount of bonds over their issue price. *Objective 4*

Effective rate. The market rate of interest at the time bonds are issued. *Objective 4*

Held-to-maturity securities. Investments in bonds or other debt securities that management intends to hold to their maturity. *Objective 8*

Premium. The excess of the issue price of bonds over the face amount. *Objective 4*

Present value. The estimated present worth of an amount of cash to be received (or paid) in the future. *Objective 3*

Present value of an annuity. The sum of the present values of a series of equal cash flows to be received at fixed intervals. *Objective 3*

Sinking fund. Assets set aside in a special fund to be used for a specific purpose. *Objective 5*

ILLUSTRATIVE PROBLEM

The fiscal year of Russell Inc., a manufacturer of acoustical supplies, ends December 31. Selected transactions for the period 1996 through 2003, involving bonds payable issued by Russell Inc., are as follows:

1996
June 30. Issued $2,000,000 of 25-year, 7% callable bonds dated June 30, 1996, for cash of $1,920,000. Interest is payable semiannually on June 30 and December 31.
Dec. 31. Paid the semiannual interest on the bonds.
31. Recorded straight-line amortization of $1,600 of discount on the bonds.
31. Closed the interest expense account.

1997
June 30. Paid the semiannual interest on the bonds.
Dec. 31. Paid the semiannual interest on the bonds.
31. Recorded straight-line amortization of $3,200 of discount on the bonds.
31. Closed the interest expense account.

2003
June 30. Recorded the redemption of the bonds, which were called at 101½. The balance in the bond discount account is $57,600 after the payment of interest and amortization of discount have been recorded. (Record the redemption only.)

Instructions

1. Journalize entries to record the preceding transactions.
2. Determine the amount of interest expense for 1996 and 1997.
3. Estimate the effective annual interest rate by dividing the interest expense for 1996 by the bond carrying amount at the time of issuance and multiplying by 2.
4. Determine the carrying amount of the bonds as of December 31, 1997.

Solution

1.

Date	Account	Debit	Credit
1996			
June 30	Cash	1,920,000	
	Discount on Bonds Payable	80,000	
	Bonds Payable		2,000,000
Dec. 31	Interest Expense	70,000	
	Cash		70,000
31	Interest Expense	1,600	
	Discount on Bonds Payable		1,600
31	Income Summary	71,600	
	Interest Expense		71,600
1997			
June 30	Interest Expense	70,000	
	Cash		70,000
Dec. 31	Interest Expense	70,000	
	Cash		70,000
31	Interest Expense	3,200	
	Discount on Bonds Payable		3,200
31	Income Summary	143,200	
	Interest Expense		143,200
2003			
June 30	Bonds Payable	2,000,000	
	Loss on Redemption of Bonds Payable	87,600	
	Discount on Bonds Payable		57,600
	Cash		2,030,000

2. a. 1996—$71,600
   b. 1997—$143,200

3. $\$71,600 \div \$1,920,000 = 3.73\%$ rate for six months of a year
   $3.73\% \times 2 = 7.46\%$ annual rate

4.

Initial carrying value of bonds	$1,920,000
Discount amortized on December 31, 1996	1,600
Discount amortized on December 31, 1997	3,200
Carrying value of bonds, December 31, 1997	$1,924,800

SELF-EXAMINATION QUESTIONS (ANSWERS AT END OF CHAPTER)

1. If a corporation plans to issue $1,000,000 of 12% bonds at a time when the market rate for similar bonds is 10%, the bonds can be expected to sell at:
   A. their face amount.
   B. a premium.
   C. a discount.
   D. a price below their face amount.

2. If the bonds payable account has a balance of $500,000 and the discount on bonds payable account has a balance of $40,000, what is the carrying value of the bonds?
   A. $460,000
   B. $500,000
   C. $540,000
   D. $580,000

3. The cash and the securities that make up the sinking fund established for the payment of bonds at maturity are classified on the balance sheet as:
   A. current assets.
   B. investments.
   C. long-term liabilities.
   D. current liabilities.

4. If a firm purchases $100,000 of bonds of X Company at 101 plus accrued interest of $2,000 and pays broker's commissions of $50, the amount debited to Investment in X Company Bonds would be:
   A. $100,000
   B. $101,050
   C. $103,000
   D. $103,050

5. The balance in the discount on bonds payable account would usually be reported in the balance sheet in the:
   A. Current Assets section.
   B. Current Liabilities section.
   C. Long-Term Liabilities section.
   D. Investments section.

DISCUSSION QUESTIONS

1. Describe the two distinct obligations incurred by a corporation when issuing bonds.
2. Explain the meaning of each of the following terms as they relate to a bond issue: (a) convertible, (b) callable, and (c) debenture.
3. What is meant by the "time value of money?"
4. What has the higher present value: (a) $2,000 to be received at the end of two years, or (b) $1,000 to be received at the end of each of the next two years?
5. If you asked your broker to purchase for you a 9% bond when the market interest rate for such bonds was 10%, would you expect to pay more or less than the face value for the bond? Explain.
6. A corporation issues $5,000,000 of 10% coupon bonds to yield interest at the rate of 9%. (a) Was the amount of cash received from the sale of the bonds greater or less than $5,000,000? (b) Identify the following terms related to the bond issue: (1) face amount, (2) market or effective rate of interest, (3) contract or coupon rate of interest, and (4) maturity amount.
7. If bonds issued by a corporation are sold at a premium, is the market rate of interest greater or less than the coupon rate?
8. The following data are related to a $900,000, 9% bond issue for a selected semiannual interest period:

Bond carrying amount at beginning of period	$925,000
Interest paid at end of period	40,500
Interest expense allocable to the period	36,500

   (a) Were the bonds issued at a discount or at a premium? (b) What is the unamortized amount of the discount or premium account at the beginning of the period? (c) What account was debited to amortize the discount or premium?
9. Assume that Espresso Co. amortizes premiums and discounts on bonds payable at the end of the year rather than when interest is paid. What accounts would be debited and credited to record (a) the amortization of a discount on bonds payable and (b) the amortization of a premium on bonds payable?
10. Would a zero-coupon bond ever sell for its face value?
11. What is the purpose of a bond sinking fund?
12. How are earnings from investments in a sinking fund reported on the income statement?
13. How are cash and securities comprising a sinking fund classified on the balance sheet?
14. Assume that two 20-year, 10% bond issues are identical, except that one bond issue is callable at its face value at the end of 10 years. Which of the two bond issues do you think will sell for a higher value?
15. Bonds Payable has a balance of $750,000, and Premium on Bonds Payable has a balance of $10,000. If the issuing corporation redeems the bonds at 105, is there a gain or loss on the bond redemption?
16. How are gains or losses on bond redemptions reported on the income statement?
17. Assume that a company purchases bonds between interest dates. What accounts would normally be debited?

18. Indicate how the following accounts should be reported on the balance sheet: (a) Premium on Bonds Payable and (b) Discount on Bonds Payable.
19. Where are investments in bonds that are classified as held-to-maturity securities reported on the balance sheet?
20. At what amount are held-to-maturity investments in bonds reported on the balance sheet?

EXERCISES

EXERCISE 16–1
Effect of financing on earnings per share
Objective 1

Harvey Co., which produces and sells skiing equipment, is financed as follows:

Bonds payable, 10% (issued at face value)	$4,000,000
Preferred $9 stock (nonparticipating), $100 par	4,000,000
Common stock, $20 par	4,000,000

Income tax is estimated at 40% of income.

Determine the earnings per share of common stock, assuming that the income before bond interest and income tax is (a) $1,200,000, (b) $2,000,000, and (c) $5,000,000.

EXERCISE 16–2
Evaluating alternative financing plans
Objective 1

Based upon the data in Exercise 16–1, discuss factors other than earnings per share that should be considered in evaluating such financing plans.

EXERCISE 16–3
Present value of amounts due
Objective 3

Determine the present value of $5,000 to be received in three years, using an interest rate of 11%, compounded annually, as follows:

a. By successive divisions. (Round to the nearest dollar.)
b. By using the present value table in Exhibit 3.

EXERCISE 16–4
Present value of annuity
Objective 3

Determine the present value of $10,000 to be received at the end of each of four years, using an interest rate of 7%, compounded annually, as follows:

a. By successive computations, using the present value table in Exhibit 3.
b. By using the present value table in Exhibit 4.

EXERCISE 16–5
Present value of an annuity
Objective 3

On January 1, 1997, you win $1,000,000 in the state lottery. The $1,000,000 prize will be paid in equal installments of $40,000 over 25 years. The payments will be made on December 31 of each year, beginning on December 31, 1997. If the current interest rate is 7%, determine the present value of your winnings. Use the present value tables in Appendix A.

EXERCISE 16–6
Present value of an annuity
Objective 3

Assume the same data as in Exercise 16–5, except that the current interest rate is 14%.

Will the present value of your winnings using an interest rate of 14% be one-half the present value of your winnings using an interest rate of 7%? Why or why not?

EXERCISE 16–7
Present value of bonds payable; discount
Objective 3

Safire Co. produces and sells bottle capping equipment for soft drink and spring water bottlers. To finance its operations, Safire Co. issued $20,000,000 of five-year, 7% bonds with interest payable semiannually at an effective interest rate of 10%. Determine the present value of the bonds payable, using the present value tables in Exhibits 3 and 4.

EXERCISE 16–8
Present value of bonds payable; premium
Objective 3

Artex Automotive Alarms Co. issued $10,000,000 of five-year, 12% bonds with interest payable semiannually, at an effective interest rate of 11%. Determine the present value of the bonds payable, using the present value tables in Exhibits 3 and 4.

EXERCISE 16–9
Bond price
Objective 4

IBM Corporation $8\frac{3}{8}$% bonds due in 2019 were reported in *The Wall Street Journal* as selling for $101\frac{5}{8}$ on March 1, 1995.

Were the bonds selling at a premium or at a discount on March 1, 1995? Explain.

EXERCISE 16–10
Entries for issuing bonds
Objective 4

Mildred Co. produces and distributes fiber optic cable for use by telecommunications companies. Mildred Co. issued $15,000,000 of 20-year, 8% bonds on April 1 of the current year, with interest payable on April 1 and October 1. The fiscal year of the company is the calendar year. Journalize the entries to record the following selected transactions for the current year:

Apr. 1. Issued the bonds for cash at their face amount.
Oct. 1. Paid the interest on the bonds.
Dec. 31. Recorded accrued interest for three months.

EXERCISE 16–11
Entries for issuing bonds and amortizing discount by straight-line method
Objective 4

On the first day of its fiscal year, Sanger Company issued $10,000,000 of five-year, 10% bonds to finance its operations of producing and selling home electronics equipment. Interest is payable semiannually. The bonds were issued at an effective interest rate of 12%, resulting in Sanger Company receiving cash of $9,264,050.

a. Journalize the entries to record the following:
   1. Sale of the bonds.
   2. First semiannual interest payment. (Amortization of discount is to be recorded annually.)
   3. Second semiannual interest payment.
   4. Amortization of discount at the end of the first year, using the straight-line method.
b. Determine the amount of the bond interest expense for the first year.

EXERCISE 16–12
Computing bond proceeds, entries for bond issuing and amortizing premium by straight-line method
Objectives 3, 4

Lido Corporation wholesales oil and grease products to equipment manufacturers. On March 1, 1997, Lido Corporation issued $1,000,000 of five-year, 12% bonds at an effective interest rate of 10%. Interest is payable semiannually on March 1 and September 1. Journalize the entries to record the following:

a. Sale of bonds on March 1, 1997. (Use the tables of present values in Exhibits 3 and 4 to determine the bond proceeds.)
b. First interest payment on September 1, 1997, and amortization of bond premium for six months, using the straight-line method. (Round to the nearest dollar.)

EXERCISE 16–13
Entries for issuing and calling bonds; loss
Objectives 4, 6

Cavalier Corp., a wholesaler of office furniture, issued $10,000,000 of 30-year, 10% callable bonds on March 1, 1997, with interest payable on March 1 and September 1. The fiscal year of the company is the calendar year. Journalize the entries to record the following selected transactions:

1997
Mar. 1. Issued the bonds for cash at their face amount.
Sep. 1. Paid the interest on the bonds.
2001
Sep. 1. Called the bond issue at 101, the rate provided in the bond indenture. (Omit entry for payment of interest.)

EXERCISE 16–14
Entries for issuing and calling bonds; gain
Objectives 4, 6

Buckle Corp. produces and sells automotive and aircraft safety belts. To finance its operations, Buckle Corp. issued $6,000,000 of 40-year, 7% callable bonds on June 1, 1996, with interest payable on June 1 and December 1. The fiscal year of the company is the calendar year. Journalize the entries to record the following selected transactions:

1996
June 1. Issued the bonds for cash at their face amount.
Dec. 1. Paid the interest on the bonds.
2002
Dec. 1. Called the bond issue at 95, the rate provided in the bond indenture. (Omit entry for payment of interest.)

EXERCISE 16–15
Reporting bonds
Objectives 5, 6, 8

At the beginning of the current year, two bond issues (C and D) were outstanding. During the year, bond issue C was redeemed and a significant loss on the redemption of bonds was reported as Other Expense on the income statement. At the end of the year, bond issue D was reported as a current liability because its maturity date was early in the following year. A sinking fund of cash and securities sufficient to pay the series D bonds was reported in the balance sheet as *Investments.*

Can you find any flaws in the reporting practices related to the two bond issues?

EXERCISE 16–16
Amortizing discount on bond investment
Objective 7

A company purchased a $1,000, 20-year zero-coupon bond for $189 to yield 8.5% to maturity. How is the interest income computed?

Source: "Technical Hotline," *Journal of Accountancy*, January 1989, p. 100.

EXERCISE 16–17
Entries for purchase and sale of investment in bonds; loss
Objective 7

Synoptic Co. sells optical supplies to opticians and ophthalmologists. Journalize the entries to record the following selected transactions of Synoptic Co.:

a. Purchased for $150,000 of Blue Co. 8% bonds at 101 plus accrued interest of $2,000.
b. Received first semiannual interest.
c. Amortized $100 on the bond investment at the end of the first year.
d. Sold the bonds at 98 plus accrued interest of $3,500. The bonds were carried at $150,750 at the time of the sale.

EXERCISE 16–18
Entries for purchase and sale of investment in bonds; gain
Objective 7

Grafix Company develops and sells graphics software for use by architects. Journalize the entries to record the following selected transactions of Grafix Company:

a. Purchased for cash $300,000 of Bly Co. 6% bonds at 98 plus accrued interest of $3,000.
b. Received first semiannual interest.
c. Amortized $267 on the bond investment at the end of the first year.
d. Sold the bonds at 99 plus accrued interest of $4,500. The bonds were carried at $296,000 at the time of the sale.

APPENDIX EXERCISE 16–19
Amortizing discount by interest method

On the first day of its fiscal year, Sanger Company issued $10,000,000 of five-year, 10% bonds to finance its operations of producing and selling home electronics equipment. Interest is payable semiannually. The bonds were issued at an effective interest rate of 12%, resulting in Sanger Company receiving cash of $9,264,050.

a. Journalize the entries to record the following:
   1. Sale of the bonds.
   2. First semiannual interest payment. (Amortization of discount is to be recorded annually.)
   3. Second semiannual interest payment.
   4. Amortization of discount at the end of the first year, using the interest method. (Round to the nearest dollar.)
b. Compute the amount of the bond interest expense for the first year.

APPENDIX EXERCISE 16–20
Amortizing premium by interest method

Lido Corporation wholesales oil and grease products to equipment manufacturers. On March 1, 1997, Lido Corporation issued $1,000,000 of five-year, 12% bonds at an effective interest rate of 10%, receiving cash of $1,077,202. Interest is payable semiannually on March 1 and September 1. Lido Corporation's fiscal year begins on March 1.

a. Journalize the entries to record the following:
   1. First interest payment on September 1, 1997. (Amortization of premium is to be recorded annually.)
   2. Second interest payment on March 1, 1998.
   3. Amortization of premium at the end of the first year, using the interest method.
b. Determine the bond interest expense for the first year.

APPENDIX EXERCISE 16–21
Computing bond proceeds, amortizing premium by interest method, and interest expense

CSX Co. produces and sells spray painting equipment for construction contractors. On the first day of its fiscal year, CSX Co. issued $20,000,000 of five-year, 11% bonds at an effective interest rate of 10%, with interest payable semiannually. Compute the following, presenting figures used in your computations.

a. The amount of cash proceeds from the sale of the bonds. (Use the tables of present values in Exhibits 3 and 4.)
b. The annual premium to be amortized for the first semiannual interest payment period, using the interest method. (Round to the nearest dollar.)
c. The amount of premium to be amortized for the second semiannual interest payment period, using the interest method. (Round to the nearest dollar.)
d. The amount of the bond interest expense for the first year.

APPENDIX EXERCISE 16–22
Computing bond proceeds; amortizing discount by interest method; and interest expense

ProMix Co. produces and sells concrete mixing equipment. On the first day of its fiscal year, ProMix Co. issued $8,000,000 of five-year, 10% bonds at an effective interest rate of 12%, with interest payable semiannually. Compute the following, presenting figures used in your computations.

a. The amount of cash proceeds from the sale of the bonds. (Use the tables of present values in Exhibits 3 and 4.)
b. The amount of discount to be amortized for the first semiannual interest payment period, using the interest method. (Round to the nearest dollar.)
c. The amount of discount to be amortized for the second semiannual interest payment period, using the interest method. (Round to the nearest dollar.)
d. The amount of the bond interest expense for the first year.

PROBLEMS SERIES A

PROBLEM 16–1A
Effect of financing on earnings per share
Objective 1

Three different plans for financing a $15,000,000 corporation are under consideration by its organizers. Under each of the following plans, the securities will be issued at their par or face amount, and the income tax rate is estimated at 40% of income.

	Plan 1	*Plan 2*	*Plan 3*
12% bonds			$ 6,250,000
Preferred $4 stock, $50 par		$ 7,500,000	5,000,000
Common stock, $30 par	$15,000,000	7,500,000	3,750,000
Total	$15,000,000	$15,000,000	$15,000,000

Instructions

1. Determine for each plan the earnings per share of common stock, assuming that the income before bond interest and income tax is $2,500,000.
2. Determine for each plan the earnings per share of common stock, assuming that the income before bond interest and income tax is $1,500,000.
3. Discuss the advantages and disadvantages of each plan.

PROBLEM 16–2A
Present value; bond premium; entries for bonds payable transactions
Objectives 3, 4

Icot Inc. produces and sells voltage regulators. On July 1, 1996, Icot Inc. issued $8,000,000 of ten-year, 10½% bonds at an effective interest rate of 10%. Interest on the bonds is payable semiannually on December 31 and June 30. The fiscal year of the company is the calendar year.

Instructions

1. Journalize the entry to record the amount of the cash proceeds from the sale of the bonds. Use the tables of present values in Appendix A to compute the cash proceeds, rounding to the nearest dollar.
2. Journalize the entries to record the following:
   a. The first semiannual interest payment on December 31, 1996, including the amortization of the bond premium, using the straight-line method.
   b. The interest payment on June 30, 1997, and the amortization of the bond premium, using the straight-line method.
3. Determine the total interest expense for 1996.
4. Will the bond proceeds always be greater than the face value of the bonds when the coupon rate is greater than the market rate of interest? Explain.

PROBLEM 16–3A
Present value; bond discount; entries for bonds payable transactions
Objectives 3, 4

On July 1, 1996, Tricon Communications Equipment Inc. issued $12,000,000 of ten-year, 8% bonds at an effective interest rate of 10%. Interest on the bonds is payable semiannually on December 31 and June 30. The fiscal year of the company is the calendar year.

Instructions

1. Journalize the entry to record the amount of the cash proceeds from the sale of the bonds. Use the tables of present values in Appendix A to compute the cash proceeds, rounding to the nearest dollar.

2. Journalize the entries to record the following:
   a. The first semiannual interest payment on December 31, 1996, and the amortization of the bond discount, using the straight-line method.
   b. The interest payment on June 30, 1997, and the amortization of the bond discount, using the straight-line method.
3. Determine the total interest expense for 1996.
4. Will the bond proceeds always be less than the face value of the bonds when the coupon rate is less than the market rate of interest? Explain.

PROBLEM 16–4A
Entries for bonds payable transactions
Objectives 4, 6

Adtex Co. produces and sells synthetic string for tennis rackets. The following transactions were completed by Adtex Co., whose fiscal year is the calendar year:

1996
July 1. Issued $20,000,000 of 10-year, 13% callable bonds dated July 1, 1996, at an effective rate of 12%, receiving cash of $21,146,997. Interest is payable semiannually on December 31 and June 30.
Dec. 31. Paid the semiannual interest on the bonds.
31. Recorded bond premium amortization of $57,350, which was determined by using the straight-line method.
31. Closed the interest expense account.

1997
June 30. Paid the semiannual interest on the bonds.
Dec. 31. Paid the semiannual interest on the bonds.
31. Recorded bond premium amortization of $114,700, which was determined by using the straight-line method.
31. Closed the interest expense account.

2002
July 1. Recorded the redemption of the bonds, which were called at 101. The balance in the bond premium account is $458,797 after the payment of interest and amortization of premium have been recorded. (Record the redemption only.)

Instructions

1. Journalize the entries to record the foregoing transactions.
2. Indicate the amount of the interest expense in (a) 1996 and (b) 1997.
3. Determine the carrying value of the bonds as of December 31, 1997.

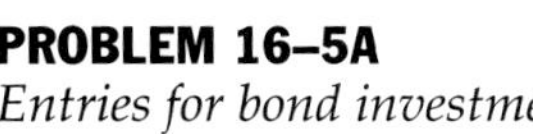

PROBLEM 16–5A
Entries for bond investments
Objective 7

The following selected transactions relate to certain securities acquired by J-Spec Blueprints Inc., whose fiscal year ends on December 31:

1996
Sep. 1. Purchased $500,000 of Schnell Company 20-year, 9% bonds dated July 1, 1996, directly from the issuing company, for $482,150 plus accrued interest of $7,500.
Dec. 31. Received the semiannual interest on the Schnell Company bonds.
31. Recorded bond discount amortization of $300 on the Schnell Company bonds. The amortization amount was determined by using the straight-line method.

(Assume that all intervening transactions and adjustments have been properly recorded and that the number of bonds owned has not changed from December 31, 1996, to December 31, 2000.)

2001
June 30. Received the semiannual interest on the Schnell Company bonds.
Oct. 31. Sold one-half of the Schnell Company bonds at 97 plus accrued interest. The broker deducted $1,350 for commission, etc., remitting the balance. Prior to the sale, $375 of discount on one-half of the bonds was amortized, increasing the carrying value of those bonds to $243,400.
Dec. 31. Received the semiannual interest on the Schnell Company bonds.
31. Recorded bond discount amortization of $450 on the Schnell Company bonds.

Instructions

Journalize the entries to record the foregoing transactions.

APPENDIX PROBLEM 16–6A
Entries for bonds payable transactions; interest method of amortizing bond premium

Icot Inc. produces and sells voltage regulators. On July 1, 1996, Icot Inc. issued $8,000,000 of ten-year, 10½% bonds at an effective interest rate of 10%, receiving proceeds of $8,249,240. Interest on the bonds is payable semiannually on December 31 and June 30. The fiscal year of the company is the calendar year.

Instructions

1. Journalize the entries to record the following:
   a. The first semiannual interest payment on December 31, 1996, and the amortization of the bond premium, using the interest method. (Round to nearest dollar.)
   b. The interest payment on June 30, 1997, and the amortization of the bond premium, using the interest method. (Round to nearest dollar.)
2. Determine the total interest expense for 1996.

APPENDIX PROBLEM 16–7A
Entries for bonds payable transactions; interest method of amortizing bond discount

On July 1, 1996, Tricon Communications Equipment Inc. issued $12,000,000 of ten-year, 8% bonds at an effective interest rate of 10%, receiving proceeds of $10,504,529. Interest on the bonds is payable semiannually on December 31 and June 30. The fiscal year of the company is the calendar year.

Instructions

1. Journalize the entries to record the following:
   a. The first semiannual interest payment on December 31, 1996, and the amortization of the bond discount, using the interest method.
   b. The interest payment on June 30, 1997, and the amortization of the bond discount, using the interest method.
2. Determine the total interest expense for 1996.

PROBLEMS SERIES B

PROBLEM 16–1B
Effect of financing on earnings per share
Objective 1

Three different plans for financing a $20,000,000 corporation are under consideration by its organizers. Under each of the following plans, the securities will be issued at their par or face amount, and the income tax rate is estimated at 40% of income.

	Plan 1	*Plan 2*	*Plan 3*
12% bonds			$10,000,000
Preferred 8% stock, $100 par		$10,000,000	5,000,000
Common stock, $20 par	$20,000,000	10,000,000	5,000,000
Total	$20,000,000	$20,000,000	$20,000,000

Instructions

1. Determine for each plan the earnings per share of common stock, assuming that the income before bond interest and income tax is $4,000,000.
2. Determine for each plan the earnings per share of common stock, assuming that the income before bond interest and income tax is $2,000,000.
3. Discuss the advantages and disadvantages of each plan.

PROBLEM 16–2B
Present value; bond premium; entries for bonds payable transactions
Objectives 3, 4

Risotto Corporation produces and sells burial vaults. On July 1, 1997, Risotto Corporation issued $10,000,000 of ten-year, 12% bonds at an effective interest rate of 10%. Interest on the bonds is payable semiannually on December 31 and June 30. The fiscal year of the company is the calendar year.

Instructions

1. Journalize the entry to record the amount of the cash proceeds from the sale of the bonds. Use the tables of present values in Appendix A to compute the cash proceeds, rounding to the nearest dollar.
2. Journalize the entries to record the following:
   a. The first semiannual interest payment on December 31, 1997, and the amortization of the bond premium, using the straight-line method.

b. The interest payment on June 30, 1998, and the amortization of the bond premium, using the straight-line method.

3. Determine the total interest expense for 1997.
4. Will the bond proceeds always be greater than the face value of the bonds when the coupon rate is greater than the market rate of interest? Explain.

PROBLEM 16–3B
Present value; bond discount; entries for bonds payable transactions
Objectives 3, 4

On July 1, 1996, Primo Corporation, a wholesaler of used robotic equipment, issued $15,000,000 of ten-year, 11% bonds at an effective interest rate of 12%. Interest on the bonds is payable semiannually on December 31 and June 30. The fiscal year of the company is the calendar year.

Instructions

1. Journalize the entry to record the amount of the cash proceeds from the sale of the bonds. Use the tables of present values in Appendix A to compute the cash proceeds, rounding to the nearest dollar.
2. Journalize the entries to record the following:
   a. The first semiannual interest payment on December 31, 1996, and the amortization of the bond discount, using the straight-line method.
   b. The interest payment on June 30, 1997, and the amortization of the bond discount, using the straight-line method.
3. Determine the total interest expense for 1996.
4. Will the bond proceeds always be less than the face value of the bonds when the coupon rate is less than the market rate of interest? Explain.

PROBLEM 16–4B
Entries for bonds payable transactions
Objectives 4, 6

The following transactions were completed by Lovin-Oven Appliances Inc., whose fiscal year is the calendar year:

1996
July 1. Issued $10,000,000 of 10-year, 9% callable bonds dated July 1, 1996, at an effective rate of 10%, receiving cash of $9,376,884. Interest is payable semiannually on December 31 and June 30.
Dec. 31. Paid the semiannual interest on the bonds.
31. Recorded bond discount amortization of $31,156, which was determined by using the straight-line method.
31. Closed the interest expense account.

1997
June 30. Paid the semiannual interest on the bonds.
Dec. 31. Paid the semiannual interest on the bonds.
31. Recorded bond discount amortization of $62,312, which was determined by using the straight-line method.
31. Closed the interest expense account.

2004
June 30. Recorded the redemption of the bonds, which were called at 99. The balance in the bond discount account is $124,620 after payment of interest and amortization of discount have been recorded. (Record the redemption only.)

Instructions

1. Journalize the entries to record the foregoing transactions.
2. Indicate the amount of the interest expense in (a) 1996 and (b) 1997.
3. Determine the carrying value of the bonds as of December 31, 1997.

PROBLEM 16–5B
Entries for bond investments
Objective 7

Data Track Inc. develops and leases databases of publicly available information. The following selected transactions relate to certain securities acquired as a long-term investment by Data Track Inc., whose fiscal year ends on December 31:

1996
Sep. 1. Purchased $600,000 of Marvel Company 10-year, 10% bonds dated July 1, 1996, directly from the issuing company, for $617,700 plus accrued interest of $10,000.
Dec. 31. Received the semiannual interest on the Marvel Company bonds.
31. Recorded bond premium amortization of $600 on the Marvel Company bonds. The amortization amount was determined by using the straight-line method.

(Assume that all intervening transactions and adjustments have been properly recorded and that the number of bonds owned has not changed from Dec. 31, 1996, to Dec. 31, 2001.)

2002

June 30. Received the semiannual interest on the Marvel Company bonds.

July 31. Sold one-half of the Marvel Company bonds at 102 plus accrued interest. The broker deducted $1,200 for commission, etc., remitting the balance. Prior to the sale, $525 of premium on one-half of the bonds is to be amortized, reducing the carrying amount of those bonds to $303,525.

Dec. 31. Received the semiannual interest on the Marvel Company bonds.

31. Recorded bond premium amortization of $900 on the Marvel Company bonds.

Instructions

Journalize the entries to record the foregoing transactions.

APPENDIX PROBLEM 16–6B
Entries for bonds payable transactions; interest method of amortizing bond premium

Risotto Corporation produces and sells burial vaults. On July 1, 1997, Risotto Corporation issued $10,000,000 of ten-year, 12% bonds at an effective interest rate of 10%, receiving proceeds of $11,246,216. Interest on the bonds is payable semiannually on December 31 and June 30. The fiscal year of the company is the calendar year.

Instructions

1. Journalize the entries to record the following:
   a. The first semiannual interest payment on December 31, 1997, and the amortization of the bond premium, using the interest method. (Round to nearest dollar.)
   b. The interest payment on June 30, 1998, and the amortization of the bond premium, using the interest method. (Round to nearest dollar.)
2. Determine the total interest expense for 1997.

APPENDIX PROBLEM 16–7B
Entries for bonds payable transactions; interest method of amortizing bond discount

On July 1, 1996, Primo Corporation, a wholesaler of used robotic equipment, issued $15,000,000 of ten-year, 11% bonds at an effective interest rate of 12%, receiving proceeds of $14,139,760. Interest on the bonds is payable semiannually on December 31 and June 30. The fiscal year of the company is the calendar year.

Instructions

1. Journalize the entries to record the following:
   a. The first semiannual interest payment on December 31, 1996, and the amortization of the bond discount, using the interest method. (Round to nearest dollar.)
   b. The interest payment on June 30, 1997, and the amortization of the bond discount, using the interest method. (Round to nearest dollar.)
2. Determine the total interest expense for 1996.

COMPREHENSIVE PROBLEM 4

Selected transactions completed by Petro Petroleum Products Inc. during the fiscal year ending July 31, 1997, were as follows:

a. Issued 10,000 shares of $25 par common stock at $42, receiving cash.
b. Issued 7,500 shares of $100 par preferred 8% stock at $115, receiving cash.
c. Issued $1,000,000 of 10-year, 10½% bonds at an effective interest rate of 10%, with interest payable semiannually. Use the present value tables in Appendix A to determine the bond proceeds. Round to the nearest dollar.
d. Declared a dividend of $0.40 per share on common stock and $2 per share on preferred stock. On the date of record, 100,000 shares of common stock were outstanding, no treasury shares were held, and 15,000 shares of preferred stock were outstanding.
e. Paid the cash dividends declared in (d).
f. Redeemed $600,000 of 8-year, 12% bonds at 101. The balance in the bond premium account is $7,900 after the payment of interest and amortization of discount have been recorded. (Record only the redemption of the bonds payable.)
g. Transferred $600,000 of the appropriation for bonded indebtedness back to retained earnings for the bonds redeemed in (f).

h. Purchased 3,000 shares of treasury common stock at $40 per share.
i. Declared a 5% stock dividend on common stock and a $2 cash dividend per share on preferred stock. On the date of declaration, the market value of the common stock was $41 per share. On the date of record, 100,000 shares of common stock were issued, 3,000 shares of treasury common stock were held, and 15,000 shares of preferred stock were outstanding.
j. Issued the stock certificates for the stock dividends declared in (i) and paid the cash dividends to the preferred stockholders.
k. Purchased $50,000 of Auxiliary Inc. 10-year, 15% bonds, directly from the issuing company, for $48,500 plus accrued interest of $1,875.
l. Sold, at $48 per share, 2,000 shares of treasury common stock purchased in (h).
m. Recorded the payment of semiannual interest on the bonds issued in (c) and the amortization of the premium for six months. The amortization was determined using the straight-line method. (Round the amortization to the nearest dollar.)
n. Appropriated $100,000 of retained earnings for bonded indebtedness.
o. Appropriated $40,000 of retained earnings for treasury stock.
p. Accrued interest for four months on the Auxiliary Inc. bonds purchased in (k). Also recorded amortization of $50.

Instructions

1. Journalize the selected transactions.
2. After all of the transactions for the year ended July 31, 1997, had been posted (including the transactions recorded in (1) and all adjusting entries), the following data were selected from the records of Petro Petroleum Products Inc.:

Income statement data:	
Advertising expense	$ 75,000
Cost of merchandise sold	3,850,000
Delivery expense	17,000
Depreciation expense—office equipment	13,100
Depreciation expense—store equipment	45,000
Gain on redemption of bonds	1,900
Income tax:	
Applicable to continuing operations	254,775
Applicable to loss from disposal of a segment of the business	21,100
Applicable to gain from redemption of bonds	500
Interest expense	68,500
Interest income	3,675
Loss from disposal of a segment of the business	80,500
Miscellaneous administrative expenses	1,600
Miscellaneous selling expenses	6,300
Office rent expense	25,000
Office salaries expense	85,000
Office supplies expense	5,300
Sales	5,100,000
Sales commissions	95,000
Sales salaries expense	180,000
Store supplies expense	9,500

Retained earnings and balance sheet data:	
Accounts payable	$ 149,500
Accounts receivable	280,500
Accumulated depreciation—office equipment	835,250
Accumulated depreciation—store equipment	2,214,750
Allowance for doubtful accounts	21,500
Bonds payable, 10½%, due 2007	1,000,000
Cash	125,500
Common stock, $25 par (400,000 shares authorized; 104,850 shares outstanding)	2,621,250

Deferred income tax payable (current portion, $4,700)	$ 25,700
Dividends:	
Cash dividends for common stock	120,000
Cash dividends for preferred stock	105,000
Stock dividends for common stock	198,850
Dividends payable	30,000
Income tax payable	55,900
Interest receivable	2,500
Investment in Auxiliary Inc. bonds (long-term)	48,550
Merchandise inventory (July 31, 1997), at lower of cost (fifo) or market	425,000
Notes receivable	77,500
Office equipment	2,410,100
Organization costs	55,000
Paid-in capital from sale of treasury stock	16,000
Paid-in capital in excess of par—common stock	325,000
Paid-in capital in excess of par—preferred stock	240,000
Preferred 8% stock, $100 par (30,000 shares authorized; 15,000 shares issued)	1,500,000
Premium on bonds payable	29,597
Prepaid expenses	15,900
Retained earnings:	
Appropriated for bonded indebtedness (August 1, 1996)	600,000
Appropriated for bonded indebtedness (July 31, 1997)	100,000
Appropriated for treasury stock (August 1, 1996)	—
Appropriated for treasury stock (July 31, 1997)	40,000
Unappropriated, August 1, 1996	2,529,303
Store equipment	8,603,950
Treasury stock (1,000 shares of common stock at cost of $40 per share)	40,000

a. Prepare a multiple-step income statement for the year ended July 31, 1997, concluding with earnings per share. In computing earnings per share, assume that the average number of common shares outstanding was 100,000 and preferred dividends were $105,000. Round to nearest cent.
b. Prepare a retained earnings statement for the year ended July 31, 1997.
c. Prepare a balance sheet in report form as of July 31, 1997.

CASES

CASE 16–1
Rapidwater Co.
Bond sinking funds

Rapidwater Co. produces and sells water slides for theme parks. Rapidwater Co. has outstanding a $40,000,000, 25-year, 10% debenture bond issue dated July 1, 1988. The bond issue is due June 30, 2013. The bond indenture requires a sinking fund, which has a balance of $10,000,000 as of July 1, 1997. Rapidwater Co. is currently experiencing a shortage of funds due to a recent plant expansion. Yonah Jones, treasurer of Rapidwater Co., has suggested using the sinking fund cash to temporarily relieve the shortage of funds. Jones' brother-in-law, who is trustee of the sinking fund, is willing to loan Rapidwater Co. the necessary funds from the sinking fund.

Discuss whether Yonah Jones is behaving in an ethical manner.

CASE 16–2
Rotan Distributors Inc.
Present values

Rotan Distributors Inc. is a wholesaler of oriental rugs. The following is a luncheon conversation between Jennifer Dobbs, the assistant controller, and Clancy Byrne, an assistant financial analyst for Rotan.

Clancy: Jenny, do you mind if I spoil your lunch and ask you an accounting question?

Jennifer: No, go ahead. This chicken salad sandwich is pretty bad. It smells like it's three days old, and I've already picked three bones out of it.

Clancy: Well, as you know, in finance we use present values for capital budgeting analysis, assessing financing alternatives, etc. It's probably the most important concept that I learned in school that I actually use.

Jennifer: So . . . ?

Clancy: I was just wondering why accountants don't use present values more.

Jennifer: What do you mean?

Clancy: Well, it seems to me that you ought to value all the balance sheet liabilities at their present values.

How would you respond if you were Jennifer?

CASE 16–3
Regis Sheats Inc.
Preferred stock vs. bonds

Regis Sheats Inc. has decided to expand its operations to owning and operating theme parks. The following is an excerpt from a conversation between the chief executive officer, JoAnn Eaves, and the vice-president of finance, Pat Seawright.

JoAnn: Pat, have you given any thought to how we're going to finance the acquisition of WaterWave Corporation?

Pat: Well, the two basic options, as I see it, are to issue either preferred stock or bonds. The equity market is a little depressed right now. The rumor is that the Federal Reserve Bank's going to increase the interest rates either this month or next.

JoAnn: Yes, I've heard the rumor. The problem is that we can't wait around to see what's going to happen. We'll have to move on this next week if we want any chance to complete the acquisition of WaterWave.

Pat: Well, the bond market is strong right now. Maybe we should issue debt this time around.

JoAnn: That's what I would have guessed as well. WaterWave's financial statements look pretty good, except for the volatility of their income and cash flows. But that's characteristic of their industry.

Discuss the advantages and disadvantages of issuing preferred stock versus bonds.

CASE 16–4
Hershey Foods Corporation
Financial analysis

A financial measure that focuses on the relative risk of the debtholders is the number of times the interest charges are earned during the year. The higher the ratio, the lower the risk that interest payments to the debtholders will not be made if earnings decrease. In other words, the higher the ratio, the greater the assurance that interest payments will be made on a continuing basis. This measure also indicates the general financial strength of the business.

The amount available to meet interest charges is not affected by taxes on income. This is because interest is deductible in determining taxable income. Thus, the number of times interest charges are earned is computed as shown below:

$$\textbf{Number of times interest charges earned} = \frac{\textbf{Income before income tax + Interest expense}}{\textbf{Interest expense}}$$

1. For Hershey Foods Corporation, determine the number of times interest charges were earned for the years ended December 31, 1993 and 1992. (The makeup of "interest expense, net" as reported on the income statement is described in Note 4 to the statements. Use only the interest on long- and short-term debt in your computation.)
2. What conclusions can be drawn from the data concerning the risk of the debtholders for the interest payments and the general financial strength of Hershey?

CASE 16–5
Summit Bottling Co.
Financing business expansion

You hold a 25% common stock interest in the family-owned business, a soft drink bottling distributorship. Your sister, who is the manager, has proposed an expansion of plant facilities at an expected cost of $1,500,000. Two alternative plans have been suggested as methods of financing the expansion. Each plan is briefly described as follows:

Plan 1. Issue $1,500,000 of 20-year, 8% notes at face amount.

Plan 2. Issue an additional 10,000 shares of $20 par common stock at $25 per share, and $1,250,000 of 20-year, 8% notes at face amount.

The balance sheet as of the end of the previous fiscal year is as follows:

Summit Bottling Co.
Balance Sheet
December 31, 19—

Assets	
Current assets	$2,350,000
Plant assets	5,150,000
Total assets	$7,500,000
Liabilities and Stockholders' Equity	
Liabilities	$2,000,000
Common stock, $20	800,000
Paid-in capital in excess of par	80,000
Retained earnings	4,620,000
Total liabilities and stockholders' equity	$7,500,000

Net income has remained relatively constant over the past several years. The expansion program is expected to increase yearly income before bond interest and income tax from $500,000 in the previous year to $600,000 for this year. Your sister has asked you, as the company treasurer, to prepare an analysis of each financing plan.

1. Prepare a table indicating the expected earnings per share on the common stock under each plan. Assume an income tax rate of 40%.
2. a. Discuss the factors that should be considered in evaluating the two plans.
   b. Which plan offers the greater benefit to the present stockholders? Give reasons for your opinion.

ANSWERS TO SELF-EXAMINATION QUESTIONS

1. **B** Since the contract rate on the bonds is higher than the prevailing market rate, a rational investor would be willing to pay more than the face amount, or a premium (answer B), for the bonds. If the contract rate and the market rate were equal, the bonds could be expected to sell at their face amount (answer A). Likewise, if the market rate is higher than the contract rate, the bonds would sell at a price below their face amount (answer D) or at a discount (answer C).
2. **A** The bond carrying amount, sometimes called the book value, is the face amount plus unamortized premium or less unamortized discount. For this question, the carrying amount is $500,000 less $40,000, or $460,000 (answer A).
3. **B** Although the sinking fund may consist of cash as well as securities, the fund is listed on the balance sheet as an investment (answer B) because it is to be used to pay the long-term liability at maturity.
4. **B** The amount debited to the investment account is the cost of the bonds, which includes the amount paid to the seller for the bonds (101% × $100,000) plus broker's commissions ($50), or $101,050 (answer B). The $2,000 of accrued interest that is paid to the seller should be debited to Interest Income, since it is an offset against the amount that will be received as interest at the next interest date.
5. **C** The balance of Discount on Bonds Payable is usually reported as a deduction from Bonds Payable in the Long-Term Liabilities section (answer C) of the balance sheet. Likewise, a balance in a premium on bonds payable account would usually be reported as an addition to Bonds Payable in the Long-Term Liabilities section of the balance sheet.

17 Statement of Cash Flows

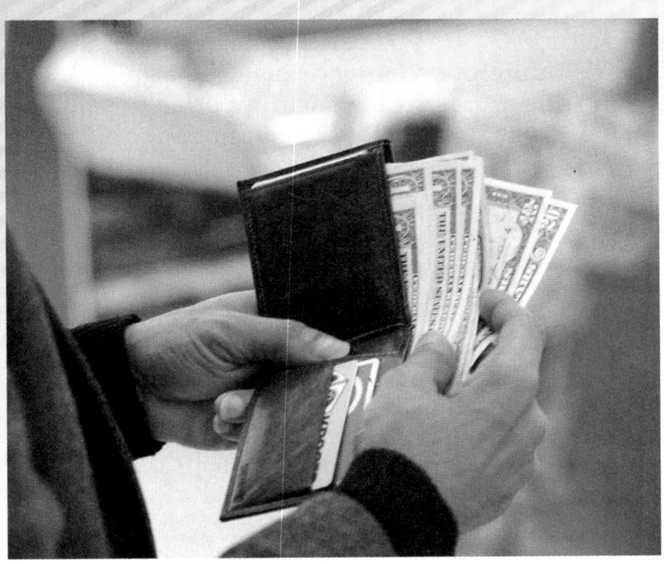

YOU AND ACCOUNTING

How much cash do you have in the bank or in your wallet or purse? How much cash did you have at the beginning of the month? The difference between these two amounts is the net change in your cash during the month. Knowing the reasons for the change in cash may be useful in evaluating whether your financial position has improved and whether you will be able to pay your bills in the future.

For example, assume that you had $200 at the beginning of the month and $550 at the end of the month. The net change in cash is $350. Based on this net change, it appears that your financial position has improved. However, this conclusion may or may not be valid, depending upon how the change of $350 was created. If you *borrowed* $1,000 during the month and spent $650 on living expenses, your cash would have increased by $350. On the other hand, if you *earned* $1,000 and spent $650 on living expenses, your cash would have also increased by $350, but your financial position is improved compared to the first scenario.

In previous chapters, we have used the income statement, balance sheet, and retained earnings statement and other information to analyze the effects of management decisions on business's revenues and costs. In this chapter, we present the basic preparation and use of the statement of cash flows.

After studying this chapter, you should be able to:

Objective 1
Explain why the statement of cash flows is one of the basic financial statements.

Objective 2
Summarize the types of cash flow activities reported in the statement of cash flows.

Objective 3
Prepare a statement of cash flows, using the indirect method.

Objective 4
Prepare a statement of cash flows, using the direct method.

Purpose of the Statement of Cash Flows

Objective 1
Explain why the statement of cash flows is one of the basic financial statements.

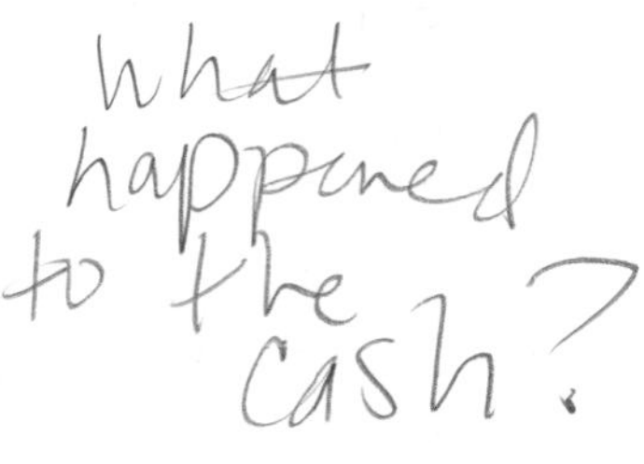
what happened to the cash?

The **statement of cash flows** reports a firm's major cash inflows and outflows for a period.[1] It provides useful information about a firm's ability to generate cash from operations, maintain and expand its operating capacity, meet its financial obligations, and pay dividends.

The statement of cash flows is one of the basic financial statements. It has been required for most businesses since 1987.[2] It is useful to managers in evaluating past operations and in planning future investing and financing activities. It is useful to investors, creditors, and others in assessing the firm's profit potential. In addition, it provides a basis for assessing the ability of the firm to pay its maturing debt.

FOCUS ON CASH FLOW

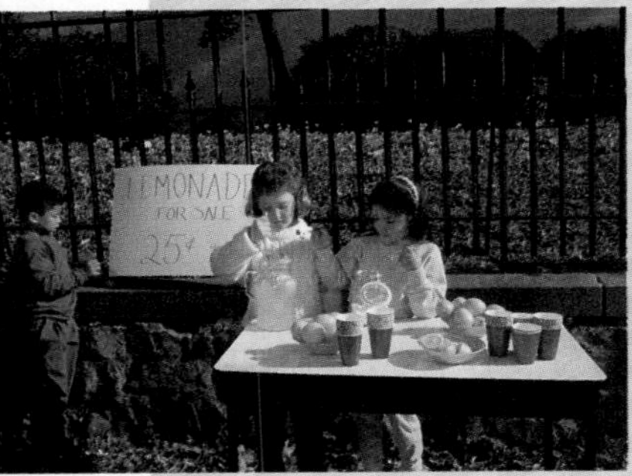

In the past, investors and creditors have relied heavily on a company's earnings information in judging the company's performance. Now, more and more investors and creditors are also focusing on cash flows for providing additional information, as described below.

As the term suggests, cash flow is basically a measure of the money flowing into—or out of—a business. If large companies were run, like lemonade stands, on a cash basis, earnings and cash flow would be identical.

Every major corporation, however, keeps its books on an accrual basis. . . . [This] can give a truer picture of corporate profitability, but sometimes it obscures important developments.

Take a company that spent $140 million on new machinery last year. If it depreciates the equipment over a seven-year period, it will be subtracting $20 million from reported profits each year.

But if the machines will stay up to date and useful for 25 years, the company's reported earnings may understate its true strength . . . .

Sometimes the reverse is true. If a company has been neglecting capital spending, its earnings may look good. But on a cash-flow basis, it will look no better. . . than its competitors.

Source: John R. Dorfman, "Stock Analysts Increase Focus on Cash Flow," *The Wall Street Journal*, February 17, 1987, Section 2, page 1.

[1] As used in this chapter, cash refers to cash and cash equivalents. Examples of cash equivalents include marketable securities, certificates of deposit, U.S. Treasury bills, and money market funds.

[2] *Statement of Accounting Standards, No. 95*, "Statement of Cash Flows," Financial Accounting Standards Board, Stamford, 1987.

Reporting Cash Flows

Objective 2
Summarize the types of cash flow activities reported in the statement of cash flows.

The statement of cash flows reports cash flows by three types of activities:[3]

1. **Cash flows from operating activities** are cash flows from transactions that affect net income. Examples of such transactions include the purchase and sale of merchandise by a retailer.
2. **Cash flows from investing activities** are cash flows from transactions that affect the investments in noncurrent assets. Examples of such transactions include the sale and purchase of plant assets, such as equipment and buildings.
3. **Cash flows from financing activities** are cash flows from transactions that affect the equity and debt of the entity. Examples of such transactions include issuing or retiring of equity and debt securities.

The cash flows from operating activities is normally presented first, followed by the cash flows from investing activities and financing activities. The total of the net cash flow from these activities is the net increase or decrease in cash for the period. The cash balance at the beginning of the period is added to the net increase or decrease in cash, and the cash balance at the end of the period is reported. The ending cash balance on the statement of cash flows equals the cash reported on the balance sheet.

Exhibit 1 shows common cash flow transactions reported in each of the three sections of the statement of cash flows. By reporting cash flows by operating, investing, and financing activities, significant relationships within and among the activities can be evaluated. For example, the cash receipts from issuing bonds can be related to repayments of borrowings when both are reported as financing activities. Also, the impact of each of the three activities (operating, investing, and financing) on cash flows can be identified. This allows investors and creditors to evaluate the effects of cash flows on a firm's profits and ability to pay debt.

Exhibit 1
Cash Flows

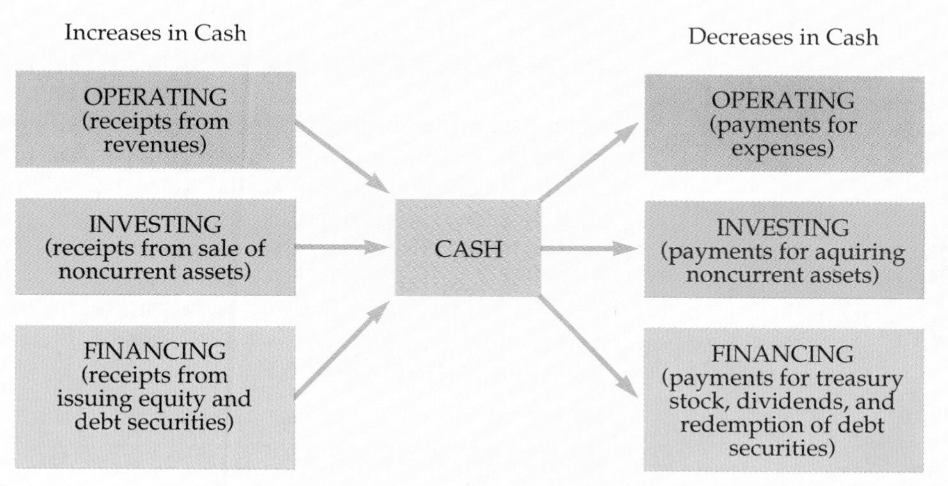

CASH FLOWS FROM OPERATING ACTIVITIES

The most frequent and often the most important cash flows of a business relate to operating activities. There are two alternative methods for reporting cash flows

[3] *Ibid.*

from operating activities in the statement of cash flows. These methods are (1) the direct method and (2) the indirect method.

The direct method reports the sources of operating cash and the uses of operating cash. The major source of operating cash is cash received from customers. The major uses of operating cash include cash paid to suppliers for merchandise and services and cash paid to employees for wages. The difference between these operating cash receipts and cash payments is the **net cash flow from operating activities.**

The primary advantage of the direct method is that it reports the sources and uses of cash in the statement of cash flows. Its primary disadvantage is that the necessary data may not be readily available and may be costly to gather.

The indirect method reports the operating cash flows by beginning with net income and adjusting it for revenues and expenses that do not involve the receipt or payment of cash. In other words, accrual net income is adjusted to determine the net amount of cash flows from operating activities.

A major advantage of the indirect method is that it focuses on the differences between net income and cash flows from operations. In this sense, it shows the relationship between the income statement, the balance sheet, and the statement of cash flows. Because the data are readily available, the indirect method is normally less costly to use than the direct method.

CASH FLOWS FROM INVESTING ACTIVITIES

Cash inflows from investing activities normally arise from selling plant assets, investments, and intangible assets. Cash outflows normally include payments to acquire plant assets, investments, and intangible assets.

Cash flows from investing activities are reported on the statement of cash flows by first listing the cash inflows. The cash outflows are then presented. If the inflows are greater than the outflows, **net cash flow provided by investing activities** is reported. If the cash inflows are less than the cash outflows, **net cash flow used for investing activities** is reported.

CASH FLOWS FROM FINANCING ACTIVITIES

Cash inflows from financing activities normally arise from issuing debt or equity securities. Examples of such inflows include issuing bonds, notes payable, and preferred and common stocks. Cash outflows from financing activities include paying cash dividends, repaying debt, and acquiring treasury stock.

Cash flows from financing activities are reported on the statement of cash flows by first listing the cash inflows. The cash outflows are then presented. If the inflows are greater than the outflows, **net cash flow provided by financing activities** is reported. If the cash inflows are less than the cash outflows, **net cash flow used for financing activities** is reported.

ILLUSTRATIONS OF THE STATEMENT OF CASH FLOWS

Exhibit 2 presents two illustrations of the statement of cash flows. Both statements are for the same accounting period for Computer King, which was used in illustrations in the first chapter of this text. The first statement reports cash flows from operating activities by the direct method. The second statement reports cash flows from operating activities by the indirect method. The same amount of net cash flow from operating activities is reported, regardless of the method. We will illustrate both methods in detail later in this chapter.

Exhibit 2
Statements of Cash Flows

Computer King
Statement of Cash Flows—Direct Method
For the Month Ended November 30, 1996

Cash flows from operating activities:		
Cash received from customers	$ 7,500	
Deduct cash payments for expenses and payment to creditors	4,600	
Net cash flow from operating activities		$ 2,900
Cash flows from investing activities:		
Cash payments for acquisition of land		(10,000)
Cash flows from financing activities:		
Cash received as owner's investment	$15,000	
Deduct cash withdrawal by owner	2,000	
Net cash flow from financing activities		13,000
Net cash flow and November 30, 1996 cash balance		$ 5,900

Computer King
Statement of Cash Flows—Indirect Method
For the Month Ended November 30, 1996

Cash flows from operating activities:		
Net income, per income statement	$ 3,050	
Add increase in accounts payable	400	
	$ 3,450	
Deduct increase in supplies	550	
Net cash flow from operating activities		$ 2,900
Cash flows from investing activities:		
Cash payments for acquisition of land		(10,000)
Cash flows from financing activities:		
Cash received as owner's investment	$15,000	
Deduct cash withdrawal by owner	2,000	
Net cash flow from financing activities		13,000
Net cash flow and November 30, 1996 cash balance		$ 5,900

NONCASH INVESTING AND FINANCING ACTIVITIES

A business may enter into investing and financing activities that do not directly involve cash. For example, it may issue common stock to retire long-term debt. Such a transaction does not have a direct effect on cash. However, the transaction does eliminate the need for future cash payments to pay interest and retire the bonds. Thus, such transactions should be reported to readers of the financial statements because of their future effect on cash flows.

When noncash investing and financing transactions occur during a period, their effect is reported in a separate schedule. This schedule accompanies the statement of cash flows. Other examples of noncash investing and financing transactions include acquiring plant assets by issuing bonds or capital stock and issuing common stock in exchange for convertible preferred stock.

CASH FLOW PER SHARE

The term *cash flow per share* is sometimes reported in the financial press. Often, the term is used to mean "cash flow from operations per share." Such reporting may be misleading to users of the financial statements. For example, users might interpret cash flow per share as the amount available for dividends. This would not be the case if most of the cash generated by operations is required for repaying loans or for reinvesting in the business. Users might also think that cash flow per share is equivalent or perhaps superior to earnings per share. For these reasons, the financial statements, including the statement of cash flows, should not report cash flow per share.

Statement of Cash Flows—The Indirect Method

Objective 3
Prepare a statement of cash flows, using the indirect method.

The indirect method of reporting cash flows from operating activities is normally less costly and more efficient than the direct method. In addition, when the direct method is used, the indirect method must also be used in preparing a supplemental reconciliation of net income with cash flows from operations. The 48th Edition (1994) of **Accounting Trends & Techniques** reported that 97% of the companies surveyed used the indirect method. For these reasons, we will discuss first the indirect method of preparing the statement of cash flows.

To collect the data for the statement of cash flows, all the cash receipts and cash payments for a period could be analyzed and then reported by purpose (operating, investing, or financing). However, this procedure is expensive and time-consuming. A more efficient approach is to analyze the changes in the noncash balance sheet accounts. The logic of this approach is that a change in any balance sheet account (including cash) can be analyzed in terms of changes in the other balance sheet accounts. To illustrate, the accounting equation is rewritten below to focus on the cash account:

Assets = Liabilities + Stockholders' Equity
Cash + Noncash Assets = Liabilities + Stockholders' Equity
Cash = Liabilities + Stockholders' Equity – Noncash Assets

Any change in the cash account results in a change in one or more noncash balance sheet accounts. That is, if the cash account changes, then a liability, stockholders' equity, or noncash asset account must also change.

Additional explanatory data are also obtained by analyzing the income statement accounts and supporting records. For example, since the net income or net loss for the period is closed to Retained Earnings, a change in the retained earnings account can be partially explained by the net income or net loss reported on the income statement.

There is no order in which the noncash balance sheet accounts must be analyzed. However, it is usually more efficient to analyze the accounts in the reverse order in which they appear on the balance sheet. Thus, the analysis of retained earnings provides the starting point for determining the cash flows from operating activities, which is the first section of the statement of cash flows.

The comparative balance sheet for Rundell Inc. on December 31, 1997 and 1996, is used to illustrate the indirect method. This balance sheet is shown in Exhibit 3. Selected ledger accounts and other data are presented as needed.[4]

RETAINED EARNINGS

The comparative balance sheet for Rundell Inc. shows that retained earnings increased $60,500 during the year. Analyzing the entries posted to the retained

[4] An appendix that discusses using a work sheet as an aid in assembling data for the statement of cash flows is presented at the end of this chapter. This appendix illustrates a work sheet that can be used with the indirect method and a work sheet that can be used with the direct method of reporting cash flows from operating activities.

Exhibit 3
Comparative Balance Sheet

Rundell Inc.
Comparative Balance Sheet
December 31, 1997 and 1996

	1997	1996	Increase Decrease*
Assets			
Cash	$ 49,000	$ 26,000	$ 23,000
Trade receivables (net)	74,000	65,000	9,000
Inventories	172,000	180,000	8,000*
Prepaid expenses	4,000	3,000	1,000
Investments (long-term)	—	45,000	45,000*
Land	90,000	40,000	50,000
Building	200,000	200,000	—
Accumulated depreciation—building	(36,000)	(30,000)	(6,000)
Equipment	290,000	142,000	148,000
Accumulated depreciation—equipment	(43,000)	(40,000)	(3,000)
Total assets	$800,000	$631,000	$169,000
Liabilities			
Accounts payable (merchandise creditors)	$ 45,000	$ 28,200	$ 16,800
Accrued expenses (operating expenses)	5,000	3,800	1,200
Income tax payable	2,500	4,000	1,500*
Dividends payable	15,000	8,000	7,000
Bonds payable	120,000	245,000	125,000*
Total liabilities	$187,500	$289,000	$101,500*
Stockholders' Equity			
Preferred stock	$150,000	—	$150,000
Paid-in capital in excess of par—preferred stock	10,000	—	10,000
Common stock	280,000	$230,000	50,000
Retained earnings	172,500	112,000	60,500
Total stockholders' equity	$612,500	$342,000	$270,500
Total liabilities and stockholders' equity	$800,000	$631,000	$169,000

earnings account indicates how this change occurred. The retained earnings account for Rundell Inc. is shown below.

ACCOUNT RETAINED EARNINGS ACCOUNT NO.

Date		Item	Debit	Credit	Balance Debit	Balance Credit
1997						
Jan.	1	Balance				112,000
Dec.	31	Net income		90,500		202,500
	31	Cash dividends	30,000			172,500

The retained earnings account must be carefully analyzed because some of the entries to retained earnings may not affect cash. For example, a decrease in retained earnings resulting from issuing a stock dividend does not affect cash. Likewise, an appropriation of retained earnings does not affect cash. Such transactions are not reported on the statement of cash flows.

For Rundell Inc., the retained earnings account indicates that the $60,500 change resulted from net income of $90,500 and cash dividends declared of $30,000. The effect of each of these items on cash flows is discussed below.

Cash Flows from Operating Activities

The net income of $90,500 reported by Rundell Inc. normally is not equal to the amount of cash generated from operations during the period. This is because net income is determined using the accrual method of accounting.

Under the accrual method of accounting, the time when revenues and expenses are recorded often differs from when cash is received or paid. For example, merchandise may be sold on account and the cash received at a later date.

Likewise, insurance expense represents the amount of insurance expired during the period. The premiums for the insurance may have been paid in a prior period. Thus, the net income reported on the income statement must be adjusted in determining cash flows from operating activities. The typical adjustments to net income are summarized in Exhibit 4.

Exhibit 4
Adjustments to Net Income—Indirect Method

Net income, per income statement		$XX
Add: Depreciation of plant assets	$XX	
Amortization of bond payable discount and intangible assets	XX	
Decreases in current assets (receivables, inventories, prepaid expenses)	XX	
Increases in current liabilities (accounts and notes payable, accrued liabilities)	XX	
Losses on disposal of assets and retirement of debt	XX	XX
Deduct: Amortization of bond payable premium	$XX	
Increases in current assets (receivables, inventories, prepaid expenses)	XX	
Decreases in current liabilities (accounts and notes payable, accrued liabilities)	XX	
Gains on disposal of assets and retirement of debt	XX	XX
Net cash flow from operating activities		$XX

Some of the adjustment items in Exhibit 4 are for expenses that affect noncurrent accounts but not cash. For example, depreciation of plant assets and amortization of intangible assets are deducted from revenue but do not affect cash. Likewise, the amortization of premium on bonds payable decreases interest expense but does not affect cash.

Some of the adjustment items in Exhibit 4 are for revenues and expenses that affect current assets and current liabilities but not cash flows. For example, a sale of $10,000 on account increases accounts receivable by $10,000. However, cash is not affected. Thus, the increase in accounts receivable of $10,000 between two balance sheet dates is deducted from net income in arriving at cash flows from operating activities.

Cash flows from operating activities should not include investing or financing transactions. For example, assume that land costing $50,000 was sold for $90,000 (a gain of $40,000). The sale should be reported as an investing activity: "Cash receipts from the sale of land, $90,000." However, the $40,000 gain on the sale of the land is included in net income on the income statement. Thus, the $40,000 gain is *deducted from* net income in determining cash flows from operations in order to avoid "double counting" the cash flow from the gain. Losses from the sale of plant assets are *added to* net income in determining cash flows from operations. Likewise, losses on the retirement of debt are added to net income and gains are deducted from net income in determining cash flows from operating activities.

The effect of dividends payable on cash flows from operating activities is omitted from Exhibit 4. Dividends payable is omitted because dividends do not affect net income. Later in the chapter, we will discuss the reporting of dividends in the statement of cash flows.

In the following paragraphs, we will discuss the adjustment of Rundell Inc.'s net income to "Cash flows from operating activities."

Depreciation

The comparative balance sheet in Exhibit 3 indicates that Accumulated Depreciation—Equipment increased by $3,000 and Accumulated Depreciation—Building by $6,000. As shown below, these two accounts indicate that depreciation for the year was $12,000 for the equipment and $6,000 for the building, or a total of $18,000.

ACCOUNT ACCUMULATED DEPRECIATION—EQUIPMENT ACCOUNT NO.

Date		Item	Debit	Credit	Balance Debit	Balance Credit
1997						
Jan.	1	Balance				40,000
May	9	Discarded, no salvage	9,000			31,000
Dec.	31	Depreciation for year		12,000		43,000

ACCOUNT ACCUMULATED DEPRECIATION—BUILDING ACCOUNT NO.

Date		Item	Debit	Credit	Balance Debit	Balance Credit
1997						
Jan.	1	Balance				30,000
Dec.	31	Depreciation for year		6,000		36,000

The $18,000 of depreciation expense reduced net income but did not require an outflow of cash. Thus, the $18,000 is added to net income in determining cash flows from operating activities, as follows:

Cash flows from operating activities:		
Net income	$90,500	
Add: Depreciation	18,000	$108,500

Current Assets and Current Liabilities

As shown in Exhibit 4, decreases in noncash current assets and increases in current liabilities are added to net income. In contrast, increases in noncash current assets and decreases in current liabilities are deducted from net income. The current asset and current liability accounts of Rundell Inc. are as follows:

	December 31		
Accounts	*1997*	*1996*	*Increase Decrease**
Trade receivables (net)	$ 74,000	$ 65,000	$ 9,000
Inventories	172,000	180,000	8,000*
Prepaid expenses	4,000	3,000	1,000
Accounts payable (merchandise creditors)	45,000	28,200	16,800
Accrued expenses (operating expenses)	5,000	3,800	1,200
Income taxes payable	2,500	4,000	1,500*

The $9,000 increase in **trade receivables** indicates that the sales on account during the year are $9,000 more than collections from customers on account. The amount reported as sales on the income statement therefore includes $9,000 that did not result in a cash inflow during the year. Thus, $9,000 is deducted from net income.

Using the indirect method of reporting cash flows, Rundell Inc. added the $8,000 decrease in inventories to net income to determine the cash flows from operating activities.

The $8,000 decrease in **inventories** indicates that the merchandise sold exceeds the cost of the merchandise purchased by $8,000. The amount deducted as cost of merchandise sold on the income statement therefore includes $8,000 that did not require a cash outflow during the year. Thus, $8,000 is added to net income. The $1,000 increase in prepaid expenses indicates that the cash payments for prepaid expenses exceed the amount deducted as an expense during the year by $1,000. Thus, $1,000 is deducted from net income.

The $16,800 increase in **accounts payable** indicates that the amount incurred during the year for merchandise purchased on account exceeds the cash payments made on account by $16,800. The amount reported on the income statement for cost of merchandise sold therefore includes $16,800 that did not require a cash outflow during the year. Thus, $16,800 is added to net income.

The $1,200 increase in **accrued expenses** indicates that the amount incurred during the year for operating expenses exceeds the cash payments by $1,200. The amount reported on the income statement for operating expenses therefore includes $1,200 that did not require a cash outflow during the year. Thus, $1,200 is added to net income.

The $1,500 decrease in **income taxes payable** indicates that the amount paid for taxes exceeds the amount owed during the year by $1,500. The amount reported on the income statement for income tax therefore is less than the amount paid by $1,500. Thus, $1,500 is deducted from net income.

The preceding adjustments to net income are summarized below.

Cash flows from operating activities:			
Net income		$ 90,500	
Add: Depreciation	$18,000		
Decrease in inventories	8,000		
Increase in accounts payable	16,800		
Increase in accrued expenses	1,200	44,000	
		$134,500	
Deduct: Increase in trade receivables	$ 9,000		
Increase in prepaid expenses	1,000		
Decrease in income taxes payable	1,500	11,500	$123,000

Gain on Sale of Investments

The ledger or income statement of Rundell Inc. indicates that the sale of long-term investments resulted in a gain of $30,000. As we discussed previously, the sale proceeds, which include the gain and the carrying value of the investments, are included in cash flows from investing activities.[5] The gain is also included in net income. Thus, to avoid double reporting, the gain of $30,000 is deducted from net income in determining cash flows from operating activities, as shown below.

Cash flows from operating activities:	
Net income	$90,500
Deduct: Gain on sale of investments	30,000

[5] The reporting of the proceeds (cash flows) from the sale of long-term investments as part of investing activities is discussed later in this chapter. Also, to simplify, we will assume that the market value of long-term investments approximates their cost.

Reporting Cash Flows from Operating Activities

We have now presented all the necessary adjustments to convert the net income to cash flows from operating activities for Rundell Inc. These adjustments are summarized in Exhibit 5 in a format suitable for the statement of cash flows.

Exhibit 5
Cash Flows from Operating Activities—Indirect Method

Cash flows from operating activities:			
Net income, per income statement		$ 90,500	
Add: Depreciation	$18,000		
Decrease in inventories	8,000		
Increase in accounts payable	16,800		
Increase in accrued expenses	1,200	44,000	
		$134,500	
Deduct: Increase in trade receivables	$ 9,000		
Increase in prepaid expenses	1,000		
Decrease in income taxes payable	1,500		
Gain on sale of investments	30,000	41,500	
Net cash flow from operating activities			$93,000

USING ACCOUNTING TO UNDERSTAND BUSINESS

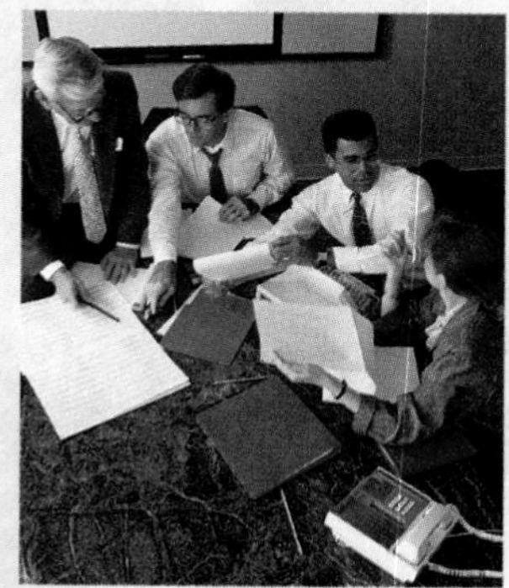

The Chief Financial Officer (CFO) of Honeywell Corporation put all managers through a financial training course in order to help them think about the cash implications of their decisions. The CFO wanted his managers to understand how cash can be tied up in current assets, such as receivables and inventory, and that growth can be achieved without significant working capital requirements. As a result, Honeywell generated cash by reducing its working capital needs from $2.2 billion to $1.6 billion, while still growing the business.

Cash Flows Used for Payment of Dividends

According to the retained earnings account of Rundell Inc., shown earlier in the chapter, cash dividends of $30,000 were declared during the year. However, the dividends payable account, shown below, indicates that dividends of only $23,000 were paid during the year.

ACCOUNT DIVIDENDS PAYABLE ACCOUNT NO.

Date		Item	Debit	Credit	Balance Debit	Balance Credit
1997						
Jan.	1	Balance				8,000
	10	Cash paid	8,000		—	—
June	20	Dividend declared		15,000		15,000
July	10	Cash paid	15,000		—	—
Dec.	20	Dividend declared		15,000		15,000

The $23,000 of dividend payments represent a cash outflow that is reported as a deduction from cash inflows in the financing activities section as follows:

Cash flows from financing activities:
Less: Cash paid for dividends $23,000

COMMON STOCK

The common stock account increased by $50,000, as shown below. This increase results from issuing stock in exchange for land valued at $50,000.

ACCOUNT COMMON STOCK ACCOUNT NO.

Date		Item	Debit	Credit	Balance Debit	Balance Credit
1997						
Jan.	1	Balance				230,000
Dec.	28	Issued at par in exchange for land		50,000		280,000

Although no inflow or outflow of cash occurred, the transaction represents a significant investing and financing activity. Such transactions, as discussed previously, are reported in a separate schedule accompanying the statement of cash flows. In this schedule, the transaction is reported as follows:

Noncash investing and financing activities:
Acquisition of land by issuance of common stock $50,000

PREFERRED STOCK

The preferred stock account increased by $150,000, and the paid-in capital in excess of par—preferred stock account increased by $10,000, as shown below. These increases result from issuing preferred stock for $160,000.

ACCOUNT PREFERRED STOCK ACCOUNT NO.

Date		Item	Debit	Credit	Balance Debit	Balance Credit
1997						
Nov.	1	30,000 shares issued for cash		150,000		150,000

ACCOUNT PAID-IN CAPTIAL IN EXCESS OF PAR—PREFERRED STOCK ACCOUNT NO.

Date		Item	Debit	Credit	Balance Debit	Balance Credit
1997						
Nov.	1	30,000 shares issued for cash		10,000		10,000

This cash inflow is reported in the financing activities section as follows:

Cash flows from financing activities:
Cash received from sale of preferred stock $160,000

BONDS PAYABLE

The bonds payable account decreased by $125,000, as shown below. This decrease results from retiring the bonds by a cash payment for their face value.

ACCOUNT BONDS PAYABLE ACCOUNT NO.

Date		Item	Debit	Credit	Balance	
					Debit	Credit
1997						
Jan.	1	Balance				245,000
June	30	Retired by payment of cash at face amount	125,000			120,000

This cash outflow is reported as a deduction from cash inflows in the financing activities section as follows:

Cash flows from financing activities:
  Less: Cash paid to retire bonds payable $125,000

EQUIPMENT

The equipment account increased by $148,000, and the accumulated depreciation—equipment account increased by $3,000, as shown below.

ACCOUNT EQUIPMENT ACCOUNT NO.

Date		Item	Debit	Credit	Balance	
					Debit	Credit
1997						
Jan.	1	Balance			142,000	
May	9	Discarded, no salvage		9,000	133,000	
Dec.	7	Purchased for cash	157,000		290,000	

ACCOUNT ACCUMULATED DEPRECIATION—EQUIPMENT ACCOUNT NO.

Date		Item	Debit	Credit	Balance	
					Debit	Credit
1997						
Jan.	1	Balance				40,000
May	9	Discarded, no salvage	9,000			31,000
Dec.	31	Depreciation for the year		12,000		43,000

The $148,000 increase in the equipment account resulted from two separate transactions. The first transaction is the discarding of equipment with a cost of $9,000. The credit of $9,000 in the equipment account and the debit of $9,000 in the accumulated depreciation—equipment account indicate that the discarded equipment was fully depreciated. In addition, the memorandum entry in the accounts indicates that no salvage was realized from the disposal of the equipment. Thus, the first transaction of discarding the equipment did not affect cash and is not reported on the statement of cash flows.

The second transaction is the purchase of equipment for cash of $157,000. This transaction is reported as a deduction from cash inflows in the investing activities section, as follows:

Cash flows from investing activities:
  Less: Cash paid for purchase of equipment $157,000

The credit of $12,000 in the accumulated depreciation account represents depreciation expense for the year. This depreciation expense of $12,000 on the equipment has already been considered as an addition to net income in determining cash flows from operating activities, as reported in Exhibit 5.

BUILDING

The comparative balance sheet in Exhibit 3 indicates no change in buildings during the year. Also, the ledger indicates that no entries were made to the building account during the year. For this reason, the account is not shown.

The credit in the accumulated depreciation—building account, shown earlier, represents depreciation expense for the year. This depreciation expense of $6,000 on the building has already been considered as an addition to net income in determining cash flows from operating activities, as reported in Exhibit 5.

LAND

The land account increased by $50,000, as shown below. This increase results from acquiring the land by issuing common stock at par.

ACCOUNT LAND ACCOUNT NO.

Date		Item	Debit	Credit	Balance Debit	Balance Credit
1997						
Jan.	1	Balance			40,000	
Dec.	28	Acquired by issuing common stock at par	50,000		90,000	

Although no inflow or outflow of cash occurred, the transaction represents a significant investing and financing activity. Such transactions, as discussed previously, are reported in a separate schedule accompanying the statement of cash flows. In this schedule, the transaction is reported as follows:

Noncash investing and financing activities:	
Acquisition of land by issuing common stock	$50,000

LONG-TERM INVESTMENTS

The investments account decreased by $45,000, as shown below. This decrease results from selling the investments for $75,000 in cash.

ACCOUNT INVESTMENTS ACCOUNT NO.

Date		Item	Debit	Credit	Balance Debit	Balance Credit
1997						
Jan.	1	Balance			45,000	
June	8	Sold for $75,000 cash		45,000	—	—

The $75,000 proceeds received from the sale of the investments is reported in the investing activities section, as follows:

Cash flows from investing activities:	
Cash received from sale of investments (includes $30,000 gain reported in net income)	$75,000

The proceeds of $75,000 include the $30,000 gain on the sale of investments and the $45,000 carrying value of the investments. As shown in Exhibit 5, the $30,000 gain is also deducted from net income in the cash flows from operating activities section. This is necessary so that the $30,000 cash inflow related to the gain is not included twice as a cash inflow.

PREPARING THE STATEMENT OF CASH FLOWS

The statement of cash flows for Rundell Inc. is prepared from the data assembled and analyzed above, using the indirect method. Exhibit 6 shows the statement of cash flows prepared by Rundell Inc. The statement indicates that the cash position increased by $23,000 during the year. The most significant increase in net cash flows, $93,000, was from operating activities. The most significant use of cash, $82,000, was for investing activities.

Exhibit 6
Statement of Cash Flows—Indirect Method

Rundell Inc.
Statement of Cash Flows
For the Year Ended December 31, 1997

Cash flows from operating activities:			
Net income, per income statement		$ 90,500	
Add: Depreciation	$ 18,000		
Decrease in inventories	8,000		
Increase in accounts payable	16,800		
Increase in accrued expenses	1,200	44,000	
		$134,500	
Deduct: Increase in trade receivables	$ 9,000		
Increase in prepaid expenses	1,000		
Decrease in income taxes payable	1,500		
Gain on sale of investments	30,000	41,500	
Net cash flow from operating activities			$93,000
Cash flows from investing activities:			
Cash received from sale of investments		$ 75,000	
Less: Cash paid for purchase of equipment		157,000	
Net cash flow used for investing activities			(82,000)
Cash flows from financing activities:			
Cash received from sale of preferred stock		$160,000	
Less: Cash paid for dividends	$ 23,000		
Cash paid to retire bonds payable	125,000	148,000	
Net cash flow provided by financing activities			12,000
Increase in cash			$23,000
Cash at the beginning of the year			26,000
Cash at the end of the year			$49,000
Schedule of Noncash Investing and Financing Activities:			
Acquisition of land by issuing common stock			$50,000

Statement of Cash Flows—The Direct Method

Objective 4
Prepare the statement of cash flows, using the direct method.

As we discussed previously, the direct method and the indirect method will report the same amount of cash flows from operating activities. In addition, the manner of reporting cash flows from investing and financing activities is the same under both methods. The methods differ in how the cash flows from operating activities data are obtained, analyzed, and reported.

To illustrate the direct method, we will use the comparative balance sheet and the income statement for Rundell Inc. In this way, we can compare the statement of cash flows under the direct method and the indirect method.

Exhibit 7 shows the changes in the current asset and liability account balances for Rundell Inc. The income statement in Exhibit 7 shows additional data for Rundell Inc.

Exhibit 7
Balance Sheet and Income Statement Data for Direct Method

Accounts	*December 31* 1997	1996	*Increase Decrease**
Cash	$ 49,000	$ 26,000	$23,000
Trade receivables (net)	74,000	65,000	9,000
Inventories	172,000	180,000	8,000*
Prepaid expenses	4,000	3,000	1,000
Accounts payable (merchandise creditors)	45,000	28,200	16,800
Accrued expenses (operating expenses)	5,000	3,800	1,200
Income taxes payable	2,500	4,000	1,500*

Rundell Inc.
Income Statement
For the Year Ended December 31, 1997

Sales		$960,000
Cost of merchandise sold		580,000
Gross profit		$380,000
Operating expenses:		
Depreciation expense	$ 18,000	
Other operating expenses	260,000	
Total operating expenses		278,000
Income from operations		$102,000
Other income:		
Gain on sale of investments	$ 30,000	
Other expense:		
Interest expense	14,000	16,000
Income before income tax		$118,000
Income tax		27,500
Net income		$ 90,500

The direct method reports cash flows from operating activities by major classes of operating cash receipts and operating cash payments. In the following paragraphs, we will describe and illustrate these classes. The difference between the major classes of total operating cash receipts and total operating cash payments is the net cash flow from operating activities.

CASH RECEIVED FROM CUSTOMERS

The $960,000 of sales for Rundell Inc. is reported by using the accrual method. To determine the cash received from sales made to customers, the $960,000 must be adjusted. The adjustments necessary to convert the sales reported on the income statement to the cash received from customers is summarized below.

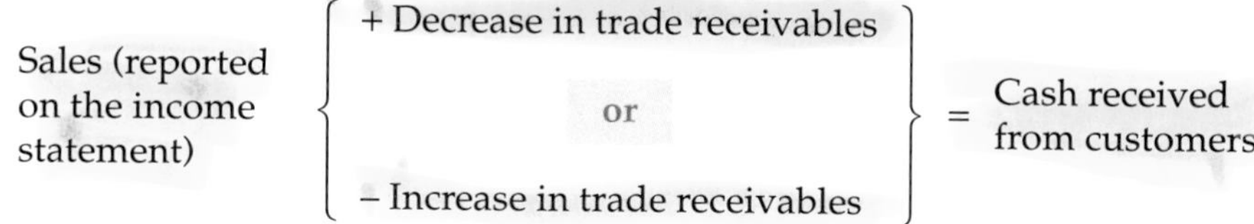

For Rundell Inc., the cash received from customers is $951,000, as shown below.

Sales	$960,000
Deduct increase in trade receivables	9,000
Cash received from customers	$951,000

The additions to **trade receivables** for sales on account during the year were $9,000 more than the amounts collected from customers on account. Sales reported on the income statement therefore included $9,000 that did not result in a cash inflow during the year. In other words, the increase of $9,000 in trade receivables during 1997 indicates that sales on account exceeded cash received from customers by $9,000. Thus, $9,000 is deducted from sales to determine the cash received from customers. The $951,000 of cash received from customers is reported in the cash flows from operating activities section of the cash flow statement.

CASH PAYMENTS FOR MERCHANDISE

The $580,000 of cost of merchandise sold is reported on the income statement for Rundell Inc., using the accrual method. The adjustments necessary to convert the cost of merchandise sold to cash payments for merchandise made during 1997 are summarized below.

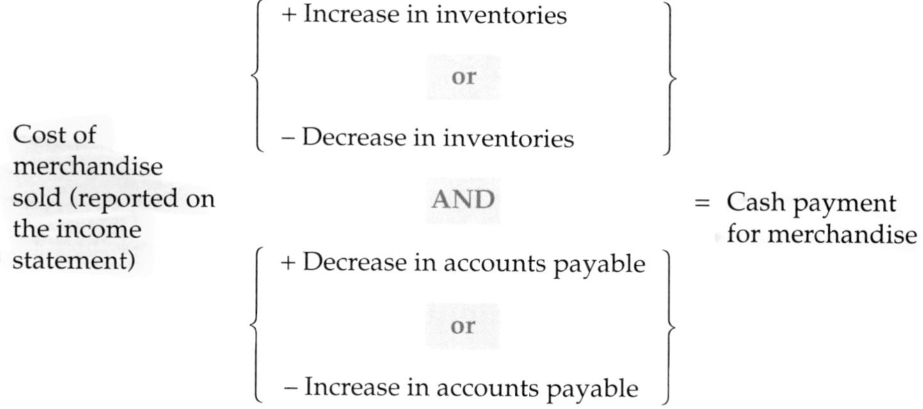

Cost of merchandise sold (reported on the income statement)
+ Increase in inventories
or
– Decrease in inventories
AND
+ Decrease in accounts payable
or
– Increase in accounts payable
= Cash payment for merchandise

For Rundell Inc., the amount of cash payments for merchandise is $555,200, as determined below.

Cost of merchandise sold		$580,000
Deduct: Decrease in inventories	$ 8,000	
Increase in accounts payable	16,800	24,800
Cash payments for merchandise		$555,200

The $8,000 decrease in **inventories** indicates that the merchandise sold exceeded the cost of the merchandise purchased by $8,000. The amount reported on the income statement for cost of merchandise sold therefore includes $8,000 that did not require a cash outflow during the year. Thus, $8,000 is deducted from the cost of merchandise sold in determining the cash payments for merchandise.

The $16,800 increase in **accounts payable** (merchandise creditors) indicates that merchandise purchases include $16,800 for which there was no cash outflow (payment) during the year. In other words, the increase in accounts payable indicates that cash payments for merchandise were $16,800 less than the purchases on account during 1997. Thus, $16,800 is deducted from the cost of merchandise sold in determining the cash payments for merchandise.

CASH PAYMENTS FOR OPERATING EXPENSES

The $18,000 of depreciation expense reported on the income statement did not require a cash outflow. Thus, under the direct method, it is not reported on the statement of cash flows. The $260,000 reported for other operating expenses is adjusted to reflect the cash payments for operating expenses, as summarized below.

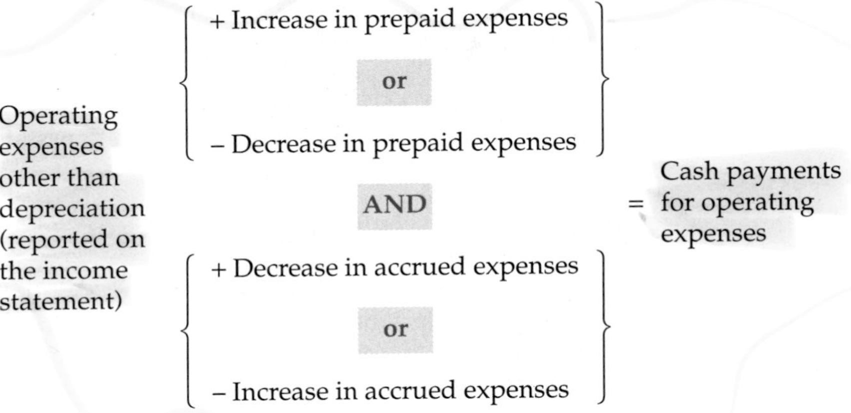

For Rundell Inc., the amount of cash payments for operating expenses is $259,800, determined as follows:

Operating expenses other than depreciation	$260,000
Add increase in prepaid expenses	1,000
	$261,000
Deduct increase in accrued expenses	1,200
Cash payments for operating expenses	$259,800

The cash outflow for **prepaid expenses** exceeded the amount deducted as an expense by $1,000 during the year. Hence, $1,000 is added to the amount of operating expenses (other than depreciation) reported on the income statement in determining the cash payments for operating expenses.

The increase in **accrued expenses** (operating expenses) indicates that operating expenses include $1,200 for which there was no cash outflow (payment) during the year. In other words, the increase in accrued expenses indicates that the cash payments for operating expenses were $1,200 less than the amount reported as an expense during the year. Thus, $1,200 is deducted from the operating expenses on the income statement in determining the cash payments for operating expenses.

GAIN ON SALE OF INVESTMENTS

The income statement for Rundell Inc. in Exhibit 7 reports a gain of $30,000 on the sale of long-term investments. As we discussed previously, the gain is included in the proceeds from the sale of investments, which is reported as part of the cash flows from investing activities.

INTEREST EXPENSE

The income statement for Rundell Inc. in Exhibit 7 reports interest expense of $14,000. The interest expense is related to the bonds payable that were outstanding during the year. We assume that interest on the bonds is paid on June 30 and December 31. Thus, $14,000 cash outflow for interest expense is reported on the statement of cash flows as an operating activity.

If interest payable had existed at the end of the year, the interest expense would be adjusted for any increase or decrease in interest payable from the beginning to the end of the year. That is, a decrease in interest payable would be added to interest expense and an increase in interest payable would be subtracted from interest expense. This is similar to the adjustment for changes in income taxes payable, which we will illustrate in the following paragraphs.

CASH PAYMENTS FOR INCOME TAXES

The adjustment to convert the income tax reported on the income statement to the cash basis is summarized below.

Income tax (reported on income statement) { + Decrease in income taxes payable or − Increase in income taxes payable } = Cash payments for income tax

For Rundell Inc., cash payments for income tax are $29,000, determined as follows:

Income tax	$27,500
Add decrease in income taxes payable	1,500
Cash payments for income tax	$29,000

The cash outflow for **income taxes** exceeded the income tax deducted as an expense during the period by $1,500. Thus, $1,500 is added to the amount of income tax reported on the income statement in determining the cash payments for income tax.

REPORTING CASH FLOWS FROM OPERATING ACTIVITIES—DIRECT METHOD

Exhibit 8 is a complete statement of cash flows for Rundell Inc., using the direct method for reporting cash flows from operating activities. The portions of this statement that differ from the indirect method are highlighted in color. Exhibit 8 also includes the separate schedule reconciling net income and net cash flow from operating activities. As we mentioned earlier, this schedule must accompany the statement of cash flows when the direct method is used. This schedule is similar to the cash flows from operating activities section of the statement of cash flows prepared using the indirect method.

Exhibit 8
Statement of Cash Flows—Direct Method

Rundell Inc.
Statement of Cash Flows
For the Year Ended December 31, 1997

Cash flows from operating activities:			
Cash received from customers		$951,000	
Deduct: Cash payments for merchandise	$555,200		
Cash payments for operating expenses	259,800		
Cash payments for interest	14,000		
Cash payments for income tax	29,000	858,000	
Net cash flow from operating activities			$ 93,000
Cash flows from investing activities:			
Cash received from sale of investments		$ 75,000	
Less: Cash paid for purchase of equipment		157,000	
Net cash flow used for investing activities			(82,000)
Cash flows from financing activities:			
Cash received from sale of preferred stock		$160,000	
Less: Cash paid for dividends	$ 23,000		
Cash paid to retire bonds payable	125,000	148,000	
Net cash flow provided by financing activities			12,000
Increase in cash			$ 23,000
Cash at the beginning of the year			26,000
Cash at the end of the year			$ 49,000
Schedule of Noncash Investing and Financing Activities:			
Acquisition of land by issuing common stock			$ 50,000
Schedule Reconciling Net Income with Cash Flows from Operating Activities:			
Net income, per income statement		$ 90,500	
Add: Depreciation	$ 18,000		
Decrease in inventories	8,000		
Increase in accounts payable	16,800		
Increase in accrued expenses	1,200	44,000	
		$134,500	
Deduct: Increase in trade receivables	$ 9,000		
Increase in prepaid expenses	1,000		
Decrease in income taxes payable	1,500		
Gain on sale of investments	30,000	41,500	
Net cash flow from operating activities		$ 93,000	

lower section exactly same as top part of 619

must add when using direct method

Appendix: Work Sheet for Statement of Cash Flows

Some accountants prefer to use a work sheet to assist them in assembling data for the statement of cash flows. Although a work sheet is not essential, it may be useful when a large number of transactions are to be analyzed. Whether or not a work sheet is used, the concepts of cash flow and the statements of cash flows presented in this chapter are not affected.

In this appendix, we will describe and illustrate the use of work sheets in preparing the statement of cash flows. We will discuss work sheets for both the indirect method and the direct method.

WORK SHEET—INDIRECT METHOD

We will use the data for Rundell Inc., presented in Exhibit 3, as a basis for illustrating the work sheet for the indirect method. The procedures used in preparing this work sheet, shown in Exhibit 9, are outlined as follows:

1. List the title of each balance sheet account in the Accounts column. For each account, enter its balance as of December 31, 1996, in the first column and its balance as of December 31, 1997, in the last column. Place the credit balances in parentheses. The column totals should equal zero, since the total of the debits in a column should equal the total of the credits in a column.
2. Analyze the change during the year in each account to determine the net increase (decrease) in cash and the cash flows from operating activities, investing activities, financing activities, and the noncash investing and financing activities. Show the effect of the change on cash flows by making entries in the Transactions columns.

Analyzing Accounts

As we discussed in this chapter, an efficient method of analyzing cash flows is to determine the type of cash flow activity that led to changes in balance sheet accounts during the period. As we analyze each noncash account, we will make entries on the work sheet for specific types of cash flow activities related to the noncash accounts. After we have analyzed all the noncash accounts, we will make an entry for the increase (decrease) in cash during the period. *These entries, however, are not posted to the ledger.* They only aid in assembling the data on the work sheet for use in preparing the statement of cash flows.

The order in which the accounts are analyzed is unimportant. However, it is more efficient to begin with the retained earnings account and proceed upward in the account listing.

RETAINED EARNINGS. The work sheet shows a Retained Earnings balance of $112,000 at December 31, 1996, and $172,500 at December 31, 1997. Thus, Retained Earnings increased $60,500 during the year. This increase resulted from two factors: (1) net income of $90,500 and (2) declaring cash dividends of $30,000. To identify the cash flows by activity, we will make two entries on the work sheet. These entries also serve to account for or explain, in terms of cash flows, the increase of $60,500.

In closing the accounts at the end of the year, the retained earnings account was credited for the net income of $90,500. The $90,500 is reported on the statement of cash flows as "cash flows from operating activities." The following entry is made in the Transactions columns on the work sheet. This entry (1) accounts for the credit portion of the closing entry (to Retained Earnings) and (2) identifies the cash flow in the bottom portion of the work sheet.

(a) Operating Activities—Net Income	90,500	
Retained Earnings		90,500

Exhibit 9
Work Sheet for Statement of Cash Flows—Indirect Method

Rundell Inc.
Work Sheet for Statement of Cash Flows
For the Year Ended December 31, 1997

Accounts	Balance, Dec. 31, 1996	Transactions Debit		Transactions Credit		Balance, Dec. 31, 1997
Cash	26,000	(s)	23,000			49,000
Trade Receivables	65,000	(r)	9,000			74,000
Inventories	180,000			(q)	8,000	172,000
Prepaid Expenses	3,000	(p)	1,000			4,000
Investments	45,000			(o)	45,000	—
Land	40,000	(n)	50,000			90,000
Building	200,000					200,000
Accumulated Depreciation—Building	(30,000)			(m)	6,000	(36,000)
Equipment	142,000	(l)	157,000	(k)	9,000	290,000
Accumulated Depreciation—Equipment	(40,000)	(k)	9,000	(j)	12,000	(43,000)
Accounts Payable	(28,200)			(h)	16,800	(45,000)
Accrued Expenses	(3,800)			(i)	1,200	(5,000)
Income Taxes Payable	(4,000)	(g)	1,500			(2,500)
Dividends Payable	(8,000)			(f)	7,000	(15,000)
Bonds Payable	(245,000)	(e)	125,000			(120,000)
Preferred Stock	—			(d)	150,000	(150,000)
Paid-In Capital in Excess of Par—Preferred Stock	—			(d)	10,000	(10,000)
Common Stock	(230,000)			(c)	50,000	(280,000)
Retained Earnings	(112,000)	(b)	30,000	(a)	90,500	(172,500)
Totals	0		405,500		405,500	0
Operating activities:						
Net income		(a)	90,500			
Decrease in income taxes payable				(g)	1,500	
Increase in accounts payable		(h)	16,800			
Increase in accrued expenses		(i)	1,200			
Depreciation of equipment		(j)	12,000			
Depreciation of building		(m)	6,000			
Gain on sale of investments				(o)	30,000	
Increase in prepaid expenses				(p)	1,000	
Decrease in inventories		(q)	8,000			
Increase in trade receivables				(r)	9,000	
Investing activities:						
Purchased equipment				(l)	157,000	
Sold investments		(o)	75,000			
Financing activities:						
Declared cash dividends				(b)	30,000	
Issued preferred stock		(d)	160,000			
Retired bonds payable				(e)	125,000	
Increase in dividends payable		(f)	7,000			
Schedule of noncash investing and financing activities:						
Acquisition of land by issuing common stock		(c)	50,000	(n)	50,000	
Net increase in cash				(s)	23,000	
Totals			426,500		426,500	

In closing the accounts at the end of the year, the retained earnings account was debited for dividends declared of $30,000. The $30,000 is reported as a financing activity on the statement of cash flows. The following entry on the work sheet (1) accounts for the debit portion of the closing entry (to Retained Earnings) and (2) identifies the cash flow in the bottom portion of the work sheet.

(b)	Retained Earnings	30,000	
	Financing Activities—Declared Cash Dividends		30,000

The $30,000 of declared dividends will be adjusted later for the actual amount of cash dividends paid during the year.

OTHER ACCOUNTS. We discussed in this chapter the analysis of the changes in the other accounts and their effect on cash flows and therefore will not repeat that discussion in this appendix. The related entries are made in the work sheet in a manner similar to entries (a) and (b). A summary of these entries is as follows:

(c)	Schedule of Noncash Investing and Financing Activities—Acquisition of Land by Issuing Common Stock	50,000	
	Common Stock		50,000
(d)	Financing Activities—Issued Preferred Stock	160,000	
	Preferred Stock		150,000
	Paid-In Capital in Excess of Par—Preferred Stock		10,000
(e)	Bonds Payable	125,000	
	Financing Activities—Retired Bonds Payable		125,000
(f)	Financing Activities—Increase in Dividends Payable	7,000	
	Dividends Payable		7,000
(g)	Income Taxes Payable	1,500	
	Operating Activities—Decrease in Income Taxes Payable		1,500
(h)	Operating Activities—Increase in Accounts Payable	16,800	
	Accounts Payable		16,800
(i)	Operating Activities—Increase in Accrued Expenses	1,200	
	Accrued Expenses		1,200
(j)	Operating Activities—Depreciation of Equipment	12,000	
	Accumulated Depreciation—Equipment		12,000
(k)	Accumulated Depreciation—Equipment	9,000	
	Equipment		9,000
(l)	Equipment	157,000	
	Investing Activities—Purchase of Equipment		157,000
(m)	Operating Activities—Depreciation of Building	6,000	
	Accumulated Depreciation—Building		6,000
(n)	Land	50,000	
	Schedule of Noncash Investing and Financing Activities—Acquisition of Land by Issuing Common Stock		50,000
(o)	Investing Activities—Sale of Investments	75,000	
	Operating Activities—Gain on Sale of Investments		30,000
	Investments		45,000
(p)	Prepaid Expenses	1,000	
	Operating Activities—Increase in Prepaid Expenses		1,000
(q)	Operating Activities—Decrease in Inventories	8,000	
	Inventories		8,000
(r)	Trade Receivables	9,000	
	Operating Activities—Increase in Trade Receivables		9,000
(s)	Cash	23,000	
	Net Increase in Cash		23,000

Completing the Work Sheet

After we have analyzed all the balance sheet accounts and made the entries on the work sheet, all the operating, investing, and financing activities are identified in the bottom portion of the work sheet. The accuracy of the work sheet entries is verified by the equality of the totals of the debit and credit Transactions columns.

Preparing the Statement of Cash Flows

The statement of cash flows prepared from the work sheet is identical to the statement in Exhibit 6. The data for the three sections of the statement are obtained from the bottom portion of the work sheet. Some of these data may not be reported exactly as they appear in the work sheet. For example, in reporting the cash flows from operating activities, the total depreciation expense ($18,000) is reported instead of the two separate amounts ($12,000 and $6,000).

In the cash flows from operating activities section, the effect of depreciation is normally presented first. The effects of increases and decreases in current assets and current liabilities are then presented. The effects of any gains and losses on operating activities are normally reported last. The cash paid for dividends is reported as $23,000 instead of the amount of dividends declared ($30,000) less the increase in dividends payable ($7,000). The issuing of the common stock for land ($50,000) is reported in a separate schedule.

WORK SHEET—DIRECT METHOD

A work sheet can also be used as an aid in assembling data for preparing a statement of cash flows under the direct method. As a basis for illustration, we will use the balance sheet data for Rundell Inc. in Exhibit 3 and the income statement data in Exhibit 7. The procedures used in preparing the work sheet shown in Exhibit 10 are outlined as follows:

1. List the title of each asset account in the Accounts column. For each account, enter its balance as of December 31, 1996, in the first column and its balance as of December 31, 1997, in the last column. Place the contra asset account balances (credit balances) in parentheses. Enter the amount of the total assets for December 31, 1996 and 1997, on the work sheet.
2. List the title of each liability and stockholders' equity account in the Accounts column. For each account, enter its balance as of December 31, 1996, in the first column and its balance as of December 31, 1997, in the last column. Enter the total liabilities and stockholders' equity for December 31, 1996 and 1997, on the work sheet. The total assets and the total liabilities and stockholders' equity should be equal for each year.
3. List the title of each income statement account and "Net Income" on the work sheet.
4. Analyze the effect of each income statement item on cash flows from operating activities. Beginning with sales, enter the balance of each item in the proper Transactions column. Complete the entry in the Transactions columns to show the effect on cash flows.
5. Analyze the change during the year in each balance sheet account to determine the net increase (decrease) in cash and the cash flows from operating activities, investing activities, financing activities, and the noncash investing and financing activities. Show the effect of the change on cash flows by making entries in the Transactions columns.

Analyzing Accounts

Under the direct method of reporting cash flows from operating activities, analyzing accounts begins with the income statement. As we analyze each income state-

Exhibit 10 *Work Sheet for Statement of Cash Flows—Direct Method*

Rundell Inc.
Work Sheet for Statement of Cash Flows
For the Year Ended December 31, 1997

Accounts	Balance, Dec. 31, 1996	Transactions: Debit	Transactions: Credit	Balance, Dec. 31, 1997
Balance Sheet				
Cash	26,000	(w) 23,000		49,000
Trade Receivables	65,000	(v) 9,000		74,000
Inventories	180,000		(u) 8,000	172,000
Prepaid Expenses	3,000	(t) 1,000		4,000
Investments	45,000		(e) 45,000	—
Land	40,000	(s) 50,000		90,000
Building	200,000			200,000
Accumulated Depreciation—Building	(30,000)		(c) 6,000	(36,000)
Equipment	142,000	(r) 157,000	(q) 9,000	290,000
Accumulated Depreciation—Equipment	(40,000)	(q) 9,000	(c) 12,000	(43,000)
Total Assets	631,000			800,000
Accounts Payable	28,200		(p) 16,800	45,000
Accrued Expenses	3,800		(o) 1,200	5,000
Income Taxes Payable	4,000	(n) 1,500		2,500
Dividends Payable	8,000		(m) 7,000	15,000
Bonds Payable	245,000	(l) 125,000		120,000
Preferred Stock	—		(k) 150,000	150,000
Paid-In Capital in Excess of Par—Preferred Stock			(k) 10,000	10,000
Common Stock	230,000		(j) 50,000	280,000
Retained Earnings	112,000	(i) 30,000	(h) 90,500	172,500
Total Liabilities and Stockholders' Equity	631,000			800,000
Income Statement				
Sales			(a) 960,000	
Cost of Merchandise Sold		(b) 580,000		
Depreciation Expense		(c) 18,000		
Other Operating Expenses		(d) 260,000		
Gain on Sale of Investments			(e) 30,000	
Interest Expense		(f) 14,000		
Income Taxes		(g) 27,500		
Net Income		(h) 90,500		
Cash Flows				
Operating activities:				
Cash received from customers		(a) 960,000	(v) 9,000	
Cash payments:				
Merchandise		(p) 16,800	(b) 580,000	
		(u) 8,000		
Operating expenses		(o) 1,200	(d) 260,000	
			(t) 1,000	
Interest expense			(f) 14,000	
Income taxes			(g) 27,500	
			(n) 1,500	
Investing activities:				
Sold investments		(e) 75,000		
Purchased equipment			(r) 157,000	
Financing activities:				
Declared cash dividends			(i) 30,000	
Issued preferred stock		(k) 160,000		
Retired bonds payable			(l) 125,000	
Increase in dividends payable		(m) 7,000		
Schedule of noncash investing & financing activities:				
Acquired land by issuing common stock		(j) 50,000	(s) 50,000	
Net increase in cash			(w) 23,000	
Totals		2,673,500	2,673,500	

ment account, we will make entries on the work sheet that show the effect on cash flows from operating activities. After we have analyzed the income statement accounts, we will analyze changes in the balance sheet accounts.

The order in which the balance sheet accounts are analyzed is unimportant. However, it is more efficient to begin with the retained earnings account and proceed upward in the account listing. As each noncash balance sheet account is analyzed, we will make entries on the work sheet for the related cash flow activities. After we have analyzed all the noncash accounts, we will make an entry for the increase (decrease) in cash during the period.

SALES. The income statement for Rundell Inc. shows sales of $960,000 for the year. Sales for cash provide cash when the sale is made. Sales on account provide cash when customers pay their bills. The entry on the work sheet is as follows:

(a) Operating Activities—Receipts from Customers	960,000	
Sales		960,000

COST OF MERCHANDISE SOLD. The income statement for Rundell Inc. shows cost of merchandise sold of $580,000 for the year. The cost of merchandise sold requires cash payments for cash purchases of merchandise. For purchases on account, cash payments are made when the invoices are due. The entry on the work sheet is as follows:

(b) Cost of Merchandise Sold	580,000	
Operating Activities—Payments for Merchandise		580,000

DEPRECIATION EXPENSE. The income statement for Rundell Inc. shows depreciation expense of $18,000. Depreciation expense does not require a cash outflow and thus is not reported on the statement of cash flows. The entry on the work sheet to fully account for the depreciation expense is as follows:

(c) Depreciation Expense	18,000	
Accumulated Depreciation—Building		6,000
Accumulated Depreciation—Equipment		12,000

OTHER ACCOUNTS. We discussed in this chapter the analysis of the changes in the other accounts and their effect on cash flows and therefore will not repeat that discussion in this appendix. The related entries are made on the work sheet in a manner similar to entries (a), (b), and (c). A summary of these entries is as follows:

(d) Other Operating Expenses	260,000	
Operating Activities—Paid Operating Expenses		260,000
(e) Investing Activities—Sold Investments	75,000	
Investments		45,000
Gain on Sale of Investments		30,000
(f) Interest Expense	14,000	
Operating Activities—Paid Interest		14,000
(g) Income Taxes	27,500	
Operating Activities—Paid Income Taxes		27,500
(h) Net Income	90,500	
Retained Earnings		90,500
(i) Retained Earnings	30,000	
Financing Activities—Declared Cash Dividends		30,000

		Debit	Credit
(j)	Schedule of Noncash Investing and Financing Activities—Acquired Land by Issuing Common Stock	50,000	
	Common Stock		50,000
(k)	Financing Activities—Issued Preferred Stock	160,000	
	Preferred Stock		150,000
	Paid-In Capital in Excess of Par—Preferred Stock		10,000
(l)	Bonds Payable	125,000	
	Financing Activities—Retired Bonds Payable		125,000
(m)	Financing Activities—Increase in Dividends Payable	7,000	
	Dividends Payable		7,000
(n)	Income Taxes Payable	1,500	
	Operating Activities—Decrease in Income Taxes Payable		1,500
(o)	Operating Activities—Cash Paid for Operating Expenses	1,200	
	Accrued Expenses		1,200
(p)	Operating Activities—Cash Paid for Merchandise	16,800	
	Accounts Payable		16,800
(q)	Accumulated Depreciation—Equipment	9,000	
	Equipment		9,000
(r)	Equipment	157,000	
	Investing Activities—Purchased Equipment		157,000
(s)	Land	50,000	
	Schedule of Noncash Investing and Financing Activities—Acquired Land by Issuing Common Stock		50,000
(t)	Prepaid Expenses	1,000	
	Operating Activities—Cash Paid for Operating Expenses		1,000
(u)	Operating Activities—Cash Paid for Merchandise	8,000	
	Inventories		8,000
(v)	Trade Receivables	9,000	
	Operating Activities—Cash Received from Customers		9,000
(w)	Cash	23,000	
	Net Increase in Cash		23,000

Completing the Work Sheet

After we have analyzed all the income statement and balance sheet accounts and have made the entries on the work sheet, all the operating, investing, and financing activities are identified in the bottom portion of the work sheet. The mathematical accuracy of the work sheet entries is verified by the equality of the totals of the debit and credit Transactions columns.

Preparing the Statement of Cash Flows

The statement of cash flows prepared from the work sheet is identical to the statement in Exhibit 8. The data for the three sections of the statement are obtained from the bottom portion of the work sheet. Some of these data may not be reported exactly as they appear on the work sheet. The cash paid for dividends is reported as $23,000 instead of the amount of dividends declared ($30,000) less the increase in dividends payable ($7,000). The issuing of the common stock for land ($50,000) is reported in a separate schedule.

KEY POINTS

Objective 1. Explain why the statement of cash flows is one of the basic financial statements.

The statement of cash flows reports useful information about a firm's ability to generate cash from operations, maintain and expand its operating capacity, meet its financial obligations, and pay dividends. This information assists investors, creditors, and others in assessing the firm's profit potential and its ability to pay its maturing debt. The statement of cash flows is also useful to managers in evaluating past operations and in planning future operating, investing, and financing activities.

Objective 2. Summarize the types of cash flow activities reported in the statement of cash flows.

The statement of cash flows reports cash receipts and cash payments by three types of activities: operating activities, investing activities, and financing activities.

Cash flows from operating activities are cash flows from transactions that affect net income. There are two methods of reporting cash flows from operating activities: (1) the direct method and (2) the indirect method.

Cash inflows from investing activities are cash flows from the sale of investments, plant assets, and intangible assets. Cash outflows generally include payments to acquire investments, plant assets, and intangible assets.

Cash inflows from financing activities include proceeds from issuing equity securities, such as preferred and common stock. Cash inflows also arise from issuing bonds, mortgage notes payable, and other long-term debt. Cash outflows from financing activities arise from paying cash dividends, purchasing treasury stock, and repaying amounts borrowed.

Investing and financing for a business may be affected by transactions that do not involve cash. The effect of such transactions should be reported in a separate schedule accompanying the statement of cash flows.

Because it may be misleading, cash flow per share is not reported in the statement of cash flows.

Objective 3. Prepare a statement of cash flows, using the indirect method.

To prepare the statement of cash flows, changes in the noncash balance sheet accounts are analyzed. This logic relies on the fact that a change in any balance sheet account can be analyzed in terms of changes in the other balance sheet accounts. Thus, by analyzing the noncash balance sheet accounts, those activities that resulted in cash flows can be identified. Although the noncash balance sheet accounts may be analyzed in any order, it is usually more efficient to begin with retained earnings. Additional data are obtained by analyzing the income statement accounts and supporting records.

Objective 4. Prepare a statement of cash flows, using the direct method.

The direct method and the indirect method will report the same amount of cash flows from operating activities. Also, the manner of reporting cash flows from investing and financing activities is the same under both methods. The methods differ in how the cash flows from operating activities data are obtained, analyzed, and reported. The direct method reports cash flows from operating activities by major classes of operating cash receipts and cash payments. The difference between the major classes of total operating cash receipts and total operating cash payments is the net cash flow from operating activities.

The data for reporting cash flows from operating activities by the direct method can be obtained by analyzing the cash flows related to the revenues and expenses reported on the income statement. The revenues and expenses are adjusted from the accrual basis of accounting to the cash basis for purposes of preparing the statement of cash flows.

When the direct method is used, a reconciliation of net income and net cash flow from operating activities is reported in a separate schedule. This schedule is similar to the cash flows from the operating activities section of the statement of cash flows prepared using the indirect method.

GLOSSARY OF KEY TERMS

Cash flows from financing activities. The section of the statement of cash flows that reports cash flows from transactions affecting the equity and debt of the entity. *Objective 2*

Cash flows from investing activities. The section of the statement of cash flows that reports cash flows from transactions affecting investments in noncurrent assets. *Objective 2*

Cash flows from operating activities. The section of the statement of cash flows that reports the cash transactions affecting the determination of net income. *Objective 2*

Direct method. A method of reporting the cash flows from operating activities as the difference between the operating cash receipts and the operating cash payments. *Objective 2*

Indirect method. A method of reporting the cash flows from operating activities as the net income from operations adjusted for all deferrals of past cash receipts and payments and all accruals of expected future cash receipts and payments. *Objective 2*

Statement of cash flows. A summary of the major cash receipts and cash payments for a period. *Objective 1*

ILLUSTRATIVE PROBLEM

The comparative balance sheet of Dowling Company for December 31, 1997 and 1996, is as follows:

Dowling Company
Comparative Balance Sheet
December 31, 1997 and 1996

	1997	*1996*
Assets		
Cash	$ 140,350	$ 95,900
Trade receivables (net)	95,300	102,300
Inventories	165,200	157,900
Prepaid expenses	6,240	5,860
Investments (long-term)	35,700	84,700
Land	75,000	90,000
Buildings	375,000	260,000
Accumulated depreciation—buildings	(71,300)	(58,300)
Machinery and equipment	428,300	428,300
Accumulated depreciation—machinery and equipment	(148,500)	(138,000)
Patents	58,000	65,000
Total assets	$1,159,290	$1,093,660
Liabilities and Stockholders' Equity		
Accounts payable (merchandise creditors)	$ 43,500	$ 46,700
Accrued expenses (operating expenses)	14,000	12,500
Income taxes payable	7,900	8,400
Dividends payable	14,000	10,000
Mortgage note payable, due 2001	40,000	0
Bonds payable	150,000	250,000
Common stock, $30 par	450,000	375,000
Excess of issue price over par—common stock	66,250	41,250
Retained earnings	373,640	349,810
Total liabilities and stockholders' equity	$1,159,290	$1,093,660

The income statement for Dowling Company is shown below.

Dowling Company
Income Statement
For the Year Ended December 31, 1997

Sales		$1,180,000
Cost of merchandise sold		790,000
Gross profit		$ 390,000
Operating expenses:		
Depreciation expense	$ 23,500	
Patent amortization	7,000	
Other operating expenses	196,000	
Total operating expenses		226,500
Income from operations		$ 163,500
Other income:		
Gain on sale of investments	$ 11,000	
Other expense:		
Interest expense	26,000	(15,000)
Income before income tax		$ 148,500
Income tax		50,000
Net income		$ 98,500

An examination of the accounting records revealed the following additional information applicable to 1997:

a. Land costing $15,000 was sold for $15,000.
b. A mortgage note was issued for $40,000.
c. A building costing $115,000 was constructed.
d. 2,500 shares of common stock were issued at 40 in exchange for the bonds payable.
e. Cash dividends declared were $74,670.

Instructions

1. Prepare a statement of cash flows, using the indirect method of reporting cash flows from operating activities.
2. Prepare a statement of cash flows, using the direct method of reporting cash flows from operating activities (without a schedule reconciling net income with cash flows from operating activities).

Solution

1.

Dowling Company
Statement of Cash Flows—Indirect Method
For the Year Ended December 31, 1997

Cash flows from operating activities:			
Net income, per income statement		$ 98,500	
Add: Depreciation	$ 23,500		
Amortization of patents	7,000		
Decrease in trade receivables	7,000		
Increase in accrued expenses	1,500	39,000	
		$137,500	
Deduct: Increase in inventories	$ 7,300		
Increase in prepaid expenses	380		
Decrease in accounts payable	3,200		
Decrease in income taxes payable	500		
Gain on sale of investments	11,000	22,380	
Net cash flow from operating activities			$115,120
Cash flows from investing activities:			
Cash received from sale of:			
Investments	$ 60,000		
Land	15,000	$ 75,000	
Less: Cash paid for construction of building		115,000	
Net cash flow used for investing activities			(40,000)
Cash flows from financing activities:			
Cash received from issuing mortgage note payable		$ 40,000	
Less: Cash paid for dividends		70,670	
Net cash flow provided by financing activities			(30,670)
Increase in cash			$ 44,450
Cash at the beginning of the year			95,900
Cash at the end of the year			$140,350

Schedule of Noncash Investing and Financing Activities:

Issued common stock to retire bonds payable	$100,000

2.

Dowling Company
Statement of Cash Flows—Direct Method
For the Year Ended December 31, 1997

Cash flows from operating activities:			
Cash received from customers[1]		$1,187,000	
Deduct: Cash paid for merchandise[2]	$800,500		
Cash paid for operating expenses[3]	194,880		
Cash paid for interest expense	26,000		
Cash paid for income tax[4]	50,500	1,071,880	
Net cash flow from operating activities			$115,120
Cash flows from investing activities:			
Cash received from sale of:			
Investments	$ 60,000		
Land	15,000	$ 75,000	
Less: Cash paid for construction of building		115,000	
Net cash flow used for investing activities			(40,000)
Cash flows from financing activities:			
Cash received from issuing mortgage note payable		$ 40,000	
Less: Cash paid for dividends[5]		70,670	
Net cash flow provided by financing activities			(30,670)
Increase in cash			$ 44,450
Cash at the beginning of the year			95,900
Cash at the end of the year			$140,350

Schedule of Noncash Investing and Financing Activities:

Issued common stock to retire bonds payable	$100,000

Computations: [1]**$1,180,000 + $7,000 = $1,187,000**
[2]**$790,000 + $3,200 + $7,300 = $800,500**
[3]**$196,000 + $380 – $1,500 = $194,880**
[4]**$50,000 + $500 = $50,500**
[5]**$74,670 + $10,000 – $14,000 = $70,670**

SELF-EXAMINATION QUESTIONS (ANSWERS AT END OF CHAPTER)

1. An example of a cash flow from an operating activity is:
   A. receipt of cash from issuing stock.
   B. receipt of cash from issuing bonds.
   C. payment of cash for dividends.
   D. receipt of cash from customers on account.

2. An example of a cash flow from an investing activity is:
   A. receipt of cash from the sale of equipment.
   B. receipt of cash from issuing stock.
   C. payment of cash for dividends.
   D. payment of cash to acquire treasury stock.

3. An example of a cash flow from a financing activity is:
   A. receipt of cash from customers on account.
   B. receipt of cash from the sale of equipment.
   C. payment of cash for dividends.
   D. payment of cash to acquire marketable securities.

4. Which of the following methods of reporting cash flows from operating activities adjusts net income for revenues and expenses not involving the receipt or payment of cash?
   A. Direct method C. Reciprocal method
   B. Purchase method D. Indirect method

5. The net income reported on the income statement for the year was $55,000, and depreciation of plant assets for the year was $22,000. The balances of the current asset and current liability accounts at the beginning and end of the year are as follows:

	End	*Beginning*
Cash	$ 65,000	$ 70,000
Trade receivables	100,000	90,000
Inventories	145,000	150,000
Prepaid expenses	7,500	8,000
Accounts payable (merchandise creditors)	51,000	58,000

The total amount reported for cash flows from operating activities in the statement of cash flows, using the indirect method, is:
   A. $33,000 C. $65,500
   B. $55,000 D. $77,000

DISCUSSION QUESTIONS

1. Which financial statement is most useful in evaluating past operations and in planning future investing and financing activities?
2. What are the three types of activities reported on the statement of cash flows?
3. Name the two alternative methods of reporting cash flows from operating activities in the statement of cash flows.
4. What is the principal disadvantage of the direct method of reporting cash flows from operating activities?
5. What are the major advantages of the indirect method of reporting cash flows from operating activities?
6. On the statement of cash flows, if the cash inflows from investing activities exceed the cash outflows, how is the difference described?
7. On the statement of cash flows, if the cash outflows from investing activities exceed the cash inflows, how is the difference described?
8. On the statement of cash flows, if the cash inflows from financing activities exceed the cash outflows, how is the difference described?
9. On the statement of cash flows, if the cash outflows from financing activities exceed the cash inflows, how is the difference described?
10. A corporation issued $200,000 of common stock in exchange for $200,000 of plant assets. Where would this transaction be reported on the statement of cash flows?
11. A corporation acquired as a long-term investment all of the stock of XL Co., valued at $5,000,000, by issuing $5,000,000 of its own common stock. Where should the transaction be reported on the statement of cash flows?
12. a. What is the effect on cash flows of declaring and issuing a stock dividend?
    b. Is the stock dividend reported on the statement of cash flows?
13. What is the effect on cash flows of appropriating retained earnings for bonded indebtedness?
14. A retail business, using the accrual method of accounting, owed merchandise creditors (accounts payable) $290,000 at the beginning of the year and $315,000 at the end of the year. How would the $25,000 increase be used to adjust net income in determining the amount of cash flows from operating activities by the indirect method? Explain.
15. If salaries payable was $75,000 at the beginning of the year and $65,000 at the end of the year, should $10,000 be added to or deducted from income to determine the amount of cash flows from operating activities by the indirect method? Explain.
16. A long-term investment in bonds with a cost of $75,000 was sold for $80,000 cash. (a) What was the gain or loss on the sale? (b) What was the effect of the transaction on cash flows? (c) How should the transaction be reported in the statement of cash flows if cash flows from operating activities are reported by the indirect method?
17. A corporation issued $5,000,000 of 20-year bonds for cash at 105. How would the transaction be reported on the statement of cash flows?
18. Fully depreciated equipment costing $55,000 was discarded. What was the effect of the transaction on cash flows if (a) $5,000 cash is received, (b) there is no salvage value?
19. For the current year, Accord Company decided to switch from the indirect method to the direct method for reporting cash flows from operating activities on the statement of cash flows. Will the change cause the amount of net cash flow from operating activities to be (a) larger, (b) smaller, or (c) the same as if the indirect method had been used? Explain.
20. Name five common major classes of operating cash receipts or operating cash payments presented on the statement of cash flows when the cash flows from operating activities are reported by the direct method.

21. In a recent annual report, PepsiCo, Inc., reported that during the year it issued treasury stock and debt of $162.7 million for acquisitions. How would this be reported on the statement of cash flows?

EXERCISES

EXERCISE 17–1
Cash flows from operating activities—net loss
Objective 2

On its income statement for the current year, Macon Company reported a net loss of $75,000 from operations. On its statement of cash flows, it reported $20,000 of cash flows from operating activities.

Explain this apparent contradiction between the loss and the positive cash flows.

EXERCISE 17–2
Effect of transactions on cash flows
Objective 2

State the effect (cash receipt or payment, and amount) of each of the following transactions, considered individually, on cash flows:

a. Sold a new issue of $100,000 of bonds at 101.
b. Sold equipment with a book value of $42,500 for $46,000.
c. Sold 5,000 shares of $30 par common stock for $45 per share.
d. Retired $500,000 of bonds, on which there was $2,500 of unamortized discount, for $501,000.
e. Purchased land for $120,000 cash.
f. Purchased 5,000 shares of $30 par common stock as treasury stock at $50 per share.
g. Paid dividends of $1.50 per share. There were 30,000 shares issued and 5,000 shares of treasury stock.
h. Purchased a building by paying $20,000 cash and issuing a $90,000 mortgage note payable.

EXERCISE 17–3
Classifying cash flows
Objective 2

Identify the type of cash flow activity for each of the following events (operating, investing, or financing):

a. Sold equipment.
b. Issued preferred stock.
c. Purchased patents.
d. Paid cash dividends.
e. Purchased treasury stock.
f. Redeemed bonds.
g. Issued bonds.
h. Net income.
i. Sold long-term investments.
j. Issued common stock.
k. Purchased buildings.

EXERCISE 17–4
Cash flows from operating activities—indirect method
Objectives 2, 3

Indicate whether each of the following would be added to or deducted from net income in determining net cash flow from operating activities by the indirect method:

a. Decrease in prepaid expenses
b. Amortization of patents
c. Decrease in salaries payable
d. Loss on disposal of plant assets
e. Decrease in accounts receivable
f. Increase in notes receivable due in 90 days
g. Amortization of discount on bonds payable
h. Increase in merchandise inventory
i. Depreciation of plant assets
j. Gain on retirement of long-term debt
k. Decrease in accounts payable
l. Increase in notes payable due in 90 days
m. Amortization of premium on bonds payable

EXERCISE 17–5
Cash flows from operating activities—indirect method
Objectives 2, 3

The net income reported on the income statement for the current year was $106,400. Depreciation recorded on equipment and a building amounted to $24,500 for the year. Balances of the current asset and current liability accounts at the beginning and end of the year are as follows:

	End of Year	Beginning of Year
Cash	$ 64,250	$ 60,500
Trade receivables (net)	98,750	92,500
Inventories	110,000	95,000
Prepaid expenses	6,400	7,650
Accounts payable (merchandise creditors)	77,200	72,700
Salaries payable	3,250	5,750

a. Prepare the cash flows from operating activities section of the statement of cash flows, using the indirect method.
b. If the direct method had been used, would the net cash flow from operating activities have been the same? Explain.

EXERCISE 17–6
Cash flows from operating activities—indirect method
Objectives 2, 3

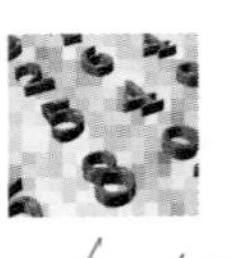

The net income reported on the income statement for the current year was $78,625. Depreciation recorded on store equipment for the year amounted to $29,250. Balances of the current asset and current liability accounts at the beginning and end of the year are as follows:

	End of Year	Beginning of Year
Cash	$ 70,150	$ 66,500
Trade receivables (net)	79,250	83,750
Merchandise inventory	110,000	102,000
Prepaid expenses	8,000	7,500
Accounts payable (merchandise creditors)	70,200	73,200
Wages payable	6,900	5,650

Prepare the cash flows from operating activities section of a statement of cash flows, using the indirect method.

EXERCISE 17–7
Determining cash payments to stockholders
Objectives 2, 3

The board of directors declared cash dividends totaling $160,000 during the current year. The comparative balance sheet indicates dividends payable of $30,000 at the beginning of the year and $40,000 at the end of the year. What was the amount of cash payments to stockholders during the year?

EXERCISE 17–8
Reporting changes in equipment on statement of cash flows
Objectives 2, 3

An analysis of the general ledger accounts indicates that office equipment, which had cost $75,000 and on which accumulated depreciation totaled $67,500 on the date of sale, was sold for $6,000 during the year. Using this information, indicate the items to be reported on the statement of cash flows.

EXERCISE 17–9
Reporting changes in equipment on statement of cash flows
Objectives 2, 3

An analysis of the general ledger accounts indicates that delivery equipment, which had cost $45,000 and on which accumulated depreciation totaled $39,000 on the date of sale, was sold for $8,000 during the year. Using this information, indicate the items to be reported on the statement of cash flows.

EXERCISE 17–10
Reporting land transactions on statement of cash flows
Objectives 2, 3

On the basis of the details of the following plant asset account, indicate the items to be reported on the statement of cash flows:

ACCOUNT LAND ACCOUNT NO.

Date		Item	Debit	Credit	Balance Debit	Balance Credit
19—						
Jan.	1	Balance			500,000	
Feb.	5	Purchased for cash	165,000		665,000	
Oct.	30	Sold for $70,000		50,000	615,000	

EXERCISE 17–11
Reporting stockholders' equity items on statement of cash flows
Objectives 2, 3

On the basis of the following stockholders' equity accounts, indicate the items, exclusive of net income, to be reported on the statement of cash flows. There were no unpaid dividends at either the beginning or the end of the year.

ACCOUNT COMMON STOCK, $10 PAR — ACCOUNT NO.

Date		Item	Debit	Credit	Balance Debit	Balance Credit
19—						
Jan.	1	Balance, 50,000 shares				500,000
Feb.	11	10,000 shares issued for cash		100,000		600,000
June	30	5,500-share stock dividend		55,000		655,000

ACCOUNT PAID-IN CAPITAL IN EXCESS OF PAR—COMMON STOCK — ACCOUNT NO.

Date		Item	Debit	Credit	Balance Debit	Balance Credit
19—						
Jan.	1	Balance				90,000
Feb.	11	10,000 shares issued for cash		40,000		130,000
June	30	Stock dividend		20,000		150,000

ACCOUNT RETAINED EARNINGS — ACCOUNT NO.

Date		Item	Debit	Credit	Balance Debit	Balance Credit
19—						
Jan.	1	Balance				275,000
June	30	Stock dividend	75,000			200,000
Dec.	30	Cash dividend	110,000			90,000
	31	Net income		195,000		285,000

EXERCISE 17–12
Reporting land acquisition for cash and mortgage note on statement of cash flows
Objectives 2, 3

On the basis of the details of the following asset account, indicate the items to be reported on the statement of cash flows:

ACCOUNT LAND — ACCOUNT NO.

Date		Item	Debit	Credit	Balance Debit	Balance Credit
19—						
Jan.	1	Balance			450,000	
Feb.	10	Purchased for cash	65,000		515,000	
Nov.	20	Purchased with long-term mortgage note	150,000		665,000	

EXERCISE 17–13
Determining net income from net cash flow from operating activities
Objectives 2, 3

Larado Inc. reported a net cash flow from operating activities of $61,250 on its statement of cash flows for the year ended December 31, 1997. The following information was reported in the cash flows from operating activities section of the statement of cash flows, using the indirect method:

Decrease in income tax payable	$ 750	Increase in accounts payable	$ 7,300
Decrease in inventories	4,500	Increase in prepaid expenses	500
Depreciation	10,600	Increase in trade receivables	4,700
Gain on sale of investments	11,750		

Determine the net income reported by Larado Inc. for the year ended December 31, 1997.

EXERCISE 17–14
Cash flows from operating activities—direct method
Objectives 2, 4

The cash flows from operating activities are reported by the direct method on the statement of cash flows. Determine the following:

a. If sales for the current year were $650,000 and trade receivables decreased by $25,000 during the year, what was the amount of cash received from customers?
b. If income tax for the current year was $80,000 and income tax payable decreased by $25,000 during the year, what was the amount of cash payments for income tax?

EXERCISE 17–15
Determining selected amounts for cash flows from operating activities—direct method
Objectives 2, 4

Selected data taken from the accounting records of D'George Company for the current year ended December 31 are as follows:

	Balance January 1	*Balance December 31*
Accrued expenses (operating expenses)	$12,000	$ 5,500
Accounts payable (merchandise creditors)	85,000	70,000
Inventories	62,500	53,500
Prepaid expenses	17,500	10,000

During the current year, the cost of merchandise sold was $940,000 and the operating expenses other than depreciation were $265,000. The direct method is used for presenting the cash flows from operating activities on the statement of cash flows.

Determine the amount reported on the statement of cash flows for (a) cash payments for merchandise and (b) cash payments for operating expenses.

EXERCISE 17–16
Cash flows from operating activities—direct method
Objectives 2, 4

The income statement of Trenton Company for the current year ended June 30 is as follows:

Sales		$995,000
Cost of merchandise sold		600,000
Gross profit		$395,000
Operating expenses:		
Depreciation expense	$ 31,500	
Other operating expenses	248,500	
Total operating expenses		280,000
Income before income tax		$115,000
Income tax		35,000
Net income		$ 80,000

Changes in the balances of selected accounts from the beginning to the end of the current year are as follows:

	*Increase Decrease**
Trade receivables (net)	$32,000*
Inventories	8,500
Prepaid expenses	1,750*
Accounts payable (merchandise creditors)	14,100*
Accrued expenses (operating expenses)	8,700
Income tax payable	5,800*

Prepare the cash flows from operating activities section of the statement of cash flows, using the direct method.

EXERCISE 17–17
Cash flows from operating activities—direct method
Objectives 2, 4

The income statement for Crowe Company for the current year ended June 30 and balances of selected accounts at the beginning and the end of the year are as follows:

Sales		$872,500
Cost of merchandise sold		500,000
Gross profit		$372,500
Operating expenses:		
Depreciation expense	$ 32,250	
Other operating expenses	213,750	
Total operating expenses		246,000
Income before income tax		$126,500
Income tax		32,500
Net income		$ 94,000

	End of Year	Beginning of Year
Trade receivables (net)	$ 90,000	$82,000
Inventories	102,500	85,000
Prepaid expenses	6,900	8,150
Accounts payable (merchandise creditors)	74,200	71,100
Accrued expenses (operating expenses)	3,750	5,850
Income tax payable	2,225	2,225

Prepare the cash flows from operating activities section of the statement of cash flows, using the direct method.

EXERCISE 17–18
Cash flows from operating activities—direct method
Objectives 2, 4

The income statement for the current year and balances of selected accounts at the beginning and end of the current year are as follows:

Sales		$1,400,000
Cost of merchandise sold		820,000
Gross profit		$ 580,000
Operating expenses:		
Depreciation expense	$ 54,000	
Other operating expenses	295,500	
Total operating expenses		349,500
Operating income		$ 230,500
Other expense:		
Interest expense		18,000
Income before income tax		$ 212,500
Income tax		78,000
Net income		$ 134,500

	End of Year	Beginning of Year
Trade receivables	$ 86,350	$ 92,450
Inventories	108,500	102,300
Prepaid expenses	8,900	8,300
Accounts payable (merchandise creditors)	81,250	88,300
Accrued expenses (operating expenses)	7,150	6,450
Interest payable	1,900	1,900
Income tax payable	4,400	5,400

Prepare the cash flows from operating activities section of the statement of cash flows, using the direct method.

EXERCISE 17–19
Cash flows from operating activities
Objectives 2, 4

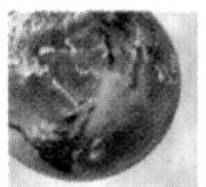

Selected data from the income statement and statement of cash flows of Toys "R" Us, Inc., for the year ending January 29, 1994, are as follows:

Income Statement Data (dollars in thousands)	
Net earnings	$482,953
Depreciation and amortization	133,370
Deferred taxes (expense)	36,534
Statement of Cash Flows Data (dollars in thousands)	
Increase in accounts receivable	$ 29,149
Increase in merchandise inventories	278,898
Increase in prepaid expenses and other operating assets	39,448
Increase in accounts payable, accrued expenses, and taxes	325,165
Increase in income tax payable	26,588

Prepare the cash flows from operating activities section of the statement of cash flows (using the indirect method) for Toys "R" Us, Inc., for the year ending January 29, 1994.

EXERCISE 17–20
Statement of cash flows
Objectives 2, 3, 4

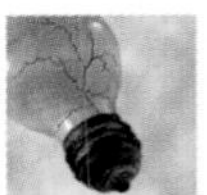

List the errors you find in the following statement of cash flows. The cash balance at the beginning of the year was $70,700. All other figures are correct.

Davenport Carpets
Statement of Cash Flows
For the Year Ended December 31, 19—

Cash flows from operating activities:			
Net income, per income statement		$100,500	
Add: Depreciation	$ 49,000		
Increase in trade receivables	9,500	58,500	
		$159,000	
Deduct: Increase in accounts payable	$ 4,400		
Increase in inventories	18,300		
Gain on sale of investments	5,000		
Decrease in accrued expenses	1,600	29,300	
Net cash flow from operating activities			$129,700
Cash flows from investing activities:			
Cash received from sale of investments		$ 85,000	
Less: Cash paid for purchase of land	$ 90,000		
Cash paid for purchase of equipment	150,100	240,100	
Net cash flow used for investing activities			(155,100)
Cash flows from financing activities:			
Cash received from sale of common stock		$107,000	
Plus cash paid for dividends		36,800	
Net cash flow provided by financing activities			143,800
Increase in cash			$118,400
Cash at the end of the year			105,300
Cash at the beginning of the year			$223,700

PROBLEMS SERIES A

PROBLEM 17–1A
Statement of cash flows—indirect method
Objective 3

The comparative balance sheet of Emerald Inc. for June 30, 1997 and 1996, is as follows:

	June 30, 1997	*June 30, 1996*
Assets		
Cash	$ 75,900	$ 69,200
Trade receivables (net)	104,800	93,500
Inventories	133,300	108,900
Investments	—	85,000
Land	112,000	—
Equipment	425,700	329,700
Accumulated depreciation	(171,800)	(137,200)
	$679,900	$549,100
Liabilities and Stockholders' Equity		
Accounts payable (merchandise creditors)	$ 71,600	$ 63,000
Accrued expenses (operating expenses)	6,100	5,000
Dividends payable	14,400	12,500
Common stock, $10 par	366,000	300,000
Paid-in capital in excess of par—common stock	31,400	19,400
Retained earnings	190,400	149,200
	$679,900	$549,100

The following additional information was taken from the records of Emerald Inc.:

a. Equipment and land were acquired for cash.
b. There were no disposals of equipment during the year.
c. The investments were sold for $100,000 cash.
d. The common stock was issued for cash.

e. There was a $94,300 credit to Retained Earnings for net income.
f. There was a $53,100 debit to Retained Earnings for cash dividends declared.

Instructions
Prepare a statement of cash flows, using the indirect method of presenting cash flows from operating activities.

PROBLEM 17–2A
Statement of cash flows—indirect method
Objective 3

The comparative balance sheet of Davis Inc. at June 30, 1997 and 1996, is as follows:

	June 30, 1997	*June 30, 1996*
Assets		
Cash	$ 43,300	$ 74,400
Trade receivables (net)	116,300	134,100
Merchandise inventory	351,200	346,400
Prepaid expenses	5,200	2,900
Plant assets	444,000	396,800
Accumulated depreciation—plant assets	(232,300)	(271,100)
	$727,700	$683,500
Liabilities and Stockholders' Equity		
Accounts payable (merchandise creditors)	$ 70,000	$ 65,400
Mortgage note payable	—	95,000
Common stock, $30 par	300,000	270,000
Paid-in capital in excess of par—common stock	39,800	34,800
Retained earnings	317,900	218,300
	$727,700	$683,500

Additional data obtained from the income statement and from an examination of the accounts in the ledger are as follows:

a. Net income, $139,600.
b. Depreciation reported on the income statement, $34,100.
c. An addition to the building was constructed at a cost of $120,100, and fully depreciated equipment costing $72,900 was discarded, with no salvage realized.
d. The mortgage note payable was not due until 2000, but the terms permitted earlier payment without penalty.
e. 1,000 shares of common stock were issued at 35 for cash.
f. Cash dividends declared and paid, $40,000.

Instructions
Prepare a statement of cash flows, using the indirect method of presenting cash flows from operating activities.

PROBLEM 17–3A
Statement of cash flows—indirect method
Objective 3

The comparative balance sheet of Olson Corporation at December 31, 1997 and 1996, is as follows:

	Dec. 31, 1997	*Dec. 31, 1996*
Assets		
Cash	$ 83,400	$ 76,800
Trade receivables (net)	94,300	100,500
Inventories	196,000	178,600
Prepaid expenses	6,400	2,900
Land	75,000	75,000
Buildings	465,300	316,800
Accumulated depreciation—buildings	(158,600)	(144,000)
Machinery and equipment	206,300	206,300
Accumulated depreciation—machinery & equip.	(92,000)	(81,300)
Patents	32,000	37,500
	$908,100	$769,100

	Dec. 31, 1997	Dec. 31, 1996
Liabilities and Stockholders' Equity		
Accounts payable (merchandise creditors)	$ 27,200	$ 38,900
Dividends payable	18,800	15,000
Salaries payable	7,900	14,600
Mortgage note payable, due 2001	105,000	—
Bonds payable	—	80,000
Common stock, $15 par	420,000	360,000
Paid-in capital in excess of par—common stock	65,000	45,000
Retained earnings	264,200	215,600
	$908,100	$769,100

An examination of the income statement and the accounting records revealed the following additional information applicable to 1997:

a. Net income, $76,100.
b. Depreciation expense reported on the income statement: buildings, $14,600; machinery and equipment, $10,700.
c. Patent amortization reported on the income statement, $5,500.
d. A building was constructed for $148,500.
e. A mortgage note for $105,000 was issued for cash.
f. 4,000 shares of common stock were issued at 20 in exchange for the bonds payable.
g. Cash dividends declared, $27,500.

Instructions
Prepare a statement of cash flows, using the indirect method of presenting cash flows from operating activities.

PROBLEM 17–4A
Statement of cash flows—indirect method
Objective 3

The comparative balance sheet of Addams Inc. at December 31, 1997 and 1996, is as follows:

	Dec. 31, 1997	Dec. 31, 1996
Assets		
Cash	$ 191,500	$ 81,400
Trade receivables (net)	165,000	151,700
Income tax refund receivable	9,000	—
Inventories	255,600	269,400
Prepaid expenses	9,300	11,100
Investments	70,000	250,000
Land	170,000	230,000
Buildings	950,000	450,000
Accumulated depreciation—buildings	(209,000)	(193,800)
Equipment	641,400	470,400
Accumulated depreciation—equipment	(234,400)	(205,700)
	$2,018,400	$1,514,500
Liabilities and Stockholders' Equity		
Accounts payable (merchandise creditors)	$ 96,000	$ 108,720
Income tax payable	—	10,880
Bonds payable	600,000	—
Discount on bonds payable	(29,000)	—
Common stock, $10 par	630,000	600,000
Paid-in capital in excess of par—common stock	81,000	72,000
Appropriation for plant expansion	280,000	230,000
Retained earnings	360,400	492,900
	$2,018,400	$1,514,500

The noncurrent asset, the noncurrent liability, and the stockholders' equity accounts for 1997 are as follows:

ACCOUNT INVESTMENTS ACCOUNT NO.

Date		Item	Debit	Credit	Balance Debit	Balance Credit
1997						
Jan.	1	Balance			250,000	
Mar.	22	Realized $240,000 cash from sale		180,000	70,000	

ACCOUNT LAND ACCOUNT NO.

Date		Item	Debit	Credit	Balance Debit	Balance Credit
1997						
Jan.	1	Balance			230,000	
April	20	Realized $70,000 cash from sale		60,000	170,000	

ACCOUNT BUILDINGS ACCOUNT NO.

Date		Item	Debit	Credit	Balance Debit	Balance Credit
1997						
Jan.	1	Balance			450,000	
April	20	Acquired for cash	500,000		950,000	

ACCOUNT ACCUMULATED DEPRECIATION—BUILDINGS ACCOUNT NO.

Date		Item	Debit	Credit	Balance Debit	Balance Credit
1997						
Jan.	1	Balance				193,800
Dec.	31	Depreciation for year		15,200		209,000

ACCOUNT EQUIPMENT ACCOUNT NO.

Date		Item	Debit	Credit	Balance Debit	Balance Credit
1997						
Jan.	1	Balance			470,400	
	26	Discarded, no salvage		35,000	435,400	
May	27	Purchased for cash	96,000		531,400	
Aug.	11	Purchased for cash	110,000		641,400	

ACCOUNT ACCUMULATED DEPRECIATION—EQUIPMENT ACCOUNT NO.

Date		Item	Debit	Credit	Balance Debit	Balance Credit
1997						
Jan.	1	Balance				205,700
	26	Equipment discarded	35,000			170,700
Dec.	31	Depreciation for year		63,700		234,400

ACCOUNT BONDS PAYABLE ACCOUNT NO.

Date		Item	Debit	Credit	Balance Debit	Balance Credit
1997						
May	1	Issued 20-year bonds		600,000		600,000

ACCOUNT DISCOUNT ON BONDS PAYABLE ACCOUNT NO.

Date		Item	Debit	Credit	Balance Debit	Balance Credit
1997						
May	1	Bonds issued	30,000		30,000	
Dec.	31	Amortization		1,000	29,000	

ACCOUNT COMMON STOCK, $10 PAR ACCOUNT NO.

Date		Item	Debit	Credit	Balance Debit	Balance Credit
1997						
Jan.	1	Balance				600,000
Dec.	7	Stock dividend		30,000		630,000

ACCOUNT PAID-IN CAPITAL IN EXCESS OF PAR—COMMON STOCK ACCOUNT NO.

Date		Item	Debit	Credit	Balance Debit	Balance Credit
1997						
Jan.	1	Balance				72,000
Dec.	7	Stock dividend		9,000		81,000

ACCOUNT APPROPRIATION FOR PLANT EXPANSION ACCOUNT NO.

Date		Item	Debit	Credit	Balance Debit	Balance Credit
1997						
Jan.	1	Balance				230,000
Dec.	31	Appropriation		50,000		280,000

ACCOUNT RETAINED EARNINGS ACCOUNT NO.

Date		Item	Debit	Credit	Balance Debit	Balance Credit
1997						
Jan.	1	Balance				492,900
Dec.	7	Stock dividend	39,000			453,900
	31	Net loss	11,500			442,400
	31	Cash dividends	32,000			410,400
	31	Appropriated	50,000			360,400

Instructions

Prepare a statement of cash flows, using the indirect method of presenting cash flows from operating activities.

PROBLEM 17–5A
Statement of cash flows—direct method
Objective 4

The comparative balance sheet of D. E. Frank Inc. for December 31, 1996 and 1997, is as follows:

	Dec. 31, 1997	*Dec. 31, 1996*
Assets		
Cash	$148,700	$ 25,500
Trade receivables (net)	92,500	80,000
Inventories	100,200	91,400
Investments	—	75,000
Land	30,000	—
Equipment	330,000	275,000
Accumulated depreciation	(156,000)	(114,000)
	$545,400	$432,900

Liabilities and Stockholders' Equity		
Accounts payable (merchandise creditors)	$ 63,000	$ 57,000
Accrued expenses (operating expenses)	4,500	7,000
Dividends payable	15,000	10,000
Common stock, $40 par	320,000	250,000
Paid-in capital in excess of par—common stock	17,000	12,000
Retained earnings	125,900	96,900
	$545,400	$432,900

The income statement for the year ended December 31, 1997, is as follows:

Sales		$956,500
Cost of merchandise sold		585,500
Gross profit		$371,000
Operating expenses:		
Depreciation expense	$ 42,000	
Other operating expenses	290,000	
Total operating expenses		332,000
Operating income		$ 39,000
Other income:		
Gain on sale of investments		15,000
Income before income tax		$ 54,000
Income tax		10,000
Net income		$ 44,000

The following additional information was taken from the records:

a. Equipment and land were acquired for cash.
b. There were no disposals of equipment during the year.
c. The investments were sold for $90,000 cash.
d. The common stock was issued for cash.
e. There was a $15,000 debit to Retained Earnings for cash dividends declared.

Instructions

Prepare a statement of cash flows, using the direct method of presenting cash flows from operating activities.

PROBLEM 17–6A
Statement of cash flows—direct method applied to Problem 17–1A
Objective 4

The comparative balance sheet of Emerald Inc. for June 30, 1997 and 1996, is as follows:

	June 30, 1997	June 30, 1996
Assets		
Cash	$ 75,900	$ 69,200
Trade receivables (net)	104,800	93,500
Inventories	133,300	108,900
Investments	—	85,000
Land	112,000	—
Equipment	425,700	329,700
Accumulated depreciation	(171,800)	(137,200)
	$679,900	$549,100
Liabilities and Stockholders' Equity		
Accounts payable (merchandise creditors)	$ 71,600	$ 63,000
Accrued expenses (operating expenses)	6,100	5,000
Dividends payable	14,400	12,500
Common stock, $10 par	366,000	300,000
Paid-in capital in excess of par—common stock	31,400	19,400
Retained earnings	190,400	149,200
	$679,900	$549,100

The income statement for the year ended June 30, 1997, is as follows:

Sales		$980,000
Cost of merchandise sold		530,000
Gross profit		$450,000
Operating expenses:		
Depreciation expense	$ 34,600	
Other operating expenses	285,000	
Total operating expenses		319,600
Operating income		$130,400
Other income:		
Gain on sale of investments		15,000
Income before income tax		$145,400
Income tax		51,100
Net income		$ 94,300

The following additional information was taken from the records of Emerald Inc.:

a. Equipment and land were acquired for cash.
b. There were no disposals of equipment during the year.
c. The investments were sold for $100,000.
d. The common stock was issued for cash.
e. There was a $53,100 debit to Retained Earnings for cash dividends declared.

Instructions

Prepare a statement of cash flows, using the direct method of presenting cash flows from operating activities.

PROBLEM 17–7A
Statement of cash flows—direct and indirect methods
Objectives 3, 4

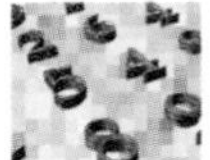

A comparative balance sheet and an income statement for Freehold Company are as follows:

Freehold Company
Comparative Balance Sheet
December 31, 1997 and 1996

	1997	*1996*
Assets		
Cash	$ 50,210	$ 66,200
Trade receivables (net)	142,900	117,800
Inventories	209,600	190,150
Prepaid expenses	5,160	6,120
Investments	69,900	93,500
Land	104,000	75,000
Buildings	425,000	225,000
Accumulated depreciation—buildings	(93,600)	(81,220)
Equipment	486,500	437,500
Accumulated depreciation—equipment	(184,500)	(149,750)
Total assets	$1,215,170	$980,300
Liabilities and Stockholders' Equity		
Accounts payable (merchandise creditors)	$ 58,715	$ 51,875
Accrued expenses (operating expenses)	12,000	10,500
Interest payable	1,875	1,875
Income tax payable	4,800	8,500
Dividends payable	15,660	12,500
Mortgage note payable	195,000	—
Bonds payable	90,000	250,000
Common stock, $25 par	450,000	375,000
Paid-in capital in excess of par—common stock	47,250	41,250
Retained earnings	339,870	228,800
Total liabilities and stockholders' equity	$1,215,170	$980,300

Freehold Company
Income Statement
For the Year Ended December 31, 1997

Sales		$1,710,000
Cost of merchandise sold		1,250,000
Gross profit		$ 460,000
Operating expenses:		
Depreciation expense	$ 47,130	
Other operating expenses	234,000	
Total operating expenses		281,130
Operating income		$ 178,870
Other income:		
Gain on sale of land	$ 19,000	
Gain on sale of investments	19,200	
	$ 38,200	
Other expense:		
Interest expense	28,000	10,200
Income before income tax		$ 189,070
Income tax		38,000
Net income		$ 151,070

The following additional information on cash flows during the year was obtained from an examination of the ledger:

a. Investments (long-term) were purchased for $53,100.
b. Investments (long-term) costing $76,700 were sold for $95,900.
c. Equipment was purchased for $49,000. There were no disposals.
d. A building valued at $200,000 and land valued at $100,000 were acquired by a cash payment of $300,000.
e. Land which cost $71,000 was sold for $90,000 cash.
f. A mortgage note payable for $195,000 was issued for cash.
g. Bonds payable of $160,000 were retired by the payment of their face amount.
h. 3,000 shares of common stock were issued for cash at 27.
i. Cash dividends of $40,000 were declared.

Instructions

1. Prepare a statement of cash flows, using the direct method of presenting cash flows from operating activities.
2. Prepare a statement of cash flows, using the indirect method of presenting cash flows from operating activities.
3. Which method of reporting cash flows from operating activities is more widely used? Explain.

PROBLEMS SERIES B

PROBLEM 17–1B
Statement of cash flows—indirect method
Objective 3

The comparative balance sheet of Jasper Inc. for December 31, 1997 and 1996, is as follows:

	Dec. 31, 1997	Dec. 31, 1996
Assets		
Cash	$ 97,500	$ 51,600
Trade receivables (net)	123,200	110,500
Inventories	146,200	128,100
Investments	—	91,000
Land	70,000	—
Equipment	874,600	724,500
Accumulated depreciation—equipment	(211,800)	(159,600)
	$1,099,700	$946,100

	Dec. 31, 1997	Dec. 31, 1996
Liabilities and Stockholders' Equity		
Accounts payable (merchandise creditors)	$ 75,000	$ 70,600
Accrued expenses (operating expenses)	4,800	7,100
Dividends payable	20,000	14,000
Common stock, $10 par	450,000	350,000
Paid-in capital in excess of par—common stock	23,800	16,800
Retained earnings	526,100	487,600
	$1,099,700	$946,100

The following additional information was taken from the records:

a. The investments were sold for $105,000 cash.
b. Equipment and land were acquired for cash.
c. There were no disposals of equipment during the year.
d. The common stock was issued for cash.
e. There was a $93,500 credit to Retained Earnings for net income.
f. There was a $55,000 debit to Retained Earnings for cash dividends declared.

Instructions

Prepare a statement of cash flows, using the indirect method of presenting cash flows from operating activities.

PROBLEM 17–2B
Statement of cash flows—indirect method
Objective 3

The comparative balance sheet of King Corporation at December 31, 1997 and 1996, is as follows:

	Dec. 31, 1997	Dec. 31, 1996
Assets		
Cash	$ 74,700	$ 77,400
Trade receivables (net)	69,300	76,200
Merchandise inventory	126,300	97,400
Prepaid expenses	7,660	4,960
Plant assets	472,440	425,240
Accumulated depreciation—plant assets	(145,100)	(157,500)
	$605,300	$523,700
Liabilities and Stockholders' Equity		
Accounts payable (merchandise creditors)	$ 68,500	$ 53,500
Mortgage note payable	—	75,000
Common stock, $25 par	300,000	250,000
Paid-in capital in excess of par—common stock	34,500	31,500
Retained earnings	202,300	113,700
	$605,300	$523,700

Additional data obtained from the income statement and from an examination of the accounts in the ledger are as follows:

a. Net income, $98,600.
b. Depreciation reported on the income statement, $41,200.
c. An addition to the building was constructed at a cost of $100,800, and fully depreciated equipment costing $53,600 was discarded, with no salvage realized.
d. The mortgage note payable was not due until 2003, but the terms permitted earlier payment without penalty.
e. 2,000 shares of common stock were issued at 26.50 for cash.
f. Cash dividends declared and paid, $10,000.

Instructions

Prepare a statement of cash flows, using the indirect method of presenting cash flows from operating activities.

PROBLEM 17–3B
Statement of cash flows—indirect method
Objective 3

The comparative balance sheet of Paxton Corporation at December 31, 1997 and 1996, is as follows:

	Dec. 31, 1997	*Dec. 31, 1996*
Assets		
Cash	$ 91,400	$ 33,400
Trade receivables (net)	86,100	68,000
Inventories	126,600	141,700
Prepaid expenses	4,500	3,100
Land	65,000	65,000
Buildings	381,500	291,500
Accumulated depreciation—buildings	(152,800)	(143,400)
Machinery and equipment	300,500	300,500
Accumulated depreciation—machinery and equipment	(105,000)	(71,500)
Patents	32,500	38,500
	$830,300	$726,800
Liabilities and Stockholders' Equity		
Accounts payable (merchandise creditors)	$ 58,800	$ 72,400
Dividends payable	9,400	8,250
Salaries payable	5,000	5,450
Mortgage note payable, due 2005	70,000	—
Bonds payable	—	110,000
Common stock, $10 par	450,000	350,000
Paid-in capital in excess of par—common stock	80,000	70,000
Retained earnings	157,100	110,700
	$830,300	$726,800

An examination of the income statement and the accounting records revealed the following additional information applicable to 1997:

a. Net income, $81,400.
b. Depreciation expense reported on the income statement: buildings, $9,400; machinery and equipment, $33,500.
c. A building was constructed for $90,000.
d. Patent amortization reported on the income statement, $6,000.
e. A mortgage note for $70,000 was issued for cash.
f. 10,000 shares of common stock were issued at 11 in exchange for the bonds payable.
g. Cash dividends declared, $35,000.

Instructions

Prepare a statement of cash flows, using the indirect method of presenting cash flows from operating activities.

PROBLEM 17–4B
Statement of cash flows—indirect method
Objective 3

The comparative balance sheet of Jenkins Inc. at December 31, 1997 and 1996, is as follows:

	Dec. 31, 1997	*Dec. 31, 1996*
Assets		
Cash	$ 31,200	$ 38,800
Trade receivables (net)	63,400	54,100
Inventories	134,250	121,000
Prepaid expenses	3,850	4,100
Investments	—	45,000
Land	28,500	28,500
Buildings	201,000	126,000
Accumulated depreciation—buildings	(47,400)	(41,400)
Equipment	296,200	239,500
Accumulated depreciation—equipment	(72,800)	(77,400)
	$638,200	$538,200

	Dec. 31, 1997	Dec. 31, 1996
Liabilities and Stockholders' Equity		
Accounts payable (merchandise creditors)	$ 39,500	$ 48,300
Income tax payable	3,600	2,800
Bonds payable	70,000	—
Discount on bonds payable	(2,900)	—
Common stock, $20 par	315,000	300,000
Paid-in capital in excess of par—common stock	40,200	33,000
Appropriation for plant expansion	50,000	30,000
Retained earnings	122,800	124,100
	$638,200	$538,200

The noncurrent asset, the noncurrent liability, and the stockholders' equity accounts for 1997 are as follows:

ACCOUNT INVESTMENTS ACCOUNT NO.

Date		Item	Debit	Credit	Balance Debit	Balance Credit
1997						
Jan.	1	Balance			45,000	
Mar.	5	Realized $38,000 cash from sale		45,000	—	—

ACCOUNT LAND ACCOUNT NO.

Date		Item	Debit	Credit	Balance Debit	Balance Credit
1997						
Jan.	1	Balance			28,500	

ACCOUNT BUILDINGS ACCOUNT NO.

Date		Item	Debit	Credit	Balance Debit	Balance Credit
1997						
Jan.	1	Balance			126,000	
July	1	Acquired for cash	75,000		201,000	

ACCOUNT ACCUMULATED DEPRECIATION—BUILDINGS ACCOUNT NO.

Date		Item	Debit	Credit	Balance Debit	Balance Credit
1997						
Jan.	1	Balance				41,400
Dec.	31	Depreciation for year		6,000		47,400

ACCOUNT EQUIPMENT ACCOUNT NO.

Date		Item	Debit	Credit	Balance Debit	Balance Credit
1997						
Jan.	1	Balance			239,500	
Mar.	1	Discarded, no salvage		21,000	218,500	
	5	Purchased for cash	50,000		268,500	
Dec.	1	Purchased for cash	27,700		296,200	

ACCOUNT ACCUMULATED DEPRECIATION—EQUIPMENT ACCOUNT NO.

Date		Item	Debit	Credit	Balance Debit	Balance Credit
1997						
Jan.	1	Balance				77,400
Mar.	1	Equipment discarded	21,000			56,400
Dec.	31	Depreciation for year		16,400		72,800

ACCOUNT BONDS PAYABLE ACCOUNT NO.

Date		Item	Debit	Credit	Balance Debit	Balance Credit
1997						
May	1	Issued 20-year bonds		70,000		70,000

ACCOUNT DISCOUNT ON BONDS PAYABLE ACCOUNT NO.

Date		Item	Debit	Credit	Balance Debit	Balance Credit
1997						
May	1	Bonds issued	3,000		3,000	
Dec.	31	Amortization		100	2,900	

ACCOUNT COMMON STOCK, $10 PAR ACCOUNT NO.

Date		Item	Debit	Credit	Balance Debit	Balance Credit
1997						
Jan.	1	Balance				300,000
June	29	Stock dividend		15,000		315,000

ACCOUNT PAID-IN CAPITAL IN EXCESS OF PAR—COMMON STOCK ACCOUNT NO.

Date		Item	Debit	Credit	Balance Debit	Balance Credit
1997						
Jan.	1	Balance				33,000
June	29	Stock dividend		7,200		40,200

ACCOUNT APPROPRIATION FOR PLANT EXPANSION ACCOUNT NO.

Date		Item	Debit	Credit	Balance Debit	Balance Credit
1997						
Jan.	1	Balance				30,000
Dec.	31	Appropriation		20,000		50,000

ACCOUNT RETAINED EARNINGS ACCOUNT NO.

Date		Item	Debit	Credit	Balance Debit	Balance Credit
1997						
Jan.	1	Balance				124,100
June	29	Stock dividend	22,200			101,900
Dec.	31	Net income		65,900		167,800
	31	Cash dividends	25,000			142,800
	31	Appropriated	20,000			122,800

Instructions
Prepare a statement of cash flows, using the indirect method of presenting cash flows from operating activities.

PROBLEM 17–5B
Statement of cash flows—direct method
Objective 4

The comparative balance sheet of D. Jacobs Co. for December 31, 1997 and 1996, is as follows:

	Dec. 31, 1997	*Dec. 31, 1996*
Assets		
Cash	$ 42,900	$ 74,900
Trade receivables (net)	94,500	80,000
Inventories	100,100	90,500
Investments	—	45,000
Land	75,000	—
Equipment	382,400	282,400
Accumulated depreciation	(144,000)	(119,000)
	$550,900	$453,800
Liabilities and Stockholders' Equity		
Accounts payable (merchandise creditors)	$ 58,400	$ 55,000
Accrued expenses (operating expenses)	5,000	4,000
Dividends payable	12,000	10,000
Common stock, $20 par	300,000	250,000
Paid-in capital in excess of par—common stock	22,000	12,000
Retained earnings	153,500	122,800
	$550,900	$453,800

The income statement for the year ended December 31, 1997, is as follows:

Sales		$940,000
Cost of merchandise sold		520,000
Gross profit		$420,000
Operating expenses:		
Depreciation expense	$ 25,000	
Other operating expenses	310,000	
Total operating expenses		335,000
Operating income		$ 85,000
Other income:		
Gain on sale of investments		10,000
Income before income tax		$ 95,000
Income tax		35,800
Net income		$ 59,200

The following additional information was taken from the records:

a. Equipment and land were acquired for cash.
b. There were no disposals of equipment during the year.
c. The investments were sold for $55,000 cash.
d. The common stock was issued for cash.
e. There was a $28,500 debit to Retained Earnings for cash dividends declared.

Instructions
Prepare a statement of cash flows, using the direct method of presenting cash flows from operating activities.

PROBLEM 17–6B
Statement of cash flows—direct method applied to Problem 17–1B
Objective 4

The comparative balance sheet of Jasper Inc. for December 31, 1997 and 1996, is as follows:

Jasper Inc.
Comparative Balance Sheet
December 31, 1997 and 1996

	Dec. 31, 1997	Dec. 31, 1996
Assets		
Cash	$ 97,500	$ 51,600
Trade receivables (net)	123,200	110,500
Inventories	146,200	128,100
Investments	—	91,000
Land	70,000	—
Equipment	874,600	724,500
Accumulated depreciation	(211,800)	(159,600)
	$1,099,700	$946,100
Liabilities and Stockholders' Equity		
Accounts payable (merchandise creditors)	$ 75,000	$ 70,600
Accrued expenses (operating expenses)	4,800	7,100
Dividends payable	20,000	14,000
Common stock, $10 par	450,000	350,000
Paid-in capital in excess of par—common stock	23,800	16,800
Retained earnings	526,100	487,600
	$1,099,700	$946,100

The income statement for the year ended December 31, 1997, is as follows:

Jasper Inc.
Income Statement
For the Year Ended December 31, 1997

Sales		$1,230,000
Cost of merchandise sold		795,300
Gross profit		$ 434,700
Operating expenses:		
Depreciation expense	$ 52,200	
Other operating expenses	255,000	
Total operating expenses		307,200
Operating income		$ 127,500
Other income:		
Gain on sale of investments		14,000
Income before income tax		$ 141,500
Income tax		48,000
Net income		$ 93,500

The following additional information was taken from the records:

a. The investments were sold for $105,000 cash at the beginning of the year.
b. Equipment and land were acquired for cash.
c. There were no disposals of equipment during the year.
d. The common stock was issued for cash.
e. There was a $55,000 debit to Retained Earnings for cash dividends declared.

Instructions

Prepare a statement of cash flows, using the direct method of presenting cash flows from operating activities.

PROBLEM 17–7B
Statement of cash flows—direct and indirect methods
Objectives 3, 4

An income statement and a comparative balance sheet for Comstock Company are as follows:

Comstock Company
Income Statement
For the Year Ended December 31, 1997

Sales		$1,350,000
Cost of merchandise sold		980,000
Gross profit		$ 370,000
Operating expenses:		
Depreciation expense	$ 27,200	
Other operating expenses	182,000	
Total operating expenses		209,200
		$ 160,800
Other income:		
Gain on sale of land	$ 35,000	
Gain on sale of investments	22,500	
	$ 57,500	
Other expense:		
Interest expense	27,500	30,000
Income before income tax		$ 190,800
Income tax		65,000
Net income		$ 125,800

Comstock Company
Comparative Balance Sheet
December 31, 1997 and 1996

	1997	*1996*
Assets		
Cash	$ 180,570	$ 60,700
Trade receivables (net)	128,500	116,700
Inventories	215,400	188,050
Prepaid expenses	5,160	6,120
Investments	40,600	93,500
Land	85,000	75,000
Buildings	425,000	225,000
Accumulated depreciation—buildings	(92,420)	(81,220)
Equipment	485,900	437,500
Accumulated depreciation—equipment	(165,750)	(149,750)
Total assets	$1,307,960	$971,600
Liabilities and Stockholders' Equity		
Accounts payable (merchandise creditors)	$ 57,200	$ 48,300
Accrued expenses (operating expenses)	12,000	11,000
Interest payable	3,000	3,000
Income tax payable	6,250	9,750
Dividends payable	15,660	12,500
Mortgage note payable	225,000	—
Bonds payable	175,000	250,000
Common stock, $25 par	450,000	375,000
Paid-in capital in excess of par—common stock	47,250	41,250
Retained earnings	316,600	220,800
Total liabilities and stockholders' equity	$1,307,960	$971,600

The following additional information on cash flows during the year was obtained from an examination of the ledger:

a. Investments (long-term) were purchased for $36,600.
b. Investments (long-term) costing $89,500 were sold for $112,000.
c. Equipment was purchased for $48,400. There were no disposals.

d. A building valued at $200,000 and land valued at $50,000 were acquired by a cash payment of $250,000.
e. Land which cost $40,000 was sold for $75,000 cash.
f. A mortgage note payable for $225,000 was issued for cash.
g. Bonds payable of $75,000 were retired by the payment of their face amount.
h. 3,000 shares of common stock were issued for cash at 27.
i. Cash dividends of $30,000 were declared.

Instructions

1. Prepare a statement of cash flows, using the direct method of presenting cash flows from operating activities.
2. Prepare a statement of cash flows, using the indirect method of presenting cash flows from operating activities.
3. Which method of reporting cash flows from operating activities is more widely used? Explain.

CASES

CASE 17–1
Fashion King Inc.
Operating cash flow per share

Ben Howard, president of Fashion King Inc., believes that reporting operating cash flow per share on the income statement would be a useful addition to the company's just completed financial statements. The following discussion took place between Ben Howard and Fashion King's controller, Kim Lang, in January, after the close of the fiscal year.

Ben: I have been reviewing our financial statements for the last year. I am disappointed that our net income per share has dropped by 10% from last year. This is not going to look good to our shareholders. Isn't there anything we can do about this?

Kim: What do you mean? The past is the past, and the numbers are in. There isn't much that can be done about it. Our financial statements were prepared according to generally accepted accounting principles, and I don't see much leeway for significant change at this point.

Ben: No, no. I'm not suggesting that we "cook the books." But look at the cash flow from operations on the statement of cash flows. The cash flow from operations has increased by 20%. This is very good news—and, I might add, useful information. The higher cash flow from operations will give our creditors comfort.

Kim: Well, the cash flow from operations is on the statement of cash flows, so I guess users will be able to see the improved cash flow figures there.

Ben: This is true, but somehow I feel that this information should be given a much higher profile. I don't like this information being "buried" in the statement of cash flows. You know as well as I do that many users will focus on the income statement. Therefore, I think we ought to include an operating cash flow per share number on the face of the income statement—someplace under the earnings per share number. In this way users will get the complete picture of our operating performance. Yes, our earnings per share dropped this year, but our cash flow from operations improved! And all the information is in one place where users can see and compare the figures. What do you think?

Kim: I've never really thought about it like that before. I guess we could put the operating cash flow per share on the income statement under the earnings per share. Users would really benefit from this disclosure. Thanks for the idea—I'll get working on it.

Ben: Glad to be of service.

How would you interpret this situation? Is Kim following professional ethics?

CASE 17–2
DiscArt Inc.
Using the statement of cash flows

You are considering an investment in a new start-up software company, DiscArt Inc. A review of the company's financial statements reveals a negative retained earnings. In addition, it appears as though the company has been running a negative cash flow from operations since the company's inception.

How is the company staying in business under these circumstances? Could this be a good investment?

CASE 17–3
Walker Company
Analysis of cash flow from operations

The Retailing Division of Walker Company provided the following information on its cash flow from operations:

Net income	$ 450,000
Increase in accounts receivable	(340,000)
Increase in inventory	(300,000)
Decrease in accounts payable	(90,000)
Depreciation	100,000
Cash flow from operations	$(180,000)

The manager of the Retailing Division provided the accompanying memo with this report:

From: Senior Vice-President, Retailing Division

I am pleased to report that we had earnings of $450,000 over the last period. This resulted in a return on invested capital of 10%, which is near our targets for this division. I have been aggressive in building the revenue volume in the division. As a result, I am happy to report that we have increased the number of new credit card customers as a result of an aggressive marketing campaign. In addition, we have found some excellent merchandise opportunities. Some of our suppliers have made some of their apparel merchandise available at a deep discount. We have purchased as much of these goods as possible in order to improve profitability. I'm also happy to report that our vendor payment problems have improved. We are nearly caught up on our overdue payables balances.

Comment on the Senior Vice-President's memo in light of the cash flow information.

CASE 17–4
Delta Air Lines
Analysis of statement of cash flows

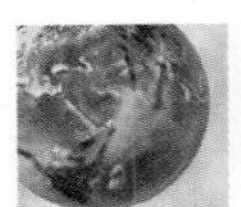

The following is a condensed version of Delta Air Line's statement of cash flows for the years ended June 30, 1990–1992.

Delta Air Lines
Statement of Cash Flows (Condensed, 000s)
For the Years Ended June 30, 1992, 1991, 1990

	1992	1991	1990
Cash Flows from Operations:			
Net Income	$ (506,318)	$ (324,380)	$ 302,783
Add: Depreciation	634,528	521,457	459,162
Increase in current liabilities	527,916	327,737	(21,772)
Other items	248,791	166,941	157,896
Deduct: Decrease (increase) in accounts receivable	(420,886)	(106,699)	26,049
Increase in prepaid expenses and other current assets	(69,108)	(72,350)	(30,510)
Gain on sale of flight equipment	(34,563)	(16,843)	(17,906)
Other items	(230,846)	(172,073)	(71,936)
Net cash provided by operations	$ 149,514	$ 323,790	$ 803,766
Cash Flows from Investing Activities:			
Property and equipment additions	$(2,481,008)	$(2,144,583)	(1,689,534)
Proceeds from sale of flight equipment	42,693	24,764	29,980
Investments in equity securities	(17)	0	(314,515)
Purchase of Pan Am	(531,000)	0	0
Purchase of leasehold and operating rights	(69,786)	(51,885)	0
Net cash provided by investing activities	$(3,039,118)	$(2,171,704)	$(1,974,069)
Cash Flows from Financing Activities:			
Issuance of long-term obligations	$ 1,500,000	$ 1,050,000	$ 781,400
Sale of treasury stock	0	476,005	0
Issuance of common stock	1,740	1,288	376,157
Net short-term borrowings	744,672	(9,331)	65,351
Repurchase of common stock	0	(220,796)	(591,154)
Payments on noncurrent obligations	(793,619)	(322,169)	(145,004)
Cash dividends	(89,372)	(83,838)	(113,647)
Proceeds from sale and leaseback transactions	812,894	1,652,000	336,000
Net cash provided by financial activities	$ 2,176,315	$ 2,543,159	$ 709,103
Net Increase (Decrease) in Cash	$ (713,289)	$ 695,245	$ (461,200)

a. 1. Is Delta Air Line's performance improving or deteriorating over the 1990–1992 time period?
2. Cash increased nearly $700 million in 1991, then fell around the same amount in 1992. What caused this reversal?
3. Explain how Delta is able to have over a $500 million loss for 1992, but still have positive cash flow from operations.
4. Why is "gain on sale of flight equipment" subtracted in determining the cash flow from operations?
5. Does Delta appear to be reducing its fleet purchases? Where is the money coming from to purchase aircraft?

b. What do you think a sale and leaseback transaction is?

CASE 17–5
A. W. Hoyt Inc.
Anaylsis of statement of cash flows

Alan Hoyt is the president and majority shareholder of A. W. Hoyt Inc., a small retail store chain. Recently, Hoyt submitted a loan application for A. W. Hoyt Inc. to Bonita National Bank. It called for a $200,000, 11%, ten-year loan to help finance the construction of a building and the purchase of store equipment, costing a total of $250,000 to enable A. W. Hoyt Inc. to open a store in Bonita. Land for this purpose was acquired last year. The bank's loan officer requested a statement of cash flows in addition to the most recent income statement, balance sheet, and retained earnings statement that Hoyt had submitted with the loan application.

As a close family friend, Hoyt asked you to prepare a statement of cash flows. From the records provided, you prepared the following statement.

A. W. Hoyt Inc.
Statement of Cash Flows
For the Year Ended December 31, 19—

Cash flows from operating activities:			
Net income, per income statement		$ 86,400	
Add: Depreciation	$31,000		
Decrease in trade receivables	11,500	42,500	
		$128,900	
Deduct: Increase in inventory	$12,000		
Increase in prepaid expenses	1,500		
Decrease in accounts payable	3,000		
Gain on sale of investments	7,500	24,000	
Net cash flow from operating activities			$104,900
Cash flows from investing activities:			
Cash received from investments sold		$ 42,500	
Less: Cash paid for purchase of store equipment		31,000	
Net cash flow from investing activities			11,500
Cash flows from financing activities:			
Cash paid for dividends		$ 40,000	
Net cash flow used for financing activities			(40,000)
Increase in cash			$ 76,400
Cash at the beginning of the year			27,500
Cash at the end of the year			$103,900
Schedule of Noncash Financing and Investing Activities:			
Issued common stock at par for land			$ 40,000

After reviewing the statement, Hoyt telephoned you and commented, "Are you sure this statement is right?" Hoyt then raised the following questions:

a. "How can depreciation be a cash flow?"
b. "The issuing of common stock for the land is listed in a separate schedule. This transaction has nothing to do with cash! Shouldn't this transaction be eliminated from the statement?"
c. "How can the gain on sale of investments be a deduction from net income in determining the cash flow from operating activities?"
d. "Why does the bank need this statement anyway? They can compute the increase in cash from the balance sheets for the last two years."

After jotting down Hoyt's questions, you assured him that this statement was "right." However, to alleviate Hoyt's concern, you arranged a meeting for the following day.

1. How would you respond to each of Hoyt's questions?
2. Do you think that the statement of cash flows enhances the chances of A. W. Hoyt Inc. receiving the loan? Discuss.

ANSWERS TO SELF-EXAMINATION QUESTIONS

1. **D** Cash flows from operating activities affect transactions that enter into the determination of net income, such as the receipt of cash from customers on account (answer D). Receipts of cash from issuing stock (answer A) and issuing bonds (answer B) and payments of cash for dividends (answer C) are cash flows from financing activities.
2. **A** Cash flows from investing activities include receipts from the sale of noncurrent assets, such as equipment (answer A), and payments to acquire noncurrent assets. Receipts of cash from issuing stock (answer B) and payments of cash for dividends (answer C) and to acquire treasury stock (answer D) are cash flows from financing activities.
3. **C** Payment of cash dividends (answer C) is an example of a financing activity. The receipt of cash from customers on account (answer A) is an operating activity. The receipt of cash from the sale of equipment (answer B) is an investing activity. The payment of cash to acquire marketable securities (answer D) is an example of an investing activity.
4. **D** The indirect method (answer D) reports cash flows from operating activities by beginning with net income and adjusting it for revenues and expenses not involving the receipt or payment of cash.
5. **C** The cash flows from operating activities section of the statement of cash flows would report net cash flow from operating activities of $65,500, determined as follows:

Net income		$55,000
Add: Depreciation	$22,000	
Decrease in inventories	5,000	
Decrease in prepaid expenses	500	27,500
		$82,500
Deduct: Increase in trade receivables	$10,000	
Decrease in accounts payable	7,000	17,000
Net cash flow from operating activities		$65,500

PART SEVEN

Managerial Accounting Principles and Systems

18. *Managerial Accounting Concepts and Principles*

19. *Job Order Cost Systems*

20. *Process Cost Systems*

18

Managerial Accounting Concepts and Principles

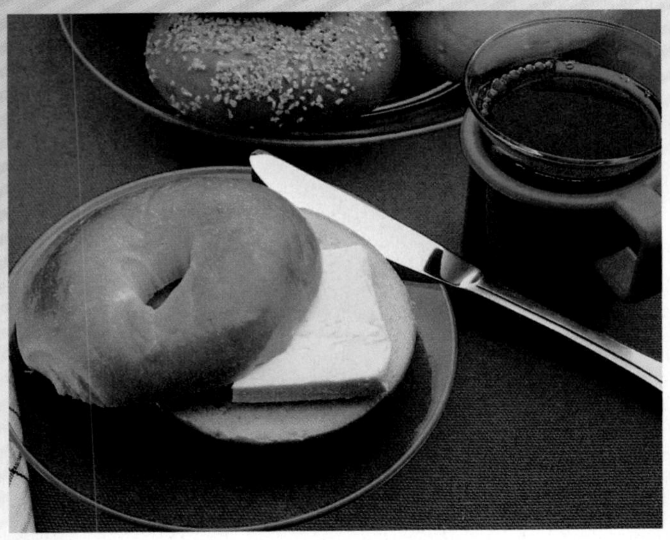

YOU AND ACCOUNTING

Suppose you go down to the local bakery and buy a bagel and coffee before class. How much should the bakery charge you? The purchase price must be greater than the costs of producing and serving the bagel and coffee. Moreover, the bakery needs to be able to answer additional questions, such as:

- How many bagels must be sold in a given period and at given prices to cover costs?
- How should the price for a single bagel differ from the price for a dozen bagels?
- How many employees should be in the shop at different times of the week?
- How much should be charged for delivery service?
- Would a larger oven be a good investment?
- Should the shop stay open 24 hours per day?

All of these questions can be answered with the aid of cost information. In this chapter you will be introduced to cost concepts used in managerial accounting, which help answer questions like those above.

We will begin this chapter by describing managerial accounting, often called management accounting, and its relationship to financial accounting. Following this overview, we will describe the management process and the role of managerial accounting in this process. We will also discuss characteristics of managerial accounting reports and various managerial accounting terms that often appear in such reports. We will conclude the chapter with a brief description of the major trends that are influencing managerial accounting and business in general.

After studying this chapter, you should be able to:

Objective 1
Explain the differences between managerial and financial accounting.

Objective 2
Evaluate the organizational and ethical roles of management accountants.

Objective 3
Describe how managerial accounting supports management's planning, directing, controlling, improving, and decision making.

Objective 4
Define and illustrate the following costs: direct and indirect, direct materials, direct labor, factory overhead, and product and period costs.

Objective 5
Describe and illustrate the financial statement elements and cost relationships for a manufacturing business.

Objective 6
Describe major trends impacting businesses and managerial accounting.

The Differences Between Managerial and Financial Accounting

Objective 1
Explain the differences between managerial and financial accounting.

Although economic information can be classified in many ways, accountants often divide accounting information into two types: financial and managerial. The diagram in Exhibit 1 illustrates the relationship between managerial accounting and financial accounting. Understanding this relationship is useful in understanding the information needs of management.

Financial accounting information is reported in statements that are useful for persons or institutions who are "outside" or external to the organization. Examples of such users include shareholders, creditors, government agencies, and the general public. To the extent that management uses the financial statements in directing current operations and planning future operations, the two areas of accounting overlap. For example, in planning future operations, management often begins by evaluating the results of past activities as reported in the financial statements. As we have discussed in previous chapters, the financial statements objectively and periodically report the results of past operations and the financial condition of the business according to **generally accepted accounting principles (GAAP).**

Managerial accounting information includes both historical and estimated data used by management in conducting daily operations, planning future operations, and developing overall business strategies. Managerial accounting reports may stress different features of the business, from high-level strategy to detailed operations. Similarly, the cost information used by management may vary, depending on the nature of the decision. We sometimes refer to this as "different costs for different purposes." Thus, usefulness guides the accountant in preparing accounting reports for management.

The characteristics of managerial accounting are influenced by the varying needs of management. First, useful managerial accounting reports provide both objective measures of past operations and subjective estimates about future decisions. Using subjective estimates in managerial accounting reports assists management in responding to business opportunities. Second, managerial reports need not be prepared according to generally accepted accounting principles. Since managerial accounting information is only used by management, the accountant can provide the information in any useful format. Third, managerial accounting reports may be provided periodically, as with financial accounting, or at any time management needs information. For example, if senior management is deciding on a geographical expansion, a managerial accounting report can be developed in a format and within a time frame to assist management in the decision. Lastly, managerial

Exhibit 1
Financial Accounting and Managerial Accounting

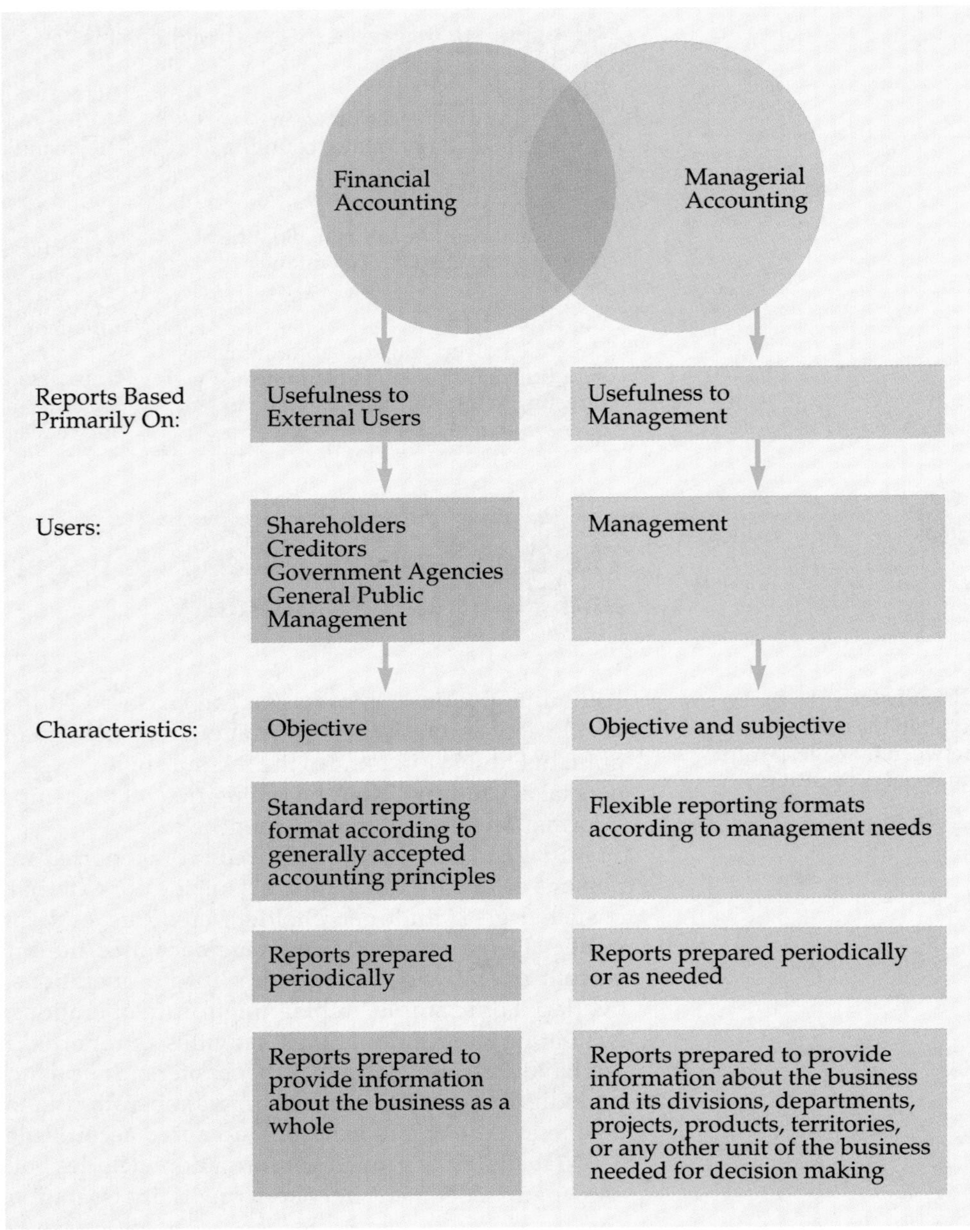

accounting reports can be prepared to report information for any unit of the business to support decision making. For example, management may request reports about a division, department, product, project, or territory of the business.

Managerial accounting is one of the most innovative areas of accounting today. There are few rules to restrict how an organization chooses to arrange its own internal data for decision making. Thus, managerial accounting provides ample opportunity for creativity and change.

The Role of the Management Accountant

Objective 2
Evaluate the organizational and ethical roles of management accountants.

The management accountant is an important member of the management team. In the next two sections, we will discuss the managerial accounting function within the organization and the ethical role of the management accountant.

WHERE DOES THE MANAGEMENT ACCOUNTANT FIT IN AN ORGANIZATION?

In most large organizations, departments or similar units are assigned responsibilities for specific functions or activities. This operating structure of an organization can be diagrammed in an **organization chart.** Exhibit 2 is an organization chart for Baker Inc., a small manufacturing firm.

Exhibit 2
Organization Chart for Baker Inc.

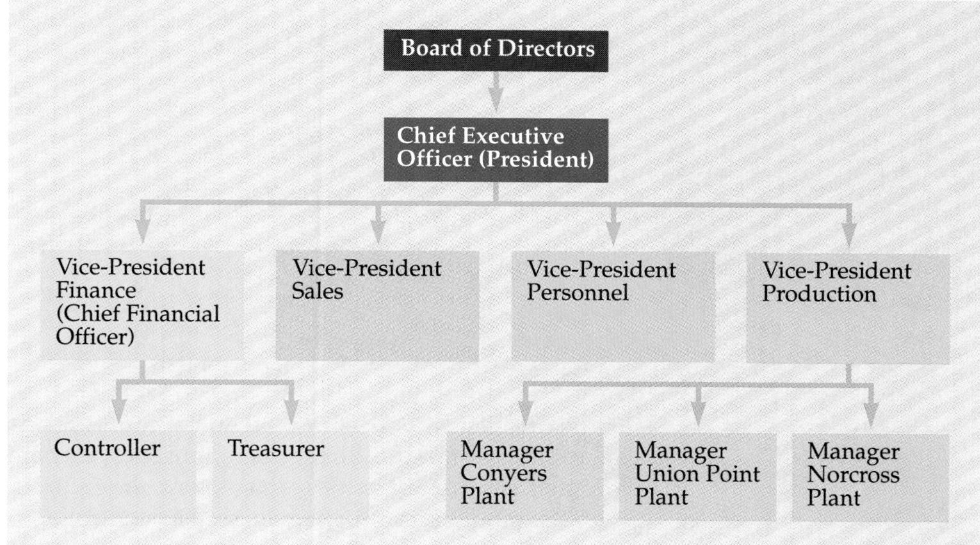

The individual reporting units in an organization can be viewed as having either (1) line responsibilities or (2) staff responsibilities. A **line** department or unit is one directly involved in the basic objectives of the organization. For Baker Inc., the vice-president of production and the managers of the Conyers Plant, the Union Plant, and the Norcross Plant occupy line positions because they are responsible for manufacturing Baker's products. Likewise, the vice-president of sales is a line position because it is directly responsible for the generation of revenues. In a hospital the doctors and nurses occupy the line positions, while in a university the faculty occupy the line positions.

A **staff** department or unit is one that provides services, assistance, and advice to the departments with line or other staff responsibilities. A staff department has no direct authority over a line department. The organization chart for Baker Inc. indicates that two staff vice-president positions report to the chief executive officer. The vice-president of personnel occupies a staff position because the Personnel Department assists line managers and others in staffing their departments. Likewise, the vice-president of finance (sometimes called the chief financial officer) occupies a staff position, to which two other staff positions—the controller and the treasurer—report. An example of a staff position in a hospital is the director of patient accounts, while a staff position at a university is the director of financial aid. In large organizations, staff positions may also exist for such functions as engineering, research and development, and marketing.

In most business organizations, the chief management accountant is called the controller.[1] The controller has a staff relationship with others in the organization.

[1] A controller may be certified by the Institute of Certified Management Accountants (ICMA) as a **Certified Management Accountant** (CMA). The CMA certificate is not a requirement for becoming a controller. The CMA is a professional designation awarded as evidence of competence in managerial accounting. The requirements for the CMA designation include education, experience, and the passing of a two-day examination.

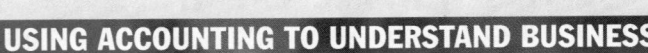

USING ACCOUNTING TO UNDERSTAND BUSINESS

The terms *line* and *staff* are often associated with manufacturing firms. However, these terms may also be applied to service organizations, such as banks, hospitals, hotels, or public accounting firms. To illustrate, what would be the line and staff positions for a professional basketball team, such as the Boston Celtics? The basketball players and coaches would be the "line" positions, since they are directly involved in the basic objectives of the organization—playing professional basketball. Staff positions would include public relations, player development and recruiting, legal staff, and accounting. These positions serve and advise the players and coaches.

The controller provides financial and accounting advice and assistance to management but assumes no direct operational responsibility. However, in providing information and analysis for management, the controller must be thoroughly familiar with the operations of the business. The controller's position provides an excellent perspective on many aspects of the business, and because of this critical role, the controller is considered a valued member of the senior management.

The controller's staff often consists of several management accountants. Each accountant is responsible for a specialized accounting function, such as systems and procedures, general accounting, budgets and budget analysis, special reports and analysis, taxes, and cost accounting.

Experience in managerial accounting is often an excellent training ground for senior management positions. A recent poll indicated that over 21% of the chief executive officers (CEOs) of the largest 1,000 companies in the United States have career paths that began with accounting or finance. More CEOs started out in these areas than in any other functional business area.[2] This is not surprising, since accounting and finance bring an individual into contact with all phases of operations.

ETHICAL ROLE OF MANAGEMENT ACCOUNTANTS

Ethics *are moral principles that guide the conduct of individuals when they are acting alone, as members of a profession, or as employees of an organization.* The Institute of Management Accountants has developed guides to professional conduct, called **Standards of Ethical Conduct for Management Accountants.**[3] These standards comprise four major categories of ethical professional conduct: (1) competence, (2) confidentiality, (3) integrity, and (4) objectivity. In addition, many companies have developed their own codes of conduct to guide their employees in performing their daily responsibilities.[4]

[2] "Corporate Elite Career Path," *Business Week,* October 11, 1993, p. 65.

[3] These standards of ethical conduct appear in Appendix B at the end of the text.

[4] An ethics case is provided at the end of each remaining chapter to focus attention on meaningful ethical situations that management accountants may encounter in practice.

Management accountants are in a unique position to influence management decision making by providing relevant information concerning alternative courses of action. In providing this information, management accountants should adhere to proper ethical conduct.

Sometimes there is pressure in organizations to manipulate earnings in order to achieve financial performance goals. However, this practice is considered unethical. To illustrate, Exhibit 3 describes three earnings manipulation scenarios. For each scenario, 11 chief financial officers (CFOs) were asked to evaluate whether the action taken in the scenario would be acceptable, questionable, or unacceptable.

Exhibit 3
Acceptability of Manipulating Earnings

Senior Financial Executives' Judgments of the Acceptability of Hypothetical Earnings Management Practices[5]

	Acceptable	*Questionable*	*Unacceptable*
Accounting Methods of Managing Earnings:			
1. Recording supplies expense in 1997 for supplies received in 1996. The supplies were mistakenly ordered in 1996. Policy requires that supplies be expensed when received.	0	1	10
2. Prepaying and recording as expenses in 1996 the costs for a 1997 trade show.	1	1	9
3. Asking a consulting firm to delay invoicing for services rendered within a low profit year until the next year.	0	0	11

Business men and women should work within an ethical framework. Although an ethical framework is formed through individual experiences and training, there are a number of sound principles that form the foundation for ethical behavior:

1. Avoid small ethical lapses. Small ethical lapses may appear harmless in and of themselves. Unfortunately, such lapses can compromise a controller's position. A controller may be reminded of small prior ethical lapses while being persuaded to commit a much larger ethical breach. In other instances, small ethical lapses can build up and lead to larger consequences at a later point in time.
2. Focus on long-term reputation. One characteristic of an ethical dilemma is that it places an individual under severe short-term pressure. The ethical dilemma is created by the stated or unstated threat that failure to "go along" may result in undesirable consequences. A controller should respond to ethical dilemmas by resisting short-term pressures and instead focusing on long-term reputation. The controller's reputation is very valuable. A controller loses effectiveness if that reputation becomes tarnished.
3. Be prepared to suffer adverse personal consequences for holding to an ethical position. In some unethical organizations, controllers have suffered personal consequences for holding to their ethical positions. Instances have been reported of controllers resigning their positions because they were unable to support management in what was perceived as unethical behavior. Thus, in the **short term,** ethical behavior can sometimes adversely affect one's career.

[5] Ken Merchant, *Rewarding Results,* Harvard Business School Press, Cambridge, 1989, pp. 178–180.

Managerial Accounting in the Management Process

Objective 3
Describe how managerial accounting supports management's planning, directing, controlling, improving, and decision making.

To explain how managerial accounting supports management actions, we will analyze the management process. The management process has five basic phases:

1. Planning
2. Directing
3. Controlling
4. Improving
5. Decision making

As shown in Exhibit 4, all five phases interact with each other. Also, they are the driving force for an organization's strategies and operations. Management's actions in the management process are, to some extent, measured by the organization's operating results.

Exhibit 4
Diagram of Management Process

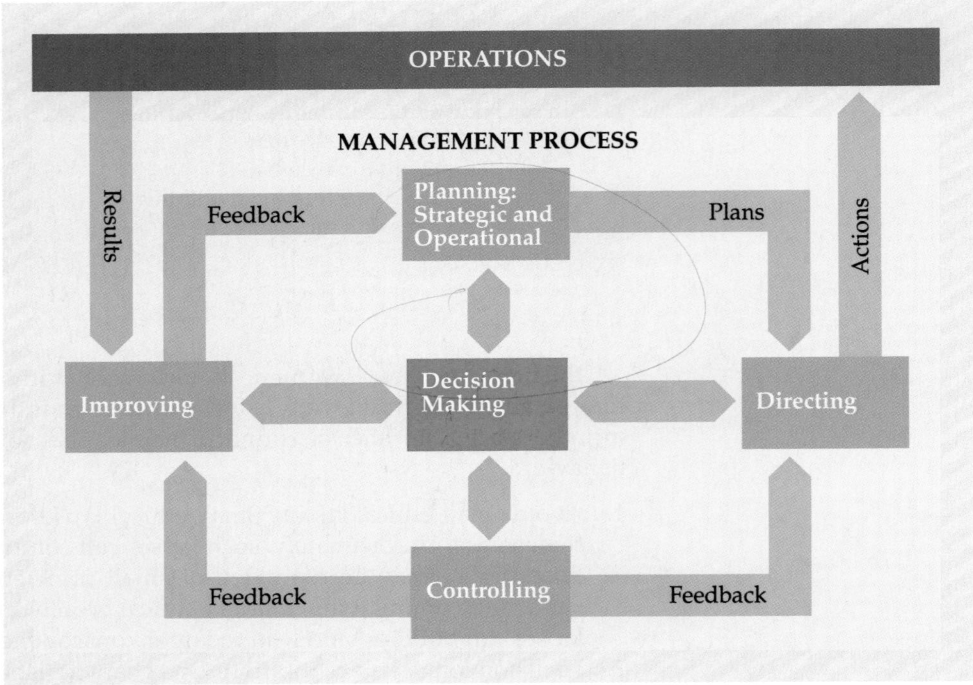

PLANNING

Planning is used by management to develop the organization's **objectives** (goals) and to translate these objectives into courses of action. For example, an organization, as part of the planning process, may set objectives to increase market share by 15% and introduce three new products. The courses of action, or means, for achieving these objectives must be established. In this example, the organization may decide to follow three courses of action: increase the advertising budget, open a new sales territory, and increase the research and development budget.

Planning can be categorized as either strategic planning or operational planning. Strategic planning is developing long-range courses of action to achieve goals. Long-range courses of action, called strategies, can often involve periods ranging from five to ten years.

Strategic plans establish business policy and priorities for such activities as research and development, marketing, financing, and plant expansion. For example, the decision by a number of Japanese automobile manufacturers to establish assembly facilities in the United States is a strategic course of action designed to capture a greater North American market share by avoiding import controls and currency fluctuations.

A strategic plan, which is normally approved by the senior management, should integrate all aspects of the business's operations necessary for achieving long-range goals. Because the strategic plan is influenced by the changing environment within which the business operates, the strategic plan should be periodically reviewed and revised. For example, rising interest rates might postpone a proposed plant expansion, or falling oil prices might postpone a business's plan to expand operations into energy-saving products. As an example of a change in strategic plans, the Tennessee Valley Authority (TVA) in the early 1980s abandoned or postponed several nuclear power construction projects because of unfavorable energy and political climates.

Operational planning, sometimes called **tactical planning,** is the short-term planning used for achieving operational goals. The goals of the operational plan should directly support the overall strategic objectives of the organization. Thus, operational plans complement the strategic plan and are typically established for short time periods ranging from days to several years.

Operational plans are typically designed to achieve quality, customer satisfaction, production, and financial goals. For example, Toyota Motor Company has a strategic plan to increase market share in North America. The operational goals may include annual production targets for their Georgetown, Kentucky, assembly plant and quality targets for their automobiles. The operational plans would identify the actions required to achieve the production and quality objectives. An example of an operational plan at Toyota may be to increase production capacity from a one-shift to a two-shift operation by hiring and training employees.

Effective communication between all levels of management within an organization is essential to coordinate day-to-day operations. An important part of communication is the various accounting and performance reports management uses in both operational and strategic planning. These reports usually include estimates showing the effects of alternative plans. The financial estimates for these plans can provide persuasive evidence for one or more of the alternatives.

USING ACCOUNTING TO UNDERSTAND BUSINESS

Merck & Co., a pharmaceutical company, is highly dependent on their research and development (R&D) effort. How are financial evaluations brought into subjective R&D decision making? Judy Lewent, Chief Financial Officer (CFO) for Merck, responds by saying that the R&D scientists must be creative and must be able to operate in an environment where they can experiment and be free to fail. "But while they are doing it [R&D], it has to be in the range where there are defined targets and objectives that make some sense over the five to 10 year period for them to pursue. Finance can offer that discipline, without getting hung up on next quarter or next year." She adds that "done properly," financial analysis "needn't pinch perspective," although "in the hands of one who has a narrow understanding, it can fall prey to that."

Source: Tim W. Ferguson, *The Wall Street Journal,* June 30, 1992, p. A17.

DIRECTING

Directing is the process by which managers, given their assigned level of responsibilities, run day-to-day operations. Examples of directing include a production supervisor's efforts to keep the production line moving smoothly throughout a work shift and the credit manager's efforts to assess the credit standing of potential customers.

Managerial accounting aids managers in directing a business by providing reports that allow them to adjust operations for changing conditions. For example, reports on the cost of defective material by vendors may aid managers in making vendor selections or improvements. Likewise, daily or weekly reports on the sales per square foot of shelf space may be used by a retail store manager in deciding which items should be stocked and where they should be displayed. In addition, managerial accounting reports are used by management to estimate the appropriate staffing and resource levels inside the formal organizational structure for achieving plans.

CONTROLLING

Once managers have planned the goals and directed the action, there comes the need to assess how well the plan is working. **Controlling** consists of monitoring the operating results of implemented plans and comparing the actual results with the expected results. This **feedback** allows management to isolate significant departures from plans for further investigation and possible remedial action. It may also lead to a revision of future plans. This philosophy of controlling is sometimes called **management by exception.** For example, if actual departmental costs incurred in maintaining a process significantly exceed expected costs, then an investigation may be conducted to determine the cause of the difference so that corrective action may be taken.

IMPROVING

Feedback can also be used by managers to support continuous process improvement. **Continuous process improvement** is the philosophy of continually improving employees, business processes, and products. Continuous improvement rejects solving individual problems with temporary solutions that fail to address the root cause of the problem. Instead, continuous process improvement uses process information to eliminate the *source* of problems in a process, so that the process delivers the right product (service) in the right quantities at the right time. This philosophy requires managers to be responsible for demonstrated process improvement.

For example, in one company the Shipping Department noticed that occasional shipments would be returned undelivered. A conventional "firefighting" approach views the undelivered shipments as isolated problems to be resolved one by one. An alternative view considers the undelivered shipments as a symptom of a broader process failure. In this case, the shipping process began with a clerk inputting shipping address data into a computer system. The system generated shipping instructions based upon the input data. An analysis of the shipment errors revealed that the errors were not random, but occurred in instances where the shipment was to be delivered "in care of" an individual. "In care of" shipments required five address lines; however, the computer system only allowed four address lines. Without the "in care of" data, the shipments would arrive at the right locations but to unrecognized individuals. As a result, the shipments were returned to the sender. The manager had the computer system changed to include a fifth address line. After this change, the number of returned shipments declined by 40%, a permanent system improvement.

Managers use a wide variety of information sources for improving operations, including managerial accounting information. For example, a purchasing manager might receive weekly or daily performance reports comparing actual materials costs with estimated costs. Significant differences between the actual and estimated costs could be identified for corrective action. Another example is a cost of quality report. A cost of quality report identifies the dollar amount of waste and work to be redone in a process. Such a report can be used by managers to prioritize and monitor improvement efforts.

USING ACCOUNTING TO UNDERSTAND BUSINESS

Gilroy Foods, Inc., a food processing division of McCormick and Company, developed a report to help management identify opportunities to improve the food-making processes. The report identified the cost of scrap, union grievances, excess waste water, customer complaints, customer returns, and excessive product movements. Each of these items represents cost improvement opportunities. Gilroy Foods was able to reduce the cost of these wasteful activities by approximately 40% within one year of adopting the new report.

DECISION MAKING

Decision making is inherent in each of the four management processes described in the preceding paragraphs. For example, in developing the strategic plan, managers must decide between alternative courses of action to achieve long-range goals and objectives. Likewise, in directing operations, managers must decide on an operating structure, procedures, training, staffing, and other aspects of day-to-day operations. In controlling and improving, managers must decide how to respond to variations in performance.

A Tour of Manufacturing Operations: Costs and Terminology

Objective 4
Define and illustrate the following costs: direct and indirect, direct materials, direct labor, factory overhead, and product and period costs.

The operations of business can be classified as service, merchandising, or manufacturing. A **service business** renders services to its customers. A **merchandising business** purchases goods in a form ready for sale and then retails the merchandise to consumers. A **manufacturing business** converts materials into a finished product through the use of machinery and labor. Most of the managerial accounting concepts and terms described in the remaining chapters of this text are applicable to all three types of businesses. In this section, however, we will tour a manufacturing firm, Goodwell Printers.

Goodwell Printers prints textbooks, like the one you are using now. Exhibit 5 provides an overview of Goodwell Printers' textbook printing operations. The Printing Department feeds large rolls of paper into printing presses to print pages. The printing machines in the Printing Department use electricity and ink to print the books. From the Printing Department, the printed pages are stacked and moved to the Binding Department. In the Binding Department, the pages are cut, separated, stacked, and bound to book covers using binding machines. A finished book is the final output of the Binding Department.

Exhibit 5
Textbook Printing Operations of Goodwell Printers

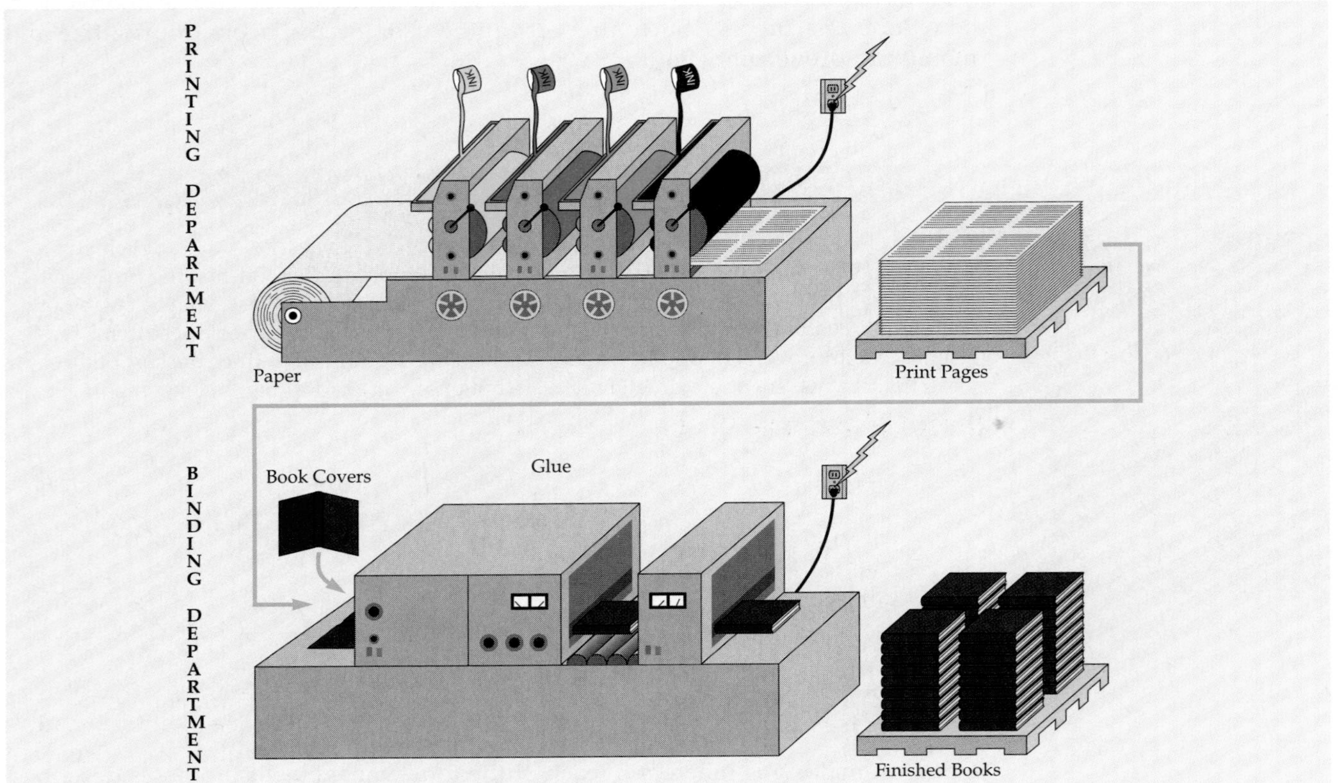

During our tour of Goodwell Printers, we will introduce the common cost terms associated with manufacturing operations. To begin, the most fundamental term is "cost." A **cost** is a payment of cash or its equivalent or the commitment to pay cash in the future for the purpose of generating revenues. For example, cash (or credit) used to purchase equipment is the cost of the equipment. Likewise, if equipment is purchased by exchanging assets other than cash, the current market value of the assets is the cost of the equipment purchased.

Costs may be classified in a number of ways, as we describe in the following sections. Understanding these classifications provides a foundation for later discussions and illustrations of more complex, decision-making situations.

DIRECT AND INDIRECT COSTS

For management's use in making decisions, costs are often classified in terms of how they relate to some object or segment of operations, often called a **cost object.** A cost object may be a product, a sales territory, a department, or some activity, such as research and development. Cost objects are determined by management according to their decision-making needs.

Costs that can be identified directly with the cost object are called **direct costs.** Costs that cannot be identified directly with a cost object are **indirect costs** for that cost object.

Classifying a cost as a direct or an indirect cost first requires that the cost object be identified by management. Next, it must be determined if the cost can be easily identified with the cost object. If so, it is a direct cost. For example, if Goodwell Printers is evaluating the cost effectiveness of its various printing machines, the cost object could be each machine. The cost of power consumed and repair parts used in operating each machine are direct costs of the machines. On the other hand, the salary of the Maintenance Department supervisor whose department repairs and maintains the machines normally cannot be identified with the individual machines. Thus, this salary cost is not direct to the machines. However, if the cost object is the Maintenance Department, the salary of the Maintenance Department supervisor would be a direct cost to the department. Likewise, a single book could be a cost object, and the cost of paper would be a direct cost of the book.

MANUFACTURING COSTS

The cost of a manufactured product includes the cost of materials used in making the product as well as the costs incurred in converting the materials into a finished product. The cost of a manufactured product normally consists of direct materials cost, direct labor cost, and factory overhead cost.

Direct Materials Cost

The cost of materials that are an integral part of the manufactured product is classified as direct materials cost. For example, the direct materials cost for Goodwell Printers, would include paper and book covers. The *cost object,* in this case, is the product (a book).

As a practical matter, a direct materials cost must not only be an integral part of the finished product, but it must also be a significant portion of the total cost of the product. For Goodwell Printers, the costs of paper and covers are a significant portion of the total cost of each book. Other examples of direct materials costs are the cost of electronic components for a TV manufacturer, lumber for a furniture manufacturer, silicon wafers for a producer of microcomputer chips, and tires for an automobile manufacturer.

Direct Labor Cost

The cost of wages of employees who are directly involved in converting materials into the manufactured product is classified as direct labor cost. As with direct materials, the *cost object* for direct labor cost is the product. For example, the direct labor cost of Goodwell Printers includes the wages of the employees who operate the printing presses. Other examples of direct labor costs are carpenters' wages for a construction contractor, mechanics' wages in an automotive repair shop, machine operators' wages in a tool manufacturing plant, and assemblers' wages in a microcomputer assembly plant.

As a practical matter, a direct labor cost must not only be an integral part of the finished product, but it must also be a significant portion of the total cost of the product. For Goodwell Printers, the printing press operators' wages are a significant portion of the total cost of each book.

Factory Overhead Cost

Costs other than direct materials cost and direct labor cost incurred in the manufacturing process are classified as factory overhead cost. Factory overhead is sometimes called **manufacturing overhead** or **factory burden.** For example, factory overhead cost includes the cost of heating and lighting the factory, repairing and maintaining factory equipment, and property taxes, insurance, and depreciation on factory plant and equipment. Factory overhead cost also includes materials and labor costs that do not enter directly into the finished product. For example, the cost of oil used to lubricate machinery is a materials cost that does not enter directly into finished products. Other examples of such costs are the wages of janitorial, supervisory, and quality control personnel. In addition, payments to employees for overtime and nonproductive time (such as idle time) are considered factory overhead because they cannot be related to a product.

As a practical matter, if the costs of direct materials or direct labor are not a significant portion of the total product cost, these costs may be classified as factory overhead. In Goodwell Printers, for example, the costs of the ink and the glue binding the pages to the cover enter directly into the manufacture of each book. However, because these costs are insignificant, they are classified as factory overhead.

Other overhead costs for Goodwell Printers would include the power to run the machines, the depreciation of the machines, and the salary of supervisors and support department personnel. For many industries, factory overhead costs are increasingly becoming a larger portion of the costs of manufacturing a product as manufacturing processes become more automated. In addition, increased automation has decreased labor costs to a level where they are a small amount of the total product cost. In this situation, direct labor costs of manufactured products are often included as part of factory overhead cost.

Prime Costs and Conversion Costs

The direct materials, direct labor, and factory overhead costs may be grouped together for analysis and reporting purposes. Two common groupings of these costs are prime costs and conversion costs. Exhibit 6 summarizes the classification of manufacturing costs into prime costs and conversion costs.

Exhibit 6
Prime Costs and Conversion Costs

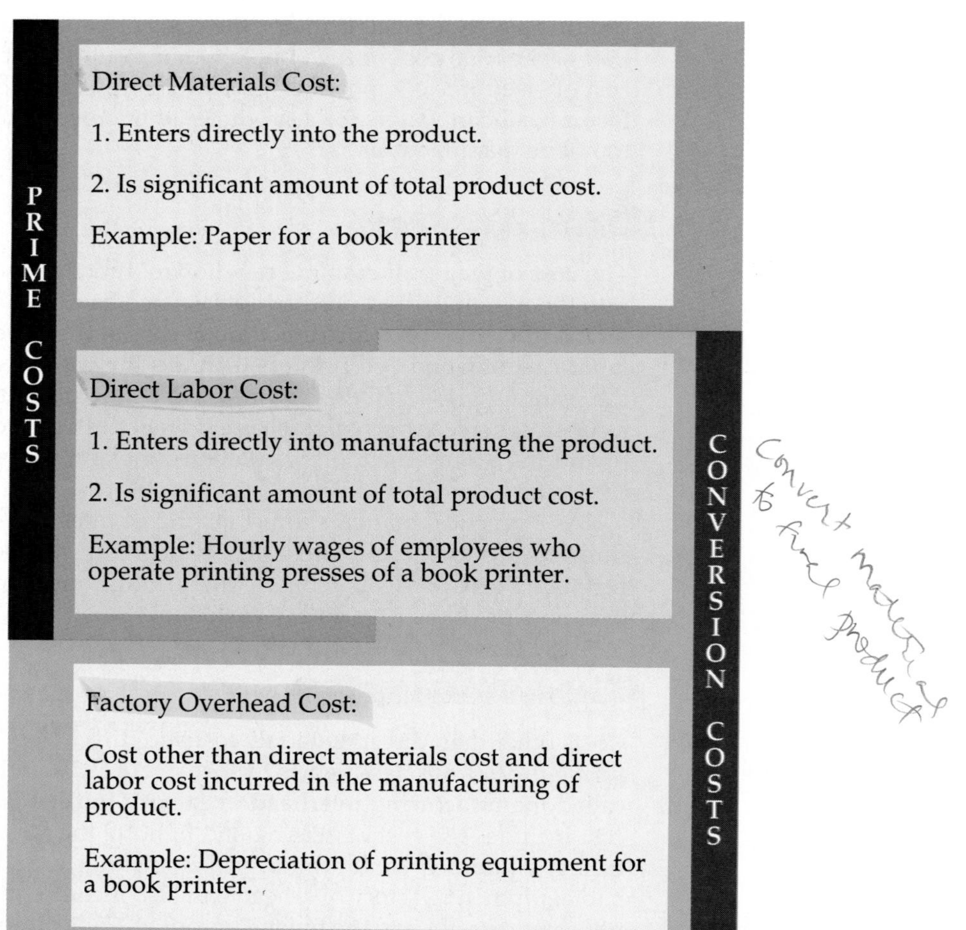

PRIME COSTS
Direct Materials Cost:
1. Enters directly into the product.
2. Is significant amount of total product cost.
Example: Paper for a book printer
Direct Labor Cost:
1. Enters directly into manufacturing the product.
2. Is significant amount of total product cost.
Example: Hourly wages of employees who operate printing presses of a book printer.
Factory Overhead Cost:
Cost other than direct materials cost and direct labor cost incurred in the manufacturing of product.
Example: Depreciation of printing equipment for a book printer.
CONVERSION COSTS

Prime costs consist of direct materials and direct labor costs. **Conversion costs** consist of direct labor and factory overhead costs. Conversion costs are the costs of converting the materials into a finished product.

PRODUCT COSTS AND PERIOD COSTS

For financial reporting purposes, costs are often classified as either product costs or period costs. **Product costs** consist of the three elements of manufacturing cost: direct materials, direct labor, and factory overhead. **Period costs** are generally classified into two categories: selling and administrative. Selling expenses are incurred in marketing the product and delivering the sold product to customers. Administrative expenses are incurred in the administration of the business and are not related to the manufacturing or selling functions. Examples of product costs and period costs for Goodwell Printers are presented in Exhibit 7.

Exhibit 7
Examples of Product Costs and Period Costs—Goodwell Printers

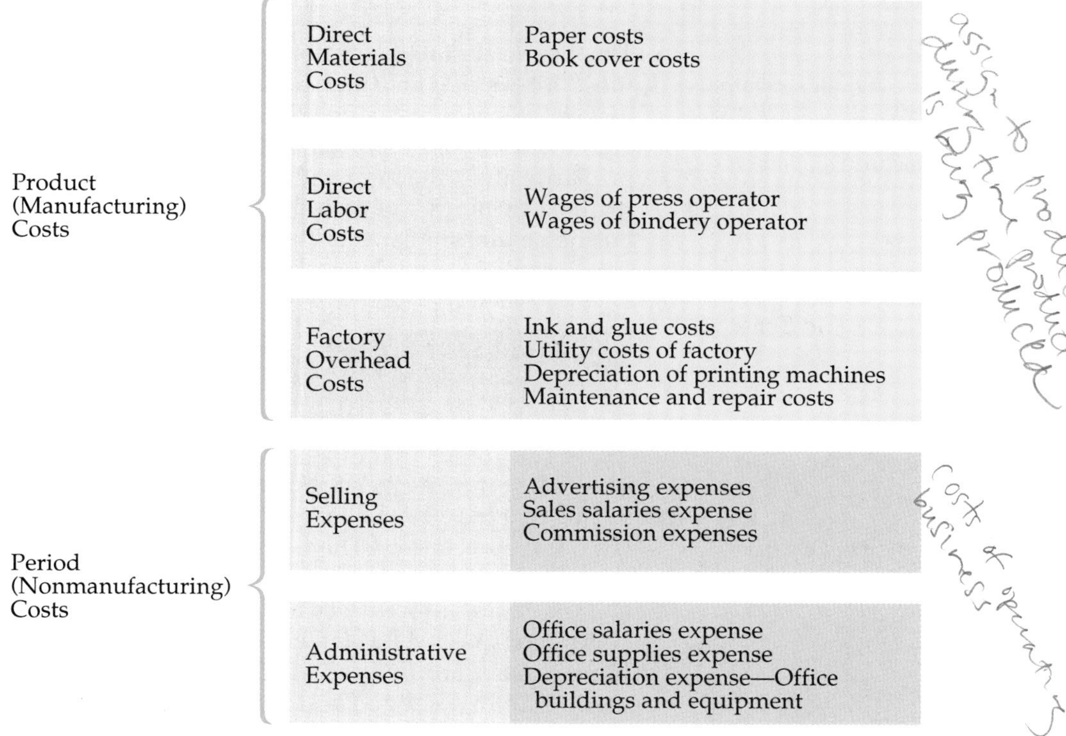

Classifying period costs as selling or administrative assists management in controlling the costs of these two major functional activities. Different levels of responsibility for these activities may be shown in managerial reports. For example, selling expenses may be reported by product, salespersons, departments, divisions, or geographic territories. Likewise, administrative expenses may be reported by functional area, such as personnel, computer services, accounting, finance, or office support.

The classification of costs as product costs and period costs is summarized in Exhibit 8. As product costs are incurred in the manufacturing process, they are accounted for as assets and reported on the balance sheet as inventory. When the inventory is sold, the direct materials, direct labor, and factory overhead costs are reported as cost of goods sold on the income statement. Period costs are recognized as expenses in the period in which they arise. In the next section, we illustrate the reporting of product costs and period costs in the financial statements of manufacturing businesses.

Exhibit 8
Product Costs and Period Costs

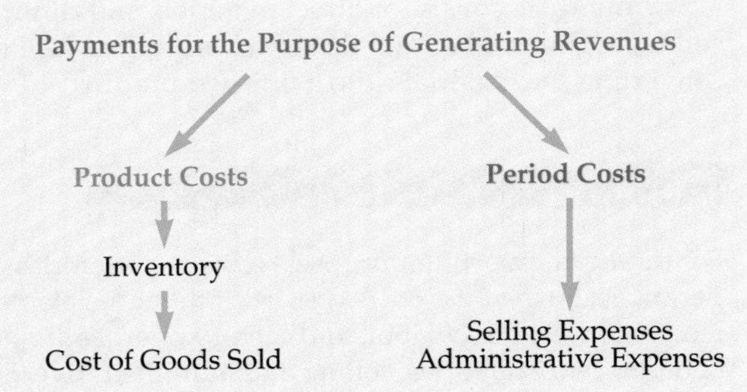

Financial Statements for Manufacturing Businesses

Objective 5
Describe and illustrate the financial statement elements and cost relationships for a manufacturing business.

The financial statements for manufacturing businesses are more complex than those for service and merchandising businesses. This is because a manufacturer makes the products that it sells. As a result, manufacturing costs must be properly accounted for and reported in the financial statements. These manufacturing costs primarily affect the preparation of the balance sheet and the income statement. The retained earnings and cash flow statements for merchandising and manufacturing businesses are similar, and therefore, we will not discuss them here.

A manufacturing business reports the following three types of inventory on its balance sheet:

1. Materials inventory
2. Work in process inventory
3. Finished goods inventory

The **materials inventory**, sometimes called raw materials inventory, consists of the costs of the direct and indirect materials that have not yet entered the manufacturing process. For Goodwell Printers, materials inventory includes paper, ink, glue, and book covers. The **work in process inventory** consists of the direct materials costs, the direct labor costs, and the factory overhead costs that have entered the manufacturing process but are associated with products that have not been completed. For Goodwell Printers, the printed pages are work in process inventory. The printed pages are "in process" because they have yet to be bound into a completed book. The **finished goods inventory** consists of the completed (or finished) products that have not been sold. For Goodwell Printers, finished goods inventory is the completed books that have yet to be sold. These three inventory balances are disclosed in the Current Assets section of the balance sheet.[6]

The major difference in the income statements for merchandising and manufacturing businesses is in the reporting of cost of products sold during the period. A merchandising business purchases merchandise (products) in a finished state for resale to customers. The cost of the product sold is generally called the **cost of merchandise sold.** Exhibit 9 illustrates the flow of costs to the balance sheet and income statement for a merchandising firm that uses a perpetual inventory system.

A manufacturer makes the products it sells, using direct materials, direct labor, and factory overhead. The cost of the product sold is generally called the **cost of goods sold.** For a manufacturer the total cost of making and finishing the product is

[6] Many companies combine materials, work in process, and finished goods as a single inventory balance on the balance sheet. When this option is chosen, a footnote is used to disclose the individual inventory balances.

Exhibit 9
Flow of Costs for a Merchandising Firm

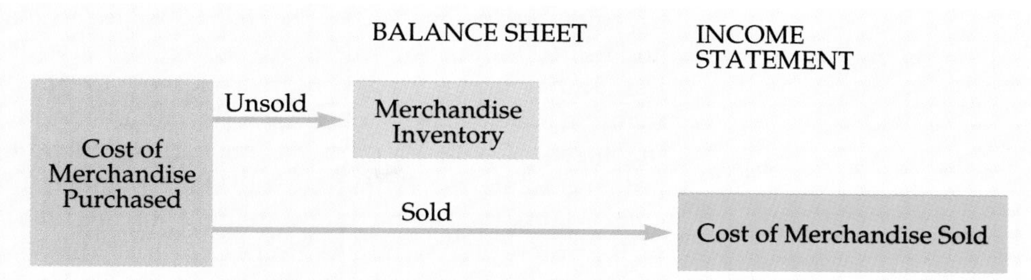

called the **cost of goods manufactured.** It is comparable to the total cost of merchandise purchased for resale in a merchandising business.

To illustrate the flow of manufacturing costs to the balance sheet and income statement for Goodwell Printers, assume the following data for January, the first month of operations:

Direct materials used in production	$ 85,000
Direct labor incurred in production	100,000
Factory overhead incurred in production	140,000
Products finished during the period (cost of goods manufactured)	250,000
Cost of goods sold	210,000
Selling expenses	80,000
Administrative expenses	50,000
Sales	400,000

On January 31, Goodwell Printers had the following inventory balances:

Materials	$35,000
Work in Process	75,000
Finished Goods	40,000

The January manufacturing costs for Goodwell Printers would flow to the financial statements as shown in Exhibit 10.

Exhibit 10
Flow of January Manufacturing Costs for Goodwell Printers

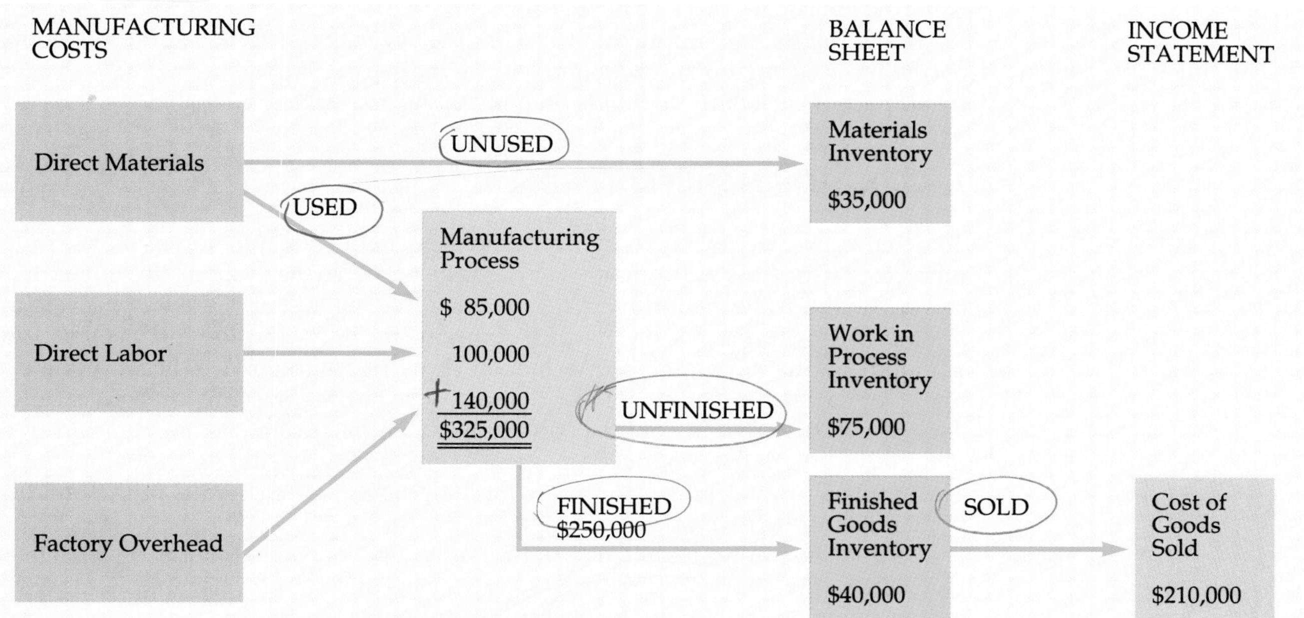

The manufacturing process uses $85,000 of direct materials, $100,000 of direct labor, and $140,000 of factory overhead during January. Of the $325,000 total cost incurred in manufacturing, $75,000 represents the work in process inventory, while the remaining $250,000 is the cost of goods manufactured. Of the total cost of goods manufactured, $210,000 represents finished production that was actually sold during January, while the remaining $40,000 represents finished goods inventory at the end of January. The income statement for the first month of operations for Goodwell Printers is shown in Exhibit 11.

Exhibit 11
Income Statement for Goodwell Printers

Goodwell Printers
Income Statement
For the Month Ended January 31, 19—

Sales		$400,000
Cost of goods sold		210,000
Gross profit		$190,000
Operating expenses:		
Selling expenses	$80,000	
Administrative expenses	50,000	
Total operating expenses		130,000
Net income		$ 60,000

Trends in Business

Objective 6
Describe major trends impacting businesses and managerial accounting.

Managerial accounting continues to evolve with changes in the business environment and management philosophies. In recent years, this evolution has been especially rapid for manufacturing businesses. Competitive worldwide pressures have forced many manufacturers to rethink their techniques and philosophies. This has led to the adoption of innovative approaches to managing and manufacturing. At the same time, the U.S. economy is becoming more and more service-oriented. This service orientation has resulted in a renewed emphasis on applying managerial accounting concepts to service businesses.

In the following paragraphs, we will look at the major trends and innovations occurring in the manufacturing and service industries. We will also briefly discuss the impact of each of these trends on managerial accounting.

JUST-IN-TIME MANUFACTURING

To achieve greater productivity and efficiency, many manufacturers have implemented **just-in-time (JIT) manufacturing systems.** These systems are sometimes called **flexible flow manufacturing systems.** In such systems, the emphasis is on manufacturing products or product components only as they are needed (demanded) by the next stage of production or by the marketplace. Because the demand initiates the manufacturing process, just-in-time systems are often called *demand-pull* systems. In contrast, traditional manufacturing systems tend to *push* materials through the production process in order to avoid idle time for employees. The emphasis on keeping the production line moving often results in the buildup of manufacturing inventories.

Because just-in-time systems produce only what is needed by the next stage of production, inventories are reduced to low or insignificant levels. Suppliers are required to deliver raw materials just in time to enter the production process. Since one of a manufacturer's goals is to respond quickly to customer orders, just-in-time systems also focus on reducing the time required to manufacture a product from the time an order is received until it is shipped to the customer. This time is called the lead time or **cycle time.** As a result, the cost of products in the process of manufacture (work in process) is reduced to a low enough level that it is often not accounted for as a separate inventory. This allows management accountants to focus more on providing information for managerial decision making, rather than measuring inventory for use in preparing financial statements.

Just-in-time manufacturing also places a greater emphasis on quality control. This is because the production line is stopped when a defective part is spotted until the part can be reworked or a new part manufactured. As mentioned above, just-in-time systems require the timely delivery of raw materials by suppliers. This requires a greater emphasis on purchasing high-quality raw materials from reliable suppliers who can meet strict production deadlines. Thus, in just-in-time systems, management accountants devote significant time and effort to measuring the costs and benefits of quality control systems, lead time, and the reliability and performance of suppliers.[7]

USING ACCOUNTING TO UNDERSTAND BUSINESS

A good example of "just-in-time" processing can be found at Wendy's Hamburgers. Wendy's will prepare a hamburger the way a customer wants it. They do this by waiting for a customer order before placing pickles, ketchup, onion, mayo, or tomato on the hamburger. As a result, the customers get exactly what they want and quickly. McDonald's, however, makes their hamburgers a standard way (pickles, onion, ketchup, and mustard). They too are able to deliver hamburgers quickly, but from an "inventory" of already-prepared hamburgers. Wendy's just-in-time approach does not require such an "inventory."

TOTAL QUALITY MANAGEMENT

A new management concept is challenging many of the conventional methods of conducting business. This new concept is termed total quality management. Total quality management (TQM) is defined by two major principles. First, the organization's primary objective is to earn the allegiance of customers by delighting them with superior products and services. Second, the organization should achieve customer loyalty by continually improving employees, business processes, and products. This latter principle we introduced previously as **continuous process improvement.** TQM advocates believe that employees who continually improve themselves and their company's processes and products will lead to more satisfying jobs, better ways to work, and better products for the customer.

Under TQM, the customer is no longer an abstract purchaser of the company's products or services, but the next employee in the process sequence is also a customer. This linking of internal customer relationships to the ultimate customer has been called "building a chain of customers."[8]

Organizations embracing total quality management philosophies are reinventing their managerial accounting systems. Many of these innovations are presented in the chapters to follow.

[7] JIT manufacturing systems are further discussed in an appendix at the end of Chapter 20.
[8] Richard J. Schonberger, *Building a Chain of Customers,* The Free Press, New York, 1990.

WHO IS MY CUSTOMER?

David Kearns, the former chairman and CEO of Xerox Corporation, realized the company was in serious trouble when Canon was selling copiers at a price less than Xerox's costs. This realization forced Xerox to completely change its corporate culture and embrace total quality management or go out of business. Kearns sums up his experience with Xerox as follows:

We've all heard a good deal about quality recently. We define it as "conforming to customer requirements"—pure and simple. It's an axiom of business that's as old as business itself, yet many of us lost sight of it. And when we speak of quality, we mean more than just product quality. We take the view that every person in the company has a customer for the work they do. For many people, the customer is someone inside the company—the person we type reports for or the person to whom we deliver parts.

It follows from this view of quality that it must work its way into the entire organization—into manufacturing, sales, service, billing, training, finance, and so on. . . .

Source: David T. Kearns, in the Foreword to *Competing Globally Through Customer Value,* Quorum Books, New York, 1991, p. x.

COMPUTER-INTEGRATED MANUFACTURING

Computer-integrated manufacturing (CIM) involves the use of automated equipment to perform routine, repetitive tasks with minimum human involvement. The automated equipment may be in the form of computer-aided machinery, such as robots. Since some automated machines perform a variety of repetitive tasks, computer-integrated manufacturing adds flexibility to the manufacturing process. This, in turn, allows manufacturers to respond quickly to changing market conditions. Computer-integrated manufacturing is often used with just-in-time manufacturing systems.

The use of automated equipment increases factory overhead costs through increases in depreciation, maintenance, repairs, and insurance. At the same time, automation normally reduces the amount of direct labor used in the manufacturing process. As a result, there has been an increased emphasis in managerial accounting on controlling and properly accounting for overhead. For example, increased emphasis has been placed on identifying activities that cause overhead to be incurred. Once identified, overhead costs for these activities are then closely monitored.

GLOBALIZATION OF BUSINESS

After World War II, the United States experienced a period of rapid growth and prosperity. Most of the industrial capacity in Europe and Japan was destroyed by the War, leaving the United States the major supplier of world markets. Whatever was produced could generally be sold either domestically or internationally.

In the decades following the 1950s, the remainder of the world slowly rebuilt its manufacturing plants. As a result, since the late 1970s and early 1980s the United States has faced increasing competition from foreign suppliers. The effects of this competition can be readily seen in retail stores throughout the United States. For example, twenty-five years ago electronics stores carried mostly U.S. brand-name products, such as GE, RCA, and Zenith. The same stores today carry many foreign products made by such companies as Sony and Sharp.

Many U.S. companies are also competing in international markets. For example, Ford and General Motors have facilities in Mexico to take advantage of lower costs as well as market opportunities in Latin America. Coca Cola derives well over 75% of its worldwide profits from international operations. Global businesses must manage resources across national borders. Managerial accounting plays an

USING ACCOUNTING TO UNDERSTAND BUSINESS

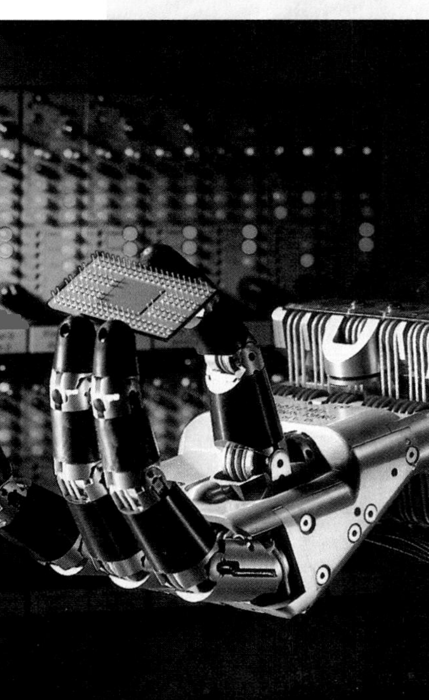

In the mid-1980s, several U.S. companies were competing with Japanese companies for what was expected to be a $2 billion business in the manufacture of factory automated equipment. By 1990, most of the U.S. companies had "quit the business, whipped by the Japanese. . ." Why?

"Saddled with high labor costs, the auto industry, particularly, saw robotics as a way to match Japan's lower car production costs." To meet this demand for factory automated equipment, U.S. companies focused on the development of hydraulic robots, while the Japanese companies stressed electric robots. The electric robot won out, partly because ". . . it cost $12,000 a year to run a hydraulic robot, but only $6,000 for electric" (even though hydraulics cost $48,000, while electric robots cost more than $70,000). Other important factors were that electric robots have 30% fewer parts and a higher reliability rate than hydraulic robots.

Source: "How U.S. Robots Lost the Market to Japan in Factory Automation," *The Wall Street Journal,* November 6, 1990.

essential role in these complex relationships by providing relevant information to management.

SERVICE INDUSTRY AWARENESS

The United States has been shifting toward a service-oriented economy over the last 50 years. Services now account for most of the new jobs created in the economy and over 60% of the gross domestic product of the industrialized world. Within the United States, 80% of the work force is employed in service companies, or service functions inside manufacturing companies.[9] Service companies provide important benefits to modern economies, such as banking, insurance, retailing, health, telecommunication, and transportation services.

Many service industries within the United States, such as the airline and trucking industries, are struggling for profits. As a result, service businesses are increasingly looking to managerial accounting for analyses that will enable them to compete more effectively. Many of the managerial accounting techniques and concepts discussed in the remainder of this text are applicable to service businesses. For example, hospital administrators need accurate cost information in order to properly bill patients for such health-care services as X-rays, nursing care, and laboratory tests. Likewise, airlines need accurate cost and revenue estimates in setting fares.

[9] "Global Service 500 Companies," *Fortune,* August 26, 1991, p. 166.

KEY POINTS

Objective 1. Explain the differences between managerial and financial accounting.
Managerial accounting and financial accounting serve different needs and, as such, have different characteristics. Managerial accounting serves the reporting needs of managers in meeting strategic and operational goals. Managerial accounting is not bound by a set of generally accepted principles, as is financial accounting. As a result, the practice of managerial accounting is as diverse as are organizations. This additional complexity in understanding the structure of managerial accounting is offset by the degree of creativity that can be applied to managerial information needs.

Objective 2. Evaluate the organizational and ethical roles of management accountants.
The financial function is generally a staff function of the organization. The chief accountant is often called the controller. The controller's function includes providing a variety of reports to support management decision making. The controller must respond to a variety of pressures in an ethical manner. Ethics are the moral principles that guide the conduct of individuals.

Objective 3. Describe how managerial accounting supports management's planning, directing, controlling, improving, and decision making.
Managerial accounting supports management actions in all phases of the management process. The five phases of the management process are:

1. Planning
2. Directing
3. Controlling
4. Improving
5. Decision making

Objective 4. Define and illustrate the following costs: direct and indirect, direct materials, direct labor, factory overhead, and product and period costs.
A direct cost can be directly traced to a cost object, while an indirect cost cannot. A manufacturer converts materials into a finished product by using machinery and labor. The cost of materials that are an integral part of the manufactured product is direct materials cost. The cost of wages of employees who are involved in converting materials into the manufactured product is direct labor cost. Costs other than direct materials and direct labor costs are factory overhead costs. Direct materials, direct labor, and factory overhead costs are associated with products and are called product costs. Selling and administrative expenses are associated with an accounting period and are called period costs.

Objective 5. Describe and illustrate the financial statement elements and cost relationships for a manufacturing business.
The balance sheets for a merchandiser and manufacturer are similar, except that a manufacturer reports materials, work in process, and finished goods inventories. The income statement of a manufacturer reports the costs of goods sold, which is the total manufacturing cost (direct materials, direct labor, and factory overhead) associated with goods sold.

Objective 6. Describe major trends impacting businesses and managerial accounting.
In just-in-time manufacturing systems, products or components are manufactured only as they are needed. Total quality management programs incorporate continuous improvement of all business processes to deliver quality products and services to customers. Computer-integrated manufacturing systems involve the use of automated equipment to perform routine, repetitive tasks. International competition and an increased service industry orientation have increased the need for managerial accounting information to guide complex decisions.

GLOSSARY OF KEY TERMS

Computer-integrated manufacturing (CIM). The use of automated equipment to perform routine, repetitive tasks with a minimum of human involvement. *Objective 6*

Continuous process improvement. A management approach that is part of the overall total quality management philosophy. The approach requires all employees to constantly improve processes of which they are a part or for which they have managerial responsibility. *Objective 3*

Controller. The chief management accountant of a business. *Objective 2*

Conversion costs. The combination of direct labor and factory overhead costs. *Objective 4*

Cost. A disbursement of cash (or a commitment to pay cash in the future) for the purpose of generating revenues. *Objective 4*

Cost object. The object or segment of operations to which costs are related for management's use, such as a product or department. *Objective 4*

Cost of goods sold. The cost of the manufactured product sold. *Objective 5*

Cost of merchandise sold. The cost of merchandise purchased by a merchandise business and sold. *Objective 5*

Cost of quality report. A report that shows the dollar cost of waste and rework in processes. The report can be used to prioritize and track the effectiveness of continuous process improvement efforts. *Objective 3*

Direct costs. Costs that can be traced directly to a cost object. *Objective 4*

Direct labor cost. Wages of factory workers who are directly involved in converting materials into a finished product. *Objective 4*

Direct materials cost. The cost of materials that are an integral part of the finished product. *Objective 4*

Factory overhead cost. All of the costs of operating the factory except for direct materials and direct labor. *Objective 4*

Feedback. Measures provided to operational employees or managers on the performance of subunits of the organization. These measures are used by employees to adjust a process or a behavior to achieve goals. See **Management by exception.** *Objective 3*

Financial accounting. The branch of accounting that is concerned with the recording of transactions using generally accepted accounting principles (GAAP) for a business or other economic unit and with a periodic preparation of various statements from such records. *Objective 1*

Finished goods inventory. The cost of finished products on hand that have not been sold. *Objective 5*

Indirect costs. Costs that cannot be traced directly to a cost object. *Objective 4*

Just-in-time (JIT) manufacturing systems. Systems of manufacturing in which a primary emphasis is on the manufacture of products only as they are needed by the next stage of production or by the marketplace. *Objective 6*

Lead time. The time required to manufacture a product from receipt of an order until it is shipped to the customer. Sometimes called cycle time. *Objective 6*

Management by exception. The philosophy of managing which involves monitoring the operating results of implemented plans and comparing the expected results with the actual results. This feedback allows management to isolate significant variations for further investigation and possible remedial action. *Objective 3*

Management process. The five basic management functions of (1) planning, (2) directing, (3) controlling, (4) improving, and (5) decision making. *Objective 3*

Managerial accounting. The branch of accounting that uses both historical and estimated data in providing information that management uses in conducting daily operations, in planning future operations, and in developing overall business strategies. *Objective 1*

Materials inventory. The cost of materials that have not yet entered into the manufacturing process. *Objective 5*

Operational planning. The development of short-term plans to achieve goals identified in a business's strategic plan. Sometimes called tactical planning. *Objective 3*

Period costs. Those costs that are used up in generating revenue during the current period and that are not involved in the manufacturing process. These costs are recognized as expenses on the current period's income statement. *Objective 4*

Prime costs. The combination of direct materials and direct labor costs. *Objective 4*

Product costs. The three components of manufacturing cost: direct materials, direct labor, and factory overhead costs. *Objective 4*

Strategic planning. The development of a long-range course of action to achieve business goals. *Objective 3*

Strategies. The means by which business goals and objectives will be achieved. *Objective 3*

Total quality management (TQM). A management approach that involves an ongoing commitment to improving product quality, starting with product design and continuing through production. *Objective 6*

Work in process inventory. The direct materials costs, the direct labor costs, and the factory overhead costs that have entered into the manufacturing process, but are associated with products that have not been finished. *Objective 5*

ILLUSTRATIVE PROBLEM

The following is a list of costs that were incurred in producing this textbook:

a. Insurance on the factory building and equipment.
b. Salary of the vice-president of finance.
c. Hourly wages of printing press operators during production.
d. Straight-line depreciation on the printing presses used to manufacture the text.
e. Electricity used to run the presses during the printing of the text.
f. Sales commissions paid to textbook representatives for each text sold.
g. Paper on which the text is printed.
h. Book covers used to bind the pages.
i. Royalties paid to the authors for each text sold.
j. Salaries of staff used to develop artwork for the text.
k. Glue used to bind pages to cover.

Instructions

With respect to the manufacture and sale of this text, classify each cost as either a product cost or a period cost. Indicate whether each product cost is a direct materials cost, a direct labor cost, or a factory overhead cost. Indicate whether each period cost is a selling expense or an administrative expense.

Solution

	Product Cost			Period Cost	
Cost	Direct Materials Cost	Direct Labor Cost	Factory Overhead Cost	Selling Expense	Administrative Expense
a.			X		
b.					X
c.		X			
d.			X		
e.			X		
f.				X	
g.	X				
h.	X				
i.					X
j.			X		
k.			X		

SELF-EXAMINATION QUESTIONS (ANSWERS AT END OF CHAPTER)

1. Which of the following best describes the difference between financial and managerial accounting?
   A. Managerial accounting provides information to support decisions, while financial accounting does not.
   B. Managerial accounting is not restricted to generally accepted accounting principles (GAAP), while financial accounting is restricted to GAAP.
   C. Managerial accounting does not result in financial reports, while financial accounting does result in financial reports.
   D. Managerial accounting is concerned solely with the future and does not record events from the past, while financial accounting records only events from past transactions.

2. Which of the following is **not** one of the five basic phases of the management process?
   A. Planning C. Decision making
   B. Controlling D. Operating

3. Which of the following is **not** considered a cost of manufacturing a product?
   A. Direct materials cost C. Sales salaries
   B. Factory overhead cost D. Direct labor cost

4. Which of the following costs would be included as part of the factory overhead costs of a microcomputer manufacturer?
   A. The cost of memory chips
   B. Depreciation of testing equipment
   C. Wages of computer assemblers
   D. The cost of disk drives

5. Which of the following trends in business is related to reducing the lead time to manufacture a product?
   A. Total quality management
   B. Just-in-time manufacturing
   C. Globalization of business
   D. Computer-integrated manufacturing

DISCUSSION QUESTIONS

1. What are the major differences between managerial accounting and financial accounting?
2. a. Differentiate between a department with line responsibility and a department with staff responsibility.
   b. In an organization that has a Sales Department and a Personnel Department, among others, which of the two departments has (1) line responsibility and (2) staff responsibility?
3. a. What is the role of the controller in a business organization?
   b. Does the controller have a line or staff responsibility?
4. Describe what proper ethical conduct implies.
5. What are the five basic phases of the management process?
6. What is the term for a plan that encompasses a period ranging from five or more years and that serves as a basis for commitment of business resources?
7. What is the process by which management runs day-to-day operations?
8. What is the process by which management assesses how well a plan is working?
9. Describe what is meant by *management by exception.*
10. What term describes a payment in cash (or its equivalent of the commitment to pay cash in the future) for the purpose of generating revenues?

11. For a company that produces microcomputers, would memory chips be considered a direct or an indirect cost of each microcomputer produced?
12. What three costs make up the cost of manufacturing a product?
13. What manufacturing cost term is used to describe the cost of materials that are an integral part of the manufactured end product?
14. If the cost of wages paid to employees who are directly involved in converting raw materials into a manufactured end product is not a significant portion of the total product cost, how would the wages cost be classified as to type of manufacturing cost?
15. Distinguish between prime costs and conversion costs.
16. What is the difference between a product cost and a period cost?
17. Name the three inventory accounts for a manufacturing business, and describe what each balance represents at the end of an accounting period.
18. What are the three categories of manufacturing costs included in the cost of finished goods and the cost of work in process?
19. For a manufacturer, what is the description of the amount that is comparable to a merchandising business's cost of merchandise sold?
20. What term is sometimes used to refer to just-in-time manufacturing systems?
21. Why are just-in-time manufacturing systems said to be demand-pull systems?
22. Does the amount of inventory normally increase or decrease with the implementation of a just-in-time manufacturing system?
23. Why does the implementation of a just-in-time manufacturing system increase the emphasis placed on quality control?
24. What are some of the implications of just-in-time manufacturing systems for managerial accounting?
25. What is meant by a total quality management system?
26. a. Why does the increased use of automated manufacturing equipment increase factory overhead costs?
    b. What is the implication of increased factory overhead costs for management accountants?
27. What is meant by globalization of business?

28. The management of Trico Products Inc., a manufacturer of windshield wipers in Buffalo, New York, was faced with a decision on whether to locate several new plants in New York or on the Mexican border. Why would management decide to locate the plants on the Mexican border?
29. Why are managers of service businesses increasingly looking to management accountants for analyses and information that will enable the business to compete more effectively?

EXERCISES

EXERCISE 18–1
Classifying costs as materials, labor, or overhead
Objective 4

Indicate whether each of the following costs of an airplane manufacturer would be classified as direct materials cost, direct labor cost, or factory overhead cost:

a. Steel used in landing gear
b. Controls for flight deck
c. Welding machinery lubricants
d. Salary of test pilot
e. Wages of assembly-line worker
f. Tires
g. Aircraft engines
h. Depreciation of welding equipment

EXERCISE 18–2
Classifying costs as product or period costs
Objective 4

For an apparel manufacturer, classify each of the following costs as either a product cost or a period cost:

a. Factory janitorial supplies
b. Depreciation on office equipment
c. Advertising expenses
d. Fabric used during production
e. Depreciation on sewing machines
f. Property taxes on factory building and equipment

g. Sales commissions
h. Wages of sewing machine operators
i. Repairs and maintenance costs for sewing machines
j. Salary of production quality control supervisor
k. Factory supervisors' salaries
l. Oil used to lubricate sewing machines
m. Travel costs of salespersons
n. Corporate controller's salary
o. Utility costs for office building
p. Research and development costs
q. Salaries of distribution center personnel

EXERCISE 18–3
Concepts and terminology
Objectives 3, 4, 5, 6

From the choices presented in parentheses, choose the appropriate term for completing each of the following sentences:

a. Feedback is often used to (improve, direct) operations
b. A product, sales territory, department, or activity to which costs are traced is called a (direct cost, cost object).
c. Payments of cash or its equivalent or the commitment to pay cash in the future for the purpose of generating revenues are (costs, expenses).
d. The balance sheet of a manufacturer would include an account for (cost of goods sold, work in process inventory).
e. Factory overhead costs combined with direct labor costs are called (prime, conversion) costs.
f. Advertising costs are usually viewed as (period, product) costs.
g. Just-in-time manufacturing uses (push, demand-pull) materials scheduling.
h. The implementation of automatic, robotic factory equipment normally (increases, decreases) the direct labor component of product costs.

EXERCISE 18–4
Concepts and terminology
Objectives 3, 4, 5, 6

From the choices presented in parentheses, choose the appropriate term for completing each of the following sentences:

a. Direct materials costs combined with direct labor costs are called (prime, conversion) costs.
b. The wages of an assembly worker are normally considered a (period, product) cost.
c. The phase of the management process associated with continuous improvement of operations is called (directing, improving).
d. Short-term plans are called (strategic, operational) plans.
e. The plant manager's salary would be considered (direct, indirect) to the product.
f. Materials for use in production are called (direct materials, materials inventory).
g. An example of factory overhead is (sales office depreciation, plant depreciation).
h. The opposite of continuous improvement is (firefighting, total quality management).

EXERCISE 18–5
Classifying costs
Objective 4

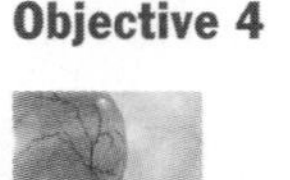

The following report was prepared for evaluating the performance of the plant manager of Miss-Take Inc. Evaluate and correct this report.

Miss-Take Inc.
Manufacturing Costs
For the Quarter Ended March 31, 1997

Direct labor (including $80,000 maintenance salaries)	$ 430,000
Materials placed into production (including $40,000 of indirect materials)	680,000
Factory overhead:	
Supervisor salaries	610,000
Heat, light, and power	140,000
Sales salaries	270,000
Promotional expenses	310,000
Insurance and property taxes—plant	160,000
Insurance and property taxes—corporate offices	210,000
Depreciation—plant and equipment	80,000
Depreciation—corporate offices	100,000
Total	$2,990,000

EXERCISE 18–6
Classifying costs in a service company
Objectives 4, 6

A partial list of the costs for Mountain Lakes Railroad, a short hauler of freight, are provided below. Classify each cost as either indirect or direct. For purposes of classifying each cost as direct or indirect, use the train as the cost object.

a. Cost to lease (rent) train locomotives
b. Wages of switch and classification yard personnel
c. Wages of train engineers
d. Cost to lease (rent) railroad cars
e. Maintenance costs of right of way, bridges, and buildings
f. Fuel costs
g. Payroll clerk salaries
h. Safety training costs
i. Salaries of dispatching and communications personnel
j. Costs of accident cleanup
k. Cost of track and bed (ballast) replacement
l. Depreciation of terminal facilities

EXERCISE 18–7
Financial statements of a manufacturing firm
Objective 5

The following events took place for Gantt Manufacturing Company during March, the first month of its operations as a producer of digital clocks:

- Purchased $65,000 of materials.
- Used $50,000 of direct materials in production.
- Incurred $75,000 of direct labor wages.
- Incurred $105,000 of factory overhead.
- Transferred $175,000 of work in process to finished goods.
- Sold goods with a cost of $140,000.
- Earned revenues of $310,000.
- Incurred $80,000 of selling expenses.
- Incurred $35,000 of administrative expenses.

a. Prepare the March income statement for Gantt Manufacturing Company. Assume that Gantt uses the perpetual inventory method.
b. Determine the inventory balances at the end of the first month of operations.

EXERCISE 18–8
Cost flow relationships
Objective 5

The following information is available for the first month of operations of Brown Company, a manufacturer of mechanical pencils:

Sales	$600,000
Gross profit	350,000
Cost of goods manufactured	300,000
Indirect labor	130,000
Indirect materials	20,000
Materials purchased	185,000
Total manufacturing costs for the period	345,000
Materials inventory	25,000

Using the above information, determine the following missing amounts:

a. Cost of goods sold
b. Finished goods inventory
c. Direct materials cost
d. Direct labor cost
e. Work in process inventory

PROBLEMS SERIES A

PROBLEM 18–1A
Classifying costs
Objective 4

The following is a list of costs that were incurred in the production and sale of boats:

a. Commissions to sales representatives, based upon the number of boats sold.
b. Cost of boat for "grand prize" promotion in local bass tournament.
c. Memberships for key executives in the Bass World Association.
d. Cost of electrical wiring for boats.

e. Cost of normal scrap from defective hulls.
f. Cost of metal hardware for boats, such as ornaments and tie-down grasps.
g. Cost of paving the employee parking lot.
h. Hourly wages of assembly-line workers.
i. Premiums on business interruption insurance in case of a natural disaster.
j. Straight-line depreciation on factory equipment.
k. Wood paneling for use in interior boat trim.
l. Steering wheels.
m. Special advertising campaign in *Bass World*.
n. Masks for use by sanders in smoothing boat hulls.
o. Power used by sanding equipment.
p. Yearly cost of maintenance contract for robotic equipment.
q. Oil to lubricate factory equipment.
r. Glue for boats.
s. Executive end-of-year bonuses.
t. Salary of shop supervisor.
u. Decals for boat hull.
v. Annual fee to pro-fisherman Jim Bo Wilks to promote the boats.
w. Paint for boats.
x. Legal department costs for the year.
y. Fiberglass for producing the boat hull.
z. Salary of president of company.

Instructions

Classify each cost as either a product cost or a period cost. Indicate whether each product cost is a direct materials cost, a direct labor cost, or a factory overhead cost. Indicate whether each period cost is a selling expense or an administrative expense. Use the following tabular headings for your answer, placing an "X" in the appropriate column.

	Product Costs			*Period Costs*	
Cost	*Direct Materials Cost*	*Direct Labor Cost*	*Factory Overhead Cost*	*Selling Expense*	*Administrative Expense*

PROBLEM 18–2A
Classifying costs
Objective 4

The following is a list of costs incurred by several businesses:

a. Cost of dyes used by a clothing manufacturer.
b. Salary of the vice-president of manufacturing logistics.
c. Wages of a machine operator on the production line.
d. Travel costs of marketing executives to annual sales meeting.
e. Cost of sewing machine needles used by a shirt manufacturer.
f. Depreciation of microcomputers used in the factory to coordinate and monitor the production schedules.
g. Pens, paper, and other supplies used by Accounting Department in preparing various managerial reports.
h. Electricity used to operate factory machinery.
i. Factory janitorial supplies.
j. Fees paid to lawn service for office grounds upkeep.
k. Wages of computer programmers for production of microcomputer software.
l. Depreciation of copying machines used by the Marketing Department.
m. Telephone charges by president's office.
n. Cost of plastic for a telephone being manufactured.
o. Oil lubricants for factory plant and equipment.
p. Cost of a 30-second television commercial.
q. Depreciation of robot used to assemble a product.
r. Wages of production quality control personnel.
s. Maintenance and repair costs for factory equipment.
t. Depreciation of tools used in production.

u. Rent for a warehouse used to store finished products.
v. Maintenance costs for factory equipment.
w. Fees charged by collection agency on past-due customer accounts.
x. Charitable contribution to United Fund.

Instructions

Classify each of the preceding costs as product costs or period costs. Indicate whether each product cost is a direct materials cost, a direct labor cost, or a factory overhead cost. Indicate whether each period cost is a selling expense or an administrative expense. Use the following tabular headings for preparing your answer, placing an "X" in the appropriate column.

	Product Costs			*Period Costs*	
Cost	*Direct Materials Cost*	*Direct Labor Cost*	*Factory Overhead Cost*	*Selling Expense*	*Administrative Expense*

PROBLEM 18–3A
Cost classifications—service company
Objectives 4, 6

A partial list of Highland Medical Center's costs are provided below.

a. Depreciation of X-ray equipment.
b. Cost of drugs used for patients.
c. Nurses' salaries.
d. Cost of new heart wing.
e. Overtime incurred in the Records Department due to a computer failure.
f. Cost of patient meals.
g. General maintenance of the hospital.
h. Salary of the nutritionist.
i. Cost of maintaining the staff and visitors cafeteria.
j. Training costs for nurses.
k. Operating room supplies used on patients (catheters, sutures, etc.).
l. Utility costs of the hospital.
m. Cost of intravenous solutions.
n. Cost of blood tests.
o. Cost of improvements on the employee parking lot.
p. Cost of laundry services for operating room personnel.
q. Depreciation on patient rooms.
r. Cost of advertising hospital services on television.
s. Cost of X-ray test.
t. Salary of intensive care personnel.
u. Doctor's fee.

Instructions

1. What would be Highland's most logical definition for the final cost object?
2. Identify how each of the costs is to be classified as either direct or indirect. Define direct costs in terms of the final cost object identified in (1).

PROBLEM 18–4A
Correcting manufacturing income statement; product cost vs. period cost
Objectives 4, 5

Holland Company makes and assembles interior door trim for the automotive industry. The owner of Holland Company, Lee Holland, was trained as a chemical engineer and has perfected an injecting molding process that makes superior plastic parts for interior door trim. The interior door trim consists of injected molded plastic pieces, ashtrays, lock and window mechanisms, armrests, and fabric. These pieces are assembled by Holland to make a completed interior door panel. Holland Company is a new business that began operations on January 1, 1997. Holland is receiving sales orders from automobile manufacturers based on the new technology.

Lee Holland prepared the following income statement for the calendar year 1997:

Holland Company
Income Statement
For the Year Ended December 31, 1997

Sales		$1,650,000
Direct materials	$ 800,000	
Direct labor	100,000	
Factory overhead	300,000	
Total incurred costs of manufacturing		$1,200,000
Selling, general, and administrative costs:		
Factory depreciation	$ 100,000	
Factory management salaries	150,000	
Selling and administrative expenses	200,000	450,000
Total incurred costs		$1,650,000
Excess of revenues over costs		$ 0

Lee Holland is very disappointed that the business did not appear to be profitable during the first year of operations. Holland's accounting training is minimal, so there is some question if the income statement is prepared properly. You have been asked to look over the Holland income statement to discover if there have been any errors in the calculations.

In the course of your examination, you have determined the correct balances for the beginning and ending inventory balances in the materials, work in process, and finished goods inventories.

	Jan. 1, 1997	*Dec. 31, 1997*
Materials inventory	$0	$ 0
Work in process inventory	0	50,000
Finished goods inventory	0	250,000

Instructions

1. Comment on the treatment of factory depreciation and factory management salaries as period costs.
2. Recast the Holland Company income statement according to generally accepted accounting principles. Provide supporting calculations.
3. Why is the net income in your recast statement different from that in Holland's statement?

PROBLEM 18–5A
Product vs. period costs, manufacturing income statement, inventories
Objectives 4, 5

Productivity Tools, Inc. (PT) is a designer, manufacturer, and distributor of software for microcomputers. The company began operations on January 1, 1997. For the first six months of operations the company spent $1,000,000 in programming a new software product. The product was ready for manufacture on July 1, 1997. On July 1, 1997, PT purchased production facilities to manufacture the final product for $1,500,000. These facilities are expected to have a 2 1/2-year life (assume straight-line depreciation and no salvage value).

Direct materials unit costs are:

Blank disk	$ 5.00
Packaging	3.00
Manual	10.00
Total	$18.00

The actual production process for the software product is fairly straightforward. The blank disks are first brought to a disk-copying machine. After the program is copied onto the disk, the disk is brought to assembly, where assembly personnel pack the disk and manual for shipping. The direct labor cost for this work is $2 per unit. The completed packages are then sold to customers through brokers, who charge PT a 15% commission on the sales price for all sales.

PT placed newspaper ads for the remainder of the year. The ads cost $10,000. Total production was 65,000 units during the year.

Other information is as follows:

General office depreciation	$500,000
Indirect labor	$120,000
Number of packages sold in 1997	50,000
Sales price per unit	$ 100

The work in process inventory on December 31, 1997, was $30,000, and the finished goods inventory was $390,000. There was no materials inventory on December 31, 1997.

Instructions

Prepare an income statement, including supporting calculations, from the information above. Note: The programming costs should be expensed.

PROBLEMS SERIES B

PROBLEM 18–1B
Classifying costs
Objective 4

The following is a list of costs that were incurred in the production and sale of lawn mowers.

a. Payroll taxes on hourly assembly-line employees.
b. Filter for spray gun used to paint the lawn mowers.
c. Cost of boxes used in packaging lawn mowers.
d. Premiums on insurance policy for factory buildings.
e. Gasoline engines used for lawn mowers.
f. Salary of factory supervisor.
g. Tires for lawn mowers.
h. Cost of advertising in a national magazine.
i. Plastic for outside housing of lawn mowers.
j. Salary of quality control supervisor who inspects each lawn mower before it is shipped.
k. Rivets, bolts, and other fasteners used in lawn mowers.
l. Cash paid to outside firm for janitorial services for factory.
m. Engine oil used in mower engines prior to shipment.
n. Attorney fees for drafting a new lease for headquarters offices.
o. Maintenance costs for new robotic factory equipment, based upon hours of usage.
p. Straight-line depreciation on the robotic machinery used to manufacture the lawn mowers.
q. License fees for use of patent for lawn mower blade, based upon the number of lawn mowers produced.
r. Telephone charges for controller's office.
s. Paint used to paint the lawn mowers.
t. Steel used in producing the lawn mowers.
u. Commissions paid to sales representatives, based upon the number of lawn mowers sold.
v. Electricity used to run the robotic machinery.
w. Factory cafeteria cashier's wages.
x. Property taxes on the factory building and equipment.
y. Salary of vice-president of marketing.
z. Hourly wages of operators of robotic machinery used in production.

Instructions

Classify each cost as either a product cost or a period cost. Indicate whether each product cost is a direct materials cost, a direct labor cost, or a factory overhead cost. Indicate whether each period cost is a selling expense or an administrative expense. Use the following tabular headings for your answer, placing an "X" in the appropriate column.

	Product Costs			*Period Costs*	
Cost	*Direct Materials Cost*	*Direct Labor Cost*	*Factory Overhead Cost*	*Selling Expense*	*Administrative Expense*

PROBLEM 18–2B
Classifying costs
Objective 4

The following is a list of costs incurred by several businesses:

a. Packing supplies for products sold.
b. Tires for an automobile manufacturer.
c. Costs for television advertisement.
d. Disk drives for a microcomputer manufacturer.
e. Executive bonus for vice-president of marketing.
f. Seed for grain farmer.
g. Wages of a machine operator on the production line.
h. Wages of controller's secretary.
i. Factory operating supplies.
j. First-aid supplies for factory workers.
k. Depreciation of factory equipment.
l. Salary of quality control supervisor.
m. Sales commissions.
n. Maintenance and repair costs for factory equipment.
o. Cost of hogs for meat processor.
p. Health insurance premiums paid for factory workers.
q. Lumber used by furniture manufacturer.
r. Paper used by commercial printer.
s. Hourly wages of warehouse laborers.
t. Paper used by computer department in processing various managerial reports.
u. Costs of operating a research laboratory.
v. Entertainment expenses for sales representatives.
w. Cost of telephone operators for a toll-free hotline to help customers operate products.
x. Protective glasses for factory machine operators.

Instructions

Classify each of the preceding costs as product costs or period costs. Indicate whether each product cost is a direct materials cost, a direct labor cost, or a factory overhead cost. Indicate whether each period cost is a selling expense or an administrative expense. Use the following tabular headings for preparing your answer. Place an "X" in the appropriate column.

	Product Costs			*Period Costs*	
Cost	*Direct Materials Cost*	*Direct Labor Cost*	*Factory Overhead Cost*	*Selling Expense*	*Administrative Expense*

PROBLEM 18–3B
Cost classifications—service company
Objectives 4, 6

A partial list of Heartland Hotel's costs are provided below.

a. Salary of the hotel president.
b. Depreciation of the hotel.
c. Cost of new carpeting.
d. Cost of soaps and shampoos for rooms.
e. Cost of food.
f. Wages of desk clerks.
g. Cost to paint lobby.
h. Cost of advertising in local newspaper.
i. Utility costs.
j. Cost of valet service.
k. General maintenance supplies.
l. Wages of maids.
m. Wages of bellhops.
n. Wages of convention setup employees.
o. Pay-for-view rental costs (in rooms).
p. Cost of room mini-bar supplies.
q. Guest room telephone costs for long-distance calls.
r. Wages of kitchen employees.
s. Cost of laundering towels and bedding.
t. Cost to replace lobby furniture.
u. Training for hotel restaurant servers.

v. Cost to mail and analyze a customer survey.
w. Champagne for guests.

Instructions

1. What would be Heartland's most logical definition for the final cost object?
2. Identify how each of the costs is to be classified as either direct or indirect. Define direct costs in terms of the final cost object identified in (1).

PROBLEM 18–4B
Correcting manufacturing income statement; product cost vs. period cost
Objectives 4, 5

Allyn Olsen started a new company to manufacture electronic testing equipment for the textile industry. This equipment tested for fiber tensile strength, color, and trash (a term used for foreign particles in the fiber) using laser technology. Olsen began this business on January 1, 1997. Olsen was not trained as an accountant, so was not sure how to construct the income statement for 1997. Olsen tracked the costs incurred in the operation since the beginning of the year. Olsen used this information to construct the following income statement:

Olsen Instruments Inc.
Income Statement
For the Year Ended December 31, 1997

Sales		$12,250,000
Direct materials	$5,400,000	
Direct labor	1,500,000	
Factory overhead:		
Production support salaries	1,200,000	
Factory utilities	400,000	
Sales office (located in factory)	800,000	
Total incurred costs of manufacturing		$ 9,300,000
Selling, general, and administrative costs:		
Factory depreciation	$ 800,000	
Factory management salaries	650,000	
General administrative expenses	1,500,000	2,950,000
Total incurred costs		$12,250,000
Excess of revenues over costs		$ 0

Allyn Olsen is disappointed that the business did not appear to be more successful than the income statement indicated. You have been asked to look over the Olsen income statement to discover if there have been any errors in the statement presentation.

In the course of your examination, you have asked for the beginning and ending inventory balances in the materials, work in process, and finished goods inventories. The following data have been provided for you:

	Jan. 1, 1997	*Dec. 31, 1997*
Materials inventory	$0	$ 0
Work in process inventory	0	200,000
Finished goods inventory	0	1,950,000

Instructions

1. Comment on the treatment of factory depreciation and factory management salaries as period costs. Comment on the treatment of the sales office expenses as a product cost.
2. Recast the Olsen Instruments income statement according to generally accepted accounting principles. Provide supporting calculations.
3. Why is the net income in your recast statement different from that in Olsen's statement?

PROBLEM 18–5B
Product vs. period costs, manufacturing income statement, inventories
Objectives 4, 5

Olympus Records is in the business of developing, promoting, and selling musical talent on compact disc (CD). The company signed a new musical act, called *Critical Mass,* on January 1, 1997. During the year, the company spent $300,000 in developing a promotional strategy for *Critical Mass.* The CD production began on January 11, 1997.

The unit direct materials cost for the CD is:

Blank CD	$4.00
Plastic package	.50
Song lyric insert	.25

The production process is straightforward. First, the blank CDs are brought to a production area where the digital soundtrack is copied on to the CD. The equipment for performing this part of the process has a cost of $200,000 and is estimated to have a four-year life (assume straight-line depreciation and no salvage value). The copying machine runs without any employee assistance.

After the CDs are copied, they are brought to an assembly area, where an employee packs the CD with a plastic package and song lyric insert. The direct labor cost is $0.40 per unit.

The CDs are sold to record stores. Each record store is given promotional materials, such as posters and aisle displays. Promotional materials cost $40 per record store. Shipping costs average $5 per sales order.

Total production was 1,300,000 units during the year. Other information is as follows:

General office depreciation	$280,000
Indirect labor	$80,000
Number of sales orders	55,000
Number of customers (record stores)	20,000
Average CDs sold per order	20
Wholesale price (to record store) per CD	$12

The work in process inventory on December 31, 1997, was $325,000, and the finished goods inventory was $1,000,000. There was no materials inventory on December 31, 1997.

Instructions

Prepare an income statement, including supporting calculations, from the information above. Note: The promotional strategy costs should be expensed.

CASES

CASE 18–1
Gulf Wing Airlines
Providing advice to top management

The following conversation took place between the newly appointed vice-president of finance (VP-Finance) and the controller of Gulf Wing Airlines.

VP-Finance: Last week, our president asked me to prepare an analysis on the feasibility of opening routes to South American cities.

Controller: I know. She has been very enthusiastic about expanding in this direction. Apparently, her trip to South America last month convinced her of the opportunity.

VP-Finance: Well, I'm going to have to give her some bad news. My analysis indicates that only in the most optimistic and unlikely scenario does the idea seem to have any chance of success.

Controller: I'm glad I'm not in your shoes! I know from past experience the president believes in Louis B. Mayer's alleged quote, "I don't want yes-men around me. Tell me what you think, even if it costs you your job." I don't think she's going to take the news well.

VP-Finance: I wonder what I should do?

The vice-president of finance has thought of three possible avenues for responding to the president:

1. Be clear in opposing the idea by referring to the analysis. This approach will likely alienate the president.
2. Take a middle road. Suggest that the idea has much promise if conditions work out just right. Show the president some of the data through a memo. Rely on the president's understanding the implications of the data and making the right decision.
3. Agree with the president. Suggest that the decision to open routes to South America is beyond financial analysis and that the only way to make the decision is by "gut feel."

Which one of these strategies comes closest to the approach you would recommend as the financial VP? Provide a detailed strategy for dealing with this dilemma.

CASE 18–2
AT&T, Apple Computer, and Kimberly Clark
Managerial accounting and the management process

Many companies are now becoming more aware of the impact their products and processes have on the environment. AT&T has invested in engineering controls and equipment that have reduced dangerous air pollution by 55%. Apple Computer Company has eliminated the use of white boxes for their products and replaced them with brown boxes to help reduce the use of bleaching agents in cardboard processing. Kimberly Clark is concerned about the biodegradability of disposable diapers on the environment and is experimenting with more biodegradable diapers.

Many environmental investments do not provide a financial return nor do they appear to provide direct customer value. Indeed, some environmentally directed decisions seem to take some value away from customers (ugly boxes, less absorbent diapers, etc.).

How does managerial accounting support environmental decisions that reflect a business's concern for customer value and return to shareholders?

CASE 18–3
Orion Division
Using managerial accounting information in the management process

The following information was prepared for the Orion Division:

Customer returns	20% of sales
Warranty claims	5% of sales
Productivity (units produced)	9,600 units
Late shipments	8%
Percent of product rejected at final inspection	12%
Cost per unit	$98
Short shipments* as a percent of total shipments	16%

*Shipments that are less than what the customer ordered due to unavailability of a particular item.

Orion had a production target of 9,500 units for the month at a target unit cost of $100 per unit.

Analyze and interpret the division's performance for the month.

CASE 18–4
Delco Company
Financial vs. managerial accounting

The following statement made by the vice-president of finance of Delco Company: "The managers of a company should use the same information as the shareholders of the firm. When managers use the same information in guiding their internal operations as shareholders use in evaluating their investments, the managers will be aligned with the stockholders' profit objectives."

Respond to the vice-president's statement.

CASE 18–5
Managerial accounting in the management process

For each of the following managers, describe how managerial accounting could be used to satisfy strategic or operational objectives:

a. The vice-president for the information system division of a bank.
b. A hospital administrator.
c. The chief executive officer of a food company. The food company is divided into three divisions: Nonalcoholic Beverage, Snack Foods, and Fast Food Restaurants.
d. The manager of the local campus copy shop.

CASE 18–6
Managerial accounting in the management process

The following situations describe decision scenarios that could use managerial accounting information.

a. The manager of Taco Castle wishes to determine the price to charge for various lunch plates.
b. By evaluating the cost of rework and scrap, the plant manager of a precision machining facility wishes to determine how effectively the plant is being run.
c. The division controller needs to determine the cost of products left in inventory.
d. The manager of a maintenance department wishes to plan next year's anticipated expenditures.

For each situation discuss how managerial accounting information could be used.

CASE 18–7
IBM
Total quality management in the accounting function

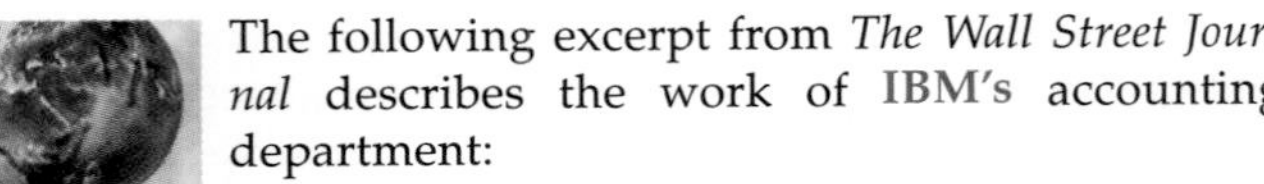

The following excerpt from *The Wall Street Journal* describes the work of IBM's accounting department:

Managers from the accounting department had three objectives in regard to their internal customers. First, they negotiated acceptable levels of accuracy for information coming into and going out of accounting. Second, they identified and developed the tools required to meet their accuracy commitments. For example, accounting provided a personal-computer software program that helped internal customers screen their own data for errors before submitting them to accounting. Third, they established feedback mechanisms by which accounting and its internal customers could identify and return erroneous information to each other and offer suggestions on how to prevent the errors from recurring.

"Managers in other parts of the company were a little surprised to have their data supply errors pointed out by accounting," [William] Eggleston [vice-president of quality] recalls. "But they quickly saw that this was the first step in a whole new process designed to help accounting provide more accurate information." The result? "We have reduced the miscoding rate to less than 1%."

Explain how the work of IBM's accounting department is an example of total quality process management.

CASE 18–8
Merck & Co.
The organizational role of a financial executive

The following interview of Judy Lewent, Chief Financial Officer (CFO) of Merck & Co. (a pharmaceutical company), is excerpted from *The Wall Street Journal* (June 30, 1992):

Corporate finance is sometimes regarded as the enemy of long-term thinking, as the enforcer of the Bottom Line at the cost of innovation and international eminence. One of the more powerful women in American business is attempting to dispel that notion. . . .

"Merck is research driven," she says, but "through the planning model, what we're able to do at finance is put in some kind of quantitative terms how we see the future of the company. . . ." Financial direction "has been helpful in terms of coming full circle and having everyone understand the unity of purpose"—that a broad and busy lab, oriented to licensing products as well as efficiently developing them, is "key to not only the success of the company but (ultimately) to funding future growth in research. . . ."

"Yes, they've got to be creative; yes, they have to be in an environment where they can experiment and fail. Without question," she says. "But while they're doing it, it has to be in the range where there are defined targets and objectives that make some sense over the five to 10 year period for them to pursue."

Finance can offer that discipline, without getting hung up on the next quarter or next year. She insists that "done properly," number crunching needn't pinch perspective, although "in the hands of one who has narrow understanding, it can fall prey to that. . . ."

Ms. Lewent goes on, "People talk about how short-termism is driven out of the fact that financial people force discounted cash-flow ROI (return on investment) down the throats of everybody, and these high-hurdle rates, this high cost of capital is what stultifies investment. I just come back and say if you really understand the business, and you're a partner with the operating members of your business, then you can marry the right kind of financial parameters to the business opportunities, and be an aid to the process, a strategic ally as opposed to the policeman."

Describe how Ms. Lewent's role as a chief financial executive supports the management process.

CASE 18–9
CCA
Trends in managerial accounting

The following is an excerpt about recent changes at CCA, a small firm in Knoxville, Tennessee:

CCA's program is based on building a participative management system and using statistical tools to monitor and improve quality. "We used to just produce a product. Our customer's wants and needs were not given the priority they are now given."

Hamilton said introducing the teamwork concept to get people involved in improving the company's processes has been the most difficult aspect of CCA's quality program. "The big problem is apathy. We are making progress, but there is still a group of people that feel this is a fad, this too will pass." Even though the company's emphasis is on participative management, CCA still falls back on the old way of doing things, an approach known as "firefighting," Hamilton said. "That's the way most of us managers were brought up on—short-term, short-lived band-aid approaches," he said. . . .

Employees have succeeded at working together as a team and have eliminated much of the old system's fingerpointing. It's probably the best thing to ever happen to American industry. Germans and Swedes jumped on the quality bandwagon well ahead of the United States. Add to that the wage pressures of developing nations and the streamlining of the European economic community, and U.S. businesses are having to scramble like never before. This competition is not a flash in the pan, quality gurus say. It's here to stay, and if U.S. companies don't adapt, they won't survive. . . .

The definition of "quality" sounds like common sense to the uninitiated. Essentially it means continuous improvement, with a constant goal of meeting the customer's needs. The "customer" means both external customers who buy the company's product or service, and the internal customers, or employees, who depend on other employees to do their jobs right.

Though it sounds simple, it actually requires a revolution in the way U.S. companies still do business, quality advocates say. "The still widespread belief . . . that a certain amount of poor quality is acceptable, and even economically necessary, has a devastating effect on efforts to improve quality, productivity, and thus customer satisfaction. . . ."

Laura Simmons, "Knox Firms Seeing Results of Quality Work," *The Knoxville News Sentinel,* January 5, 1992, p. D1.

Identify the major management trends that are being reflected in CCA. What are some possible impacts on managerial accounting?

CASE 18–10

England Engine Company

The management process and total quality management

England Engine Company assembles engines. A major part of the process is to assemble the pistons into their appropriate cylinders. The outside diameter of the pistons must nearly match the inside diameters of the cylinders so that very little gas escapes during the firing of the pistons. However, there must be no interference between the fit, or else the piston will damage the inside walls of the cylinders. The tolerance (engineering specification) for the gap between the cylinder walls and piston are very tight.

England finds that cylinders and pistons do not always match perfectly. In fact, pistons must be sorted into diameter categories that differ by fractions of centimeters. England has ten different categories ranging from 10.5 cm to 10.7 cm. In addition, cylinders are not exactly the same from cylinder to cylinder. Because of this subtle variation between cylinders and pistons, assemblers attempt to match pistons with cylinders in order to get proper "fit." This process is much like a jigsaw puzzle where different pieces are attempted before the correctly fitting piece is discovered. This sorting and matching process is time-consuming but necessary in order to build engines that maintain their compression.

When an engine is completed, it is tested by being run for one hour. Every engine is tested in this manner to guarantee a well-functioning engine. About 5% of the engines fail this final test. When an engine fails this test, it is disassembled and reassembled properly. England believes that it is much too expensive to just scrap the engine and that this rework process is cost effective. Frequently, engine failure is the result of compression loss, stuck valves, and engine overheating. Further analysis reveals that 25% of the reworked engines must again be reworked to eliminate defects.

England sells engines to major automobile manufacturers. England prides itself in its customer satisfaction and product quality ratings. England guarantees 100% satisfaction by replacing any defective engine found at the automobile manufacturer and any defective engine found in a customer's car after one year. In fact, out of the last 5,000 engines shipped, only one engine was returned defective from the plant. Of the 100,000 engines shipped during the last year, only 160 have been returned defective from automobile customers.

1. England believes that they are following the principles of total quality management (TQM) because their customers are satisfied and their defects have been under 0.2%. Do you agree or disagree? Why?
2. What forces may require England to reconsider the way it is presently conducting business?
3. If you were an operating manager of the England engine plant, what operational plans would you propose? How could you use managerial accounting data in implementing these plans through the management process?

CASE 18–11

Speedy TV Repairs

Classifying costs

Speedy TV Repairs provides TV repair services for the community. Gail Sherwood's TV was not working, and she called Speedy for a home repair visit. The Speedy technician arrived at 2:00 P.M. to begin work. By 4:00 P.M. the problem was diagnosed as a failed circuit board. Unfortunately, the technician did not have a new circuit board in the truck, since the technician's previous customer had the same problem, and a board was used on that visit. Replacement boards were available back at the Speedy shop. Therefore, the technician drove back to the shop to retrieve a replacement board. From 4:00 to 5:00 P.M. the Speedy technician drove the round trip to retrieve the replacement board from the shop.

At 5:00 P.M. the technician was back on the job at Sherwood's home. The replacement procedure is somewhat complex, since a variety of tests must be performed once the board is installed. The job was completed at 6:00 P.M.

Gail Sherwood's repair bill showed the following:

Circuit board	$ 80
Labor charges	210
Total	$290

Gail Sherwood was surprised at the size of the bill and asked for some greater detail supporting the calculations. Speedy responded with the following explanations.

Cost of Materials	
Purchase price of circuit board	$60
Mark-up on purchase price to cover storage and handling	20
Total materials charge	$80

The labor charge per hour is detailed as follows:

Labor Charges	
2:00–3:00 P.M.	$ 50
3:00–4:00 P.M.	30
4:00–5:00 P.M.	70
5:00–6:00 P.M.	60
Total labor charge	$210

Further explanations in the differences in the hourly rates are as follows:

First hour:		
Base labor rate	$20	
Fringe benefits	5	
Administrative overhead	5	
Hourly labor rate		$30
Additional charge for first hour of any job to cover the cost of vehicle depreciation, fuel, and employee time in transit. A 30-minute transit time is assumed.		20
		$50
Third hour:		
Hourly labor rate		$30
The trip back to the shop includes depreciation and fuel; therefore, a charge was added to the hourly rate to cover these costs. The charge was calculated at twice the first-hour base charge, since the round trip took an hour.		40
		$70
Fourth hour:		
Hourly labor rate		$30
Overtime premium for time worked in excess of an eight-hour day (starting at 5:00 P.M.) is double time.		30
		$60

1. If you were in Gail Sherwood's position, how would you respond to the bill? Are there parts of the bill that appear incorrect to you? If so, what logic would you employ to convince Speedy that the bill is too high?
2. Use the headings below to construct a table. Fill in the table by first listing the costs identified in the case in the left-hand column. For each cost, place a check mark in the appropriate column identifying the **correct** cost classification. Assume the cost object is a service call.

Cost	*Direct Materials*	*Direct Labor*	*Overhead*

ANSWERS TO SELF-EXAMINATION QUESTIONS

1. **B** Both financial and managerial accounting support decision making (answer A). Financial accounting is mostly concerned with the decision making of external users, while managerial accounting supports decision making of management. Both financial and managerial accounting can result in financial reports (answer C). Managerial accounting reports are developed for internal use by managers at various levels in the organization. Both managerial and financial accounting record events from the past (answer D); however, managerial accounting can also include information about the future in the form of budgets and cash flow projections. It is true that managerial accounting is not restricted to generally accepted accounting principles, as is financial accounting (answer B).
2. **D** The five basic phases of the management process are planning (answer A), directing (not listed), controlling (answer B), improving (not listed), and decision making (answer C). Operating (answer D) is not one of the five basic phases, but operations are the object of managers' attention.
3. **C** Sales salaries (answer C) is a selling expense and is not considered a cost of manufacturing a product. Direct materials cost (answer A), factory overhead cost (answer B), and direct labor cost (answer D) are costs of manufacturing a product.
4. **B** Depreciation of testing equipment (answer B) is included as part of the factory overhead costs of the microcomputer manufacturer. The cost of memory chips (answer A) and the cost of disk drives (answer D) are both considered a part of direct materials cost. The wages of microcomputer assemblers (answer C) are part of direct labor costs.
5. **B** Just-in-time manufacturing (answer B) is concerned with reducing inventories, lead time, and waste in manufacturing processes. Total quality management (answer A) is concerned with the continuous improvement of people, processes, and products. Globalization of business (answer C) concerns increasing competition from international businesses in the United States, and increasing involvement of U.S.-based companies in international markets. Computer-integrated manufacturing (answer D) concerns the use of computers to design and manufacture products.

19 Job Order Cost Systems

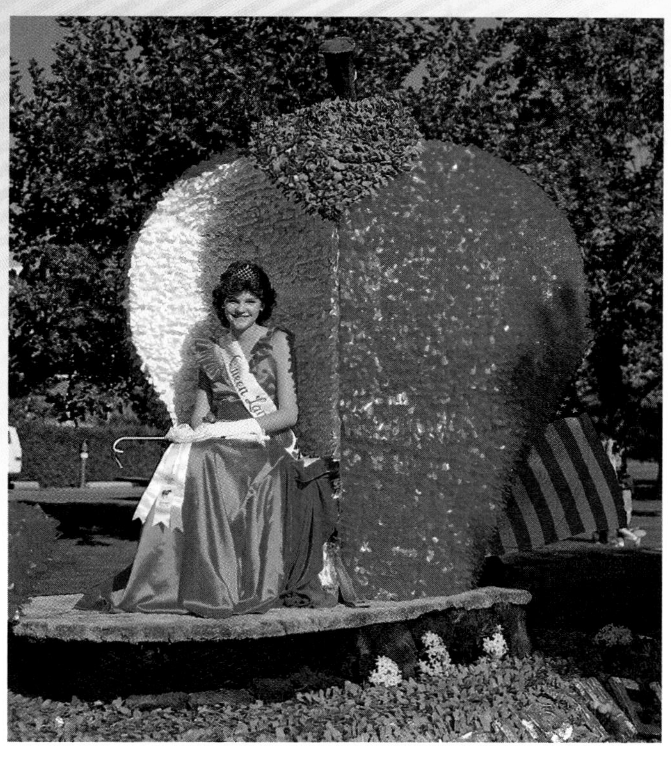

YOU AND ACCOUNTING

At the beginning of the school year, your accounting club budgeted $500 for constructing a float for the annual holiday parade. You have volunteered to lead the float project. Since only $500 is available for this project, you have decided to keep a detailed record of all costs related to the float. Initial costs were for lumber, hardware, paint, and artistic supplies. As these costs were incurred, you recorded them in a notebook. The notebook provided you a running total of costs incurred to date. Sometimes a club member would have an idea for the float that would add significantly to the cost. The notebook allowed you to make decisions regarding whether new ideas for the float could be accepted, given the amount spent to date compared to the $500 limitation.

Additional costs included in the notebook were the cost of renting a tractor to pull the float in the parade, the fees for an electrician to perform electrical wiring and testing, an entry fee, refreshments for the work team, and some supplies.

After the float was complete and all expenses were incurred, the total costs recorded in the notebook were $460. The club members decided that the last $40 would be spent on a post-parade pizza party.

Business organizations can also accumulate costs according to the work being performed on a quantity of a product or a project. In this chapter, you will study the principles of accounting systems that accumulate costs in this manner.

After studying this chapter, you should be able to:

Objective 1
Give examples of the usefulness of product costs.

Objective 2
Categorize accounting systems used by manufacturing businesses.

Objective 3
Describe and prepare summary journal entries for a job order cost accounting system.

Objective 4
Summarize the cost flows for a job order cost accounting system.

Objective 5
Use job order cost information for decision making.

Objective 6
Diagram the flow of costs for a service business that uses a job order cost accounting system.

Usefulness of Product Costs

Objective 1
Give examples of the usefulness of product costs.

The primary function of managerial accounting is to provide useful information to managers for planning and controlling operations. Much of this information is developed in the process of accounting for product costs.

Product costs are used by managers for a wide variety of purposes. For example, the unit cost of a finished product is useful for establishing product prices. Product costs are also useful in deciding whether to make a component of a product or to purchase the component from an outside source. Accurate product costs also enable managers to effectively and efficiently manage operations. Throughout the remainder of this text, we discuss a variety of other managerial decisions requiring the use of product costs.

Product costs are also used in preparing the financial statements of the business. Product costs are necessary for valuing work in process and finished goods inventories on the balance sheet and in determining the cost of goods sold on the income statement.

Cost Accounting System Overview

Objective 2
Categorize accounting systems used by manufacturing businesses.

The financial statements of a manufacturing business are prepared from the general ledger. The **general ledger** is the principal ledger that contains all the balance sheet and income statement accounts. The **cost accounting system** accumulates the product costs, originating with inventory and ending with the cost of goods sold. Thus, the cost accounting system contributes to developing financial statements by providing inventory and cost of goods sold balances. In addition, the cost accounting system improves control by supplying data on the costs incurred by each manufacturing department or process. Such systems not only provide useful data for minimizing costs, but also may provide management with other valuable data. For example, cost accounting systems may provide information to support production planning and control decisions.

There are two main types of cost accounting systems for manufacturing operations: job order and process cost systems. Each of the two systems is widely used, and any one manufacturer may use more than one type.

A job order cost system provides a separate record for the cost of each quantity of product that passes through the factory. A particular quantity of product is termed a **job.** A job order cost system is best suited to industries that manufacture custom goods to fill special orders from customers or that produce a high variety of products for stock. Manufacturers that use a job order cost system are sometimes called **job shops.** An example of a job shop would be an apparel manufacturer, such as Levi Strauss.

Many service firms also use job order cost systems to accumulate the costs associated with providing client services. For example, a law firm will accumulate all of the costs associated with a particular client engagement, such as lawyer time, copying charges, filing fees, and overhead. Recording costs in this manner helps the law firm control costs during a client engagement and determine client billing and profitability.

USING ACCOUNTING TO UNDERSTAND BUSINESS

Major electric utilities such as Tennessee Valley Authority, Consolidated Edison, or Pacific Gas and Electric use job order accounting to control the costs associated with major repairs and overhauls that occur during forced or planned outages. A forced outage is an unexpected shutdown of a power plant, whereas a planned outage is a scheduled shutdown. During an outage, the power plant stops generating electricity while maintenance crews perform extensive repairs. The materials, labor, and overhead costs of these repairs are controlled by accumulating these costs by the various tasks that make up a repair job. Typically, such jobs can last several months. Management maintains records of all repair jobs by type of repair. In this way, management can develop trend data and cost experience that can support cost planning and control in future projects.

Under a process cost system, costs are accumulated for each of the departments or processes within the factory. A process system is best suited for manufacturers of like units of product that are not distinguishable from each other during a continuous production process. An example would be a cookie processor. In a cookie company, cookies are mixed, baked, and packed in a continuous stream through the mixing, baking, and packing departments. The cost of the cookies is determined by summing the costs consumed within each department during the production process.

Exhibit 1 summarizes a survey of manufacturers, showing the breakdown between the use of job order and process costing. Exhibit 1 indicates that job order costing is used by approximately 20% of all the respondents, whereas 23% indicate they use process costing approaches. This leaves over 50% of the respondents that use some other type of cost system. Although not indicated in this survey, these other respondents probably use a hybrid system that combines features of a pure job order or pure process cost system.

Exhibit 1
Cost Accounting Practices by Major Industries

Industry Group	*% Using Job Order Costing*	*% Using Process Costing*
Metal, chemical, oil, gas, paper	21	41
Machinery	35	15
Automobile	11	8
Aerospace	45	10
Electronics	24	15
High technology	33	43
Other industrial products	13	23
Consumer products	2	33
Diverse products	50	31
Average of all respondents	20%	23%

Source: R. A. Howell, J. D. Brown, S. R. Soucy, and A. H. Seed, *Management Accounting in the New Manufacturing Environment*, IMA/CAM-I, 1987, p. 36.

In this chapter, we will illustrate the job order cost system. In the next chapter, we will illustrate the process cost system.

Job Order Cost Systems for Manufacturing Businesses

Objective 3
Describe and prepare summary journal entries for a job order cost accounting system.

In the following paragraphs, we discuss the source documents that serve as the basis for the entries in the job order cost system. We will focus on the flow of information and how it is used in planning and controlling operations. In addition, we discuss how predetermined overhead rates are used to allocate factory overhead costs.

COST FLOW OVERVIEW—JOB ORDER COST SYSTEM

In a cost accounting system, perpetual inventory controlling accounts and subsidiary ledgers are maintained for materials, work in process, and finished goods inventories. Each inventory account is debited for all additions and is credited for all deductions. The balance of each account thus represents the inventory on hand.

Exhibit 2 shows the cost flow through the perpetual inventory accounts. Costs follow the flow of production. As we discussed previously, both materials and labor used in production can be classified as either direct or indirect. Direct materials and direct labor are debited to Work in Process (a and c). Indirect materials and indirect labor are debited to Factory Overhead (b and d). Examples of indirect materials are oils and greases, abrasives and polishes, cleaning supplies, gloves, and brushes. Examples of indirect labor are salaries of supervisors, inspectors, material handlers, security guards, and janitors. Other costs debited to factory overhead (e) include depreciation, property taxes, and insurance.

Factory overhead cost is allocated (applied) to the product manufactured by using a rate determined at the beginning of the period. The applied factory overhead cost is debited to Work in Process (f). The costs of the goods finished are transferred from Work in Process to Finished Goods (g). When the goods are sold, their costs are transferred from Finished Goods to Cost of Goods Sold (h).

Exhibit 2
Flow of Costs Through Perpetual Inventory Accounts

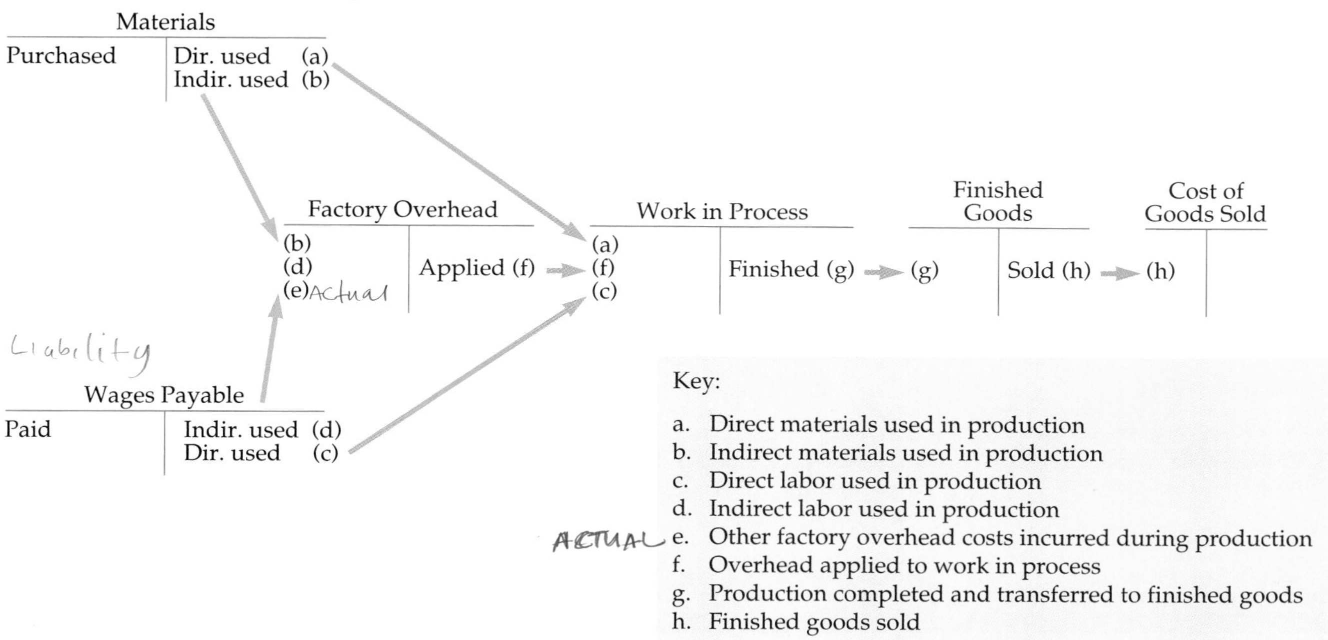

MATERIALS

The procedures used to purchase, store, and issue materials to production often differ among manufacturers. In the following discussion, we emphasize the basic principles rather than minor variations and details. Exhibit 3 shows the basic information and cost flows for the paper received and issued to production by Goodwell Printers, the book printing company introduced in the previous chapter.

Prior to producing a given item, a **bill of materials** is prepared, listing all materials necessary to manufacture an item. The Production Scheduling Department informs the Purchasing Department that materials will be needed. The request for materials is accomplished through a **purchase requisition.** The Purchasing Department then issues the necessary **purchase orders** to suppliers. After the materials have been received and inspected, the Receiving Department personnel prepare a **receiving report,** showing the quantity received and its condition. Some organizations now use bar code scanning devices in place of receiving reports to record and electronically transmit incoming materials data. When the supplier's **invoice** is received, the quantities, unit costs, and total costs of the materials billed are compared with the purchase order and the receiving report. This comparison, which can also be done electronically, verifies that the amount billed agrees with the materials ordered and received. After the invoice has been approved, it is recorded as a debit to Materials and a credit to Accounts Payable. The journal entry to record the Receiving Report 196 in Exhibit 3 is:

a. Materials purchased during December.	Materials	10,500	
	Accounts Payable		10,500

The materials account in the general ledger is a controlling account. A separate account for each type of material is maintained in a subsidiary ledger called the **materials ledger.** Details as to quantity and cost of materials received are recorded

Exhibit 3
Materials Information and Cost Flows

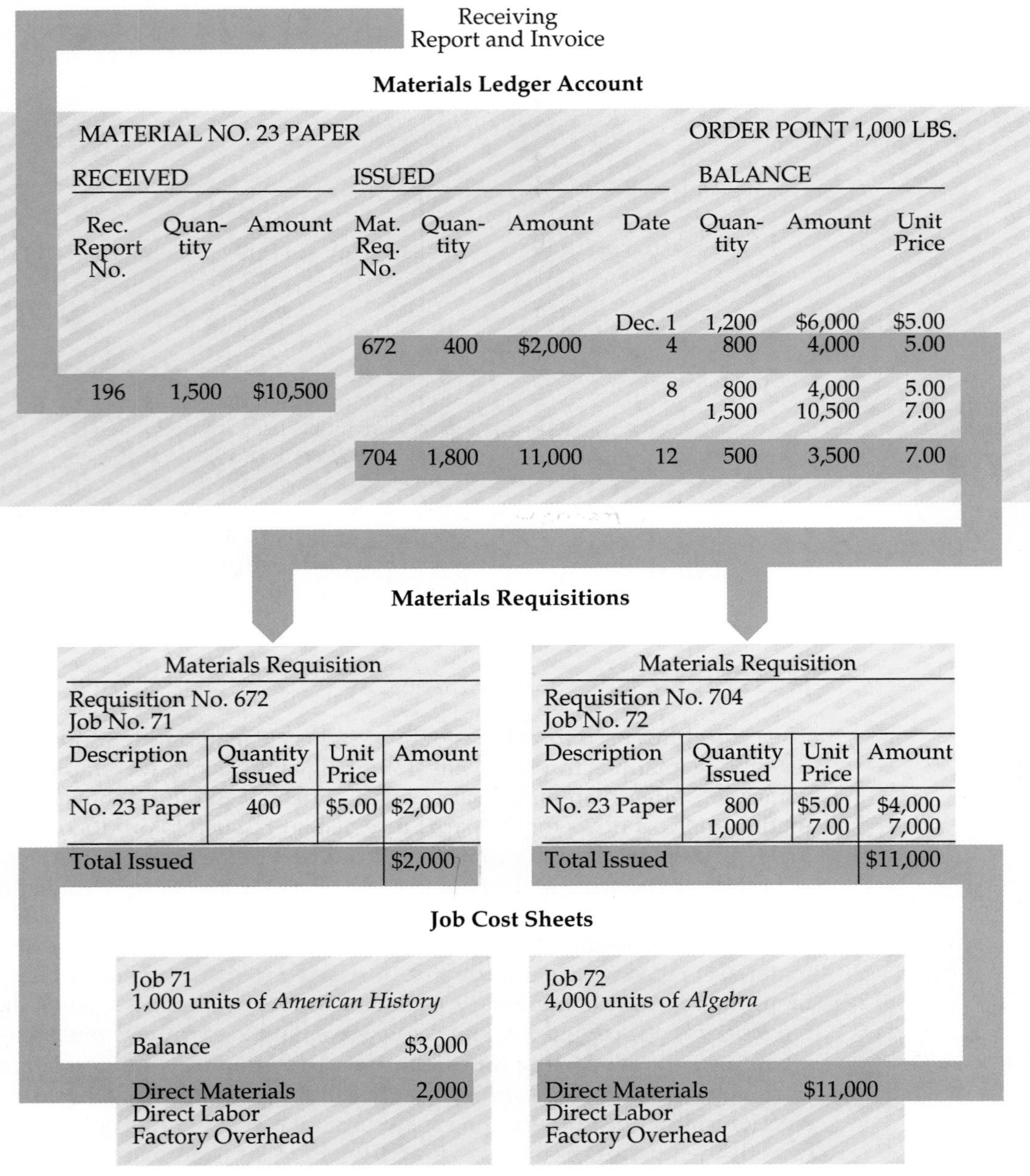

MATERIAL NO. 23 PAPER — ORDER POINT 1,000 LBS.

RECEIVED			ISSUED				BALANCE		
Rec. Report No.	Quantity	Amount	Mat. Req. No.	Quantity	Amount	Date	Quantity	Amount	Unit Price
						Dec. 1	1,200	$6,000	$5.00
			672	400	$2,000	4	800	4,000	5.00
196	1,500	$10,500				8	800 1,500	4,000 10,500	5.00 7.00
			704	1,800	11,000	12	500	3,500	7.00

Materials Requisition
Requisition No. 672
Job No. 71

Description	Quantity Issued	Unit Price	Amount
No. 23 Paper	400	$5.00	$2,000
Total Issued			$2,000

Materials Requisition
Requisition No. 704
Job No. 72

Description	Quantity Issued	Unit Price	Amount
No. 23 Paper	800 1,000	$5.00 7.00	$4,000 7,000
Total Issued			$11,000

Job 71
1,000 units of *American History*

Balance	$3,000
Direct Materials	2,000
Direct Labor	
Factory Overhead	

Job 72
4,000 units of *Algebra*

Direct Materials	$11,000
Direct Labor	
Factory Overhead	

in the materials ledger on the basis of the purchase invoices or receiving reports. A typical form of a materials ledger account is illustrated in Exhibit 3.

The materials ledger may also be used to aid in maintaining proper inventory quantities. Comparing quantities on hand with predetermined order points enables management to avoid idle time caused by lack of materials.

Materials are released from the storeroom to the factory in response to **materials requisitions.** An illustration of a materials requisition is in Exhibit 3. Materials requisitions may be issued by the Production or Scheduling Department. Storeroom personnel record the physical quantity of the issuances on the materials requisition form. A copy of the materials requisition is then routed to the materials ledger clerk, who inserts unit prices and amounts.

The completed requisition for each job serves as the basis for posting quantities and dollar data to the job cost sheets in the case of direct materials or to factory overhead in the case of indirect materials. Job cost sheets, which are illustrated in Exhibit 3, are the work in process subsidiary ledger to the work in process controlling account. For Goodwell Printers, Job 71 is for 1,000 textbooks titled *American History,* while Job 72 is for 4,000 textbooks titled *Algebra.*

Often the job cost sheet will actually travel with the particular job through the production process. Information is posted to the sheet as the job progresses through production.

In Exhibit 3, the first-in, first-out costing method is used. A summary of the materials requisitions completed during the month is the basis for transferring the cost of the materials from the materials account in the general ledger to the controlling account for work in process. The flow of materials from the materials storeroom into production in Exhibit 3 ($2,000 + $11,000) is recorded by the following entry:

b. Materials requisitioned to jobs.	Work in Process	13,000	
	Materials		13,000

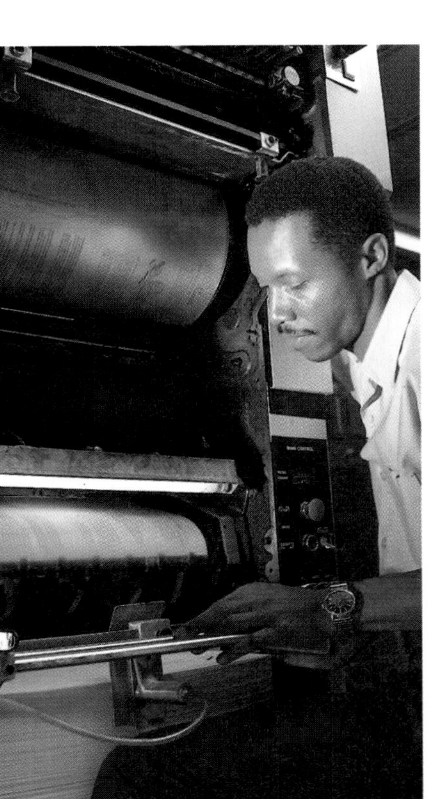

At Goodwell Printers, the job cost sheet with information about materials and labor will accompany each job as it progresses through production.

This accounting for the flow of materials may be a manual or an automated process. Many organizations are using automated information processes that use computer technology to account for the flow of materials. In automated settings, a worker would place a requisition for materials into a computer at the work location. Requisition information would be received electronically by the storeroom. Materials would then be transferred from the storeroom to the work location by a materials handler. The storeroom manager would record the release of materials into a computer, which would automatically update the subsidiary materials records.

The perpetual inventory system for materials has three important advantages. First, it provides for prompt and accurate charging of materials to production. This allows managers to know when materials are in short supply and need to be reordered. Second, it permits the work of counting inventory to be spread out rather than concentrated at the end of a fiscal period. Third, it aids in disclosing inventory shortages or other irregularities. When the physical quantities of the various materials are counted, they are compared with the balances in the subsidiary ledger. Any major differences between the two inventory amounts should be promptly investigated so that any necessary actions can be taken.

FACTORY LABOR

There are two primary objectives in accounting for factory labor. One objective is to determine the correct amount to be paid each employee for each payroll period. A second objective is to properly allocate factory labor costs to factory overhead and individual job orders.

The amount of time spent by an employee in the factory is usually recorded on **clock cards.** These cards are sometimes called **in-and-out cards.** The amount of time spent by each employee and the labor cost incurred for each individual job, or for factory overhead, are recorded on time tickets. Exhibit 4 shows typical time ticket forms and cost flows for labor for Goodwell Printers.

The time tickets are completed for all the different workers, days, and tasks required to complete the job. A summary of the time tickets at the end of each month is the basis for recording the direct and indirect labor costs incurred in production. Direct labor is posted to each job cost sheet, while indirect labor is debited to Factory Overhead. Goodwell Printers incurred 850 direct labor hours on Jobs 71 and 72 during December. The total direct labor costs were $11,000, divided into $3,500 for Job 71 and $7,500 for Job 72. The labor costs that flow into production are recorded by the following summary entry to the work in process controlling account:

c. Factory labor used in production of jobs.	Work in Process	11,000	
	Wages Payable		11,000

Exhibit 4 *Labor Information and Cost Flows*

Job 71 Time Tickets

TIME TICKET

No. 4521

Employee Name D. McInnis

Date Dec. 13, 19–

Work Description: Binding

Job No. 71

Start Time	Finish Time	Hours Worked	Hourly Rate	Cost
8:00	12:00	4	$10.00	$40.00
1:00	3:00	2	10.00	20.00

Total Cost $60.00

Approved by T.D.

December Job 71 Hours 350
December Job 71 Labor Costs: $3,500

Job 72 Time Tickets

TIME TICKET

No. 2311

Employee Name S. Andrews

Date Dec. 26, 19–

Work Description: Printing

Job No. 72

Start Time	Finish Time	Hours Worked	Hourly Rate	Cost
9:00	12:00	3	$15.00	$45.00
1:00	6:00	5	15.00	75.00

Total Cost $120.00

Approved by A.M.

December Job 72 Hours 500
December Job 72 Labor Costs: $7,500

Job Cost Sheets

Job 71
1,000 Units of *American History*

Balance	$3,000
Direct Materials	2,000
Direct Labor	3,500
Factory Overhead	

Job 72
4,000 Units of *Algebra*

Direct Materials	11,000
Direct Labor	7,500
Factory Overhead	

As with recording materials, many organizations are automating the recording and labor distribution process. In automated information processing settings, direct labor employees record their time for a particular job or nonproduction task into a computer at their work location. The labor is then distributed to jobs and overhead automatically.[1] In companies that build very large products, such as submarines, jet aircraft, or space vehicles, direct labor employees can be given magnetic cards, much like credit cards. These cards can be used to log in and log out of particular work assignments on particular jobs by running the card through a magnetic reader at any number of remote terminals. Shell Oil Company uses such a magnetic system to track the work of maintenance crews in its refineries.

FACTORY OVERHEAD

Factory overhead includes all manufacturing costs except direct materials and direct labor. Examples of factory overhead costs, in addition to indirect materials and

[1] There are a variety of methods for recording and distributing labor costs. In the approach illustrated in this chapter, we assume that labor costs are automatically distributed to jobs and factory overhead when incurred. Alternatively, wages could be first debited to "factory labor" when incurred, and then later distributed to jobs and factory overhead.

indirect labor, are depreciation, electricity, fuel, insurance, and property taxes. It is normal to have a factory overhead controlling account in the general ledger. Details of the individual overhead costs are then accumulated in a subsidiary ledger.

Debits to Factory Overhead come from various sources. For example, the cost of indirect materials is obtained from the summary of the materials requisitions. For Goodwell Printers, indirect materials are the glue and ink used in producing textbooks. The cost of indirect labor is obtained from the summary of the time tickets. The cost of electricity and water are obtained from invoices. The cost of depreciation and expired insurance may be recorded as adjustments at the end of the accounting period. For example, the factory overhead of $4,600 incurred in December for Goodwell Printers would be recorded as follows:

d. Factory overhead incurred in production.	Factory Overhead	4,600	
	Materials		500
	Wages Payable		2,000
	Utilities Payable		900
	Accumulated Depreciation		1,200

Factory overhead is an essential component of manufacturing costs. As factories have become more highly automated, factory overhead has become a larger part of the total product cost.

Allocating Factory Overhead

Overhead is much different from direct labor and direct materials because it is indirect to the jobs. How, then, do the jobs get assigned a portion of overhead costs? The answer is through cost allocation. **Cost allocation** is the process of assigning indirect costs to a cost object, such as a job. The indirect costs are assigned to the jobs on the basis of some known measure about each job. The known measure of each job "carries" the overhead to the job. The measure used to allocate overhead is frequently called an **activity base** or **activity driver.** The estimated activity base should be a measure that reflects the consumption or use of factory overhead cost. For example, the direct labor is recorded for each job, using time tickets. Thus, direct labor could be used to allocate, or carry, production-related overhead cost, such as supervisory salaries, to each job. Likewise, direct materials costs are known about each job through the materials requisitions. Thus, materials-related overhead, such as purchasing department salaries, could logically be allocated to the job on the basis of materials cost.

Predetermined Factory Overhead Rate

In order that job costs may be currently available, factory overhead may be allocated or applied to production using a **predetermined factory overhead rate.** The predetermined factory overhead rate is calculated by dividing the estimated amount of factory overhead for the forthcoming year by the estimated activity base, such as machine hours, direct labor costs, or direct labor hours.

To illustrate calculating a predetermined overhead rate, assume that Goodwell Printers estimates the total factory overhead cost to be $50,000 for the year and the activity base to be 10,000 direct labor hours. The predetermined factory overhead rate would be calculated as $5 per direct labor hour, as follows:

$$\textbf{Predetermined factory overhead rate} = \frac{\textbf{Estimated total factory overhead costs}}{\textbf{Estimated activity base}}$$

$$\textbf{Predetermined factory overhead rate} = \frac{\$50{,}000}{\textbf{10,000 direct labor hours}} = \textbf{\$5 per direct labor hour}$$

Why is the predetermined overhead rate calculated from estimated numbers at the beginning of the period? The answer hinges on the tradeoff between accuracy and timeliness. If a company waited until the end of an accounting period, when all overhead costs are known, the allocated factory overhead would be accurate but not timely. If the cost system is to have maximum usefulness, cost data should be available as each job is completed, even though there may be a small sacrifice in accuracy. Only through timely reporting can management make needed adjustments in pricing or in manufacturing methods and achieve the best possible combination of revenue and cost on future jobs.

Recording Factory Overhead

As factory overhead costs are incurred, they are debited to the factory overhead account. Factory overhead is applied to production as illustrated in Exhibit 5. For Goodwell Printers, factory overhead costs are applied to production at the rate of $5 per direct labor hour. The amount of factory overhead applied to each job would be recorded in the job cost sheets. For example, the 850 direct labor hours used in Goodwell's December operations would all be traced to individual jobs. Job 71 used 350 labor hours, so $1,750 (350 × $5) of overhead would be applied to Job 71. Similarly, $2,500 (500 × $5) of overhead would be applied to Job 72. The factory overhead costs applied to production are periodically credited to the factory overhead account and debited to the work in process account. The summary entry to apply the $4,250 ($1,750 + $2,500) of factory overhead is as follows:

e. Factory overhead applied to jobs according to the predetermined overhead rate.	Work in Process	4,250	
	Factory Overhead		4,250

The factory overhead costs applied and the actual factory overhead costs incurred during a period will usually differ. If the amount applied exceeds the actual costs incurred, the factory overhead account will have a credit balance. This credit is described as overapplied or **overabsorbed** factory overhead. If the amount applied is less than the actual costs incurred, the account will have a debit balance. This debit is described as underapplied or **underabsorbed** factory overhead. Both cases are illustrated in the following account for Goodwell Printers:

ACCOUNT FACTORY OVERHEAD ACCOUNT NO.

Date		Item	Debit	Credit	Balance Debit	Balance Credit
Dec.	1	Balance				200
	31	Factory overhead cost incurred	4,600		4,400	
	31	Factory overhead cost applied		4,250	150	

Underapplied balance (150)
Overapplied balance (200)

Disposal of Factory Overhead Balance

The balance in the factory overhead account is carried forward from month to month until the end of the year. The balance is reported on interim balance sheets as a deferred debit or credit.

The balance in the factory overhead account (underapplied or overapplied), as well as the amount, may change during the year. If the balance increases in only one direction and the balance becomes large, the balance and the overhead rate should be investigated. For example, if a large balance is caused by changes in manufacturing methods or in production goals, the factory overhead rate should be re-

Exhibit 5
Assigning Factory Overhead to Jobs

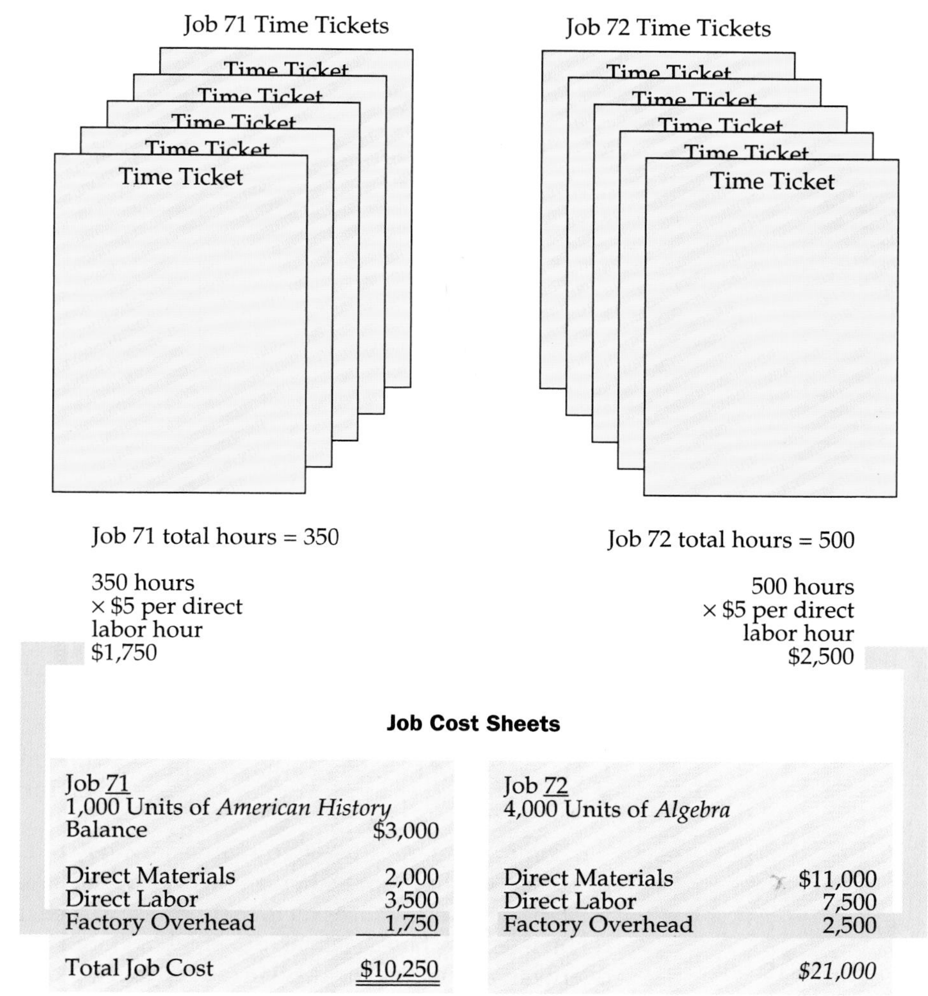

vised. On the other hand, a large underapplied balance may indicate a serious control problem caused by inefficiencies in production methods, excessive costs, or a combination of factors.

Regardless of how carefully the predetermined overhead rate is estimated, Factory Overhead will usually have a balance at the end of the fiscal year. Since this balance applies to the operations of the year just ended, it should not be carried over to the next year and reported as a deferred item on the balance sheet.

One approach for disposing of the balance of factory overhead at the end of the year is to transfer the entire overapplied or underapplied balance to the cost of goods sold account.[2] To illustrate, the journal entry to eliminate Goodwell Printers' underapplied overhead balance of $150 at the end of the calendar year would be:

f. Closing underapplied factory overhead to cost of goods sold.	Cost of Goods Sold	150	
	Factory Overhead		150

Selecting an Activity Base

A variety of allocation bases may be used to allocate factory overhead to jobs. Exhibit 6 reports the results of a survey on the allocation bases used by manufacturers.

[2] Alternatively, the balance may be allocated among the work in process, finished goods, and cost of goods sold balances. This approach brings the accounts into agreement with the costs actually incurred. Since this approach is a more complex calculation that adds little accuracy, it will not be used in this text.

Exhibit 6
Overhead Allocation Bases (Activity Drivers)[3]

Description of Activity Base (Driver)	*Percentage of Survey Respondents Indicating Usage**
Direct labor hours	61%
Direct labor dollars	54
Machine hours	54
Direct materials	26
Other	25

*Note: The percentages total more than 100% because many firms use more than one activity base in different parts of their operations.

As you can see, direct labor measures dominate the survey. Often companies use direct labor dollars instead of direct labor hours, because the labor rates are different throughout the plant. The underlying logic is that products using labor with high direct labor rates are associated with greater overhead support. A widely used alternative activity base in highly automated settings is machine hours. For example, Amerock Corporation, a manufacturer of cabinet and decorative hardware, began replacing their direct-labor-based allocation rate with a machine-hour-based allocation rate as manufacturing processes became more automated.

The predetermined overhead rate under machine hours is calculated in much the same way as for direct labor hours, as follows:

$$\textbf{Predetermined factory overhead rate} = \frac{\textbf{Estimated factory overhead costs}}{\textbf{Estimated machine hours}}$$

Some companies use two overhead rates to allocate factory overhead to products.[4] Under this approach, one factory overhead rate is used to allocate production-related overhead, such as factory supervision. The rate used is based on a production-related activity base, such as direct labor hours or machine hours. A second factory overhead rate is used to allocate materials-related factory overhead, such as materials management or purchasing salaries. This rate is based on a materials-related activity base, such as direct materials dollars, as shown in the following equation:

$$\begin{array}{l}\textbf{Predetermined materials-related} \\ \textbf{factory overhead rate}\end{array} = \frac{\textbf{Estimated materials-related factory overhead}}{\textbf{Estimated direct materials dollars}}$$

A number of companies are using a new product-costing approach called activity-based costing.[5] Activity-based costing is a method of accumulating and allocating factory overhead costs to products, using many overhead rates. Each rate is related to separate factory activities, such as inspecting, moving, and machining. Activity-based costing is discussed and illustrated in the appendix to this chapter.

WORK IN PROCESS

Costs incurred for the various jobs are debited to Work in Process. Goodwell Printers' job costs described in the preceding sections may be summarized as follows:

[3] James A. Hendricks, "Applying Cost Accounting to Factory Automation," *Management Accounting*, December 1988, pp. 24–30.
[4] Over 60% of the firms surveyed by Hendricks (see footnote 3) used more than one factory overhead rate to allocate factory overhead to products.
[5] A recent survey conducted by the Cost Management Group of the Institute for Management Accountants found that 11% of U.S. companies are using activity-based costing and 19% are considering it.

- **Direct materials, $13,000**—Work in Process debited and Materials credited; data obtained from summary of materials requisitions.
- **Direct labor, $11,000**—Work in Process debited and Wages Payable credited; data obtained from summary of time tickets.
- **Factory overhead, $4,250**—Work in Process debited and Factory Overhead credited; data obtained from summary of time tickets.

The details concerning the costs incurred on each job order are accumulated in the job cost sheets. Exhibit 7 illustrates the relationship between the job cost sheets and the work in process controlling account.

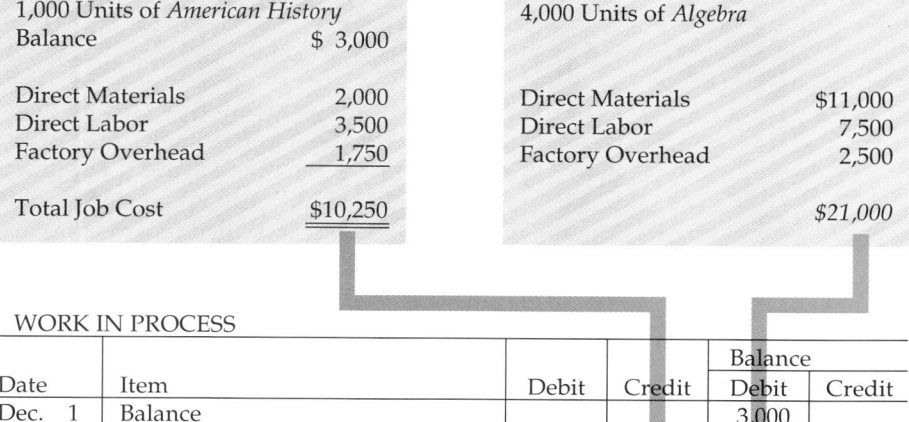

Exhibit 7
Job Cost Sheets and the Work in Process Controlling Account

Job Cost Sheets

Job 71	
1,000 Units of *American History*	
Balance	$ 3,000
Direct Materials	2,000
Direct Labor	3,500
Factory Overhead	1,750
Total Job Cost	$10,250

Job 72	
4,000 Units of *Algebra*	
Direct Materials	$11,000
Direct Labor	7,500
Factory Overhead	2,500
	$21,000

WORK IN PROCESS

Date		Item	Debit	Credit	Balance Debit	Balance Credit
Dec.	1	Balance			3,000	
	31	Direct materials	13,000		16,000	
	31	Direct labor	11,000		27,000	
	31	Factory overhead	4,250		31,250	
	31	Jobs completed		10,250	21,000	

In this example, Job 71 was started in November and completed in December. The beginning December balance represents the costs carried over from the end of November. Job 72 was started in December but was not yet completed at the end of the month. Thus, the ending balance on December 31 is the cost associated with the incomplete Job 72 that will be carried over to January.

When Job 71 was completed, the direct materials costs, the direct labor costs, and the factory overhead costs were totaled and divided by the number of units produced to determine the cost per unit. If we assume 1,000 units of a textbook titled *American History* were produced for Job 71, then the unit cost would be $10.25 ($10,250 ÷ 1,000).

Upon completing Job 71, the job cost sheet was removed from the cost ledger and filed for future reference. At the end of the accounting period (December), the total costs for all completed jobs during the period are determined, and the following entry is made:

g. Job 71 completed in December.	Finished Goods	10,250	
	Work in Process		10,250

FINISHED GOODS AND COST OF GOODS SOLD

The finished goods account is a controlling account. Its related subsidiary ledger, which has an account for each product, is called the **finished goods ledger** or **stock**

ledger. Each account in the finished goods ledger contains cost data for the units manufactured, units sold, and units on hand. Exhibit 8 illustrates an account in the finished goods ledger.

Exhibit 8
Finished Goods Ledger Account

Item: *American History*

Manufactured			Shipped				Balance		
Job Order No.	Quantity	Amount	Ship Order No.	Quantity	Amount	Date	Quantity	Amount	Unit Cost
						Dec. 1	2,000	$20,000	$10.00
			643	2,000	$20,000	9	—	—	—
71	1,000	10,250				31	1,000	10,250	10.25

Just as there are various methods of costing materials entering into production, there are various methods of determining the cost of the finished goods sold. In Exhibit 8, the first-in, first-out method is used. The quantities shipped are posted to the finished goods ledger from a copy of the shipping order or another memorandum. The finished goods ledger clerk then records on the copy of the shipping order the unit cost and the total amount of the textbooks sold. A summary of the cost data on these shipping orders ($20,000) becomes the basis for the following entry:

h. Cost of 2,000 *American History* textbooks sold.	Cost of Goods Sold	20,000	
	Finished Goods		20,000

SALES

For each sale of finished goods, a record of both the cost and the selling price of the goods sold must be maintained. As we previously stated, the cost data may be recorded on the shipping orders. As each sale occurs, the cost of the goods is recorded by debiting Cost of Goods Sold and crediting Finished Goods. The selling price of the goods sold is recorded by debiting Accounts Receivable (or Cash) and crediting Sales. To illustrate, assume that Goodwell Printers sold to the publisher the 2,000 *American History* textbooks for $14 per unit.[6] The entry to the accounts receivable controlling account would be:

i. Revenue received from textbooks sold.	Accounts Receivable	28,000	
	Sales		28,000

Summary of Cost Flows for Goodwell Printers

Objective 4
Summarize the cost flows for a job order cost accounting system.

Exhibit 9 shows the cost flow through the manufacturing accounts, together with summary details of the subsidiary ledgers for Goodwell Printers. Entries in the accounts are identified by letters that refer to the summary journal entries introduced in the preceding section.

[6] The $14 price of the textbook is the amount paid by the textbook publisher for printing the book. The publisher must also pay royalties, development and production costs, and selling expenses. Thus, the price of the textbook to you or another final user will be higher than $14.

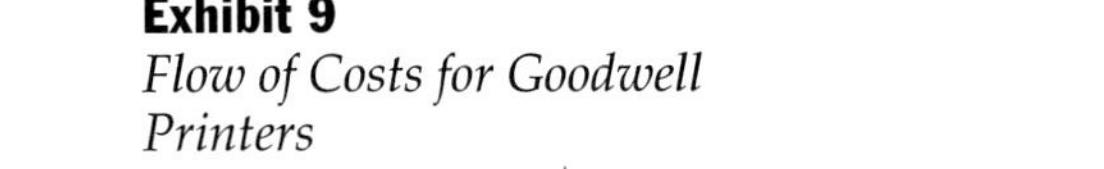

Exhibit 9
Flow of Costs for Goodwell Printers

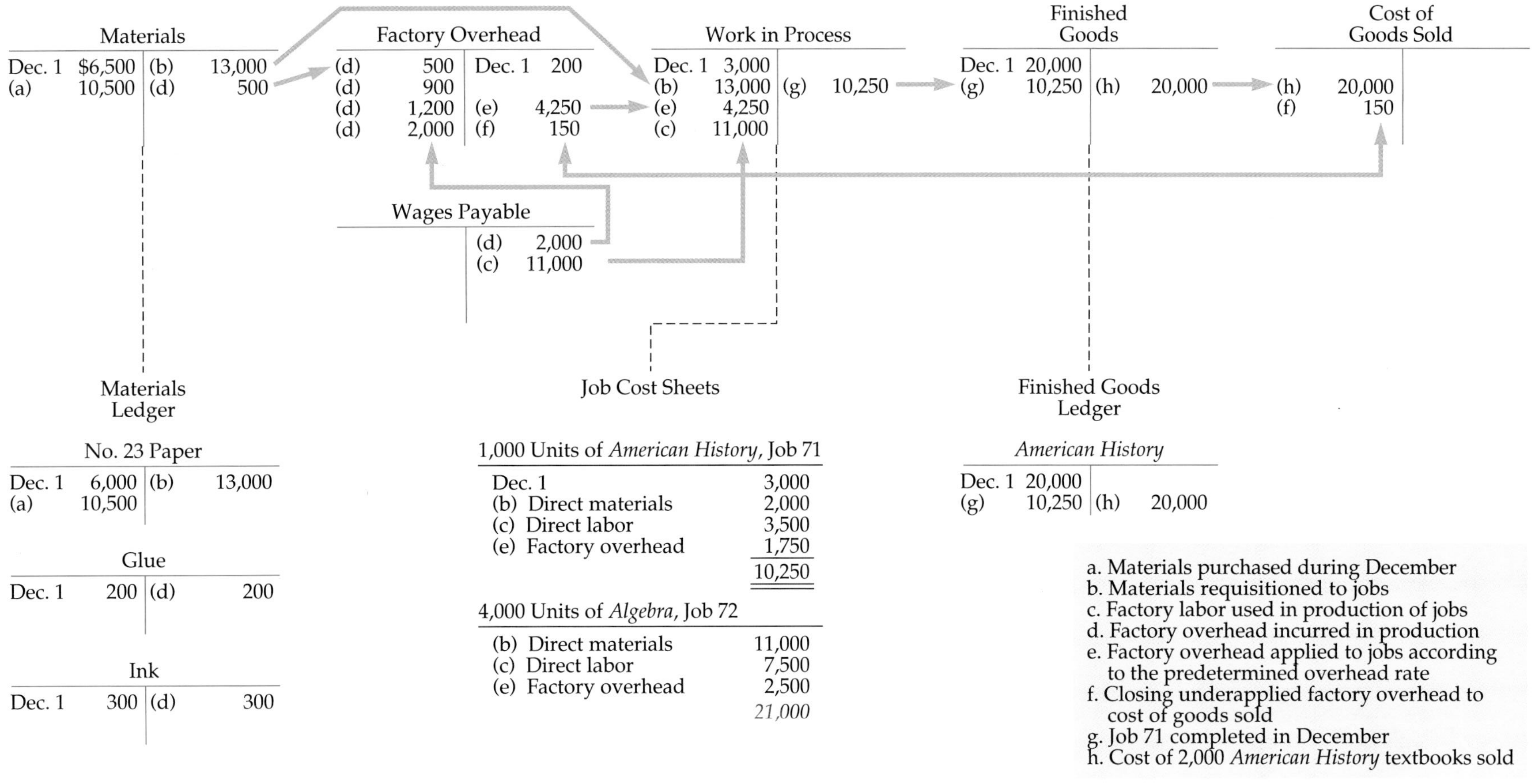

Materials

Dec. 1	$6,500	(b)	13,000
(a)	10,500	(d)	500

Factory Overhead

(d)	500	Dec. 1	200
(d)	900		
(d)	1,200	(e)	4,250
(d)	2,000	(f)	150

Work in Process

Dec. 1	3,000		
(b)	13,000	(g)	10,250
(e)	4,250		
(c)	11,000		

Finished Goods

Dec. 1	20,000		
(g)	10,250	(h)	20,000

Cost of Goods Sold

(h)	20,000		
(f)	150		

Wages Payable

		(d)	2,000
		(c)	11,000

Materials Ledger

No. 23 Paper

Dec. 1	6,000	(b)	13,000
(a)	10,500		

Glue

Dec. 1	200	(d)	200

Ink

Dec. 1	300	(d)	300

Job Cost Sheets

1,000 Units of *American History*, Job 71

Dec. 1	3,000
(b) Direct materials	2,000
(c) Direct labor	3,500
(e) Factory overhead	1,750
	10,250

4,000 Units of *Algebra*, Job 72

(b) Direct materials	11,000
(c) Direct labor	7,500
(e) Factory overhead	2,500
	21,000

Finished Goods Ledger

American History

Dec. 1	20,000		
(g)	10,250	(h)	20,000

a. Materials purchased during December
b. Materials requisitioned to jobs
c. Factory labor used in production of jobs
d. Factory overhead incurred in production
e. Factory overhead applied to jobs according to the predetermined overhead rate
f. Closing underapplied factory overhead to cost of goods sold
g. Job 71 completed in December
h. Cost of 2,000 *American History* textbooks sold

The balances of the three inventory accounts—Finished Goods ($10,250), Work in Process ($21,000), and Materials ($3,500)—represent the respective ending inventories of December 31. The balances of the general ledger controlling accounts should be supported by their respective subsidiary ledgers.

Job Order Costing for Decision Making

Objective 5
Use job order cost information for decision making.

The job order cost system that we developed in the previous sections can be used to evaluate an organization's cost performance. The unit costs for similar jobs can be compared over time to determine if costs are staying within expected ranges. If costs increase for some unexpected reason, the details in the job cost sheets can provide clues to discovering why costs are not as expected.

To illustrate, consider the job cost sheets for Jobs 144 and 163 in Exhibit 10. Job 144 was for **200** folding chairs, and Job 163 was for **400** folding chairs. The direct materials, direct labor, and factory overhead are identified in detail on the job cost sheets for these chairs. As you can see, the materials used to produce the chairs include lumber and fabric, whereas direct labor includes cutting, sanding, and assembly.

The supervisor has arranged to compare these two job cost sheets because both job sheets refer to the same product. Thus, the supervisor expects the unit costs to be about the same. Unfortunately, the cost per chair for Job 163 is $82.45, whereas Job 144 had a cost per chair of $72.75. For some reason, costs have increased since folding chairs were produced for Job 144. The supervisor can use the job cost sheets to investigate possible reasons for the increased cost.

First, the supervisor should note that the rates for direct materials and direct labor did not change. Thus, the cost increase is not related to increasing prices. Second, the supervisor should review the direct materials quantities and direct labor hours required to perform each job. Job 163 resulted in twice as many chairs as did Job 144. Thus, the supervisor should expect the direct materials and direct labor quantities to be approximately twice as much for Job 163 as for Job 144. A close review of the fabric quantities, sanding time, and assembly time reveals that this is indeed the case. For example, Job 144 required 600 square yards of fabric to make 200 chairs, and Job 163 required 1,200 square yards to make 400 chairs. The same is true for sanding and assembly time. These relationships would be expected.

What about the wood consumption and the cutting time? These two items tell a different story. The quantity of wood used to produce 200 chairs in Job 144 is 1,600 board feet. However, Job 163 required *more* than twice this amount to make 400 chairs. Specifically, Job 163 required 4,000 board feet, which is 800 board feet greater than the 3,200 board feet expected for Job 163. Likewise, Job 144 required 100 hours of cutting time, yet Job 163 required 260 cutting hours, which is 60 hours more than the 200 hours that might be expected. As a result of 60 more hours of direct labor, there will be a corresponding increase in factory overhead applied. How are these cost increases to be explained? Most likely, the excess wood consumption and cutting time can be explained together. Any one of the following explanations are possible and could be investigated further:

1. There was a new employee that was not adequately trained for cutting the wood for chairs. As a result, the employee improperly cut and scrapped many pieces.
2. The lumber was of poor quality. As a result, the cutting operator ended up using and scrapping additional pieces of lumber and incurred time sorting lumber to find good pieces.
3. The cutting tools were in need of repair. As a result, the cutting operators miscut and scrapped many pieces of wood.
4. The operator was careless. As a result of poor work, many pieces of cut wood had to be scrapped and new pieces cut.

Exhibit 10
Comparative Job Cost Sheets

Job 144

Item: 200 folding chairs

Direct materials	*Materials Quantity*	*Materials Price*	*Amount*
Wood (board feet)	1,600	$ 3.50	$ 5,600
Fabric (square yards)	600	.50	300
Total direct materials			$ 5,900
Direct labor	*Labor Hours*	*Labor Rate*	*Amount*
Cutting	100	$ 8.00	$ 800
Sanding	150	9.00	1,350
Assembly	200	10.00	2,000
Total direct labor	450		$ 4,150
	Total Labor Hours	*Factory Overhead Rate*	*Amount*
Factory overhead ($10 per direct labor hour)	450	$ 10	$ 4,500
Total cost			$14,550
Total units			÷ 200
Unit cost			$ 72.75

Job 163

Item: 400 folding chairs

Direct materials	*Materials Quantity*	*Materials Price*	*Amount*
Wood (board feet)	4,000	$ 3.50	$14,000
Fabric (square yards)	1,200	.50	600
Total direct materials			$14,600
Direct labor	*Labor Hours*	*Labor Rate*	*Amount*
Cutting	260	$ 8.00	$ 2,080
Sanding	300	9.00	2,700
Assembly	400	10.00	4,000
Total direct labor	960		$ 8,780
	Total Labor Hours	*Factory Overhead Rate*	*Amount*
Factory overhead ($10 per direct labor hour)	960	$ 10	$ 9,600
Total cost			$32,980
Total units			÷ 400
Unit cost			$ 82.45

5. The instructions attached to the job were incorrect. The operator cut wood according to the instructions but discovered that the pieces would not fit. As a result, many pieces had to be scrapped, and the operator had to start from the beginning.

You should note that many of these explanations are not necessarily related to operator error. Poor cost performance may be the result of root causes that are outside the control of the operator.

Job cost sheets can provide information to managers on unit cost trends, the cost impact of continuous improvement in the manufacturing process, the cost impact of materials changes, and the cost impact of direct materials price or direct labor rate changes over time. All these analyses can be used by managers to price products and to guide and improve operations.

USING ACCOUNTING TO UNDERSTAND BUSINESS

Smithfield Precision Machining Company uses a job order cost system to track the cost of various custom machine parts manufactured for the aerospace industry. The system allows management to evaluate the benefits of advanced manufacturing technology and to assess cost trends for manufacturing selected parts over time. This information is used by the company to price bids for new jobs, to improve operating performance of computer numerical control machines, and to value inventories.

Warner Bros. and other movie studios use job order cost systems to accumulate movie production and distribution costs. Costs such as actor salaries, production costs, movie print costs, and marketing costs are accumulated in a job account for a particular movie. Cost information from the job cost report can be used to control the costs of the movie while it is being produced and to determine the profitability of the movie after it has been exhibited.

Job Order Cost Systems for Service Businesses

Objective 6
Diagram the flow of costs for a service business that uses a job order cost accounting system.

A job order cost accounting system may be useful to the management of a service business in planning and controlling operations. For example, an advertising agency, an attorney, and a physician all share the common characteristic of rendering services to individual customers, clients, or patients. In such cases, the customer, client, or patient can be viewed as an individual job for which costs are accumulated.

Since the "product" of a service business is service, management's focus is on direct labor and overhead costs. The cost of any materials or supplies used in rendering services for a client is usually small and is normally included as part of the overhead.

The direct labor and overhead costs of rendering services to clients are accumulated in a work in process account. This account is supported by a cost ledger. A job cost sheet is used to accumulate the costs for each client's job. When a job is completed and the client is billed, the costs are transferred to a cost of services account. This account is similar to the cost of merchandise sold account for a merchandising business or the cost of goods sold account for a manufacturing business. A finished goods account and related finished goods ledger are not necessary, since the revenues associated with the services are recorded after the services have been rendered. The flow of costs through a service business using a job order cost accounting system is shown in Exhibit 11.

Exhibit 11
Flow of Costs Through a Service Business

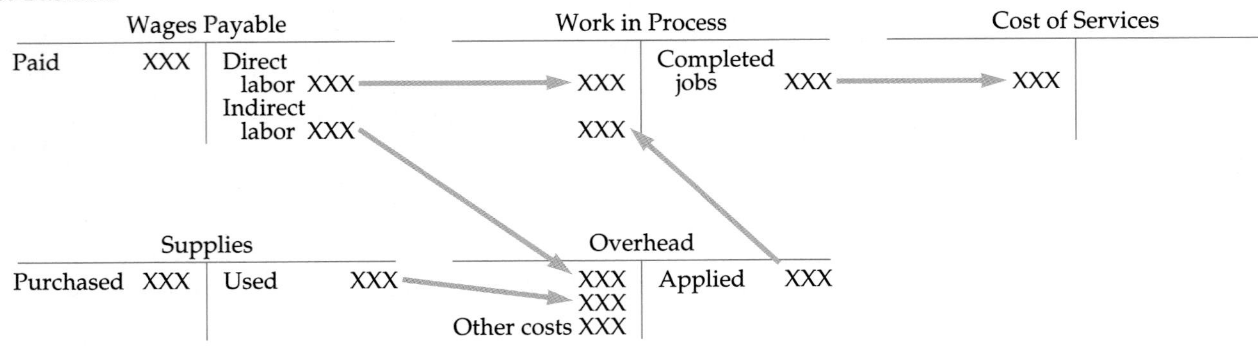

In practice, additional accounting considerations unique to service businesses may need to be considered. For example, a service business may bill clients on a weekly or monthly basis rather than waiting until a job is completed. In these situations, a portion of the costs related to each billing should be transferred from the work in process account to the cost of services account. This treatment is similar to the percentage-of-completion method used by construction contractors. A service business may also have advance billings that would be accounted for as deferred revenue until the services have been completed.

Appendix: Activity-Based Costing

As discussed in this chapter, factory overhead costs may be allocated to jobs by using predetermined rates. The following paragraphs further discuss and illustrate how activity-based costing may provide more accurate and useful product cost data.

Exhibit 12 illustrates the activity-based costing framework for Ruiz Company. In the Exhibit, five activities are used in manufacturing Products A and B: machining, assembly, setup, quality control, and engineering changes. These activites can be defined as follows:

- **Machining—**The activity of cutting metal in order to properly shape a product. This activity is machine-intensive and, for this reason, costs more than does assembly.
- **Assembly—**The activity of manually assembling machined pieces into a final product. This activity is labor-intensive.
- **Setup**—The activity of changing tooling in a machine to prepare for making a new product. Thus, each customer order requires a setup.
- **Quality control**—The activity of inspecting the product for conformance to specifications.
- **Engineering changes**—The activity of processing changes in design or process specifications of a product. The document that initiates the administrative process to change the requirements of a product or process is called the **engineering change order (ECO).**

Exhibit 12
Activity-Based Costing—Ruiz Company

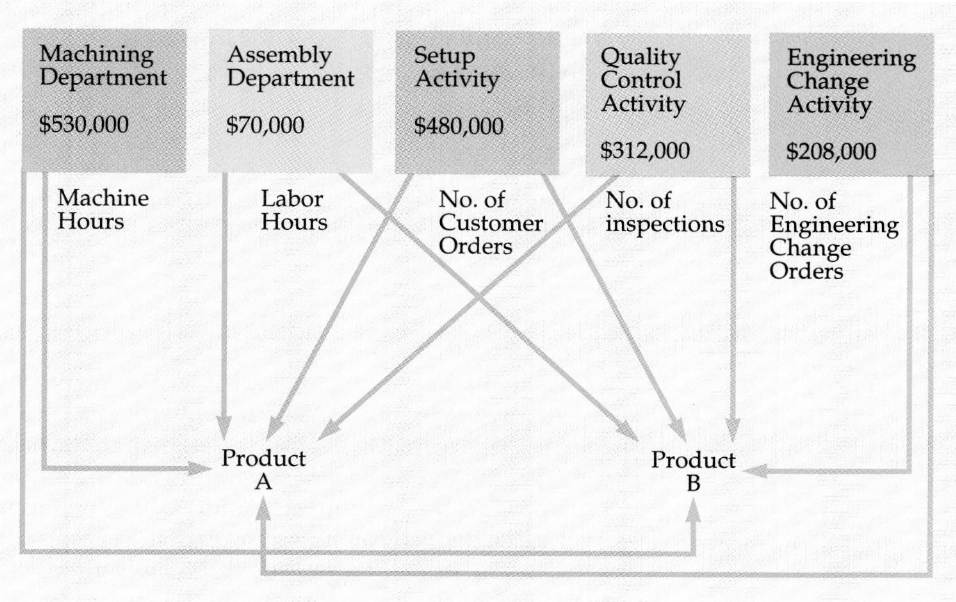

Assume the following additional information about the two products for Ruiz Company:

- **Product A** is a new machine-intensive product. The design is not very stable, meaning that the engineers are still tinkering with design changes. Product A is viewed by customers as a specialized product. Thus, customers order Product A in small order sizes, which average ten units per order. Each order must be set up for production. Every order for Product A must be sampled and inspected before being shipped because Ruiz has had quality problems with Product A. The total annual demand for Product A is 1,000 units.
- **Product B** is a mature, stable and labor-intensive product that has been produced by Ruiz for many years. Product B is viewed by customers as a standardized product. Thus, customers purchase Product B in large order sizes, which average 50 units per order. Each order must be set up for production. Only 20% of the orders are sampled and inspected because Ruiz has had few quality problems with Product B. The total anticipated annual demand for Product B is 1,000 units.

Exhibit 13 shows the activity driver quantities associated with each product. These quantities reflect the underlying differences noted in the paragraphs above.

Exhibit 13
Activity Driver Quantities—Ruiz Company

Activity	*Activity Driver*	*Budgeted Activity Driver Quantity*		
		Product A	*Product B*	*Total*
Machining	Machine hours	8,000	2,000	10,000
Assembly	Direct labor hours	2,000	8,000	10,000
Setup	Number of customer orders	100	20	120
Quality control inspections	Number of inspections	100	4	104
Engineering changes	Number of engineering change orders (ECOs)	12	4*	16

*20 orders × 20%

The activity driver rates for Ruiz can be determined by dividing the estimated activity costs (Exhibit 12) by the total estimated activity driver quantities (Exhibit 13), as follows:

Machining	\$530,000 ÷ 10,000 mh	= \$53 per machine hour
Assembly	\$ 70,000 ÷ 10,000 dlh	= \$7 per direct labor hour
Setup	\$480,000 ÷ 120 orders	= \$4,000 per order
Quality control inspections	\$312,000 ÷ 104 inspections	= \$3,000 per inspection
Engineering changes	\$208,000 ÷ 16 ECOs	= \$13,000 per engineering change order

Using these activity rates, we can calculate the overhead costs for Product A and B, as shown in Exhibit 14. The activity driver rate, multiplied by the activity quantity for each department or activity, results in the overhead cost allocated to each product. The unit overhead cost is determined by dividing the overhead cost allocated to each product by the number of units budgeted for manufacture in the period.

Under the activity-based approach, each product consumed factory overhead activities in different proportions. Namely, Product A consumed a large majority of the machining, setup, quality control inspection, and engineering change activities,

Exhibit 14
Activity-Based Overhead Cost Calculations—Ruiz Company

	Overhead Allocated			
Activity	*Product A*		*Product B*	
Machining	8,000 × $53 =	$ 424,000	2,000 × $53 =	$106,000
Assembly	2,000 × $7 =	14,000	8,000 × $7 =	56,000
Setup	100 × $4,000 =	400,000	20 × $4,000 =	80,000
Quality control inspections	100 × $3,000 =	300,000	4 × $3,000 =	12,000
Engineering changes	12 × $13,000 =	156,000	4 × $13,000 =	52,000
Total overhead cost		$1,294,000		$306,000
Units		÷ 1,000		÷ 1,000
Unit overhead cost		$ 1,294		$ 306

while Product B consumed lesser quantities of these activities. Only under the activity-based approach are these differences between the products reflected in the product cost.

When differences in products are not reflected in the overhead cost allocations, management's strategies may be flawed. To illustrate, Rockwell International conducted a special activity-based costing study after one of its best-selling axles had begun losing market share. The study found that incorrect factory overhead cost allocations had "overcosted" its highest-volume axle by roughly 20%, while underestimating the cost of low-volume axles by as much as 40%. Since sales prices were based on these estimated costs, Rockwell had underpriced its low-volume axles and overpriced its high-volume axle. Competitors had begun to lure customers away from Rockwell's best-selling, high-volume axles. This was the result of mispricing the products, due to lack of accurate product cost information. Without the special study, Rockwell could well have discovered that they were gradually being squeezed out of the high-volume axle business—not as a strategic choice, but because of poor product costing.[7]

USING ACCOUNTING TO UNDERSTAND BUSINESS

Hewlett-Packard abandoned its conventional direct labor-based product costing system for decision-making purposes in favor of activity-based costing. The manufacturing manager stated, "We had a gulf between cost accounting information and actual incurred costs which would be useful for decision making. . . . Going to cost pools and drivers allowed the physical process to be modeled closer to reality." The activity-based costing system was used by the Research & Development staff to predict the cost of alternative product designs by referring to activity rates.

[7] "Accounting Bores You? Wake Up," Fred S. Worthy, *Fortune*, October 12, 1987.

KEY POINTS

Objective 1. Give examples of the usefulness of product costs.

Product costs are useful to managers for preparing financial statements. Product costs are also needed by management for a wide variety of decisions, such as setting long-term product prices. Without accurate product cost information, managers could not effectively manage product strategy.

Objective 2. Categorize accounting systems used by manufacturing businesses.

A cost accounting system accumulates costs used in manufacturing products. The cost accounting system is used by management to determine the proper product cost for inventory valuation on the financial statements, to support product pricing decisions, and to identify opportunities for cost reduction and improved production efficiency. The two primary cost accounting systems are job order and process cost systems.

Objective 3. Describe and prepare summary journal entries for a job order cost accounting system.

A job order cost system provides for a separate record of the cost of each particular quantity of product that passes through the factory. The product costs are accumulated in a subsidiary cost ledger, in which each account is represented by a job cost sheet. Work in Process is the controlling account for the cost ledger. As a job is finished, its costs are transferred to the finished goods ledger, for which Finished Goods is the controlling account.

Objective 4. Summarize the cost flows for a job order cost accounting system.

The cost flows for a job order cost accounting system for Goodwell Printers is presented in this chapter.

Objective 5. Use job order cost information for decision making.

The job order cost information can support pricing and cost analysis. Managers can use job cost information to identify areas for cost improvement.

Objective 6. Diagram the flow of costs for a service business that uses a job order cost accounting system.

A diagram of the flow of costs for a service business using a job order cost accounting system is shown in Exhibit 11. For a service business, the cost of materials or supplies used is normally included as part of the overhead. The direct labor and overhead costs of rendering services are accumulated in a work in process account. When a job is completed and the client is billed, the costs are transferred to a cost of services account.

GLOSSARY OF KEY TERMS

Activity base. A measure of activity that is related to changes in cost. Used in analyzing and classifying cost behavior. Activity bases are also used in the denominator in calculating the predetermined factory overhead rate to assign overhead costs to cost objects. *Objective 3*

Activity-based costing. An accounting framework based on determining the cost of activities. The activity cost is then related to products for product costing. *Objective 3*

Bill of materials. A list of all the materials required to manufacture a product. *Objective 3*

Cost accounting system. A branch of managerial accounting concerned with accumulating manufacturing costs for financial reporting and decision-making purposes. *Objective 2*

Cost allocation. The process of assigning indirect cost to a cost object, such as a job. *Objective 3*

Finished goods ledger. The subsidiary ledger that contains the individual accounts for each kind of commodity or product produced. *Objective 3*

General ledger. The principal ledger, when used in conjunction with subsidiary ledgers, that contains all the balance sheet and income statement accounts. *Objective 2*

Job cost sheet. An account in the work in process subsidiary ledger in which the costs charged to a particular job order are recorded. *Objective 3*

Job order cost system. A type of cost accounting system that provides for a separate record of the cost of each particular quantity of product that passes through the factory. *Objective 2*

Materials ledger. The subsidiary ledger containing the individual accounts for each type of material. *Objective 3*

Materials requisitions. The form or electronic transmission used by a manufacturing department to authorize the issuance of materials from the storeroom. *Objective 3*

Overapplied factory overhead. The amount of factory overhead applied in excess of the actual factory overhead costs incurred for production during a period. *Objective 3*

Predetermined factory overhead rate. The rate used to apply factory overhead costs to the goods manufactured. The rate is determined from budgeted overhead cost and activity usage data at the beginning of the fiscal period. *Objective 3*

Process cost system. A type of cost accounting system that accumulates costs for each of the various departments or processes within a manufacturing facility. *Objective 2*

Purchase requisitions. The form or electronic transmission used to inform the Purchasing Department that purchased items or services are needed for a business purpose. *Objective 3*

Receiving report. The form or electronic transmission used by the receiving personnel to indicate that materials have been received and inspected. *Objective 3*

Time tickets. The form on which the amount of time spent by each employee and the labor cost incurred for each individual job, or for factory overhead, are recorded. *Objective 3*

Underapplied factory overhead. The amount of actual factory overhead in excess of the factory overhead applied to production during a period. *Objective 3*

ILLUSTRATIVE PROBLEM

Derby Music Company specializes in producing and packaging compact discs (CDs) for the music recording industry. Derby uses a job order cost system. The following data summarize the operations related to production for March, the first month of operations:

a. Materials purchased on account, $15,500.
b. Materials requisitioned and labor used:

	Materials	*Factory Labor*
Job No. 100	$2,650	$1,770
Job No. 101	1,240	650
Job No. 102	980	420
Job No. 103	3,420	1,900
Job No. 104	1,000	500
Job No. 105	2,100	1,760
For general factory use	450	650

c. Factory overhead costs incurred on account, $2,700.
d. Depreciation of machinery, $1,750.
e. The factory overhead is applied at 70% of direct labor cost.
f. Jobs completed: Nos. 100, 101, 102, 104.
g. Jobs 100, 101, and 102 were shipped, and customers were billed for $8,100, $3,800, and $3,500, respectively.

Instructions

1. Journalize the entries to record the transactions identified above.
2. Determine the account balances for Work in Process and Finished Goods.
3. Prepare a schedule of unfinished jobs to support the balance in the work in process account.
4. Prepare a schedule of completed jobs on hand to support the balance in the finished goods account.

Solution

1. a. Materials	15,500	
Accounts Payable		15,500
b. Work in Process	11,390	
Materials		11,390
Work in Process	7,000	
Wages Payable		7,000
Factory Overhead	1,100	
Materials		450
Wages Payable		650
c. Factory Overhead	2,700	
Accounts Payable		2,700
d. Factory Overhead	1,750	
Accumulated Depreciation—Machinery		1,750
e. Work in Process	4,900	
Factory Overhead (70% of $7,000)		4,900
f. Finished Goods	11,548	
Work in Process		11,548

Computation of the cost of jobs finished:

Job	*Direct Materials*	*Direct Labor*	*Factory Overhead*	*Total*
Job No. 100	$2,650	$1,770	$1,239	$ 5,659
Job No. 101	1,240	650	455	2,345
Job No. 102	980	420	294	1,694
Job No. 104	1,000	500	350	1,850
				$11,548

g. Accounts Receivable	15,400	
Sales		15,400
Cost of Goods Sold	9,698	
Finished Goods		9,698

Cost of jobs sold computation:

Job No. 100	$5,659
Job No. 101	2,345
Job No. 102	1,694
	$9,698

2. Work in Process: $11,742 ($11,390 + $7,000 + 4,900 – $11,548)
   Finished Goods: $1,850 ($11,548 – $9,698)

3.

Job	*Schedule of Unfinished Jobs*			*Total*
	Direct Materials	*Direct Labor*	*Factory Overhead*	
Job No. 103	$3,420	$1,900	$1,330	$ 6,650
Job No. 105	2,100	1,760	1,232	5,092
Balance of Work in Process, March 31				$11,742

4.

Schedule of Completed Jobs	
Job No. 104:	
Direct materials	$1,000
Direct labor	500
Factory overhead	350
Balance of Finished Goods, March 31	$1,850

SELF-EXAMINATION QUESTIONS (ANSWERS AT END OF CHAPTER)

1. The account maintained by a manufacturing business for inventory of goods in the process of manufacture is:
   A. Finished Goods.
   B. Materials.
   C. Work in Process.
   D. Merchandise Inventory.

2. For a manufacturing business, finished goods inventory includes:
   A. direct materials costs.
   B. direct labor costs.
   C. factory overhead costs.
   D. all of the above.

3. An example of a factory overhead cost is:
   A. wages of factory assembly-line workers.
   B. salaries for factory plant supervisors.
   C. bearings for electric motors being manufactured.
   D. all of the above.

4. For which of the following would the job order cost system be appropriate?
   A. Antique furniture repair shop
   B. Rubber manufacturer
   C. Coal manufacturer
   D. All of the above

5. If the factory overhead account has a credit balance, factory overhead is said to be:
   A. underapplied.
   B. overapplied.
   C. underabsorbed.
   D. in error.

DISCUSSION QUESTIONS

1. How is product cost information used by managers?
2. a. Name two principal types of cost accounting systems.
   b. Which system provides for a separate record of each particular quantity of product that passes through the factory?
   c. Which system accumulates the costs for each department or process within the factory?
3. What kind of firm would use a job order cost system?

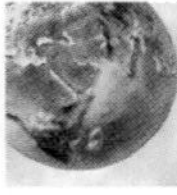

4. Hewlett-Packard Company manufactures printed circuit boards in which a high volume of standardized units are circuit etched, hole punched, assembled, and tested. Is the job order cost system appropriate in this situation?

5. Which account is used in a job order cost system to accumulate direct materials, direct labor, and factory overhead applied to production costs for individual jobs?
6. Distinguish between the purchase requisition and the purchase order used in the procurement of materials.
7. What purpose is served by a bill of materials?
8. Briefly discuss how the purchase order, purchase invoice, and receiving report can be used to assist in controlling cash paid for materials acquired.
9. What document is the source for (a) debiting the accounts in the materials ledger and (b) crediting the accounts in the materials ledger?
10. Briefly discuss how the accounts in the materials ledger can be used as an aid in maintaining appropriate inventory quantities of stock items.
11. What is the job cost sheet?
12. How does use of the materials requisition help control the issuance of materials from the storeroom?
13. Discuss the major advantages of a perpetual inventory system over a periodic system for materials.
14. a. Differentiate between the clock card and the time ticket.
    b. Why should the total time reported on an employee's time tickets for a payroll period be compared with the time reported on the employee's clock cards for the same period?
15. Discuss how the predetermined factory overhead rate can be used in job order cost accounting to assist management in pricing jobs.
16. a. How is a predetermined factory overhead rate calculated?
    b. Name three common bases used in calculating the rate.
17. a. What is (1) overapplied factory overhead and (2) underapplied factory overhead?
    b. If the factory overhead account has a debit balance, was factory overhead underapplied or overapplied?
    c. If the factory overhead account has a credit balance at the end of the first month of the fiscal year, where will the amount of this balance be reported on the interim balance sheet?
18. At the end of the fiscal year, there was a relatively minor balance in the factory overhead account. What procedure can be used for disposing of the balance in the account?
19. What document serves as the basis for posting to (a) the direct materials section of the job cost sheet and (b) the direct labor section of the job cost sheet?
20. Describe the source of the data for debiting Work in Process for (a) direct materials, (b) direct labor, and (c) factory overhead.
21. What account is the controlling account for (a) the materials ledger, (b) the job cost sheets, and (c) the finished goods ledger or stock ledger?
22. How can job cost information be used to identify cost improvement opportunities?

EXERCISES

EXERCISE 19–1
Transactions in a job order cost system
Objective 3

Five selected transactions for the current month are indicated by letters in the following T accounts in a job order cost accounting system:

Materials	
	(a)

Work in Process	
(a) (b) (c)	(d)

Wages Payable	
	(b)

Finished Goods	
(d)	(e)

Factory Overhead	
(a) (b)	(c)

Cost of Goods Sold	
(e)	

Describe each of the 5 transactions.

EXERCISE 19–2
Classifying overhead costs
Objective 3

Which of the following items are properly classified as part of factory overhead?

a. Amortization of patents on factory processes
b. Interest expense
c. Factory supplies used
d. Direct materials
e. Sales commissions
f. Property taxes on factory buildings
g. Plant manager's salary
h. Consultant's fees for surveying production employee morale
i. Chief Financial Officer's salary

EXERCISE 19–3
Cost of materials issuances by fifo method
Objectives 3, 4

An incomplete subsidiary ledger of Material F for May is as follows:

RECEIVED			ISSUED				BALANCE		
Receiving Report Number	Quantity	Price	Materials Requisition Number	Quantity	Amount	Date	Quantity	Amount	Unit Price
						May 1	240	$9,600	$40.00
23	600	$42.00				May 3			
			104	360		May 5			
29	480	$42.60				May 12			
			117	300		May 19			
35	360	$43.20				May 29			
			123	400		May 30			

a. Complete the materials issuances and balances for Material F under FIFO.
b. Determine the balance of Material F at the end of May.
c. Journalize the summary entry to transfer materials to work in process.
d. Explain how the materials ledger might be used as an aid in maintaining inventory quantities on hand.

EXERCISE 19–4
Entry for issuing materials
Objectives 3, 4

Materials issued for the current month are as follows:

Requisition No.	*Material*	*Job No.*	*Amount*
711	A-06	511	$ 9,620
712	I-70	514	4,830
713	B-11	526	10,600
714	F-12	Abrasives	700
715	W-29	533	7,500

Journalize the summary entry to record the issuances of materials.

EXERCISE 19–5
Entries for materials
Objectives 3, 4

Franklin Company manufactures furniture. Franklin uses a job order cost system. Balances on June 1 from the materials ledger are as follows:

Fabric	$ 45,000
Polyester filling	15,000
Lumber	85,000
Glue	5,000

The materials purchased during June are summarized from the receiving reports as follows:

Fabric	$315,000
Polyester filling	390,000
Lumber	628,000
Glue	10,000

Materials were requisitioned to individual jobs as follows:

	Fabric	*Polyester Filling*	*Lumber*	*Total*
Job 111	$110,000	$140,000	$215,000	$ 465,000
Job 112	85,000	100,000	146,000	331,000
Job 113	145,000	150,000	285,400	580,400
Factory overhead—indirect materials				12,000
Total	$340,000	$390,000	$646,400	$1,388,400

The glue is not a significant cost, so it is treated as indirect materials (factory overhead).

a. Journalize the entry to record the purchase of materials in June.
b. Journalize the entry to record the requisition of materials in June.
c. Determine the June 30 balances as would be shown in the materials ledger accounts.

EXERCISE 19–6
Entry for factory labor costs
Objectives 3, 4

A summary of the time tickets for the current month follows:

Job No.	*Amount*	*Job No.*	*Amount*
101	$ 4,650	141	$ 3,260
122	11,260	Indirect labor	11,120
133	5,200	143	8,940
139	1,110	147	6,000

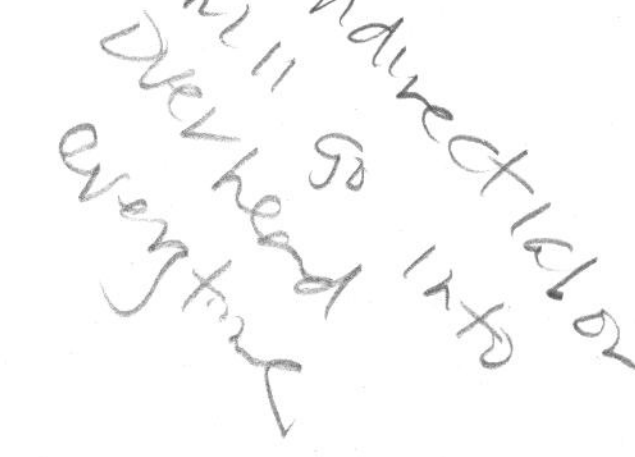

Journalize the entry to record the factory labor costs.

EXERCISE 19–7
Entries for direct labor and factory overhead
Objectives 3, 4

Huffy Enterprises Inc. manufactures log homes. Huffy uses a job order cost system. The time tickets from September jobs are summarized below:

Job 502	$1,440
Job 503	1,104
Job 504	2,496
Job 505	3,300
Factory supervision	2,400

Factory overhead is applied to jobs on the basis of a predetermined overhead rate of $26 per direct labor hour. The direct labor rate is $12 per hour.

a. Journalize the entry to record the factory labor costs.
b. Journalize the entry to apply factory overhead to production for September.

EXERCISE 19–8
Factory overhead rates, entries, and account balance
Objectives 3, 4

Oxford Company, which operates two consumer appliance factories, applies factory overhead to jobs on the basis of machine hours in Factory 1 and on the basis of direct labor costs in Factory 2. Estimated factory overhead costs, direct labor costs, and machine hours for April are as follows:

	Factory 1	*Factory 2*
Estimated factory overhead cost for year	$85,000	$294,400
Estimated direct labor costs for year		$640,000
Estimated machine hours for year	25,000	
Actual factory overhead costs for April	$ 6,900	$ 23,500
Actual direct labor costs for April		$ 51,500
Actual machine hours for April	2,000	

a. Determine the factory overhead rate for Factory 1.
b. Determine the factory overhead rate for Factory 2.
c. Journalize the entries to apply factory overhead to production in each factory for April.
d. Determine the balances of the overhead accounts for each factory as of April 30, and indicate whether the amounts represent overapplied or underapplied factory overhead.

EXERCISE 19–9
Factory overhead rates and entry to apply factory overhead
Objectives 3, 4

Boxer Company manufactures custom kitchen cabinets. The budgeted factory overhead for the year was as follows:

Purchasing Department salaries	$ 175,000
Materials management salaries	225,000
Production management salaries	360,000
Depreciation	400,000
Production supplies	80,000
Total	$1,240,000

The estimated activity for the year is as follows:

Direct labor	$ 700,000
Direct materials	$1,250,000

Boxer uses two overhead rates. One rate is determined for materials-related overhead (Purchasing and Materials management salaries) based on estimated direct material cost. The other rate is determined for production-related overhead, based on direct labor cost.

Boxer Company has worked on and completed two jobs during April. The following job cost sheets have been prepared for the two jobs before April's factory overhead has been applied to jobs:

Job 123	
Balance, April 1	$ 8,000
Direct materials	72,000
Direct labor	36,000
Factory overhead	

Job 165	
Direct materials	$36,000
Direct labor	30,000
Factory overhead	

a. Determine the materials-related overhead rate.
b. Determine the production-related overhead rate.
c. Determine the factory overhead to be applied to each job.
d. Journalize the entry to record the overhead applied during April.

EXERCISE 19–10
Entry for jobs completed; cost of unfinished jobs
Objectives 3, 4

The following account appears in the ledger after only part of the postings have been completed for March:

Work in Process	
Balance, March 1	18,500
Direct Materials	47,250
Direct Labor	67,500
Factory Overhead	37,000

Jobs finished during March are summarized as follows:

Job 320	$25,400	Job 327	$43,600
Job 326	46,100	Job 350	26,100

a. Journalize the entry to record the jobs completed.
b. Determine the cost of the unfinished jobs at March 31.

EXERCISE 19–11
Entries for factory costs and jobs completed
Objectives 3, 4

Mack Printing Inc. began manufacturing operations on April 1. Jobs 1 and 2 were completed during the month, and all costs applicable to them were recorded on the related cost sheets. Jobs 3 and 4 are still in process at the end of the month, and all applicable costs except factory overhead have been recorded on the related cost sheets. In addition to the materials and labor charged directly to the jobs, $9,100 of indirect materials and $24,900 of indirect labor were used during the month. The cost sheets for the four jobs entering production during the month are as follows, in summary form:

Job 1		*Job 2*	
Direct materials	16,500	Direct materials	28,200
Direct labor	12,600	Direct labor	20,160
Factory overhead	7,560	Factory overhead	12,096
Total	36,660	Total	60,456

Job 3		*Job 4*	
Direct materials	21,400	Direct materials	5,500
Direct labor	17,640	Direct labor	8,000
Factory overhead		Factory overhead	

Journalize the entry to record each of the following operations for the month (one entry for each operation):

a. Direct and indirect materials used.
b. Direct and indirect labor used.
c. Factory overhead applied (a single overhead rate is used based on direct labor cost).
d. Completion of Jobs 1 and 2.

EXERCISE 19–12
Reconciling the job cost sheets with the control account
Objectives 3, 4

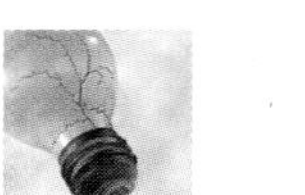

Rachel Company completed January's production of electric kiddie cars and discovered that the job cost sheets did not reconcile with the balance in the work in process account. Factory overhead is applied to jobs at a rate of 70% of direct labor cost. Jobs 11 and 12 were completed during the period. The work in process account and associated job cost sheets are shown below:

ACCOUNT WORK IN PROCESS ACCOUNT NO.

Date		Item	Debit	Credit	Balance Debit	Balance Credit
1996						
Jan.	1	Balance			10,000	
	31	Materials requisitioned	110,000		120,000	
	31	Factory labor	90,000		210,000	
	31	Factory overhead incurred	60,000		270,000	
	31	Jobs completed		200,000	70,000	

Job Cost Sheets

Job 11	
Jan. 1, Balance	$ 10,000
Direct materials	40,000
Direct labor	36,000
Factory overhead	25,200
	$111,200

Job 12	
Direct materials	$ 37,800
Direct labor	30,000
Factory overhead	21,000
	$ 88,800

Job 13	
Direct materials	$ 30,000
Direct labor	20,000
Factory overhead	14,000
	$ 64,000

Jobs 11 and 12 are completed. The job costs sheets were posted from the total materials requisitions and total labor used in the factory:

Total of materials requisitions:	
Material Req. No. 23 (Job 13)	$ 30,000
Material Req. No. 24 (Job 11)	40,000
Material Req. No. 25*	2,200
Material Req. No. 26 (Job 12)	37,800
Total	$110,000

*Material Req. No. 25 is indirect.

Total time tickets:	
Ticket 1 (Job 11)	$ 36,000
Ticket 2 (Job 12)	30,000
Ticket 3 (Job 13)	20,000
Ticket 4*	4,000
	$ 90,000

*Ticket 4 was for indirect labor.

Correct the entry titles and numbers in the work in process control account, based on the information provided.

EXERCISE 19–13
Decision making with job order costs
Objectives 1, 5

Yomani Manufacturing Company is a job shop. The management of Yomani wished to use the cost information from the job sheets to assess their cost performance. Information on the total cost, product type, and quantity of selected items produced is as follows:

Date	*Job No.*	*Quantity*	*Product Type*	*Total Cost*
Jan. 1	1	100	XXY	$ 2,000
Jan. 29	26	800	AAB	10,000
Feb. 15	43	1,200	AAB	15,600
Mar. 10	64	200	XXY	5,000
Mar. 31	75	1,500	MM	45,000
May 10	91	300	MM	7,500
June 20	104	1,000	XXY	30,000
Aug. 2	112	600	MM	12,000
Sept. 20	114	100	AAB	1,250
Nov. 1	126	500	XXY	18,000
Dec. 3	133	1,000	MM	17,000

a. Use this information to determine Yomani's unit cost of each product type over time.
b. What additional information would you require to investigate Yomani's cost performance more precisely?

EXERCISE 19–14
Labor and overhead entries for a law firm
Objectives 3, 6

The law firm of Steiner and Jenkins uses a job order cost system to accumulate client-related costs. The overhead rate is 40% of direct labor charges. Staff lawyer time is charged at a rate of $60 per hour. Partner time is charged at a rate of $140 per hour. The following time was charged to a particular case involving Green Acres Development Company, a firm client:

Staff	45 hours
Partners	15 hours

Journalize the summary entry to record:

a. Direct labor cost charged to the Green Acres Development Company case.
b. Overhead applied to the Green Acres Development Company case.

EXERCISE 19–15
Job order cost accounting entries for a service business
Objectives 3, 6

Epoch Advertising provides media services for clients across the nation. Epoch is presently working on four projects, each for a different client. Epoch accumulates costs for each account (client) on the basis of both direct costs and allocated indirect costs. The direct costs include the charged time of professional personnel and media purchases (air time and ad space). Overhead is allocated to each project as a percentage of media purchases. The predetermined overhead rate is 30% of media purchases.

On March 1, the four advertising projects had the following accumulated costs:

	March 1 Balances
Stone Beverage	$140,000
Hampshire Bank	25,000
All-Right Rentals	260,000
SleepEzz Hotel	90,000

During March, Epoch incurred the following personnel and media purchase costs related to preparing advertising for each of the four accounts:

	Personnel Salaries	*Media Purchases*
Stone Beverage	$ 45,000	$100,000
Hampshire Bank	60,000	320,000
All-Right Rentals	20,000	140,000
SleepEzz Hotel	30,000	80,000
Total	$155,000	$640,000

At the end of March, both the Hampshire Bank and All-Right Rentals campaigns were completed. Hampshire Bank was billed for $900,000, and All-Right Rentals was billed for $700,000. The cost of completed campaigns are debited to the cost of services account.

Journalize the summary entry to record each of the following for the month:

a. Direct personnel costs.
b. Media purchases.
c. Overhead applied.
d. Completion of Hampshire and All-Right campaigns.
e. Revenues from the Hampshire and All-Right campaigns.

APPENDIX EXERCISE 19–16
Activity-based product costing and product cost distortion

Wind Song Company is considering a change to activity-based product costing. The company produces two products, Products T and U, in a single production department. The factory overhead can be divided into two activities as follows:

Setup	$ 720,000
Production-related overhead	$1,080,000

The following information about Products T and U was determined from the corporate records:

	Number of Setups	Direct Labor Hours	Units
Product T	50	20,000	5,000
Product U	450	20,000	5,000
Total	500	40,000	10,000

a. Determine the activity rates under activity-based costing, assuming that the setup activity uses number of setups as an activity driver, and the production-related overhead uses direct labor hours as an activity driver.
b. Determine the overhead costs allocated to Products T and U, using activity-based costing.
c. Why are the overhead costs per unit of Product T and U different?

PROBLEMS SERIES A

PROBLEM 19–1A
Entries for costs in a job order cost system
Objectives 3, 4

Tallent Company uses a job order cost system. The following data summarize the operations related to production for June:

a. Materials purchased on account, $104,150.
b. Materials requisitioned, $98,650, of which $2,900 was for general factory use.
c. Factory labor used, $84,000, of which $11,500 was factory overhead.
d. Other costs incurred on account were for factory overhead, $17,150; selling expenses, $10,500; and administrative expenses, $9,000.
e. Prepaid expenses expired for factory overhead were $950; for selling expenses, $250; and for administrative expenses, $150.
f. Depreciation of factory equipment was $9,100; of office equipment, $400; and of store equipment, $300.
g. Factory overhead costs applied to jobs, $40,910.
h. Jobs completed, $208,800.
i. Cost of goods sold, $197,250.

Instructions
Journalize the entries to record the summarized operations.

PROBLEM 19–2A
Entries and schedules for unfinished and completed jobs
Objectives 3, 4

Weaver Printing Inc. uses a job order cost system. The following data summarize the operations related to production for April, the first month of operations:

a. Materials purchased on account, $125,610.
b. Materials requisitioned and factory labor used:

	Materials	Factory Labor
Job 601	$15,840	$ 9,500
Job 602	12,410	8,140
Job 603	13,900	5,100
Job 604	21,860	14,220
Job 605	11,440	6,680
Job 606	7,400	3,000
For general factory use	2,300	1,760

c. Factory overhead costs incurred on account, $21,200.
d. Depreciation of machinery and equipment, $7,760.
e. The factory overhead rate is $15 per machine hour. Machine hours used:

Job 601	510
Job 602	352
Job 603	240
Job 604	669
Job 605	344
Job 606	145
Total	2,260

f. Jobs completed: 601, 602, 603, and 605.
g. Jobs were shipped and customers were billed as follows: Job 601, $49,250; Job 602, $31,100; and Job 605, $31,280.

Instructions

1. Journalize the entries to record the summarized operations.
2. Post the appropriate entries to T accounts for Work in Process and Finished Goods, using the identifying letters as dates. Insert memorandum account balances as of the end of the month.
3. Prepare a schedule of unfinished jobs to support the balance in the work in process account.
4. Prepare a schedule of completed jobs on hand to support the balance in the finished goods account.

PROBLEM 19–3A
Job order cost sheet
Objectives 3, 4, 5

If the working papers correlating with this textbook are not used, omit Problem 19–3A.

Judy Snow repairs, refinishes, and reupholsters furniture. Snow uses a job order cost system.

When a prospective customer asks for a price quote on a job, the estimated cost data are inserted on an unnumbered job cost sheet. If the offer is accepted, a number is assigned to the job and the costs incurred are recorded in the usual manner on the job cost sheet. After the job is completed, reasons for the variances between the estimated and actual costs are noted on the sheet. The data are then available to management in evaluating the efficiency of operations and in preparing quotes on future jobs.

On September 9, an estimate of $924 for reupholstering a chair and couch was given to Brian Bales. The estimate was based on the following data:

Estimated direct materials:	
12 meters at $10 per meter	$120
Estimated direct labor:	
24 hours at $15 per hour	360
Estimated factory overhead (50% of direct labor cost)	180
Total estimated costs	$660
Markup (40% of production costs)	264
Total estimate	$924

On September 12, the chair and couch were picked up from the residence of Brian Bales, 1927 Oak Tree Way, Columbus, with a commitment to return it on September 28. The job was completed on September 24.

The related materials requisitions and time tickets are summarized as follows:

Materials Requisition No.	*Description*	*Amount*
3480	12 meters at $10	$120
3492	3 meters at $10	30

Time Ticket No.	*Description*	*Amount*
H143	20 hours at $15	$300
H151	8 hours at $15	120

Instructions

1. Complete that portion of the job order cost sheet that would be prepared when the estimate is given to the customer.
2. Assign number R4-15 to the job, record the costs incurred, and complete the job order cost sheet. Comment on the reasons for the variances between actual costs and estimated costs. For this purpose, assume that 3 meters of materials were spoiled, the factory overhead rate has been proved to be satisfactory, and an inexperienced employee performed the work.

PROBLEM 19–4A
Analyze manufacturing cost accounts
Objectives 3, 4

Banta Sporting Goods Company manufactures golf clubs in a wide variety of lengths and weights. The following incomplete ledger accounts refer to transactions that are summarized for August:

Materials

Aug. 1	Balance	6,000	Aug. 31	Requisitions	(A)
Aug. 31	Purchases	235,000			

Work in Process

Aug. 1	Balance	(B)	Aug. 31	Completed jobs	(F)
Aug. 31	Direct materials	(C)			
Aug. 31	Direct labor	(D)			
Aug. 31	Factory overhead applied	(E)			

Finished Goods

Aug. 1	Balance	0	Aug. 31	Cost of goods sold	(H)
Aug. 31	Completed jobs	(G)			

Wages Payable

			Aug. 31	Wages incurred	170,000

Factory Overhead

Aug. 1	Balance	3,000	Aug. 31	Factory overhead applied	(J)
Aug. 31	Indirect labor	(I)			
Aug. 31	Indirect materials	2,800			
Aug. 31	Other overhead	112,000			

In addition, the following information is available:

a. Materials and direct labor were applied to six jobs in August:

Job No.	*Style*	*Quantity*	*Direct Materials*	*Direct Labor*
Job 111	DL-8's	100	$ 39,000	$ 30,000
Job 112	DL-18's	50	39,200	16,000
Job 113	DL-11's	100	38,200	51,000
Job 114	SL-101's	150	4,800	14,000
Job 115	SL-110's	100	91,000	35,000
Job 116	DL-14's	75	18,000	15,000

b. Factory overhead is applied to each job at a rate of 80% of direct labor cost.
c. The August 1 Work in Process balance consisted of two jobs, as follows:

Job No.	*Style*	*Work in Process, Aug. 1*
Job 111	DL-8's	$22,000
Job 112	DL-18's	40,000

d. Customer jobs completed and units sold in August were as follows:

Job No.	*Style*	*Completed in August*	*Units sold in August*
Job 111	DL-8's	X	95
Job 112	DL-18's	X	30
Job 113	DL-11's	X	80
Job 114	SL-101's		
Job 115	SL-110's	X	60
Job 116	DL-14's		

Instructions

1. Determine the missing amounts associated with each letter. Provide supporting calculations.
2. Determine the August 31 balances for each of the inventory accounts and factory overhead.

PROBLEM 19–5A
Hospital job order costing
Objectives 3, 5, 6

East Lansing Medical Center determines the amount to bill each patient, based upon the cost of each patient's use of Medical Center services during hospital visits. Each patient bill is broken into the following categories:

Medicine—a direct materials cost
Surgeon fees—a direct labor cost
Operating room charge per hour—indirect cost allocated by operating room hours
General and administrative overhead—indirect cost allocated by days per stay

The operating room and general and administrative overhead are determined at the beginning of each year (January 1), based on estimated operating room hours and patient-days (a measure explained below). A portion of the estimated cost was determined for the Medical Center on January 1 as follows:

Operating room costs	$ 432,000
General and administrative costs	16,644,000
Total	$17,076,000

On January 1 the financial staff estimated that the Medical Center would have 43,800 patient-days for the year, which is the average number of patients per day (120) multiplied by the number of calendar days in the year (365). The financial staff also estimated the operating room to be used for 1,800 hours during the next year.

Martha and Harry Briggs were both hospitalized on January 10. Martha Briggs entered the hospital for required rest, while Harry entered for cardiac surgery. Martha had a 30-day stay. Harry required 6 hours of operating room usage and had a 15-day stay.

A partial bill for Martha and Harry is reproduced below:

Martha Briggs	*Billed Amount*	*Harry Briggs*	*Billed Amount*
Medicine	$1,650	Medicine	$1,550
Surgeon fees	0	Surgeon fees	4,500
Operating room charges	(A)	Operating room charges	(D)
General and administrative overhead	(B)	General and administrative overhead	(E)
Total	(C)		(F)

When the Briggs's received their hospital bills, the totals didn't make sense to them.

Instructions

1. Determine the predetermined overhead rates for the operating room charges and general and administrative overhead.
2. Determine the missing amounts, lettered (A) through (F), in the Briggs's hospital bills.
3. What didn't seem right about the Briggs's bills? Why?
4. Compare how the cost accounting in a hospital is similar to a manufacturing job shop.

APPENDIX PROBLEM 19–6A
Activity-based costing

Mohawk Industries manufactures two products, C and D, which involves four overhead activities—production setup, procurement, quality control, and materials management. An activity analysis of the overhead revealed the following estimated costs for these activities:

Production setup	$ 44,000
Procurement	160,000
Quality control	175,000
Materials management	150,000
Total	$529,000

The appropriate activity drivers and the estimated amount of each activity driver for the two products are as follows:

Activity	*Activity Driver*
Production setup	Number of setups
Procurement	Number of production work orders
Quality control	Number of inspections
Materials management	Number of components

	Setups	*Work Orders*	*Inspections*	*Components*	*Unit Volume*
Product C	1,000	3,000	6,000	80	10,000
Product D	100	200	1,000	20	10,000
Total	1,100	3,200	7,000	100	20,000

Instructions

1. Determine an activity rate for each activity.
2. Assign activity costs to each product, and determine the estimated unit activity cost, using the activity rates from (1).
3. Determine the estimated total and unit activity cost for each product if overhead is allocated on the basis of production volume.
4. Explain why the answers in (2) and (3) are different.

PROBLEMS SERIES B

PROBLEM 19–1B
Entries for costs in a job order cost system
Objectives 3, 4

Kingston Industries uses a job order cost system. The following data summarize the operations related to production for June:

a. Materials purchased on account, $94,200.
b. Materials requisitioned, $83,150, of which $2,900 was for general factory use.
c. Factory labor used, $160,000, of which $7,500 was factory overhead.
d. Other costs incurred on account were for factory overhead, $105,150, selling expenses, $9,500, and administrative expenses, $7,500.
e. Prepaid expenses expired for factory overhead were $750; for selling expenses, $250, and for administrative expenses, $150.
f. Depreciation of factory equipment was $8,100, of office equipment, $500, and of store equipment, $300.
g. Factory overhead costs applied to jobs, $123,000.
h. Jobs completed, $305,500.
i. Cost of goods sold, $308,200.

Instructions

Journalize the entries to record the summarized operations.

PROBLEM 19–2B
Entries and schedules for unfinished jobs and completed jobs
Objectives 3, 4

Hammond Printing Company uses a job order cost system. The following data summarize the operations related to production for April, the first month of operations:

a. Materials purchased on account, $61,410.
b. Materials requisitioned and factory labor used:

	Materials	*Factory Labor*
Job 101	$10,550	$8,960
Job 102	3,400	1,960
Job 103	9,060	4,840
Job 104	4,280	1,900
Job 105	6,620	2,600
Job 106	6,180	4,610
For general factory use	1,310	3,000

c. Factory overhead costs incurred on account, $8,300.
d. Depreciation of machinery and equipment, $5,400.
e. The factory overhead rate is $14 per machine hour. Machine hours used:

Job 101	457.5
Job 102	104.0
Job 103	234.5
Job 104	88.0
Job 105	140.0
Job 106	245.5
Total	1,269.5

f. Jobs completed: 101, 102, 104, and 105.
g. Jobs were shipped and customers were billed as follows: Job 101, $36,200; Job 102, $8,400; Job 104, $10,350.

Instructions

1. Journalize the entries to record the summarized operations.
2. Post the appropriate entries to T accounts for Work in Process and Finished Goods, using the identifying letters as dates. Insert memorandum account balances as of the end of the month.
3. Prepare a schedule of unfinished jobs to support the balance in the work in process account.
4. Prepare a schedule of completed jobs on hand to support the balance in the finished goods account.

PROBLEM 19–3B
Job order cost sheet
Objectives 3, 4, 5

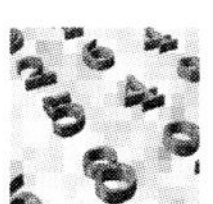

If the working papers correlating with this textbook are not used, omit Problem 19–3B.
Draper Furniture Company refinishes and reupholsters furniture. Draper uses a job order cost system. When a prospective customer asks for a price quote on a job, the estimated cost data are inserted on an unnumbered job cost sheet. If the offer is accepted, a number is assigned to the job, and the costs incurred are recorded in the usual manner on the job cost sheet. After the job is completed, reasons for the variances between the estimated and actual costs are noted on the sheet. The data are then available to management in evaluating the efficiency of operations and in preparing quotes on future jobs. On May 5, an estimate of $425.10 for reupholstering a chair and couch was given to Ted O'Brien. The estimate was based on the following data:

Estimated direct materials:	
8 meters at $12 per meter	$ 96.00
Estimated direct labor:	
11 hours at $15 per	165.00
Estimated factory overhead (40% of direct labor cost)	66.00
Total estimated costs	$327.00
Markup (30% of production costs)	98.10
Total estimate	$425.10

On May 9, the chair and couch were picked up from the residence of Ted O'Brien, 979 Park Shore Dr., Ft. Myers, with a commitment to return it on May 26. The job was completed on May 23.

The related materials requisitions and time tickets are summarized as follows:

Materials Requisition No.	*Description*	*Amount*
U642	8 meters at $12	$ 96
U651	3 meters at $12	36

Time Ticket No.	*Description*	*Amount*
1519	9 hours at $15	$135
1520	3 hours at $15	45

Instructions

1. Complete that portion of the job order cost sheet that would be prepared when the estimate is given to the customer.
2. Assign number 96-15-1 to the job, record the costs incurred, and complete the job order cost sheet. Comment on the reasons for the variances between actual costs and estimated costs. For this purpose, assume that 3 meters of materials were spoiled, the factory overhead rate has been proved to be satisfactory, and an inexperienced employee performed the work.

PROBLEM 19–4B
Analyzing manufacturing cost accounts
Objectives 3, 4

Kay-Two Company manufactures snow skis in a wide variety of lengths and styles. The following incomplete ledger accounts refer to transactions that are summarized for January:

Materials

Jan. 1	Balance	10,000	Jan. 31	Requisitions	(A)
Jan. 31	Purchases	134,000			

Work in Process

Jan. 1	Balance	(B)	Jan. 31	Completed jobs	(F)
Jan. 31	Direct materials	(C)			
Jan. 31	Direct labor	(D)			
Jan. 31	Factory overhead applied	(E)			

Finished Goods

Jan. 1	Balance	0	Jan. 31	Cost of goods sold	(H)
Jan. 31	Completed jobs	(G)			

Wages Payable

			Jan. 31	Wages incurred	175,000

Factory Overhead

Jan. 1	Balance	4,000	Jan. 31	Factory overhead applied	(J)
Jan. 31	Indirect labor	(I)			
Jan. 31	Indirect materials	3,000			
Jan. 31	Other overhead	165,000			

In addition, the following information is available:

a. Materials and direct labor were applied to six jobs in January:

Job No.	*Style*	*Quantity*	*Direct Materials*	*Direct Labor*
Job 51	V-100	50	$ 10,000	$ 12,000
Job 52	V-200	68	13,000	18,000
Job 53	V-500	100	30,000	45,000
Job 54	A-200	200	30,000	28,000
Job 55	V-400	150	40,000	50,000
Job 56	A-100	100	7,000	5,000

b. Factory overhead is applied to each job at a rate of 120% of direct labor cost.
c. The January 1 Work in Process balance consisted of two jobs, as follows:

Job No.	*Style*	*Work in Process, Jan. 1*
Job 51	V-100	$ 8,000
Job 52	V-200	12,000

d. Customer jobs completed and units sold in January were as follows:

Job No.	*Style*	*Completed in January*	*Units sold in January*
Job 51	V-100	X	40
Job 52	V-200	X	60
Job 53	V-500		
Job 54	A-200	X	175
Job 55	V-400	X	60
Job 56	A-100		

Instructions

1. Determine the missing amounts associated with each letter. Provide supporting calculations.
2. Determine the January 31 balances for each of the inventory accounts and factory overhead.

PROBLEM 19–5B
Veterinary hospital job order costing
Objectives 3, 5, 6

Hillsdale Veterinary Hospital determines the amount to bill each animal owner, based upon the cost of each animal's use of Hillsdale services during veterinary visits. Each bill is broken into the following categories:

Medicine—a direct materials cost
Veterinary fees—a direct labor cost
Operating room charges per hour—indirect cost allocated to animal patients per operating room hours
General and administrative overhead—indirect cost allocated to animal patients per day

The operating room and general and administrative overhead are determined at the beginning of each year (January 1), based on estimated operating room hours and animal patient-days (a measure explained below). A portion of the estimated cost was determined for the hospital on January 1 as follows:

Operating room costs	$ 264,000
General and administrative costs	2,372,500
Total	$2,636,500

On January 1, the financial staff estimated that the hospital would have 9,125 animal-days, which is the average number of animal patients per day (25) multiplied by the number of calendar days in the period (365). The financial staff also estimated the operating room to be used for 1,200 hours during the next period.

Harvey Weatherspoon delivered a cow and his dog to the hospital on March 15. The cow entered the hospital for a difficult calf delivery, while the dog entered for a broken leg. The cow required no operating room time and had a 3-day stay. The dog required 2 hours of operating room usage and had a 20-day stay while the leg healed.

A partial bill for the cow and dog is reproduced as follows:

Weatherspoon Cow	*Billed Amount*	*Weatherspoon Dog*	*Billed Amount*
Medicine	$ 70	Medicine	$340
Veterinary fees	800	Veterinary fees	750
Operating room charges	(A)	Operating room charges	(D)
General and administrative overhead	(B)	General and administrative overhead	(E)
Total cost of services	(C)	Total cost of services	(F)

When Harvey Weatherspoon received the hospital bills, the totals didn't seem right.

Instructions

1. Determine the predetermined overhead rates for the operating room charges and general and administrative overhead.
2. Determine the missing amounts, lettered (A) through (F), in the Weatherspoon hospital bills.
3. What didn't seem right about the Weatherspoon bills? Why?
4. Compare how the cost accounting in a veterinary hospital is similar to a manufacturing job shop.

APPENDIX PROBLEM 19–6B
Activity-based costing
Objective 4

Hydro Technologies Inc. manufactures two products, F and G, which involves four overhead activities—raw materials receiving, setup, design engineering, and finished goods shipping. An activity analysis of the overhead revealed the following estimated costs for these activities:

Raw materials receiving	$ 50,000
Setup	202,000
Design engineering	300,000
Finished goods shipping	96,000
Total	$648,000

The appropriate activity drivers and the estimated amount of each activity driver for the two products are as follows:

Activity	*Activity Driver*
Raw materials receiving	Number of raw materials shipments
Setup	Number of setups
Design engineering	Number of engineering change orders
Finished goods shipping	Number of customer orders

	Shipments	*Setups*	*Engineering Changes*	*Customer Orders*	*Unit Volume*
Product F	200	500	45	1,000	25,000
Product G	50	5	5	200	25,000
Total	250	505	50	1,200	50,000

Instructions

1. Determine an activity rate for each activity.
2. Assign activity costs to each product and determine the estimated unit activity cost, using the activity rates from (1).
3. Determine the estimated total and unit activity cost for each product if overhead is allocated on the basis of production volume.
4. Explain why the answers in (2) and (3) are different.

CASES

CASE 19–1
Boswell Manufacturing Enterprises
Materials costs

Boswell Manufacturing Enterprises allows employees to purchase, at cost, manufacturing materials, such as metal and lumber, for personal use. To purchase materials for personal use, an employee must complete a materials requisition form, which must then be approved by the employee's immediate supervisor. Cheryl Long, an assistant cost accountant, charges the employee an amount based on Boswell's net purchase cost.

Cheryl Long is in the process of replacing a deck on her home and has requisitioned lumber for personal use, which has been approved in accordance with company policy. In computing the cost of the lumber, Long reviewed all the purchase invoices for the past year. She then used the lowest price to compute the amount due the company for the lumber.

Discuss whether Cheryl behaved in an ethical manner.

CASE 19–2
Manfield Molding Company
Managerial analysis

The controller of the plant of Manfield Molding Company prepared a graph of the unit costs from the job cost reports for Product XD. The graph appeared as follows:

How would you interpret this information? What further information would you request?

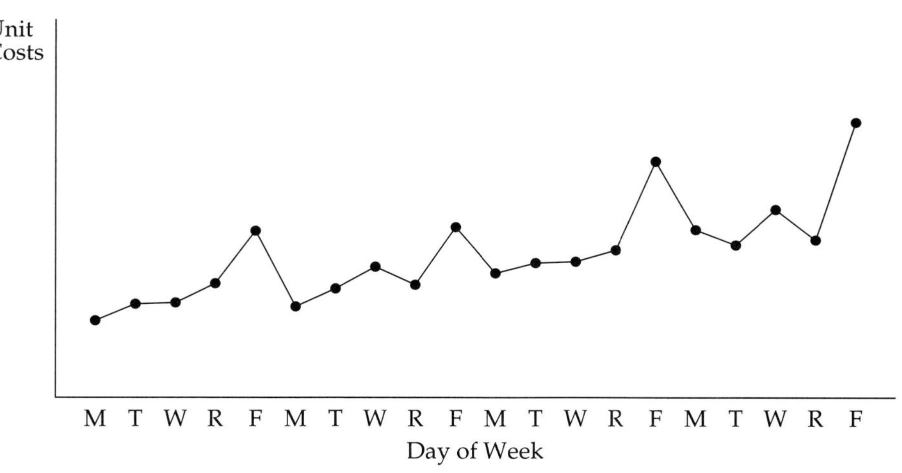

CASE 19–3
Pacific Instruments Inc.
Factory overhead rate

Pacific Instruments Inc., an electronics instrument manufacturer, uses a job order costing system. The overhead is allocated to jobs on the basis of direct labor hours. The overhead rate is now $1,000 per direct labor hour. The design engineer thinks that this is illogical. The design engineer has stated the following:

Our accounting system doesn't make any sense to me. It tells me that every labor hour carries an additional burden of $1,000. This means that direct labor makes up only 5% of our total product cost, yet it drives all our costs. In addition, these rates give my design engineers incentives to "design out" direct labor by using machine technology. Yet, over the past years as we have had less and less direct labor, the overhead rate keeps going up and up. I won't be surprised if next year the rate is $1,200 per direct labor hour. I'm also concerned because small errors in our estimates of the direct labor content can have a large impact on our estimated costs. Just a 30-minute error in our estimate of assembly time is worth $500. Small mistakes in our direct labor time estimates really swing our bids around. I think this puts us at a disadvantage when we are going after business.

1. What is the engineer's concern about the direct labor rate going "up and up?"
2. What did the engineer mean about the large overhead rate being a disadvantage when placing bids and seeking new business?
3. What do you think is a possible solution?

CASE 19–4

Maytime Company

Recording manufacturing costs

Jeff Flowers just began working as a cost accountant for the Maytime Company. Maytime manufactures gift items. Flowers is preparing to record summary journal entries for the month. Flowers begins by recording the factory wages as follows:

Wages Expense	15,000	
Wages Payable		15,000

Then the factory depreciation:

Depreciation Expense—Factory Machinery	4,000	
Accumulated Depreciation—Factory Machinery		4,000

Flower's supervisor, Hanna Tully, walks by and notices the entries. The following conversation takes place.

Hanna: That's a very unusual way to record our factory wages and depreciation for the month.

Jeff: What do you mean? This is exactly the way we were taught to record wages and depreciation in school. You know, debit an expense and credit Cash or payables, or in the case of depreciation, credit Accumulated Depreciation.

Hanna: Well, it's not the credits I'm concerned about. It's the debits—I don't think you've recorded the debits correctly. I wouldn't mind if you were recording the administrative wages or office equipment depreciation this way, but I've got real questions about recording factory wages and factory machinery depreciation this way.

Jeff: Now I'm really confused. You mean this is correct for administrative costs, but not for factory costs? Well, what am I supposed to do—and why?

Answer Jeff's questions. Why would Hanna accept the journal entries if they were for administrative costs?

CASE 19–5

Palentino Company

Job order decision making and rate deficiencies

Palentino Company makes attachments, such as backhoes and grader and bulldozer blades, for construction equipment. The company uses a job order cost system. Management is concerned about cost performance and evaluates the job cost sheets to learn more about the cost effectiveness of the operations. To facilitate a comparison, the cost sheet for Job 500 (15 Type Z bulldozer blades completed in March) was compared with Job 750, which was for 25 Type Z bulldozer blades completed in September. The two job cost sheets are shown.

Job 500

Item: 15 Type Z bulldozer blades

Materials:	Direct Materials Quantity	×	Direct Materials Price	=	Amount
Steel (tons)	30		$800.00		$24,000
Steel components (pieces)	225		3.00		675
Total materials					$24,675
Direct labor	Direct Labor Hours	×	Direct Labor Rate	=	Amount
Foundry	180.0		$ 14.00		$ 2,520
Welding	120.0		16.00		1,920
Shipping	22.5		10.00		225
Total direct labor	322.5				$ 4,665
	Direct Total Labor Cost	×	Factory Overhead Rate	=	Amount
Factory overhead (400% of direct labor dollars)	$4,665	×	400%		$18,660
Total cost					$48,000
Total units					÷ 15
Unit cost					$ 3,200

Job 750

Item: 25 Type Z bulldozer blades

Materials:	Direct Materials Quantity	×	Direct Materials Price	=	Amount
Steel (tons)	58		$750.00		$43,500
Steel components	375		3.00		1,125
Total materials					$44,625
Direct labor	**Direct Labor Hours**	**×**	**Direct Labor Rate**	**=**	**Amount**
Foundry	325.0		14.00		$ 4,550
Welding	250.0		16.00		4,000
Shipping	37.5		10.00		375
Total direct labor	612.5				$ 8,925
	Direct Total Labor Cost	**×**	**Factory Overhead Rate**	**=**	**Amount**
Factory overhead (400% of direct labor dollars)	$8,925	×	400%		$35,700
Total cost					$89,250
Total units					÷ 25
Unit cost					$ 3,570

Management is concerned with the increase in unit costs over the months from March to September. To understand what has occurred, management interviewed the purchasing manager and quality manager.

Purchasing Manager: "Prices have been holding steady for our raw materials during the first half of the year. I found a new supplier for our bulk steel that was willing to offer a better price than we received in the past. I saw these lower steel prices and jumped at them, knowing that a reduction in steel prices would have a very favorable impact on our costs."

Quality Manager: "Something happened around mid-year. All of a sudden, we were experiencing problems with respect to the quality of our steel. As a result, we've been having all sorts of problems on the shop floor in our foundry and welding operation."

1. Analyze the two job cost sheets, and identify why the unit costs have changed for the Type Z bulldozer blades. Complete the following schedule to help you in your analysis:

Item	*Input Quantity per Unit—Job 500*	*Input Quantity per Unit—Job 750*
Steel		
Foundry labor		
Welding labor		

2. How would you interpret what has happened in light of your analysis and the interviews?

CASE 19–6
Lyle Industries
Predetermined overhead rates

As an assistant cost accountant for Lyle Industries, you have been assigned to review the activity driver for the predetermined factory overhead rate. The president, Calvin Adler, has expressed concern that the over- or underapplied overhead has fluctuated excessively over the years.

An analysis of the company's operations and use of the current overhead base (direct materials usage) has narrowed the possible alternative overhead bases to direct labor cost and machine hours. For the past five years, the following data have been gathered:

	1997	*1996*	*1995*	*1994*	*1993*
Actual overhead	$ 650,000	$ 700,000	$ 500,000	$ 600,000	$ 550,000
Applied overhead	616,000	722,000	526,000	569,000	589,000
(Over) underapplied overhead	$ 34,000	$ (22,000)	$ (26,000)	$ 31,000	$ (39,000)
Direct labor cost	$2,150,000	$2,350,000	$1,630,000	$2,040,000	$1,830,000
Machine hours	52,600	61,300	44,100	48,700	43,300

1. Calculate a predetermined factory overhead rate for each alternative base, assuming that the rates would have been determined by relating the amount of factory overhead for the past five years to the base.
2. For each of the past five years, determine the over- or underapplied overhead, based on the two predetermined overhead rates developed in (1).
3. Which predetermined overhead rate would you recommend? Discuss the basis for your recommendation.

ANSWERS TO SELF-EXAMINATION QUESTIONS

1. **C** Inventory accounts are maintained by manufacturing businesses for (1) goods in the process of manufacture (Work in Process—answer C), (2) goods in the state in which they are to be sold (Finished Goods—answer A), and (3) goods in the state in which they were acquired (Materials—answer B). Merchandise Inventory (answer D) is not a type of manufacturing inventory but is inventory for a merchandising business.
2. **D** The finished goods inventory comprises three categories of manufacturing costs: direct materials (answer A), direct labor (answer B), and factory overhead (answer C).
3. **B** Factory overhead includes all manufacturing costs, except direct materials and direct labor. Salaries of plant supervisors (answer B) is an example of a factory overhead item. Wages of factory assembly-line workers (answer A) is a direct labor item, and bearings for electric motors (answer C) are direct materials.
4. **A** Job order cost systems are best suited to businesses manufacturing for special orders from customers, such as would be the case for a repair shop for antique furniture (answer A). A process cost system is best suited for manufacturers of homogeneous units of product, such as rubber (answer B) and coal (answer C).
5. **B** If the amount of factory overhead applied during a particular period exceeds the actual overhead costs, the factory overhead account will have a credit balance and is said to be overapplied (answer B) or overabsorbed. If the amount applied is less than the actual costs, the account will have a debit balance and is said to be underapplied (answer A) or underabsorbed (answer C). Since an "estimated" predetermined overhead rate is used to apply overhead, a credit balance does not necessarily represent an error (answer D).

20 Process Cost Systems

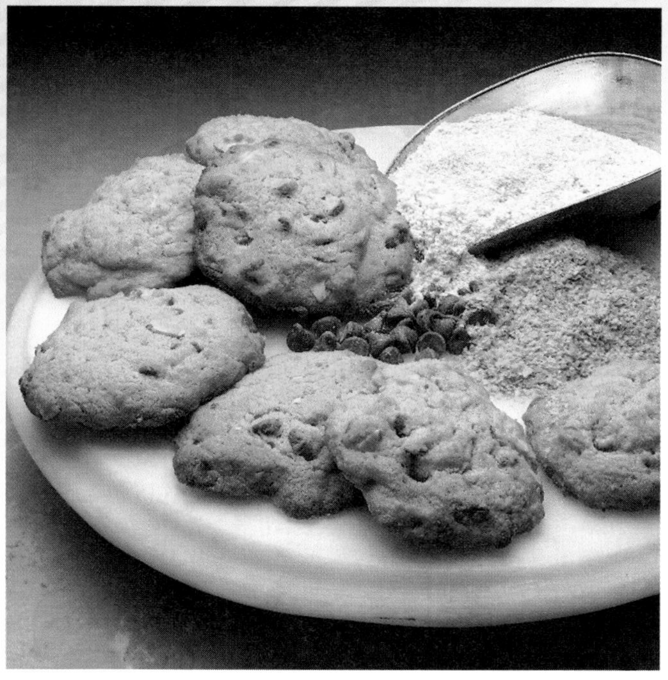

YOU AND ACCOUNTING

If you bake cookies, the ingredients would include flour, sugar, and water. These ingredients would all be added at the beginning of the baking process by mixing them in a bowl. After mixing, do you have cookies? No. Why? Because they aren't baked (converted). But are they 100% complete with respect to materials? Yes, all the materials have been added to the baking process. When will they be cookies? When they are 100% complete with respect to materials *and* baking.

Now, assume that you ask the question, "How much cost have I incurred in baking cookies after 15 minutes (out of 30 minutes) of baking time?" The answer would require that you separate the ingredients and the electricity costs. These two costs are incurred in the baking process at different rates, and so it is convenient to identify them separately. The ingredient costs have all been incurred, since they were all introduced at the beginning of the process. The electricity costs, however, are a different story. Since the baking is only 50% complete, only 50% of the electricity costs (for the oven) have been incurred in the baking process. Therefore, the answer to the question is that all the materials costs and half the electricity costs have been incurred in the baking process after 15 minutes of baking.

In this chapter, we apply these concepts to manufacturers that use a process cost system. After introducing process costing, we discuss decision making with process cost system reports. We conclude the chapter with a brief discussion of just-in-time cost systems.

After studying this chapter, you should be able to:

Objective 1
Distinguish between job order costing and process costing systems.

Objective 2
Explain and illustrate the physical flows and cost flows for a process manufacturer.

Objective 3
Calculate and interpret the accounting for completed and partially completed units under the fifo method.

Objective 4
Prepare a cost of production report.

Objective 5
Prepare journal entries for transactions of a process manufacturer.

Objective 6
Use cost of production reports for decision making.

Objective 7
Contrast just-in-time processing with conventional manufacturing practices.

Comparing Job Order Costing and Process Costing

Objective 1
Distinguish between job order costing and process costing systems.

As we discussed in the previous chapter, the job order cost system is best suited to industries that fill special orders from customers or manufacture a variety of different products in batches. Industries that may use job order cost systems include special-order printing, custom-made tailoring, furniture manufacturing, shipbuilding, aircraft building, and construction. The process manufacturing environment is different from the job shop. **Process manufacturers** typically use large machines to process a continuous flow of raw materials into a finished state. For example, crude oil is processed through numerous refining steps to produce higher grades of oil until eventually gasoline is produced. The cost accounting system used by process manufacturers is called the **process cost system.** Industries that may use process cost systems include chemicals, oil, metals, food, paper, and pharmaceuticals. Examples of companies that would use a process cost system include **DuPont, International Paper,** and **Alcoa.**

In many ways, the process cost and job order cost systems are similar. Both systems accumulate product costs—direct materials, direct labor, and factory overhead—and allocate these costs to the units produced. Additionally, both systems maintain perpetual inventory accounts with subsidiary ledgers for materials, work in process, and finished goods. Both systems also provide product cost data to management for planning, directing, improving, controlling, and decision making. The main difference between the two systems is the format in which the product costs are accumulated and reported.

Exhibit 1 graphically illustrates the main differences between the job order and process cost systems. In a job order cost system, product costs are accumulated for individual jobs and are summarized on job cost sheets. The job cost sheets provide unit cost information and can be used by management for product pricing, cost control, and inventory valuation. The process manufacturer does not manufacture according to individual "jobs," as do job shops. Thus, costs cannot be accumulated for job orders. In the process cost system, costs are accumulated by department. Each unit of product that passes through the department is similar. Thus, the production costs reported by each department provide unit cost information that can be used by management for cost control. In a job order cost system, the work in process inventory at the end of the accounting period is the sum of the job cost sheets for partially completed jobs. In a process cost system, the amount of work in process inventory is determined by allocating costs between completed and partially completed units within a department.

Exhibit 1
Job Order and Process Cost Systems Compared

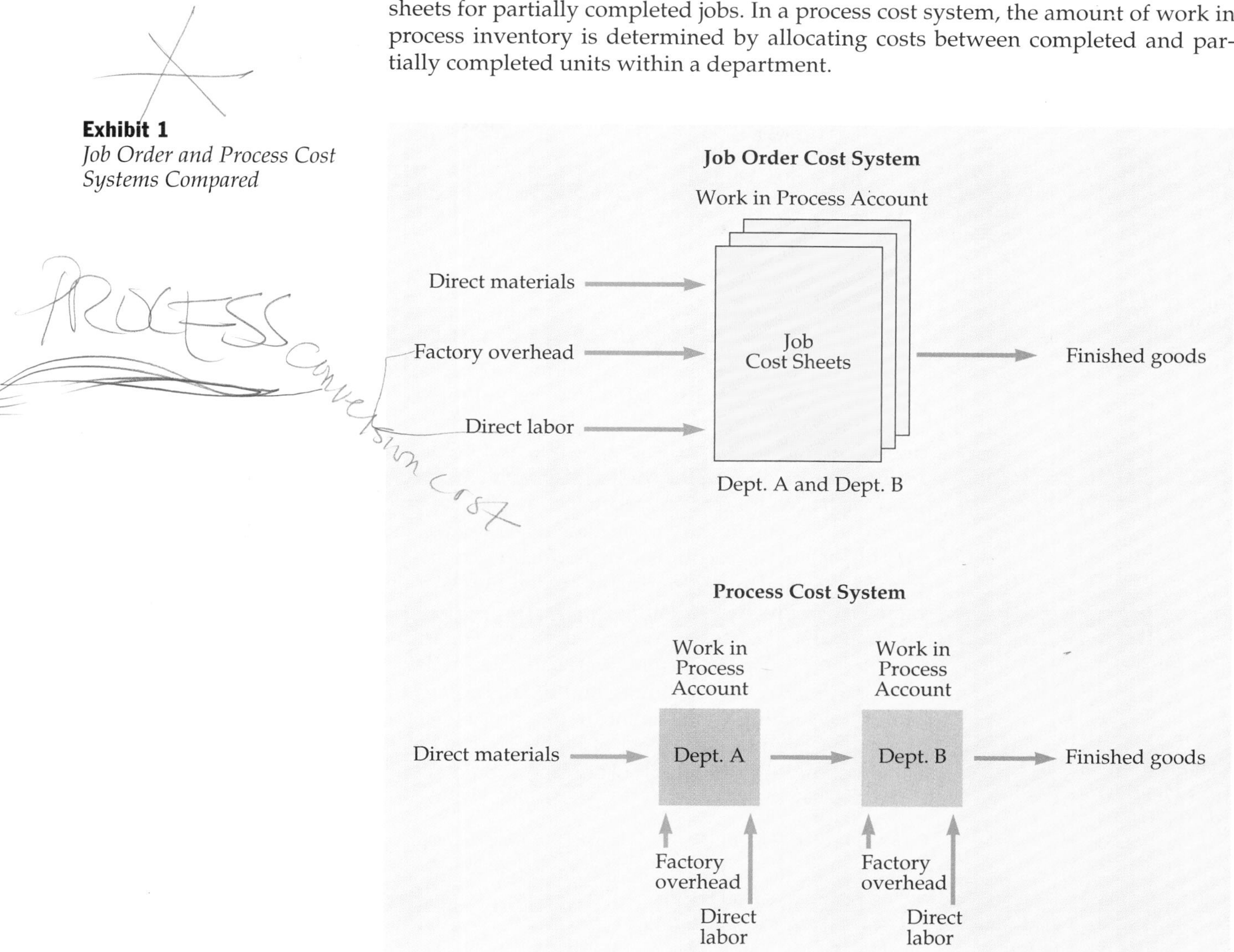

Physical Flows and Cost Flows for a Process Manufacturer

Objective 2
Explain and illustrate the physical flows and cost flows of a process manufacturer.

Process manufacturers are noted for being materials intensive; i.e., materials costs are a large portion of the cost structure. Thus, accounting for materials costs is very important.

Exhibit 2 illustrates the physical flow of materials for a steel processor. Direct materials in the form of scrap metal are placed into a furnace in the Melting Department. The Melting Department uses conversion costs (direct labor and factory overhead) during the melting process. The molten metal is then transferred to the Casting Department, where it is poured into an ingot casting. The Casting Department also uses conversion costs during the casting process. The ingot castings are transferred to the finished goods inventory for shipment to customers.

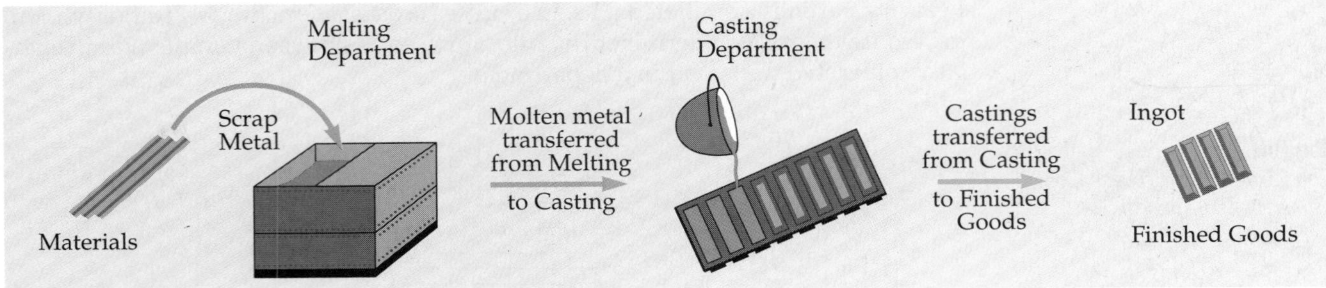

Exhibit 2
Physical Flows for a Process Manufacturer

The cost flows in a process cost system reflect the physical materials flows and are illustrated in Exhibit 3. Purchased materials are debited to Materials (a) and credited to Accounts Payable (not shown). Direct materials (scrap metal) used by the Melting Department are debited to Work in Process—Melting and credited to Materials (b). In addition, indirect materials and other overhead incurred are debited to department factory overhead accounts and credited to Materials (d) and other accounts. Direct labor in the Melting Department is debited to the department's work in process account (c) and credited to Wages Payable (not shown). Applied factory overhead is debited to Work in Process—Melting, using a predetermined overhead rate (e). The cost of completed production from the Melting Department is transferred to the Casting Department by debiting Work in Process—Casting and crediting Work in Process—Melting (f). The transferred costs include the direct materials and conversion costs for completed production of the Melting Department. The direct labor and applied factory overhead costs in the Casting Department are debited to Work in Process—Casting (g and h). The cost of the finished ingots is transferred out of the Casting Department by debiting Finished Goods and crediting Work in Process—Casting (i). The cost of ingots sold to customers is transferred out of finished goods with a debit to Cost of Goods Sold and a credit to Finished Goods (j).

Exhibit 3
Cost Flows for a Process Manufacturer

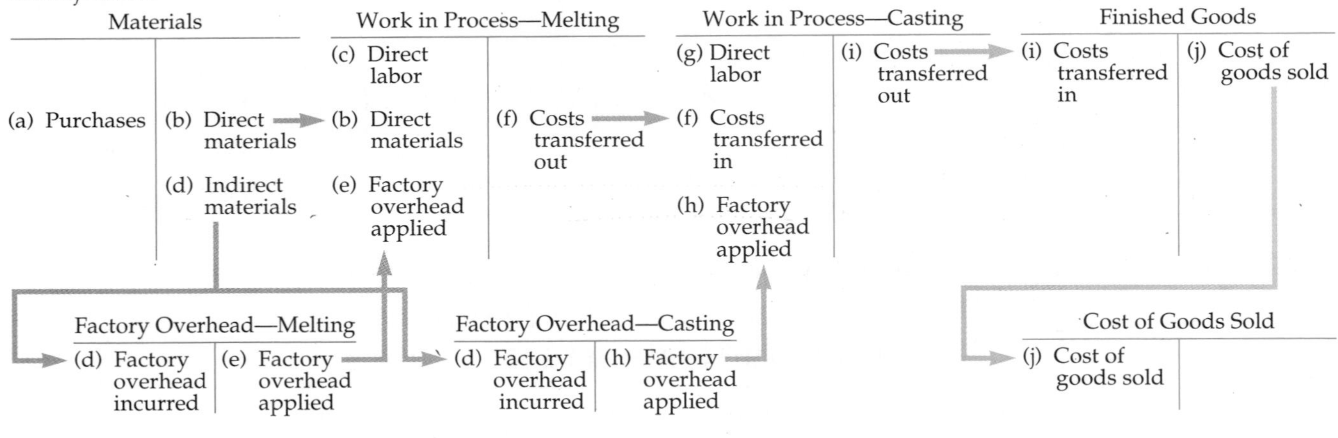

The First-In, First-Out (Fifo) Method

Objective 3
Calculate and interpret the accounting for completed and partially completed units under the fifo method.

In a process cost system, the accountant must determine the cost transferred out and thus the amount remaining in inventory for each department. For many manufacturing processes, materials are added at the beginning of production, and the units are moved through the production processes in a **first-in, first-out (fifo)** flow. That is, the first units entering the production process are the first to be completed.[1]

[1] An alternative method—the average cost method—is discussed in advanced textbooks.

Steel manufacturers melt scrap metal and pour the molten metal into an ingot casting. For many manufacturing processes such as this, materials are added at the beginning of production, and units are moved through the production processes in a fifo flow.

Most process manufacturers have more than one department. In the illustrations that follow, McDermott Steel Inc. has two departments, Melting and Casting. McDermott melts scrap metal and then pours the molten metal into an ingot casting.

To illustrate the first-in, first-out method for a process manufacturer, we will simplify by using only the Melting Department of McDermott Steel Inc. The following data for the Melting Department are available for July of the current year:

Inventory in process, July 1, 500 tons:		
Direct materials cost, for 500 tons	$24,550	
Conversion costs, for 500 tons, 70% completed	3,600	
Total inventory in process, July 1		$28,150
Direct materials cost for July, 1,000 tons		50,000
Conversion costs for July		9,690
Goods finished in July (includes units in process on July 1), 1,100 tons		?
Inventory in process, July 31, 400 tons, 25% completed as to conversion costs		?

We will assume that all materials used in the department are added at the beginning of the process, and conversion costs (direct labor and factory overhead) are incurred evenly throughout the melting process. The company's objective is to determine the cost of goods completed and the ending inventory valuation, which are represented by the question marks. We will determine these amounts by using the following four steps:

1. Determine the units to be assigned costs.
2. Calculate equivalent units of production.
3. Determine the cost per equivalent unit.
4. Allocate costs to transferred and partially completed units.

STEP 1: DETERMINE THE UNITS TO BE ASSIGNED COSTS

The first step in our illustration is to determine the units to be assigned costs. A unit can be any measure of completed production, such as tons, gallons, pounds, barrels, or cases. We will use tons as the definition for units in McDermott Steel.

McDermott Steel had 1,500 tons of direct materials charged to production in the Melting Department for July, as shown below.

Total tons charged to production:	
In process, July 1	500 tons
Received from materials storeroom	1,000
Total units accounted for by the Melting Department	1,500 tons

There are three categories of units to be assigned cost for an accounting period: (a) units in beginning in-process inventory, (b) units started and completed during the period, and (c) units in ending in-process inventory. Exhibit 4 illustrates these categories in the Melting Department for July. The 500-ton beginning inventory (a) was completed and transferred to the Casting Department. McDermott Steel started another 1,000 tons of material into the process during July. Of the 1,000 tons introduced in July, 400 tons were left incomplete at the end of the month (c). Thus, only 600 of the 1,000 tons were actually started and completed in July (b).

Exhibit 4
July Units To Be Costed—Melting Department

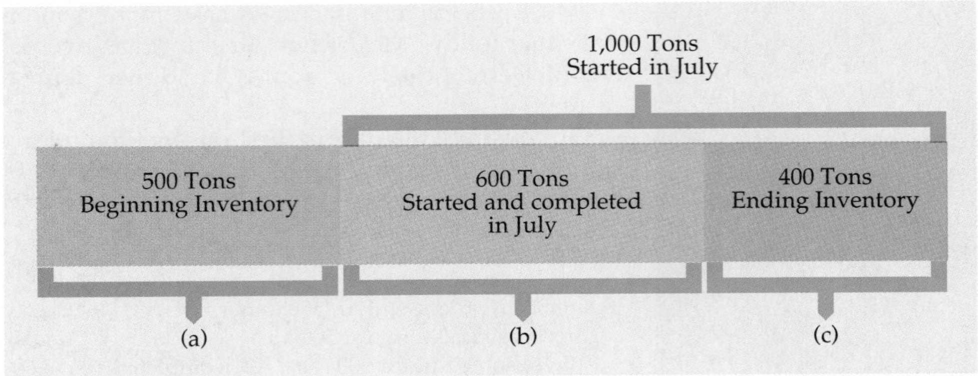

The total units (tons) to be assigned costs for McDermott Steel can be summarized as shown below.

Inventory in process, July 1, completed in July	500 tons
Started and completed in July	600
Transferred out in July to the Casting Department	1,100
Inventory in process, July 31	400
Total tons to be assigned costs	1,500 tons

Notice that the total tons to be assigned costs equals the total tons accounted for by the department. The three unit categories (a, b, and c) are used in the remaining steps to determine the cost transferred to the Casting Department and the cost remaining in work in process inventory at the end of the period.

STEP 2: CALCULATE EQUIVALENT UNITS OF PRODUCTION

Process manufacturers often have some partially processed materials remaining in production at the end of a period. In these cases, the costs of production must be allocated between the units that have been completed and transferred to the next process (or finished goods) and those that are only partially completed and remain within the department. This allocation can be determined by using the equivalent units of production.

The **equivalent units of production** are the number of units that could have been completed within a given accounting period with respect to direct materials and conversion costs. In contrast, **whole units** are the number of units in production during a period, whether or not completed. For example, assume that 800 whole units are in work in process at the end of a period. If the units are 60% complete, the number of equivalent units in process is 480 (800 × 60%).

Materials and conversion costs are frequently separated in determining equivalent units because they are often introduced at different times or different rates in the production process. On the other hand, direct labor and factory overhead are combined together as conversion costs because they are often incurred in production at the same time and rate.

Materials Equivalent Units

To allocate materials costs between the completed and partially completed units, it is necessary to determine how materials are added during the manufacturing process. In the case of McDermott Steel, the materials are added at the beginning of the melting process. In other words, the melting process cannot begin without the scrap metal. The equivalent unit computation for materials in July is as follows:

	Direct Materials Equivalent Units in July		
	Total Whole Units	*Percent Materials Added in July*	*Equivalent Units for Direct Materials*
Inventory in process, July 1	500	0%	0
Started and completed in July (1,100 – 500)	600	100%	600
Transferred out to Casting Dept. in July	1,100	—	600
Inventory in process, July 31	400	100%	400
Total tons to be assigned cost			1,000

The whole units from Step 1 are multiplied by the percentage of materials that are added in July for the in-process inventories and units started and completed. The equivalent units for direct materials are illustrated in Exhibit 5.

Exhibit 5
Direct Materials Equivalent Units

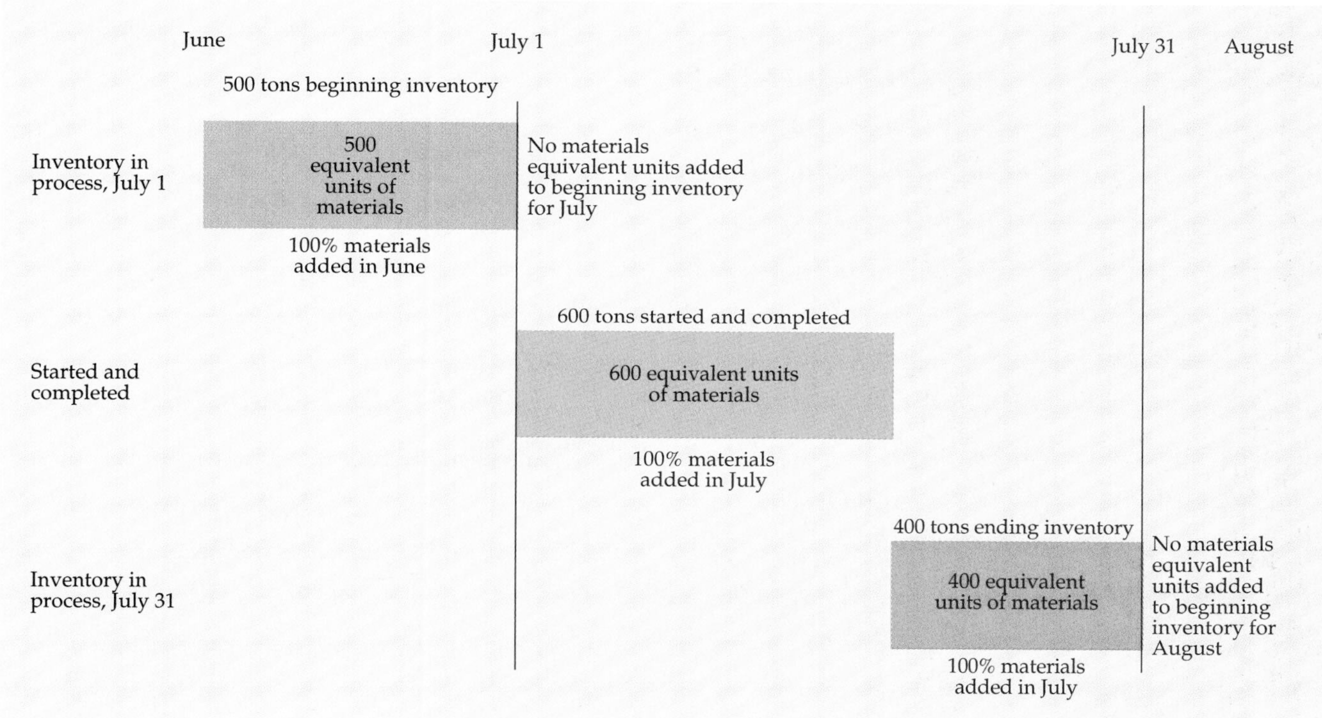

The direct materials for the 500 tons of July 1 in-process inventory were introduced in June. Thus, no materials units were added in July for the inventory in process on July 1. All of the 600 tons started and completed in July were 100% complete with respect to materials. Thus, 600 equivalent units of materials were added in July. All the materials for the July 31 in-process inventory were introduced at the beginning of the process. Thus, 400 equivalent units of material for the July 31 in-process inventory were added in July.

Conversion Equivalent Units

The conversion costs are usually incurred evenly throughout a process. For example, direct labor, utilities, and machine depreciation are usually used uniformly during processing. Thus, the conversion equivalent units are added in July in direct relation to the percentage of processing completed in July. The computations for July are as follows:

	Conversion Equivalent Units in July		
	Total Whole Units	*Percent Conversion Completed in July*	*Equivalent Units for Conversion*
Inventory in process, July	500	30%	150
Started and completed in July (1,100 – 500)	600	100%	600
Transferred out to Casting Dept. in July	1,100	—	750
Inventory in process, July 31	400	25%	100
Total tons to be assigned cost			850

The whole units from Step 1 are multiplied by the percentage of conversion completed in July for the in-process inventories and units started and completed. The equivalent units for conversion are illustrated in Exhibit 6.

Exhibit 6
Conversion Equivalent Units

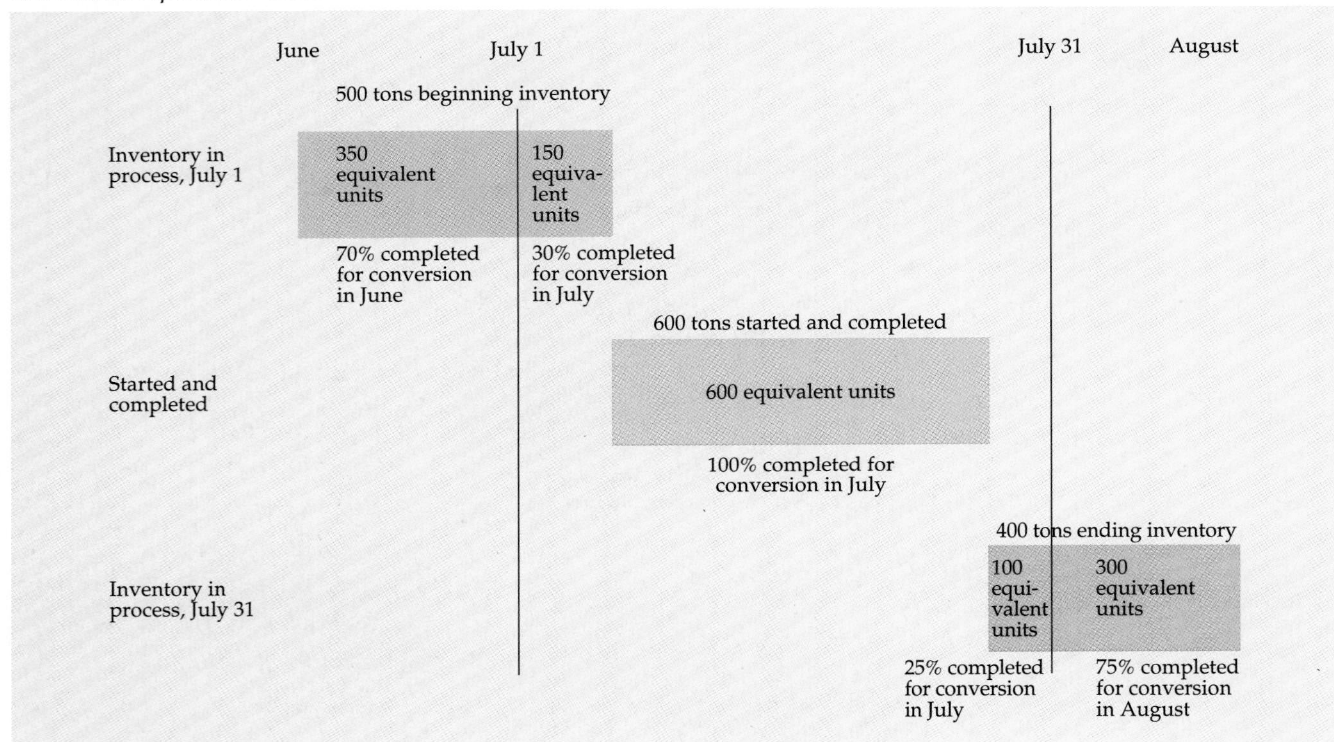

The conversion equivalent units of the July 1 in-process inventory are 30% of the 500 tons, or 150 equivalent units. Since 70% of the conversion had been completed on July 1, only 30% of the conversion effort for these tons was incurred in July. All the units started and completed used converting effort in July. Thus, conversion equivalent units are 100% of these tons. The equivalent units for the July 31 in-process inventory are 25% of the tons because only 25% of the converting has been completed with respect to these tons in July.

STEP 3: DETERMINE THE COST PER EQUIVALENT UNIT

In Step 3, we calculate the cost per equivalent unit. The July equivalent unit totals for McDermott Steel's Melting Department are reproduced from Step 2 as follows:

	Equivalent Units	
	Direct Materials	*Conversion*
Inventory in process, July 1	0	150
Started and completed in July (1,100 – 500)	600	600
Transferred out to Casting Dept. in July	600	750
Inventory in process, July 31	400	100
Total tons to be assigned cost	1,000	850

The cost per equivalent unit is determined by dividing the direct materials and conversion costs incurred in July by the respective total equivalent units for direct materials and conversion costs. The direct materials and conversion costs were given at the beginning of this illustration. These calculations are as follows:

Equivalent unit cost for direct materials:

$$\frac{\textbf{\$50,000 direct materials cost}}{\textbf{1,000 direct materials equivalent units}} = \textbf{\$50.00 per equivalent unit of direct materials}$$

Equivalent unit cost for conversion:

$$\frac{\textbf{\$9,690 conversion cost}}{\textbf{850 conversion equivalent units}} = \textbf{\$11.40 per equivalent unit of conversion}$$

We will use these rates in the final step to allocate the direct materials and conversion costs to the completed and partially completed units.

STEP 4: ALLOCATE COSTS TO TRANSFERRED AND PARTIALLY COMPLETED UNITS

In Step 4, we multiply the equivalent unit rates by their respective equivalent units of production in order to determine the cost of transferred and partially completed units. First, we must determine the cost of the July 1 in-process inventory, completed and transferred out to the Casting Department, as follows:

	Direct Materials Costs	*Conversion Costs*	*Total Costs*
Inventory in process, July 1 balance			$28,150
Equivalent units for completing the July 1 in-process inventory	0	150	
Equivalent unit cost	× $50.00	× $11.40	
Cost of completed July 1 in-process inventory	0	$1,710	1,710
Cost of July 1 in-process inventory transferred to Casting			$29,860

The July 1 in-process inventory cost of $28,150 is carried over from June and will be transferred to Casting. The cost required to finish the July 1 in-process inventory is $1,710, consisting of conversion costs required to complete the remaining 30% of the processing. This total does not include direct materials costs, since these costs were added at the beginning of the process in June. The conversion costs required to complete the beginning inventory are added to the balance carried over from the previous month to yield a total cost of the completed July 1 in-process inventory of $29,860.

The 600 units started and completed in July get 100% of their direct materials and conversion costs in July. The costs associated with the units started and completed are determined by multiplying the equivalent units in Step 2 by the unit costs in Step 3, as follows:

	Direct Materials Costs	*Conversion Costs*	*Total Costs*
Units started and completed in July	600	600	
Equivalent unit cost	× $50.00	× $11.40	
Cost to complete the units started and completed in July	$ 30,000	$ 6,840	$36,840

The total cost transferred to the Casting Department is the sum of the beginning inventory cost from the previous period ($28,150), the additional costs incurred in July to complete the beginning inventory ($1,710), and the costs incurred for the units started and completed in July ($36,840). Thus, the total cost transferred to Casting is $66,700.

The units of ending inventory have not been transferred, so they must be valued at July 31. The costs associated with the partially completed units in the ending inventory are determined by multiplying the equivalent units in Step 2 by the unit costs in Step 3, as follows:

	Direct Materials Costs	*Conversion Costs*	*Total Costs*
Equivalent units in ending inventory	400	100	
Equivalent unit cost	× $50.00	× $11.40	
Cost of ending inventory	$ 20,000	$ 1,140	$21,140

The units in the ending inventory have received 100% of their materials in July. Thus, the materials cost incurred in July for the ending inventory is $20,000, or 400 equivalent units of materials multiplied by $50. The conversion cost incurred in July for the ending inventory is $1,140, which is 100 equivalent units of conversion (400 units, 25% complete) for the ending inventory multiplied by $11.40. Summing the conversion and materials costs, the total ending inventory cost is $21,140.

USING ACCOUNTING TO UNDERSTAND BUSINESS

GPP's Gencorp Polymer Products designed their process cost accounting system not only to provide cost of goods sold information for financial reporting, but also to help managers improve the cost of their operations. They discovered that the primary drivers influencing the cost of packaging materials included poor use of machine capacities, complex material formulations, long processing times, machine cleaning time, and the frequency of cleaning. These insights led management to simplify product formulations, to reduce cleaning time, and to change their pricing strategies to reflect the cost of using machine capacity.

Bringing It All Together: The Cost of Production Report

Objective 4
Prepare a cost of production report.

A cost of production report is normally prepared for each processing department at periodic intervals. This report summarizes the four previous steps by providing the following production quantity and cost data:

1. The units for which the department is accountable and the disposition of those units.

2. The production costs incurred by the department and the allocation of those costs between completed and partially completed units.

The cost of production report is also used to control costs. Each department manager is responsible for the units entering production and the costs incurred in the department. Any failure to account for all costs and any significant differences in unit product costs from one month to another should be investigated.

The July cost of production report for McDermott Steel's Melting Department is shown in Exhibit 7.

Exhibit 7
Cost of Production Report for McDermott Steel's Melting Department—FIFO

McDermott Steel Inc.
Cost of Production Report—Melting Department
For the Month Ended July 31, 19—

UNITS	Whole Units (Step 1)	Equivalent Units (Step 2)		
		Direct Materials	Conversion	
Units charged to production:				
Inventory in process, July 1	500			
Received from materials storeroom	1,000			
Total units accounted for by the Melting Dept.	1,500			
Units to be assigned costs:				
Inventory in process, July 1 (70% completed)	500	0	150	
Started and completed in July	600	600	600	
Transferred to Casting Department in July	1,100	600	750	
Inventory in process, July 31 (25% complete)	400	400	100	
Total units to be assigned cost	1,500	1,000	850	
COSTS		Costs		
		Direct Materials	Conversion	Total Costs
Unit costs (Step 3):				
Total costs for July in Melting Dept.		$50,000	$9,690	
Total equivalent units (from Step 2 above)		÷ 1,000	÷ 850	
Cost per equivalent unit		$ 50.00	$11.40	
Costs charged to production:				
Inventory in process, July 1				$28,150
Costs incurred in July				59,690
Total costs accounted for by the Melting Dept.				$87,840
Costs allocated to completed and partially completed units (Step 4):				
Inventory in process, July 1—balance				$28,150
To complete inventory in process, July 1		$ 0	$1,710[a]	1,710
Started and completed in July		30,000[b]	6,840[c]	36,840
Transferred to Casting Dept. in July				$66,700
Inventory in process, July 31		$20,000[d]	$1,140[e]	21,140
Total costs assigned by the Melting Dept.				$87,840

[a]150 units × $11.40 = $1,710
[b]600 units × $50.00 = $30,000
[c]600 units × $11.40 = $6,840
[d]400 units × $50.00 = $20,000
[e]100 units × $11.40 = $1,140

Journal Entries for a Process Cost System

Objective 5
Prepare journal entries for transactions of a process manufacturer.

To illustrate the journal entries to record the cost flows in a process costing system, we will use the July transactions for McDermott Steel. The transactions in summary form and the entries are shown below. In practice, transactions would be recorded daily.

Transaction	Account	Debit	Credit
a. Materials purchased on account, $62,000.	Materials	62,000	
	Accounts Payable		62,000
b. Materials requisitioned by: Melting, $50,000 direct and $4,000 indirect materials; Casting, $3,000 indirect materials.	Work in Process—Melting	50,000	
	Factory Overhead—Melting	4,000	
	Factory Overhead—Casting	3,000	
	Materials		57,000
c. Direct labor used by: Melting, $5,000; Casting, $4,500.	Work in Process—Melting	5,000	
	Work in Process—Casting	4,500	
	Wages Payable		9,500
d. Depreciation expenses: Melting, $1,000; Casting, $7,000.	Factory Overhead—Melting	1,000	
	Factory Overhead—Casting	7,000	
	Accumulated Depreciation		8,000
e. Factory overhead applied: Melting, $4,690; Casting, $9,640.	Work in Process—Melting	4,690	
	Work in Process—Casting	9,640	
	Factory Overhead—Melting		4,690
	Factory Overhead—Casting		9,640
f. Melting Department transferred $66,700 to Casting Department (from Exhibit 7); Casting Department transferred $78,600 to Finished Goods.	Work in Process—Casting	66,700	
	Work in Process—Melting		66,700
	Finished Goods	78,600	
	Work in Process—Casting		78,600
g. Goods sold at a cost of $73,700.	Cost of Goods Sold	73,700	
	Finished Goods		73,700

Exhibit 8
McDermott Steel's Cost Flows

Exhibit 8 shows the flow of costs according to the lettered transactions. Note that the highlighted amounts in Exhibit 8 were determined from assigning the costs

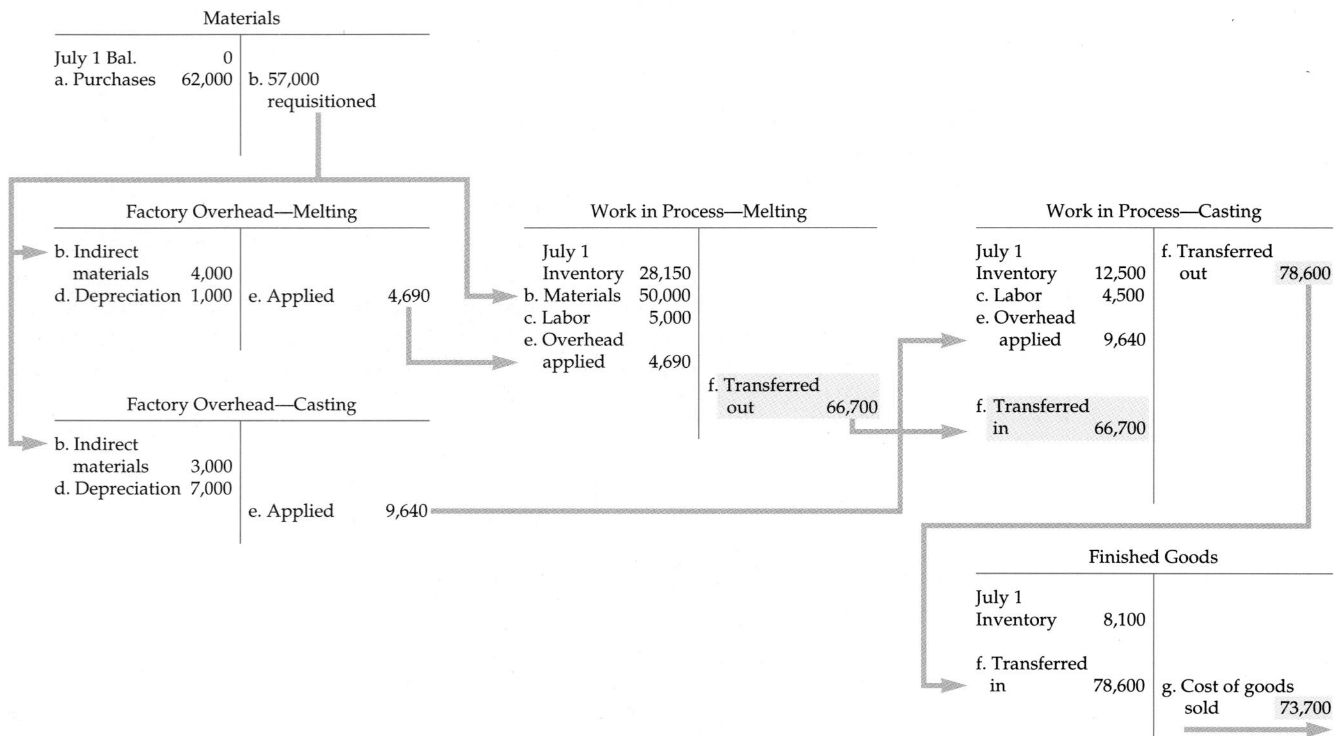

charged to production in the Melting Department. These amounts were calculated in the previous section and are shown at the bottom of the cost of production report for the Melting Department in Exhibit 7. Likewise, the amount transferred out of the Casting Department to Finished Goods would have also been determined from a cost of production report for the Casting Department.

Using the Cost of Production Report for Decision Making

Objective 6
Use cost of production reports for decision making.

The cost of production report is one source of information that may be used by managers to control and improve operations. A cost of production report will normally list costs in greater detail than we've shown previously in order to help management isolate problems and opportunities. To illustrate, assume that the Blending Department of Holland Beverage Company prepared comparative cost of production reports for April and May. In addition, assume, for simplicity, that the Blending Department had no beginning or ending work in process inventory for either month. Thus, there is no need to determine equivalent units of production for allocating costs between completed and partially completed units. The cost of production report for April and May in the Blending Department is as follows:

Cost of Production Reports
Holland Beverage Company—Blending Department
For the Months Ended April 30 and May 31, 19—

	April	May
Direct materials	$ 20,000	$ 40,600
Direct labor	15,000	29,400
Energy	8,000	20,000
Repairs	4,000	8,000
Tank cleaning	3,000	8,000
Total	$ 50,000	$ 106,000
Units completed	÷ 100,000	÷ 200,000
Cost per unit	$0.50	$0.53

Notice that this listing provides more cost detail than simply reporting direct materials and conversion costs. The May results indicate that total unit costs have increased from $0.50 to $0.53, or 6% from the previous month. What caused this increase? To determine the possible causes for this increase, the cost of production report can be restated in per-unit terms. This helps the analyst isolate changes in each cost category after removing the influence of volume changes. The following information reflects this restatement by dividing each cost category by the units completed:

BLENDING DEPARTMENT PER-UNIT EXPENSE COMPARISONS

	April	*May*	*% Change*
Direct materials	$0.200	$0.203	1.50%
Direct labor	0.150	0.147	–2.00%
Energy	0.080	0.100	25.00%
Repairs	0.040	0.040	0.00%
Tank cleaning	0.030	0.040	33.33%
Total	$0.500	$0.530	6.00%

Apparently, both energy and tank cleaning costs have increased dramatically in May. Thus, these costs are the major cause of the month-to-month per-unit cost increase. Further investigation should focus on the energy and tank cleaning costs. For example, an increasing trend in energy may indicate that the machines are losing fuel efficiency, thereby requiring the company to purchase an increasing amount of fuel. Thus, this unfavorable trend could motivate management to repair the machines. The tank cleaning costs could be investigated in a similar fashion.

In addition to unit production cost trends, managers of process manufacturers are also concerned about yield trends. Yield is the ratio of the materials output quantity to the input quantity. A yield less than one occurs when the output quantity is less than the input quantity due to materials losses during the process. For example, if 1,000 pounds of sugar entered the packing operation, and only 980 pounds of sugar were packed, the yield would be 98%. Two percent or 20 pounds of sugar were lost or spilled during the packing process.

USING ACCOUNTING TO UNDERSTAND BUSINESS

American National Can Company uses cost reporting information by container specification and by run size. One way container specifications can differ is by the type of printing on the outside. Some cans have multiple colors (litho runs) and designs, whereas others have single designs with few colors. The cost system provides information to help schedule the best run size and litho print sequencing to minimize the cost impact of color changes.

Just-in-Time Processing

Objective 7
Contrast just-in-time processing with conventional manufacturing practices.

As we mentioned in Chapter 18, many companies are now recognizing the need to simultaneously produce products with high quality, low cost, and instant availability. Accomplishing these objectives has required a revolution in the science of manufacturing methods. One approach to achieving these objectives is a new philosophy termed just-in-time (JIT) processing. Just-in-time processing is a business philosophy that focuses on reducing time and cost and eliminating poor quality within manufacturing and nonmanufacturing processes. A JIT system attempts to achieve production efficiencies and flexibility by reorganizing the traditional production process.

In a traditional production process, a product moves from process to process as each function or step is completed. Each worker is assigned a specific job, which is performed repeatedly as unfinished products are received from the preceding department. For example, a furniture manufacturer might use seven production departments to perform the operating functions necessary to manufacture furniture, as shown in the diagram in Exhibit 9.

For the furniture maker in the illustration, manufacturing would begin in the Cutting Department, where the wood would be cut to design specifications. Next, the Drilling Department would perform the drilling function, after which the Sanding Department would sand the wood, the Staining Department would stain the furniture, and the Varnishing Department would apply varnish and other protective coatings. Then, the Upholstery Department would add fabric and other materials. Finally, the Assembly Department would assemble the furniture to complete the manufacturing process.

In the traditional production process, production supervisors attempt to enter enough materials into the manufacturing process to keep all the manufacturing

Exhibit 9
Traditional Production Line—Furniture Manufacturer

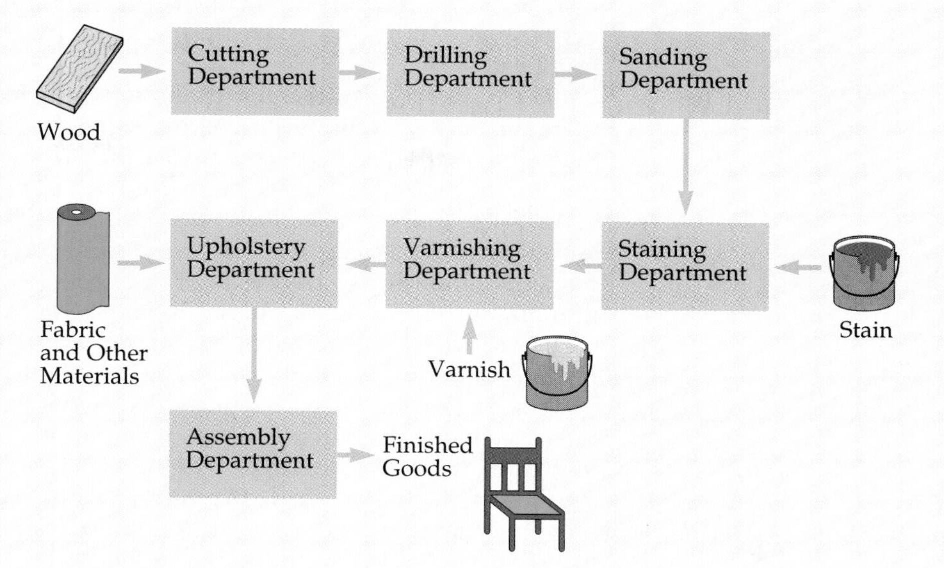

departments operating. Some departments, however, may process materials more rapidly than others. In addition, if one department stops production because of machine breakdowns, for example, the preceding departments usually continue production in order to avoid idle time. This unevenness may result in a build-up of work in some departments. Furthermore, if bottlenecks occur, the entire production line slows or stops because the unfinished product is not passed on to the next department.

In a just-in-time system, processing functions are combined into work centers, sometimes called **manufacturing cells.** For example, the seven departments illustrated above for the furniture manufacturer might be reorganized into three work centers. As shown in the diagram in Exhibit 10, Work Center One would perform the cutting, drilling, and sanding functions, Work Center Two would perform the staining and varnishing functions, and Work Center Three would perform the upholstery and assembly functions.

In the traditional production line, as described previously, a worker typically performs only one function on a continuous basis. However, in a work center in which several manufacturing functions take place, the workers are often cross-trained to perform more than one function. Research has indicated that workers

Exhibit 10
Just-in-Time Production Line—Furniture Manufacturer

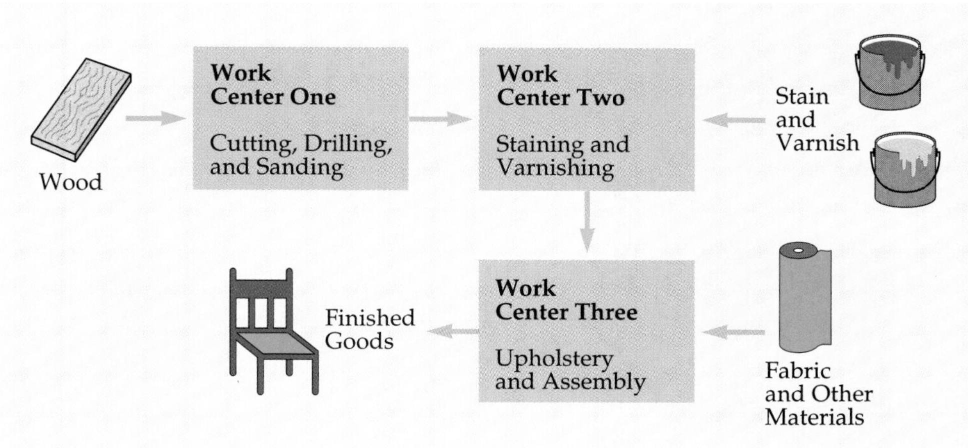

who perform several manufacturing functions identify better with the end product. This identification creates pride in the product and improves quality and productivity.

The JIT reorganization of the manufacturing departments may also result in a reorganization of activities involving services to these departments. Specifically, the service activities may be assigned to individual work centers, rather than to traditional centralized service departments. For example, each work center may be assigned the responsibility for the repair and maintenance of its machinery and equipment. Accepting this responsibility creates an environment in which workers gain a better understanding of the production process and machinery limitations. In turn, workers tend to take better care of the machinery, which decreases repairs and maintenance costs, reduces machine downtime, and improves product quality.

In a JIT system, the non-value-added activity of moving the product and materials is reduced. The product is often placed on a movable carrier that is centrally located in the work center. After the workers in a work center have completed their activities with the product, the entire carrier and any additional materials are moved to the next work center just in time to be completed and to satisfy the demand or need of that work center. In this sense, the product is said to be "pulled through." Each work center is linked with supplier work centers through information that communicates a work center's need for material. This information is sometimes called Kanban, which is a Japanese term for cards.

The experience of Caterpillar Inc. illustrates the impact of JIT. Caterpillar discovered before implementing JIT that an average transmission would travel 10 miles through the factory and require 1,000 pieces of paper for materials, labor, and movement transactions. After implementing JIT, Caterpillar improved manufacturing so that an average transmission traveled only 200 feet and required only 10 pieces of paper.

In summary, the primary benefit of JIT systems is the increased efficiency of operations, which is achieved by eliminating waste and reducing or eliminating non-value-added activities. At the same time, JIT systems emphasize continuous improvement in the manufacturing process and the improvement of product quality.

USING ACCOUNTING TO UNDERSTAND BUSINESS

Before adopting a just-in-time philosophy, Oregon Cutting Systems, a supplier of cutting tools to the wood products industry, used a complex process cost system with over 46 manufacturing departments. Each department required transactions to transfer materials and labor whenever a product moved between any two departments. After implementing JIT, the company was able to radically simplify its accounting system by reducing the number of departments and transactions. As a result, the company was able to eliminate waste, reduce lead times, reduce inventory, and improve quality.

KEY POINTS

Objective 1. Distinguish between job order costing and process costing systems.
The process cost system is best suited for industries that mass-produce identical units of a product that often have passed through a sequence of processes on a continuous basis. In process cost accounting, costs are charged to processing departments, and the cost of the finished unit is determined by dividing the total cost incurred in each process by the number of units produced.

Objective 2. Explain and illustrate the physical flows and cost flows for a process manufacturer.
Materials are introduced, converted, and passed through from one department to the next department or to finished goods. The accumulated costs transferred from preceding departments and the costs of direct materials and direct labor incurred in each processing department are debited to the related work in process account in a process cost system. Each work in process account is also debited for the factory overhead applied.

Objective 3. Calculate and interpret the accounting for completed and partially completed units under the fifo method.
Frequently, partially processed materials remain in various stages of production in a department at the end of a period. In this case, the manufacturing costs must be allocated between the units that have been completed and those that are only partially completed and remain within the department. To allocate processing costs between the output completed and the inventory of goods within the department under fifo, it is necessary to determine the number of equivalent units of production during the period for the beginning inventory, units started and completed currently, and the ending inventory.

Objective 4. Prepare a cost of production report.
A cost of production report is prepared periodically for each processing department. It summarizes (1) the units for which the department is accountable and the disposition of those units and (2) the production costs incurred by the department and the allocation of those costs. The report is used to control costs and improve the process.

Objective 5. Prepare journal entries for transactions of a process manufacturer.
Summary journal entries for common process manufacturer transactions are illustrated for McDermott Steel in the text. Basic entries include debiting direct materials, direct labor, and applied factory overhead to the processing department work in process account for costs incurred in production. Costs for completed units are credited to the transferring department's work in process account and debited to the receiving department's work in process account.

Objective 6. Use cost of production reports for decision making.
The cost of production report provides information for controlling and improving operations. Most cost of production reports include the detailed manufacturing costs incurred for completing production during the period. Analyzing trends in each of these costs over time can provide insights about process performance.

Objective 7. Contrast just-in-time processing with conventional manufacturing practices.
The just-in-time processing philosophy focuses on reducing time, cost, and poor quality within the process. This is accomplished by combining process functions into work centers, assigning overhead services directly to the cells, involving the employees in process improvement efforts, eliminating wasteful activities, and reducing the amount of work in process inventory required to fulfill production targets.

GLOSSARY OF KEY TERMS

Cost of production report. A report prepared periodically by a processing department, summarizing (1) the units for which the department is accountable and the disposition of those units and (2) the costs incurred by the department and the allocation of those costs between completed and incomplete production. *Objective 4*

Equivalent units of production. The number of units that could have been completed within a given accounting period with respect to direct materials and conversion costs. Equivalent units are used to allocate departmental costs incurred during the period between completed units and in-process units at the end of the period. *Objective 3*

First-in, first-out (fifo) cost method. A method of inventory costing that assumes the unit product costs should be determined separately for each period in the order in which the costs were incurred. *Objective 3*

Just-in-time processing. A processing approach that focuses on reducing time and cost and eliminating poor quality within manufacturing processes. *Objective 7*

Process manufacturers. Manufacturers that use machines to process a continuous flow of raw materials through various stages of completion into a finished state. An example is an oil refinery. *Objective 1*

Yield. A measure of materials usage efficiency. Yield measures the ratio of the materials output quantity to the materials input quantity. Yields less than 1.0 are the result of materials losses in the process. *Objective 6*

ILLUSTRATIVE PROBLEM

Southern Aggregate Company manufactures concrete by a series of four processes. All materials are introduced in Crushing. From Crushing, the materials pass through Sifting, Baking, and Mixing, emerging as finished concrete. All inventories are costed by the first-in, first-out method.

The balances in the accounts Work in Process—Mixing and Finished Goods were as follows on May 1:

Work in Process—Mixing (2,000 units, 1/4 completed)	$13,700
Finished Goods (1,800 units at $8.00 a unit)	14,400

The following costs were charged to Work in Process—Mixing during May:

Direct materials transferred from Baking:	
15,200 units at $6.50 a unit	$98,800
Direct labor	17,200
Factory overhead	11,780

During May, 16,000 units of concrete were completed, and 15,800 units were sold. Inventories on May 31 were as follows:

Work in Process—Mixing: 1,200 units, 1/2 completed
Finished Goods: 2,000 units

Instructions

1. Prepare a cost of production report for the Mixing Department.
2. Determine the cost of goods sold (indicate number of units and unit costs).
3. Determine the finished goods inventory, May 31.

Solution

1.

Southern Aggregate Company
Cost of Production Report—Mixing Department
For the Month Ended May 31, 19—

UNITS		Equivalent Units	
	Whole Units	Direct Materials	Conversion
Units charged to production:			
Inventory in process, May 1	2,000		
Received from Baking	15,200		
Total units accounted for by the Mixing Dept.	17,200		
Units to be assigned costs:			
Inventory in process, May 1 (25% completed)	2,000	0	1,500
Started and completed in May	14,000	14,000	14,000
Transferred to finished goods in May	16,000	14,000	15,500
Inventory in process, May 31 (50% complete)	1,200	1,200	600
Total units to be assigned cost	17,200	15,200	16,100

COSTS	Costs		
	Direct Materials	Conversion	Total Costs
Unit costs:			
Total cost for May in Mixing	$98,800	$28,980	
Total equivalent units (from above)	÷15,200	÷16,100	
Cost per equivalent unit	$ 6.50	$ 1.80	
Costs charged to production:			
Inventory in process, May 1			$ 13,700
Costs incurred in May			127,780
Total costs accounted for by the Mixing Dept.			$141,480

	Direct Materials	Conversion	Total Costs
Costs allocated to completed and partially completed units:			
Inventory in process, May 1—balance			$ 13,700
To complete inventory in process, May 1	$ 0	$ 2,700 (a)	2,700
Started and completed in May	91,000 (b)	25,200 (c)	116,200
Transferred to finished goods in May			$132,600
Inventory in process, May 31	$ 7,800 (d)	$ 1,080 (e)	8,880
Total costs assigned by the Mixing Department			$141,480

(a) 1,500 × $1.80 = $2,700 (c) 14,000 × $1.80 = $25,200 (e) 600 × $1.80 = $1,080
(b) 14,000 × $6.50 = $91,000 (d) 1,200 × $6.50 = $7,800

2. Cost of goods sold:

1,800 units at $8.00	$ 14,400	(from finished goods beginning inventory)
2,000 units at $8.20*	16,400	(from work in process beginning inventory)
12,000 units at $8.30**	99,600	(from May production)
15,800 units	$130,400	

* $16,400 ÷ 2,000
** $116,200 ÷ 14,000

3. Finished goods inventory, May 31:

2,000 units at $8.30 $ 16,600

SELF-EXAMINATION QUESTIONS (ANSWERS AT END OF CHAPTER)

1. For which of the following businesses would the process cost system be most appropriate?
   A. Custom furniture manufacturer
   B. Commercial building contractor
   C. Crude oil refinery
   D. Automobile repair shop

2. There were 2,000 pounds in process at the beginning of the period in the Packing Department. The Blending Department transferred 24,000 pounds to the Packing Department during the month, of which 3,000 pounds were in process at the end of the month. How many pounds were completed and transferred to finished goods from the Packing Department?
   A. 23,000 C. 26,000
   B. 24,000 D. 29,000

3. Information relating to production in Department A for May is as follows:

May 1	Balance, 1,000 units, 3/4 completed	$22,150
31	Direct materials, 5,000 units	75,000
31	Direct labor	32,500
31	Factory overhead	16,250

   If 500 units were one-fourth completed at May 31, 5,500 units were completed during May, and inventories are costed by the first-in, first-out method, what was the number of equivalent units of production with respect to conversion costs for May?
   A. 4,500 C. 5,500
   B. 4,875 D. 6,000

4. Based on the data presented in Question 3, what is the conversion cost per equivalent unit?
   A. $10 C. $25
   B. $15 D. $32

5. Information from the accounting system revealed the following:

	Day 1	*Day 2*	*Day 3*	*Day 4*	*Day 5*
Materials	$20,000	$18,000	$22,000	$20,000	$20,000
Electricity	2,500	3,000	3,500	4,000	4,700
Maintenance	4,000	3,800	3,400	3,000	2,800
Total costs	$26,500	$24,800	$28,900	$27,000	$27,500
Pounds produced	÷10,000	÷ 9,000	÷11,000	÷10,000	÷10,000
Cost per unit	$ 2.65	$ 2.75	$ 2.63	$ 2.70	$ 2.75

   Which of the following statements best interprets this information?
   A. The total costs are out of control.
   B. The product costs have steadily increased because of higher electricity costs.
   C. Electricity costs have steadily increased because of lack of maintenance.
   D. The unit costs reveal a significant operating problem.

DISCUSSION QUESTIONS

1. Which type of cost system, process or job order, would be best suited for each of the following: (a) oil refinery, (b) custom jewelry manufacturer, (c) paper manufacturer, (d) automobile repair shop, (e) building contractor, (f) lumber manufacturer? Give reasons for your answers.
2. Are perpetual inventory accounts for materials, work in process, and finished goods generally used for (a) job order and (b) process cost systems?
3. In job order cost accounting, the three elements of manufacturing cost are charged directly to job orders. Why is it not necessary to charge manufacturing costs in process cost accounting to job orders?
4. In a job order cost system, direct labor and factory overhead applied are debited to individual jobs. How are these items treated in a process cost system and why?
5. What two groups of manufacturing costs are referred to as conversion costs?
6. What are transferred-out materials?
7. What account for a production department receives the debit for "transferred-in materials?"
8. What are the four steps for determining the cost of goods completed and the ending work in process inventory?
9. What is meant by the term *equivalent units?*
10. Why is the cost per equivalent unit often determined separately for direct materials and conversion costs?
11. What is the purpose for determining the cost per equivalent unit?
12. Domingo Company is a process manufacturer with two production departments, Departments A and B. All direct materials are introduced to Department A from the materials storeroom. What is included in the cost transferred into Department B?
13. How is actual factory overhead accounted for in a process manufacturer?
14. What data are summarized in the two principal sections of the cost of production report?
15. What is the most important purpose of the cost of production report?
16. How are cost of production reports used for controlling and improving operations?
17. How is "yield" determined for a process manufacturer?
18. What is just-in-time processing?
19. How does just-in-time processing differ from the conventional manufacturing process?

EXERCISES

EXERCISE 20–1
Flowchart of accounts related to processing departments
Objective 2

Domino Co. manufactures metal sheet products. Direct materials are entered in the Shearing Department. The entire output of the Shearing Department is transferred to the Slitting Department. Part of the fully processed goods from the Slitting Department are sold as uncoated sheet, and the remainder of the goods are transferred to the Coating Department for further processing into coated sheet.

Prepare a chart of the flow of costs from materials and the processing department accounts into the finished goods accounts and then into the cost of goods sold account. The relevant accounts are as follows:

Cost of Goods Sold	Finished Goods—Uncoated Sheet
Materials	Finished Goods—Coated Sheet
Factory Overhead—Shearing Department	Work in Process—Shearing Department
Factory Overhead—Slitting Department	Work in Process—Slitting Department
Factory Overhead—Coating Department	Work in Process—Coating Department

EXERCISE 20–2
Entries for flow of factory costs for process cost system
Objectives 2, 5

Juniper Company manufactures a sugar product by a continuous process, involving three production departments. The records indicate that direct materials, direct labor, and applied factory overhead during the period for the first department, Refining, were $118,000, $85,000, and $27,600, respectively. Also, work in process in the department at the beginning of the period totaled $45,000, and work in process at the end of the period totaled $52,000.

Journalize the entries to record (a) the flow of costs into the Refining Department during the period for (1) direct materials, (2) direct labor, and (3) factory overhead, and (b) the transfer of production costs to the second department, Sifting.

EXERCISE 20–3
Factory overhead rate, entry for applying factory overhead, and factory overhead account balance
Objectives 2, 5

The chief cost accountant for Monique Co. estimates total factory overhead cost for the Blending Department for the year at $27,000 and total direct labor costs at $90,000. During April, the actual direct labor cost totaled $7,600, and factory overhead cost incurred totaled $2,300.

a. What is the predetermined factory overhead rate based on direct labor cost?
b. Journalize the entry to apply factory overhead to production for April.
c. What is the April 30 balance of the account Factory Overhead—Blending Department?
d. Does the balance in (c) represent overapplied or underapplied factory overhead?

EXERCISE 20–4
Equivalent units of production
Objective 3

Department 3 of Hazelmount Co. had 500 units in work in process at the beginning of the period, which were 40% complete. During the period, 6,000 units were completed and transferred to Department 4. There were 1,000 units in process at the end of the period, which were 60% complete. Direct materials are placed into the process at the beginning of production. Determine the number of equivalent units of production with respect to direct materials and conversion costs.

EXERCISE 20–5
Equivalent units of production
Objective 3

Units of production data for two departments for August of the current fiscal year are as follows:

	Stamping Department	*Polishing Department*
Work in process, August 1	5,000 units, 40% completed	2,000 units, 25% completed
Completed and transferred to next processing department during August	30,000 units	28,000 units
Work in process, August 31	3,000 units, 80% completed	4,000 units, 60% completed

If all direct materials are placed in process at the beginning of production, determine the direct materials and conversion equivalent units of production for August for (a) the Stamping Department and (b) the Polishing Department.

EXERCISE 20–6
Equivalent units of production
Objectives 2, 3

The following information concerns production in the Painting Department for March. All direct materials are placed into production at the beginning of production.

ACCOUNT WORK IN PROCESS—PAINTING DEPARTMENT ACCOUNT NO.

Date		Item	Debit	Credit	Balance Debit	Balance Credit
Mar.	1	Bal., 6,000 units, 3/4 completed			9,500	
	31	Direct materials, 15,000 units	7,500		17,000	
	31	Direct labor	14,450		31,450	
	31	Factory overhead	7,225		38,675	
	31	Goods finished, 13,500 units		28,550	10,125	
	31	Bal. —— units, 3/5 completed			10,125	

a. Determine the number of units in work in process inventory at the end of the month.
b. Determine the equivalent units of production for direct materials and conversion costs in March.

EXERCISE 20–7
Costs per equivalent unit
Objective 3

Epoch Manufacturing Company completed and transferred 1,000 units of production from the Pressing Department. There was no beginning inventory in process in the department. The ending in-process inventory was 200 units, which were 75% complete as to conversion cost. All materials are added at the beginning of the process. Direct materials cost incurred was $39,600, direct labor cost incurred was $14,000, and factory overhead applied was $9,000. Determine the following for the Pressing Department:

a. Total conversion cost
b. Conversion cost per equivalent unit
c. Direct materials cost per equivalent unit

EXERCISE 20–8
Equivalent units of production and related costs
Objective 3

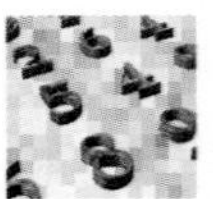

The charges to Work in Process—Finishing Department for a period, together with information concerning production, are as follows. All direct materials are placed in process at the beginning of production.

Work in Process—Finishing Department

4,000 units, 70% completed	105,000	To Finished Goods, 12,400 units	301,800
Direct materials, 8,400 at $12	100,800		
Direct labor	78,000		
Factory overhead	18,000		

Determine the following:

a. Equivalent units of production for direct materials and conversion.
b. Costs per equivalent unit for direct materials and conversion.

EXERCISE 20–9
Errors in equivalent unit computation
Objective 3

The Tri-State Oil Refining Company processes gasoline. At May 1 of the current year, 4,000 units were 1/5 completed in the Blending Department. During May, 10,500 units entered the Blending Department from the Refining Department. During May, the units in process at the beginning of the month were completed. Of the 10,500 units entering the department, all were completed except 3,300 units that were 1/3 completed. The equivalent units of production for conversion costs in the Blending Department were computed as follows:

Equivalent units of production in May:	
To process units in inventory on May 1:	
$4{,}000 \times 1/5$	800
To process units started and completed in May:	
$10{,}500 - 4{,}000$	6,500
To process units in inventory on May 31:	
$3{,}300 \times 1/3$	1,100
Equivalent units of production	8,400

List the errors in the computation of equivalent units of production for the Blending Department for May.

EXERCISE 20–10
Cost per equivalent unit
Objectives 2, 3

The following information concerns production in the Forging Department for April. All direct materials are placed into the process at the beginning of production, and conversion costs are incurred evenly throughout the process. The beginning inventory consists of $42,000 of direct materials and $20,000 of conversion costs.

ACCOUNT WORK IN PROCESS—FORGING DEPARTMENT ACCOUNT NO.

Date		Item	Debit	Credit	Balance Debit	Balance Credit
April	1	Bal., 1,200 units, 80% completed			62,000	
	30	Direct materials, 4,800 units	150,000		212,000	
	30	Direct labor	39,960		251,960	
	30	Factory overhead	39,960		291,920	
	30	Goods transferred, 5,000 units		253,470		
	30	Bal., 1,000 units, 40% completed			38,450	

Determine the cost per equivalent unit of direct materials and conversion.

EXERCISE 20–11
Cost of production report
Objective 4

The debits to Work in Process—Melting Department for Walters Company for January, together with information concerning production, are as follows:

Work in process, January 1, 3,500 units, 60% completed	$245,000
Materials added during January, 14,000 units	280,000
Conversion costs during January	340,000
Work in process, January 31, 2,000 units, 10% completed	—
Goods finished during January, 15,500 units	—

All direct materials are placed in process at the beginning of the process. Prepare a cost of production report, presenting the following computations:

a. Direct materials and conversion equivalent units of production for the period.
b. Direct materials and conversion cost per equivalent unit for the period.
c. Cost of goods finished during the period.
d. Cost of work in process at the end of the period.

EXERCISE 20–12
Cost of production report
Objective 4

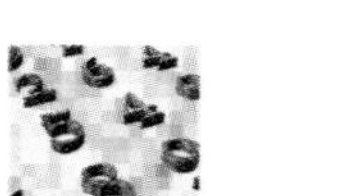

Prepare a cost of production report for the Forming Department of Gunther Company for May of the current fiscal year, using the following data:

Inventory, May 1, 6,000 units, 80% completed	$ 90,000
Materials from the Sanding Department, 22,000 units	264,000
Direct labor for May	200,000
Factory overhead for May	136,000
Goods finished during May (includes units in process, May 1), 26,000 units	—
Inventory, May 31, 2,000 units, 60% completed	—

EXERCISE 20–13
Decision making
Objective 6

Westman Kodiac Company produces film products for cameras. One of the processes for this operation is a coating (solvent spreading) operation, where chemicals are coated on to film stock. There has been some concern about the cost performance of this operation. As a result, you have begun an investigation. You first discover that all input prices have not changed for the last six months. If there is a problem, it is related to the quantity of input. You have discovered three possible problems from some of the operating personnel, whose quotes follow:

Operator 1: "I've been keeping an eye on my operating room instruments. I feel as though our energy consumption is becoming less efficient."
Operator 2: "Every time the coating machine goes down, we produce waste on shutdown and subsequent startup. It seems like during the last half year we have had more unscheduled machine shutdowns than in the past. Thus, I feel as though our yields must be dropping."
Operator 3: "My sense is that our coating costs are going up. It seems to me like we are spreading a thicker coating than we should. Perhaps the coating machine needs to be recalibrated."

In addition, you have determined that the Coating Department had no beginning or ending inventories for any month during the study period. The following data are also made available.

	January	*February*	*March*	*April*	*May*	*June*
Transferred-in materials	$10,000	$11,250	$ 9,500	$10,000	$11,250	$11,000
Coating cost	5,000	5,625	5,035	5,500	6,525	6,600
Conversion cost (incl. energy)	4,000	4,500	3,800	4,000	4,500	4,400
Pounds input to the process	40,000	45,000	38,000	40,000	45,000	44,000
Pounds transferred out	36,000	40,500	34,200	36,000	40,500	39,600

Use the preceding information to analyze each operator's explanation.

EXERCISE 20–14
Just-in-time processing
Objective 7

The following are some quotes provided by a number of managers at Western Sprocket Company regarding the company's planned move toward a just-in-time processing system:

Director of Purchasing: *I'm very concerned about moving to a just-in-time system for materials. What would happen if one of our suppliers were unable to make a shipment due to a strike or a plant fire? Without some safety stock in our materials, our whole plant would shut down.*

Director of Manufacturing: *If we go to just-in-time, I think our factory output will drop. We need in-process inventory in order to "smooth out" the inevitable problems that occur during manufacturing. For example, we have machines dedicated to various products. Assume a machine that is used to process product A breaks down. If I have in-process inventory that can be used to make product B on a different machine, then I won't lose production while the product A machine is being fixed. Thus, the in-process inventories give me a safety valve that I can use to keep things running when things go wrong.*

Director of Sales: *I'm afraid we'll miss some sales if we don't keep a large stock of items on hand just in case demand increases. It only makes sense to me to keep large inventories in order to assure product availability for our customers.*

How would you respond to these managers?

PROBLEMS SERIES A

PROBLEM 20–1A
Entries for process cost system
Objectives 2, 5

Kato Company manufactures carpets. Cotton is placed in process in the Spinning Department, where it is spun into yarn. The output of the Spinning Department is transferred to the Tufting Department, where carpet backing is added at the beginning of the process and the process is completed. On October 1, Kato Company had the following inventories:

Finished Goods	$82,000
Work in Process—Spinning Department	—
Work in Process—Tufting Department	23,600
Materials	14,500

Departmental accounts are maintained for factory overhead, and both have zero balances on October 1.

Manufacturing operations for October are summarized as follows:

a. Materials purchased on account	$ 48,800
b. Materials requisitioned for use:	
Cotton	$ 39,600
Carpet backing	11,200
Indirect materials—Spinning Department	3,450
Indirect materials—Tufting Department	600
c. Labor used:	
Direct labor—Spinning Department	$ 57,000
Direct labor—Tufting Department	46,700
Indirect labor—Spinning Department	5,600
Indirect labor—Tufting Department	2,400
d. Depreciation charged on plant assets:	
Spinning Department	$ 27,670
Tufting Department	22,700
e. Expired prepaid insurance:	
Spinning Department	$ 1,200
Tufting Department	900
f. Applied factory overhead:	
Spinning Department	$ 38,500
Tufting Department	26,200
g. Production costs transferred from Spinning Dept. to Tufting Dept.	$128,600
h. Production costs transferred from Tufting Dept. to finished goods	$215,000
i. Cost of goods sold during the period	$229,500

Instructions:

1. Journalize the entries to record the operations, identifying each entry by letter.
2. Compute the October 31 balances of the inventory accounts.
3. Compute the October 31 balances of the factory overhead accounts.

PROBLEM 20–2A
Entries for process cost system
Objectives 2, 5

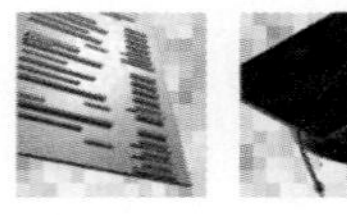

Denver Company manufactures cookies. Materials are placed in production in the Baking Department and after processing are transferred to the Packing Department, where more materials are added. The finished products emerge from the Packing Department.

There were no inventories of work in process at the beginning or at the end of March. Finished goods inventory at March 1 was 20,000 cases of cookies at a total cost of $300,000.

Transactions related to manufacturing operations for March are summarized as follows:

a. Materials purchased on account, $186,400.
b. Materials requisitioned for use: Baking Department, $128,500 ($122,300 entered directly into the product); Packing Department, $55,300 ($51,100 entered directly into the product).
c. Labor costs incurred: Baking Department, $97,700 ($85,200 entered directly into the product); Packing Department, $63,100 ($53,400 entered directly into the product).
d. Miscellaneous costs and expenses incurred on account: Baking Department, $32,400; Packing Department, $26,200.
e. Depreciation charged on plant assets: Baking Department, $52,400; Packing Department, $41,100.
f. Expiration of various prepaid expenses: Baking Department, $3,400; Packing Department, $3,000.
g. Factory overhead applied to production, based on machine hours: $105,000 for Baking and $85,000 for Packing.
h. Output of Baking Department: 31,375 cases.
i. Output of Packing Department: 31,375 cases of cookies.
j. Sales on account: 40,000 cases of cookies at $25. Credits to the finished goods account are to be made according to the first-in, first-out method.

Instructions

Journalize the entries to record the transactions, identifying each by letter. Include as an explanation for entry (j) the number of cases and the cost per case of cookies sold.

PROBLEM 20–3A
Cost of production report
Objectives 3, 4

Lawler Company roasts and packs coffee beans. The process begins by placing coffee beans into the Roasting Department. From the Roasting Department, coffee beans are then transferred to the Packing Department. The following is a partial work in process account of the Roasting Department at March 31:

ACCOUNT WORK IN PROCESS—ROASTING DEPARTMENT ACCOUNT NO.

Date		Item	Debit	Credit	Balance Debit	Balance Credit
Mar.	1	Bal., 20,000 units, 3/5 completed			46,000	
	31	Direct materials, 432,000 units	864,000		910,000	
	31	Direct labor	185,000		1,095,000	
	31	Factory overhead	74,680		1,169,680	
	31	Goods completed and transferred, 440,000 units		?		
	31	Bal., —— units, 2/5 completed			?	

Instructions

Prepare a cost of production report, and identify the missing amounts for the work in process—Roasting Department account.

PROBLEM 20–4A
Equivalent units and related costs; cost of production report; entries
Objectives 3, 4, 5

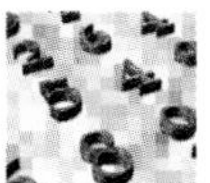

Picard Company manufactures newsprint by a series of four processes, all materials being introduced in the Chipping Department. From the Chipping Department, the materials pass through the Pulping, Papermaking, and Converting Departments, emerging as finished newsprint.

The balance in the account Work in Process—Converting Department was as follows on July 1:

Work in Process—Converting Department (1,400 units, 3/5 completed)	$10,100

The following costs were charged to Work in Process—Converting Department during July:

Direct materials transferred from Papermaking Department: 10,600 units at $5.50 a unit	$58,300
Direct labor	31,800
Factory overhead	20,000

During July, 10,400 units of newsprint were completed. Work in Process on July 31 was as follows:

Work in Process—Converting Department: 1,600 units, 1/2 completed

Instructions

1. Prepare a cost of production report for the Converting Department for July.
2. Journalize the entries for costs transferred from Papermaking to Converting and the cost of goods transferred from Converting to finished goods.
3. Discuss the uses of the cost of production report.

PROBLEM 20–5A
Work in process account data for two months and cost of production reports
Objectives 2, 3, 4, 5

Zidek Company uses a process cost system to record the costs of processing soup, which requires a series of three processes. The inventory of Work in Process—Filling (the last process) on July 1 and debits to the account during July were as follows:

Balance, 1,000 units, 3/4 completed	$13,100
From Cooking Department, 7,000 units	58,800
Direct labor	30,000
Factory overhead	18,280

During July, 1,000 units in process on July 1 were completed, and of the 7,000 units entering the department, all were completed except 600 units that were 1/4 completed. Charges to Work in Process—Filling for August were as follows:

From Cooking Department, 7,800 units	$69,420
Direct labor	36,000
Factory overhead	21,470

During August, the units in process at the beginning of the month were completed, and of the 7,800 units entering the department, all were completed except 200 units that were 4/5 completed.

Instructions

1. Enter the balance as of July 1 in a four-column account for Work in Process—Filling. Record the debits and the credits in the account for July. Construct a cost of production report, and present computations for determining (a) equivalent units of production for materials and conversion, (b) equivalent costs per unit, (c) cost of goods finished, differentiating between units started in the prior period and units started and finished in July, and (d) work in process inventory.
2. Provide the same information for August by recording the August transactions in the four-column work in process account. Construct a cost of production report, and present the August computations (a through d) listed in (1).

PROBLEMS SERIES B

PROBLEM 20–1B
Entries for process cost system
Objectives 2, 5

Tidy Soap Company manufactures powdered detergent. Phosphate is placed in process in the Making Department, where it is granularized. The output of Making is transferred to the Packing Department, where packaging is added at the beginning of the process. On July 1, Tidy Soap Company had the following inventories:

Finished Goods	$18,900
Work in Process—Making	1,400
Work in Process—Packing	12,400
Materials	23,500

Departmental accounts are maintained for factory overhead, which both have zero balances on July 1.

Manufacturing operations for July are summarized as follows:

a. Materials purchased on account	$ 79,400
b. Materials requisitioned for use:	
Phosphate	$ 56,700
Packaging	23,200
Indirect materials—Making	2,500
Indirect materials—Packing	1,400
c. Labor used:	
Direct labor—Making	$ 85,800
Direct labor—Packing	65,200
Indirect labor—Making	6,800
Indirect labor—Packing	4,500
d. Depreciation charged on plant assets:	
Making Department	$ 34,600
Packing Department	29,000
e. Expired prepaid insurance:	
Making Department	$ 2,500
Packing Department	1,400
f. Applied factory overhead:	
Making Department	$ 45,000
Packing Department	38,000
g. Production costs transferred from Making to Packing	$180,000
h. Production costs transferred from Packing to finished goods	$310,000
i. Cost of goods sold during the period	$318,500

Instructions

1. Journalize the entries to record the operations, identifying each entry by letter.
2. Compute the July 31 balances of the inventory accounts.
3. Compute the July 31 balances of the factory overhead accounts.

PROBLEM 20–2B
Entries for process cost system
Objectives 2, 5

Irvin Manufacturing Inc. manufactures aluminum cans. Materials are placed in production in the Blanking Department and after processing are transferred to the Forming Department, where more materials (coatings) are added. The finished product emerges from the Forming Department.

There were no inventories of work in process at the beginning or at the end of July. Finished goods inventory at July 1 was 5,000 cases of aluminum cans at a total cost of $110,000.

Transactions related to manufacturing operations for July are summarized as follows:

a. Materials purchased on account, $126,000.
b. Materials requisitioned for use: Blanking, $50,600 ($45,400 entered directly into the product); Forming, $66,000 ($62,200 entered directly into the product).
c. Labor costs incurred: Blanking, $69,000 ($63,600 entered directly into the product); Forming, $108,500 ($97,300 entered directly into the product).
d. Miscellaneous costs and expenses incurred on account: Blanking, $12,600; Forming, $18,600.
e. Expiration of various prepaid expenses: Blanking, $2,400; Forming, $3,000.
f. Depreciation charged on plant assets: Blanking, $21,100; Forming, $27,500.
g. Factory overhead applied to production, based on machine hours: $46,000 for Blanking and $65,000 for Forming.
h. Output of Blanking: 15,000 cases.
i. Output of Forming: 15,000 cases of aluminum cans.
j. Sales on account: 18,000 cases of aluminum cans at $40. Credits to the finished goods account are to be made according to the first-in, first-out method.

Instructions

Journalize the entries to record the transactions, identifying each by letter. Include as an explanation for entry (j) the number of cases and the cost per case of cans sold.

PROBLEM 20–3B
Cost of production report
Objectives 3, 4

Venus Chocolate Company processes chocolate into candy bars. The process begins by placing direct materials (raw chocolate, milk, and sugar) into the Blending Department. All materials are placed into production at the beginning of the blending process. After blending, the milk chocolate is then transferred to the Molding Department, where the milk chocolate is formed into candy bars. The following is a partial work in process account of the Blending Department at December 31:

ACCOUNT WORK IN PROCESS—BLENDING DEPARTMENT ACCOUNT NO.

Date		Item	Debit	Credit	Balance	
					Debit	Credit
Dec.	1	Bal., 32,000 units, 4/5 completed			9,350	
	31	Direct materials, 851,000 units	170,200		179,550	
	31	Direct labor	60,000		239,550	
	31	Factory overhead	42,258		281,808	
	31	Goods completed and transferred, 862,000 units	?			
	31	Bal., —— units, 3/4 completed			?	

Instructions

Prepare a cost of production report and identify the missing amounts for the work in process—Blending Department account.

PROBLEM 20–4B
Equivalent units and related costs; cost of production report; entries
Objectives 3, 4, 5

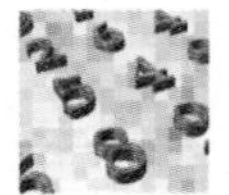

Moore Company manufactures specialty chemicals by a series of three processes, all materials being introduced in the Blending Department. From the Blending Department, the materials pass through the Reaction and Filling Departments, emerging as finished chemicals.

The balance in the account Work in Process—Filling was as follows on March 1:

Work in Process—Filling Department (6,000 units, 1/5 completed)	$155,000

The following costs were charged to Work in Process—Filling Department during March:

Direct materials transferred from Reaction Department:	
39,000 units at $22.50 a unit	$877,500
Direct labor	660,000
Factory overhead	209,400

During March, 41,000 units of specialty chemicals were completed. Work in Process on March 31 was as follows:

Work in Process—Filling Department: 4,000 units, 2/5 completed

Instructions

1. Prepare a cost of production report for the Filling Department for March.
2. Journalize the entries for costs transferred from Reaction to Filling, and the costs transferred from Filling to finished goods.
3. Discuss the uses of the cost of production report.

PROBLEM 20–5B
Work in process account data for two months and cost of production reports
Objectives 2, 3, 4, 5

Bailey Company uses a process cost system to record the costs of manufacturing aluminum, which requires a series of five processes. The inventory of Work in Process—Rolling (the last process) on September 1 and debits to the account during September were as follows:

Balance, 1,200 units, 3/4 completed	$31,500
From Smelting, 4,900 units	44,100
Direct labor	70,000
Factory overhead	37,100

During September, 1,200 units in process on September 1 were completed, and of the 4,900 units entering the department, all were completed except 400 units that were 3/4 completed.

Charges to Work in Process—Rolling for October were as follows:

From Smelting, 5,000 units	$47,500
Direct labor	65,000
Factory overhead	36,640

During October, the units in process at the beginning of the month were completed, and of the 5,000 units entering the department, all were completed except 800 units that were 2/5 completed.

Instructions

1. Enter the balance as of September 1 in a four-column account for Work in Process—Rolling. Record the debits and the credits in the account for September. Construct a cost of production report and present computations for determining (a) equivalent units of production for materials and conversion, (b) equivalent costs per unit, (c) cost of goods finished, differentiating between units started in the prior period and units started and finished in September, and (d) work in process inventory.
2. Provide the same information for October by recording the October transactions in the four-column work in process account. Construct a cost of production report, and present the October computations (a through d) listed in (1).

CASES

CASE 20–1
Crunchy Cookie Company
Effect of change in materials costs

You are the division controller for the Crunchy Cookie Company. Crunchy introduced a chocolate chip cookie called Chock Full of Chips. The new cookie was a success. As a result, the product manager responsible for the launch of this new cookie was promoted to division vice-president and became your boss. A new product manager, Davis, has been brought in to replace the promoted manager. Davis notices that the Chock Full of Chips cookie uses a lot of chips, which increases the cost of the cookie. As a result, Davis has ordered that the amount of chips used in the cookies be reduced by 5%. The manager's thinking is that this reduction in chips will not be noticed by the marketplace but will reduce costs and hence improve margins. The increased margins would help Davis meet profit targets for the period.

You are looking over some cost of production reports segmented by cookie line. You notice that there is a drop in the materials costs for Chock Full of Chips. On further investigation, you discover why the chip costs have declined (fewer chips). Both you and Davis report to the division vice-president, who was the original product manager for Chock Full of Chips. You are trying to decide what to do, if anything.

Discuss the options you might consider.

CASE 20–2
International Paper, Inc.
Accounting for materials costs

In paper-making operations for companies such as International Paper, Inc., wet pulp is fed into paper machines, which press and dry pulp into a continuous sheet of paper. The paper is formed at very high speeds (60 mph). Once the paper is formed, the paper is rolled onto a reel at the back end of the paper machine. One of the characteristics of paper making is the creation of "broke" paper. Broke is paper that fails to satisfy quality standards and is therefore rejected for final shipment to customers. Broke is recycled back to the beginning of the process by combining the recycled paper with virgin (new) pulp material. The combination of virgin pulp and recycled broke is sent to the paper machine for paper making. Broke is fed into this recycle process continuously from all over the facility.

In this industry it is typical to charge the paper-making operation with the cost of direct materials, which is a mixture of virgin materials and broke. Broke has a much lower cost than does virgin pulp. Therefore, the more broke in the mixture, the lower the average cost of direct materials to the department. Paper-making managers will frequently comment on the importance of broke for keeping their direct materials costs down.

a. How do you react to this accounting procedure?
b. What does the accountant fail to consider in accounting for broke in this way?

CASE 20–3

Forever Fresh Can Company

Managerial analysis

The Forever Fresh Can Company manufactures cans for the canned food industry. The operations manager of a can manufacturing operation wants to conduct a cost study investigating the relationship of tin content in the material (can stock) to the energy cost for enameling the cans. The enameling was necessary to prepare the cans for labeling. Differences in materials unit costs were entirely related to the amount of tin content. The percentage of tin content in the can stock increases the cost of material. The operations manager believed there was a relationship between the tin content and energy costs for enameling. During the analysis period the amount of tin content in the steel can stock increased for every week, from week 1 to week 6. The summary production reports available from the controller are shown in a table below.

Interpret this information and report to the operations manager your recommendations with respect to tin content.

	Week 1	*Week 2*	*Week 3*	*Week 4*	*Week 5*	*Week 6*
Energy	$ 1,300	$ 2,880	$ 2,420	$ 1,400	$ 1,620	$ 1,500
Materials	1,200	3,000	2,860	1,890	2,520	2,900
Total cost	$ 2,500	$ 5,880	$ 5,280	$ 3,290	$ 4,140	$ 4,400
Units produced	÷10,000	÷24,000	÷22,000	÷14,000	÷18,000	÷20,000
Cost per unit	$ 0.250	$ 0.245	$ 0.240	$ 0.235	$ 0.230	$ 0.220

CASE 20–4

Diaz Co.

Cost of production report and decision making

Diaz Co. manufactures castings by a series of four processes. All materials are placed in production in the Molding Department and, after processing, are transferred to the Dipping, Casting, and Machining Departments, emerging as a finished casting.

On June 1, the balance in the account Work in Process—Machining was $35,600, determined as shown:

Direct materials: 8,000 units	$ 32,000
Direct labor: 8,000 units, 1/4 completed	2,200
Factory overhead: 8,000 units, 1/4 completed	1,400
Total	$ 35,600

The following costs were charged to Work in Process—Machining during June:

Direct materials transferred from Casting Dept., 88,600 units	$380,980
Direct labor	104,080
Factory overhead	79,600

During June, 92,000 castings were completed and transferred to Finished Goods. On June 30, the inventory in the Machining Department consisted of 4,600 units, two-fifths completed. All inventories are costed by the first-in, first-out method.

As a new cost accountant for Diaz Co., you have just received a phone call from Norma Jenkins, the superintendent of the Machining Department. She was extremely upset with the cost of production report. In addition, she commented:

"I give up! These reports are a waste of time. My department has always been the best department in the plant, so why should I bother with these reports? Just what purpose do they serve?"

1. Based on the data for June, prepare a cost of production report for the Machining Department.
2. Assuming that all costs reported in the work in process account on June 1 were incurred in the preceding month, determine the unit direct materials cost and the unit conversion cost for May.
3. Based on (2), determine the change in the unit direct materials cost and unit conversion cost for June as compared to May.
4. Based on (3), what are some possible explanations for the changing unit costs?
5. Describe how you would explain to Jenkins that cost of production reports are useful.

CASE 20–5
Winner Paper Company
Decision making

Alex Greenbar, plant manager of Winner Paper Company's paper-making mill, was looking over the cost of production reports for October and November for the Paper-making Department. The reports revealed the following:

	October	*November*
Pulp and chemicals	$300,000	$307,000
Conversion cost	150,000	153,000
Total cost	$450,000	$460,000
Number of tons	÷ 625	÷ 575
Cost per ton	$ 720	$ 800

Alex was concerned about the growth in the cost per ton from the output of the department. As a result, he asked the plant controller to perform a study to help explain these results. The controller, Alicia Bond, began the analysis by performing some interviews of key plant personnel in order to understand what the problem might be. Excerpts from an interview with Niles Gilbert, a paper machine operator, follow:

Niles: We have two paper-making machines in the department. I have no data, but I think paper machine 1 is applying too much pulp, and thus is wasting both conversion and materials resources. We haven't had repairs on paper machine 1 in a while. Maybe this is the problem.

Alicia: How does too much pulp result in wasted resources?

Niles: Well, you see, if too much pulp is applied, then we will waste pulp material. The customer will not pay for the extra weight. Thus, we just lose that amount of material. Also, when there is too much pulp, the machine must be slowed down in order to complete the drying process. This results in a waste of conversion costs.

Alicia: Do you have any other suspicions?

Niles: Well, as you know, we have two products—red paper and blue paper. They are identical except for the color. The color is added to the paper-making process in the paper machine. I think that during November these two color papers have been behaving very differently. I don't have any data, but it just seems as though the amount of waste associated with the red paper has increased.

Alicia: Why is this?

Niles: I understand that there has been a change in specifications for the red paper near the beginning of November. This change could be causing the machines to run poorly when making red paper. If this is the case, the cost per ton would increase for red paper.

Alicia also asked for a computer printout providing greater detail on November's operating results.

Computer run: 42
December 4
Requested by: Alicia Bond
Paper-making Department—November detail

Paper Machine	*Color*	*Materials Costs*	*Conversion Costs*	*Tons*
1	Red	35,800	17,400	60
1	Blue	41,700	21,200	70
1	Red	44,600	22,500	75
1	Blue	36,100	18,100	60
2	Red	38,300	18,800	80
2	Blue	41,300	19,900	85
2	Red	35,600	18,100	75
2	Blue	33,600	17,000	70
Total		307,000	153,000	575

Assuming that you're Alicia Bond, write a memo to Alex Greenbar with a recommendation to management. You should analyze the November data to determine whether the paper machine or the paper color explains the increase in the unit cost from October. Include any supporting schedules that are appropriate.

ANSWERS TO SELF-EXAMINATION QUESTIONS

1. **C** The process cost system is most appropriate for a business where manufacturing is conducted by continuous operations and involves a series of uniform production processes, such as the processing of crude oil (answer C). The job order cost system is most appropriate for a business where the product is made to customer's specifications, such as custom furniture manufacturing (answer A), commercial building construction (answer B), or automobile repair shop (answer D).
2. **A** The total pounds transferred to finished goods are the 2,000 in-process pounds at the beginning of the period plus the number of pounds started and completed during the month, 21,000 (24,000 – 3,000). Answer B incorrectly assumes that the beginning inventory is not transferred during the month. Answer C assumes that all 24,000 pounds started during the month are transferred to finished goods, instead of only the portion started and *completed*. Answer D incorrectly adds all the numbers together.
3. **B** The number of units that could have been produced from start to finish during a period is termed equivalent units. The 4,875 equivalent units (answer B) is determined as follows:

To process units in inventory on May 1: 1,000 × 1/4	250
To process units started and completed in May: 5,500 units – 1,000 units	4,500
To process units in inventory on May 31: 500 units × 1/4	125
Equivalent units of production in May	4,875

4. **A** The conversion costs (direct labor and factory overhead) totaling $48,750 are divided by the number of equivalent units (4,875) to determine the unit conversion cost of $10 (answer A).

5. **C** The electricity costs have increased, and maintenance costs have decreased. Answer C would be a reasonable explanation for these results. The total costs, materials costs, and costs per unit do not reveal any type of pattern over the time period. In fact, the materials costs have stayed at exactly $2.00 per pound over the time period. This demonstrates that aggregated numbers can sometimes hide underlying information that can be used to improve the process.

PART EIGHT

Planning and Control

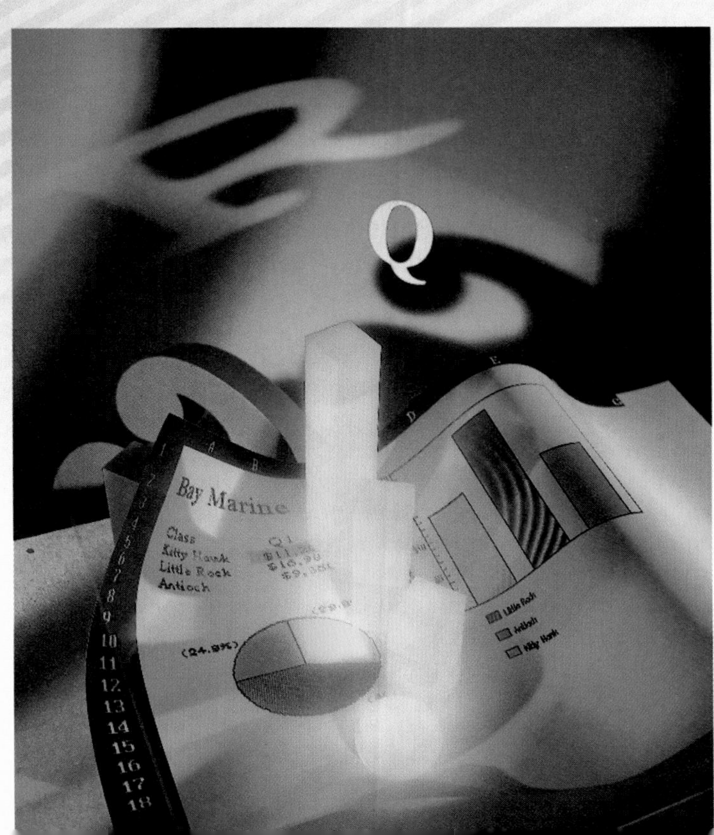

21 Cost Behavior and Cost-Volume-Profit Analysis

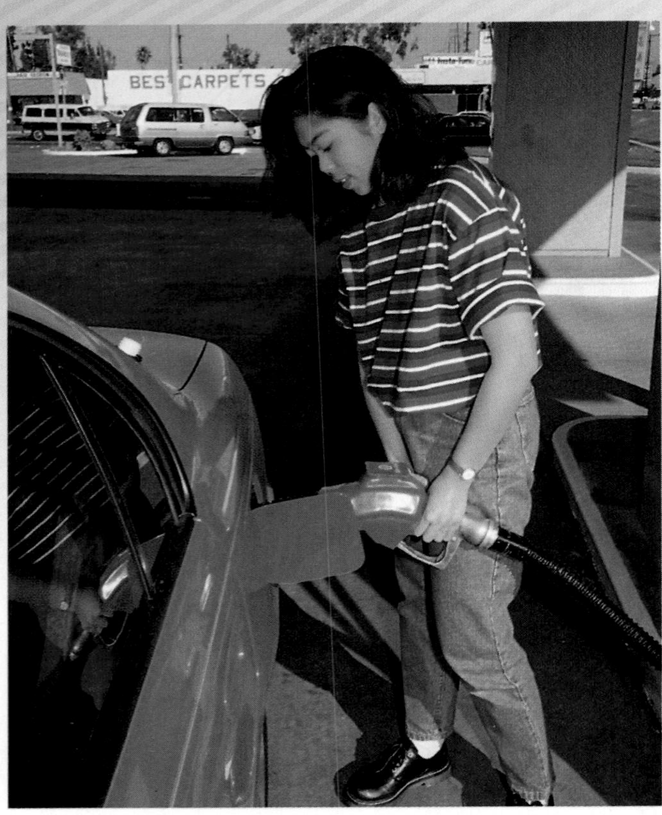

YOU AND ACCOUNTING

What are the costs of operating your car? You will normally pay a license plate (tag) fee once a year. This cost does not change, regardless of the number of miles you drive. On the other hand, the total amount you spend on gasoline during the year changes on a day-to-day basis as you drive. The more you drive, the more you spend on gasoline.

How does such operating cost information affect you? Information on how your car's operating costs behave could be relevant in planning a summer vacation. For example, you might be trying to decide between taking an airline flight or driving your car to your vacation destination. In this case, your license plate fee and annual car insurance costs will not change, regardless of whether you drive your car or fly. Thus, these costs would not affect your decision. However, the estimated cost of gasoline and routine maintenance would affect your decision.

As in operating your car, all of the costs of operating a business do not behave in the same way. In this chapter, we discuss commonly used methods for classifying costs according to how they change. We also discuss how management uses cost-volume-profit analysis as a tool in making decisions.

After studying this chapter, you should be able to:

Objective 1
Classify costs by their behavior as:

Variable costs
Fixed costs
Mixed costs

Objective 2
Compute the contribution margin, the contribution margin ratio, and the unit contribution margin, and explain how they may be useful to managers.

Objective 3
Using the unit contribution margin, determine the break-even point and the volume necessary to achieve a target profit.

Objective 4
Using a cost-volume-profit chart and a profit-volume chart, determine the break-even point and the volume necessary to achieve a target profit.

Objective 5
Calculate the break-even point for a business selling more than one product.

Objective 6
Compute the margin of safety and the operating leverage, and explain how managers use these concepts.

Objective 7
List the assumptions underlying cost-volume-profit analysis.

Cost Behavior

Objective 1
Classify costs by their behavior as:

Variable costs
Fixed costs
Mixed costs

Cost behavior refers to the manner in which a cost changes as a related activity changes.[1] Knowledge of how costs behave is useful to management for a variety of purposes. For example, knowledge as to how costs behave allows managers to predict profits as sales and production volumes change. Knowledge of how costs behave is also useful for estimating costs. Estimated costs, in turn, affect a variety of management decisions, such as whether to use excess machine capacity to produce and sell a product at a reduced price.

To understand the behavior of a cost, two factors that are related to the cost must be considered. First, we must identify the activities that are thought to cause the cost to be incurred. Such activities are called activity bases (or activity drivers). Second, we must specify the range of activity over which the changes in the cost are of interest to management. This range of activity is often called the relevant range.

To illustrate, hospital administrators must plan and control hospital food costs. To fully understand why food costs change, the activity that causes cost to be incurred must be identified. In the case of food costs, the feeding of patients is a major cause of these costs. The number of patients *treated* by the hospital would not be a good activity base, since some patients are outpatients who do not stay in the hospital. The number of patients who *stay* in the hospital, however, is an appropriate activity base for studying food costs. Once the proper activity base is identified, food costs can then be analyzed over the range of the number of patients who normally stay in the hospital (the relevant range).

Three of the most common ways in which costs are classified by behavior for management decision making are variable costs, fixed costs, and mixed costs. We discuss each of these cost classifications below.

VARIABLE COSTS

Variable costs are costs that vary in total in proportion to changes in the level of activity. When the level of activity is measured in units produced, direct materials and direct labor costs are generally classified as variable costs. For example, assume

[1] In this chapter, the term *costs* is often used as a convenience to represent both *costs* and *expenses*.

that Jason Inc. produces stereo sound systems under the brand name of J-Sound. The parts for the stereo systems are purchased from outside suppliers for $10 per unit and are assembled in Jason Inc.'s Waterloo plant. The direct materials costs for Model JS-12 for the relevant range of 5,000 to 30,000 units of production are shown below.

Number of Units of Model JS-12 Produced	*Direct Materials Cost per Unit*	*Total Direct Materials Cost*
5,000 units	$10	$ 50,000
10,000	10	100,000
15,000	10	150,000
20,000	10	200,000
25,000	10	250,000
30,000	10	300,000

Variable costs are constant per unit, while the total variable cost changes in proportion to changes in the activity base. For Model JS-12, for example, the direct materials cost for 10,000 units ($100,000) is twice the direct materials cost for 5,000 units ($50,000). The total direct materials cost varies in proportion to the number of units produced because the direct materials cost per unit ($10) is the same for all levels of production. Thus, producing 20,000 additional units of JS-12 will increase the direct materials cost by $200,000 (20,000 × $10), producing 25,000 additional units will increase the materials cost by $250,000, and so on.

Exhibit 1 illustrates how the variable costs for direct materials for Model JS-12 behave in total and on a per-unit basis as production changes.

Exhibit 1
Variable Cost Graphs

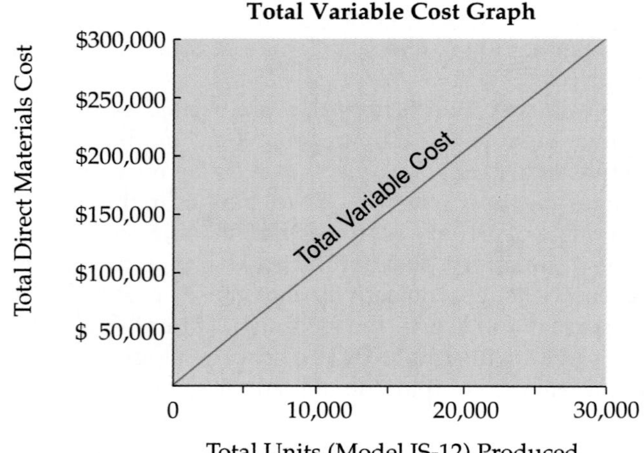

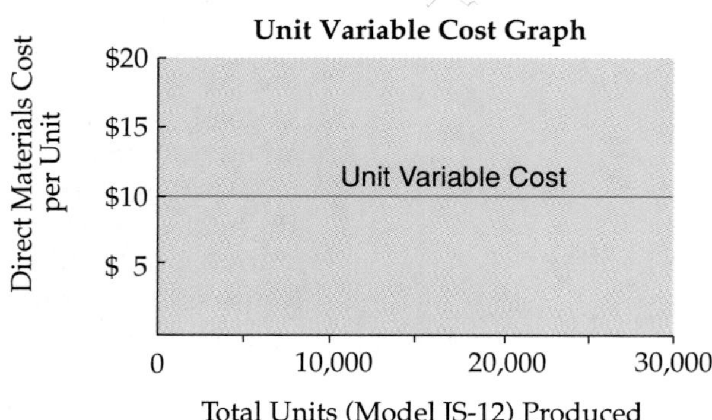

There are a wide variety of activity bases used by managers for evaluating cost behavior. The list below provides some examples of these bases, along with their related cost categories for a variety of businesses.

Type of Business	*Cost Category*	*Activity Base*
University	Faculty salaries	Number of classes
Passenger airline	Fuel	Number of miles flown
Manufacturing	Direct materials	Number of units produced
Hospital	Nurse wages	Number of patients
Hotel	Maid wages	Number of guests
Bank	Teller wages	Number of banking transactions
Insurance	Claim processing salaries	Number of claims

Managers can use activity bases to estimate the impact of activity volume changes on costs. Such information is useful for planning and controlling operations.

FIXED COSTS

Fixed costs are costs that remain the same in total dollar amount as the level of activity changes. When units produced is the measure of activity, examples of fixed manufacturing costs include straight-line depreciation of factory equipment, insurance on factory plant and equipment, and salaries of factory supervisors.

To illustrate, assume that Minton Inc. manufactures, bottles, and distributes La Fleur Perfume at its Los Angeles plant. The production supervisor at the Los Angeles plant is Jane Sovissi, who is paid a salary of $75,000 per year. The relevant range of activity for a year is 50,000 to 300,000 bottles of perfume. Sovissi's salary is a fixed cost that does not vary with the number of units produced. Regardless of the number of bottles produced within the range of 50,000 to 300,000 bottles, Sovissi will still receive a salary of $75,000.

Although the total fixed cost remains the same as the number of bottles produced changes, the fixed cost per bottle changes. As more bottles are produced, the total fixed costs are spread over a larger number of bottles, and thus the fixed cost per bottle decreases. This relationship is shown below for Jane Sovissi's $75,000 salary.

Number of Bottles of Perfume Produced	*Total Salary for Jane Sovissi*	*Salary per Bottle of Perfume Produced*
50,000 bottles	$75,000	$1.500
100,000	75,000	.750
150,000	75,000	.500
200,000	75,000	.375
250,000	75,000	.300
300,000	75,000	.250

Exhibit 2 illustrates how the fixed cost of Jane Sovissi's salary behaves graphically in total and on a per-unit basis as production changes.

Exhibit 2
Fixed Cost Graphs

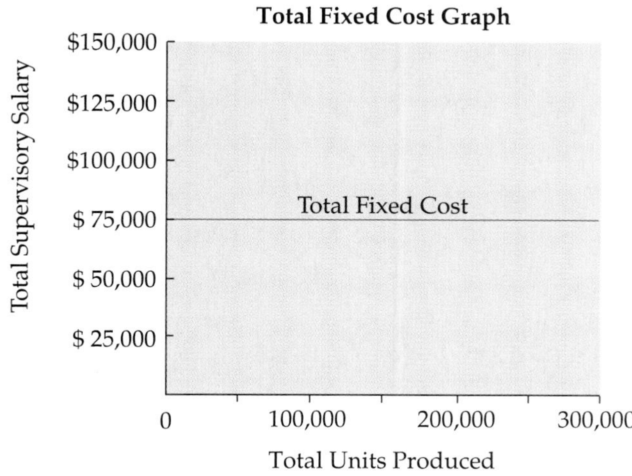

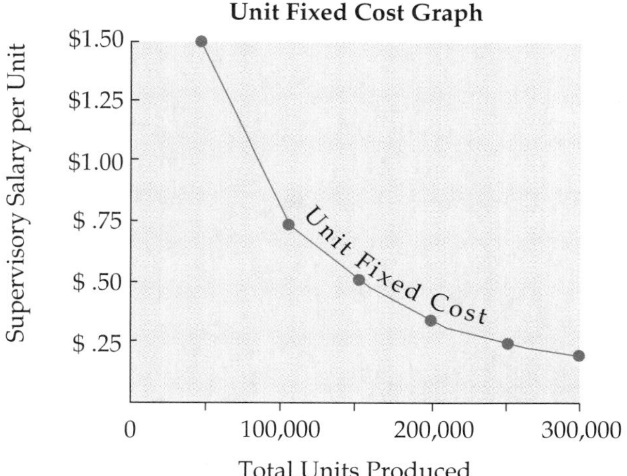

MIXED COSTS

A **mixed cost** has characteristics of both a variable and a fixed cost. For example, over one range of activity, the total mixed cost may remain the same. It thus behaves as a fixed cost. Over another range of activity, the mixed cost may change in

USING ACCOUNTING TO UNDERSTAND BUSINESS

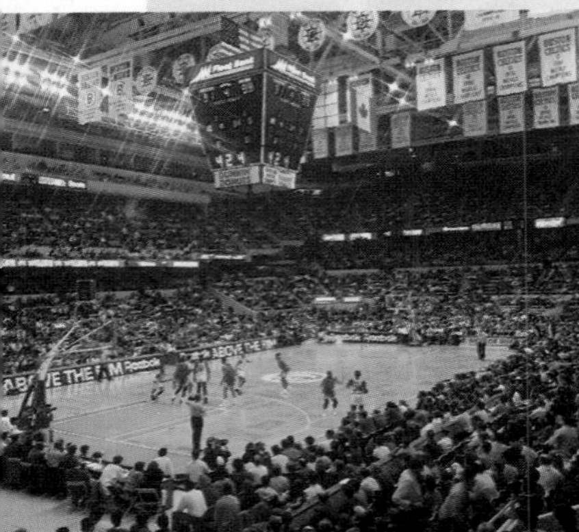

The Boston Celtics Partnership owns the Boston Celtics professional basketball team. A large portion of the Boston Celtics Partnership costs are fixed to the activity base (fan attendance). For example, the Boston Celtics would incur all the costs to play a season, such as players' and coaches' salaries, lease payments on the Boston Garden, and transportation costs for away games, regardless of the number of fans that paid to see the games. Only a small portion of costs, such as concession costs, are variable to fan attendance. Thus, the Boston Celtics management must focus its energies on generating revenues instead of reducing costs, given that many of the costs are fixed.

proportion to changes in the level of activity. It thus behaves as a variable cost. Mixed costs are sometimes called *semivariable* or *semifixed costs.*

To illustrate, assume that Simpson Inc. manufactures sails, using rented machinery. The rental charges are $15,000 per year, plus $1 for each machine hour used over 10,000 hours. If the machinery is used 8,000 hours, the total rental charge is $15,000. If the machinery is used 20,000 hours, the total rental charge is $25,000 [$15,000 + (10,000 hours × $1)], and so on. Thus, if the level of activity is measured in machine hours and the relevant range is 0 to 40,000 hours, the rental charges are a fixed cost up to 10,000 hours and a variable cost thereafter. This mixed cost behavior is shown graphically in Exhibit 3.

Exhibit 3
Mixed Costs

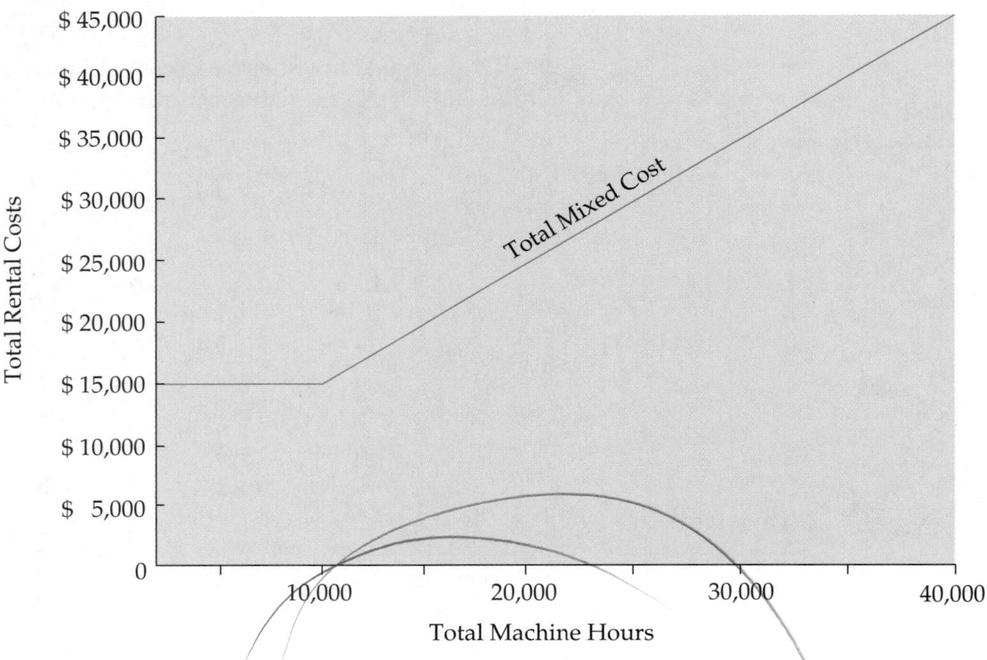

In practice, mixed costs are usually separated into their fixed and variable components for management analysis. The high-low method is a cost estimation technique that may be used for this purpose.[2] The high-low method uses the highest

[2] Other methods of estimating costs, such as the scattergraph method and the least squares method, are discussed in cost accounting textbooks.

and lowest activity levels and their related costs to estimate the variable cost per unit and the fixed cost component of mixed costs.

To illustrate, assume that the Equipment Maintenance Department of Kason Inc. incurred the following costs during the past 5 months:

	Production	*Total Cost*
June	1,000 units	$45,550
July	1,500	52,000
August	2,100	61,500
September	1,800	57,500
October	750	41,250

The number of units produced is the measure of activity, and the number of units produced between June and October represents the relevant range of production. For Kason Inc., the difference between the number of units produced and the difference between the total cost at the highest and lowest levels of production are as follows:

	Production	*Total Cost*
Highest level	2,100 units	$61,500
Lowest level	750	41,250
Difference	1,350 units	$20,250

Since the total fixed cost does not change with changes in volume of production, the $20,250 difference in the total cost represents the change in the total variable cost. Hence, dividing the difference in the total cost by the difference in production provides an estimate of the variable cost per unit. For Kason Inc., the variable cost per unit is $15, as shown below.

$$\text{Variable cost per unit} = \frac{\text{Difference in total cost}}{\text{Difference in production}}$$

$$\text{Variable cost per unit} = \frac{\$20{,}250}{1{,}350 \text{ units}} = \$15$$

The fixed cost will be the same at both the highest and the lowest levels of production. Thus, the fixed cost can be estimated at either of these levels. This is done by subtracting the estimated total variable cost from the total cost, using the following total cost equation:

Total cost = (Variable cost per unit × Units of production) + Fixed cost

Highest level:
$61,500 = ($15 × 2,100 units) + Fixed cost
$61,500 = $31,500 + Fixed cost
$30,000 = Fixed Cost
Lowest level:
$41,250 = ($15 × 750 units) + Fixed cost
$41,250 = $11,250 + Fixed cost
$30,000 = Fixed cost

The total equipment maintenance cost for Kason Inc. can thus be analyzed as a $30,000 fixed cost and a $15-per-unit variable cost. Using these amounts in the total cost equation above, the total equipment maintenance cost at other levels of production can be estimated.

SUMMARY OF COST BEHAVIOR CONCEPTS

As we indicated in the preceding paragraphs, costs can be classified as variable costs, fixed costs, or mixed costs. For purposes of analysis, mixed costs are generally separated into their variable and fixed cost components. The following table summarizes the cost behavior attributes of variable costs and fixed costs:

	Effect of Changing Activity Level	
Cost	*Total Amount*	*Per-Unit Amount*
Variable	Increases and decreases proportionately with activity level.	Remains the same regardless of activity level.
Fixed	Remains the same regardless of activity level.	Increases and decreases inversely with activity level.

Examples of common variable, fixed, and mixed costs for a manufacturing business when the number of units produced is the activity base is provided in the following table:

Variable Cost	*Fixed Cost*	*Mixed Cost*
Direct materials	Depreciation expense	Quality Control Department salaries
Direct labor	Property taxes	Purchasing Department salaries
Utility expense	Officer salaries	Maintenance expenses
Sales commissions	Insurance expense	Warehouse expenses

The mixed costs in this table result from the requirement that there be a minimum effort in these areas within an operating plant, which is the fixed portion. In addition, there is a variable portion related to the amount of production in the plant.

REPORTING VARIABLE AND FIXED COSTS

Separating costs into their variable and fixed components for reporting purposes can be useful for management decision making. One method of reporting variable and fixed costs is called variable costing or **direct costing.** Under variable costing, only the variable manufacturing costs (direct materials, direct labor, and variable factory overhead) are included in the product cost. The fixed factory overhead is an expense of the period in which it is incurred.[3]

Cost-Volume-Profit Relationships

Objective 2
Compute the contribution margin, the contribution margin ratio, and the unit contribution margin, and explain how they may be useful to managers.

After costs have been classified as fixed and variable, their effect on revenues, volume, and profits can be studied by using cost-volume-profit analysis. Cost-volume-profit analysis is the systematic examination of the relationships among selling prices, sales and production volume, costs, expenses, and profits.

Cost-volume-profit analysis is a commonly used tool that provides management with information for decision making. For example, cost-volume-profit analysis may be used in setting selling prices, selecting the mix of products to sell, choosing among marketing strategies, and analyzing the effects of changes in costs on profits. In today's manufacturing and marketing environment, management must make such decisions quickly and accurately. As a result, the importance of cost-volume-profit analysis has increased in recent years.

[3] The variable costing concept is discussed more fully in the appendix at the end of this chapter.

CONTRIBUTION MARGIN CONCEPT

One relationship among cost, volume, and profit is the contribution margin. The **contribution margin** is the excess of sales revenues over variable costs. The contribution margin concept is especially useful in business planning because it gives insight into the profit potential of a firm. To illustrate, the income statement of Lambert Inc. in Exhibit 4 has been prepared in a contribution margin format.

Exhibit 4
Contribution Margin Income Statement

Sales	$1,000,000
Variable costs	600,000
Contribution margin	$ 400,000
Fixed costs	300,000
Operating income	$ 100,000

The contribution margin of $400,000 is available to cover the fixed costs of $300,000. Once the fixed costs are covered, any remaining amount adds directly to the operating income of the company. Think of the fixed costs as a bucket and the contribution margin as water filling the bucket. Once the bucket is filled, the overflow represents operating income. Up until the point of overflow, however, the contribution margin contributes to fixed costs (filling the bucket).

Contribution Margin Ratio

The contribution margin can also be expressed as a percentage. The **contribution margin ratio,** sometimes called the **profit-volume ratio,** indicates the percentage of each sales dollar available to cover the fixed costs and to provide operating income. For Lambert Inc., the contribution margin ratio is 40%, as computed below.

$$\text{Contribution margin ratio} = \frac{\text{Sales} - \text{Variable costs}}{\text{Sales}}$$

$$\text{Contribution margin ratio} = \frac{\$1{,}000{,}000 - \$600{,}000}{\$1{,}000{,}000} = 40\%$$

The contribution margin ratio measures the effect on operating income of an increase or a decrease in sales volume. For example, assume that the management of Lambert Inc. is studying the effect of adding $80,000 in sales orders. Multiplying the contribution margin ratio (40%) by the change in sales volume ($80,000) indicates that operating income will increase $32,000 if the additional orders are obtained. The validity of this analysis is illustrated by the following contribution margin income statement of Lambert Inc.:

Sales	$1,080,000
Variable costs ($1,080,000 × 60%)	648,000
Contribution margin ($1,080,000 × 40%)	$ 432,000
Fixed costs	300,000
Operating income	$ 132,000

Variable costs as a percentage of sales are equal to 100% minus the contribution margin ratio. Thus, in the above income statement, the variable costs are 60% (100% – 40%) of sales, or $648,000 ($1,080,000 × 60%). The total contribution margin, $432,000, can also be computed directly by multiplying the sales by the contribution margin ratio ($1,080,000 × 40%).

In using the contribution margin ratio in an analysis, factors other than sales volume are assumed to remain constant. If such factors as the amount of fixed costs, the percentage of variable costs to sales, and the unit sales price are not constant, the effect of any change must be considered.

The contribution margin ratio is also useful in setting business policy. For example, if the contribution margin ratio of a firm is large and production is at a level below 100% capacity, a comparatively large increase in operating income can be expected from an increase in sales volume. A firm in such a position might decide to devote more effort to additional sales promotion because of the large change in operating income that will result from changes in sales volume. In contrast, a firm with a small contribution margin ratio will probably want to give more attention to reducing costs before attempting to promote sales.

Unit Contribution Margin

Similar to the contribution margin ratio, the unit contribution margin is also useful for analyzing the profit potential of proposed projects. The **unit contribution margin** represents the dollars from each unit of sales available to cover fixed costs and provide operating profits. For example, if Lambert Inc.'s unit selling price is $20 and its unit variable cost is $12, the unit contribution margin is $8 ($20 – $12).

The contribution margin ratio is most useful when the increase or decrease in sales volume is measured in sales dollars. The unit contribution margin is most useful when the increase or decrease in sales volume is measured in sales units (quantities). To illustrate, assume that Lambert Inc. sold 50,000 units. Its operating income is $100,000, as shown in the following contribution margin income statement:

Sales (50,000 units × $20)	$1,000,000
Variable costs (50,000 × $12)	600,000
Contribution margin (50,000 units × $8)	$ 400,000
Fixed costs	300,000
Operating income	$ 100,000

If Lambert Inc.'s sales could be increased by 15,000 units, from 50,000 units to 65,000 units, its operating income would increase by $120,000 (15,000 units × $8), as shown below.

Sales (65,000 units × $20)	$1,300,000
Variable costs (65,000 × $12)	780,000
Contribution margin (65,000 units × $8)	$ 520,000
Fixed costs	300,000
Operating income	$ 220,000

Unit contribution margin analyses can provide useful information for managers. The preceding illustration indicates, for example, that Lambert could spend up to $120,000 for special advertising or other product promotions to increase sales by 15,000 units.

Mathematical Approach to Cost-Volume-Profit Analysis

Objective 3
Using the unit contribution margin, determine the break-even point and the volume necessary to achieve a target profit.

Accountants use various approaches for expressing the relationship of costs, sales (volume), and operating income (profit). The mathematical approach is one approach that is used frequently in practice.

The mathematical approach to cost-volume-profit analysis uses equations (1) to determine the units of sales necessary to achieve the break-even point in operations or (2) to determine the units of sales necessary to achieve a target or desired profit. In the paragraphs that follow, we will describe and illustrate these equations and their use by management in profit planning.

BREAK-EVEN POINT

The break-even point is the level of operations at which a business's revenues and expired costs are exactly equal. At this level of operations, a business will neither realize an operating income nor incur an operating loss. The break-even point is useful in guiding business planning, especially when either expanding or declining operations is expected.

To illustrate the computation of the break-even point, assume that the fixed costs for Barker Corporation are estimated to be $90,000. The unit selling price, unit variable cost, and unit contribution margin for Barker Corporation are as follows:

Unit selling price	$25
Unit variable cost	15
Unit contribution margin	$10

The break-even point is 9,000 units, which can be computed by using the following equation:

$$\text{Break-even sales (units)} = \frac{\text{Fixed costs}}{\text{Unit contribution margin}}$$

$$\text{Break-even sales (units)} = \frac{\$90{,}000}{\$10} = 9{,}000 \text{ units}$$

The following income statement verifies the preceding computation:

Sales (9,000 units × $25)	$225,000
Variable costs (9,000 units × $15)	135,000
Contribution margin	$ 90,000
Fixed costs	90,000
Operating income	$ 0

The break-even point is affected by changes in the fixed costs, unit variable costs, and the unit selling price. In the following paragraphs, we will briefly describe the effect of each of these factors on the break-even point.

Effect of Changes in Fixed Costs

Although fixed costs do not change in total with changes in the level of activity, they may change because of such factors as changes in property tax rates or salary increases given to factory supervisors. Increases in fixed costs will raise the break-even point. Likewise, decreases in fixed costs will lower the break-even point. For example, General Motors closed 21 plants and eliminated 74,000 jobs to lower its break-even from approximately 7 million to 5 million automobiles through the mid-1990s.

To illustrate, assume that Bishop Co. is evaluating a proposal to budget an additional $100,000 for advertising. Fixed costs before the additional advertising are estimated at $600,000, and the unit contribution margin is $20. The break-even point before the additional expense is 30,000 units, computed as follows:

$$\text{Break-even sales (units)} = \frac{\text{Fixed costs}}{\text{Unit contribution margin}}$$

$$\text{Break-even sales (units)} = \frac{\$600{,}000}{\$20} = 30{,}000 \text{ units}$$

If the additional amount is spent, the fixed costs will increase by \$100,000 and the break-even point will increase to 35,000 units, computed as follows:

$$\text{Break-even sales (units)} = \frac{\text{Fixed costs}}{\text{Unit contribution margin}}$$

$$\text{Break-even sales (units)} = \frac{\$700{,}000}{\$20} = 35{,}000 \text{ units}$$

The increased fixed cost of \$100,000 increases the break-even point by 5,000 units of sales. The break-even point changes because, for each unit sold, the unit contribution margin of \$20 is available to cover fixed costs. An increase in the fixed costs of \$100,000 will require an additional 5,000 units (\$100,000 ÷ \$20) of sales to break even. In other words, an increase in sales of 5,000 units is required in order to generate an additional \$100,000 of total contribution margin (5,000 units × \$20) to cover the increased fixed costs.

Effect of Changes in Unit Variable Costs

Although unit variable costs are not affected by changes in volume of activity, they may be affected by such factors as changes in the price of direct materials and increases in wages for factory workers providing direct labor. Increases in unit variable costs will raise the break-even point. Likewise, decreases in unit variable costs will lower the break-even point. For example, when fuel prices rise or decline, there is a direct impact on the break-even passenger load for American Airlines.

To illustrate, assume that Park Co. is evaluating a proposal to pay an additional 2% commission to its sales representatives as an incentive to increase sales. Fixed costs are estimated at \$840,000, and the unit selling price, unit variable cost, and unit contribution margin before the additional 2% commission are as follows:

Unit selling price	\$250
Unit variable cost	145
Unit contribution margin	\$105

The break-even point is 8,000 units, computed as follows:

$$\text{Break-even sales (units)} = \frac{\text{Fixed costs}}{\text{Unit contribution margin}}$$

$$\text{Break-even sales (units)} = \frac{\$840{,}000}{\$105} = 8{,}000 \text{ units}$$

If the sales commission proposal is adopted, variable costs will increase by \$5 per unit (\$250 × 2%). This increase in the variable costs will decrease the unit contribution margin by \$5 (from \$105 to \$100). Thus, the break-even point is raised to 8,400 units, computed as follows:

$$\text{Break-even sales (units)} = \frac{\text{Fixed costs}}{\text{Unit contribution margin}}$$

$$\text{Break-even sales (units)} = \frac{\$840{,}000}{\$100} = 8{,}400 \text{ units}$$

The additional 2% sales commission increases the break-even point by 400 units. The break-even point changes because, at the original break-even point of 8,000 units, the new unit contribution margin of \$100 would provide only \$800,000 to cover fixed costs of \$840,000. Thus, an additional 400 units of sales will be required in order to provide the additional \$40,000 (400 units × \$100) contribution margin necessary to break even.

Effect of Changes in the Unit Selling Price

Increases in the unit selling price will lower the break-even point, while decreases in the unit selling price will raise the break-even point. Thus, for example, computer price reductions for Apple Computers increased its break-even point.

To illustrate, assume that Graham Co. is evaluating a proposal to increase the unit selling price of its product from $50 to $60. The following data have been gathered:

	Current	*Proposed*
Unit selling price	$ 50	$ 60
Unit variable cost	30	30
Unit contribution margin	$ 20	$ 30
Total fixed costs	$600,000	$600,000

The break-even point based on the current selling price is 30,000 units, computed as follows:

$$\text{Break-even sales (units)} = \frac{\text{Fixed costs}}{\text{Unit contribution margin}}$$

$$\text{Break-even sales (units)} = \frac{\$600,000}{\$20} = 30,000 \text{ units}$$

If the selling price is increased by $10 per unit, the break-even point is decreased to 20,000 units, computed as follows:

$$\text{Break-even sales (units)} = \frac{\text{Fixed costs}}{\text{Unit contribution margin}}$$

$$\text{Break-even sales (units)} = \frac{\$600,000}{\$30} = 20,000 \text{ units}$$

The increase of $10 per unit in the selling price increases the unit contribution margin by $10. Thus, the break-even point decreases by 10,000 units (from 30,000 units to 20,000 units).

Summary of Effects of Changes on Break-Even Point

The break-even point in sales (units) moves in the same direction as changes in the variable cost per unit and fixed costs. In contrast, the break-even point in sales (units) moves in the opposite direction to changes in the sales price per unit. A summary of the impact of these changes on the break-even point in sales (units) is shown below.

Type of Change	*Direction of Change*	*Effect of Change on Break-Even Sales (Units)*
Fixed cost	Increase	Increase
	Decrease	Decrease
Variable cost per unit	Increase	Increase
	Decrease	Decrease
Unit sales price	Increase	Decrease
	Decrease	Increase

TARGET PROFIT

At the break-even point, sales and costs are exactly equal. However, the break-even point is not the goal for the future operations of most businesses. Rather, managers seek to achieve profit by attaining the largest volume of possible sales above the

USING ACCOUNTING TO UNDERSTAND BUSINESS

The airline and hotel portions of the travel industry use break-even analysis extensively. In the hotel industry, individual hotels determine break-even occupancy over a span of time. Occupancy is the percentage of available room space that has been used by guests. Depending on room rates, a typical hotel will need to exceed 60% occupancy to remain profitable. Airlines also determine the break-even passenger load for particular routes. Thus, for example, an airline may determine how many seats must be sold in order for a flight from New York to Chicago to be profitable. In the highly competitive airline industry, break-even passenger loads are approaching 70%-80% on some routes.

break-even point. By modifying the break-even equation, the sales volume required to earn a target or desired amount of profit may be estimated. For this purpose, a factor for target profit is added to the standard break-even equation as shown below.

$$\text{Sales (units)} = \frac{\text{Fixed costs} + \text{Target profit}}{\text{Unit contribution margin}}$$

To illustrate, assume that fixed costs are estimated at $200,000, and the desired profit is $100,000. The unit selling price, unit variable cost, and unit contribution margin are as follows:

Unit selling price	$75
Unit variable cost	45
Unit contribution margin	$30

The sales volume necessary to earn the target profit of $100,000 is 10,000 units, computed as follows:

$$\text{Sales (units)} = \frac{\text{Fixed costs} + \text{Target profit}}{\text{Unit contribution margin}}$$

$$\text{Sales (units)} = \frac{\$200{,}000 + \$100{,}000}{\$30} = 10{,}000 \text{ units}$$

The following income statement verifies this computation:

Sales (10,000 units × $75)	$750,000
Variable costs (10,000 units × $45)	450,000
Contribution margin (10,000 units × $30)	$300,000
Fixed costs	200,000
Operating income	$100,000

Graphic Approach to Cost-Volume-Profit Analysis

Objective 4
Using a cost-volume-profit chart and a profit-volume chart, determine the break-even point and the volume necessary to achieve a target profit.

Cost-volume-profit analysis can be presented graphically as well as in equation form. Many managers prefer the graphic format because the operating profit or loss for any given level of sales can be visually determined. In the following paragraphs, we describe two graphic approaches that managers find useful.

COST-VOLUME-PROFIT (BREAK-EVEN) CHART

A cost-volume-profit chart, sometimes called a **break-even chart,** may assist management in understanding relationships among costs, sales, and operating profit or loss. To illustrate, the cost-volume-profit chart in Exhibit 5 is based on the following data.

Unit selling price	$ 50
Unit variable cost	30
Unit contribution margin	$ 20
Total fixed costs	$100,000

Exhibit 5
Cost-Volume-Profit Chart

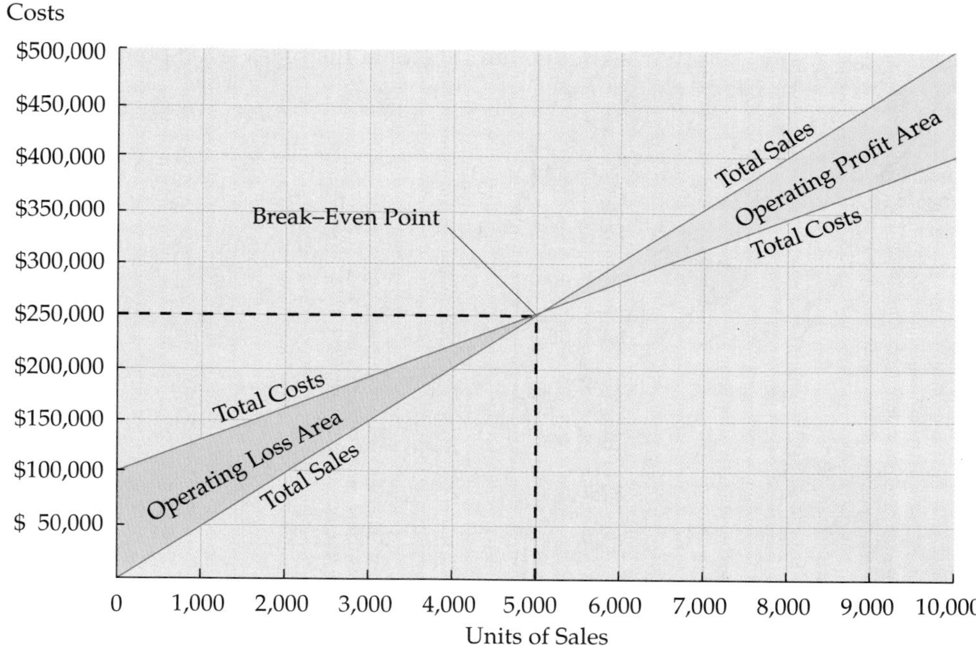

We constructed the cost-volume-profit chart in Exhibit 5 as follows:

1. Volume expressed in units of sales is indicated along the horizontal axis. The range of volume shown on the horizontal axis should reflect the relevant range in which the business expects to operate. Dollar amounts representing total sales and costs are indicated along the vertical axis.
2. A sales line is plotted by beginning at zero on the left corner of the graph. A second point is determined by multiplying any units of sales on the horizontal axis by the unit sales price of $50. For example, for 10,000 units of sales, the total sales would be $500,000 (10,000 units × $50). The sales line is drawn upward to the right from zero through the $500,000 point.
3. A cost line is plotted by beginning with total fixed costs, $100,000, on the vertical axis. A second point is determined by multiplying any units of sales on the horizontal axis by the unit variable costs and adding the fixed costs. For example, for 10,000 units of sales, the total estimated costs would be $400,000 [(10,000 units × $30) + $100,000]. The cost line is drawn upward to the right from $100,000 on the vertical axis through the $400,000 point.
4. Horizontal and vertical lines are drawn at the point of intersection of the sales and cost lines, which is the break-even point, and the areas representing operating profit and operating loss are identified.

In Exhibit 5, the dotted lines drawn from the point of intersection of the total sales line and the total cost line identify the break-even point in total sales dollars and units. The break-even point is $250,000 of sales, which represents a sales volume of 5,000 units. Operating profits will be earned when sales levels are to the right of the break-even point (operating profit area). Operating losses will be incurred when sales levels are to the left of the break-even point (operating loss area).

Changes in the unit selling price, total fixed costs, and unit variable costs can be analyzed by using a cost-volume-profit chart. Using the data in Exhibit 5, assume that a proposal to reduce fixed costs by $20,000 is to be evaluated. In this case, the total fixed costs would be $80,000 ($100,000 – $20,000). As shown in Exhibit 6, the total cost line should be redrawn, starting at the $80,000 point (total fixed costs) on the vertical axis. A second point is determined by multiplying any units of sales on the horizontal axis by the unit variable costs and adding the fixed costs. For example, for 10,000 units of sales, the total estimated costs would be $380,000 [(10,000 units × $30) + $80,000]. The cost line is drawn upward to the right from $80,000 on the vertical axis through the $380,000 point. The revised cost-volume-profit chart in Exhibit 6 indicates that the break-even point decreases to $200,000 or 4,000 units of sales.

Exhibit 6
Revised Cost-Volume-Profit Chart

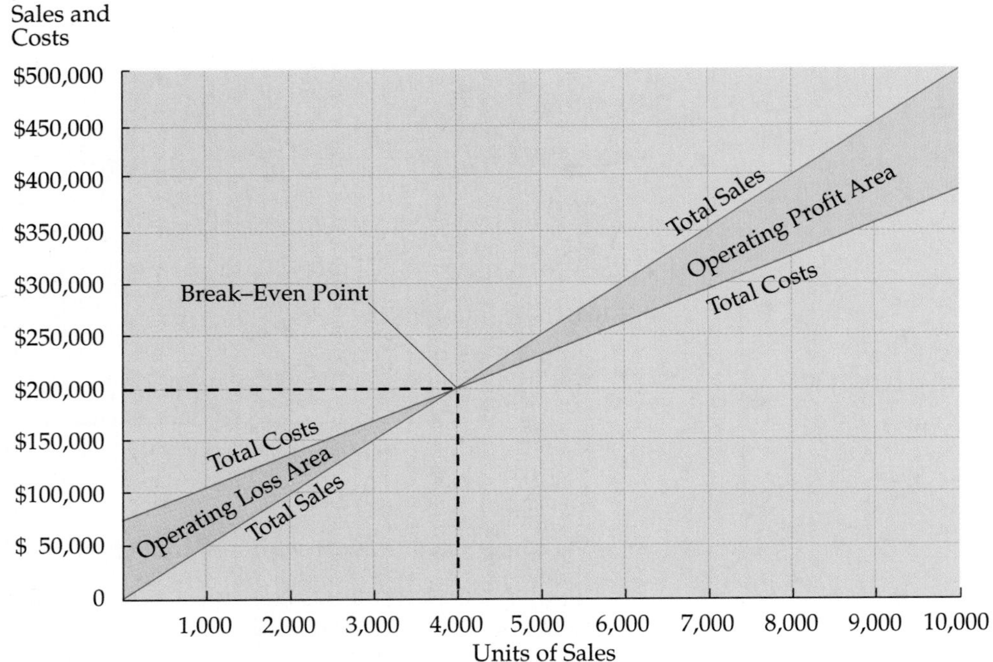

PROFIT-VOLUME CHART

Another graphic approach to cost-volume-profit analysis, the **profit-volume chart,** focuses on profits. This is in contrast to the cost-volume-profit chart, which focuses on sales and costs. The profit-volume chart plots only the difference between total sales and total costs or profits. In this way, the profit-volume chart allows managers to determine the operating profit (or loss) for various levels of operations.

To illustrate, assume the profit-volume chart in Exhibit 7 is based on the same data as used in Exhibit 5. These data are as follows:

Unit selling price	$ 50
Unit variable cost	30
Unit contribution margin	$ 20
Total fixed costs	$100,000

The maximum operating loss is equal to the fixed costs of $100,000. Assuming that the maximum unit sales within the relevant range is 10,000 units, the maximum operating profit is $100,000, computed as follows:

Sales (10,000 units × $50)	$500,000
Variable costs (10,000 units × $30)	300,000
Contribution margin (10,000 units × $20)	$200,000
Fixed costs	100,000
Operating profit	$100,000

Exhibit 7
Profit-Volume Chart

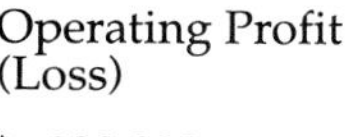

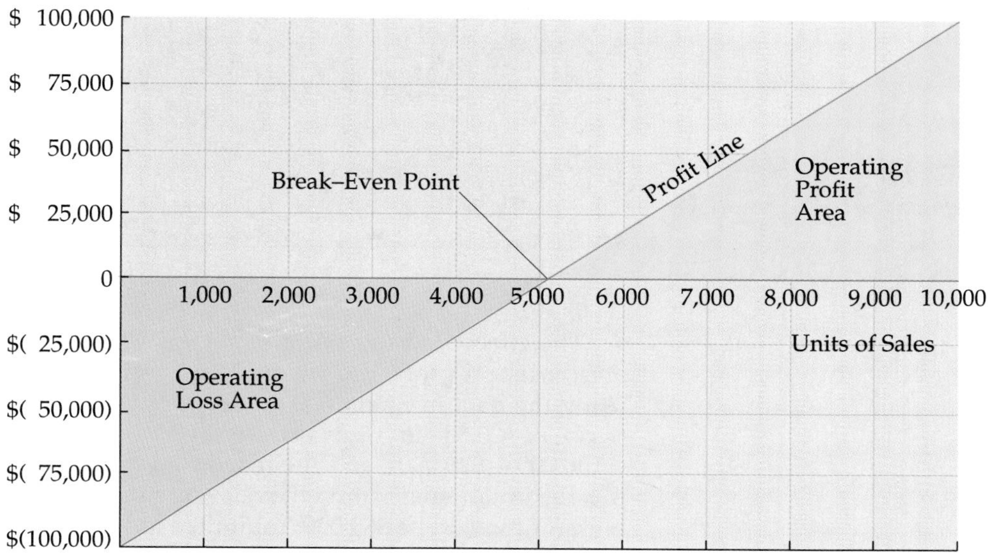

We constructed the profit-volume chart in Exhibit 7 as follows:

1. Volume expressed in units of sales is indicated along the horizontal axis. The range of volume shown on the horizontal axis should reflect the relevant range in which the business expects to operate. In this illustration, the maximum number of sales units within the relevant range is assumed to be 10,000 units. Dollar amounts indicating operating profits and losses are shown along the vertical axis.
2. A point representing the maximum operating loss is plotted on the vertical axis at the left. This loss is equal to the total fixed costs at the zero level of sales.
3. A point representing the maximum operating profit within the relevant range is plotted on the right.
4. A diagonal profit line is drawn connecting the maximum operating loss point with the maximum operating profit point.
5. The profit line intersects the horizontal axis at the break-even point expressed in units of sales, and the areas indicating operating profit and loss are identified.

In Exhibit 7, the break-even point is 5,000 units of sales, which is equal to total sales of $250,000 (5,000 units × $50). Operating profit will be earned when sales levels are to the right of the break-even point (operating profit area). Operating losses will be incurred when sales levels are to the left of the break-even point (operating loss area). For example, at sales of 8,000 units, an operating profit of $60,000 will be earned, as shown in Exhibit 8.

Exhibit 8
Operating Profit Plotted on Profit-Volume Chart

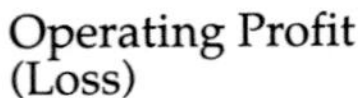

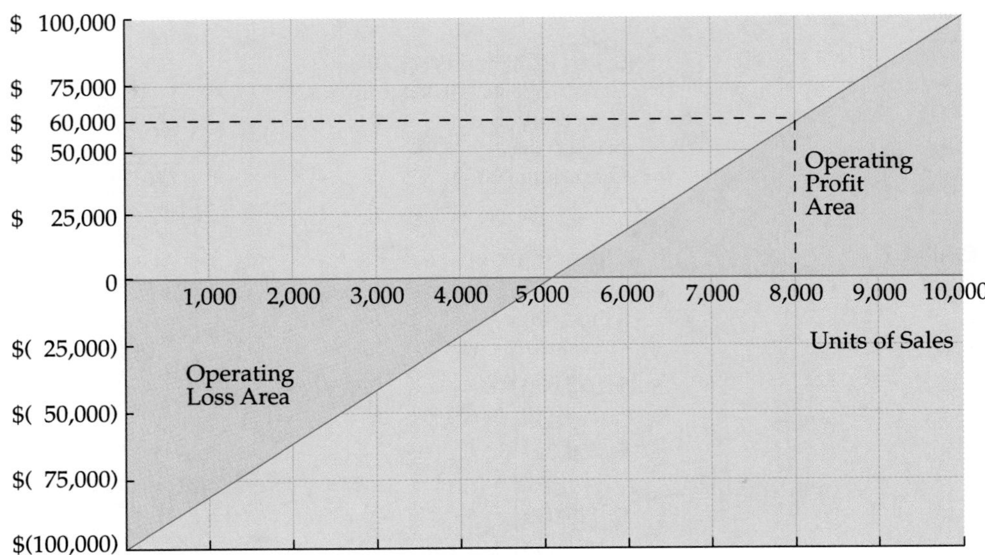

The effect of changes in the unit selling price, total fixed costs, and unit variable costs on profit can be analyzed using a profit-volume chart. To illustrate, using the data in Exhibits 7 and 8, we will evaluate the effect on profit of an increase of $20,000 in fixed costs. In this case, the total fixed costs would be $120,000 ($100,000 + $20,000), and the maximum operating loss would also be $120,000. If the maximum sales within the relevant range is 10,000 units, the maximum operating profit would be $80,000, computed as follows:

Sales (10,000 units × $50)	$500,000
Variable costs (10,000 units × $30)	300,000
Contribution margin (10,000 units × $20)	$200,000
Fixed costs	120,000
Operating profit	$ 80,000

A revised profit-volume chart is constructed by plotting the maximum operating loss and maximum operating profit points and drawing the revised profit line. The original and the revised profit-volume charts are shown in Exhibit 9.

The revised profit-volume chart indicates that the break-even point is 6,000 units of sales. This is equal to total sales of $300,000 (6,000 units × $50). The operating loss area of the chart has increased, while the operating profit area has decreased under the proposed change in fixed costs.

USE OF COMPUTERS IN COST-VOLUME-PROFIT ANALYSIS

The graphic approach as well as the mathematical approach to cost-volume-profit analysis are becoming increasingly easy to use, since most managers have access to computer terminals or microcomputers. With the aid of computer software, managers can vary assumptions regarding selling prices, costs, and volume and can immediately see the effects of each change on the break-even point and profit. Such an analysis is called a **"what if"** or **sensitivity analysis.**

Exhibit 9
Original Profit-Volume Chart and Revised Profit-Volume Chart

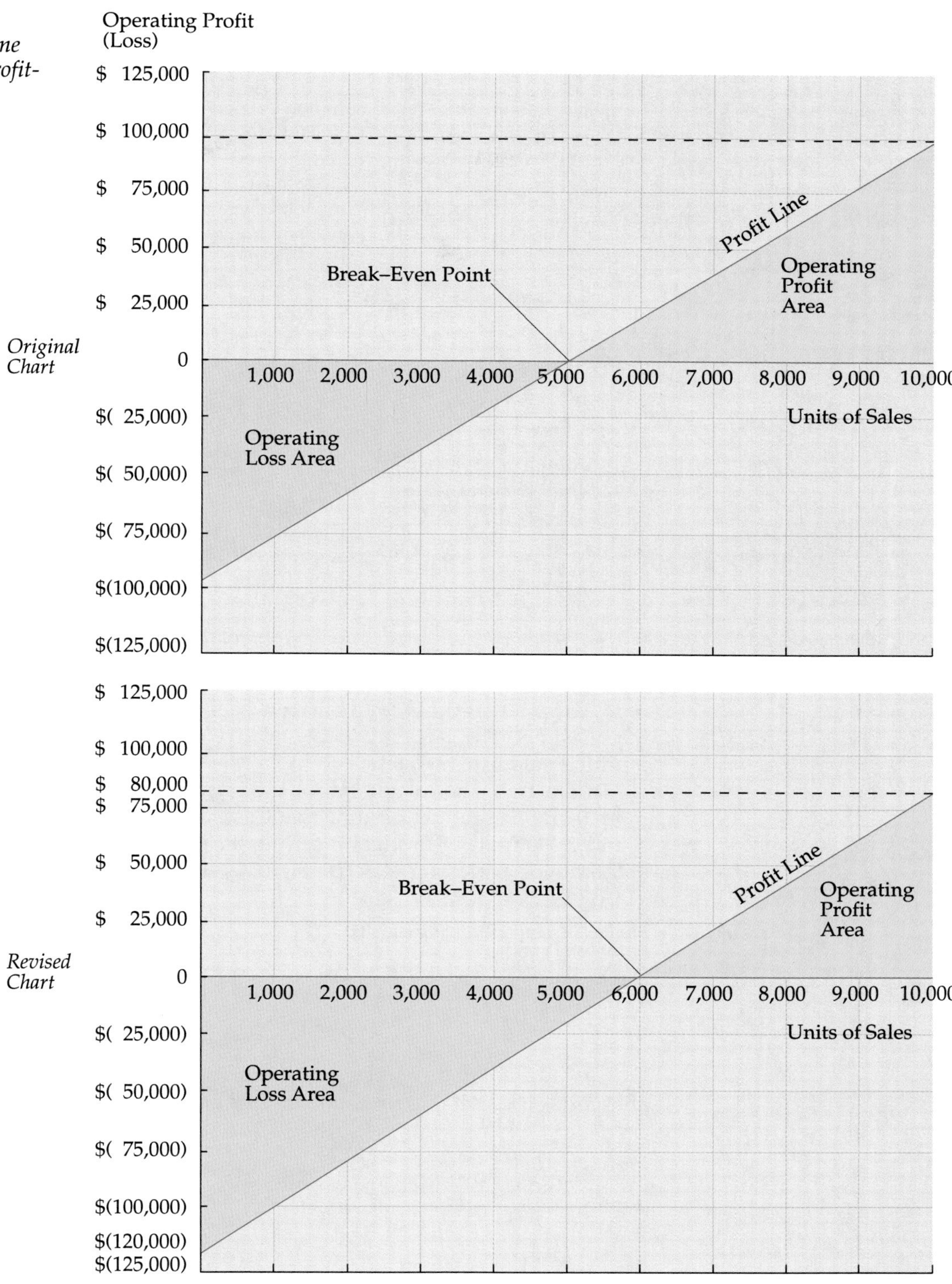

Sales Mix Considerations

Objective 5
Calculate the break-even point for a business selling more than one product.

In most businesses, more than one product is sold at varying selling prices. In addition, the products often have different unit variable costs, and each product makes a different contribution to profits. Thus, the sales volume necessary to break even

USING ACCOUNTING TO UNDERSTAND BUSINESS

A break-even analysis based on a multidimensional approach, rather than the traditional two-dimensional approach, was described in an article in *The Journal of Accountancy.* Such an approach is used by The Motor Convoy Inc., (now known as Allied Systems) a Georgia-based common carrier operating primarily in the southeastern U.S. The Motor Convoy Inc.'s chief financial officer prepared the break-even chart at the left.

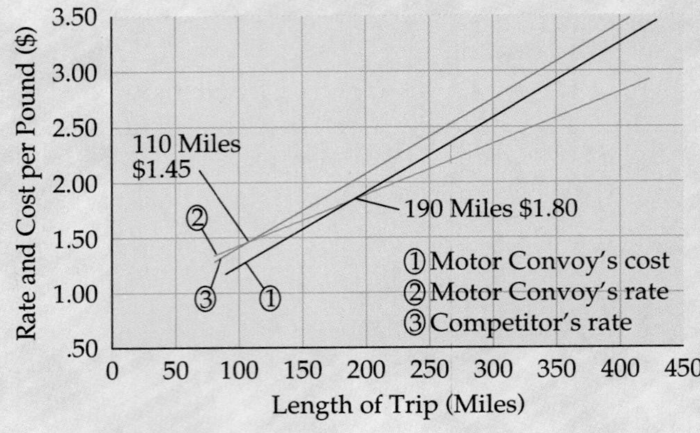

The chart illustrates a typical break-even analysis at The Motor Convoy for a normal load of 2,000 pounds over a relevant range of trips—from about 100 miles to 450 miles. The rate and cost per pound are plotted along the vertical axis, while the length of the trip (in miles) is plotted along the horizontal axis. The rate charged by The Motor Convoy's primary competitor is also graphed, so that the company can assess the effect of competition on developing its operating strategy.

In the above chart, the rate and cost curves are drawn only in the relevant range. The competitor's rate curve is parallel to The Motor Convoy's cost curve, and both rate curves cross at 110 miles. At this volume, The Motor Convoy's business should be concentrated on trips between 110 miles and 190 miles. On shorter trips, the competition is cheaper than The Motor Convoy. On longer trips, The Motor Convoy is losing money.

Source: "Multidimensional Break-even Analysis," *The Journal of Accountancy,* January 1987, pp. 132–133.

or to earn a target profit for a business selling two or more products depends upon the sales mix. The **sales mix** is the relative distribution of sales among the various products sold by a business.

To illustrate the calculation of the break-even point for a company that sells more than one product, assume that Cascade Company sold 8,000 units of Product A and 2,000 units of Product B during the past year. The sales mix for products A and B can be expressed as percentages, as shown below, or as a ratio (80:20).

Product	*Units Sold*	*Sales Mix*
A	8,000	80%
B	2,000	20
	10,000	100%

Cascade Company's fixed costs are $200,000. The unit selling prices, unit variable costs, and unit contribution margins for products A and B are as follows:

Product	*Unit Selling Price*	*Unit Variable Cost*	*Unit Contribution Margin*
A	$ 90	$70	$20
B	140	95	45

To compute the break-even point, it is useful to think of the individual products as components of one overall product. For Cascade Company, this overall product is called C. We can think of the unit selling price of C as equal to the total of the unit selling prices of products A and B, multiplied by their sales mix percentages. Likewise, we can think of the unit variable cost and unit contribution margin of C as equal to the total of the unit variable costs and unit contribution margins of products A and B, multiplied by the sales mix percentages. These computations are as follows:

Unit selling price of C:	($90 × .8) + ($140 × .2) = $100
Unit variable cost of C:	($70 × .8) + ($ 95 × .2) = $ 75
Unit contribution margin of C:	($20 × .8) + ($ 45 × .2) = $ 25

The break-even point of 8,000 units of C can be determined in the normal manner as follows:

$$\text{Break-even sales (units)} = \frac{\text{Fixed costs}}{\text{Unit contribution margin}}$$

$$\text{Break-even sales (units)} = \frac{\$200{,}000}{\$25} = 8{,}000 \text{ units}$$

Since the sales mix for products A and B is 80% and 20%, the break-even quantity of A is 6,400 units (8,000 units × 80%) and B is 1,600 units (8,000 units × 20%). This analysis can be verified in the following income statement:

	Product A	*Product B*	*Total*
Sales:			
6,400 units × $90	$576,000		$576,000
1,600 units × $140		$224,000	224,000
Total sales	$576,000	$224,000	$800,000
Variable costs:			
6,400 units × $70	$448,000		$448,000
1,600 units × $95		$152,000	152,000
Total variable costs	$448,000	$152,000	$600,000
Contribution margin	$128,000	$ 72,000	$200,000
Fixed costs			200,000
Operating profit			$ 0

The effects of changes in the sales mix on the break-even point can be determined by repeating the above analysis, assuming a different sales mix.

USING ACCOUNTING TO UNDERSTAND BUSINESS

The break-even point for many industries is influenced by the mix of products sold. For example, the daily break-even attendance at Universal Studios theme areas depends on how many tickets were sold at an advance purchase discount rate vs. the full gate rate. Likewise, the break-even point for an overseas flight of Delta Airlines will be influenced by the number of first class, business class, and tourist class tickets sold for the flight. The weekly break-even number of long distance minutes for AT&T depends on the number of minutes called during day, evening, and weekend rates.

Special Cost-Volume-Profit Relationships

Objective 6
Compute the margin of safety and the operating leverage, and explain how managers use these concepts.

Additional relationships can be developed from cost-volume-profit data. Two of these relationships that are especially useful to managers are the margin of safety and operating leverage.

MARGIN OF SAFETY

The **margin of safety** is the difference between the current sales revenue and the sales at the break-even point. It indicates the possible decrease in sales that may occur before an operating loss results. For example, if the margin of safety is low, even a small decline in sales revenue may result in an operating loss.

The margin of safety, stated as a percentage of sales, is computed using the following formula:

$$\text{Margin of safety} = \frac{\text{Sales} - \text{Sales at break-even point}}{\text{Sales}}$$

If sales are $250,000, the unit selling price is $25, and sales at the break-even point are $200,000, the margin of safety is 20%, as computed below.

$$\text{Margin of safety} = \frac{\$250{,}000 - \$200{,}000}{\$250{,}000} = 20\%$$

The margin of safety may also be stated in terms of units. In this illustration, for example, the margin of safety of 20% is equivalent to $50,000 ($250,000 × 20%). In units, the margin of safety is 2,000 units ($50,000 ÷ $25). Thus, the current sales of $250,000 may decline $50,000 or 2,000 units before an operating loss occurs.

OPERATING LEVERAGE

Operating leverage is a measure of the relative mix of a business's variable costs and fixed costs. It is computed as follows:

$$\text{Operating leverage} = \frac{\text{Contribution margin}}{\text{Operating income}}$$

Since the difference between contribution margin and operating income is fixed costs, companies with large amounts of fixed costs will generally have a high operating leverage. Thus, companies in capital-intensive industries, such as the airline and automotive industries, will generally have a high operating leverage. A low operating leverage is normal for companies in industries that are labor-intensive, such as some service industries.

Managers can use operating leverage to measure the impact of changes in sales on operating income. A high operating leverage indicates that a small increase in sales will yield a large percentage increase in operating income. In contrast, a low operating leverage indicates that a large increase in sales is necessary to significantly increase operating income. To illustrate, assume the following operating data for Jones Inc. and Wilson Inc.:

	Jones Inc.	*Wilson Inc.*
Sales	$400,000	$400,000
Variable costs	300,000	300,000
Contribution margin	$100,000	$100,000
Fixed costs	80,000	50,000
Operating income	$ 20,000	$ 50,000

Both companies have the same sales, the same variable costs, and the same contribution margin. Jones Inc. has larger fixed costs than Wilson Inc. and, as a result, a lower operating income and a higher operating leverage. The operating leverage for each company is computed as follows:

Jones Inc.

$$\text{Operating leverage} = \frac{\$100{,}000}{\$20{,}000} = 5$$

Wilson Inc.

$$\text{Operating leverage} = \frac{\$100{,}000}{\$50{,}000} = 2$$

Jones Inc.'s operating leverage indicates that, for each percentage point change in sales, operating income will change five times that percentage. In contrast, for each percentage point change in sales, the operating income of Wilson Inc. will only change two times that percentage. For example, if sales increased by 10% ($40,000) for each company, operating income will increase by 50% (10% × 5), or $10,000 (50% × $20,000), for Jones Inc. The sales increase of $40,000 will increase operating income by only 20% (10% × 2), or $10,000 (20% × $50,000), for Wilson Inc. The validity of this analysis is shown as follows:

	Jones Inc.	*Wilson Inc.*
Sales	$440,000	$440,000
Variable costs	330,000	330,000
Contribution margin	$110,000	$110,000
Fixed costs	80,000	50,000
Operating income	$ 30,000	$ 60,000

For Jones Inc., even a small increase in sales will generate a large percentage increase in operating income. Thus, managers may be motivated to think of ways to increase sales. In contrast, managers of Wilson Inc. might attempt to increase Wilson's operating leverage by reducing variable costs and thereby change the cost structure.

Assumptions of Cost-Volume-Profit Analysis

Objective 7
List the assumptions underlying cost-volume-profit analysis.

The reliability of cost-volume-profit analysis depends upon the validity of several assumptions. The primary assumptions are as follows:

1. Total sales and total costs can be represented by straight lines.
2. Within the relevant range of operating activity, the efficiency of operations does not change.
3. Costs can be accurately divided into fixed and variable components.
4. The sales mix is constant.
5. There is no change in the inventory quantities during the period.

The above assumptions simplify cost-volume-profit analysis. Since the assumptions are often valid for the relevant range of operations under consideration, cost-volume-profit analysis is often used by managers as an aid to decision making. The impact of violating these assumptions is discussed in advanced accounting texts.

Appendix: Variable Costing

For financial reporting to external users, the cost of manufactured products normally consists of direct materials, direct labor, and factory overhead. The reporting of all these costs as product costs, called **absorption costing,** is required under generally accepted accounting principles. However, the **variable costing** or **direct costing** reporting format may be used for managerial decision making. In this appendix, we will describe and illustrate this format.

In variable costing, the cost of goods manufactured is composed only of variable costs. Variable costs normally include direct materials, direct labor, and variable factory overhead, when the level of activity is measured in units produced. Fixed factory overhead costs are related to the productive capacity of the manufacturing plant and are normally not affected by the number of units produced. Thus, in a variable costing income statement, fixed factory overhead costs do not become a part of the cost of goods manufactured. Instead, fixed factory overhead costs are treated as an expense of the period.

Exhibit 10 highlights the difference between absorption costing and variable costing. The difference between the two costing concepts is in the treatment of the fixed manufacturing costs, which consist of the fixed factory overhead costs.

Exhibit 10
Absorption Costing Compared to Variable Costing

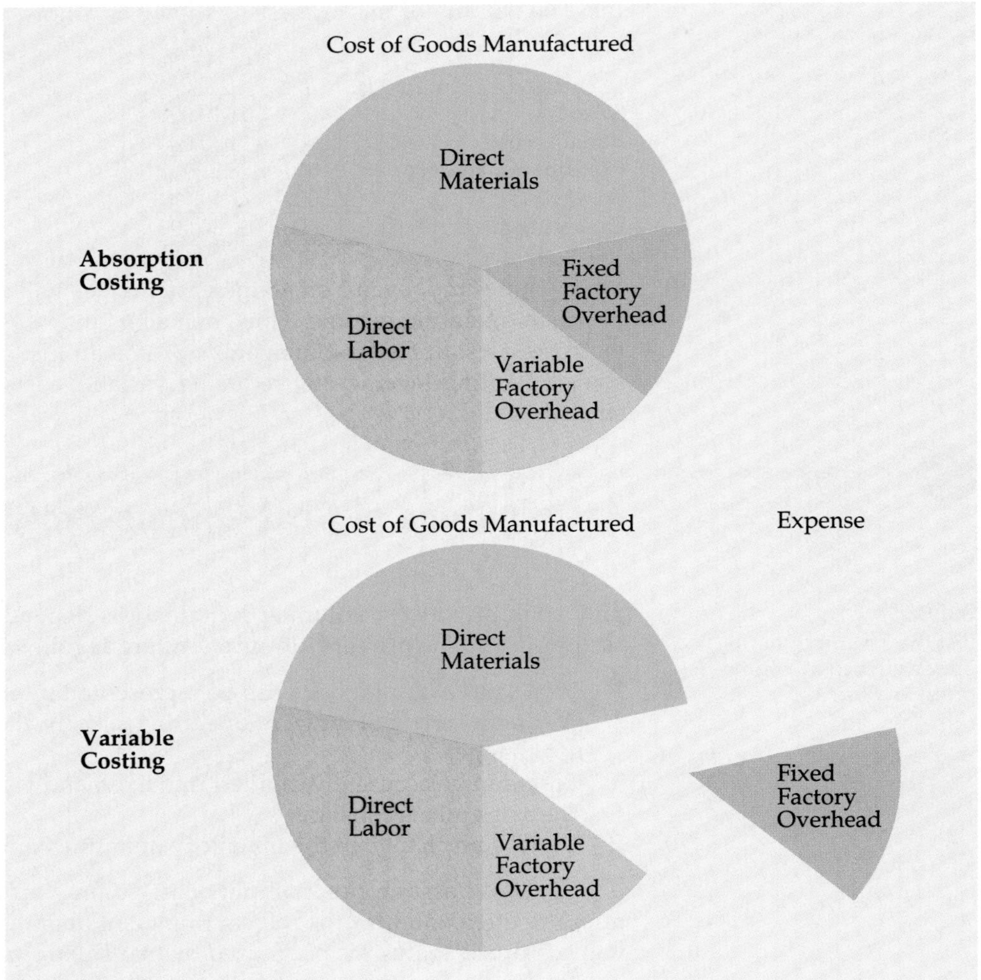

To illustrate preparing a variable costing income statement, assume that 15,000 units were manufactured and sold at a price of $50 and the costs were as follows:

	Total Cost	*Number of Units*	*Unit Cost*
Manufacturing costs:			
Variable	$375,000	15,000	$25
Fixed	150,000	15,000	10
Total	$525,000		$35
Selling and administrative expenses:			
Variable ($5 per unit sold)	$ 75,000		
Fixed	50,000		
Total	$125,000		

Exhibit 11 shows the variable costing income statement prepared from the preceding data. The computations are shown in parentheses.

Exhibit 11
Variable Costing Income Statement

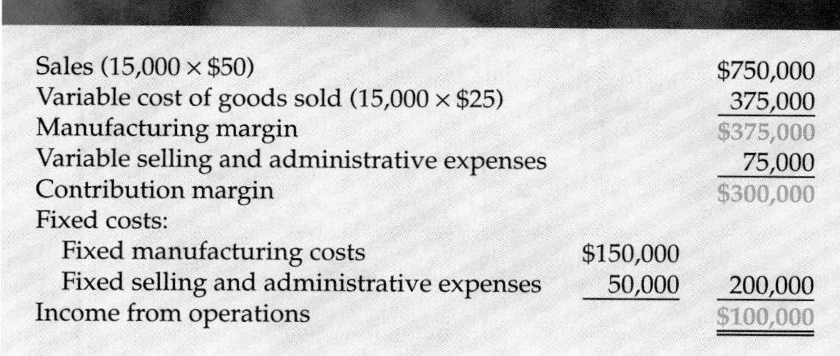

Sales (15,000 × $50)		$750,000
Variable cost of goods sold (15,000 × $25)		375,000
Manufacturing margin		$375,000
Variable selling and administrative expenses		75,000
Contribution margin		$300,000
Fixed costs:		
Fixed manufacturing costs	$150,000	
Fixed selling and administrative expenses	50,000	200,000
Income from operations		$100,000

In a variable costing income statement, the **manufacturing margin** is the excess of sales over the variable cost of goods sold. In Exhibit 11, the manufacturing margin is $375,000 ($750,000 sales – $375,000 variable cost of goods sold). The variable selling and administrative expenses of $75,000 are deducted from the manufacturing margin to yield the contribution margin of $300,000. Income from operations of $100,000 is then determined by deducting fixed costs from the contribution margin.

Exhibit 12 shows the absorption costing income statement prepared from the same data. The absorption costing income statement does not distinguish between variable and fixed costs. All manufacturing costs are included in the cost of goods sold. Deducting the cost of goods sold from sales yields the gross profit. Deducting the selling and administrative expenses from gross profit yields the income from operations.

Exhibit 12
Absorption Costing Income Statement

Sales (15,000 × $50)	$750,000
Cost of goods sold (15,000 × $35)	525,000
Gross profit	$225,000
Selling and administrative expenses ($75,000 + $50,000)	125,000
Income from operations	$100,000

In the preceding illustration, 15,000 units were manufactured and sold. Both the absorption and the variable costing income statements reported the same income from operations of $100,000. Assuming no other changes, operating income will be the same under both methods when the number of units manufactured equals the number of units sold. When the number of units manufactured and the number of units sold are not equal, the operating incomes will differ as shown below.

Units manufactured:	
Exceed units sold	Variable costing income is less than absorption costing income.
Less than units sold	Variable costing income is greater than absorption costing income.

As noted above, if the number of units manufactured exceeds the number of units sold, the operating income reported under variable costing will be less than the operating income reported under absorption costing. To illustrate, assume that in the preceding example only 12,000 units of the 15,000 units manufactured were sold. Exhibit 13 shows the two income statements that result.

Exhibit 13
Units Manufactured Exceed Units Sold

Variable Costing Income Statement		
Sales (12,000 × $50)		$600,000
Variable cost of goods sold:		
Variable cost of goods manufactured (15,000 × $25)	$375,000	
Less ending inventory (3,000 × $25)	75,000	
Variable cost of goods sold		300,000
Manufacturing margin		$300,000
Variable selling and administrative expenses		60,000
Contribution margin		$240,000
Fixed costs:		
Fixed manufacturing costs	$150,000	
Fixed selling and administrative expenses	50,000	200,000
Income from operations		$ 40,000

Absorption Costing Income Statement		
Sales (12,000 × $50)		$600,000
Cost of goods sold:		
Cost of goods manufactured (15,000 × $35)	$525,000	
Less ending inventory (3,000 × $35)	105,000	
Cost of goods sold		420,000
Gross profit		$180,000
Selling and administrative expenses [(12,000 × $5) + $50,000]		110,000
Income from operations		$ 70,000

The $30,000 difference in the amount of income from operations ($70,000 – $40,000) is due to the different treatment of the fixed manufacturing costs. The entire amount of the $150,000 of fixed manufacturing costs is included as an expense of the period in the variable costing statement. The ending inventory in the absorption costing statement includes $30,000 (3,000 × $10) of fixed manufacturing costs. This $30,000, by being included in inventory, is thus excluded from the current cost of goods sold and deferred to another period.

A similar analysis verifies that operating income under variable costing is greater than operating income under absorption costing when the units manufactured are less than the units sold. In both cases where sales and production differ, finished goods inventory will also be different under absorption costing and variable costing. As a result, increases or decreases in operating income due to changes in inventory levels could be misinterpreted by managers using absorption costing income statements as operating efficiencies or inefficiencies. This is one of the reasons that variable costing rather than absorption costing is used by managers for decision-making purposes.

Variable costing is especially useful to managers for cost control, product pricing, and production planning purposes. Such uses of variable costing are discussed in advanced accounting texts.

KEY POINTS

Objective 1. Classify costs by their behavior as variable costs, fixed costs, or mixed costs.

Cost behavior refers to the manner in which a cost changes as a related activity changes. Variable costs are costs that vary in total in proportion to changes in the level of activity. Fixed costs are costs that remain the same in total dollar amount as the level of activity changes. A mixed cost has attributes of both a variable and a fixed cost.

Objective 2. Compute the contribution margin, the contribution margin ratio, and the unit contribution margin, and explain how they may be useful to managers in planning and controlling operations.
The contribution margin concept is useful in business planning because it gives insight into the profit potential of a firm. The contribution margin is the excess of sales revenues over variable costs. The contribution margin ratio is computed as follows:

$$\text{Contribution margin ratio} = \frac{\text{Sales} - \text{Variable costs}}{\text{Sales}}$$

The unit contribution margin is the excess of the unit selling price over the unit variable cost.

Objective 3. Using the unit contribution margin, determine the break-even point and the volume necessary to achieve a target profit.
The mathematical approach to cost-volume-profit analysis uses the unit contribution margin concept and the following equations to determine the break-even point and the volume necessary to achieve a target profit for a business:

$$\text{Break-even sales (units)} = \frac{\text{Fixed costs}}{\text{Unit contribution margin}}$$

$$\text{Sales (units)} = \frac{\text{Fixed costs} + \text{Target profit}}{\text{Unit contribution margin}}$$

Objective 4. Using a cost-volume-profit chart and a profit-volume chart, determine the break-even point and the volume necessary to achieve a target profit.
A cost-volume-profit chart focuses on the relationships among costs, sales, and operating profit or loss. Preparing and using a cost-volume-profit chart to determine the break-even point and the volume necessary to achieve a target profit are illustrated in this chapter.

The profit-volume chart focuses on profits rather than on revenues and costs. Preparing and using a profit-volume chart to determine the break-even point and the volume necessary to achieve a target profit are illustrated in this chapter.

Objective 5. Calculate the break-even point for a business selling more than one product.
Calculating the break-even point for a business selling two or more products is based upon a specified sales mix. Given the sales mix, the break-even point can be computed, using the methods illustrated for Cascade Company in this chapter.

Objective 6. Compute the margin of safety and the operating leverage, and explain how managers use these concepts.
The margin of safety as a percentage of current sales is computed as follows:

$$\text{Margin of safety} = \frac{\text{Sales} - \text{Sales at break-even point}}{\text{Sales}}$$

The margin of safety is useful in evaluating past operations and in planning future operations. For example, if the margin of safety is low, even a small decline in sales revenue will result in an operating loss.

Operating leverage is computed as follows:

$$\text{Operating leverage} = \frac{\text{Contribution margin}}{\text{Operating income}}$$

Operating leverage is useful in measuring the impact of changes in sales on operating income without preparing formal income statements. For example, a high operating leverage indicates that a small increase in sales will yield a large percentage increase in operating income.

Objective 7. List the assumptions underlying cost-volume-profit analysis.
The primary assumptions underlying cost-volume-profit analysis are as follows:

1. Total sales and total costs can be represented by straight lines.
2. Within the relevant range of operating activity, the efficiency of operations does not change.
3. Costs can be accurately divided into fixed and variable components.
4. The sales mix is constant.
5. There is no change in the inventory quantities during the period.

GLOSSARY OF KEY TERMS

Activity bases (drivers). A measure of activity that is thought to cause the incurrence of cost. Used in analyzing and classifying cost behavior. *Objective 1*

Break-even point. The level of business operations at which revenues and expired costs are equal. *Objective 3*

Contribution margin. Sales less variable costs and variable selling and administrative expenses. *Objective 2*

Contribution margin ratio. The percentage of each sales dollar that is available to cover the fixed costs and provide an operating income. *Objective 2*

Cost behavior. The manner in which a cost changes in relation to its activity base (driver). *Objective 1*

Cost-volume-profit analysis. The systematic examination of the relationships among selling prices, volume of sales and production, costs, expenses, and profits. *Objective 2*

Cost-volume-profit chart. A chart used to assist management in understanding the relationships among costs, expenses, sales, and operating profit or loss. *Objective 4*

Fixed costs. Costs that tend to remain the same in amount, regardless of variations in the level of activity. *Objective 1*

High-low method. A technique that uses the highest and lowest total costs as a basis for estimating the variable cost per unit and the fixed cost component of a mixed cost. *Objective 1*

Margin of safety. The difference between current sales revenue and the sales at the break-even point. *Objective 6*

Mixed cost. A cost with both variable and fixed characteristics, sometimes called a semivariable or semifixed cost. *Objective 1*

Operating leverage. A measure of the relative mix of a business's variable costs and fixed costs, computed as contribution margin divided by operating income. *Objective 6*

Profit-volume chart. A chart used to assist management in understanding the relationship between profit and volume. *Objective 4*

Relevant range. The range of activity over which changes in cost are of interest to management. *Objective 1*

Sales mix. The relative distribution of sales among the various products available for sale. *Objective 5*

Unit contribution margin. The dollars available from each unit of sales to cover fixed costs and provide operating profits. *Objective 2*

Variable costing. A method of reporting variable and fixed costs that includes only the variable manufacturing costs in the cost of the product. *Objective 1*

Variable costs. Costs that vary in total dollar amount as the level of activity changes. *Objective 1*

ILLUSTRATIVE PROBLEM

Wyatt Inc. expects to maintain the same inventories at the end of the year as at the beginning of the year. The estimated fixed costs for the year are $288,000, and the estimated variable costs per unit are $14. It is expected that 60,000 units will be sold at a price of $20 per unit. Maximum sales within the relevant range are 70,000 units.

Instructions

1. What is (a) the contribution margin ratio and (b) the unit contribution margin?
2. Determine the break-even point in units.
3. Construct a cost-volume-profit chart, indicating the break-even point.
4. Construct a profit-volume chart, indicating the break-even point.
5. What is the margin of safety?

Solution

1. a. $$\text{Contribution margin ratio} = \frac{\text{Sales} - \text{Variable costs}}{\text{Sales}}$$

$$\text{Contribution margin ratio} = \frac{(60{,}000 \text{ units} \times \$20) - (60{,}000 \text{ units} \times \$14)}{(60{,}000 \text{ units} \times \$20)}$$

$$\text{Contribution margin ratio} = \frac{\$1{,}200{,}000 - \$840{,}000}{\$1{,}200{,}000} = \frac{\$360{,}000}{\$1{,}200{,}000}$$

$$\text{Contribution margin ratio} = 30\%$$

b. Unit contribution margin = Unit selling price – Unit variable costs

Unit contribution margin = $20 – $14 = $6

2. $$\text{Break-even sales (units)} = \frac{\text{Fixed costs}}{\text{Unit contribution margin}}$$

$$\text{Break-even sales (units)} = \frac{\$288{,}000}{\$6} = 48{,}000 \text{ units}$$

3\.

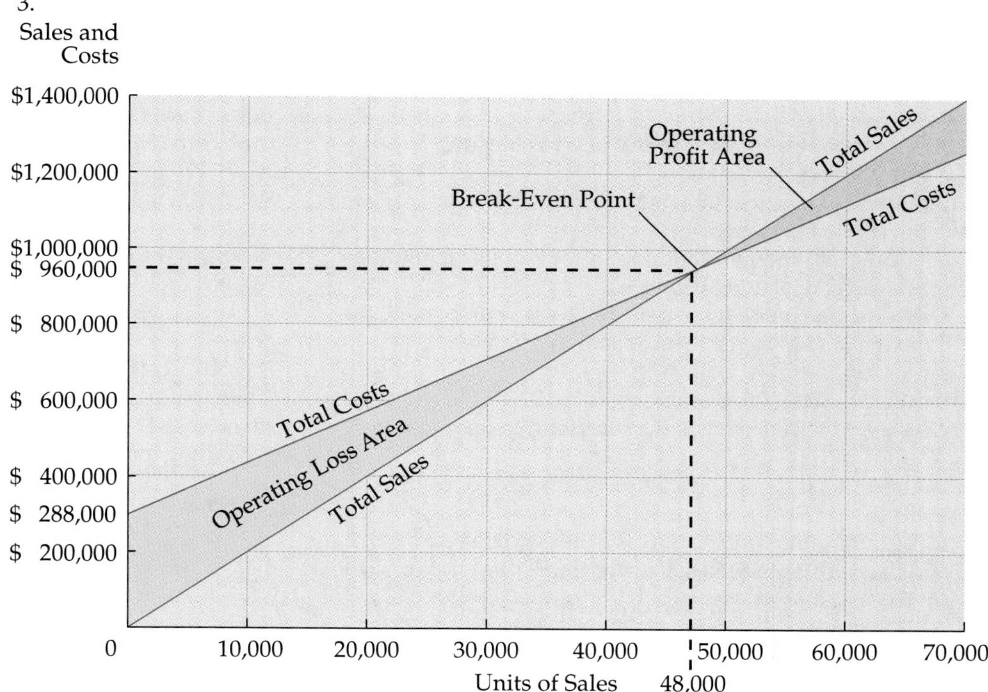

4\.

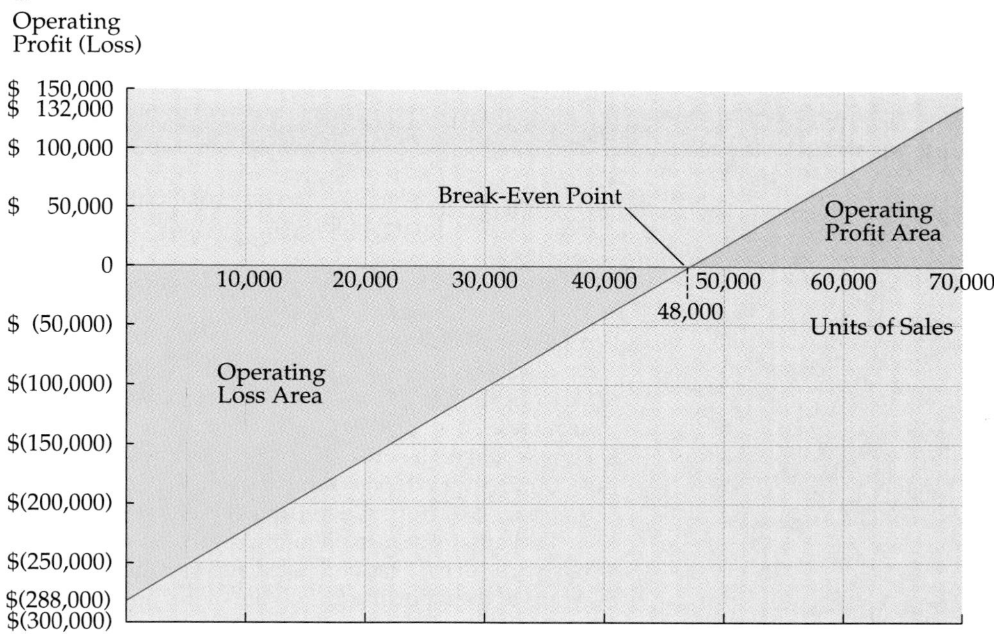

5\. Margin of safety:

Expected sales (60,000 units × $20)	$1,200,000
Break-even point (48,000 units × $20)	960,000
Margin of safety	$ 240,000

or

$$\text{Margin of safety} = \frac{\text{Sales} - \text{Sales at break-even point}}{\text{Sales}}$$

$$\text{Margin of safety} = \frac{\$240,000}{\$1,200,000} = 20\%$$

SELF-EXAMINATION QUESTIONS (ANSWERS AT END OF CHAPTER)

1. Which of the following statements describes variable costs?
   A. Costs that vary on a per-unit basis as the level of activity changes.
   B. Costs that vary in total in direct proportion to changes in the level of activity.
   C. Costs that remain the same in total dollar amount as the level of activity changes.
   D. Costs that vary on a per-unit basis, but remain the same in total as the level of activity changes.

2. If sales are $500,000, variable costs are $200,000, and fixed costs are $240,000, what is the contribution margin ratio?
   A. 40% C. 52%
   B. 48% D. 60%

3. If the unit selling price is $16, the unit variable cost is $12, and fixed costs are $160,000, what are the break-even sales (units)?
   A. 5,714 units C. 13,333 units
   B. 10,000 units D. 40,000 units

4. Based on the data presented in Question 3, how many units of sales would be required to realize an operating profit of $20,000?
   A. 11,250 units C. 20,000 units
   B. 15,000 units D. 45,000 units

5. Based on the following operating data, what is the operating leverage?

Sales	$600,000
Variable costs	240,000
Contribution margin	$360,000
Fixed costs	160,000
Operating income	$200,000

   A. 0.8 C. 1.8
   B. 1.2 D. 4.0

DISCUSSION QUESTIONS

1. What are the three most common classifications of cost behavior?
2. Describe how total variable cost and unit variable costs behave with changes in the level of activity.
3. How would each of the following costs be classified if units produced is the activity base?
   a. Direct labor costs
   b. Direct materials cost
   c. Electricity costs of $.20 per kilowatt-hour
4. Describe the behavior of (a) total fixed costs and (b) unit fixed costs as the level of activity increases.
5. How would each of the following costs be classified if units produced is the activity base?
   a. Straight-line depreciation of plant and equipment
   b. Salary of factory supervisor ($80,000 per year)
   c. Property insurance premiums of $5,000 per month on plant and equipment
6. What type of cost has both fixed and variable cost characteristics?
7. Which of the following graphs illustrates how total variable costs behave with changes in total units produced?

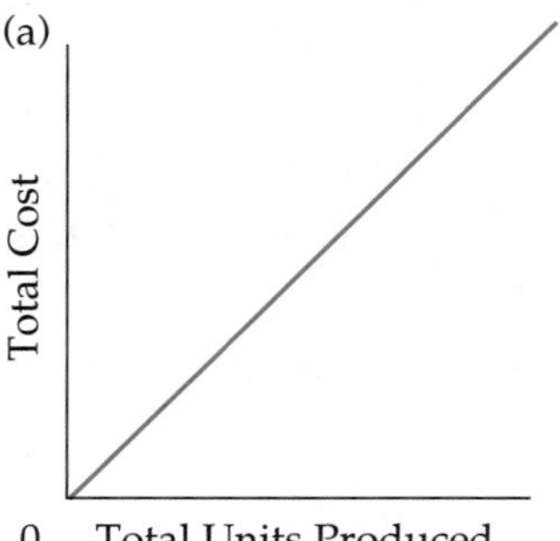

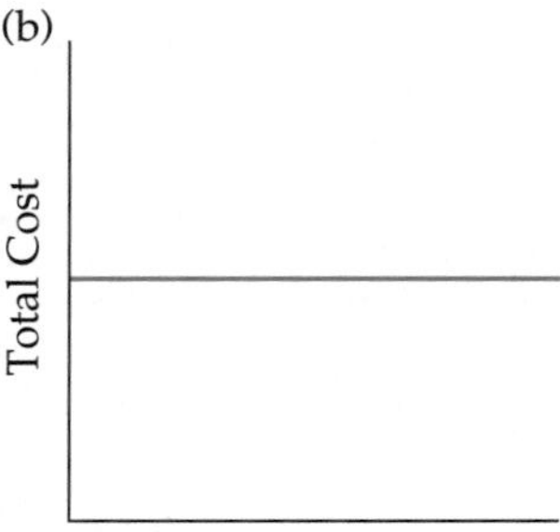

8. Which of the following graphs illustrates how unit variable costs behave with changes in total units produced?

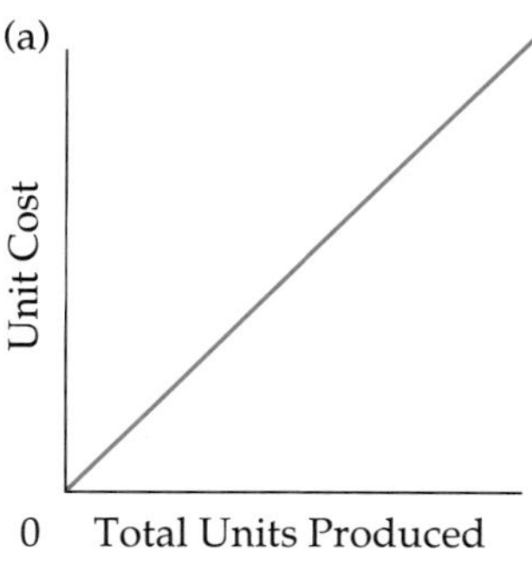

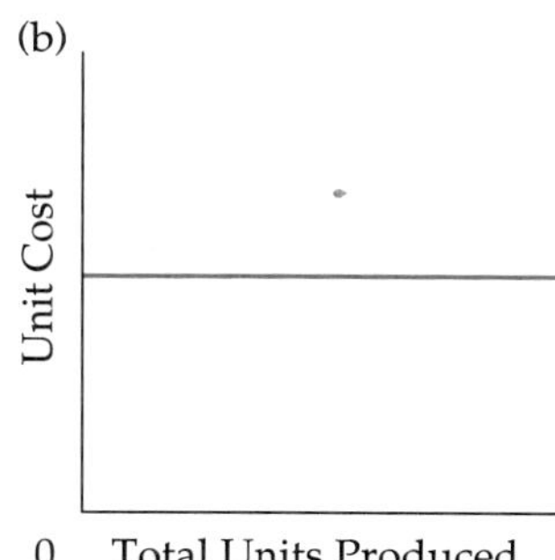

9. Which of the following graphs best illustrates fixed costs per unit as the activity base changes?

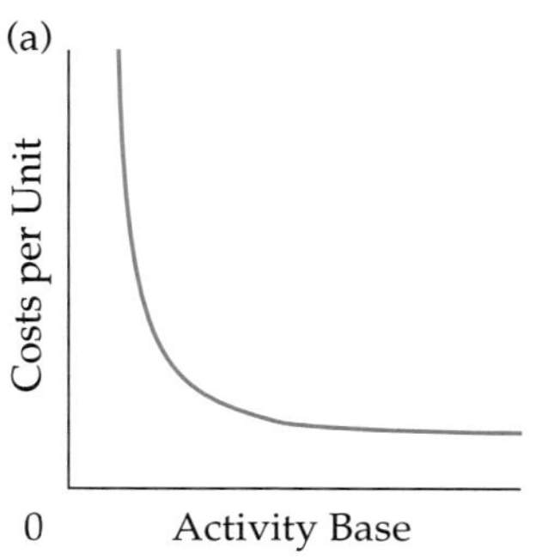

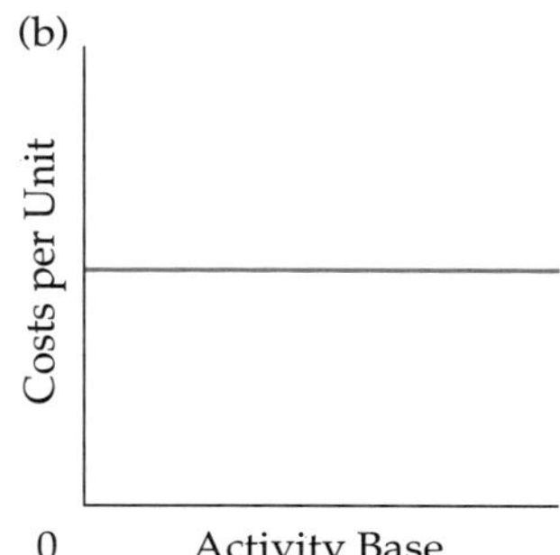

10. In applying the high-low method of cost estimation, how is the total fixed cost estimated?
11. What is contribution margin?
12. If fixed costs increase, what would be the impact on the (a) contribution margin? (b) operating profit?
13. An examination of the accounting records of Hudson Company disclosed a high contribution margin ratio and production at a level below maximum capacity. Based on this information, suggest a likely means of improving operating profit. Explain.
14. a. What is the break-even point?
    b. What equation is used to determine the break-even point in sales units?
15. If the unit cost of direct materials is decreased, what effect will this change have on the break-even point?
16. If insurance rates are increased, what effect will this change in fixed costs have on the break-even point?
17. Both Simmons Company and Pate Company had the same sales, total costs, and operating profit for the current fiscal year; yet Simmons Company had a lower break-even point than Pate Company. Explain the reason for this difference in break-even points.
18. What is meant by sales mix?
19. What is meant by the margin of safety?
20. a. How is operating leverage computed?
    b. What does operating leverage measure?

EXERCISES

EXERCISE 21–1
Classifying costs
Objective 1

Following is a list of various costs incurred in producing pencils. With respect to the manufacture and sale of pencils, classify each cost as either variable, fixed, or mixed.

1. Number 2 1/2 lead.
2. Property insurance premiums, $1,000 per month plus $.005 for each dollar of property over $2,000,000.

3. Straight-line depreciation on the factory equipment.
4. Hourly wages of machine operators.
5. Salary of the plant superintendent.
6. Red paint.
7. Erasers.
8. Janitorial costs, $2,000 per month.
9. Property taxes on factory building and equipment.
10. Metal to hold the eraser on the end of the pencil.
11. Pension cost, $.20 per employee hour on the job.
12. Wood costs.
13. Electricity costs, $.025 per kilowatt-hour.
14. Oils used to lubricate machinery.
15. Rent on warehouse, $3,000 per month plus $2 per square foot of storage used.

EXERCISE 21–2
Identifying cost graphs
Objective 1

The following cost graphs illustrate various types of cost behavior:

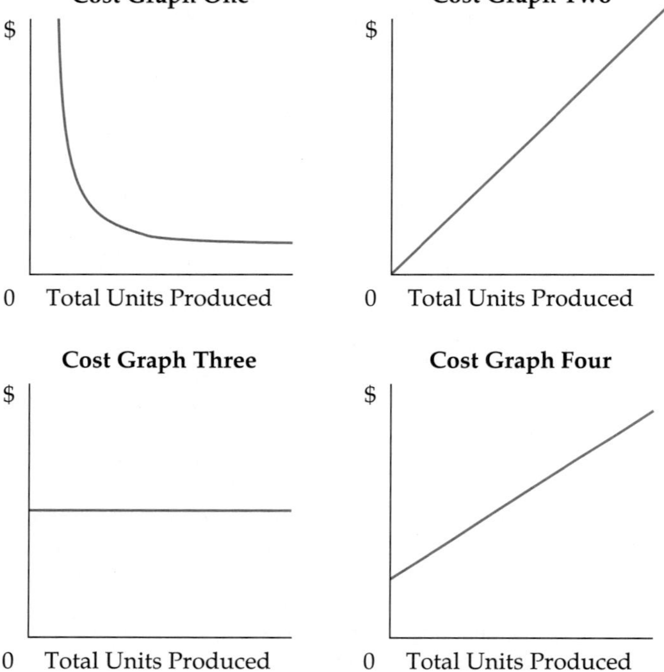

For each of the following costs, identify the cost graph that best illustrates its cost behavior as the number of units produced increases.

a. Salary of quality control supervisor, $4,000 per month.
b. Total direct materials cost.
c. Per-unit direct labor cost.
d. Electricity costs of $2,000 per month plus $.02 per kilowatt-hour.
e. Per-unit cost of straight-line depreciation on factory equipment.

EXERCISE 21–3
Identifying activity bases
Objective 1

For Tree Wizard Inc., match each cost in the following table with the activity base most appropriate to it. An activity base may be used more than once.

Cost:	Activity Base:
1. Fertilizer	a. Number of fields
2. Sales commissions	b. Number of trees shipped
3. The cost of water used to water the trees	c. Number of trees planted in the fields
4. Dirt for packaging materials for shipping mature trees	d. Dollar amount of trees planted in the fields
5. Field managers' salaries	e. Dollar amount of trees sold

EXERCISE 21–4
Identifying activity bases
Objective 1

From the following list of activity bases for an automobile dealership, select the base that would be most appropriate for each of these costs: (1) preparation costs (cleaning, oil, and gasoline costs) for each car received, (2) salespersons' commission of 3% for each car sold, and (3) property taxes at the end of the year.

Activity Base:
a. Number of cars received
b. Number of cars sold
c. Number of cars ordered
d. Number of cars on hand
e. Dollar amount of cars received
f. Dollar amount of cars sold
g. Dollar amount of cars ordered
h. Dollar amount of cars on hand

EXERCISE 21–5
Identifying fixed and variable costs
Objective 1

Dutch Pantry Inc. operates full-service family restaurants in the eastern states. To ensure consistent quality, many of the items served in the restaurants are prepared in a central food-processing plant. Classify each of the following costs and expenses of the food-processing plant as either variable or fixed:

a. Monthly garbage collection expense
b. Salad dressing
c. Office salaries
d. Depreciation of equipment (straight-line method)
e. Cooking oil
f. Experimental costs (includes salaries of nutritionists)
g. Cleaning supplies
h. Spices
i. Water
j. Property taxes
k. Electricity

EXERCISE 21–6
Relevant range and computing fixed and variable costs
Objective 1

Fritz Inc. manufactures tool sets within a relevant range of 100,000 to 300,000 sets a year. Within this range, the following partially completed manufacturing cost schedule has been prepared:

Tool sets produced	100,000	200,000	300,000
Total costs:			
Total variable costs	$400,000	(d)	(j)
Total fixed costs	150,000	(e)	(k)
Total costs	$550,000	(f)	(l)
Cost per unit:			
Variable cost per unit	(a)	(g)	(m)
Fixed cost per unit	(b)	(h)	(n)
Total cost per unit	(c)	(i)	(o)

Complete the cost schedule, identifying each cost by the appropriate letter (a) through (o).

EXERCISE 21–7
Estimating costs, using the high-low method
Objective 1

Dunn Industries has decided to use the high-low method to estimate the total cost and the fixed and variable cost components of the total cost. The data for the highest and lowest levels of production are as follows:

	Units Produced	*Total Costs*
Highest level	200,000	$850,000
Lowest level	50,000	400,000

a. Determine the variable cost per unit and the fixed cost.
b. Based on (a), estimate the total cost for 60,000 units of production.

EXERCISE 21–8
Estimating costs, using the high-low method
Objective 1

Sheppard Hotel decided to use the high-low method and operating data from the past six months to estimate the total cost and the fixed and variable components of total cost. The activity base used by Sheppard Hotel is a measure of room occupancy, termed "room-nights," which is the number of days multiplied by the number of rooms used by guests.

	Total Costs	*Room-Nights*
March	$405,000	4,300
April	$392,000	3,200
May	$421,000	5,400
June	$380,000	3,000
July	$376,000	2,400
August	$416,000	5,200

Determine the variable cost per unit and the fixed cost.

EXERCISE 21–9
Contribution margin ratio
Objective 2

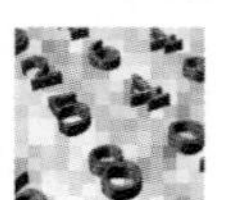

(a) Malkovicz Company budgets sales of $1,200,000, fixed costs of $150,000, and variable costs of $456,000. What is the anticipated contribution margin ratio? (b) If the contribution margin ratio for Stein Company is 32%, sales were $750,000, and fixed costs were $125,000, what was the operating income?

EXERCISE 21–10
Contribution margin and contribution margin ratio
Objective 2

For the year just ended, DeGeorge Company had sales of $500,000, variable costs of $230,000, fixed costs of $170,000, and an operating income of $100,000. DeGeorge sold 100,000 units during the year. DeGeorge is planning on a $150,000 increase in sales for next year, with no change in the contribution margin ratio or fixed costs.

a. What is the contribution margin ratio for the year just ended?
b. What is the unit contribution margin for the year just ended?
c. How much will operating income increase if sales increase as planned?

EXERCISE 21–11
Break-even sales and sales to realize operating profit
Objective 3

For the current year ending March 31, Baxter Company expects fixed costs of $492,000, a unit variable cost of $118, and a unit selling price of $200.

a. Compute the anticipated break-even sales (units).
b. Compute the sales (units) required to realize an operating income of $65,600.

EXERCISE 21–12
Break-even sales
Objective 3

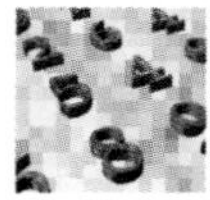

For the past year, Gentry Company had fixed costs of $150,000 and a unit variable cost of $25. All revenues and costs are expected to remain constant for the coming year, except that property taxes are expected to increase by $30,000 during the year. The selling price is $40 per unit.

a. Compute the break-even sales (units) for the past year.
b. Compute the anticipated break-even sales (units) for the coming year.

EXERCISE 21–13
Break-even sales
Objective 3

Currently, the unit selling price of a product is $25, the unit variable cost is $15, and the total fixed costs are $180,000. A proposal is being evaluated to decrease the unit selling price to $24.

a. Compute the current break-even sales (units).
b. Compute the anticipated break-even sales (units), assuming that the unit selling price is decreased and all costs remain constant.

EXERCISE 21–14
Cost-volume-profit chart
Objective 4

For the coming year, Dillard Inc. anticipates fixed costs of $800,000, a unit variable cost of $60, and a unit selling price of $100. The maximum sales within the relevant range are $4,000,000.

a. Construct a cost-volume-profit chart.
b. Estimate the break-even sales (dollars) by using the cost-volume-profit chart constructed in (a).
c. What is the main advantage of presenting the cost-volume-profit analysis in graphic form rather than equation form?

EXERCISE 21–15
Profit-volume chart
Objective 4

Using the data for Dillard Inc. in Exercise 21–14, (a) determine the maximum possible operating loss, (b) compute the maximum possible operating income, (c) construct a profit-volume chart, and (d) estimate the break-even sales (units) by using the profit-volume chart constructed in (c).

EXERCISE 21–16
Break-even chart
Objective 4

Name the following chart, and identify the items represented by the letters a through f.

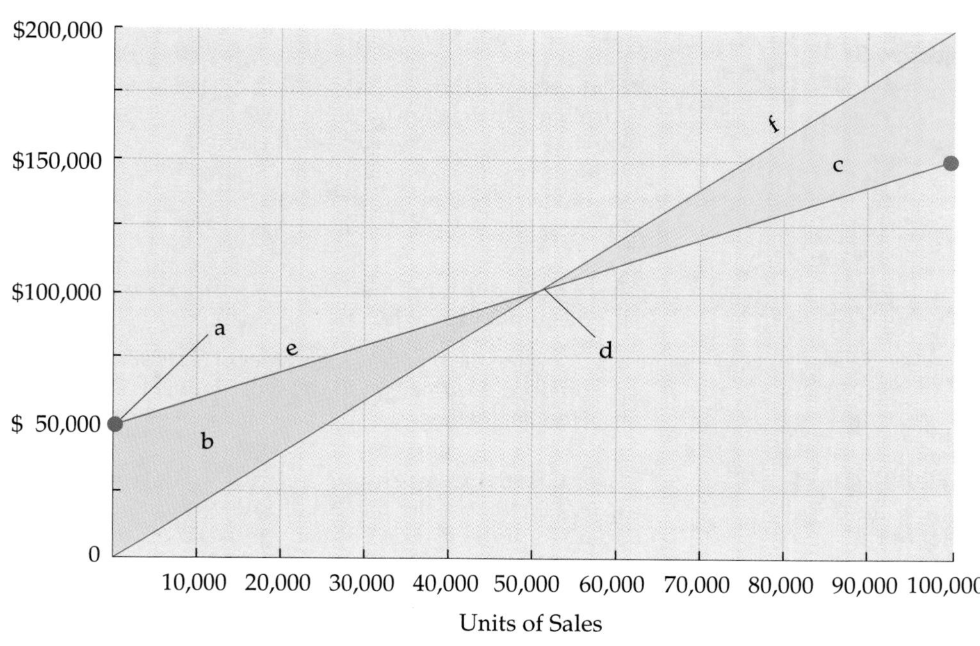

EXERCISE 21–17
Break-even chart
Objective 4

Name the following chart, and identify the items represented by the letters a through f.

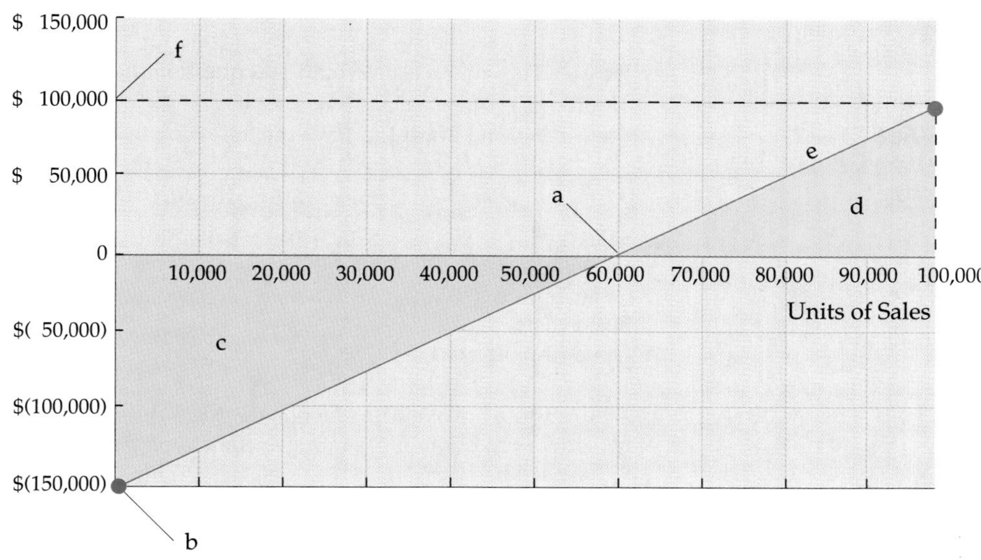

EXERCISE 21–18
Sales mix and break-even sales
Objective 5

Brinkley Inc. manufacturers and sells two products, C and D. The fixed costs are $248,000, and the sales mix is 60% C and 40% D. The unit selling price and the unit variable cost for each product are as follows:

Product	Unit Selling Price	Unit Variable Cost
C	$ 50	$ 30
D	150	100

a. Compute the break-even sales (units) for the overall product, E.
b. How many units of each product, C and D, would be sold at the break-even point?

EXERCISE 21–19
Break-even sales and sales mix for a service company
Objective 5

Blue Sky Airways provides air transportation services between New York and Miami. A single New York to Miami round trip flight has the following operating statistics:

Fuel	$16,500
Flight crew salaries	3,300
Airplane depreciation (straight-line)	13,200
Variable cost per passenger—first class	30
Variable cost per passenger—tourist class	20
Round trip ticket price—first class	440
Round trip ticket price—tourist class	330

It is assumed that the fuel and crew salaries are fixed, regardless of the number of seats sold for the round trip flight.

a. Compute the break-even number of seats sold on a single round trip flight for the overall product. Assume that the overall product is 20% first class and 80% tourist class tickets.
b. How many first class and tourist class seats would be sold at the break-even point?

EXERCISE 21–20
Margin of safety
Objective 6

(a) If Garland Company, with a break-even point at $530,000 of sales, has actual sales of $689,000, what is the margin of safety expressed (1) in dollars and (2) as a percentage of sales? (b) If the margin of safety for Jackson Company was 20%, fixed costs were $400,000, and variable costs were 75% of sales, what was the amount of actual sales (dollars)?

EXERCISE 21–21
Break-even and margin of safety relationships
Objectives 4, 6

At a recent staff meeting, the question of discontinuing Product Q from the product line was being discussed. The chief financial analyst reported the following current monthly data for Product Q:

Units of sales	20,000
Break-even units	23,000
Margin of safety in units	3,000

For what reason would you question the validity of these data?

EXERCISE 21–22
Operating leverage
Objective 6

Brewer Inc. and Ward Inc. have the following operating data:

	Brewer Inc.	Ward Inc.
Sales	$700,000	$400,000
Variable costs	300,000	120,000
Contribution margin	$400,000	$280,000
Fixed costs	80,000	260,000
Operating income	$320,000	$ 20,000

a. Compute the operating leverage for Brewer Inc. and Ward Inc.
b. How much would operating income increase for each company if the sales of each increased by 10%?
c. Why is there a difference in the increase in operating income for the two companies? Explain.

APPENDIX EXERCISE 21–23
Items on variable costing income statement

In the following equations, based on the variable costing income statement, identify the items designated by "X":

a. Net sales – X = Manufacturing margin

b. Manufacturing margin – X = Contribution margin
c. Contribution margin – X = Income from operations

APPENDIX EXERCISE 21–24
Variable costing income statement

On July 31, the end of the first month of operations, Anthony Company prepared the following income statement, based on the absorption costing concept:

Sales (4,400 units)		$72,000
Cost of goods sold:		
Cost of goods manufactured	$45,000	
Less ending inventory (600 units)	5,400	
Cost of goods sold		39,600
Gross profit		$32,400
Selling and administrative expenses		19,200
Income from operations		$13,200

Prepare a variable costing income statement, assuming that the fixed manufacturing costs were $20,000 and the variable selling and administrative expenses were $8,200.

APPENDIX EXERCISE 21–25
Absorption costing income statement

On June 30, the end of the first month of operations, Schott Company prepared the following income statement, based on the variable costing concept:

Sales (18,000 units)		$410,000
Variable cost of goods sold:		
Variable cost of goods manufactured	$200,000	
Less ending inventory (2,000 units)	20,000	
Variable cost of goods sold		180,000
Manufacturing margin		$230,000
Variable selling and administrative expenses		36,000
Contribution margin		$194,000
Fixed costs:		
Fixed manufacturing costs	$ 30,000	
Fixed selling and administrative expenses	21,000	51,000
Income from operations		$143,000

Prepare an absorption costing income statement.

APPENDIX EXERCISE 21–26
Income statements under absorption costing and variable costing

Lancaster Company began operations on July 1 and operated at 100% of capacity during the first month. The following data summarize the results for July:

Sales (12,000 units)		$580,000
Production costs (15,000 units):		
Direct materials	$150,000	
Direct labor	135,000	
Variable factory overhead	45,000	
Fixed factory overhead	75,000	405,000
Selling and administrative expenses:		
Variable selling and administrative expenses	$ 50,000	
Fixed selling and administrative expenses	18,000	68,000

a. Prepare an absorption costing income statement.
b. Prepare a variable costing income statement.
c. What is the reason for the difference in the amount of operating income reported in (a) and (b)?

PROBLEMS SERIES A

PROBLEM 21–1A
Classifying costs
Objective 1

H&B manufactures sofas for distribution to several major retail chains. The following costs are incurred in the production and sale of sofas:

a. Rental costs of warehouse, $10,000 per month.
b. Cartons used to ship sofas.
c. Rent on experimental equipment, $25 for every sofa produced.
d. Salary of production vice-president.
e. Salary of designers.
f. Hourly wages of sewing machine operators.
g. Springs.
h. Fabric for sofa coverings.
i. Consulting fee of $15,000 paid to efficiency specialists.
j. Electricity costs of $.02 per kilowatt-hour.
k. Property taxes on property, plant, and equipment.
l. Legal fees paid to attorneys in defense of the company in a patent infringement suit, $10,000 plus $75 per hour.
m. Straight-line depreciation on factory equipment.
n. Wood for framing the sofas.
o. Insurance premiums on property, plant, and equipment, $5,000 per year plus $20 per $10,000 of insured value over $8,000,000.
p. Foam rubber for cushion fillings.
q. Sewing supplies.
r. Employer's FICA taxes on controller's salary of $75,000.
s. Salesperson's salary, $12,000 plus 5% of the selling price of each sofa sold.
t. Janitorial supplies, $10 for each sofa produced.

Instructions

Classify the preceding costs as either fixed, variable, or mixed. Use the following tabular headings and place an "X" in the appropriate column. Identify each cost by letter in the Cost column.

Cost	*Fixed Cost*	*Variable Cost*	*Mixed Cost*

PROBLEM 21–2A
Break-even sales under present and proposed conditions
Objectives 2, 3

Grayson Inc., operating at full capacity, sold 50,000 units at a price of $65 per unit during 1997. Its income statement for 1997 is as follows:

Sales		$3,250,000
Cost of goods sold		2,000,000
Gross profit		$1,250,000
Operating expenses:		
Selling expenses	$500,000	
Administrative expenses	200,000	
Total operating expenses		700,000
Operating income		$ 550,000

The division of costs between fixed and variable is as follows:

	Fixed	*Variable*
Cost of sales	25%	75%
Selling expenses	30%	70%
Administrative expenses	25%	75%

Management is considering a plant expansion program that will permit an increase of $975,000 in yearly sales. The expansion will increase fixed costs by $240,000, but will not affect the relationship between sales and variable costs.

Instructions

1. Determine for 1997 the total fixed costs and the total variable costs.
2. Determine for 1997 (a) the unit variable cost and (b) the unit contribution margin.
3. Compute the break-even sales (units) for 1997.
4. Compute the break-even sales (units) under the proposed program.
5. Determine the amount of sales (units) that would be necessary under the proposed program to realize the $550,000 of operating income that was earned in 1997.
6. Determine the maximum operating income possible with the expanded plant.
7. If the proposal is accepted and sales remain at the 1997 level, what will the operating income or loss be for 1998?
8. Based on the data given, would you recommend accepting the proposal? Explain.

PROBLEM 21–3A
Break-even sales and cost-volume-profit chart
Objectives 3, 4

For the coming year, Ladd Company anticipates a unit selling price of $20, a unit variable cost of $14, and fixed costs of $84,000.

Instructions

1. Compute the anticipated break-even sales (units).
2. Compute the sales (units) required to realize an operating income of $36,000.
3. Construct a cost-volume-profit chart, assuming maximum sales of 25,000 units within the relevant range.
4. Determine the probable operating income (loss) if sales total 13,500 units.

PROBLEM 21–4A
Break-even sales and cost-volume-profit chart
Objectives 3, 4

Last year, Sierra Company had sales of $600,000, based upon a unit selling price of $800. The variable cost per unit was $480, and fixed costs were $128,000. The maximum sales within Sierra Company's relevant range are 1,000 units. Sierra Company is considering a proposal to spend an additional $32,000 on billboard advertising during the current year in an attempt to increase sales and utilize unused capacity.

Instructions

1. Construct a cost-volume-profit chart indicating the break-even sales for last year.
2. Using the cost-volume-profit chart prepared in (1), determine (a) the operating income for last year and (b) the maximum operating income that could have been realized during the year.
3. Construct a cost-volume-profit chart indicating the break-even sales for the current year, assuming that a noncancellable contract is signed for the additional billboard advertising. No changes are expected in the unit selling price or other costs.
4. Using the cost-volume-profit chart prepared in (3), determine (a) the operating income if sales total 750 units and (b) the maximum operating income that could be realized during the year.

PROBLEM 21–5A
Sales mix and break-even sales
Objective 5

Data related to the expected sales of products P and Q for Gonzalez Inc. for the current year, which are typical of recent years, are as follows:

Product	*Selling Price per Unit*	*Variable Cost per Unit*	*Sales Mix*
P	$150	$110	80%
Q	340	100	20

The estimated fixed costs for the current year are $114,000.

Instructions

1. Determine the estimated units of sales of the overall product necessary to reach the break-even point for the current year.
2. Based on the break-even sales (units) in (1), determine the unit sales of both P and Q for the current year.
3. Assume the sales mix was 20% P and 80% Q. Compare the break-even point with that in (1). Why is it so different?

PROBLEM 21–6A
Contribution margin, break-even sales, cost-volume-profit chart, margin of safety, and operating leverage
Objectives 2, 3, 4, 6

Downey Company expects to maintain the same inventories at the end of 1997 as at the beginning of the year. The total of all production costs for the year is therefore assumed to be equal to the cost of goods sold. With this in mind, the various department heads were asked to submit estimates of the costs for their departments during 1997. A summary report of these estimates is as follows:

	Estimated Fixed Cost	*Estimated Variable Cost (per unit sold)*
Production costs:		
Direct materials	—	$ 32.00
Direct labor	—	40.00
Factory overhead	$200,000	22.90
Selling expenses:		
Sales salaries and commissions	140,000	3.50
Advertising	70,000	—
Travel	44,000	—
Miscellaneous selling expense	14,000	.50
Administrative expenses:		
Office and officers salaries	100,000	—
Supplies	23,000	.60
Miscellaneous administrative expense	9,000	.50
Total	$600,000	$100.00

It is expected that 8,000 units will be sold at a price of $200 a unit. Maximum sales within the relevant range are 15,000 units.

Instructions

1. Prepare an estimated income statement for 1997.
2. What is the expected contribution margin ratio?
3. Determine the break-even sales in units.
4. Construct a cost-volume-profit chart indicating the break-even sales.
5. What is the expected margin of safety?
6. Determine the operating leverage.

PROBLEMS SERIES B

PROBLEM 21–1B
Classifying costs
Objective 1

Helms Inc. manufactures blue jeans for distribution to several major retail chains. The following costs are incurred in the production and sale of blue jeans:

a. Rent on experimental equipment, $25,000 per year.
b. Salary of production vice-president.
c. Blue denim fabric.
d. Salesperson's salary, $12,000 plus 3% of the total sales.
e. Janitorial supplies, $2,000 per month.
f. Consulting fee of $50,000 paid to industry specialist for marketing advice.
g. Legal fees paid to attorneys in defense of the company in a patent infringement suit, $20,000 plus $100 per hour.
h. Brass buttons.
i. Thread.
j. Hourly wages of sewing machine operators.
k. Insurance premiums on property, plant, and equipment, $10,000 per year plus $3 per $10,000 of insured value over $5,000,000.
l. Salary of designers.
m. Leather for patches identifying each jean style.
n. Rental costs of warehouse, $2,000 per month plus $1 per square foot of storage used.
o. Property taxes on property, plant, and equipment.
p. Shipping boxes used to ship orders.
q. Sewing supplies.

r. Electricity costs of $.07 per kilowatt-hour.
s. Straight-line depreciation on sewing machines.
t. Blue dye.

Instructions

Classify the preceding costs as either fixed, variable, or mixed. Use the following tabular headings and place an "X" in the appropriate column. Identify each cost by letter in the cost column.

Cost	*Fixed Cost*	*Variable Cost*	*Mixed Cost*

PROBLEM 21–2B
Break-even sales under present and proposed conditions
Objectives 2, 3

McIntyre Inc., operating at full capacity, sold 100,000 units at a price of $71 per unit during 1997. Its income statement for 1997 is as follows:

Sales		$7,100,000
Cost of goods sold		4,000,000
Gross profit		$3,100,000
Operating expenses:		
Selling expenses	$1,000,000	
Administrative expenses	500,000	
Total operating expenses		1,500,000
Operating income		$1,600,000

The division of costs between fixed and variable is as follows:

	Fixed	*Variable*
Cost of sales	25%	75%
Selling expenses	30%	70%
Administrative expenses	60%	40%

Management is considering a plant expansion program that will permit an increase of $1,420,000 in yearly sales. The expansion will increase fixed costs by $400,000, but will not affect the relationship between sales and variable costs.

Instructions

1. Determine for 1997 the total fixed costs and the total variable costs.
2. Determine for 1997 (a) the unit variable cost and (b) the unit contribution margin.
3. Compute the break-even sales (units) for 1997.
4. Compute the break-even sales (units) under the proposed program.
5. Determine the amount of sales (units) that would be necessary under the proposed program to realize the $1,600,000 of operating income that was earned in 1997.
6. Determine the maximum operating income possible with the expanded plant.
7. If the proposal is accepted and sales remain at the 1997 level, what will the operating income or loss be for 1998?
8. Based on the data given, would you recommend accepting the proposal? Explain.

PROBLEM 21–3B
Break-even sales and cost-volume-profit chart
Objectives 3, 4

For the coming year, Dugan Company anticipates a unit selling price of $120, a unit variable cost of $85, and fixed costs of $420,000.

Instructions

1. Compute the anticipated break-even sales (units).
2. Compute the sales (units) required to realize an operating income of $98,000.
3. Construct a cost-volume-profit chart, assuming maximum sales of 25,000 units within the relevant range.
4. Determine the probable operating income (loss) if sales total 13,500 units.

PROBLEM 21–4B
Break-even sales and cost-volume-profit chart
Objectives 3, 4

Last year, Yee Company had sales of $2,000,000, based upon a unit selling price of $32. The variable cost per unit was $24, and fixed costs were $360,000. The maximum sales within Yee Company's relevant range are 100,000 units. Yee Company is considering a proposal to spend an additional $120,000 on billboard advertising during the current year in an attempt to increase sales and utilize unused capacity.

Instructions

1. Construct a cost-volume-profit chart indicating the break-even sales for last year.
2. Using the cost-volume-profit chart prepared in (1), determine (a) the operating income for last year and (b) the maximum operating income that could have been realized during the year.
3. Construct a cost-volume-profit chart indicating the break-even sales for the current year, assuming that a noncancellable contract is signed for the additional billboard advertising. No changes are expected in the unit selling price or other costs.
4. Using the cost-volume-profit chart prepared in (3), determine (a) the operating income if sales total 62,500 units and (b) the maximum operating income that could be realized during the year.

PROBLEM 21–5B
Sales mix and break-even sales
Objective 5

Data related to the expected sales of products A and B for Girard Inc. for the current year, which are typical of recent years, are as follows:

Product	*Selling Price per Unit*	*Variable Cost per Unit*	*Sales Mix*
A	$420	$280	75%
B	260	200	25

The estimated fixed costs for the current year are $420,000.

Instructions

1. Determine the estimated units of sales of the overall product necessary to reach the break-even point for the current year.
2. Based on the break-even sales (units) in (1), determine the unit sales of both A and B for the current year.
3. Assume the sales mix was 25% A and 75% B. Compare the break-even point with that in (1). Why is it so different?

PROBLEM 21–6B
Contribution margin, break-even sales, cost-volume-profit chart, margin of safety, and operating leverage
Objectives 2, 3, 4, 6

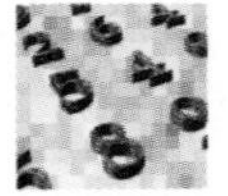

Gemini Company expects to maintain the same inventories at the end of 1997 as at the beginning of the year. The total of all production costs for the year is therefore assumed to be equal to the cost of goods sold. With this in mind, the various department heads were asked to submit estimates of the costs for their departments during 1997. A summary report of these estimates is as follows:

	Estimated Fixed Cost	*Estimated Variable Cost (per unit sold)*
Production costs:		
Direct materials	—	$2.10
Direct labor	—	2.50
Factory overhead	$ 75,000	1.10
Selling expenses:		
Sales salaries and commissions	25,000	.15
Advertising	20,000	—
Travel	6,500	—
Miscellaneous selling expense	1,350	.06
Administrative expenses:		
Office and officers salaries	20,000	—
Supplies	1,650	.07
Miscellaneous administrative expense	500	.02
Total	$150,000	$6.00

It is expected that 160,000 units will be sold at a price of $7.50 a unit. Maximum sales within the relevant range are 200,000 units.

Instructions

1. Prepare an estimated income statement for 1997.
2. What is the expected contribution margin ratio?
3. Determine the break-even sales in units.
4. Construct a cost-volume-profit chart indicating the break-even sales.
5. What is the expected margin of safety?
6. Determine the operating leverage. Round to one decimal place.

CASES

CASE 21–1
Real Assets Inc.
Break-even disclosures

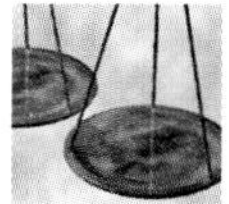

Howard Skinner is a financial consultant to Real Assets Inc., a real estate syndicate. Real Assets Inc. finances and develops commercial real estate (office buildings). The completed projects are then sold as limited partnership interests to individual investors. The syndicate makes a profit on the sale of these partnership interests. Howard provides financial information for the offering prospectus, which is a document that provides the financial and legal details of the limited partnership offerings. In one of the projects, the bank has financed the construction of a commercial office building at a rate of 6% for the first 4 years, after which time the rate jumps to 10% for the remaining 26 years of the mortgage. The interest costs are one of the major ongoing costs of a real estate project. Howard has reported prominently in the prospectus that the break-even occupancy for the first four years is 60%. This is the amount of office space that must be leased to cover the interest and general upkeep costs over the first four years. The 60% break-even is very low and thus communicates a low risk to potential investors. Howard uses the 60% break-even rate as a major marketing tool in selling the limited partnership interests. Deep in the fine print of the prospectus, there is additional information that would allow an astute investor to determine that the break-even occupancy will jump to 85% after the fourth year because of the contracted increase in the mortgage interest rate. Howard believes prospective investors are adequately informed as to the risk of the investment.

Comment on the ethical considerations of this situation.

CASE 21–2
U.S. Airlines
Break-even sales, contribution margin

"For a student, a grade of 65 percent is nothing to write home about. But for the airline . . . [industry], filling 65 percent of the seats . . . is the difference between profit and loss. For [this] hard-pressed [industry], simply breaking even this year would seem like a moral victory. . .

The [economy] might be just strong enough to sustain all the carriers on a cash basis, but not strong enough to bring any significant profitability to the industry. . . For the airlines still flying, the emphasis will be on trying to consolidate routes and raise ticket prices. . ."

Do you think that the strategy to consolidate routes and raise ticket prices is reasonable? What would make this strategy succeed or fail? Why?

Source: Edwin McDowell, "Empty Seats, Empty Beds, Empty Pockets," *New York Times*, January 6, 1992, p. C3.

CASE 21–3
Creative Arts Company
Managerial analysis

Creative Arts Company has finished a new VCR movie offering, *Keeping in Balance*. Management is now considering its marketing strategies. The following information is available:

Anticipated sales price per unit	$25
Variable cost per unit*	$5
Anticipated volume	750,000
Movie production costs	$10,000,000
Anticipated advertising	$5,000,000

*The cost of the VCR tape, packaging, and copying costs.

Two managers, Ann Wilson and John Harris, had the following discussion of ways to increase the profitability of this new offering.

Ann: I think we need to think of some way to increase our profitability. Do you have any ideas?

John: Well, I think the best strategy would be to become aggressive on price.

Ann: How aggressive?

John: If we drop the price to $20 per unit and maintain our advertising budget at $5,000,000, I think we will generate sales of 1,600,000 units.

Ann: I think that's the wrong way to go. You're giving too much up on price. Instead, I think we need to follow an aggressive advertising strategy.

John: How aggressive?

Ann: If we increase our advertising to a total of $8,000,000, we should be able to increase sales volume to 1,500,000 units without any change in price.

John: I don't think that's reasonable. We'll never cover the increased advertising costs.

Which strategy is best: Do nothing? Follow the advice of Ann Wilson? Or follow John Harris's strategy?

CASE 21–4
Shirt Prints
Variable costs and activity bases in decision making

The owner of Shirt Prints, a T-shirt printing company, is planning direct labor needs for the upcoming year. The owner has provided you with the following information for next year's plans:

	One Color	*Two Color*	*Three Color*	*Four Color*	*Total*
Number of T-shirts	300	800	900	1,000	3,000

Each color on the T-shirt must be printed one at a time. Thus, for example, a four-color T-shirt will require a T-shirt to be run through the silk screen operation four separate times. The total production volume *last* year was 2,000 T-shirts, as shown below:

	One Color	*Two Color*	*Three Color*	*Total*
Number of T-shirts	300	800	900	2,000

As you can see, the four-color T-shirt is a new product offering for the upcoming year. The owner believes that the expected 1,000-unit increase in volume from last year means that direct labor expenses should increase by 50% (1,000/2,000).

What do you think?

CASE 21–5
Wolfe Company
Variable costs and activity bases in decision making

Sales volume has been dropping at Wolfe Company. During this time, however, the Shipping Department manager has been under severe financial constraints. The manager knows that most of the Shipping Department's effort is related to pulling inventory from the warehouse for each order and performing the paperwork. The paperwork involves preparing shipping documents for each order. Thus, the pulling and paperwork effort associated with each sales order is essentially the same, regardless of the size of the order. The Shipping Department manager has discussed the financial situation with senior management. Senior management has responded by pointing out that sales volume has been dropping, so that the amount of work in the Shipping Department should be dropping. Thus, senior management told the Shipping Department manager that costs should be decreasing in the department.

The Shipping Department manager prepared the following information:

Month	*Sales Volume*	*Number of Customer Orders*	*Sales Volume per Order*
January	$95,000	500	$190
February	93,600	520	180
March	90,100	530	170
April	90,000	600	150
May	89,900	620	145
June	85,000	625	136
July	81,900	630	130
August	80,000	640	125

Given this information, how would you respond to senior management?

CASE 21–6
Woodley Company
Break-even sales

Woodley Company manufactures Product X, which sold for $72 per unit in 1997. For the past several years, sales and operating income have been declining. On sales of 11,000 units in 1996, the company operated near the break-even point and used only 40% of its productive capacity. Walter Woodley, your father-in-law, is considering several proposals to reverse the trend of declining sales and operating income, and to more fully use production facilities. One proposal under consideration is to reduce the unit selling price to $60.

Your father-in-law has asked you to aid him in assessing the proposal to reduce the sales price by $12. For this purpose, he provided the following summary of the estimated fixed and variable costs for 1997, which are unchanged from 1996:

Variable costs:	
Production costs	$24.00 per unit
Selling expenses	12.50 per unit
Administrative expenses	8.50 per unit
Fixed costs:	
Production costs	$115,000
Selling expenses	75,000
Administrative expenses	80,000

1. Determine the break-even sales for 1997 in units, assuming (a) no change in sales price and (b) the proposed sales price.
2. How much additional sales are necessary for Woodley Company to break even in 1997 under the proposal?
3. Determine the operating income for 1997, assuming (a) no change in sales price and volume from 1996 and (b) the new sales price and no change in volume from 1996.
4. Determine the maximum operating income for 1997, assuming the proposed sales price.
5. Briefly list factors that you would discuss with your father-in-law in evaluating the proposal.

ANSWERS TO SELF-EXAMINATION QUESTIONS

1. **B** Variable costs vary in total in direct proportion to changes in the level of activity (answer B). Costs that vary on a per-unit basis as the level of activity changes (answer A) or remain constant in total dollar amount as the level of activity changes (answer C), or both (answer D), are fixed costs.
2. **D** The contribution margin ratio indicates the percentage of each sales dollar available to cover the fixed costs and provide operating income and is determined as follows:

$$\text{Contribution margin ratio} = \frac{\text{Sales} - \text{Variable costs}}{\text{Sales}}$$

$$\text{Contribution margin ratio} = \frac{\$500{,}000 - \$200{,}000}{\$500{,}000} = 60\%$$

3. **D** The break-even sales of 40,000 units (answer D) is computed as follows:

$$\text{Break-even sales (units)} = \frac{\text{Fixed costs}}{\text{Unit contribution margin}}$$

$$\text{Break-even sales (units)} = \frac{\$160{,}000}{\$4} = 40{,}000 \text{ units}$$

4. **D** Sales of 45,000 units are required to realize an operating income of $20,000, computed as follows:

$$\text{Sales (units)} = \frac{\text{Fixed costs} + \text{Target profit}}{\text{Unit contribution margin}}$$

$$\text{Sales (units)} = \frac{\$160{,}000 + \$20{,}000}{\$4} = 45{,}000 \text{ units}$$

5. **C** The operating leverage is 1.8, computed as follows:

$$\text{Operating leverage} = \frac{\text{Contribution margin}}{\text{Operating income}}$$

$$\text{Operating leverage} = \frac{\$360{,}000}{\$200{,}000} = 1.8$$

22 Budgeting

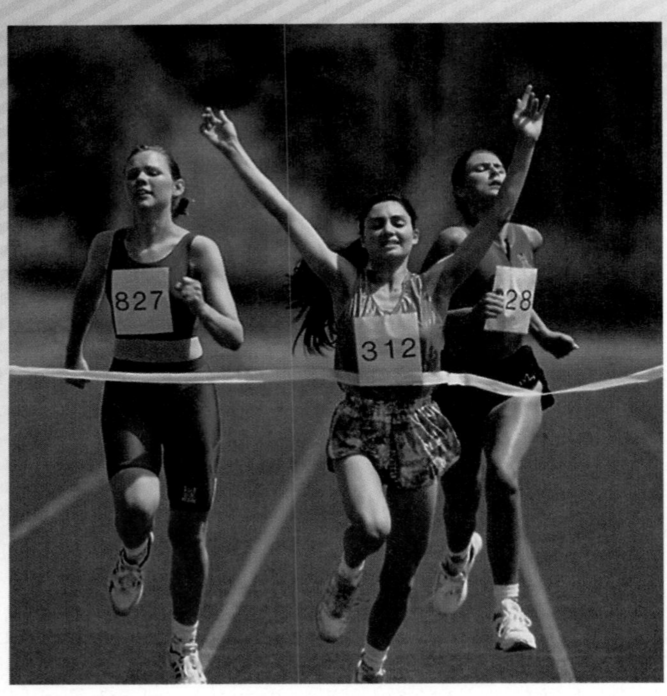

YOU AND ACCOUNTING

If you are a runner, you probably set goals for yourself. You may also have goals for other areas of your life. To achieve some of these goals, it is sometimes necessary to plan for future expenses. For example, you may consider taking a part-time job to save money for school expenses for the coming school year. How much money would you need to earn and save in order to provide for these expenses? One way to answer this question would be to estimate next year's expenses by using a budget. For example, a budget would estimate the expenses associated with school, such as tuition, fees, and books. In addition, you would have expenses for day-to-day living, such as rent, food, and clothing. You might also have expenses for travel and entertainment. Once the school year is underway, you can use the budget as a tool for guiding your spending priorities during the year.

The budget is used in businesses in much the same way as it can be used in personal life. For example, **Chrysler Corporation** uses budgeting to determine the number of cars to be produced, number of shifts to operate, number of employees to be employed, and amount of material to be purchased for the upcoming year. The budget provides the company a "game plan" for the year. In this chapter, you will see how the budget can be used to plan and control expenditures.

After studying this chapter, you should be able to:

Objective 1
Describe budgeting, its objectives, and its impact on human behavior.

Objective 2
Describe the basic elements of the budget process, the two major types of budgeting, and the use of computers in budgeting.

Objective 3
Describe the master budget for a manufacturing business.

Objective 4
Prepare the basic income statement budgets for a manufacturing business.

Objective 5
Prepare balance sheet budgets for a manufacturing business.

Nature and Objectives of Budgeting

Objective 1
Describe budgeting, its objectives, and its impact on human behavior.

If you were to go on a driving vacation across the country, you might wish to plan the trip with the aid of a road map. The road map would lay out your route across the country, identify stopping opportunities, and minimize your chances of getting lost. In the same way, a **budget** charts a course of future action for a business by outlining the plans of the business in financial terms. Like the road map, the budget can help a company successfully navigate through the year and help avoid unwelcome outcomes.

Although budgets are commonly associated with profit-making businesses, they also play an important role in operating most units of government. For example, budgets are important in managing rural school districts and small villages as well as agencies of the federal government. Budgets are also important for managing the operations of churches, hospitals, and other nonprofit institutions. Individuals and families also use budgeting techniques in managing their financial resources. In this chapter, we discuss the principles of budgeting in the context of a manufacturing business organized for profit.

OBJECTIVES OF BUDGETING

Budgeting involves (1) establishing specific goals for future operations, (2) executing plans to achieve the goals, and (3) periodically comparing actual results with the goals. These goals include both the overall goals of the business as well as the specific goals for the individual units within the business. Establishing specific goals for future operations is part of the *planning* function of management, while executing actions to meet the goals is the *directing* function of management. Periodically comparing actual results with these goals encompasses the *control* function of management.

Planning

As in most activities in life, a set of goals is often necessary to guide and focus individual and group actions. For example, students set academic goals, athletes set athletic goals, employees set career goals, and businesses set financial goals. These goals, in turn, motivate individuals and groups to perform at high levels. In the same way, budgeting supports the planning process by requiring all organizational units to establish their goals for the upcoming period. The process is similar to a football team establishing team goals at the beginning of the season. The process of establishing goals through the budget increases the motivation of managers and employees by providing an agreed-upon set of expectations. For example, Florida Power and Light (FP&L), an electric utility, announced plans to reduce costs by 8% of their total budget in order to maintain their target profitability. Using the budget to communicate these expectations throughout the organization helped FP&L to reach its target. Without the budget establishing this clear expectation, these results would have been very difficult to achieve.

Planning not only motivates employees to attain goals, but also improves overall decision making. During the planning phase of the budget process, all viewpoints are considered, options identified, and cost reduction opportunities calculated. This effort leads to better decision making for the organization. As a result, the budget process may unveil opportunities or expose threats that were not widely known prior to the budget planning process. For example, the financial planning process helped General Motors identify the high costs associated with its far-flung parts operations. As a result, GM decided to sell over 45 lines of businesses (radiator caps, vacuum pumps, electric motors, etc.) in order to focus on the core auto-making business.

Directing

Once the budget plans are in place, they can be used to direct and coordinate operations during the period in order to achieve the stated goals. A student's goal to receive an "A" in a course would result in directing and coordinating certain activities, such as reading the book, completing assignments, participating in class, and studying for exams. Such actions are fairly easy to direct and coordinate. A business, however, is much more complex and requires more formal direction and coordination. The budget provides one way to direct and coordinate a variety of activities to achieve stated goals. This is accomplished by preparing the budget for the complete organization and all units of the organization, such as divisions, plants, and departments. The budgetary units of an organization are called **responsibility centers.** Each responsibility center is led by a manager who has both the authority over and responsibility for the unit's performance.

If there is a change in the external environment, the budget process can also be used by unit managers to readjust the operations. For example, SKI Ltd. uses weather information to plan expenditures at its Killington and Mt. Snow ski resorts in Vermont. When the weather is forecasted to turn cold and dry, the company increases expenditures in snow-making activities and adds to the staff in order to serve a greater number of skiers.

Controlling

Once a period of time has passed, the actual performance of the operation can be compared against the planned goals. The benefit of this is to provide prompt feedback to employees about their performance relative to the goal. Such feedback can be used by employees, if necessary, to adjust their activities in the future. For example, a salesperson may be given a quota to achieve $100,000 in sales for the period. If the actual sales are only $75,000, then feedback about this underperformance can be used by the salesperson to change sales tactics in order to improve future sales. Feedback is not only helpful to individuals, but can also redirect a complete organization. For example, Euro Disney, the company that operates Euro Disneyland theme park outside of Paris, France, estimated 11 million visitors per year when it first opened, but drew only 9.6 million the first year. As a result, the theme park lost money. Management responded to this feedback with new budget plans that reflected lower ticket prices (from $38 to $30), lower hotel prices, 900 fewer jobs, and six new attractions. As a result of implementing these plans, Euro Disney began earning an operating profit.

Comparing actual results to the plan also helps prevent unplanned expenditures. Businesses have limited resources, so the budget encourages employees to establish their spending priorities. For example, departments in universities have budgets to support faculty travel to conferences and meetings. The travel budget communicates to the faculty the upper limit on travel. Often, desired travel exceeds the budget. Thus, the budget requires the faculty to prioritize travel-related opportunities. In the next chapter, we will discuss using the budget to compare actual costs with budgeted costs in greater detail.

USING ACCOUNTING TO UNDERSTAND BUSINESS

Georgia Tech introduced what it terms a "responsibility center approach" (RCA) to financial management in the athletic department. The approach requires each sport to be responsible for its own budgeted revenues and outlays. Thus, for example, budgeted outlays for operating costs, scholarships, staff salaries, and recruiting were compared to budgeted revenues to determine anticipated surplus and deficits in each sport. The new RCA provides coaches with incentives to control costs and seek revenue possibilities. For example, under the new approach, the baseball program took advantage of revenue-generating opportunities by developing the "Grand Slam Club," leasing scoreboard advertising, and increasing baseball yearbook advertising. These extra revenues could be used by the baseball program to support additional expenditures for promotions, recruiting, and operating costs.

Source: C. David Strupeck, Ken Milani, and James E. Murphy, "Financial Management at Georgia Tech," *Management Accounting,* February 1993, pp. 58–63.

HUMAN BEHAVIOR AND BUDGETING

In the budgeting process, business, team, and individual goals are established. Human behavior problems can arise if (1) the budget goal is unachievable (too tight), (2) the budget goal is very easy to achieve (too loose), or (3) the budget goals established for the business conflict with the objectives of employees (goal conflict). Each of these problems is discussed in the following paragraphs.

Setting Budget Goals Too Tightly

Sometimes people become discouraged if performance expectations are set too high. For example, would you be inspired or discouraged by a guitar instructor expecting you to play like Eric Clapton after only a few lessons? You'd probably be discouraged. The same kinds of human behavior problems can develop in businesses if employees view budget goals as unrealistic or unachievable. In such a case, employees may become discouraged as well as uncommitted to achieving the goals. As a result, the budget becomes less effective as a tool for planning and controlling operations. On the other hand, goals set within a range that employees consider attainable are likely to inspire employees to achieve the goals. Therefore, it is important that employees (managers and non-managers) be involved in establishing budget estimates.

Involving all employees fosters cooperation both within and among departments. It also heightens awareness of each department's importance to the overall objectives of the company. There is also evidence that employees view budgeting more positively when they have an opportunity to participate in the budget-setting process. This is because employees with a greater sense of control over the budget process will have a greater behavioral stake in the outcomes of the operation. In such an environment, the budget is a planning tool that will favorably affect human behavior and increase the possibility of achieving the goals.

Setting Budget Goals Too Loosely

Although it's desirable to establish attainable goals, it is undesirable to plan lower goals than may be possible. Such budget "padding" is termed **budgetary slack.** An example of budgetary slack is budgeting employees that aren't needed. Employees may plan slack in the budget in order to provide a "cushion" for unexpected events or improve the appearance of performance. Budgetary slack can be avoided if lower and mid-level managers are required to support all of their spending requirements with specific operational plans.

Budgetary slack may cause the company to become less competitive than possible because employees are not motivated to use resources efficiently. In addition, slack budgets can cause employees to develop a "spend it or lose it" mentality. This often occurs at the end of the budget period when actual spending is much less than the budget. Employees may attempt to quickly, and potentially wastefully, spend the remaining budget (purchase equipment, hire consultants, purchase supplies) in order to avoid having the budget cut next period.

Setting Conflicting Budget Goals

Goal conflict occurs when individual objectives are in conflict with business objectives. Goal conflict can cause employees to pursue their own self-interests to the detriment of the overall organization's objectives. To illustrate, the manager of the Transportation Department of one company was instructed to stay within the department's budget. To meet the budget goal, the manager stopped transporting all shipments for the last two weeks of the period. Though the Transportation Department budget was met, customers were upset because they did not receive their orders. As a result, many customers stopped doing business with the company or demanded price discounts that far exceeded the additional transportation costs that should have been spent. In this example, the budget pressure caused the Transportation Department manager to make a decision that appeared correct from the department's perspective, but was harmful from an organizational perspective. Goal conflict can be avoided if budget goals are carefully designed for consistency across all areas of the organization.

Budgeting Systems

Objective 2
Describe the basic elements of the budget process, the two major types of budgeting, and the use of computers in budgeting.

The details of budgeting systems vary among businesses. They are affected by such factors as the type and complexity of operations, the organizational structure of the business, and management's philosophy. Differences among budgeting systems are even more significant among different types of businesses, such as manufacturers and service businesses. The details of a budgeting system used by an automobile manufacturer such as Ford would obviously differ from a service company such as American Airlines. However, the basic budgeting concepts illustrated in the following paragraphs apply to all types of businesses and organizations.

The budgetary period for operating activities normally includes the fiscal year of a business. A year is short enough to make dependable estimates of future operations, yet long enough to view the future in a broad context. However, to achieve effective control, the annual budgets are usually subdivided into shorter time periods, such as quarters of the year, months, or weeks.

A variation of fiscal-year budgeting, called continuous budgeting, maintains a twelve-month projection into the future. The twelve-month budget is continually revised by removing the data for the period just ended and adding estimated budget data for the same period next year.

Developing budgets for the next fiscal year usually begins several months prior to the end of the current year. The responsibility for initially developing the budget is normally assigned to a committee. Such a committee often consists of the budget director and such high-level executives as the controller, treasurer, the production manager, and the sales manager. Once the budget has been approved, the budget process is often monitored and summarized by the Accounting Department, under the oversight of the budget committee.

There are several methods of developing budget estimates. One method, termed zero-based budgeting, requires all levels of management to start from zero and estimate sales, production, and other operating data as though operations are being started for the first time. This approach has the benefit of taking a "clean slate" view of the operations. A more common approach is to start with last year's budget and revise it for actual results and expected changes for the coming year. Two major budgets using this approach are the static budget and the flexible budget.

USING ACCOUNTING TO UNDERSTAND BUSINESS

Lockheed Martin Corporation used a zero-based budgeting approach, called risk-based budgeting, to identify cost savings during the downsizing of some of its military and weapons programs. Martin Marietta divided its operations into core and supplemental activities. Core activities were spared from deep budget cuts, but supplemental activities were evaluated for possible budget reductions.

STATIC BUDGET

A static budget shows the expected results of a responsibility center for only one activity level. Once the budget has been determined, it is not changed, even if the underlying activity changes. Static budgeting is used by many service companies and in many administrative and support functions of manufacturing companies, such as purchasing, engineering, and information services. For example, the Engineering Department manager for Micro Motors Inc. prepared the static budget shown in Exhibit 1, based on the amount of staff time, supplies, travel, and training expected to be required for the upcoming year.

Exhibit 1
Static Budget

Micro Motors Inc.
Engineering Department Budget
For the Year Ending December 31, 1997

Salaries	$435,000
Supplies	45,000
Travel	85,000
Training	35,000
Total	$600,000

A disadvantage of static budgets is that they do not show possible changes in underlying activity levels. For example, assume that the actual amounts spent by the Engineering Department of Micro Motors Inc. totaled $840,000, which is $240,000 or 40% ($240,000 ÷ $600,000) more than budgeted. Is this good news or bad news? At first you might think that this is a negative result. However, this conclusion may not be valid, since performance relative to static budget goals may be difficult to interpret. To illustrate, assume that the engineering manager constructed the budget based on plans to design five new products during the year. However, ten products were actually designed. Ten product designs represent twice as much work as expected. Should the additional $240,000 in spending in excess of budget be considered "bad news" under this scenario? Probably not. The Engineering Department provided 100% more output for only 40% additional cost.

FLEXIBLE BUDGET

Unlike static budgets, **flexible budgets** show the expected results of a responsibility center for several activity levels. The flexible budget is, in effect, a series of static budgets for different levels of activity. Such budgets are especially useful in estimating and controlling factory costs and operating expenses. Exhibit 2 is a flexible budget for the Assembly Department of Colter Manufacturing Company.

Exhibit 2
Flexible Budget

Colter Manufacturing Company
Assembly Department Budget
For the Month Ending July 31, 1997

Units of production	*8,000*	*9,000*	*10,000*
Variable cost:			
Direct labor ($5 per unit)	$40,000	$45,000	$50,000
Electric power ($0.50 per unit)	4,000	4,500	5,000
Total variable cost	$44,000	$49,500	$55,000
Fixed cost:			
Electric power	$ 1,000	$ 1,000	$ 1,000
Supervisor salaries	15,000	15,000	15,000
Total fixed cost	$16,000	$16,000	$16,000
Total department costs	$60,000	$65,500	$71,000

When constructing a flexible budget, we first identify the relevant activity levels to be budgeted. In Exhibit 2, these are 8,000, 9,000, and 10,000 units of production. Alternative activity bases, such as machine hours or direct labor hours, may be used in measuring the volume of activity. Second, we identify the fixed and variable cost components of the costs being budgeted. For example, in Exhibit 2 the electric power cost is separated between its fixed cost ($1,000 per month) and variable cost ($0.50 per unit). Lastly, we prepare the budget for each activity level by multiplying the variable cost per unit by the activity level and then adding the monthly fixed cost.

With a flexible budget, the department manager can be evaluated by comparing actual expenses to the budgeted amount for actual activity. For example, if Colter Manufacturing Company's Assembly Department actually spent $70,000 to produce 10,000 units, the manager would be considered under budget by $1,000 ($71,000 – $70,000). However, if the Assembly Department actually spent $70,000 to produce 9,000 units, the manager would be considered over budget by $4,500 ($70,000 – $65,500).

COMPUTERIZED BUDGETING SYSTEMS

In developing budgets, many firms use computerized budgeting systems. Such systems can not only speed up the budgeting process, but they can also reduce the cost of budget preparation. This is especially true when large quantities of data need to be processed. Computers are particularly useful in continuous budgeting. Reports that compare actual results with amounts budgeted can also be prepared on a timely basis through the use of computerized systems.

Managers can mathematically represent the operating and budget relationships on a computer spreadsheet or simulation model. By using computer simulation models, the impact of various operating alternatives on the budget can be assessed. For example, the impact of a proposed change in direct labor wage rates can be assessed and the budget revised to reflect the new rates. Likewise, the effects on the budget of a proposal to add a new product line can be quickly determined.

A common objective of using computer-based budgeting is to link all the budgets of the organization together. In the next section we will illustrate how a company links budgets together to develop a complete plan for an organization.

USING ACCOUNTING TO UNDERSTAND BUSINESS

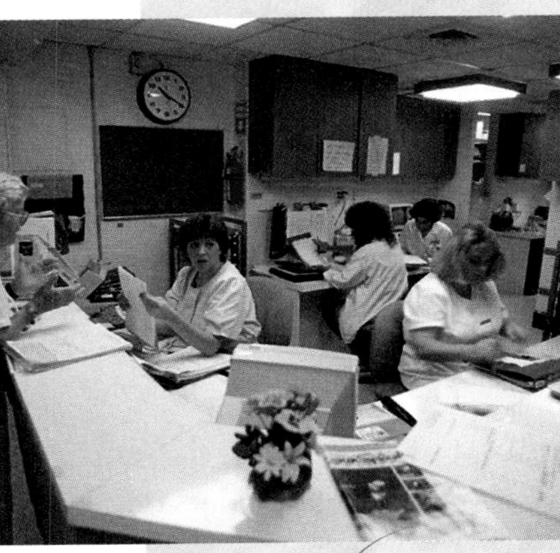

Many hospitals use simulations to plan the optimal number of nurses to be used on the patient floors. These simulations use a measure termed "relative value units." A relative value unit is a measure of effort related to a nursing activity, such as feeding the patient or verifying vital signs. The total relative value units for a floor can be determined from a computer simulation, based on the number of patients on the floor and the severity of their illnesses. Naturally, the more patients and the more severe their illnesses, the higher the total relative value units. The total relative units can then be translated into the number of nurses required to provide the effort estimated by the simulation.

Master Budget

Objective 3
Describe the master budget for a manufacturing business.

Manufacturing operations require a series of budgets that are linked together in a **master budget.** The major parts of the master budget are as follows:

Budgeted income statement
Sales budget
Cost of goods sold budget
Production budget
Direct materials purchases budget
Direct labor cost budget
Factory overhead cost budget
Operating expenses budget

Budgeted balance sheet
Cash budget
Capital expenditures budget

Exhibit 3 shows the relationship among the income statement budgets. The budget process is started by estimating sales. The sales information is then provided to the various administrative units for estimating the production and operating expense budgets. The production budgets are used to prepare the direct materials purchases, direct labor cost, and factory overhead cost budgets. These three budgets are used to develop the cost of goods sold budget. Once these budgets have been completed, the budgeted income statement can be prepared.

Exhibit 3
Income Statement Budgets

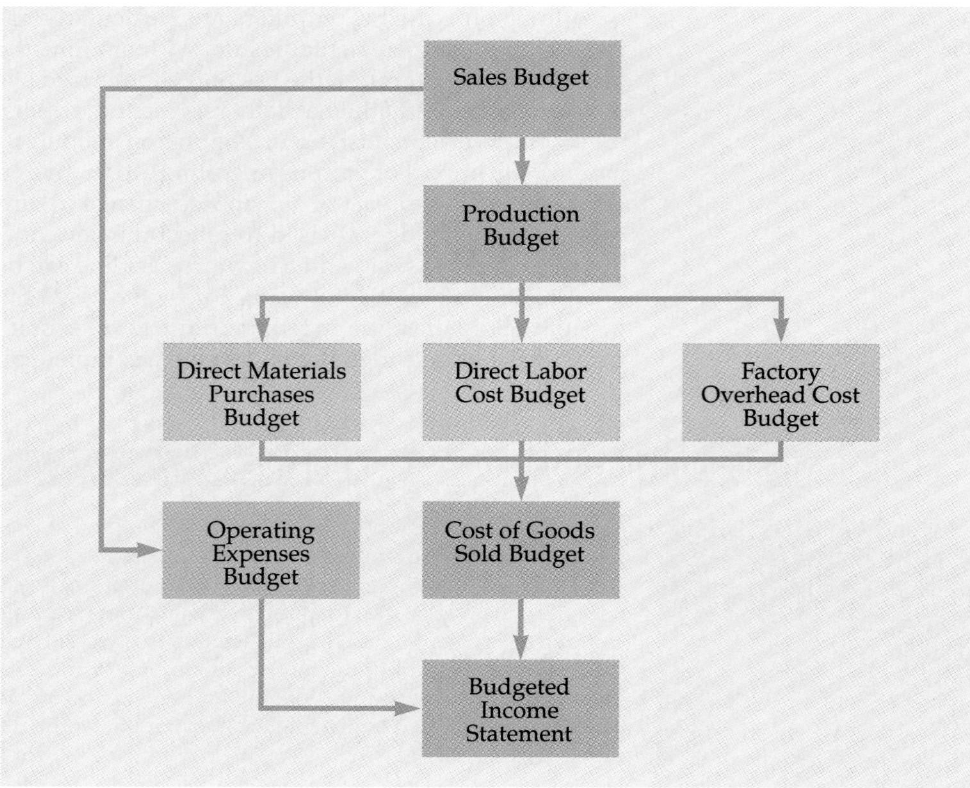

After the budgeted income statement has been developed, the budgeted balance sheet can be prepared. Two major budgets comprising the budgeted balance sheet are the cash budget and the capital expenditures budget.

Income Statement Budgets

Objective 4
Prepare the basic income statement budgets for a manufacturing business.

In the following sections, we will illustrate the major elements of the income statement budget. We will use a small manufacturing business, Sanchez Inc.

SALES BUDGET

The sales budget normally indicates for each product (1) the quantity of estimated sales and (2) the expected unit selling price. These data are often classified by regions or by sales representatives.

In estimating the quantity of sales for each product, past sales volumes are often used as a starting point. These amounts are revised for factors expected to affect future sales. Such factors include a backlog of unfilled sales orders, planned advertising and promotion, expected industry and general economic conditions, productive capacity, projected pricing policy, and findings of market research studies. Statistical analysis can be used in this process to evaluate the effects of these factors on past sales volume. Such analysis can provide a mathematical association between past sales and the several variables expected to affect future sales.

Once an estimate of sales volume is obtained, the expected sales revenue can then be determined by multiplying the volume by the expected unit sales price. Exhibit 4 is the sales budget for Sanchez Inc.

Exhibit 4
Sales Budget

Sanchez Inc. Sales Budget For the Year Ending December 31, 1997			
Product and Region	**Unit Sales Volume**	**Unit Selling Price**	**Total Sales**
Product X:			
Region A	208,000	$ 9.90	$2,059,200
Region B	162,000	9.90	1,603,800
Region C	158,000	9.90	1,564,200
Total	528,000		$5,227,200
Product Y:			
Region A	111,600	$16.50	$1,841,400
Region B	78,800	16.50	1,300,200
Region C	89,600	16.50	1,478,400
Total	280,000		$4,620,000
Total revenue from sales			$9,847,200

For control purposes, management can use comparisons between actual sales and budgeted sales by product, region, or sales representative. Management would investigate any significant differences and take possible corrective actions.

PRODUCTION BUDGET

Production should be carefully coordinated with the sales budget to ensure that production and sales are kept in balance during the period. The number of units to be manufactured to meet budgeted sales and inventory needs for each product is set forth in the production budget. The budgeted volume of production is determined as follows:

Expected units of sales
\+ **Desired units in ending inventory**
− **Estimated units in beginning inventory**
Total units to be produced

Exhibit 5 is the production budget for Sanchez Inc.

Exhibit 5
Production Budget

Sanchez Inc. Production Budget For the Year Ending December 31, 1997		
	Units	
	Product X	Product Y
Sales	528,000	280,000
Plus desired ending inventory, December 31, 1997	80,000	60,000
Total	608,000	340,000
Less estimated beginning inventory, January 1, 1997	88,000	48,000
Total production	520,000	292,000

DIRECT MATERIALS PURCHASES BUDGET

The production budget provides the starting point for determining the estimated quantities of direct materials to be purchased. Multiplying these quantities, determined as shown here, by the expected unit purchase price determines the total cost of direct materials to be purchased.

Materials needed for production
\+ **Desired ending materials inventory**
– **Estimated beginning materials inventory**
Direct materials to be purchased

In Sanchez Inc.'s production operations, Materials A and C are required for Product X, and Materials A, B, and C are required for Product Y. The quantities of direct materials expected to be used for each unit of product are as follows:

Product X:
Material A: .75 pound per unit
Material C: 1.00 pound per unit
Product Y:
Material A: .50 pound per unit
Material B: 1.00 pound per unit
Material C: 1.10 pounds per unit

Based on these requirements and the production budget, the direct materials purchases budget is prepared. As shown in the budget in Exhibit 6, for Sanchez Inc. to produce 520,000 units of Product X, 390,000 pounds (520,000 units × .75 lb. per unit) of Material A are needed. Likewise, to produce 292,000 units of Product Y, 146,000 pounds (292,000 units × .50 lb. per unit) of Material A are needed. We can compute the requirements for Material B and Material C in a similar manner. Then adding the desired ending inventory for each material and deducting the estimated beginning inventory arrives at the amount of each material to be purchased. Multiplying these amounts by the estimated cost per pound yields the total materials purchase cost.

Exhibit 6
Direct Materials Purchases Budget

Sanchez Inc.
Direct Materials Purchases Budget
For the Year Ending December 31, 1997

	Direct Materials			
	A	B	C	Total
Units required for production:				
Product X (Note A)	390,000 lbs.	—	520,000 lbs.	
Product Y (Note B)	146,000	292,000 lbs.	321,200	
Plus desired inventory,				
December 31, 1997	80,000	40,000	120,000	
Total	616,000 lbs.	332,000 lbs.	961,200 lbs.	
Less estimated inventory,				
Jan. 1, 1997	80,000	44,000	141,200	
Total units to be purchased	536,000 lbs.	288,000 lbs.	820,000 lbs.	
Unit price	× $.60	× $1.70	× $1.00	
Total direct materials purchases	$321,600	$489,600	$820,000	$1,631,200

Note A: Material A: 520,000 units × .75 lb. per unit = 390,000 lbs.
Material C: 520,000 units × 1 lb. per unit = 520,000 lbs.

Note B: Material A: 292,000 units × .5 lb. per unit = 146,000 lbs.
Material B: 292,000 units × 1 lb. per unit = 292,000 lbs.
Material C: 292,000 units × 1.1 lb. per unit = 321,200 lbs.

The direct materials purchases budget is useful for assisting management in maintaining inventory levels within reasonable limits. For this purpose, the timing of the direct materials purchases should be closely coordinated between the purchasing and production departments.

DIRECT LABOR COST BUDGET

The production budget also provides the starting point for preparing the direct labor cost budget. For Sanchez Inc., the labor requirements for each unit of product are estimated as follows:

Product X:
- Department 1: .1 hour per unit
- Department 2: .08 hour per unit

Product Y:
- Department 1: .1 hour per unit
- Department 2: .16 hour per unit

Based on the preceding labor requirements and the production budget, Sanchez Inc. prepares the direct labor budget. As shown in the budget in Exhibit 7, for Sanchez Inc. to produce 520,000 units of Product X, 52,000 hours (520,000 units × .1 hour per unit) of labor in Department 1 are required. Likewise, to produce 292,000 units of Product Y, 29,200 hours (292,000 units × .1 hour per unit) of labor in Department 1 are required. In a similar manner, we can determine the direct labor hours needed in Department 2 to meet the budgeted production. Multiplying the direct labor hours for each department by the estimated department hourly rate yields the total direct labor cost for each department.

Exhibit 7
Direct Labor Cost Budget

Sanchez Inc.
Direct Labor Cost Budget
For the Year Ending December 31, 1997

	Department 1	Department 2	Total
Hours required for production:			
Product X (Note A)	52,000	41,600	
Product Y (Note B)	29,200	46,720	
Total	81,200	88,320	
Hourly rate	× $ 15	× $ 20	
Total direct labor cost	$1,218,000	$1,766,400	$2,984,400

Note A: Department 1: 520,000 units × .1 hour per unit = 52,000 hours
Department 2: 520,000 units × .08 hour per unit = 41,600 hours

Note B: Department 1: 292,000 units × .1 hour per unit = 29,200 hours
Department 2: 292,000 units × .16 hour per unit = 46,720 hours

The direct labor requirements should be closely coordinated between the production and personnel departments. This ensures that there will be enough labor available to meet production needs. Efficient manufacturing operations minimize idle time and labor shortages.

FACTORY OVERHEAD COST BUDGET

The estimated factory overhead costs necessary to meet production make up the factory overhead cost budget. This budget usually includes the total estimated cost for each item of factory overhead, as shown in Exhibit 8.

Exhibit 8
Factory Overhead Cost Budget

Sanchez Inc. Factory Overhead Cost Budget For the Year Ending December 31, 1997	
Indirect factory wages	$ 732,800
Supervisory salaries	360,000
Power and light	306,000
Depreciation of plant and equipment	288,000
Indirect materials	182,800
Maintenance	140,280
Insurance and property taxes	79,200
Total factory overhead cost	$2,089,080

Supplemental schedules are often prepared to present the factory overhead cost, broken down by fixed and variable cost elements, for each individual department. Such schedules enable department supervisors to direct attention to those costs for which each is solely responsible. They also aid managers in evaluating performance in each department.

COST OF GOODS SOLD BUDGET

The direct materials purchases budget, direct labor cost budget, and factory overhead cost budget provide the starting point for preparing the cost of goods sold budget. The desired ending inventory and the estimated beginning inventory data are combined with these data to determine the budgeted cost of goods sold.

To illustrate, the cost of goods sold budget shown in Exhibit 9 is based on the following work in process and finished goods inventories for Sanchez Inc.:

Estimated inventories on January 1, 1997:	
Finished goods	$1,095,600
Work in process	214,400
Desired inventories on December 31, 1997:	
Finished goods	$1,565,000
Work in process	220,000

OPERATING EXPENSES BUDGET

The operating expenses budget is made up of the estimated selling and administrative expenses. The sales budget is often used as the basis for estimating these expenses. Exhibit 10 is an operating expenses budget for Sanchez Inc.

Detailed supporting schedules for each department are often prepared for major items in the operating expenses budget. For example, an advertising expense schedule for the Marketing Department should include the advertising media to be used (newspaper, direct mail, television), quantities (column inches, number of pieces, minutes), and the cost per unit. Careful attention to such details will result in realistic budgets. Effective control will result from assigning responsibility for achieving the budget to department supervisors.

BUDGETED INCOME STATEMENT

The budgets for sales, cost of goods sold, and operating expenses, combined with the data on other income, other expense, and income tax provide the basis for preparing the budgeted income statement. Exhibit 11 is a budgeted income statement for Sanchez Inc.

Exhibit 9
Cost of Goods Sold Budget

Sanchez Inc.
Cost of Goods Sold Budget
For the Year Ending December 31, 1997

Finished goods inventory, January 1, 1997			$1,095,600
Work in process inventory, January 1, 1997		$ 214,400	
Direct materials:			
Direct materials inventory, January 1, 1997 (Note A)	$ 264,000		
Direct materials purchases (from Exhibit 6)	1,631,200		
Cost of direct materials available for use	$1,895,200		
Less direct materials inventory, December 31, 1997 (Note B)	236,000		
Cost of direct materials placed in production	$1,659,200		
Direct labor (from Exhibit 7)	2,984,400		
Factory overhead (from Exhibit 8)	2,089,080		
Total manufacturing costs		6,732,680	
Total work in process during period		$6,947,080	
Less work in process inventory, December 31, 1997		220,000	
Cost of goods manufactured			6,727,080
Cost of finished goods available for sale			$7,822,680
Less finished goods inventory, December 31, 1997			1,565,000
Cost of goods sold			$6,257,680

Note A:	Material A: 80,000 units at $ .60	$ 48,000
	Material B: 44,000 units at $1.70	74,800
	Material C: 141,200 units at $1.00	141,200
	Direct materials inventory, January 1, 1997	$264,000
Note B:	Material A: 80,000 units at $ .60	$ 48,000
	Material B: 40,000 units at $1.70	68,000
	Material C: 120,000 units at $1.00	120,000
	Direct materials inventory, December 31, 1997	$236,000

Exhibit 10
Operating Expenses Budget

Sanchez Inc.
Operating Expenses Budget
For the Year Ending December 31, 1997

Selling expenses:		
Sales salaries expense	$595,000	
Advertising expense	360,000	
Travel expense	115,000	
Telephone expense—selling	95,000	
Miscellaneous selling expense	25,000	
Total selling expenses		$1,190,000
Administrative expenses:		
Officers' salaries expense	$360,000	
Office salaries expense	105,000	
Heating and lighting expense	75,000	
Taxes expense	60,000	
Depreciation expense—office equipment	27,000	
Telephone expense—administrative	18,000	
Insurance expense	17,500	
Office supplies expense	7,500	
Miscellaneous administrative expenses	25,000	
Total administrative expenses		695,000
Total operating expenses		$1,885,000

Exhibit 11
Budgeted Income Statement

Sanchez Inc.
Budgeted Income Statement
For the Year Ending December 31, 1997

Revenue from sales		$9,847,200
Cost of goods sold		6,257,680
Gross profit		$3,589,520
Operating expenses:		
Selling expenses	$1,190,000	
Administrative expenses	695,000	
Total operating expenses		1,885,000
Income from operations		$1,704,520
Other income:		
Interest income	$ 98,000	
Other expense:		
Interest expense	90,000	8,000
Income before income tax		$1,712,520
Income tax		240,000
Net income		$1,472,520

The budgeted income statement condenses the estimates of all profit-making phases of operations. This allows management to assess the effects of the individual budgets on profits for the year. If the budgeted net income is too low, management could review and revise operating plans in an attempt to improve income.

USING ACCOUNTING TO UNDERSTAND BUSINESS

Emerson Electric is well-regarded for its state-of-the-art financial planning. The CEO at Emerson, Charles F. Knight, blocks out at least 50% of his time for planning activities. One tool used by Emerson Electric is the "5-back-by-5-forward" income statement. This statement both reports five years of Emerson's history and projects five years of expected operating results. The rigorous planning practiced at Emerson fosters teamwork, communication, and improved skills among its managers. As Knight states, "We want proof that a division is stretching to reach its goals, and we want to see the details of the actions division management believes will yield improved results. Our expectations are high, and the discussions are intense. A division president who comes to a planning conference poorly prepared has made a serious mistake."

Source: Charles F. Knight, "Emerson Electric: Consistent Profits, Consistently," *Harvard Business Review* (January-February 1992), pp. 57–70.

Balance Sheet Budgets

Objective 5
Prepare balance sheet budgets for a manufacturing business.

Balance sheet budgets are used by managers to plan financing, investing, and cash objectives for the firm. The balance sheet budgets illustrated for Sanchez Inc. in the following sections are the cash budget and the capital expenditures budget.

CASH BUDGET

The cash budget is one of the most important elements of the budgeted balance sheet. The cash budget presents the expected receipts (inflows) and payments (outflows) of cash for a day, a week, a month, or a longer period.

Information from the various operating budgets, such as the sales budget, the direct materials purchases budget, and the operating expenses budget, affect the cash budget. In addition, the capital expenditures budget, dividend policies, and plans for equity or long-term debt financing also affect the cash budget.

We will illustrate the preparation of the cash budget for January, February, and March, 1997 for Sanchez Inc. by developing the estimated cash receipts and estimated cash payments portion of the cash budget separately.

Estimated Cash Receipts

Estimated cash receipts are planned additions to cash from sales and other sources, such as issuing securities or collecting interest. A supporting schedule for determining collections from sales can be useful. To illustrate this schedule, assume the following information for Sanchez Inc.:

Accounts receivable, January 1, 1997 $295,800

	January	*February*	*March*
Budgeted sales	$840,000	$925,000	$575,000

Sanchez Inc. expects to sell 20% of its merchandise for cash. Of the remaining 80% of the sales on account, 60% are expected to be collected in the month of the sale and the remainder in the following month.

Using this information, we can prepare the schedule of collections from sales shown in Exhibit 12. The cash receipts from sales on account are determined by summing the amounts collected from sales earned in the current period (60%) and the amounts accrued from sales in the previous period as a receivable (40%).

Exhibit 12
Schedule of Collections from Sales

Sanchez Inc.
Schedule of Collections from Sales
For the Three Months Ending March 31, 1997

	January	February	March
Receipts from cash sales:			
Cash sales (20% × current month's sales—Note A)	$168,000	$185,000	$115,000
Receipts from sales on account:			
Collections from prior month's sales (40% of previous month's credit sales—Note B)	$295,800	$268,800	$296,000
Collections from current month's sales (60% of current month's credit sales—Note C)	403,200	444,000	276,000
Total receipts from sales on account	$699,000	$712,800	$572,000

Note A: $168,000 = $840,000 × 20%
$185,000 = $925,000 × 20%
$115,000 = $575,000 × 20%

Note B: $295,800, given as January 1, 1997 balance of Accounts Receivable
$268,800 = $840,000 × 80% × 40%
$296,000 = $925,000 × 80% × 40%

Note C: $403,200 = $840,000 × 80% × 60%
$444,000 = $925,000 × 80% × 60%
$276,000 = $575,000 × 80% × 60%

Estimated Cash Payments

Estimated cash payments are planned reductions in cash from manufacturing costs, operating expenses, capital expenditures, and other sources, such as buying securities or paying interest or dividends. As in the cash receipts portion of the cash budget, supporting schedules can be used in determining the cash payments portion of the cash budget. To illustrate the schedule of payments for operations, assume the following information for Sanchez Inc.:

Accounts payable, January 1, 1997			$110,000
Accrued expenses payable, January 1, 1997			31,000

	January	*February*	*March*
Budgeted cost information:			
Manufacturing costs	$555,000	$575,000	$545,000
Operating expenses	150,000	154,000	138,000

Depreciation expense on machines is estimated to be $15,000 per month and is included in the manufacturing costs. The accounts payable were incurred for manufacturing costs, and the accrued expenses were incurred for operating expenses. Sanchez Inc. expects to pay 75% of the manufacturing costs and operating expenses in the month in which they are incurred and the balance in the following month.

Using this information, we can prepare the schedule of payments for manufacturing costs and operating expenses, as shown in Exhibit 13.

Exhibit 13
Schedule of Payments for Manufacturing Costs and Operating Expenses

Sanchez Inc.
Schedule of Payments for Manufacturing Costs and Operating Expenses
For the Three Months Ending March 31, 1997

	January	February	March
Payments for manufacturing costs:			
Payments of prior month's manufacturing costs (25% × previous month's manufacturing costs (less depreciation))—(Note A)	$110,000	$135,000	$140,000
Payment of current month's manufacturing costs (75% × current month's manufacturing costs (less depreciation))—(Note B)	405,000	420,000	397,500
Total payments	$515,000	$555,000	$537,500
Payments for operating expenses:			
Payments of prior month's operating expenses (25% × previous month's operating expenses—Note C)	$ 31,000	$ 37,500	$ 38,500
Payment of current month's operating expenses (75% × current month's manufacturing costs—Note D)	112,500	115,500	103,500
Total payments	$143,500	$153,000	$142,000

Note A: $110,000, given as January 1, 1997 balance of Accounts Payable
$135,000 = ($555,000 – $15,000) × 25%
$140,000 = ($575,000 – $15,000) × 25%

Note B: $405,000 = ($555,000 – $15,000) × 75%
$420,000 = ($575,000 – $15,000) × 75%
$397,500 = ($545,000 – $15,000) × 75%

Note C: $31,000, given as January 1, 1997 balance of Accrued Expenses
$37,500 = $150,000 × 25%
$38,500 = $154,000 × 25%

Note D: $112,500 = $150,000 × 75%
$115,500 = $154,000 × 75%
$103,500 = $138,000 × 75%

In Exhibit 13, the cash payments are determined by summing the amounts paid from costs incurred in the current period (75%) and the amounts accrued as a liability from costs in the previous period (25%). For the manufacturing costs, the $15,000 of depreciation must be excluded from all calculations, since depreciation is a noncash expense that should not be included in the cash budget.

Completing the Cash Budget

To complete the cash budget for Sanchez Inc., as shown in Exhibit 14, assume that Sanchez Inc. is expecting to pay income taxes of $20,000 each month, to pay $27,000 of interest on January 10, to purchase plant and equipment for $274,000 in February, to receive $25,000 in interest in March, and to repay a $140,000 note on March 20. The cash balance on January 1 is $280,000.

Exhibit 14
Cash Budget

Sanchez Inc.
Cash Budget
For the Three Months Ending March 31, 1997

	January	February	March
Estimated cash receipts from:			
Cash sales	$168,000	$ 185,000	$ 115,000
Collections of accounts receivable	699,000	712,800	572,000
Other sources (issuance of securities, interest, etc.)	—	—	25,000
Total cash receipts	$867,000	$ 897,800	$ 712,000
Estimated cash payments for:			
Manufacturing costs	$515,000	$ 555,000	$ 537,500
Operating expenses	143,500	153,000	142,000
Capital expenditures	—	274,000	—
Other purposes (notes, income taxes, interest, etc.)	47,000	20,000	160,000
Total cash payments	$705,500	$1,002,000	$ 839,500
Cash increase (decrease)	$161,500	$ (104,200)	$(123,500)
Cash balance at beginning of month	280,000	441,500	337,300
Cash balance at end of month	$441,500	$ 337,300	$ 209,800
Minimum cash balance	300,000	300,000	300,000
Excess (deficiency)	$141,500	$ 37,300	$ (90,200)

We can compare the estimated cash balance at the end of the period with the minimum balance required by operations. Assuming that the minimum cash balance for Sanchez Inc. is $300,000, we can then determine any expected excess or deficiency. This is illustrated for Sanchez Inc. in Exhibit 14.

The minimum cash balance provides a safety buffer for variations in estimates and for unexpected emergencies. The amount stated as the minimum balance need not remain fixed. It could be larger during periods of "peak" business activity than during "slow" periods. In addition, for effective cash management, much of the minimum cash balance should be deposited in income-producing securities that can be readily converted to cash. U.S. Treasury Bills or Notes are examples of such securities.

CAPITAL EXPENDITURES BUDGET

The capital expenditures budget summarizes plans for acquiring plant assets. Such expenditures are necessary as machinery and other plant assets wear out, become obsolete, or for other reasons fall below minimum standards of efficiency. In addition, expanding plant facilities may be necessary to meet increasing demand for a company's product.

The useful life of many plant assets extends over relatively long periods of time. In addition, the amount of the expenditures for such assets may change significantly from year to year. The normal practice is to project the plans for a number of periods into the future in preparing the capital expenditures budget. Exhibit 15 is a five-year capital expenditures budget for Sanchez Inc.

Exhibit 15
Capital Expenditures Budget

Sanchez Inc.
Capital Expenditures Budget
For the Five Years Ending December 31, 2001

Item	1997	1998	1999	2000	2001
Machinery—Department 1	$400,000			$280,000	$360,000
Machinery—Department 2	180,000	$260,000	$560,000	200,000	
Office equipment		90,000			60,000
Total	$580,000	$350,000	$560,000	$480,000	$420,000

The capital expenditures budget should be considered in preparing the other operating budgets. For example, the estimated depreciation of new equipment affects the factory overhead cost budget and the operating expenses budget. The plans for financing the capital expenditures may also affect the cash budget.

BUDGETED BALANCE SHEET

The budgeted balance sheet estimates the financial condition at the end of a budget period. The budgeted balance sheet assumes that all operating budgets and financing plans are met. It is similar to a balance sheet based on actual data in the accounts. Thus, we do not illustrate a budgeted balance sheet for Sanchez Inc. If the budgeted balance sheet indicates a weakness in financial position, revising the financing plans or other plans may be necessary. For example, an excessive amount of long-term debt in relation to stockholders' equity might require revising financing plans for capital expenditures. Such revisions might include issuing equity rather than debt.

KEY POINTS

Objective 1. Describe budgeting, its objectives, and its impact on human behavior.
Budgeting involves (1) establishing specific goals for future operations, (2) directing and coordinating activities toward the goals, and (3) periodically comparing actual results with these goals. In addition, budget goals should be established to avoid problems in human behavior. Thus, budgets should not be set too tightly, too loosely, or with goal conflict.

Objective 2. Describe the basic elements of the budget process, the two major types of budgeting, and the use of computers in budgeting.
The budget process is initiated by a budget committee. The annual estimates received by the budget committee should be carefully studied, analyzed, revised, and finally integrated together into the budget. Two major types of budgets are the static budget and the flexible budget. The static budget does not adjust with changes in activity, while the flexible budget does adjust with changes in activity. Computers can be useful in speeding up the budgetary process and in preparing timely budget performance reports. In addition, simulation models can be used to determine the impact of operating alternatives on various budgets.

Objective 3. Describe the master budget for a manufacturing business.
The master budget consists of the budgeted income statement and budgeted balance sheet. These two budgets are developed from detailed budgets that are described in the next two objectives.

Objective 4. Prepare the basic income statement budgets for a manufacturing business.
The basic income statement budgets of the master budget are the sales budget, production budget, direct materials purchases budget, direct labor cost budget, factory overhead cost budget, cost of goods sold budget, and operating expense budget.

Objective 5. Prepare balance sheet budgets for a manufacturing business.
Both the cash budget and the capital expenditures budget can be used in preparing the budgeted balance sheet. The cash budget consists of budgeted cash receipts and budgeted cash payments. The capital expenditures budget is an important tool for planning expenditures for plant and equipment.

GLOSSARY OF KEY TERMS

Budget. An outline of a business's future plans, stated in financial terms. A budget is used to plan and control operational departments and divisions. *Objective 1*

Capital expenditures budget. The budget summarizing future plans for acquiring plant facilities and equipment. *Objective 5*

Continuous budgeting. A method of budgeting that provides for maintaining a twelve-month projection into the future. *Objective 2*

Flexible budget. A budget that adjusts for varying rates of activity. *Objective 2*

Master budget. The comprehensive budget plan encompassing all the individual budgets related to sales, cost of goods sold, operating expenses, capital expenditures, and cash. *Objective 3*

Responsibility center. An organizational unit for which a manager is assigned responsibility for the unit's performance. *Objective 1*

Static budget. A budget that does not adjust to changes in activity levels. *Objective 2*

Zero-based budgeting. A concept of budgeting that requires all levels of management to start from zero and estimate budget data as if there had been no previous activities in their unit. *Objective 2*

ILLUSTRATIVE PROBLEM

Selected information concerning sales and production for Cabot Co. for July of the current year are summarized as follows:

a. Estimated sales:
Product K: 40,000 units at $30.00 per unit
Product L: 20,000 units at $65.00 per unit

b. Estimated inventories, July 1, 19—:

Material A: 4,000 lbs.	Product K 3,000 units at $17 per unit	$ 51,000
Material B: 3,500 lbs.	Product L 2,700 units at $35 per unit	94,500
	Total	$145,500

There were no work in process inventories estimated for July 1, 19—.

c. Desired inventories at July 31, 19—:

Material A: 3,000 lbs.	Product K 2,500 units at $17 per unit	$ 42,500
Material B: 2,500 lbs.	Product L 2,000 units at $35 per unit	70,000
	Total	$112,500

There were no work in process inventories desired for July 31, 19—.

d. Direct materials used in production:

	Product K	*Product L*
Material A:	0.7 lb. per unit	3.5 lbs. per unit
Material B:	1.2 lbs. per unit	1.8 lbs. per unit

e. Unit costs for direct materials:

Material A:	$4.00 per lb.
Material B:	$2.00 per lb.

f. Direct labor requirements:

	Department 1	*Department 2*
Product K	0.4 hour per unit	0.15 hour per unit
Product L	0.6 hour per unit	0.25 hour per unit

g.

	Department 1	*Department 2*
Direct labor rate	$12.00 per hour	$16.00 per hour

h. Estimated factory overhead costs for July:

Indirect factory wages	$200,000
Depreciation of plant and equipment	40,000
Power and light	25,000
Indirect materials	34,000
Total	$299,000

Instructions

1. Prepare a sales budget for July.
2. Prepare a production budget for July.
3. Prepare a direct materials purchases budget for July.
4. Prepare a direct labor cost budget for July.
5. Prepare a cost of goods sold budget for July.

Solution

1.

CABOT CO.
Sales Budget
For the Month Ending July 31, 19—

Product	*Unit Sales Volume*	*Unit Selling Price*	*Total Sales*
Product K	40,000	$30.00	$1,200,000
Product L	20,000	65.00	1,300,000
Total revenue from sales			$2,500,000

2.

CABOT CO.
Production Budget
For the Month Ending July 31, 19—

	Units *Product K*	*Product L*
Sales	40,000	20,000
Plus desired inventories at July 31, 19—	2,500	2,000
Total	42,500	22,000
Less estimated inventories, July 1, 19—	3,000	2,700
Total production	39,500	19,300

3.

CABOT CO.
Direct Materials Purchases Budget
For the Month Ending July 31, 19—

	Direct Materials *Material A*	*Material B*	*Total*
Units required for production:			
Product K (39,500 × lbs. per unit)	27,650 lbs.*	47,400 lbs.*	
Product L (19,300 × lbs. per unit)	67,550**	34,740**	
Plus desired units of inventory, July 31, 19—	3,000	2,500	
Total	98,200 lbs.	84,640 lbs.	
Less estimated units of inventory, July 1, 19—	4,000	3,500	
Total units to be purchased	94,200 lbs.	81,140 lbs.	
Unit price	$ 4.00	$ 2.00	
Total direct materials purchases	$376,800	$162,280	$539,080

*27,650 = 39,500 × 0.7 47,400 = 39,500 × 1.2
**67,550 = 19,300 × 3.5 34,740 = 19,300 × 1.8

4.

CABOT CO.
Direct Labor Cost Budget
For the Month Ending July 31, 19—

	Department 1	*Department 2*	*Total*
Hours required for production:			
Product K (39,500 × hours per unit)	15,800*	5,925*	
Product L (19,300 × hours per unit)	11,580**	4,825**	
Total	27,380	10,750	
Hourly rate	$ 12.00	$ 16.00	
Total direct labor cost	$328,560	$172,000	$500,560

*15,800 = 39,500 × .4 5,925 = 39,500 × .15
**11,580 = 19,300 × .6 4,825 = 19,300 × .25

5.

CABOT CO.
Cost of Goods Sold Budget
For the Month Ending July 31, 19—

Finished goods inventory, July 1, 19—		$ 145,500
Direct materials:		
Direct materials inventory, July 1, 19— (Note A)	$ 23,000	
Direct materials purchases	539,080	
Cost of direct materials available for use	$562,080	
Less direct materials inventory, July 31, 19— (Note B)	17,000	
Cost of direct materials placed in production	$545,080	
Direct labor	500,560	
Factory overhead	299,000	
Cost of goods manufactured		1,344,640
Cost of finished goods available for sale		$1,490,140
Less finished goods inventory, July 31, 19—		112,500
Cost of goods sold		$1,377,640

Note A:

Material A	4,000 lbs.	at $4.00 per lb.	$16,000
Material B	3,500 lbs.	at $2.00 per lb.	7,000
Direct materials inventory, July 1, 19—			$23,000

Note B:

Material A	3,000 lbs.	at $4.00 per lb.	$12,000
Material B	2,500 lbs.	at $2.00 per lb.	5,000
Direct materials inventory, July 31, 19—			$17,000

SELF-EXAMINATION QUESTIONS (ANSWERS AT END OF CHAPTER)

1. The system that "builds in" the effect of fluctuations in the level of activity into the various budgets is called:
   A. static budgeting. C. flexible budgeting.
   B. zero-based budgeting. D. cash budgeting.

2. Budgeting of operating activities to provide at all times for maintaining a twelve-month projection into the future is called:
   A. static budgeting. C. continuous budgeting.
   B. flexible budgeting. D. zero-based budgeting.

3. The budget that summarizes future plans for acquiring of plant facilities and equipment is the:
   A. cash budget. C. capital expenditures budget.
   B. sales budget. D. production budget.

4. The total estimated units of sales for the coming year is 250,000. The estimated inventory at the beginning of the year is 22,500 units, and the desired inventory at the end of the year is 30,000 units. The total production indicated in the production budget is:
   A. 242,500 units. C. 280,000 units.
   B. 257,500 units. D. 302,500 units.

5. Dixon Company expects $650,000 of credit sales in March and $800,000 of credit sales in April. Dixon historically collects 70% of its sales in the month of sale and 30% in the following month. How much cash does Dixon expect to collect in April?
   A. $800,000 C. $755,000
   B. $560,000 D. $1,015,000

DISCUSSION QUESTIONS

1. What is a budget?
2. What is continuous budgeting?
3. What is the manager's role in a responsibility center?
4. What are the three major objectives of budgeting?
5. Why should all levels of management and all departments participate in preparing and submitting budget estimates?
6. Briefly describe the type of human behavior problems that might arise if budget goals are set too tightly.
7. What behavioral problems are associated with setting a budget too loosely?
8. Give an example of budgetary slack.
9. What behavioral problems are associated with establishing conflicting goals within the budget?
10. When would a company use zero-based budgeting?
11. Under what circumstances would a static budget be appropriate?
12. What is a flexible budget?
13. How do computerized budgeting systems aid firms in the budgeting process?
14. What is the first step in preparing a master budget?
15. Why should the production requirements as set forth in the production budget be carefully coordinated with the sales budget?
16. Why should the timing of direct materials purchases be closely coordinated with the production budget?
17. In preparing the budget for the cost of goods sold, what are the three budgets from which data on relevant estimates of quantities and costs are combined with data on estimated inventories?
18. a. Discuss the purpose of the cash budget.
    b. If the cash for the first quarter of the fiscal year indicates excess cash at the end of each of the first two months, how might the excess cash be used?
19. How does a schedule of collections from sales assist in preparing the cash budget?
20. What is the capital expenditures budget?

EXERCISES

EXERCISE 22–1
Personal cash budget
Objectives 2, 5

At the beginning of the school year, Sheldon Allman decided to prepare a cash budget for the months of September, October, November, and December. The following information relates to the budget.

Cash balance, September 1	$4,100
Purchase season football tickets in September	200
Additional entertainment for each month	150
Pay semester tuition on September 3	3,000
Pay rent at the beginning of each month	450
Pay for food each month	250
Pay apartment deposit on September 2 (to be returned December 15)	300
Part-time job earnings each month	600

a. Prepare a cash budget for September, October, November, and December.
b. Are the budgets prepared as static budgets or flexible budgets?
c. What are the budget implications for Sheldon Allman?

EXERCISE 22–2
Flexible budget for operating expenses
Objectives 2, 4

Biddle Furniture Company uses flexible budgets that are based on the following data:

Sales commissions	4% of sales
Advertising expense	8% of sales
Miscellaneous selling expense	$800 plus 1 1/2% of sales
Office salaries expense	$4,000 per month
Office supplies expense	1/2% of sales
Miscellaneous administrative expense	$200 per month plus 1/4% of sales

Prepare a flexible operating expenses budget for May of the current year for sales volumes of $80,000, $120,000, and $160,000. (Note: Use Exhibit 2 as a model for this budget.)

EXERCISE 22–3
Static budget vs. flexible budget
Objectives 2, 4

The production supervisor of Department 4 for Arnez Bindery Company agreed to the following monthly static budget for the upcoming year:

Arnez Bindery Company
Department 4
Monthly Production Budget

Wages	$252,000
Utilities	144,000
Depreciation	35,000
Total	$431,000

The actual amount spent for the first three months of the year in Department 4 was as follows:

January	$360,000
February	320,000
March	300,000

The Department 4 supervisor has been very pleased with this performance, since actual expenditures have been less than the monthly budget. However, the plant manager believes the budget should not remain fixed for every month, but should "flex" or adjust to the volume of work that is produced in Department 4. Additional information for Department 4 is as follows:

Wages per hour	$14.00
Utility cost per direct labor hour	$ 8.00
Direct labor hours per unit	0.4
Units produced	45,000

The actual units produced in Department 4 were as follows:

January	36,000 units
February	32,000
March	28,000

a. Prepare a flexible budget for the actual units produced for January, February, and March in Department 4.
b. Compare the flexible budget with the actual expenditures for the first three months. What does this comparison suggest?

EXERCISE 22–4
Sales and production budgets
Objective 4

Baldwin Company manufactures two models of clock radios, R4 and R8. Based on the following production and sales data for September of the current year, prepare (a) a sales budget and (b) a production budget.

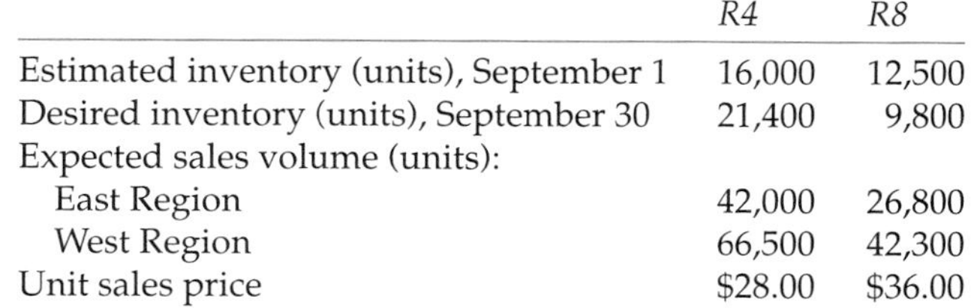

	R4	*R8*
Estimated inventory (units), September 1	16,000	12,500
Desired inventory (units), September 30	21,400	9,800
Expected sales volume (units):		
East Region	42,000	26,800
West Region	66,500	42,300
Unit sales price	$28.00	$36.00

EXERCISE 22–5
Professional fees budget
Objective 4

Levitt and Lyle, CPAs, offer three types of services to clients: auditing, tax, and computer consulting. Based on experience and projected growth, the following billable hours have been estimated for the year ending December 31, 1997:

	Billable Hours
Audit Department:	
Staff	48,000
Partners	8,600
Tax Department:	
Staff	36,500
Partners	6,400
Computer Consulting Department:	
Staff	29,400
Partners	4,600

The average billing rate for staff is $90 per hour, and the average billing rate for partners is $160 per hour.

Prepare a professional fees budget for Levitt and Lyle, CPAs, for the year ending December 31, 1997, using the following column headings and showing the estimated professional fees by type of service rendered:

Billable Hours	*Hourly Rate*	*Total Revenue*

EXERCISE 22–6
Professional labor cost budget
Objective 4

Based on the data in Exercise 22–5 and assuming that the average compensation per hour for staff is $45 and for partners is $120, prepare a direct labor cost budget for Levitt and Lyle, CPAs, for the year ending December 31, 1997. Use the following column headings:

Billable Hours Required	
Staff	*Partners*

EXERCISE 22–7
Direct materials purchases budget
Objective 4

Tucker Machine Company has determined from its production budget the following estimated production volumes for products DD-1 and DD-5 for August:

	Units	
	DD-1	*DD-5*
Budgeted production volume	56,300	24,700

There are three direct materials used in producing DD-1 and DD-5. The quantities of direct materials expected to be used for each unit of product are as follows:

	DD-1	*DD-5*
Direct materials:		
Material 1	0.25 lb. per unit	0.2 lb. per unit
Material 2	0.8	0.7
Material 3	1.5	1.2

In addition, Tucker has determined the following information about each material:

	Material 1	*Material 2*	*Material 3*
Estimated inventory, August 1, 19—	600	1,200	980
Desired inventory, August 31, 19—	800	1,350	1,000
Price per pound	$5.60	$3.40	$1.20

Prepare a direct materials purchases budget for Tucker.

EXERCISE 22–8
Direct materials purchases budget
Objective 4

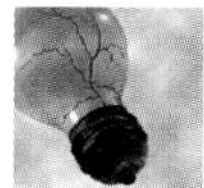

Anticipated sales for Gulliver Battery Co. were 10,000 units of Product A and 20,000 units of Product B. There were no anticipated beginning finished goods inventories for either product. The planned ending finished goods inventories were 2,000 units for each product. Materials X and Y are used in producing Products A and B according to the following table:

	Product A	*Product B*
Material X	0.5 lb. per unit	1 lb. per unit
Material Y	1.5 lbs. per unit	2 lbs. per unit

The purchase prices of Materials X and Y are $5.00 and $8.00 per pound, respectively. The desired ending inventories of Materials X and Y are 4,000 and 6,000 pounds, respectively. The estimated beginning inventories for Materials X and Y are 7,000 and 5,000 pounds, respectively.

The following materials purchases budget was prepared for Gulliver Battery Company:

Gulliver Battery Company
Direct Materials Purchases Budget
For the Year Ending December 31, 19—

	Material X	*Material Y*	*Total*
Units required for production:			
Product A	5,000 lbs.	10,000 lbs.	
Product B	15,000	40,000	
Total	20,000 lbs.	50,000 lbs.	
Unit price	$ 5.00	$ 8.00	
Total direct materials purchases	$100,000	$400,000	$500,000

Correct the direct materials purchases budget for Gulliver Battery Company.

EXERCISE 22–9
Direct labor cost budget
Objective 4

Edberg Sporting Goods Company manufactures two types of tennis rackets, the Junior and Pro-Striker models. The production budget for November for the two rackets is as follows:

	Junior	*Pro-Striker*
Production budget	19,800 units	76,500 units

Both rackets are produced in two departments, Molding and Finishing. The direct labor hours required for each racket are estimated as follows:

	Molding Department	*Finishing Department*
Junior	0.75 hour per unit	0.3 hour per unit
Pro-Striker	1.2 hours per unit	0.8 hour per unit

The direct labor rate for each department is as follows:

Molding Department	$12.50 per hour
Finishing Department	$16.80 per hour

Prepare the direct labor cost budget for November.

EXERCISE 22–10
Cost of goods sold budget
Objective 4

The controller of Hillcrest Pottery Company wishes to prepare a cost of goods sold budget for June. The controller assembled the following information for constructing the cost of goods sold budget:

Direct materials:

	Material D	*Material E*	*Material F*	*Total*
Total direct material purchases budgeted for June	$12,300	$23,350	$4,780	$40,430
Estimated inventory, June 1, 19—	1,870	2,675	450	4,995
Desired inventory, June 30, 19—	1,500	3,120	380	5,000

Direct labor cost:

	Department 1	*Department 2*	*Total*
Total direct labor cost budgeted for June	$47,700	$29,650	$77,350

Finished goods inventories:

	Product J-11	*Product J-21*	*Product J-31*	*Total*
Estimated inventory, June 1, 19—	$2,580	$3,310	$1,900	$7,790
Desired inventory, June 30, 19—	2,670	3,190	2,040	7,900

Work in process inventories:

Estimated inventory, June 1, 19—	$1,670
Desired inventory, June 30, 19—	1,890

Budgeted factory overhead costs for June:

Indirect factory wages	$25,700
Depreciation of plant and equipment	5,860
Power and light	8,400
Indirect materials	12,460
Total	$52,420

Use the information assembled above to prepare a cost of goods sold budget for June.

EXERCISE 22–11
Schedule of cash collections of accounts receivable
Objective 5

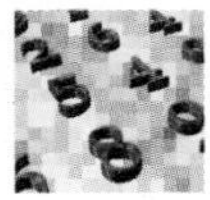

Moore Company was organized on March 1 of the current year. Projected sales for each of the first three months of operations are as follows:

March	$240,000
April	255,000
May	290,000

The company expects to sell 20% of its merchandise for cash. Of sales on account, 50% are expected to be collected in the month of the sale, 30% in the month following the sale, and the remainder in the following month. Prepare a schedule indicating cash collections of accounts receivable for March, April, and May.

EXERCISE 22–12
Schedule of cash payments
Objective 5

Ackerman Company was organized on May 31 of the current year. Projected operating expenses for each of the first three months of operations are as follows:

June	$ 64,000
July	81,000
August	104,500

Depreciation, insurance, and property taxes represent $15,000 of the estimated monthly operating expenses. The annual insurance premium was paid on May 31, and property taxes for the year will be paid in December. Three-fourths of the remainder of the operating expenses are expected to be paid in the month in which they are incurred, with the balance to be paid in the following month.

Prepare a schedule indicating cash payments for operating expenses for June, July, and August.

EXERCISE 22–13
Schedule of cash payments
Objective 5

The Sharman Hotel is planning its cash payments for operations for the fourth quarter (October-December). The Accrued Expenses Payable balance on October 1 is $65,000. The budgeted operating expenses for the next three months are as follows:

	October	*November*	*December*
Salaries	$ 90,000	$120,000	$ 70,000
Utilities	8,000	9,000	7,500
Other operating expenses	45,000	50,000	40,000
Total	$143,000	$179,000	$117,500

Other Operating Expenses include $24,000 of monthly depreciation expense and $2,000 of monthly insurance expense that was prepaid for the year on March 1 of the current year. The remaining operating expenses are 70% paid in the month in which they are incurred, with the remainder paid in the following month. The Accrued Expenses Payable balance on October 1 relates to the expenses incurred in September.

Prepare a schedule of cash payments for operations for October, November, and December.

EXERCISE 22–14
Capital expenditures budget
Objective 5

On January 1, 1996, the controller of Gerry Manufacturing Company is planning capital expenditures for the years 1996–1999. The following interviews helped the controller collect the necessary information for the capital expenditures budget.

Director of Facilities: A construction contract was signed in late 1995 for the construction of a new factory building at a contract cost of $10,000,000. The construction is scheduled to begin in 1996 and be 60% complete at the end of 1996. Construction will be completed in 1997.

Vice-President of Manufacturing: When the new factory building is finished, we plan to purchase $2.5 million in equipment. I expect that an additional $500,000 will be needed early in the following year to test and install the equipment before we can begin production. If sales continue to grow, I expect we'll need to invest another million in equipment in 1999.

Vice-President of Marketing: We have really been growing lately. I wouldn't be surprised if we need to expand the size of our new factory building in 1999 at a cost of $4,000,000. Fortunately, we expect inflation to have minimal impact on construction costs over the next four years.

Director of Information Systems: We need to upgrade our information systems to local area network (LAN) technology. It doesn't make sense to do this until after the new factory building is completed and producing product. Once the factory is up and running, we should equip the whole facility with LAN technology. I think it would cost us $2,000,000 today to install the technology. However, prices have been dropping by 20% per year, so it should be less expensive at a later date.

President: I am excited about our long-term prospects. My only short-term concern is financing the $6,000,000 of construction costs on the portion of the new factory building scheduled to be completed in 1996.

Use the interview information above to prepare a capital expenditures budget for Gerry Manufacturing Company for the years 1996–1999.

PROBLEMS SERIES A

PROBLEM 22–1A
Forecast sales volume and sales budget
Objective 4

Parkin Frame Company prepared the following sales budget for the current year:

Parkin Frame Company
Sales Budget
For the Year Ending December 31, 1997

Product and Area	*Unit Sales Volume*	*Unit Selling Price*	*Total Sales*
Product A:			
East	30,000	$15.00	$ 450,000
Central	25,000	15.00	375,000
West	15,000	15.00	225,000
Total	70,000		$1,050,000
Product B:			
East	36,000	$20.00	$ 720,000
Central	18,000	20.00	360,000
West	32,000	20.00	640,000
Total	86,000		$1,720,000
Total revenue from sales			$2,770,000

At the end of September 1997, the following unit sales data were reported for the first nine months of the year:

	Unit Sales	
	Product A	*Product B*
East	23,400	28,620
Central	18,000	13,365
West	11,025	22,800

For the year ending December 31, 1998, unit sales are expected to follow the patterns established during the first nine months of the year ending December 31, 1997. The unit selling price for Product A is expected to increase to $25, and the unit selling price for Product B is expected to be increased to $23, effective January 1, 1998.

Instructions

1. Compute the increase or decrease of actual unit sales for the nine months ended September 30, 1997, over expectations for this nine-month period. Since sales have historically occurred evenly throughout the year, budgeted sales for the first nine months of a year would be 75% of the year's budgeted sales. Comparison of this amount with actual sales will indicate the percentage increase or decrease of actual sales for the nine months over budgeted sales for the nine months. (Round percent changes to the nearest whole percent.) Place your answers in a columnar table with the following format:

	Unit Budgeted Sales			*Increase (Decrease)*	
	Year	*Nine Months*	*Actual Sales for Nine Months*	*Amount*	*Percent*
Product A					
East					
Central					
West					
Product B					
East					
Central					
West					

2. Assuming that the trend of sales indicated in (1) is to continue in 1998, compute the unit sales volume to be used for preparing the sales budget for the year ending December 31, 1998. Place your answers in a columnar table with the following format:

	1997 Budgeted Units	*Percentage Increase (Decrease)*	*1998 Budgeted Units*
Product A			
East			
Central			
West			
Product B			
East			
Central			
West			

3. Prepare a sales budget for the year ending December 31, 1998.

PROBLEM 22–2A
Sales, production, direct materials, and direct labor budgets
Objective 4

The budget director of Drisco Chair Company requests estimates of sales, production, and other operating data from the various administrative units every month. Selected information concerning sales and production for May of the current year is summarized as follows:

a. Estimated sales for May by sales territory:
East:
Product K-1: 12,000 units at $45 per unit
Product LS-5: 16,000 units at $80 per unit
Midwest:
Product K-1: 35,000 units at $40 per unit
Product LS-5: 42,500 units at $75 per unit
West:
Product K-1: 21,600 units at $48 per unit
Product LS-5 23,400 units at $85 per unit

b. Estimated inventories at May 1:
Direct materials:
Material P: 500 lbs. Material R: 740 lbs.
Material Q: 1,150 lbs. Material S: 270 lbs.
Finished products:
Product K-1: 3,000 units Product LS-5: 2,700 units

c. Desired inventories at May 31:
Direct materials:
Material P: 710 lbs. Material R: 720 lbs.
Material Q: 980 lbs. Material S: 340 lbs.
Finished products:
Product K-1: 3,100 units Product LS-5: 2,000 units

d. Direct materials used in production:
In manufacture of Product K-1:
Material Q: 0.9 lb. per unit of product
Material R: 1.4 lbs. per unit of product
Material S: 2.7 lbs. per unit of product
In manufacture of Product LS-5:
Material P: 3.5 lbs. per unit of product
Material Q: 1.8 lbs. per unit of product
Material S: 0.7 lb. per unit of product

e. Anticipated purchase price for direct materials:
Material P: $1.80 per lb. Material R: $4.00 per lb.
Material Q: $2.50 per lb. Material S: $0.60 per lb.

f. Direct labor requirements:
Product K-1:
Department 10: .5 hour at $9 per hour
Department 30: .25 hour at $11 per hour
Product LS-5:
Department 10: .3 hour at $9 per hour
Department 20: .85 hour at $12 per hour

Instructions

1. Prepare a sales budget for May.
2. Prepare a production budget for May.
3. Prepare a direct materials purchases budget for May.
4. Prepare a direct labor cost budget for May.

PROBLEM 22–3A
Budgeted income statement and supporting budgets
Objective 4

The budget director of Asada Inc., with the assistance of the controller, treasurer, production manager, and sales manager, has gathered the following data for use in developing the budgeted income statement for June:

a. Estimated sales for June:
Product E: 96,000 units at $18 per unit
Product F: 43,500 units at $26 per unit

b. Estimated inventories at June 1:
Direct materials:
Material TY-1: 2,500 lbs.
Material AA-5: 3,200 lbs.
Finished products:
Product E: 5,400 units at $11 per unit
Product F: 2,100 units at $15 per unit

c. Desired inventories at June 30:

Direct materials:		Finished products:	
Material TY-1:	2,800 lbs.	Product E:	6,000 units at $11 per unit
Material AA-5:	3,050 lbs.	Product F:	2,350 units at $15 per unit

d. Direct materials used in production:
   In manufacture of Product E:
      Material TY-1: 0.9 lb. per unit of product
      Material AA-5: 0.4 lb. per unit of product
   In manufacture of Product F:
      Material AA-5: 1.2 lbs. per unit of product

e. Anticipated cost of purchases and beginning and ending inventory of direct materials:
      Material TY-1: $1.30 per lb.
      Material AA-5: $3.20 per lb.

f. Direct labor requirements:
   Product E:
      Department 100: .2 hour at $10 per hour
      Department 200: .25 hour at $15 per hour
   Product F:
      Department 100: .5 hour at $10 per hour
      Department 300: .2 hour at $13 per hour

g. Estimated factory overhead costs for June:

Indirect factory wages	$185,000
Depreciation of plant and equipment	28,000
Supervisory salaries	85,500
Power and light	12,800
Indirect materials	32,000
Maintenance	26,400
Insurance and property taxes	8,400

h. Estimated operating expenses for June:

Sales salaries expense	$144,300
Officers salaries expense	90,500
Advertising expense	111,900
Office salaries expense	65,800
Depreciation expense—office equipment	4,600
Telephone expense—selling	3,250
Telephone expense—administrative	1,400
Travel expense—selling	24,300
Travel expense—administrative	12,600
Office supplies expense	3,200
Miscellaneous selling expense	6,860
Miscellaneous administrative expense	4,570

i. Estimated other income and expense for June:

Interest income	$15,700
Interest expense	11,350

j. Estimated tax rate: 40%.

Instructions

1. Prepare a sales budget for June.
2. Prepare a production budget for June.
3. Prepare a direct materials purchases budget for June.
4. Prepare a direct labor cost budget for June.
5. Prepare a factory overhead cost budget for June.
6. Prepare a cost of goods sold budget for June. Work in process at the beginning of June is estimated to be $28,500, and work in process at the end of June is estimated to be $34,200.
7. Prepare an operating expenses budget for June. Classify the expenses as either selling or administrative expenses.
8. Prepare a budgeted income statement for June.

PROBLEM 22–4A
Cash budget
Objective 5

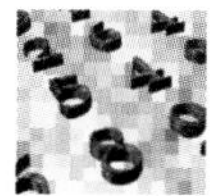

The treasurer of Bradly Lawn Equipment Company instructs you to prepare a monthly cash budget for the next three months. You are presented with the following budget information:

	August	*September*	*October*
Sales	$310,000	$390,000	$366,000
Manufacturing costs	190,000	240,000	215,000
Operating expenses	56,000	71,000	65,000
Capital expenditures	—	24,000	—

The company expects to sell about 20% of its merchandise for cash. Of sales on account, 70% are expected to be collected in full in the month following the sale and the remainder the following month. Depreciation, insurance, and property taxes represent $20,000 of the estimated monthly manufacturing costs and $4,000 of the probable monthly operating expenses. The annual insurance premium is paid in July, and the annual property taxes are paid in November. Of the remainder of the manufacturing costs and operating expenses, 80% are expected to be paid in the month in which they are incurred and the balance in the following month.

Current assets as of August 1 comprise cash of $32,000, marketable securities of $40,000, and accounts receivable of $261,800 ($220,000 from July sales and $41,800 from June sales). Current liabilities as of August 1 comprise a $60,000, 12%, 60-day note payable due September 20, $30,000 of accounts payable incurred in July for manufacturing costs, and accrued liabilities of $9,500 incurred in July for operating expenses.

It is expected that $1,500 in dividends will be received in August. An estimated income tax payment of $21,000 will be made in September. Bradly's regular quarterly dividend of $10,000 is expected to be declared in September and paid in October. Management desires to maintain a minimum cash balance of $25,000.

Instructions

1. Prepare a monthly cash budget for August, September, and October.
2. On the basis of the cash budget prepared in (1), what recommendation should be made to the treasurer?

PROBLEM 22–5A
Budgeted income statement and balance sheet
Objectives 4, 5

As a preliminary to requesting budget estimates of sales, costs, and expenses for the fiscal year beginning January 1, 1997, the following tentative trial balance as of December 31 of the preceding year is prepared by the Accounting Department of Carcello Seatcover Company:

Cash	46,000	
Accounts Receivable	54,000	
Finished Goods	110,000	
Work in Process	23,550	
Materials	42,100	
Prepaid Expenses	3,560	
Plant and Equipment	410,000	
Accumulated Depreciation—Plant and Equipment		240,000
Accounts Payable		36,400
Common Stock, $10 par		250,000
Retained Earnings		162,810
	689,210	689,210

Factory output and sales for 1997 are expected to total 70,000 units of product, which are to be sold at $18 per unit. The quantities and costs of the inventories (lifo method) at December 31, 1997, are expected to remain unchanged from the balances at the beginning of the year.

Budget estimates of manufacturing costs and operating expenses for the year are summarized as follows:

	Estimated Costs and Expenses	
	Fixed (Total for Year)	Variable (Per Unit Sold)
Cost of goods manufactured and sold:		
Direct materials	—	$7.20
Direct labor	—	3.65
Factory overhead:		
Depreciation of plant and equipment	$25,000	—
Other factory overhead	8,000	1.75
Selling expenses:		
Sales salaries and commissions	46,000	.80
Advertising	22,000	—
Miscellaneous selling expense	3,500	.20
Administrative expenses:		
Office and officers salaries	54,000	.08
Supplies	3,100	.04
Miscellaneous administrative expense	1,400	.02

Balances of accounts receivable, prepaid expenses, and accounts payable at the end of the year are expected to differ from the beginning balances by only insignificant amounts.

Federal income tax of $31,400 on 1997 taxable income will be paid during 1997. Regular quarterly cash dividends of $0.25 a share are expected to be declared and paid in March, June, September, and December. It is anticipated that plant and equipment will be purchased for $90,000 cash in May.

Instructions

1. Prepare a budgeted income statement for 1997.
2. Prepare a budgeted balance sheet as of December 31, 1997.

PROBLEM 22–6A
Static vs. flexible budgets for factory overhead costs
Objectives 2, 4

Binder Plastics Company prepared the following June factory overhead cost budget for the Molding Department, based on the actual expenditures for May 1997:

Binder Plastics Company
Factory Overhead Cost Budget—Molding Department
For the Month Ending June 30, 1997

Variable cost:		
Indirect factory wages	$28,200	
Indirect materials	16,200	
Power and light	3,240	
Total variable cost		$47,640
Fixed cost:		
Supervisory salaries	$12,570	
Indirect factory wages	8,900	
Depreciation of plant and equipment	3,570	
Insurance	2,790	
Power and light	3,670	
Property taxes	1,560	
Total fixed cost		33,060
Total factory overhead		$80,700

There were 24,000 machine hours used in the Molding Department in May. The June actual results are shown at the top of the next page. The actual June cost was less than the June budget by $3,740. The plant manager was prepared to take the department out for a celebration, until noticing that there were only 20,000 machine hours used in June.

Binder Plastics Company
Factory Overhead Actual Costs—Molding Department
For the Month Ending June 30, 1997

Variable cost:		
Indirect factory wages	$24,900	
Indirect materials	15,100	
Power and light	3,900	
Total variable cost		$43,900
Fixed cost:		
Supervisory salaries	$12,570	
Indirect factory wages	8,900	
Depreciation of plant and equipment	3,570	
Insurance	2,790	
Power and light	3,670	
Property taxes	1,560	
Total fixed cost		33,060
Total factory overhead		$76,960

Instructions

1. Prepare a flexible budget for the Molding Department for 20,000 machine hours.
2. Determine the difference between the flexible budget prepared in (1) and the actual cost for the Molding Department in June.
3. Should the May static budget or flexible budget be used for controlling June's cost? Why?

PROBLEMS SERIES B

PROBLEM 22–1B
Forecast sales volume and sales budget
Objective 4

Lincoln Security Alarm Company prepared the following sales budget for the current year:

Lincoln Security Alarm Company
Sales Budget
For the Year Ending December 31, 1996

Product and Area	*Unit Sales Volume*	*Unit Selling Price*	*Total Sales*
Product E:			
East	25,000	$32	$ 800,000
Central	32,000	32	1,024,000
West	20,000	32	640,000
Total	77,000		$2,464,000
Product F:			
East	20,000	$40	$ 800,000
Central	26,000	40	1,040,000
West	12,000	40	480,000
Total	58,000		$2,320,000
Total revenue from sales			$4,784,000

At the end of September 1996, the following unit sales data were reported for the first nine months of the year:

	Unit Sales	
	Product E	*Product F*
East	19,875	15,900
Central	23,520	19,695
West	14,550	8,550

For the year ending December 31, 1997, unit sales are expected to follow the patterns established during the first nine months of the year ending December 31, 1996. The unit selling price for Product E is expected to be increased to $35, and the unit selling price for Product F is expected to be increased to $44, effective January 1, 1997.

Instructions

1. Compute the increase or decrease of actual unit sales for the nine months ended September 30, 1996, over expectations for this nine-month period. Since sales have historically occurred evenly throughout the year, budgeted sales for the first nine months of a year would be 75% of the year's budgeted sales. Comparison of this amount with actual sales will indicate the percentage increase or decrease of actual sales for the nine months over budgeted sales for the nine months. Place your answers in a columnar table with the following format:

	Unit Budgeted Sales			*Increase (Decrease)*	
	Year	*Nine Months*	*Actual Sales for Nine Months*	*Amount*	*Percent*
Product E					
East					
Central					
West					
Product F					
East					
Central					
West					

2. Assuming that the trend of sales indicated in (1) is to continue in 1997, compute the unit sales volume to be used for preparing the sales budget for the year ending December 31, 1997. Place your answers in a columnar table with the following format:

	1996 Budgeted Units	*Percentage Increase (Decrease)*	*1997 Budgeted Units*
Product E			
East			
Central			
West			
Product F			
East			
Central			
West			

3. Prepare a sales budget for the year ending December 31, 1997.

PROBLEM 22–2B
Sales, production, direct materials, and direct labor budgets
Objective 4

The budget director of Lin Mower Company requests estimates of sales, production, and other operating data from the various administrative units every month. Selected information concerning sales and production for May of the current year is summarized as follows:

a. Estimated sales for May by sales territory:
   North:
      Product X: 1,650 units at $620 per unit
      Product Y: 2,310 units at $450 per unit
   Southeast:
      Product X: 2,340 units at $620 per unit
      Product Y: 1,870 units at $460 per unit
   Southwest:
      Product X: 860 units at $600 per unit
      Product Y: 1,140 units at $440 per unit

b. Estimated inventories at May 1:
   Direct materials:
      Material A: 860 lbs. Material C: 460 lbs.
      Material B: 980 lbs. Material D: 300 lbs.

Finished products:
Product X: 80 units   Product Y: 100 units

c. Desired inventories at May 31:
Direct materials:
Material A: 940 lbs.   Material C: 510 lbs.
Material B: 1,050 lbs.   Material D: 280 lbs.
Finished products:
Product X: 110 units   Product Y: 75 units

d. Direct materials used in production:
In manufacture of Product X:
Material A: 1.9 lbs. per unit of product
Material B: 2.4 lbs. per unit of product
Material C: 0.8 lb. per unit of product
In manufacture of Product Y:
Material B: 1.8 lbs. per unit of product
Material D: 0.4 lb. per unit of product

e. Anticipated purchase price for direct materials:
Material A: $85 per lb.   Material C: $120 per lb.
Material B: $60 per lb.   Material D: $100 per lb.

f. Direct labor requirements:
Product X:
Department 2: 1.5 hours at $16 per hour
Department 3: .8 hour at $14 per hour
Product Y:
Department 1: 2.4 hours at $12 per hour
Department 2: .6 hour at $16 per hour

Instructions

1. Prepare a sales budget for May.
2. Prepare a production budget for May.
3. Prepare a direct materials purchases budget for May.
4. Prepare a direct labor cost budget for May.

PROBLEM 22–3B
Budgeted income statement and supporting budgets
Objective 4

The budget director of O'Leary Inc., with the assistance of the controller, treasurer, production manager, and sales manager, has gathered the following data for use in developing the budgeted income statement for March:

a. Estimated sales for March:
Product K-1: 8,500 units at $290 per unit
Product K-22: 11,900 units at $165 per unit

b. Estimated inventories at March 1:
Direct materials:
Material K: 1,350 lbs.
Material L: 860 lbs.
Finished products:
Product K-1: 560 units at $180 per unit
Product K-22: 430 units at $100 per unit

c. Desired inventories at March 31:
Direct materials:
Material K: 1,050 lbs.
Material L: 900 lbs.
Finished products:
Product K-1: 610 units at $180 per unit
Product K-22: 420 units at $100 per unit

d. Direct materials used in production:
In manufacture of Product K-1:
Material K: 1.8 lbs. per unit of product
Material L: 2.8 lbs. per unit of product
In manufacture of Product K-22:
Material L: 1.9 lbs. per unit of product

e. Anticipated cost of purchases and beginning and ending inventory of direct materials:
Material K: $25 per lb.
Material L: $40 per lb.

f. Direct labor requirements:
   Product K-1:
      Department 10: .4 hour at $8 per hour
      Department 11: .3 hour at $14 per hour
   Product K-22:
      Department 10: .4 hour at $8 per hour
      Department 12: .5 hour at $10 per hour

g. Estimated factory overhead costs for March:

Indirect factory wages	$210,000
Depreciation of plant and equipment	21,500
Supervisory salaries	95,600
Power and light	8,500
Indirect materials	23,400
Maintenance	11,100
Insurance and property taxes	3,200

h. Estimated operating expenses for March:

Sales salaries expense	$326,700
Officers salaries expense	432,700
Advertising expense	243,000
Office salaries expense	85,200
Depreciation expense—office equipment	6,200
Telephone expense—selling	4,250
Telephone expense—administrative	1,750
Travel expense—selling	32,100
Travel expense—administrative	16,300
Office supplies expense	2,700
Miscellaneous selling expense	5,790
Miscellaneous administrative expense	2,430

i. Estimated other income and expense for March:

Interest income	$17,300
Interest expense	13,500

j. Estimated tax rate: 35%. (Round to nearest dollar.)

Instructions

1. Prepare a sales budget for March.
2. Prepare a production budget for March.
3. Prepare a direct materials purchases budget for March.
4. Prepare a direct labor cost budget for March.
5. Prepare a factory overhead cost budget for March.
6. Prepare a cost of goods sold budget for March. Work in process at the beginning of March is estimated to be $34,200, and work in process at the end of March is estimated to be $31,600.
7. Prepare an operating expenses budget for March. Classify the expenses as either selling or administrative expenses.
8. Prepare a budgeted income statement for March.

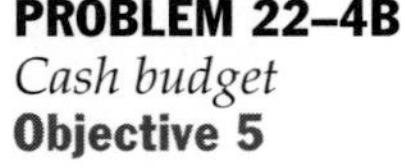

PROBLEM 22–4B
Cash budget
Objective 5

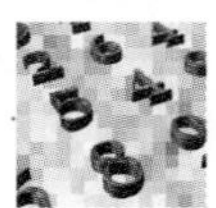

The treasurer of Bright Star Light Company instructs you to prepare a monthly cash budget for the next three months. You are presented with the following budget information:

	April	*May*	*June*
Sales	$160,000	$220,000	$190,000
Manufacturing costs	90,000	125,000	115,000
Operating expenses	52,000	68,200	63,000
Capital expenditures	—	28,000	—

The company expects to sell about 25% of its merchandise for cash. Of sales on account, 80% are expected to be collected in full in the month following the sale and the remainder the following month. Depreciation, insurance, and property taxes represent $15,000 of the estimated monthly manufacturing costs and $6,000 of the probable monthly operating expenses. The annual insurance premium and the annual property taxes are paid in December. Of the remainder of the manufacturing costs and operating expenses, 70% are expected to be paid in the month in which they are incurred and the balance in the following month.

Current assets as of April 1 comprise cash of $28,000, marketable securities of $80,000, and accounts receivable of $166,500 ($135,000 from March sales and $31,500 from February sales). Current liabilities as of April 1 comprise a $40,000, 12%, 60–day note payable due May 20, $26,000 of accounts payable incurred in March for manufacturing costs, and accrued liabilities of $16,400 incurred in March for operating expenses.

It is expected that $2,000 in dividends will be received in April. An estimated income tax payment of $17,000 will be made in May. Bright Star Light Company's regular quarterly dividend of $12,000 is expected to be declared in May and paid in June. Management desires to maintain a minimum cash balance of $25,000.

Instructions

1. Prepare a monthly cash budget for April, May, and June.
2. On the basis of the cash budget prepared in (1), what recommendation should be made to the treasurer?

PROBLEM 22–5B
Budgeted income statement and balance sheet
Objectives 4, 5

As a preliminary to requesting budget estimates of sales, costs, and expenses for the fiscal year beginning January 1, 1997, the following tentative trial balance as of December 31 of the preceding year is prepared by the Accounting Department of Chadwick Glass Company:

Cash	22,400	
Accounts Receivable	36,200	
Finished Goods	18,400	
Work in Process	4,350	
Materials	12,900	
Prepaid Expenses	4,230	
Plant and Equipment	267,500	
Accumulated Depreciation—Plant and Equipment		145,700
Accounts Payable		18,650
Common Stock, $25 par		50,000
Retained Earnings		151,630
	365,980	365,980

Factory output and sales for 1997 are expected to total 120,000 units of product, which are to be sold at $12.50 per unit. The quantities and costs of the inventories (lifo method) at December 31, 1997, are expected to remain unchanged from the balances at the beginning of the year.

Budget estimates of manufacturing costs and operating expenses for the year are summarized as follows:

	Estimated Costs and Expenses	
	Fixed (Total for Year)	*Variable (Per Unit Sold)*
Cost of goods manufactured and sold:		
Direct materials	—	$5.50
Direct labor	—	2.75
Factory overhead:		
Depreciation of plant and equipment	$19,000	—
Other factory overhead	6,000	1.40
Selling expenses:		
Sales salaries and commissions	23,500	.90
Advertising	12,800	—
Miscellaneous selling expense	1,560	.30
Administrative expenses:		
Office and officers salaries	31,300	.10
Supplies	2,400	.06
Miscellaneous administrative expense	800	.03

Balances of accounts receivable, prepaid expenses, and accounts payable at the end of the year are expected to differ from the beginning balances by only insignificant amounts.

Federal income tax of $28,500 on 1997 taxable income will be paid during 1997. Regular quarterly cash dividends of $.50 a share are expected to be declared and paid in March, June, September, and December. It is anticipated that plant and equipment will be purchased for $60,000 cash in December.

Instructions

1. Prepare a budgeted income statement for 1997.
2. Prepare a budgeted balance sheet as of December 31, 1997.

PROBLEM 22–6B
Static vs. flexible budgets for factory overhead costs
Objectives 2, 4

D'Angelo Metals Company prepared the following factory July overhead cost budget for the Machining Department, based on the actual expenditures for June, 1997.

D'Angelo Metals Company
Factory Overhead Cost Budget—Machining Department
For the Month Ending July 31, 1997

Variable cost:		
Indirect factory wages	$37,800	
Indirect materials	25,200	
Power and light	1,740	
Total variable cost		$64,740
Fixed cost:		
Supervisory salaries	$ 9,460	
Indirect factory wages	2,570	
Depreciation of plant and equipment	5,700	
Insurance	1,760	
Power and light	5,230	
Property taxes	2,020	
Total fixed cost		26,740
Total factory overhead		$91,480

There were 30,000 machine hours used in the Machining Department in June. The July actual results appeared as follows:

D'Angelo Metals Company
Factory Overhead Actual Costs—Machining Department
For the Month Ending July 31, 1997

Variable cost:		
Indirect factory wages	$33,600	
Indirect materials	23,150	
Power and light	1,605	
Total variable cost		$58,355
Fixed cost:		
Supervisory salaries	$ 9,460	
Indirect factory wages	2,570	
Depreciation of plant and equipment	5,700	
Insurance	1,760	
Power and light	5,230	
Property taxes	2,020	
Total fixed cost		26,740
Total factory overhead		$85,095

The actual July cost was less than the July budget by $6,385. The plant manager was prepared to take the department out for a celebration, until noticing that there were only 26,000 machine hours used in July.

Instructions

1. Prepare a flexible budget for the Machining Department for 26,000 machine hours.
2. Determine the difference between the flexible budget prepared in (1) and the actual cost for the Machining Department in July.

3. Should the June static budget or flexible budget be used for controlling July's cost? Why?

CASES

CASE 22–1
Quick Solutions Software Company
Human behavior and budgets

The director of marketing for Quick Solutions Software Company, Ron Keller, had the following discussion with the company controller, Jo Johnson, on July 26th of the current year:

Ron: Jo, it looks like I'm going to spend much less than my July budget.

Jo: I'm glad to hear it.

Ron: Well, I'm not so sure it's good news. I'm concerned that the president will see that I'm under budget and reduce my budget in the future. The only reason that I look good is that we've delayed an advertising campaign. Once the campaign hits in September, I'm sure my actual figures will go up. You see, we are also having our sales convention in September. Having the advertising campaign and the convention at the same time is going to kill my September numbers.

Jo: I don't think that's anything to worry about. We all expect some variation in actual spending month to month. What's really important is staying within the budgeted targets for the year. Does that look like it's going to be a problem?

Ron: I don't think so, but just the same, I'd like to be on the safe side.

Jo: What do you mean?

Ron: Well, this is what I'd like to do. I want to pay the convention-related costs in advance this month. I'll pay the hotel for room and convention space and purchase the airline tickets in advance. In this way I can charge all these expenditures to July's budget. This would cause my actual expenses to come close to budget for July. Moreover, when the big advertising campaign hits in September, I won't have to worry about expenditures for the convention on my September budget as well. The convention costs will already be paid. Thus, my September expenses should be pretty close to budget.

Jo: I can't tell you when to make your convention purchases, but I'm not too sure that it should be expensed on July's budget.

Ron: What's the problem? It looks like "no harm, no foul" to me. I can't see that there's anything wrong with this—it's just smart management.

How should Jo Johnson respond to Ron Keller's request to expense the advance payments for convention-related costs against July's budget?

CASE 22–2
Elgin Sweeper Company
Evaluating budgeting systems

In the mid-1980s, Elgin Sweeper Company began an overhaul of its planning and control system. This overhaul is described in the following excerpt from an article in *Management Accounting:*

How could we bring responsibility for and management of costs to the individual department managers? For two years before we began our efforts the annual budget had been prepared substantially by the accounting department with little [responsibility] for results felt by persons outside top management.

Our first step was to modify the budget responsibility reports to reflect only those costs controllable by the department manager.

. . . The next step was [to change] the actual budget preparation. . . . [Under the old method, expense] accounts did not segregate variable and fixed costs. When volume-adjusted numbers were required for either budget preparation or budget-to-actual comparison, we merely would use an "executive judgment" percentage to adjust the appropriate expenses. Needless to say, this system resulted in some unusual variations, which sometimes required "innovative" explanations.

Source: J. P. Callan, W. N. Tredup, and R. S. Wisinger, "Elgin Sweeper Company's Journey Toward Cost Management," *Management Accounting*, July 1991, pp. 24–27.

What are the behavioral ramifications of including expenses within a responsibility center for which a manager has no control? Did Elgin previously use static budgeting or flexible budgeting? What type of budgeting will Elgin use in the future?

CASE 22–3
Pyramid Bancorp.
Service company static budget; decision making

A bank manager of Pyramid Bancorp. uses the managerial accounting system to track the costs of operating the various departments within the bank. The departments include Cash Management, Trust, Commercial Loans, Mortgage Loans, Operations, Credit Card, and Branch Services. The budget and actual results for the Operations Department are as follows:

Resources	*Budget*	*Actual*
Salaries	$150,000	$150,000
Benefits	30,000	30,000
Supplies	45,000	42,000
Travel	20,000	30,000
Training	25,000	30,000
Overtime	25,000	20,000
Total	$295,000	$302,000
Excess of actual over budget	$ 7,000	

a. What information is provided by the budget? Specifically, what questions can the bank manager ask of the Operations Department manager?

b. What information does the budget fail to provide? Specifically, could the budget information be presented differently to provide even more insight for the bank manager?

CASE 22–4
Dell Computer Company
Objectives of the master budget

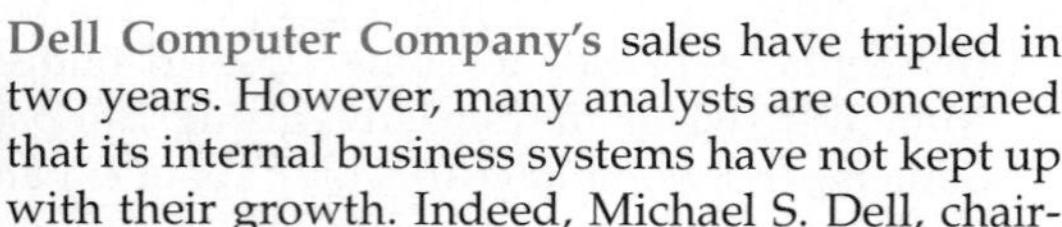

Dell Computer Company's sales have tripled in two years. However, many analysts are concerned that its internal business systems have not kept up with their growth. Indeed, Michael S. Dell, chairman and chief executive officer, said, "The systems and processes in the company didn't grow as fast as the business." As a result, one Dell official stated, "This is like building a high-performance car while going around the racetrack." Some analysts are concerned that the lack of internal systems may harm Dell's future growth. Mr. Dell stated, "I believe the issues the company faces are quite serious."

Source: *Wall Street Journal*, June 19, 1993, p. B4.

How would a master budget support planning, directing, and control in Dell Computer Company?

CASE 22–5
SRC
Behavioral aspects of financial goals

One aspect of motivating line employees is to provide them financial improvement targets. The following excerpt describes this approach:

For managers and line workers to be similarly focused on bottom-line issues, it's critical that all employees are first well-trained in understanding the financials. . . While training is important, what makes Bottom Line Powered Management so powerful is that financial and performance data are presented to employees to be used as direct, practical feedback for operations. At SRC, for example, financial and performance data become critical to individual performance when the profit-and-loss statement is broken down for all operations—that is, for all employee teams and work groups. Each employee team then knows if it is on target and can make the appropriate corrections. If sales to a particular customer are off track, that is immediately investigated. If the team's overhead is above the projection, that is attacked. Moreover, this information is provided weekly, letting the employees quickly pounce on any problem. . . . To ensure that financial data are actually used, (they are given) numbers the employees can understand and influence.

Source: Willard I. Zangwill, "Focusing All Eyes on the Bottom Line," *Wall Street Journal*, March 21, 1994, p. A12.

Identify and explain what critical characteristics of the Bottom Line Powered Management (BLPM) approach appear to affect human behavior.

CASE 22–6
Joy Williamson
Objectives of budgeting

At the beginning of the academic year, Joy Williamson decided to prepare a cash budget for the year, based upon anticipated cash receipts and payments. The estimates in the budget represent a "best guess." The budget is as follows:

Expected annual cash receipts:		
Salary from part-time job	$10,000	
Salary from summer job	4,000	
Total receipts		$14,000
Expected annual cash payments:		
Tuition	$ 4,500	
Books	400	
Rent	3,500	
Food	2,500	
Utilities	800	
Entertainment	4,000	
Total payments		15,700
Net change in cash		$ (1,700)

1. What does this budget suggest? In what ways is this useful information to Joy?
2. a. Some items in the budget are more certain than are others. Which items are the most certain? Which items are the most uncertain? What are the implications of these different levels of certainty to Joy's planning?
   b. Some payment items are more adjustable than others. Assuming that Joy plans to go to school, classify the items as adjustable, partially adjustable or not adjustable. What are the implications of adjustable items to planning?
3. What actions could Joy take in order to avoid having the anticipated shortfall of $1,700 at the end of the year?
4. What does this budget fail to consider, and what are the implications of these omissions to Joy's planning?

ANSWERS TO SELF-EXAMINATION QUESTIONS

1. **C** Flexible budgeting (answer C) provides a series of budgets for varying rates of activity and thereby builds into the budgeting system the effect of fluctuations in the level of activity. Static budgeting (answer A) does not take into account changes in activity level. Zero-based budgeting (answer B) determines budget priorities by requiring managers to start from zero and assume operations are being started for the first time. Cash budgeting (answer D) is one of the elements of balance sheet budgeting.
2. **C** Continuous budgeting (answer C) is a type of budgeting that continually provides for maintaining a twelve-month projection into the future.
3. **C** The capital expenditures budget (answer C) summarizes the plans for acquiring plant facilities and equipment for a number of years into the future. The cash budget (answer A) presents the expected inflow and outflow of cash for a budget period, and the sales budget (answer B) presents the expected sales for the budget period. The production budget (answer D) translates the expected sales into unit production requirements.
4. **B** The total production indicated in the production budget is 257,500 units (answer B), which is computed as follows:

Sales	250,000 units
Plus desired ending inventory	30,000 units
Total	280,000 units
Less estimated beginning inventory	22,500 units
Total production	257,500 units

5. **C** Dixon expects to collect 70% of April sales ($560,000) plus 30% of the March sales ($195,000) in April, for a total of $755,000 (answer C). Answer A is 100% of April sales. Answer B is 70% of April sales. Answer D adds 70% of both March and April sales.

23 Performance Evaluation Using Variances from Standard Costs

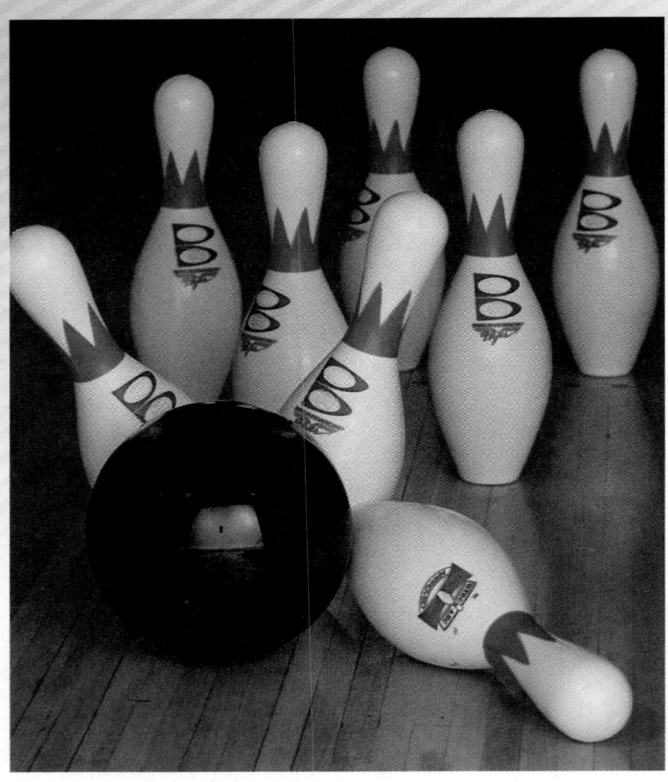

YOU AND ACCOUNTING

When you play a sport, you are evaluated with respect to how well you perform compared to a standard or to a competitor. In bowling, for example, your score is compared to a perfect score of 300 or to the score of your competitors. In this class, you are evaluated according to performance standards, which are often described in terms of letter grades. These grades provide a measure of how well you achieved the class objectives. On your job, you are evaluated according to performance standards.

Just as your class performance is evaluated, managers are evaluated with respect to how well they perform relative to the plan established at the beginning of the year. Performance is often measured as the difference between actual results and budgeted results. In this chapter, we will discuss and illustrate the ways in which companies evaluate business performance.

After studying this chapter, you should be able to:

Objective 1
Describe the types of standards and how they are established for businesses.

Objective 2
Explain and illustrate how standards are used in flexible budgeting.

Objective 3
Calculate and interpret direct materials price and quantity variances.

Objective 4
Calculate and interpret direct labor rate and time variances.

Objective 5
Calculate and interpret factory overhead controllable and volume variances.

Objective 6
Journalize the entries for recording standards in the accounts and prepare an income statement that includes variances from standard.

Objective 7
Explain how standards may be used for nonmanufacturing expenses.

Objective 8
Explain and provide examples of nonfinancial performance measures.

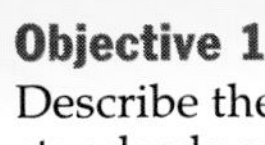

Standards

Objective 1
Describe the types of standards and how they are established for businesses.

What are standards? **Standards** are performance benchmarks. Service, merchandising, and manufacturing businesses may all use standards to evaluate and control operations. For example, long-haul drivers for United Parcel Service are expected to drive a standard distance per day. Salespersons for The Limited are expected to exceed sales standards in order to earn bonuses.

In The Limited stores, salespersons earn bonuses by exceeding the sales standards.

The widest use of standards is by manufacturing businesses. Manufacturers normally establish standard costs for each of the three categories of manufacturing costs: direct materials, direct labor, and factory overhead.

Accounting systems that use standards for each element of manufacturing cost entering into the finished product are called standard cost systems. Standard cost systems are widely used in industry in conjunction with job order and process systems. One survey of manufacturing firms reported that 87% of the firms use some form of standard cost accounting.[1]

Standard cost systems enable management to determine how much a product should cost (standard cost), how much it does cost (actual cost), and the causes of any difference (variance from standard) between the two. Standard costs thus serve as a device for measuring efficiency.

When actual costs are compared with standard costs, only the exceptions or variances are reported for cost control. This reporting by the *principle of exceptions* allows management to focus on the cause and correction of the variances. Thus, using standard costs assists management in controlling costs and in motivating employees to become more cost-conscious.

Automated manufacturing operations can integrate standard cost data with the computerized system that directs operations. The system then detects and reports variances automatically and makes adjustments to operations in progress.

SETTING STANDARDS

Setting standards is both an art and a science. Although the standard-setting process varies among businesses, it normally requires the joint efforts of accountants,

[1] B. R. Gaumnitz and F. P. Kollaritsch, "Manufacturing Variances: Current Trends and Practice," *Journal of Cost Management*, Spring 1991, pp. 58–63.

engineers, and other management personnel. The management accountant plays an essential role by expressing the results of judgments and studies in dollars and cents. Engineers contribute to the standard-setting process by identifying the materials, labor, and machine requirements needed to produce the product. For example, engineers can determine the direct materials requirements by studying such factors as the materials specifications for the product and estimating normal spoilage in production. Time and motion studies may be used to determine the length of time required for each of the various manufacturing operations. Engineering studies may also be used to determine standards for some of the elements of factory overhead, such as the amount of power needed to operate machinery.

Setting standards often begins with analyzing past operations. However, standards are not just an extension of past costs, and caution must be used in relying on past cost data. For example, inefficiencies may be contained within past costs. In addition, changes in technology, machinery, or production methods may make past costs irrelevant for future operations.

TYPES OF STANDARDS

Implicit in using standards is the concept of an acceptable level of production efficiency. One of the major objectives in setting this performance level is to motivate workers to achieve the most efficient operations.

Like the budgets we discussed earlier, standards that are too high, that is, standards that are unrealistic, may have a negative impact on performance. This is because workers may become frustrated with their inability to meet the standards and, therefore, may not be motivated to do their best. Such standards represent levels of performance that can be achieved only under perfect operating conditions, such as no idle time, no machine breakdowns, and no materials spoilage. These standards, often called **theoretical standards** or **ideal standards,** are not widely used.

Standards that are too low might not motivate employees to perform at their best. This is because the standard level of performance can be reached too easily. As a result, productivity may be lower than what could be achieved.

Most companies use **currently attainable standards** (sometimes called **normal standards**). These standards represent levels of operation that can be attained with reasonable effort. Such standards allow for reasonable production difficulties and mistakes, such as normal materials spoilage and machine breakdowns. When reasonable standards are used, employees become more cost-conscious. They often put forth their best efforts to achieve the best operating results at the lowest possible cost. Further, if employees are given bonuses for exceeding normal standards, the standards may be even more effective in motivating employees.

An example from the game of golf illustrates the distinction between ideal and normal standards. In golf, "par" is an *ideal* standard for most players. Each player's USGA (United States Golf Association) handicap is the player's *normal* standard. The motivation of average players is to beat their handicaps because they may view beating par as unrealistic.

REVIEWING AND REVISING STANDARDS

Standard costs should be continuously reviewed, and when they no longer reflect operating conditions, they should be revised. Inaccurate standards may have a harmful effect on management decision making and may weaken management's ability to plan and control operations.

Standards should not be revised, however, just because they differ from actual costs. They should be revised only when they no longer reflect the operating conditions that they were intended to measure. For example, the direct labor standard would not be revised simply because workers were unable to meet properly determined standards. On the other hand, standards should be revised when prices, product designs, labor rates, or manufacturing methods change to such an extent that current standards are no longer a useful measure of performance. For example, when aluminum beverage cans were redesigned to taper slightly at the top, manufacturers reduced the standard amount of aluminum per can because less aluminum was required for the tapered can.

SUPPORT AND CRITICISM OF STANDARDS

In business, standards are used to support inventory valuation for financial statements, to plan costs through flexible budgets, and to control costs through comparing standards to actual performance. As evidence of the increasing importance of standards, one survey indicates that companies are now using standards to assess performance at lower levels of the organization, for shorter accounting periods, and for an increasing number of costs.[2]

Using standards for performance evaluation has been criticized. The critics assert that standards limit continuous improvement of operations by discouraging improvement beyond the standard. Regardless of this criticism, standards are widely used. One survey reports that managers strongly support standard cost systems and that they regard standards as critical for running large businesses efficiently.[3]

Flexible Budgeting and Control

Objective 2
Explain and illustrate how standards are used in flexible budgeting.

As we discussed in the previous chapter, the master budget assists a company in planning, directing, and controlling performance. In the remainder of this chapter, we will discuss using the master budget to control plans. The control function, or **budgetary performance evaluation,** compares the actual performance against the budget.

We will illustrate budget performance evaluation using Western Rider Inc., a manufacturer of blue jeans. Western Rider Inc. uses standard manufacturing costs in its budgets. The standards for direct materials, direct labor, and factory overhead are separated into two components: (1) a price standard and (2) a quantity standard. Multiplying these two elements together yields the standard cost per unit for a given manufacturing cost category, as shown for style XL jeans in Exhibit 1.

The standard price and quantity are separated because the means of controlling them are frequently different. For example, the direct materials price per square

Exhibit 1
Standard Cost for XL Jeans

Manufacturing Costs	*Standard Price*	×	*Standard Quantity per Pair*	=	*Standard Cost per Pair of XL Jeans*
Direct materials	$5.00 per square yard		1.5 square yards		$ 7.50
Direct labor	$9.00 per hour		.80 hour per pair		7.20
Factory overhead	$6.00 per hour		.80 hour per pair		4.80
Total standard cost per pair					$19.50

[2] *Ibid.*
[3] C. Graham, D. Lydall, and A. G. Puxty, "Cost Control: The Manager's Perspective," *Management Accounting*, UK, October 1992, pp. 26–27.

Western Rider Inc., a manufacturer of blue jeans, uses standard manufacturing costs for materials, labor, and factory overhead when preparing its master budget.

yard is controlled by the Purchasing Department, and the direct materials quantity per pair is controlled by the Production Department.

Western Rider Inc. uses flexible budgeting in preparing its master budget. This means that the budgeted materials purchases, direct labor, and factory overhead are determined at the beginning of the period by multiplying the standard cost by different estimates of production. Thus, for example, the June 1997 flexible budget for Western Rider for planned volumes of 4,600 and 5,000 pairs of XL jeans is as follows:

Manufacturing Costs	*Flexible Budget at Planned Volume (4,600 Pairs of XL Jeans)**	*Flexible Budget at Planned Volume (5,000 Pairs of XL Jeans)***
Direct materials	$34,500	$37,500
Direct labor	33,120	36,000
Factory overhead	22,080	24,000
Total budgeted manufacturing costs	$89,700	$97,500

*4,600 pairs × $7.50 per pair = $34,500
4,600 pairs × $7.20 per pair = $33,120
4,600 pairs × $4.80 per pair = $22,080

**5,000 pairs × $7.50 per pair = $37,500
5,000 pairs × $7.20 per pair = $36,000
5,000 pairs × $4.80 per pair = $24,000

The budgeted costs at planned volumes are included in the master budget at the beginning of the period, as illustrated in the previous chapter. The actual production costs for the period should be compared to the flexible budget at *actual* volumes of production. To illustrate, assume that Western Rider produced and sold 5,000 pairs of XL jeans in June 1997, for the following actual production costs:

Manufacturing Costs	*Actual Costs for 5,000 Pairs*
Direct materials	$ 40,150
Direct labor	38,500
Factory overhead	22,400
Total actual manufacturing costs	$101,050

These costs should be compared to the flexible budget for 5,000 pairs of jeans. The difference between the actual cost and the flexible budget at the actual volume is called a **cost variance.** A *favorable* cost variance occurs when actual cost is less than budgeted cost (at actual volumes). An *unfavorable* variance occurs when actual cost exceeds budgeted cost (at actual volumes).

Cost variances can be summarized in a budget performance report, prepared periodically. A **budget performance report** compares actual results with the budgeted amounts for the level of production achieved. This feedback enables management to investigate significant differences and to take corrective action. A budget performance report for Western Rider Inc. is shown in Exhibit 2.

Exhibit 2
Budget Performance Report

Western Rider Inc.
Budget Performance Report
For the Month Ended June 30, 1997

Manufacturing Costs	Actual Costs	Flexible Budget at Actual Volume (5,000 pairs of XL Jeans)	Cost Variance—(Favorable) Unfavorable
Direct materials	$ 40,150	$37,500	$2,650
Direct labor	38,500	36,000	2,500
Factory overhead	22,400	24,000	(1,600)
Total manufacturing costs	$101,050	$97,500	$3,550

The cause of cost variances should be determined. In Exhibit 2, for example, the direct materials cost variance is an unfavorable $2,650. There are two possible explanations for this variance: (1) the amount of blue denim used per pair of blue jeans was different than expected, and/or (2) the purchase price of blue denim was different than expected. In the next sections, we will illustrate how to separate the cost variances for direct materials, direct labor, and factory overhead.

Direct Materials Variances

Objective 3
Calculate and interpret direct materials price and quantity variances.

What caused Western Rider Inc.'s unfavorable materials variance of $2,650, determined in the previous section? Recall that the direct materials standards from Exhibit 1 are as follows:

Price standard: $5.00 per square yard
Quantity standard: 1.5 square yards per pair of XL jeans

To determine the number of standard square yards of denim budgeted, multiply the actual production for June 1997 (5,000 pairs) by the quantity standard (1.5 square yards per pair). Then multiply the standard square yards by the standard price per square yard ($5.00) to determine the standard budgeted cost at the actual volume. The calculation is shown as follows:

Standard square yards per pair of jeans	1.5 sq. yards
Actual units produced	× 5,000 pairs of jeans
Standard square yards of denim budgeted for actual production	7,500 sq. yards
Standard price per square yard	× $5.00
Standard direct materials cost at actual production (same as Exhibit 2)	$37,500

This calculation assumes that there is no change in the beginning and ending inventories for materials. Thus, the amount of materials budgeted for production is also equal to the amount budgeted to be purchased.

Assume that the actual total cost for denim used during June 1997 was as follows:

Actual quantity of denim used in production	7,300 sq. yards
Actual price per square yard	× $5.50
Total actual direct materials cost (same as Exhibit 2)	$40,150

The total unfavorable cost variance $2,650 ($40,150 – $37,500) results from an excess price per square yard of $.50 per square yard and using 200 fewer square yards of denim. These two reasons can be reported as two separate variances, as shown in the next sections.

DIRECT MATERIALS PRICE VARIANCE

The **direct materials price variance** is the difference between the actual price per unit ($5.50) and the standard price per unit ($5.00), multiplied by the actual quantity used (7,300 square yards). If the actual price per unit exceeds the standard price per unit, the variance is unfavorable, as shown for Western Rider Inc. If the actual price per unit is less than the standard price per unit, the variance is favorable. The calculation for Western Rider Inc. is as follows:

Price variance:	
Actual price per unit	\$5.50 per square yard
Standard price per unit	5.00 per square yard
Price variance—unfavorable	\$ .50 per square yard × actual qty., 7,300 sq. yds. = \$3,650

DIRECT MATERIALS QUANTITY VARIANCE

The **direct materials quantity variance** is the difference between the actual quantity used (7,300 square yards) and the standard quantity at actual production (7,500 square yards), multiplied by the standard price per unit (\$5.00). If the actual quantity of materials used exceeds the standard quantity budgeted, the variance is unfavorable. If the actual quantity of materials used is less than the standard quantity, the variance is favorable, as shown for Western Rider Inc.:

Quantity variance:	
Actual quantity	7,300 square yards
Standard quantity at actual production	7,500
Quantity variance—favorable	(200) square yards × standard price, \$5.00 = (\$1,000)

DIRECT MATERIALS VARIANCE RELATIONSHIPS

The direct materials variances can be illustrated by making three calculations and relating them as shown in Exhibit 3. The three calculations are:

1. Determine the actual cost: *actual quantity × actual price.*
2. Determine the actual quantity at the standard price: *actual quantity × standard price.*
3. Determine the standard materials cost at actual production: *standard quantity × standard price.*

The difference between the first and second columns is the price variance, while the difference between the second and third columns is the quantity variance. The difference between the first and third columns is the total cost variance.

Exhibit 3
Direct Materials Variance Relationships

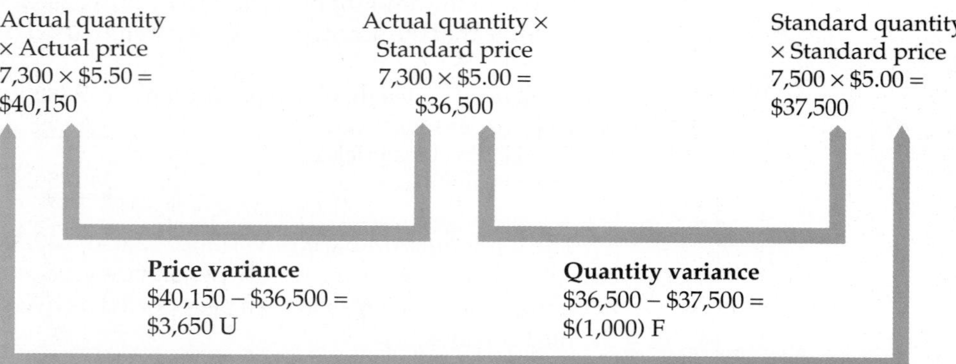

Total direct materials cost variance: \$40,150 – \$37,500 = \$2,650 U

REPORTING DIRECT MATERIALS VARIANCES

The direct materials quantity variance should be reported to the proper operating management level for possible corrective action. For example, excessive amounts of direct materials might have been used because of the malfunction of equipment that has not been properly maintained or operated. However, an unfavorable direct materials quantity variance may not always be the responsibility of an operating department. For example, the excess materials usage may be caused by purchasing inferior raw materials. In this case, the Purchasing Department should be held responsible.

The direct materials price variance should normally be reported to the Purchasing Department, which may or may not be able to control this variance. If materials of the same quality could have been purchased from another supplier at the standard price, the variance was controllable. On the other hand, if the variance resulted from a marketwide price increase, the variance may not be subject to control.

Direct Labor Variances

Objective 4
Calculate and interpret direct labor rate and time variances.

The direct labor cost variance can also be separated into two parts. Recall that the direct labor standards from Exhibit 1 are as follows:

Rate standard: $9.00 per hour
Time standard: .80 hour per pair of XL jeans

The actual production (5,000 pairs) is multiplied by the time standard (.80 hour per pair) to determine the number of standard direct labor hours budgeted. The standard direct labor hours are then multiplied by the standard rate per hour ($9.00) to determine the budgeted direct labor cost at actual volumes. The calculation is shown as follows:

Standard direct labor hours per pair of XL jeans	.80 direct labor hours
Actual units produced	× 5,000 pairs of jeans
Standard direct labor hours budgeted for actual production	4,000 direct labor hours
Standard rate per direct labor hour	× $9.00
Standard direct labor cost at actual production (same as Exhibit 2)	$36,000

Assume that the actual total cost for direct labor during June 1997 was as follows:

Actual direct labor hours used in production	3,850 direct labor hours
Actual rate per direct labor hour	× $10.00
Total actual direct labor cost (same as Exhibit 2)	$ 38,500

The total unfavorable cost variance $2,500 ($38,500 – $36,000) results from an excess direct labor rate of $1.00 per direct labor hour and using 150 fewer direct labor hours. These two reasons can be reported as two separate variances, as shown in the next sections.

DIRECT LABOR RATE VARIANCE

The **direct labor rate variance** is the difference between the actual rate per hour ($10.00) and the standard rate per hour ($9.00), multiplied by the actual hours worked (3,850 hours). If the actual rate per hour exceeds the standard rate per hour, the variance is unfavorable, as for Western Rider Inc. If the actual rate per hour is less than the standard rate per hour, the variance is favorable. The calculation for Western Rider Inc. is as follows:

Rate variance:	
Actual rate	$10.00 per hour
Standard rate	9.00
Rate variance—unfavorable	$ 1.00 per hour × actual time, 3,850 hours = $3,850

DIRECT LABOR TIME VARIANCE

The direct labor time variance is the difference between the actual hours worked (3,850 hours) and the standard hours at actual production (4,000 hours), multiplied by the standard rate per hour ($9.00). If the actual hours worked exceed the standard hours, the variance is unfavorable. If the actual hours worked are less than the standard hours, the variance is favorable, as shown below for Western Rider Inc.

Time variance:	
Actual hours	3,850 direct labor hours
Standard hours at actual production	4,000
Time variance—favorable	(150) direct labor hours × standard rate, $9.00 = ($1,350)

DIRECT LABOR VARIANCE RELATIONSHIPS

The direct labor variances can be illustrated by making three calculations and relating them as shown in Exhibit 4. The three calculations are:

1. Determine the actual cost: *actual hours × actual rate.*
2. Determine the actual hours at the standard rate: *actual hours × standard rate.*
3. Determine the standard direct labor cost at actual production: *standard hours × standard rate.*

The difference between the first and second columns is the rate variance, while the difference between the second and third columns is the time variance. The difference between the first and third columns is the total cost variance.

Exhibit 4
Direct Labor Variance Relationships

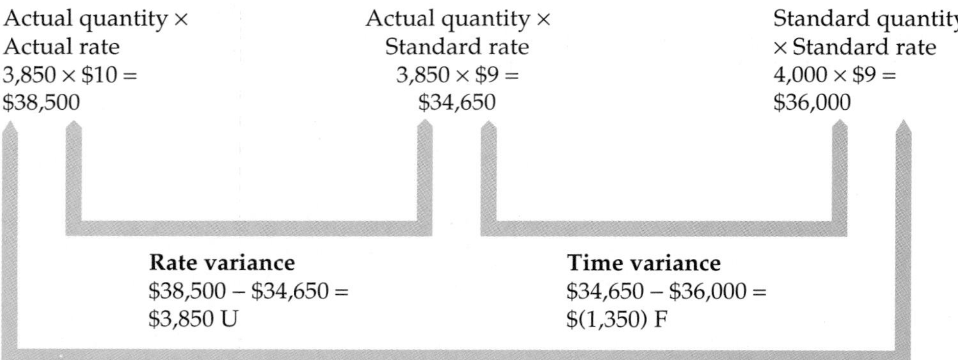

Total direct labor cost variance: $38,500 – $36,000 = $2,500 U

REPORTING DIRECT LABOR VARIANCES

Controlling direct labor cost is often the responsibility of the production supervisors. To aid them, periodic reports analyzing the cause of any direct labor variance may be prepared. Comparing standard direct labor hours and actual direct labor hours provides the basis for investigating any major time variances. For example, a major time variance may be incurred because of the shortage of skilled workers. Such variances may be uncontrollable unless they are related to unusually high turnover rates among employees, in which case the cause of the high turnover should be investigated.

Comparing the rates paid for direct labor with the standard rates provides a basis for investigating any major rate variances. For example, unfavorable rate variances may be caused by the improper scheduling and use of workers. In such cases, skilled, highly paid workers may be used in jobs that are normally performed by unskilled, lower paid workers. If this is the case, the unfavorable rate variance should be reported for corrective action to the level of management responsible for scheduling work assignments.

USING ACCOUNTING TO UNDERSTAND BUSINESS

SCM Corporation identified its business units as either "harvest" or "build." Harvest business units contained mature products, whereas build business units depended on developing and growing new product markets. The budget system reflected the differences between these two types of business units. Harvest business units were concerned about maintaining cost competitiveness. Thus, performance against budget was the primary control tool. Build business units were concerned about launching successful products. Thus, performance against budget was a minor control tool. Instead, the budget for build businesses was used for short-term planning to help manage rapidly changing business conditions.

SCM Corporation is a diversified company which identifies its business units, such as Allied Paper Co., as either "harvest" or "build."

Source: G. E. Hall, "Reflections on Running a Diversified Company," *Harvard Business Review,* January-February 1987.

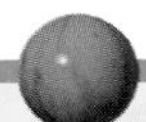

Factory Overhead Variances

Objective 5
Calculate and interpret factory overhead controllable and volume variances.

Factory overhead costs are more difficult to manage than are direct labor and materials costs because the relationship between production volume and indirect costs is not as easy to determine. For example, when production is increased, the direct materials will increase. But what about the Engineering Department overhead? The relationship between production volume and costs is less clear for the Engineering Department. Companies normally respond to this difficulty by separating factory overhead into variable and fixed costs. For example, manufacturing supplies would be considered variable to production volume, whereas straight-line plant depreciation would be considered fixed. In the following sections, we will discuss the performance evaluation approaches used when factory overhead is separated into fixed and variable components.

THE FACTORY OVERHEAD FLEXIBLE BUDGET

A flexible budget may be used to determine the impact of production volume changes on fixed and variable factory overhead. The standard overhead rate is determined by dividing the budgeted factory overhead costs by the standard amount of productive activity, such as direct labor hours. Exhibit 5 is a flexible factory overhead budget for Western Rider Inc., showing the standard factory overhead rate for a month.

Exhibit 5
Factory Overhead Cost Budget Indicating Standard Factory Overhead Rate

Western Rider Inc.
Factory Overhead Cost Budget
For the Month Ending June 30, 1997

Percent of normal capacity	80%	90%	100%	110%
Direct labor hours	4,000	4,500	5,000	5,500
Budgeted factory overhead:				
Variable costs:				
Indirect factory wages	$ 8,000	$ 9,000	$10,000	$11,000
Power and light	4,000	4,500	5,000	5,500
Indirect materials	2,400	2,700	3,000	3,300
Total variable cost	$14,400	$16,200	$18,000	$19,800
Fixed costs:				
Supervisory salaries	$ 5,500	$ 5,500	$ 5,500	$ 5,500
Depreciation of plant and equipment	4,500	4,500	4,500	4,500
Insurance and property taxes	2,000	2,000	2,000	2,000
Total fixed cost	$12,000	$12,000	$12,000	$12,000
Total factory overhead cost	$26,400	$28,200	$30,000	$31,800

Factory overhead rate per direct labor hour, $30,000 ÷ 5,000 = $6.00

In this illustration, the standard factory overhead cost rate is determined on the basis of the currently attainable standard for the level of expected business activity of 100% of normal capacity. The standard rate is $6.00 per direct labor hour. This rate can be subdivided into $3.60 per hour for variable factory overhead ($18,000 ÷ 5,000 hours) and $2.40 per hour for fixed factory overhead ($12,000 ÷ 5,000 hours).

Variances from standard for factory overhead cost result from:

1. Incurring a total amount of variable factory overhead cost greater or less than the amount of variable factory overhead budgeted for actual production.
2. Operating at a level above or below 100% of normal capacity.

The first factor results in the controllable variance with respect to variable overhead costs. The second factor results in a volume variance with respect to fixed overhead costs. We will discuss each of these variances in the following sections.

VARIABLE FACTORY OVERHEAD CONTROLLABLE VARIANCE

The variable factory overhead **controllable variance** is the difference between the actual amount of variable overhead incurred and the amount of budgeted variable overhead for actual production. The controllable variance measures the *efficiency* of using variable overhead resources. Thus, if the budgeted variable overhead exceeds the actual variable overhead, the variance is favorable. If the budgeted variable overhead is less than the actual variable overhead, the variance is unfavorable.

To illustrate, recall that Western Rider Inc. produced 5,000 pairs of XL jeans in June. Each pair requires .80 standard labor hour for production. As a result, Western Rider Inc. had 4,000 standard hours at actual production (5,000 × .80). This represents 80% of normal productive capacity. The standard variable overhead at 4,000 hours worked, according to the budget in Exhibit 5, was $14,400 (4,000 direct labor hours × $3.60). The following actual factory overhead costs were incurred in June:

Actual costs:	
Variable factory overhead	$10,400
Fixed factory overhead	12,000
Total actual factory overhead	$22,400

The controllable variance can be calculated as follows:

Controllable variance:	
Actual variable factory overhead	$10,400
Budgeted variable factory overhead for	
actual amount produced (4,000 hrs. × $3.60)	14,400
Variance—favorable	$ (4,000)

The variable factory overhead controllable variance indicates management's ability to keep the factory overhead costs within the limits set forth in the budget. Since variable factory overhead costs are normally controllable at the department level, responsibility for controlling this variance usually rests with department supervisors.

FIXED FACTORY OVERHEAD VOLUME VARIANCE

Western Rider Inc. set its budgeted normal capacity at 5,000 direct labor hours.

As we noted in the previous section, the efficiency of variable factory overhead can be evaluated with the controllable variance. This leaves the question of how to measure the variance related to fixed factory overhead. Using currently attainable standards, Western Rider Inc. set its budgeted normal capacity at 5,000 direct labor hours. This is the amount of expected manufacturing capacity that management believes will be used under normal business conditions. You should note that this amount may be much less than the total available capacity if management believes demand will be low.

The fixed factory overhead **volume variance** is the difference between the budgeted fixed overhead at 100% of normal capacity and the standard fixed overhead for the actual production achieved during the period. The volume variance measures the utilization of fixed overhead resources. If the standard fixed overhead exceeds the budgeted overhead at 100% of normal capacity, the variance is favorable. Thus, the firm has received greater utilization from its plant and equipment than would be expected under normal operating conditions. If the standard fixed overhead is less than the budgeted overhead at 100% of normal capacity, the variance is unfavorable. Thus, the company has received less utilization from its plant and equipment than would be expected under normal operating conditions.

The volume variance for Western Rider Inc. is shown in the following calculation:

100% of normal capacity	5,000	direct labor hours
Standard hours at actual production	4,000	
Capacity not used	1,000	direct labor hours
Standard fixed overhead rate	× $2.40	
Volume variance—unfavorable	$ 2,400	

Exhibit 6 is a graph illustrating the volume variance for Western Rider Inc. The budgeted fixed overhead is $12,000 at all levels. Therefore, the standard fixed overhead at 5,000 hours is also $12,000. This is the point at which the standard fixed overhead line intersects the budgeted fixed cost line. For actual volume greater than 100% of normal capacity, the volume variance is favorable. For volume at less than 100% volume, the volume variance is unfavorable. For Western Rider Inc., the volume variance is unfavorable because the actual volume is 4,000 hours, or 80% of normal volume. The amount of the volume variance, $2,400, can be viewed as the cost of the unused capacity (1,000 hours).

Exhibit 6
Graph of Fixed Overhead Volume Variance

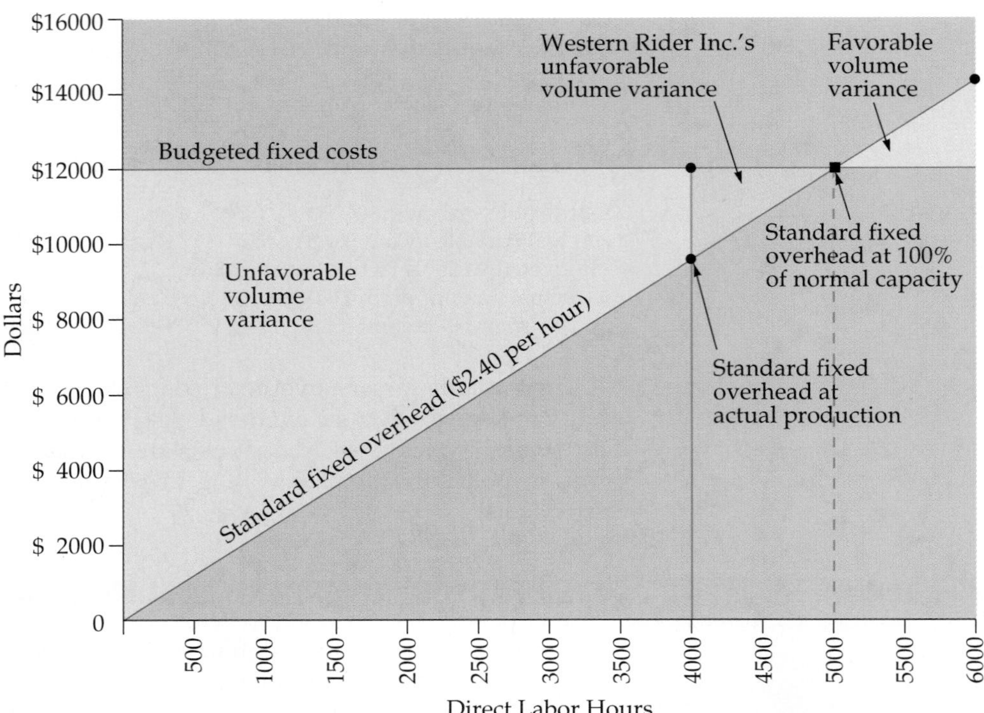

The idle time that resulted in an unfavorable volume variance may be due to such factors as failure to maintain an even flow of work, machine breakdowns, repairs causing work stoppages, and failure to obtain enough sales orders to keep the factory operating at normal capacity. Management should determine the causes of the idle time and consider taking corrective action. A volume variance caused by supervisors failing to maintain an even flow of work, for example, can be remedied by changing operating procedures. Volume variances caused by lack of sales orders may be corrected through increased advertising or other sales effort. It may also be advisable to develop other means of using the excess plant capacity.

Volume variances may encourage manufacturing managers to run the factory above the normal capacity. This is favorable when the additional production can be sold. However, if the additional production cannot be sold and must be stored as inventory, favorable volume variances may actually be harmful. For example, one paper company ran paper machines above normal volume in order to create favorable volume variances. Unfortunately, this practice eventually created a six months' supply of finished goods inventory that had to be stored in public warehouses. The "savings" from the favorable volume variances were exceeded by the additional inventory carrying and obsolescence costs. In this example, the volume variances produced goal conflict by creating incentives for manufacturing managers to overproduce.

REPORTING FACTORY OVERHEAD VARIANCES

The total factory overhead cost variance is the difference between the actual factory overhead and the total overhead applied to production, using the predetermined factory overhead rate. This calculation is as follows:

Total actual factory overhead	$22,400
Factory overhead applied (4,000 hours × $6.00 per hour)	24,000
Total factory overhead cost variance—favorable	$ (1,600)

The factory overhead cost variance can be verified for each variable factory overhead cost and fixed factory overhead cost element in a **factory overhead cost variance report.** Such a report, which can be used by management to control costs, is shown in Exhibit 7 for Western Rider Inc. The report indicates both the controllable variance and the volume variance.

Exhibit 7
Factory Overhead Cost Variance Report

Western Rider Inc.
Factory Overhead Cost Variance Report
For the Month Ended June 30, 1997

Productive capacity for the month (100% of normal)		5,000 hours		
Actual production for the month		4,000 hours		
			Variances	
	Budget (at Actual Production)	Actual	Favorable	Unfavorable
Variable factory overhead costs:				
Indirect factory wages	$ 8,000	$ 5,100	$2,900	
Power and light	4,000	4,200		$ 200
Indirect materials	2,400	1,100	1,300	
Total variable factory overhead cost	$14,400	$10,400		
Fixed factory overhead costs:				
Supervisory salaries	$ 5,500	$ 5,500		
Depreciation of plant and equipment	4,500	4,500		
Insurance and property taxes	2,000	2,000		
Total fixed factory overhead cost	12,000	12,000		
Total factory overhead cost	$26,400	$22,400		
Total controllable variances			$4,200	$ 200
Net controllable variance—favorable				$4,000
Volume variance—unfavorable:				
Idle hours at the standard rate for fixed factory overhead—1,000 × $2.40				2,400
Total factory overhead cost variance—favorable				$1,600

It is possible to break down many of the individual factory overhead cost variances into quantity and price variances, similar to the analysis for direct materials and direct labor. For example, the indirect factory wages variance may include both time and rate variances. Likewise, the indirect materials variance may include both a quantity variance and a price variance. Such variances are illustrated in advanced textbooks.

Recording and Reporting Variances from Standards

Objective 6
Journalize the entries for recording standards in the accounts and prepare an income statement that includes variances from standards.

Standard costs can be used solely as a management tool apart from the accounts in the general ledger. However, many companies include both standard costs and variances, in addition to actual costs, in their accounts. In doing so, one approach is to record the standard costs and variances at the same time the actual manufacturing costs are recorded in the accounts. To illustrate, assume that Western Rider Inc. purchased, on account, the 7,300 square yards of blue denim used at $5.50 per square yard. The standard price for direct materials is $5.00 per square yard. The entry to record the purchase and the unfavorable direct materials price variance is as follows:

Materials (7,300 sq. yds. × $5.00)	36,500	
Direct Materials Price Variance	3,650	
Accounts Payable (7,300 sq. yds. × $5.50)		40,150

The materials account is debited for the actual quantity purchased at the standard price, $36,500 (7,300 square yards × $5.00). The unfavorable direct materials price variance is $3,650 [($5.50 actual price per square yard – $5.00 standard price per square yard) × 7,300 square yards purchased]. The variance is recorded by debiting Direct Materials Price Variance for $3,650. If the variance had been favorable, Direct Materials Price Variance would have been credited for the amount of the variance.

The direct materials quantity variance is recorded in a similar manner. For example, Western Rider Inc. used 7,300 square yards of blue denim to produce 5,000 pairs of XL jeans with a standard of 7,500 square yards. The entry to record the materials used is as follows:

Work in Process (7,500 sq. yds. × $5.00)	37,500	
Direct Materials Quantity Variance		1,000
Materials (7,300 sq. yds. × $5.00)		36,500

The work in process account is debited for the standard price of the standard amount of direct materials required, $37,500 (7,500 square yards × $5.00). Materials is credited for the actual amount of materials used at the standard price, $36,500 (7,300 square yards × $5.00). The favorable direct materials quantity variance of $1,000 [(7,500 standard square yards – 7,300 actual square yards) × $5.00 standard price per square yard] is credited to Direct Materials Quantity Variance. If the variance had been unfavorable, Direct Materials Quantity Variance would have been debited for the amount of the variance.

The entries for direct labor are recorded in a manner similar to direct materials. The work in process account is debited for the standard cost of direct labor and factory overhead as well as direct materials. Likewise, the work in process account is credited for the standard cost of the product completed and transferred to the finished goods account.

In a given period, it is possible to have both favorable and unfavorable variances. At the end of the period, the balances of the variance accounts will indicate the net favorable or unfavorable variance for the period.

Variances from standard costs are usually not reported to stockholders and others outside management. If standards are recorded in the accounts, however, the variances are often reported in income statements prepared for use by management. Exhibit 8 is an example of such an income statement prepared for Western Rider Inc.'s internal use. In this exhibit, we assume a sales price of $28 per pair, selling expenses of $14,500, and administrative expenses of $11,225.

At the end of the fiscal year, the variances from standard are usually transferred to the cost of goods sold account. However, if the variances are significant or if many of the products manufactured are still on hand, the variances should be allocated to the work in process, finished goods, and cost of goods sold accounts. The result of such an allocation is to convert these account balances from standard cost to actual cost.

Standards for Nonmanufacturing Expenses

Objective 7
Explain how standards may be used for nonmanufacturing expenses.

The use of standards for nonmanufacturing expenses is not as common as the use of standards for manufacturing costs. A major reason for this is due in part to the fact that many nonmanufacturing expenses often cannot be readily associated with a unit of product or other measure of activity. For example, the manufacturing costs associated with an Assembly Department can be measured and related to

Exhibit 8
Variances from Standards in Income Statement

Western Rider Inc.
Income Statement
For the Month Ended June 30, 1997

	Favorable	Unfavorable	
Sales			$140,000[1]
Cost of goods sold—at standard			97,500[2]
Gross profit—at standard			$ 42,500
Less variances from standard cost:			
Direct materials price		$ 3,650	
Direct materials quantity	$1,000		
Direct labor rate		3,850	
Direct labor time	1,350		
Factory overhead controllable	4,000		
Factory overhead volume		2,400	3,550
Gross profit			$ 38,950
Operating expenses:			
Selling expenses		$14,500	
Administrative expenses		11,225	25,725
Income before income tax			$ 13,225

[1] 5,000 × $28
[2] $37,500 + $36,000 + $24,000 (from Exhibit 2), or 5,000 × $19.50 (from Exhibit 1)

the product. On the other hand, the expenses associated with the work of the office manager are not easily related to a unit of activity.

When nonmanufacturing activities are repetitive and produce a common output, the concept of standards can be applied. In these cases, the process of estimating and using standards is similar to that described for a manufactured product. For example, standards can be applied to the work of office personnel who process sales orders. A standard cost for processing a sales order could be developed. The variance between the actual cost of processing a sales order and the standard cost could then be used to control sales order processing costs.

In practice, using standards for nonmanufacturing expenses is becoming more widely used. This is partially because managers have begun to direct more attention to controlling nonmanufacturing expenses. When standards are not used, such expenses are normally controlled by using static budgets.

Nonfinancial Performance Measures

Objective 8
Explain and provide examples of nonfinancial performance measures.

Many managers believe that financial performance measures, such as variances from standard, should be supplemented with nonfinancial measures of performance. Measuring both financial and nonfinancial performance helps employees consider multiple, and sometimes conflicting, performance objectives. For example, one company had a machining operation that was measured according to a direct labor time standard. Employees did their work quickly in order to create favorable direct labor time variances. Unfortunately, the fast work resulted in poor machining quality that, in turn, created difficulty in the assembly operation. The company decided to measure performance using both a labor time standard *and* a quality standard in order to cause employees to consider both the speed and quality of their work.

In another example, a company placed its 1–800 customer service phone representatives on labor time standards that required completing a given number of phone calls per hour. As a result, representatives became more concerned with completing phone calls than delivering customer service. The company added another performance measure focusing on satisfying customer requests correctly and completely. As a result, both the efficiency and quality of the response were considered in controlling the 1–800 customer service operation.

In both of these examples, nonfinancial performance measures brought additional perspectives, such as quality of work, to evaluating performance. Additional examples of nonfinancial performance measures for manufacturing firms are as follows:

Nonfinancial Performance Measures[4]
Inventory turnover (82%)
On-time delivery (41%)
Elapsed time between a customer order and product delivery (35%)
Customer preference rankings compared to competitors
Response time to a service call
Time to develop new products
Employee satisfaction
Number of customer complaints

KEY POINTS

Objective 1. Describe the types of standards and how they are established for businesses.
Standards represent performance benchmarks that can be compared to actual results in evaluating performance. Standards are developed, reviewed, and revised by accountants and engineers, based upon studies of operations. Standards are established so that they are neither too high nor too low, but are attainable.

Objective 2. Explain and illustrate how standards are used in flexible budgeting.
Flexible budgets are prepared by multiplying the standard cost per unit by the planned production. To measure performance, the standard cost per unit is multiplied by the actual number of units produced, and the actual results are compared with the flexible budget at actual volumes (cost variance).

Objective 3. Calculate and interpret direct materials price and quantity variances.
The direct materials cost variance can be separated into a direct materials price and quantity variance. The direct materials price variance is calculated by multiplying the actual quantity by the difference between the actual and standard price. The direct materials quantity variance is calculated by multiplying the standard price by the difference between the actual materials used and the budgeted materials at actual volumes.

Objective 4. Calculate and interpret direct labor rate and time variances.
The direct labor cost variance can be separated into a direct labor rate and time variance. The direct labor rate variance is calculated by multiplying the actual hours worked by the difference between the actual labor rate and the standard labor rate. The direct labor time variance is calculated by multiplying the standard labor rate by the difference between the actual labor hours worked and the labor hours budgeted at actual volumes.

Objective 5. Calculate and interpret factory overhead controllable and volume variances.
The factory overhead cost variance can be separated into a variable factory overhead controllable variance and a fixed factory overhead volume variance. The controllable variance is calculated by subtracting the actual variable factory overhead from the budgeted variable factory overhead at actual volumes. The volume variance is determined by multiplying the fixed factory overhead rate by the difference between the normal budgeted hours and the standard hours used at actual production.

Objective 6. Journalize the entries for recording standards in the accounts and prepare an income statement that includes variances from standard.
Standard costs and variances can be recorded in the accounts at the same time the manufacturing costs are recorded in the

[4] The first three examples indicate the percentage of firms using the nonfinancial performance measure taken from a survey by Forrest B. Green and Felix E. Amenkhienan, "Accounting Innovations: A Cross-Sectional Survey of Manufacturing Firms," *Journal of Cost Management*, Spring 1992, pp. 58–64.

accounts. For example, the purchase of direct materials on account is recorded as a debit to Materials for the standard cost of materials and a credit to Accounts Payable for the actual cost. Any difference is debited or credited to the direct materials price variance account.

The entries for direct labor, factory overhead, and other variances are recorded in a manner similar to the entries for direct materials. The work in process account is debited for the standard costs of direct labor and factory overhead as well as direct materials. Likewise, the work in process account is credited for the standard cost of the product completed and transferred to the finished goods account.

Under a standard cost system, the cost of goods sold will be reported at standard cost. Manufacturing variances can be disclosed on the income statement to adjust the gross profit at standard to the actual gross profit. Such a disclosure is generally limited for use by management.

Objective 7. Explain how standards may be used for nonmanufacturing expenses.

Standards may be used for nonmanufacturing expenses when nonmanufacturing activities are repetitive and related to an activity base. Such standards may be useful to managers in planning, directing, and controlling nonmanufacturing expenses.

Objective 8. Explain and provide examples of nonfinancial performance measures.

Many companies use a combination of financial and nonfinancial measures in order for multiple perspectives to be incorporated in evaluating performance. Combining financial and nonfinancial measures helps employees balance cost efficiency with quality and customer service performance.

GLOSSARY OF KEY TERMS

Budget performance report. A report comparing actual results with budget figures. *Objective 2*

Controllable variance. The difference between the actual amount of variable factory overhead cost incurred and the amount of variable factory overhead budgeted for the standard product. *Objective 5*

Cost variance. The difference between actual cost and the flexible budget at actual volumes. *Objective 2*

Currently attainable standards. Standards that represent levels of operation that can be attained with reasonable effort. *Objective 1*

Direct labor rate variance. The cost associated with the difference between the standard rate and the actual rate paid for direct labor used in producing a commodity. *Objective 4*

Direct labor time variance. The cost associated with the difference between the standard hours and the actual hours of direct labor spent producing a commodity. *Objective 4*

Direct materials price variance. The cost associated with the difference between the standard price and the actual price of direct materials used in producing a commodity. *Objective 3*

Direct materials quantity variance. The cost associated with the difference between the standard quantity and the actual quantity of direct materials used in producing a commodity. *Objective 3*

Standard cost. A detailed estimate of what a product should cost. *Objective 1*

Standard cost systems. Accounting systems that use standards for each element of manufacturing cost entering into the finished product. *Objective 1*

Theoretical standards. Standards that represent levels of performance that can be achieved only under perfect operating conditions. *Objective 1*

Variance from standard. The difference between standard cost and actual cost. *Objective 1*

Volume variance. The difference between the budgeted fixed overhead at 100% of normal capacity and the standard fixed overhead for the actual production achieved during the period. *Objective 5*

ILLUSTRATIVE PROBLEM

Hawley Inc. manufactures Product S for national distribution. The standard costs for the manufacture of Product S were as follows:

	Standard Costs	*Actual Costs*
Direct materials	1,500 pounds at $35	1,600 pounds at $32
Direct labor	4,800 hours at $11	4,500 hours at $11.80
Factory overhead	Rates per labor hour, based on 100% of normal capacity of 5,500 labor hours:	
	Variable cost, $2.40	$12,300 variable cost
	Fixed cost, $3.50	$19,250 fixed cost

Instructions

1. Determine the quantity variance, price variance, and total direct materials cost variance for Product S.
2. Determine the time variance, rate variance, and total direct labor cost variance for Product S.
3. Determine the controllable variance, volume variance, and total factory overhead cost variance for Product S.

Solution

1. **Direct Materials Cost Variance**

Quantity variance:		
Actual quantity	1,600 pounds	
Standard quantity	1,500	
Variance—unfavorable	100 pounds × standard price, $35	$3,500
Price variance:		
Actual price	$32.00 per pound	
Standard price	35.00	
Variance—favorable	($3.00) per pound × actual quantity, 1,600	(4,800)
Total direct materials cost variance—favorable		$(1,300)

2. **Direct Labor Cost Variance**

Time variance:		
Actual time	4,500 hours	
Standard time	4,800 hours	
Variance—favorable	(300) hours × standard rate, $11	$(3,300)
Rate variance:		
Actual rate	11.80	
Standard rate	11.00	
Variance—unfavorable	.80 per hour × actual time, 4,500 hrs.	3,600
Total direct labor cost variance—unfavorable		$ 300

3. **Factory Overhead Cost Variance**

Variable factory overhead—controllable variance:		
Actual variable factory overhead cost incurred	$12,300	
Budgeted variable factory overhead for 4,800 hours	11,520*	
Variance—unfavorable		$ 780
Fixed factory overhead—volume variance:		
Budgeted hours at 100% of normal capacity	5,500 hours	
Standard hours for actual production	4,800	
Productive capacity not used	700 hours	
Standard fixed factory overhead cost rate	× $3.50	
Variance—unfavorable		2,450
Total factory overhead cost variance—unfavorable		$ 3,230

*4,800 hrs. × $2.40 = $11,520

SELF-EXAMINATION QUESTIONS (ANSWERS AT END OF CHAPTER)

1. The actual and standard direct materials costs for producing a specified quantity of product are as follows:

Actual:	51,000 pounds at $5.05	$257,550
Standard:	50,000 pounds at $5.00	$250,000

The direct materials price variance is:

A. $50 unfavorable
B. $2,500 unfavorable
C. $2,550 unfavorable
D. $7,550 unfavorable

2. Bower Company produced 4,000 units of product. Each unit requires 0.5 standard hour. The standard labor rate is $12 per hour. Actual direct labor for the period was $22,000 (2,200 hours × $10 per hour). The direct labor time variance is:

A. 200 hours unfavorable
B. $2,000 unfavorable
C. $4,000 favorable
D. $2,400 unfavorable

3. The actual and standard factory overhead costs for producing a specified quantity of product are as follows:

Actual:	Variable factory overhead	$72,500	
	Fixed factory overhead	40,000	$112,500
Standard:	19,000 hours at $6		
	($4 variable and $2 fixed)		114,000

If 1,000 hours were unused, the fixed factory overhead volume variance would be:

A. $1,500 favorable C. $4,000 unfavorable
B. $2,000 unfavorable D. $6,000 unfavorable

4. Ramathan Company produced 6,000 units of product Y, which is 80% of capacity. Each unit required 0.25 standard machine hour for production. The standard variable factory overhead rate is $5.00 per machine hour. The actual variable factory overhead incurred during the period was $8,000. The variable factory overhead controllable variance is:

A. $500 favorable C. $1,875 favorable
B. $500 unfavorable D. $1,875 unfavorable

5. Applegate Company has a normal budgeted capacity of 200 machine hours. Applegate produced 600 units. Each unit requires a standard 0.2 machine hour to complete. The standard fixed factory overhead is $12.00 per hour, determined at normal capacity. The fixed factory overhead volume variance is:

A. $4,800 unfavorable C. $960 favorable
B. $4,800 favorable D. $960 unfavorable

DISCUSSION QUESTIONS

1. What are the basic objectives in the use of standard costs?
2. How can standards be used by management to help control costs?
3. What is a variance, as the term is used in reference to standard costs?
4. What is meant by reporting by the "principle of exceptions," as the term is used in reference to cost control?
5. How often should standards be revised?
6. How are standards used in flexible budgeting?
7. What is a budget performance report?
8. a. What are the two variances between the actual cost and the standard cost for direct materials?
   b. Discuss some possible causes of these variances.
9. The materials cost variance report for Nickols Inc. indicates a large favorable materials price variance and a significant unfavorable materials quantity variance. What might have caused these offsetting variances?
10. a. What are the two variances between the actual cost and the standard cost for direct labor?
    b. Who generally has control over the direct labor cost?
11. A new assistant controller recently was heard to remark: "All the assembly workers in this plant are covered by union contracts, so there should be no labor variances." Was the controller's remark correct? Discuss.
12. a. Describe the two variances between the actual costs and the standards costs for factory overhead.
    b. What is a factory overhead cost variance report?
13. What are budgeted fixed costs at normal volume?
14. If variances are recorded in the accounts at the time the manufacturing costs are incurred, what does a debit balance in Direct Materials Price Variance represent?
15. If variances are recorded in the accounts at the time the manufacturing costs are incurred, what does a credit balance in Direct Materials Quantity Variance represent?
16. Are variances from standard costs usually reported in financial statements issued to stockholders and others outside the firm?
17. Assuming that the variances from standards are not significant at the end of the period, to what account are they transferred?
18. Would the use of standards be appropriate in a nonmanufacturing setting, such as a fast food restaurant?
19. Briefly explain why firms might use nonfinancial performance measures.

20. During the ten-year period 1983–1993, the ratio of cost of products sold to sales for Hershey Foods Corporation decreased from 66% to 57%. During this same period, the sales of Hershey Foods Corporation increased by almost 272%. As sales increase, why would management normally expect the ratio of cost of products sold to sales to decrease?

EXERCISES

EXERCISE 23–1
Standard direct materials cost per unit
Objective 2

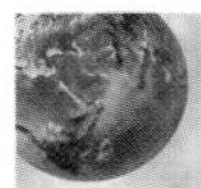

Concrete Pipe & Products Co. Inc. manufactures concrete pipe in its operations in Richmond, Virginia. The primary materials used in producing concrete are cement, sand, and gravel. The costs for a batch of concrete weighing 13,250 pounds are as follows:

	Pounds per Batch	*Price per Pound*
Cement	2,200	$ .0400
Sand	7,200	.0030
Gravel	4,500	.0024
	13,900	

Assuming 5% waste, compute the standard cost per pound for concrete, rounding to five decimal places. Use the following column headings for organizing the computations:

	Pounds per Batch	*Price per Pound*	*Batch Cost*	*5% Waste*	*Total Batch Cost*	*Cost per Pound*
Cement	2,200	$.0400				
Sand	7,200	.0030				
Gravel	4,500	.0024				
	13,900					

EXERCISE 23–2
Standard product cost
Objective 2

Marcello Company produces and sells speaker wire for audio equipment. Marcello Company uses a standard cost system. The direct labor, direct materials, and factory overhead standards for 18-gauge wiring are as follows:

Direct labor:	standard rate	$12.00 per hour
	standard time per unit	.40 hour per 100 yards
Direct materials (copper):	standard price	$ 1.20 per pound
	standard quantity	4.5 pounds per 100 yards
Variable factory overhead:	standard rate	$10.50 per hour
Fixed factory overhead:	standard rate	$ 6.00 per hour

Determine the standard cost per 100 yards of electrical wiring.

EXERCISE 23–3
Budget performance report
Objective 2

Calloway Container Company (CCC) manufactures plastic 2-liter bottles for the beverage industry. The cost standards per 100 2-liter bottles are as follows:

Cost Category	*Standard Cost per 100 2-Liter Bottles*
Direct labor	$3.70
Direct materials	0.90
Factory overhead	5.20
Total	$9.80

At the beginning of April, CCC management planned to produce 400,000 bottles. The actual number of bottles produced for April was 480,000 bottles. The actual costs for April were as follows:

Cost Category	*Actual Cost for the Month Ended April 30, 19—*
Direct labor	$19,300
Direct materials	4,700
Factory overhead	27,200
Total	$51,200

a. Prepare the manufacturing cost budget (direct labor, direct materials, and factory overhead) for CCC for April.
b. Prepare a budget performance report for manufacturing costs for CCC for April.
c. Interpret the budget performance report.

EXERCISE 23–4
Direct materials variances
Objective 3

The following data relate to the direct materials cost for the production of 15,000 units of product:

Actual:	69,500 pounds at $1.11	$77,145
Standard:	68,000 pounds at $1.04	$70,720

a. Determine the price variance, quantity variance, and total direct materials cost variance.
b. To whom should the unfavorable variances be reported for analysis and control? Discuss.

EXERCISE 23–5
Standard direct materials cost per unit from variance data
Objectives 2, 3

The following data relating to direct materials cost for August of the current year are taken from the records of Judd Company, a brick manufacturer:

Quantity of direct materials used	24,000 pounds
Actual unit price of direct materials	$3.00 per pound
Units of finished product manufactured	33,500 units
Standard direct materials per unit of finished product	.75 pound
Direct materials quantity variance—favorable	$3,210
Direct materials price variance—unfavorable	$3,600

Determine the standard direct materials cost per unit of finished product, assuming that there was no inventory of work in process at either the beginning or the end of the month.

EXERCISE 23–6
Direct labor variances
Objective 4

The following data relate to direct labor cost for the production of 5,000 units of product:

Actual:	16,600 hours at $14.50	$240,700
Standard:	16,000 hours at $15.00	$240,000

a. Determine the rate variance, time variance, and total direct labor cost variance.
b. The rate variance is favorable, and the time variance is unfavorable. Discuss what might have caused these offsetting variances.

EXERCISE 23–7
Direct materials and direct labor variances
Objectives 2, 3, 4

At the beginning of April, Marquis Textile Company budgeted 5,000 units of production for April at direct materials and direct labor costs as follows:

Direct materials	$36,000
Direct labor	54,000
Total	$90,000

The standard materials price is $1.50 per pound. The standard direct labor rate is $12 per hour. At the end of April, the actual direct materials and direct labor costs were as follows:

Actual direct materials	$ 40,500
Actual direct labor	62,700
Total	$103,200

There were no direct materials price or direct labor rate variances for April. In addition, assume no changes in the direct materials inventory balances in April. Marquis Textile Company actually produced 6,000 units during April.

Determine the direct materials quantity and direct labor time variances.

EXERCISE 23–8
Overhead flexible budget
Objective 5

Summit Equipment Company prepared the following factory overhead cost budget for the Welding Department for August of the current year, during which it expected to require 15,000 hours of productive capacity in the department:

Variable overhead cost:		
Indirect factory labor	$42,000	
Power and light	4,500	
Indirect materials	24,000	
Total variable cost		$ 70,500
Fixed overhead cost:		
Supervisory salaries	$64,200	
Depreciation of plant and equipment	23,100	
Insurance and property taxes	3,700	
Total fixed cost		91,000
Total factory overhead cost		$161,500

Assuming that the estimated costs for September are the same as for August, prepare a flexible factory overhead cost budget for the Welding Department for September for 12,000, 15,000, and 18,000 hours of production.

EXERCISE 23–9
Factory overhead cost variances
Objective 5

The following data relate to factory overhead cost for the production of 20,000 units of product:

Actual:	Variable factory overhead	$149,900
	Fixed factory overhead	48,000
Standard:	40,000 hours at $4.50	180,000

If productive capacity of 100% was 60,000 hours and the factory overhead cost budgeted at the level of 40,000 standard hours was $180,000, determine the variable factory overhead controllable variance, fixed factory overhead volume variance, and total factory overhead cost variance. The fixed factory overhead rate was $0.80 per hour.

EXERCISE 23–10
Factory overhead cost variances
Objective 5

Pinnacle Fabrics Corporation began March with a budget for 75,000 hours of production in the Weaving Department. The department has a full capacity of 90,000 hours under normal business conditions. The budgeted overhead at the planned volumes at the beginning of March was as follows:

Variable overhead	$337,500
Fixed overhead	126,000
Total	$463,500

The actual factory overhead was $480,000 for March. The actual fixed factory overhead was as budgeted. During March, the Weaving Department had standard hours at actual production volume of 85,000 hours.

a. Determine the variable factory overhead controllable variance.
b. Determine the fixed factory overhead volume variance.

EXERCISE 23–11
Factory overhead cost variance report
Objective 5

Platinum Bearing Company prepared the following factory overhead cost budget for the Finishing Department for May of the current year, during which it expected to use 40,000 hours for production:

Variable overhead cost:		
Indirect factory labor	$68,000	
Power and light	10,000	
Indirect materials	96,000	
Total variable cost		$174,000
Fixed overhead cost:		
Supervisory salaries	$75,300	
Depreciation of plant and equipment	12,400	
Insurance and property taxes	4,800	
Total fixed cost		92,500
Total factory overhead cost		$266,500

Platinum Bearing Company has available 50,000 hours of monthly productive capacity in the Finishing Department under normal business conditions. During May, the Finishing Department actually used 36,000 hours for production. The actual fixed costs were as budgeted. The actual variable overhead for May was as follows:

Actual variable factory overhead cost:	
Indirect factory labor	$ 66,800
Power and light	9,200
Indirect materials	85,100
Total variable cost	$161,100

Construct a factory overhead cost variance report for the Finishing Department for May.

EXERCISE 23–12
Recording standards in accounts
Objective 6

Gerry Manufacturing Company incorporates standards in the accounts and identifies variances at the time the manufacturing costs are incurred. Journalize the entries to record the following transactions:

a. Purchased 500 units of direct material A on account at $20.40 per unit. The standard price is $20 per unit.
b. Used 190 units of direct material A in the process of manufacturing 50 units of finished product. Four units of material A are required, at standard, to produce a finished unit.

EXERCISE 23–13
Income statement indicating standard cost variance
Objective 6

The following data were taken from the records of Hazemount Company for January of the current year:

Administrative expenses	$ 40,000
Cost of goods sold (at standard)	775,000
Direct materials quantity variance—favorable	2,200
Direct materials price variance—favorable	700
Direct labor time variance—unfavorable	3,000
Direct labor rate variance—unfavorable	1,800
Fixed factory overhead volume variance—unfavorable	11,000
Variable factory overhead controllable variance—favorable	3,800
Interest expense	1,900
Sales	950,000
Selling expenses	71,500

Prepare an income statement for presentation to management.

EXERCISE 23–14
Variance calculations
Objectives 3, 4, 5

The data related to Reel 'N Line Sporting Goods Company's factory overhead cost for the production of 75,000 units of product are as follows:

Actual:	Variable factory overhead	$168,300
	Fixed factory overhead	122,500
Standard:	30,000 hours at $9 ($5.50 for variable factory overhead)	270,000

Productive capacity at 100% of normal was 35,000 hours, and the factory overhead cost budgeted at the level of 30,000 standard hours was $287,500. Based upon these data, the chief cost accountant prepared the following variance analysis:

Variable factory overhead controllable variance:		
Actual variable factory overhead cost incurred	$168,300	
Budgeted variable factory overhead for 30,000 hours	165,000	
Variance—unfavorable		$ 3,300
Fixed factory overhead volume variance:		
Normal productive capacity at 100%	35,000 hours	
Standard for amount produced	30,000	
Productive capacity not used	5,000 hours	
Standard variable factory overhead rate	× $5.50	
Variance—unfavorable		27,500
Total factory overhead cost variance—unfavorable		$30,800

Identify the errors in the factory overhead cost variance analysis.

EXERCISE 23–15
Standards for nonmanufacturing expenses
Objective 7

Hope Hospital began using standards to evaluate its Admissions Department. The standard was broken into two types of admissions as follows:

Type of Admission	*Standard Time to Complete Admission Record*
Unscheduled admission	40 minutes
Scheduled admission	15 minutes

The unscheduled admission took longer, since name, address, and insurance information needed to be determined at the time of admission. Information was collected on scheduled admissions prior to the admissions, which was less time consuming.

The Admissions Department employs two full-time people (40 productive hours per week) at $10.50 per hour. For the most recent week, the department handled 50 unscheduled and 160 scheduled admissions.

a. How much was actually spent on labor for the week?
b. What is the flexible budget for the actual volume for the week?
c. Calculate a time variance, and report how well the department performed for the week.

EXERCISE 23–16
Standards for nonmanufacturing operations
Objectives 2, 4, 7

One of the operations in the U.S. Post Office is a mechanical mail sorting operation. In this operation, letter mail is sorted at a rate of one letter per second. The letter is mechanically sorted from a three-digit code input by an operator sitting at a keyboard. The manager of the mechanical sorting operation wishes to determine the number of temporary employees to hire for December. The manager estimates that there will be an additional 27 million pieces of mail in December, due to the upcoming holiday season.

Assume the following:

1. Each operator receives a paid 10-minute break per hour.
2. The sorting operators are temporary employees. The union contract requires that temporary employees be hired for one month at a time. A temporary employee is hired for 180 hours in the month.

a. How many temporary employees should the manager hire for December?
b. If each employee earns a standard $18 per hour, what would be the labor time variance if there were only 24.3 million additional letters sorted in December?

PROBLEMS SERIES A

PROBLEM 23–1A
Direct materials and direct labor variance analysis
Objectives 3, 4

Erickson Company manufactures silk dresses in a small manufacturing facility. Manufacturing consists of eight employees, who are paid $9.60 per hour. Each employee presently provides 40 hours of productive labor per week. Information about a production week is as follows:

Standard wage per hour	$9.00
Standard labor time per dress	25 minutes
Standard number of yards of silk per dress	4 yards
Standard price per yard of silk	$3.50
Actual price per yard of silk	$3.80
Actual yards of silk used during the week	3,080 yards
Number of dresses produced during the week	780

Instructions

Determine (a) the standard cost per dress for direct materials and direct labor, (b) the price variance, quantity variance, and total direct materials cost variance, and (c) the rate variance, time variance, and total direct labor cost variance.

PROBLEM 23–2A
Flexible budgeting and variance analysis
Objectives 2, 3, 4

Terrace Hill Company makes dark chocolate and light chocolate. Both products require cocoa and sugar. The following planning information has been made available:

	Standard Quantity		
	Dark Chocolate	*Light Chocolate*	*Standard Price*
Cocoa	3 lbs.	2 lbs.	$8.00
Sugar	2 lbs.	4 lbs.	$4.00
Standard labor time	0.2 hr.	0.25 hr.	
Planned production	2,550 units	3,600 units	
Standard labor rate	$12.00 per hour	$12.00 per hour	

Terrace Hill does not expect there to be any beginning or ending inventories of cocoa or sugar.

At the end of the budget year, Terrace Hill had the following actual results:

	Dark Chocolate	*Light Chocolate*
Actual production	3,500	3,200

	Actual Price	*Actual Quantity Purchased and Used*
Cocoa	$10.00	17,200
Sugar	6.00	18,500

	Actual Labor Rate	*Actual Labor Hours Used*
Dark chocolate	$10.00	750
Light chocolate	10.00	760

Instructions

1. Prepare the following variance analyses, based on the actual results and production levels at the end of the budget year:
   a. Direct materials price, quantity, and total variance.
   b. Direct labor rate, time, and total variance.
2. Why are the standard amounts in (1) based on the actual production for the year instead of the planned production for the year?

PROBLEM 23–3A
Direct materials, direct labor, and factory overhead cost variance analysis
Objectives 3, 4, 5

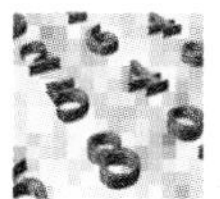

Standard costs and actual costs for direct materials, direct labor, and factory overhead incurred for the manufacture of 2,000 units of product were as follows:

	Standard Costs	*Actual Costs*
Direct materials	2,000 pounds at $12.50	1,940 pounds at $12.80
Direct labor	8,000 hours at $14	8,180 hours at $15
Factory overhead	Rates per machine hour, based on 100% of normal capacity of 10,000 machine hours:	
	Variable cost, $1.80	$15,200 variable cost
	Fixed cost, $2.50	$25,000 fixed cost

Four machine hours are required per unit.

Instructions

Determine (a) the price variance, quantity variance, and total direct materials cost variance, (b) the rate variance, time variance, and total direct labor cost variance, and (c) variable factory overhead controllable variance, the fixed factory overhead volume variance, and total factory overhead cost variance.

PROBLEM 23–4A
Standard factory overhead variance report
Objective 5

San Gabriel Inc., a manufacturer of garden equipment, prepared the following factory overhead cost budget for Department A for May of the current year. The company expected to operate the department at 100% of normal capacity of 12,000 hours.

Variable costs:		
Indirect factory wages	$43,200	
Power and light	4,800	
Indirect materials	61,200	
Total variable cost		$109,200
Fixed costs:		
Supervisory salaries	$84,500	
Depreciation of plant and equipment	12,200	
Insurance and property taxes	2,300	
Total fixed cost		99,000
Total factory overhead cost		$208,200

During May, the department operated at 10,400 hours, and the factory overhead costs incurred were: indirect factory wages, $36,980; power and light, $4,250; indirect materials, $52,830; supervisory salaries, $84,500; depreciation of plant and equipment, $12,200; and insurance and property taxes, $2,300.

Instructions

Prepare a factory overhead cost variance report for May. To be useful for cost control, the budgeted amounts should be based on 10,400 hours.

PROBLEM 23–5A
Flexible factory overhead cost budget and variance report
Objective 5

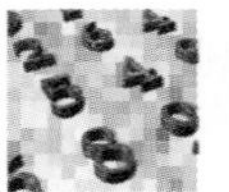

COM-TEK Inc., a manufacturer of furniture, prepared the following factory overhead cost budget for the Shaping Department for May production of the current year:

COM-TEK Inc.
Factory Overhead Cost Budget—Shaping Department
For the Month Ending May 31, 19—

Machine hours:		
Productive capacity of 100%		40,000
Hours budgeted		46,000
Variable costs:		
Indirect factory wages	$289,800	
Indirect materials	188,600	
Power and light	55,200	
Total variable cost		$ 533,600
Fixed costs:		
Supervisory salaries	$326,700	
Indirect factory wages	124,300	
Depreciation of plant and equipment	34,000	
Insurance	12,200	
Power and light	6,400	
Property taxes	10,400	
Total fixed cost		514,000
Total factory overhead cost		$1,047,600

During May, the Shaping Department was operated for 46,000 machine hours, and the following factory overhead costs were incurred:

Indirect factory wages	$ 416,700
Supervisory salaries	326,700
Indirect materials	184,300
Power and light	60,500
Depreciation of plant and equipment	34,000
Insurance	12,200
Property taxes	10,400
Total factory overhead cost incurred	$1,044,800

Instructions

1. Prepare a flexible budget for May, indicating capacities of 28,000, 34,000, 40,000, and 46,000 machine hours and determining a standard factory overhead rate per machine hour.
2. Prepare a factory overhead cost variance report for May. Assume that the actual fixed factory overhead was as budgeted.

PROBLEM 23–6A
Standards for nonmanufacturing expenses
Objectives 4, 7, 8

QuickSoft Company does software development. One important activity in software development is writing software code. The manager of the Venus Development Team determined that the average software programmer could write 20 lines of code in an hour. The plan for the first week in July called for 3,100 lines of code to be written on the Venus product. The Venus Team has four programmers. Each programmer is hired from a temporary employment firm that requires that temporary employees be hired for a minimum of a 40-hour week. Programmers are paid $20.00 per hour. The manager offered a bonus if the team could generate at least 3,375 lines for the week, without overtime. Due to a project emergency, the programmers wrote more code in the first week of July than planned. The actual amount of code written in the first week of July was 3,400 lines without overtime. As a result, the bonus caused the average programmer's hourly rate to increase to $24.00 per hour during the first week in July.

Instructions

1. If the team generated 3,100 lines of code according to the original plan, what would have been the labor time variance?
2. What was the actual labor time variance as a result of generating 3,400 lines of code?
3. What was the labor rate variance as a result of the bonus?
4. The manager is trying to determine if a better decision would have been to hire a temporary programmer to meet the higher programming demand in the first week of July, rather than paying out the bonus. If another employee was hired from the temporary services firm, what would have been the labor time variance in the first week?
5. Which decision is better, paying the bonus or hiring another programmer?
6. Are there any performance-related issues that the labor time and rate variances fail to consider? Explain.

PROBLEMS SERIES B

PROBLEM 23–1B
Direct materials and direct labor variance analysis
Objectives 2, 3, 4

Corso Company manufactures faucets in a small manufacturing facility. The faucets are made from zinc. Manufacturing consists of 12 employees, who are paid $15 per hour. Each employee presently provides 36 hours of labor per week. Information about a production week is as follows:

Standard wage per hour	$12.00
Standard labor time per faucet	15 minutes
Standard number of pounds of zinc	3 pounds
Standard price per pound of zinc	$6.20
Actual price per pound of zinc	$6.00
Actual pounds of zinc used during the week	5,400 lbs.
Number of faucets produced during the week	1,680

Instructions

Determine (a) the standard cost per unit for direct materials and direct labor, (b) the price variance, quantity variance, and total direct materials cost variance, and (c) the rate variance, time variance, and total direct labor cost variance.

PROBLEM 23–2B
Flexible budgeting and variance analysis
Objectives 2, 3, 4

Hubble Company makes women's and men's coats. Both products require leather and lining material. The following planning information has been made available:

	Standard Quantity		
	Women's Coats	*Men's Coats*	*Standard Price per Unit*
Leather	2 yds.	4 yds.	$25.00
Liner	3 yds.	2 yds.	$ 5.00
Standard labor time	0.1 hr.	0.2 hr.	
Planned production	2,800 units	2,600 units	
Standard labor rate	$14.00 per hour	$14.00 per hour	

Hubble does not expect there to be any beginning or ending inventories of leather and lining material.

At the end of the budget year, Hubble experienced the following actual results:

	Women's Coat	*Men's Coat*
Actual production	2,400	3,400

	Actual Price	*Actual Quantity Purchased and Used*
Leather	$28.00	19,000
Liner	4.00	13,600

	Actual Labor Rate	*Actual Labor Hours Used*
Woman's Coat	$16.00	250
Man's Coat	16.00	640

The expected beginning inventory and desired ending inventory were realized.

Instructions

1. Prepare the following variance analyses, based on the actual results and production levels at the end of the budget year:
   a. Direct materials price, quantity, and total variance.
   b. Direct labor rate, time, and total variance.
2. Why are the standard amounts in (1) based on the actual production at the end of the year instead of the planned production at the beginning of the year?

PROBLEM 23–3B
Direct materials, direct labor, and factory overhead cost variance analysis
Objectives 3, 4, 5

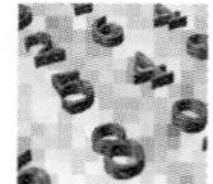

Standard costs and actual costs for direct materials, direct labor, and factory overhead incurred for the manufacture of 2,500 units of product were as follows:

	Standard Costs	*Actual Costs*
Direct materials	8,000 pounds at $4.50	7,850 pounds at $4.20
Direct labor	5,000 hours at $18	5,250 hours at $19.00
Factory overhead	Rates per machine hour, based on 100% of normal capacity of 6,000 machine hours:	
	Variable cost, $2.30	$11,750 variable cost
	Fixed cost, $.90	$ 5,400 fixed cost

Two machine hours are required per unit.

Instructions

Determine (a) the price variance, quantity variance, and total direct materials cost variance, (b) the rate variance, time variance, and total direct labor cost variance, and (c) variable factory overhead controllable variance, the fixed factory overhead volume variance, and total factory overhead cost variance.

PROBLEM 23–4B
Standard factory overhead variance report
Objective 5

Spire Company, a manufacturer of hardware, prepared the following factory overhead cost budget for Department C for June of the current year. The company expected to operate the department at 100% of normal capacity of 40,000 hours.

Variable costs:		
Indirect factory wages	$76,000	
Power and light	24,000	
Indirect materials	92,000	
Total variable cost		$192,000
Fixed costs:		
Supervisory salaries	$66,700	
Depreciation of plant and equipment	7,500	
Insurance and property taxes	1,400	
Total fixed cost		75,600
Total factory overhead cost		$267,600

During June, the department operated at 34,000 hours, and the factory overhead costs incurred were: indirect factory wages, $62,970; power and light, $21,120; indirect materials, $77,720; supervisory salaries, $66,700; depreciation of plant and equipment, $7,500; and insurance and property taxes, $1,400.

Instructions

Prepare a factory overhead variance report for June. To be useful for cost control, the budgeted amounts should be based on 34,000 hours.

PROBLEM 23–5B
Flexible factory overhead cost budget and variance report
Objective 5

Winslow Inc., a manufacturer of silverware, prepared the following factory overhead cost budget for the Polishing Department for July production of the current year:

Machine hours:		
Productive capacity of 100%		50,000
Hours budgeted		57,500
Variable costs:		
Indirect factory wages	$224,250	
Indirect materials	304,750	
Power and light	46,000	
Total variable cost		$ 575,000
Fixed costs:		
Supervisory salaries	$297,800	
Indirect factory wages	96,600	
Depreciation of plant and equipment	25,600	
Insurance	7,500	
Power and light	8,600	
Property taxes	9,900	
Total fixed cost		446,000
Total factory overhead cost		$1,021,000

During July, the Polishing Department was operated for 57,500 machine hours, and the following factory overhead costs were incurred:

Indirect factory wages	$389,000
Supervisory salaries	297,800
Indirect materials	184,300
Power and light	62,700
Depreciation of plant and equipment	25,600
Insurance	7,500
Property taxes	9,900
Total factory overhead cost incurred	$976,800

Instructions

1. Prepare a flexible budget for July, indicating capacities of 35,000, 42,500, 50,000, and 57,500 machine hours and determining a standard factory overhead rate per machine hour.
2. Prepare a factory overhead cost variance report for July. Assume that the actual fixed factory overhead was as budgeted.

PROBLEM 23–6B
Standards for nonmanufacturing expenses
Objectives 4, 7, 8

TestRite Company provides quality testing services for the mining industry. One important activity in quality testing is transcribing tape-recorded analysis of mineral samples into a written report. The manager of the Transcription Department determined that the average transcriptionist could type 350 lines of a report in an hour. The plan for the first week in May called for 40,600 typed lines to be written. The Transcription Department has three transcriptionists. Each transcriptionist is hired from a temporary employment firm that requires that temporary employees be hired for a minimum of a 40-hour week. Transcriptionists are paid $12.00 per hour. The manager offered a bonus if the department could type at least 45,000 lines for the week, without overtime. Due to high customer testing service demands, the transcriptionists typed more lines in the first week of May than planned. The actual amount of lines typed in the first week of May was 45,500 lines, without overtime. As a result, the bonus caused the average transcriptionist hourly rate to increase to $15.00 per hour during the first week in May.

Instructions

1. If the department typed 40,600 lines according to the original plan, what would have been the labor time variance?
2. What was the actual labor time variance as a result of typing 45,500 lines?
3. What was the labor rate variance as a result of the bonus?
4. The manager is trying to determine if a better decision would have been to hire a temporary transcriptionist to meet the higher typing demands in the first week of May, rather than paying out the bonus. If another employee was hired from the temporary services firm, what would have been the labor time variance in the first week?
5. Which decision is better, paying the bonus or hiring another transcriptionist?
6. Are there any performance-related issues that the labor time and rate variances fail to consider? Explain.

CASES

CASE 23–1
Big Rock Insurance Company
Establishing standards in nonmanufacturing

Dan Hendrix is a cost analyst with Big Rock Insurance Company. Big Rock is applying standards to their claims payment operation. Claims payment is a repetitive operation that could be evaluated with standards. Dan used time and motion studies to identify a theoretical standard of 25 claims processed per hour. The Claims Processing Department manager, Angie Street, has rejected this standard and has argued that the standard should be 20 claims processed per hour. Angie and Dan were unable to agree, so they decided to discuss this matter openly at a joint meeting with the Vice-President of Operations, who would arbitrate a final decision. Prior to the meeting, Dan wrote the following memo to the VP.

Discuss the ethical and professional issues in this situation.

To: Kim Jan, Vice-President of Operations
From: Dan Hendrix
Re: Standards in the Claims Processing Department

As you know, Angie and I are scheduled to meet with you to discuss our disagreement with respect to the appropriate standards for the Claims Processing Department. I have conducted time and motion studies and have determined that the theoretical standard is 25 claims processed per hour. Angie argues that 20 claims processed per hour would be more appropriate. I believe she is trying to "pad" the budget with some slack. I'm not sure what she is trying to get away with, but I believe a tight standard will drive efficiency up in her area. I hope you will agree when we meet with you next week.

CASE 23–2
Silverman Company
Nonfinancial performance measures

The senior management of Silverman Company has proposed the following three performance measures for the company:

1. Net income as a percent of stockholders' equity
2. Revenue growth
3. Employee satisfaction

Management believes these three measures combine both financial and nonfinancial measures and are thus superior to using just financial measures.

Comment on Silverman Company's new performance measurement system.

CASE 23–3
Rogers Corporation
Nonfinancial performance measures

At the Soladyne Division of Rogers Corporation, the controller used a number of measures to provide managers information about the performance of a just-in-time (JIT) manufacturing operation. Three measures used by the company are:

Orders Past Due: Sales dollar value of orders that were scheduled for shipment, but were not shipped during the period.

Buyer Misery Index: Number of different customers that have orders that are late (scheduled for shipment, but not shipped).

Scrap Index: The sales dollar value of scrap for the period.

1. How is the "orders past due" measure different from the "buyer's misery index"? Or are the two measures just measuring the same thing?
2. Why do you think the scrap index is measured at sales dollar value, rather than at cost?

Source: John W. Schmitthenner, "Metrics," *Management Accounting*, May 1993, pp. 27–30.

CASE 23–4
Kass Co.
Variance interpretation

You have been asked to investigate some cost problems in the Assembly Department of Kass Co., a consumer electronics company. To begin your investigation, you have obtained the following budget performance report for the department for the last quarter.

Kass Co.—Assembly Department
Quarterly Budget and Performance Report

	Standard Quantity at Standard Rates	*Actual Quantity at Standard Rates*	*Quantity Variances*
Direct labor	$ 45,000	$ 65,000	$20,000 U
Direct materials	85,000	110,000	25,000 U
Total	$130,000	$175,000	$45,000 U

The following reports were also obtained:

Kass Co.—Purchasing Department
Quarterly Budget and Performance Report

	Actual Quantity at Standard Rates	*Actual Quantity at Actual Rates*	*Price Variance*
Direct materials	$125,000	$110,000	$15,000 F

Kass Co.—Fabrication Department
Quarterly Budget and Performance Report

	Standard Quantity at Standard Rates	*Actual Quantity at Standard Rates*	*Quantity Variances*
Direct labor	$ 70,000	$ 58,000	$12,000 F
Direct materials	40,000	40,000	0
Total	$110,000	$ 98,000	$12,000 F

You also interviewed the Assembly Department supervisor. Excerpts from the interview follow.

Q: "What explains the poor performance in your department?"

A: "Listen, you've got to understand what it's been like in this department recently. Lately, it seems no matter how hard we try, we can't seem to make the standards. I'm not sure what is going on, but we've been having a lot of problems lately."

Q: "What kind of problems?"

A: "Well, for instance, all this quarter we've been requisitioning purchased parts from the material storeroom, and the parts just didn't fit together very well. I'm not sure what is going on, but during most of this quarter we've had to scrap and sort purchased parts—just to get our assemblies put together. Naturally, all this takes time and material. And that's not all."

Q: "Go on."

A: "All this quarter, the work that we've been receiving from the Fabrication Department has been shoddy. I mean, maybe around 20% of the stuff that comes in from Fabrication just can't be assembled. The fabrication is all wrong. As a result, we've had to scrap and rework a lot of the stuff. Naturally, this has just shot our quantity variances."

Interpret the variance reports in light of the comments by the Assembly Department supervisor.

CASE 23–5
Juniper Company
Variance interpretation

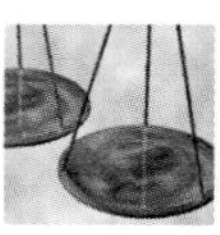

Juniper Company is a small manufacturer of electronic musical instruments. The plant manager received the following variable factory overhead report for the period:

	Actual	*Budgeted Variable Factory Overhead at Actual Production*
Supplies	$21,000	$20,000
Power and light	9,000	8,000
Indirect factory wages	50,000	40,000
Total	$80,000	$68,000

Actual units produced: 4,000 (90% of practical capacity)

The plant manager is not pleased with the $12,000 unfavorable variable factory overhead controllable variance and has come to discuss the matter with the controller. The following discussion occurred:

Plant Manager: I just received this factory report for the latest month of operation. I'm not very pleased with these figures. Before these numbers go to headquarters, you and I will need to reach an understanding.

Controller: Go ahead, what's the problem?

Plant Manager: What's the problem? Well, everything. Look at the variance. It's too large. If I understand your accounting approach being used here, you are assuming that my costs are variable to the units produced. Thus, as the production volume declines, so should these costs. Well, I don't believe that these costs are variable at all. I think that they are fixed costs. As a result, when we operate below capacity, the costs really don't go down at all. I'm being penalized for costs I really have no control over at all. I really need this report to be redone to reflect this fact. If anything, the difference between actual and budget is really a volume variance. Listen, I know that you're a team player. You really need to reconsider your assumptions on this one.

If you were in the controller's position, how would you respond to the plant manager?

CASE 23–6
Paragon Company
Comprehensive variance analysis

Paragon Company operates a plant in Ramsey, New Jersey, where you have been assigned as the new cost analyst. To familiarize yourself with your new responsibilities, you have gathered the cost variance data for July shown on the next page. During July, 6,000 units of product were manufactured.

After your review of the July cost variance data, you arranged a meeting with the factory superintendent to discuss manufacturing operations. During this meeting, the factory superintendent made the following comment:

"Why do you have to compute a factory overhead volume variance? I don't have any control over the level of operations. I can control only costs for the level of production at which I am told to operate. Why not just eliminate the volume variance from the factory overhead cost variance report?"

You next discussed the direct materials variance analyses with the Purchasing Department manager, who made the following comment:

"The materials price variance is computed incorrectly. The computations should be actual price minus standard price times the standard quantity of materials for the amount produced. By multiplying the difference in the actual and standard price by the actual quantity of materials used, my department is being penalized for the inefficiencies of the Production Department."

During August the standard costs were not changed, normal capacity was 15,000 hours, and the following data were taken from the records for the production of 7,000 units of product:

Quantity of direct materials used	5,450 pounds	
Cost of direct materials	$26.70 per pound	
Quantity of direct labor used	14,600 hours	
Cost of direct labor	$17.50 per hour	
Factory overhead costs:		
Indirect factory wages		$25,900
Power and light		13,150
Indirect materials		33,550
Maintenance		11,150
Supervisory salaries		22,500
Depreciation of plant and equipment		15,000
Insurance and property taxes		11,250

Factory Overhead Cost Variance Report

Normal capacity for the month	15,000 hours			
Standard for amount produced during month	12,000 hours			

			Variances	
	Budget	*Actual*	*Favorable*	*Unfavorable*
Variable costs:				
Indirect factory wages	$ 21,600	$ 21,900		$ 300
Power and light	10,800	11,150		350
Indirect materials	28,800	28,700	$100	
Maintenance	9,600	9,550	50	
Total variable cost	$ 70,800	$ 71,300		
Fixed costs:				
Supervisory salaries	$ 22,500	$ 22,500		
Depreciation of plant and equipment	15,000	15,000		
Insurance and property taxes	11,250	11,250		
Total fixed cost	$ 48,750	$ 48,750		
Total factory overhead cost	$119,550	$120,050		
Total controllable variances			$150	$ 650
Net controllable variance—unfavorable				$ 500
Volume variance—unfavorable:				
Idle hours at the standard rate for fixed factory overhead—3,000 × $3.25				9,750
Total factory overhead cost variance—unfavorable				$10,250

Direct Materials Cost Variance

Price variance:		
Actual price	$26.50 per pound	
Standard price	25.00 per pound	
Variance—unfavorable	$ 1.50 per pound × actual quantity, 4,600	$ 6,900
Quantity variance:		
Actual quantity	4,600 pounds	
Standard quantity	4,500 pounds	
Variance—unfavorable	100 pounds × standard price, $25.00	2,500
Total direct materials cost variance—unfavorable		$ 9,400

Direct Labor Cost Variance

Rate variance:		
Actual rate	$17.60 per hour	
Standard rate	18.00 per hour	
Variance—favorable	$ (.40) per hour × actual hours, 12,200	$(4,880)
Time variance:		
Actual time	12,200 hours	
Standard time	12,000 hours	
Variance—unfavorable	200 hours × standard rate, $18	3,600
Total direct labor cost—favorable		$(1,280)

1. Prepare a factory overhead cost variance report for August.
2. Determine (a) the price variance, quantity variance, and total direct materials cost variance, and (b) the rate variance, time variance, and total direct labor cost variance for August.
3. Based upon the cost variances for July and August, what areas of operations would you investigate and why?
4. How would you respond to the comment by the factory superintendent?
5. How would you respond to the comment by the manager of the Purchasing Department?

ANSWERS TO SELF-EXAMINATION QUESTIONS

1. **C** The unfavorable direct materials price variance of $2,550 (answer C) is determined as follows:

Actual price	$5.05 per pound
Standard price	5.00
Price variance—unfavorable	$ .05 per pound

$.05 × 51,000 actual pounds = $2,550

2. **D**

Actual direct labor time	2,200	
Standard direct labor time	2,000	
Direct labor time variance—unfavorable		200 × $12 standard rate = $2,400

3. **B** The unfavorable factory overhead volume variance of $2,000 (answer B) is determined as follows:

Productive capacity not used	1,000 hours
Standard fixed factory overhead cost rate	× $2
Factory overhead volume variance—unfavorable	$2,000

4. **B** The controllable variable factory overhead variance is determined as:

6,000 units × .25 hour = 1,500 hours
1,500 hours × $5.00 per hour = $7,500

Actual variable overhead:	$8,000
Less: budgeted variable overhead at actual volume	7,500
Unfavorable controllable variance	$ 500

The $1,875 variance (answers C and D) is the difference between 100% of capacity (7,500 units) and 6,000 units, which is a calculation used for the volume variance.

5. **D** The fixed factory overhead volume variance can be determined as follows:

Actual production in standard hours:
600 units × .2 machine hour = 120 machine hours

Practical capacity	200 machine hours
Standard hours at actual production	120
Idle capacity	80 machine hours

80 hours × $12.00 = $960 unfavorable volume variance.

24 Performance Evaluation for Decentralized Operations

YOU AND ACCOUNTING

Have you ever noticed how large retail stores, such as J.C. Penney Co. and Sears, are divided into departments? Some typical departments are the Men's Department, Women's Department, Appliances Department, Home Entertainment Department, and Sporting Goods Department.

In many cases, each department is the responsibility of a department manager. The manager of the Sporting Goods Department, for example, is responsible for the financial performance of that department. The particular store may be the responsibility of a store manager, and a group of stores within a particular geographic area may be the responsibility of a division manager. If you were to be hired by a department store chain, you would probably begin your career in a department. Running a department would be a valuable experience before becoming responsible for a complete store. Likewise, responsibility for a complete store provides excellent training for a more responsible position.

In this chapter, we will focus on the role of accounting in assisting managers in planning and controlling organizational units, such as divisions, stores, and departments.

After studying this chapter, you should be able to:

Objective 1
List and explain the advantages and disadvantages of decentralized operations.

Objective 2
Prepare a responsibility accounting report for a cost center.

Objective 3
Prepare responsibility accounting reports for a profit center, using the following income concepts:

Operating income
Controllable operating income

Objective 4
Compute and interpret the rate of return on investment and the residual income for an investment center.

Objective 5
Explain how the following transfer pricing approaches may be used by decentralized segments of a business:

Market price approach
Negotiated price approach
Cost price approach

Centralized and Decentralized Operations

Objective 1
List and explain the advantages and disadvantages of decentralized operations.

A completely **centralized** business is one in which all major planning and operating decisions are made by top management. For example, a one-person, owner/manager-operated business is centralized because all plans and decisions are made by one person. In a small owner/manager-operated business, centralization may be desirable. This is because the owner/manager's close supervision ensures that the business will be operated in the way the owner/manager wishes.

Separating a business into divisions or operating units and delegating responsibility for these units to managers is called decentralization. In a decentralized business, the unit managers are responsible for planning and controlling operations. These managers have the authority to make decisions without first seeking the approval of top management.

Divisions are often structured around common functions, products, customers, or regions. For example, Delta Air Lines is organized around *functions,* such as the Flight Operations Division. The Procter & Gamble Company is organized around common *products,* such as the Soap Division, which sells a wide array of cleaning products. Boeing Corporation has organized divisions around the *customer.* The commercial aircraft division makes jet aircraft for airlines, and the aerospace/defense division contracts military aircraft with the U.S. Department of Defense. IBM-Japan is an example of a *regional* division of IBM.

The amount of decentralization varies significantly, and there is no one best level of decentralization for all businesses. In some companies, for example, division managers have authority over all plant operations, including plant asset acquisitions and retirements. In other companies, a division manager may have authority only for scheduling production and for controlling the costs of direct materials, direct labor, and factory overhead. The proper amount of decentralization for a company depends on the advantages and disadvantages of decentralization as they apply to a company's unique circumstances.

ADVANTAGES OF DECENTRALIZATION

As a business grows, it becomes more difficult for top management to maintain close daily contact with all operations. In such cases, delegating authority to managers closest to the operations usually results in better decisions. These managers often anticipate and react to operating data more quickly than could top management. In addition, as a company expands into a wide range of products and services, it becomes more difficult for top management to maintain operating expertise in all

USING ACCOUNTING TO UNDERSTAND BUSINESS

PepsiCo has decentralized its operations into three major divisions: Beverages, Snack Foods, and Restaurant. The Beverages Division sells Pepsi Cola, the Snack Foods Division sells Frito-Lay food products, and the Restaurant Division consists of Pizza Hut, Taco Bell and Kentucky Fried Chicken. These divisions are treated as three separate businesses, with their own financial performance targets. A trend among large international companies is to decentralize into smaller customer-focused units, while maintaining the advantages of a big company. For example Siemens, the giant $45 billion German electronics company, divided responsibility into 16 minicorporations, each with its own CEO and board of directors. Johnson and Johnson has a network of over 150 highly decentralized health care businesses that are overseen by a relatively small corporate staff. Xerox Corporation has redesigned its organization into what CEO Paul Allaire calls "microenterprise units" that are focused on customer needs. Aluminum Company of America (Alcoa) recently restructured its centrally managed divisions into 22 autonomous business units in order to streamline decision making and enhance financial accountability.

product lines and services. Decentralization allows managers to focus on acquiring expertise in their areas of responsibility. For example, in a company that maintains operations in insurance, banking, and health care, managers could become "experts" in the areas of their operations and responsibility.

Decentralized decision making also provides excellent training for managers. This may be a factor in enabling a company to retain quality managers. Since the art of management is best acquired through experience, delegating responsibility allows managers to acquire and develop managerial expertise early in their careers.

Businesses that work closely with customers are often decentralized. This enables managers to respond quickly to customers' needs, which helps create good customer relations. In addition, because managers of decentralized operations tend to identify with customers and with operations, they are often more creative in suggesting operating and product improvements.

DISADVANTAGES OF DECENTRALIZATION

A primary disadvantage of decentralized operations is that decisions made by one manager may affect other managers in such a way that the profitability of the entire company may suffer. For example, the *Coke* manager may engage in price cutting to win customers. However, this may cause *Diet Coke* to lose customers, which may prompt the *Diet Coke* manager to cut prices. As a result, the overall company profit may be less than it might have been if the price cutting had not occurred.

Another potential disadvantage of decentralized operations is duplicating assets and costs in operating divisions. For example, each manager of a product line might have a separate sales force and administrative office staff. Centralizing these personnel could save money.

RESPONSIBILITY ACCOUNTING

In a decentralized business, an important function of the management accountant is to assist individual managers in evaluating and controlling their areas of responsibility, called **responsibility centers.** Responsibility accounting is the process of measuring and reporting operating data by responsibility center. Three common types of responsibility centers are cost centers, profit centers, and investment centers. In the following sections, we will briefly describe the responsibility accounting for these three types of centers.

Responsibility Accounting for Cost Centers

Objective 2
Prepare a responsibility accounting report for a cost center.

In a cost center, the department or division manager has responsibility and authority for controlling the costs incurred. For example, the supervisor of the Power Department has responsibility for the costs incurred in providing power. A cost center manager does not make decisions concerning sales or the amount of plant assets invested in the center. Cost centers may vary in size from a small department to an entire manufacturing plant. In addition, cost centers may exist within other cost centers. For example, we could view an entire state university as a cost center, and the individual departments within the university can also be cost centers. Since managers of cost centers have responsibility for and authority over costs, responsibility accounting for cost centers focuses on costs. As a basis for illustrating responsibility accounting for cost centers, Exhibit 1 shows an organization chart for a business's manufacturing operations. This business has three cost center levels. The lowest level is the department, the next-highest level is the plant, and the vice-president of production is at the highest level.

Exhibit 1
Organization Chart—Management Responsibility for Production

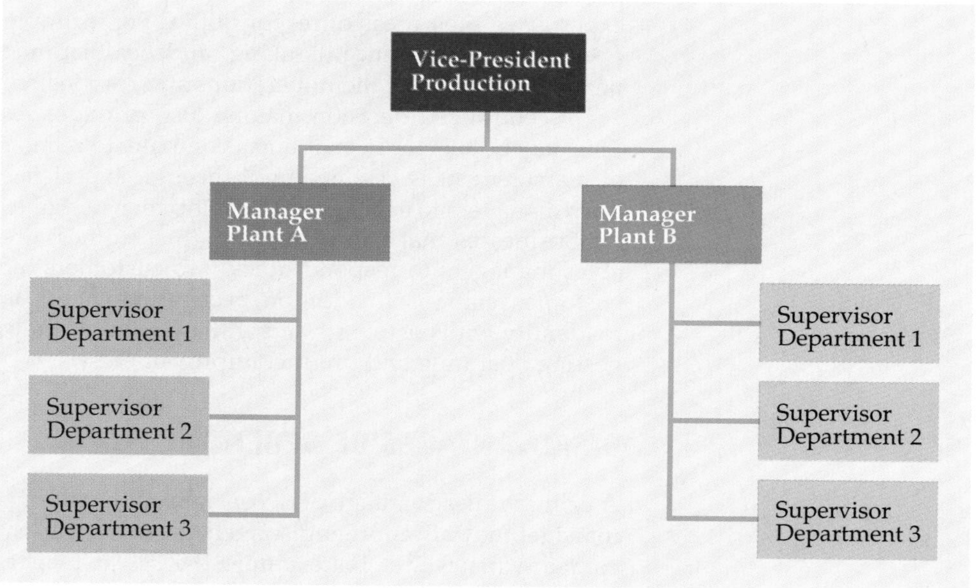

The budget performance reports in Exhibit 2 are part of a responsibility accounting system for the business shown in Exhibit 1. These reports can aid each management level in controlling costs.

In Exhibit 2, the reports prepared for the department supervisors show the budgeted and actual manufacturing costs for their departments. The supervisors can use these reports and other, more detailed information to focus on the items that created significant differences, such as the difference between the budgeted and actual costs for materials. For example, the supervisor of Department 1 in Plant A may use information from a scrap report to determine why materials are over budget. Such a report might show that materials were scrapped as a result of machine malfunctions, improper use of machines by employees, or substandard materials.

For higher levels of management, responsibility accounting reports are usually more summarized than for lower levels of management. In Exhibit 2, for example, the budget performance report for the plant manager summarizes budget and actual

Exhibit 2
Responsibility Accounting Reports for Cost Centers

Budget Performance Report
Vice-President, Production
For the Month Ended October 31, 1997

	Budget	Actual	Over Budget	Under Budget
Administration	$ 19,500	$ 19,700	$ 200	
Plant A	467,475	470,330	2,855	
Plant B	395,225	394,300		$925
	$882,200	$884,330	$3,055	$925

Budget Performance Report
Manager, Plant A
For the Month Ended October 31, 1997

	Budget	Actual	Over Budget	Under Budget
Administration	$ 17,500	$ 17,350		$150
Department 1	109,725	111,280	$1,555	
Department 2	190,500	192,600	2,100	
Department 3	149,750	149,100		650
	$467,475	$470,330	$3,655	$800

Budget Performance Report
Supervisor, Department 1—Plant A
For the Month Ended October 31, 1997

	Budget	Actual	Over Budget	Under Budget
Factory wages	$ 58,100	$ 58,000		$100
Materials	32,500	34,225	$1,725	
Supervisory salaries	6,400	6,400		
Power and light	5,750	5,690		60
Depreciation of plant and equipment	4,000	4,000		
Maintenance	2,000	1,990		10
Insurance and property taxes	975	975		
	$109,725	$111,280	$1,725	$170

cost data for the departments under the manager's supervision. This report enables the plant manager to identify the department supervisors responsible for major differences. Likewise, the report for the vice-president of production summarizes the cost data for each plant. The plant managers can thus be held responsible for major differences in budgeted and actual costs in their plants.

Responsibility Accounting for Profit Centers

Objective 3
Prepare responsibility accounting reports for a profit center, using the following income concepts:

Operating income
Controllable operating income

In a profit center, the manager has the responsibility and the authority to make decisions that affect both costs and revenues (and thus profits). Profit centers may be divisions, departments, or products. For example, a consumer products company might organize its brands (product lines) as divisional profit centers. The manager of each brand could have responsibility for product manufacturing cost and decisions regarding revenues, such as determining sales prices. The manager of a profit center does not make decisions concerning the plant assets invested in the center.

For example, the brand manager of a consumer products company could not make a decision to expand the plant capacity for the brand.

Profit centers are often viewed as an excellent training assignment for new managers. For example, Lester B. Korn, Chairman and Chief Executive Officer of Korn/Ferry International, offered the following strategy for young executives en route to top management positions:

Get Profit-Center Responsibility—Obtain a position where you can prove yourself as both a specialist with particular expertise and a generalist who can exercise leadership, authority, and inspire enthusiasm among colleagues and subordinates.

Responsibility accounting reports for profit centers are normally in the form of income statements. These income statements usually report revenues, expenses, and operating income by profit center. The profit center income statement should include only revenues and expenses that are controlled by the manager. Controllable revenues are revenues earned by the profit center and are generally easy to determine. Controllable expenses are costs that can be influenced (controlled) by the decisions of profit center managers. For example, the manager of the Sporting Goods department at Sears would not control the property taxes of the store, but would control the salaries of department personnel.

OPERATING INCOME

We will illustrate profit center income and performance reporting for the Nova Entertainment Group (NEG). Assume that NEG is a diversified entertainment company with two operating divisions organized as profit centers: the Theme Park Division and the Movie Production Division. The operating income for the two divisions is shown in Exhibit 3. The operating income is determined by subtracting operating expenses from revenues. Operating expenses incurred only for the benefit of a particular profit center are direct expenses. An example of an operating expense for the Theme Park Division would be salaries of theme park employees.

Exhibit 3
Divisional Operating Income for NEG

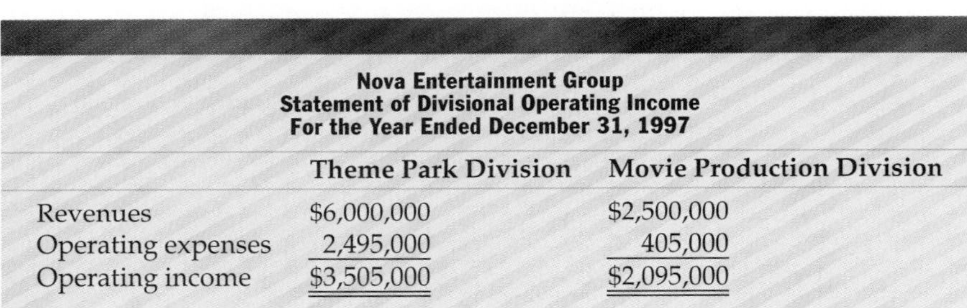

Nova Entertainment Group
Statement of Divisional Operating Income
For the Year Ended December 31, 1997

	Theme Park Division	Movie Production Division
Revenues	$6,000,000	$2,500,000
Operating expenses	2,495,000	405,000
Operating income	$3,505,000	$2,095,000

The operating income for the Movie Production Division of NEG is determined by subtracting operating expenses from revenues.

For a profit center that sells products rather than services, the cost of goods sold would be subtracted from net sales in order to determine the gross profit. From this amount, the selling and administrative expenses of the profit center would be subtracted in order to determine the operating income, as follows:

Net sales
– Cost of goods sold
Gross profit
– Selling and administrative expenses
Operating income

SERVICE DEPARTMENT CHARGES

Services may be provided more efficiently by internal **service departments** than by outside service firms. For example, a company may establish a Payroll Department to provide payroll services because it has easy access to employee records. Other examples of service departments include the following:

Research and Development	Employee Relations
Government Relations	Purchasing
Legal	Information Systems
Telecommunications	Employee Travel Support
Publications and Graphics	Transportation
Facilities Management	Personnel Administration

When the costs of services are charged to a profit center, based on its use of those services, they are called **service department charges.** Service department charges are indirect expenses to a profit center. They are expenses that have been incurred by the service department in providing services to the profit center. They are similar to the expenses that would be incurred if the profit center had purchased the services from a source outside the company. A profit center manager has control over such expenses if he or she is free to choose *how much* service is used from the service department.

To illustrate service department charges, assume that the Nova Entertainment Group has three service departments: Purchasing, Payroll Accounting, and Legal. The budget for the year ended December 31, 1997, for each department is as follows:

Purchasing	$400,000
Payroll Accounting	255,000
Legal	250,000
Total	$905,000

The **activity base** of the service departments will be used to charge service expenses to the Theme Park and Movie Production Divisions. The activity base for each of the service departments is a measure of the services performed, such as purchase requisitions for Purchasing, number of payroll checks for Payroll Accounting, and number of billed hours for Legal. The estimated usage of services by the Theme Park and Movie Production Divisions is shown as follows:

	Estimated Service Usage		
	Purchasing	*Payroll Accounting*	*Legal*
Theme Park Division	25,000 purchase requisitions	12,000 payroll checks	100 billed hours
Movie Production Division	15,000	3,000	900
Total	40,000 purchase requisitions	15,000 payroll checks	1,000 billed hours

The rates at which services are charged to each division are called **service department charge rates.** These rates are determined by dividing each service department's budget by the total estimated service usage as follows:

$$\textbf{Purchasing: } \frac{\$400{,}000}{40{,}000 \text{ purchase requisitions}} = \$10 \text{ per purchase requisition}$$

$$\textbf{Payroll Accounting: } \frac{\$255{,}000}{15{,}000 \text{ payroll checks}} = \$17 \text{ per payroll check}$$

$$\textbf{Legal: } \frac{\$250{,}000}{1{,}000 \text{ hours}} = \$250 \text{ per hour}$$

The estimated usage of services by the Theme Park and Movie Production Divisions can now be multiplied by the service department charge rates to determine the charges to each division, as shown in Exhibit 4.

Exhibit 4
Service Department Charges to NEG Divisions

Nova Entertainment Group
Service Department Charges to NEG Divisions
For the Year Ended December 31, 1997

Service Department	Theme Park Division	Movie Production Division
Purchasing (Note A)	$250,000	$150,000
Payroll Accounting (Note B)	204,000	51,000
Legal (Note C)	25,000	225,000
Total service department charges	$479,000	$426,000

Note A:
25,000 purchase requisitions × $10 per purchase requisition = $250,000
15,000 purchase requisitions × $10 per purchase requisition = $150,000
Note B:
12,000 payroll checks × $17 per check = $204,000
3,000 payroll checks × $17 per check = $51,000
Note C:
100 hours × $250 per hour = $25,000
900 hours × $250 per hour = $225,000

The Theme Park Division employs many temporary and part-time employees that are paid weekly. This is in contrast to the Movie Production Division, which has a more permanent payroll that is paid on a monthly basis. As a result, the Theme Park Division requires 12,000 payroll checks. This results in a large service charge from Payroll Accounting to the Theme Park Division. The Movie Production Division uses a greater amount of legal services for contract negotiations, compared to the Theme Park Division. Thus, there is a large service charge from Legal to the Movie Production Division.

USING ACCOUNTING TO UNDERSTAND BUSINESS

Several companies were asked in a survey to indicate their service department charging practices. The percentages of respondents that charged various service department expenses on the basis of service usage are shown below.

Service Department	*Usage-Based Service Charge*
Accounting and Finance	35%
Legal	35
Electronic Data Processing	63
General Marketing Services	35
Advertising	50

Service Department	*Usage-Based Service Charge*
Market Research	36%
Public Relations	24
Industrial Relations	32
Personnel Administration	35
Real Estate	37
Operations Research	47
Purchasing	40
Top Management Overhead	13
Corporate Planning	20

Source: Richard F. Vancil, *Decentralization: Managerial Ambiguity by Design*, Dow Jones Irwin, Homewood, Illinois, 1979, p. 251.

CONTROLLABLE OPERATING INCOME

The divisional income statements for NEG are presented in Exhibit 5. These statements show the service department charges to the divisions. The operating income less the service department charges is called **controllable operating income.**

Exhibit 5
Divisional Income Statements—Nova Entertainment Group

Nova Entertainment Group
Divisional Income Statements
For the Year Ended December 31, 1997

	Theme Park Division	Movie Production Division
Revenues	$6,000,000	$2,500,000
Operating expenses	2,495,000	405,000
Operating income	$3,505,000	$2,095,000
Less service department charges:		
Purchasing	$ 250,000	$ 150,000
Payroll Accounting	204,000	51,000
Legal	25,000	225,000
Total service department charges	$ 479,000	$ 426,000
Controllable operating income	$3,026,000	$1,669,000

The controllable operating income is an accepted measure of the manager's performance. In evaluating the profit center manager, the controllable operating income should be compared to historical performance or to the budget. It should not be compared across profit centers, since the profit centers are likely different in terms of size, products, and customers.

Responsibility Accounting for Investment Centers

Objective 4
Compute and interpret the rate of return on investment and the residual income for an investment center.

In an investment center, the manager has the responsibility and the authority to make decisions that affect not only costs and revenues but also the assets invested in the center. Investment centers are widely used in highly diversified companies. Typically, investment centers are organized as divisions.

The manager of an investment center has more authority and responsibility than the manager of either a cost center or a profit center. The manager of an investment center occupies a position similar to that of a chief operating officer or president of a separate company. As such, an investment center manager is evaluated in much the same way as a manager of a separate company.

Since investment center managers have responsibility for revenues and expenses, controllable operating income is an essential part of investment center reporting. In addition, because the manager has responsibility for the assets invested in the center, two additional measures of performance are often used: the rate of return on investment and residual income. Top management may use comparisons of these measures across investment centers as a basis for rewarding performance and ranking investment in the centers.

To illustrate the analysis of profitability of investment centers, assume that Baldwin Company has three regional divisions, Northern, Central, and Southern. Condensed divisional income statements for the investment centers are shown in Exhibit 6.

Exhibit 6
Divisional Income Statements—Baldwin Company

Baldwin Company
Divisional Income Statements
For the Year Ended December 31, 1997

	Northern Division	Central Division	Southern Division
Revenues	$560,000	$672,000	$750,000
Operating expenses	336,000	470,400	562,500
Operating income	$224,000	$201,600	$187,500
Service department charges	154,000	117,600	112,500
Controllable operating income	$ 70,000	$ 84,000	$ 75,000

Based on the amount of controllable operating income, the Central Division is the most profitable division. However, controllable operating income does not reflect the amount of assets invested in each center. For example, if the amount of assets invested in the Central Division is twice that of the other divisions, then the Central Division would be the least profitable in terms of the rate of return on these assets.

RATE OF RETURN ON INVESTMENT

Since investment center managers also control the amount of assets invested in their centers, it is logical that they should also be held accountable for the use of these assets. One measure that considers the amount of assets invested is the **rate of return on investment (ROI)** or **rate of return on assets**. It is one of the most widely used measures of divisional performance for investment centers and is computed as follows:

$$\text{Rate of Return on Investment (ROI)} = \frac{\text{Controllable Operating Income}}{\text{Invested Assets}}$$

The rate of return on investment is useful because the three factors subject to control by divisional managers (revenues, expenses, and invested assets) are considered in its computation. By measuring profitability relative to the amount of assets invested in each division, the rate of return on investment can be used to compare divisions. The higher the rate of return on investment, the more effectively the division is utilizing its assets to generate income. To illustrate, the rate of return on investment for each division of Baldwin Company, based on the book value of invested assets, is as follows:

	Northern Division	*Central Division*	*Southern Division*
Controllable operating income	\$ 70,000	\$ 84,000	\$ 75,000
Invested assets	\$350,000	\$700,000	\$500,000
Rate of return on investment	20%	12%	15%

Although the Central Division generated the largest controllable operating income, its rate of return on investment (12%) is the lowest. Hence, relative to the assets invested, the Central Division is the least profitable division. In comparison, the rate of return on investment of the Northern Division is 20% and the Southern Division is 15%. These differences in the rates of return on investment can be analyzed using an expanded formula for the rate of return on investment.

In the expanded formula, the rate of return on investment is the product of two factors. The first factor is the ratio of controllable operating income to sales, often called the **profit margin**. The second factor is the ratio of sales to invested assets, often called the **investment turnover**. As shown here, using this expanded expression yields the same rate of return on investment for the Northern Division, 20%, as computed previously.

$$\text{Rate of Return on Investment (ROI)} = \text{Profit Margin} \times \text{Investment Turnover}$$

$$\text{Rate of Return on Investment (ROI)} = \frac{\text{Controllable Operating Income}}{\text{Sales}} \times \frac{\text{Sales}}{\text{Invested Assets}}$$

$$\text{Division A ROI} = \frac{\$\ 70{,}000}{\$560{,}000} \times \frac{\$560{,}000}{\$350{,}000}$$

$$\text{ROI} = 12.5\% \times 1.6$$

$$\text{ROI} = 20\%$$

The expanded expression for the rate of return on investment is useful in evaluating and controlling decentralized operations. This is because the profit margin and the investment turnover focus on the underlying operating relationships of each division. The profit margin component focuses on profitability by indicating the rate of profit earned on each sales dollar. If a division's profit margin increases, and all other factors remain the same, the division's rate of return on investment will increase. For example, a division might add more profitable products to its sales mix and thereby increase its overall profit margin and rate of return on investment.

The investment turnover component focuses on efficiency in using assets and indicates the rate at which sales are generated for each dollar of invested assets. The more sales per dollar invested, the greater the efficiency in using the assets. If a division's investment turnover increases, and all other factors remain the same, the division's rate of return on investment will increase. For example, a division might attempt to increase sales through special sales promotions or reduce inventory assets by employing just-in-time principles, either of which would increase investment turnover.

The rate of return on investment, using the expanded expression for each division of Baldwin Company, is summarized as follows:

$$\textbf{Rate of Return on Investment (ROI)} = \frac{\textbf{Controllable Operating Income}}{\textbf{Sales}} \times \frac{\textbf{Sales}}{\textbf{Invested Assets}}$$

$$\textbf{Northern Division (ROI)} = \frac{\$\ 70{,}000}{\$560{,}000} \times \frac{\$560{,}000}{\$350{,}000}$$

ROI = 12.5% × 1.6
ROI = 20%

$$\textbf{Central Division (ROI)} = \frac{\$\ 84{,}000}{\$672{,}000} \times \frac{\$672{,}000}{\$700{,}000}$$

ROI = 12.5% × .96
ROI = 12%

$$\textbf{Southern Division (ROI)} = \frac{\$\ 75{,}000}{\$750{,}000} \times \frac{\$750{,}000}{\$500{,}000}$$

ROI = 10% × 1.5
ROI = 15%

Although the Northern and Central Divisions have the same profit margins, the Northern Division investment turnover is larger than that of the Central Division (1.6 to .96). Thus, by more efficiently utilizing its invested assets, the Northern Division's rate of return on investment is higher than the Central Division's. The Southern Division's profit margin of 10% and investment turnover of 1.5 are lower than those of the Northern Division. The product of these factors results in a return on investment of 15% for the Southern Division compared to 20% for the Northern Division.

To determine possible ways of increasing the rate of return on investment, the profit margin and investment turnover for a division may be analyzed. For example, if the Northern Division is in a highly competitive industry where the profit margin cannot be easily increased, the division manager might focus on increasing the investment turnover. To illustrate, assume that the revenues of the Northern Division could be increased by $56,000 through increasing advertising expenditures. The operating expenses will increase to $385,000, and the Northern Division's controllable operating income will increase from $70,000 to $77,000, as shown:

Revenues ($560,000 + $56,000)	$616,000
Operating expenses	385,000
Operating income	$231,000
Service department charges	154,000
Controllable operating income	$ 77,000

The rate of return on investment for the Northern Division, using the expanded expression, is recomputed as follows:

$$\textbf{Rate of Return on Investment (ROI)} = \frac{\textbf{Controllable Operating Income}}{\textbf{Sales}} \times \frac{\textbf{Sales}}{\textbf{Invested Assets}}$$

$$\textbf{Northern Division Revised ROI} = \frac{\$\ 77{,}000}{\$616{,}000} \times \frac{\$616{,}000}{\$350{,}000}$$

$$\textbf{ROI} = 12.5\% \times 1.76$$

$$\textbf{ROI} = 22\%$$

Although the Northern Division's profit margin remains the same (12.5%), the investment turnover has increased from 1.6 to 1.76, an increase of 10% (.16 ÷ 1.6). The 10% increase in investment turnover also increases the rate of return on investment by 10% (from 20% to 22%).

The major advantage of using the rate of return on investment instead of operating income as a divisional performance measure is that the amount of divisional investment is directly considered. Thus, divisional performances can be compared, even though the sizes of the divisions may vary significantly.

In addition to using it as a performance measure, the rate of return on investment can assist management in other ways. For example, in considering a decision to expand the operations of Baldwin Company, management might consider giving priority to the Northern Division because it earns the highest rate of return on investment. If the current rates of return on investment are maintained in the future, an investment in the Northern Division will return 20 cents (20%) on each dollar invested. In contrast, investments in the Central Division will earn only 12 cents per dollar invested, and investments in the Southern Division will return only 15 cents per dollar.

A disadvantage of the rate of return on investment as a performance measure is that it may lead divisional managers to reject new investments that could be profitable for the company as a whole. For example, assume that Division W of Struck Inc. has an overall rate of return on investment of 25%. The average rate of return on investment for Struck Inc., with all divisions considered, is 15%. The manager of Division W has the opportunity of investing in a new project that is estimated will earn a 20% rate of return. If the manager of Division W invests in the project, however, Division W's overall rate of return will decrease from 25%. Thus, the division manager might decide to reject the project, even though the investment would increase Struck Inc.'s overall rate of return of 15%.

USING ACCOUNTING TO UNDERSTAND BUSINESS

Mars, Inc. candy company uses ROI as a measure of responsibility center performance. In its equation, total assets are measured at replacement cost instead of book value. As a result, it believes that its ROI gives management an incentive to replace equipment with the latest technology. In other words, adding new equipment does not penalize the ROI with a larger denominator, since the denominator already is expressed at replacement cost. For example, at a Mars facility in Germany, a perfectly good machine was replaced with state-of-the-art technology. Using the latest technology provides the company with highly efficient production processes that are able to adjust quickly to changes in product demand.

RESIDUAL INCOME

An additional measure of evaluating divisional performance—residual income—is useful in overcoming some of the disadvantages associated with the rate of return on investment. **Residual income** is the excess of controllable operating income over a minimum amount of desired controllable operating income. The minimum amount of desired controllable operating income is set by top management, based on such factors as the cost of financing the operations of the business. It is normally computed by multiplying a minimum rate of return for the invested assets by the amount of divisional assets. To illustrate, assume that Baldwin Company has established 10% as the minimum rate of return on divisional assets. The residual incomes for the three divisions are shown as follows:

	Northern Division	*Central Division*	*Southern Division*
Controllable operating income	$70,000	$84,000	$75,000
Minimum amount of controllable operating income as a percent of assets:			
$350,000 × 10%	35,000		
$700,000 × 10%		70,000	
$500,000 × 10%			50,000
Residual income	$35,000	$14,000	$25,000

The Northern Division has more residual income than the other divisions, even though it has the least amount of controllable operating income. This is because the Northern Division has fewer assets on which to earn a minimum rate of return than the other divisions.

The major advantage of residual income as a performance measure is that it considers both the minimum rate of return and the total amount of the controllable operating income earned by each division. Residual income encourages division managers to maximize controllable operating income in excess of a minimum threshold. This provides an incentive to accept any project that is expected to have a rate of return in excess of the minimum rate of return. Thus, the residual income number supports both divisional and corporate objectives.

Residual income is growing in popularity as a performance measure. For example, companies such as **Quaker Oats Company** and **Coca Cola Company** are using it. As a measure of "economic value added," these companies use residual income to guide their strategic investment decisions and to measure managers' abilities to return profits from the assets entrusted to them.

NONFINANCIAL DIVISIONAL PERFORMANCE MEASUREMENT

In practice, most companies use a variety of divisional performance measures. For example, a survey of manufacturers found that 70% of the respondents used operating income as a percent of sales, 62% used rate of return on investment, and 13% used residual income as performance measures in setting company goals.[1] In addition, some companies are relying on nonfinancial measures that take into account customer perspectives and innovativeness. Examples include measures of product quality, customer complaints, warranty experience, customer retention rates, product availability, on-time performance, customer satisfaction, new product time to market, and market share. These newer nonfinancial measures combined with conventional financial measures can provide the organization with a balanced perspective with respect to performance.

[1] Robert A. Howell, James D. Brown, Stephen R. Soucy, and Allen H. Seed, *Management Accounting in the New Manufacturing Environment*, National Association of Accountants, Montvale, New Jersey, 1987.

USING ACCOUNTING TO UNDERSTAND BUSINESS

Analog Devices, an electronic components manufacturer, requires each division manager to be evaluated on a scorecard that includes financial results (such as ROI), new product results (such as number of new products delivered on time), and quality improvement (such as defects). Each of these three areas is given equal weight. However, there is some conflict between these three performance areas. The founder of the company, Ray Stata, states, "Another problem with management information systems is that they are strongly biased toward reporting financial information . . . . Unless quality improvement and other more fundamental performance measures are elevated to the same level of importance as financial measures, when conflict arises, financial considerations win out." Analog Devices is attempting to balance the focus between financial and nonfinancial performance.

Source: R. A. Howell, J. K. Shank, S. R. Soucy, and J. Fisher, *Cost Management for Tomorrow: Seeking the Competitive Edge*, FEFR, Morristown, New Jersey, 1992.

Transfer Pricing

Objective 5
Explain how the following transfer pricing approaches may be used by decentralized segments of a business:

Market price approach
Negotiated price approach
Cost price approach

When decentralized divisions transfer products or render services to each other, a **transfer price** is used to charge for the products or services. Since transfer prices affect the goals for both divisions, setting these prices is a sensitive matter for division managers.

The objective of transfer pricing is to encourage each division manager to transfer goods and services between divisions if overall company income can be increased by doing so. As we will illustrate, however, transfer prices may be misused in such a way that overall company income suffers.

In the following paragraphs, we discuss various approaches to setting transfer prices. Exhibit 7 shows the range of prices that result from common approaches to setting transfer prices.[2] Transfer prices can be set as low as variable cost per unit or as high as market price. Often, transfer prices are negotiated at some point between variable cost per unit and market price.

Exhibit 7
Commonly Used Transfer Prices

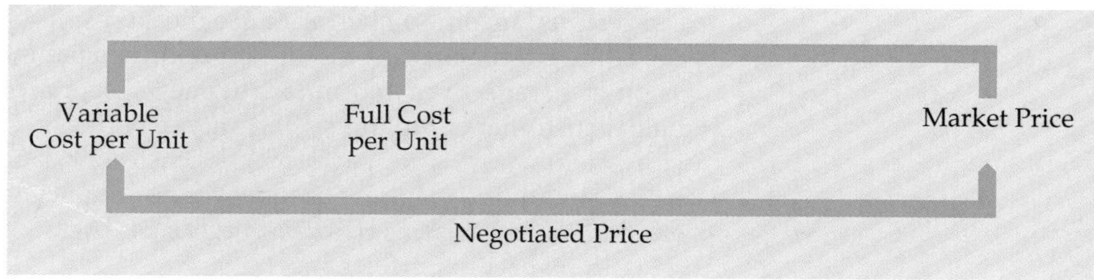

[2] The discussion in this chapter highlights the essential concepts of transfer pricing. In-depth discussion of transfer pricing can be found in advanced texts.

A survey of transfer pricing practices has reported the following frequency of use:

Cost price (variable or full)	46%
Negotiated price	17
Market price	37

Source: Roger Y. W. Tang, "Transfer Pricing in the 1990's," *Management Accounting*, February 1992, pp. 22–26.

Transfer prices may be used when decentralized units are organized as cost, profit, or investment centers. For purposes of illustration, we will use a diversified company (Wilson Company) with no service departments and two operating divisions (M and N) organized as investment centers. Condensed divisional income statements for Wilson Company, assuming no transfers between divisions, are shown in Exhibit 8.

Exhibit 8
Income Statement—No Transfers Between Divisions

Wilson Company
Divisional Income Statements
For the Year Ended December 31, 1997

	Division M	Division N	Total
Sales:			
50,000 units × $20 per unit	$1,000,000		$1,000,000
20,000 units × $40 per unit		$800,000	800,000
			$1,800,000
Expenses:			
Variable:			
50,000 units × $10 per unit	$ 500,000		$ 500,000
20,000 units × $30* per unit		$600,000	600,000
Fixed	300,000	100,000	400,000
Total expenses	$ 800,000	$700,000	$1,500,000
Controllable operating income	$ 200,000	$100,000	$ 300,000

*$20 of the $30 per unit represents materials costs, and the remaining $10 per unit represents other expenses incurred within Division N.

MARKET PRICE APPROACH

Under the market price approach, the transfer price is the price at which the product or service transferred could be sold to outside buyers. If an outside market exists for the product or service transferred, the current market price at which the purchasing division could buy the product or service may be an appropriate transfer price.

To illustrate, assume that materials used by Wilson Company in producing Division N's product are currently purchased from an outside supplier at $20 per unit. The same materials are produced by Division M. Division M is operating at full capacity of 50,000 units and can sell all it produces to either Division N or to outside buyers. A transfer price of $20 per unit (the market price) has no effect on the income of Division M or total company income. Division M will earn revenues of $20 per unit on all its production and sales, regardless of who buys its product. Likewise, Division N will pay $20 per unit for materials (the market price). Thus, the use of the market price as the transfer price has no effect on the income of Division M or total company income. In this situation, the use of the market price as the transfer price is appropriate. The condensed divisional income statements for Wilson Company under such circumstances would be as shown in Exhibit 8.

NEGOTIATED PRICE APPROACH

If unused or excess capacity exists in the supplying division (Division M), and the transfer price is equal to the market price, total company profit may not be maximized. This is because the manager of Division N will be indifferent as to whether to purchase the materials from Division M or from outside suppliers. Thus, Division N may purchase the materials from outside suppliers. If, however, Division N purchases the materials from Division M, the difference between the market price of $20 and the variable costs of Division M can cover fixed costs and contribute to company profits. When the negotiated price approach is used in this situation, the manager of Division N is encouraged to purchase the materials from Division M.

The **negotiated price approach** allows the managers of decentralized units to agree (negotiate) among themselves as to the transfer price. The only constraint on the negotiations is that the transfer price be less than the market price but greater than the supplying division's variable costs per unit. If agreement cannot be reached between the division managers, the company's top management may intervene to set the transfer price.

To illustrate the use of the negotiated price approach, assume that instead of a capacity of 50,000 units, Division M's capacity is 70,000 units. In addition, assume that Division M can continue to sell only 50,000 units to outside buyers. A transfer price less than $20 would encourage the manager of Division N to purchase from Division M. This is because Division N's materials cost per unit would decrease, and its controllable operating income would increase. At the same time, a transfer price above Division M's variable costs per unit of $10 (from Exhibit 8) would encourage the manager of Division M to use the excess capacity to supply materials to Division N. In doing so, Division M's controllable operating profits would increase.

To continue the illustration with the aid of Exhibit 9, assume that Wilson Company's division managers agree to a transfer price of $15 for Division M's product. By purchasing from Division M, Division N's materials cost would be $5 per unit less. At the same time, Division M would increase its sales by $300,000 (20,000 units × $15 per unit) and increase its income by $100,000 ($300,000 sales – $200,000 variable costs). The effect of reducing Division N's materials cost by $100,000 (20,000 units × $5 per unit) is to increase its income by $100,000. Therefore, Wilson Company's income is increased by $200,000 ($100,000 reported by Division M and $100,000 reported by Division N), as shown in the condensed income statements in Exhibit 9.

In this illustration, any transfer price less than the market price of $20 but greater than Division M's unit variable costs of $10 would increase each division's income and would increase overall company profit by $200,000. By establishing a range of $20 to $10 for the transfer price, each division manager will have an incentive to negotiate the transfer of the materials.

Exhibit 9
Income Statements—Negotiated Transfer Price

Wilson Company
Divisional Income Statements
For the Year Ended December 31, 1997

	Division M	Division N	Total
Sales:			
50,000 units × $20 per unit	$1,000,000		$1,000,000
20,000 units × $15 per unit	300,000		300,000
20,000 units × $40 per unit		$800,000	800,000
	$1,300,000	$800,000	$2,100,000
Expenses:			
Variable:			
70,000 units × $10 per unit	$ 700,000		$ 700,000
20,000 units × $25* per unit		$500,000	500,000
Fixed	300,000	100,000	400,000
Total expenses	$1,000,000	$600,000	$1,600,000
Controllable operating income	$ 300,000	$200,000	$ 500,000

*$10 of the $25 is incurred solely within Division N, and $15 per unit represents the transfer price per unit from Division M.

COST PRICE APPROACH

Under the cost price approach, cost is used as the basis for setting transfer prices. With this approach, a variety of cost concepts may be used. For example, cost may refer to either total product cost per unit or variable product cost per unit. If total product cost per unit is used, direct materials, direct labor, and factory overhead are included in the transfer price. If variable product cost per unit is used, the fixed factory overhead component of total product cost is excluded from the transfer price.

Either actual costs or standard (budgeted) costs may be used in applying the cost price approach. If actual costs are used, inefficiencies of the producing division are transferred to the purchasing division. Thus, there is little incentive for the producing division to control costs carefully. For this reason, most companies use standard costs in the cost price approach. In this way, differences between actual and standard costs are isolated in the producing divisions for cost control purposes.

When division managers have responsibility for cost centers, the cost price approach to transfer pricing is appropriate and is often used. The cost price approach may not be appropriate, however, for decentralized operations organized as profit or investment centers. In profit and investment centers, division managers have responsibility for both revenues and expenses. The use of cost as a transfer price ignores the supplying division manager's responsibility for revenues. When a supplying division's sales are all intracompany transfers, for example, the use of the cost price approach would prevent the supplying division from reporting any operating income. A cost-based transfer price may therefore not motivate the division manager to make intracompany transfers, even though they are in the best interests of the company.

KEY POINTS

Objective 1. List and explain the advantages and disadvantages of decentralized operations.

The advantages of decentralization may include better decisions by the managers closest to the operations, more time for top management to focus on strategic planning, training for managers, improved ability to serve customers and respond to their needs, and improved manager morale. The disadvantages of decentralization may include failure of the company to maximize profits because decisions made by one manager may affect other managers in such a way that the profitability of the entire company may suffer.

Objective 2. Prepare a responsibility accounting report for a cost center.

Since managers of cost centers have responsibility and authority to make decisions regarding costs, responsibility accounting for cost centers focuses on costs. The primary accounting tools for planning and controlling costs for a cost center are budgets and budget performance reports. An example of a budget performance report is shown in Exhibit 2.

Objective 3. Prepare responsibility accounting reports for a profit center, using the following income concepts:

Operating income
Controllable operating income

In preparing a profitability report for a profit center, operating expenses are subtracted from revenues in order to determine the operating income. From operating income, service department charges are subtracted in order to determine the controllable operating income of the profit center. An example of a divisional income statement is shown in Exhibit 5.

Objective 4. Compute and interpret the rate of return on investment and the residual income for an investment center.

The rate of return on investment for an investment center is the controllable operating income divided by invested assets. The rate of return on investment may also be computed as the product of (1) the profit margin and (2) the investment turnover. Residual income for an investment center is the excess of controllable operating income over a minimum amount of desired controllable operating income.

Objective 5. Explain how the following transfer pricing approaches may be used by decentralized segments of a business:

Market price approach
Negotiated price approach
Cost price approach

Under the market price approach, the transfer price is the price at which the product or service transferred could be sold to outside buyers. Market price should be used when the supplier division is able to sell to outsiders and is operating at capacity.

Under the negotiated price approach, the managers of decentralized units agree (negotiate) among themselves as to the transfer price. Negotiated prices should be used when the supplier division is operating below capacity.

Under the cost price approach, cost is used as the basis for setting transfer prices. A variety of cost concepts may be used, such as total product cost per unit or variable product cost per unit. In addition, actual costs or standard (budgeted) costs may be used. The cost price approach should be used for supplier divisions that are organized as cost centers.

GLOSSARY OF KEY TERMS

Controllable expenses. Costs that can be influenced by the decisions of a manager. *Objective 3*

Controllable operating income. The operating income that is the responsibility of a profit or investment center manager. It is computed as operating income less service department charges. *Objective 3*

Cost center. A decentralized unit in which the department or division manager has responsibility for the control of costs incurred and the authority to make decisions that affect these costs. *Objective 2*

Cost price approach. An approach to transfer pricing that uses cost as the basis for setting the transfer price. *Objective 5*

Decentralization. The separation of a business into more manageable operating units. *Objective 1*

Division. A decentralized organizational unit that is structured around a common function, product, customer, or geographical territory. Divisions can be cost, profit, or investment centers. *Objective 1*

Investment center. A decentralized unit in which the manager has the responsibility and authority to make decisions that affect not only costs and revenues but also the plant assets available to the center. *Objective 4*

Investment turnover. A component of the rate of return on investment, computed as the ratio of sales to invested assets. *Objective 4*

Market price approach. An approach to transfer pricing that uses the price at which the product or service transferred could be sold to outside buyers as the transfer price. *Objective 5*

Negotiated price approach. An approach to transfer pricing that allows managers of decentralized units to agree (negotiate) among themselves as to the transfer price. *Objective 5*

Operating income. Revenues less operating expenses for a profit or investment center. *Objective 3*

Profit center. A decentralized unit in which the manager has the responsibility and the authority to make decisions that affect both costs and revenues (and thus profits). *Objective 3*

Profit margin. A component of the rate of return on investment, computed as the ratio of controllable operating income to sales. *Objective 4*

Rate of return on investment (ROI). A measure of managerial efficiency in the use of investments in assets, computed as controllable operating income divided by invested assets. *Objective 4*

Residual income. The excess of controllable operating income over a "minimum" amount of desired controllable operating income. *Objective 4*

Service department charges. The costs of services provided by an internal service department and transferred to a responsibility center. *Objective 3*

Responsibility accounting. The process of measuring and reporting operating data by areas of responsibility. *Objective 1*

Transfer price. The price charged one decentralized unit by another for the goods or services provided. *Objectives 3 and 5*

ILLUSTRATIVE PROBLEM

Quinn Company has two divisions, A and B. Invested assets and condensed income statement data for each division for the past year ended December 31 are as follows:

	Division A	*Division B*
Revenues	$675,000	$480,000
Operating expenses	450,000	372,400
Service department charges	90,000	50,000
Invested assets	600,000	384,000

Instructions

1. Prepare condensed income statements for the past year for each division.
2. Using the expanded expression, determine the profit margin, investment turnover, and rate of return on investment for each division.

3. If management desires a minimum rate of return of 10%, determine the residual income for each division.

Solution

1.

Quinn Company
Divisional Income Statements
For the Year Ended December 31, 19—

	Division A	*Division B*
Revenues	$675,000	$480,000
Operating expenses	450,000	372,400
Operating income	$225,000	$107,600
Service department charges	90,000	50,000
Controllable operating income	$135,000	$ 57,600

2. **Rate of Return on Investment (ROI) = Profit Margin × Investment Turnover**

$$\text{Rate of Return on Investment (ROI)} = \frac{\text{Controllable Operating Income}}{\text{Sales}} \times \frac{\text{Sales}}{\text{Invested Assets}}$$

$$\text{Division A: ROI} = \frac{\$135{,}000}{\$675{,}000} \times \frac{\$675{,}000}{\$600{,}000}$$

$$\text{ROI} = 20\% \times 1.125$$
$$\text{ROI} = 22.5\%$$

$$\text{Division B: ROI} = \frac{\$\ 57{,}600}{\$480{,}000} \times \frac{\$480{,}000}{\$384{,}000}$$

$$\text{ROI} = 12\% \times 1.25$$
$$\text{ROI} = 15\%$$

3. Division A: $75,000 [$135,000 – (10% × $600,000)]
Division B: $19,200 [$57,600 – (10% × $384,000)]

SELF-EXAMINATION QUESTIONS (ANSWERS AT END OF CHAPTER)

1. When the manager has the responsibility and authority to make decisions that affect costs and revenues, but no responsibility for or authority over assets invested in the department, the department is called:
   A. a cost center
   B. a profit center
   C. an investment center
   D. a service department

2. The Accounts Payable Department has a budget of $600,000 and expects to make 150,000 payments to the various vendors who provide products and services to the divisions. Division A has operating income of $900,000 and requires 60,000 payments to vendors. If the Accounts Payable Department incurs expenses that are only service department charges, what is Division A's controllable operating income?
   A. $300,000
   B. $900,000
   C. $660,000
   D. $540,000

3. Division A of Kern Co. has sales of $350,000, cost of goods sold of $200,000, operating expenses of $30,000, and invested assets of $600,000. What is the rate of return on investment for Division A?
   A. 20%
   B. 25%
   C. 33%
   D. 40%

4. Division L of Liddy Co. has a rate of return on investment of 24% and an investment turnover of 1.6. What is the profit margin?
   A. 6%
   B. 15%
   C. 24%
   D. 38%

5. Which approach to transfer pricing uses the price at which the product or service transferred could be sold to outside buyers?
   A. Cost price approach
   B. Negotiated price approach
   C. Market price approach
   D. Standard cost approach

DISCUSSION QUESTIONS

1. What is responsibility accounting?
2. Name three common types of responsibility centers for decentralized operations.
3. Differentiate between a cost center and a profit center.
4. Differentiate between a profit center and an investment center.
5. In what major respect would budget performance reports prepared for the use of plant managers of a manufacturing business with cost centers differ from those prepared for the use of the various department supervisors who report to the plant managers?
6. How do service department charges and direct expenses differ with respect to a responsibility center?
7. What is a service department?
8. What are service department charges?
9. How is a service department charge rate determined?

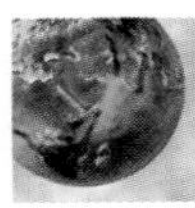

10. Weyerhaeuser Company developed a system that assigns service department expenses to user divisions on the basis of actual services consumed by the division. Here are a number of Weyerhaeuser's activities in its central financial services department:

    Payroll
    Accounts payable
    Accounts receivable
    Database administration—report preparation

    For each activity, identify an output measure that could be used to charge user divisions for service.
11. What term is applied to the dollar amount representing the focal point of profit center responsibility?
12. Name two performance measures useful in evaluating investment centers.
13. What is the major shortcoming of using controllable operating income as a performance measure for investment centers?
14. Why should the factors under the control of the investment center manager (revenues, expenses, and invested assets) be considered in computing the rate of return on investment?
15. What are two ways of expressing the rate of return on investment?
16. In evaluating investment centers, what does multiplying the profit margin by the investment turnover equal?
17. In a decentralized company in which the divisions are organized as investment centers, how could a division be considered the least profitable, even though it earned the largest amount of controllable operating income?
18. Which component of the rate of return on investment (profit margin or investment turnover) focuses on efficiency in the use of assets and indicates the rate at which sales are generated for each dollar of invested assets?
19. How does using the rate of return on investment facilitate comparability between divisions of decentralized companies?
20. The rates of return on investment for Harmon Co.'s three divisions, A, B, and C, are 20%, 17%, and 15%, respectively. In expanding operations, which of Harmon Co.'s divisions should be given priority? Explain.
21. What term is used to describe the excess of controllable operating income over a minimum amount of desired controllable operating income?
22. Why would a firm use nonfinancial measures in evaluating divisional performance?
23. What is the objective of transfer pricing?
24. What approach uses as the transfer price the price at which the product or service transferred could be sold to outside buyers?
25. When is the negotiated price approach preferred over the market price approach in setting transfer prices?
26. If division managers cannot agree among themselves on a transfer price when using the negotiated price approach, how is the transfer price established?
27. When using the negotiated price approach to transfer pricing, within what range should the transfer price be established?

EXERCISES

EXERCISE 24–1
Budget performance report for a cost center
Objective 2

The budget for Department 3 of Plant D for the current month ended March 31 is as follows:

Factory wages	$190,300
Materials	165,700
Power and light	64,000
Supervisory salaries	36,000
Depreciation of plant and equipment	21,300
Maintenance	24,200
Insurance and property taxes	12,000

During March, the costs incurred in Department 3 of Plant D were as follows:

Factory wages	$190,700
Materials	171,900
Power and light	63,700
Supervisory salaries	36,000
Depreciation of plant and equipment	21,300
Maintenance	24,600
Insurance and property taxes	12,000

a. Prepare a budget performance report for the supervisor of Department 3, Plant D, for the month of March.

b. For what significant variations in costs might the supervisor be expected to request supplemental reports?

EXERCISE 24–2
Budget performance reports for cost centers
Objective 2

Partially completed budget performance reports of Klondike Company, a manufacturer of air conditioners, are provided below:

Klondike Company
Budget Performance Report—Vice-President, Production
For the Month Ended April 30, 19—

	Budget	*Actual*	*Over Budget*	*Under Budget*
Plant A	$430,000	$450,000	$20,000	
Plant B	320,000	310,000		$10,000
Plant C	g.	h.	i.	
	j.	k.	l.	$10,000

Klondike Company
Budget Performance Report—Manager, Plant C
For the Month Ended April 30, 19—

	Budget	*Actual*	*Over Budget*	*Under Budget*
Department 1	a.	b.	c.	
Department 2	175,000	190,000	15,000	
Department 3	100,000	100,000		
	d.	e.	f.	

Klondike Company
Budget Performance Report—Supervisor, Department 1, Plant C
For the Month Ended April 30, 19—

	Budget	*Actual*	*Over Budget*	*Under Budget*
Factory wages	$ 75,000	$ 95,000	$20,000	
Materials	45,000	50,000	5,000	
Power and light	25,000	25,000		
Maintenance	80,000	150,000	70,000	
	$225,000	$320,000	$95,000	

a. Complete the budget performance reports by determining the correct amounts for the lettered spaces.
b. Compose a memo to Harold Poling, vice-president of production of Klondike Company, explaining the performance of the production division for April.

EXERCISE 24–3
Divisional income statements
Objective 3

The following data were summarized from the accounting records for Dell Company for the current year ended June 30:

Cost of goods sold:	
Division C	$170,500
Division D	237,000
Administrative expenses:	
Division C	88,000
Division D	119,200
Service department charges:	
Division C	23,500
Division D	31,200
Net sales:	
Division C	380,000
Division D	620,000

Prepare divisional income statements for Dell Company.

EXERCISE 24–4
Service department charges
Objective 3

In income statements prepared for Gibson Instruments Company, Payroll Department expenses are charged to user divisions on the basis of the number of checks, and Purchasing Department expenses are charged on the basis of the number of purchase requisitions. The Payroll Department had a budgeted cost of $146,380, and the Purchasing Department had a budgeted cost of $196,000 for the year. The following annual data for Able, Baker, and Charley Divisions were estimated:

	Able	*Baker*	*Charley*
Sales	$2,500,000	$2,200,000	$3,000,000
Number of employees:			
Weekly payroll (52 weeks per year)	25	100	50
Monthly payroll	100	30	50
Number of purchase requisitions per year	400	700	300

a. Determine the amount of payroll and purchasing service department expenses charged to the Able, Baker, and Charley Divisions.
b. Why does Baker Division have a larger service department charge than the other two divisions, even though its sales are lower?

EXERCISE 24–5
Service department charges and activity bases
Objective 3

For each of the following expenses, identify an activity base that could be used for charging the expense to the profit center.

a. Telecommunications
b. Electronic data processing
c. Central purchasing
d. Accounts receivable
e. Duplication services

EXERCISE 24–6
Activity bases for service department charges
Objective 3

For each of the following service departments, select the activity base listed that is most appropriate for charging service expenses to responsible units.

Service Department	*Activity Base*
a. Employee Travel	1. Number of publications
b. Central Purchasing	2. Number of employees trained
c. Publications Group	3. Number of telephone lines
d. Training	4. Number of sales invoices
e. Telecommunications	5. Number of conference attendees
f. Conferences	6. Number of purchase requisitions
g. Accounts Receivable	7. Number of travel claims
h. Payroll Accounting	8. Number of payroll checks

EXERCISE 24–7
Divisional income statements with service department charges
Objective 3

Salvatori Company has two divisions, K and L, and two corporate service departments, Legal and Accounts Payable, with expenses budgeted for the year ended December 31 as follows:

Legal Department	$250,000
Accounts Payable Department	145,000

The Legal Department charges the divisions for services rendered, based on hours, and the Accounts Payable Department charges divisions for services, based on the number of checks issued. The usage of service by the two divisions is as follows:

	Legal Department	*Accounts Payable Department*
Division K	1,000 hours	2,800 checks
Division L	4,000	5,200
Total	5,000 hours	8,000 checks

The service department charges of the Legal Department and the Accounts Payable Department are considered controllable by the divisions. The revenues and operating expenses of the two divisions are as follows:

	Division K	*Division L*
Revenues	$2,100,000	$900,000
Operating expenses	900,000	500,000

Prepare the divisional income statements for the two divisions.

EXERCISE 24–8
Corrections to service department charges
Objective 3

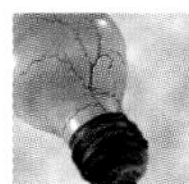

Pegasus Airlines Inc. has two divisions organized as profit centers, the Passenger Division and the Cargo Division. The following divisional income statements were prepared:

Pegasus Airlines Inc.
Divisional Income Statements
For the Year Ended October 31, 19—

	Passenger Division		*Cargo Division*	
Revenues		$5,000,000		$5,000,000
Operating expenses		3,500,000		3,000,000
Operating income		$1,500,000		$2,000,000
Less service department charges:				
Training	$180,000		$180,000	
Flight scheduling	220,000		220,000	
Reservations	400,000	800,000	400,000	800,000
Controllable operating income		$ 700,000		$1,200,000

The service department charge rate for the service department costs was based on revenues. Since the revenues of the two divisions were the same, the service department charges to each division were also the same.

The following additional information is available:

	Passenger Division	*Cargo Division*	*Total*
Number of flight personnel trained	240	60	300
Number of flights	160	240	400
Number of reservations requested	30,000	0	30,000

a. Does the reported controllable operating income for the two divisions accurately measure performance?
b. Correct the divisional income statements, using the activity bases provided above in revising the service department charges.

EXERCISE 24–9
Profit center responsibility reporting
Objective 3

Dubinski Sporting Goods Co. operates two divisions—Division C for camping equipment and Division S for skiing equipment. The following partial trial balance was prepared as of June 30, the end of the current fiscal year, after all adjustments were recorded and posted:

Sales—Division C		560,000
Sales—Division S		240,000
Cost of Goods Sold—Division C	169,300	
Cost of Goods Sold—Division S	101,950	
Selling Expense—Division C	70,000	
Selling Expense—Division S	24,600	
Administrative Expense—Division C	83,000	
Administrative Expense—Division S	46,500	
Advertising Expense	11,000	
Transportation Expense	33,490	
Accounts Receivable Collection Expense	3,717	
Warehouse Expense	45,000	

The bases to be used in charging services, together with other essential information, are as follows:

a. Advertising—incurred at headquarters, charged to divisions on the basis of usage: Division C, $7,200; Division S, $3,800.
b. Transportation—charged to divisions at a transfer price of $6.80 per bill of lading: Division C, 2,325 bills of lading; Division S, 2,600 bills of lading.
c. Accounts receivable collection—incurred at headquarters, charged to divisions at a transfer price of $2.10 per invoice: Division C, 860 sales invoices; Division S, 910 sales invoices.
d. Warehouse—charged to divisions on the basis of floor space used in storing division products: Division C, 10,000 square feet; Division S, 5,000 square feet.

Prepare a divisional income statement with two column headings: Division C and Division S. Provide supporting schedules for determining service department charges.

EXERCISE 24–10
Rate of return on investment
Objective 4

The controllable operating income and the amount of invested assets in each division of Kincaid Dairy Company are as follows:

	Controllable Operating Income	*Invested Assets*
Division A	$256,000	$800,000
Division B	100,800	360,000
Division C	217,000	620,000

a. Compute the rate of return on investment for each division.
b. Which division is the most profitable per dollar invested?

EXERCISE 24–11
Residual income
Objective 4

Based on the data in Exercise 24–10, assume that management has established a 15% minimum rate of return for invested assets.

a. Determine the residual income for each division.
b. Based on residual income, which of the divisions is the most profitable?

EXERCISE 24–12
Determining missing items in rate of return computation
Objective 4

One item is omitted from each of the following computations of the rate of return on investment:

Rate of Return on Investment	= Profit Margin	× Investment Turnover
30%	= 25%	× (a)
(b)	= 20%	× 1.1
18%	= (c)	× 1.5
24%	= 8%	× (d)
(e)	= 15%	× 1.4

Determine the missing items, identifying each by the appropriate letter.

EXERCISE 24–13
Profit margin, investment turnover, and rate of return on investment
Objective 4

The condensed income statement for Division B of Glickman Company is as follows (assuming no service department charges):

Sales	$800,000
Cost of goods sold	550,000
Gross profit	$250,000
Operating expenses	60,000
Controllable operating income	$190,000

The manager of Division B is considering ways to increase the rate of return on investment.

a. Using the expanded expression for rate of return on investment, determine the profit margin, investment turnover, and rate of return on investment of Division B, assuming that $500,000 of assets have been invested in Division B.
b. If expenses could be reduced by $18,000 without decreasing sales, what would be the impact on the profit margin, investment turnover, and rate of return on investment for Division B?

EXERCISE 24–14
Determining missing items in rate of return and residual income computations
Objective 4

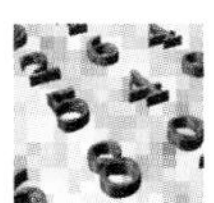

Data for Hyde Company is presented in the following table of rates of return on investment and residual incomes:

Invested Assets	*Controllable Operating Income*	*Rate of Return on Investment*	*Minimum Rate of Return*	*Minimum Amount of Controllable Operating Income*	*Residual Income*
$750,000	$105,000	(a)	12%	(b)	(c)
$420,000	(d)	18%	(e)	$63,000	$12,600
$640,000	(f)	(g)	(h)	$57,600	$19,200
$300,000	$ 27,000	(i)	10%	(j)	(k)

Determine the missing items, identifying each item by the appropriate letter.

EXERCISE 24–15
Determining missing items from computations
Objective 4

Data for Divisions 1, 2, 3, and 4 of Florence Marine Company are as follows:

	Sales	*Controllable Operating Income*	*Invested Assets*	*Rate of Return on Investment*	*Profit Margin*	*Investment Turnover*
Division 1	$720,000	$230,400	$1,152,000	(a)	(b)	(c)
Division 2	$440,000	(d)	$ 220,000	16%	(e)	(f)
Division 3	(g)	$144,000	(h)	(i)	12%	1.5
Division 4	$850,000	(j)	(k)	28%	7%	(l)

a. Determine the missing items, identifying each by the letters (a) through (l).
b. Determine the residual income for each division, assuming that the minimum rate of return established by management is 14%.
c. Which division is the most profitable in terms of (a) return on investment and (b) residual income?

EXERCISE 24–16
Decision on transfer pricing
Objective 5

Materials used by Division S of Chambers Company are currently purchased from outside suppliers at a cost of $80 per unit. However, the same materials are available from Division D. Division D has unused capacity and can produce the materials needed by Division S at a variable cost of $55 per unit.

a. If a transfer price of $66 per unit is established and 50,000 units of materials are transferred, with no reduction in Division D's current sales, how much would Chambers Company's total operating income increase?
b. How much would Division S's operating income increase?
c. How much would Division D's operating income increase?

EXERCISE 24–17
Decision on transfer pricing
Objective 5

Based on the Chambers Company data in Exercise 24–16, assume that a transfer price of $75 has been established and 50,000 units of materials are transferred, with no reduction in Division D's current sales.

a. How much would Chambers Company's total operating income increase?
b. How much would Division S's operating income increase?
c. How much would Division D's operating income increase?
d. If the negotiated price approach is used, what would be the range of acceptable transfer prices and why?

PROBLEMS SERIES A

PROBLEM 24–1A
Profit center responsibility reporting
Objective 3

Trans Coast Railroad has six regional divisions organized as profit centers. The Northwest (NW) and Western (W) Regions are being considered for sale to a competing railroad. The board of directors believes that it is now time to consider retaining or selling these two divisions. If sold, Trans Coast does not expect to realize a gain on the sale. The following condensed trial balance was prepared as of October 31, the end of the first month of the current fiscal year. October is considered to be a typical month.

Current Assets	576,780	
Equipment	3,350,000	
Accumulated Depreciation—Equipment		365,000
Current Liabilities		165,000
Common Stock		390,000
Retained Earnings		2,900,000
Cash Dividends	840,000	
Sales—NW Region		540,000
Sales—W Region		480,000
Sales—Other Regions		4,980,000
Operating Expenses—NW Region	320,000	
Operating Expenses—W Region	270,000	
Operating Expenses—Other Regions	2,340,000	
Operating Expenses—Internal Auditing	140,000	
Operating Expenses—Dispatching	164,640	
Operating Expenses—Equipment	853,580	
General Corporate Officers' Salaries	420,000	
Interest Expense	545,000	
Total	9,820,000	9,820,000

The company operates three service departments: the Dispatching Department, the Equipment Department, and the Internal Auditing Department. The Dispatching Department manages the scheduling and releasing of trains. The Equipment Department manages the railroad car inventories. It makes sure the right freight cars are at the right place at the right time. The Internal Auditing Department conducts a variety of services for the company as a whole. The following additional information has been gathered:

	Northwest	*Western*	*Other Regions*
Number of scheduled trains	114	172	890
Number of railroad cars in inventory	3,628	4,360	16,400

Instructions

1. Prepare income statements for the month ended October 31, with three column headings: Northwest, Western, and Other Regions.
2. State your recommendations for retaining or selling either the Northwest or Western Divisions, and give reasons for your answer.

PROBLEM 24–2A
Profit center responsibility reporting
Objective 3

Wilson Food Corporation is organized as two regional profit centers, the southern (S) and northern (N) regions. Each region consists of a single packaging plant, distribution center, and sales office. The following information is available:

a. Composite work for newspaper ads (advertising expense) is conducted at the headquarters—charged to each region based on usage: Region N, $12,000; Region S, $18,000.
b. Payroll accounting is conducted at the headquarters—charged at a transfer price of $4.20 per issued payroll check. Payroll checks issued for Region N are 350, and Region S, 450.
c. Accounts payable accounting is conducted at the headquarters—charged at a transfer price of $1.80 per invoice paid. Invoices paid for Region N are 2,350, and Region S, 3,200.
d. Property tax expense is paid at the headquarters—charged to the regions at a rate of a half cent per dollar of valuation. Valuation is determined as the sum of the book values of plant and equipment and inventories. The sum of the book values of plant and equipment and inventories was $560,000 for Region N and $876,000 for Region S.

The following revenue and expense data are selected from the Wilson ledger on September 30, the end of the current fiscal year:

Sale—Region N		440,000
Sales—Region S		660,000
Cost of Goods Sold—Region N	190,000	
Cost of Goods Sold—Region S	280,000	
Selling Expense—Region N	65,000	
Selling Expense—Region S	105,000	
Administrative Expense—Region N	78,000	
Administrative Expense—Region S	98,000	
Advertising Expense	30,000	
Payroll Expense	3,360	
Accounts Payable Accounting Expense	9,990	
Property Tax Expense	7,180	

Instructions

1. Provide schedules for the service department charges for advertising, payroll, accounts payable, and property tax.
2. Prepare a profit center income statement with two column headings for the North and South Divisions.

PROBLEM 24–3A
Divisional income statements and rate of return on investment analysis
Objective 4

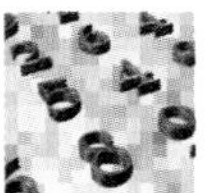

Patel Company is a diversified electronics company with three operating divisions organized as investment centers. Condensed data taken from the records of the three divisions for the year ended December 31 are as follows:

	Division U	*Division V*	*Division W*
Sales	$360,000	$ 925,000	$710,000
Cost of goods sold	170,000	535,000	420,000
Operating expenses	82,000	168,000	176,400
Invested assets	720,000	1,156,250	443,750

The management of Patel Company is evaluating each division as a basis for planning a future expansion of operations.

Instructions

1. Prepare condensed divisional income statements for Divisions U, V, and W, assuming that there were no service department charges.
2. Using the expanded expression for rate of return on investment, compute the profit margin, investment turnover, and rate of return on investment for each division.
3. If available funds permit the expansion of operations of only one division, which of the divisions would you recommend for expansion, based on (1) and (2)? Explain.

PROBLEM 24–4A
Effect of proposals on divisional performance
Objective 4

A condensed income statement for Division K of Amigo Company for the year ended January 31 is as follows:

Sales	$4,500,000
Cost of goods sold	3,250,000
Gross profit	$1,250,000
Operating expenses	800,000
Controllable operating income	$ 450,000

Assume that Division K received no charges from service departments.

The president of Amigo Company is concerned with Division K's rate of return on invested assets of $3,000,000 and has indicated that the division's rate of return on investment must be increased to at least 18% by the end of the next year if operations are to continue. The division manager is considering the following three proposals:

Proposal 1: Reduce invested assets by discontinuing a product line. This action would eliminate sales of $300,000, cost of goods sold of $260,000, and operating expenses of $52,000. Assets of $600,000 would be transferred to other divisions at no gain or loss.

Proposal 2: Purchase new and more efficient machinery and thereby reduce the cost of goods sold by $112,500. Sales would remain unchanged, and the old machinery, which has no remaining book value, would be scrapped at no gain or loss. The new machinery would increase invested assets by $750,000 for the year.

Proposal 3: Transfer equipment with a book value of $500,000 to other divisions at no gain or loss and lease similar equipment. The annual lease payments would exceed the amount of depreciation expense on the old equipment by $22,500. This increase in expense would be included as part of the cost of goods sold. Sales would remain unchanged.

Instructions

1. Using the expanded expression for rate of return on investment, determine the profit margin, investment turnover, and rate of return on investment for Division K for the past year.
2. Prepare condensed estimated income statements for Division K for each proposal.
3. Using the expanded expression for rate of return on investment, determine the profit margin, investment turnover, and rate of return on investment for Division K under each proposal.
4. Which of the three proposals would meet the required 18% rate of return on investment?
5. If Division K were in an industry where the profit margin could not be increased, how much would the investment turnover have to increase to meet the president's required 18% rate of return on investment?

PROBLEM 24–5A
Divisional performance analysis and evaluation
Objective 4

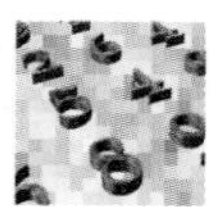

The vice-president of operations of Martino Company is evaluating the performance of two divisions organized as investment centers. Division D has the highest rate of return on investment but generates the smallest amount of controllable operating income. Division Z generates the largest controllable operating income but has the lowest rate of return on investment. Invested assets and condensed income statement data for the past year for each division are as follows:

	Division D	*Division Z*
Sales	$4,200,000	$ 8,800,000
Cost of goods sold	1,600,000	5,200,000
Operating expenses	2,012,000	1,400,000
Invested assets	2,800,000	13,750,000

Instructions

1. Prepare condensed divisional income statements for the year ended July 31, assuming that there were no service department charges.
2. Using the expanded expression for rate of return on investment, determine the profit margin, investment turnover, and rate of return on investment for each division.
3. If management desires a minimum rate of return of 12%, determine the residual income for each division.
4. Discuss the evaluation of Divisions D and Z, using the performance measures determined in (1), (2), and (3).

PROBLEM 24–6A
Transfer pricing
Objective 5

Edison Company is a diversified aerospace company, with two operating divisions, T and V. Condensed divisional income statements, which involve no intracompany transfers and which include a breakdown of expenses into variable and fixed components, are as follows:

Edison Company
Divisional Income Statements
For the Year Ended December 31, 19—

	Division T	*Division V*	*Total*
Sales:			
90,000 units × $30 per unit	$2,700,000		$2,700,000
70,000 units × $70 per unit		$4,900,000	4,900,000
			$7,600,000
Expenses:			
Variable:			
90,000 units × $16 per unit	$1,440,000		$1,440,000
70,000 units × $38* per unit		$2,660,000	2,660,000
Fixed	460,000	750,000	1,210,000
Total expenses	$1,900,000	$3,410,000	$5,310,000
Controllable operating income	$ 800,000	$1,490,000	$2,290,000

*$30 of the $38 per unit represents materials costs, and the remaining $8 per unit represents other expenses incurred within Division V.

Division T is operating at three-fourths of capacity of 120,000 units. Materials used in producing Division V's product are currently purchased from outside suppliers at a price of $30 per unit. The materials used by Division V are produced by Division T. Except for the possible transfer of materials between divisions, no changes are expected in sales and expenses.

Instructions

1. Would the market price of $30 per unit be an appropriate transfer price for Edison Company? Explain.
2. If Division V purchases 30,000 units from Division T and a transfer price of $25 per unit is negotiated between the managers of Divisions T and V, how much would the controllable operating income of each division and total company controllable operating income increase?
3. Prepare condensed divisional income statements for Edison Company, based on the data in (2).
4. If a transfer price of $20 per unit is negotiated, how much would the controllable operating income of each division and total company income increase?
5. a. What is the range of possible negotiated transfer prices that would be acceptable for Edison Company?
   b. Assuming that the managers of Divisions T and V cannot agree on a transfer price, what price would you suggest as the transfer price?

PROBLEMS SERIES B

PROBLEM 24–1B
Profit center responsibility reporting
Objective 3

Mid-West Bancorp has ten branches organized as profit centers. The board of directors believes that it is now time to consider retaining or closing Branches 9 and 10. If sold, Mid-West Bancorp does not expect to realize a gain on the sale. The following condensed trial balance was prepared as of March 31, the end of the first month of the current fiscal year. March is considered to be a typical month.

Current Assets	61,022	
Noncurrent Assets	8,500,000	
Noncurrent Liabilities		6,000,000
Current Liabilities		21,000
Common Stock		550,000
Retained Earnings		1,992,452
Cash Dividends	8,500	
Net Interest and Fee Income—Branch 9		18,900
Net Interest and Fee Income—Branch 10		23,100
Net Interest and Fee Income—Other Branches		168,000
Operating Expenses—Branch 9	9,600	
Operating Expenses—Branch 10	14,900	
Operating Expenses—Other Branches	97,500	
Operating Expenses—Corporate Relations	9,000	
Operating Expenses—Loan Department	23,180	
Operating Expenses—Central Accounting	18,950	
General Corporate Officers' Salaries	26,000	
Interest Expense—Corporate Loans	4,800	
Total	8,773,452	8,773,452

The company operates three service departments, the Loan Department, the Central Accounting Department, and the Corporate Relations Department. The Loan Department evaluates all loan applications submitted from the branches. The Central Accounting Department provides daily, weekly, and monthly reports for branch management. Central Accounting believes that its work is driven by the number of reports. The Corporate Relations Department conducts a variety of public relations services for the company as a whole. The following additional information has been gathered:

	Branch 9	*Branch 10*	*Other Branches*
Number of loan applications	133	197	890
Number of reports per day (22 business days in March)	9	14	75
Number of reports per week (4 weeks in March)	24	32	250
Number of monthly reports	55	45	310

Instructions

1. Prepare income statements for the month ended March 31, with three column headings: Branch 9, Branch 10, and Other Branches.
2. State your recommendations for retaining or selling either Branch 9 or Branch 10, and give reasons for your answer.

PROBLEM 24–2B
Profit center responsibility reporting
Objective 3

Reigle Restaurant Corporation has a headquarters facility and two restaurants (a seafood restaurant and a steak restaurant) in the same city, each organized as a profit center. The following information is available:

a. Advertising—charged to each restaurant based on usage: Seafood, $4,895; Steak, $4,005.
b. Payroll accounting is conducted at the headquarters—charged at a transfer price of $3.20 per issued check. Payroll checks issued for Seafood are 250, and Steak, 175.
c. Property tax expense is paid at the headquarters—charged to the restaurants at a rate of a 3/4 cent per dollar of valuation. Valuation is determined as the sum of the book values of

facilities and equipment. The sum of the book values of facilities and equipment was $350,000 for Seafood and $280,000 for Steak.

d. Accounts payable accounting is conducted at the headquarters—charged at a transfer price of $2.40 per invoice paid. Invoices paid for Seafood are 625, and Steak, 575.

The following revenue and expense data are selected from the Reigle ledger on January 31, the end of the current fiscal year:

Sales—Seafood		231,000
Sales—Steak		189,000
Operating Expenses—Seafood	84,500	
Operating Expenses—Steak	66,400	
Advertising Expense	8,900	
Payroll Expense	1,360	
Property Tax Expense	4,725	
Accounts Payable Accounting Expense	2,880	

Instructions

1. Provide schedules for the service department charges for advertising, payroll, accounts payable, and property tax.
2. Prepare a profit center income statement with two column headings for the Seafood and Steak Restaurants.

PROBLEM 24–3B
Divisional income statements and rate of return on investment analysis
Objective 4

Lyonnes Company is a diversified food products company with three operating divisions organized as investment centers. Condensed data taken from the records of the three divisions for the year ended June 30 are as follows:

	Division 1	*Division 2*	*Division 3*
Sales	$1,200,000	$560,000	$ 860,000
Cost of goods sold	850,000	310,000	420,000
Operating expenses	206,000	210,800	225,000
Invested assets	600,000	140,000	1,075,000

The management of Lyonnes Company is evaluating each division as a basis for planning a future expansion of operations.

Instructions

1. Prepare condensed divisional income statements for Divisions 1, 2, and 3, assuming that there were no service department charges.
2. Using the expanded expression for rate of return on investment, compute the profit margin, investment turnover, and rate of return on investment for each division.
3. If available funds permit the expansion of operations of only one division, which of the divisions would you recommend for expansion based on (1) and (2)? Explain.

PROBLEM 24–4B
Effect of proposals on divisional performance
Objective 4

A condensed income statement for Division R of Joshua Company for the year ended December 31 is as follows:

Sales	$1,600,000
Cost of goods sold	550,000
Gross profit	$1,050,000
Operating expenses	450,000
Controllable operating income	$ 600,000

Assume that Division R received no charges from service departments. The president of Joshua Company is concerned with Division R's rate of return on invested assets of $3,200,000 and has indicated that the division's rate of return on investment must be increased to at least 20% by the end of the next year if operations are to continue. The division manager is considering the following three proposals:

Proposal 1: Reduce invested assets by discontinuing a product line. This action would eliminate sales of $200,000, cost of goods sold of $115,000, and operating expenses of $17,000. Assets of $400,000 would be transferred to other divisions at no gain or loss.

Proposal 2: Purchase new and more efficient machinery and thereby reduce the cost of goods sold by $160,000. Sales would remain unchanged, and the old machinery, which has no remaining book value, would be scrapped at no gain or loss. The new machinery would increase invested assets by $800,000 for the year.

Proposal 3: Transfer equipment with a book value of $1,200,000 to other divisions at no gain or loss, and lease similar equipment. The annual lease payments would exceed the amount of depreciation expense on the old equipment by $120,000. This increase in expense would be included as part of the cost of goods sold. Sales would remain unchanged.

Instructions

1. Using the expanded expression for rate of return on investment, determine the profit margin, investment turnover, and rate of return on investment for Division R for the past year.
2. Prepare condensed estimated income statements for Division R for each proposal.
3. Using the expanded expression for rate of return on investment, determine the profit margin, investment turnover, and rate of return on investment for Division R under each proposal.
4. Which of the three proposals would meet the required 20% rate of return on investment?
5. If Division R were in an industry where the profit margin could not be increased, how much would the investment turnover have to increase to meet the president's required 20% rate of return on investment?

PROBLEM 24–5B
Divisional performance analysis and evaluation
Objective 4

The vice-president of operations of Little Company is evaluating the performance of two divisions organized as investment centers. Division B generates the largest amount of controllable operating income but has the lowest rate of return on investment. Division A has the highest rate of return on investment but generates the smallest controllable operating income. Invested assets and condensed income statement data for the past year for each division are as follows:

	Division A	*Division B*
Sales	$6,500,000	$5,400,000
Cost of goods sold	2,900,000	2,100,000
Operating expenses	2,820,000	2,490,000
Invested assets	3,250,000	4,500,000

Instructions

1. Prepare condensed divisional income statements for the year ended December 31, assuming there were no service department charges.
2. Using the expanded expression for rate of return on investment, determine the profit margin, investment turnover, and rate of return on investment for each division.
3. If management desires a minimum rate of return of 15%, determine the residual income for each division.
4. Discuss the evaluation of Divisions A and B, using the performance measures determined in (1), (2), and (3).

PROBLEM 24–6B
Transfer pricing
Objective 5

Wills Company is a diversified office products company, with two operating divisions, X and Y. Condensed divisional income statements, which involve no intracompany transfers and which include a breakdown of expenses into variable and fixed components, are as follows:

Wills Company
Divisional Income Statements
For the Year Ended December 31, 19—

	Division X	*Division Y*	*Total*
Sales:			
60,000 units × $17 per unit	$1,020,000		$1,020,000
100,000 units × $45 per unit		$4,500,000	4,500,000
			$5,520,000
Expenses:			
Variable:			
60,000 units × $5 per unit	$ 300,000		$ 300,000
100,000 units × $23* per unit		$2,300,000	2,300,000
Fixed	180,000	460,000	640,000
Total expenses	$ 480,000	$2,760,000	$3,240,000
Controllable operating income	$ 540,000	$1,740,000	$2,280,000

*$17 of the $23 per unit represents materials costs, and the remaining $6 per unit represents other expenses incurred within Division Y.

Division X is operating at two-thirds of capacity of 90,000 units. Materials used in producing Division Y's product are currently purchased from outside suppliers at a price of $17 per unit. The materials used by Division Y are produced by Division X. Except for the possible transfer of materials between divisions, no changes are expected in sales and expenses.

Instructions

1. Would the market price of $17 per unit be an appropriate transfer price for Wills Company? Explain.
2. If Division Y purchases 30,000 units from Division X and a transfer price of $14 per unit is negotiated between the managers of Divisions X and Y, how much would the controllable operating income of each division and total company controllable operating income increase?
3. Prepare condensed divisional income statements for Wills Company, based on the data in (2).
4. If a transfer price of $10 per unit is negotiated, how much would the controllable operating income of each division and total company income increase?
5. a. What is the range of possible negotiated transfer prices that would be acceptable for Wills Company?
   b. Assuming that the managers of Divisions X and Y cannot agree on a transfer price, what price would you suggest as the transfer price?

CASES

CASE 24–1
Benjamin Company
Transfer pricing

Benjamin Company has two divisions, the Can Division and the Food Division. The Food Division may purchase cans from the Can Division or from outside suppliers. The Can Division sells can products both internally and externally. The market price for cans is $100 per 1,000 cans. Lee Tazwell is the controller of the Food Division, and Tracy Ford is the controller of the Can Division. The following conversation took place between Lee and Tracy:

Lee: I hear you are having problems selling cans out of your division. Maybe I can help.

Tracy: You've got that right. We're only producing and selling at 70% of our capacity to outsiders. Last year we were selling all we could make. It would help a great deal if your division would divert some of your purchases to our division so we could use up our capacity. After all, we are part of the same company.

Lee: What kind of price could you give me?

Tracy: Well, you know as well as I that we are under strict profit responsibility in our divisions, so I would expect to get market price, $100 for 1,000 cans.

Lee: I'm not so sure we can swing that. I was expecting a price break from a "sister" division.

Tracy: Hey, I can only take this "sister" stuff so far. If I give you a price break, our profits will fall from last year's levels. I don't think I could explain that. I'm sorry, but I must remain firm—market price. After all, it's only fair—that's what you would have to pay from an external supplier.

Lee: Fair or not, I think we'll pass. Sorry we couldn't have helped.

Was Lee behaving ethically by trying to force the Can Division into a price break? Comment on Tracy's reactions.

CASE 24–2
Farnsworth University
Service department charges

The Accounting Department of Farnsworth University asked the Publications Department to prepare a brochure for the Masters of Accountancy program. The Publications Department delivered the brochures and charged the Accounting Department a rate that was 20% higher than could be obtained from an outside printing company. The policy of the University required the Accounting Department to use the internal publications group for brochures. The Publications Department claimed that they had a drop in demand for their services during the fiscal year, so had to charge higher prices in order to recover their payroll and fixed costs.

Should the cost of the brochure be transferred to the Accounting Department in order to hold the department head accountable for the cost of the brochure? What changes in policy would you recommend?

CASE 24–3
Wonder Media Enterprises
Evaluating divisional performance

The three divisions of Wonder Media Enterprises are Publications, Broadcasting, and Music. The divisions are structured as investment centers. The following responsibility reports were prepared for the three divisions for the prior year:

1. Which division is making the best use of invested assets and thus should be given priority for future capital investments?
2. Assuming the expected rate of return on new projects is 10%, would all investments that produce a return in excess of 10% be accepted by the divisions?
3. Can you identify opportunities for improving the company's financial performance?

	Publications	*Broadcasting*	*Music*
Revenues	$ 600,000	$1,400,000	$500,000
Operating expenses	240,000	800,000	100,000
Operating income	$ 360,000	$ 600,000	$400,000
Service department charges:			
Promotion	$ 100,000	$ 200,000	$200,000
Legal	50,000	40,000	80,000
	$ 150,000	$ 240,000	$280,000
Controllable operating income	$ 210,000	$ 360,000	$120,000
Invested assets	$1,500,000	$3,000,000	$800,000

CASE 24–4
Gleason Foods Inc.
Evaluating division performance over time

The Snack Foods Division of Gleason Foods Inc. has been experiencing revenue and profit growth during the years 1996–1998. The divisional income statements are provided below.

Assume that there are no charges from service departments. The vice-president of the division, Harlan Tyson, is proud of his division's performance over the last three years. The president of Gleason Foods, Janice Gleason, is discussing the division's performance with Harlan, as follows:

Harlan: As you can see, we have had a successful three years in the Snack Foods Division.

Gleason Foods Inc.
Divisional Income Statements, Snack Foods Division
For the Years Ended December 31, 1996–1998

	1996	*1997*	*1998*
Revenues	$360,000	$480,000	$610,000
Cost of goods sold	180,000	216,000	244,000
Gross profit	$180,000	$264,000	$366,000
Operating expenses	108,000	134,400	152,500
Controllable operating income	$ 72,000	$129,600	$213,500

Janice: I'm not too sure.

Harlan: What do you mean? Look at our results. Our controllable operating income has nearly tripled, while our profit margins are improving.

Janice: I am looking at your results. However, your income statements fail to include one very important piece of information; namely, the invested assets. You have been investing a great deal of assets into the division. You had $240,000 in invested assets in 1996, $518,400 in 1997, and $1,067,500 in 1998.

Harlan: You are right. I've needed the assets in order to upgrade our technologies and expand our operations. The additional assets is one reason we have been able to grow and improve our profit margins. I don't see that this is a problem.

Janice: The problem is that we must maintain a 20% rate of return on invested assets.

1. Determine the profit margins for the Snack Foods Division for 1996–1998.
2. Calculate the investment turnover for the Snack Foods Division for 1996–1998.
3. Calculate the rate of return on investment for the Snack Foods Division for 1996–1998.
4. Evaluate the division's performance over the 1996–1998 time period. Why was Janice concerned about the performance?

CASE 24–5
Ontario Company
Evaluating division performance

Your father is the president of Ontario Company, a privately held, diversified company with five separate divisions organized as investment centers. A condensed income statement for the Sporting Goods Division for the past year, assuming no service department charges, is as follows:

Ontario Company—Sporting Goods Division
Income Statement
For the Year Ended December 31, 19—

Sales	$16,000,000
Cost of goods sold	10,100,000
Gross profit	$ 5,900,000
Operating expenses	1,900,000
Controllable operating income	$ 4,000,000

The manager of the Sporting Goods Division was recently presented with the opportunity to add an additional product line, which would require invested assets of $12,000,000. A projected income statement for the new product line is as follows:

New Product Line
Projected Income Statement
For the Year Ended December 31, 19—

Sales	$ 7,500,000
Cost of goods sold	4,200,000
Gross profit	$ 3,300,000
Operating expenses	2,100,000
Controllable operating income	$ 1,200,000

The Sporting Goods Division currently has $20,000,000 in invested assets, and Ontario Company's overall rate of return on investment, including all divisions, is 8%. Each division manager is evaluated on the basis of divisional rate of return on investment, and a bonus equal to $5,000 for each percentage point by which the division's rate of return on investment exceeds the company average is awarded each year.

Your father is concerned that the manager of the Sporting Goods Division rejected the addition of the new product line, when all estimates indicated that the product line would be profitable and would increase overall company income. You have been asked to analyze the possible reasons why the Sporting Goods Division manager rejected the new product line.

1. Determine the rate of return on investment for the Sporting Goods Division for the past year.
2. Determine the Sporting Goods Division manager's bonus for the past year.
3. Determine the estimated rate of return on investment for the new product line.
4. Why might the manager of the Sporting Goods Division decide to reject the new product line?
5. Can you suggest an alternative performance measure for motivating division managers to accept new investment opportunities that would increase the overall company income and rate of return on investment?

ANSWERS TO SELF-EXAMINATION QUESTIONS

1. **B** The manager of a profit center (answer B) has responsibility for and authority over costs and revenues. If the manager has responsibility for only costs, the department is called a cost center (answer A). If the responsibility and authority extend to the investment in assets as well as costs and revenues, it is called an investment center (answer C). A service department (answer D) provides services to other departments. A service department could be a cost center, profit center, or investment center.
2. **C** $600,000 ÷ 150,000 = $4 per payment. Division A anticipates 60,000 payments or $240,000 (60,000 × $4) in service department charges from the Accounts Payable

Department. Controllable operating income is thus \$900,000 – \$240,000, or \$660,000. Answer A assumes that all of the service department overhead is assigned to Division A, which would be incorrect, since Division A does not use all of the accounts payable service. Answer B incorrectly assumes that there are no service department charges from Accounts Payable.

3. **A** The rate of return on investment for Division A is 20% (answer A), computed as follows:

$$\textbf{Rate of Return on Investment (ROI)} = \frac{\textbf{Operating Income}}{\textbf{Invested Assets}}$$

$$\textbf{ROI} = \frac{\textbf{\$350,000} - \textbf{\$200,000} - \textbf{\$30,000}}{\textbf{\$600,000}} = \textbf{20\%}$$

4. **B** The profit margin for Division L of Liddy Co. is 15% (answer B), computed as follows:

$$\textbf{Rate of Return on Investment (ROI)} = \textbf{Profit Margin} \times \textbf{Investment Turnover}$$

$$\textbf{24\%} = \textbf{Profit Margin} \times \textbf{1.6}$$

$$\textbf{15\%} = \textbf{Profit Margin}$$

5. **C** The market price approach (answer C) to transfer pricing uses the price at which the product or service transferred could be sold to outside buyers. The cost price approach (answer A) uses cost as the basis for setting transfer prices. The negotiated price approach (answer B) allows managers of decentralized units to agree (negotiate) among themselves as to the proper transfer price. The standard cost approach (answer D) is a version of the cost price approach that uses standard costs in setting transfer prices.

PART NINE

Decision Making

25. *Differential Analysis and Product Pricing*

26. *Capital Investment Analysis*

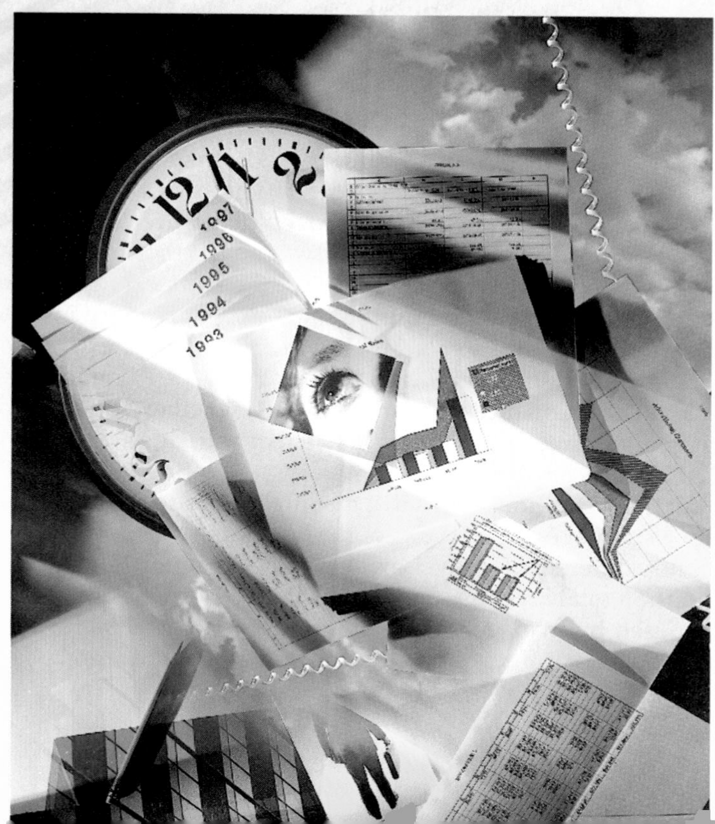

25 Differential Analysis and Product Pricing

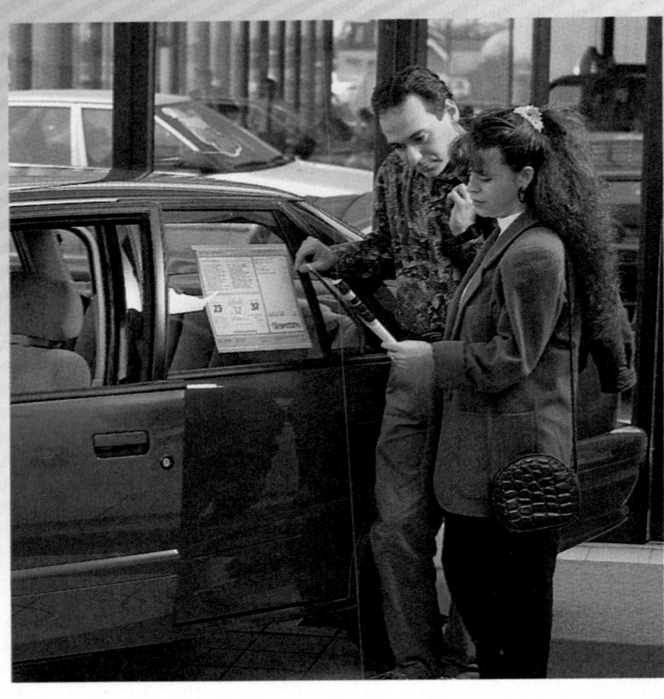

YOU AND ACCOUNTING

Most of us will buy an automobile at some time. But rather than buying a car, would it be better to lease one?

To answer this question, you need to carefully consider the costs of owning the car versus the costs of leasing the car. For example, if you own the car, you will need to pay the license fees, insurance, and maintenance and repair costs. How many of these costs you need to pay to lease the car depends on the specific lease contract. For example, the lease contract may require you to purchase a minimum amount of liability insurance. The lease contract will also require a monthly payment. In addition, if you drive the car more than a maximum number of miles (for example, 15,000 miles per year), you may be charged an additional cost per mile. Finally, whether you intend to keep the car or trade it in after three or four years may affect your decision.

The decision to buy or lease a car depends on comparing the estimated costs of each alternative. Likewise, managers must consider the effects of alternative decisions on the short- and long-term operating results of the business.

In this chapter, we discuss differential analysis, which provides reports on the effects of alternative decisions on total revenues and costs. We also describe and illustrate practical approaches used by managers in setting product prices. Finally, we discuss how production bottlenecks influence product mix and pricing decisions.

After studying this chapter, you should be able to:

Objective 1
Prepare a differential analysis report for decisions involving:

Leasing or selling equipment.
Discontinuing an unprofitable segment.
Manufacturing or purchasing a needed part.
Replacing usable plant assets.
Processing further or selling an intermediate product.
Accepting additional business at a special price.

Objective 2
Determine the selling price of a product, using the total cost, product cost, and variable cost concepts.

Objective 3
Calculate the relative profitability of products in bottleneck production environments.

Differential Analysis

Objective 1
Prepare a differential analysis report for decisions involving:

Leasing or selling equipment.
Discontinuing an unprofitable segment.
Manufacturing or purchasing a needed part.
Replacing usable plant assets.
Processing further or selling an intermediate product.
Accepting additional business at a special price.

Planning for future operations chiefly involves decision making. For some decisions, revenue and cost data taken from the general ledger and other accounting records may be useful. However, the revenue and cost data needed to evaluate courses of future operations or to choose among competing alternatives are often not available in the accounting records and often must be estimated.

Consider the following decisions:

- The decision by Apple Computer to purchase its laser printer engine from Canon instead of making it internally.
- The decision by Mercedes to expand manufacturing operations into the United States (Alabama).
- The decision by Sears to sell its Allstate Insurance unit.

Differential analysis is important when making decisions about future operations, such as Mercedes' decision to expand manufacturing operations in the U.S.

In each of these decisions, the estimated revenues and costs were **relevant.** The relevant revenues and costs focus on the differences between the alternatives being considered. Costs that have been incurred in the past are not relevant to the decision. These costs are called sunk costs.

Differential revenue is the amount of increase or decrease in revenue expected from a course of action as compared with an alternative. To illustrate, assume that certain equipment is being used to manufacture Product M, which is expected to provide revenue of $150,000. If the equipment could be used to make Product T, which would provide revenue of $175,000, the differential revenue from making and selling Product T is $25,000.

Differential cost is the amount of increase or decrease in cost that is expected from a particular course of action as compared with an alternative. For example, if an increase in advertising expenditures from $100,000 to $150,000 is being considered, the differential cost of the action is $50,000.

Differential income or loss is the difference between the differential revenue and the differential costs. Differential income indicates that a particular decision is expected to be profitable, while a differential loss indicates the opposite.

Differential analysis focuses on the effect of alternative courses of action on the relevant revenues and costs. For example, if a manager must decide between two alternatives, differential analysis would involve comparing the differential revenues of the two alternatives with the differential costs, as shown in Exhibit 1. Differential analysis thus emphasizes the significant factors affecting a decision, clarifies the issues, and saves the time of the decision maker. It can aid management in making decisions on a variety of alternatives.

Exhibit 1
Differential Analysis

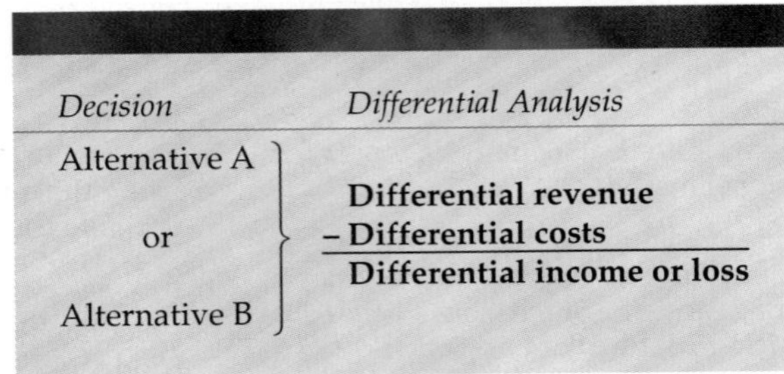

Decision	*Differential Analysis*
Alternative A or Alternative B	**Differential revenue** **– Differential costs** **Differential income or loss**

In the following paragraphs, we will discuss the use of differential analysis in analyzing the following alternatives:

1. Leasing or selling equipment.
2. Discontinuing an unprofitable segment.
3. Manufacturing or purchasing a needed part.
4. Replacing usable plant assets.
5. Processing further or selling an intermediate product.
6. Accepting additional business at a special price.

COST BENEFIT ANALYSIS IN EVERYDAY LIVING

The following excerpt of an article discusses how using differential analysis and recognizing the irrelevancy of sunk costs can lead to superior decision making in individual life decisions:

Cost-benefit analysis pays off in everyday living, a University of Michigan team concludes.

Richard Nisbett and two colleagues quizzed Michigan faculty members and university seniors on such questions as how often they walk out on a bad movie, refuse to finish a bad meal, start over on a weak term paper or abandon a research project that no longer looks promising. They believe that people who cut their losses this way are following sound economic rules: calculating the net benefits of alternative courses of action, writing off past costs that can't be recovered and weighing the opportunity to use future time and effort more profitably elsewhere.

They find that among faculty members, those who use cost-benefit reasoning in this fashion—being more likely to give up on research that isn't getting anywhere or using labor-saving devices as often as possible—have higher salaries relative to their age and departments. Not surprisingly, economists are more likely to apply the approach than professors of humanities or biology.

Among students, those who have learned to use cost-benefit analysis frequently are apt to have far better grades than their Scholastic Aptitude Test scores would have predicted. Again, the more economics courses the students have, the more likely they are to apply cost-benefit analysis outside the classroom.

Dr. Nisbett concedes that for many Americans, cost-benefit rules often appear to conflict with such traditional principles as "never give up" and "waste not, want not."

Source: Alan L. Otten, "Economic Perspective Produces Steady Yields" from People Patterns, *The Wall Street Journal,* March 31, 1992, p. B1.

LEASE OR SELL

Management may have a choice between leasing or selling a piece of equipment that is no longer needed in the business. In deciding which option is best, management may use differential analysis. To illustrate, assume that Marcus Company is considering disposing of equipment that cost $200,000 and has $120,000 of accumulated depreciation to date. Marcus Company can sell the equipment through a broker for $100,000 less a 6% commission. Alternatively, Potamkin Company (the lessee) has offered to lease the equipment for five years for a total of $160,000. At the end of the fifth year of the lease, the equipment is expected to have no residual value. During the period of the lease, Marcus Company (the lessor) will incur repair, insurance, and property tax expenses estimated at $35,000. Exhibit 2 shows Marcus Company's analysis of whether to lease or sell the equipment.

Exhibit 2
Differential Analysis Report—Lease or Sell

Proposal to Lease or Sell Equipment
June 22, 1997

Differential revenue from alternatives:		
Revenue from lease	$160,000	
Revenue from sales	100,000	
Differential revenue from lease		$60,000
Differential cost of alternatives:		
Repair, insurance, and property tax expenses	$ 35,000	
Commission expense on sale	6,000	
Differential cost of lease		29,000
Net differential income from the lease alternative		$31,000

In the preceding analysis, the $80,000 book value ($200,000 – $120,000) of the equipment is a sunk cost and is not considered in the analysis. The $80,000 is a cost that resulted from a previous decision. It will not be affected by the alternatives now being considered in leasing or selling the equipment. The relevant factors to be considered are the differential revenues and differential costs associated with the lease or sell decision. The undepreciated cost of the equipment is irrelevant. This analysis is verified by the traditional analysis in Exhibit 3.

Exhibit 3
Traditional Analysis

Lease or Sell

Lease alternative:			
Revenue from lease		$160,000	
Depreciation expense	$80,000		
Repair, insurance, and property tax expenses	35,000	115,000	
Net gain			$45,000
Sell alternative:			
Sales price		$100,000	
Book value of equipment	$80,000		
Commission expense	6,000	86,000	
Net gain			14,000
Net differential income from the lease alternative			$31,000

The alternatives presented in Exhibits 2 and 3 were relatively uncomplicated. Regardless of the complexity, the approach to differential analysis is essentially the same. Two additional factors that often need to be considered are (1) differential revenue from investing the funds generated by the alternatives and (2) any income tax differential. In Exhibit 2, there could be differential revenue related to the investment of the $94,000 net proceeds ($100,000 – $6,000) from the sale over the investment of the yearly net proceeds from the lease arrangement. Any income tax differential would be related to the differences in timing of the income from the alternatives and the differences in the amount of investment income.

DISCONTINUE A SEGMENT OR PRODUCT

When a product or a department, branch, territory, or other segment of a business is generating losses, management may consider eliminating the product or segment. It is often assumed, sometimes in error, that the total operating income of a business would be increased if the operating loss could be eliminated. Discontinuing the product or segment usually eliminates all of the product or segment's variable costs (direct materials, direct labor, sales commissions, and so on). However, if the product or segment is a relatively small part of the business, the fixed costs (depreciation, insurance, property taxes, and so on) may not be decreased by discontinuing it. It is possible in this case for the total operating income of a company to decrease rather than increase by eliminating the product or segment. To illustrate, the income statement for Mandel Inc. presented in Exhibit 4 is for a normal year ending August 31, 1997.

Exhibit 4
Income (Loss) by Product

Mandel Inc.
Condensed Income Statement
For the Year Ended August 31, 1997

	Product			
	A	B	C	Total
Sales	$100,000	$400,000	$500,000	$1,000,000
Cost of goods sold:				
Variable costs	$ 60,000	$200,000	$220,000	$ 480,000
Fixed costs	20,000	80,000	120,000	220,000
Total cost of goods sold	$ 80,000	$280,000	$340,000	$ 700,000
Gross profit	$ 20,000	$120,000	$160,000	$ 300,000
Operating expenses:				
Variable expenses	$ 25,000	$ 60,000	$ 95,000	$ 180,000
Fixed expenses	6,000	20,000	25,000	51,000
Total operating expenses	$ 31,000	$ 80,000	$120,000	$ 231,000
Income (loss) from operations	$ (11,000)	$ 40,000	$ 40,000	$ 69,000

Because Product A incurs annual losses, management is considering discontinuing it. An increase in annual operating income to $80,000 (Product B, $40,000; Product C, $40,000) might seem to be indicated by the income statement in Exhibit 4 if Product A is discontinued.

Discontinuing Product A, however, would actually decrease operating income by $15,000, to $54,000 ($69,000 – $15,000). This is shown by the differential analysis report in Exhibit 5, in which we assume that discontinuing Product A would have no effect on fixed costs and expenses.

Exhibit 5
Differential Analysis Report—Discontinue an Unprofitable Segment

Proposal to Discontinue Product A
September 29, 1997

Differential revenue from annual sales of product:		
Revenue from sales		$100,000
Differential cost of annual sales of product:		
Variable cost of goods sold	$60,000	
Variable operating expenses	25,000	85,000
Annual differential income from sales of Product A		$ 15,000

The traditional analysis in Exhibit 6 verifies the preceding differential analysis. In Exhibit 6, only the short-term (one year) effects of discontinuing Product A are considered. In decisions involving eliminating a product or segment, management should also consider the long-term effects. For example, the plant capacity made available by discontinuing Product A might be eliminated. This could reduce fixed costs. Some employees may have to be laid off, and others may have to be re-

Exhibit 6
Traditional Analysis

Proposal to Discontinue Product A
September 29, 1997

	Current Operations			
	Product A	Products B and C	Total	Discontinuing Product A
Sales	$100,000	$900,000	$1,000,000	$900,000
Cost of goods sold:				
Variable costs	$ 60,000	$420,000	$ 480,000	$420,000
Fixed costs	20,000	200,000	220,000	220,000
Total cost of goods sold	$ 80,000	$620,000	$ 700,000	$640,000
Gross profit	$ 20,000	$280,000	$ 300,000	$260,000
Operating expenses:				
Variable expenses	$ 25,000	$155,000	$ 180,000	$155,000
Fixed expenses	6,000	45,000	51,000	51,000
Total operating expenses	$ 31,000	$200,000	$ 231,000	$206,000
Income (loss) from operations	$ (11,000)	$ 80,000	$ 69,000	$ 54,000

located and retrained. Further, there may be a related decrease in sales of more profitable products to those customers who were attracted by the discontinued product.

MAKE OR BUY

The assembly of many parts is often a major element in manufacturing some products, such as automobiles. These parts may be made by the product's manufacturer, or they may be purchased. For example, some of the parts for an automobile, such as the motor, may be produced by the automobile manufacturer. Other parts, such as tires, may be purchased from other manufacturers. In addition, in manufacturing motors, such items as spark plugs and nuts and bolts may be acquired from suppliers.

Management uses differential costs to decide whether to make or buy a part or component. For example, if a part is purchased, management has concluded that it is less costly to buy the part than to manufacture it. Make or buy options often arise when a manufacturer has excess productive capacity in the form of unused equipment, space, and labor.

The differential analysis is similar, whether management is considering making a part that is currently being purchased or purchasing a part that is currently being made. To illustrate, assume that a manufacturer has been purchasing a component, Part X, for $5 a unit. The factory is currently operating at 80% of capacity, and no major increase in production is expected in the near future. The cost per unit of manufacturing Part X, including fixed costs, is estimated as follows:

Direct materials	$1
Direct labor	2
Factory overhead (150% of direct labor cost)	3
Total cost per unit	$6

If the *make* price of $6 is simply compared with the *buy* price of $5, the decision is to buy the part. However, if unused capacity could be used in manufacturing the part, there would be no increase in the total amount of fixed factory overhead costs. Thus, only the variable factory overhead costs need to be considered. Assume that variable factory overhead costs, such as power and maintenance, are estimated at $1.30 per unit. The relevant costs are summarized in the differential report in Exhibit 7.

Exhibit 7
Differential Analysis Report—Make or Buy

Proposal to Manufacture Part X
February 15, 1997

Purchase price of part		$5.00
Differential cost to manufacture part:		
Direct materials	$1.00	
Direct labor	2.00	
Variable factory overhead	1.30	4.30
Cost savings from manufacturing Part X		$ .70

Other possible effects of a decision to manufacture the part should also be considered. For example, one consideration is that increasing production in the future might require using the currently idle capacity. The possible effect of decisions on employees and on future business relations with the supplier of Part X should also be considered. For example, the supplier of Part X may also provide other essential components that cannot be readily manufactured within the company. A decision to manufacture Part X might jeopardize the timely delivery of these other essential parts.

USING ACCOUNTING TO UNDERSTAND BUSINESS

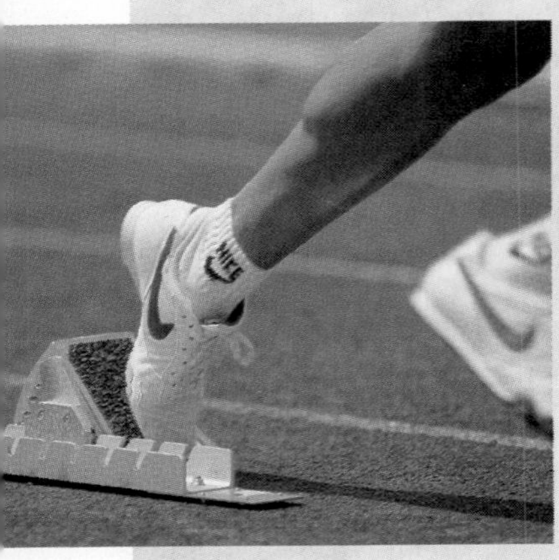

The make or buy decision is an important strategic decision. Many companies are focusing efforts on those aspects of the business that can earn superior returns. For example, Nike, Inc., the largest supplier of athletic shoes, believes that its strengths are in designing, marketing, distributing, and selling athletic shoes. Nike, Inc. doesn't manufacture shoes, but purchases 100% of its shoe manufacturing from outside suppliers. Thus, Nike is able to remain focused on the parts of the business where it believes it adds the greatest value to the customer, and thus the greatest profitability to the company.

REPLACE EQUIPMENT

The usefulness of plant assets may be impaired long before they are considered to be worn out. Equipment may no longer be efficient for the purpose for which it is used. On the other hand, the equipment may not have reached the point of complete inadequacy. Decisions to replace usable plant assets should be based on studies of relevant costs. The relevant costs are the future costs of continuing to use the equipment versus replacement. The book values of the plant assets being replaced are sunk costs and are irrelevant.

To illustrate, assume that a business is considering disposing of several identical machines having a total book value of $100,000 and an estimated remaining life of five years. The old machines can be sold for $25,000. They can be replaced by a single high-speed machine at a cost of $250,000. The new machine has an estimated useful life of five years and no residual value. Analyses indicate an estimated annual reduction in variable manufacturing costs from $225,000 with the old machine to $150,000 with the new machine. No other changes in the manufacturing costs or the operating expenses are expected. The relevant costs are summarized in the differential report in Exhibit 8.

Exhibit 8
Differential Analysis Report—Replace Equipment

Proposal to Replace Equipment
November 28, 1997

Annual variable costs—present equipment	$225,000	
Annual variable costs—new equipment	150,000	
Annual differential decrease in cost	$ 75,000	
Number of years applicable	× 5	
Total differential decrease in cost	$375,000	
Proceeds from sale of present equipment	25,000	$400,000
Cost of new equipment		250,000
Net differential decrease in cost, 5-year total		$150,000
Annual net differential decrease in cost—new equipment		$ 30,000

Additional factors are often involved in equipment replacement decisions. For example, differences between the remaining useful life of the old equipment and the estimated life of the new equipment could exist. In addition, the new equipment might improve the overall quality of the product, resulting in an increase in sales volume. Other factors that could be significant include the time value of money and other uses for the cash needed to purchase the new equipment.[1]

The amount of income that is forgone from an alternative use of cash is called opportunity cost. Although the opportunity cost does not appear as a part of historical accounting data, it is useful in analyzing alternative courses of action. To illustrate, assume that the cash outlay of $250,000 for the new equipment, less the $25,000 proceeds from the sale of the present equipment, could be invested to yield a 10% return. Thus, the opportunity cost related to the purchase of the new equipment is $22,500 (10% × $225,000).

PROCESS OR SELL

When a product is manufactured, it progresses through various stages of production. Often a product can be sold at an intermediate stage of production, or it can be processed further and then sold. In deciding whether to sell a product at an intermediate stage or to process it further, differential analysis is useful. The differential revenues from further processing are compared to the differential costs of further processing. The costs of producing the intermediate product do not change, regardless of whether the intermediate product is sold or processed further. Thus, these costs are not differential costs and are irrelevant to the decision to process further.

To illustrate, assume that a business produces Product Y in batches of 4,000 gallons. Standard quantities of 4,000 gallons of direct materials are processed, which cost $1.20 per gallon. Product Y can be sold without further processing for $2 per gallon. Product Y can be processed further to yield Product Z, which can be sold for $5 per gallon. Product Z requires additional processing costs of $5,760 per batch, and 20% of the gallons of Product Y will evaporate during production. Exhibit 9 summarizes the differential revenues and costs in deciding whether to process Product Y to produce Product Z.

[1] The importance of the time value of money in equipment replacement decisions is discussed later in this text.

Exhibit 9
Differential Analysis Report—Process or Sell

Proposal to Process Product Y Further
October 1, 1997

Differential revenue from further processing per batch:		
Revenue from sale of Product Z [(4,000 gallons – 800 gallons evaporation) × $5]	$16,000	
Revenue from sale of Product Y (4,000 gallons × $2)	8,000	
Differential revenue		$8,000
Differential cost per batch:		
Additional cost of producing Product Z		5,760
Differential income from further processing Product Y per batch		$2,240

The differential income from further processing Product Y into Product Z is $2,240 per batch. The initial cost of producing the intermediate Product Y, $4,800 (4,000 gallons × $1.20), is not considered in deciding whether to process Product Y further. This initial cost will be incurred, regardless of whether Product Z is produced.

USING ACCOUNTING TO UNDERSTAND BUSINESS

An example of a decision to process further is the decision to release a produced movie as VHS video tape for the home VCR market. Items that are relevant to this decision are the copying and packaging costs for the VHS tape, marketing costs associated with promoting the tape, and anticipated revenues from selling the tape. The original movie production costs are not relevant to the decision.

ACCEPT BUSINESS AT A SPECIAL PRICE

Differential analysis is also useful in deciding whether to accept additional business at a special price. The differential revenue that would be provided from the additional business is compared to the differential costs of producing and delivering the product to the customer. If the company is operating at full capacity, any additional production will increase both fixed and variable production costs. If, however, the normal production of the company is below full capacity, additional business may be undertaken without increasing fixed production costs. In this case, the differential costs of the additional production are the variable manufacturing costs. If operating expenses increase because of the additional business, these expenses should also be considered.

To illustrate, assume that the monthly capacity of a business is 12,500 units of Product H. Current sales and production are averaging 10,000 units of Product H per month. The current manufacturing cost of $20 per unit consists of variable costs of $12.50 and fixed costs of $7.50. The normal selling price of the product in the domestic market is $30. The manufacturer receives an offer from an exporter for 5,000 units of the product at $18 each. Production can be spread over a three-month period without interfering with normal production or incurring overtime costs. Pricing policies in the domestic market will not be affected. Simply comparing the sales price of $18 with the present unit manufacturing cost of $20 indicates that the offer should be rejected. However, by focusing only on the differential cost, which in this case is the variable cost, the decision is different. Exhibit 10 shows the differential analysis report for this decision.

Proposals to sell a product in the domestic market at prices lower than the normal price may require additional considerations. For example, it may be unwise to

Exhibit 10
Differential Analysis Report—Sell at Special Price

Proposal to Sell Product H to Exporter
March 10, 1997

Differential revenue from accepting offer:	
Revenue from sale of 5,000 additional units at $18	$90,000
Differential cost of accepting offer:	
Variable costs of 5,000 additional units at $12.50	62,500
Differential income from accepting offer	$27,500

increase sales volume in one territory by price reductions if sales volume is lost in other areas. Manufacturers must also conform to the Robinson-Patman Act, which prohibits price discrimination within the United States unless differences in prices can be justified by different costs of serving different customers.

USING ACCOUNTING TO UNDERSTAND BUSINESS

Companies must be very careful when accepting business at a special price. There are times when customers may expect the "special price" to be in effect all the time. For example, the airline industry has offered special discount summer fares when it was difficult to fill seats at the regular price. In the short term, filling seats with discount fare customers added differential income. However, airline passengers began to expect the special discount pricing. As a result, airlines had to continue offering special discounts throughout the year. Thus, the special discount periods became a normal part of operations and a fierce revenue drain for the industry.

Setting Normal Product Selling Prices

Objective 2
Determine the selling price of a product, using the total cost, product cost, and variable cost concepts.

Differential analysis may be useful in deciding to lower selling prices for special short-run decisions, such as whether to accept business at a price lower than the normal price. In such cases, the minimum short-run price is set high enough to cover all variable costs. Any price above this minimum price will improve profits in the short run. In the long run, however, the normal selling price must be set high enough to cover all costs and expenses (both fixed and variable) and provide a reasonable profit. Otherwise, the business may not survive.

The normal selling price can be viewed as the target selling price to be achieved in the long run. Exhibit 11 shows the two basic approaches to setting the normal selling price—market methods and cost-plus methods.

Under the market methods, managers refer to the external market to determine the price. Managers using demand-based methods set the price according to the

Exhibit 11
Setting a Normal Selling Price

Setting a Normal Selling Price	
Market Methods	*Cost-Plus Methods*
1. Demand-based methods.	1. Total cost concept
2. Competition-based methods.	2. Product cost concept
	3. Variable cost concept

demand for the product. If there is high demand for the product, then the price may be set high, while lower demand may require the price to be set low. An example of setting different prices according to the demand for the product is found in the telecommunications industry, with low weekend rates and high business day rates for long-distance telephone calls.

Managers using competition-based methods set the price according to the price offered by competitors. For example, if a competitor reduces the price, then management may be required to adjust the price to meet the competition. The market-based pricing approaches are discussed in greater detail in marketing courses, so we will not expand upon them here.

Under the cost-plus methods, managers identify a target profit and price the product in order to achieve the target profit. Using this approach, managers determine product prices by adding to a cost amount a plus, called a **markup,** so that all costs plus a profit are included in the selling price. The size of the markup determines the target profit. Three cost concepts often used in applying the cost-plus approach are: (1) total cost, (2) product cost, and (3) variable cost. In the following paragraphs, we describe and illustrate each of these cost concepts.

USING ACCOUNTING TO UNDERSTAND BUSINESS

One industry in which pricing plays a significant role is the airline industry. The fine tuning involved in pricing fares depends to a large extent upon how many business travelers will be expected on the flight. Business travelers who book flights with little advance notice are more likely to pay full coach fare, while those that plan ahead can receive a discount. Thus, for example, airlines reserve a larger block of full fare seats during high business demand times, such as late Friday afternoon, compared to mid-day flights. The following table indicates the difference between the number of seats sold at each fare for a Wednesday and Friday flight of **American Airlines.** Both examples are based on one-way fares for actual American Airlines flights from LaGuardia to Dallas/Fort Worth on a DC-10, which has coach capacity of 258 passengers.

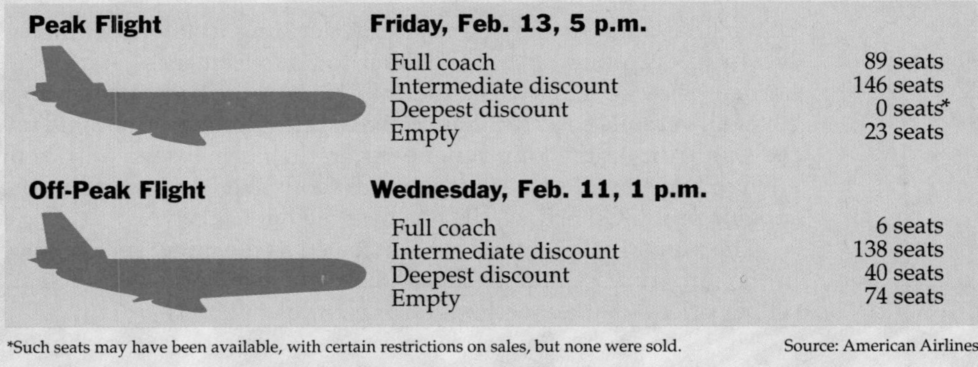

Peak Flight	**Friday, Feb. 13, 5 p.m.**	
	Full coach	89 seats
	Intermediate discount	146 seats
	Deepest discount	0 seats*
	Empty	23 seats
Off-Peak Flight	**Wednesday, Feb. 11, 1 p.m.**	
	Full coach	6 seats
	Intermediate discount	138 seats
	Deepest discount	40 seats
	Empty	74 seats

*Such seats may have been available, with certain restrictions on sales, but none were sold.

Source: American Airlines

Source: Eric Schmitt, "The Art of Devising Air Fares," *The New York Times,* March 4, 1987, sec. D, p. 1.

TOTAL COST CONCEPT

Using the total cost concept, all costs of manufacturing a product plus the selling and administrative expenses are included in the cost amount to which the markup is added. Since all costs and expenses are included in the cost amount, the dollar amount of the markup equals the desired profit.

The first step in applying the total cost concept is to determine the total cost of manufacturing the product. This cost, which includes the costs of direct materials, direct labor, and factory overhead, should be available from the accounting records that support the cost accounting system. The next step is to add the estimated selling and administrative expenses to the total cost of manufacturing the product. The cost amount per unit is then computed by dividing the total costs by the total units expected to be produced and sold.

After the cost amount per unit has been determined, the dollar amount of the markup is determined. For this purpose, the markup is expressed as a percentage of cost. This percentage is then multiplied by the cost amount per unit. The dollar amount of the markup is then added to the cost amount per unit to arrive at the selling price.

The markup percentage for the total cost concept is determined by applying the following formula:

$$\textbf{Markup Percentage} = \frac{\textbf{Desired Profit}}{\textbf{Total Costs}}$$

The numerator of the markup percentage formula includes only the desired profit. This is because all costs and expenses are included in the cost amount to which the markup is added. The denominator of the formula is the total costs.

To illustrate, assume that the costs for Product R of Pellit Co. are as follows:

Variable costs:	
Direct materials	$ 3.00 per unit
Direct labor	10.00
Factory overhead	1.50
Selling and administrative expenses	1.50
Total	$ 16.00 per unit
Fixed costs:	
Factory overhead	$50,000
Selling and administrative expenses	20,000

Pellit Co. desires a profit equal to a 20% rate of return on assets, $800,000 of assets are devoted to producing Product R, and 100,000 units are expected to be produced and sold. The cost amount for Product R is $1,670,000, or $16.70 per unit, computed as follows:

Variable costs ($16.00 × 100,000 units)		$1,600,000
Fixed costs:		
Factory overhead	$50,000	
Selling and administrative expenses	20,000	70,000
Total costs		$1,670,000
Cost amount per unit ($1,670,000 ÷ 100,000 units)		$16.70

The desired profit is $160,000 (20% × $800,000), and the markup percentage for Product R is 9.6%, computed as follows:

$$\textbf{Markup Percentage} = \frac{\textbf{Desired Profit}}{\textbf{Total Costs}}$$

$$\textbf{Markup Percentage} = \frac{\$160{,}000}{\$1{,}670{,}000} = 9.6\%$$

Based on the cost amount per unit and the markup percentage for Product R, Pellit Co. would price Product R at $18.30 per unit. The price computation is shown below.

Cost amount per unit	$16.70
Markup ($16.70 × 9.6%)	1.60
Selling price	$18.30

The ability of the selling price of $18.30 to generate the desired profit of $160,000 is verified by the following income statement:

Pellit Co.
Income Statement
For the Year Ended December 31, 1997

Sales (100,000 units × $18.30)		$1,830,000
Expenses:		
Variable (100,000 units × $16.00)	$1,600,000	
Fixed ($50,000 + $20,000)	70,000	1,670,000
Income from operations		$ 160,000

The total cost concept of applying the cost-plus approach to product pricing is often used by contractors who sell products to government agencies. In many cases, government contractors are required by law to be reimbursed for their products on a total-cost-plus-profit basis.

PRODUCT COST CONCEPT

Using the product cost concept, only the costs of manufacturing the product, termed the product cost, are included in the cost amount to which the markup is added. Estimated selling expenses, administrative expenses, and profit are included in the markup. The markup percentage is determined by applying the following formula:

$$\text{Markup Percentage} = \frac{\text{Desired Profit} + \text{Total Selling and Administrative Expenses}}{\text{Total Manufacturing Costs}}$$

The numerator of the markup percentage formula includes the desired profit plus the total selling and administrative expenses. Selling and administrative expenses must be included in the markup, since they are not included in the cost amount to which the markup is added. The denominator of the formula includes the costs of direct materials, direct labor, and factory overhead.

To illustrate, assume the same data used in the preceding illustration. The cost amount for Pellit Co.'s Product R is $1,500,000, or $15 per unit, computed as follows:

Direct materials ($3 × 100,000 units)		$ 300,000
Direct labor ($10 × 100,000 units)		1,000,000
Factory overhead:		
Variable ($1.50 × 100,000 units)	$150,000	
Fixed	50,000	200,000
Total manufacturing costs		$1,500,000
Cost amount per unit ($1,500,000 ÷ 100,000 units)		$15

The desired profit is $160,000 (20% × $800,000), and the total selling and administrative expenses are $170,000 [(100,000 units × $1.50 per unit) + $20,000]. The markup percentage for Product R is 22%, computed as follows:

$$\text{Markup Percentage} = \frac{\text{Desired Profit + Total Selling and Administrative Expenses}}{\text{Total Manufacturing Costs}}$$

$$\text{Markup Percentage} = \frac{\$160{,}000 + \$170{,}000}{\$1{,}500{,}000}$$

$$\text{Markup Percentage} = \frac{\$330{,}000}{\$1{,}500{,}000} = 22\%$$

Based on the cost amount per unit and the markup percentage for Product R, Pellit Co. would price Product R at $18.30 per unit. The price computation is shown below.

Cost amount per unit	$15.00
Markup ($15 × 22%)	3.30
Selling price	$18.30

VARIABLE COST CONCEPT

The variable cost concept emphasizes the distinction between variable and fixed costs in product pricing. Using the variable cost concept, only variable costs are included in the cost amount to which the markup is added. All variable manufacturing costs, as well as variable selling and administrative expenses, are included in the cost amount. Fixed manufacturing costs, fixed selling and administrative expenses, and profit are included in the markup.

The markup percentage is determined by applying the following formula:

$$\text{Markup Percentage} = \frac{\text{Desired Profit + Total Fixed Costs}}{\text{Total Variable Costs}}$$

The numerator of the markup percentage formula includes the desired profit plus the total fixed manufacturing costs and the total fixed selling and administrative expenses. Fixed manufacturing costs and fixed selling and administrative expenses must be included in the markup, since they are not included in the cost amount to which the markup is added. The denominator of the formula includes the total variable costs.

To illustrate, assume the same data used in the two preceding illustrations. The cost amount for Product R is $1,600,000, or $16.00 per unit, computed as follows:

Variable costs:	
Direct materials ($3 × 100,000 units)	$ 300,000
Direct labor ($10 × 100,000 units)	1,000,000
Factory overhead ($1.50 × 100,000 units)	150,000
Selling and administrative expenses ($1.50 × 100,000 units)	150,000
Total variable costs	$1,600,000
Cost amount per unit ($1,600,000 ÷ 100,000 units)	$16.00

The desired profit is $160,000 (20% × $800,000), the total fixed manufacturing costs are $50,000, and the total fixed selling and administrative expenses are $20,000. The markup percentage for Product R is 14.4%, computed as follows:

$$\text{Markup Percentage} = \frac{\text{Desired Profit + Total Fixed Costs}}{\text{Total Variable Costs}}$$

$$\text{Markup Percentage} = \frac{\$160{,}000 + \$50{,}000 + \$20{,}000}{\$1{,}600{,}000}$$

$$\text{Markup Percentage} = \frac{\$230{,}000}{\$1{,}600{,}000} = 14.4\%$$

Based on the cost amount per unit and the markup percentage for Product R, Pellit Co. would price Product R at $18.30 per unit. The price computation is shown below.

Cost amount per unit	$16.00
Markup ($16.00 × 14.4%)	2.30
Selling price	$18.30

CHOOSING A COST-PLUS APPROACH COST CONCEPT

The three cost concepts commonly used in applying the cost-plus approach to product pricing are summarized below.

Cost Concept	*Covered in Cost Amount*	*Covered in Markup*
Total cost	Total costs	Desired profit
Product cost	Total manufacturing costs	Desired profit + Total selling and administrative expenses
Variable cost	Total variable costs	Desired profit + Total fixed costs

All three cost concepts produced the same selling price ($18.30) for the Pellit Co. illustration. In practice, however, the three cost concepts are usually not viewed as alternatives. The following paragraphs discuss factors normally considered in choosing among the preceding cost concepts.

Each cost concept requires different estimates of costs and expenses. The complexity of the manufacturing operations and the difficulty of estimating costs and expenses should be considered in choosing a cost concept.

To reduce the costs of gathering data, estimated (standard) costs rather than actual costs may be used with any of the three cost concepts. However, management should exercise caution when using estimated costs in applying the cost-plus approach. The estimates should be based on normal (attainable) operating levels and not theoretical (ideal) levels of performance. In product pricing, the use of estimates based on ideal- or maximum-capacity operating levels might lead to setting product prices too low. In this case, the costs of such factors as normal spoilage or normal periods of idle time might not be considered.

The decision-making needs of management are also an important factor in selecting a cost concept for product pricing. For example, managers who often make special pricing decisions are more likely to use the variable cost concept. In contrast, a government defense contractor would be more likely to use the total cost concept.

The following survey results show the pricing strategies used by manufacturers and service companies.[2] As you can see, cost-plus approaches to pricing dominate practice, and the product (or total) cost approach dominates the cost-plus approaches. In addition, there is little difference between manufacturing and service companies in their pricing approaches.

	Manufacturing	*Service Companies*
Basic methods:		
Cost-plus	71%	68%
Market-related	17	11
Combination	12	21
Total	100%	100%
Cost-plus:		
Variable cost	27%	28%
Product or total cost	59	45
Other	14	27
Total	100%	100%

[2] R. W. Mills, and C. Sweeting, *Pricing Decisions in Practice*, London: CIMA, 1988.

A variation of the cost concepts discussed in the preceding paragraphs is the target cost concept. Under this concept, which was pioneered by the Japanese, the selling price is assumed to be set by the marketplace. Thus, the target cost is determined by subtracting a satisfactory profit from a given selling price. Managers design, manufacture, and sell the product to achieve its target cost. In contrast, the three cost concepts discussed previously start with a given product cost and add a markup to determine the selling price. Some argue that the target cost concept may be superior to the cost-plus approaches in highly competitive markets that require continual product cost reductions to remain competitive.

ACTIVITY-BASED COSTING

As illustrated in the preceding paragraphs, costs are an important consideration in setting product prices. To more accurately measure the costs of producing and selling products, some companies have implemented activity-based costing. Activity-based costing (ABC) focuses on identifying and tracing activities to specific products.

Activity-based costing may be useful in making product pricing decisions where diverse and complex manufacturing operations involve large amounts of factory overhead. In such cases, conventional overhead allocation using activity bases such as units produced or machine hours may yield inaccurate cost allocations. This, in turn, may result in distorted product costs and product prices. By providing more accurate product cost allocations, activity-based costing aids in setting product prices that will cover costs and expenses.[3]

Product Profitability and Pricing Under Production Bottlenecks

Objective 3
Calculate the relative profitability of products in bottleneck production environments.

An important consideration in setting production volumes and prices is the influence of production bottlenecks. A production bottleneck (or **constraint**) occurs when the demand for the company's product exceeds the ability to produce the product. The theory of constraints (TOC) is a manufacturing strategy that focuses on reducing the influence of bottlenecks on a process. A company operating under production bottlenecks will be operating a segment of the production process at full capacity.

PRODUCT PROFITABILITY UNDER PRODUCTION BOTTLENECKS

When a company has a bottleneck in its production process, it should attempt to maximize its profitability, subject to the influence of the bottleneck. To illustrate, assume that Snapp-Off Tool Company makes products A, B, and C. All three products are processed through a heat treatment operation, which hardens the steel tools. Snapp-Off Tool's heat treatment process is operating at full capacity and is a production bottleneck. Exhibit 12 shows the product contribution margin per unit information.

Exhibit 12
Product Contribution Margin per Unit

	Product A	*Product B*	*Product C*
Sales price per unit	$130	$140	$160
Variable cost per unit	40	40	40
Contribution margin per unit	$ 90	$100	$120

[3] Activity-based costing is further discussed and illustrated in an appendix at the end of the job order cost systems chapter.

In addition, assume the following information about the number of hours used by each product in the heat treatment (bottleneck) operation:

	Product A	*Product B*	*Product C*
Heat treatment hours per unit	1	4	8

In Exhibit 12, Product C appears the most profitable product, because its contribution margin per unit is the greatest. However, the contribution margin per unit can be a misleading indicator of profitability in a bottleneck operation. The correct measure of performance is the value of each bottleneck hour, or the contribution margin per bottleneck hour. Using this measure, each product has a much different profitability than compared to the contribution margin per unit information, as shown in Exhibit 13.

Exhibit 13
Contribution Margin per Bottleneck Hour

	Product A	*Product B*	*Product C*
Sales price	$130	$140	$160
Variable cost per unit	40	40	40
Contribution margin per unit	$ 90	$100	$120
Bottleneck (heat treatment) hours per unit	÷ 1	÷ 4	÷ 8
Contribution margin per bottleneck hour	$ 90	$ 25	$ 15

Product A produces the most contribution margin per bottleneck (heat treatment) hour used, while Product C produces the smallest profit per bottleneck (heat treatment) hour. Thus, Product A is the most profitable product. This information is opposite to that implied by the unit contribution margin profit reports.

PRODUCT PRICING UNDER PRODUCTION BOTTLENECKS

Each hour of a bottleneck delivers profit to the company. When a company has a production bottleneck, the contribution margin per hour of bottleneck provides a measure of the product's relative profitability. This information can also be used to adjust the product price to better reflect the value of the product's use of a bottleneck. Products that use a large number of bottleneck hours per unit require more margin than products that use few bottleneck hours per unit. For example, Snapp-Off Tool Company should increase the price of Product C in order to deliver more contribution margin per bottleneck hour.

To determine the price of Product C that would equate its profitability to Product A, we need to solve the following equation:

$$\textbf{Contribution Margin per Bottleneck Hour of A} = \frac{\textbf{Revised Price of C} - \textbf{Variable Cost per Unit of C}}{\textbf{Bottleneck Hours per Unit of C}}$$

$$\$90 = \frac{\text{Revised Price of C} - \$40}{8}$$

$$\$720 = \text{Revised Price of C} - \$40$$

$$\text{Revised Price of C} = \$760$$

Product C's price would need to be increased to $760 in order to deliver the same contribution margin per bottleneck hour as does Product A, as shown below.

Revised price of Product C	$760
Less: Variable cost per unit of Product C	40
Contribution margin per unit of Product C	$720
Bottleneck hours per unit of Product C	÷ 8
Revised contribution margin per bottleneck hour	$ 90

At a price of $760, the company would be indifferent between producing and selling Product A or Product C, all else being equal. This analysis assumes that there is unlimited demand for the products. If the market were unwilling to purchase Product C at this price, then the company should produce Product A.

USING ACCOUNTING TO UNDERSTAND BUSINESS

Wharton Manufacturing Company, a fabricator of steel structures, originally priced product according to a markup on full cost. However, the company discovered that there was a bottleneck in its operation. As such, the company used "throughput value per bottleneck hour" as a gauge of relative product profitability. The throughput value (contribution margin) per bottleneck hour information was used by the company to quote prices according to the hours used by the products on the bottleneck. In addition, the company discovered there were products that appeared only marginally profitable under the traditional accounting system, but that had, in fact, a high throughput value per bottleneck hour. As a result, these products were emphasized in the company's marketing plans.

Source: *Cases from Management Accounting Practice:* Vol. 8, IMA, 1992.

KEY POINTS

Objective 1. Prepare a differential analysis report for decisions involving:

Leasing or selling equipment.
Discontinuing an unprofitable segment.
Manufacturing or purchasing a needed part.
Replacing usable plant assets.
Processing further or selling an intermediate product.
Accepting additional business at a special price.

Differential analysis reports for leasing or selling, discontinuing a segment or product, making or buying, replacing equipment, processing or selling, and accepting business at a special price are illustrated in the text. Each analysis focuses on the differential revenues and/or costs of the alternative courses of action.

Objective 2. Determine the selling price of a product, using the total cost, product cost, and variable cost concepts.

The three cost concepts commonly used in applying the cost-plus approach to product pricing are summarized below:

Cost Concept	*Covered in Cost Amount*	*Covered in Markup*
Total cost	Total costs	Desired profit
Product cost	Total manufacturing costs	Desired profit + Total selling and administrative expenses
Variable cost	Total variable costs	Desired profit + Total fixed costs

The markup percentages used in applying each cost concept are as follows:

Total cost concept:

$$\text{Markup Percentage} = \frac{\text{Desired Profit}}{\text{Total Costs}}$$

Product cost concept:

$$\text{Markup Percentage} = \frac{\text{Desired Profit + Total Selling and Administrative Expenses}}{\text{Total Manufacturing Costs}}$$

Variable cost concept:

$$\text{Markup Percentage} = \frac{\text{Desired Profit + Total Fixed Costs}}{\text{Total Variable Costs}}$$

Objective 3. Calculate the relative profitability of products in bottleneck production environments.

The profitability of a product in a bottleneck production environment may not be accurately shown in the contribution margin product report. Instead, the best measure of profitability is determined by dividing the contribution margin per unit by the bottleneck hours per unit. The resulting measure indicates the product's profitability per hour of bottleneck use. This information can be used to support product pricing decisions.

GLOSSARY OF KEY TERMS

Activity-based costing. A cost allocation method that identifies activities causing the incurrence of costs and allocates these costs to products (or other cost objects) based upon activity drivers (bases). *Objective 2*

Bottleneck. A condition that occurs when product demand exceeds production capacity. The bottleneck resource is a portion of the production process that is operating at 100% of capacity and is unable to meet product demand. *Objective 3*

Differential analysis. The area of accounting concerned with the effect of alternative courses of action on revenues and costs. *Objective 1*

Differential cost. The amount of increase or decrease in cost expected from a particular course of action as compared with an alternative. *Objective 1*

Differential revenue. The amount of increase or decrease in revenue expected from a particular course of action as compared with an alternative. *Objective 1*

Markup. An amount that is added to a "cost" amount to determine product price. *Objective 2*

Opportunity cost. The amount of income forgone from an alternative to a proposed use of cash or its equivalent. *Objective 1*

Product cost concept. A concept used in applying the cost-plus approach to product pricing in which only the costs of manufacturing the product, termed the product cost, are included in the cost amount to which the markup is added. *Objective 2*

Sunk cost. A cost that is not affected by subsequent decisions. *Objective 1*

Target cost concept. A concept used to design and manufacture a product at a cost that will deliver a target profit for a given market-determined price. *Objective 2*

Theory of constraints (TOC). A manufacturing strategy that attempts to remove the influence of bottlenecks (constraints) on a process. *Objective 3*

Total cost concept. A concept used in applying the cost-plus approach to product pricing in which all the costs of manufacturing the product plus the selling and administrative expenses are included in the cost amount to which the markup is added. *Objective 2*

Variable cost concept. A concept used in applying the cost-plus approach to product pricing in which only the variable costs are included in the cost amount to which the markup is added. *Objective 2*

ILLUSTRATIVE PROBLEM

Inez Company recently began production of a new product, M, which required the investment of $1,600,000 in assets. The costs of producing and selling 80,000 units of Product M are estimated as follows:

Variable costs:	
Direct materials	$ 10.00 per unit
Direct labor	6.00
Factory overhead	4.00
Selling and administrative expenses	5.00
Total	$ 25.00 per unit
Fixed costs:	
Factory overhead	$800,000
Selling and administrative expenses	400,000

Inez Company is currently considering establishing a selling price for Product M. The president of Inez Company has decided to use the cost-plus approach to product pricing and has indicated that Product M must earn a 10% rate of return on invested assets.

Instructions

1. Determine the amount of desired profit from the production and sale of Product M.
2. Assuming that the total cost concept is used, determine (a) the cost amount per unit, (b) the markup percentage, and (c) the selling price of Product M.
3. Assuming that the product cost concept is used, determine (a) the cost amount per unit, (b) the markup percentage, and (c) the selling price of Product M.
4. Assuming that the variable cost concept is used, determine (a) the cost amount per unit, (b) the markup percentage, and (c) the selling price of Product M.
5. Assume that for the current year, the selling price of Product M was $42 per unit. To date, 60,000 units have been produced and sold, and analysis of the domestic market

indicates that 15,000 additional units are expected to be sold during the remainder of the year. Recently, Inez Company received an offer from Wong Inc. for 4,000 units of Product M at $28 each. Wong Inc. will market the units in Korea under its own brand name, and no additional selling and administrative expenses associated with the sale will be incurred by Inez Company. The additional business is not expected to affect the domestic sales of Product M, and the additional units could be produced during the current year, using existing capacity. (a) Prepare a differential analysis report of the proposed sale to Wong Inc. (b) Based upon the differential analysis report in (a), should the proposal be accepted?

Solution

1. $160,000 ($1,600,000 × 10%)

2. a. Total costs:

Variable ($25 × 80,000 units)	$2,000,000
Fixed ($800,000 + $400,000)	1,200,000
Total	$3,200,000

Cost amount per unit: $3,200,000 ÷ 80,000 units = $40.00

b. $$\textbf{Markup Percentage} = \frac{\textbf{Desired Profit}}{\textbf{Total Costs}}$$

$$\textbf{Markup Percentage} = \frac{\$160{,}000}{\$3{,}200{,}000} = 5\%$$

c.

Cost amount per unit	$40.00
Markup ($40 × 5%)	2.00
Selling price	$42.00

3. a. Total manufacturing costs:

Variable ($20 × 80,000 units)	$1,600,000
Fixed factory overhead	800,000
Total	$2,400,000

Cost amount per unit: $2,400,000 ÷ 80,000 units = $30.00

b. $$\textbf{Markup Percentage} = \frac{\textbf{Desired Profit + Total selling and administrative expenses}}{\textbf{Total manufacturing costs}}$$

$$\textbf{Markup Percentage} = \frac{\$160{,}000 + \$400{,}000 + (\$5 \times 80{,}000 \text{ units})}{\$2{,}400{,}000}$$

$$\textbf{Markup Percentage} = \frac{\$160{,}000 + \$400{,}000 + \$400{,}000}{\$2{,}400{,}000}$$

$$\textbf{Markup Percentage} = \frac{\$960{,}000}{\$2{,}400{,}000} = 40\%$$

c.

Cost amount per unit	$30.00
Markup ($30 × 40%)	12.00
Selling price	$42.00

4. a. Variable cost amount per unit: $25
Total variable costs: $25 × 80,000 units = $2,000,000

b. $$\textbf{Markup Percentage} = \frac{\textbf{Desired Profit + Total fixed costs}}{\textbf{Total variable costs}}$$

$$\textbf{Markup Percentage} = \frac{\$160{,}000 + \$800{,}000 + \$400{,}000}{\$2{,}000{,}000}$$

$$\textbf{Markup Percentage} = \frac{\$1{,}360{,}000}{\$2{,}000{,}000} = 68\%$$

c.

Cost amount per unit	$25.00
Markup ($25 × 68%)	17.00
Selling price	$42.00

5. a.

Proposal to Sell to Wong Inc.

Differential revenue from accepting offer:	
Revenue from sale of 4,000 additional units at $28	$112,000
Differential cost from accepting offer:	
Variable production costs of 4,000 additional units at $20	80,000
Differential income from accepting offer	$ 32,000

b. The proposal should be accepted.

SELF-EXAMINATION QUESTIONS (ANSWERS AT END OF CHAPTER)

1. The amount of increase or decrease in cost that is expected from a particular course of action as compared with an alternative is called:
   A. differential cost C. sunk cost
   B. replacement cost D. opportunity cost

2. Victor Company is considering disposing of equipment that was originally purchased for $200,000 and has $150,000 of accumulated depreciation to date. The same equipment would cost $310,000 to replace. What is the sunk cost?
   A. $50,000 C. $200,000
   B. $150,000 D. $310,000

3. The amount of income that would result from the best available alternative to a proposed use of cash or its equivalent is called:
   A. actual cost C. opportunity cost
   B. historical cost D. sunk cost

4. For which cost concept used in applying the cost-plus approach to product pricing are fixed manufacturing costs, fixed selling and administrative expenses, and desired profit allowed for in determining the markup?
   A. Total cost C. Variable cost
   B. Product cost D. Standard cost

5. Mendosa Company produces three products. The three products all use a furnace operation, which is a production bottleneck. The following information is available:

	Product 1	*Product 2*	*Product 3*
Unit volume—March	1,000	1,500	1,000
Per unit information:			
Sales price	$35	$33	$29
Variable cost	15	15	15
Contribution margin	$20	$18	$14
Furnace hours	4	3	2

From a profitability perspective, which product should be emphasized in April's advertising campaign?
   A. Product 1 C. Product 3
   B. Product 2 D. All three

DISCUSSION QUESTIONS

1. What term is applied to the type of analysis that emphasizes the difference between the revenues and costs for proposed alternative courses of action?
2. Explain the meaning of (a) differential revenue, (b) differential cost, and (c) differential income.
3. What is meant by opportunity cost?

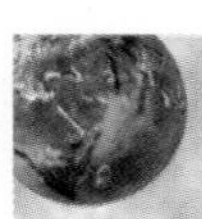

4. In February 1993, *Fortune* reported that **Exabyte,** a fast growing (100-fold in four years) Colorado marketer of tape drives has decided to purchase key components of their product from others. For example, **Sony** provides Exabyte with mechanical decks and **Solectron** provides circuitboards. Exabyte's chief executive officer, Peter Behrendt states, "If we'd tried to build our own plants we could never have grown that fast or maybe survived." The decision to purchase key product components is an example of what type of decision illustrated in this chapter?
5. In the long run, the normal selling price must be set high enough to cover what factors?
6. What are the two primary methods of setting prices?
7. What are three cost concepts commonly used in applying the cost-plus approach to product pricing?
8. In using the product cost concept of applying the cost-plus approach to product pricing, what factors are included in the markup?
9. The variable cost concept used in applying the cost-plus approach to product pricing includes what costs in the cost amount to which the markup is added?

10. In determining the markup percentage for the variable cost concept of applying the cost-plus approach, what is included in the denominator?
11. Why might the use of ideal standards in applying the cost-plus approach to product pricing lead to setting product prices that are too low?
12. Although the cost-plus approach to product pricing may be used by management as a general guideline, what are some examples of other factors that managers should also consider in setting product prices?
13. What method of product cost plus markup may be appropriate in settings where the manufacturing process is complex?
14. How does target costing differ from cost-plus approaches?
15. What is a production bottleneck?
16. What is the appropriate measure of a product's value when a firm is operating under production bottlenecks?

EXERCISES

EXERCISE 25–1
Lease or sell decision
Objective 1

Haslam Corporation is considering selling excess machinery with a book value of $200,000 (original cost of $325,000 less accumulated depreciation of $125,000) for $140,000 less a 10% brokerage commission. Alternatively, the machinery can be leased for a total of $165,000 for five years, after which it is expected to have no residual value. During the period of the lease, Haslam Corporation's costs of repairs, insurance, and property tax expenses are expected to be $35,000.

a. Prepare a differential analysis report, dated January 3 of the current year, for the lease or sell decision.
b. On the basis of the data presented, would it be advisable to lease or sell the machinery? Explain.

EXERCISE 25–2
Differential analysis report for a discontinued product
Objective 1

A condensed income statement by product line for Fontana Co. indicated the following for Product S for the past year:

Sales	$130,000
Cost of goods sold	80,000
Gross profit	$ 50,000
Operating expenses	60,000
Loss from operations	$ (10,000)

It is estimated that 20% of the cost of goods sold represents fixed factory overhead costs and that 25% of the operating expenses are fixed. Since Product S is only one of many products, the fixed costs will not be materially affected if the product is discontinued.

a. Prepare a differential analysis report, dated January 3 of the current year, for the proposed discontinuance of Product S.
b. Should Product S be retained? Explain.

EXERCISE 25–3
Differential analysis report for a discontinued product
Objective 1

The condensed product line income statement for Rogers Company for the current year is as follows:

Rogers Company
Product Line Income Statement
For the Year Ended December 31, 19—

	Product A	*Product B*	*Product C*
Sales	$120,000	$145,000	$210,000
Cost of goods sold	80,000	95,000	145,000
Gross profit	$ 40,000	$ 50,000	$ 65,000
Selling and administrative expenses	30,000	45,000	90,000
Income from operations	$ 10,000	$ 5,000	$ (25,000)

Fixed costs are 40% of the cost of goods sold and 20% of the selling and administrative expenses. Rogers assumes that fixed costs would not be materially affected if Product C were discontinued.

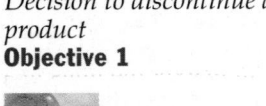

a. Prepare a differential analysis report for all three products for the current year.
b. Should Product C be retained? Explain.

EXERCISE 25–4
Decision to discontinue a product
Objective 1

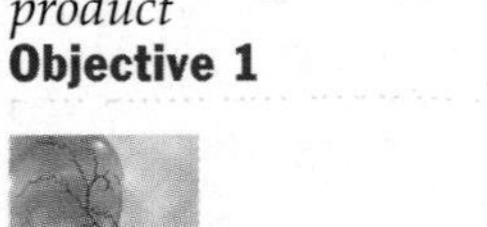

On the basis of the following data, the general manager decided to discontinue Product X because it reduced income from operations by $17,000. What is the flaw in this decision?

Condensed Income Statement
For the Year Ended August 31, 19—

	Product X	*Product Y*	*Product Z*	*Total*
Sales	$100,000	$300,000	$500,000	$900,000
Costs of goods sold:				
Variable costs	$ 65,000	$150,000	$220,000	$435,000
Fixed costs	20,000	60,000	120,000	200,000
Total cost of goods sold	$ 85,000	$210,000	$340,000	$635,000
Gross profit	$ 15,000	$ 90,000	$160,000	$265,000
Operating expenses:				
Variable expenses	$ 25,000	$ 45,000	$ 95,000	$165,000
Fixed expenses	7,000	20,000	25,000	52,000
Total operating expenses	$ 32,000	$ 65,000	$120,000	$217,000
Income (loss) from operations	$ (17,000)	$ 25,000	$ 40,000	$ 48,000

EXERCISE 25–5
Make or buy decision
Objective 1

Cheney Company has been purchasing carrying cases for its portable typewriters at a delivered cost of $25 per unit. The company, which is currently operating below full capacity, charges factory overhead to production at the rate of 40% of direct materials cost. The costs to produce comparable carrying cases are expected to be $12 per unit for direct materials and $8 per unit for direct labor. If Cheney Company manufactures the carrying cases, fixed factory overhead costs will not increase and variable factory overhead costs associated with the cases are expected to be 20% of the direct materials costs.

a. Prepare a differential analysis report, dated June 5 of the current year, for the make or buy decision.
b. On the basis of the data presented, would it be advisable to make or to continue buying the carrying cases? Explain.

EXERCISE 25–6
Machine replacement decision
Objective 1

A company is considering replacing an old piece of machinery, which cost $500,000 and has $420,000 of accumulated depreciation to date, with a new machine that costs $460,000. The old equipment could be sold for $100,000. The variable production costs associated with the old machine are estimated to be $125,000 for six years. The variable production costs for the new machine are estimated to be $40,000 for six years.

a. Determine the differential annual income or loss from replacing the old machine.
b. What is the sunk cost in this situation?

EXERCISE 25–7
Differential analysis report for machine replacement
Objective 1

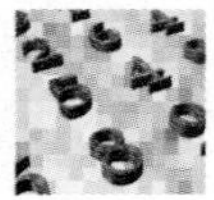

Gatlin Company produces wood chips by applying a machine and direct labor to logs (direct materials). The original cost of the machine is $300,000, the accumulated depreciation is $190,000, its remaining useful life is 10 years, and its salvage value is negligible. On January 20, a proposal was made to replace the present manufacturing procedure with a fully automatic machine that will cost $400,000. The automatic machine has an estimated useful life of 10 years and no significant salvage value. For use in evaluating the proposal, the accountant accumulated the following annual data on present and proposed operations:

	Present Operations	*Proposed Operations*
Sales	$595,000	$595,000
Direct materials	285,000	285,000
Direct labor	119,600	—
Power and maintenance	20,400	52,300
Taxes, insurance, etc.	13,200	22,900
Selling and administrative expenses	45,000	45,000

a. Prepare a differential analysis report for the proposal to replace the machine. Include in the analysis both the net differential decrease in costs anticipated over the 10 years and the net annual differential decrease in costs anticipated.
b. Based only on the data presented, should the proposal be accepted?
c. What are some of the other factors that should be considered before a final decision is made?

EXERCISE 25–8
Decision on accepting additional business
Objective 1

Leon Glass Company has a plant capacity of 60,000 units, and current production is 45,000 units. Monthly fixed costs are $200,000, and variable costs are $19 per unit. The present selling price is $25 per unit. On May 18, the company received an offer from Barker Company for 10,000 units of the product at $21 each. The Barker Company will market the units in a foreign country under its own brand name. The additional business is not expected to affect the regular selling price or quantity of sales of Leon Glass Company.

a. Prepare a differential analysis report for the proposed sale to Barker Company.
b. Briefly explain the reason why accepting this additional business will increase operating income.
c. What is the minimum price per unit that would produce a contribution margin?

EXERCISE 25–9
Sell or process further
Objective 1

Lakeside Lumber Company incurs a cost of $85 per thousand board feet in processing certain "rough-cut" lumber, which it sells for $120 per thousand board feet. An alternative is to produce a "finished-cut" at a total processing cost of $115 per thousand board feet, which can be sold for $170 per thousand board feet. For each alternative, what is the amount of (a) the differential revenue and (b) differential cost?

EXERCISE 25–10
Sell or process further
Objective 1

Irving Coffee Company produces Product A in batches of 8,000 pounds. The standard quantity of materials required in the process are 8,000 pounds, which cost $5.80 per pound. Product A can be sold without further processing for $10 per pound. Product A can also be processed further to yield Product T, which can be sold for $14 per pound. The processing into Product T requires additional processing costs of $30,200 per batch. The additional processing will also cause a 5% loss of product due to evaporation.

a. Prepare a differential analysis report for the decision to sell or process further.
b. Should Irving sell Product A or process further and sell Product T?
c. Determine the price of Product T that would cause neither an advantage or disadvantage for processing further and selling Product T.

EXERCISE 25–11
Accepting business at a special price
Objective 1

McNelly Company expects to operate at 90% of productive capacity during May. The total manufacturing costs for May for the production of 15,000 batteries are budgeted as follows:

Direct materials	$136,000
Direct labor	55,000
Variable factory overhead	19,000
Fixed factory overhead	40,000
Total manufacturing costs	$250,000

The company has an opportunity to submit a bid for 1,000 batteries to be delivered by May 31 to a government agency. If the contract is obtained, it is anticipated that the additional activity will not interfere with normal production during May or increase the selling or administrative expenses. What is the unit cost below which McNelly Company should not go in bidding on the government contract?

EXERCISE 25–12
Total cost concept of product costing
Objective 2

Draper Company uses the total cost concept of applying the cost-plus approach to product pricing. The costs of producing and selling 2,500 units of Product B are as follows:

Variable costs:		Fixed costs:	
Direct materials	$ 80.00 per unit	Factory overhead	$120,000
Direct labor	54.40	Selling and adm. exp.	60,000
Factory overhead	9.60		
Selling and adm. exp.	24.00		
Total	$168.00 per unit		

Draper Company desires a profit equal to a 28.5% rate of return on invested assets of $400,000.

a. Determine the amount of desired profit from the production and sale of Product B.
b. Determine the total costs and the cost amount per unit for the production and sale of 2,500 units of Product B.
c. Determine the markup percentage for Product B.
d. Determine the selling price of Product B.

EXERCISE 25–13
Product cost concept of product pricing
Objective 2

Based on the data presented in Exercise 25–12, assume that Draper Company uses the product cost concept of applying the cost-plus approach to product pricing.

a. Determine the total manufacturing costs and the cost amount per unit for the production and sale of 2,500 units of Product B.
b. Determine the markup percentage for Product B.
c. Determine the selling price of Product B.

EXERCISE 25–14
Variable cost concept of product pricing
Objective 2

Based on the data presented in Exercise 25–12, assume that Draper Company uses the variable cost concept of applying the cost-plus approach to product pricing.

a. Determine the variable costs and the cost amount per unit for the production and sale of 2,500 units of Product B.
b. Determine the markup percentage for Product B.
c. Determine the selling price of Product B.

EXERCISE 25–15
Product decisions under bottlenecked operations
Objective 3

Pitts Glass Company manufactures three types of safety plate glass: Large, Medium, and Small. All three products have high demand. Thus, Pitts is able to sell all the safety glass that it can make. The production process includes an autoclave operation, which is an oil spray heat treatment. The autoclave is a production bottleneck. Fixed costs are $250,000. In addition, the following information is available about the three products:

	Large	*Medium*	*Small*
Sales price per unit	$ 140	$ 90	$ 60
Variable cost per unit	80	40	15
Contribution margin per unit	$ 60	$ 50	$ 45
Autoclave hours per unit	10	8	6
Total process hours per unit	20	18	15
Budgeted units of production	2,000	2,000	2,000

a. Determine the total company net income for the budgeted units of production.
b. Prepare an analysis showing which product is the most profitable per bottleneck hour.

EXERCISE 25–16
Product pricing under bottlenecked operations
Objective 3

Based on the data presented in Exercise 25–15, assume that Pitts wanted to price all products so that they produced the same profit potential as the highest profit product. What would be the prices of all three products that would produce the largest profit?

PROBLEMS SERIES A

PROBLEM 25–1A
Differential analysis report involving opportunity costs
Objective 1

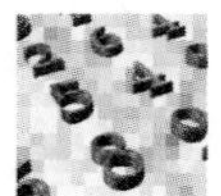

On July 1, Jupiter Storage Company is considering leasing a building and purchasing the necessary equipment to operate a public warehouse. The project would be financed by selling $650,000 of 12% U.S. Treasury bonds that mature in 20 years. The bonds were purchased at face value and are currently selling at face value. The following data have been assembled:

Cost of equipment	$650,000
Life of equipment	20 years
Estimated residual value of equipment	$120,000
Yearly costs to operate the warehouse, in addition to depreciation of equipment	$ 60,000
Yearly expected revenues—years 1–10	$180,000
Yearly expected revenues—years 11–20	$160,000

Instructions

1. Prepare a report presenting a differential analysis of the proposed operation of the warehouse for the 20 years as compared with present conditions.
2. Based on the results disclosed by the differential analysis, should the proposal be accepted?
3. If the proposal is accepted, what is the total estimated income from operation of the warehouse for the 20 years?

PROBLEM 25–2A
Differential analysis report for machine replacement decision
Objective 1

Columbus Printing Company is considering replacing a machine that has been used in its factory for four years. Relevant data associated with the operations of the old machine and the new machine, neither of which has any estimated residual value, are as follows:

Old Machine	
Cost of machine, 12-year life	$ 250,000
Annual depreciation (straight-line)	20,833
Annual manufacturing costs, exclusive of depreciation	525,000
Annual nonmanufacturing operating expenses	390,000
Annual revenue	1,350,000
Current estimated selling price	180,000

New Machine	
Cost of machine, 8-year life	$ 700,000
Annual depreciation (straight-line)	87,500
Estimated annual manufacturing costs, exclusive of depreciation	397,900

Annual nonmanufacturing operating expenses and revenue are not expected to be affected by purchase of the new machine.

Instructions

1. Prepare a differential analysis report as of August 11 of the current year, comparing operations utilizing the new machine with operations using the present equipment. The analysis should indicate the total differential income that would result over the 8-year period if the new machine is acquired.
2. List other factors that should be considered before a final decision is reached.

PROBLEM 25–3A
Differential analysis report for sales promotion proposal
Objective 1

Sentell Cosmetics Company is planning a one-month campaign for May to promote sales of one of its two cosmetics products. A total of $60,000 has been budgeted for advertising, contests, redeemable coupons, and other promotional activities. The following data have been assembled for their possible usefulness in deciding which of the products to select for the campaign:

	Product T	*Product Z*
Unit selling price	$52	$90
Unit production costs:		
Direct materials	$15	$40
Direct labor	9	26
Variable factory overhead	4	6
Fixed factory overhead	5	2
Total unit production costs	$33	$74
Unit variable operating expenses	5	5
Unit fixed operating expenses	6	1
Total unit costs	$44	$80
Operating income per unit	$ 8	$10

No increase in facilities would be necessary to produce and sell the increased output. It is anticipated that 10,000 additional units of Product T or 12,000 additional units of Product Z could be sold without changing the unit selling price of either product.

Instructions

1. Prepare a differential analysis report as of April 5 of the current year, presenting the additional revenue and additional costs anticipated from the promotion of Product T and Product Z.
2. The sales manager had tentatively decided to promote Product Z, estimating that operating income would be increased by $60,000 ($10 operating income per unit for 12,000 units, less promotion expenses of $60,000). The manager also believed that the selection of Product T would increase operating income by only $20,000 ($8 operating income per unit for 10,000 units, less promotion expenses of $60,000). State briefly your reasons for supporting or opposing the tentative decision.

PROBLEM 25–4A
Differential analysis report for further processing
Objective 1

The management of HDI Company is considering whether to process further Product L into Product W. Product W can be sold for $80 per pound, and Product L can be sold without further processing for $45 per pound. Product L is produced in batches of 650 pounds by processing 800 pounds of raw material, which costs $15 per pound. Product W will require additional processing costs of $17 per pound of Product L, and 1.25 pounds of Product L will produce 1 pound of Product W.

Instructions

1. Prepare a report as of May 30, presenting a differential analysis of the further processing of Product L to produce Product W.
2. Briefly report your recommendations.

PROBLEM 25–5A
Product pricing using the cost-plus approach concepts; differential analysis report for accepting additional business
Objectives 1, 2

Vision Inc. recently began production of a new product, L, which required the investment of $1,600,000 in assets. The costs of producing and selling 50,000 units of Product L are estimated as follows:

Variable costs per unit:	
Direct materials	$ 16.80
Direct labor	9.20
Factory overhead	4.00
Selling and administrative expenses	2.00
Total	$ 32.00
Fixed costs:	
Factory overhead	$300,000
Selling and administrative expenses	100,000

Vision Inc. is currently considering establishing a selling price for Product L. The president of Vision Inc. has decided to use the cost-plus approach to product pricing and has indicated that Product L must earn a 19% rate of return on invested assets.

Instructions

1. Determine the amount of desired profit from the production and sale of Product L.
2. Assuming that the total cost concept is used, determine (a) the cost amount per unit, (b) the markup percentage, and (c) the selling price of Product L.
3. Assuming that the product cost concept is used, determine (a) the cost amount per unit, (b) the markup percentage, and (c) the selling price of Product L.
4. Assuming that the variable cost concept is used, determine (a) the cost amount per unit, (b) the markup percentage, and (c) the selling price of Product L.
5. Comment on any additional considerations that could influence establishing of the selling price for Product L.
6. Assume that as of September 1, 40,000 units of Product L have been produced and sold during the current year. Analysis of the domestic market indicates that 6,500 additional units are expected to be sold during the remainder of the year at the normal product price determined under the total cost concept. On September 3, Vision Inc. received an offer from Kimble Company for 3,000 units of Product L at $31 each. Kimble Company will market the units in Canada under its own brand name, and no additional selling and administrative expenses associated with the sale will be incurred by Vision Inc. The

additional business is not expected to affect the domestic sales of Product L, and the additional units could be produced using existing capacity.

a. Prepare a differential analysis report of the proposed sale to Kimble Company.
b. Based upon the differential analysis report in (a), should the proposal be accepted?

PROBLEM 25–6A
Product pricing and profit analysis with bottleneck operations
Objectives 1, 3

Bright Star Steel Company produces three grades of steel, X, Y, and Z. Each of these products (grades) has high demand in the market, and Bright Star is able to sell as much as it can produce of all three. The furnace operation is a bottleneck in the process and is running at 100% of capacity. Bright Star is attempting to determine how to improve profitability for the steel operations. The variable conversion cost is $5 per process hour. The fixed cost is $1,440,000. In addition, the cost analyst was able to determine the following information about the three products:

	Product X	*Product Y*	*Product Z*
Budgeted units produced	3,000	3,000	3,000
Total process hours per unit	30	25	25
Furnace hours per unit	20	10	5
Price per unit	$590	$525	$485
Direct materials cost per unit	$140	$150	$160

The furnace operation is part of the total process for each of these three products. So, for example, 10 of the 25 hours required to process Product Y and 5 of the 25 hours to process Product Z are associated with the furnace.

Instructions

1. Determine the contribution margin per unit for each product.
2. Provide an analysis to determine the relative product profitabilities.
3. Assume management wishes to improve profitability by increasing prices on selected products. At what price would Products X and Y need to be offered in order to produce the same relative profitability as Product Z?

PROBLEMS SERIES B

PROBLEM 25–1B
Differential analysis report involving opportunity costs
Objective 1

On December 1, Spurrier Distribution Company is considering leasing a building and buying the necessary equipment to operate a public warehouse. The project would be financed by selling $900,000 of 7% U.S. Treasury bonds that mature in 16 years. The bonds were purchased at face value and are currently selling at face value. The following data have been assembled:

Cost of equipment	$900,000
Life of equipment	16 years
Estimated residual value of equipment	$ 90,000
Yearly costs to operate the warehouse, in addition to depreciation of equipment	$ 80,000
Yearly expected revenues—years 1–8	$210,000
Yearly expected revenues—years 9–16	$195,000

Instructions

1. Prepare a report presenting a differential analysis of the proposed operation of the warehouse for the 16 years as compared with present conditions.
2. Based on the results disclosed by the differential analysis, should the proposal be accepted?
3. If the proposal is accepted, what is the total estimated income from operation of the warehouse for the 16 years?

PROBLEM 25–2B
Differential analysis report for machine replacement proposal
Objective 1

Cades Tooling Company is considering replacing a machine that has been used in its factory for three years. Relevant data associated with the operations of the old machine and the new machine, neither of which has any estimated residual value, are as follows:

Old Machine	
Cost of machine, 9-year life	$480,000
Annual depreciation (straight-line)	53,333
Annual manufacturing costs, exclusive of depreciation	325,000
Annual nonmanufacturing operating expenses	164,000
Annual revenue	730,000
Current estimated selling price	145,000

New Machine	
Cost of machine, 6-year life	$540,000
Annual depreciation (straight-line)	90,000
Estimated annual manufacturing costs, exclusive of depreciation	240,000

Annual nonmanufacturing operating expenses and revenue are not expected to be affected by purchase of the new machine.

Instructions

1. Prepare a differential analysis report as of March 22 of the current year, comparing operations utilizing the new machine with operations using the present equipment. The analysis should indicate the differential income that would result over the 6-year period if the new machine is acquired.
2. List other factors that should be considered before a final decision is reached.

PROBLEM 25–3B
Differential analysis report for sales promotion proposal
Objective 1

Chevez Shoe Company is planning a one-month campaign for April to promote sales of one of its two shoe products. A total of $20,000 has been budgeted for advertising, contests, redeemable coupons, and other promotional activities. The following data have been assembled for their possible usefulness in deciding which of the products to select for the campaign.

	Product A	*Product L*
Unit selling price	$39	$55
Unit production costs:		
Direct materials	$12	$18
Direct labor	7	18
Variable factory overhead	4	5
Fixed factory overhead	5	2
Total unit production costs	$28	$43
Unit variable operating expenses	2	4
Unit fixed operating expenses	4	1
Total unit costs	$34	$48
Operating income per unit	$ 5	$ 7

No increase in facilities would be necessary to produce and sell the increased output. It is anticipated that 6,000 additional units of Product A or 7,000 additional units of Product L could be sold without changing the unit selling price of either product.

Instructions

1. Prepare a differential analysis report as of March 3 of the current year, presenting the additional revenue and additional costs anticipated from the promotion of Product A and Product L.
2. The sales manager had tentatively decided to promote Product L, estimating that operating income would be increased by $29,000 ($7 operating income per unit for 7,000 units, less promotion expenses of $20,000). The manager also believed that the selection of Product A would increase operating income by only $10,000 ($5 operating income per unit for 6,000 units, less promotion expenses of $20,000). State briefly your reasons for supporting or opposing the tentative decision.

PROBLEM 25–4B
Differential analysis report for further processing
Objective 1

The management of Joy Oil Company is considering whether to process further Product A into Product Y. Product Y can be sold for $58 per pound, and Product A can be sold without further processing for $24 per pound. Product A is produced in batches of 420 pounds by processing 500 pounds of raw material, which costs $12 per pound. Product Y will require additional processing costs of $6 per pound of Product A, and 2 pounds of Product A will produce 1 pound of Product Y.

Instructions

1. Prepare a report as of February 20, presenting a differential analysis associated with the further processing of Product A to produce Product Y.
2. Briefly report your recommendations.

PROBLEM 25–5B
Product pricing using the cost-plus approach concepts; differential analysis report for accepting additional business
Objectives 1, 2

Maxwell Company recently began production of a new product, C, which required the investment of $1,000,000 in assets. The costs of producing and selling 25,000 units of Product C are estimated as follows:

Variable costs per unit:	
Direct materials	$ 10.00
Direct labor	6.50
Factory overhead	3.50
Selling and administrative expenses	4.00
Total	$ 24.00
Fixed costs:	
Factory overhead	$140,000
Selling and administrative expenses	60,000

Maxwell Company is currently considering establishing a selling price for Product C. The president of Maxwell Company has decided to use the cost-plus approach to product pricing and has indicated that Product C must earn a 28% rate of return on invested assets.

Instructions

1. Determine the amount of desired profit from the production and sale of Product C.
2. Assuming that the total cost concept is used, determine (a) the cost amount per unit, (b) the markup percentage, and (c) the selling price of Product C.
3. Assuming that the product cost concept is used, determine (a) the cost amount per unit, (b) the markup percentage, and (c) the selling price of Product C. Round to the nearest cent.
4. Assuming that the variable cost concept is used, determine (a) the cost amount per unit, (b) the markup percentage, and (c) the selling price of Product C.
5. Comment on any additional considerations that could influence establishing the selling price for Product C.
6. Assume that as of May 1, 6,500 units of Product C have been produced and sold during the current year. Analysis of the domestic market indicates that 14,500 additional units of Product C are expected to be sold during the remainder of the year at the normal product price determined under the total cost concept. On May 5, Maxwell Company received an offer from Yee Inc. for 1,000 units of Product C at $19.50 each. Yee Inc. will market the units in Japan under its own brand name, and no additional selling and administrative expenses associated with the sale will be incurred by Maxwell Company. The additional business is not expected to affect the domestic sales of Product C, and the additional units could be produced using existing capacity.
   a. Prepare a differential analysis report of the proposed sale to Yee Inc.
   b. Based upon the differential analysis report in (a), should the proposal be accepted?

PROBLEM 25–6B
Product pricing and profit analysis with bottleneck operations
Objectives 1, 3

Dew Point Chemical Company produces three products, A, B, and C. Each of these products has high demand in the market, and Dew Point is able to sell as much as it can produce of all three. The reaction operation is a bottleneck in the process and is running at 100% of capacity. Dew Point is attempting to determine how to improve profitability for the chemical operations. The variable conversion cost is $3 per process hour. The fixed cost is $768,000. In addition, the cost analyst was able to determine the following information about the three products:

	Product A	Product B	Product C
Budgeted units produced	1,500	1,500	1,500
Total process hours per unit	20	20	24
Reactor hours per unit	4	8	16
Price per unit	$318	$348	$392
Direct materials cost per unit	42	56	64

The reaction operation is part of the total process for each of these three products. So, for example, four of the 20 hours required to process Product A and eight of the 20 hours to process Product B are associated with reaction.

Instructions

1. Determine the contribution margin per unit for each product.
2. Provide an analysis to determine the relative product profitabilities.
3. Assume Dew Point wishes to improve profitability by increasing prices on selected products. At what price would Products B and C need to be offered in order to produce the same relative profitability as Product A?

CASES

CASE 25–1
Morton Enterprises
Product pricing

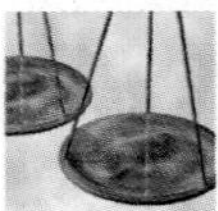

Lee Davis is a cost accountant for Morton Enterprises. Ann Yeager, vice-president of marketing, has asked Lee to meet with representatives of Morton's major competitor to discuss product cost data. Yeager indicates that the sharing of these data will enable Morton to determine a fair and equitable price for its products.

Would it be ethical for Davis to attend the meeting and share the relevant cost data?

CASE 25–2
Ralley Sporting Goods Company
Decision on accepting additional business

A manager of Ralley Sporting Goods Company is considering accepting an order from an overseas customer. This customer has requested an order for 20,000 dozen golf balls at a price of $10.00 per dozen. The variable cost to manufacture a dozen golf balls is $8.00 per dozen. The full cost is $12.00 per dozen. Ralley has a normal selling price of $18.00 per dozen. Ralley's plant has just enough excess capacity on the second shift to make the overseas order.

What are some considerations in accepting or rejecting this order?

CASE 25–3
Almont Hotel
Business decisions with contribution margin

The management of the Almont Hotel is evaluating a proposal for a 100-person convention in the hotel. The professional society sponsoring the convention insists on a $50 per night room rate. The variable cost per guest is $15 per night. However, the full operating cost of the hotel per guest is $60 per night, including fixed costs such as hotel depreciation and management salaries. The convention is scheduled for a weekend, when the hotel will be empty.

Should Almont management accept the business? Discuss.

CASE 25–4
Owens Company
Product profitability with production constraints

Owens Company produces glass products for the automobile industry. The company produces three types of products: small, medium, and large windows. One of the process steps in glass making involves a furnace operation. Presently, the furnace runs 24 hours per day, seven days per week. The following information is available about the three major product lines:

	Small Window	*Medium Window*	*Large Window*
Sales price per unit	$14.00	$24.00	$32.00
Variable cost per unit	6.00	14.00	18.00
Contribution margin	$ 8.00	$10.00	$14.00
Furnace hours per unit	2	4	5

The product manager of Owens Company believes that the company should increase incremental sales effort on the large window, since the contribution margin per unit is the highest. Respond to this suggestion. What recommendations would you suggest to improve profitability?

CASE 25–5
Hull Company
Make or buy decision

The president of Hull Company, Jason Sheppard, asked the controller, Gil Adkins, to provide an analysis of a make vs. buy decision for material TS-101. The material is presently processed in Hull Company's Roanoke facility. TS-101 is used in processing of final products in the facility. Adkins determined the following unit production costs for the material as of March 15, 1997:

Unit production costs:	
Direct materials	$ 6.70
Direct labor	2.50
Variable factory overhead	1.20
Fixed factory overhead	2.00
Total production costs per unit	$12.40

In addition, material TS-101 requires special hazardous material handling. This special handling adds an additional cost of $1.40 for each unit produced.

Material TS-101 can be purchased from an overseas supplier. The supplier does not presently do business with Hull Company. This supplier promises monthly delivery of the material at a price of $9.00 per unit, plus transportation cost of $.40 per unit. In addition, Hull would need to incur additional administrative costs to satisfy import regulations for hazardous material. This additional administrative cost is estimated to be $.80 per purchased unit. Each purchased unit would also require special hazardous material handling of $1.40 per unit.

a. Prepare a differential analysis report to support Adkins recommendation on whether to continue making material TS-101 or whether to purchase the material from the overseas supplier.
b. What additional considerations should Adkins address in the recommendation?

CASE 25–6
3T Company
Cost-plus and target costing concepts

The following conversation took place between Alex Myers, vice-president of marketing, and Jill Jacoby, controller of 3T Company:

Alex: I am really excited about our new computer coming out. I think it will be a real market success.

Jill: I'm really glad you think so. I know that our price is one variable that will determine if it's a success. If our price is too high, our competitors will be the ones with the market success.

Alex: Don't worry about it. We'll just mark our product cost up by 25% and it will all work out. I know we'll make money at those markups. By the way, what does the estimated product cost look like?

Jill: Well, there's the rub. The product cost looks like its going to come in at around $2,400. With a 25% markup, that will give us a selling price of $3,000.

Alex: I see your concern. That's a little high. Our research indicates that computer prices are dropping by about 20% per year, and that this type of computer should be selling for around $2,500 when we release it to the market.

Jill: I'm not sure what to do.

Alex: Let me see if I can help. How much of the $2,400 is fixed cost?

Jill: About $400.

Alex: There you go. The fixed cost is sunk. We don't need to consider it in our pricing decision. If we reduce the product cost by $400, the new price with a 25% markup would be right at $2,500. Boy, I was really worried for a minute there. I knew something wasn't right.

a. If you were Jill, how would you respond to Alex's solution to the pricing problem?
b. How might target costing be used to help solve this pricing dilemma?

CASE 25–7
Schoolcraft Motors
Decision to sell at a special price

You operate a family-owned automotive dealership. Recently, the city government has requested bids on the purchase of eight sedans for use by the city police department. Although the city prefers to purchase from local dealerships, state law requires accepting the lowest bid. The past several contracts for automotive purchases have been granted to dealerships from surrounding communities.

The following data were taken from the dealership records for the normal sale of the automobile for which current bids have been requested:

Retail list price of sedan	$21,000
Costs allocated to normal sale:	
Dealer cost from manufacturer	18,000
Fixed overhead	900
Shipping charges from manufacturer	500
Preparation charges	150
Sales commission based on selling price	6%

In the past, you have always bid $300 above the total cost (including fixed overhead). No sales commissions will be paid if the bid is accepted, and the bid price must contribute at least $300 per car to the profits of the dealership.

a. Do you think that you have used good bidding procedures for prior contracts?

b. What should be the bid price, based upon your profit objectives?

c. Explain why the bid price determined in (b) would not be an acceptable price for normal customers.

ANSWERS TO SELF-EXAMINATION QUESTIONS

1. **A** Differential cost (answer A) is the amount of increase or decrease in cost that is expected from a particular course of action compared with an alternative. Replacement cost (answer B) is the cost of replacing an asset at current market prices. Sunk cost (answer C) is a past cost that will not be affected by subsequent decisions. Opportunity cost (answer D) is the amount of income that would result from the best available alternative to a proposed use of cash or its equivalent.
2. **A** A sunk cost is not affected by later decisions. For Victor Company, the sunk cost is the $50,000 (answer A) book value of the equipment, which is equal to the original cost of $200,000 (answer C) less the accumulated depreciation of $150,000 (answer B).
3. **C** The amount of income that could have been earned from the best available alternative to a proposed use of cash is called opportunity cost (answer C). Actual cost (answer A) or historical cost (answer B) is the cash or equivalent outlay for goods or services actually acquired. Sunk cost (answer D) is a cost that is not affected by later decisions.
4. **C** Under the variable cost concept of product pricing (answer C), fixed manufacturing costs, fixed administrative and selling expenses, and desired profit are allowed for in determining the markup. Only desired profit is allowed for in the markup under the total cost concept (answer A). Under the product cost concept (answer B), total selling and administrative expenses and desired profit are allowed for in determining the markup. Standard cost (answer D) can be used under any of the cost-plus approaches to product pricing.
5. **C** Product 3 has the highest unit contribution margin per bottleneck hour ($14 ÷ 2 = $7). Product 1 (Answer A) has the largest contribution margin per unit, but the lowest unit contribution per bottleneck hour ($20 ÷ 4 = $5), so it is the least profitable product in the constrained environment. Product 2 (Answer B) has the highest total profitability in March (1,500 units × $18), but this does not suggest that it has the highest profit potential. Product 2's unit contribution per bottleneck hour ($18 ÷ 3 = $6) is between Products 1 and 3. Answer D is not true, since the products all have different profit potential in terms of unit contribution margin per bottleneck hour.

26 Capital Investment Analysis

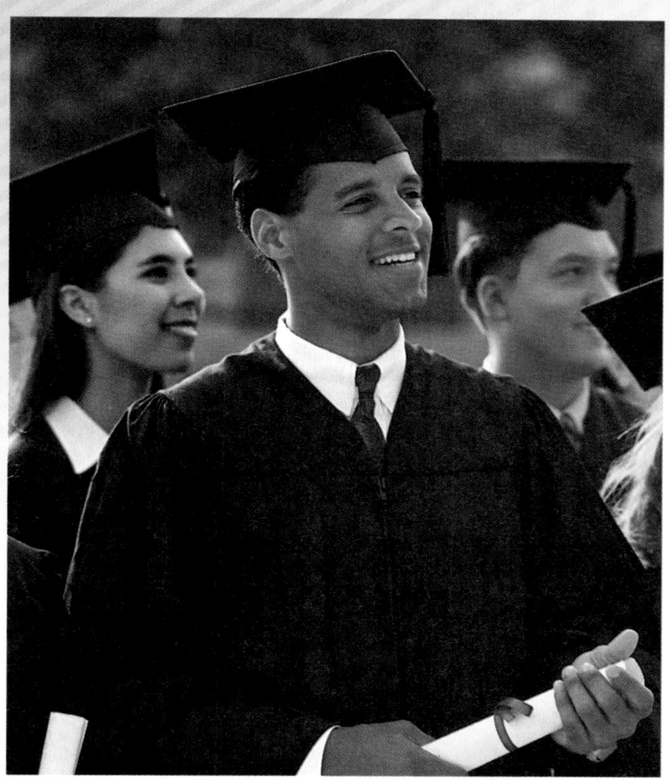

YOU AND ACCOUNTING

Why are you paying tuition and spending time on a higher education? Most people believe that the money and time spent now on an education will return them a higher income in the future. In other words, the money and time spent now on a higher education are an investment in future earning ability. How would you know if the investment in higher education is worth it? One method would be to compare the present cost of attaining your education against the estimated future benefits in increased earning power. The more your future estimated increased earnings exceed the investment, the more attractive the investment. As you will see in this chapter, the same is true for business investments in plant assets. Business organizations analyze potential capital investments by using various methods that compare investment expenditures to future earnings and cash flows.

In this chapter, we will describe analyses useful for making investment decisions, which may involve thousands, millions, or even billions of dollars. We will emphasize the similarities and differences among the most commonly used methods of evaluating investment proposals, as well as the uses of each method. We will also discuss qualitative considerations affecting investment analyses. Finally, we will briefly discuss considerations complicating investment analyses and the process of allocating available investment funds among competing proposals.

After studying this chapter, you should be able to:

Objective 1
Explain the nature and importance of capital investment analysis.

Objective 2
Evaluate capital investment proposals, using the following methods:

Average rate of return
Cash payback
Net present value
Internal rate of return

Objective 3
List examples of qualitative considerations in capital investment analysis, especially as related to today's manufacturing environment.

Objective 4
List and describe factors that complicate capital investment analysis.

Objective 5
Diagram the capital rationing process.

Nature of Capital Investment Analysis

Objective 1
Explain the nature and importance of capital investment analysis.

How do companies decide to make significant investments such as the following?

- Toyota Motor Company doubles its annual production capacity to 400,000 cars at its Georgetown, Kentucky assembly plant.
- General Electric invests over $1 billion on new kitchen appliance products from 1993–1995.
- Hilton Hotels builds a new 3,642-room hotel/casino at the site of the old Flamingo hotel in Las Vegas, Nevada.

Toyota Motor Company doubled its annual production capacity at its Georgetown, Kentucky assembly plant. Capital investment analysis is useful in evaluating such long-term investments.

Companies use capital investment analysis to help evaluate these long-term investments. Capital investment analysis (or **capital budgeting**) is the process by which management plans, evaluates, and controls investments in plant assets. Since capital investments involve a long-term commitment of funds, they affect operations for many years. These investments must earn a reasonable rate of return, so that the business can meet its obligations to creditors and provide dividends to stockholders. Because capital investment decisions are some of the most important decisions that management makes, capital investment analysis must be carefully developed and implemented.

A capital investment program should include a plan for encouraging employees at all levels of the business to submit proposals for capital investments. The plan should provide for communicating to employees the long-range goals of the business, so that useful proposals are submitted. In addition, the plan may reward employees whose proposals are accepted. All reasonable proposals should be given serious consideration, and the economic costs and benefits expected from these proposals should be identified.

Methods of Evaluating Capital Investment Proposals

Objective 2
Evaluate capital investment proposals, using the following methods:

Average rate of return
Cash payback
Net present value
Internal rate of return

The methods of evaluating capital investment proposals can be grouped into the following two general categories:

1. Methods that do not use present values
2. Methods that use present values

The two methods that do not use present values in evaluating capital investment proposals are (1) the average rate of return method and (2) the cash payback method. The two methods that use present values are (1) the net present value method and (2) the internal rate of return method. These methods consider the time value of money. The time value of money concept recognizes that an amount of cash invested today will earn income and therefore has value over time.

Management often uses a combination of methods in evaluating capital investment proposals. A survey of business practices in a variety of industries reported the following use of capital investment analysis methods:[1]

Method	*Percentage of Respondents Using the Method*
Average rate of return method	46%
Cash payback method	71
Net present value method	64
Internal rate of return method	69

Each of the preceding methods has advantages and disadvantages. In addition, some of the computations can become complex. Computers, however, can perform the calculations quickly and easily. More importantly, computers can be used to develop models that indicate the effect of changes in key estimates on the evaluation of capital investment proposals.

METHODS THAT IGNORE PRESENT VALUE

The average rate of return and the cash payback methods of evaluating capital investment proposals are easy to use. These methods are often used initially to screen proposals. Management normally sets minimum standards for accepting proposals, and those not meeting these standards are dropped from further consideration. If a proposal meets the minimum standards, it is often subject to further analysis.

The methods that ignore present value are often useful in evaluating capital investment proposals that have relatively short useful lives. In such cases, the timing of the cash flows is less important. Management can thus focus attention on the amount of income expected to be earned from the investment and the total net cash flows to be received from the investment.

Average Rate of Return Method

The expected average rate of return, sometimes called the **accounting rate of return,** measures the expected income from an investment in plant assets. The expected income from the investment is the annual average income over the useful life of the investment. The amount of the investment is the original cost of the investment less depreciation taken over the useful life. Thus, the investment gradually declines from the original cost to the estimated residual value at the end of its useful life. If straight-line depreciation and no residual value are assumed, the average investment over the useful life is equal to one-half of the original cost.[2]

[1] Robert A. Howell, James D. Brown, Stephen R. Soucy, and Allen H. Seed, *Management Accounting in the New Manufacturing Environment,* National Association of Accountants and Computer Aided Manufacturing International, Montvale, New Jersey, 1987.

[2] The average investment is the midpoint of the depreciable cost of the asset. Since a plant asset is never depreciated below its residual value, this midpoint is determined by adding the original cost of the asset to the estimated residual value and dividing by 2.

To illustrate, assume that management is considering the purchase of a machine at a cost of \$500,000. The machine is expected to have a useful life of 4 years, with no residual value, and to yield total income of \$200,000. The estimated average annual income is therefore \$50,000 (\$200,000 ÷ 4), and the average investment is \$250,000 [(\$500,000 + \$0 residual value) ÷ 2]. Thus, the expected average rate of return on the average investment is 20%, computed as follows:

$$\textbf{Average rate of return} = \frac{\textbf{Estimated average annual income}}{\textbf{Average investment}}$$

$$\text{Average rate of return} = \frac{\$200{,}000 \div 4}{(\$500{,}000 + \$0) \div 2} = 20\%$$

The expected average rate of return of 20% should be compared with the rate set by management as the minimum rate for such investments. If the expected average rate of return equals or exceeds the minimum rate, the machine is desirable for investment purposes.

When several alternative capital investment proposals are considered, the proposals can be ranked by their average rates of return. The higher the average rate of return, the more desirable the proposal. For example, assume that management is considering the following alternative capital investment proposals and has computed the indicated average rates of return:

	Proposal A	*Proposal B*
Estimated average annual income	\$ 30,000	\$ 36,000
Average investment	\$120,000	\$180,000
Average rate of return:		
\$30,000 ÷ \$120,000	25%	
\$36,000 ÷ \$180,000		20%

If only the average rate of return is considered, Proposal A, with an average rate of return of 25%, would be preferred over Proposal B.

In addition to its ease of computation, the average rate of return method has several advantages. One advantage is that it includes the amount of income earned over the entire life of the proposal. In addition, it emphasizes accounting income, which is commonly used by investors and creditors in evaluating management performance. Its main disadvantage is that it does not directly consider the expected cash flows from the proposal and the timing of these cash flows.

Cash Payback Method

Cash flows are important because cash coming from an investment can be reinvested in other income-producing activities. Very simply, the capital investment uses cash, and must therefore return cash in the future in order to be successful.

The expected period of time that will pass between the date of an investment and the complete recovery in cash (or equivalent) of the amount invested is the cash payback period. To simplify the analysis, the revenues and operating expenses related to operating plant assets, other than depreciation, are assumed to be all in the form of cash. The excess of the cash flowing in from revenue over the cash flowing out for expenses is termed **net cash flow.** The time required for the net cash flow to equal the initial outlay for the plant asset is the payback period.

To illustrate, assume that the proposed investment in a plant asset with an 8-year life is \$200,000 and that the annual net cash flow is expected to be \$40,000. The estimated cash payback period for the investment is 5 years, computed as follows:

$$\frac{\$200{,}000}{\$\ 40{,}000} = \text{5-year cash payback period}$$

In this illustration, the annual net cash flows are equal ($40,000 per year). If these annual net cash flows are not equal, the cash payback period is determined by adding the annual net cash flows until the cumulative sum equals the amount of the proposed investment. To illustrate, assume that for a proposed investment of $400,000, the annual net cash flows and the cumulative net cash flows over the proposal's 6-year life are as follows:

Year	*Net Cash Flow*	*Cumulative Net Cash Flow*
1	$ 60,000	$ 60,000
2	80,000	140,000
3	105,000	245,000
4	155,000	400,000
5	100,000	500,000
6	90,000	590,000

The cumulative net cash flow at the end of the fourth year equals the amount of the investment, $400,000. Thus, the payback period is 4 years. If the amount of the proposed investment had been $450,000, the cash payback period would occur during the fifth year. If the net cash flows are uniform throughout the period, the cash payback period in this case would be 4 1/2 years.

The cash payback method is widely used in evaluating proposals for investments in new projects. A relatively short payback period is desirable, because the sooner the cash is recovered, the sooner it becomes available for reinvestment in other projects. In addition, there is less possibility of losses from changes in economic conditions, obsolescence, and other unavoidable risks when the payback period is short. The cash payback period is also important to bankers and other creditors who may be depending upon net cash flow for repaying debt related to the capital investment. The sooner the cash is recovered, the sooner the debt or other liabilities can be paid. Thus, the cash payback method is especially useful to managers whose primary concern is liquidity.

USING ACCOUNTING TO UNDERSTAND BUSINESS

Capital investment analysis is best used for decisions that have productivity improvements or cost savings that can be easily estimated. For example, capital investment analysis is used for many equipment investment decisions. New equipment can be evaluated with respect to its higher productivity, labor savings, energy savings, and the like. For example, the Procter & Gamble Company used capital investment analysis to evaluate investments in a new packaging line technology. A new line can package detergent faster and with less labor cost than the older lines. These benefits were easily compared to the original investment cost to determine if the investment met an acceptable minimum return or cash payback period.

One of the disadvantages of the cash payback method is its failure to include in the analysis the cash flows occurring after the payback period. In addition, the cash payback method does not use present value concepts in valuing cash flows occurring in different periods. In the next section, we will review present value concepts and introduce capital investment analyses that use present value methods.

PRESENT VALUE METHODS

An investment in plant and equipment may be viewed as acquiring a series of net cash flows over a period of time. The period of time over which these net cash flows will be received may be an important factor in determining the value of an investment. Present value methods use both the amount and the timing of net cash flows in determining the acceptability of an investment.

Before illustrating how present value methods are used in capital investment analysis, we will review basic present value concepts.[3]

Present Value Concepts

Present value concepts can be divided into the present value of an amount and the present value of an annuity. In the next two sections, we will describe and illustrate these two concepts.

PRESENT VALUE OF AN AMOUNT. If you were given the choice, would you prefer to receive $1 now or $1 three years from now? You should prefer to receive $1 now, because you could invest the $1 and earn interest for three years. As a result, the amount you would have after three years would be greater than $1.

At the present time on the time line in Exhibit 1, assume you invest $1 in an account that earns 12% interest compounded annually. After one year, the $1 will grow to $1.12, because interest of 12¢ is added to the investment ($1 × 1.12). The $1.12 earns 12% interest for the second year. Interest earning interest is called **compounding.** By the end of the second year, the investment has grown to $1.254 ($1.12 × 1.12). By the end of the third year, the investment has grown to $1.404 ($1.254 × 1.12). Thus, if money is worth 12%, you would be equally satisfied with $1 today or $1.404 three years in the future.

Exhibit 1
Time Line for $1 Compounded at 12%

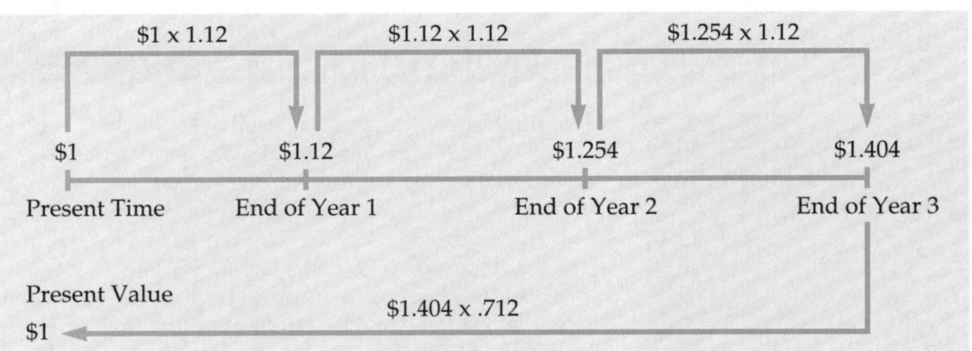

Referring again to Exhibit 1, what is the present value of $1.404 to be received three years hence? This is a present value question. The solution can be determined with the aid of a present value of $1 table. For example, the partial table in Exhibit 2

[3] Present value calculations were introduced in accounting for bond liabilities. Present value concepts are developed again here in order to reinforce that introduction.

indicates that the present value of $1 to be received three years hence, with earnings compounded at the rate of 12% a year, is .712. Multiplying .712 by $1.404 yields $1, which is the present value that started the compounding process.[4]

Exhibit 2
Partial Present Value of $1 Table

Present Value of $1 at Compound Interest

Year	6%	10%	12%	15%	20%
1	.943	.909	.893	.870	.833
2	.890	.826	.797	.756	.694
3	.840	.751	.712	.658	.579
4	.792	.683	.636	.572	.482
5	.747	.621	.567	.497	.402
6	.705	.564	.507	.432	.335
7	.665	.513	.452	.376	.279
8	.627	.467	.404	.327	.233
9	.592	.424	.361	.284	.194
10	.558	.386	.322	.247	.162

PRESENT VALUE OF AN ANNUITY. An annuity is a series of equal net cash flows at fixed time intervals. Annuities are very common in business. For example, rental, salary, and bond interest cash flows are all examples of annuities. The present value of an annuity is the sum of the present values of each cash flow. In other words, the present value of an annuity is the amount of cash that is needed today to yield a series of equal net cash flows at fixed time intervals in the future.

Exhibit 3 illustrates the present value of an annuity concept. The present value of a $100 annuity for five periods at 12% could be determined by using the present value factors in Exhibit 2. Each $100 net cash flow could be multiplied by the present value of $1 at 12% factor for the appropriate period and summed to determine a present value of $360.50.

Exhibit 3
Time Line of Present Value of a $100 Annuity at 12%

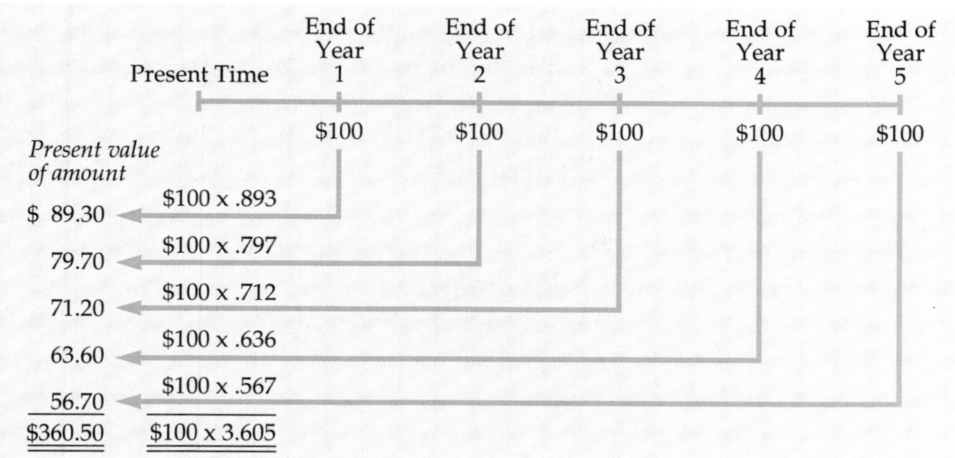

Using a present value of an annuity table is a simpler approach. Exhibit 4 is a partial table of present value of annuity factors.[5] These factors are merely the sum

[4] The present value factors in the table are rounded to three decimal places. More complete tables of both present values and future values are in Appendix A.

[5] Expanded tables for the present value of an annuity are in Appendix A.

of the present value of $1 factors in Exhibit 2 for the number of annuity periods. Thus, 3.605 in the annuity table (Exhibit 4) is the sum of the individual present value of $1 factors, as shown in Exhibit 3.

Exhibit 4 indicates that the present value of net cash flows of $1 at the end of each of five years, earning interest at 12% per year, is $3.605. Multiplying $100 by 3.605 yields the same amount ($360.50) that was determined in the preceding illustration by five successive multiplications.

Exhibit 4
Partial Present Value of an Annuity Table

Present Value of an Annuity of $1 at Compound Interest

Year	6%	10%	12%	15%	20%
1	.943	.909	.893	.870	.833
2	1.833	1.736	1.690	1.626	1.528
3	2.673	2.487	2.402	2.283	2.106
4	3.465	3.170	3.037	2.855	2.589
5	4.212	3.791	3.605	3.353	2.991
6	4.917	4.355	4.111	3.785	3.326
7	5.582	4.868	4.564	4.160	3.605
8	6.210	5.335	4.968	4.487	3.837
9	6.802	5.759	5.328	4.772	4.031
10	7.360	6.145	5.650	5.019	4.192

Net Present Value Method

The **net present value method** analyzes capital investment proposals by comparing the initial cash investment with the present value of the net cash flows. It is sometimes called the **discounted cash flow method.** The interest rate (return) used in net present value analysis is established by management. This rate is often based upon such factors as the nature of the business and its relative profitability, the purpose of the capital investment, the cost of securing funds for the investment, and the minimum desired rate of return. If the net present value of the cash flows expected from a proposed investment at the selected rate equals or exceeds the amount of the initial investment, the proposal is desirable.

To illustrate, assume a proposal to acquire $200,000 of equipment with an expected useful life of five years (no residual value) and a minimum desired rate of return of 10%. Exhibit 5 shows the expected cash flow for each of the five years on a time line. The present values of the cash flows are also shown.

Exhibit 5
Time Line of Net Present Value

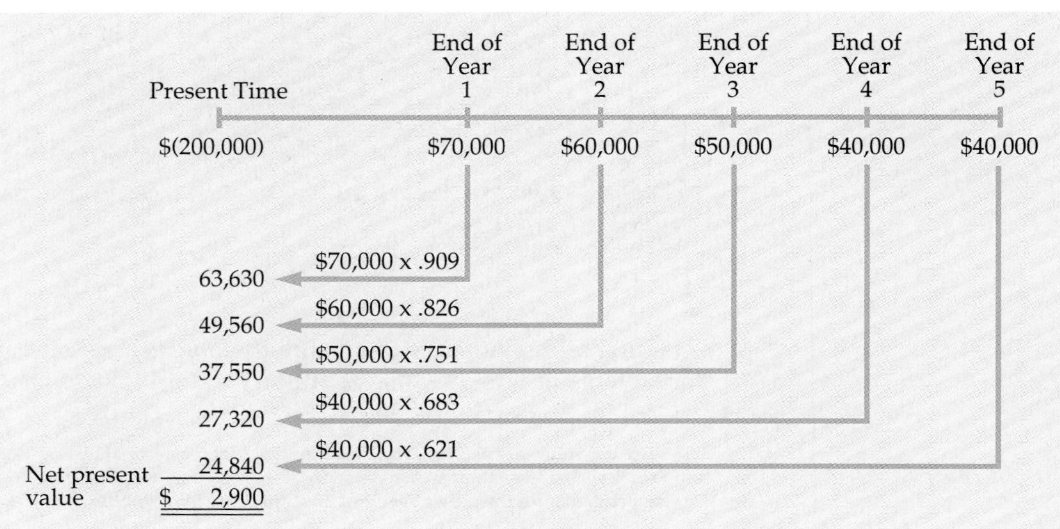

The present value of the net cash flow for each year is computed by multiplying the net cash flow for the year by the present value factor of $1 for that year. Using the data in Exhibit 5, the net cash flow of $70,000 to be received at the end of year 1 is multiplied by the present value of $1 for one year at 10% (.909). Thus, the present value of the $70,000 is $63,630. Likewise, the net cash flow at the end of the second year, $60,000, is multiplied by the present value of $1 for two years at 10% (.826) to yield $49,560, and so on. As shown in Exhibit 6, the amount to be invested, $200,000, is then subtracted from the total present value of the net cash flows $202,900, to determine the net present value, $2,900. The net present value indicates that the proposal is expected to recover the investment and provide more than the minimum rate of return of 10%.

Exhibit 6
Net Present Value Analysis at 10%

Year	*Present Value of $1 at 10%*	*Net Cash Flow*	*Present Value of Net Cash Flow*
1	.909	$ 70,000	$ 63,630
2	.826	60,000	49,560
3	.751	50,000	37,550
4	.683	40,000	27,320
5	.621	40,000	24,840
Total		$260,000	$202,900
Less: Amount to be invested			200,000
Net present value			$ 2,900

When capital investment funds are limited and several alternative investment proposals of the same amount are being considered, the one with the largest net present value is the most desirable. If the alternative proposals involve different amounts of investment, it is useful to prepare a relative ranking of the proposals by using a present value index. The **present value index** is computed by dividing the total present value of the net cash flow by the amount to be invested. The present value index for the investment in Exhibit 6 is computed as follows:

$$\textbf{Present value index} = \frac{\textbf{Total present value of net cash flow}}{\textbf{Amount to be invested}}$$

$$= \frac{\$202{,}900}{\$200{,}000} = 1.0145$$

To further illustrate, assume that the total present values of the net cash flow and the amounts to be invested for three alternative proposals are as follows:

	Proposal A	*Proposal B*	*Proposal C*
Total present value of net cash flow	$107,000	$86,400	$93,600
Amount to be invested	100,000	80,000	90,000
Net present value	$ 7,000	$ 6,400	$ 3,600

The present value index for each proposal is as follows:

	Present Value Index
Proposal A	1.07 ($107,000 ÷ $100,000)
Proposal B	1.08 ($ 86,400 ÷ $ 80,000)
Proposal C	1.04 ($ 93,600 ÷ $ 90,000)

Although Proposal A has the largest net present value, the present value indexes indicate that it is not as desirable as Proposal B. In other words, Proposal B returns 1.08 present value per dollar invested, whereas Proposal A returns only

1.07. Proposal B requires an investment of $80,000, compared to an investment of $100,000 for Proposal A. Management should consider the possible use of the $20,000 difference between Proposal A and Proposal B investments before making a final decision.

An advantage of the net present value method is that it considers the time value of money. A disadvantage is that the computations are more complex than those for the methods that ignore present value. In addition, the net present value method assumes that the cash received from the proposal during its useful life can be reinvested at the rate of return used in computing the present value of the proposal. Because of changing economic conditions, this assumption may not always be reasonable.

USING ACCOUNTING TO UNDERSTAND BUSINESS

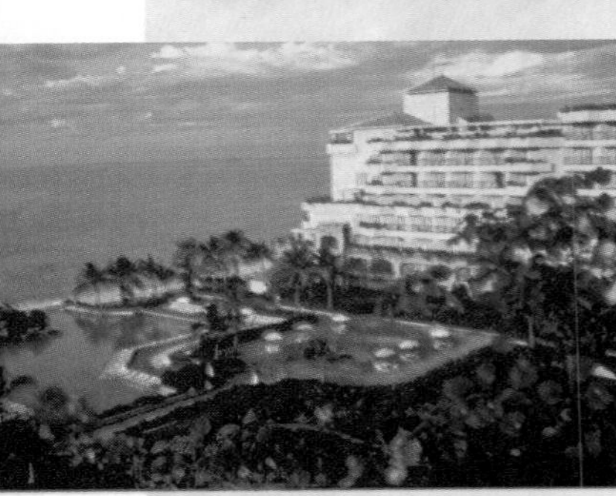

How does a company like Marriott Corporation determine when and where to build a new hotel? Marriott will first identify a likely site for the hotel. The site could be in a city (Warsaw, Poland), in a tourist location (Walt Disney World), or in a resort location (Cancun, Mexico). The site will be evaluated with respect to the estimated cash flows from business and vacation-related demand for hotel rooms. In addition, the company needs to balance the cash flows against the cost of building the hotel. For example, Marriott built a "western" style hotel in Warsaw, Poland at a modest cost, due to favorable land and construction costs. As eastern Europe opened up to business opportunities, this hotel has been booked to capacity, providing a positive net present value on Marriott's investment.

Internal Rate of Return Method

The internal rate of return method uses present value concepts to compute the rate of return from the net cash flows expected from capital investment proposals. This method is sometimes called the **time-adjusted rate of return method.** It is similar to the net present value method, in that it focuses on the present value of the net cash flows. However, the internal rate of return method starts with the net cash flows and, in a sense, works backwards to determine the rate of return expected from the proposal.

To illustrate, assume that management is evaluating a proposal to acquire equipment costing $33,530, which is expected to provide annual net cash flows of $10,000 per year for five years. If we assume a rate of return of 12%, we can compute the present value of the net cash flows, using the present value of an annuity table in Exhibit 4. These computations are shown in Exhibit 7.

Exhibit 7
Net Present Value Analysis at 12%

Annual net cash flow (at the end of each of five years)	$10,000
Present value of an annuity of $1 at 12% for 5 years (Exhibit 4)	× 3.605
Present value of annual net cash flows	$36,050
Less: Amount to be invested	33,530
Net present value	$ 2,520

In Exhibit 7, the $36,050 present value of the cash inflows, based on a 12% rate of return, is greater than the $33,530 to be invested. Therefore, the internal rate of return must be greater than 12%. Exhibit 8 indicates that 15% is the rate of return that equates the $33,530 cost of the investment with the present value of the net cash flows.

Exhibit 8
Net Present Value Analysis at 15%

Annual net cash flow (at the end of each of five years)	$10,000
Present value of an annuity of $1 at 15% for 5 years (Exhibit 4)	× 3.353
Present value of annual net cash flows	$33,530
Less: Amount to be invested	33,530
Net present value	$ 0

In the above illustration, a rate of 12% was assumed before the internal rate of return of 15% was identified. Such trial-and-error procedures are time-consuming. When equal annual net cash flows are expected from a proposal, as in the illustration, the computations are simplified by using the procedures summarized below.[6]

1. Determine a present value factor for an annuity of $1 by dividing the amount to be invested by the equal annual net cash flows. This computation is expressed by the following formula:

$$\textbf{Present value factor for an annuity of \$1} = \frac{\textbf{Amount to be invested}}{\textbf{Equal annual net cash flows}}$$

2. In the present value of an annuity of $1 table, locate the present value factor determined in (1). First locate the number of years of expected useful life of the investment in the Year column, and then proceed horizontally across the table until you find the present value factor computed in (1).
3. Identify the internal rate of return by the heading of the column in which the present value factor in (2) is located.

To illustrate these procedures, assume that management is considering a proposal to acquire equipment costing $97,360. The equipment is expected to provide equal annual net cash flows of $20,000 for seven years. The present value factor for an annuity of $1 is 4.868, computed as follows:

$$\text{Present value factor for an annuity of \$1} = \frac{\text{Amount to be invested}}{\text{Equal annual net cash flows}}$$

$$= \frac{\$97{,}360}{\$20{,}000} = 4.868$$

For a period of seven years, the partial present value of an annuity of $1 table indicates that the factor 4.868 is related to a percentage of 10%, as shown below. Thus, 10% is the internal rate of return for this proposal.

Present Value of an Annuity of $1 at Compound Interest

Year	6%	10%	12%
1	.943	.909	.893
2	1.833	1.736	1.690
3	2.673	2.487	2.402
4	3.465	3.170	3.037
5	4.212	3.791	3.605
6	4.917	4.355	4.111
7	5.582	4.868	4.564
8	6.210	5.335	4.968
9	6.802	5.759	5.328
10	7.360	6.145	5.650

[6] In Exhibits 7 and 8, equal annual net cash flows were assumed in order to simplify the illustration. If the annual net cash flows are not equal, the computations are more complex, but the basic concepts are the same.

If the minimum acceptable rate of return for similar proposals is 10% or less, then the proposed investment should be considered desirable. When several proposals are considered, management often ranks the proposals by their internal rates of return. The proposal with the highest rate is considered the most desirable.

The primary advantage of the internal rate of return method is that the present values of the net cash flows over the entire useful life of the proposal are considered. In addition, by determining a rate of return for each proposal, all proposals are placed on a common basis for comparison. The primary disadvantage of the internal rate of return method is that the computations are more complex than for some of the other methods. However, spreadsheet programs have internal rate of return functions that can be used to simplify the calculation. Also, like the net present value method, this method assumes that the cash received from a proposal during its useful life will be reinvested at the internal rate of return. Because of changing economic conditions, this assumption may not always be reasonable.

Qualitative Considerations in Capital Investment Analysis

Objective 3
List examples of qualitative considerations in capital investment analysis, especially as related to today's manufacturing environment.

The methods we described and illustrated in the preceding paragraphs focused on the quantitative aspects of capital investment analysis. For example, in evaluating a proposal to purchase new equipment, we compared the expected cash flows with the amount of cash to be invested. However, some benefits of capital investments are qualitative in nature and cannot be readily estimated in dollar terms. If management does not consider these qualitative considerations, the quantitative analyses may suggest rejecting a worthy investment.

Qualitative considerations in capital investment analysis are most appropriate for strategic investments. Strategic investments are those that are designed to affect a company's long-term ability to generate profits. Frequently, strategic investments have many uncertainties and intangible benefits. Unlike capital investments that are designed to cut costs, strategic investments have very few "hard" savings. Instead, they may affect future revenues, which are difficult to estimate. An example of a strategic investment is **Nucor's** decision to be the first to invest in a new continuous casting technology that had the potential to make thin gauge sheet steel and thus open new product markets. Nucor's new investment was justified more on the strategic importance of the investment than on the economic analysis. As it turned out, the investment was very successful.

Qualitative considerations that may influence capital investment analysis also include the impact of investment proposals on product quality, manufacturing flexibility, employee morale, manufacturing productivity, and manufacturing control. Many of these qualitative factors may be as important, if not more important, than the results of quantitative analysis in today's manufacturing environment. The new manufacturing environment is characterized by investments in redesigning the manufacturing process and implementing manufacturing systems such as just-in-time manufacturing and computer-integrated manufacturing. In this environment, qualitative factors may be especially important in capital investment analysis.

Factors That Complicate Capital Investment Analysis

Objective 4
List and describe factors that complicate capital investment analysis.

In the preceding discussion, we described the basic concepts for four widely used methods of evaluating capital investment proposals. In practice, additional factors may have an impact on the outcome of a capital investment decision. In the following paragraphs, we discuss some of the most important of these factors. These factors include the federal income tax, unequal lives of alternative proposals, leasing, uncertainty, and changes in price levels.

USING ACCOUNTING TO UNDERSTAND BUSINESS

Capital investment analysis is not especially useful in evaluating all investments. Such investments are usually strategic decisions involving a high degree of uncertainty. Often the investments have no historical precedent, so benefits are very difficult to estimate. An example would be Matsushita's (JVC and Panasonic brand names) fifteen-year quest to develop the video cassette recorder and VHS tape. Such a long-term decision was probably not evaluated using conventional capital investment analysis. The product and market didn't even exist when Matsushita began its investments. Thus, the size of the potential market would be difficult to estimate. Indeed, Matsushita states that this investment was based on its belief that customers would value "time shifting." In other words, customers would value a product that would allow viewing times for their favorite movies or TV shows to be shifted to times that would suit them. As it turns out, this strategic investment eventually paid off handsomely for Matsushita.

The importance of considering qualitative aspects of capital investments is best summarized by John H. McConnell, Chairman of Worthington Industries, who stated, "We try to find the best technology, stay ahead of the competition, and serve the customer . . . We'll make any investment that will pay back quickly . . . but if it is something that we really see as a must down the road, payback is not going to be that important."[7]

INCOME TAX

In many cases, the impact of the federal income tax on capital investment decisions can be material. In determining depreciation for federal income tax purposes, useful lives that are much shorter than the actual useful lives can often be used. Also, depreciation can be calculated by methods that approximate the 200-percent declining-balance method. Thus, depreciation for tax purposes often exceeds the depreciation for financial statement purposes in the early years of an asset's use. The tax reduction in these early years is offset by higher taxes in the later years, so that accelerated depreciation does not result in a long-run saving in taxes. However, the timing of the cash outflows for income taxes can have a significant impact on capital investment analysis.[8]

UNEQUAL PROPOSAL LIVES

In the preceding discussion, the illustrations of the methods of analyzing capital investment proposals were based on the assumption that alternative proposals had the same useful lives. In practice, however, alternative proposals may have unequal lives. To illustrate, assume that alternative proposals X and Y are being compared. Each proposal requires an initial investment of $100,000 and has the following expected cash flow and useful life:

	Net Cash Flows	
Year	*Proposal X*	*Proposal Y*
1	$30,000	$30,000
2	30,000	30,000
3	25,000	30,000
4	20,000	30,000
5	15,000	35,000
6	15,000	—
7	10,000	—
8	10,000	—

[7] Joseph Morone and Albert Paulson, "Cost of Capital: The Managerial Perspective," *California Management Review,* Summer 1991, pp. 9–32.
[8] The impact of income taxes on capital investment analysis is described and illustrated in advanced textbooks.

If the desired rate of return is 10%, each proposal's net present value could be determined as shown in Exhibit 9. Because of the unequal useful lives of the two proposals, the net present values in Exhibit 9 are not comparable. To make them comparable for the analysis, the proposals can be adjusted to end at the same time. This can be done by assuming that Proposal X is to be terminated at the end of 5 years and the asset sold. This assumption requires that the residual value of Proposal X be estimated at the end of 5 years and that this value be included as a cash flow at that date. Both proposals will then cover 5 years, and net present value analysis can be used to compare the two proposals over the same 5-year period.

Exhibit 9
Net Present Value Analysis

Proposal X

Year	*Present Value of $1 at 10%*	*Net Cash Flow*	*Present Value of Net Cash Flow*
1	.909	$ 30,000	$ 27,270
2	.826	30,000	24,780
3	.751	25,000	18,775
4	.683	20,000	13,660
5	.621	15,000	9,315
6	.564	15,000	8,460
7	.513	10,000	5,130
8	.467	10,000	4,670
Total		$155,000	$112,060
Amount to be invested			100,000
Net present value			$ 12,060

Proposal Y

Year	*Present Value of $1 at 10%*	*Net Cash Flow*	*Present Value of Net Cash Flow*
1	0.909	$ 30,000	$ 27,270
2	0.826	30,000	24,780
3	0.751	30,000	22,530
4	0.683	30,000	20,490
5	0.621	35,000	21,735
Total		$155,000	$116,805
Amount to be invested			100,000
Net present value			$ 16,805

To illustrate, assume that Proposal X has an estimated residual value of $40,000 at the end of year 5. For Proposal X, the excess of the present value over the amount to be invested is $18,640 for a 5-year life, as shown in Exhibit 10.

Exhibit 10
Net Present Value Analysis

Year	*Present Value of $1 at 10%*	*Net Cash Flow*	*Present Value of Net Cash Flow*
1	.909	$ 30,000	$ 27,270
2	.826	30,000	24,780
3	.751	25,000	18,775
4	.683	20,000	13,660
5	.621	15,000	9,315
5 (Residual value)	.621	40,000	24,840
Total		$160,000	$118,640
Amount to be invested			100,000
Net present value			$ 18,640

If a 5-year life is used for both proposals, the net present value for Proposal X (Exhibit 10) exceeds the net present value for Proposal Y (Exhibit 9) by $1,835 ($18,640 – $16,805). Therefore, Proposal X may be viewed as the more attractive of the two proposals.

LEASE VERSUS CAPITAL INVESTMENT

Leasing plant assets has become common in many industries. For example, hospitals often lease diagnostic and other medical equipment. Leasing allows a business to acquire the use of plant assets without using large amounts of cash to purchase them. In addition, management may believe that a plant asset has a high degree of risk of becoming obsolete before the end of its useful life. In this case, the risk of obsolescence may be reduced by leasing rather than purchasing the asset. Finally, the *Internal Revenue Code* allows the lessor (the owner of the asset) to pass tax deductions on to the lessee (the party leasing the asset). These provisions of the tax law have made leasing assets more attractive. For example, a company that pays $50,000 per year for leasing a $200,000 plant asset with a life of 8 years is permitted to deduct from taxable income the annual lease payments.

In many cases, before a final decision is made, management should consider the possibility of leasing assets instead of purchasing them. Normally, leasing assets is more costly than purchasing because the lessor must include in the rental price not only the costs associated with owning the assets but also a profit. Nevertheless, using the methods of evaluating capital investment proposals, management should consider whether it is more profitable to lease rather than purchase an asset.

UNCERTAINTY

All capital investment analyses rely on factors that are uncertain. For example, the estimates related to revenues, expenses, and cash flows are uncertain. The long-term nature of capital investments suggests that some estimates are likely to involve uncertainty. Errors in one or more of the estimates could lead to incorrect decisions.

CHANGES IN PRICE LEVELS

Periods of increasing price levels are described as periods of **inflation.** In recent years, the rates of inflation have varied widely, making the estimation of future revenues, expenses, and cash flows even more difficult. Management should, however, attempt to anticipate future price levels and consider their effects on the estimates used in capital investment analyses. Changes in anticipated price levels could significantly affect the analyses.

Capital Rationing

Objective 5
Diagram the capital rationing process.

Capital rationing is the process by which management allocates available investment funds among competing capital investment proposals. Normally, management uses various combinations of the evaluation methods described in this chapter in developing an effective approach to capital rationing.

In capital rationing, an initial screening of alternative proposals is usually performed by establishing minimum standards for the cash payback and the average rate of return methods. The proposals that survive this initial screening are further analyzed, using the net present value and internal rate of return methods. Throughout the capital rationing process, qualitative factors related to each proposal should also be considered. For example, the acquisition of new, more efficient equipment that eliminates several jobs could lower employee morale to a level that could decrease overall plant productivity. Alternatively, new equipment might improve the quality of the product and thus increase consumer satisfaction and sales.

The final step in the capital rationing process is to rank the proposals according to management's criteria, compare the proposals with the funds available, and select the proposals to be funded. The unfunded proposals may be reconsidered if funds later become available. The flowchart in Exhibit 11 portrays the capital rationing decision process.

Exhibit 11
Capital Rationing Decision Process

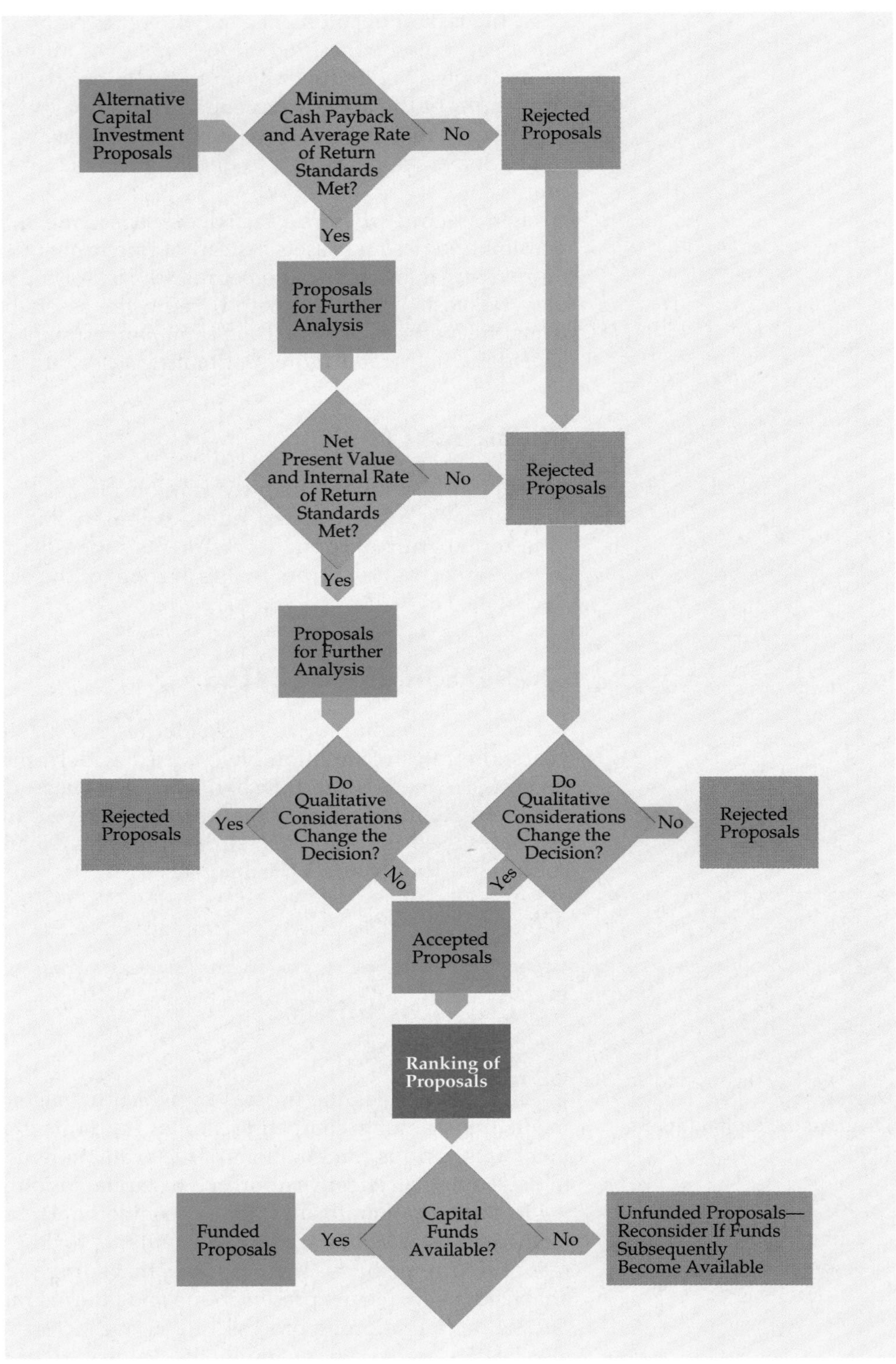

Proposals that are funded in the capital rationing process are included in the **capital expenditures budget** to aid the planning and financing of operations. This budget, as discussed in a prior chapter, should be integrated with the master budget.

KEY POINTS

Objective 1. Explain the nature and importance of capital investment analysis.

Capital investment analysis is the process by which management plans, evaluates, and controls investments involving plant assets. Capital investment analysis is important to a business because such investments affect profitability for a long period of time.

Objective 2. Evaluate capital investment proposals, using the following methods: average rate of return, cash payback, net present value, and internal rate of return.

The average rate of return method measures the expected profitability of an investment in plant assets. It is computed using the following formula:

$$\text{Average rate of return} = \frac{\text{Estimated average annual income}}{\text{Average investment}}$$

The expected period of time that will pass between the date of an investment and the complete recovery in cash (or equivalent) of the amount invested is the cash payback period. Investment proposals with the shortest cash payback are considered the most desirable.

The net present value method uses present values to compute the net present value of the cash flows expected from a proposal. The net present value of the cash flows are then compared across proposals. The present value of a cash flow is computed by looking up the present value of $1 from a table of present values and multiplying it by the amount of the future cash flow, as shown in the text.

The internal rate of return method uses present values to compute the rate of return from the net cash flows expected from capital investment proposals. When equal annual net cash flows are expected from a proposal, the computations are simplified by using a table of the present value of an annuity, as shown in the text.

Objective 3. List examples of qualitative considerations in capital investment analysis, especially as related to today's manufacturing environment.

Some benefits of capital investment analysis, which are especially important in today's manufacturing environment, cannot be readily estimated in dollar terms. Some examples of such considerations include improvements in product quality, manufacturing flexibility, employee morale, and manufacturing productivity and control.

Objective 4. List and describe factors that complicate capital investment analysis.

Factors that may complicate capital investment analysis include the impact of the federal income tax, unequal lives of alternative proposals, leasing, uncertainty, and changes in price levels. A brief description of the effect of each of these factors appears in the text.

Objective 5. Diagram the capital rationing process.

Capital rationing refers to the process by which management allocates available investment funds among competing capital investment proposals. A diagram of the capital rationing process appears in the text.

GLOSSARY OF KEY TERMS

Annuity. A series of equal cash flows at fixed intervals. *Objective 2*

Average rate of return. A method of evaluating capital investment proposals that focuses on the expected profitability of the investment. *Objective 2*

Capital investment analysis. The process by which management plans, evaluates, and controls long-term capital investments involving property, plant, and equipment. *Objective 1*

Capital rationing. The process by which management allocates available investment funds among competing capital investment proposals. *Objective 5*

Cash payback period. The expected period of time that will elapse between the date of a capital expenditure and the complete recovery in cash (or equivalent) of the amount invested. *Objective 2*

Inflation. A period when prices in general are rising and the purchasing power of money is declining. *Objective 4*

Internal rate of return method. A method of analysis of proposed capital investments that focuses on using present value concepts to compute the rate of return from the net cash flows expected from the investment. *Objective 2*

Net present value method. A method of analysis of proposed capital investments that focuses on the present value of the cash flows expected from the investments. *Objective 2*

Present value concept. Cash to be received (or paid) in the future is not the equivalent of the same amount of money received at an earlier date. *Objective 2*

Present value index. An index computed by dividing the total present value of the net cash flow to be received from a proposed capital investment by the amount to be invested. *Objective 2*

Present value of an annuity. The sum of the present values of a series of equal cash flows to be received at fixed intervals. *Objective 2*

Time value of money concept. The concept that an amount of money invested today will earn income. *Objective 2*

ILLUSTRATIVE PROBLEM

The capital investment committee of Hopewell Company is currently considering two projects. The estimated operating income and net cash flows expected from each project are as follows:

	Project A		*Project B*	
Year	*Operating Income*	*Net Cash Flow*	*Operating Income*	*Net Cash Flow*
1	$ 6,000	$ 22,000	$13,000	$ 29,000
2	9,000	25,000	10,000	26,000
3	10,000	26,000	8,000	24,000
4	8,000	24,000	8,000	24,000
5	11,000	27,000	3,000	19,000
	$44,000	$124,000	$42,000	$122,000

Each project requires an investment of $80,000. Straight-line depreciation will be used, and no residual value is expected. The committee has selected a rate of 15% for purposes of the net present value analysis.

Instructions

1. Compute the following:
   a. The average rate of return for each project, giving effect to depreciation on the investment.
   b. The net present value for each project. Use the present value of $1 table appearing in this chapter.
2. Why is the net present value of Project B greater than Project A, even though its average rate of return is less?
3. Prepare a summary for the capital investment committee, advising it on the relative merits of the two projects.

Solution

1. a. Average rate of return for Project A:

$$\frac{\$44{,}000 \div 5}{(\$80{,}000 + \$0) \div 2} = 22\%$$

Average rate of return for Project B:

$$\frac{\$42{,}000 \div 5}{(\$80{,}000 + \$0) \div 2} = 21\%$$

b. Net present value analysis:

		Net Cash Flow		*Present Value of Net Cash Flow*	
Year	*Present Value of $1 at 15%*	*Project A*	*Project B*	*Project A*	*Project B*
1	0.870	$ 22,000	$ 29,000	$19,140	$25,230
2	0.756	25,000	26,000	18,900	19,656
3	0.658	26,000	24,000	17,108	15,792
4	0.572	24,000	24,000	13,728	13,728
5	0.497	27,000	19,000	13,419	9,443
Total		$124,000	$122,000	$82,295	$83,849
Amount to be invested				80,000	80,000
Net present value				$ 2,295	$ 3,849

2. Project B has a lower average rate of return than Project A because Project B's total operating income for the five years is $42,000, which is $2,000 less than Project A's. Even so, the net present value of Project B is greater than that of Project A, because Project B has higher cash flows in the early years.

3. Both projects exceed the selected rate established for the net present value analysis. Project A has a higher average rate of return, but Project B offers a larger net present value. Thus, if only one of the two projects can be accepted, Project B would be the more attractive.

SELF-EXAMINATION QUESTIONS (ANSWERS AT END OF CHAPTER)

1. Methods of evaluating capital investment proposals that ignore present value include:
   A. average rate of return.
   B. cash payback.
   C. both A and B.
   D. neither A nor B.

2. Management is considering a $100,000 investment in a project with a 5-year life and no residual value. If the total income from the project is expected to be $60,000 and recognition is given to the effect of straight-line depreciation on the investment, the average rate of return is:
   A. 12%.
   B. 24%.
   C. 60%.
   D. 75%.

3. As used in the analysis of proposed capital investments, the expected period of time that will elapse between the date of a capital investment and the complete recovery of the amount of cash invested is called:
   A. the average rate of return period.
   B. the cash payback period.
   C. the net present value period.
   D. the internal rate of return period.

4. Which method of analyzing capital investment proposals determines the total present value of the cash flows expected from the investment and compares this value with the amount to be invested?
   A. Average rate of return
   B. Cash payback
   C. Net present value
   D. Internal rate of return

5. The process by which management allocates available investment funds among competing capital investment proposals is called:
   A. capital rationing.
   B. present value indexing.
   C. leasing.
   D. uncertainty.

DISCUSSION QUESTIONS

1. Which two methods of capital investment analysis ignore present value?
2. Which two methods of capital investment analysis can be described as present value methods?
3. What is the time value of money concept?
4. How is the average rate of return computed for capital investment analysis, assuming that the effect of straight-line depreciation on the amount of the investment is considered?
5. What are the principal objections to the use of the average rate of return method in evaluating capital investment proposals?
6. a. As used in analyses of proposed capital investments, what is the cash payback period?
   b. Discuss the principal limitations of the cash payback method for evaluating capital investment proposals.
7. What is an annuity?
8. Which method of evaluating capital investment proposals reduces their expected future net cash flows to present values and compares the total present values to the amount of the investment?
9. A net present value analysis used to evaluate a proposed equipment acquisition indicated a $9,750 net present value. What is the meaning of the $9,750 as it relates to the desirability of the proposal?
10. How is the present value index for a proposal determined?
11. What are the major disadvantages of the use of the net present value method of analyzing capital investment proposals?
12. What are the major disadvantages of the use of the internal rate of return method of analyzing capital investment proposals?
13. Give an example of a qualitative factor that should be considered in a capital investment analysis related to acquiring automated factory equipment.

14. Monsanto, a large chemical and fibers company, invested $37 million in state-of-the-art systems to improve process control, laboratory automation, and local area network communications. The investment was not justified merely on cost savings but was also justified on the basis of qualitative considerations. Monsanto management viewed the

investment as a critical element toward achieving its vision of the future. What qualitative and quantitative considerations do you believe Monsanto would have considered in its strategic evaluation of these investments?
15. What provision of the Internal Revenue Code is especially important to consider in analyzing capital investment proposals?
16. What method can be used to place two capital investment proposals with unequal useful lives on a comparable basis?
17. What are the major advantages of leasing a plant asset rather than purchasing it?
18. What is capital rationing?

EXERCISES

EXERCISE 26–1
Average rate of return
Objective 2

The following data are accumulated by O'Brien Company in evaluating two competing capital investment proposals:

	Proposal C	*Proposal D*
Amount of investment	$800,000	$720,000
Useful life	8 years	5 years
Estimated residual value	-0-	-0-
Estimated total income	$640,000	$450,000

Determine the expected average rate of return for each proposal, giving effect to straight-line depreciation on each investment.

EXERCISE 26–2
Average rate of return—cost savings
Objective 2

Russell Company is considering an investment in equipment that will replace direct labor. The equipment has a cost of $120,000, with a $30,000 residual value and 10-year life. The equipment will replace one employee who has an average wage of $35,000 per year. In addition, the equipment will have operating and energy costs of $14,000 per year. Determine the average rate of return on the equipment.

EXERCISE 26–3
Calculating cash flows
Objective 2

Humvee Company is planning to invest $180,000 in a new garden product that is expected to generate additional sales of 10,000 units at $24 a piece. The $180,000 investment at the beginning of the current year includes $60,000 for initial launch-related expenses and $120,000 for equipment that has a 15-year life and a $7,500 residual value. Selling expenses related to the new product are expected to be 5% of sales revenue. The cost to manufacture the product includes the following per unit costs:

Direct labor	$ 5.00
Direct materials	8.00
Fixed factory overhead—depreciation	0.75
Variable factory overhead	2.00
Total	$15.75

Determine the annual net cash flows for the first year of the project, years 2-14, and for the last year of the project.

EXERCISE 26–4
Cash payback period
Objective 2

Elk Insurance Company is evaluating two capital investment proposals, each requiring an investment of $240,000 and each with an 8-year life and expected total net cash flows of $320,000. Proposal 1 is expected to provide equal annual net cash flows of $40,000, and Proposal 2 is expected to have the following unequal annual net cash flows:

Year 1	$100,000	Year 5	20,000
Year 2	60,000	Year 6	20,000
Year 3	40,000	Year 7	20,000
Year 4	40,000	Year 8	20,000

Determine the cash payback period for both proposals.

EXERCISE 26–5
Cash payback method
Objective 2

Diego Entertainment Group is considering an investment in one of two competing projects. The investment required for either project is $120,000. The net cash flows associated with each project are as follows:

	Project 1	*Project 2*
Year 1	$ 60,000	$ 30,000
2	40,000	30,000
3	20,000	30,000
4	20,000	30,000
5	20,000	30,000
6	20,000	30,000
Total	$180,000	$180,000

a. Recommend a project to Diego Entertainment Group, based on the cash payback period for each project.
b. Why is one project preferred over the other, even though they both have the same total net cash flows through six periods?

EXERCISE 26–6
Net present value method
Objective 2

The following data are accumulated by Likert Company in evaluating the purchase of $160,000 of equipment, having a 4-year useful life:

	Net Income	*Net Cash Flow*
Year 1	$40,000	$80,000
Year 2	10,000	50,000
Year 3	5,000	45,000
Year 4	2,000	42,000

a. Assuming that the desired rate of return is 12%, determine the net present value for the proposal. Use the table of the present value of $1 appearing in this chapter.
b. Would management be likely to look with favor on the proposal? Explain.

EXERCISE 26–7
Net present value method—annuity
Objective 2

Wu Construction Company is planning an investment of $140,000 for a bulldozer. The bulldozer is expected to operate for 1,200 hours per year for five years. Customers will be charged $75 per hour for bulldozer work. The bulldozer operator is paid an hourly wage of $24 per hour. The bulldozer is expected to require annual maintenance costing $4,000. The bulldozer uses fuel that is expected to cost $15 per hour of bulldozer operation.

a. Determine the equal annual net cash flows from operating the bulldozer.
b. Determine the net present value of the investment, assuming that the desired rate of return is 10%. Use the table of present values of an annuity of $1 in the chapter.
c. Should Wu Construction Company invest in the bulldozer, based on this analysis?

EXERCISE 26–8
Net present value—unequal lives
Objective 2

Song Development Company has two competing investments, Proposal Y and Proposal Z. Proposal Y and Z have an initial investment of $120,000. The net cash flows estimated for the two investments are as follows:

	Net Cash Flow	
Year	*Proposal Y*	*Proposal Z*
1	$32,000	$50,000
2	30,000	40,000
3	28,000	35,000
4	20,000	30,000
5	18,000	
6	15,000	
7	10,000	
8	5,000	

The estimated residual value of Proposal Y at the end of year four is $50,000.

Determine which proposal should be favored by comparing the net present values of the two investments, assuming a minimum rate of return of 12%.

EXERCISE 26–9
Net present value method and present value index
Objective 2

Apollo Sporting Goods Company is considering an investment in one of two machines. Machine A will increase productivity from sewing 120 baseballs per hour to sewing 150 per hour. The contribution margin is $.50 per baseball. Assume that any increased production of baseballs can be sold. Machine B is an automatic packaging machine for the golf ball line. The packaging machine will reduce packing labor cost. The labor cost saved is equivalent to $16 per hour. Machine A will cost $137,000, have an eight-year life, and will operate for 2,100 hours per year. Machine B will cost $125,000, have an eight-year life, and will operate for 1,800 hours per year. Apollo seeks a minimum rate of return of 15% on its investments.

a. Determine the net present value for the two machines.
b. Determine the present value index for the two machines.
c. If Apollo only has sufficient funds for one of the machines, and qualitative factors are equal between the two machines, in which machine should it invest?

EXERCISE 26–10
Present value index
Objective 2

Conrad Company has computed the net present value for capital expenditure proposals A and B, using the net present value method. Relevant data related to the computation are as follows:

	Proposal A	*Proposal B*
Total present value of net cash flow	$214,000	$343,000
Amount to be invested	200,000	350,000
Net present value	$ 14,000	$ (7,000)

Determine the present value index for each proposal.

EXERCISE 26–11
Average rate of return, cash payback period, net present value method
Objective 2

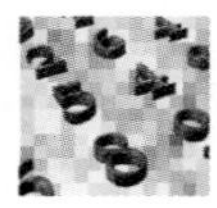

Tonaka Forging Company is considering acquiring equipment at a cost of $800,000. The equipment has an estimated life of 8 years and no residual value. It is expected to provide yearly income of $100,000 and yearly net cash flows of $200,000. The company's minimum desired rate of return for net present value analysis is 12%. Compute the following:

a. The average rate of return, giving effect to straight-line depreciation on the investment.
b. The cash payback period.
c. The net present value. Use the table of the present value of an annuity of $1 appearing in this chapter.

EXERCISE 26–12
Internal rate of return method
Objective 2

The internal rate of return method is used by Spielman Stamping Company in analyzing a capital expenditure proposal that involves an investment of $832,700 and annual net cash flows of $220,000 for each of the 6 years of useful life.

a. Determine a present value factor for an annuity of $1 which can be used in determining the internal rate of return.
b. Using the factor determined in (a) and the present value of an annuity of $1 table appearing in this chapter, determine the internal rate of return for the proposal.

EXERCISE 26–13
Net present value method and internal rate of return method
Objective 2

Watson Inc. is evaluating a proposed expenditure of $182,220 on a 4-year project whose estimated net cash flows are $60,000 for each of the four years.

a. Compute the net present value, using a rate of return of 15%.
b. Based on the analysis prepared in (a), is the rate of return (1) more than 15%, (2) 15%, or (3) less than 15%? Explain.
c. Determine the internal rate of return by computing a present value factor for an annuity of $1 and using the table of the present value of an annuity of $1 presented in the text.

EXERCISE 26–14
Identifying error in capital investment analysis calculations
Objective 2

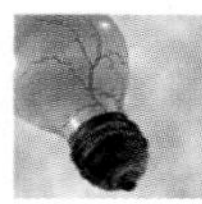

Rodgers Company is considering the purchase of automated machinery that is expected to have a useful life of 5 years and no residual value. The average rate of return on the average investment has been computed to be 20%, and the cash payback period was computed to be 5.2 years.

Do you see any reason to question the validity of the data presented? Explain.

PROBLEMS SERIES A

PROBLEM 26–1A
Average rate of return method, net present value method, and analysis
Objective 2

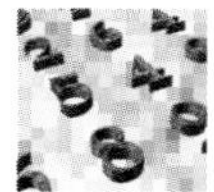

The capital investment committee of Spillman Development Company is considering two projects. The estimated operating income and net cash flows from each project are as follows:

	Project A		*Project X*	
Year	*Operating Income*	*Net Cash Flow*	*Operating Income*	*Net Cash Flow*
1	$21,000	$ 61,000	$13,000	$ 53,000
2	15,000	55,000	13,000	53,000
3	12,000	52,000	12,000	52,000
4	10,000	50,000	13,000	53,000
5	7,000	47,000	14,000	54,000
	$65,000	$265,000	$65,000	$265,000

Each project requires an investment of $200,000. Straight-line depreciation will be used, and no residual value is expected. The committee has selected a rate of 10% for purposes of the net present value analysis.

Instructions

1. Compute the following:
   a. The average rate of return for each project, giving effect to depreciation on the investment.
   b. The net present value for each project. Use the present value of $1 table appearing in this chapter.
2. Prepare a brief report for the capital investment committee, advising it on the relative merits of the two projects.

PROBLEM 26–2A
Cash payback period, net present value method, and analysis
Objective 2

Wong Company is considering two projects. The estimated net cash flows from each project are as follows:

Year	*Project E*	*Project F*
1	$100,000	$200,000
2	300,000	200,000
3	100,000	100,000
4	80,000	70,000
5	50,000	60,000
Total	$630,000	$630,000

Each project requires an investment of $400,000, with no residual value expected. A rate of 20% has been selected for the net present value analysis.

Instructions

1. Compute the following for each project:
   a. Cash payback period.
   b. The net present value. Use the present value of $1 table appearing in this chapter.
2. Prepare a brief report advising management on the relative merits of each of the two projects.

PROBLEM 26–3A
Net present value method, present value index, and analysis
Objective 2

Pinnacle Power and Light Company wishes to evaluate three capital investment proposals by using the net present value method. Relevant data related to the proposals are summarized as follows:

	Proposal X	*Proposal Y*	*Proposal Z*
Amount to be invested	$150,000	$150,000	$250,000
Annual net cash flows:			
Year 1	110,000	90,000	160,000
Year 2	65,000	50,000	140,000
Year 3	40,000	40,000	45,000

Instructions

1. Assuming that the desired rate of return is 15%, prepare a net present value analysis for each proposal. Use the present value of $1 table appearing in this chapter.
2. Determine a present value index for each proposal.
3. Which proposal offers the largest amount of present value per dollar of investment? Explain.

PROBLEM 26–4A
Net present value method, internal rate of return method, and analysis
Objective 2

Management is considering two capital investment projects. The estimated net cash flows from each project are as follows:

Year	*Project B*	*Project C*
1	$40,000	$15,000
2	40,000	15,000
3	40,000	15,000
4	40,000	15,000

Project B requires an investment of $121,480, while Project C requires an investment of $42,825. No residual value is expected from either project.

Instructions

1. Compute the following for each project:
   a. The net present value. Use a rate of 10% and the present value of an annuity of $1 table appearing in this chapter.
   b. A present value index.
2. Determine the internal rate of return for each project by (a) computing a present value factor for an annuity of $1 and (b) using the present value of an annuity of $1 table appearing in this chapter.
3. What advantage does the internal rate of return method have over the net present value method in comparing projects?

PROBLEM 26–5A
Evaluation of alternative capital investment decisions
Objectives 2, 4

The investment committee of Jeffries Stores Inc. is evaluating two projects. The projects have different useful lives, but each requires an investment of $250,000. The estimated net cash flows from each project are as follows:

	Net Cash Flows	
Year	*Project I*	*Project II*
1	$70,000	$95,000
2	70,000	95,000
3	70,000	95,000
4	70,000	95,000
5	70,000	
6	70,000	

The committee has selected a rate of 15% for purposes of net present value analysis. It also estimates that the residual value at the end of each project's useful life is $0, but at the end of the fourth year, Project I's residual value would be $130,000.

Instructions

1. For each project, compute the net present value. Use the present value of an annuity of $1 table appearing in this chapter. (Ignore the unequal lives of the projects.)
2. For each project, compute the net present value, assuming that Project I is adjusted to a four-year life for purposes of analysis. Use the present value of $1 table appearing in this chapter.
3. In reporting to the investment committee, what advice would you give on the relative merits of the two projects?

PROBLEM 26–6A
Capital rationing decision involving six proposals
Objectives 2, 5

Dixon Investment Company is considering allocating a limited amount of capital investment funds among six proposals. The amount of proposed investment, estimated operating income, and net cash flow for each proposal are as follows:

	Investment	*Year*	*Operating Income*	*Net Cash Flow*
Proposal A:	$140,000	1	$ 52,000	$ 80,000
		2	32,000	60,000
		3	12,000	40,000
		4	7,000	35,000
		5	2,000	30,000
Proposal B:	$ 90,000	1	$ 12,000	$ 30,000
		2	12,000	30,000
		3	12,000	30,000
		4	11,000	29,000
		5	10,000	28,000
Proposal C:	$ 80,000	1	$ 9,000	$ 25,000
		2	9,000	25,000
		3	(1,000)	15,000
		4	(1,000)	15,000
		5	(1,000)	15,000
Proposal D:	$600,000	1	$130,000	$250,000
		2	30,000	150,000
		3	(20,000)	100,000
		4	(20,000)	100,000
		5	(15,000)	105,000
Proposal E:	$800,000	1	$240,000	$400,000
		2	40,000	200,000
		3	40,000	200,000
		4	40,000	200,000
		5	(10,000)	150,000
Proposal F:	$250,000	1	$ 10,000	$ 60,000
		2	10,000	60,000
		3	10,000	60,000
		4	10,000	60,000
		5	10,000	60,000

The company's capital rationing policy requires a minimum cash payback period of 4 years for projects of $100,000 and over and a minimum cash payback period of 3 years for projects under $100,000. In addition, a minimum average rate of return of 10% is required on all projects. If the preceding minimum standards are met, the net present value method and present value indexes are used to rank the remaining proposals.

Instructions

1. Compute the cash payback period for each of the six proposals.
2. Giving effect to straight-line depreciation on the investments and assuming no estimated residual value, compute the average rate of return for each of the six proposals.
3. Using the following format, summarize the results of your computations in (1) and (2). By placing a check mark in the appropriate column at the right, indicate which proposals should be accepted for further analysis and which should be rejected.

Proposal	*Cash Payback Period*	*Average Rate of Return*	*Accept for Further Analysis*	*Reject*
A				
B				
C				
D				
E				
F				

continued

4. For the proposals accepted for further analysis in (3), compute the net present value. Use a rate of 10% and the present value of $1 table appearing in this chapter.
5. Compute the present value index for each of the proposals in (4).
6. Rank the proposals from most attractive to least attractive, based on the present values of net cash flows computed in (4).
7. Rank the proposals from most attractive to least attractive, based on the present value indexes computed in (5).
8. Based upon the analyses, comment on the relative attractiveness of the proposals ranked in (6) and (7).

PROBLEMS SERIES B

PROBLEM 26–1B
Average rate of return method, net present value method, and analysis
Objective 2

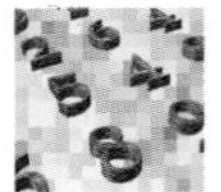

The capital investment committee of Soft Solutions Inc., a software development company, is considering two projects. The estimated operating income and net cash flows from each project are as follows:

	Project P		*Project Q*	
Year	*Operating Income*	*Net Cash Flow*	*Operating Income*	*Net Cash Flow*
1	$ 26,000	$ 90,000	$ 45,000	$109,000
2	27,000	91,000	37,000	101,000
3	27,000	91,000	29,000	93,000
4	28,000	92,000	16,000	80,000
5	28,000	92,000	9,000	73,000
	$136,000	$456,000	$136,000	$456,000

Each project requires an investment of $320,000. Straight-line depreciation will be used, and no residual value is expected. The committee has selected a rate of 12% for purposes of the net present value analysis.

Instructions

1. Compute the following:
   a. The average rate of return for each project, giving effect to depreciation on the investment.
   b. The net present value for each project. Use the present value of $1 table appearing in this chapter.
2. Prepare a brief report for the capital investment committee, advising it on the relative merits of the two projects.

PROBLEM 26–2B
Cash payback period, net present value method, and analysis
Objective 2

Triple-A Company is considering two projects. The estimated net cash flows from each project are as follows:

Year	*Project G*	*Project R*
1	$150,000	$110,000
2	100,000	140,000
3	50,000	30,000
4	40,000	30,000
5	40,000	70,000
Total	$380,000	$380,000

Each project requires an investment of $250,000, with no residual value expected. A rate of 15% has been selected for the net present value analysis.

Instructions

1. Compute the following for each project:
   a. Cash payback period.

b. The net present value. Use the present value of $1 table appearing in this chapter.

2. Prepare a brief report advising management on the relative merits of each of the two projects.

PROBLEM 26–3B
Net present value method, present value index, and analysis
Objective 2

Compu-Tech Inc. wishes to evaluate three capital investment projects by using the net present value method. Relevant data related to the projects are summarized as follows:

	Project C	*Project D*	*Project E*
Amount to be invested	$600,000	$300,000	$300,000
Annual net cash flows:			
Year 1	400,000	200,000	80,000
Year 2	300,000	145,000	125,000
Year 3	120,000	75,000	180,000

Instructions

1. Assuming that the desired rate of return is 20%, prepare a net present value analysis for each project. Use the present value of $1 table appearing in this chapter.
2. Determine a present value index for each project.
3. Which project offers the largest amount of present value per dollar of investment? Explain.

PROBLEM 26–4B
Net present value method, internal rate of return method, and analysis
Objective 2

Management is considering two capital investment projects. The estimated net cash flows from each project are as follows:

Year	*Project I*	*Project II*
1	$25,000	$160,000
2	25,000	160,000
3	25,000	160,000
4	25,000	160,000

Project I requires an investment of $64,725, while Project II requires an investment of $456,800. No residual value is expected from either project.

Instructions

1. Compute the following for each project:
   a. The net present value. Use a rate of 12% and the present value of an annuity of $1 table appearing in this chapter.
   b. A present value index.
2. Determine the internal rate of return for each project by (a) computing a present value factor for an annuity of $1 and (b) using the present value of an annuity of $1 table appearing in this chapter.
3. What advantage does the internal rate of return method have over the net present value method in comparing projects?

PROBLEM 26–5B
Evaluating alternative capital investment decisions
Objectives 2, 4

The investment committee of North Central Bancorp is evaluating two projects. The projects have different useful lives, but each requires an investment of $180,000. The estimated net cash flows from each project are as follows:

	Net Cash Flows	
Year	*Project A*	*Project B*
1	$50,000	$67,000
2	50,000	67,000
3	50,000	67,000
4	50,000	67,000
5	50,000	
6	50,000	

The committee has selected a rate of 15% for purposes of net present value analysis. It also estimates that the residual value at the end of each project's useful life is $0, but at the end of the fourth year, Project A's residual value would be $90,000.

Instructions

1. For each project, compute the net present value. Use the present value of an annuity of $1 table appearing in this chapter. (Ignore the unequal lives of the projects.)
2. For each project, compute the net present value, assuming that Project A is adjusted to a four-year life for purposes of analysis. Use the present value of $1 table appearing in this chapter.
3. In reporting to the investment committee, what advice would you give on the relative merits of the two projects?

PROBLEM 26–6B
Capital rationing decision involving six proposals
Objectives 2, 5

Western Insurance Company is considering allocating a limited amount of capital investment funds among six proposals. The amount of proposed investment, estimated operating income, and net cash flow for each proposal are as follows:

	Investment	*Year*	*Operating Income*	*Net Cash Flow*
Proposal A:	$140,000	1	$ 52,000	$ 80,000
		2	32,000	60,000
		3	12,000	40,000
		4	7,000	35,000
		5	2,000	30,000
Proposal B:	$ 90,000	1	$ 12,000	$ 30,000
		2	12,000	30,000
		3	12,000	30,000
		4	11,000	29,000
		5	10,000	28,000
Proposal C:	$200,000	1	$ 10,000	$ 50,000
		2	10,000	50,000
		3	10,000	50,000
		4	10,000	50,000
		5	0	40,000
Proposal D:	$500,000	1	$ 20,000	$120,000
		2	20,000	120,000
		3	20,000	120,000
		4	40,000	140,000
		5	20,000	120,000
Proposal E:	$800,000	1	$240,000	$400,000
		2	40,000	200,000
		3	40,000	200,000
		4	40,000	200,000
		5	(10,000)	150,000
Proposal F:	$ 70,000	1	$ 5,000	$ 19,000
		2	5,000	19,000
		3	2,000	16,000
		4	2,000	16,000
		5	0	14,000

The company's capital rationing policy requires a minimum cash payback period of 4 years for projects of $100,000 and over and a minimum cash payback period of 3 years for projects under $100,000. In addition, a minimum average rate of return of 10% is required on all projects. If the preceding minimum standards are met, the net present value method and present value indexes are used to rank the remaining proposals.

Instructions

1. Compute the cash payback period for each of the six proposals.
2. Giving effect to straight-line depreciation on the investments and assuming no estimated residual value, compute the average rate of return for each of the six proposals.
3. Using the following format, summarize the results of your computations in (1) and (2). By placing a check mark in the appropriate column at the right, indicate which proposals should be accepted for further analysis and which should be rejected.

Proposal	*Cash Payback Period*	*Average Rate of Return*	*Accept for Further Analysis*	*Reject*
A				
B				
C				
D				
E				
F				

4. For the proposals accepted for further analysis in (3), compute the net present value. Use a rate of 10% and the present value of $1 table appearing in this chapter.
5. Compute the present value index for each of the proposals in (4).
6. Rank the proposals from most attractive to least attractive, based on the present values of net cash flows computed in (4).
7. Rank the proposals from most attractive to least attractive, based on the present value indexes computed in (5).
8. Based upon the analyses, comment on the relative attractiveness of the proposals ranked in (6) and (7).

CASES

CASE 26–1
J. H. Binder Company
Net present value analysis

Roland Dale was recently hired as a cost analyst by J. H. Binder Company. One of Roland's first assignments was to perform a net present value analysis for a new warehouse. Roland performed the analysis and calculated a present value index of .75. The plant manager, I. M. Madd, is very intent on purchasing the warehouse because he believes that more storage space is needed. I. M. Madd asks Roland into his office and the following conversation takes place.

I. M.: Dale, you're new here, aren't you?

Roland: Yes, sir.

I. M.: Well, Dale, let me tell you something. I'm not at all pleased with the capital investment analysis that you performed on this new warehouse. I need that warehouse for my production. If I don't get it, where am I going to place our output?

Roland: Hopefully with the customer, sir.

I. M.: Now don't get smart with me, young man.

Roland: No, really, I was being serious. My analysis does not support constructing a new warehouse. There is no way that I can get the numbers to make this a favorable investment. In fact, it seems to me that purchasing a warehouse does not add much value to the business. We need to be producing product to customer orders, not to inventory.

I. M.: Listen, you need to understand something. The headquarters people will not allow me to build the warehouse if the numbers don't add up. I know as well as you that many assumptions go into your net present value analysis. Why don't you relax some of your assumptions so that the financial savings will offset the cost?

Roland: I'm willing to discuss my assumptions with you. Maybe I overlooked something.

I. M.: Good. Here's what I want you to do. I see in your analysis that you don't project greater sales as a result of the warehouse. It seems to me, if we can store more goods, then we will have more to sell. Thus, logically, a larger warehouse translates into more sales. If you incorporate this into your analysis, I think you'll see that the numbers will work out. Why don't you work it through and come back with a new analysis. I'm really counting on you on this one. Let's get off to a good start together and see if we can get this project accepted.

What is your advice to Roland?

CASE 26–2
Federal Mogul
Qualitative considerations

Some companies have attempted to respond to competitive pressure by relying solely on automation. For example, Federal Mogul, a parts supplier to the automotive industry, invested in robots, production line computers, and automated materials movement systems in order to regain a cost advantage that it lost to the Japanese. Unfortunately, this automation not only failed to lower costs, but caused the plant to become much less flexible than required by its customers. The high technology could not be "changed over" quickly from one product to another. In addition, Federal Mogul found that the new automation reduced employee motivation. As indicated by one of the managers, "Very clearly, we made some poor decisions. One of them was that high-tech was the answer."

Why might relying solely on automation lead to lower profits?

CASE 26–3
Yum Yum Candy Company
Investment analysis and qualitative considerations

The plant manager of Yum Yum Candy Company is considering the purchase of a new robotic assembly plant. The new robotic line will cost $1,000,000. The manager believes that the new investment will result in direct labor savings of $250,000 per year for ten years.

1. What is the payback period on this project?
2. What is the net present value, assuming a 10% rate of return?
3. Has the manager omitted anything in the analysis?

CASE 26–4
Worthington Industries, Amgen, and Merck & Co.
Qualitative issues in investment analysis

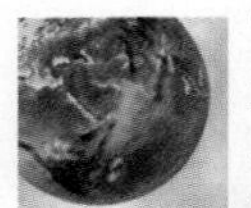

The following are some selected quotes from senior executives:

John H. McConnel, CEO, Worthington Industries (a high technology steel company): "We try to find the best technology, stay ahead of the competition, and serve the customer. . . . We'll make any investment that will pay back quickly . . . but if it is something that we really see as a must down the road, payback is not going to be that important."

George Rathmann, Chairman Emeritus of Amgen (a biotech company): "You cannot really run the numbers, do net present value calculations, because the uncertainties are really gigantic . . . You decide on a project you want to run, and then you run the numbers [as a reality check on your assumptions]. Success in a business like this is much more dependent on tracking rather than on predicting, much more dependent on seeing results over time, tracking and adjusting and readjusting, much more dynamic, much more flexible."

Judy Lewent, Chief Financial Officer of Merck & Co. (a pharmaceutical company): ". . . at the individual product level—the development of a successful new product requires on the order of $230 million in R&D, spread over more than a decade—discounted cash flow style analysis does not become a factor until development is near the point of manufacturing scale-up effort. Prior to that point, given the uncertainties associated with new product development, it would be lunacy in our business to decide that we know exactly what's going to happen to a product once it gets out."

Explain the role of capital investment analysis for these companies.

(Joseph Morone and Albert Paulson, "Cost of Capital: The Managerial Perspective," *California Management Review,* Summer 1991, pp. 9–32).

CASE 26–5
Stabler Industries Inc.
Analyzing cash flows

You are considering an investment of $360,000 in either Project K or Project L. In discussing the two projects with an advisor, you decided that, for the risk involved, a return of 12% on the cash investment would be required. For this purpose, you estimated the following economic factors for the projects:

	Project K	*Project L*
Useful life	4 years	4 years
Residual value	-0-	-0-
Net income:		
Year 1	$ 65,000	$ 25,000
2	50,000	40,000
3	40,000	58,000
4	25,000	64,200
Net cash flows:		
Year 1	$155,000	$115,000
2	140,000	130,000
3	130,000	148,000
4	115,000	154,200

Although the average rate of return exceeded 12% on both projects, you have tentatively decided to invest in Project L because the rate was higher for Project L. You noted that the total net cash flow from Project L is $547,200, which exceeds that of Project K by $7,200.

1. Determine the average rate of return for both projects.
2. How would you justify the importance of net cash flows in the analysis of investment projects? Include a specific example to demonstrate the importance of net cash flows and their timing to these two projects.

ANSWERS TO SELF-EXAMINATION QUESTIONS

1. **C** Methods of evaluating capital investment proposals that ignore the time value of money are categorized as methods that ignore present value. This category includes the average rate of return method (answer A) and the cash payback method (answer B).
2. **B** The average rate of return is 24% (answer B), determined by dividing the expected average annual earnings by the average investment, as follows:

$$\frac{\$60{,}000 \div 5}{(\$100{,}000 + \$0) \div 2} = 24\%$$

3. **B** Of the four methods of analyzing proposals for capital investments, the cash payback period (answer B) refers to the expected period of time required to recover the amount of cash to be invested. The average rate of return (answer A) is a measure of the anticipated profitability of a proposal. The net present value method (answer C) reduces the expected future net cash flows originating from a proposal to their present values. The internal rate of return method (answer D) uses present value concepts to compute the rate of return from the net cash flows expected from the investment.
4. **C** The net present value method (answer C) uses the concept of present value to determine the total present value of the cash flows expected from a proposal and compares this value with the amount to be invested. The average rate of return method (answer A) and the cash payback method (answer B) ignore present value. The internal rate of return method (answer D) uses present value concepts to determine the internal rate of return expected from the proposal.
5. **A** Capital rationing (answer A) is the process by which management allocates available investment funds among competing capital investment proposals. The present value index (answer B) is a tool that may aid in ranking alternative proposals as part of the capital rationing process. Leasing (answer C) is an alternative that management should consider before making a final decision on acquiring assets. Uncertainty (answer D) complicates capital investment analysis because of the need to rely upon estimates in evaluating alternative proposals.

APPENDICES

A. *Interest Tables*

B. *Codes of Ethics*

C. *Alternate Methods of Recording Deferrals*

D. *Periodic Inventory Systems for Merchandising Businesses*

E. *Periodic Inventory Systems for Manufacturing Businesses*

F. *Annual Reports and Financial Statement Analysis*

Appendix A Interest Tables

Present Value of $1 at Compound Interest Due in n Periods: $p_{\overline{n}|i} = \frac{1}{(1+i)^n}$

n \ i	5%	5.5%	6%	6.5%	7%	8%
1	0.952381	0.94787	0.943396	0.93897	0.934580	0.925926
2	0.907029	0.89845	0.889996	0.88166	0.873439	0.857339
3	0.863838	0.85161	0.839619	0.82785	0.816298	0.793832
4	0.822702	0.80722	0.792094	0.77732	0.762895	0.735030
5	0.783526	0.76513	0.747258	0.72988	0.712986	0.680583
6	0.746215	0.72525	0.704961	0.68533	0.666342	0.630170
7	0.710681	0.68744	0.665057	0.64351	0.622750	0.583490
8	0.676839	0.65160	0.627412	0.60423	0.582009	0.540269
9	0.644609	0.61763	0.591898	0.56735	0.543934	0.500249
10	0.613913	0.58543	0.558395	0.53273	0.508349	0.463193
11	0.584679	0.55491	0.526788	0.50021	0.475093	0.428883
12	0.556837	0.52598	0.496969	0.46968	0.444012	0.397114
13	0.530321	0.49856	0.468839	0.44102	0.414964	0.367698
14	0.505068	0.47257	0.442301	0.41410	0.387817	0.340461
15	0.481017	0.44793	0.417265	0.38883	0.362446	0.315242
16	0.458112	0.42458	0.393646	0.36510	0.338735	0.291890
17	0.436297	0.40245	0.371364	0.34281	0.316574	0.270269
18	0.415521	0.38147	0.350344	0.32189	0.295864	0.250249
19	0.395734	0.36158	0.330513	0.30224	0.276508	0.231712
20	0.376889	0.34273	0.311805	0.28380	0.258419	0.214548
21	0.358942	0.32486	0.294155	0.26648	0.241513	0.198656
22	0.341850	0.30793	0.277505	0.25021	0.225713	0.183941
23	0.325571	0.29187	0.261797	0.23494	0.210947	0.170315
24	0.310068	0.27666	0.246979	0.22060	0.197147	0.157699
25	0.295303	0.26223	0.232999	0.20714	0.184249	0.146018
26	0.281241	0.24856	0.219810	0.19450	0.172195	0.135202
27	0.267848	0.23560	0.207368	0.18263	0.160930	0.125187
28	0.255094	0.22332	0.195630	0.17148	0.150402	0.115914
29	0.242946	0.21168	0.184557	0.16101	0.140563	0.107328
30	0.231377	0.20064	0.174110	0.15119	0.131367	0.099377
31	0.220359	0.19018	0.164255	0.14196	0.122773	0.092016
32	0.209866	0.18027	0.154957	0.13329	0.114741	0.085200
33	0.199873	0.17087	0.146186	0.12516	0.107235	0.078889
34	0.190355	0.16196	0.137912	0.11752	0.100219	0.073045
35	0.181290	0.15352	0.130105	0.11035	0.093663	0.067635
40	0.142046	0.11746	0.097222	0.08054	0.066780	0.046031
45	0.111297	0.08988	0.072650	0.05879	0.047613	0.031328
50	0.087204	0.06877	0.054288	0.04291	0.033948	0.021321

Present Value of \$1 at Compound Interest Due in n Periods: $p_{\overline{n}|i} = \dfrac{1}{(1+i)^n}$

$n \diagdown i$	9%	10%	11%	12%	13%	14%
1	0.917431	0.909091	0.90090	0.892857	0.88496	0.87719
2	0.841680	0.826446	0.81162	0.797194	0.78315	0.76947
3	0.772183	0.751315	0.73119	0.711780	0.69305	0.67497
4	0.708425	0.683013	0.65873	0.635518	0.61332	0.59208
5	0.649931	0.620921	0.59345	0.567427	0.54276	0.51937
6	0.596267	0.564474	0.53464	0.506631	0.48032	0.45559
7	0.547034	0.513158	0.48166	0.452349	0.42506	0.39964
8	0.501866	0.466507	0.43393	0.403883	0.37616	0.35056
9	0.460428	0.424098	0.39092	0.360610	0.33288	0.30751
10	0.422411	0.385543	0.35218	0.321973	0.29459	0.26974
11	0.387533	0.350494	0.31728	0.287476	0.26070	0.23662
12	0.355535	0.318631	0.28584	0.256675	0.23071	0.20756
13	0.326179	0.289664	0.25751	0.229174	0.20416	0.18207
14	0.299246	0.263331	0.23199	0.204620	0.18068	0.15971
15	0.274538	0.239392	0.20900	0.182696	0.15989	0.14010
16	0.251870	0.217629	0.18829	0.163122	0.14150	0.12289
17	0.231073	0.197845	0.16963	0.145644	0.12522	0.10780
18	0.211994	0.179859	0.15282	0.130040	0.11081	0.09456
19	0.194490	0.163508	0.13768	0.116107	0.09806	0.08295
20	0.178431	0.148644	0.12403	0.103667	0.08678	0.07276
21	0.163698	0.135131	0.11174	0.092560	0.07680	0.06383
22	0.150182	0.122846	0.10067	0.082643	0.06796	0.05599
23	0.137781	0.111678	0.09069	0.073788	0.06014	0.04911
24	0.126405	0.101526	0.08170	0.065882	0.05323	0.04308
25	0.115968	0.092296	0.07361	0.058823	0.04710	0.03779
26	0.106393	0.083905	0.06631	0.052521	0.04168	0.03315
27	0.097608	0.076278	0.05974	0.046894	0.03689	0.02908
28	0.089548	0.069343	0.05382	0.041869	0.03264	0.02551
29	0.082155	0.063039	0.04849	0.037383	0.02889	0.02237
30	0.075371	0.057309	0.04368	0.033378	0.02557	0.01963
31	0.069148	0.052099	0.03935	0.029802	0.02262	0.01722
32	0.063438	0.047362	0.03545	0.026609	0.02002	0.01510
33	0.058200	0.043057	0.03194	0.023758	0.01772	0.01325
34	0.053395	0.039143	0.02878	0.021212	0.01568	0.01162
35	0.048986	0.035584	0.02592	0.018940	0.01388	0.01019
40	0.031838	0.022095	0.01538	0.010747	0.00753	0.00529
45	0.020692	0.013719	0.00913	0.006098	0.00409	0.00275
50	0.013449	0.008519	0.00542	0.003460	0.00222	0.00143

Present Value of Ordinary Annuity of $1 per Period: $P_{\overline{n}|i} = \dfrac{1 - \dfrac{1}{(1+i)^n}}{i}$

n \ i	5%	5.5%	6%	6.5%	7%	8%
1	0.952381	0.94787	0.943396	0.93897	0.934579	0.925926
2	1.859410	1.84632	1.833393	1.82063	1.808018	1.783265
3	2.723248	2.69793	2.673012	2.64848	2.624316	2.577097
4	3.545951	3.50515	3.465106	3.42580	3.387211	3.312127
5	4.329477	4.27028	4.212364	4.15568	4.100197	3.992710
6	5.075692	4.99553	4.917324	4.84101	4.766540	4.622880
7	5.786373	5.68297	5.582381	5.48452	5.389289	5.206370
8	6.463213	6.33457	6.209794	6.08875	5.971299	5.746639
9	7.107822	6.95220	6.801692	6.65610	6.515232	6.246888
10	7.721735	7.53763	7.360087	7.18883	7.023582	6.710081
11	8.306414	8.09254	7.886875	7.68904	7.498674	7.138964
12	8.863252	8.61852	8.383844	8.15873	7.942686	7.536078
13	9.393573	9.11708	8.852683	8.59974	8.357651	7.903776
14	9.898641	9.58965	9.294984	9.01384	8.745468	8.224237
15	10.379658	10.03758	9.712249	9.40267	9.107914	8.559479
16	10.837770	10.46216	10.105895	9.76776	9.446649	8.851369
17	11.274066	10.86461	10.477260	10.11058	9.763223	9.121638
18	11.689587	11.24607	10.827603	10.43247	10.059087	9.371887
19	12.085321	11.60765	11.158116	10.73471	10.335595	9.603599
20	12.462210	11.95038	11.469921	11.01851	10.594014	9.818147
21	12.821153	12.27524	11.764077	11.28498	10.835527	10.016803
22	13.163003	12.58317	12.041582	11.53520	11.061241	10.200744
23	13.488574	12.87504	12.303379	11.77014	11.272187	10.371059
24	13.798642	13.15170	12.550358	11.99074	11.469334	10.528758
25	14 093945	13.41393	12.783356	12.19788	11.653583	10.674776
26	14.375185	13.66250	13.003166	12.39237	11.825779	10.809978
27	14.643034	13.89810	13.210534	12.57500	11.986709	10.935165
28	14.898127	14.12142	13.406164	12.74648	12.137111	11.051078
29	15.141074	14.33310	13.590721	12.90749	12.277674	11.158406
30	15.372451	14.53375	13.764831	13.05868	12.409041	11.257783
31	15.592811	14.72393	13.929086	13.20063	12.531814	11.349799
32	15.802677	14.90420	14.084043	13.33393	12.646555	11.434999
33	16.002549	15.07507	14.230230	13.45909	12.753790	11.513888
34	16.192904	15.23703	14.368141	13.57661	12.854009	11.586934
35	16.374194	15.39055	14.498246	13.68696	12.947672	11.654568
40	17.159086	16.04612	15.046297	14.14553	13.331709	11.924613
45	17.774070	16.54773	15.455832	14.48023	13.605522	12.108402
50	18.255925	16.93152	15.761861	14.72452	13.800746	12.233485

Present Value of Ordinary Annuity of $1 per Period: $P_{\overline{n}|i} = \dfrac{1 - \dfrac{1}{(1+i)^n}}{i}$

n \ i	9%	10%	11%	12%	13%	14%
1	0.917431	0.909091	0.90090	0.892857	0.88496	0.87719
2	1.759111	1.735537	1.71252	1.690051	1.66810	1.64666
3	2.531295	2.486852	2.44371	2.401831	2.36115	2.32163
4	3.239720	3.169865	3.10245	3.037349	2.97447	2.91371
5	3.889651	3.790787	3.69590	3.604776	3.51723	3.43308
6	4.485919	4.355261	4.23054	4.111407	3.99755	3.88867
7	5.032953	4.868419	4.71220	4.563757	4.42261	4.28830
8	5.534819	5.334926	5.14612	4.967640	4.79677	4.63886
9	5.995247	5.759024	5.53705	5.328250	5.13166	4.94637
10	6.417658	6.144567	5.88923	5.650223	5.42624	5.21612
11	6.805191	6.495061	6.20652	5.937699	5.68694	5.45273
12	7.160725	6.813692	6.49236	6.194374	5.91765	5.66029
13	7.486904	7.103356	6.74987	6.423548	6.12181	5.84236
14	7.786150	7.366687	6.96187	6.628168	6.30249	6.00207
15	8.060688	7.606080	7.19087	6.810864	6.46238	6.14217
16	8.312558	7.823709	7.37916	6.973986	6.60388	6.26506
17	8.543631	8.021553	7.54879	7.119630	6.72909	6.37286
18	8.755625	8.201412	7.70162	7.249670	6.83991	6.46742
19	8.950115	8.364920	7.83929	7.365777	6.93797	6.55037
20	9.128546	8.513564	7.96333	7.469444	7.02475	6.62313
21	9.292244	8.648694	8.07507	7.562003	7.10155	6.68696
22	9.442425	8.771540	8.17574	7.644646	7.16951	6.74294
23	9.580207	8.883218	8.26643	7.718434	7.22966	6.79206
24	9.706612	8.984744	8.34814	7.784316	7.28288	6.83514
25	9.822580	9.077040	8.42174	7.843139	7.32998	6.87293
26	9.928972	9.160945	8.48806	7.895660	7.37167	6.90608
27	10.026580	9.237223	8.54780	7.942554	7.40856	6.93515
28	10.116128	9.306567	8.60162	7.984423	7.44120	6.96066
29	10.198283	9.369606	8.65011	8.021806	7.47009	6.98304
30	10.273654	9.426914	8.69379	8.055184	7.49565	7.00266
31	10.342802	9.479013	8.73315	8.084986	7.51828	7.01988
32	10.406240	9.526376	8.76860	8.111594	7.53830	7.03498
33	10.464441	9.569432	8.80054	8.135352	7.55602	7.04823
34	10.517835	9.608575	8.82932	8.156564	7.57170	7.05985
35	10.566821	9.644159	8.85524	8.175504	7.58557	7.07005
40	10.757360	9.779051	8.95105	8.243777	7.63438	7.10504
45	10.881197	9.862808	9.00791	8.282516	7.66086	7.12322
50	10.961683	9.914814	9.04165	8.304498	7.67524	7.13266

Future Amount of $1 at Compound Interest Due in n Periods: $a_{\overline{n}|i} = (1 + i)^n$

$n \backslash i$	5%	5.5%	6%	6.5%	7%	8%
1	1.050000	1.05500	1.060000	1.06500	1.070000	1.080000
2	1.102500	1.11303	1.123600	1.13423	1.144900	1.166400
3	1.157625	1.17424	1.191016	1.20795	1.225043	1.259712
4	1.215506	1.23882	1.262477	1.28647	1.310796	1.360489
5	1.276282	1.30696	1.338226	1.37009	1.402552	1.469328
6	1.340096	1.37884	1.418519	1.45914	1.500730	1.586874
7	1.407100	1.45468	1.503630	1.55399	1.605781	1.713824
8	1.543469	1.53469	1.593848	1.65500	1.718186	1.850930
9	1.551328	1.61909	1.689479	1.76257	1.838459	1.999005
10	1.628895	1.70814	1.790848	1.87714	1.967151	2.158925
11	1.710339	1.80209	1.898299	1.99915	2.104852	2.331639
12	1.795856	1.90121	2.012196	2.12910	2.252192	2.518170
13	1.885649	2.00577	2.132928	2.26749	2.409845	2.719624
14	1.979932	2.11609	2.260904	2.41487	2.578534	2.937194
15	2.078928	2.23248	2.396558	2.57184	2.759032	3.172169
16	2.182875	2.35526	2.540352	2.73901	2.952164	3.425943
17	2.292018	2.48480	2.692773	2.91705	3.158815	3.700018
18	2.406619	2.62147	2.854339	3.10665	3.379932	3.996019
19	2.526950	2.76565	3.025600	3.30859	3.616528	4.315701
20	2.653298	2.91776	3.207135	3.52365	3.869684	4.660957
21	2.785963	3.07823	3.399564	3.75268	4.140562	5.033834
22	2.925261	3.24754	3.603537	3.99661	4.430402	5.436540
23	3.071524	3.42615	3.819750	4.25639	4.740530	5.871464
24	3.225100	3.61459	4.048935	4.53305	5.072367	6.341181
25	3.386355	3.81339	4.291871	4.82770	5.427433	6.848475
26	3.555673	4.02313	4.549383	5.14150	5.807353	7.396353
27	3.733456	4.24440	4.822346	5.47570	6.213868	7.988061
28	3.920129	4.47784	5.111687	5.83162	6.648838	8.627106
29	4.116136	4.72412	5.418388	6.21067	7.114257	9.317275
30	4.321942	4.98395	5.743491	6.61437	7.612255	10.062657
31	4.538039	5.25807	6.088101	7.04430	8.145113	10.867669
32	4.764941	5.54726	6.453387	7.50218	8.715271	11.737083
33	5.003189	5.85236	6.840590	7.98982	9.325340	12.676050
34	5.253348	6.17424	7.251025	8.50916	9.978114	13.690134
35	5.516015	6.51383	7.686087	9.06225	10.676581	14.785344
40	7.039989	8.51331	10.285718	12.41607	14.974458	21.724521
45	8.985008	11.12655	13.764611	17.01110	21.002452	31.920449
50	11.467400	14.54196	18.420154	23.30668	29.457025	46.901613

Future Amount of \$1 at Compound Interest Due in n Periods: $a_{\overline{n}|i} = (1 + i)^n$

$n \backslash i$	9%	10%	11%	12%	13%	14%
1	1.090000	1.100000	1.11000	1.120000	1.13000	1.14000
2	1.188100	1.210000	1.23210	1.254400	1.27690	1.29960
3	1.295029	1.331000	1.36763	1.404926	1.44290	1.48154
4	1.411582	1.464100	1.51807	1.573519	1.63047	1.68896
5	1.538624	1.610510	1.68506	1.762342	1.84244	1.92541
6	1.677100	1.771561	1.87041	1.973823	2.08195	2.19497
7	1.828039	1.948717	2.07616	2.210681	2.35261	2.50227
8	1.992563	2.143589	2.30454	2.475963	2.65844	2.85259
9	2.171893	2.357948	2.55804	2.773079	3.00404	3.25195
10	2.367364	2.593742	2.83942	3.105848	3.39457	3.70722
11	2.580426	2.853117	3.15176	3.478550	3.83586	4.22623
12	2.812665	3.138428	3.49845	3.895976	4.33452	4.81790
13	3.065805	3.452271	3.88328	4.363493	4.89801	5.49241
14	3.341727	3.797498	4.31044	4.887112	5.53475	6.26135
15	3.642482	4.177248	4.78459	5.473566	6.25427	7.13794
16	3.970306	4.594973	5.31089	6.130394	7.06733	8.13725
17	4.327633	5.054470	5.89509	6.866041	7.98608	9.27646
18	4.717120	5.559917	6.54355	7.689966	9.02427	10.57517
19	5.141661	6.115909	7.26334	8.612762	10.19742	12.05569
20	5.604411	6.727500	8.06231	9.646293	11.52309	13.74349
21	6.108808	7.400250	8.94917	10.803848	13.02109	15.66758
22	6.658600	8.140275	9.93357	12.100310	14.71383	17.86104
23	7.257874	8.954302	11.02627	13.552347	16.62663	20.36158
24	7.911083	9.849733	12.23916	15.178629	18.78809	23.21221
25	8.623081	10.834706	13.58546	17.000064	21.23054	26.46192
26	9.399158	11.918177	15.07986	19.040072	23.99051	30.16658
27	10.245082	13.109994	16.73865	21.324881	27.10928	34.38991
28	11.167140	14.420994	18.57990	23.883866	30.63349	39.20449
29	12.172182	15.863093	20.62369	26.749930	34.61584	44.69312
30	13.267678	17.449402	22.89230	29.959922	39.11590	50.95016
31	14.461770	19.194342	25.41045	33.555113	44.20096	58.08318
32	15.763329	21.113777	28.20560	37.581726	49.94709	66.21483
33	17.182028	23.225154	31.30821	42.091533	56.44021	75.48490
34	18.728411	25.547670	34.75212	47.142517	63.77744	86.05279
35	20.413968	28.102437	38.57485	52.799620	72.06851	98.10018
40	31.409420	45.259256	65.00087	93.050970	132.78155	188.88351
45	48.327286	72.890484	109.53024	163.987604	244.64140	363.67907
50	74.357520	117.390853	184.56483	289.002190	450.73593	700.23299

Future Amount of Ordinary Annuity of $1 per Period: $A_{\overline{n}|i} = \frac{(1+i)^n - 1}{i}$

$n \backslash i$	5%	5.5%	6%	6.5%	7%	8%
1	1.000000	1.00000	1.000000	1.00000	1.000000	1.000000
2	2.050000	2.05500	2.060000	2.06500	2.070000	2.080000
3	3.152500	3.16802	3.183600	3.19922	3.214900	3.246400
4	4.310125	4.34227	4.374616	4.40717	4.439943	4.506112
5	5.525631	5.58109	5.637093	5.69364	5.750740	5.866601
6	6.801913	6.88805	6.975319	7.06373	7.153291	7.335929
7	8.142008	8.26689	8.393838	8.52287	8.654021	8.922803
8	9.549109	9.72157	9.897468	10.07688	10.259803	10.636628
9	11.026564	11.25626	11.491316	11.73185	11.977989	12.487558
10	12.577893	12.87535	13.180795	13.49442	13.816448	14.486562
11	14.206787	14.58350	14.971843	15.37156	15.783599	16.645487
12	15.917127	16.38559	16.869941	17.37071	17.888451	18.977126
13	17.712983	18.28680	18.882138	19.49981	20.140643	21.495297
14	19.598632	20.29257	21.015066	21.76730	22.550488	24.214920
15	21.578564	22.40866	23.275970	24.18217	25.129022	27.152114
16	23.657492	24.64114	25.672528	26.75401	27.888054	30.324283
17	25.840366	28.99640	28.212880	29.49302	30.840217	33.750226
18	28.132385	29.48120	30.905653	32.41007	33.999033	37.450244
19	30.539004	32.10267	33.759992	35.51672	37.378965	41.446263
20	33.065954	34.86832	36.785591	38.82531	40.995492	45.761964
21	35.719252	37.78608	39.992727	42.34895	44.865177	50.422921
22	38.505214	40.86431	43.392290	46.10164	49.005739	55.456755
23	41.430475	44.11185	46.995828	50.09824	53.436141	60.893296
24	44.501999	47.53800	50.815577	54.35463	58.176671	66.764759
25	47.727099	51.15259	54.864512	58.88768	63.249038	73.105940
26	51.113454	54.96598	59.156383	63.71538	68.676470	79.954415
27	54.669126	58.98911	63.705766	68.85688	74.483823	87.350768
28	58.402583	63.23351	68.528112	74.33257	80.697691	95.338830
29	62.322712	67.71135	73.629798	80.16419	87.346529	103.965936
30	66.438848	72.43548	79.058186	86.37486	94.460786	113.283211
31	70.760790	77.41943	84.801677	92.98923	102.073041	123.345868
32	75.298829	82.67750	90.889778	100.03353	110.218154	134.213537
33	80.063771	88.22476	97.343165	107.53571	118.933425	145.950620
34	85.066959	94.07712	104.183755	115.52553	128.258765	158.626670
35	90.320307	100.25136	111.434780	124.03469	138.236878	172.316804
40	120.799774	136.60561	154.761966	175.63192	199.635112	259.056519
45	159.700156	184.11917	212.743514	246.32459	285.749311	386.505617
50	209.347996	246.21748	290.335905	343.17967	406.528929	573.770156

Future Amount of Ordinary Annuity of $1 per Period: $A_{\overline{n}|i} = \frac{(1+i)^n - 1}{i}$

n \ i	9%	10%	11%	12%	13%	14%
1	1.000000	1.000000	1.00000	1.000000	1.00000	1.00000
2	2.090000	2.100000	2.11000	2.120000	2.13000	2.14000
3	3.278100	3.310000	3.34210	3.374400	3.40690	3.43960
4	4.573129	4.641000	4.70973	4.779328	4.84980	4.92114
5	5.984711	6.105100	6.22780	6.352847	6.48027	6.61010
6	7.523335	7.715610	7.91286	8.115189	8.32271	8.53552
7	9.200435	9.487171	9.78327	10.089012	10.40466	10.73049
8	11.028474	11.435888	11.85943	12.299693	12.75726	13.23276
9	13.021036	13.579477	14.16397	14.775656	15.41571	16.08535
10	15.192930	15.937425	16.72201	17.548735	18.41975	19.33730
11	17.560293	18.531167	19.56143	20.654583	21.81432	23.04452
12	20.140720	21.384284	22.71319	24.133133	25.65018	27.27075
13	22.953385	24.522712	26.21164	28.029109	29.98470	32.08865
14	26.019189	27.974983	30.09492	32.392602	34.88271	37.58107
15	29.360916	31.772482	34.40536	37.279715	40.41746	43.84241
16	33.003399	35.949730	39.18995	42.753280	46.67173	50.98035
17	36.973705	40.544703	44.50084	48.883674	53.73906	59.11760
18	41.301338	45.599173	50.39594	55.749715	61.72514	68.39407
19	46.018458	51.159090	56.93949	63.439681	70.74941	78.96923
20	51.160120	57.274999	64.20283	72.052442	80.94683	91.02493
21	56.764530	64.002499	72.26514	81.698736	92.46992	104.76842
22	62.873338	71.402749	81.21431	92.502584	105.49101	120.43600
23	69.531939	79.543024	91.14788	104.602894	120.20484	138.29704
24	76.789813	88.497327	102.17415	118.155241	136.83147	158.65862
25	84.700896	98.347059	114.41331	133.333870	155.61956	181.87083
26	93.323977	109.181765	127.99877	150.333934	176.85010	208.33274
27	102.723135	121.099942	143.07864	169.374007	200.84061	238.49933
28	112.968217	134.209936	159.81729	190.698887	227.94989	272.88923
29	124.135356	148.630930	178.39719	214.582754	258.58338	312.09373
30	136.307539	164.494023	199.02088	241.332684	293.19922	356.78685
31	149.575217	181.943425	221.91317	271.292606	332.31511	407.73701
32	164.036987	201.137767	247.32362	304.847719	376.51608	465.82019
33	179.800315	222.251544	275.52922	342.429446	426.46317	532.03501
34	196.982344	245.476699	306.83744	384.520979	482.90338	607.51991
35	215.710755	271.024368	341.58955	431.663496	546.68082	693.57270
40	337.882445	442.592556	581.82607	767.091420	1013.70424	1342.02510
45	525.858734	718.904837	986.63856	1358.230032	1874.16463	2590.56480
50	815.083556	1163.908529	1668.77115	2400.018249	3459.50712	4994.52135

Appendix B: Codes of Professional Ethics for Accountants

In recent years, governments, businesses, and the public have given increased attention to ethical conduct. They have insisted upon a level of human behavior that goes beyond that required by laws and regulations. Thus many businesses, as well as professional groups (such as accountants) and governmental organizations, have established standards of ethical conduct. This text emphasizes the ethical conduct of accountants, who serve various business interests as well as the public.

This appendix sets forth the standards of professional conduct expected of accountants in public accounting and private accounting. For accountants employed in public accounting, the American Institute of Certified Public Accountants' *Code of Professional Conduct* is presented.[1] For accountants employed in private accounting, the Institute of Management Accountants' *Standards of Ethical Conduct for Management Accountants* is presented as a guide to professional conduct.[2]

Supplementing the codes of professional ethics are ethics discussion cases that appear at the end of each chapter. These cases represent "real world" examples of ethical issues facing accountants. It should be noted that codes of professional ethics are general guides to good behavior and their application to specific situations often requires the exercise of professional judgment. In some cases, the line between right and wrong may be quite fine, and reasonable people may disagree. In addition, business is dynamic and everchanging, and what society considers to be acceptable behavior changes from time to time.

CODE OF PROFESSIONAL CONDUCT

Composition, Applicability, and Compliance

The Code of Professional Conduct of the American Institute of Certified Public Accountants consists of two sections—(1) the Principles and (2) the Rules. The Principles provide the framework for the Rules, which govern the performance of professional services by members. The Council of the American Institute of Certified Public Accountants is authorized to designate bodies to promulgate technical standards under the Rules, and the bylaws require adherence to those Rules and standards.

The Code of Professional Conduct was adopted by the membership to provide guidance and rules to all members—those in public practice, in industry, in government, and in education—in the performance of their professional responsibilities.

Compliance with the Code of Professional Conduct, as with all standards in an open society, depends primarily on members' understanding and voluntary actions, secondarily on reinforcement by peers and public opinion, and ultimately on disciplinary proceedings, when necessary, against members who fail to comply with the Rules.

Other Guidance

The Principles and Rules as set forth herein are further amplified by interpretations and rulings contained in *AICPA Professional Standards* (Volume 2).

Interpretations of Rules of Conduct consists of interpretations which have been adopted, after exposure to state societies, state boards, practice units and other in-

[1] *Code of Professional Conduct* (New York: American Institute of Certified Public Accountants, 1994), pp. 3–8.
[2] *Standards of Ethical Conduct for Management Accountants,* Institute of Management Accountants, Montvale, New Jersey, 1994, pp. 1–2.

terested parties, by the professional ethics division's executive committee to provide guidelines as to the scope and application of the Rules but are not intended to limit such scope or application. A member who departs from such guidelines shall have the burden of justifying such departure in any disciplinary hearing.

Ethics Rulings consist of formal rulings made by the professional ethics division's executive committee after exposure to state societies, state boards, practice units and other interested parties. These rulings summarize the application of Rules of Conduct and interpretations to a particular set of factual circumstances. Members who depart from such rulings in similar circumstances will be requested to justify such departures.

Publication of an interpretation or ethics ruling in the *Journal of Accountancy* constitutes notice to members. Hence, the effective date of the pronouncement is the last day of the month in which the pronouncement is published in the *Journal of Accountancy*. The professional ethics division will take into consideration the time that would have been reasonable for the member to comply with the pronouncement.

Members should also consult, if applicable, the ethical standards of their state CPA society, state board of accountancy, the Securities and Exchange Commission, and any other governmental agency which may regulate their client's business or use their reports to evaluate the client's compliance with applicable laws and related regulations.

SECTION I—PRINCIPLES

Preamble

Membership in the American Institute of Certified Public Accountants is voluntary. By accepting membership, a certified public accountant assumes an obligation of self-discipline above and beyond the requirements of laws and regulations.

These Principles of the Code of Professional Conduct of the American Institute of Certified Public Accountants express the profession's recognition of its responsibilities to the public, to clients, and to colleagues. They guide members in the performance of their professional responsibilities and express the basic tenets of ethical and professional conduct. The Principles call for an unswerving commitment to honorable behavior, even at the sacrifice of personal advantage.

Article I—Responsibilities

In carrying out their responsibilities as professionals, members should exercise sensitive professional and moral judgments in all their activities.

As professionals, certified public accountants perform an essential role in society. Consistent with that role, members of the American Institute of Certified Public Accountants have responsibilities to all those who use their professional services. Members also have a continuing responsibility to cooperate with each other to improve the art of accounting, maintain the public's confidence, and carry out the profession's special responsibilities for self-governance. The collective efforts of all members are required to maintain and enhance the traditions of the profession.

Article II—The Public Interest

Members should accept the obligation to act in a way that will serve the public interest, honor the public trust, and demonstrate commitment to professionalism.

A distinguishing mark of a profession is acceptance of its responsibility to the public. The accounting profession's public consists of clients, credit grantors, governments, employers, investors, the business and financial community, and others who rely on the objectivity and integrity of certified public accountants to maintain the orderly functioning of commerce. This reliance imposes a public interest responsibility on certified public accountants. The public interest is defined as the collective well-being of the community of people and institutions the profession serves.

In discharging their professional responsibilities, members may encounter conflicting pressures from among each of those groups. In resolving those conflicts, members should act with integrity, guided by the precept that when members fulfill their responsibility to the public, clients' and employers' interests are best served.

Those who rely on certified public accountants expect them to discharge their responsibilities with integrity, objectivity, due professional care, and a genuine interest in serving the public. They are expected to provide quality services, enter into fee arrangements, and offer a range of services—all in a manner that demonstrates a level of professionalism consistent with these Principles of the Code of Professional Conduct.

All who accept membership in the American Institute of Certified Public Accountants commit themselves to honor the public trust. In return for the faith that the public reposes in them, members should seek continually to demonstrate their dedication to professional excellence.

Article III—Integrity

To maintain and broaden public confidence, members should perform all professional responsibilities with the highest sense of integrity.

Integrity is an element of character fundamental to professional recognition. It is the quality from which the public trust derives and the benchmark against which a member must ultimately test all decisions.

Integrity requires a member to be, among other things, honest and candid within the constraints of client confidentiality. Service and the public trust should not be subordinated to personal gain and advantage. Integrity can accommodate the inadvertent error and the honest difference of opinion; it cannot accommodate deceit or subordination of principle.

Integrity is measured in terms of what is right and just. In the absence of specific rules, standards, or guidance, or in the face of conflicting opinions, a member should test decisions and deeds by asking: "Am I doing what a person of integrity would do? Have I retained my integrity?" Integrity requires a member to observe both the form and the spirit of technical and ethical standards; circumvention of those standards constitutes subordination of judgment.

Integrity also requires a member to observe the principles of objectivity and independence and of due care.

Article IV—Objectivity and Independence

A member should maintain objectivity and be free of conflicts of interest in discharging professional responsibilities. A member in public practice should be independent in fact and appearance when providing auditing and other attestation services.

Objectivity is a state of mind, a quality that lends value to a member's services. It is a distinguishing feature of the profession. The principle of objectivity imposes the obligation to be impartial, intellectually honest, and free of conflicts of interest. Independence precludes relationships that may appear to impair a member's objectivity in rendering attestation services.

Members often serve multiple interests in many different capacities and must demonstrate their objectivity in varying circumstances. Members in public practice render attest, tax, and management advisory services. Other members prepare financial statements in the employment of others, perform internal auditing services, and serve in financial and management capacities in industry, education, and government. They also educate and train those who aspire to admission into the profession. Regardless of service or capacity, members should protect the integrity of their work, maintain objectivity, and avoid any subordination of their judgment.

For a member in public practice, the maintenance of objectivity and independence requires a continuing assessment of client relationships and public responsibility. Such a member who provides auditing and other attestation services should be independent in fact and appearance. In providing all other services, a member should maintain objectivity and avoid conflicts of interest.

Although members not in public practice cannot maintain the appearance of independence, they nevertheless have the responsibility to maintain objectivity in rendering professional services. Members employed by others to prepare financial statements or to perform auditing, tax, or consulting services are charged with the same responsibility for objectivity as members in public practice and must be scrupulous in their application of generally accepted accounting principles and candid in all their dealings with members in public practice.

Activity V—Due Care

A member should observe the profession's technical and ethical standards, strive continually to improve competence and the quality of services, and discharge professional responsibility to the best of the member's ability.

The quest for excellence is the essence of due care. Due care requires a member to discharge professional responsibilities with competence and diligence. It imposes the obligation to perform professional services to the best of a member's ability with concern for the best interest of those for whom the services are performed and consistent with the profession's responsibility to the public.

Competence is derived from a synthesis of education and experience. It begins with a mastery of the common body of knowledge required for designation as a certified public accountant. The maintenance of competence requires a commitment to learning and professional improvement that must continue throughout a member's professional life. It is a member's individual responsibility. In all engagements and in all responsibilities, each member should undertake to achieve a level of competence that will assure that the quality of the member's services meets the high level of professionalism required by these Principles.

Competence represents the attainment and maintenance of a level of understanding and knowledge that enables a member to render services with facility and acumen. It also establishes the limitations of a member's capabilities by dictating that consultation or referral may be required when a professional engagement exceeds the personal competence of a member or a member's firm. Each member is responsible for assessing his or her own competence—of evaluating whether education, experience, and judgment are adequate for the responsibility to be assumed.

Members should be diligent in discharging responsibilities to clients, employers, and the public. Diligence imposes the responsibility to render services promptly and carefully, to be thorough, and to observe applicable technical and ethical standards.

Due care requires a member to plan and supervise adequately any professional activity for which he or she is responsible.

Article VI—Scope and Nature of Services

A member in public practice should observe the Principles of the Code of Professional Conduct in determining the scope and nature of services to be provided.

The public interest aspect of certified public accountants' services requires that such services be consistent with acceptable professional behavior for certified public accountants. Integrity requires that service and the public trust not be subordinated to personal gain and advantage. Objectivity and independence require that members be free from conflicts of interest in discharging professional responsibilities. Due care requires that services be provided with competence and diligence.

Each of these Principles should be considered by members in determining whether or not to provide specific services in individual circumstances. In some instances, they may represent an overall constraint on the nonaudit services that might be offered to a specific client. No hard-and-fast rules can be developed to help members reach these judgments, but they must be satisfied that they are meeting the spirit of the Principles in this regard.

In order to accomplish this, members should

- Practice in firms that have in place internal quality-control procedures to ensure that services are competently delivered and adequately supervised.
- Determine, in their individual judgments, whether the scope and nature of other services provided to an audit client would create a conflict of interest in the performance of the audit function for that client.
- Assess, in their individual judgments, whether an activity is consistent with their role as professionals (for example, Is such activity a reasonable extension or variation of existing services offered by the member or others in the profession?).

STANDARDS OF ETHICAL CONDUCT FOR MANAGEMENT ACCOUNTANTS

Management accountants have an obligation to the organizations they serve, their profession, the public, and themselves to maintain the highest standards of ethical conduct. In recognition of this obligation, the Institute of Management Accountants has promulgated the following standards of ethical conduct for management accountants. Adherence to these standards is integral to achieving the *Objectives of Management Accounting*.[3] Management accountants shall not commit acts contrary to these standards nor shall they condone the commission of such acts by others within their organizations.

Competence

Management accountants have a responsibility to:

- Maintain an appropriate level of professional competence by ongoing development of their knowledge and skills.
- Perform their professional duties in accordance with relevant laws, regulations, and technical standards.
- Prepare complete and clear reports and recommendations after appropriate analyses of relevant and reliable information.

Confidentiality

Management accountants have a responsibility to:

- Refrain from disclosing confidential information acquired in the course of their work except when authorized, unless legally obligated to do so.
- Inform subordinates as appropriate regarding the confidentiality of information acquired in the course of their work and monitor their activities to assure the maintenance of that confidentiality.
- Refrain from using or appearing to use confidential information acquired in the course of their work for unethical or illegal advantage either personally or through third parties.

[3] National Association of Accountants, *Statements on Management Accounting: Objectives of Management Accounting*, Statement No. 1B, New York, N.Y., June 17, 1982.

Integrity

Management accountants have a responsibility to:

- Avoid actual or apparent conflicts of interest and advise all appropriate parties of any potential conflict.
- Refrain from engaging in any activity that would prejudice their ability to carry out their duties ethically.
- Refuse any gift, favor, or hospitality that would influence or would appear to influence their actions.
- Refrain from either actively or passively subverting the attainment of the organization's legitimate and ethical objectives.
- Recognize and communicate professional limitations or other constraints that would preclude responsible judgment or successful performance of an activity.
- Communicate unfavorable as well as favorable information and professional judgments or opinions.
- Refrain from engaging in or supporting any activity that would discredit the profession.

Objectivity

Management accountants have a responsibility to:

- Communicate information fairly and objectively.
- Disclose fully all relevant information that could reasonably be expected to influence an intended user's understanding of the reports, comments, and recommendations presented.

Appendix C: Alternative Methods of Recording Deferrals

As discussed in Chapter 3, deferrals are created by recording a transaction in a way that delays or defers the recognition of an expense or a revenue. Deferrals may be either deferred expenses (prepaid expenses) or deferred revenues (unearned revenues).

In Chapter 2, deferred expenses (prepaid expenses) were debited to an *asset* account at the time of payment. As an alternative, deferred expenses may be debited to an *expense* account at the time of payment. In Chapter 2, deferred revenues (unearned revenues) were credited to a *liability* account at the time of receipt. As an alternative, deferred revenues may be credited to a *revenue* account at the time of receipt. This appendix describes and illustrates these alternative methods of recording deferred expenses and deferred revenues.

DEFERRED EXPENSES (PREPAID EXPENSES)

As a basis for illustrating the alternative methods of recording deferred expenses, the insurance premium paid by Computer King in Chapter 2 is used. The amounts related to this insurance are as follows:

Prepayment of insurance for 24 months, starting December 1	$2,400
Insurance premium expired during December	100
Unexpired insurance premium at the end of December	$2,300

Based on the above data, the entries to account for the deferred expense (prepaid insurance) recorded initially as an *asset* are shown in the journal and T accounts in Exhibit 1. The adjusting entry in Exhibit 1 was shown in Chapter 3. The entries to account for the prepaid insurance recorded initially as an *expense* are shown in the journal and T accounts in Exhibit 2.

Exhibit 1

Prepaid Expense Recorded Initially as Asset

Initial entry (to record initial payment):

Dec. 1	Prepaid Insurance	2,400	
	Cash		2,400

Adjusting entry (to transfer amount **used** to proper expense account):

Dec. 31	Insurance Expense	100	
	Prepaid Insurance		100

Closing entry (to close income statement accounts with debit balances):

Income Summary	XXXX	
Supplies Expense		XXXX
~~		
Insurance Expense		100

Prepaid Insurance

Dec. 1		2,400	Dec. 31	Adjusting	100

Insurance Expense

Dec. 31	Adjusting	100	Dec. 31	Closing	100

Exhibit 2

Prepaid Expense Recorded Initially as Expense

Initial entry (to record initial payment):

Dec. 1	Insurance Expense	2,400	
	Cash		2,400

Adjusting entry (to transfer amount **unused** to the proper asset account):

Dec. 31	Prepaid Insurance	2,300	
	Insurance Expense		2,300

Closing entry (to close income statement accounts with debit balances):

Income Summary	XXXX	
Supplies Expense		XXXX
~~		
Insurance Expense		100

Prepaid Insurance

Dec. 31	Adjusting	2,300			

Insurance Expense

Dec. 1		2,400	Dec. 31	Adjusting	2,300
			31	Closing	100

Either of the two methods of recording deferred expenses (prepaid expenses) may be used. As illustrated in Exhibits 1 and 2, both methods result in the same account balances after the adjusting entries have been recorded. Therefore, the amounts reported as expenses in the income statement and as assets on the balance sheet will not be affected by the method used. To avoid confusion, the method used by a business for each kind of prepaid expense should be followed consistently from year to year.

Some businesses record all deferred expenses using one method. Other businesses use one method to record the prepayment of some expenses and the other method for other expenses. Initial debits to the asset account are logical for prepayments of insurance, which are usually for periods of one to three years. On the other hand, rent on a building may be prepaid on the first of each month. The prepaid rent will expire by the end of the month. In this case, it is logical to record the payment of rent by initially debiting an expense account rather than an asset account.

DEFERRED REVENUES (UNEARNED REVENUES)

As a basis for illustrating the alternative methods of recording deferred revenues, the rent received by Computer King in Chapter 2 is used. Computer King rented land on December 1 to a local retailer for use as a parking lot for three months and received \$360 for the entire three months. On December 31, \$120 (1/3 × \$360) of the rent has been earned, and \$240 (2/3 × \$360) of the rent is still unearned.

Based on the above data, the entries to account for the deferred revenue (unearned rent) recorded initially as a liability are shown in the journal and ledger in Exhibit 3. The adjusting entry in Exhibit 3 was shown in Chapter 3. The entries to account for the unearned rent recorded initially as revenue are shown in the journal and ledger in Exhibit 4.

Exhibit 3

Unearned Revenue Recorded Initially as Liability

Initial entry (to record initial receipt):

Dec. 1	Cash	360	
	Unearned Rent		360

Adjusting entry (to transfer amount **earned** to proper **revenue** account):

Dec. 31	Unearned Rent	120	
	Rent Income		120

Closing entry (to close income statement accounts with credit balances):

Dec. 31	Fees Earned	XXXX	
	~		
	Rent Income	120	
	Income Summary		XXXX

Unearned Rent

Dec. 31	Adjusting	120	Dec. 1		360

Rent Income

Dec. 31	Closing	120	Dec. 31	Adjusting	120

Exhibit 4

Unearned Revenue Recorded Initially as Revenue

Initial entries (to record initial receipt):

Dec. 1	Cash	360	
	Rent Income		360

Adjusting entry (to transfer amount **unearned** to proper **liability** account):

Dec. 31	Rent Income	240	
	Unearned Rent		240

Closing entry (to close income statement accounts with credit balances):

Dec. 31	Fees Earned	XXXX	
	~		
	Rent Income	120	
	Income Summary		XXXX

Unearned Rent

			Dec. 31	Adjusting	240

Rent Income

Dec. 31	Adjusting	240	Dec. 1		360
Dec. 31	Closing	120			

As illustrated in Exhibits 3 and 4, both methods result in the same account balances after the adjusting entries have been recorded. Therefore, the amounts reported as revenues in the income statement and as liabilities on the balance sheet will not be affected by the method used. Either of the methods may be used for all revenues received in advance. Alternatively, the first method may be used for advance receipts of some kinds of revenue and the second method for other kinds. To avoid confusion, the method used by a business for each kind of unearned revenue should be followed consistently from year to year.

REVERSING ENTRIES FOR DEFERRALS

As discussed in the appendix at the end of Chapter 4, the use of reversing entries is optional. However, the use of reversing entries generally simplifies the analysis of transactions and reduces the likelihood of errors in the subsequent recording of transactions. Normally, reversing entries are prepared for deferrals in the following two cases:

1. When a deferred expense (prepaid expense) is initially recorded as an expense.
2. When a deferred revenue (unearned revenue) is initially recorded as a revenue.

The entry to reverse the adjustment to record the prepaid insurance in Exhibit 2 is as follows:

Jan.	1	Insurance Expense	2,300	
		Prepaid Insurance		2,300

The entry to reverse the adjustment to record the unearned rent in Exhibit 4 is as follows:

Jan.	1	Unearned Rent	240	
		Rent Income		240

EXERCISES

EXERCISE C–1
Adjusting entries for office supplies

The office supplies purchased during the year total $3,450, and the amount of office supplies on hand at the end of the year is $830.

a. Record the following transactions directly in T accounts for Office Supplies and Office Supplies Expense, using the system of initially recording supplies as an asset: (1) purchases for the period; (2) adjusting entry at the end of the period. Identify each entry by number.
b. Record the following transactions directly in T accounts for Office Supplies and Office Supplies Expense, using the system of initially recording supplies as an expense: (1) purchases for the period; (2) adjusting entry at the end of the period. Identify each entry by number.

EXERCISE C–2
Adjusting entries for prepaid insurance

During the first year of operations, insurance premiums of $7,300 were paid. At the end of the year, unexpired premiums totaled $2,750. Journalize the adjusting entry at the end of the year, assuming that (a) prepaid expenses were initially recorded as assets and (b) prepaid expenses were initially recorded as expenses.

EXERCISE C–3
Adjusting entries for advertising revenue

The advertising revenues received during the year total $160,000, and the unearned advertising revenue at the end of the year is $22,000.

a. Record the following transactions directly in T accounts for Unearned Advertising Revenue and Advertising Revenue, using the system of initially recording advertising fees as a liability: (1) revenues received during the period; (2) adjusting entry at the end of the period. Identify each entry by number.
b. Record the following transactions directly in T accounts for Unearned Advertising Revenue and Advertising Revenue, using the system of initially recording advertising fees as revenue: (1) revenues received during the period; (2) adjusting entry at the end of the period. Identify each entry by number.

EXERCISE C–4
Year-end entries for deferred revenues

In their first year of operation, Snyder Publishing Co. received $530,000 from advertising contracts and $875,000 from magazine subscriptions, crediting the two amounts to Unearned Advertising Revenue and Circulation Revenue, respectively. At the end of the year, the unearned advertising revenue amounts to $175,000, and the unearned circulation revenue amounts to $240,000. Journalize the adjusting entries that should be made at the end of the year.

Appendix D: Periodic Inventory Systems for Merchandising Businesses

In this text, we emphasize the perpetual inventory system of accounting for purchases and sales of merchandise. Not all merchandise businesses, however, use perpetual inventory systems. For example, some managers/owners of small merchandise businesses, such as locally owned hardware stores, may feel more comfortable using manually kept records. Because a manual perpetual inventory system is time-consuming and costly to maintain, the periodic inventory system is often used in these cases.

MERCHANDISE TRANSACTIONS IN A PERIODIC INVENTORY SYSTEM

In a periodic inventory system, the revenues from sales are recorded when sales are made in the same manner as in a perpetual inventory system. However, no attempt is made on the date of sale to record the cost of the merchandise sold. Instead, the merchandise inventory on hand at the end of the period is counted. This physical inventory is then used to determine (1) the cost of merchandise sold during the period and (2) the cost of merchandise on hand at the end of the period.

In a periodic inventory system, purchases of inventory are recorded in a purchases account rather than in a merchandise inventory account. No attempt is made to keep a detailed record of the amount of inventory on hand at any given time.

The purchases account is normally debited for the amount of the invoice before considering any purchases discounts. Purchases discounts are normally recorded in a separate purchases discounts account.[1] The balance of this account is reported as a deduction from the amount initially recorded in Purchases for the period. Thus, the purchases discounts account is viewed as a contra (or offsetting) account to Purchases.

Purchases returns and allowances are recorded in a similar manner as purchases discounts. A separate account is used to keep a record of the amount of purchases returns and allowances during a period. Purchases returns and allowances are reported as a deduction from the amount initially recorded as Purchases. Like Purchases Discounts, the purchases returns and allowances account is a contra (or offsetting) account to Purchases.

When merchandise is purchased FOB shipping point, the buyer is responsible for paying the freight charges. In a periodic inventory system, freight charges paid when purchasing merchandise FOB shipping point are debited to Transportation In, Freight In, or a similarly titled account.

To illustrate the recording of merchandise transactions in a periodic system, we will use the following selected transactions for Taylor Co. We will also explain how the transaction would have been recorded under a perpetual system.

June 5. Purchased $30,000 of merchandise on account from Owen Clothing, terms 2/10, n/30.

Purchases	30,000	
Accounts Payable		30,000

Under the perpetual inventory system, such purchases would be recorded in the merchandise inventory account at their net cost, $29,400.

June 8. Returned merchandise purchased on account from Owen Clothing on June 5, $500.

Accounts Payable	500	
Purchases Returns and Allowances		500

[1] Some businesses prefer to credit the purchases account. If this alternative is used, the balance of the purchases account will be a net amount—the total purchases less the total purchases discounts for the period.

Under the perpetual inventory system, returns would be recorded as a credit to the merchandise inventory account at their net cost of $490.

June 15. Paid Owen Clothing for purchase of June 5, less return of $500 and discount of $590 [($30,000 – $500) × 2%].

Accounts Payable	29,500	
Cash		28,910
Purchases Discounts		590

Under a perpetual inventory system, purchases are recorded at their net cost, and thus a purchases discount account is not used.

June 18. Sold merchandise on account to Jones Co., $12,500, 1/10, n/30. The cost of the merchandise sold was $9,000.

Accounts Receivable	12,500	
Sales		12,500

The entry to record the sale is the same under both systems. Under the perpetual inventory system, the cost of merchandise sold and the reduction in merchandise inventory would also be recorded on the date of sale.

June 21. Received merchandise returned on account from Jones Co., $4,000. The cost of the merchandise returned was $2,800.

Sales Returns and Allowances	4,000	
Accounts Receivable		4,000

The entry to record the sales return is the same under both systems. In addition, the cost of the merchandise returned would be debited to the merchandise inventory account and credited to the cost of merchandise sold account under the perpetual inventory system.

June 22. Purchased merchandise from Norcross Clothiers, $15,000, terms FOB shipping point, 2/15, n/30, with prepaid transportation charges of $750 added to the invoice.

Purchases	15,000	
Transportation In	750	
Accounts Payable		15,750

This entry is similar to the June 5 entry for the purchase of merchandise. Since the transportation terms were FOB shipping point, the prepaid freight charges of $750 must be added to the invoice cost of $15,000. Under the perpetual inventory system, the purchase is recorded in the merchandise inventory account at the net cost of $15,450 (invoice price less discount plus transportation).

June 28. Received $8,415 as payment on account from Jones Co., less return of June 21 and less discount of $85 [($12,500 – $4,000) × 1%].

Cash	8,415	
Sales Discounts	85	
Accounts Receivable		8,500

This entry is the same under the perpetual inventory system.

June 29. Received $19,600 from cash sales. The cost of the merchandise sold was $13,800.

Cash	19,600	
Sales		19,600

The entry to record the sale is the same under both systems. Under the perpetual inventory system, the cost of merchandise sold and the reduction in merchandise inventory would also be recorded on the date of sale.

COST OF MERCHANDISE SOLD

Under the periodic inventory system, the cost of merchandise sold during a period is reported in a separate section in the income statement. To illustrate, assume that on January 3, 1997, Computer King opened a merchandising outlet selling microcomputers and software. During 1997, Computer King purchased $340,000 of merchandise. The inventory on December 31, 1997, is $59,700. The cost of merchandise sold during 1997 is reported as follows:

Cost of merchandise sold:	
Purchases	$340,000
Less merchandise inventory, December 31, 1997	59,700
Cost of merchandise sold	$280,300

To continue the example, assume that during 1998 Computer King purchased additional merchandise of $521,980. Computer King also received credit for purchases returns and allowances of $9,100, took purchases discounts of $2,525, and paid transportation costs of $17,400. The purchases returns and allowances and the purchases discounts are deducted from the total purchases to yield the net purchases. The transportation costs are then added to the net purchases to yield the cost of merchandise purchased. These amounts are reported in the cost of merchandise sold section of the Computer King income statement for 1998 as follows:

Purchases		$521,980	
Less: Purchases returns and allowances	$9,100		
Purchases discounts	2,525	11,625	
Net purchases		$510,355	
Add transportation in		17,400	
Cost of merchandise purchased			$527,755

The ending inventory of Computer King on December 31, 1997, $59,700, becomes the beginning inventory for 1998. In the cost of merchandise sold section of the income statement for 1998, this beginning inventory is added to the cost of merchandise purchased to yield the merchandise available for sale. The ending inventory on December 31, 1998, $62,150, is then subtracted from the merchandise available for sale to yield the cost of merchandise sold. Exhibit 1 shows the cost of merchandise sold during 1998.

Exhibit 1
Cost of Merchandise Sold—Periodic Inventory System

Cost of merchandise sold:				
Merchandise inventory, January 1, 1998			$ 59,700	
Purchases		$521,980		
Less: Purchases returns and allowances	$9,100			
Purchases discounts	2,525	11,625		
Net purchases		$510,355		
Add transportation in		17,400		
Cost of merchandise purchased			527,755	
Merchandise available for sale			$587,455	
Less merchandise inventory, December 31, 1998			62,150	
Cost of merchandise sold				$525,305

The multiple-step income statement under the periodic inventory system is illustrated in Exhibit 2. The multiple-step income statement under a perpetual inventory system is similar, except that the cost of merchandise sold is reported as a single amount.

Exhibit 2
Multiple-Step Income Statement—Periodic Inventory System

Computer King
Income Statement
For the Year Ended December 31, 1998

Revenue from sales:				
Sales			$720,185	
Less: Sales returns and allowances		$ 6,140		
Sales discounts		5,790	11,930	
Net sales				$708,255
Cost of merchandise sold:				
Merchandise inventory January 1, 1998			$ 59,700	
Purchases		$521,980		
Less: Purchases returns and allowances	$9,100			
Purchases discounts	2,525	11,625		
Net purchases		$510,355		
Add transportation in		17,400		
Cost of merchandise purchased			527,755	
Merchandise available for sale			$587,455	
Less merchandise inventory, December 31, 1998			62,150	
Cost of merchandise sold				525,305
Gross profit				$182,950
Operating expenses:				
Selling expenses:				
Sales salaries expense		$ 60,030		
Advertising expense		10,860		
Depreciation expense—store equipment		3,100		
Miscellaneous selling expense		630		
Total selling expenses			$ 74,620	
Administrative expenses:				
Office salaries expense		$ 21,020		
Rent expense		8,100		
Depreciation expense—office equipment		2,490		
Insurance expense		1,910		
Office supplies expense		610		
Miscellaneous administrative expense		760		
Total administrative expenses			34,890	
Total operating expenses				109,510
Income from operations				$ 73,440
Other income:				
Interest income		$ 3,800		
Rent income		600		
Total other income			$ 4,400	
Other expense:				
Interest expense			2,440	1,960
Net income				$ 75,400

CHART OF ACCOUNTS FOR A PERIODIC INVENTORY SYSTEM

Exhibit 3 is the chart of accounts for Computer King when a periodic inventory system is used. The periodic inventory accounts related to merchandising transactions are shown in color.

Exhibit 3
Chart of Accounts—Periodic Inventory System

Balance Sheet Accounts		*Income Statement Accounts*	
	100 Assets		400 Revenues
110	Cash	410	Sales
111	Notes Receivable	411	Sales Returns and Allowances
112	Accounts Receivable	412	Sales Discounts
113	Interest Receivable		500 Costs and Expenses
115	Merchandise Inventory	510	Purchases
116	Office Supplies	511	Purchases Returns and Allowances
117	Prepaid Insurance	512	Purchases Discounts
120	Land	513	Transportation In
123	Store Equipment	520	Sales Salaries Expenses
124	Accumulated Depreciation—Store Equipment	521	Advertising Expense
125	Office Equipment	522	Depreciation Expense—Store Equipment
126	Accumulated Depreciation—Office Equipment	529	Miscellaneous Selling Expense
	200 Liabilities	530	Office Salaries Expense
210	Accounts Payable	531	Rent Expense
211	Salaries Payable	532	Depreciation Expense—Office Equipment
212	Unearned Rent	533	Insurance Expense
215	Notes Payable	534	Office Supplies Expense
	300 Owner's Equity	539	Misc. Administrative Expense
310	Pat King, Capital		600 Other Income
311	Pat King, Drawing	610	Rent Income
312	Income Summary	611	Interest Income
			700 Other Expense
		710	Interest Expense

END-OF-PERIOD PROCEDURES IN A PERIODIC INVENTORY SYSTEM

The end-of-period procedures are generally the same for the periodic and perpetual inventory systems. In the remainder of this appendix, we will discuss the differences in procedures for the two systems which affect the work sheet, the adjusting entries, and the closing entries. As the basis for illustrations, we will use the data for Computer King, presented in Chapter 6.

WORK SHEET

The differences in the work sheet for a merchandising business that uses the periodic inventory system are highlighted in the work sheet for Computer King in Exhibit 4. As we illustrated earlier, accounts for purchases, purchases returns and allowances, purchases discounts, and transportation in are used in a periodic inventory system.

Under the periodic inventory system, the merchandise inventory account, throughout the accounting period, shows the inventory at the beginning of the period. As shown in Exhibit 1, the merchandise inventory on January 1, 1998, $59,700, is a part of the merchandise available for sale. At the end of the period, the beginning inventory amount in the ledger is replaced with the ending inventory amount. To update the inventory account, two adjusting entries are used.[2] The first adjusting entry transfers the beginning inventory balance to Income Summary. This entry,

[2] Another method of updating the merchandise inventory account at the end of the period is called the *closing method*. This method adjusts the merchandise inventory through the use of closing entries. This method may not be appropriate for use in computerized accounting systems. Since the financial statements are the same under both methods and since computerized accounting systems are used by most businesses, the closing method is not illustrated.

Exhibit 4
Work Sheet—Periodic Inventory System

Computer King
Work Sheet
For the Year Ended December 31, 1998

	Trial Balance		Adjustments		Adjusted Trial Balance		Income Statement		Balance Sheet	
Account Title	**Dr.**	**Cr.**	**Dr.**	**Cr.**	**Dr.**	**Cr.**	**Dr.**	**Cr.**	**Dr.**	**Cr.**
Cash	52,950				52,950				52,950	
Notes Receivable	40,000				40,000				40,000	
Accounts Receivable	60,880				60,880				60,880	
Interest Receivable			(a) 200		200				200	
Merchandise Inventory	59,700		(c)62,150	(b)59,700	62,150				62,150	
Office Supplies	1,090			(d) 610	480				480	
Prepaid Insurance	4,560			(e) 1,910	2,650				2,650	
Land	10,000				10,000				10,000	
Store Equipment	27,100				27,100				27,100	
Accum. Depr.—Store Equipment		2,600		(f) 3,100		5,700				5,700
Office Equipment	15,570				15,570				15,570	
Accum. Depr.—Office Equipment		2,230		(g) 2,490		4,720				4,720
Accounts Payable		22,420				22,420				22,420
Salaries Payable				(h) 1,140		1,140				1,140
Unearned Rent		2,400	(i) 600			1,800				1,800
Notes Payable (final payment, 2000)		25,000				25,000				25,000
Pat King, Capital		153,800				153,800				153,800
Pat King, Drawing	18,000				18,000				18,000	
Income Summary			(b)59,700	(c)62,150	59,700	62,150	59,700	62,150		
Sales		720,185				720,185		720,185		
Sales Returns and Allowances	6,140				6,140		6,140			
Sales Discounts	5,790				5,790		5,790			
Purchases	521,980				521,980		521,980			
Purchases Returns & Allowances		9,100				9,100		9,100		
Purchases Discounts		2,525				2,525		2,525		
Transportation In	17,400				17,400		17,400			
Sales Salaries Expense	59,250		(h) 780		60,030		60,030			
Advertising Expense	10,860				10,860		10,860			
Depr. Expense—Store Equipment			(f) 3,100		3,100		3,100			
Miscellaneous Selling Expense	630				630		630			
Office Salaries Expense	20,660		(h) 360		21,020		21,020			
Rent Expense	8,100				8,100		8,100			
Depr. Expense—Office Equipment			(g) 2,490		2,490		2,490			
Insurance Expense			(e) 1,910		1,910		1,910			
Office Supplies Expense			(d) 610		610		610			
Misc. Administrative Expense	760				760		760			
Rent Income				(i) 600		600		600		
Interest Income		3,600		(a) 200		3,800		3,800		
Interest Expense	2,440				2,440		2,440			
	943,860	943,860	131,900	131,900	1,012,940	1,012,940	722,960	798,360	289,980	214,580
Net Income							75,400			75,400
							798,360	798,360	289,980	289,980

(a) Interest earned but not received on notes receivable, $200.
(b) Beginning merchandise inventory, $59,700.
(c) Ending merchandise inventory, $62,150.
(d) Office supplies used, $610 ($1,090 – $480).
(e) Insurance expired, $1,910.
(f) Depreciation of store equipment, $3,100.
(g) Depreciation of office equipment, $2,490.
(h) Salaries accrued but not paid (sales salaries, $780; office salaries, $360), $1,140.
(i) Rent earned from amount received in advance, $600.

shown below, has the effect of increasing the cost of merchandise sold and decreasing net income.

Dec. 31	Income Summary	59,700	
	Merchandise Inventory		59,700

After the first adjusting entry has been recorded and posted, the balance of the merchandise inventory account is zero. The second adjusting entry records the cost of the merchandise on hand at the end of the period by debiting Merchandise Inventory. Since the merchandise inventory at December 31, 1998, $62,150, is subtracted from the cost of merchandise available for sale in determining the cost of merchandise sold, Income Summary is credited. This credit has the effect of decreasing the cost of merchandise available for sale during the period, $587,455, by the cost of the unsold merchandise. The second adjusting entry is shown below.

Dec. 31	Merchandise Inventory	62,150	
	Income Summary		62,150

After the second adjusting entry has been recorded and posted, the balance of the merchandise inventory account is the amount of the ending inventory. The accounts for Merchandise Inventory and Income Summary after both entries have been posted would appear in T account form as follows:

Merchandise Inventory

1998					
Jan. 1	Beginning inventory	59,700	Dec. 31	Beginning inventory	59,700
Dec. 31	Ending inventory	62,150			

Income Summary

Dec. 31	Beginning inventory	59,700	Dec. 31	Ending inventory	62,150

No separate adjusting entry can be made for merchandise inventory shrinkage in a periodic inventory system. This is because no perpetual inventory records are available to show what inventory should be on hand at the end of the period. One disadvantage of the periodic inventory system is that inventory shrinkage cannot be measured.[3]

COMPLETING THE WORK SHEET

After all of the necessary adjustments have been entered on the work sheet, the work sheet is completed in the normal manner. An exception to the usual practice of extending only account balances is Income Summary. Both the debit and credit amounts for Income Summary are extended to the Adjusted Trial Balance columns. Extending both amounts aids in the preparation of the income statement because the debit adjustment (the beginning inventory of $59,700) and the credit adjustment (the ending inventory of $62,150) are reported as part of the cost of merchandise sold.

The purchases, purchases discounts, purchases returns and allowances, and transportation in accounts are extended to the Income Statement Columns of the work sheet, since they are used in computing the cost of merchandise sold. You should note that the two merchandise inventory amounts in Income Summary are extended to the Income Statement columns. After all of the items have been extended to the statement columns, the four columns are totaled and the net income or net loss is determined.

[3] Any inventory shrinkage that does exist is part of the cost of merchandise sold and is reported on the income statement, since a smaller ending inventory is deducted from other merchandise available for sale.

FINANCIAL STATEMENTS

The financial statements for Computer King are essentially the same under both the perpetual and periodic inventory systems.[4] The main difference is that the cost of goods is reported as a single amount under the perpetual system. Exhibit 2 illustrates the manner in which cost of merchandise sold is reported in a multiple-step income statement when the periodic inventory system is used.[5]

ADJUSTING AND CLOSING ENTRIES

The adjusting entries are the same under both inventory systems, except for merchandise inventory. As indicated previously, two adjusting entries for beginning and ending merchandise inventory are necessary in a periodic inventory system.

The closing entries differ in the periodic inventory system in that there is no cost of merchandise sold account to be closed to Income Summary. Instead, the purchases, purchases discounts, purchases returns and allowances, and transportation in accounts are closed to Income Summary.[6] To illustrate, the adjusting and closing entries under a periodic inventory system for Computer King are shown below.

JOURNAL — **PAGE 16**

Date		Description	Post. Ref.	Debit	Credit
		Adjusting Entries			
1998 Dec.	31	Interest Receivable	113	200 00	
		Interest Income	611		200 00
	31	Income Summary	312	59 700 00	
		Merchandise Inventory	115		59 700 00
	31	Merchandise Inventory	115	62 150 00	
		Income Summary	312		62 150 00
	31	Office Supplies Expense	534	610 00	
		Office Supplies	116		610 00
	31	Insurance Expense	533	1 910 00	
		Prepaid Insurance	117		1 910 00
	31	Depreciation Expense—Store Equip.	522	3 100 00	
		Accumulated Depr.—Store Equip.	124		3 100 00
	31	Depreciation Expense—Office Equip.	532	2 490 00	
		Accumulated Depr.—Office Equip.	126		2 490 00
	31	Sales Salaries Expense	520	780 00	
		Office Salaries Expense	530	360 00	
		Salaries Payable	211		1 140 00
	31	Unearned Rent	212	600 00	
		Rent Income	610		600 00

[4] To simplify the discussion, we assume that the accounts payable for Computer King on December 31, 1998, were not subject to any cash discounts.
[5] The single-step income statement would be the same for both the perpetual and the periodic inventory systems.
[6] The balance of Income Summary, after the merchandise inventory adjustments and the first two closing entries have been posted, is the net income or net loss for the period.

JOURNAL **PAGE 17**

Date		Description	Post. Ref.	Debit	Credit
		Closing Entries			
1998 Dec.	31	Sales	410	720 1 8 5 00	
		Purchases Returns and Allowances	511	9 1 0 0 00	
		Purchases Discounts	512	2 5 2 5 00	
		Rent Income	610	6 0 0 00	
		Interest Income	611	3 8 0 0 00	
		Income Summary	312		736 2 1 0 00
	31	Income Summary	312	663 2 6 0 00	
		Sales Returns and Allowances	411		6 1 4 0 00
		Sales Discounts	412		5 7 9 0 00
		Purchases	510		521 9 8 0 00
		Transportation In	513		17 4 0 0 00
		Sales Salaries Expense	520		60 0 3 0 00
		Advertising Expense	521		10 8 6 0 00
		Depreciation Exp.—Store Equip.	522		3 1 0 0 00
		Miscellaneous Selling Expense	529		6 3 0 00
		Office Salaries Expense	530		21 0 2 0 00
		Rent Expense	531		8 1 0 0 00
		Depreciation Exp.—Office Equip.	532		2 4 9 0 00
		Insurance Expense	533		1 9 1 0 00
		Office Supplies Expense	534		6 1 0 00
		Miscellaneous Administrative Exp.	539		7 6 0 00
		Interest Expense	710		2 4 4 0 00
	31	Income Summary	312	75 4 0 0 00	
		Pat King, Capital	310		75 4 0 0 00
	31	Pat King, Capital	310	18 0 0 0 00	
		Pat King, Drawing	311		18 0 0 0 00

EXERCISES

EXERCISE D–1
Purchases-related transactions—periodic inventory system

Journalize entries for the following related transactions, assuming the Sports "R" Us Co. uses the periodic inventory system.

a. Purchased $10,000 of merchandise from Nikon Co. on account, terms 2/10, n/30.
b. Discovered that some of the merchandise was defective and returned items with an invoice price of $1,000, receiving credit.
c. Paid the amount owed on the invoice within the discount period.
d. Purchased $6,000 of merchandise from Shick Co. on account, terms 1/10, n/30.
e. Paid the amount owed on the invoice within the discount period.

EXERCISE D–2
Sales-related transactions—periodic inventory system

Journalize entries for the following related transactions, assuming that Suzuki Company uses the periodic inventory system.

Mar. 8 Sold merchandise to a customer for $12,000, terms FOB shipping point, 2/10, n/30.
8 Paid the transportation charges of $230, debiting the amounts to Accounts Receivable.
12 Issued a credit memorandum for $1,800 to a customer for merchandise returned.
18 Received a check for the amount due from the sale.

EXERCISE D–3
Adjusting entries for merchandise inventory—periodic inventory system

Data assembled for preparing the work sheet for T. C. Hardy's Co. for the fiscal year ended December 31, 1996, included the following:

Merchandise inventory as of January 1, 1996	$155,000
Merchandise inventory as of December 31, 1996	$187,500

Journalize the two adjusting entries for merchandise inventory that would appear on the work sheet, assuming that the periodic inventory system is used.

EXERCISE D–4
Identification of missing items from income statement—periodic inventory system

For (a) through (i), identify the items designated by "X".

a. Sales – (X + X) = Net sales
b. Purchases – (X + X) = Net purchases
c. Net purchases + X = Cost of merchandise purchased
d. Merchandise inventory (beginning) + cost of merchandise purchased = X
e. Merchandise available for sale – X = Cost of merchandise sold
f. Net sales – cost of merchandise sold = X
g. X + X = Operating expenses
h. Gross profit – operating expenses = X
i. Income from operations + X – X = Net income

EXERCISE D–5
Multiple-step income statement—periodic inventory system

Selected data for Cabinet Company for the current year ended December 31 are as follows:

Merchandise inventory, January 1	$ 45,000
Merchandise inventory, December 31	67,500
Purchases	662,000
Purchases discounts	8,000
Purchases returns and allowances	15,500
Sales	805,000
Sales discounts	6,500
Sales returns and allowances	8,700
Transportation in	22,500

Prepare a multiple-step income statement through gross profit for Cabinet Company for the current year ended December 31.

EXERCISE D–6
Adjusting and closing entries—periodic inventory system

Selected account titles and related amounts appearing in the Income Statement and Balance Sheet columns of the work sheet of Las Posas Company for the year ended December 31 are listed in alphabetical order as follows:

Administrative Expenses	$ 69,500
Building	312,500
Cash	58,500
Interest Expense	2,500
J. Sanchez, Capital	472,580
J. Sanchez, Drawing	45,000
Merchandise Inventory (1/1)	325,000
Merchandise Inventory (12/31)	280,000
Notes Payable	25,000
Office Supplies	10,600
Purchases	750,000
Purchases Discounts	6,000
Purchases Returns and Allowances	7,000
Salaries Payable	4,220
Sales	1,375,000
Sales Discounts	10,200
Sales Returns and Allowances	44,300
Selling Expenses	232,700
Store Supplies	7,700
Transportation In	21,300

All selling expenses have been recorded in the account entitled Selling Expenses, and all administrative expenses have been recorded in the account entitled Administrative Expenses. Assuming that Las Posas Company uses the periodic inventory system, journalize (a) the adjusting entries for merchandise inventory and (b) the closing entries.

PROBLEMS

PROBLEM D–1
Sales-related and purchase-related transactions—periodic inventory system

The following were selected from among the transactions completed by The Accessories Company during April of the current year:

Apr. 3. Purchased office supplies for cash, $320.
4. Purchased merchandise on account from Anchor Co., list price $15,000, trade discount 40%, terms FOB destination, 2/10, n/30.
5. Sold merchandise for cash, $3,950.
7. Purchased merchandise on account from Mattox Co., $6,400, terms FOB shipping point, 2/10, n/30, with prepaid transportation costs of $190 added to the invoice.
7. Returned merchandise purchased on April 4 from Anchor Co., $2,500.
11. Sold merchandise on account to Bowles Co., list price $2,250, trade discount 20%, terms 1/10, n/30.
14. Paid Anchor Co. on account for purchase of April 4, less return of April 7 and discount.
15. Sold merchandise on nonbank credit cards and reported accounts to the card company, $5,850.
17. Paid Mattox Co. on account for purchase of April 7, less discount.
20. Purchased merchandise for cash, $6,500.
21. Received cash on account from sale of April 11 to Bowles Co., less discount.
25. Sold merchandise on account to Clemons Co., $3,200, terms 1/10, n/30.
28. Received cash from card company for nonbank credit card sales of April 15, less $280 service fee.
30. Received merchandise returned by Clemons Co. from sale on April 25, $1,700.

Instructions
Journalize the transactions for The Accessories Co. in a two-column general journal.

PROBLEM D–2
Sales-related and purchase-related transactions—periodic inventory system

The following were selected from among the transactions completed by Stevens Company during March of the current year:

Mar. 2. Purchased merchandise on account from Doyle Co., list price $15,000, trade discount 20%, terms FOB shipping point, 2/10, n/30, with prepaid transportation costs of $720 added to the invoice.
4. Purchased merchandise on account from Annex Co., $6,000, terms FOB destination, 1/10, n/30.
6. Sold merchandise on account to C. F. Howell Co., list price $4,000, trade discount 30%, terms 2/10, n/30.
7. Purchased office supplies for cash, $350.
9. Returned merchandise purchased on March 4 from Annex Co., $1,300.
12. Paid Doyle Co. on account for purchase of March 2, less discount.
13. Purchased merchandise for cash, $18,500.
14. Paid Annex Co. on account for purchase of March 4, less return of March 9 and discount.
16. Received cash on account from sale of March 6 to C. F. Howell Co., less discount.
19. Sold merchandise on nonbank credit cards and reported accounts to the card company, $3,450.
22. Sold merchandise on account to Comer Co., $3,480, terms 2/10, n/30.
24. Sold merchandise for cash, $4,350.
25. Received merchandise returned by Comer Co. from sale on March 22, $1,480.
31. Received cash from card company for nonbank credit card sales of March 19, less $340 service fee.

Instructions
Journalize the transactions for Stevens Co. in a two-column general journal.

PROBLEM D–3
Sales-related and purchase-related transactions for seller and buyer—periodic inventory system

The following selected transactions were completed during July between Spivey Company and C. K. Barker.

July 3. Spivey Company sold merchandise on account to C. K. Barker Co., $9,500, terms FOB destination, 2/15, n/eom.
3. Spivey Company paid transportation costs of $400 for delivery of merchandise sold to C. K. Barker Co. on July 3.
10. Spivey Company sold merchandise on account to C. K. Barker Co., $12,000, terms FOB shipping point, n/eom.
11. C. K. Barker Co. returned merchandise purchased on account on July 3 from Spivey Company, $2,000.
14. C. K. Barker Co. paid transportation charges of $200 on July 10 purchase from Spivey Company.
17. Spivey Company sold merchandise on account to C. K. Barker Co., $18,000, terms FOB shipping point, 1/10, n/30. Spivey prepaid transportation costs of $1,500, which were added to the invoice.
18. C. K. Barker Co. paid Spivey Company for purchase of July 3, less discount and less return of July 11.
27. C. K. Barker Co. paid Spivey Company on account for purchase of July 17, less discount.
31. C. K. Barker Co. paid Spivey Company on account for purchase of July 10.

Instructions
Journalize the July transactions for (1) Spivey Company and for (2) C. K. Barker Co.

PROBLEM D–4
Preparation of work sheet, financial statements, and adjusting and closing entries—periodic inventory system

The accounts and their balances in the ledger of The Bag Co. on December 31 of the current year are as follows:

Cash	$ 38,175
Accounts Receivable	112,500
Merchandise Inventory	180,000
Prepaid Insurance	9,700
Store Supplies	4,250
Office Supplies	2,100
Store Equipment	132,000
Accumulated Depreciation—Store Equipment	40,300
Office Equipment	50,000
Accumulated Depreciation—Office Equipment	17,200
Accounts Payable	66,700
Salaries Payable	—
Unearned Rent	1,200
Note Payable (final payment, 2008)	105,000
C. Tote, Capital	175,510
C. Tote, Drawing	40,000
Income Summary	—
Sales	895,000
Sales Returns and Allowances	11,900
Sales Discounts	7,100
Purchases	535,000
Purchases Returns and Allowances	10,100
Purchases Discounts	4,900
Transportation In	6,200
Sales Salaries Expense	76,400
Advertising Expense	25,000
Depreciation Expense—Store Equipment	—
Store Supplies Expense	—
Miscellaneous Selling Expense	1,335
Office Salaries Expense	44,000
Rent Expense	26,000
Insurance Expense	—
Depreciation Expense—Office Equipment	—

Office Supplies Expense	—
Miscellaneous Administrative Expense	$ 1,650
Rent Income	—
Interest Expense	12,600

The data needed for year-end adjustments on December 31 are as follows:

Merchandise inventory on December 31		$220,000
Insurance expired during the year		6,260
Supplies on hand on December 31:		
Store supplies		1,300
Office supplies		750
Depreciation for the year:		
Store equipment		7,500
Office equipment		3,800
Salaries payable on December 31:		
Sales salaries	$3,750	
Office salaries	1,150	4,900
Unearned rent on December 31		400

Instructions

1. Prepare a work sheet for the fiscal year ended December 31, listing all accounts in the order given.
2. Prepare a multiple-step income statement.
3. Prepare a statement of owner's equity.
4. Prepare a report form of balance sheet, assuming that the current portion of the note payable is $15,000.
5. Journalize the adjusting entries.
6. Journalize the closing entries.

Appendix E: Periodic Inventory Systems for Manufacturing Businesses

In this text, we illustrated the perpetual inventory system for manufacturing businesses. However, not all manufacturing businesses use the perpetual inventory system. The periodic inventory system is used by smaller manufacturers whose manufacturing operations are fairly simple. This might be the case when a single product or several similar products are manufactured.

MANUFACTURING TRANSACTIONS IN A PERIODIC INVENTORY SYSTEM

In a periodic inventory system for manufacturers, no attempt is made to record materials purchases or requisitions in the materials account, to record manufacturing costs in the work in process account, or to record the completion or sale of goods in the finished goods account. The three manufacturing inventory accounts are debited or credited when adjusting entries are recorded at the end of an accounting period.

We will use the January transactions for Lincoln Log Company, a manufacturer of pre-cut unassembled log homes, to illustrate the periodic inventory system for a manufacturer. We will also illustrate how the transactions would have been recorded under a perpetual inventory system.

January 2. Purchased $430,000 in logs from Tandy Logging Company, terms net 30.

Periodic Inventory Method			Perpetual Inventory Method		
Purchases	430,000		Materials	430,000	
Accounts Payable		430,000	Accounts Payable		430,000

Explanation. As illustrated in Appendix D for merchandise businesses, purchases are debited to the purchases account under the periodic inventory method. No attempt is made to keep a detailed record of the amount of materials inventory on hand at any given time.

January 4. Requisitioned $380,000 of logs from materials for constructing log home kits.

Periodic Inventory Method			Perpetual Inventory Method		
No entry			Work in Process	380,000	
			Materials		380,000

Explanation. Logs that are requisitioned from Materials are not recorded, since no attempt is made to maintain perpetual materials and work in process inventory balances.

January 16. Advertising is purchased for $180,000.

Periodic Inventory Method			Perpetual Inventory Method		
Advertising Expense	180,000		Advertising Expense	180,000	
Cash		180,000	Cash		180,000

Explanation. The advertising expense entry is the same under the periodic and perpetual inventory methods. Advertising expense is a period cost. Thus, it does not affect inventory accounts.

January 31. Log home kits were sold to customers for $1,210,000 on account. From perpetual finished goods inventory records, the cost of the sold kits could be determined to be $692,000.

Periodic Inventory Method			Perpetual Inventory Method		
Accounts Receivable	1,210,000		Accounts Receivable	1,210,000	
Sales		1,210,000	Sales		1,210,000
No entry			Cost of Goods Sold	692,000	
			Finished Goods		692,000

Explanation. Both the periodic and perpetual methods record the sale and associated receivable. However, only under the perpetual method is the cost of the sale recorded. The cost of the sale is not recorded under the periodic method because perpetual information for the finished goods inventory is not maintained.

January 31. Paid January direct labor of $165,000.

Periodic Inventory Method			Perpetual Inventory Method		
Direct Labor	165,000		Work in Process	165,000	
Cash		165,000	Cash		165,000

Explanation. The direct labor account is debited under the periodic inventory method. Direct labor is a manufacturing expense. Debits for direct labor are not made to Work in Process, as would be the case under the perpetual inventory method, since work in process perpetual balances are not maintained.

January 31. Lincoln Log Company recorded a $32,000 adjusting entry for January factory depreciation.

Periodic Inventory Method			Perpetual Inventory Method		
Factory Depreciation Expense	32,000		Factory Depreciation Expense	32,000	
Accumulated Depreciation		32,000	Accumulated Depreciation		32,000

January 31. Factory utilities incurred during January, $18,000.

Periodic Inventory Method			Perpetual Inventory Method		
Factory Utility Expense	18,000		Factory Utility Expense	18,000	
Accounts Payable		18,000	Accounts Payable		18,000

January 31. Indirect factory labor salaries paid for January, $105,000.

Periodic Inventory Method			Perpetual Inventory Method		
Indirect Labor	105,000		Indirect Labor	105,000	
Cash		105,000	Cash		105,000

Explanation. The last three factory overhead entries are the same under the periodic and perpetual inventory systems.

INVENTORY ADJUSTING ENTRIES—PERIODIC METHOD

Assume that Lincoln Log Company uses the periodic inventory method and had unadjusted inventory balances on January 31, 1997, as shown below.

Inventories (unadjusted), January 31, 1997:

Materials	$65,000
Work in process	42,000
Finished goods	86,000

These unadjusted balances were determined from the physical count that was completed on December 31, 1996, and are thus the beginning inventory balances for January. At the end of January, a new physical count is multiplied by the estimated cost of the counted items in order to value the ending inventories. Assume that the balances for the three inventories on January 31, 1997, were determined as shown below.

Inventories, January 31, 1997:

Materials	$115,000
Work in process	56,000
Finished goods	80,000

The unadjusted materials inventory (beginning-of-the-period inventory) is transferred to a manufacturing summary account, which is an account used at the end of the period to summarize manufacturing costs. Likewise, the ending materials inventory must be established. The adjusting entries for the beginning and ending materials inventory are shown below.

January 31. Transfer the beginning materials inventory to Manufacturing Summary.

Manufacturing Summary	65,000	
Materials		65,000

January 31. Establish the ending inventory.

Materials	115,000	
Manufacturing Summary		115,000

Like the materials inventory, the work in process inventory is adjusted in the same manner. These entries are illustrated below.

January 31. Transfer the beginning work in process inventory to Manufacturing Summary.

Manufacturing Summary	42,000	
Work in Process		42,000

January 31. Establish the ending work in process inventory.

Work in Process	56,000	
Manufacturing Summary		56,000

The finished goods inventory account is adjusted by using the income summary account in the same manner as the merchandise inventory of a merchandising business (as shown in Appendix D).

January 31. Transfer the beginning finished goods inventory to Income Summary.

Income Summary	86,000	
Finished Goods		86,000

January 31. Establish the ending finished goods inventory.

Finished Goods	80,000	
Income Summary		80,000

CLOSING ENTRIES—PERIODIC METHOD

The closing entries are recorded in the journal immediately following the adjusting entries. The manufacturing accounts are closed to Manufacturing Summary. The balance in Manufacturing Summary is closed to Income Summary, along with the other nonmanufacturing expense accounts. The remaining accounts are closed in the normal manner. The closing entries for Lincoln Log Company are shown below.

January 31. Closing entries.		
Manufacturing Summary	750,000	
Purchases		430,000
Direct Labor		165,000
Factory Depreciation Expense		32,000
Factory Utility Expense		18,000
Indirect Labor		105,000
Sales	1,210,000	
Income Summary		1,210,000
Income Summary	866,000	
Advertising Expense		180,000
Manufacturing Summary		686,000
Income Summary	338,000	
Retained Earnings		338,000

The January manufacturing summary and income summary accounts for Lincoln Log Company are shown in Exhibit 1.

Exhibit 1
Manufacturing and Income Summary Accounts

Manufacturing Summary

Jan. 31	Materials inventory, Jan. 1	65,000	Jan. 31	Materials inventory, Jan. 31	115,000
	Work in process inventory, Jan. 1	42,000		Work in process inventory, Jan. 31	56,000
	Closing	750,000		To Income Summary	686,000

Income Summary

Jan. 31	Finished goods inventory, Jan. 1	86,000	Jan. 31	Finished goods inventory, Jan. 31	80,000
	Closing	866,000		Sales	1,210,000
	To Retained Earnings	338,000			

MANUFACTURING AND INCOME STATEMENTS—PERIODIC METHOD

At the end of the period, the manufacturing costs are reported in the statement of cost of goods manufactured. This statement is illustrated for Lincoln Log Company in Exhibit 2.

The cost of goods manufactured of $686,000 represents the total cost of the manufactured items during the period. The cost of goods manufactured is included in the income statement of a manufacturing business in the same way that merchandise purchases are included in the income statement of a merchandise business under the periodic inventory method. The income statement for Lincoln Log Company is illustrated in Exhibit 3. As you can see in the exhibit, the cost of goods sold is determined by adding the cost of goods manufactured to the beginning finished goods inventory, and then subtracting the ending finished goods inventory. This approach to determining the cost of goods sold is similar to the approach used for determining the cost of merchandise sold for a merchandising business under the periodic inventory method, as illustrated in Appendix D.

Exhibit 2
Statement of Cost of Goods Manufactured

Lincoln Log Company
Statement of Cost of Goods Manufactured
For the Month Ended January 31, 1997

Work in process inventory, January 1, 1997			$ 42,000
Materials:			
Inventory, January 1, 1997	$ 65,000		
Purchases	430,000		
Cost of materials available for use	$495,000		
Less inventory, January 31, 1997	115,000		
Cost of materials placed into production		$380,000	
Direct labor		165,000	
Factory overhead:			
Factory depreciation	$ 32,000		
Factory utilities	18,000		
Indirect labor	105,000		
Total factory overhead		155,000	
Total manufacturing costs			700,000
Total work in process during period			$742,000
Less work in process inventory, January 31, 1997			56,000
Cost of goods manufactured			$686,000

Exhibit 3
Income Statement for a Manufacturing Business—Periodic Method

Lincoln Log Company
Income Statement
For the Month Ended January 31, 1997

Sales		$1,210,000
Cost of goods sold:		
Finished goods inventory, January 1, 1997	$ 86,000	
Cost of goods manufactured	686,000	
Cost of finished goods available for sale	$772,000	
Less finished goods inventory, January 31, 1997	80,000	
Cost of goods sold		692,000
Gross profit		$ 518,000
Advertising expense		180,000
Net income		$ 338,000

PROBLEMS

PROBLEM E–1
Recording transactions under the periodic inventory method

Huan Garment Company cuts and assembles fabric to manufacture men's pants. The following transactions occurred during March.

Mar. 1. Purchased fabric for $245,000 from Dixon Textile Company, terms net 30.
2. Garments were sold to Birch Department Stores Inc. for $345,000 on account.
6. Requisitioned $124,000 from materials for production.
15. Paid $37,000 wages to sewing machine operators.
16. Garments were sold to Winslow Department Stores for $258,000 on account.
20. Requisitioned $138,000 from materials for production.
22. Purchased fabric for $90,000 from Wu Textiles Inc., terms net 30.
26. Received an invoice for $4,000 from Industrial Cleaners Services for factory cleaning services rendered during March.
31. Paid $40,000 wages to sewing machine operators.
31. Paid $65,000 salaries to factory indirect labor.
31. Recorded $29,000 factory depreciation for March.

Instructions
Journalize the entries, assuming that Huan Garment Company uses the periodic inventory method to value inventories.

PROBLEM E–2
Factory adjusting and closing entries

The June 30, 1997 unadjusted trial balance for Baynard Furniture Company, a manufacturer of wood end tables, is shown below.

Baynard Furniture Company
Trial Balance
June 30, 1997

Cash	48,000	
Accounts Receivable	76,000	
Materials	123,000	
Work in Process	51,000	
Finished Goods	169,000	
Equipment	120,000	
Accumulated Depreciation		31,000
Accounts Payable		55,000
Common Stock		50,000
Paid-In Capital in Excess of Par		150,000
Retained Earnings		252,000
Sales		244,000
Purchases	90,000	
Direct Labor	43,000	
Indirect Labor	31,000	
Factory Utility Expense	4,000	
Selling Expenses	11,000	
Administrative Expenses	16,000	
	782,000	782,000

In addition, the following information is given for making the month-end adjustments:

a. The equipment has a 10-year life and no salvage value, and is depreciated by the straight-line method.
b. Direct labor incurred but not paid on June 30, 1997, is $8,000.
c. The inventories are valued per physical count on June 30, 1997, as follows:

Materials	$112,000
Work in Process	65,000
Finished Goods	152,000

Instructions

1. Journalize the month-end adjusting entries.
2. Journalize the month-end closing entries.

PROBLEM E–3
Statement of cost of goods manufactured; cost of goods sold

The following accounts related to the manufacturing operations of Mundy Inc. were selected from the pre-closing trial balance at October 31, 1997, the end of the current fiscal year:

Depreciation of Factory Buildings	$ 60,000
Depreciation of Factory Equipment	75,200
Direct Labor	590,000
Factory Supplies Expense	17,200
Finished Goods Inventory	220,000
Heat, Light, and Power	80,500
Indirect Labor	132,000
Insurance Expense—Factory	25,400
Materials	132,000
Miscellaneous Factory Expenses	13,500
Property Taxes—Factory	35,000
Purchases	746,000
Work in Process Inventory	170,000

Inventories at October 31 were as follows:

Materials	$128,000
Finished Goods	260,000
Work in Process	175,000

Instructions

1. Prepare a statement of cost of goods manufactured.
2. Prepare the cost of goods sold section of the income statement.

PROBLEM E–4
Factory adjusting and closing entries; statement of cost of goods manufactured

The May 31, 1997 unadjusted trial balance for Yale Box Company, a manufacturer of corrugated cardboard boxes, is shown below.

Yale Box Company
Trial Balance
May 31, 1997

Cash	62,000	
Accounts Receivable	81,000	
Materials	162,000	
Work in Process	45,000	
Finished Goods	201,000	
Equipment	240,000	
Accumulated Depreciation		80,000
Accounts Payable		69,000
Common Stock		100,000
Paid-In Capital in Excess of Par		200,000
Retained Earnings		208,000
Sales		635,000
Purchases	185,000	
Direct Labor	125,000	
Indirect Labor	86,000	
Factory Utility Expense	8,000	
Selling Expense	42,000	
Administrative Expense	55,000	
	1,292,000	1,292,000

In addition, the following information is made available for making the month-end adjustments:

a. The equipment has a 10-year life and no salvage value, and is depreciated by the straight-line method.
b. Direct labor incurred but not paid on May 31, 1997, is $15,000.
c. The inventories are valued per physical count on May 31, 1997, as follows:

Materials	$170,000
Work in Process	39,000
Finished Goods	191,000

Instructions

1. Journalize the month-end adjusting entries.
2. Journalize the month-end closing entries.
3. Prepare the May statement of cost of goods manufactured.
4. Prepare the May income statement.

Appendix F: Annual Reports and Financial Statement Analysis

CORPORATE ANNUAL REPORTS

Corporations normally issue annual reports to their stockholders and other interested parties. Such reports summarize the corporation's operating activities for the past year and plans for the future. There are many variations in the order and form for presenting the major sections of annual reports. However, one section of the annual report is devoted to the financial statements, including the accompanying notes. In addition, annual reports usually include the following sections:

1. Financial Highlights
2. President's Letter to the Stockholders
3. Management Report
4. Independent Auditors' Report
5. Historical Summary

In the following paragraphs, we describe these sections. Each section, as well as the financial statements, is illustrated in the 1993 annual report for **Hershey Foods Corporation.**

Financial Highlights

The Financial Highlights section summarizes the operating results for the last year or two. It is sometimes called Results in Brief. It is usually presented on the first one or two pages of the annual report.

There are many variations in format and content of the Financial Highlights section. Such items as sales, net income, net income per common share, cash dividends paid, cash dividends per common share, and the amount of capital expenditures are typically presented. In addition to these data, information about the financial position at the end of the year may be presented. As shown in the Financial Highlights section for Hershey Foods Corporation on page F–3, such information may include the year-end amounts of stockholders' equity, common shares outstanding, book value per share, and the price per share.

President's Letter to the Stockholders

A letter from the company president (and often the chairperson of the board of directors) to the stockholders is also presented in most annual reports. These letters usually discuss such items as reasons for an increase or decrease in net income, changes in existing plants, purchase or construction of new plants, significant new financing commitments, social responsibility issues, and future plans. The president's letter to Hershey Foods Corporation's stockholders is shown on pages F–4-5.

Management Report

The management of the corporation is responsible for the corporation's accounting system and financial statements. The Management Report section normally includes the following:

1. A statement that the financial statements are management's responsibility and that they have been prepared according to generally accepted accounting principles.

2. Management's assessment of the company's internal accounting control system.
3. Comments on any other relevant matters related to the accounting system, the financial statements, and the examination by the independent auditor.

Hershey's management report is shown on page F–28.

Independent Auditors' Report

Before issuing annual statements, all publicly held corporations are required to have an independent audit (examination) of their financial statements. For the financial statements of most companies, the CPAs who conduct the audit render an opinion on the fairness of the statements, as shown for Hershey Foods Corporation on page F–28. Such an opinion is called an *unqualified* or *clean opinion.*

Historical Summary

The Historical Summary section reports selected financial and operating data of past periods, usually for five or ten years. It is usually presented in close proximity to the financial statements for the current year. There are wide variations in the types of data reported and the title of this section. In the annual report for Hershey Foods Corporation, this section is called the "Eleven-Year Consolidated Financial Summary." This summary is shown on pages F–30-31.

Other Information

Some annual reports may include other financial information. For example, some reports may include management's financial review, forecasts that indicate financial plans, and expectations for the year ahead and other supplemental data.

Contents

About Hershey Foods Corporation

Hershey Foods Corporation and its subsidiaries are engaged in the manufacture, distribution and sale of consumer food products. The Corporation, primarily through its Hershey Chocolate U.S.A., Hershey Grocery, Hershey International and Hershey Pasta Group divisions and its Hershey Canada Inc. subsidiary, produces and distributes a broad line of chocolate, confectionery, grocery and pasta products. While these products are primarily manufactured and sold in North America, the Corporation also has manufacturing operations in Germany, the Netherlands, Belgium and Italy.

Financial Highlights

(in thousands of dollars except shares and per share amounts)

	1993	1992	Percent Change
Net sales	$3,488,249	$3,219,805	+8
Income before cumulative effect of accounting changes	297,233[a]	242,598	+23
Net cumulative effect of accounting changes	(103,908)	—	—
Net income	193,325	242,598	−20
Income per share[b]:			
Before accounting changes	3.31[a]	2.69	+23
Net cumulative effect of accounting changes	(1.16)	—	—
Net income	2.15	2.69	−20
Cash dividends paid per share:			
Common Stock	1.140	1.030	+11
Class B Common Stock	1.035	.935	+11
Cash dividends paid	100,499	91,444	+10
Capital additions	211,621	249,795	−15
Stockholders' equity at year-end	1,412,344	1,465,279	−4
Net book value per share at year-end	16.12	16.25	−1
Price per share of Common Stock at year-end	49	47	+4
Outstanding shares at year-end[b]	87,613,236	90,186,336	−3

(a) Income before cumulative effect of accounting changes and income per share before accounting changes for 1993 included an after-tax gain of $40.6 million and $.45 per share, respectively, on the sale of the Corporation's investment interest in Freia Marabou a.s.

(b) Income per share has been computed based on weighted average outstanding shares of 89,757,135 for 1993 and 90,186,336 for 1992. Excluding treasury stock, outstanding shares as of December 31, 1993, consisted of 72,359,957 shares of Common Stock and 15,253,279 shares of Class B Common Stock.

Letter to Stockholders

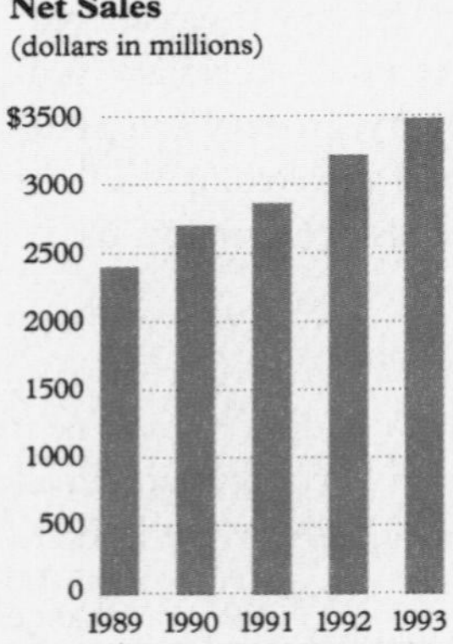

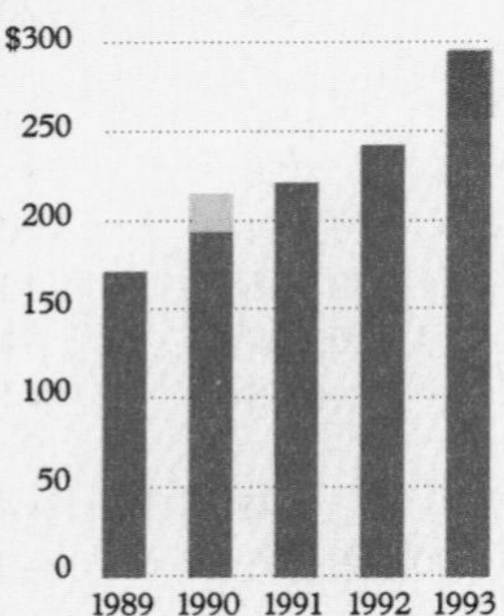

Nineteen ninety-three was an excellent, but challenging year for Hershey Foods Corporation. Excluding mandated accounting changes, the Corporation achieved record sales and earnings from operations despite a weak consumer market and higher federal income taxes. In addition, Hershey Chocolate U.S.A., Hershey Pasta Group and Hershey Canada Inc. made significant market share gains.

Throughout the year, the Corporation continued to utilize its manufacturing, sales, marketing, distribution and financial strengths to achieve its business objectives. All divisions achieved strong volume growth in sales. Most of Hershey Chocolate U.S.A.'s sales growth was provided by successful new products such as *Hershey's Hugs* chocolates, *Hershey's Cookies 'n' Mint* chocolate bar and *Amazin' Fruit* gummy bears. Hershey Pasta Group and Hershey Canada Inc. also made substantial volume gains during the year, although Hershey Canada's results were blunted somewhat by a decline in the value of the Canadian dollar. Hershey International's sales benefited from two acquisitions, as well as from excellent volume growth in its export business.

Pursuing its strategy to enhance our worldwide confectionery position, Hershey International acquired a leading non-chocolate confectionery business in Italy, Sperlari S.r.l., as well as a Dutch confectionery concern, Overspecht B.V. operating as OZF Jamin, which manufactures both chocolate and non-chocolate confectionery products. In the United States, Hershey Pasta Group acquired the Ideal Macaroni and Weiss Noodle companies which operate in the Cleveland market.

Despite the Corporation's strong earnings growth from operations, its net income for 1993 was below the prior year as a result of a change in accounting for post-retirement benefits and income taxes as required by the adoption of Statements of Financial Accounting Standards No. 106 and No. 109, respectively. This non-cash, one-time net charge was partially offset by a gain on the sale of the Corporation's 18.6 percent interest in Freia Marabou a.s. In addition, the Corporation's effective income tax rate was increased retroactively to January 1, 1993, by passage of the 1993 Revenue Reconciliation Act, lowering earnings per share.

The Corporation initiated a stock repurchase program in July 1993 to acquire up to $200 million of its Common Stock. By the end of the year, approximately two-thirds of this program had been completed. Throughout the year substantial investments were made to increase manufacturing capacity for existing and new products, as well as to modernize and improve the efficiency of manufacturing facilities. The Corporation's higher-cost, long-term debt position was significantly reduced, thereby lowering its interest expense.

Two capital projects of particular importance were the West Hershey chocolate-processing plant and finished goods facility in Hershey, Pa., and the Winchester, Va., pasta plant. The completion of the chocolate processing facility provided the Corporation with a new, state-of-the-art manufacturing operation and the finished goods facility provided the capacity for the production of *Hershey's Hugs* chocolates, one of the most successful new products in the Corporation's history. The Winchester plant is a highly efficient pasta production facility and provides Hershey Pasta Group with greater manufacturing capacity at a significantly lower cost-per-pound.

Despite the high aggregate level of investment made in acquisitions, the stock repurchase program, capital additions and debt retirement, the Corporation's financial condition remained strong, and dividends paid to stockholders were increased for the 19th consecutive year. The 11.1 percent increase in the dividend rate was consistent with the Corporation's practice of paying approximately one-third of income from continuing operations to stockholders in the form of dividends.

Significant management changes were made during the year at both the corporate and divisional levels. Richard A. Zimmerman, Chairman of the Board and Chief Executive Officer, retired December 31, 1993, after 35 years of service. Succeeding him as Chairman of the Board and Chief Executive Officer was Kenneth L. Wolfe. Joseph P. Viviano succeeded Mr. Wolfe as President and Chief Operating Officer of the Corporation. Michael F. Pasquale replaced Mr. Viviano as President of Hershey Chocolate U.S.A., and William F. Christ, previously President of Hershey International, was named to succeed Mr. Pasquale as Senior Vice President and Chief Financial Officer.

Mr. Christ's successor at Hershey International was Jay F. Carr, previously Vice President of Marketing for Hershey Chocolate U.S.A. In addition, a new division called Hershey Grocery was formed to market and sell grocery products. Dennis N. Eshleman, previously Director of Marketing for Hershey Chocolate U.S.A., was named General Manager of this new division. These executive changes were part of a planned, orderly succession.

Additional executive changes occurred at Hershey Chocolate U.S.A. as a result of those discussed above, as well as an important reorganization of the business. The focus on markets was sharpened by creating three separate business units with responsibility for chocolate confectionery, non-chocolate confectionery and special market categories such as vending, concession, fund-raising and novelties.

Bonnie Guiton Hill, Dean, McIntire School of Commerce, University of Virginia, was elected to the Board of Directors on August 3, 1993. We welcome the wealth of knowledge and experience she brings.

While 1993 was another record year for the Corporation, it was characterized by intense competition in all of our markets. A highly skilled, dedicated workforce is required to meet the increasing challenges of the competitive marketplace. Hershey Foods is blessed with a team of talented individuals who possess the skills necessary to enable the Corporation to achieve its goals. We thank all of our employees for their superb performance during 1993 and look forward to meeting the challenges of 1994, our Centennial year.

Kenneth L. Wolfe
Chairman of the Board and
Chief Executive Officer

Joseph P. Viviano
President and
Chief Operating Officer

Hershey Foods Corporation

Management's Discussion and Analysis—Financial Review

Summary of Consolidated Operating Results

The Corporation achieved increased sales in 1993 and 1992. Net sales during this two-year period increased at a compound annual rate of 10%, primarily reflecting volume growth from new product introductions, existing confectionery and pasta products, international acquisitions, and modest confectionery and pasta price increases. Consolidated net sales during the last half of 1993 were heavily influenced by volume growth from new domestic confectionery products, acquisitions and promotional activities. These factors more than offset the effects of sluggish demand for existing brands in most of the Corporation's domestic and international markets which began late in the first quarter of 1993 and has continued to sporadically affect sales and income into early 1994.

Effective January 1, 1993, the Corporation adopted Statements of Financial Accounting Standards No. 106 "Employers' Accounting for Post-retirement Benefits Other Than Pensions" (FAS No. 106) and No. 109 "Accounting for Income Taxes" (FAS No. 109) by means of catch-up adjustments. The net charge associated with these changes in accounting had the effect of decreasing net income by approximately $103.9 million, or $1.16 per share.

In March 1993, the Corporation recorded a pre-tax gain of $80.6 million on the sale of its 18.6% investment interest in Freia Marabou a.s (Freia) which had the effect of increasing net income by $40.6 million.

In March 1992, Hershey Chocolate U.S.A. increased the wholesale price of its line of packaged candy products by approximately 5%, the first increase since 1984. This product line represented approximately 15% of the Corporation's annual sales in 1992. The price increase was intended to cover the rising costs of certain raw materials, petroleum-based packaging materials, fuel and employee benefits.

Income, excluding the 1993 catch-up adjustments for accounting changes and the impact of the after-tax gain on the sale of the Freia investment, increased at a compound annual rate of 8% during the two-year period. This increase was a result of the growth in sales and an improved gross profit margin, partially offset by higher selling, marketing and administrative expenses and an increase in the effective income tax rate.

Summary of Financial Position and Liquidity

The Corporation's financial position remained strong during 1993. The capitalization ratio (total short-term and long-term debt as a percent of stockholders' equity, short-term and long-term debt) was 27% as of December 31, 1993 and 1992. The ratio of current assets to current liabilities was 1.1:1 as of December 31, 1993 and 1.3:1 as of December 31, 1992. The decrease in the current ratio reflects the sale of the Corporation's $179.1 million investment in Freia, and short-term borrowings for acquisitions and a share repurchase program, partially offset by the early repayment of long-term debt, which was classified as current as of December 31, 1992.

Historically, the Corporation's major source of financing has been cash generated from operations. Generally, seasonal working capital needs peak during the summer months and have been met by issuing commercial paper.

During the three-year period ended December 31, 1993, the Corporation's cash and cash equivalents decreased by $10.7 million. Total debt, including debt assumed, increased by $218.6 million during this same period reflecting the financing needs for several business acquisitions and a share repurchase program.

Capital Additions
(dollars in millions)

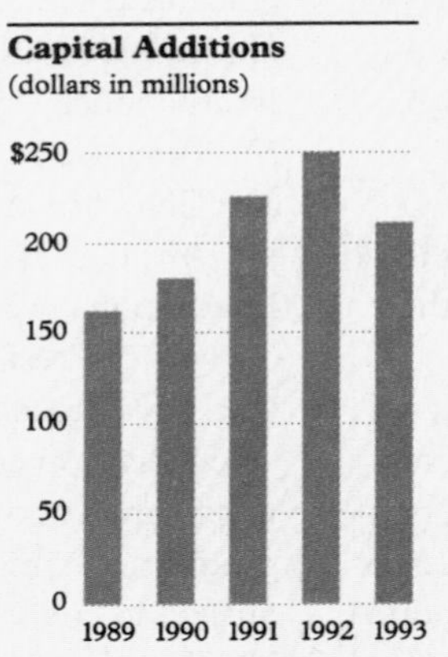

The Corporation anticipates that capital expenditures will be in the range of $200 million per annum during the next several years as a result of capacity expansion to support new products and continued modernization of existing facilities. As of December 31, 1993, the Corporation's principal capital commitments included manufacturing capacity expansion and modernization.

Gross proceeds from the sale of the Corporation's Freia investment interest in the amount of $259.7 million were received in April 1993 and a portion thereof was used for the early repayment of long-term debt.

In the second quarter of 1993, the Corporation's Board of Directors approved a share repurchase program to acquire from time to time through open market or privately negotiated transactions up to $200 million of its Common Stock. During 1993, a total of 2,573,100 shares of Common Stock were acquired under the share repurchase program, of which 264,000 shares were retired and the remaining 2,309,100 shares were held as treasury stock as of December 31, 1993.

As of December 31, 1993, $100 million of debt securities remained available for issuance under a Form S-3 Registration Statement which was declared effective in June 1990. In November 1993, the Corporation filed another Form S-3 Registration Statement under which it may offer, on a delayed or continuous basis, up to $400 million of additional debt securities. Proceeds from any offering of the $500 million of debt securities available under these shelf registrations may be used to reduce existing commercial paper borrowings, finance capital additions, and fund the share repurchase program and future business acquisitions.

In 1991, the Corporation established an employee stock ownership trust (ESOP) to serve as the primary vehicle for the Corporation's contributions to its existing employee savings and stock investment plan for participating domestic salaried and hourly employees. The ESOP was funded by a 7.75% loan of $47.9 million from the Corporation. The proceeds from this loan were used to purchase 1,193,816 shares of the Corporation's Common Stock which it had previously acquired through open market purchases.

Acquisitions and Divestiture

Operating results during the period were impacted by the following:

- October 1993—Completed the purchase of the outstanding shares of Overspecht B.V. (OZF Jamin) for approximately $20.2 million, plus the assumption of approximately $13.4 million in debt. OZF Jamin manufactures chocolate and non-chocolate confectionery products, cookies, biscuits and ice cream for distribution primarily to customers in the Netherlands and Belgium.

- September 1993—Completed the acquisition of the Italian confectionery business of Heinz Italia S.p.A. (Sperlari) for approximately $130.0 million. Sperlari is a leader in the Italian non-chocolate confectionery market and manufactures and distributes a wide range of confectionery products, including sugar candies and traditional products for special occasions such as nougat and gift boxes. Products are marketed under the *Sperlari, Dondi, Scaramellini* and other brands.

- March 1993—Acquired certain assets of the Cleveland area Ideal Macaroni and Weiss Noodle companies (Ideal/Mrs. Weiss) for approximately $14.6 million.

- April 1992—Completed the sale of Hershey do Brasil Participacoes Ltda., a holding company which owned a 41.7% equity interest in Petybon S.A., to the Bunge & Born Group for approximately $7.0 million. Petybon S.A., located in Brazil, is a producer of pasta, biscuits and margarine products.

- October 1991—Purchased the shares of Nacional de Dulces, S. A. de C.V. (subsequently renamed Hershey Mexico, S. A. de C.V.) owned by its joint venture partner, Grupo Carso, S. A. de C.V. Prior to this transaction, the Corporation owned 50% of the stock. Hershey Mexico produces, imports and markets chocolate products for the Mexican market under the *Hershey's* brand name.

Contribution to Net Sales of Businesses Acquired 1991-1993
(dollars in millions)

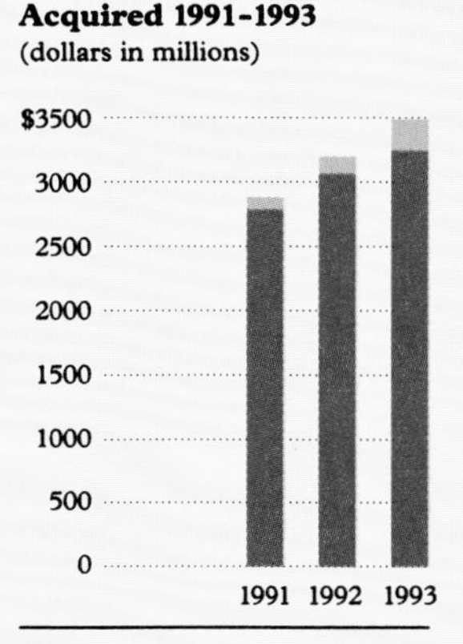

- May 1991—Acquired from Dairymen, Inc. certain assets of its ultra-high temperature fluid milk-processing business (aseptically-packaged drink business), including a Savannah, Georgia manufacturing facility.

- May 1991—Completed the acquisition of the Gubor Schokoladen GmbH and Gubor Schokoladenfabrik GmbH (Gubor) chocolate business from H. Bahlsens Keksfabrik KG. Gubor, which operates two manufacturing plants in Germany, produces and markets high-quality assorted pralines and seasonal chocolates under the *Gubor* brand name. The transaction was effective as of January 1, 1991.

A further discussion of these acquisitions and divestiture can be found in Note 2 to the consolidated financial statements.

Other Items

The Corporation's net sales, net income and cash flows are affected by business acquisitions, new product introductions, the timing of promotional activities and price increases. These factors generally benefited financial results in 1993. However, sluggish demand for existing brands and an increasingly seasonal sales bias resulted in a decline in net sales and net income in the second quarter of 1993 and, to the extent these conditions continue, has the potential to similarly impact financial results as the Corporation enters 1994.

The most significant raw material used in the production of the Corporation's chocolate and confectionery products is cocoa beans. Generally, the Corporation has been able to offset the effects of increases in the cost of this raw material through selling price increases or reductions in product weights. Conversely, declines in the cost of cocoa beans have served as a source of funds to maintain selling price stability, enhance consumer value through increases in product weights, respond to competitive activity, develop new products and markets, and offset rising costs of other raw materials and expenses.

The cost of cocoa beans and the prices for the related commodity futures contracts historically have been subject to wide fluctuations attributable to a variety of factors, including the effect of weather on crop yield, other imbalances between supply and demand, currency exchange rates and speculative influences. During the past decade, the market prices of cocoa beans and cocoa futures trended lower as a result of the worldwide cocoa bean crop exceeding demand during most years. However, cocoa crops for the most recent three years fell somewhat short of demand resulting in supply deficits.

Prices in 1993 were relatively stable because of the excess stocks produced earlier in the decade, but may begin to trend upward in 1994 as stocks decline further. The Corporation's costs during 1994 will not necessarily reflect market price fluctuations because of its forward purchasing practices, premiums and discounts reflective of relative values, varying delivery times, and supply and demand for specific varieties and grades of cocoa beans.

The major raw material used in the manufacture of pasta products is semolina milled from durum wheat. The Corporation purchases semolina from commercial millers and is also engaged in custom milling arrangements to obtain sufficient quantities of high-quality semolina. A decrease in plantings and adverse weather conditions in the Midwest reduced the quantity and quality of the 1993 durum wheat crop, resulting in substantial cost increases. Supplies are expected to remain tight and prices may continue at the recent high levels pending the outcome of the new crop harvest in the fall of 1994.

Capital Structure

The Corporation has two classes of stock outstanding, Common Stock and Class B Common Stock (Class B Stock). The Common Stock and the Class B Stock generally vote together without regard to class on matters submitted to stockholders, including the election of directors, with the Common Stock having one vote per share and the Class B Stock having ten votes per share. However, the Common Stock, voting separately as a class, is entitled to elect one-sixth of the Board of Directors. With respect to dividend rights, the Common Stock is entitled to cash dividends 10% higher than those declared and paid on the Class B Stock.

The Corporation's Common Stock is listed on the New York Stock Exchange (NYSE), which has a rule generally prohibiting dual classes of common stock. The Corporation's dual class structure has been grandfathered under this rule. In February 1994, the NYSE released for public comment a new uniform voting rights policy proposed by the Chairman of the Securities and Exchange Commission and agreed to by the American Stock Exchange and the National Association of Securities Dealers. The policy would provide that the voting rights of existing holders of publicly traded common stock cannot be disparately reduced or restricted through any corporate action or issuance. Under the proposed policy the Corporation's and other listed companies' existing dual class structures would be grandfathered.

Market Prices and Dividends

Cash dividends paid on the Corporation's Common Stock and Class B Stock were $100.5 million in 1993 and $91.4 million in 1992. The annual dividend rate on the Common Stock is $1.20 per share, an increase of 11% over the 1992 rate of $1.08 per share. The 1993 dividend represented the 19th consecutive year of Common Stock dividend increases.

Dividends Paid Per Share of Common Stock
(dollars)

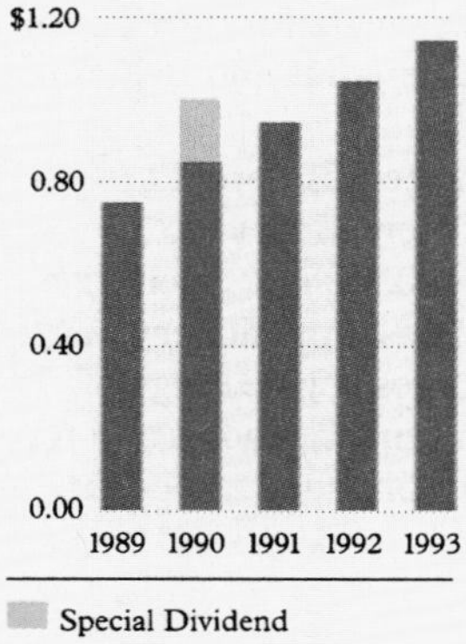

$1.20
0.80
0.40
0.00
1989 1990 1991 1992 1993

Special Dividend

On February 8, 1994, the Corporation's Board of Directors declared a quarterly dividend of $.30 per share of Common Stock payable on March 15, 1994, to stockholders of record as of February 25, 1994. It is the Corporation's 257th consecutive Common Stock dividend. A quarterly dividend of $.2725 per share of Class B Stock was also declared.

Hershey Foods Corporation's Common Stock is listed and traded principally on the NYSE under the ticker symbol "HSY." Approximately 29.3 million shares of the Corporation's Common Stock were traded during 1993.

The closing price of the Common Stock on December 31, 1993 was $49. The Class B Stock is not publicly traded. There were 32,859 stockholders of record of the Common Stock and the Class B Stock as of December 31, 1993.

The following table shows the dividends paid per share of Common Stock and Class B Stock and the price range of the Common Stock for each quarter of the past two years:

	Dividends Paid Per Share		Common Stock Price Range*	
	Common Stock	Class B Stock	High	Low
1993				
1st Quarter	$ .270	$ .2450	$55⅞	$46½
2nd Quarter	.270	.2450	54⅝	45¾
3rd Quarter	.300	.2725	51⅞	43½
4th Quarter	.300	.2725	54¾	48⅝
Total	$1.140	$1.0350		
1992				
1st Quarter	$ .245	$ .2225	$45¼	$39⅞
2nd Quarter	.245	.2225	42⅛	38¼
3rd Quarter	.270	.2450	45½	41⅝
4th Quarter	.270	.2450	48⅜	43½
Total	$1.030	$ .9350		

*NYSE - Composite Quotations for Common Stock by calendar quarter.

Operating Return on Average Stockholders' Equity

The Corporation's operating return on average stockholders' equity was 17.8% in 1993. Over the most recent five-year period, the return has ranged from 16.1% in 1989 to 17.8% in 1993. For the purpose of calculating operating return on average stockholders' equity, earnings is defined as net income, excluding the after-tax gain on business restructuring in 1990, and both the catch-up adjustment for accounting changes and the after-tax gain on the sale of the investment in Freia in 1993.

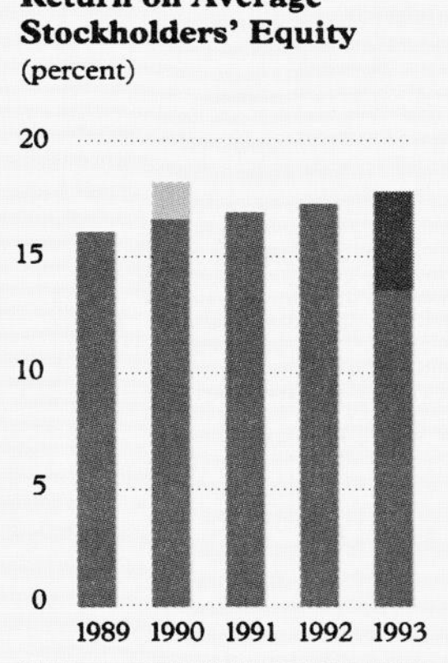

Gain on Business Restructuring, Net

Catch-up Adjustment for Accounting Changes and Gain on Sale of Investment Interest

Operating Return on Average Invested Capital

The Corporation's operating return on average invested capital was 15.0% in 1993. Over the most recent five-year period, the return has ranged from 13.2% in 1989 to 15.0% in 1993. Average invested capital consists of the annual average of beginning and ending balances of long-term debt, deferred income taxes and stockholders' equity. For the purpose of calculating operating return on average invested capital, earnings is defined as net income, excluding the after-tax gains on business restructuring and the sale of the investment in Freia, the catch-up adjustment for accounting changes, and the after-tax effect of interest on long-term debt.

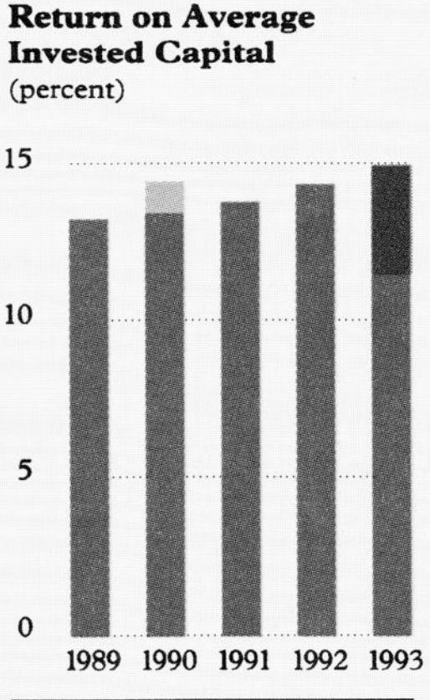

Gain on Business Restructuring, Net

Catch-up Adjustment for Accounting Changes and Gain on Sale of Investment Interest

Hershey Foods Corporation

Consolidated Statements of Income

(in thousands of dollars except per share amounts)

For the years ended December 31,	1993	1992	1991
Net Sales	$3,488,249	$3,219,805	$2,899,165
Costs and Expenses:			
Cost of sales	1,995,502	1,833,388	1,694,404
Selling, marketing and administrative	1,035,519	958,189	814,459
Total costs and expenses	3,031,021	2,791,577	2,508,863
Gain on Sale of Investment Interest	80,642	—	—
Income before Interest, Income Taxes and Accounting Changes	537,870	428,228	390,302
Interest expense, net	26,995	27,240	26,845
Income before Income Taxes and Accounting Changes	510,875	400,988	363,457
Provision for income taxes	213,642	158,390	143,929
Income before Cumulative Effect of Accounting Changes	297,233	242,598	219,528
Net cumulative effect of accounting changes	(103,908)	—	—
Net Income	$ 193,325	$ 242,598	$ 219,528
Income Per Share:			
Before accounting changes	$ 3.31	$ 2.69	$ 2.43
Net cumulative effect of accounting changes	(1.16)	—	—
Net income	$ 2.15	$ 2.69	$ 2.43

Cash Dividends Paid Per Share:			
Common Stock	$ 1.140	$ 1.030	$ .940
Class B Common Stock	1.035	.935	.850

The notes to consolidated financial statements are an integral part of these statements.

Hershey Foods Corporation

Management's Discussion and Analysis—Results of Operations

Net Sales

Net sales rose $268.4 million or 8% in 1993 and $320.6 million or 11% in 1992. The increase in 1993 primarily reflected volume growth from new products and business acquisitions, and pasta selling price increases, which more than offset the effects of sluggish demand for existing brands in most of the Corporation's domestic and international markets. The increase in 1992 was due to volume growth from existing brands, sales of new products, confectionery price increases and the consolidation of Hershey Mexico, the remaining shares of which were acquired in late 1991.

Costs and Expenses

Cost of sales as a percent of net sales decreased from 58.4% in 1991 to 56.9% in 1992 but increased to 57.2% in 1993. The decrease in gross margin in 1993 reflected higher manufacturing costs related to new products, incremental manufacturing, shipping and depreciation costs associated with the completion and start-up of new manufacturing and distribution facilities, and recurring expenses associated with a change in accounting for post-retirement benefits. These higher costs and expenses were partially offset by lower costs for certain major raw materials and pasta price increases. The increase in gross margin in 1992 was primarily due to lower costs for certain major raw materials, confectionery price increases and manufacturing efficiencies.

Selling, marketing and administrative costs increased in 1993 primarily as a result of higher promotion expenses, associated with the sales volume growth and the introduction of new products, and incremental selling expenses related to business acquisitions. Selling, marketing and administrative costs increased in 1992, primarily as a result of higher promotion and advertising expenses related to sales volume growth and the introduction of new products.

Gain on Sale of Investment Interest

In March 1993, the Corporation sold its 18.6% investment interest in Freia to Kraft General Foods Holdings Norway, Inc. and recorded a pre-tax gain of $80.6 million. This gain had the effect of increasing net income by $40.6 million.

Interest Expense, Net

Net interest expense decreased by $.2 million in 1993 as lower long-term interest expense, reflecting lower debt balances, and higher interest income more than offset a decrease in capitalized interest. Interest income increased due in part to interim investments of a portion of the proceeds from the sale of the investment in Freia. Capitalized interest was below the prior year reflecting the completion of major long-term construction projects in late 1992 and early 1993 and a corresponding reduction in expenditures qualifying for interest capitalization in 1993.

Net interest expense was $.4 million higher in 1992 than 1991, due to higher levels of short-term borrowings, offset partially by lower short-term interest rates, lower long-term interest expense and an increase in capitalized interest. The increase in short-term debt was a result of the Corporation's May 1992 purchase of its 18.6% investment interest in Freia and interim borrowings to finance capital additions. Long-term interest expense was below 1991 reflecting repayments of long-term debt. A cumulative increase in capital expenditures resulted in significantly higher capitalized interest in 1992 versus 1991.

Provision for Income Taxes

The Corporation's effective income tax rate was 41.8%, 39.5% and 39.6% in 1993, 1992 and 1991, respectively. The increase in 1993 was largely a result of the relatively high income taxes associated with the gain on the sale of the Corporation's Freia investment and an increase in the Federal statutory income tax rate as provided for in the Revenue Reconciliation Act of 1993, which reduced net income by $5.5 million. The effective income tax rate was lower in 1992 than in 1991 as a tax benefit associated with the sale of the Corporation's equity interest in its Brazilian joint venture more than offset the full-year impact in 1992 of a mid-1991 increase in the Pennsylvania corporate income tax rate.

Net Cumulative Effect of Accounting Changes

Effective January 1, 1993, the Corporation adopted FAS No. 106 and FAS No. 109 by means of catch-up adjustments. These changes in accounting had the effect of decreasing net income by approximately $103.9 million or $1.16 per share.

Net Income

Net income decreased by 20% in 1993. Excluding the impact of the after-tax gain on the 1993 sale of the Freia investment and the 1993 catch-up adjustments for accounting changes, income increased $14.1 million or 6% in 1993. Net income increased $23.1 million or 11% in 1992. Income as a percent of net sales, after excluding the 1993 net cumulative effect of accounting changes and the after-tax gain on the sale of the investment interest in Freia, was 7.4% in 1993, 7.5% in 1992, and 7.6% in 1991.

Hershey Foods Corporation

Consolidated Statements of Cash Flows

(in thousands of dollars)

For the years ended December 31,	1993	1992	1991
Cash Flows Provided from (Used by) Operating Activities			
Net income	$ 193,325	$ 242,598	$ 219,528
Adjustments to reconcile net income to net cash provided from operations:			
Net cumulative effect of accounting changes	103,908	—	—
Depreciation and amortization	113,064	97,087	85,413
Deferred income taxes	11,047	21,404	20,654
Gain on sale of investment interest	(80,642)	—	—
Changes in assets and liabilities, net of effects from business acquisitions:			
Accounts receivable—trade	(100,957)	(13,841)	(6,404)
Inventories	32,347	(20,262)	(43,949)
Accounts payable	(12,809)	(10,715)	4,070
Other assets and liabilities	110,259	(20,707)	94,270
Other, net	9,399	649	(26,242)
Net Cash Provided from Operating Activities	378,941	296,213	347,340
Cash Flows Provided from (Used by) Investing Activities			
Capital additions	(211,621)	(249,795)	(226,071)
Business acquisitions	(164,787)	—	(44,108)
Sale (purchase) of investment interest	259,718	(179,076)	—
Other, net	(1,947)	6,581	(1,510)
Net Cash (Used by) Investing Activities	(118,637)	(422,290)	(271,689)
Cash Flows Provided from (Used by) Financing Activities			
Net increase in short-term debt	67,485	201,425	56,489
Long-term borrowings	1,130	1,259	23,620
Repayment of long-term debt	(104,792)	(32,173)	(27,861)
Loan to ESOP	—	—	(47,902)
Proceeds from sale of Common Stock to ESOP	—	—	47,902
Cash dividends paid	(100,499)	(91,444)	(83,401)
Repurchase of Common Stock	(131,783)	—	—
Net Cash Provided from (Used by) Financing Activities	(268,459)	79,067	(31,153)
Increase (Decrease) in Cash and Cash Equivalents	(8,155)	(47,010)	44,498
Cash and Cash Equivalents as of January 1	24,114	71,124	26,626
Cash and Cash Equivalents as of December 31	$ 15,959	$ 24,114	$ 71,124
Interest Paid	$ 32,073	$ 29,515	$ 24,468
Income Taxes Paid	171,586	151,490	119,038

The notes to consolidated financial statements are an integral part of these statements.

Hershey Foods Corporation

Management's Discussion and Analysis—Cash Flows

Summary

Over the past three years, cash provided from operating activities and the net cash from the purchase and subsequent sale of the Corporation's investment interest in Freia exceeded cash requirements for capital additions and dividend payments by $140.3 million. Total debt, including debt assumed, increased during the period by $218.6 million, reflecting the financing needs for several business acquisitions and a share repurchase program. Cash and cash equivalents decreased by $10.7 million during the period.

The Corporation's income and, consequently, cash provided from operations during the year is affected by seasonal sales patterns, the timing of new product introductions, business acquisitions and price increases. Chocolate, confectionery and grocery seasonal and holiday-related sales have typically been highest during the third and fourth quarters of the year, representing the principal seasonal effect. Generally, the Corporation's seasonal working capital needs peak during the summer months and have been met by issuing commercial paper.

Operating Activities

During the past three years, depreciation and amortization have increased significantly as a result of continuous investment in capital additions and business acquisitions. Cash requirements for accounts receivable and inventories have tended to fluctuate during the three-year period based on sales during December and inventory management practices. The change in cash required for or provided from other assets and liabilities between the years was primarily related to commodities transactions, the timing of payments for accrued liabilities, including income taxes, and a corporate-owned life insurance program.

Investing Activities

Investing activities included capital additions, several business acquisitions, and the purchase and subsequent sale of an 18.6% investment interest in Freia in 1992 and 1993, respectively. The income taxes paid in 1993 on the Freia gain were included in operating activities. Capital additions during the past three years included the purchase of manufacturing equipment, construction of new manufacturing and office facilities and expansion of existing facilities. Businesses acquired during the past three years included OZF Jamin, Sperlari and Ideal/Mrs. Weiss in 1993, and Gubor, the aseptically-packaged drink business and Hershey Mexico in 1991. Cash used for business acquisitions represented the purchase price paid and consisted of the current assets, property, plant and equipment, and intangibles acquired, net of liabilities assumed.

Financing Activities

Financing activities included debt borrowings and repayments, payment of dividends, the repurchase of Common Stock in 1993, and ESOP transactions in 1991. During the past three years, short-term borrowings in the form of commercial paper or bank borrowings were used to fund seasonal working capital requirements, business acquisitions, the purchase of the Freia investment interest and a share repurchase program. A portion of the proceeds received from the sale of the Freia investment was used to repay long-term debt in 1993. In February 1991, the Corporation issued $100 million of Debentures under its Form S-3 Registration Statement which was declared effective in June 1990. A portion of the proceeds from issuance of the Debentures was used to repay $76.7 million of domestic commercial paper borrowings which were classified as long-term debt as of December 31, 1990.

During the second quarter of 1993, the Corporation's Board of Directors approved a share repurchase program to acquire from time to time through open market or privately negotiated transactions up to $200 million of Common Stock. During 1993, a total of 2,573,100 shares were repurchased at an average price of $51 per share.

During 1991, the Corporation established an ESOP to serve as the primary vehicle for the Corporation's contributions to its existing employee savings and stock investment plan for participating domestic salaried and hourly employees. The ESOP was funded by a 7.75% loan of $47.9 million from the Corporation. The proceeds from this loan were used to purchase, at a market price of $40⅛ per share, 1,193,816 shares of the Corporation's Common Stock which it had previously acquired through open market purchases.

Hershey Foods Corporation

Consolidated Balance Sheets

(in thousands of dollars)

December 31,	1993	1992
ASSETS		
Current Assets:		
Cash and cash equivalents	$ 15,959	$ 24,114
Accounts receivable—trade	294,974	173,646
Inventories	453,442	457,179
Deferred income taxes	85,548	46,451
Prepaid expenses and other	39,073	59,515
Investment interest	—	179,076
Total current assets	888,996	939,981
Property, Plant and Equipment, Net	1,460,904	1,295,989
Intangibles Resulting from Business Acquisitions	473,408	399,768
Other Assets	31,783	37,171
Total assets	$2,855,091	$2,672,909
LIABILITIES AND STOCKHOLDERS' EQUITY		
Current Liabilities:		
Accounts payable	$ 125,658	$ 127,175
Accrued liabilities	301,989	240,816
Accrued income taxes	35,603	5,682
Short-term debt	337,286	259,045
Current portion of long-term debt	13,309	104,224
Total current liabilities	813,845	736,942
Long-term Debt	165,757	174,273
Other Long-term Liabilities	290,401	92,950
Deferred Income Taxes	172,744	203,465
Total liabilities	1,442,747	1,207,630
Stockholders' Equity:		
Preferred Stock, shares issued: none in 1993 and 1992	—	—
Common Stock, shares issued: 74,669,057 in 1993 and 74,929,057 in 1992	74,669	74,929
Class B Common Stock, shares issued: 15,253,279 in 1993 and 15,257,279 in 1992	15,253	15,257
Additional paid-in capital	51,196	52,129
Cumulative foreign currency translation adjustments	(13,905)	2,484
Unearned ESOP compensation	(41,515)	(44,708)
Retained earnings	1,445,609	1,365,188
Treasury—Common Stock shares, at cost: 2,309,100 in 1993 and none in 1992	(118,963)	—
Total stockholders' equity	1,412,344	1,465,279
Total liabilities and stockholders' equity	$2,855,091	$2,672,909

Hershey Foods Corporation

Management's Discussion and Analysis—Financial Condition

Assets

Total assets increased $182.2 million or 7% as of December 31, 1993, primarily as a result of capital additions and intangibles from business acquisitions, offset somewhat by a decrease in current assets.

Current assets decreased by $51.0 million as a result of the sale of the $179.1 million investment interest in Freia, which was classified as a current asset as of December 31, 1992. This decrease was partially offset by increases in accounts receivable, resulting from inclusion of the accounts receivable of acquired businesses and the timing and payment terms associated with sales occurring toward the end of the year, and current deferred income taxes.

The $164.9 million net increase in property, plant and equipment included $65.6 million of assets acquired through business acquisitions. Capital additions totaled $211.6 million in 1993, while depreciation amounted to $100.1 million.

The increase in intangibles resulting from business acquisitions as of December 31, 1993, principally reflected the preliminary accounting for 1993 business acquisitions partially offset by amortization of intangibles.

Liabilities

Total liabilities increased by $235.1 million or 19% as of December 31, 1993, primarily due to higher long-term liabilities associated with the adoption of FAS No. 106 and higher current liabilities.

Current liabilities increased by $76.9 million principally as a result of liabilities assumed as part of business acquisitions and increases in accrued liabilities related to marketing promotions, benefits, compensation, and timing of income tax payments. A decline in current portion of long-term debt more than offset an increase in short-term debt. Current portion of long-term debt decreased by $90.9 million, reflecting the early retirement of $95.2 million of long-term debt which had been classified as current as of December 31, 1992. The increase in short-term debt was a result of commercial paper borrowings to finance capital additions and the share repurchase program.

The deferred income tax liability as of December 31, 1993 was provided using the liability method as required by FAS No. 109, which was adopted by the Corporation effective January 1, 1993. The decrease of $30.7 million reflected the impact of adopting FAS No. 109 and deferred income tax benefits associated with the adoption of FAS No. 106.

Stockholders' Equity

Total stockholders' equity declined by 4% in 1993 primarily due to the repurchase of Common Stock. Total stockholders' equity has increased at a compound annual rate of 9% over the past ten years.

Hershey Foods Corporation

Consolidated Statements of Stockholders' Equity

(in thousands of dollars)

	Preferred Stock	Common Stock	Class B Common Stock	Additional Paid-in Capital	Cumulative Foreign Currency Translation Adjustments	Unearned ESOP Compen-sation	Retained Earnings	Treasury Common Stock	Total Stockholders' Equity
Balance as of January 1, 1991	$—	$74,910	$15,276	$49,249	$26,195	$ —	$1,077,907	$ —	$1,243,537
Net income							219,528		219,528
Dividends:									
Common Stock, $.940 per share							(70,426)		(70,426)
Class B Common Stock, $.850 per share							(12,975)		(12,975)
Foreign currency translation adjustments					229				229
Conversion of Class B Common Stock into Common Stock		11	(11)						—
Incentive plan transactions				(446)					(446)
Employee stock ownership trust transactions				3,706		(47,902)			(44,196)
Balance as of December 31, 1991	—	74,921	15,265	52,509	26,424	(47,902)	1,214,034	—	1,335,251
Net income							242,598		242,598
Dividends:									
Common Stock, $1.030 per share							(77,174)		(77,174)
Class B Common Stock, $.935 per share							(14,270)		(14,270)
Foreign currency translation adjustments					(23,940)				(23,940)
Conversion of Class B Common Stock into Common Stock		8	(8)						—
Incentive plan transactions				(741)					(741)
Employee stock ownership trust transactions				361		3,194			3,555
Balance as of December 31, 1992	—	74,929	15,257	52,129	2,484	(44,708)	1,365,188	—	1,465,279
Net income							193,325		193,325
Dividends:									
Common Stock, $1.140 per share							(84,711)		(84,711)
Class B Common Stock, $1.035 per share							(15,788)		(15,788)
Foreign currency translation adjustments					(16,389)				(16,389)
Conversion of Class B Common Stock into Common Stock		4	(4)						—
Incentive plan transactions				(1,269)					(1,269)
Employee stock ownership trust transactions				487		3,193			3,680
Repurchase of Common Stock		(264)		(151)			(12,405)	(118,963)	(131,783)
Balance as of December 31, 1993	$—	$74,669	$15,253	$51,196	$(13,905)	$(41,515)	$1,445,609	$(118,963)	$1,412,344

The notes to consolidated financial statements are an integral part of these statements.

Hershey Foods Corporation

Notes to Consolidated Financial Statements

1. Summary of Significant Accounting Policies

Significant accounting policies employed by the Corporation are discussed below and in other notes to the consolidated financial statements. Certain reclassifications have been made to prior year amounts to conform to the 1993 presentation.

Principles of Consolidation

The consolidated financial statements include the accounts of the Corporation and its subsidiaries after elimination of intercompany accounts and transactions. Investments in affiliated companies are accounted for using the equity method.

Cash Equivalents

All highly liquid debt instruments purchased with a maturity of three months or less are classified as cash equivalents.

Commodities Futures and Options Contracts

In connection with the purchasing of major commodities (principally cocoa and sugar) for anticipated manufacturing requirements, the Corporation enters into commodities futures and options contracts as deemed appropriate to reduce the risk of future price increases. These futures and options contracts are accounted for as hedges and, accordingly, gains and losses are deferred and recognized in cost of sales as part of the product cost.

Property, Plant and Equipment

Property, plant and equipment are stated at cost. Depreciation of buildings, machinery and equipment is computed using the straight-line method over the estimated useful lives.

Intangibles Resulting from Business Acquisitions

Intangible assets resulting from business acquisitions principally consist of the excess of the acquisition cost over the fair value of the net assets of businesses acquired (goodwill). Goodwill is amortized on a straight-line basis over 40 years. Other intangible assets are amortized on a straight-line basis over their estimated useful lives.

Accumulated amortization of intangible assets resulting from business acquisitions was $73.4 million and $61.2 million as of December 31, 1993 and 1992, respectively.

Foreign Currency Translation

Results of operations for international entities are translated using the average exchange rates during the period. For international entities operating in non-highly inflationary economies, assets and liabilities are translated to U.S. dollars using the exchange rates in effect at the balance sheet date. Resulting translation adjustments are recorded in a separate component of stockholders' equity, "Cumulative Foreign Currency Translation Adjustments."

Foreign Exchange Contracts

The Corporation enters into foreign exchange contracts to hedge transactions denominated in international currencies and to hedge payment of intercompany transactions with its non-domestic subsidiaries. Gains and losses are accounted for as part of the underlying transactions. In entering into these contracts the Corporation has assumed the risk which might arise from the possible inability of counterparties to meet the terms of their contracts. The Corporation does not expect any losses as a result of counterparty defaults.

As of December 31, 1993, the Corporation had contracts maturing in 1994 and 1995 to purchase $39.1 million in foreign currency at contracted forward rates, primarily British sterling and Canadian dollars, and to sell $3.6 million in foreign currency at contracted forward rates. As of December 31, 1992, the Corporation had contracts maturing in 1993 and 1994 to purchase $57.2 million in foreign currency at contracted forward rates, primarily Canadian dollars and British sterling, and to sell $238.9 million in foreign currency at contracted forward rates, related to Norwegian kroner to be received from the sale of the Corporation's investment interest in Freia Marabou a.s (Freia) as discussed below.

License Agreements

The Corporation has entered into license agreements under which it has access to proprietary technology and manufactures and/or markets and distributes certain products. The rights under these agreements are extendable on a long-term basis at the Corporation's option subject to certain conditions, including minimum sales levels. License fees and royalties, payable under the terms of the agreements, are expensed as incurred.

2. Acquisitions and Divestiture

In October 1993, the Corporation completed the purchase of the outstanding shares of Overspecht B.V. (OZF Jamin) for approximately $20.2 million, plus the assumption of approximately $13.4 million in debt. OZF Jamin manufactures chocolate and non-chocolate confectionery products, cookies, biscuits and ice cream for distribution primarily to customers in the Netherlands and Belgium.

In September 1993, the Corporation completed the acquisition of the Italian confectionery business of Heinz Italia S.p.A. (Sperlari) for approximately $130.0 million. Sperlari is a leader in the Italian non-chocolate confectionery market and manufactures and distributes a wide range of confectionery products, including sugar candies and traditional products for special occasions such as nougat and gift boxes. Products are marketed under the *Sperlari, Dondi, Scaramellini* and other brands.

In March 1993, the Corporation acquired certain assets of the Cleveland area Ideal Macaroni and Weiss Noodle companies for approximately $14.6 million.

In October 1991, the Corporation purchased the shares of Nacional de Dulces, S. A. de C.V. (NDD) owned by its joint venture partner, Grupo Carso, S. A. de C.V., for $10.0 million. Prior to the acquisition, the Corporation owned 50% of the outstanding stock of NDD. Subsequent to the acquisition, NDD was renamed Hershey Mexico, S. A. de C.V. (Hershey Mexico). Hershey Mexico produces, imports and markets chocolate products for the Mexican market under the *Hershey's* brand name.

In May 1991, the Corporation purchased certain assets of Dairymen, Inc.'s ultra-high temperature fluid milk-processing business, including a Savannah, Georgia manufacturing facility for $2.2 million, plus the assumption of $8.5 million in debt.

Also in May 1991, the Corporation completed the acquisition of the Gubor Schokoladen GmbH and Gubor Schokoladenfabrik GmbH (Gubor) chocolate business from H. Bahlsens Keksfabrik KG for $31.9 million, plus the assumption of $9.0 million in debt. Gubor manufactures and markets high-quality assorted pralines and seasonal chocolates in Germany. The acquisition was effective as of January 1, 1991.

In accordance with the purchase method of accounting, the purchase prices of the acquisitions summarized above were allocated to the underlying assets and liabilities at the date of acquisition based on their estimated respective fair values which may be revised at a later date. Total liabilities assumed, including debt, were $54.0 million in 1993 and $40.4 million in 1991. Results subsequent to the dates of acquisition are included in the consolidated financial statements. Had the results of these acquisitions been included in consolidated results for the entire length of each period presented, the effect would not have been material.

In April 1992, the Corporation completed the sale of Hershey do Brasil Participacoes Ltda., a holding company which owned a 41.7% equity interest in Petybon S. A., to the Bunge & Born Group for approximately $7.0 million. Petybon S. A., located in Brazil, is a producer of pasta, biscuits and margarine products. The sale resulted in a modest pre-tax gain and a reduction in the effective income tax rate of .8% for 1992.

3. Gain on Sale of Investment Interest

In May 1992, the Corporation completed the acquisition of an 18.6% investment interest in Freia for $179.1 million. The investment was accounted for under the cost method in 1992. In October 1992, the Corporation tendered its investment interest in response to a Kraft General Foods Holdings Norway, Inc. (KGF) bid to acquire Freia subject to certain conditions, including approval by the Norwegian government.

KGF received approval of its ownership and, in March 1993, the Corporation recorded a pre-tax gain of $80.6 million on the sale of its Freia investment. This gain had the effect of increasing net income by $40.6 million. Gross proceeds from the sale in the amount of $259.7 million were received in April 1993.

4. Interest Expense

Interest expense, net consisted of the following:

For the years ended December 31, *(in thousands of dollars)*	1993	1992	1991
Long-term debt and lease obligations	$23,016	$ 30,435	$ 32,252
Short-term debt	11,854	11,328	7,403
Capitalized interest	(4,646)	(12,055)	(10,386)
	30,224	29,708	29,269
Interest income	(3,229)	(2,468)	(2,424)
Interest expense, net	$26,995	$ 27,240	$ 26,845

5. Short-term Debt

Generally, the Corporation's short-term borrowings are in the form of commercial paper or bank loans with an original maturity of three months or less. The Corporation maintained lines of credit arrangements with domestic and international commercial banks, under which it could borrow in various currencies up to $560 million as of December 31, 1993 and up to $377 million as of December 31, 1992 at the lending banks' prime commercial interest rates or lower. These lines of credit, which may be used to support commercial paper borrowings, may be terminated at the option of the Corporation. The Corporation had combined domestic commercial paper borrowings and short-term international bank loans against these lines of credit of $337.3 million and $259.0 million as of December 31, 1993 and 1992, respectively.

Lines of credit were supported by commitment fee arrangements. The fees were generally ⅛% per annum of the commitment. There were no significant compensating balance agreements which legally restricted these funds.

As a result of maintaining a consolidated cash management system, the Corporation maintains overdraft positions at certain banks. Such overdrafts, which were included in accounts payable, were $17.2 million and $22.0 million as of December 31, 1993 and 1992, respectively.

6. Long-term Debt

Long-term debt consisted of the following:

December 31, *(in thousands of dollars)*	1993	1992
Medium-term Notes, 8.45% to 9.92%, due 1994–1998	$ 55,400	$ 55,400
9.5% Sinking Fund Debentures due 2009	—	42,000
9.125% Sinking Fund Debentures due 2016	—	50,000
8.8% Debentures due 2021	100,000	100,000
Other obligations, net of unamortized debt discount	23,666	31,097
Total long-term debt	179,066	278,497
Less—current portion	13,309	104,224
Long-term portion	$165,757	$174,273

As of December 31, 1992, current portion of long-term debt included $95.2 million of debt which, in 1993, the Corporation retired early using a portion of the proceeds from the sale of its investment interest in Freia.

Aggregate annual maturities during the next five years are: 1994, $13.3 million; 1995, $7.8 million; 1996, $2.1 million; 1997, $15.9 million; and 1998, $25.5 million. The Corporation's debt is principally unsecured and of equal priority. None of the debt is convertible into stock of the Corporation. The Corporation is in compliance with all covenants included in the related debt agreements.

7. Income Taxes

Effective January 1, 1993, the Corporation adopted Statement of Financial Accounting Standards No. 109 "Accounting for Income Taxes" (FAS No. 109), which requires the use of the liability method of accounting for deferred income taxes. This change in accounting as of January 1, 1993, which was recorded as a catch-up adjustment, increased net income by $8.2 million or $.09 per share.

The provision for income taxes, which included the effect of an increase in the Federal statutory income tax rate as provided for in the Revenue Reconciliation Act of 1993 but excluded the FAS No. 109 catch-up adjustment, was as follows:

For the years ended December 31, *(in thousands of dollars)*	1993	1992	1991
Current:			
Federal	$141,541	$104,223	$ 96,074
State	37,358	30,968	25,128
International	23,696	1,795	2,073
Current provision for income taxes	202,595	136,986	123,275
Deferred:			
Federal	2,949	11,770	12,618
State	1,764	4,579	6,111
International	6,334	5,055	1,925
Deferred provision for income taxes	11,047	21,404	20,654
Total provision for income taxes	$213,642	$158,390	$143,929

The tax effects of the significant temporary differences which comprised the deferred tax assets and liabilities were as follows:

December 31, 1993 *(in thousands of dollars)*	Deferred Income Tax Assets	Deferred Income Tax (Liabilities)	Net Deferred Income Tax Assets (Liabilities)
Current:			
Post-retirement benefit obligations	$ 3,478	$ —	
Accrued expenses and other reserves	70,678	—	
Other	16,555	(5,163)	
Total current deferred income taxes	90,711	(5,163)	$ 85,548
Non-current:			
Depreciation	—	(214,566)	
Post-retirement benefit obligations	78,190	—	
Accrued expenses and other reserves	24,800	—	
Other	10,744	(71,912)	
Total non-current deferred income taxes	113,734	(286,478)	(172,744)
Total deferred income taxes	$204,445	$(291,641)	$ (87,196)

The following table reconciles the Federal statutory income tax rate with the Corporation's effective income tax rate:

For the years ended December 31,	1993	1992	1991
Federal statutory tax rate	35.0%	34.0%	34.0%
Increase (reduction) resulting from:			
State income taxes, net of Federal income tax benefits	6.2	6.0	5.5
Sale of investment interest	1.5	—	—
Non-deductible acquisition costs	0.6	0.9	1.0
Sale of equity interest	—	(0.8)	—
Corporate-owned life insurance	(1.0)	(1.0)	(1.1)
Other, net	(0.5)	0.4	0.2
Effective income tax rate	41.8%	39.5%	39.6%

8. Retirement Plans

The Corporation and its subsidiaries sponsor several defined benefit retirement plans covering substantially all employees. Plans covering most domestic salaried and hourly employees provide retirement benefits based on individual account balances which are increased annually by pay-related and interest credits. Plans covering certain non-domestic employees provide retirement benefits based on career average pay, final pay, or final average pay as defined within the provisions of the individual plans. The Corporation also participates in several multi-employer retirement plans which provide defined benefits to employees covered under certain collective bargaining agreements.

The Corporation's policy is to fund domestic pension liabilities in accordance with the minimum and maximum limits imposed by the Employee Retirement Income Security Act of 1974 and Federal income tax laws, respectively. Non-domestic pension liabilities are funded in accordance with applicable local laws and regulations. Plan assets are invested in a broadly diversified portfolio consisting primarily of domestic and international common stocks and fixed income securities.

Pension expense included the following components:

For the years ended December 31, *(in thousands of dollars)*	1993	1992	1991
Service cost	$ 27,835	$ 22,858	$ 20,056
Interest cost on projected benefit obligations	26,423	24,098	22,148
Investment return on plan assets	(46,232)	(12,331)	(53,627)
Net amortization and deferral	18,519	(15,245)	30,161
Corporate sponsored plans	26,545	19,380	18,738
Multi-employer plans	612	580	1,231
Other	678	630	645
Total pension expense	$ 27,835	$ 20,590	$ 20,614

The funded status and amounts recognized in the consolidated balance sheets for the retirement plans were as follows:

(in thousands of dollars)	December 31, 1993		December 31, 1992	
	Assets Exceeded Accumulated Benefits	Accumulated Benefits Exceeded Assets	Assets Exceeded Accumulated Benefits	Accumulated Benefits Exceeded Assets
Actuarial present value of:				
Vested benefit obligations	$144,608	$204,861	$1,643	$319,635
Accumulated benefit obligations	$155,838	$221,867	$1,987	$344,091
Actuarial present value of projected benefit obligations	$185,926	$231,972	$3,255	$375,715
Plan assets at fair value	166,727	181,813	2,566	305,255
Plan assets less than projected benefit obligations	19,199	50,159	689	70,460
Net gain (loss) unrecognized at date of transition	(5,440)	4,381	79	(1,306)
Prior service cost and amendments not yet recognized in earnings	94	(11,556)	(6)	(12,815)
Unrecognized net loss from past experience different than that assumed	(7,171)	(13,948)	(708)	(29,664)
Minimum liability adjustment	—	14,866	—	18,999
Accrued pension liability	$ 6,682	$ 43,902	$ 54	$ 45,674

The projected benefit obligations for the plans were determined principally using a discount rate of 7.0% as of December 31, 1993 and 1992. For both 1993 and 1992 the assumed long-term compensation increase rate and the assumed long-term rate of return on plan assets were primarily 6.0% and 9.5%, respectively.

9. Post-retirement Benefits

The Corporation and its subsidiaries provide certain health care and life insurance benefits for retired employees subject to pre-defined limits. Substantially all of the Corporation's domestic employees become eligible for these benefits at retirement with a pre-defined benefit being available at an early retirement date. The post-retirement medical benefit is contributory for pre-Medicare retirees and for most post-Medicare retirees retiring on or after February 1, 1993. Retiree contributions are based upon a combination of years of service and age at retirement. The post-retirement life insurance benefit is non-contributory.

Effective January 1, 1993, the Corporation adopted Statement of Financial Accounting Standards No. 106 "Employers' Accounting for Post-retirement Benefits Other Than Pensions" (FAS No. 106) which requires that the cost of post-retirement benefits be accrued during employees' working careers. The Corporation elected to adopt FAS No. 106 by means of a catch-up adjustment which had the effect of decreasing net income by $112.2 million, or $1.25 per share, after a deferred tax benefit of $76.3 million.

Prior to 1993, the Corporation accounted for such benefits as an expense as paid. Expense recognized under FAS No. 106 during 1993, incrementally reduced net income by $5.9 million and consisted of the following components (in thousands of dollars):

Service cost	$ 3,997
Interest cost on projected benefit obligations	12,897
Amortization	(280)
Total	$16,614

Obligations are unfunded and the actuarial present value of accumulated post-retirement benefit obligations recognized in the consolidated balance sheet as of December 31, 1993 was as follows (in thousands of dollars):

Retirees	$ 87,765
Fully eligible active plan participants	31,852
Other active plan participants	65,069
Total	184,686
Plan amendments	5,746
Unrecognized net gain from past experience different than that assumed	7,976
Accrued post-retirement benefits	$198,408

The accumulated post-retirement benefit obligations were determined using a discount rate of 7.5% as of December 31, 1993. The assumed average health care cost trend rate used in measuring the accumulated post-retirement benefit obligations as of December 31, 1993 was principally 12% in 1993, gradually declining to approximately 7% over ten years. A one percentage point increase in the average health care cost trend rate would increase the accumulated post-retirement benefit obligations as of December 31, 1993 by $18.3 million and the sum of the service and interest costs by $2.2 million.

As part of its long-range financing plans, the Corporation, in 1989, implemented a corporate-owned life insurance program covering most of its domestic employees. After paying employee death benefits, proceeds from this program will be available for general corporate purposes and may be used to offset future employee benefits costs, including retiree medical benefits. The Corporation's investment in corporate-owned life insurance policies was recorded net of policy loans in other assets, and interest accrued on the policy loans was included in accrued liabilities as of December 31, 1993. Net life insurance expense, including interest expense, was included in selling, marketing and administrative expenses.

10. Employee Stock Ownership Trust

In 1991, the Corporation established an employee stock ownership trust (ESOP) to serve as the primary vehicle for the Corporation's contributions to its existing employee savings and stock investment plan for participating domestic salaried and hourly employees. The ESOP was funded by a 15-year 7.75% loan of $47.9 million from the Corporation. The proceeds from this loan were used to purchase, at a market price of $40⅛ per share, 1,193,816 shares of the Corporation's Common Stock which it had previously acquired through open market purchases.

During 1993 and 1992, the ESOP received a combination of dividends on unallocated shares and contributions from the Corporation equal to the amount required to meet its principal and interest payments under the loan. Simultaneously, the ESOP allocated to participants 79,588 shares of Common Stock each year. As of December 31, 1993 the ESOP held 152,406 of allocated shares and 1,034,640 of unallocated shares.

The Corporation recognized net compensation expense equal to the shares allocated multiplied by the original cost of $40⅛ per share less dividends received by the ESOP on unallocated shares. Compensation expense related to the ESOP for 1993 and 1992 was $2.0 million and $2.3 million, respectively. Dividends paid on unallocated ESOP shares were $1.2 million in 1993 and $.9 million in 1992. The unearned ESOP compensation balance of $41.5 million as of December 31, 1993 represented deferred compensation expense to be recognized by the Corporation in future years as additional shares are allocated to participants.

11. Capital Stock and Net Income Per Share

As of December 31, 1993, the Corporation had 530,000,000 authorized shares of capital stock. Of this total, 450,000,000 shares were designated as Common Stock, 75,000,000 shares as Class B Common Stock (Class B Stock), and 5,000,000 shares as Preferred Stock, each class having a par value of one dollar per share. As of December 31, 1993, a combined total of 89,922,336 shares of both classes of common stock had been issued of which 87,613,236 shares were outstanding. No shares of the Preferred Stock were issued or outstanding during the three-year period ended December 31, 1993.

The Common Stock and the Class B Stock generally vote together without regard to class on matters submitted to stockholders, including the election of directors, with the Common Stock having one vote per share and the Class B Stock having ten votes per share. However, the Common Stock, voting separately as a class, is entitled to elect one-sixth of the Board of Directors. With respect to dividend rights, the Common Stock is entitled to cash dividends 10% higher than those declared and paid on the Class B Stock.

Class B Stock can be converted into Common Stock on a share-for-share basis at any time. During 1993, 1992 and 1991, a total of 4,000, 7,775, and 11,350 shares, respectively, of Class B Stock were converted into Common Stock.

Hershey Trust Company, as Trustee for Milton Hershey School (Hershey Trust), as institutional fiduciary for estates and trusts unrelated to Milton Hershey School, and as direct owner of investment shares, held a total of 21,398,312 shares of the Common Stock, and as Trustee for Milton Hershey School, held 15,153,003 shares of the Class B Stock as of December 31, 1993, and was entitled to cast approximately 77% of the total votes of both classes of the Corporation's common stock. Hershey Trust must approve the issuance of shares of Common Stock or any other action which would result in the Hershey Trust not continuing to have voting control of the Corporation.

During the second quarter of 1993, the Corporation's Board of Directors approved a share repurchase program to acquire from time to time through open market or privately negotiated transactions up to $200 million of Common Stock. During 1993, a total of 2,573,100 shares were repurchased at an average price of $51 of which 264,000 shares were retired and the remaining 2,309,100 shares were held as treasury stock as of December 31, 1993. Of the total purchased, 2,000,000 shares were acquired from Hershey Trust for approximately $103.1 million.

Net income per share has been computed based on the weighted average number of shares of the Common Stock and the Class B Stock outstanding during the year. Average shares outstanding were 89,757,135 for 1993 and 90,186,336 for 1992 and 1991.

12. Incentive Plan

The long-term portion of the 1987 Key Employee Incentive Plan (Plan) provides for grants or awards to senior executives and key employees of one or more of the following: performance stock units, non-qualified stock options (stock options), stock appreciation rights and restricted stock units. The Plan also provides for the deferral of performance stock unit awards by participants.

As of December 31, 1993, a total of 190,855 contingent performance stock units and restricted stock units had been granted for potential future distribution, primarily related to three-year cycles ending December 31, 1993, 1994 and 1995. Deferred performance stock units and accumulated dividend amounts totaled 255,288 shares as of December 31, 1993.

Stock options are granted at exercise prices of not less than 100% of the fair market value of a share of Common Stock at the time the option is granted and are exercisable for periods no longer than ten years from the date of grant. Each option may be used to purchase one share of Common Stock. No compensation expense is recognized under the stock options portion of the Plan.

No stock appreciation rights had been granted or awarded as of December 31, 1993. Stock option activity was as follows:

	Shares under Options	
	Number of Shares	Option Price per Share
Outstanding—January 1, 1991	834,960	$23¾ to 35⅜
Granted	59,800	$36¼
Exercised	(30,135)	$23¾ to 28
Cancelled	(7,500)	$35⅜
Outstanding—December 31, 1991	857,125	$23¾ to 36¼
Granted	939,000	$41⅛ to 44¾
Exercised	(69,650)	$23¾ to 35⅜
Cancelled	(9,500)	$44¾
Outstanding—December 31, 1992	1,716,975	$25⅜ to 44¾
Granted	116,600	$47 to 53
Exercised	(82,850)	$25⅜ to 35⅜
Cancelled	(20,300)	$44¾
Outstanding—December 31, 1993	1,730,425	$25⅜ to 53

13. Supplemental Income Statement Information

Supplemental income statement information is provided in the table below. These costs were expensed in the year incurred.

For the years ended December 31, *(in thousands of dollars)*	1993	1992	1991
Promotion	$444,546	$398,577	$325,465
Advertising	130,009	137,631	117,049
Maintenance and repairs	85,845	79,563	72,192
Depreciation expense	100,124	84,434	72,735
Rent expense	24,524	23,960	23,288
Research and development	26,151	24,203	22,770

Rent expense pertains to all operating leases which were principally related to certain administrative buildings, distribution facilities and transportation equipment. Future minimum rental payments under non-cancellable operating leases with a remaining term in excess of one year as of December 31, 1993, were: 1994, $12.3 million; 1995, $12.0 million; 1996, $11.4 million; 1997, $11.1 million; 1998, $10.7 million; 1999 and beyond, $102.8 million.

Amounts for taxes other than payroll and income taxes, amortization of intangibles resulting from business acquisitions, and royalties were less than 1% of net sales.

14. Supplemental Balance Sheet Information

Accounts Receivable—Trade

In the normal course of business, the Corporation extends credit to customers which satisfy pre-defined credit criteria. The Corporation believes that it has little concentration of credit risk due to the diversity of its customer base. Receivables, as shown on the consolidated balance sheets, were net of allowances and anticipated discounts of $12.5 million and $10.4 million as of December 31, 1993 and 1992, respectively.

Inventories

The Corporation values the majority of its inventories under the last-in, first-out (LIFO) method and the remaining inventories at the lower of first-in, first-out (FIFO) cost or market. LIFO cost of inventories valued using the LIFO method was $310.6 million as of December 31, 1993 and $350.4 million as of December 31, 1992 and all inventories were stated at amounts that did not exceed realizable values.

Total inventories were as follows:

December 31, *(in thousands of dollars)*	1993	1992
Raw materials	$209,570	$243,243
Goods in process	37,261	30,965
Finished goods	265,616	231,313
Inventories at FIFO	512,447	505,521
Adjustment to LIFO	(59,005)	(48,342)
Total inventories	$453,442	$457,179

Property, Plant and Equipment

Property, plant and equipment balances included construction in progress of $171.1 million and $196.9 million as of December 31, 1993 and 1992, respectively. Major classes of property, plant and equipment were as follows:

December 31, *(in thousands of dollars)*	1993	1992
Land	$ 48,239	$ 40,163
Buildings	430,199	385,545
Machinery and equipment	1,563,326	1,371,729
	2,041,764	1,797,437
Accumulated depreciation	580,860	501,448
Property, plant and equipment, net	$1,460,904	$1,295,989

Accrued Liabilities

Accrued liabilities were as follows:

December 31, *(in thousands of dollars)*	1993	1992
Payroll and other compensation	$ 81,909	$ 63,088
Advertising and promotion	89,819	72,735
Other	130,261	104,993
Total accrued liabilities	$301,989	$240,816

Other Long-term Liabilities

Other long-term liabilities were as follows:

December 31, *(in thousands of dollars)*	1993	1992
Accrued post-retirement benefits	$189,959	$ —
Other	100,442	92,950
Total other long-term liabilities	$290,401	$92,950

15. Segment Information

The Corporation operates in a single consumer foods line of business, encompassing the domestic and international manufacture, distribution and sale of chocolate, confectionery, grocery and pasta products.

Operations in Canada and Europe represent the majority of the Corporation's international business. Historically, transfers of product between geographic areas have not been significant. Net sales, income before interest, income taxes and accounting changes, and identifiable assets by geographic segment were as follows:

For the years ended December 31, *(in thousands of dollars)*	1993	1992	1991
Net sales:			
Domestic	$3,080,329	$2,871,438	$2,566,448
International	407,920	348,367	332,717
Total	$3,488,249	$3,219,805	$2,899,165
Income before interest, income taxes and accounting changes:			
Domestic	$ 446,565	$ 419,317	$ 381,549
International	10,663	8,911	8,753
Gain on sale of investment interest	80,642	—	—
Total	$ 537,870	$ 428,228	$ 390,302
Identifiable assets as of December 31:			
Domestic	$2,281,766	$2,353,230	$2,003,425
International	573,325	319,679	338,397
Total	$2,855,091	$2,672,909	$2,341,822

16. Quarterly Data (Unaudited)

Summary quarterly results were as follows:
(in thousands of dollars except per share amounts)

Year 1993	First	Second	Third	Fourth
Net sales	$ 897,788	$618,430	$935,662	$1,036,369
Gross profit	387,019	254,834	390,846	460,048
Income before cumulative effect of accounting changes	105,055	26,025	73,971	92,182
Net cumulative effect of accounting changes	(103,908)	—	—	—
Net income	1,147[(a)]	26,025	73,971	92,182
Income per share[(b)]:				
Before accounting changes	1.16	.29	.82	1.04
Net cumulative effect of accounting changes	(1.15)	—	—	—
Net income	.01	.29	.82	1.04
Weighted average shares outstanding	90,186	90,186	90,124	88,489

Year 1992	First	Second	Third	Fourth
Net sales	$ 800,967	$621,840	$827,475	$ 969,523
Gross profit	337,529	266,791	352,792	429,305
Net income	58,924	34,475	66,880	82,319
Net income per share	.65	.39	.74	.91
Weighted average shares outstanding	90,186	90,186	90,186	90,186

(a) Net income for the first quarter and year 1993 included the net cumulative effect of accounting changes for post-retirement benefits and income taxes of $(103.9) million and an after-tax gain on the sale of the investment interest in Freia of $40.6 million. Net income per share was similarly impacted.

(b) Quarterly income per share amounts for 1993 do not total to annual amounts due to the changes in weighted average shares outstanding during the year.

Responsibility for Financial Statements

Hershey Foods Corporation is responsible for the financial statements and other financial information contained in this report. The Corporation believes that the financial statements have been prepared in conformity with generally accepted accounting principles appropriate under the circumstances to reflect in all material respects the substance of applicable events and transactions. In preparing the financial statements, it is necessary that management make informed estimates and judgments. The other financial information in this annual report is consistent with the financial statements.

The Corporation maintains a system of internal accounting controls designed to provide reasonable assurance that financial records are reliable for purposes of preparing financial statements and that assets are properly accounted for and safeguarded. The concept of reasonable assurance is based on the recognition that the cost of the system must be related to the benefits to be derived. The Corporation believes its system provides an appropriate balance in this regard. The Corporation maintains an Internal Audit Department which reviews the adequacy and tests the application of internal accounting controls.

The financial statements have been audited by Arthur Andersen & Co., independent public accountants, whose appointment was ratified by stockholder vote at the stockholders' meeting held on April 26, 1993. Their report expresses an opinion that the Corporation's financial statements are fairly stated in conformity with generally accepted accounting principles, and they have indicated to us that their examination was performed in accordance with generally accepted auditing standards which are designed to obtain reasonable assurance about whether the financial statements are free of material misstatement.

The Audit Committee of the Board of Directors of the Corporation, consisting solely of outside directors, meets regularly with the independent public accountants, internal auditors and management to discuss, among other things, the audit scopes and results. Arthur Andersen & Co. and the internal auditors both have full and free access to the Audit Committee, with and without the presence of management.

Report of Independent Public Accountants

To the Stockholders and Board of Directors
of Hershey Foods Corporation:

We have audited the accompanying consolidated balance sheets of Hershey Foods Corporation (a Delaware Corporation) and subsidiaries as of December 31, 1993 and 1992, and the related consolidated statements of income, stockholders' equity and cash flows for each of the three years in the period ended December 31, 1993, appearing on pages 20, 22, 24, 26, and 27 through 36. These financial statements are the responsibility of the Corporation's management. Our responsibility is to express an opinion on these financial statements based on our audits.

We conducted our audits in accordance with generally accepted auditing standards. Those standards require that we plan and perform the audit to obtain reasonable assurance about whether the financial statements are free of material misstatement. An audit includes examining, on a test basis, evidence supporting the amounts and disclosures in the financial statements. An audit also includes assessing the accounting principles used and significant estimates made by management, as well as evaluating the overall financial statement presentation. We believe that our audits provide a reasonable basis for our opinion.

In our opinion, the financial statements referred to above present fairly, in all material respects, the financial position of Hershey Foods Corporation and subsidiaries as of December 31, 1993 and 1992, and the results of their operations and cash flows for each of the three years in the period ended December 31, 1993 in conformity with generally accepted accounting principles.

As discussed in Notes 7 and 9 to the consolidated financial statements, effective January 1, 1993, the Corporation changed its methods of accounting for income taxes and post-retirement benefits other than pensions.

Arthur Andersen & Co.

New York, N.Y.
January 28, 1994

Investor Information

Stockholders

As of December 31, 1993, Hershey Foods Corporation had outstanding 72,359,957 shares of Common Stock and 15,253,279 shares of Class B Common Stock.

Year	Year-end Common Stock and Class B Common Stock Holders	Approximate Annual Composite Trading Volume
1993	32,859	29,338
1992	31,642	24,146
1991	31,029	27,975
1990	30,052	31,024
1989	29,998	41,220

Stock Market Data

Hershey Foods Corporation's Common Stock is listed and traded principally on the New York Stock Exchange under the ticker symbol "HSY." Class B Common Stock is not listed for trading. The stock tables of most financial publications list the Corporation as "Hershey." Options on the Corporation's Common Stock are traded on the American Stock Exchange.

Common Stock Profile

	Common Stock Price			Dividends Paid	
1993 (calendar quarter)	High	Low	Close	Common	Class B
1st Quarter	$55⅞	$46½	$53⅝	$.270	$.2450
2nd Quarter	54⅝	45¾	47⅛	.270	.2450
3rd Quarter	51⅞	43½	49⅞	.300	.2725
4th Quarter	54¾	48⅝	49	.300	.2725

Dividend Policy

Dividends on Hershey Foods Corporation's Common Stock and Class B Common Stock are declared by the Board of Directors, and are normally paid in the months of March, June, September and December.

The dividend to be paid on the Common Stock in March 1994 will be the 257th consecutive regular dividend paid by the Corporation. The dividend rate has been increased annually for 19 consecutive years. Historically, the Corporation has targeted approximately one-third of income from continuing operations as dividends to stockholders.

Dividend Reinvestment Service

The Corporation offers an Automatic Dividend Reinvestment Service to registered holders of Hershey Foods Common Stock. This service provides a convenient method of increasing share ownership without paying brokerage commissions or service fees. The Corporation pays all commissions and fees associated with stock purchases made with reinvested dividends. However, under Internal Revenue Service regulations, any fees paid on behalf of stockholders are considered taxable income and will be included on their Form 1099-DIV Statement of Dividends and Distributions. Participants also may make voluntary cash payments of up to $20,000 annually, for which there are only nominal brokerage commissions and service fees. Approximately one-third of Hershey Foods Corporation's registered stockholders are enrolled in this Automatic Dividend Reinvestment Service. For more information, contact:

Chemical Bank
Dividend Reinvestment Department
P.O. Box 3069
Church Street Station
New York, NY 10116-3069
(800) 851-4216

Safekeeping of Stock Certificates

Your stock certificate is a valuable document and should be kept in a safe place such as a safe deposit box. Stock certificates should not be signed until sold or transferred to another person. For tax purposes, please keep a record of each certificate, including the original cost. This record should be kept in a separate place from the certificates.

Stockholder Inquiries

Questions relating to stockholder records, change of ownership, change of address and dividend payments should be sent to the Corporation's Transfer Agent, Chemical Bank, listed on page 41.

Financial Information

Security analysts, investment managers and stockholders should direct financial information inquiries to the Investor Relations contact listed on page 41.

Hershey Foods Corporation

Eleven-Year Consolidated Financial Summary

(all dollar and share amounts in thousands except market price and per share statistics)

	10-Year Compound Growth Rate	1993	1992	1991	1990	1989
Summary of Operations[a]						
Net Sales	10.5%	$3,488,249	3,219,805	2,899,165	2,715,609	2,420,988
Cost of Sales	9.0%	$1,995,502	1,833,388	1,694,404	1,588,360	1,455,612
Selling, Marketing and Administrative	14.4%	$1,035,519	958,189	814,459	776,668	655,040
Gain on Business Restructuring, Net		$ —	—	—	35,540	—
Gain on Sale of Investment Interest		$ 80,642	—	—	—	—
Interest Expense, Net	6.3%	$ 26,995	27,240	26,845	24,603	20,414
Income Taxes	11.8%	$ 213,642	158,390	143,929	145,636	118,868
Income from Continuing Operations Before Accounting Changes	13.9%	$ 297,233	242,598	219,528	215,882	171,054
Net Cumulative Effect of Accounting Changes		$ (103,908)	—	—	—	—
Discontinued Operations		$ —	—	—	—	—
Net Income	6.8%	$ 193,325	242,598	219,528	215,882	171,054
Income Per Share:						
From Continuing Operations Before Accounting Changes[b]	14.4%	$ 3.31[g]	2.69	2.43	2.39[h]	1.90
Net Cumulative Effect of Accounting Changes		$ (1.16)	—	—	—	—
Net Income[b]	7.2%	$ 2.15[g]	2.69	2.43	2.39[h]	1.90
Weighted Average Shares Outstanding[b]		89,757	90,186	90,186	90,186	90,186
Dividends Paid on Common Stock	9.4%	$ 84,711	77,174	70,426	74,161[d]	55,431
Per Share[b]	12.0%	$ 1.140	1.030	.940	.990[d]	.740
Dividends Paid on Class B Common Stock		$ 15,788	14,270	12,975	13,596[d]	10,161
Per Share[b]		$ 1.035	.935	.850	.890[d]	.665
Income from Continuing Operations Before:						
Interest, Income Taxes and Accounting Changes as a Percent of Net Sales		13.1%[c]	13.3%	13.5%	12.9%[e]	12.8%
Accounting Changes as a Percent of Net Sales		7.4%[c]	7.5%	7.6%	7.2%[e]	7.1%
Depreciation	18.3%	$ 100,124	84,434	72,735	61,725	54,543
Advertising	7.8%	$ 130,009	137,631	117,049	146,297	121,182
Promotion	18.9%	$ 444,546	398,577	325,465	315,242	256,237
Payroll	9.2%	$ 469,564	433,162	398,661	372,780	340,129
Year-end Position and Statistics[a]						
Working Capital	(8.9)%	$ 75,151	203,039	273,747	320,552	281,821
Capital Additions	11.4%	$ 211,621	249,795	226,071	179,408	162,032
Total Assets	12.0%	$2,855,091	2,672,909	2,341,822	2,078,828	1,814,101
Long-term Portion of Debt	4.5%	$ 165,757	174,273	282,933	273,442	216,108
Stockholders' Equity	9.0%	$1,412,344	1,465,279	1,335,251	1,243,537	1,117,050
Current Ratio		1.1:1	1.3:1	1.6:1	1.9:1	2.0:1
Capitalization Ratio		27%	27%	22%	19%	17%
Net Book Value Per Share[b]	9.8%	$ 16.12	16.25	14.81	13.79	12.39
Operating Return on Average Stockholders' Equity		17.8%	17.3%	17.0%	16.6%	16.1%
Operating Return on Average Invested Capital		15.0%	14.4%	13.8%	13.4%	13.2%
Full-time Employees at Year-end		14,300	13,700	14,000	12,700	11,800
Stockholders' Data						
Outstanding Shares of Common Stock and Class B Common Stock at Year-end[b]		87,613	90,186	90,186	90,186	90,186
Market Price of Common Stock at Year-end[b]	16.7%	$ 49	47	44 3/8	37 1/2	35 7/8
Range During Year[b]		$55 7/8–43 1/2	48 3/8–38 1/4	44 1/2–35 1/8	39 5/8–28 1/4	36 7/8–24 3/4

Notes:

(a) All amounts for years prior to 1988 have been restated for discontinued operations, where applicable. Operating Return on Average Stockholders' Equity and Operating Return on Average Invested Capital have been computed using Net Income, excluding the 1988 gain and 1985 loss on disposal included in Discontinued Operations, the 1993 Net Cumulative Effect of Accounting Changes, and the after-tax impacts of the 1990 Gain on Business Restructuring, Net, and the 1993 Gain on Sale of Investment Interest in Freia Marabou a.s (Freia).

(b) All shares and per share amounts have been adjusted for the three-for-one stock split effective September 15, 1986 and the two-for-one stock split effective September 15, 1983.

(c) Calculated percent excludes the Gain on Sale of Investment Interest in Freia. Including the gain, Income from Continuing Operations Before Interest, Income Taxes and Accounting Changes as a Percent of Net Sales was 15.4% and Income from Continuing Operations Before Accounting Changes as a Percent of Net Sales was 8.5%.

(d) Amounts included a special dividend for 1990 of $11.2 million or $.15 per share of Common Stock and $2.1 million or $.135 per share of Class B Common Stock.

1988	1987	1986	1985	1984	1983
2,168,048	1,863,816	1,635,486	1,526,584	1,423,396	1,280,379
1,326,458	1,149,663	1,032,061	982,370	934,817	844,488
575,515	468,062	387,227	345,299	309,587	270,472
—	—	—	—	—	—
—	—	—	—	—	—
29,954	22,413	8,061	10,240	8,325	14,602
91,615	99,604	100,931	91,910	82,986	70,123
144,506	124,074	107,206	96,765	87,681	80,694
—	—	—	—	—	—
69,443	24,097	25,558	15,462	21,001	19,472
213,949	148,171	132,764	112,227	108,682	100,166
1.60	1.38	1.15	1.03	.93	.86
—	—	—	—	—	—
2.37	1.64	1.42	1.19	1.16	1.07
90,186	90,186	93,508	94,011	94,011	94,011
49,433	43,436	40,930	37,386	37,073	34,470
.660	.580	.520	.475	.413	.367
9,097	8,031	7,216	6,556	1,607	—
.595	.525	.472	.428	.105	—
12.3%	13.2%	13.2%	13.0%	12.6%	12.9%
6.7%	6.7%	6.6%	6.3%	6.2%	6.3%
43,721	35,397	31,254	28,348	22,725	18,594
99,082	97,033	83,600	77,135	71,070	61,274
230,187	171,162	122,508	105,401	94,921	78,773
298,483	263,529	238,742	222,267	208,395	195,254
273,716	190,069(f)	174,147	225,345	187,642	191,435
101,682	68,504	74,452	61,361	45,258	71,697
1,764,665	1,544,354	1,262,332	1,116,074	1,052,161	920,329
233,025	280,900	185,676	86,986	103,155	106,543
1,005,866	832,410	727,941	727,899	660,928	596,037
1.8:1	1.7:1(f)	2.0:1	2.4:1	2.1:1	2.6:1
22%	27%	21%	12%	14%	16%
11.15	9.23	8.07	7.74	7.03	6.34
17.5%	19.0%	18.2%	17.2%	17.3%	17.8%
13.3%	13.5%	13.5%	13.5%	13.5%	13.8%
12,100	10,540	10,210	10,380	10,150	9,630
90,186	90,186	90,186	94,011	94,011	94,011
26	24 1/2	24 5/8	17 1/8	12 7/8	10 1/2
28 5/8–21 7/8	37 3/4–20 3/4	30–15 1/2	18 3/8–11 5/8	13 3/4–9 3/8	11 5/8–8 1/8

(e) Calculated percent excludes the Gain on Business Restructuring, Net. Including the gain, Income from Continuing Operations Before Interest and Income Taxes as a Percent of Net Sales was 14.2% and Income from Continuing Operations as a Percent of Net Sales was 7.9%.

(f) Amounts exclude net assets of discontinued operations.

(g) Income Per Share from Continuing Operations Before Accounting Changes and Net Income Per Share for 1993 included a $.45 per share gain on the sale of the investment interest in Freia. Excluding the impact of this gain, Income Per Share from Continuing Operations Before Accounting Changes would have been $2.86.

(h) Income Per Share from Continuing Operations and Net Income Per Share for 1990 included a $.22 per share Gain on Business Restructuring, Net. Excluding the impact of this gain, Income Per Share from Continuing Operations Before Accounting Changes and Net Income Per Share would have been $2.17.

FINANCIAL STATEMENT ANALYSIS

The basic financial statements provide much of the information users need to make economic decisions about businesses. In the following paragraphs, we discuss various ways in which financial statement data are analyzed.

BASIC ANALYTICAL PROCEDURES

The analytical measures obtained from financial statements are often expressed as ratios or percentages. For example, the relationship of $300,000 to $200,000 ($300,000/$200,000, or $300,000:$200,000) may be expressed as 1.5, 1.5:1, or 150%.

Analytical procedures may be used to compare items on a current statement with related items on earlier statements. For example, cash of $150,000 on the current balance sheet may be compared with cash of $100,000 on the balance sheet of a year earlier. The current year's cash may be expressed as 1.5 or 150% of the earlier amount or as an increase of 50% or $50,000.[1]

Analytical procedures are also widely used to examine relationships within a financial statement. To illustrate, assume that cash of $50,000 and inventories of $250,000 are included in the total assets of $1,000,000 on a balance sheet. In relative terms, the cash balance is 5% of the total assets, and the inventories are 25% of the total assets.

In the following discussion, we emphasize the importance of each of the various analytical measures illustrated. The measures are not ends in themselves; they are only guides in evaluating financial and operating data. Many other factors, such as trends in the industry and general economic conditions, should also be considered.

Horizontal Analysis

The percentage analysis of increases and decreases in related items in comparative financial statements is called **horizontal analysis.** The amount of each item on the most recent statement is compared with the related item on one or more earlier statements. The amount of increase or decrease in the item is listed, along with the percent of increase or decrease.

Horizontal analysis may include a comparison between two statements. In this case, the earlier statement is used as the base. Horizontal analysis may also include three or more comparative statements. In this case, the earliest date or period may be used as the base for comparing all later dates or periods. Alternatively, each statement may be compared to the immediately preceding statement. Exhibit 1 is a condensed comparative balance sheet for two years for Lincoln Company, with horizontal analysis.

We cannot fully evaluate the significance of the various increases and decreases in the items shown in Exhibit 1 without additional information. Although total assets at the end of 1997 were $91,000 (7.4%) less than at the beginning of the year, liabilities were reduced by $133,000 (30%), and stockholders' equity increased $42,000 (5.3%). It appears that the reduction of $100,000 in long-term liabilities was achieved mostly through the sale of long-term investments.

The balance sheet in Exhibit 1 may be expanded to include the details of the various categories of assets and liabilities. An alternative is to present the details in separate schedules. Exhibit 2 is a supporting schedule with horizontal analysis.

[1] Increases or decreases in items may be expressed in percentage terms only when the initial or base amount is positive. If the base amount is zero or a negative value, the amount of change cannot be expressed as a percentage.

Exhibit 1
Comparative Balance Sheet—Horizontal Analysis

Lincoln Company
Comparative Balance Sheet
December 31, 1997 and 1996

	1997	1996	Increase (Decrease)	
			Amount	Percent
Assets				
Current assets	$ 550,000	$ 533,000	$ 17,000	3.2%
Long-term investments	95,000	177,500	(82,500)	(46.5%)
Plant assets (net)	444,500	470,000	(25,500)	(5.4%)
Intangible assets	50,000	50,000	—	
Total assets	$1,139,500	$1,230,500	$ (91,000)	(7.4%)
Liabilities				
Current liabilities	$ 210,000	$ 243,000	$ (33,000)	(13.6%)
Long-term liabilities	100,000	200,000	(100,000)	(50.0%)
Total liabilities	$ 310,000	$ 443,000	$(133,000)	(30.0%)
Stockholders' Equity				
Preferred 6% stock, $100 par	$ 150,000	$ 150,000	—	—
Common stock, $10 par	500,000	500,000	—	—
Retained earnings	179,500	137,500	$ 42,000	30.5%
Total stockholders' equity	$ 829,500	$ 787,500	$ 42,000	5.3%
Total liabilities and stockholders' equity	$1,139,500	$1,230,500	$ (91,000)	(7.4%)

Exhibit 2
Comparative Schedule of Current Assets—Horizontal Analysis

Lincoln Company
Comparative Schedule of Current Assets
December 31, 1997 and 1996

	1997	1996	Increase (Decrease)	
			Amount	Percent
Cash	$ 90,500	$ 64,700	$25,800	39.9%
Marketable securities	75,000	60,000	15,000	25.0%
Accounts receivable (net)	115,000	120,000	(5,000)	(4.2%)
Inventories	264,000	283,000	(19,000)	(6.7%)
Prepaid expenses	5,500	5,300	200	3.8%
Total current assets	$550,000	$533,000	$17,000	3.2%

The decrease in accounts receivable may be due to changes in credit terms or improved collection policies. Likewise, a decrease in inventories during a period of increased sales may indicate an improvement in the management of inventories.

The changes in the current assets in Exhibit 2 appear favorable. This assessment is supported by the 24.8% increase in net sales shown in Exhibit 3.

An increase in net sales may not have a favorable effect on operating performance. The percentage increase in Lincoln Company's net sales is accompanied by a greater percentage increase in the cost of goods (merchandise) sold. This has the effect of reducing gross profit. Selling expenses increased significantly, and administrative expenses increased slightly. Overall operating expenses increased by 20.7%, whereas gross profit increased by only 19.7%.

The increase in operating income and in net income is favorable. However, a study of the expenses and additional analyses and comparisons should be made before reaching a conclusion.

Exhibit 4 illustrates a comparative retained earnings statement with horizontal analysis. It reveals an increase of 30.5% in retained earnings for the year. The increase is due to net income of $91,000 for the year less dividends of $49,000.

Exhibit 3
Comparative Income Statement—Horizontal Analysis

Lincoln Company
Comparative Income Statement
December 31, 1997 and 1996

	1997	1996	Increase (Decrease)	
			Amount	Percent
Sales	$1,530,500	$1,234,000	$296,500	24.0%
Sales returns and allowances	32,500	34,000	(1,500)	(4.4%)
Net sales	$1,498,000	$1,200,000	$298,000	24.8%
Cost of goods sold	1,043,000	820,000	223,000	27.2%
Gross profit	$ 455,000	$ 380,000	$ 75,000	19.7%
Selling expenses	$ 191,000	$ 147,000	$ 44,000	29.9%
Administrative expenses	104,000	97,400	6,600	6.8%
Total operating expenses	$ 295,000	$ 244,400	$ 50,600	20.7%
Operating income	$ 160,000	$ 135,600	$ 24,400	18.0%
Other income	8,500	11,000	(2,500)	(22.7%)
	$ 168,500	$ 146,600	$ 21,900	14.9%
Other expense	6,000	12,000	(6,000)	(50.0%)
Income before income tax	$ 162,500	$ 134,600	$ 27,900	20.7%
Income tax	71,500	58,100	13,400	23.1%
Net income	$ 91,000	$ 76,500	$ 14,500	19.0%

Exhibit 4
Comparative Retained Earnings Statement—Horizontal Analysis

Lincoln Company
Comparative Retained Earnings Statement
December 31, 1997 and 1996

	1997	1996	Increase (Decrease)	
			Amount	Percent
Retained earnings, January 1	$137,500	$100,000	$37,500	37.5%
Net income for the year	91,000	76,500	14,500	19.0%
Total	$228,500	$176,500	$52,000	29.5%
Dividends:				
On preferred stock	$ 9,000	$ 9,000	—	—
On common stock	40,000	30,000	$10,000	33.3%
Total	$ 49,000	$ 39,000	$10,000	25.6%
Retained earnings, December 31	$179,500	$137,500	$42,000	30.5%

Vertical Analysis

A percentage analysis may also be used to show the relationship of each component to the total within a single statement. This type of analysis is called **vertical analysis.** Like horizontal analysis, the statements may be prepared in either detailed or condensed form. In the latter case, additional details of the changes in individual items may be presented in supporting schedules. In such schedules, the percentage analysis may be based on either the total of the schedule or the statement total. Although vertical analysis is limited to an individual statement, its significance may be improved by preparing comparative statements.

In vertical analysis of the balance sheet, each asset item is stated as a percent of the total assets. Each liability and stockholders' equity item is stated as a percent of the total liabilities and stockholders' equity. Exhibit 5 is a condensed comparative balance sheet with vertical analysis for Lincoln Company.

The major percentage changes in Lincoln Company's assets are in the current asset and long-term investment categories. In the Liabilities and Stockholders'

Exhibit 5
Comparative Balance Sheet—Vertical Analysis

Lincoln Company
Comparative Balance Sheet
December 31, 1997 and 1996

	1997		1996	
	Amount	Percent	Amount	Percent
Assets				
Current assets	$ 550,000	48.3%	$ 533,000	43.3%
Long-term investments	95,000	8.3	177,500	14.4
Plant assets (net)	444,500	39.0	470,000	38.2
Intangible assets	50,000	4.4	50,000	4.1
Total assets	$1,139,500	100.0%	$1,230,500	100.0%
Liabilities				
Current liabilities	$ 210,000	18.4%	$ 243,000	19.7%
Long-term liabilities	100,000	8.8	200,000	16.3
Total liabilities	$ 310,000	27.2%	$ 443,000	36.0%
Stockholders' Equity				
Preferred 6% stock, $100 par	$ 150,000	13.2%	$ 150,000	12.2%
Common stock, $10 par	500,000	43.9	500,000	40.6
Retained earnings	179,500	15.7	137,500	11.2
Total stockholders' equity	$ 829,500	72.8%	$ 787,500	64.0%
Total liabilities and stockholders' equity	$1,139,500	100.0%	$1,230,500	100.0%

Equity sections of the balance sheet, the greatest percentage changes are in long-term liabilities and retained earnings. Stockholders' equity increased from 64% to 72.8% of total liabilities and stockholders' equity in 1997. There is a comparable decrease in liabilities.

In a vertical analysis of the income statement, each item is stated as a percent of net sales. Exhibit 6 is a condensed comparative income statement with vertical analysis for Lincoln Company.

Exhibit 6
Comparative Income Statement—Vertical Analysis

Lincoln Company
Comparative Income Sheet
December 31, 1997 and 1996

	1997		1996	
	Amount	Percent	Amount	Percent
Sales	$1,530,500	102.2%	$1,234,000	102.8%
Sales returns and allowances	32,500	2.2	34,000	2.8
Net sales	$1,498,000	100.0%	$1,200,000	100.0%
Cost of goods sold	1,043,000	69.6	820,000	68.3
Gross profit	$ 455,000	30.4%	$ 380,000	31.7%
Selling expenses	$ 191,000	12.8%	$ 147,000	12.3%
Administrative expenses	104,000	6.9	97,400	8.1
Total operating expenses	$ 295,000	19.7%	$ 244,400	20.4%
Operating income	$ 160,000	10.7%	$ 135,600	11.3%
Other income	8,500	0.6	11,000	0.9
	$ 168,500	11.3%	$ 146,600	12.2%
Other expense	6,000	0.4	12,000	1.0
Income before income tax	$ 162,500	10.9%	$ 134,600	11.2%
Income tax	71,500	4.8	58,100	4.8
Net income	$ 91,000	6.1%	$ 76,500	6.4%

We must be careful when judging the significance of differences between percentages for the two years. For example, the decline of the gross profit rate from 31.7% in 1996 to 30.4% in 1997 is only 1.3 percentage points. In terms of dollars of potential gross profit, however, it represents a decline of approximately $19,500 (1.3% × $1,498,000).

Common-Size Statements

Horizontal and vertical analyses with both dollar and percentage amounts are useful in assessing relationships and trends in financial conditions and operations of a business. Vertical analysis with both dollar and percentage amounts is also useful in comparing one company with another or with industry averages. Such comparisons are easier to make with the use of common-size statements. In a **common-size statement,** all items are expressed in percentages.

Common-size statements are useful in comparing the current period with prior periods, individual businesses, or one business with industry percentages. Industry data are often available from trade associations and financial information services. Exhibit 7 is a comparative common-size income statement for two businesses.

Exhibit 7
Common-Size Income Statement

Lincoln Company and Madison Corporation
Condensed Common-Size Income Statement
For the Year Ended December 31, 1997

	Lincoln Company	Madison Corporation
Sales	102.2%	102.3%
Sales returns and allowances	2.2	2.3
Net sales	100.0%	100.0%
Cost of goods sold	69.6	70.0
Gross profit	30.4%	30.0%
Selling expenses	12.8%	11.5%
Administrative expenses	6.9	4.1
Total operating expenses	19.7%	15.6%
Operating income	10.7%	14.4%
Other income	0.6	0.6
	11.3%	15.0%
Other expense	0.4	0.5
Income before income tax	10.9%	14.5%
Income tax	4.8	5.5
Net income	6.1%	9.0%

Exhibit 7 indicates that Lincoln Company has a slightly higher rate of gross profit than Madison Corporation. However, this advantage is more than offset by Lincoln Company's higher percentage of selling and administrative expenses. As a result, the operating income of Lincoln Company is 10.7% of net sales, compared with 14.4% for Madison Corporation—an unfavorable difference of 3.7 percentage points.

Other Analytical Measures

In addition to the preceding analyses, other relationships may be expressed in ratios and percentages. Often, these items are taken from the financial statements and thus are a type of vertical analysis. Comparison of these items with items from earlier periods is a type of horizontal analysis.

FINANCIAL STATEMENT ANALYSES OF SOLVENCY AND PROFITABILITY

Some aspects of a business's financial condition and operations are of greater importance to some users than others. However, all users are interested in the ability of a business to pay its debts as they are due and to earn income. These two aspects of a business are called factors of **solvency** and **profitability.**

A business that cannot pay its debts on a timely basis may experience difficulty in obtaining credit. A lack of available credit may, in turn, lead to a decline in the business's profitability. Eventually, the business may be forced into bankruptcy. Likewise, a business that is less profitable than its competitors is likely to be at a disadvantage in obtaining credit or new capital from stockholders. Thus, the factors of solvency and profitability are interrelated.

Analyses of historical data are useful in assessing the past performance of a business and in forecasting its future performance. The results of financial analyses may be even more useful when they are compared with those of competing businesses and with industry averages.

In the following paragraphs, we discuss various types of financial analyses that are useful in evaluating the solvency and profitability of a business. The examples are based on Lincoln Company's financial statements presented earlier. In some cases, data from Lincoln Company's financial statements of the preceding year and from other sources are also used.

SOLVENCY ANALYSIS

Solvency is the ability of a business to meet its financial obligations (debts) as they are due. Solvency analysis, therefore, focuses on the ability of a business to pay or otherwise satisfy its current and noncurrent liabilities. This ability is normally assessed by examining balance sheet relationships. Major analyses used in assessing solvency include the following:

1. Current position analysis
2. Accounts receivable analysis
3. Inventory analysis
4. The ratio of plant assets to long-term liabilities
5. The ratio of liabilities to stockholders' equity
6. The number of times interest charges are earned

Current Position Analysis

To be useful in assessing solvency, a ratio or other financial measure must relate to a business's ability to pay or otherwise satisfy its liabilities. The use of such measures to assess the ability of a business to pay its current liabilities is called **current position analysis.** Such analysis is of special interest to short-term creditors.

An analysis of a firm's current position normally includes determining the working capital, the current ratio, and the acid-test ratio. The current and acid-test ratios are most useful when analyzed together and compared to previous periods and other firms in the industry.

WORKING CAPITAL. The excess of the current assets of a business over its current liabilities is called **working capital.** *The working capital is often used in evaluating a company's ability to meet currently maturing debts.* It is especially useful in making monthly or other period-to-period comparisons for a company. However, amounts of working capital are difficult to assess when comparing companies of different sizes or in comparing such amounts with industry figures. For example, working capital of $250,000 may be adequate for a small residential contractor, but it may be inadequate for a large commercial contractor.

CURRENT RATIO. Another means of expressing the relationship between current assets and current liabilities is the **current ratio.** This ratio is sometimes called the **working capital ratio** or **bankers' ratio.** The ratio is computed by dividing the total current assets by the total current liabilities. For Lincoln Company, working capital and the current ratio for 1997 and 1996 are as follows:

	1997	*1996*
Current assets	$550,000	$533,000
Current liabilities	210,000	243,000
Working capital	$340,000	$290,000
Current ratio	2.6:1	2.2:1

The current ratio is a more reliable indicator of solvency than is working capital. To illustrate, assume that as of December 31, 1997, the working capital of a competitor is much greater than $340,000, but its current ratio is only 1.3:1. Considering these facts alone, Lincoln Company, with its current ratio of 2.6:1, is in a more favorable position to obtain short-term credit than the competitor, which has the **greater** amount of working capital.

ACID-TEST RATIO. The working capital and the current ratio do not consider the makeup of the current assets. To illustrate the importance of this consideration, the current position data for Lincoln Company and Jefferson Corporation as of December 31, 1997, are as follows:

	Lincoln Company	*Jefferson Corporation*
Current assets:		
Cash	$ 90,500	$ 45,500
Marketable securities	75,000	25,000
Accounts receivable (net)	115,000	90,000
Inventories	264,000	380,000
Prepaid expenses	5,500	9,500
Total current assets	$550,000	$550,000
Current liabilities	210,000	210,000
Working capital	$340,000	$340,000
Current ratio	2.6:1	2.6:1

Both companies have a working capital of $340,000 and a current ratio of 2.6:1. But the ability of each company to pay its current debts is significantly different. Jefferson Corporation has more of its current assets in inventories. Some of these inventories must be sold and the receivables collected before the current liabilities can be paid in full. Thus, a large amount of time may be necessary to convert these inventories into cash. Declines in market prices and a reduction in demand could also impair its ability to pay current liabilities. In contrast, Lincoln Company has cash and current assets (marketable securities and accounts receivable) that can generally be converted to cash rather quickly to meet its current liabilities.

A ratio that measures the "instant" debt-paying ability of a company is called the **acid-test ratio** or **quick ratio.** It is the ratio of the total quick assets to the total current liabilities. **Quick assets** are cash and other current assets that can be quickly converted to cash. Quick assets normally include cash, marketable securities, and receivables. The acid-test ratio data for Lincoln Company are as follows:

	1997	*1996*
Quick assets:		
Cash	$ 90,500	$ 64,700
Marketable securities	75,000	60,000
Accounts receivable (net)	115,000	120,000
Total	$280,500	$244,700
Current liabilities	$210,000	$243,000
Acid-test ratio	1.3:1	1.0:1

Accounts Receivable Analysis

The size and makeup of accounts receivable change constantly during business operations. Sales on account increase accounts receivable, whereas collections from customers decrease accounts receivable. Firms that grant long credit terms usually have larger accounts receivable balances than those granting short credit terms. Increases or decreases in the volume of sales also affect the balance of accounts receivable.

It is desirable to collect receivables as promptly as possible. The cash collected from receivables improves solvency. In addition, the cash generated by prompt collections from customers may be used in operations for such purposes as purchasing merchandise in large quantities at lower prices. The cash may also be used for payment of dividends to stockholders or for other investing or financing purposes. Prompt collection also lessens the risk of loss from uncollectible accounts.

ACCOUNTS RECEIVABLE TURNOVER. The relationship between credit sales and accounts receivable may be stated as the **accounts receivable turnover.** This ratio is computed by dividing net sales on account by the average net accounts receivable. It is desirable to base the average on monthly balances, which allows for seasonal changes in sales. When such data are not available, it may be necessary to use the average of the accounts receivable balance at the beginning and the end of the year. If there are trade notes receivable as well as accounts, the two may be combined. The accounts receivable turnover data for Lincoln Company are as follows. All sales were made on account.

	1997	*1996*
Net sales on account	$1,498,000	$1,200,000
Accounts receivable (net):		
Beginning of year	$ 120,000	$ 140,000
End of year	115,000	120,000
Total	$ 235,000	$ 260,000
Average	$ 117,500	$ 130,000
Accounts receivable turnover	12.7	9.2

The increase in the accounts receivable turnover for 1997 indicates that there has been an improvement in the collection of receivables. This may be due to a change in the granting of credit or the collecting practices or both.

NUMBER OF DAYS' SALES IN RECEIVABLES. Another measure of the relationship between credit sales and accounts receivable is the **number of days' sales in receivables.** This ratio is computed by dividing the net accounts receivable at the end of the year by the average daily sales on account. Average daily sales on account is determined by dividing net sales on account by 365 days. The number of days' sales in receivables is computed for Lincoln Company as follows:

	1997	*1996*
Accounts receivable (net), end of year	$ 115,000	$ 120,000
Net sales on account	$1,498,000	$1,200,000
Average daily sales on account	$ 4,104	$ 3,288
Number of days' sales in receivables*	28.0	36.5

*Accounts receivable ÷ Average daily sales on account

The number of days' sales in receivables is an estimate of the length of time the accounts receivable have been outstanding. Comparing this measure with the credit terms provides information on the efficiency in collecting receivables. For example, assume that the number of days' sales in receivables for Grant Inc. is 40. If Grant Inc.'s credit terms are n/45, then its collection process appears to be efficient. On the other hand, if Grant Inc.'s credit terms are n/30, its collection process does not appear to be efficient. A comparison with other firms in the same industry and with prior years also provides useful information. Such comparisons may indicate efficiency of collection procedures and trends in credit management.

Inventory Analysis

A business should keep enough inventory on hand to meet the needs of its customers and its operations. At the same time, however, an excessive amount of inventory reduces solvency by tying up funds. Excess inventories also increase insurance expense, property taxes, storage costs, and other related expenses. These expenses further reduce funds that could be used elsewhere to improve operations. Finally, excess inventory also increases the risk of losses because of price declines or obsolescence of the inventory. Two measures that are useful for evaluating the management of inventory are the inventory turnover and the number of days' sales in inventory.

INVENTORY TURNOVER. The relationship between the volume of goods (merchandise) sold and inventory may be stated as the **inventory turnover.** It is computed by dividing the cost of goods sold by the average inventory. If monthly data are not available, the average of the inventories at the beginning and the end of the year may be used. The inventory turnover for Lincoln Company is computed as follows:

	1997	*1996*
Cost of goods sold	$1,043,000	$820,000
Inventories:		
Beginning of year	$ 283,000	$311,000
End of year	264,000	283,000
Total	$ 547,000	$594,000
Average	$ 273,500	$297,000
Inventory turnover	3.8	2.8

The inventory turnover improved for Lincoln Company because of an increase in the cost of goods sold and a decrease in the average inventories. Differences across inventories, companies, and industries are too great to allow a general statement on what is a good inventory turnover. For example, a firm selling food should have a higher turnover than a firm selling furniture or jewelry. Likewise, the perishable foods department of a supermarket should have a higher turnover than the soaps and cleansers department. However, for each business or each department within a business, there is a reasonable turnover rate. A turnover lower than this rate could mean that inventory is not being managed properly.

NUMBER OF DAYS' SALES IN INVENTORY. Another measure of the relationship between the cost of goods sold and inventory is the **number of days' sales in inventory.** This measure is computed by dividing the inventory at the end of the year by the average daily cost of goods sold (cost of goods sold divided by 365). The number of days' sales in inventory for Lincoln Company is computed as follows:

	1997	*1996*
Inventories, end of year	$ 264,000	$283,000
Cost of goods sold	$1,043,000	$820,000
Average daily cost of goods sold	$ 2,858	$ 2,247
Number of days' sales in inventory	92.4	125.9
(Inventories ÷ avg. daily cost of goods sold)		

The number of days' sales in inventory is a rough measure of the length of time it takes to acquire, sell, and replace the inventory. For Lincoln Company, there is a major improvement in the number of days' sales in inventory during 1997. However, a comparison with earlier years and similar firms would be useful in assessing Lincoln Company's overall inventory management.

Ratio of Plant Assets to Long-Term Liabilities

Long-term notes and bonds are often secured by mortgages on plant assets. The **ratio of total plant assets to long-term liabilities** *is a solvency measure that indicates the margin of safety of the noteholders or bondholders. It also indicates the ability of the business to borrow additional funds on a long-term basis.* The ratio of plant assets to long-term liabilities for Lincoln Company is as follows:

	1997	*1996*
Plant assets (net)	$444,500	$470,000
Long-term liabilities	$100,000	$200,000
Ratio of plant assets to long-term liabilities	4.4:1	2.4:1

The major increase in this ratio at the end of 1997 is mainly due to liquidating one-half of Lincoln Company's long-term liabilities. If the company needs to borrow additional funds on a long-term basis in the future, it is in a strong position to do so.

Ratio of Liabilities to Stockholders' Equity

Claims against the total assets of a business are divided into two groups: (1) claims of creditors and (2) claims of owners. *The relationship between the total claims of the creditors and owners is a solvency measure that indicates the margin of safety for creditors. It also indicates the ability of the business to withstand adverse business conditions.* When the claims of creditors are large in relation to the equity of the stockholders, there are usually significant interest payments. If earnings decline to the point where the company is unable to meet its interest payments, the business may be taken over by the creditors.

The relationship between creditor and stockholder equity is shown in the vertical analysis of the balance sheet. For example, the balance sheet of Lincoln Company in Exhibit 5 indicates that on December 31, 1997, liabilities represented 27.2% and stockholders' equity represented 72.8% of the total liabilities and stockholders' equity (100.0%). Instead of expressing each item as a percent of the total, this relationship may be expressed as a ratio of one to the other, as follows:

	1997	1996
Total liabilities	$310,000	$443,000
Total stockholders' equity	$829,500	$787,500
Ratio of liabilities to stockholders' equity	0.37:1	0.56:1

The balance sheet of Lincoln Company shows that the major factor affecting the change in the ratio was the $100,000 decrease in long-term liabilities during 1997. The ratio at the end of both years shows a large margin of safety for the creditors.

Number of Times Interest Charges Earned

Corporations in some industries, such as public utilities, normally have high ratios of debt to stockholders' equity. For such corporations, *the relative risk of the debtholders is normally measured as the* **number of times the interest charges are earned** during the year. The higher the ratio, the lower the risk that interest payments will not be made if earnings decrease. In other words, the higher the ratio, the greater the assurance that interest payments will be made on a continuing basis. *This measure also indicates the general financial strength of the business, which is of interest to stockholders and employees as well as creditors.*

The amount available to meet interest charges is not affected by taxes on income. This is because interest is deductible in determining taxable income. For example, the number of times interest charges are earned for Adams Co. is computed as shown.

	1997	1996
Income before income tax	$ 900,000	$ 800,000
Add interest expense	300,000	250,000
Amount available to meet interest charges	$1,200,000	$1,050,000
Number of times interest charges earned	4	4.2

Analysis such as this can also be applied to dividends on preferred stock. In such a case, net income is divided by the amount of preferred dividends to yield the number of times preferred dividends are earned. This measure indicates the risk that dividends to preferred stockholders may not be paid.

PROFITABILITY ANALYSIS

Profitability is the ability of an entity to earn profits. This ability to earn profits depends on the effectiveness and efficiency of operations as well as resources available to the business. Profitability analysis, therefore, focuses primarily on the relationship between operating results as reported in the income statement and resources available to the business as reported in the balance sheet. Major analyses used in assessing profitability include the following:

1. Ratio of net sales to assets
2. Rate earned on total assets
3. Rate earned on stockholders' equity
4. Rate earned on common stockholders' equity
5. Earnings per share on common stock
6. Price-earnings ratio
7. Dividend yield

Ratio of Net Sales to Assets

The **ratio of net sales to assets** *is a profitability measure that shows how effectively a firm utilizes its assets.* For example, two competing businesses have equal amounts of assets. If the sales of one are twice the sales of the other, the business with the higher sales is making better use of its assets.

In computing the ratio of net sales to assets, any long-term investments are excluded from total assets. This is because such investments are unrelated to normal operations involving the sale of goods or services. Assets may be measured as the total at the end of the year, the average at the beginning and end of the year, or the average of monthly totals. The basic data and the computation of this ratio for Lincoln Company are as follows:

	1997	*1996*
Net sales	$1,498,000	$1,200,000
Total assets (excluding long-term investments):		
Beginning of year	$1,053,000	$1,010,000
End of year	1,044,500	1,053,000
Total	$2,097,500	$2,063,000
Average	$1,048,750	$1,031,500
Ratio of net sales to assets	1.4:1	1.2:1

There was an improvement in this ratio during 1997. This was primarily due to an increase in sales volume. A comparison with similar companies or industry averages would be helpful in assessing the effectiveness of Lincoln Company's use of its assets.

Rate Earned on Total Assets

The **rate earned on total assets** *measures the profitability of total assets, without considering how the assets are financed.* This rate is therefore not affected by whether the assets are financed primarily by creditors or stockholders.

The rate earned on total assets is computed by adding interest expense to net income and dividing this sum by the average total assets. The addition of interest expense to net income eliminates the effect of whether the assets are financed by debt or equity. The rate earned by Lincoln Company on total assets is computed as follows:

	1997	*1996*
Net income	$ 91,000	$ 76,500
Plus interest expense	6,000	12,000
Total	$ 97,000	$ 88,500
Total assets:		
Beginning of year	$1,230,500	$1,187,500
End of year	1,139,500	1,230,500
Total	$2,370,000	$2,418,000
Average	$1,185,000	$1,209,000
Rate earned on total assets	8.2%	7.3%

The rate earned on total assets of Lincoln Company during 1997 improved over that of 1996. A comparison with similar companies and industry averages would be useful in evaluating Lincoln Company's profitability on total assets.

Sometimes it may be desirable to compute the rate of operating income to total assets. This is especially true if significant amounts of nonoperating income and expense are reported on the income statement. In this case, any assets related to the nonoperating income and expense items should be excluded from total assets in computing the rate. In addition, using operating income (which is before tax) has the advantage of eliminating the effects of any changes in the tax structure on the rate of earnings. When evaluating published data on rates earned on assets, you should be careful to determine the exact nature of the measure that is reported.

Rate Earned on Stockholders' Equity

Another measure of profitability is the **rate earned on stockholders' equity.** It is computed by dividing net income by average total stockholders' equity. In contrast to the rate earned on total assets, *this measure emphasizes the rate of income earned on the amount invested by the stockholders.*

The total stockholders' equity may vary throughout a period. For example, a business may issue or retire stock, pay dividends, and earn net income. If monthly amounts are not available, the average of the stockholders' equity at the beginning and the end of the year is normally used to compute this rate. For Lincoln Company, the rate earned on stockholders' equity is computed as follows:

	1997	*1996*
Net income	$ 91,000	$ 76,500
Stockholders' equity:		
Beginning of year	$ 787,500	$ 750,000
End of year	829,500	787,500
Total	$1,617,000	$1,537,500
Average	$ 808,500	$ 768,750
Rate earned on stockholders' equity	11.3%	10.0%

The rate earned by a business on the equity of its stockholders is usually higher than the rate earned on total assets. This occurs when the amount earned on assets acquired with creditors' funds is more than the interest paid to creditors. This difference in the rate on stockholders' equity and the rate on total assets is called **leverage.**

Lincoln Company's rate earned on stockholders' equity for 1997, 11.3%, is greater than the rate of 8.2% earned on total assets. The leverage of 3.1% (11.3% – 8.2%) for 1997 compares favorably with the 2.7% (10.0% – 7.3%) leverage for 1996. Exhibit 8 shows the 1997 and 1996 leverages for Lincoln Company.

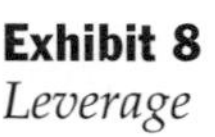

Exhibit 8
Leverage

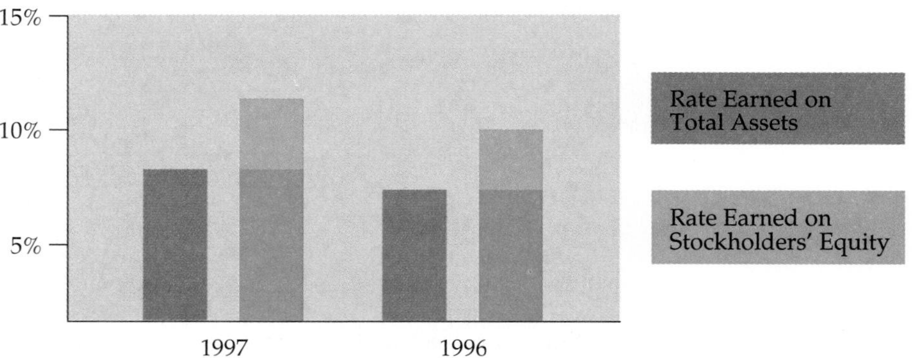

Rate Earned on Common Stockholders' Equity

A corporation may have both preferred and common stock outstanding. In this case, the common stockholders have the residual claim on earnings. The **rate earned on common stockholders' equity** focuses only on the rate of profits earned on the amount invested by the common stockholders. It is computed by subtracting preferred dividend requirements from the net income and dividing by the average common stockholders' equity.

Lincoln Company has $150,000 of 6% nonparticipating preferred stock outstanding on December 31, 1997 and 1996. Thus, the annual preferred dividend requirement is $9,000 ($150,000 × 6%). The common stockholders' equity equals the total stockholders' equity, including retained earnings, less the par of the preferred stock ($150,000). The basic data and the rate earned on common stockholders' equity for Lincoln Company are as follows:

	1997	1996
Net income	$ 91,000	$ 76,500
Preferred dividends	9,000	9,000
Remainder—identified with common stock	$ 82,000	$ 67,500
Common stockholders' equity:		
Beginning of year	$ 637,500	$ 600,000
End of year	679,500	637,500
Total	$1,317,000	$1,237,500
Average	$ 658,500	$ 618,750
Rate earned on common stockholders' equity	12.5%	10.9%

The rate earned on common stockholders' equity differs from the rates earned by Lincoln Company on total assets and total stockholders' equity. This occurs if there are borrowed funds and also preferred stock outstanding, which rank ahead of the common shares in their claim on earnings. Thus, the concept of leverage, as we discussed in the preceding section, can also be applied to the use of funds from the sale of preferred stock as well as borrowing. Funds from both sources can be used in an attempt to increase the return on common stockholders' equity.

Earnings Per Share on Common Stock

One of the profitability measures most commonly quoted by the financial press is **earnings per share (EPS)** on common stock. It is also normally reported in the income statement in corporate annual reports. If a company has issued only one class of stock, the earnings per share is computed by dividing net income by the number of shares of stock outstanding. If preferred and common stock are outstanding, the net income is first reduced by the amount of preferred dividend requirements.

The data on the earnings per share of common stock for Lincoln Company are as follows:

	1997	1996
Net income	$91,000	$76,500
Preferred dividends	9,000	9,000
Remainder—identified with common stock	$82,000	$67,500
Shares of common stock outstanding	50,000	50,000
Earnings per share on common stock	$1.64	$1.35

Since earnings are the primary basis for dividends, earnings per share and dividends per share on common stock are commonly used by investors in assessing alternative stock investments. Earnings per share can be reported with dividends per share to indicate the relationship between earnings and dividends. A comparison of these two per share amounts indicates the extent to which the corporation is retaining its earnings for use in operations. Exhibit 9 shows these relationships for Lincoln Company.

Price-Earnings Ratio

Another profitability measure commonly quoted by the financial press is the **price earnings (P/E) ratio** on common stock. *The price-earnings ratio is an indicator of a*

Exhibit 9
Earnings and Dividends per Share of Common Stock

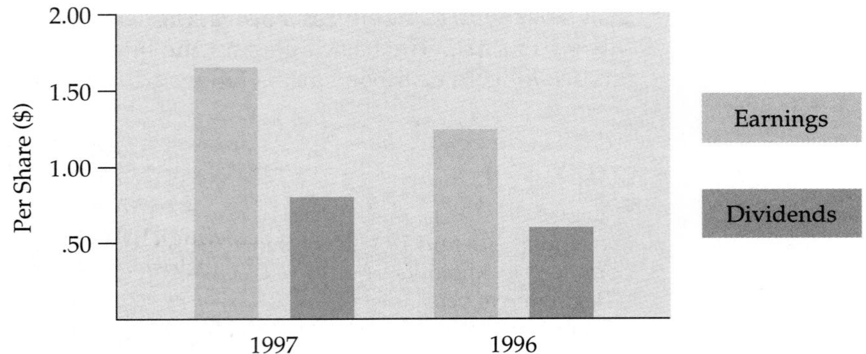

firm's future earnings prospects. It is computed by dividing the market price per share of common stock at a specific date by the annual earnings per share. To illustrate, assume that the market prices per common share are 20 1/2 at the end of 1997 and 13 1/2 at the end of 1996. The price-earnings ratio on common stock of Lincoln Company is computed as follows:

	1997	*1996*
Market price per share of common stock	$20.50	$13.50
Earnings per share on common stock	$ 1.64	$ 1.35
Price-earnings ratio on common stock	12.5	10.0

The price-earnings ratio indicates that a share of common stock of Lincoln Company was selling for 10 times the amount of earnings per share at the end of 1996. At the end of 1997, the common stock was selling for 12.5 times the amount of earnings per share.

Dividend Yield

The **dividend yield** on common stock is a profitability measure that shows the rate of return to common stockholders in terms of cash dividends. It is of special interest to investors whose main investment objective is to receive current returns (dividends) on an investment rather than an increase in the market price of the investment. The dividend yield is computed by dividing the annual dividends paid per share of common stock by the market price per share on a specific date. To illustrate, assume that dividends were $0.80 per common share and the market price was 20 1/2 at the end of 1997. Dividends were $0.60 per share, and the market price was 13 1/2 at the end of 1996. The dividend yield on common stock of Lincoln Company is as follows:

	1997	*1996*
Dividends per share of common stock	$ 0.80	$ 0.60
Market price per share of common stock	$20.50	$13.50
Dividend yield on common stock	3.9%	4.4%

SUMMARY OF ANALYTICAL MEASURES

Exhibit 10 presents a summary of the analytical measures that we have discussed. These measures can be computed for most medium-size businesses. Depending on the specific business being analyzed, some measures might be omitted or additional measures could be developed. The type of industry, the capital structure, and the diversity of the business's operations usually affect the measures used. For example, analysis for an airline might include revenue per passenger mile and cost per available seat as measures. Likewise, analysis for a hotel might focus on occupancy rates.

Percentage analyses, ratios, turnovers, and other measures of financial position and operating results are useful analytical measures. They are helpful in assessing a business's past performance and predicting its future. They are not, however, a substitute for sound judgment. In selecting and interpreting analytical measures, conditions peculiar to a business or its industry should be considered. In addition, the influence of the general economic and business environment should be considered.

In determining trends, the interrelationship of the measures used in assessing a business should be carefully studied. Comparable indexes of earlier periods should also be studied. Data from competing businesses may be useful in assessing the efficiency of operations for the firm under analysis. In making such comparisons, however, the effects of differences in the accounting methods used by the businesses should be considered.

Exhibit 10
Summary of Analytical Measures

	Method of Computation	*Use*
Solvency measures:		
Working capital	Current assets – Current liabilities	**To indicate the ability to meet currently maturing obligations**
Current ratio	$\frac{\text{Current assets}}{\text{Current liabilities}}$	
Acid-test ratio	$\frac{\text{Quick assets}}{\text{Current liabilities}}$	**To indicate instant debt-paying ability**
Accounts receivable turnover	$\frac{\text{Net sales on account}}{\text{Average accounts receivable}}$	**To assess the efficiency in collecting receivables and in the management of credit**
Number of days' sales in receivables	$\frac{\text{Accounts receivable, end of year}}{\text{Average daily sales on account}}$	
Inventory turnover	$\frac{\text{Cost of goods sold}}{\text{Average inventory}}$	**To assess the efficiency in the management of inventory**
Number of days' sales in inventory	$\frac{\text{Inventory, end of year}}{\text{Average daily cost of goods sold}}$	
Ratio of plant assets to long-term liabilities	$\frac{\text{Plant assets (net)}}{\text{Long-term liabilities}}$	**To indicate the margin of safety to long-term creditors**
Ratio of liabilities to stockholders' equity	$\frac{\text{Total liabilities}}{\text{Total stockholders' equity}}$	**To indicate the margin of safety to creditors**
Number of times interest charges earned	$\frac{\text{Income before income tax + Interest expense}}{\text{Interest expense}}$	**To assess the risk to debtholders in terms of number of times interest charges were earned**
Profitability measures:		
Ratio of net sales to assets	$\frac{\text{Net sales}}{\text{Average total assets (excluding long-term investments)}}$	**To assess the effectiveness in the use of assets**
Rate earned on total assets	$\frac{\text{Net income + Interest expense}}{\text{Average total assets}}$	**To assess the profitability of the assets**
Rate earned on stockholders' equity	$\frac{\text{Net income}}{\text{Average total stockholders' equity}}$	**To assess the profitability of the investment by stockholders**

Exhibit 10 *continued*

	Method of Computation	*Use*
Profitability measures:		
Rate earned on common stockholders' equity	Net income – Preferred dividends / Average common stockholders' equity	**To assess the profitability of the investment by common stockholders**
Earnings per share on common stock	Net income – Preferred dividends / Shares of common stock outstanding	
Dividends per share of common stock	Dividends / Shares of common stock outstanding	**To indicate the extent to which earnings are being distributed to common stockholders**
Price-earnings ratio	Market price per share of common stock / Earnings per share of common stock	**To indicate future earnings prospects, based on the relationship between market value of common stock and earnings**
Dividend yield	Dividends per share of common stock / Market price per share of common stock	**To indicate the rate of return to common stockholders in terms of dividends**

PROBLEMS

PROBLEM F–1
Horizontal analysis for income statement

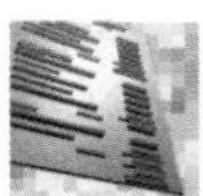

For 1997, Olympic Athletic Company reported its most significant increase in net income in years. At the end of the year, Joan Garcia, the president, is presented with the following condensed comparative income statement:

Olympic Athletic Company
Comparative Income Statement
For the Years Ended December 31, 1997 and 1996

	1997	*1996*
Sales	$717,200	$652,000
Sales returns and allowances	3,200	2,000
Net sales	$714,000	$650,000
Cost of goods sold	408,000	364,000
Gross profit	$306,000	$286,000
Selling expenses	$ 90,000	$120,000
Administrative expenses	60,000	50,000
Total operating expenses	$150,000	$170,000
Operating income	$156,000	$116,000
Other income	2,000	1,000
Income before income tax	$158,000	$117,000
Income tax	65,600	40,000
Net income	$ 92,400	$ 77,000

Instructions

1. Prepare a comparative income statement with horizontal analysis for the two-year period, using 1996 as the base year.
2. To the extent the data permit, comment on the significant relationships revealed by the horizontal analysis prepared in (1).

PROBLEM F–2
Vertical analysis for income statement

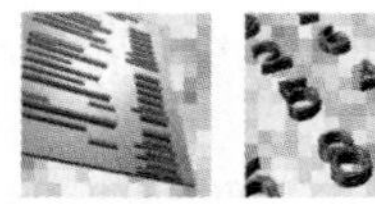

For 1997, Sunrise Dairy Inc. initiated an extensive sales promotion campaign that included the expenditure of an additional $50,000 for advertising. At the end of the year, Ann Hartley, the president, is presented with the following condensed comparative income statement:

Sunrise Dairy Inc.
Comparative Income Statement
For the Years Ended December 31, 1997 and 1996

	1997	*1996*
Sales	$955,500	$679,800
Sales returns and allowances	45,500	19,800
Net sales	$910,000	$660,000
Cost of goods sold	400,400	264,000
Gross profit	$509,600	$396,000
Selling expenses	$145,600	$ 92,400
Administrative expenses	72,800	66,000
Total operating expenses	$218,400	$158,400
Operating income	$291,200	$237,600
Other income	2,730	2,640
Income before income tax	$293,930	$240,240
Income tax	127,400	92,400
Net income	$166,530	$147,840

Instructions

1. Prepare a comparative income statement for the two-year period, presenting an analysis of each item in relationship to net sales for each of the years.
2. To the extent the data permit, comment on the significant relationships revealed by the vertical analysis prepared in (1).

PROBLEM F–3
Common-size income statement

Revenue and expense data for the current calendar year for Diamond Publishing Company and for the publishing industry are as follows. The Diamond Publishing Company data are expressed in dollars; the publishing industry averages are expressed in percentages.

	Diamond Publishing Company	*Publishing Industry Average*
Sales	$4,030,000	100.5%
Sales returns and allowances	30,000	0.5
Cost of goods sold	2,840,000	69.0
Selling expenses	312,000	9.0
Administrative expenses	256,000	8.2
Other income	24,000	0.6
Other expense	60,000	1.4
Income tax	196,000	5.0

Instructions

1. Prepare a common-size income statement comparing the results of operations for Diamond Publishing Company with the industry average.
2. As far as the data permit, comment on significant relationships revealed by the comparisons.

PROBLEM F–4
Effect of transactions on current position analysis

Data pertaining to the current position of Steel N' Brass Hardware Company are as follows:

Cash	$164,000
Marketable securities	64,000
Accounts and notes receivable (net)	292,000
Inventories	520,500
Prepaid expenses	29,500
Accounts payable	287,500
Notes payable (short-term)	79,000
Accrued expenses	33,500

Instructions

1. Compute (a) the working capital, (b) the current ratio, and (c) the acid-test ratio.
2. List the following captions on a sheet of paper:

Transaction	*Working Capital*	*Current Ratio*	*Acid-Test Ratio*

Compute the working capital, the current ratio, and the acid-test ratio after each of the following transactions, and record the results in the appropriate columns. Consider each transaction separately, and assume that only that transaction affects the data given.

a. Sold marketable securities, $60,000.
b. Paid accounts payable, $120,000.
c. Purchased goods on account, $100,000.
d. Paid notes payable, $60,000.
e. Declared a cash dividend, $90,000.
f. Declared a common stock dividend on common stock, $62,500.
g. Borrowed cash from bank on a long-term note, $140,000.
h. Received cash on account, $180,000.
i. Issued additional shares of stock for cash, $200,000.
j. Paid cash for prepaid expenses, $40,000.

PROBLEM F–5
Effect of errors on current position analysis

Prior to approving an application for a short-term loan, Citizens National Bank required that Traction Tire Company provide evidence of working capital of at least $300,000, a current ratio of at least 2.0:1, and an acid-test ratio of at least 1.5:1. The chief accountant of Traction Tire Company compiled the following data pertaining to the current position:

Traction Tire Company
Schedule of Current Assets and Current Liabilities
December 31, 1996

Current assets:		Current liabilities:	
Cash	$119,500	Accounts payable	$240,000
Marketable securities	94,250	Notes payable	60,000
Accounts receivable	280,250	Total current liabilities	$300,000
Notes receivable	100,000		
Interest receivable	6,000		
Inventories	132,000		
Supplies	18,000		
Total current assets	$750,000		

Instructions

1. Compute (a) the working capital, (b) the current ratio, and (c) the acid-test ratio.
2. At the request of the bank, a firm of independent auditors was hired to examine data submitted with the loan application. This examination disclosed several errors. Prepare correcting entries for each of the following errors:
   a. A canceled check indicates that a bill for $20,000 for repairs on factory equipment had not been recorded in the accounts.
   b. Accounts receivable of $30,250 are uncollectible and should be immediately written off. In addition, it was estimated that of the remaining receivables, 5% would eventually become uncollectible. An allowance should be made for these future uncollectible accounts.
   c. Six months' interest had been accrued on the $100,000, 12%, six-month note receivable dated October 1, 1996.
   d. Supplies on hand at December 31, 1996, total $11,000.
   e. The marketable securities portfolio includes $40,000 of Porter Company stock that is held as a long-term investment.
   f. The notes payable account consists of a 12%, 90-day note dated November 1, 1996. No interest had been accrued on the note.
   g. Accrued wages as of December 31, 1996, totaled $45,000.
   h. Rental Income had been credited on receipt of $58,000, which was the full amount of a year's rent for warehouse space leased to C. Pena and Son, effective July 1, 1996.

3. Considering each of the preceding errors separately and assuming that only that error affects the current position of Traction Tire Company, compute (a) the working capital, (b) the current ratio, and (c) the acid-test ratio. Use the following column headings for recording your answers:

Error	*Working Capital*	*Current Ratio*	*Acid-Test Ratio*

4. Prepare a revised schedule of working capital as of December 31, 1996, and recompute the current ratio and the acid-test ratio, considering the corrections of all the preceding errors.
5. Discuss the action you would recommend that the bank take regarding the pending loan application.

PROBLEM F–6
Eighteen measures of solvency and profitability

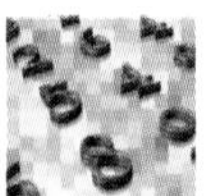

The comparative financial statements of White Cloud Flour Co. are as follows. The market price of White Cloud Flour Co. common stock was $24.50 on December 31, 1996, and $36 on December 31, 1997.

White Cloud Flour Co.
Comparative Balance Sheet
December 31, 1997 and 1996

	1997	*1996*
Assets		
Current assets:		
Cash	$ 100,000	$ 90,000
Marketable securities	195,000	165,000
Accounts receivable (net)	535,000	359,000
Inventories	680,600	428,400
Prepaid expenses	35,400	26,600
Total current assets	$1,546,000	$1,069,000
Long-term investments	300,000	200,000
Plant assets (net)	3,442,000	2,945,000
Total assets	$5,288,000	$4,214,000
Liabilities		
Current liabilities	$ 720,000	$ 426,000
Long-term liabilities:		
Mortgage note payable, 10%, due 2001	$ 400,000	
Bonds payable, 15%, due 2009	800,000	$ 800,000
Total long-term liabilities	$1,200,000	$ 800,000
Total liabilities	$1,920,000	$1,226,000
Stockholders' Equity		
Preferred $6 stock, $100 par	$ 500,000	$ 500,000
Common stock, $10 par	1,000,000	1,000,000
Retained earnings	1,868,000	1,488,000
Total stockholders' equity	$3,368,000	$2,988,000
Total liabilities and stockholders' equity	$5,288,000	$4,214,000

White Cloud Flour Co.
Comparative Retained Earnings Statement
For the Years Ended December 31, 1997 and 1996

	1997	*1996*
Retained earnings, January 1	$1,488,000	$1,261,000
Add net income for year	500,000	327,000
Total	$1,988,000	$1,588,000
Deduct dividends:		
On preferred stock	$ 30,000	$ 30,000
On common stock	90,000	70,000
Total	$ 120,000	$ 100,000
Retained earnings, December 31	$1,868,000	$1,488,000

White Cloud Flour Co.
Comparative Income Statement
For the Years Ended December 31, 1997 and 1996

	1997	*1996*
Sales (all on account)	$4,360,000	$2,550,000
Sales returns and allowances	92,000	58,000
Net sales	$4,268,000	$2,492,000
Cost of goods sold	2,050,000	1,180,000
Gross profit	$2,218,000	$1,312,000
Selling expenses	$ 705,000	$ 410,000
Administrative expenses	497,000	248,000
Total operating expenses	$1,202,000	$ 658,000
Operating income	$1,016,000	$ 654,000
Other income	84,000	63,000
	$1,100,000	$ 717,000
Other expense (interest)	160,000	120,000
Income before income tax	$ 940,000	$ 597,000
Income tax	440,000	270,000
Net income	$ 500,000	$ 327,000

Instructions

Determine the following measures for 1997.

1. Working capital.
2. Current ratio.
3. Acid-test ratio.
4. Accounts receivable turnover.
5. Number of days' sales in receivables.
6. Inventory turnover.
7. Number of days' sales in inventory.
8. Ratio of plant assets to long-term liabilities.
9. Ratio of liabilities to stockholders' equity.
10. Number of times interest charges earned.
11. Number of times preferred dividends earned.
12. Ratio of net sales to assets.
13. Rate earned on total assets.
14. Rate earned on stockholders' equity.
15. Rate earned on common stockholders' equity.
16. Earnings per share on common stock.
17. Price-earnings ratio.
18. Dividend yield.

Glossary

A

Accelerated depreciation method. A depreciation method that provides for a high depreciation expense in the first year of use of an asset and a gradually declining expense thereafter. (353)

Account. The form used to record additions and deductions for each individual asset, liability, owner's equity, revenue, and expense. (43)

Account form of balance sheet. A form of balance sheet with assets on the left-hand side and liabilities and owner's equity on the right-hand side. (22, 222)

Account payable. A liability created by a purchase made on credit. (17)

Account receivable. A claim against a customer for services rendered or goods sold on credit. (17)

Accounting. The process of identifying, measuring, and communicating economic information to permit informed judgments and decisions by users of the information. (9)

Accounting cycle. The sequence of basic accounting procedures during a fiscal period. (135)

Accounting equation. The expression of the relationship between assets, liabilities, and owner's equity; it is most commonly stated as Assets = Liabilities + Owner's Equity. (16)

Accounting period concept. An accounting principle that requires accounting reports be prepared at periodic intervals. (90)

Accounting system. The methods and procedures used by a business to record and report financial data for use by management and external users. (163)

Accounts payable subsidiary ledger. The subsidiary ledger containing the individual accounts with suppliers (creditors). (172)

Accounts receivable subsidiary ledger. The subsidiary ledger containing the individual accounts with customers (debtors). (172)

Accrual basis. Revenues are recognized in the period earned, and expenses are recognized in the period incurred in the process of generating revenues. (90)

Accruals. Expenses that have been incurred or revenues that have been earned but have not been recorded. (92)

Accrued expenses. Expenses that have been incurred but not recorded in the accounts. Sometimes called accrued liabilities. (92)

Accrued revenues. Revenues that have been earned but not recorded in the accounts. Sometimes called accrued assets. (92)

Accumulated depreciation account. The contra asset account used to accumulate the depreciation recognized to date on plant assets. (99)

Activity base. A measure of activity that is related to changes in cost. Used in analyzing and classifying cost behavior. Activity bases are also used in the denominator in calculating the predetermined factory overhead rate to assign overhead costs to cost objects. (707)

Activity bases (drivers). A measure of activity that is thought to cause the incurrence of cost. Used in analyzing and classifying cost behavior. (777)

Activity-based costing. A cost allocation method that identifies activities causing the incurrence of costs and allocates these costs to products (or other cost objects) based upon activity drivers (bases). An accounting framework based on determining the cost of activities. The activity cost is then related to products for product costing. (710, 949)

Adequate disclosure. The concept that financial statements and their accompanying footnotes should contain all of the pertinent data believed essential to the reader's understanding of a business's financial status. (438)

Adjusting entries. Entries required at the end of an accounting period to bring the ledger up to date. (91)

Adjusting process. The process of updating the accounts at the end of a period. (90)

Administrative expenses. Expenses incurred in the administration or general operations of a business. (219)

Aging the receivables. The process of analyzing the accounts receivable and classifying them according to various age groupings, with the due date being the base point for determining age. (289)

Allowance method. A method of accounting for uncollectible receivables, whereby advance provision for the uncollectibles is made. (285)

Amortization. The periodic expense attributed to the decline in usefulness of an intangible asset. (364)

Annuity. A series of equal cash flows at fixed intervals. (577, 973)

Appropriation. The amount of a corporation's retained earnings that has been restricted and therefore is not available for distribution to shareholders as dividends. (514)

Assets. Physical items (tangible) or rights (intangible) that have value and that are owned by the business entity. (14, 43)

Available-for-sale security. A debt or equity security that is not classified as either a held-to-maturity or a trading security. (296)

Average cost method. The method of inventory costing that is based on the assumption that costs should be charged against revenue in accordance with the weighted average unit costs of the items sold. (321)

Average rate of return. A method of evaluating capital investment proposals that focuses on the expected profitability of the investment. (969)

B

Balance of the account. The amount of difference between the debits and the credits that have been entered into an account. (45)

Balance sheet. A financial statement listing the assets, liabilities, and owner's equity of a business entity as of a specific date. (20)

Bank reconciliation. The analysis that details the items responsible for the difference between the cash balance reported in the bank statement and the balance of the cash account in the ledger. (261)

Betterment. An expenditure that increases operating efficiency or capacity for the remaining useful life of a plant asset. (357)

Bill of materials. A list of all the materials required to manufacture a product. (703)

Bond. A form of interest-bearing note employed by corporations to borrow on a long-term basis. (573)

Bond indenture. The contract between a corporation issuing bonds and the bondholders. (574)

Book value of the asset. The difference between the balance of a plant asset account and its related accumulated depreciation account. (100, 352)

Boot. The balance owed the supplier when an old asset is traded for a new asset. (360)

Bottleneck. A condition that occurs when product demand exceeds production capacity. The bottleneck resource is a portion of the production process that is operating at 100% of capacity and is unable to meet product demand. (949)

Break-even point. The level of business operations at which revenues and expired costs are equal. (785)

Budget. An outline of a business's future plans, stated in financial terms. A budget is used to plan and control operational departments and divisions. (821)

Budget performance report. A report comparing actual results with budget figures. (866)

Business entity concept. The concept that assumes that accounting applies to individual economic units and that each unit is separate and distinct from the persons who supply its assets. (14, 431)

Business transaction. The occurrence of an economic event or a condition that must be recorded in the accounting records. (14)

C

Capital expenditures. Costs that add to the usefulness of assets for more than one accounting period. (357)

Capital expenditures budget. The budget summarizing future plans for acquiring plant facilities and equipment. (837)

Capital investment analysis. The process by which management plans, evaluates, and controls long-term capital investments involving property, plant, and equipment. (968)

Capital leases. Leases that include one or more of four provisions that result in treating the leased assets as purchased assets in the accounts. (362)

Capital rationing. The process by which management allocates available investment funds among competing capital investment proposals. (981)

Carrying value. The amount at which a long-term investment or a long-term liability is reported on the balance sheet; also called basis or book value. (582)

Cash. Coins, currency (paper money), checks, money orders, and money on deposit that is available for unrestricted withdrawal from banks or other financial institutions. (251)

Cash basis. Revenue is recognized in the period cash is received, and expenses are recognized in the period cash is paid. (90)

Cash dividend. A cash distribution of earnings by a corporation to its shareholders. (511)

Cash equivalents. Highly liquid investments that are usually reported on the balance sheet with cash. (264)

Cash flows from financing activities. The section of the statement of cash flows that reports cash flows from transactions affecting the equity and debt of the entity. (607)

Cash flows from investing activities. The section of the statement of cash flows that reports cash flows from transactions affecting investments in noncurrent assets. (607)

Cash flows from operating activities. The section of the statement of cash flows that reports the cash transactions affecting the determination of net income. (607)

Cash payback period. The expected period of time that will elapse between the date of a capital expenditure and the complete recovery in cash (or equivalent) of the amount invested. (970)

Cash payments journal. The journal in which all cash payments are recorded. (179)

Cash receipts file. Listing of customer cash receipts information. (184)

Cash receipts journal. The journal in which all cash receipts are recorded. (176)

Chart of accounts. The system of accounts that make up the ledger for a business. (43)

Closing entries. Entries necessary to eliminate the balances of temporary accounts in preparation for the following accounting period. (128A)

Common stock. The basic ownership class of corporate stock. (503)

Completed-contract method. The method that recognizes revenue from long-term construction contracts when the project is completed. (437)

Computer-integrated manufacturing (CIM). The use of automated equipment to perform routine, repetitive tasks with a minimum of human involvement. (680)

Conservatism. The concept that dictates that in selecting among alternatives, the method or procedure that yields the lesser amount of net income or asset value should be selected. (445)

Consistency. The concept that assumes that the same generally accepted accounting principles have been applied in preparing successive financial statements. (443)

Consolidated statements. Financial statements resulting from combining parent and subsidiary company statements. (554)

Consolidation. The creation of a new corporation by the transfer of assets and liabilities from two or more existing corporations. (553)

Constant dollar data. Historical costs that have been converted into dollars of constant value through the use of a price-level index. (434)

Contingent liabilities. Potential obligations that will materialize only if certain events occur in the future. (294)

Continuous budgeting. A method of budgeting that provides for maintaining a twelve-month projection into the future. (825)

Continuous process improvement. A management approach that is part of the overall total quality management philosophy. The approach requires all employees to constantly improve processes of which they are a part or for which they have managerial responsibility. (670)

Contra accounts. Accounts that are offset against other accounts. (99)

Contract rate. The interest rate specified on a bond; sometimes called the coupon rate of interest. (577)

Contribution margin ratio. The percentage of each sales dollar that is available to cover the fixed costs and provide an operating income. (783)

Contribution margin. Sales less variable costs and variable selling and administrative expenses. (783)

Controllable expenses. Costs that can be influenced by the decisions of a manager. (902)

Controllable operating income. The operating income that is the responsibility of a profit or investment center manager. It is computed as operating income less service department charges. (904)

Controllable variance. The difference between the actual amount of variable factory overhead cost incurred and the amount of variable factory overhead budgeted for the standard product. (872)

Controller. The chief management accountant of a business. (665)

Controlling account. The account in the general ledger that summarizes the balances of the accounts in a subsidiary ledger. (172)

Conversion costs. The combination of direct labor and factory overhead costs. (675)

Corporation. A separate legal entity that is organized in accordance with state or federal statutes and in which ownership is divided into shares of stock. (14)

Cost. A disbursement of cash (or a commitment to pay cash in the future) for the purpose of generating revenues. (672)

Cost accounting system. A branch of managerial accounting concerned with accumulating manufacturing costs for financial reporting and decision-making purposes. (700)

Cost allocation. The process of assigning indirect cost to a cost object, such as a job. (707)

Cost behavior. The manner in which a cost changes in relation to its activity base (driver). (777)

Cost center. A decentralized unit in which the department or division manager has responsibility for the control of costs incurred and the authority to make decisions that affect these costs. (900)

Cost method. A method of accounting for an investment in common stock, by which the investor recognizes as income its share of cash dividends of the investee. (551)

Cost object. The object or segment of operations to which costs are related for management's use, such as a product or department. (672)

Cost of goods sold. The cost of the manufactured product sold. (676)

Cost of merchandise sold. The cost of merchandise purchased by a merchandise business and sold. (676)

Cost of production report. A report prepared periodically by a processing department, summarizing (1) the units for which the department is accountable and the disposition of those units and (2) the costs incurred by the department and the allocation of those costs between completed and incomplete production. (752)

Cost of quality report. A report that shows the dollar cost of waste and rework in processes. The report can be used to prioritize and track the effectiveness of continuous process improvement efforts. (671)

Cost price approach. An approach to transfer pricing that uses cost as the basis for setting the transfer price. (913)

Cost principle. The principle that the monetary record for properties and services purchased by a business should be maintained in terms of actual cost. (14)

Cost variance. The difference between actual cost and the flexible budget at actual volumes. (866)

Cost-volume-profit analysis. The systematic examination of the relationships among selling prices, volume of sales and production, costs, expenses, and profits. (782)

Cost-volume-profit chart. A chart used to assist management in understanding the relationships among costs, expenses, sales, and operating profit or loss. (789)

Credit. (1) The right side of an account; (2) the amount entered on the right side of an account; (3) to enter an amount on the right side of an account. (45)

Credit memorandum. The form issued by a seller to inform a buyer that a credit has been posted to the buyer's account receivable. (212)

Cumulative preferred stock. Preferred stock that is entitled to current and past dividends before dividends may be paid on common stock. (504)

Current assets. Cash or other assets that are expected to be converted to cash or sold or used up, usually within a year or less, through the normal operations of a business. (127)

Current cost. The amount of cash that would have to be paid currently to acquire assets of the same age and in the same condition as existing assets. (434)

Current liabilities. Liabilities that will be due within a short time (usually one year or less) and that are to be paid out of current assets. (128)

Currently attainable standards. Standards that represent levels of operation that can be attained with reasonable effort. (864)

D

Debit. (1) The left side of an account; (2) the amount entered on the left side of an account; (3) to enter an amount on the left side of an account. (45)

Debit memorandum. The form issued by a buyer to inform a seller that a debit has been posted to the seller's account payable. (209)

Debt security. A security that represents an obligation between a creditor and the business issuing the obligation. (295)

Decentralization. The separation of a business into more manageable operating units. (898)

Declining-balance depreciation method. A method of depreciation that provides declining periodic depreciation expense over the estimated life of an asset. (352)

Deferrals. Delays in the recognition of expenses that have been incurred or revenues that have been received. (91)

Deferred expenses. Items that are initially recorded as assets but are expected to become expenses over time or through the normal operations of the business. Sometimes called prepaid expenses. (92)

Deferred revenues. Items that are initially recorded as liabilities but are expected to become revenues over time or through the normal operations of the business. Sometimes called unearned revenues. (92)

Deficiency. The debit balance in the owner's equity account of a partner. (480)

Deficit. A debit balance in the retained earnings account. (502)

Defined benefit plan. A pension plan that promises employees a fixed annual pension benefit at retirement, based on years of service and compensation levels. (401)

Defined contribution plan. A pension plan that requires a fixed amount of money to be invested for the employee's behalf during the employee's working years. (401)

Depletion. The cost of metal ores and other minerals removed from the earth. (363)

Depreciation. In a general sense, the decrease in usefulness of plant assets other than land. In accounting, refers to the systematic allocation of a plant asset's cost to expense. (99, 349)

Differential analysis. The area of accounting concerned with the effect of alternative courses of action on revenues and costs. (935)

Differential cost. The amount of increase or decrease in cost expected from a particular course of action as compared with an alternative. (935)

Differential revenue. The amount of increase or decrease in revenue expected from a particular course of action as compared with an alternative. (935)

Direct costs. Costs that can be traced directly to a cost object. (672)

Direct labor cost. Wages of factory workers who are directly involved in converting materials into a finished product. (673)

Direct labor rate variance. The cost associated with the difference between the standard rate and the actual rate paid for direct labor used in producing a commodity. (869)

Direct labor time variance. The cost associated with the difference between the standard hours and the actual hours of direct labor spent producing a commodity. (870)

Direct materials cost. The cost of materials that are an integral part of the finished product. (673)

Direct materials price variance. The cost associated with the difference between the standard price and the actual price of direct materials used in producing a commodity. (867)

Direct materials quantity variance. The cost associated with the difference between the standard quantity and the actual quantity of direct materials used in producing a commodity. (868)

Direct method. A method of reporting the cash flows from operating activities as the difference between the operating cash receipts and the operating cash payments. (608)

Direct write-off method. A method of accounting for uncollectible receivables, whereby an expense is recognized only when specific accounts are judged to be uncollectible. (285)

Discontinued operations. The operations of a business segment that has been disposed of. (541)

Discount. The excess of par value of stock over its sales price. The excess of the face amount of bonds over their issue price. The interest deducted from the maturity value of a note receivable. (294, 404, 506, 577)

Discount rate. The rate used in computing the interest to be deducted from the maturity value of a note. (404)

Dishonored note receivable. A note that the maker fails to pay on its due date. (295)

Division. A decentralized organizational unit that is structured around a common function, product, customer, or geographical territory. Divisions can be cost, profit, or investment centers. (898)

Double-entry accounting. A system for recording transactions, based on recording increases and decreases in accounts so that debits always equal credits. (49)

Drawing. The amount of withdrawals made by the owner of a sole proprietorship. (43)

E

Earnings per share (EPS). The profitability ratio of net income available to common shareholders to the number of common shares outstanding. (543)

Effective rate. The market rate of interest at the time bonds are issued. (579)

Electronic funds transfer (EFT). A payment system that uses computerized electronic impulses rather than paper (money, checks, etc.) to effect a cash transaction. (264)

Employee's earnings record. A detailed record of each employee's earnings. (395)

Equity method. A method of accounting for investments in common stock, by which the investment account is adjusted for the investor's share of periodic net income and property dividends of the investee. (552)

Equity per share. The ratio of stockholders' equity to the related number of shares of stock outstanding. (550)

Equity security. A security that represents ownership in a business, such as stock in a corporation. Preferred or common stock. (295, 549)

Exchange rate. The rate at which one currency can be converted into another currency. (546)

Expense. The amount of assets or services used in the process of earning revenue. (17, 44)

Extraordinary items. Events or transactions that are unusual and infrequent. (542)

Extraordinary repair. An expenditure that increases the useful life of an asset beyond the original estimate. (357)

Equivalent units of production. The number of units that could have been completed within a given accounting period with respect to direct materials and conversion costs. Equivalent units are used to allocate departmental costs incurred during the period between completed units and in-process units at the end of the period. (748)

F

Factory overhead cost. All of the costs of operating the factory except for direct materials and direct labor. (673)

Feedback. Measures provided to operational employees or managers on the performance of subunits of the organization. These measures are used by employees to adjust a process or a behavior to achieve goals. See **Management by exception.** (670)

FICA tax. Federal Insurance Contributions Act tax used to finance federal programs for old-age and disability benefits (social security) and health insurance for the aged (Medicare). (388)

Financial accounting. The branch of accounting that is concerned with the recording of transactions using generally accepted accounting principles (GAAP) for a business or other economic unit and with a periodic preparation of various statements from such records. (663)

Financial Accounting Standards Board (FASB). The current authoritative body for the development of accounting principles for all entities except state and municipal governments. (13, 427)

Finished goods inventory. The cost of finished products on hand that have not been sold. (676)

Finished goods ledger. The subsidiary ledger that contains the individual accounts for each kind of commodity or product produced. (711)

First-in, first-out (fifo) method. A method of inventory costing based on the assumption that the costs of merchandise sold should be charged against revenue in the order in which the costs were incurred. (318, 746)

Fiscal year. The annual accounting period adopted by a business. (134)

Fixed costs. Costs that tend to remain the same in amount, regardless of variations in the level of activity. (779)

Flexible budget. A budget that adjusts for varying rates of activity. (826)

FOB destination. Terms of agreement between buyer and seller whereby ownership passes when merchandise is received by the buyer, and the seller pays the transportation costs. (214)

FOB shipping point. Terms of agreement between buyer and seller whereby ownership passes when merchandise is delivered to the freight carrier, and the buyer pays the transportation costs. (214)

Funded. An appropriation of retained earnings accompanied by a segregation of cash or marketable securities. (515)

G

General journal. The two-column form used for entries that do not "fit" in any of the special journals. (174)

General ledger. The primary ledger, when used in conjunction with subsidiary ledgers, that contains all of the balance sheet and income statement accounts. (172)

Generally accepted accounting principles (GAAP). Generally accepted guidelines for the preparation of financial statements. (12)

Going concern concept. The concept that assumes that a business entity has a reasonable expectation of continuing in business at a profit for an indefinite period of time. (431)

Goodwill. An intangible asset of a business due to such favorable factors as location, product superiority, reputation, and managerial skill. (365)

Gross pay. The total earnings of an employee for a payroll period. (388)

Gross profit. The excess of net sales over the cost of merchandise sold. (214)

Gross profit method. A means of estimating inventory based on the relationship of gross profit to sales. (330)

General ledger. The principal ledger, when used in conjunction with subsidiary ledgers, that contains all the balance sheet and income statement accounts. (700)

H

Held-to-maturity securities. Investments in bonds or other debt securities that management intends to hold to their maturity. (296, 587)

High-low method. A technique that uses the highest and lowest total costs as a basis for estimating the variable cost per unit and the fixed cost component of a mixed cost. (780)

I

Income from operations. The excess of gross profit over total operating expenses. (219)

Income statement. A summary of the revenues and expenses of a business entity for a specific period of time. (20)

Income Summary. The account used in the closing process for transferring the revenue and expense account balances to the owner's capital account at the end of the period. (128A)

Indirect costs. Costs that cannot be traced directly to a cost object. (672)

Indirect method. A method of reporting the cash flows from operating activities as the net income from operations adjusted for all deferrals of past cash receipts and payments and all accruals of expected future cash receipts and payments. (608)

Inflation. A period when prices in general are rising and the purchasing power of money is declining. (981)

Installment method. The method of recognizing revenue, whereby each receipt of cash from installment sales is considered to be part cost of merchandise sold and part gross profit. (436)

Intangible assets. Long-lived assets that are useful in the operations of a business, are not held for sale, and are without physical qualities. (364)

Internal control framework. Consists of five major elements: (1) the control environment, (2) risk assessment, (3) control procedures, (4) monitoring, and (5) information and communication. (166)

Internal controls. The detailed policies and procedures used to direct operations, assure accurate reports, and assure compliance with laws and regulations. (166)

Internal rate of return method. A method of analysis of proposed capital investments that focuses on using present value concepts to compute the rate of return from the net cash flows expected from the investment. (976)

International Accounting Standards Committee (IASC). The primary body leading the effort in developing uniform international accounting standards. (429)

Inventory shrinkage. Loss of inventory due to shoplifting, employee theft, or errors in recording or counting inventory. (221)

Investment center. A decentralized unit in which the manager has the responsibility and authority to make decisions that affect not only costs and revenues but also the plant assets available to the center. (905)

Investment turnover. A component of the rate of return on investment, computed as the ratio of sales to invested assets. (906)

Invoice. The bill provided by the seller (who refers to it as a sales invoice) to a buyer (who refers to it as a purchase invoice) for items purchased. (207)

Invoice file. An electronic listing of customer billing information in a computer. (183)

J

Job cost sheet. An account in the work in process subsidiary ledger in which the costs charged to a particular job order are recorded. (705)

Job order cost system. A type of cost accounting system that provides for a separate record of the cost of each particular quantity of product that passes through the factory. (701)

Journal. The initial record in which the effects of a transaction on accounts are recorded. (46)

Journalizing. The process of recording a transaction in a journal. (46)

Just-in-time (JIT) manufacturing systems. Systems of manufacturing in which a primary emphasis is on the manufacture of products only as they are needed by the next stage of production or by the marketplace. (678)

Just-in-time processing. A processing approach that focuses on reducing time and cost and eliminating poor quality within manufacturing and nonmanufacturing processes. (756)

L

Last-in, first-out (lifo) method. A method of inventory costing based on the assumption that the most recent merchandise costs incurred should be charged against revenue. (320)

Ledger. The group of accounts used by a business. (43)

Lead time. The time required to manufacture a product from receipt of an order until it is shipped to the customer. Sometimes called cycle time. (679)

Liabilities. Debts of a business owed to outsiders (creditors). (14, 43)

Liquidating dividend. A distribution out of paid-in capital when a corporation permanently reduces its operations or winds up its affairs completely. (514)

Liquidation. The winding-up process when a partnership goes out of business. (477)

Long-term liabilities. Liabilities that are not due for a long time (usually more than one year). (128)

Lower-of-cost-or-market method. A method of valuing inventory that reports the inventory at the lower of its cost or current market value (replacement cost). (326)

M

Management by exception. The philosophy of managing which involves monitoring the operating results of implemented plans and comparing the expected results with the actual results. This feedback allows management to isolate significant variations for further investigation and possible remedial action. (670)

Management process. The five basic management functions of (1) planning, (2) directing, (3) controlling, (4) improving, and (5) decision making. (668)

Managerial accounting. The branch of accounting that uses both historical and estimated data in providing information that management uses in conducting daily operations, in planning future operations, and in developing overall business strategies. (663)

Margin of safety. The difference between current sales revenue and the sales at the break-even point. (796)

Market price approach. An approach to transfer pricing that uses the price at which the product or service transferred could be sold to outside buyers as the transfer price. (911)

Marketable securities. Investments in securities that can be readily sold when cash is needed. (295)

Markup. An amount that is added to a "cost" amount to determine product price. (944)

Master budget. The comprehensive budget plan encompassing all the individual budgets related to sales, cost of goods sold, operating expenses, capital expenditures, and cash. (827)

Materials inventory. The cost of materials that have not yet entered into the manufacturing process. (676)

Materials ledger. The subsidiary ledger containing the individual accounts for each type of material. (703)

Materials requisitions. The form or electronic transmission used by a manufacturing department to authorize the issuance of materials from the storeroom. (704)

Matching concept. The concept that expenses incurred in generating revenue should be matched against the revenue in determining the net income or net loss for the period. (20, 90, 435)

Materiality. The concept that recognizes that small or insignificant deviations from generally accepted accounting principles can be treated in the easiest manner. (444)

Maturity value. The amount due (face value plus interest) at the maturity or due date of a note. (293)

Merchandise inventory. Merchandise on hand and available for sale to customers. (206)

Merger. The combining of two corporations by the acquisition of the properties of one corporation by another, with the dissolution of one of the corporations. (553)

Minority interest. The portion of a subsidiary corporation's stock that is not owned by the parent corporation. (555)

Mixed cost. A cost with both variable and fixed characteristics, sometimes called a semivariable or semifixed cost. (779)

Multiple-step income statement. An income statement with several sections, subsections, and subtotals. (218)

N

Natural business year. A year that ends when a business's activities have reached the lowest point in its annual operating cycle. (134)

Negotiated price approach. An approach to transfer pricing that allows managers of decentralized units to agree (negotiate) among themselves as to the transfer price. (912)

Net income. The final figure in the income statement when revenues exceed expenses. (20)

Net loss. The final figure in the income statement when expenses exceed revenues. (20)

Net pay. Gross pay less payroll deductions; the amount the employer is obligated to pay the employee. (388)

Net present value method. A method of analysis of proposed capital investments that focuses on the present value of the cash flows expected from the investments. (974)

Net realizable value. The amount at which merchandise that can be sold only at prices below cost should be valued; it is determined as the estimated selling price less any direct cost of disposal. (327)

Nominal accounts. Revenue or expense accounts that are periodically closed to the income summary account; temporary owner's equity accounts. (128A)

Nonparticipating preferred stock. Preferred stock with a limited dividend preference. (503)

Note receivable. A written promise to pay, representing an amount to be received by a business. (283)

O

Operating income. Revenues less operating expenses for a profit or investment center. (902)

Operating leases. Leases that do not meet the criteria for capital leases and thus are accounted for as operating expenses. (363)

Operating leverage. A measure of the relative mix of a business's variable costs and fixed costs, computed as contribution margin divided by operating income. (796)

Operational planning. The development of short-term plans to achieve goals identified in a business's strategic plan. Sometimes called tactical planning. (669)

Opportunity cost. The amount of income forgone from an alternative to a proposed use of cash or its equivalent. (941)

Other expense. An expense that cannot be traced directly to operations. (220)

Other income. Revenue from sources other than the primary operating activity of a business. (220)

Outstanding stock. The stock that is in the hands of stockholders. (502)

Overapplied factory overhead. The amount of factory overhead applied in excess of the actual factory overhead costs incurred for production during a period. (708)

Owner's equity. The owner's right to the assets of the business after the total liabilities are deducted. (14, 43)

P

Paid-in capital. The capital acquired from stockholders. (502)

Par. The monetary amount printed on a stock certificate. (502)

Parent company. The company owning a majority of the voting stock of another corporation. (553)

Partnership. An unincorporated business of two or more persons to carry on as co-owners a business for profit. (14, 467)

Partnership agreement. The formal written contract creating a partnership. (468)

Payroll. The total amount paid to employees for a certain period. (387)

Payroll register. A multicolumn form used to assemble and summarize payroll data at the end of each payroll period. (392)

Percentage-of-completion method. The method of recognizing revenue from long-term contracts over the entire life of the contract. (437)

Period costs. Those costs that are used up in generating revenue during the current period and that are not involved in the manufacturing process. These costs are recognized as expenses on the current period's income statement. (675)

Periodic inventory system. A system of inventory accounting in which only the revenue from sales is recorded each time a sale is made. The cost of merchandise on hand at the end of a period is determined by a detailed listing (physical inventory) of the merchandise on hand. (207)

Perpetual inventory system. A system of inventory accounting in which both the revenue from sales and the cost of merchandise sold are recorded each time a sale is made, so that the records continually disclose the amount of the inventory on hand. (207)

Petty cash fund. A special cash fund used to pay relatively small amounts. (256)

Physical inventory. The detailed listing of merchandise on hand. (207, 315)

Plant assets. Tangible assets that are owned by a business, are permanent or have a long life, and are used in the business. (99, 347)

Point-of-sale method. The method of recognizing revenue, whereby the revenue is determined to be realized at the time that title passes to the buyer. (436)

Pooling-of-interests method. A method of accounting for an affiliation of two corporations resulting from an exchange of voting stock of one corporation for substantially all the voting stock of the other corporation. (554)

Post-closing trial balance. A trial balance prepared after all of the temporary accounts have been closed. (133)

Posting. The process of transferring debits and credits from a journal to the accounts. (50)

Postretirement benefits. Rights to benefits that employees earn during their term of employment for themselves and their dependents after they retire. (402)

Predetermined factory overhead rate. The rate used to apply factory overhead costs to the goods manufactured. The rate is determined from budgeted overhead cost and activity usage data at the beginning of the fiscal period. (707)

Preemptive right. The right of each shareholder to maintain the same fractional interest in the corporation by purchasing shares of any additional issuances of stock. (503)

Preferred stock. A class of stock with preferential rights over common stock. (503)

Premium. The excess of the issue price of bonds over the face amount. The excess of the sales price of stock over its par amount. (506, 580)

Prepaid expenses. Purchased commodities or services that have not been used up at the end of an accounting period. (17)

Present value. The estimated present worth of an amount of cash to be received (or paid) in the future. (576)

Present value concept. Cash to be received (or paid) in the future is not the equivalent of the same amount of money received at an earlier date. (972)

Present value index. An index computed by dividing the total present value of the net cash flow to be received from a proposed capital investment by the amount to be invested. (974)

Present value of an annuity. The sum of the present values of a series of equal cash flows to be received at fixed intervals. (577, 973)

Price-earnings ratio. The ratio, often called the P/E ratio, computed by dividing the market price per share of common stock at a specific date by the company's earnings per share on common stock. (549)

Price-level index. The ratio of the total cost of a group of commodities prevailing at a particular time to the total cost of the same group of commodities at an earlier base time. (434)

Prime costs. The combination of direct materials and direct labor costs. (675)

Prior-period adjustments. Corrections of material errors related to a prior period or periods, excluded from the determination of net income. (548)

Private accounting. The profession whose members are accountants employed by a business firm or not-for-profit organization. (10)

Proceeds. The net amount available from discounting a note. (294, 404)

Process cost system. A type of cost accounting system that accumulates costs for each of the various departments or processes within a manufacturing facility. (701)

Process manufacturers. Manufacturers that use machines to process a continuous flow of raw materials through various stages of completion into a finished state. An example is an oil refinery. (744)

Product cost concept. A concept used in applying the cost-plus approach to product pricing in which only the costs of manufacturing the product, termed the product cost, are included in the cost amount to which the markup is added. (946)

Product costs. The three components of manufacturing cost: direct materials, direct labor, and factory overhead costs. (675)

Profit center. A decentralized unit in which the manager has the responsibility and the authority to make decisions that affect both costs and revenues (and thus profits). (901)

Profit margin. A component of the rate of return on investment, computed as the ratio of controllable operating income to sales. (906)

Profit-volume chart. A chart used to assist management in understanding the relationship between profit and volume. (790)

Promissory note. A written promise to pay a sum in money on demand or at a definite time. (283)

Public accounting. The profession whose members render accounting services on a fee basis. (10)

Purchase method. The accounting method employed when a parent company acquires a controlling share of the voting stock of a subsidiary other than by the exchange of voting common stock. (554)

Purchases discounts. An available discount taken by a buyer for early payment of an invoice. (208)

Purchases journal. The journal in which all items purchased on account are recorded. (178)

Purchases returns and allowances. Reductions in purchases, resulting from merchandise being returned to the seller or from the seller's reduction in the original purchase price. (209)

Purchase requisitions. The form or electronic transmission used to inform the Purchasing Department that purchased items or services are needed for a business purpose. (703)

R

Rate of return on investment (ROI). A measure of managerial efficiency in the use of investments in assets, computed as controllable operating income divided by invested assets. (906)

Real accounts. Balance sheet accounts. (128A)

Realization. The sale of assets when a partnership is being liquidated. (477)

Receiving report. The form or electronic transmission used by the receiving personnel to indicate that materials have been received and inspected. (703)

Relevant range. The range of activity over which changes in cost are of interest to management. (777)

Report form of balance sheet. A form of balance sheet with the liabilities and owner's equity sections below the assets section. (22, 222)

Residual income. The excess of controllable operating income over a "minimum" amount of desired controllable operating income. (909)

Residual value. The estimated recoverable cost of a depreciable asset as of the time of its removal from service. (349)

Responsibility accounting. The process of measuring and reporting operating data by areas of responsibility. (899)

Responsibility center. An organizational unit for which a manager is assigned responsibility for the unit's performance. (822)

Retail inventory method. A means of estimating inventory based on the relationship of the cost and the retail price of merchandise. (329)

Retained earnings. Net income retained in a corporation. (501)

Revenue expenditures. Expenditures that benefit only the current period. (357)

Revenue journal. The journal in which all sales of services on account are recorded. (174)

Revenue recognition principle. The principle by which revenues are recognized in the period in which they are earned. (90)

Revenues. Increases in owner's equity as a result of providing services or selling products to customers. (17, 43)

S

Sales discounts. An available discount granted by a seller for early payment of an invoice; a contra account to Sales. (211)

Sales mix. The relative distribution of sales among the various products available for sale. (794)

Sales returns and allowances. Reductions in sales, resulting from merchandise being returned by customers or from the seller's reduction in the original sales price; a contra account to Sales. (212)

Selling expenses. Expenses incurred directly in the sale of merchandise. (218)

Service department charges. The costs of services provided by an internal service department and transferred to a responsibility center. (903)

Single-step income statement. An income statement in which the total of all expenses is deducted in one step from the total of all revenues. (220)

Sinking fund. Assets set aside in a special fund to be used for a specific purpose. (582)

Slide. The erroneous movement of all digits in a number, one or more spaces to the right or the left, such as writing $542 as $5,420. (63)

Sole proprietorship. An unincorporated business owned by one individual. (14)

Special journals. Journals designed to be used for recording a single type of transaction. (173)

Standard cost. A detailed estimate of what a product should cost. (863)

Standard cost systems. Accounting systems that use standards for each element of manufacturing cost entering into the finished product. (863)

Stated value. A value approved by the board of directors of a corporation for no-par stock. Similar to par value. (502)

Statement of cash flows. A summary of the major cash receipts and cash payments for a period. (20, 606)

Statement of owner's equity. A summary of the changes in the owner's equity of a business that have occurred during a specific period of time. (20)

Statement of stockholders' equity. A summary of the changes in the stockholders' equity of a corporation that have occurred during a specific period of time. (517)

Static budget. A budget that does not adjust to changes in activity levels. (825)

Stock. Shares of ownership of a corporation. (499)

Stock dividend. Distribution of a company's own stock to its shareholders. (512)

Stock split. A reduction in the par or stated value of a share of common stock and the issuance of a proportionate number of additional shares. (510)

Stockholders. The owners of a corporation. (499)

Stockholders' equity. The equity of the shareholders in a corporation. (501)

Straight-line depreciation method. A method of depreciation that provides for equal periodic depreciation expense over the estimated life of an asset. (351)

Strategic planning. The development of a long-range course of action to achieve business goals. (668)

Strategies. The means by which business goals and objectives will be achieved. (668)

Subsidiary company. The corporation that is controlled by a parent company. (553)

Subsidiary ledger. A ledger containing individual accounts with a common characteristic. (172)

Sum-of-the-years-digits depreciation method. A method of depreciation that provides for declining periodic depreciation expense over the estimated life of an asset. (367)

Sunk cost. A cost that is not affected by subsequent decisions. (935)

T

T account. A form of account resembling the letter T. (45)

Target cost concept. A concept used to design and manufacture a product at a cost that will deliver a target profit for a given market-determined price. (949)

Taxable income. The base on which the amount of income tax is determined. (539)

Temporary accounts. Revenue or expense accounts that are periodically closed to the income summary account; nominal accounts. (128A)

Temporary differences. Differences between income before income tax and taxable income created by items that are recognized in one period for income statement purposes and in another period for tax purposes. Such differences reverse, or turn around, in later years. (539)

Temporary investments. Investments in securities that can be readily sold when cash is needed. (295)

Theoretical standards. Standards that represent levels of performance that can be achieved only under perfect operating conditions. (864)

Theory of constraints (TOC). A manufacturing strategy that attempts to remove the influence of bottlenecks (constraints) on a process. (949)

Time tickets. The form on which the amount of time spent by each employee and the labor cost incurred for each individual job, or for factory overhead, are recorded. (705)

Time value of money concept. The concept that an amount of money invested today will earn income. (969)

Total cost concept. A concept used in applying the cost-plus approach to product pricing in which all the costs of manufacturing the product plus the selling and administrative expenses are included in the cost amount to which the markup is added. (945)

Total quality management (TQM). A management approach that involves an ongoing commitment to improving product quality, starting with product design and continuing through production. (679)

Trade discounts. Special discounts from published list prices offered by sellers to certain classes of buyers. (214)

Trade-in allowance. The amount a seller grants a buyer for a plant asset that is traded in for similar asset. (360)

Trading security. A debt or equity security that management intends to actively trade for profit. (296)

Transfer price. The price charged one decentralized unit by another for the goods or services provided. (910)

Transposition. The erroneous arrangement of digits in a number, such as writing $542 as $524. (63)

Treasury stock. A corporation's own outstanding stock that has been reacquired. (505)

Trial balance. A summary listing of the titles and balances of the accounts in the ledger. (61)

U

Underapplied factory overhead. The amount of actual factory overhead in excess of the factory overhead applied to production during a period. (708)

Unit contribution margin. The dollars available from each unit of sales to cover fixed costs and provide operating profits. (784)

Units-of-production depreciation method. A method of depreciation that provides for depreciation expense based on the expected productive capacity of an asset. (351)

V

Variable cost concept. A concept used in applying the cost-plus approach to product pricing in which only the variable costs are included in the cost amount to which the markup is added. (947)

Variable costing. A method of reporting variable and fixed costs that includes only the variable manufacturing costs in the cost of the product. (782)

Variable costs. Costs that vary in total dollar amount as the level of activity changes. (777)

Variance from standard. The difference between standard cost and actual cost. (863)

Volume variance. The difference between the budgeted fixed overhead at 100% of normal capacity and the standard fixed overhead for the actual production achieved during the period. (873)

Voucher. A document that serves as evidence of authority to pay cash. (254)

Voucher system. Records, methods, and procedures used in verifying and recording liabilities and paying and recording cash payments. (254)

W

Work sheet. A working paper used to summarize adjusting entries and assist in the preparation of financial statements. (100)

Work in process inventory. The direct materials costs, the direct labor costs, and the factory overhead costs that have entered into the manufacturing process, but are associated with products that have not been finished. (676)

Y

Yield. A measure of materials usage efficiency. Yield measures the ratio of the materials output quantity to the materials input quantity. Yields less than 1.0 are the result of materials losses in the process. (756)

Z

Zero-based budgeting. A concept of budgeting that requires all levels of management to start from zero and estimate budget data as if there had been no previous activities in their unit. (825)

Index

A

D

E

T

INDEX OF REAL COMPANIES

Check Figures for Selected Problems

Prob.	Check Figure
1–1A	1. June 30, cash, $25,270
1–2A	1. Net income, $36,655
1–3A	1. Net income, $4,350
1–4A	2. Net income, $6,250
1–5A	3. Net income, $2,350
1–6A	1. Net income, $65,900
1–1B	1. March 31, cash, $12,295
1–2B	1. Net income, $25,300
1–3B	1. Net income, $2,470
1–4B	2. Net income, $3,075
1–5B	3. Net income, $1,775
1–6B	1. Net income, $103,375
Cont. Prob.	2. Net income, $140
2–1A	3. Total credits, $39,160
2–2A	3. Total debits, $35,350
2–3A	3. Total debits, $32,350
2–4A	4. Total credits, $237,865
2–5A	7. Total debits, $33,338.10
2–6A	1. Total credits, $78,190
2–1B	3. Total debits, $46,100
2–2B	3. Total credits, $33,400
2–3B	3. Total debits, $34,815
2–4B	4. Total credits, $323,350
2–5B	7. Total credits, $33,338.10
2–6B	1. Total debits, $103,090
Cont. Prob.	Trial balance, total debits, $11,945
3–3A	1. Adjusted trial balance totals, $88,380
3–6A	3. Adjusted trial balance totals, $482,270
3–3B	1. Adjusted trial balance totals, $88,380
3–6B	3. Adjusted trial balance totals, $467,000
Cont. Prob.	Adjusted trial balance, total debits, $12,515
4–1A	2. Net income, $7,610
4–2A	2. Net income, $32,295; 3. Ending capital, $56,140
4–3A	2. Net income, $4,541.11
4–4A	2. Net income, $44,870
4–5A	3. Net income, $23,407
4–1B	2. Net income, $23,490
4–2B	2. Net income, $21,780; 3. Ending capital, $126,680
4–3B	2. Net income, $4,166.11
4–4B	2. Net income, $37,930
4–5B	3. Net income, $17,705
Cont. Prob.	2. Net income, $1,522; Post-closing trial balance, total debits, $8,042
Comp. Prob. 1	4. Net income, $6,770; Post-closing trial balance, total credits, $23,070
5–1A	1. Total fees earned, $15,045
5–2A	3. Total cash receipts, $76,910
5–3A	3. Total accounts payable credit, $37,310
5–4A	1. Total cash payments, $56,590
5–5A	2. Total cash receipts, $40,100
5–1B	1. Total fees earned, $15,045
5–2B	3. Total cash receipts, $73,150
5–3B	3. Total accounts payable credit, $41,090
5–4B	1. Total cash payments, $48,040
5–5B	2. Total cash receipts, $51,390
6–5A	1. Net income, $90,000
6–6A	3. Total assets, $470,000
6–7A	1. Net income, $176,855
6–5B	1. Net income, $122,490
6–6B	3. Total assets, $360,200
6–7B	1. Net income, $149,965
Comp. Prob. 2	6. Net income, $69,657; 7. Total debits, $268,020
7–4A	1. Adjusted balance, $17,764.30
7–5A	1. Adjusted balance, $20,879.87
7–6A	1. Adjusted balance, $9,650.02
7–4B	1. Adjusted balance, $20,645.00
7–5B	1. Adjusted balance, $17,091.88
7–6B	1. Adjusted balance, $12,646.09
8–1A	3. $413,500
8–2A	1. Balance of Allowance, Year 4, $8,450
8–4A	2. Note 3, (d) $15,045
8–1B	3. $752,300
8–2B	1. Balance of Allowance, Year 4, $11,650
8–4B	2. Note 2, (d) $10,021.44
9–1A	1. Sept. 30 inventory, 10,000 at $6 = $60,000
9–2A	1. Sept. 30 inventory, 5,000 at $ 6.10 = $30,500; 5,000 at $6.05 = $30,250
9–3A	1. $8,681; 3. $8,339
9–4A	LCM, $55,065
9–5A	1. $157,500; 2. a. $122,500
9–1B	1. June 28 inventory, 1 at $235 = $235; 15 at $240 = $3,600
9–2B	1. June 28 inventory, 10 at $ 220 = $2,200; 2 at $225 = $450; 4 at $240 = $960
9–3B	1. $11,247; 3. $11,024
9–4B	LCM, $54,395
9–5B	1. $171,500; 2. a. $372,550
10–2A	a. 1996: $100,000; b. 1996: $75,000; c. 1996: $210,000
10–3A	a. 1996: $17,000; b. 1996: $14,400; c. 1996: $36,000
10–4A	2. $201,680; 6. $212,680
10–7A	4. a. $11,175
10–8A	1. a. $70,000; 1. b. $12,500; 1. c. $3,750
10–9A	1996: $150,000
10–10A	1996: $25,500
10–2B	a. 1996: $30,000; b. 1996: $18,000; c. 1996: $65,000
10–3B	a. 1996: $12,000; b. 1996: $15,300; c. 1996: $25,000
10–4B	2. $170,000; 6. $190,000
10–7B	4. a. $3,750
10–8B	1. a. $93,750; 1. b. $12,000; 1. c. $4,675
10–9B	1996: $48,000
10–10B	1996: $18,000
11–1A	2. a. FICA Tax Payable, credit $10,200
11–2A	3. Payroll Tax Expense, debit $628.62
11–3A	1. Total FICA withheld, $20,529
11–4A	1. Total net amount paid, $4,852.59
11–1B	2. a. FICA Tax Payable, credit $12,000
11–2B	3. Payroll Tax Expense, debit $ 621.48
11–3B	1. Total FICA withheld, $20,979
11–4B	1. Total net amount paid, $4,940.77
Comp. Prob. 3	5. Total assets, $1,042,230
12–1A	2. Third year net income, $35,100
12–2A	3. Gain, $32
12–3A	1997 income, $1,375,000
12–4A	Third year net income, $96,230
12–1B	2. Third year net income, $95,510
12–2B	3. Loss, $224
12–3B	1997 income, $1,085,000
12–4B	Third year net income, $184,250
13–1A	3. Tsao net income, $ 40,000
13–2A	1. f. Haddox net income, $93,000
13–3A	2. Strange year-end capital balance, $91,000
13–4A	3. Total assets, $232,600
13–6A	2. e. Mentzer Capital debit, $9,000
13–1B	3. Hall net income, $35,200
13–2B	1. f. Garland net income, $36,000
13–3B	2. Hepburn year-end capital balance, $67,000
13–4B	3. Total assets, $202,220

Prob.	Check Figure
13–6B	2. e. Mentzer Capital debit, $12,000
14–1A	2. Common stock, $1.20 per share
14–2A	2. Total stockholders' equity, $3,145,000
14–3A	2. Total stockholders' equity, $1,804,000
14–4A	3. Total stockholders' equity, 12/31, $2,879,840
14–5A	Nov. 30, Stock Dividends Distributable, $48,750 (cr.)
14–6A	Retained earnings, 12/31, $1,275,000
14–1B	2. Common stock, $.43 per share
14–2B	2. Total stockholders' equity, $3,871,000
14–3B	2. Total stockholders' equity, $8,972,000
14–4B	3. Total stockholders' equity, 12/31, $2,026,870
14–5B	July 23, Stock Dividends Distributable, $14,000 (cr.)
14–6B	Retained earnings, 12/31, $860,000
15–1A	1. Year-end balance, 4th year, $42,300
15–2A	Net income, $19,600
15–4A	D. Common stock, $28.50
15–1B	1. Year-end balance, 4th year, $25,500
15–2B	Net income, $90,000
15–4B	D. Common stock, $19.67
16–1A	1. Plan 2, $3.60 eps
16–2A	1. Proceeds, $8,249,240
16–3A	1. Proceeds, $10,504,529
16–4A	2. a. $1,242,650; 3. $20,974,947
16–5A	Oct. 31: Loss, $2,250
16–6A	1. a. Interest expense, $412,462
16–7A	1. a. Interest expense, $525,226
16–1B	1. Plan 2, $3.20 eps
16–2B	1. Proceeds, $11,246,216
16–3B	1. Proceeds, $14,139,760
16–4B	2. a. $481,156; 3. $9,470,352
16–5B	July 31: Gain, $1,275
16–6B	1. a. Interest expense, $562,311
16–7B	1. a. Interest expense, $848,386
Comp. Prob. 4	1. (c) Proceeds of $1,031,155; 2. a. Net income, $314,600; 2. c. Total assets, $8,973,000
17–1A	Net cash flow from operating activities, $87,900
17–2A	Net cash flow from operating activities, $189,000
17–3A	Net cash flow from operating activities, $73,800
17–4A	Net cash flow from operating activities, $(31,900)
17–5A	Net cash flow from operating activities, $53,200
17–6A	Net cash flow from operating activities, $87,900
17–7A	1. Net cash flow from operating activities, $121,050
17–1B	Net cash flow from operating activities, $103,000
17–2B	Net cash flow from operating activities, $130,100
17–3B	Net cash flow from operating activities, $111,850
17–4B	Net cash flow from operating activities, $65,100
17–5B	Net cash flow from operating activities, $54,500
17–6B	Net cash flow from operating activities, $103,000
17–7B	1. Net cash flow from operating activities, $63,710
18–4A	2. Cost of Goods Sold, $1,150,000
18–5A	Cost of Goods Sold, $1,300,000
18–4B	2. Cost of Goods Sold, $7,800,000
18–5B	Cost of Goods Sold, $5,500,000
19–2A	1.f. Finished Goods debit, $104,700
19–3A	Total actual cost, $780
19–4A	1. H. Cost of goods sold, $370,450
19–5A	2. C Total amount billed to Martha Briggs, $13,050
19–6A	2. Product C unit cost, $46
19–2B	1. f. Finished Goods debit, $51,323
19–3B	Total actual cost, $384
19–4B	1. H. Cost of goods sold, $232,670
19–5B	2. C Total amount billed to Weatherspoon cow, $1,650
19–6B	2. Product F unit cost, $23.60
20–3A	Costs transferred to Packing Department, $1,142,800
20–4A	1. Costs transferred to finished goods, $107,400
20–5A	1. Costs transferred to finished goods, July 31, $114,075
20–3B	Costs transferred to Molding Department, $275,718
20–4B	1. Total equivalent units for conversion, 41,400
20–5B	1. Conversion cost per equivalent unit, September, $21.00
21–2A	4. Break-even in sales units, 37,600
21–3A	1. Break-even in sales units, 14,000
21–4A	2. a. Operating income, $112,000
21–5A	1. Break-even in sales units, 1,425
21–6A	3. Break-even in sales units, 6,000
21–2B	3. Break-even in sales units, 50,000
21–3B	1. Break-even in sales units, 12,000
21–4B	2. a. Operating income, $140,000
21–5B	1. Break-even in sales units, 3,500
21–6B	3. Break-even in sales units, 100,000
22–1A	3. Total revenue, $3,734,240
22–2A	3. Direct material P purchases, $511,938
22–3A	6. Cost of goods sold, $1,654,670
22–4A	1. October excess cash, $80,400
22–5A	1. Net income, $103,800
22–6A	1. Total factory overhead, $72,760
22–1B	3. Total revenue, $5,293,940
22–2B	3. Direct material A purchases, $794,920
22–3B	6. Cost of goods sold, $2,774,658
22–4B	1. June excess cash, $22,700
22–5B	1. Net income, $49,340
22–6B	1. Total factory overhead, $82,848
23–1A	b. Direct materials quantity variance, $140 favorable
23–2A	b. Direct labor rate variance, $3,020 favorable
23–3A	b. Direct labor time variance, $2,520 unfavorable
23–4A	Volume variance, $13,200
23–5A	2. Net factory overhead controllable variance, $2,800 favorable
23–6A	3. Direct labor rate variance, $640 unfavorable
23–1B	b. Direct materials quantity variance, $2,232 unfavorable
23–2B	b. Direct labor rate variance, $1,780 unfavorable
23–3B	b. Direct labor time variance, $4,500 unfavorable
23–4B	Volume variance, $11,340 unfavorable
23–5B	2. Net factory overhead controllable variance, $44,200 favorable
23–6B	3. Direct labor rate variance, $360 unfavorable
24–1A	1. Controllable operating income, Northwest Division, $77,060
24–2A	2. Controllable operating income, North, $86,500
24–3A	2. ROI, Division U, 15%
24–4A	1. ROI, 15%
24–5A	2. Division Z ROI, 16%
24–6A	3. Controllable operating income, Division T, $1,070,000
24–1B	1. Controllable operating income, Branch 9, $5,028
24–2B	2. Controllable operating income, Seafood, $136,680
24–3B	2. ROI, Division 1, 24%
24–4B	1. ROI, 18.75%
24–5B	2. ROI, 18%
24–6B	3. Controllable operating income, Division X, $810,000
25–1A	3. Total estimated income from operating warehouse, $1,670,000
25–2A	1. Differential income from replacement, $496,800
25–3A	1. Differential income for sales campaign, Product T, $130,000
25–4A	1. Differential income from further processing of Product L, $1,300
25–5A	2. c. $46.08
25–6A	2. Contribution margin per furnace hour, Product X, $15
25–1B	3. Total estimated income from operating warehouse, $1,150,000
25–2B	1. Differential income from replacement, $115,000
25–3B	1. Differential income for sales campaign, Product A, $64,000
25–4B	1. Differential loss from further processing of Product A, $(420)
25–5B	2. c. $43.20
25–6B	2. Contribution margin per reactor hour, Product A, $54
26–1A	1. b. Net present value, Project A, $3,268
26–2A	1. b. Net present value, Project E, $8,060
26–3A	1. Net present value, Proposal X, $21,160
26–4A	2. b. Internal rate of return, Project B, 12%
26–5A	2. Net present value, Project I, $24,280
26–6A	4. Net present value, Proposal A, $54,855
26–1B	1. b. Net present value, Project P, $8,365
26–2B	1. b. Net present value, Project G, $31,760
26–3B	1. Net present value, Proposal C, $10,880
26–4B	2. b. Internal rate of return, Project I, 20%
26–5B	2. Net present value, Project A, $14,280
26–6B	4. Net present value, Proposal A, $54,855

Abbreviations and Acronyms Commonly Used in Business and Accounting

AAA	American Accounting Association
ABC	Activity-based costing
ACRS	Accelerated Cost Recovery System
AICPA	American Institute of Certified Public Accountants
CIA	Certified Internal Auditor
CIM	Computer-integrated manufacturing
CMA	Certified Management Accountant
CPA	Certified Public Accountant
Cr.	Credit
Dr.	Debit
EFT	Electronic funds transfer
EPS	Earnings per share
FAF	Financial Accounting Foundation
FASB	Financial Accounting Standards Board
FEI	Financial Executives Institute
FICA tax	Federal Insurance Contributions Act tax
FIFO	First-in, first-out
FOB	Free on board
GAAP	Generally accepted accounting principles
GASB	Governmental Accounting Standards Board
GNP	Gross National Product
IMA	Institute of Management Accountants
IRC	Internal Revenue Code
IRS	Internal Revenue Service
JIT	Just-in-time
LIFO	Last-in, first-out
Lower of C or M	Lower of cost or market
MACRS	Modified Accelerated Cost Recovery System
n/30	Net 30
n/eom	Net, end-of-month
P/E Ratio	Price-earnings ratio
POS	Point of sale
ROI	Return on investment
SEC	Securities and Exchange Commission
TQC	Total quality control

Classification of Accounts

Account Title	*Account Classification*	*Normal Balance*	*Financial Statement*
Accounts Payable	Current liability	Credit	Balance sheet
Accounts Receivable	Current asset	Debit	Balance sheet
Accumulated Depreciation	Plant asset	Credit	Balance sheet
Accumulated Depletion	Plant asset	Credit	Balance sheet
Advertising Expense	Operating expense	Debit	Income statement
Allowance for Doubtful Accounts	Current asset	Credit	Balance sheet
Amortization Expense	Operating expense	Debit	Income statement
Appropriation for ________	Stockholders' equity	Credit	Retained earnings statement/ Balance sheet
Bonds Payable	Long-term liability	Credit	Balance sheet
Building	Plant asset	Debit	Balance sheet
________ Capital	Owners' equity	Credit	Statement of owner's equity/ Balance sheet
Capital Stock	Stockholders' equity	Credit	Balance sheet
Cash	Current asset	Debit	Balance sheet
Cash Dividends	Stockholders' equity	Debit	Retained earnings statement
Cash Dividends Payable	Current liability	Credit	Balance sheet
Common Stock	Stockholders' equity	Credit	Balance sheet
Cost of Merchandise (Goods) Sold	Cost of merchandise (goods sold)	Debit	Income statement
Deferred Income Tax	Current liability/Long-term liability	Credit	Balance sheet
Depletion Expense	Operating expense	Debit	Income statement
Discount on Bonds Payable	Long-term liability	Debit	Balance sheet
Discounts Lost	Other expense	Debit	Income statement
Dividend Income	Other income	Credit	Income statement
Dividends	Stockholders' equity	Debit	Retained earnings statement
Donated Capital	Stockholders' equity	Credit	Balance sheet
Employees Federal Income Tax Payable	Current liability	Credit	Balance sheet
Equipment	Plant asset	Debit	Balance sheet
Exchange Gain	Other income	Credit	Income statement
Exchange Loss	Other expense	Debit	Income statement
Factory Overhead (Overapplied)	Deferred credit	Credit	Balance sheet (interim)
Factory Overhead (Underapplied)	Deferred debit	Debit	Balance sheet (interim)
Federal Income Tax Payable	Current liability	Credit	Balance sheet
Federal Unemployment Tax Payable	Current liability	Credit	Balance sheet
FICA Tax Payable	Current liability	Credit	Balance sheet
Finished Goods	Current asset	Debit	Balance sheet
Gain on Disposal of Plant Assets	Other income	Credit	Income statement
Gain on Redemption of Bonds	Extraordinary item	Credit	Income statement
Gain on Sale of Investments	Other income	Credit	Income statement
Goodwill	Intangible asset	Debit	Balance sheet
Income Tax	Income tax	Debit	Income statement
Income Tax Payable	Current liability	Credit	Balance sheet
Insurance Expense	Operating expense	Debit	Income statement
Interest Expense	Other expense	Debit	Income statement
Interest Income	Other income	Credit	Income statement
Interest Receivable	Current asset	Debit	Balance sheet
Investment in Bonds	Investment	Debit	Balance sheet
Investment in Stocks	Investment	Debit	Balance sheet
Investment in Subsidiary	Investment	Debit	Balance sheet